Indon

D0789624

THE ROUGH GUIDE

There are more than one hundred Rough Guide titles
covering destinations from Amsterdam to Zimbabwe

Forthcoming titles include
Dominican Republic • Melbourne • Laos • South India

Rough Guide Reference Series
Classical Music • European Football • The Internet • Jazz
Opera • Reggae • Rock Music • World Music

Rough Guide Phrasebooks
Czech • Dutch • French • German • Greek • Hindi & Urdu • Hungarian
Indonesian • Italian • Japanese • Mandarin Chinese • Mexican Spanish
Polish • Portuguese • Russian • Spanish • Thai • Turkish • Vietnamese
European Languages

Rough Guides on the Internet
www.roughguides.com

ROUGH GUIDE CREDITS

Text editor: Helena Smith
Series editor: Mark Ellingham
Editorial: Martin Dunford, Jonathan Buckley, Jo Mead, Kate Berens, Paul Gray, Amanda Tomlin, Ann-Marie Shaw, Chris Schüler, Judith Bamber, Kieran Falconer, Orla Duane, Olivia Eccleshall, Ruth Blackmore, Sophie Martin, Geoff Howard, Claire Saunders, Anna Sutton, Gavin Thomas, Alexander Mark Rogers, Joe Staines, Lisa Nellis, Andrew Tomicić (UK); Andrew Rosenberg (US)
Production: Susanne Hillen, Andy Hilliard, Link Hall, Helen Ostick, Julia Bovis, Michelle Draycott, Anna Wray, Katie Pringle

Cartography: Melissa Flack, Maxine Burke, Nichola Goodliffe, Ed Wright
Picture research: Eleanor Hill, Louise Boulton
Online editors: Alan Spicer, Kate Hands (UK); Kelly Cross (US)
Finance: John Fisher, Katy Miesiaczek, Gary Singh, Ed Downey
Marketing & publicity: Richard Trillo, Simon Carloss, Niki Smith, David Wearn (UK); Jean-Marie Kelly, Myra Campolo (US)
Administration: Tania Hummel, Charlotte Marriott, Demelza Dallow

PUBLISHING INFORMATION

This first edition published June 1999 by Rough Guides Ltd, 62–70 Shorts Gardens, London WC2H 9AB.
Distributed by the Penguin Group:
Penguin Books Ltd, 27 Wrights Lane, London W8 5TZ
Penguin Books USA Inc., 375 Hudson Street, New York 10014, USA
Penguin Books Australia Ltd, 487 Maroondah Highway, PO Box 257, Ringwood, Victoria 3134, Australia
Penguin Books Canada Ltd, 10 Alcorn Avenue, Toronto, Ontario, Canada M4V 1E4
Penguin Books (NZ) Ltd, 182–190 Wairau Road, Auckland 10, New Zealand
Typeset in Linotron Univers and Century Old Style to an original design by Andrew Oliver
Printed in England by Clays Ltd, St Ives PLC
Illustrations in Part One and Part Three by Edward Briant
Illustrations on p.1 & p.945 by Henry Iles

Indonesia

THE ROUGH GUIDE

written and researched by

Stephen Backshall, David Leffman, Lesley Reader and Henry Stedman

with additional contributions by

Lucy Ridout

and

Colin Bass, Jessica Eveleigh, Jenny Heaton and Simon Steptoe

THE ROUGH GUIDES

THE ROUGH GUIDES

TRAVEL GUIDES • PHRASEBOOKS • MUSIC AND REFERENCE GUIDES

 We set out to do something different when the first Rough Guide was published in 1982. Mark Ellingham, just out of university, was travelling in Greece. He brought along the popular guides of the day, but found they were all lacking in some way. They were either strong on ruins and museums but went on for pages without mentioning a beach or taverna. Or they were so conscious of the need to save money that they lost sight of Greece's cultural and historical significance. Also, none of the books told him anything about Greece's contemporary life – its politics, its culture, its people and how they lived.

So, with no job in prospect, Mark decided to write his own guidebook, one which aimed to provide practical information that was second to none, detailing the best beaches and the hottest clubs and restaurants, while also giving hard-hitting accounts of every sight, both famous and obscure, and providing up-to-the-minute information on contemporary culture. It was a guide that encouraged independent travellers to find the best of Greece, and was a great success, getting shortlisted for the Thomas Cook travel guide award, and encouraging Mark, along with three friends, to expand the series.

The Rough Guide list grew rapidly and the letters flooded in, indicating a much broader readership than had been anticipated, but one which uniformly appreciated the Rough Guide mix of practical detail and humour, irreverence and enthusiasm. Things haven't changed. The same four friends who began the series are still the caretakers of the Rough Guide mission today: to provide the most reliable, up-to-date and entertaining information to independent-minded travellers of all ages, on all budgets.

We now publish more than a hundred titles and have offices in London and New York. The travel guides are written and researched by a dedicated team of more than a hundred authors, based in Britain, Europe, the USA and Australia. We have also created a unique series of phrasebooks to accompany the travel series, along with an acclaimed series of music guides, and a best-selling pocket guide to the Internet and World Wide Web. We also publish comprehensive travel information on our Web site:

www.roughguides.com

HELP US UPDATE

We've gone to a lot of effort to ensure that this first edition of *The Rough Guide to Indonesia* is accurate and up-to-date. However, things change – places get "discovered", opening hours are notoriously fickle, restaurants and rooms raise prices or lower standards. If you feel we've got it wrong or left something out, we'd like to know, and if you can remember the address, the price, the time, the phone number, so much the better.

We'll credit all contributions, and send a copy of the next edition (or any other Rough Guide if you prefer) for the best letters. Please mark letters: "Rough Guide Indonesia Update" and send to:
Rough Guides, 62–70 Shorts Gardens, London WC2H 9AB, or Rough Guides, 375 Hudson St, 9th floor, New York, NY 10014.
Or send email to: mail@roughguides.co.uk
Online updates about this book can be found on Rough Guides' Web site at www.roughguides.com

THE AUTHORS

Stephen Backshall spent three years travelling around Asia, and lived for a year in Japan, studying martial arts. He now writes and researches television programmes, in between indulging a passion for every sport, from rugby to rock climbing.

David Leffman is the co-author of *The Rough Guide to Australia* and *The Rough Guide to China*, and has travelled throughout Asia. When not on the road, he spends much of his time scuba diving near his home in Queensland.

Lesley Reader has lived and worked in Bhutan and Thailand and travelled widely in Asia. She is co-author, with Lucy Ridout, of *First-Time Asia* and *The Rough Guide to Bali and Lombok*, and has contributed to *The Rough Guide to China*.

Henry Stedman graduated from the University of Bristol in 1991, and headed for Asia, in an attempt to rid himself of a particularly virulent travel bug. This treatment proved unsuccessful, and for the last four years he has been a freelance travel writer. This is his second guidebook, his first for Rough Guides.

ACKNOWLEDGEMENTS

The editor would like to thank the following people at Rough Guides, for all their help in planning and producing this title: Jo Mead and Kate Berens; Louise Boulton, Maxine Burke, Michelle Draycott, Eleanor Hill, Susanne Hillen, Cathy McElhinney, James Morris and Katie Pringle. Also Nick Thomson, the Map Studio (Romsey, Hants), Lisa Pusey for picture research and Nikky Tywman and Russell Walton for expert proofreading.

Stephen: Specially for Mum and Dad – thanks for keeping me solvent and sane, to Kristina, Aguus and all the Delta Gecko-ers, to Pak Johannes for dragging me around Savu on his motorbike, to Guru Ben, Abdul Muis, Mark and Bernie at the judo club, the boys, and everyone in Indonesia, who've done so much to make my time there a joy.

David: For Narrell and Jim, who trekked, dived, got soaked, drank *sopi*, and ate cassowary like champions; and Leaf and Max, who had to put up with just hearing about it all. And a huge tip of the *topi* to Peter Veth, for pointing the way on Aru. Thanks to: Aud Mari and Odd Ivar; David Carr; Emil, Oce, and Hans; Jessica and Anneka; Sarkani Gambi; Elizabeth Humphries at Paddy Pallin; Lesley and Lucy for original Basics material; Georg and Judit Mayer; Bruce Moore; Odie Rusdianor; Supian; Ronie Tomiansyah; Wim; Gerhard Wohlman; Rudi Yanto; Marguarite Young; Muhammad Yusuf.

Lesley: Many thanks to the staff in the tourist offices and national park offices who answered queries so patiently, especially Nyoman Suwela and the Buleleng Tourist Office, Dr Mathur Riady and the Provincial Tourism Office of west Nusa Tenggara, especially Dahlia, the East Java Government Tourism Service in Surabaya, everyone in the offices in Padang, Bukittinggi, Bengkulu, Bandar Lampung, Jambi, Surabaya, Tanjung Pinang and Cici in Malang. In addition, to the people I met on the road who were great company – special mentions to Neddy, Jane, Angela, Iwan, Komang, Inengah Parni, Made Suliter, Nyoman Ardana and family, Toké, Sue and Bob in Bali, Amang on Madura, Debbie Martyr and her colleagues in Sungaipenuh, Antok and Helios in Malang, Yosi in Bengkulu and staff at Yasumi. Also many thanks to Gill Cook and Jerry for Jakarta hospitality and Max and Dom and fellow sufferers on the "flight from hell". Back in the UK, thanks to Liz at Down to Earth, Yau Sang Man and, as always, Barbara Unger for everything.

Henry: Jean Grindley – for making Central Java so enjoyable; Petra – for making Jakarta bearable; Claudine King, Conor Wall and Mervyn for the blarney; Sarah Hampson for the book; Tal Ben-Hur for the karaoke; Stuart Adamson for the attitude, Rudi, Marsono, Johnno at Ella's and Denson Noven Sudiyo Girsang, for their help along the way; and Mel Konizi, for making the bits in between the travelling so much fun.

CONTENTS

Introduction xiii

• CHAPTER 3: CENTRAL JAVA 153–231

• CHAPTER 4: EAST JAVA 232–288

• CHAPTER 5: NORTH SUMATRA AND ACEH 289–350

● CHAPTER 13: IRIAN JAYA 900–944

PART THREE CONTEXTS 945

LIST OF MAPS

MAP SYMBOLS

═══	Main road	✺	Crater
══	Road	⌁	Rocks
═	Minor road		Hill
──▶	One way street (town maps)	∧	Mountains
----	Path	▲	Mountain peak
▬▬	Railway	⋇	Viewpoint
──	River	◠	Cave
──	Ferry/hydrofoil route	⋇	Marsh
▪▬▬	International boundary	ϒ	Spring
▪▬▬	Provincial boundary	⌒	Surf area
▬▬▬	Chapter division boundary	(i)	Information office
✗	Airport	(S)	Bank
★	Bus stop	⊠	Post office
◉	Accommodation	(C)	Telephone
▣	Restaurant	⊞	Hospital
▲	Campsite	ⅲⅲⅲ	Steps
⚖	Market	──	Wall
⚑	Mosque	■	Building
▲	Temple	+	Church
♦	Museum	+₊+	Cemetery
♨	Fort	⸸	Muslim cemetery
◆	Point of interest		Park
∴	Ruins	▨	National park/nature reserve
⅄	Lighthouse	⸬	Beach
∩	Arch	▧	Swamp
⇊	Waterfall		

INTRODUCTION

For sheer size, scale and variety, **Indonesia** is pretty much unbeatable. The country is so enormous that nobody is really sure quite how big it is; there are between 13,000 and 17,000 islands. It's certainly the largest archipelago in the world, spreading over 5200km between the Asian mainland and Australia, all of it within the tropics and with huge areas of ocean separating the landmasses. Not surprisingly, Indonesia's ethnic, cultural and linguistic diversity is correspondingly great – the best estimate is of 500 languages and dialects spoken by around 200 million people.

The largely volcanic nature of the islands has created tall cloud-swept mountains swathed in the green of rice terraces or rainforest, dropping to blindingly bright beaches and vivid blue seas, the backdrop for Southeast Asia's biggest wilderness areas and wildlife sanctuaries. All of this provides an endless resource for adventurous trekking, surfing, scuba diving, or just lounging by a pool in a five-star resort. You'll find that the Indonesians themselves are one of the best reasons to visit the country – despite recent troubles, people are generally very open and welcoming, whether they're sophisticated city dwellers or remote island villagers who hunt game and maintain traditional beliefs. The ethnic mix is overwhelming: this is the world's largest Muslim country, but with a distinct local flavour, and there are also substantial populations of Christians, Hindus and animists, whose forms of worship, customs and lifestyles have been influencing each other for centuries.

The area which now comprises modern Indonesia was once a multitude of kingdoms, empires and states, many of which controlled vast areas, some into mainland Asia. Strong foreign influences helped define the rich religious and cultural pattern of the islands: located on the shortest sea route between Europe and the Far East, they have long been visited and settled by traders. Merchants from India brought Hinduism along with the goods they traded as early as the third century, Islam was imported from the subcontinent in the fifth century and, by 1511, the Portuguese had established the immensely lucrative trade in spices. Their grip on the region was loosened by the Dutch, who, in 1602, formed the Dutch East India Company which monopolized trade in the region – then known as the Dutch East Indies – until the end of the eighteenth century. The British had a brief tenure in the archipelago, but were supplanted by the Dutch in 1816, who faced gathering opposition to their rule. During World War II, nationalist ideals took hold across the islands, and led to the Declaration of Independence on August 17, 1945, read by Achmed Sukarno. The War for Independence lasted until December 1949, when the Republic of Indonesia was formed, with Sukarno as its first president. His achievements and miscalculations remain to be fully assessed, but his rule was strongly characterized by both: he managed to introduce a semblance of democracy to the country and to unite its extraordinarily diverse peoples, but failed to control the economy – as well as embarking on a fruitless and costly confrontation with Malaysia. He was toppled by Suharto in 1965, whose successful handling of the economy and commitment to pluralism went hand in hand with increasing authoritarianism and rampant corruption and nepotism. The currency crisis that battered Southeast Asia towards the end of 1997 crystallized the growing dissatisfaction with Suharto's regime, and he was swept from power in 1998.

Much of the recent news about Indonesia has emphasized the fragility of the state. As the old order of ex-president Suharto is dismantled and the current leadership struggles to cope with an ailing economy, some sort of fragmentation seems inevitable:

East Timor has recently been promised independence (though whether this will materialize is uncertain), while Aceh, in North Sumatra, continues to press for a greater degree of autonomy. These two provinces lie at the geographical extremes of the archipelago, and it's tempting to think that, if successful, their break from Indonesia will have little adverse effect on the rest of the country. More worrying, however, are the religious and racial ructions that threaten to unravel the very fabric of Indonesian society. Recent riots in many parts of the country have pitched Muslims against their Christian neighbours, while deep-rooted anti-Chinese sentiment surfaced in particularly bloody fashion in 1998. More localized ethnic violence has its source in the transmigration policies of the Indonesian government, whose aim was to settle far-flung areas such as Kalimantan with migrants from overpopulated regions including Java and Madura, often without local consultation and with little heed given to traditional land rights. Unsurprisingly, resentment and violence have sometimes boiled over. Whilst the economy remains on the point of collapse, these tensions will continue to reverberate, and further turmoil can be expected.

In spite of this unrest, the dangers of a trip to Indonesia shouldn't be exaggerated: violence of the sort witnessed on the streets of Jakarta in 1998 remains extremely rare, and has largely been confined to a couple of big cities on Java, although serious ethnic violence flared up in Maluku in early 1999. Keeping an ear to the ground for developments and acting with a degree of common sense and sensitivity should be enough to ensure that your own trip to the country is a safe one.

Travel across the archipelago is pretty unforgettable, in tiny fragile planes, rusty ferries and careering buses – their drivers with one eye on the road, the other on the Jean-Claude Van Damme movie blaring in the background. Give yourself plenty of time to cover the large distances; if you only have a couple of weeks, you'll have a better time if you restrict yourself to exploring a small area properly rather than hopping across 3000km to see your top ten sights. If you do have longer, try to plan a trip that doesn't involve too much doubling back, consider an open-jaw international plane ticket, and try to intersperse lengthy journeys with a few days of relaxation in peaceful surroundings. Also, leave yourself some leeway – if you're in a hurry with a vital plane to catch, something is bound to go wrong. Having said all this, the places which are hardest to reach are often well worth the effort. Some of the most rewarding experiences come when you least expect them: under the surface of the least inspiring place there's always something interesting going on. An enforced day's malinger between transport in an apparently dull town might end with an invitation to watch an exorcism, or to examine a collection of ancestor skulls over coffee and cigarettes.

Just as you should give yourself more time than you think you'll need, allow yourself more than the rock-bottom **budget** – even if it means a shorter trip. Indonesia can be very economical, but there's plenty to spend your money on: watching every last rupiah will detract from the enjoyment.

Where to go

Java, with the country's largest cities, industries and highest concentration of people – over sixty percent of the population live here – is the epicentre of modern Indonesia, but also a place of great beauty, its lush volcanic landscape harbouring stately old settlements and splendid temples. Towards the western end of the island is **Jakarta**, the country's capital and the home of over ten million of its people. Overgrown, inefficient and polluted, it does, though, contain some of Indonesia's finest museums – including the massive and comprehensive National Museum – as well as a delightful colonial quarter. Outside Jakarta, West Java features upmarket beach resorts giving access to the infamous **Krakatau** volcano; rolling tea plantations around the Puncak Pass; the cultural centre of **Bandung**, where dramatic ram fights take place to the sound of Sundanese flutes and drums; and the popular coastal haven of **Pangandaran**. Moving across the island, Central Java is the heartland of ethnic Javanese art, education and language. **Surakarta** and **Yogyakarta** (more often known as Solo and Yogya) are the ancient capital cities of Central Java's royal families – both fabulously evocative, and steeped in a refined and elaborate culture. The province also boasts the finest classical ruins in the archipelago, from the huge **Borobudur** (Buddhist) and **Prambanan** (Hindu) temples, to the enigmatic ruins of the **Dieng plateau**. Most tourists head to East Java for the awesome volcanic scenery around smoking **Gunung Bromo**, while the marvellous rolling uplands of the **Ijen Plateau** and the idiosyncratic backwater of **Pulau Madura** are luring increasing numbers of visitors. Whilst nothing could entice most people to the monster metropolis of **Surabaya**, the nearby university city of **Malang** is a cool, attractive alternative for exploring the area.

The sixth largest island in the world, over 1800km long, **Sumatra** has everything in abundance and nothing in miniature: its mountain ranges, lakes and national parks are vast, its cities overwhelming, its roads long and arduous, and it even plays host to a couple of the largest flowers in the world. While there is little appeal to **Medan**, the main city of the island, the rest of the province of North Sumatra is becoming a poplar tourist destination, thanks to attractions such as the wonderful **orang-utan sanctuary** at Bukit Lawang, the resorts of **Danau Toba** (home to the Toba Batak people, whose reputation for aggression and occasional cannibalism kept explorers at bay for centuries), the surfers' mecca of **Nias** and the chilly little hill resort of **Berastagi**. **Aceh**, the fiercely Islamic (by Indonesian standards) autonomous province to the north, features the **Gunung Leuser national park** – the largest park in Southeast Asia, with such exotic inhabitants as the clouded leopard, marbled cat and sun bear – and a number of exquisite paradise islands, including **Pulau Weh**, the northernmost island in Indonesia. Further south, the area around **Bukittinggi** is best known as the homeland of the **Minangkabau** people, with their distinctive matrilineal culture, flamboyant architecture and dances, colourful costume and unique cuisine. **Danau Maninjau** is developing as a laid-back resort, and many people use the west coast port of Padang as a jumping-off point to the richly forested **Mentawai Islands**, where the inhabitants still maintain their subsistence economy, living in communal longhouses in intimate harmony with the natural world. However, many travellers hurtle through the southern half of Sumatra in their headlong rush to Yogyakarta, and miss the highlights of the **Kerinci-Seblat national park**, with Sumatra's highest mountain and brilliant trekking; the strange megaliths of the upland Pagaralam area; the remote and idyllic coast around Krui; and the mountains of the South Bukit Barisan national park, which shelter rhinos and tigers – although a few visitors do make it to the remarkable elephant training school in the **Way Kambas national park**. Over to the east of Sumatra, the extensive, scattered **Riau Islands** are an economical route into Indonesia from Singapore and, for adventurers with time to spare, the lovely **Lingga Islands** to the south are attractive possibilities, as are sleepy, undeveloped **Pulau Bangka** and **Pulau Belitung**, off the southeast coast.

Just east of Java, the Hindu island of **Bali**, the longtime jewel in the crown of Indonesian tourism, continues to draw over a million visitors each year to its shores. While some of the island is undeniably concrete jungle, its appeal is still very evident – in pristine beaches, elegant temples studding the fabulous verdant landscape of the interior, and some of the loveliest hotels in Indonesia. Bali has facilities for every pocket, plus beautiful art, dance, music and textiles and colourful religious festivals. The most popular areas are the hectic and happening coastal resorts of **Kuta** and **Legian** in the south, **Lovina** in the north, where you can snorkel, dive and dolphin-watch from the black-sand beach, and the cultural centre of **Ubud**, where painting, carving, dancing and music-making is the lifeblood of the area. Further afield, the central volcanoes provide great hiking away from the crowds, whilst the main temple and spiritual heart of the island, **Besakih**, is firmly on the tourist trail but dramatically located on the slopes of **Gunung Agung**, Bali's highest mountain.

The up-and-coming region for visitors are the arcs of islands which comprise **Nusa Tenggara**. The beautiful beaches and temples of **Lombok** have provided an overflow for Bali for over a decade, but visitors who brave an erratic ferry service are discovering the delights of remote and intriguing islands such as divided **Timor**, and **Sumba**, where intricate fabrics are produced and grand funeral ceremonies punctuate the religious calendar. Nusa Tenggara's main attraction is its immense variety: neighbouring islands can be as different as if they were on separate continents. Star attractions, in addition to great surfing, include the coloured crater lakes of Keli Mutu on **Flores** and the world's largest lizards – **Komodo dragons**. However, Nusa Tenggara's most lasting impression comes from the traditional animist lifestyles of its peoples, and festivals such as the *pasola*, where hundreds of brightly dressed horsemen attack each other with spears in a wild and exuberant ritual battle.

Kalimantan is Indonesia's lion share of the island of Borneo, and, though the romance associated with the name is often confounded by the effects of natural and man-made calamities, there are still some wild corners left to explore. The pick of these are at **Tanjung Puting**, a southwestern fragment of protected riverine forest offering guaranteed close contact with orang-utans; the **Bentuang Karimun national park** on the border with Sarawak, where a vast area of rainforest remains virtually untouched; the **Gunung Palung Reserve**, home to a large population of proboscis monkeys; and – much harder to reach – traditional **Dayak villages** in Kalimantan's unspoilt central mountains and jungles. There's also the chance to make some monumental river journeys by following either the western Kapuas or eastern Mahakam upstream to the centre of the island, where the truly hardy can hike between the sources and follow the opposite flow down to the far coast. Kalimantan's cities are generally functional, purpose-built places, though the Muslim port of **Banjarmasin**, complete with floating markets and nearby diamond mines, has at least some character.

The geography of **Sulawesi** has divided the island into three areas which, despite recent road-building, remain distinct. The southern third is split between the coastal

Bugis – famous seafarers and infamous pirates, with a lively history and excellent ship-building skills – and highland Torajans, one of Indonesia's most self-confident and out-going ethnic groups. Central Sulawesi's attractions range from the easy scenery of the **Togian Islands** and **Danau Poso**, to hard-core hiking in the mountainous fringes in search of elusive megalithic cultures. Meanwhile, the north of the island contains untouched rainforest, with Indonesia's best scuba diving to be found around **Pulau Bunaken**, out from the easygoing city of **Manado**.

Fragmented as it is, **Maluku** remains one of the country's least travelled regions, as getting around is notoriously time-consuming. It's worth the effort, however: focused on the small island-capital of **Ambon**, the central island group includes truly wild and virtually unexplored mountain forests on **Pulau Seram** and **Pulau Buru**, famed for their birdlife and reclusive inhabitants, along with the picturesque volcanoes and seascapes of the Banda Islands, only an overnight boat ride away. In northern Maluku, the twin islands of **Ternate** and **Tidore** house the remains of formerly powerful sultanates, while roads across neighbouring **Halmahera** lead past rusting relics of the World War II Japanese occupation and take you within striking distance of **Morotai**, a distant island outpost with pivotal wartime associations. Most remote of all, Maluku's southeastern islands include superb beaches and the fragmentary cultural relics of the **Kei** and **Tanimbar** groups, while **Aru** is one of the least touched areas in all Indonesia, with birds of paradise amongst its mix of Asian and Australasian wildlife.

In the far east of Indonesia, **Irian Jaya**, located to the west of Papua New Guinea on one of the world's largest islands, is a Holy Grail for explorers: great areas of its rainforests, mountains and valleys remain untouched by Western incursion. Most visitors will plan their trips around this inhospitable but fascinating region from the capital city **Jayapura**, or from **Pulau Biak**, which has fabulous birds and coral reefs. Planes penetrate to the **Baliem Valley**, the highland home of the Dani people, who hunt with bows and arrows and wear penis gourds and feathered headdresses. In the south, the **Asmat region** has a rich artistic tradition, producing expressively carved shields, masks and totem poles. On the **Bird's Head Peninsula, Fak Fak** features stunning ancient cave paintings, **Manokwari** and **Nabire** have gorgeous lakes, and the **Cenderawasih National Reserve** is fringed by delicate reefs, perfect for divers. There are a multitude of other exciting destinations in Irian, but they are the preserve of modern-day Marco Polos and occasional missionaries.

When to go

Indonesia's **climate** is highly complex. The whole archipelago is tropical, with temperatures at sea level always between 21°C and 33°C, although cooler in the mountains. In theory, the year divides into a wet and dry season depending on the effects of the two major winds, the **monsoons**, that drive wet or dry air towards the islands. However, in many places it's pretty hard to tell the difference between wet and dry, and the heat and humidity can be extremely oppressive at any time of the year. Very roughly, in much of the country November to April are the wet months (January and February the wettest) and May through to October are dry. However, in northern Sumatra and central and northern Maluku, this pattern is effectively reversed.

The whole picture becomes even more difficult when you take into account the local microclimates that pattern the islands, moderating the overall picture due to mountains and winds, and sea breezes can temper even the most oppressive climate. Generally, in purely practical terms, the best time to visit is outside the **rainy season**; during the rains, you can expect transport, especially ferries and small planes, to be disrupted, roads and rivers to flood, and mountain-climbing to become both dangerous and unrewarding. In the gaps between downpours, though, the newly washed landscape is at its most dazzlingly beautiful.

Another factor to take into account is the wealth of **local festivals** (see p.50), many of which are movable against the Western calendar. The **peak tourist season** across the islands is between mid-June and mid-September and again over the Christmas and New Year season for Western visitors. This is particularly relevant in the major resorts, where prices rocket and rooms can be fully booked for days, and sometimes weeks, on end. Bear in mind also that there is a large domestic tourist market; major Indonesian holidays see everyone moving to their favourite spot, and the end of Ramadan brings national chaos, with many people travelling to visit their families.

AVERAGE DAILY TEMPERATURES (°C, MAX AND MIN) AND MONTHLY RAINFALL (MM)											
	Jan	Feb	March	April	May	June	July	Aug	Sept	Oct	Nov	Dec
Ambon (Maluku)												
Max (°C)	31	31	31	30	29	28	27	27	28	29	31	31
Min (°C)	24	24	24	24	24	23	23	23	23	23	24	24
Rainfall (mm)	127	119	135	279	516	638	602	401	241	155	114	132
Balikpapan (Kalimantan)												
Max (°C)	29	30	30	29	29	29	28	29	29	29	29	29
Min (°C)	23	23	23	23	23	23	23	23	23	23	23	23
Rainfall (mm)	201	175	231	208	231	193	180	163	140	132	168	206
Jakarta (Java)												
Max (°C)	29	29	30	31	31	31	31	31	31	31	30	29
Min (°C)	23	23	23	24	24	23	23	23	23	23	23	23
Rainfall (mm)	300	300	211	147	114	97	64	43	66	112	142	203
Makassar (Sulawesi)												
Max (°C)	29	29	29	30	31	30	30	31	31	31	30	29
Min (°C)	23	24	23	23	23	22	21	21	21	22	23	23
Rainfall (mm)	686	536	424	150	89	74	36	10	15	43	178	610
Padang (Sumatra)												
Max (°C)	31	31	31	31	31	31	31	31	30	30	30	30
Min (°C)	23	23	23	24	24	23	23	23	23	23	23	23
Rainfall (mm)	351	259	307	363	315	307	277	348	152	495	518	480

PART ONE

THE

BASICS

GETTING THERE FROM BRITAIN AND IRELAND

Java's Sukarno-Hatta airport in Jakarta, and Bali's Ngurah Rai airport at the regional capital, Denpasar, are the major international gateways to Indonesia. The most expensive time to fly to Indonesia is during high season, which on most airlines runs from the beginning of July through to the end of August and also includes most of December. During these peak months, a discounted flight is likely to cost you around £700; flights get booked solid and should be reserved several weeks in advance. Prices drop considerably at other times of the year, when you should be able to find a fare for under £550.

AIRLINES

Aeroflot, 70 Piccadilly, London W1V 9HH (☎0171/355 2233; www.aeroflotl.com); Dublin Airport (☎01/844 6166) Shannon Airport (☎061/472 299). Once a week from Heathrow to Jakarta via Moscow.

British Airways, 156 Regent St, London W1R 5TA (www.british-airways.com); 101–102 Cheapside, London EC2V 6DT; Victoria Place, Victoria Station, London SW1W 9SJ; 146 New St, Birmingham B2 4HN; 19–21 St Mary's Gate, Market St, Manchester M1 1PU; 66 New Broadmead, Bristol BS1 2DL; 66 Gordon St, Glasgow G1 3RS; 32 Frederick St, Edinburgh EH2 2JR; 209 Union St, Aberdeen AB1 2BA (all enquiries ☎0345/222111); 1 Fountain Centre, College St, Belfast BT1 6ET (☎0345/222 111). Direct flights from Heathrow to Jakarta six times a week.

Cathay Pacific, 7 Appletree Yard, Duke of York St, London SW1Y 6LD (☎0171/747 8888; www.cathaypacific.com). Daily flights to Jakarta and Bali via Hong Kong, with an overnight stay in Hong Kong.

Garuda Indonesia, 35 Duke St, London W1M 5DF (☎0171/486 3010; www.garuda.co.id). Three flights a week from London to Bali, with connections to elsewhere in Indonesia.

KLM, reservations (☎0990/750 900; www.klm.nl/); ticket office at Terminal 4, Heathrow. Daily flights to Bali, via Amsterdam and either Singapore or Jakarta. Good connections with regional airports, especially Manchester and Glasgow.

Lauda Air, Units 1 & 2, 123 Buckingham Palace Rd, London SW1W 9SH (☎0171/630 5924; www.laudaair.com). Inexpensive flights from London to Denpasar via Vienna, but currently only operates once a week.

Malaysia Airlines, 61 Piccadilly, London W1V 9HL (☎0171/341 2020; www.malaysiaair.com); 20 Upper Merrion St, Dublin 2 (☎01/676 1561 or 676 2131). Daily flights to Ujung Pandang, Bali, and Jakarta via Kuala Lumpur.

Qantas, Travel Shop, 182 The Strand, London WC2R 1ET (☎0345/747767; www.qantas.com.au). Three flights weekly to Bali and Jakarta via Singapore.

Royal Brunei Airlines, 49 Cromwell Rd, London SW7 2ED (☎0171/584 6660). Inexpensive flights to Bali, Surabaya, Jakarta and Balikpapan, often involving long waits in Brunei, but with good connection times once a week.

Silk Air, see "Singapore Airlines" (www.silkair.com). Daily flights from Singapore to Mataram (Lombok), and twice a week to Manado in north Sulawesi.

Singapore Airlines, 143–147 Regent St, London W1R 7LB (☎0181/747 0007; www.singaporeair.com); 3rd Floor, 29 Dawson St, Dublin 2 (☎01/671 0722). Fast daily flights via Singapore to Bali; longer connecting times for onward flights to Lombok.

Thai International, 41 Albemarle St, London W1X 4LE (☎0171/499 9113; www.thaiair.com). Daily flights to Jakarta or Bali via Bangkok.

If you're flying from a **regional British airport** or **from Ireland**, you'll need to add on the return fare to London, as there are no direct flights to Indonesia from any of these departure points.

With a long-haul destination such as Indonesia, it's always worth considering stopping off for a few days en route – an option offered free of charge by a number of Asian airlines – or putting together a more extensive Circle Asia or Round-the-World itinerary (see p.10).

TO JAVA AND BALI

From London, there are direct flights to **Jakarta** with British Airways, and to **Bali** with Garuda; otherwise, the fastest and most comfortable way of reaching Java or Bali from Britain is with either Singapore Airlines, Malaysia Airlines or Qantas, all of which make the journey in around eighteen hours, including an hour or two's wait in either Singapore or Kuala Lumpur.

Other airlines (see box on p.3) have longer connection times in either Europe or Asia, which add several hours to the journey, though they do sometimes slice a fair bit off the price. Currently, Lauda Air and Royal Brunei are quoting the cheapest **fares**, at around £450 low season and £510 during high season. Garuda also offers a good deal during the low season, with a similar fare, but their peak-season rate jumps to over £700.

TO PROVINCIAL INDONESIA

If you're prepared to change planes along the way, you can take a Garuda flight from London to Bali, and then on via Jakarta to Medan (**Sumatra** £550 low season/£700 high season return) or anywhere else that Garuda fly to Indonesia.

Another option is to use a different Southeast Asian carrier and fly into provincial Indonesia via a stopover elsewhere in the region. For example, you can fly direct from Britain to Singapore with Singapore Airlines and then change onto its subsidiary Silk Air for direct flights so either Mataram (**Lombok** £500/680) or Manado (**Sulawesi** £500/635). Alternatively, Malaysia Airways flies to Sulawesi's capital, **Ujung Pandang**, via Kuala Lumpur (£475/650), and Royal Brunei offers flights to Balikpapan in **Kalimantan**, and **Surabaya** in Java (from £580 and £455 low season respectively) via Brunei.

VISIT INDONESIA PASS

Those flying to Indonesia on Garuda Airways might want to make use of the **Visit Indonesia Pass**, available either when you buy your international ticket, or from Garuda agents once you've arrived in Indonesia. For £190/US$300 you get three coupons, each valid for a single domestic flight on Garuda; you can also buy up to another three coupons for £60/US$100 each. If you don't have an international fare with Garuda, the first three coupons cost £280/US$450, with subsequent coupons at £90/US$150 each.

While this can be a good deal if you plan to cross the country at some stage, check that Garuda actually flies to where you want to go – Merpati and other services have taken over many of their domestic routes – and whether the fare might cost less than £60/US$100 if purchased within Indonesia.

BUYING A TICKET

Booking a scheduled ticket direct with the airline is the most expensive way to fly. Generally, you're best off booking through an established **discount agent**, which can usually undercut airline prices by a significant amount. See the box on p.5 for a list of recommended agents, all of which are members of official travel organizations such as ABTA or IATA, which means that you'll get a refund on your fare should the company go bust. Bucket-shop adverts in national Sunday papers, London's *Evening Standard* newspaper or *Time Out* magazine, or in major regional newspapers and listings magazines, may give even better deals, but possibly lack ABTA/IATA affiliation.

If you are a **student** or **under 26**, you may be able to get further discounts on flight prices, especially through agents like Usit CAMPUS or STA Travel (see opposite). However, for this part of the world, there's often little difference between a youth fare and a regular discounted one.

STOPOVERS, OPEN JAWS AND ROUND-THE-WORLD TICKETS

If you want to make full use of all that flying time and **stop over** on the way there or back, you'll probably have to go with the associated national airline – for example, Malaysia Airlines for stops in Kuala Lumpur or Thai International for a break in Bangkok – for which service there should be no extra charge. Garuda offer free stopovers in either Bangkok or Singapore (depending on the routing) and, for a

DISCOUNT FLIGHT AGENTS

Bridge the World, 47 Chalk Farm Rd, London NW1 8AN (☎0171/911 0900). Specializing in Round-the-World tickets, with good deals aimed at the backpacker market.

Cheap Flights (*www.cheapflights.co.uk*). Online service that lists the day's cheapest flight deals available from subscribing UK flight agents.

Co-op Travel Care, 35 Belmont Rd, Belfast 4 (☎01232/471717). Advertises ten percent discount off listed fares or free travel insurance on all bookings.

Council Travel, 28a Poland St, London W1V 3DB (☎0171/437 7767). Flights and student discounts.

Flightbookers, 177–178 Tottenham Court Rd, London W1P 0LX (☎0171/757 2444); Gatwick Airport, south terminal, British Rail station (daily 7am–10pm; ☎01293/568300); 34 Argyle Arcade, off Buchanan St, Glasgow G1 1RS (☎0141/204 1919). Low fares on an extensive offering of scheduled flights.

Joe Walsh Tours, 34 Grafton St, Dublin 2 (☎01/671 8751); 69 Upper O'Connell St, Dublin 2 (☎01/872 2555); 8–11 Baggot St, Dublin 2 (☎01/676 3053); 117 St Patrick St, Cork (☎021/277959). Budget-fares agent.

The London Flight Centre, 131 Earls Court Rd, London SW5 9RH (☎0171/244 6411); 47 Notting Hill Gate, London W11 3JS (☎0171/727 4290); Shop 33, The Broadway.Centre, Hammersmith tube, London W6 9YE (☎0181/748 6777). Long-established agent dealing in discount flights.

North South Travel, Moulsham Mill Centre, Parkway, Chelmsford CM2 7PX (☎01245/492882). Friendly, competitive travel agency, offering discounted fares worldwide – profits are used to support projects in the developing world, especially the promotion of sustainable tourism.

Quest Worldwide, 10 Richmond Rd, Kingston KT2 5HL (☎0181/547 3322). Specialists in Round-the-World and Australasian discount fares.

STA Travel, 86 Old Brompton Rd, London SW7 3LH; 117 Euston Rd, London NW1 2SX; 38 Store St, London WC1E 7BZ (☎0171/361 6262); 25 Queens Rd, Bristol BS8 1QE (☎0117/929 4399); 38 Sidney St, Cambridge CB2 3HX (☎01223/366966); 75 Deansgate, Manchester M3 2BW (☎0161/834 0668); 88 Vicar Lane, Leeds LS1 7JH (☎0113/244 9212); 36 George St, Oxford OX1 2OJ

(☎01865/792800); and branches in Aberdeen, Birmingham, Canterbury, Cardiff, Coventry, Durham, Glasgow, Loughborough, Nottingham, Warwick and Sheffield. Worldwide specialists in low-cost flights and tours for students and under-26s, though other customers welcome.

Trailfinders, 42–50 Earls Court Rd, London W8 6FT (☎0171/938 3366); 194 Kensington High St, London W8 7RG (☎0171/938 3939); 58 Deansgate, Manchester M3 2FF (☎0161/839 6969); 254–284 Sauchiehall St, Glasgow G2 3EH (☎0141/353 2224); 22–24 The Priory Queensway, Birmingham B4 6BS (☎0121/236 1234); 48 Corn St, Bristol BS1 1HQ (☎0117/929 9000); 4–5 Dawson St, Dublin 2 (☎01/677 7888). One of the best-informed and most efficient agents for independent travellers.

Travel Bag, 52 Regent St, London W1R 6DX; 373–375 The Strand, opposite the *Savoy Hotel*, London WC2R 0JF; 12 High St, Alton GU34 1BN (☎0171/287 5558). Discount flights; official Qantas agent.

The Travel Bug, 125a Gloucester Rd, London SW7 4SF (☎0171/835 2000); 597 Cheetham Hill Rd, Manchester M8 5EJ (☎0161/721 4000). Large range of discounted tickets.

Usit, Fountain Centre, College St, Belfast BT1 6ET (☎01232/324073); 10–11 Market Parade, Patrick St, Cork (☎021/270900); 33 Ferryquay St, Derry (☎01504/371888); 19 Aston Quay, Dublin 2 (☎01/602 1700); Victoria Place, Eyre Square, Galway (☎091/565177); Central Buildings, O'Connell St, Limerick (☎061/415064); 36–37 Georges St, Waterford (☎051/872601). Student and youth specialists.

Usit CAMPUS, 52 Grosvenor Gardens, London SW1W 0AG (☎0171/730 8111); 541 Bristol Rd, Selly Oak, Birmingham B29 6AU (☎0121/414 1848); 61 Ditchling Rd, Brighton BN1 4SD (☎01273/570226); 37–39 Queens Rd, Bristol BS8 1QE (☎0117/929 2494); 5 Emmanuel St, Cambridge CB1 1NE (☎01223/324283); 53 Forest Rd, Edinburgh EH1 2QP (☎0131/225 6111, telesales ☎668 3303); 122 George St, Glasgow G1 1RS (☎0141/553 1818); 166 Deansgate, Manchester M3 3FE (☎0161/273 1721); 105–106 St Aldates, Oxford OX1 1DD (☎01865/242067). Student/youth travel specialists, with branches also in YHA shops and on university campuses all over Britain.

nominal supplement, will allow an extra stop within Indonesia, at Jakarta, Yogyakarta or Medan. If you want to make several stops within the archipelago, it's well worth buying a domestic **air pass** before leaving Britain (see p.10 for details).

Open-jaw tickets are return fares where you make your own way between different arrival and departure points – perfect if you want to avoid retracing your steps. Because many airlines "common-rate" all fares within the region, the cost of an open-jaw ticket may also not be appreciably higher than a return fare. One drawback in Indonesia, however, is that almost all the major airlines – Garuda's domestic connections making it the exception – use only one gateway, though you could fly into Manado or Mataram and leave from Bali on Silk Air/Singapore, while Royal Brunei offer the option of flying into Balikpapan and leaving from Bali, Suarabaya or Jakarta.

If you're thinking of continuing on to Australia, you'll find it much cheaper to buy a through-ticket to Perth or Sydney on Garuda with a stopover in Denpasar (£750–950 depending on the season). Alternatively, consider investing in a **Round-the-World ticket**, which allows you several stops in Asia or elsewhere. For example, a one-year open ticket from London taking in Bangkok, Bali, Brunei, Brisbane/Melbourne, Auckland and New York starts for as little as £750, rising to around £1000 if you add stops in India and the South Pacific.

ORGANIZED TOURS AND PACKAGE HOLIDAYS

Inevitably more expensive and less spontaneous than if you travelled independently, **package tours** to Indonesia are nonetheless worth investigating if you have limited time or a specialist interest. They include resort-based trips through to overland trekking excursions, cruises and specialist surfing or diving expeditions. It's also sometimes possible to use them as a starting point to your holiday, allowing you to get the feel of the place with minimal hassles – just check before booking that you can stay on independently and fly back at a later date. Your local travel agent should be able to book any tour for you at no additional cost.

A large chunk of the holiday price goes on the flight, so anything below £750 for room-only rates is good value; many companies are quoting for five-night trips now, rather than a full week, so be vigilant when reading brochures. If you are planning a **hotel-based holiday**, the range of accommodation on offer will be limited and generally towards the top end of the market.

For a more varied and energetic experience, several companies offer **overland trips**, ranging from bussing between Java and Bali via the main sights, to hard-core hiking through Irian Jaya or Kalimantan. The range of **cruises** on offer is huge,

SPECIALIST TOUR OPERATORS

Abercrombie & Kent, Sloane Square House, Holbein Place, London SW1W 8NS (☎0171/730 9600, fax 730 9376; *www.abercrombiekent.com*). Top-of-the-range trips (they are specialists in tailor-made trips) using luxury hotels. Some are based in Bali, others are part of extensive tours through Indonesia including Sumatra, Java or Sulawesi. Prices for a week in the *Oberoi* in Bali start at £1070.

Airwaves, 10 Becktive Place, London SW15 2PZ (☎0181/875 1188). Beach-based holidays in Bali and Lombok (from £773 for five nights) plus a variety of combinations with other Far Eastern destinations including Hong Kong and Beijing (from £1490).

Arc Journeys, 102 Stanley Rd, Cambridge CB5 8LB (☎01223 779200, fax 779090; *ArcJourney@aol.com*). Tailor-made specialists with a large portfolio of suggestions for trips to Indonesia. They also have "The Spice Islands", a

series of seven-day tours of Bali, Maluku, Sulawesi and Flores that can be combined for an individual trip (£550 per week excluding flights) and "Volcanoes and Beaches", a fifteen-day trip (£850).

Bales, Bales House, Junction Rd, Dorking RH4 3HB (☎01306/885991, fax 740048). Ten-day escorted tour through Java and Bali, from £995, with optional extensions in Sulawesi, Lombok or on the *Bali Sea Dancer* for the seven-night Spice Island cruise east to Maluku.

Earthwatch Institute, Belsyre Court, 57 Woodstock Rd, Oxford OX2 6HU (☎01865/311600, fax 311383; *info@uk. earthwatch.org*). Volunteer work on ever-changing Indonesia-wide projects, including assisting locally based archeologists or biologists, or helping in community programmes. Groups are small and you tend to stay with local people rather than in hotels; costs – excluding flights – start at around £1000 for two weeks.

Exodus, 9 Weir Rd, London SW12 0LT (☎0181/675 5550, fax 673 0779; *sales@exodustravels.co.uk*, *www.exodustravels.co.uk*). "Java, Bali and Lombok" is a seventeen-day trip (from £1120) from Jakarta, which includes Ubud and Tirtagangga in Bali and Tetebatu and Sengiggi on Lombok. There is also a seven-week "South East Asia Overland" trip (from £1090) between Bangkok and Bali. All prices exclude flights.

Explore, 1 Frederick St, Aldershot GU11 1LQ (☎01252/319448, fax 343170; *infor@explore.co.uk*, *www.explore.co.uk*). A variety of adventure holidays are available, including a 31-day overland trip from Medan to Bali (from £1090 without flights, £1885 with flights), also available in shorter segments, and a fifteen-day East Indies *Seatrek* sailing from Bali to Flores (from £1295 without flights, £1760 with flights).

Footprint Adventures, 5 Malham Drive, Lincoln LN6 0XD (☎01522 690852, fax 501392; *sales@footventure.co.uk* *www.footventure.co.uk*). This company is a trekking and wildlife specialist and the trips include the twelve-day "Sumatra Expedition", taking in Bukit Lawang, the Kerinci-Seblat national park and Krakatau (twelve days from £1250), the five-day "Rinjani Adventure" including the climb to the summit (five days from £185), and Ujung Kulon national park (seven days from £700). All prices exclude flights.

Guerba, Wessex House, 40 Station Rd, Westbury BA13 3JN (☎01373 858956, fax 858351). This well-established overland tour company offers a two-week trip from Jakarta to Bali, from £750 excluding flights.

Hayes and Jarvis, Hayes House, 152 King St, London W6 0QU (☎0181/748 5050). A range of south Bali and Lombok (Senggigi) holidays, from £718 for one island and £828 if you combine Bali and Lombok, plus a fourteen-night Java to Bali overland trip (from £1289).

Imaginative Traveller, 14 Barley Mow Passage, London W4 4PH (☎0181/742 8612, fax 742 3045; *info@imaginative-traveller.com*, *www.imaginative-traveller.com*). Broad selection of tours to less-travelled parts of the island, including walking, cycling, camping and snorkelling. Trips start from around £500, excluding airfares.

Kuoni Worldwide, Kuoni House, Dorking RH5 4AZ (☎01306/740500). Hotel-based holidays in Indonesia from £598 for five nights. Plenty of chances for add-ons too, from island cruises to tours taking in other destinations in Southeast Asia.

Magic of the Orient, 2 Kingsland Court, Three Bridges Rd, Crawley RH10 1HL (☎01293/537700, fax 537888). Hotel-based holidays in the southern resorts on Bali, Senggigi or the Oberoi on Lombok from £760 for five nights including flights, with optional add-ons in Ubud or cruising east on the *Oceanic Odyssey* or *Bali Sea Dancer*.

Noble Caledonia Limited, 11 Charles St, London W1X 8LE (☎0171/409 0376, fax 409 0834). Luxury cruise line that includes a sixteen-day "Beyond Borobodur" trip from Singapore to Bali, including visits to the Tambelan and Kangean islands. From £3690 all-inclusive.

Silverbird, 4 Northfields Prospect, Putney Bridge Rd, London SW18 1PE (☎0181/875 9090, fax 875 1874). Far East specialist offering tailor-made holidays including Bali and/or Lombok. They occasionally advertise "Golden Opportunities", which are extremely good-value special deals for a limited period – for example, ten days in Sanur from £699 (flights and room only).

Steppes East, Castle Eaton, Cricklade SN6 6JU (☎01285/810267, fax 810693; *sales@steppeseast.co.uk*, *www.steppeseast.co.uk*). A top-of-the-range company, specializing in tailor-made trips throughout Indonesia which are available all year, but also offering small-group trips such as "By Boat on the River of Diamonds", a fourteen-day trip in Central Kalimantan (from £2200).

Thomas Cook Holidays, PO Box 36, Thorpe Wood, Peterborough PE3 6SB (☎01733/332255). Wide choice of hotel-based holidays, primarily in Bali and Java. From £850 for seven days.

Travelbag Adventures, 15 Turk St, Alton GU34 1AG (☎0171/287 7744, fax 01420/541022; *www.travelbag-adventures.co.uk*). Offers a small-group trip (maximum twelve people) from Jakarta to Bali taking seventeen days and costing from £1095 with flights. There is also an option without flights.

World Dreams, 3rd Floor, Waterloo House, 11–17 Chertsey Rd, Woking GU21 5AB (☎01483/726699, fax 721919). A huge range of Bali beach-based holidays (five nights from £741 including flights), with extensions to take in Lombok or cruises eastwards.

from two- or three-day tasters to much longer voyages taking in a wider area of Asia; be sure to check how long you have ashore at specific stops if you plan to explore anywhere in particular.

Sold as the ultimate in romantic destinations, several companies, including Thomas Cook Holidays, Kuoni Worldwide and Airwaves, offer packages catering for those intending to **get married on Bali**. You will have to complete certain formalities at the British Embassy in Jakarta

and be resident in Indonesia for ten working days before the marriage. Men must be at least 23 years old and women 21 and they must be of the same religion. On top of the standard holiday you book with the tour operator, you should count on an extra £750–1000 for the Jakarta practicalities and some wedding decorations, flowers and champagne – deals vary slightly, so it is important to check exactly what is and is not included.

GETTING THERE FROM THE USA AND CANADA

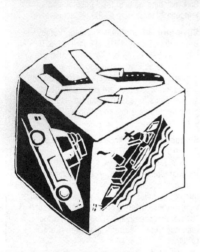

At the time of writing, all flights from North America to Indonesia on the national airline Garuda have been suspended due to Asia's economic crisis; call the number given in the airlines box (p.9) to check current status. From the US and Canada there's a choice of flights on other carriers, either flying across the Pacific or the Atlantic.

Prices quoted are round-trip, assume midweek travel (where there's a difference in price), exclude taxes (roughly US$45/CAN$30) and are subject to availability and change.

FLIGHTS FROM THE US

While a number of airlines (see box on p.5) will fly you **from the US** to Jakarta (on Java) or Denpasar (on Bali), if your destination is one of the other

islands then you'll probably find it most convenient to take Singapore Airlines, whose subsidiary, Silk Air, operates connections to Sumatra, Lombok, Kalimantan and Sulawesi. You might also want to bear in mind that most of the Asian national airlines allow one free stopover each way (additional stopovers cost extra). On Malaysia Airlines flying westward, for example, you could spend a few days in Tokyo, Taipei or Kuala Lumpur.

Singapore Airlines currently offer the best value on published fares to **Jakarta** or **Denpasar**. Their round-trip APEX fares from LA to Denpasar are US$1150 (low season)/US$1395 (high season); from LA to Jakarta, US$1080 (low)/US$1420 (high); from New York to Denpasar, US$900 (low)/US$1350 (high); from New York to Jakarta, US$1070 (low)/US$1350 (high).

However, you should first shop around for a better price from **discount agents** (see p.9) or your local travel agent. At the time of writing, for instance, low-season fares to Bali were available for as little as US$750 (New York–Denpasar) or US$850 (LA–Denpasar). As with all long-haul flights involving a possible change of planes, complex scheduling and big time differences, you'd be well advised to double-check the details of any lay-overs involved in the various routings.

FLIGHTS FROM CANADA

From Canada your best option is a flight on one of the Asian airlines. Cathay Pacific's published APEX fares from Toronto to either Jakarta or Denpasar are currently CAN$2233 (low season)/CAN$2507 (high). From Vancouver their rates to both cities are CAN$1977 (low) or CAN$2271 (high). Once again, you'll most likely

AIRLINES

Cathay Pacific (☎800/233-2742; *www.cathay-usa.com*). Flies via Hong Kong daily from New York, Los Angeles, Vancouver and Toronto to Denpasar and Jakarta, and twice weekly to Surabaya.

China Airlines (☎800/227-5118; *www.china-airlines.com*). Daily flights from Los Angeles and San Francisco and Monday, Wednesday, Friday, Saturday and Sunday flights from New York to Denpasar and Jakarta. All via Taiwan.

Garuda Indonesia (US ☎800/342-7832, Canada ☎800/663-2254; *www.garuda.co.id*). All Garuda flights from North America to Indonesia are currently suspended.

Japan Airlines (☎800/525-3663; *www.jal.co.jp*). Daily flights, via Tokyo, from New York, Chicago, Atlanta, San Francisco , Los Angeles and Vancouver to Denpasar and Jakarta.

Northwest/KLM (☎800/447-4747; *www.klm.nl*). Daily flights to Denpasar or Jakarta from Los Angeles or New York via Tokyo and Singapore.

Malaysia Airlines (☎800/552-9264; *www.malaysiaairlines.com.my*). Flies to Jakarta and Denpasar westward from Los Angeles (via Taipei, Tokyo or Kuala Lumpur) every day except Tuesday or eastward from Newark, New Jersey (via Kuala Lumpur or Dubai) each Tuesday, Friday and Sunday.

Singapore Airlines (☎800/742-3333; *www.singaporeair.com*). Daily flights to Denpasar, Jakarta and Surabaya from Los Angeles and San Francisco (via the Pacific) and New York (via Europe). Also flights from Vancouver three times a week. All flights are via Singapore, from where, on certain days of the week, you can also connect on Singapore Airlines' sister company Silk Air to Padang, Pekanbaru, Medan, Lombok, Balikpapan,Ujung Panang, Manado and Solo.

Thai Airways International (US ☎800/426-5204, Canada ☎800/668-8103; *www.thaiair.com*). Daily flights to Jakarta and Denpasar from Los Angeles via Osaka and Bangkok.

get better deals from a discount outfit or even your local travel agent. At the time of writing, there were return fares to Jakarta from Toronto for around CAN$1280 (low season)/CAN$1760 (high) and from Vancouver for CAN$1350 (low)/CAN$1890 (high).

BUYING A TICKET

Barring special offers, the cheapest of the airlines' published fares is usually an **Apex ticket**, although this will carry certain restrictions. You will, most likely, have to book – and pay – 21 days before departure, spend at least seven days abroad (maximum stay three months), and you tend to get penalized if you change your schedule. Some airlines also issue **Special Apex** tickets to people younger than 24, often extending the maximum stay to a year, as well as **youth or student fares** to under-26s – a passport or driving licence is sufficient proof of age, though these tickets are subject to availability and can have eccentric booking conditions. It's worth remembering that most cheap return fares involve spending at least one Saturday night away and that many will only give a percentage refund if you need to cancel or alter your journey, so make sure you check the restrictions carefully before buying a ticket.

Fares vary depending on the **season**; on flights to Asia there are usually only two seasons to choose from – high and low – although you may find (especially on flights from Canada) a third "shoulder" season complicating matters. Generally speaking, however, fares are highest from June through August and lowest from January through May and September through mid-December. Be prepared for a price hike around the Christmas holiday period. Note also that flying on weekends may mean US$70–/CAN$100 extra on the round-trip fare.

CONSOLIDATORS, DISCOUNT AGENTS AND COURIER FLIGHTS

You can normally cut costs by going through a specialist flight agent – either a **consolidator**, who buys up blocks of tickets from the airlines and sells them at a discount, or a **discount agent**, who, in addition to dealing with discounted flights, may also offer special student and youth fares and a range of other travel-related services such as travel insurance, rail passes, car rentals, tours and the like. Bear in mind, though, that penalties for changing your plans can be stiff. Remember, too, that these companies make their money by dealing in bulk – don't expect them to

CONSOLIDATORS, DISCOUNT AGENTS AND TRAVEL CLUBS

Air Brokers International, 150 Post St, Suite 620, San Francisco, CA 94108 (☎800/883-3273 or 415/397-1383; www.airbrokers.com). Consolidator and specialist in RTW tickets.

Air Courier Association, 15000 W 6th Ave, Suite 203, Golden, CO 80401 (☎800/282-1202 or 303/215-0900; www.aircourier.org). Courier flight broker.

Airtech, 588 Broadway, Suite 204, New York, NY 10017 (☎800/575-8324 or 212/219-7000; www.airtech.com). Standby-seat broker; also deals in consolidator fares and courier flights.

Council Travel, Head Office, 205 E 42nd St, New York, NY 10017 (☎800/226-8624, 888/COUNCIL or 212/822-2700); 530 Bush St, Suite 700, San Francisco, CA 94108 (☎415/421-3473); 10904 Lindbrook Drive, Los Angeles, CA 90024 (☎310/208 3551); 1138 13th St, Boulder, CO 80302 (☎303/447-8101); 3300 M St NW, 2nd Floor, Washington, DC 20007 (☎202/337-6464); 1153 N Dearborn St, Chicago, IL 60610 (☎312/951-0585); 273 Newbury St, Boston, MA 02116 (☎617/266-1926). Nationwide specialists in student and youth travel.

Educational Travel Center, 438 N Frances St, Madison, WI 53703 (☎800/747-5551). Student/youth discount agent.

High Adventure Travel, 353 Sacramento St, Suite 600, San Francisco, CA 94111 (☎800/350-0612 or 415/912-5600; www.highadv.com). Round-the-World and Circle Pacific tickets. Their Web site features an interactive database that lets you build and price your own RTW itinerary.

International Association of Air Travel Couriers, 8 South J St, PO Box 1349, Lake Worth, FL 33460 (☎561/582-8320; www.courier.org). Courier flight broker.

Now Voyager, 74 Varick St, Suite 307, New York, NY 10013 (☎212/431-1616). Courier flight broker and consolidator.

STA Travel, 10 Downing St, New York, NY 10014 (☎800/777-0112 or 212/627-3111); 7202 Melrose Ave, Los Angeles, CA 90046 (☎213/934-8722); 51 Grant Ave, San Francisco, CA 94108 (☎415/391-8407); 297 Newbury St, Boston, MA 02115 (☎617/266-6014); 429 S. Dearborn St, Chicago, IL 60605 (☎312/786-9050); 3730 Walnut St, Philadelphia, PA 19104 (☎215/382-2928); 317 14th Ave SE, Minneapolis, MN 55414 (☎612/615-1800). Worldwide specialists in student and youth travel.

Travel Avenue, 10 S Riverside Plaza, Suite 1404, Chicago, IL 60606 (☎800/333-3335). Discount travel company.

Travel Cuts, 187 College St, Toronto, ON M5T 1P7 (☎800/667-2887 or 416/979-2406; ☎888/238-2887 from US). 180 MacEwan Student Centre, University of Calgary, Calgary, AB T2N 1N4 (☎403/282-7687); 12304 Jasper Ave, Edmonton, AB T5N 3K5 (☎403/488-8487); 1613 Rue St Denis, Montréal, PQ H2X 3K3 (☎514/843-8511); 555 W 8th Ave, Vancouver, BC V5Z 1C6 (☎888/FLY-CUTS or 604/822-6890); University Centre, University of Manitoba, Winnipeg, MB R3T 2N2 (☎204/269-9530). Canadian student travel organization.

answer lots of questions. Some agents specialize in charter flights, which may be cheaper than scheduled flights, but again departure dates are fixed and withdrawal penalties are high (check the refund policy). If you travel a lot, **discount travel clubs** are another option – the annual membership fee may be worth it for benefits such as cut-price air tickets and car rental.

Don't automatically assume that tickets purchased through a travel specialist will be cheapest – once you get a quote, check with the airlines and you may turn up an even better deal. Be advised also that the pool of travel companies is swimming with sharks – exercise caution and never deal with a company that demands cash up front or refuses to accept payment by credit card.

A further possibility is to see if you can arrange a **courier flight**, although the hit-or-miss nature of these makes them most suitable for the single traveller who travels light and has a very flexible schedule. In return for shepherding a parcel through customs and possibly giving up your baggage allowance, you can expect to get a very inexpensive ticket. However, it's unlikely you'll find a courier flight direct to Indonesia. Your nearest option would probably be to go Hong Kong, from where you might be able to pick up another courier flight to Jakarta. A couple of courier flight brokers are listed in the box above.

CIRCLE PACIFIC, ROUND-THE-WORLD TICKETS AND AIR PASSES

If Indonesia is only one stop on a longer journey, you might want to consider buying a **Round-the-World** (RTW) or **Circle Pacific** ticket. Some travel agents can sell you an "off-the-shelf"

SAMPLE ITINERARIES

Circle Pacific

San Francisco–Hong Kong–Bangkok–Jakarta–Denpasar–Los Angeles for US$1150; Los Angeles–Sydney–Auckland–Denpasar–Singapore–Bangkok–Tokyo–San Francisco for US$1820; New York–Hong Kong–Bangkok–Jakarta–Denpasar–Los Angeles–New York for US$1440; New York–Taipei–Singapore–Denpasar–Brisbane/overland on your own/Sydney–Christchurch/overland on your own/Auckland–Nadi (Fiji)–Rarotonga (Cooks)–Papeete (Tahiti)–Los Angeles–New York for US$1950.

RTW

Los Angeles–Denpasar–Jakarta–Singapore–Madras–Delhi–Paris–Los Angeles for US$1710; Los Angeles–Denpasar–Bangkok–Kathmandu–Delhi–Bombay–Nairobi–Cairo–Athens–London–Los Angeles for US$2540; New York–Los Angeles–Denpasar–Bangkok–Rome/overland on your own/Milan–London–New York for US$1640; New York–Tokyo–Hong Kong–Bangkok–Singapore–Jakarta–Yogyakarta–Denpasar–Darwin/overland on your own/Sydney–Kuala Lumpur–Amsterdam–New York for US$2700.

RTW/Circle Pacific ticket that will have you touching down in about half a dozen cities (Denpasar and/or Jakarta are on several itineraries); other agents will assemble one for you, which can be tailored to your needs but is apt to be more expensive. See the box above for sample itineraries.

Another possibility is Cathay Pacific's **All Asia Pass**, which flies you from either LA or New York to Hong Kong, then gives you thirty days of flights to a choice of seventeen different cities – all for US$999.

SPECIALIST TOURS

You'll find **tour packages** to Indonesia to suit any budget. Asia Transpacific Journeys, with perhaps the widest variety to choose from, offers premium trips such as a 24-day trip to see the "Lost Tribes of Irian Jaya" priced from US$3495, along with a line of cut-rate options like a one-week "Flores Adventure" for US$695 (both land only). Walking and hiking tours have become especially popular on Bali. Backroads offers a ten-day walking tour

for US$2398 and a ten-day bicycling tour for US$2298, plus US$180 bike rental (both land only). Some of the best packages are small-group tours focusing on the art and culture of the area. Asian Pacific Adventures offers a fifteen-day "Bali Through an Artist's Eye" trip, led by an Indonesian textiles expert, visiting woodcarvers, weavers and basketmakers for US$2540, and a ten-day "Romantic Bali-Lombok Honeymoon" combining beaches and rainforest hikes with traditional music, dance, silverwork, *ikat* weaving and batik from US$1325 (both land only).

Remember to check if any **internal airfares** are included in the quoted price of a holiday package. And make sure you're clear about the number of days – once you've taken into account the time difference between North America and Asia – that you'll actually be spending in Indonesia.

All prices quoted in the box (below and on p.12) **exclude taxes** and are subject to change. Accommodation is based on single person/double occupancy. Unless stated otherwise, return flights are from the West Coast.

SPECIALIST OPERATORS

Abercrombie & Kent International, Inc., 1520 Kensington Rd, Oak Brook, IL 60523 (☎800/323-7308 or 630/954-2944; *www.abercrombiekent.com*). Upmarket tour packages plus customized travel. "Exploring Irian Java" fifteen-day cruise from US$4745 (land only).

Adventure Center, 1311 63rd St, Suite 200, Emeryville, CA 94608 (☎800/227-8747 or 510/654-1879; *www.adventure-travel.com*). "Tribal Sumatra" consists of fifteen days'

exploring rainforests, volcanoes and tribal culture from US$860; "East Indies Seatrek" is a fifteen-day beach-hotel-and-schooner cruise from US$2250 (both land only).

Adventures Abroad, 2148-20800 Westminster Hwy, Richmond, BC V6V 2W3 (☎800/665-3998 or 604/303-1099, fax 604/303-1076; *www.adventures-abroad.com*). Small-group tours with a cultural focus. Three weeks on Sumatra, Java, Lombok and Bali from US$3796 (land/air). *continues over/*

Asian Pacific Adventures, 826 South Sierra Bonita Ave, Los Angeles, CA 90036 (☎213/935-3156). Customized tours and arts and culture packages. "Fire, Water, Earth & Tribal Life – A Cultural Odyssey" comprises twenty days on Bali, Sulawesi/Toraja, Flores and Sumba from US$3803 (land and internal flights only).

Asia Transpacific Journeys, 3055 Center Green Drive, Boulder, CO 80301 (☎800/642-2742; *www.southeastasia.com*). Offers a wide range of Indonesia packages.

Backroads, 801 Cedar St, Berkeley, CA 94710-1800 (☎800/462-2848 or 510/527-1555; *www.backroads.com*). Active-holiday specialists.

Garuda Indonesia Vacations, 9841 Airport Blvd, Suite 300, Los Angeles, CA 90045 (☎800/342-7832). Formerly Garuda Orient Holidays, now a tour subsidiary of Garuda Indonesia Airlines. Wide range of packages with activities such as bicycling, diving, white-water rafting, *wakalouka* land cruises and Spice Island cruises.

Geographic Expeditions (aka Inner Asia) 2627 Lombard St, San Francisco, CA 94123 (☎800/777-8183 or 415/922-0448; *www.goex.com*). Twelve days' "Sailing the Savu Seas" from US$3495; eight days in Sulawesi's Tanah Torajda from US$1995 (both land only).

Himalayan Travel, 110 Prospect St, Stamford, CT 06901 (☎800/225-2380; *www.gorp.com//himtravel.htm*). Customized tours plus a variety of packages. Four days on Bali for US$245, plus the "The Dragons of Komodo" tour – three days for US$625 (both land only).

International Gay Travel Association (☎800/448-8550). Trade group with lists of gay-owned or gay-friendly travel agents, accommodation and other travel businesses.

Mountain Travel Sobek, 6420 Fairmount Ave, El Cerrito, CA 94530 (☎888/MTSOBEK; *www.mtsobek.com*). The "Heart of Indonesia" trip comprises fifteen days (twelve in Indonesia) of hiking, biking, rafting and music-making in Bali, Sulawesi and Java from US$2590 (land only).

Saga Holidays, 222 Berkeley St, Boston, MA 02116 (☎800/343-0273). Specialists in group travel for seniors. Sixteen nights at the Balinese resort of Sanur from US$1699 (land/air).

Wilderness Travel, 1102 9th St, Berkeley, CA 94710-1211 (☎800/368-2794 or 510/558-2488; *www.wildernesstravel.com*). "East of Bali" is an eleven-day cultural/natural history cruise from US$2705; "Magical Indonesia" comprises eleven days of cultural exploration, hiking and performing arts on Sulawesi, Java and Bali from US$2680 (both including internal flights).

GETTING THERE FROM AUSTRALIA AND NEW ZEALAND

Despite continual rumours of imminent ferry services, flying is at present the only scheduled way to reach Indonesia from Australia and New Zealand. Low-season fares operate February to March, and October 16 to November 30; shoulder season is January 16–31, April to June and July 1 to October 15; and high season is December 1 to January 15. When buying your ticket, discount agents listed in the box opposite can fill you in on the latest deals and usually give up to a ten percent discount on student and under-26s fares.

FLIGHTS FROM AUSTRALIA

Garuda, Ansett and Qantas all have direct, similarly priced flights several times a week **to**

Denpasar and **Jakarta**. Fares to Denpasar from Sydney, Melbourne, Brisbane, Cairns or Adelaide are common-rated at A$999 (low season) and A$1199 (high season). From Perth it will cost you A$799/A$999, and from Darwin A$699/A$850. For Jakarta, prices from all starting points are around A$100 lower.

For a direct route into provincial Indonesia, catch Merpati's weekly flight from **Darwin to Kupang** in Timor for A$350/A$450, from where you can island-hop west through Nusa Tenggara to Bali, or cruise northeast to Maluku and Irian Jaya. The down side here is reaching Darwin: flights from Perth, the south, or east coasts cost around A$600 return, and Darwin is a very long coach trip from anywhere.

Royal Brunei offers the cheapest **indirect flights** from Australia to Indonesia, flying to Jakarta or Balikpapan from Brisbane (A$850/A$1099 to either), Darwin (A$650/A$899), or Perth (A$750/A$999), via a night in Brunei's capital, Bandar Seri Begawan. Other Southeast Asian airlines stop in Indonesia en route to their home cities, which, while more expensive than direct

AIRLINES

Air New Zealand, Australia ☎13 2476, New Zealand ☎09/357 3000. To Denpasar and Jakarta from Auckland, twice weekly direct and twice weekly via Singapore; from Christchurch and Wellington, twice a week via Auckland.

Ansett Australia, Australia ☎13 1767, New Zealand ☎09/796 409 (*www.ansett.com*). Several direct flights a week to Denpasar and Jakarta from Darwin, Perth and Sydney, plus once a week from Melbourne.

Garuda, Australia ☎02/9334 9944 or 1800/800 873, New Zealand ☎09/366 1855 (*www.garuda.co.id/*). To Denpasar and Jakarta, direct several times a week from Brisbane, Sydney, Melbourne, Perth, Darwin and Auckland.

Malaysia Airlines, Australia ☎13 2627, New Zealand ☎09/373 2741 (*www.malaysiaair.com*). Several flights a week from Australasian capital cities to Kuala Lumpur, via permitted stopovers in Denpasar and Jakarta.

Merpati Nusantara, Australia ☎08/8941 1606 or 1800/060188; no New Zealand office. Weekly direct flights to Kupang from Darwin.

Qantas, Australia ☎13 1211; New Zealand ☎9/357 8900 or 0800/808 767 (*www.qantas.com.au*). Several direct flights a week to Denpasar and Jakarta from Darwin, Melbourne, Sydney and Perth; indirect flights from other cities via Sydney, Melbourne and Darwin.

Royal Brunei, Australia ☎02/9223 1566; no New Zealand office. Twice a week from Brisbane and Darwin to Balikpapan (Kalimantan) via an overnight stopover in Bandar Seri Begawan.

Singapore Airlines, 17 Bridge St, Sydney (☎13 1011); corner of Albert and Fanshawe streets, Auckland (☎09/379 3209; *www.singaporeair.com*). Several flights a week from Australasian capital cities to Singapore via Denpasar and Jakarta.

DISCOUNT FLIGHT AGENTS

Brisbane Discount Travel, 260 Queen St, Brisbane (☎07/3229 9211). Good-value discounter offering flight-and-accommodation packages.

Destinations Unlimited, 3 Milford Rd, Auckland (☎09/373 4033). Long-time operator with experience in Indonesia.

Flight Centres Australia, 82 Elizabeth St, Sydney, plus branches nationwide (☎13 1600); 205 Queen St, Auckland (☎09/309 6171), plus branches nationwide. Good discounts on fares, plus a comprehensive range of tours, cruises and accommodation packages.

STA Travel, 702 Harris St, Ultimo, Sydney; 256 Flinders St, Melbourne; other offices in state capitals and major universities (nearest branch ☎13 1776, fastfare telesales ☎1300/360 960); 10 High St, Auckland (☎09/309 0458, fastfare telesales ☎09/366 6673); plus branches in Wellington, Christchurch, Dunedin, Palmerston North, Hamilton and at major universities; *traveller@statravelaus.com.au*. *www.statravelaus.com.au* Fare discounts for students and under-26s.

Thomas Cook, 175 Pitt St, Sydney; 257 Collins St, Melbourne; plus branches in other state capitals (local branch ☎13 1771; Thomas Cook Direct telesales ☎1800/063 913); 96 Anzac Ave, Auckland (☎09/379 3920). Travellers' cheques and tours.

Tymtro Travel, Level 8, 130 Pitt St, Sydney (☎02/9223 2211 or 1300/652 969). Competitive discounts on fares.

SPECIALIST TUUR OPERATORS

Adventure Specialists, Floor 1, 69 Liverpool St, Sydney (☎02/9261 2927). Agents for adventure wholesalers such as Explore, Peregrine and Exodus.

Adventure World, 73 Walker St, North Sydney (☎1800/221 931); 8 Victoria Ave, Perth (☎08/9221 2300); 101 Great South Rd, Remuera, Auckland (☎09/524 5118). Agents for Explore's escorted packages, which include fifteen to twenty days' investigating different cultures in Java, Sumatra, Bali and Sulawesi, and a fourteen-day "East India Seatrek", sailing between Bali and Flores aboard a bugis schooner (A$1899/NZ$2150). Prices include hotel accommodation, meals and domestic airfares.

Bali Travel Service, 302 Pitt St, Sydney (☎02/9264 5895). Huge range of ever-changing accommodation package deals; phone for details.

Destinations Adventure, 2nd Premier Building, corner of Queen and Durham streets, East Auckland (☎09/309 0464). NZ agents for Peregrine.

Earthwatch, 1st Floor, 453–457 Elizabeth St, Melbourne (☎03/9600 9100; *gilmour@creative.access.com.au*). Volunteer-staffed research programmes ranging from distributing solar-powered ovens to timber-poor villages in Nusa Tenggara, to archeological surveys in Maluku and wildlife studies in Komodo and Kalimantan. Costs A$1600–1900 for two weeks, including food and accommodation.

Exodus, Top Deck Adventure, 8th Floor, 350 Kent St, Sydney (☎02/9299 8844; *topdeck@s054.aone.net.au*). Small escorted groups for a 24-day trip by minibus, boat and plane from Bali, east through the Lesser Sunda islands, exploring villages, volcanoes and coral reefs. A$3699/NZ$4299, including accommodation, meals and airfare from Denpasar to Flores. Aug–Oct.

Garuda Indonesia Holidays (booking through travel agents). Offers three- to five-day leisure, culture and adventure packages everywhere between downtown Jakarta and the highlands of Irian.

Go Travel, 151 Victoria St West, Auckland (☎09/379 5520). General travel agent offering accommodation packages to Indonesia.

Intrepid, 246 Brunswick St, Fitzroy, VIC (☎03/9416 2655). Ever-changing range of expeditions to untouristy destinations across the archipelago, some with local guides. Options include fifteen days between Bali and Jakarta exploring coral reefs, lagoons, nature reserves and historical sites (A$990/NZ$1190), and a two-week river-and-jungle trek across Kalimantan from Samarinda to Pangkalanbun (A$1140/NZ$1370).

Padi Travel Network, 4/372 Eastern Valley Way, Chatswood, Sydney (☎02/9417 2800 or 1800/678 100; *ptn_aust@padi.com.au*). Tailored diving packages to sites in Bali and Lombok.

Peregrine, 258 Lonsdale St, Melbourne (☎03/9663 8611); Sydney (☎02/9290 2770); 407 Great South Rd, Penrose, Auckland (☎09/525 3074). Escorted fifteen-day overland bus trip from Jakarta to Bali taking in the local customs and food along the way (A$1450/NZ$1650); October to February.

Pro Dive Travel, Dymocks Building, 428 George St, Sydney (☎02/9232 5733). Diving packages in Bali and Lombok including airfares, accommodation, diving gear and transport to diving sites – seven nights in Kuta with six dives from A$1299 twin share.

San Michele Travel, 81 York St, Sydney (☎1800/222 244); also offices in Melbourne and Perth. Extensive range of adventure tours and transport–accommodation packages from this Indonesian specialist.

Suntravel, PO Box 12-424, Penrose, Auckland (☎09/525 3047). Agents for Intrepid (see above).

Surf Travel Company, 12 Cronulla Plaza, Cronulla Beach, Sydney (☎02/9527 4722; *www.surftravel.com.au*); Kirra Surf Centre, corner of Gold Coast Highway and Coolangatta Rd, Kirra, Queensland (☎075/5599 2818); 6 Danbury Drive, Torbay, Auckland (☎09/473 8388). Airfares, 4WD rental, accommodation, camping and yacht/surf packages to Bali, Lombok and throughout Indonesia for both beginners and experienced surfers.

GAY AND LESBIAN

The following both offer comprehensive booking services and travel arrangements for gay and lesbian travellers:

Pride Travel, 254 Bay St, Brighton, Melbourne (☎03/9596 3566 or 1800/061 427).

Silke's Travel, 263 Oxford St, Darlinghurst, Sydney (☎02/9380 5835; *www.magna.com.au./~silba*).

returns to Indonesia, are worth considering if you're planning a long trip which will involve leaving Indonesia briefly to renew your visa (see p.17). Singapore Airlines and Malaysian Airlines, for example, offer returns via Denpasar and Jakarta to Singapore and Kuala Lumpur respectively for around A$1399/A$1499 from eastern Australian cities, and A$1199/A$1299 from Perth.

For details of the **Visit Indonesia Pass**, see p.4.

FLIGHTS FROM NEW ZEALAND

From **Auckland**, there are direct flights to Denpasar and Jakarta with Garuda for NZ$1299 (low season) and NZ$1499 (high season) and Air New Zealand (NZ$1399/$NZ1599). Add on NZ$300 return from **Christchurch** and **Wellington**, or you can fly indirectly via Australia with Qantas, Ansett or Air New Zealand at the added cost of the domestic fare from New Zealand (NZ$450/NZ$690 to Sydney or Brisbane).

ROUND-THE-WORLD TICKETS

Qantas, Ansett and Air New Zealand combine with a variety of carriers to offer tailored, unlimited stopover, **Round-the-World** (RTW) fares from A$4500/NZ$4800, as well as more restrictive global packages, that take you via Denpasar and Jakarta. Air New Zealand-KLM-Northwest's "World Navigator", Malaysia Airlines' "Global Experience" and Qantas-BA's "Global Explorer" all start from A$2599/NZ$3089, including limited backtracking and six stopovers worldwide, with additional stopovers for A$100/NZ$120 each.

PACKAGE HOLIDAYS

Garuda, Qantas and Air New Zealand, in conjunction with several wholesalers, offer flight/accommodation **packages** – mostly to Bali – costing little more than the airfare, with airport transfers thrown in. Other operators (see box opposite) might also offer car or jeep rental at around A$50/NZ$60 a day, including insurance. Bookings can be made from most travel agents, but before you book ask about any special conditions or hidden costs that may apply.

There is also a wide range of **surfing** and **diving** packages. Pro Dive Travel is one of the biggest diving operators; they offer seven nights and six dives in Bali departing from Sydney for A$1285. Alternatively, you can surf your way from Kupang to Kuta on an eight-day yacht charter from A$2099 with the Surf Travel Company.

GETTING THERE FROM SOUTHEAST ASIA

If you've the time, there are numerous ways to reach Indonesia through adjacent countries. When planning such a route, bear in mind that if you don't already have an Indonesian visa you must enter the country through an official gateway – see the box on p.16. Coming from the US or Europe, one advantage is that flights to Indonesia's neighbours are often cheaper than services direct to Jakarta or Bali, and that lax government controls mean that many Southeast Asian travel agents offer good deals on airfares – handy if you're planning to stay in Indonesia longer than sixty days and will therefore need to leave the country to renew your visa (see p.17). Generally, however, you'll rarely save once additional accommodation and overland transport is added in, but the routes allow a broader taste of the region, as well as delivering you to some less-travelled parts of Indonesia.

FROM THAILAND VIA THE MALAY PENINSULA

Discounted return flights to the Thai capital, **Bangkok**, cost from about £400 from London, or US$800 from Los Angeles. Buses and trains from Bangkok run down through the Malaysian peninsula to Singapore, from where you can travel by boat to Indonesia. There's a choice of routes between Bangkok and Singapore, going via Penang or the Malaysian capital, Kuala Lumpur. One Malaysia-bound train leaves Bangkok's Hualamphong station every day (book at least a day in advance from the station ticket office or designated agencies), arriving at Butterworth (for Penang) 21 hours later; tickets cost about £25/US$40 first class. If continuing to Singapore you'll need to change trains here for the remaining fifteen-hour journey (a through first-class ticket costs around £70/US$105). Alternatively, you could take one of the four daily trains from Bangkok to Thailand's main southern terminal at Hat Yai (16hr) and change onto the once-daily Hat Yai–Kuala Lumpur train (14hr). Through-fares to Kuala Lumpur are approximately £55/US$80 first class and from here you can travel on to Singapore for around £65/US$90. Buses and share-taxis from Hat Yai to Penang run throughout the day, take six hours and cost about £5/US$8 per person. Buses from Hat Yai take eighteen hours to Singapore.

There are **direct flights** from **Kuala Lumpur** to Jakarta, Denpasar, and Ujung Pandang in southern Sulawesi, and **from Singapore** to Jakarta, Denpasar, Mataram on Lombok and Manado in northern Sulawesi. A much cheaper option is the range of **sea routes** into Indonesia from southern Malaysia and Singapore. A variety of ferries and speedboats depart from **Penang** daily for Medan in northern Sumatra (4–14hr), and daily services run between **Melaka** and Dumai, south of Medan (2hr 30min), though this is not an official immigration gateway (see box below). You can also reach Batam, Bintan and Karimun islands, in Indonesia's Riau archipelago, from **Johor Bahru** in far southern Malaysia or from Singapore.

FROM BORNEO

The island of **Borneo** is split between the tiny Sultanate of Brunei and the Malaysian states of Sabah and Sarawak in the north, and Indonesian

OFFICIAL IMMIGRATION GATEWAYS INTO INDONESIA

When planning your overland trip, check that your proposed ports of entry and exit are officially recognized **immigration gateways** where sixty-day tourist visas can be issued; if not, you'll need to buy an **Indonesian visa** before you arrive in the country. See below for a current list of gateways, and opposite for full visa requirements, though it's always worth checking with the Indonesian embassy for any recent or temporary alterations.

AIRPORTS

Bali Ngurah Rai, Denpasar.

Irian Jaya Frans Kaisiepo, Biak.

Java Sukarno-Hatta, Jakarta; Adi Sumarmo, Solo; Juanda, Surabaya.

Kalimantan Sepinggan, Balikpapan; Soepadio, Pontianak.

Lombok Selaparang, Mataram.

Maluku Pattimura, Ambon.

Riau Hang Nadim, Pulau Batam.

Sulawesi Sam Ratulangi, Manado; Hasanuddin, Ujung Pandang.

Sumatra Polonia, Medan; Simpang Tiga, Pekanbaru; Tabing, Padang.

Timor El Tari, Kupang.

SEAPORTS

Bali Benoa, Sanur; Padang Bai.

Java Tanjung Priok, Jakarta; Tanjung Perak, Surabaya; Tanjung Mas, Semarang.

Maluku Yos Sudarso, Ambon.

Riau Batu Ampar, Pulau Batam; Sekupang, Pulau Batam; Tanjung Pinang, Pulau Bintan.

Sulawesi Bitung, Manado.

Sumatra Belawan, Medan.

LAND BORDERS

Kalimantan Etikong.

Kalimantan in the south. You can fly directly to **Bandar Seri Begawan**, the capital of Brunei, on Royal Brunei from London or Australia (£455/A$850 low season), and on Malaysian Airways via Kuala Lumpur to **Kuching** in Sarawak (£475/US$900/A$1000) or Sabah's **Kota Kinabalu** (£525/US$950/A$1200). These three cities are linked by road, so all make a viable starting point for a crossing into Indonesia.

Indonesia's only open **land border** is 40km southwest of Kuching at **Etikong**. Buses from Kuching regularly run over the border into Kalimantan and across to the city of Pontianak. Alternatively, you can cross from Sabah by catching a ferry from **Tewau**, a full two days' bus ride southeast of Kota Kinabalu, to Pulau Nunukan in northeastern Kalimantan – see Chapter Ten for more details. With about a month to spare, you could even use these crossings to make a complete circuit of Borneo.

FROM THE PHILIPPINES AND PAPUA NEW GUINEA

Discounted return fares to the Philippine capital, **Manila**, start at around £550/US$1000/A$900. From Manila, it's possible to island-hop through the Philippine archipelago to **Davao**, port for the southern island of Mindanao. Every two weeks, the Indonesian Pelni ferry *Tilongkabila* calls in here, taking 36 hours to cross south to Bitung in Sulawesi via Lirung and Tahuna in the Sangihe-Talaud group (see p.852).

Until recently, the crossing **from Vanimo in Papua New Guinea** to Jayapura in Irian Jaya was a guaranteed adventure, not so much for the crossing itself – a forty-minute flight – but simply for the effort needed to reach Vanimo from the PNG capital, Port Moresby. Though the border is presently closed due to political upheavals, check with Air Niugini in Cairns, Australia (☎07/4035 9109) to see if their weekly Vanimo–Jayapura flight (US$65) has started up again.

VISAS AND RED TAPE

Citizens of Britain, Ireland, most of Europe, Australia, New Zealand, Canada and the USA do not need a visa to enter Indonesia if intending to stay for less than sixty days, and if entering and exiting via one of the designated gateways. There are currently 28 of these ports in the Indonesian archipelago – sixteen major airports, eleven seaports and one land border – at which you can get a free, non-extendable sixty-day visa on arrival (see the box opposite for the full list). Note that "sixty days" includes the date of entry – it's best not to overstay your visa.

In addition, your passport must be valid for at least six months and you must be able to show **proof of onward travel** or sufficient funds to buy a ticket. Some international airlines may ask to be shown proof of onward travel before letting you board a flight into Indonesia, and they may request to see relevant documents such as visas (for Australia, for example) – if you don't have the right documents you'll probably have to sign a form waiving the airline's responsibility.

If you need to stay more than two months, or are entering via a non-designated gateway, then you'll need to obtain a visa through the nearest Indonesian consulate or embassy before entering Indonesia. Simplest to obtain, **tourist visas** are initially valid for four weeks, and cost £10 in the UK, US$25 in the USA, CAN$40 in Canada, A$100 in Australia and NZ$110 in New Zealand. **Business visas** involve a fair amount of paperwork, including supporting letters from your current employer and a sponsor in Indonesia, and are

INDONESIAN EMBASSIES AND CONSULATES ABROAD

Australia 8 Darwin Ave, Yarralumla, Canberra, ACT 2600 (☎02/6250 8600); 20 Harry Chan Ave, Darwin, NT 5784 (☎089/41 0048); 72 Queen Rd, Melbourne, VIC 3004 (☎03/9525 2755); 134 Adelaide Terrace, East Perth, WA 6004 (☎08/9221 5858); 236–238 Maroubra Rd, Maroubra, NSW 2035 (☎02/9344 9933).

Canada 287 Maclaren St, Ottawa, ON K2P 0L9 (☎613/237-7403); 425 University Ave, Toronto, ON M5G 1T6 (☎416/360-1220).

Ireland see UK and Ireland.

Malaysia 233 JL Tun Razak, 50400 Kuala Lumpur (☎03/984 2011); JL Kemajuan, Karamunsing, 88817 Kota Kinabulu, Sabah (☎088/218 600); 467 JL Burma, 10350 Penang (☎04/374 686).

New Zealand 70 Glen Rd, Kelburn, Wellington, PO Box 3543 (☎04/475 8697).

Singapore 7 Chatsworth Rd, Singapore 1024 (☎737 7422).

Thailand 600–602 Petchaburi Rd, Bangkok 10400 (☎02/252 3135–40).

UK and Ireland 38 Grosvenor Square, London W1X 9AD (☎0891/171210).

USA 2020 Massachusetts Ave NW, Washington, DC 20036 (☎202/775-5200); 5 E 68th St, New York, NY 10021 (☎212/879-0600); 72 E Randolph St, Chicago, IL 60601 (☎312/345-9300); 3457 Wilshire Blvd, Los Angeles, CA 90010 (☎213/383-5126).

valid for five weeks; they cost £22 in the UK and the same price as a tourist visa elsewhere. Both tourist and business visas can be extended for up to six months at immigration offices in Indonesia, if you can convince the authorities that your need is legitimate – this is not necessarily easy.

However, it's quite simple, if expensive, to get yourself a **new sixty-day visa** by leaving the country for a few hours and then coming straight back in through a designated port of entry. Most people choose to go to Singapore; numerous unofficial expat "residents" do the Singapore hop

on a regular basis and immigration officials don't seem too bothered by this. Penalties for **overstaying your visa** are quite severe: on departure, you'll be fined Rp20,000 for every day that you've exceeded the limit, up to a maximum of fourteen days. If you've exceeded the fourteen-day overtime limit, you'll get blacklisted from Indonesia for two years.

Should you need to contact the government **immigration offices** (*kantor immigrasi*), you'll find them listed in the "Listings" sections of the large city entries.

TRAVEL INSURANCE

Bank and credit cards often have certain levels of travel insurance included, if you use them to pay for your trip. Though some anticipate anything from lost or stolen baggage to missed connections, for medical reasons alone it's advisable to take out comprehensive travel insurance before visiting Indonesia.

When shopping around for a policy, ensure that there is a **24-hour emergency contact number**, in case you need medical evacuation. The per-article limit for loss or theft should cover your most valuable possession (a camera, for example) but, conversely, don't pay for cover you don't need. Check the fine print for the level of **excess** – the initial amount of any claim that you have to pay for – and any **exclusions**; policies tend to prohibit **dangerous sports** such as scuba diving or mountain climbing, but these can often be added for an extra charge.

To **claim**, you will need an on-the-spot police report in the event of loss or theft of your goods, and receipts for any medical expenses. Note that very few insurers arrange for immediate payments in any circumstances; you will usually be reimbursed only after going home.

UK INSURANCE

Most travel agents and tour operators will offer you insurance when you book your flight or holiday, but it pays to shop around and check what cover you may already have. If you have a good "all risks" **home insurance policy** it may well cover your possessions against loss or theft even when overseas, or you can extend cover through your household contents insurer. Many private medical schemes also cover you when abroad.

In **Britain and Ireland**, travel insurance schemes are sold by almost every travel agent or bank, and by **specialist insurance companies**. The cost will depend on what you want to be insured for, and for how long: for around £35–50, you should find a policy offering two weeks' cover for the cost of cancellation and curtailment of flights, medical expenses, travel delay, accident, missed departures, lost baggage, lost passport, personal liability and legal expenses. For an extended trip, however, you're looking at up to £360 for a full year's comprehensive coverage, though exclude certain items – your baggage, money or missed flights, for example – and you can find policies from as low as £185.

Some insurance companies refuse to cover travellers over 65, or stop at 69 or 74 years of age, and

most that do charge hefty premiums. The best policies for **older travellers**, with no upper age limit, are offered by Age Concern (☎01883/346964).

In **Ireland** travel insurance is best obtained through a travel specialist such as Usit (see box on p.5). Their policies cost £44 for six to ten days worldwide (£63 for one month). Discounts are offered to students of any age and anyone under 35.

NORTH AMERICAN INSURANCE

Before buying an **insurance policy**, check that you're not already covered. Canadian provincial health plans typically provide some overseas medical coverage, although they are unlikely to pick up the full tab in the event of a mishap. Holders of official **student/teacher/youth cards** are entitled to accident coverage and hospital inpatient benefits – the annual membership is far less than the cost of comparable insurance. Students may also find that their student health coverage extends during the vacations and for one term beyond the date of last enrolment. Bank and credit cards (particularly American Express) often provide certain levels of medical or other insurance, and travel insurance may also be included if you use a major credit or charge card to pay for your trip. Homeowners' or renters' insurance often covers theft or loss of documents, money and valuables while overseas.

After exhausting the possibilities above, you might want to contact a specialist travel insurance company: your travel agent can usually recommend one, or see the box on p.20.

Travel insurance policies vary: some are comprehensive, while others cover only certain risks (accidents, illnesses, delayed or lost luggage, cancelled flights and so on). In particular, ask whether the policy pays medical costs up front or reimburses you later, and whether it provides for medical evacuation to your home country.

The best premiums are usually to be had through student/youth travel agencies – STA policies, for example, come in two forms: with or without **medical coverage**. The current rates are US$45/35 (for up to seven days); US$60/45 (eight to fifteen days); US$110/85 (one month); US$140/115 (45 days); US$165/135 (two months); US$50/35 (for each extra month). If you're planning to do any "dangerous sports" (such as skiing or mountaineering), be sure to ask whether these activities are covered: some companies levy a surcharge.

TRAVEL INSURANCE COMPANIES IN BRITAIN

Campus ☎0171/730 8111.
Columbus Travel Insurance ☎0171/375 0011.
Endsleigh Insurance ☎0171/436 4451.
Marcus Hearne & Co Ltd ☎0171/739 3444.
STA ☎0171/361 6262.
Worldwide ☎01732/773366.

IRELAND
Usit See p.5.

Most North American travel policies apply only
to items lost, stolen or damaged while in the cus-
tody of an identifiable, responsible third party –
hotel porter, airline or luggage consignment. Even in
these cases you will have to contact the local police

within a certain time limit to have a complete report
made out so that your insurer can process the claim.

AUSTRALASIAN INSURANCE

Travel insurance in **Australia** and **New Zealand**
is available from most travel agents or direct from
insurance companies (see the box below), for
periods ranging from a few days to six months.
Most policies appear similar in premium, but
there's some variation as to which will automatically cover valuables, or high-risk activities – both
applicable to scuba divers, for instance. Expect to
pay around A$90/NZ$100 for two weeks,
A$130/NZ$145 for one month, A$190/NZ$210 for
two months and A$298/NZ$330 for six months.

TRAVELLERS WITH DISABILITIES

**Indonesia makes few provisions for its own
disabled citizens, which clearly affects travellers with disabilities. Simply at the physical level, pavements are usually high and
often uneven with all sorts of obstacles, and
only rarely have slopes for you to get on or off
them; access to most public places involves
steps and very few have ramps. Public transport is inaccessible to wheelchair users, and
the few pedestrian crossings on major roads
have no audible signal. On the positive side,
however, some accommodation comprises
bungalows in extensive grounds, with spacious bathrooms, and the more upmarket
hotels are increasingly aware of the requirements of disabled travellers.**

For all of these reasons, it may be worth considering an **organized tour** – the contacts in the box
opposite will help you start researching trips to
Indonesia. If you want to be more independent, it's
important to know where you must be self-reliant
and where you may expect help, especially regarding transport and accommodation. It is also vital to

be honest – with travel agencies, insurance companies and travel companions. If you do not use a
wheelchair all the time but your walking capabili-
ties are limited, remember that you are likely to
need to cover greater distances while travelling
(often over rougher terrain and in hotter temperatures) than you are used to. If you use a wheelchair,
have it serviced before you go and carry a repair kit.

Read your travel **insurance** small print carefully to make sure that people with an existing
medical condition are not excluded. And use your
travel agent to make your journey simpler: airlines
can cope better if they are expecting you, with a
wheelchair provided at airports and staff primed
to help. A **medical certificate** of your fitness to
travel, provided by your doctor, is also extremely
useful; some airlines or insurance companies may
insist on it. Take a backup prescription including
the generic name of any drugs in case of emergency. Carry spares of any clothing or equipment
that might be hard to find and, if there's an association representing people with your disability,
contact them early in the planning process.

CONTACTS FOR TRAVELLERS WITH DISABILITIES

BRITAIN

Holiday Care Service, 2nd Floor, Imperial Building, Victoria Rd, Horley RH6 7PZ (☎01293/774535, fax 784647; minicom ☎01293/776943). Provides information on all aspects of travel, although they have no specific information on Indonesia.

RADAR (Royal Association for Disability and Rehabilitation), 12 City Forum, 250 City Rd, London EC1V 8AF (☎0171/250 3222; minicom ☎0171/250 4119). Their guide, *Holidays and Travel Abroad: A Guide for Disabled People* (£5), is an essential source book providing information country by country, as well as information on airports, flying, where to get advice, and commercial companies and hotel chains offering specialist services.

Tripscope, The Courtyard, Evelyn Rd, London W4 5JL (☎0181/994 9294, fax 994 3618). This registered charity provides a national telephone information service offering free advice on UK and international transport and travel for those with a mobility problem.

IRELAND

The places below offer information about access for disabled travellers abroad.

Disability Action Group, 2 Annadale Ave, Belfast BT7 3JH (☎01232/491 011).

Irish Wheelchair Association, Blackheath Drive, Clontarf, Dublin 3 (☎01/833 8241, fax 833 3873; email *iwa@iol.ie*).

NORTH AMERICA

Jewish Rehabilitation Hospital, 3205 Place Alton Goldbloom, Montréal, PQ H7V 1R2 (☎514/688-9550, ext 226). Guidebooks and travel info.

Mobility International USA, PO Box 10767, Eugene, OR 97440 (☎541/343-1284). Information and referral services, access guides, tours and exchange programmes. Annual membership US$35 (includes quarterly newsletter).

Society for the Advancement of Travel for the Handicapped (SATH), 347 5th Ave, Suite 610, New York, NY 10016 (☎212/447-7284). Non-profit-making travel industry referral service that passes queries onto its members as appropriate.

Travel Information Service (☎215/456-9603). Telephone-only information and referral service for disabled travellers.

Twin Peaks Press, Box 129, Vancouver, WA 98666 (☎206/694-2462 or 800/637-2256). Publisher of: the *Directory of Travel Agencies for the Disabled* ($19.95), listing more than 370 agencies worldwide; *Travel for the Disabled* ($19.95); the *Directory of Accessible Van Rentals* ($9.95); and *Wheelchair Vagabond* ($14.95), loaded with personal tips.

AUSTRALIA

ACROD (Australian Council for Rehabilitation of the Disabled), PO Box 60, Curtin, ACT 2605 (☎02/6282 4333). Good source of information about disabled organizations within Australia.

NICAN, PO Box 407, Curtin, ACT 2605 (☎02/6285 3713). Compiles a database on disabled-friendly travel companies.

NEW ZEALAND

Disabled Persons Assembly, 173–175 Victoria St, Wellington (☎04/811 9100).

Make sure that you take sufficient supplies of any **medications**, and – if they're essential – carry the complete supply with you whenever you travel (including on buses and planes), in case of loss or theft. It's also a good idea to carry a doctor's letter about your drug prescriptions with you at all times – particularly when passing through airport customs – as this will ensure you don't get hauled up for narcotics transgressions. If your medication has to be kept cool, buy a thermal insulation bag and a couple of freezer blocks before you leave home. That way you can refreeze one of the two blocks every day while the other is in use; staff in most hotels, restaurants and bars should be happy to let you use their freezer compartment for a few hours. You may also be able to store your medication in hotel and guest-house refrigerators, though obviously you wouldn't want it to go missing, so make a considered judgement about security first.

Based in the US, **Access Able Travel** is a first-rate **Web site** for disabled travellers, with bulletin boards for passing on tips and accounts of accessible attractions, accommodation, guides and resources around the globe. As yet, there's no information posted on Indonesia, but Access Able is fairly new and growing fast – check the site at *www.access-able.com* (or email *carol@access-able.com*) for the latest.

COSTS, MONEY AND BANKS

In a country where the average daily wage is about £1.50/US$2, it's hardly surprising that expenses in Indonesia are low for most travellers, and that even upmarket services in relatively costly places such as Jakarta are good value compared to what you would pay at home.

Standards of living for Indonesians – particularly urban Indonesians – have, however, plummeted as a result of the archipelago's recent **economic crisis** (see Contexts, p.959). There were severe price hikes for daily necessities after the rupiah devalued by 600 percent in the twelve months from August 1997. As wages haven't increased proportionately, hotels, restaurants, and services aimed primarily at Indonesians have been slow to raise their rates for fear of pricing out customers. Strictly tourist businesses, however, have responded by charging for their goods and services in **US dollars**, a practice that was already standard policy for upmarket hotels throughout Indonesia, as well as for some diving operators, tour agents and car-rental outlets. Even where

---

DOLLARS AND RUPIAH

Due to Indonesia's fluctuating financial situation, all accommodation prices in this guide are given in their more stable **US dollar** equivalents, even for places where you are not required to pay in this currency. Prices quoted **in rupiah** for transport and other services were correct at the time of research and have been retained to give a relative idea of costs, though in practice the price of many of these things will be higher than those quoted in the Guide.

---

prices are displayed in US dollars, though, you're usually given the option of paying with cash, travellers' cheques, credit card or rupiah, and it's worth checking the dollar exchange rate as it can be very good.

CURRENCY

The Indonesian currency is the **rupiah** (abbreviated to "Rp"), for which there are no smaller units. **Notes** are the main form of exchange and come in denominations of Rp100, Rp500, Rp1000, Rp5000, Rp10,000, Rp20,000 and Rp50,000, increasing in size according to value. Be warned that most people won't accept ripped or badly worn banknotes, so *you* shouldn't either. **Coins**, mainly used for public telephones and bemo rides, come in Rp25, Rp50, Rp100, Rp500 and Rp1000 denominations, though you'll very rarely see the lower values nowadays.

Officially, rupiah are available outside of Indonesia, but its volatile value means that very few banks carry it at present. You can check the latest exchange rate through a bank, or with **Oanda**, an **online currency converter** at *www.oanda.com/cgi-bin/ncc*, which gives you the day's rate for 164 currencies and compiles free, wallet-sized conversion tables for travellers to print out and use on the ground.

COSTS

With the currency in free fall, and **prices** for different services responding at varying speeds, it's difficult to make exact predictions of how much Indonesia costs on a daily basis. Things will also depend greatly on where you visit, how much you move around and how much discomfort you're prepared to endure. You'll keep all costs to a minimum if you concentrate on Java, Sumatra, Bali and Lombok, where it's possible to travel on cheap, land-based transport, and there's usually a good range of services – though you'll find that there's also plenty to spend money on, too. In the outer islands such as Kalimantan, Sulawesi, Maluku and Irian Jaya, severe geography and a lack of infrastructure may mean flying or cruising between places are the only options for travel, while the cost of goods imported from elsewhere in Indonesia will be that much higher.

Taking all this into account, if you're happy to eat where the locals do, use the cheapest forms of public transport and stay in simple accommodation, you could manage on a **daily budget** of £6.50/US$10 per person. For around £20/US$30 a day (less if you share a room), you'll get a few extra comforts, like hot water and air-conditioning in your accommodation, bigger meals, a few beers, and the ability to travel in better style from time to time. Staying in luxury hotels and eating at the flashiest restaurants, expect to spend upwards of £75/US$115 per day.

There's generally a **fee** to enter museums, archeological sites and – in Bali – temples, which can range from a small donation (before which you're often shown a register recording grossly inflated amounts given by previous visitors) to several thousand rupiah. **Youth and student reductions** are very rarely offered at these places, but student discounts were previously available on some **airlines** within Indonesia, and are worth inquiring about if you hold a valid international student card.

BARGAINING

One of the most obvious ways of lowering your everyday costs, **bargaining** is an art which requires not only a sense of humour but also a fair amount of tact – it's easy to forget that you're quibbling over amounts which mean a lot more to an Indonesian than to you. Pretty much everything is negotiable, from cigarettes and woodcarvings to car-rental and accommodation rates. The first price given is rarely the real one, and most stallholders and shopkeepers engage in some financial banter before finalizing the sale. Have a look at what others are paying first, but expect to pay more than locals, and to make a few blunders before getting a feel for the game; on average, buyers will start their counterbid at about 25 percent of the vendor's opening price, and the bartering continues from there.

Places that are focused towards the upmarket tourist trade usually don't like to bargain, and many such hotels and shops display "fixed price" notices on their walls. Even here it's worth asking about "low-season discounts", however, and there are some tourist-oriented services – such as diving – where putting up a struggle will still net you substantial savings.

BANKS AND EXCHANGE

You'll find **banks** capable of handling foreign exchange in provincial capitals and bigger cities

BANKS AND THE CRISIS

Having invested huge amounts of money in dubious development schemes – not to mention some directors simply channelling bank funds into their private coffers – Indonesia's **economic crisis** has hit the **banks** extremely hard. While none had officially closed down at the time of writing, it's very possible that many specific branches mentioned in the guide chapters – especially the BCA, BNI and Bank Danamon – may no longer exist by the time you reach the country, so be careful to carry enough rupiah with you if you're travelling to any region with a limited banking system.

throughout Indonesia, with privately run **moneychangers** in major tourist centres. Where there's a choice, it's always worth shopping around: moneychangers sometimes offer better rates than banks, and you'll often find big differences not just between separate institutions, but also individual branches of the same bank. As a rule of thumb, Indonesian **banking hours** are Monday to Friday 8am to 3pm and Saturday 8am to 1pm, but these can vary, with restricted hours for foreign-exchange transactions. If available, moneychangers open early and close late.

Always time-consuming, the **exchange process** is straightforward enough in banks, though there may be minimum or maximum **limits** to transactions, or you may be asked to supply a **photocopy** of your passport, or the **receipt** (or proof of purchase) that you get when you buy your travellers' cheques. With moneychangers, always establish any **commissions** before signing cheques; many display promising rates, but charge a hefty fee or only give that rate for big transactions. Always count your money carefully, as it's not unknown for unscrupulous dealers to rip you off, either by folding notes over to make it look as if you're getting twice as much as you actually are, or by distracting you and then whipping away a few notes from your pile.

TRAVELLERS' CHEQUES, CASH AND PLASTIC

Travellers' cheques, available through banks and travel agents before you leave home, are the best way to carry the bulk of your funds around. Though you get a slightly poorer rate than for cash, they can be replaced if lost or stolen (keep a list of the serial numbers separate from the cheques). Stick to major brands such as American Express and Visa, in US dollars, as outside Bali and Java you'll have trouble cashing anything else. Larger denominations are preferable too, as you tend to get better rates. If you're planning a trip to less-travelled regions of Indonesia, you'll find that many provincial banks incapable of cashing travellers' cheques have no such qualms over **US dollar notes**. In emergencies, it's not unknown for small-town businesses or even village stores (generally Chinese-run) to exchange dollars, though at poor rates. Notes do need to be in perfect condition, however. **Credit cards** are also invaluable, and not just for paying for more upmarket services and accommodation: banks – especially in the provinces – are beginning to set **exchange-rate ceilings** of around Rp7500 to the US dollar, irrespective of the official value, and over-the-counter **cash advances** on Visa can be used for obtaining the full international rate. A growing number of bank **ATMs** across the country also have **Cirrus-Maestro** connections, allowing you to draw funds direct from your home account, again at international rates – check with your bank for details.

WIRING MONEY

Wiring money through a specialist agent (see the box above) is a fast but expensive way to send and receive money abroad. The money wired should be available for collection, usually in local currency, from the company's local agent within twenty minutes of being sent via Western Union or Moneygram; both charge on a sliding scale, so sending larger amounts of cash is better value. Ask the agents for a list of their Indonesian representatives where the cash can be collected.

It's also possible to have money wired **directly from a bank** in your home country to a bank in Indonesia, although this is somewhat less reliable

---

WIRING MONEY

From the UK

American Express Moneygram
☎0800/894 887.
Western Union ☎0800/833 833.

From North America

American Express Moneygram
☎800/543-4080.
Western Union ☎800/325-6000.

From Australia

American Express Moneygram
☎1800/230 100.
Western Union ☎1800/649 565.

From New Zealand

American Express Moneygram
☎09/379 8243 or 0800/262 263.
Western Union ☎09/302 0143.

---

because it involves two separate institutions. Most banks will allow account holders to nominate almost any branch of any bank as a collection point, though if this is not the central bank that they usually deal with it will take longer than normal. It is therefore a good idea to check with your bank before travelling to see with which branch of which bank they have reciprocal arrangements. Your home bank will need the address of the branch bank where you want to pick up the money, and the address and telex number of the Indonesian head office, which will act as the clearing house; money wired this way will take at least two working days to arrive, and costs around £25/US$40 per transaction.

HEALTH

The vast majority of travellers to Indonesia suffer nothing more than an upset stomach; generally, hygiene and health standards are improving. If you have a minor ailment, it's usually best to head to a pharmacy or apotik – most have a decent idea of how to treat common ailments and can provide many medicines without prescription.

Otherwise, ask for the nearest *doktor, doktor gigi* (dentist) or *rumah sakit* (hospital). If you have a serious accident or illness then you will need to be evacuated home or to Singapore, which has the best medical provision in Asia. It is, therefore, vital to arrange **health insurance** before you leave home.

BEFORE YOU GO

Immunizations are not required for visitors to Indonesia, but several are strongly recommended. Typhus, hepatitis A, tetanus and polio are the most important ones, and rabies, hepatitis B, Japanese encephalitis, diphtheria and TB are all worth considering if you're planning trips outside of Java or Bali.

For up-to-the-minute **information**, make an appointment at a travel clinic (see box on p.26), although immunizations can be costly, as these clinics are private. They also sell travel accessories, including mosquito nets and first-aid kits.

In the UK, pick up the Department of Health's free publication, *Health Advice for Travellers*, a comprehensive **booklet** available at the post office, or by calling the Health Literature Line on ☎0800/555777. The content of the booklet, which contains immunization advice, is constantly updated on pages 460–464 of CEEFAX. Most general practitioners in the UK can give advice and certain vaccines on prescription, though they may not administer some of the less common immunizations, and only some immunizations are free under the NHS. A doctor should be consulted at least two months in advance of your departure date, as not all immunizations can be given at the same time, and some take a while to become effective (hepatitis B, for example, can take six months to provide full protection).

PRECAUTIONS

Prevention is always better than cure. Remember that most **water** that comes out of taps has had very little treatment, and can contain a whole range of bacteria and viruses. These micro-organisms cause diseases such as diarrhoea, gastroenteritis, typhus, cholera, dysentery, poliomyelitis, hepatitis A and giardia, and can be present even when water looks clean and safe to drink. The only water you should ever put in your mouth, and that includes brushing your teeth, should be bottled, boiled or sterilized. Fortunately, except in the furthest-flung corners of the archipelago, **bottled water** is on sale everywhere. You should be careful about cutlery, plates, salads and vegetables that have been washed in tap water and are still wet. Bear in mind that while **ice** is made in government-run plants from sterilized water, its methods of transport are not the most hygienic – it's best avoided.

If you're planning to head off the beaten track or don't fancy shelling out daily for bottled water, you should consider taking a **water purifier** with you. While boiling water for ten minutes kills most micro-organisms, it's not the most convenient method. Sterilization with **iodine tablets** is effective, but the resulting liquid doesn't taste very pleasant – though flavouring with cordial can mask this slightly – and you'll probably want to filter the water as well. (Iodine is unsafe for pregnant women, babies and people with thyroid complaints.) Portable water purifiers, which sterilize and filter the water, give the most complete treatment. A low-cost and highly recommended range made by Pre-Mac is available in the UK from British Airways Travel Clinics (see box, p.26) and specialist outdoor-equipment retailers. Contact Pre-Mac for details of local stockists and specialist advice: (Unit 5, Morewood Close, Sevenoaks, Kent TN13 1UH ☎01732/460333, fax 460222; *www.pre-mac.com*). In Ireland, contact All Water Systems Ltd (Unit 12, Western Parkway Business Centre, Lower Ballymount Road, Dublin 12; ☎01/456 4933).

An estimated eighty percent of the indigenous population of rural Indonesia carry intestinal parasites, flukes and worms, contracted either through water, poorly cooked fish, pork or beef, or from walking around barefoot. Should you pick up flukes or worms, they may be very difficult to diagnose. Your best bet is to have a full checkup at your home country's tropical diseases hospital on your return; parasites can usually be killed off quickly and easily with a short course of tablets.

TRAVEL CLINICS AND INFORMATION LINES

BRITAIN

British Airways Travel Clinic, 156 Regent St, London W1 7RA (Mon–Fri 9.30am–5.15pm, Sat 10am–4pm; ☎0171/439 9584), no appointment necessary; a walk-in service is also offered at the clinic within Flightbookers at 177 Tottenham Court Rd, London W1P 0LX (Mon–Fri 9.30am–6.30pm, Sat 10am–2pm; ☎0171/757 2504), though appointments are available at both. There are appointment-only branches at 101 Cheapside, London EC2 (Mon–Fri 9–11.45am & 12.15–4.45pm; ☎0171/606 2977), and at the BA terminal in London's Victoria station (8.15–11.45am & 12.30–4pm; ☎0171/233 6661). BA also operates around forty regional clinics throughout the country (call ☎0171/831 5333 for the one nearest to you), plus airport locations at Gatwick and Heathrow.

Hospital for Tropical Diseases, St Pancras Hospital, 4 St Pancras Way, London NW1 0PE (☎0171/388 9600). Travel clinic and recorded message service (☎0839/337733; 49p per min) which gives hints on hygiene and illness prevention as well as listing appropriate immunizations.

MASTA (Medical Advisory Service for Travellers Abroad), London School of Hygiene and Tropical Medicine. Operates a prerecorded 24hr Travellers' Health Line (☎0891/224100; 50p per min), giving written information tailored to your journey by return of post.

IRELAND

All of these places offer medical advice before a trip and medical help afterwards in the event of a tropical disease.

Travel Medicine Services, PO Box 254, 16 College St, Belfast 1 (☎01232/315 220).

Tropical Medical Bureau, Grafton Street Medical Centre, 34 Grafton St, Dublin 2 (☎01/671 9200).

Tropical Medical Bureau, Dun Laoghaire Medical Centre, 5 Northumberland Ave, Dun Laoghaire, Co. Dublin (☎01/280 4996, fax 280 5603; *tropical@iol.ie; www.iol.ie/-tmb*).

NORTH AMERICA

Canadian Society for International Health, 170 Laurier Ave W, Suite 902, Ottawa, ON K1P 5V5 (☎613/230-2654). Distributes a free pamphlet, *Health Information for Canadian Travellers*, containing an extensive list of travel health centres in Canada.

Centers for Disease Control, 1600 Clifton Rd NE, Atlanta, GA 30333 (☎404/639-3311; *www.cdc.gov/travel/travel.html*). Publishes outbreak warnings, suggested inoculations, precautions and other background information for travellers. Their Web site is very useful.

International Association for Medical Assistance to Travellers (IAMAT), 417 Center St, Lewiston, NY 14092 (☎716/754-4883; *www.sentex.net/~iamat*); 40 Regal Rd, Guelph, ON N1K 1B5 (☎519/836-0102). A non-profit organization supported by donations, it can provide a list of English-speaking doctors, climate charts and leaflets on various diseases and inoculations.

International SOS Assistance, PO Box 11568, Philadelphia, PA 19116 (☎800/523-8930). Members receive pre-trip medical referral information, as well as overseas emergency services designed to complement travel insurance coverage.

Travel Medicine, 351 Pleasant St, Suite 312, Northampton, MA 01060 (☎800/872-8633). Sells first-aid kits, mosquito netting, water filters and other health-related travel products.

Travelers Medical Center, 31 Washington Square, New York, NY 10011 (☎212/982-1600). Consultation service on immunizations and treatment of diseases for people travelling to developing countries.

AUSTRALIA

Travellers' Medical and Vaccination Centre, 7/428 George St, Sydney (☎02/9221 7133); 3/393 Little Bourke St, Melbourne (☎03/9602 5788); 6/29 Gilbert Place, Adelaide (☎08/8212 7522); 6/247 Adelaide St, Brisbane (☎07/3221 9066); 1 Mill St, Perth (☎08/9321 1977); *www.tmvc.com.au*

NEW ZEALAND

Travellers' Medical and Vaccination Centre, Level 1, Canterbury Arcade, 170 Queen St, Auckland 1 (☎09/373 3531; *www.tmvc.com.au*).

FIRST-AID KIT

Some of the items listed below can be purchased more easily and cheaply in Indonesian **apotik**; Imodium and dental/sterile surgical kits will need to be bought before you leave home.

Antiseptic cream
Insect repellent
Antihistamine
Plasters/band aids
Water sterilization tablets or water purifier
Lint and sealed bandages
A course of flagyl antibiotics
Anti-fungal/athletes-foot cream
Imodium (Lomotil) for emergency diarrhoea treatment
Paracetamol/aspirin
Anti-inflammatory/Ibuprofen
Multivitamin and mineral tablets
Rehydration salts
Emergency dental kit with temporary fillings
Hypodermic and intravenous needles, sutures and sterilized skin wipes
Condoms and other contraceptives

Though the Indonesian government would have the international community believe that **AIDS** is not yet a problem, this could not be further from the truth. Using latex **condoms** during sex reduces the risks. Bring a supply of them with you, take special care with expiry dates and bear in mind that condoms don't last as long when kept in the heat. Blood transfusions, intravenous drug use, acupuncture, dentistry, tattooing and body piercing are high-risk. Get a dental checkup before you leave home, and carry a sterile needles kit for medical emergencies.

PHARMACIES AND DOCTORS

You'll find **pharmacies** (*apotik*) in towns and cities selling a wide range of medicines, many of which you would need a prescription to buy back home. Only in the main tourist areas will assistants speak English; in the village health posts, staff are generally interested and well-meaning, but ill equipped to cope with serious illness.

If you need an English-speaking **doctor**, seek advice at your hotel (some of the luxury ones have an in-house doctor) or at the local tourist office. For more serious problems, you'll find a public **hospital** in major cities and towns, and in some

places these are supplemented by private hospitals, many of which operate an accident and emergency department.

TUMMY TROUBLES AND VIRUSES

If you travel in Asia for an extended period of time, you are likely to come down with some kind of stomach bug. For most this is just a case of **diarrhoea**, caught through bad hygiene, unfamiliar or affected food, and is generally over in a couple of days if treated properly; dehydration is one of the main concerns if you have diarrhoea, so **rehydration salts** dissolved in clean water provide the best treatment. **Gastroenteritis** is a more extreme version, but can still be cured with the same blend of rest and rehydration. Oralit is the most frequently available brand in pharmacies, but you can make up your own by mixing three teaspoons of sugar and one of salt to a litre of water. You will need to drink as much as three litres a day to stave off dehydration. Eat non-spicy, non-greasy foods such as **young coconut**, unbuttered toast, rice, **bananas** and noodles, and steer away from alcohol, coffee, milk and most fruits. Charcoal tablets work wonders for some people, and there are blocking medicines, Lomotil and Imodium. Since diarrhoea purges the body of the bugs, taking them is not recommended unless you have some urgent reason to be mobile. Antibiotics are a worse idea, as they can wipe out friendly bacteria in the bowel and render you far more susceptible to future attacks.

The next step up from gastroenteritis is **dysentery**, diagnosable from blood and mucus in the (often blackened) stool. Dysentery is either amoebic or bacillary. The latter is caused by a bacteria causing a high fever and vomiting, and serious attacks will require antibiotics. Amoebic dysentery shares the above symptoms except for the fever and vomiting. It can last for weeks and recur, and therefore must always be treated, preferably in hospital.

Giardia can be diagnosed by foul-smelling farts and burps, abdominal distension, evil-smelling stools that float, and diarrhoea without blood or pus. Don't be over eager with your diagnosis though, and treat it as normal diarrhoea for at least 24 hours before seeking out some Flagl antibiotics.

Hepatitis A or E is a waterborne viral infection spread through water and food. It causes jaundice, loss of appetite and nausea and can leave you feeling wiped out for months. Seek immediate medical help if you think you may have contracted hepatitis. The new Havrix vaccination lasts for several years, provided you have a booster the year after your first jabs. Hepatitis B is transmitted by bodily fluids, during unprotected sex or by intravenous drug use.

Cholera and **typhus** both occur in Indonesia, though you are unlikely to come into contact with them. They are infectious diseases, generally spread when communities rely on sparse water supplies. It's worth getting vaccinated against typhus, but the World Health Organization now reckons the cholera vaccine is only about fifty percent effective.

MALARIA AND DENGUE FEVER

Indonesia is within a **malarial zone**, although in the developed tourist resorts of Bali, for example, there is little risk. If you are visiting any other areas, even in transit, you should take full precautions and, in any case, check the advice of your doctor before you travel, as information regarding malaria is constantly being updated. The latest information shows an increase in infections of the most serious form of the illness and there are reports of resistance to certain drug treatments by some strains. Pregnant women and children need particular advice on dosage and the different drugs available.

Malaria is caused by a parasite in the saliva of the anopheles mosquito which is passed into the human when bitten by the mosquito. There are various prophylactic drug regimes available, depending on your destination, all of which must be taken according to a strict timetable, beginning one week before you go and continuing four weeks after leaving the area. If you don't do this, you are in danger of developing the illness once you have returned home. One drug, Mefloquine (sold as Larium) has received some very critical media coverage; in some people it appears to produce disorientation, depression and sleep disturbance, although it suits other people very well. If you're intending to use Larium you should begin to take it two weeks before you depart to see whether it will agree with your metabolism. Anyone planning to scuba-dive should discuss the use of Larium very carefully with their medical advisers as there has been some indication of an increased risk of the "bends".

None of the drugs is one hundred per cent effective and it is equally important to the prevention of

malaria to stop the mosquitoes biting you: sleep under a net, burn mosquito coils and use repellent on exposed skin when the mosquitoes are around, mostly after dark.

The symptoms of malaria are fever, headache and shivering, similar to a severe dose of flu and often coming in cycles, but a lot of people have additional symptoms. Don't delay in seeking help fast: malaria can be fatal. You will need a blood test to confirm the illness and the doctor will prescribe the most effective treatment locally. If you develop flu-like symptoms any time up to a year after returning home, you should inform a doctor of the areas you have been travelling in and ask for a blood test.

Another important reason to avoid getting bitten is **dengue fever**, a virus carried by a different species of mosquito, which bites during the day. There is no vaccine or tablet available to prevent the illness, which causes fever, headache and joint and muscle pains among the least serious symptoms, and internal bleeding and circulatory-system failure among the most serious, and there is no specific drug to cure it. Reports, rather worryingly, indicate that the disease is on the increase across Asia and hundreds died from it in Indonesia in 1998. It is vital to get an early medical diagnosis and get treatment.

OTHER THINGS THAT BITE OR STING

The most common irritations for travellers come from tiny pests whose most serious evil is to wreck a good night's sleep. **Fleas**, **lice** and **bed bugs** thrive in run-down guest houses, and adore grimy sheets. Examine your bedding carefully, air and beat the offending articles and then coat yourself liberally in insect repellent.

Ticks are nasty pea-shaped bloodsuckers which usually attach themselves to you if you walk through long grass. A dab of petrol, alcohol, tiger balm or insect repellent, or a lit cigarette, should convince them to leave; if not, then grab hold of their head with tweezers and twist them off. **Leeches** are generally only a problem in the jungle and in fresh water. These relatives of the earthworm attach themselves to the skin, apply an anticoagulant and anaesthetic and then proceed to gulp blood. They will eventually fall off when replete, but you won't want to leave them that long. Salt, applied directly, is the best remedy, but all the anti-tick treatments also work. **Deet** is an effective deterrent, and applying it at the tops of your boots and around the lace-holes is a good idea. Always wear shoes, and, for trekking, boots with socks tucked into your trousers. With all of these irritants, there is a danger of infection to or through the bitten area, so keep bites clean and wash with antiseptic soap.

Indonesia has many species of both land and sea **snakes**, and encounters in wilder places are fairly common. Contrary to popular belief, however, most snakes do their best to avoid people, and will generally get out of your way long before you know they are there. Not all are venomous, but three to watch out for are: **cobras**, fast, nervous snakes who become aggressive if startled; boldly striped **kraits**, which are sluggish and so slow to move on at your approach; and **pit vipers**, whose cryptic coloration and habitual immobility make them a potentially dangerous inhabitant of thick undergrowth. If confronted, back off; if **bitten**, apply a pressure bandage as tightly as you would for a sprain, splint the affected limb, keep it below the level of the heart and try to stay still – the idea is to slow the venom's entry into the bloodstream – and get to hospital as soon as possible. Tourniquets, cutting open the bite and trying to suck the venom out have long been discredited.

Indonesia's other venomous beasts – which include the world's only poisonous bird in Irian Jaya – are mostly on the small side. **Scorpions** are found in a range of habitats and range from large, black varieties capable of painful but otherwise minor stings, to smaller and more dangerous species. If stung, avoid the temptation to cool the stung area (as this intensifies the pain), avoid rubbing, keep the wound warm and get to hospital quickly.

Crocodiles and **sharks** occupy far more time in travellers' nightmares than their realities. You will see sharks if you spend any amount of time snorkelling or diving on Asia's reefs: they are inquisitive but rarely aggressive. The most dangerous species such as the tiger and mako are rare sights for snorkellers, the former liking muddy estuaries and the latter the open sea.

Rabies is transmitted to humans by the bite of carrier animals, who have the disease in their saliva; **tetanus** is an additional danger from such bites. All animals should be treated with caution, but particularly monkeys, cats and dogs. Be extremely cautious with wild animals that seem inexplicably tame, as this can be a symptom. If you do get bitten, scrub the wound with a strong antiseptic and then alcohol – whisky will do – and get to a hospital as soon as possible. Do not attempt to close the wound. The incubation period for the disease can be as much as a year or as little as a few days; once the disease has taken hold it will be fatal.

HEAT PROBLEMS

Travellers who are unused to tropical climates regularly suffer from **sunburn** and **dehydration**. Limit your exposure to the sun in the hours around midday, use high-factor sunscreen and wear dark glasses and a sunhat. You'll be sweating a great deal in the heat, so the important thing is to make sure that you drink enough (see p.25 for advice on water). If you are urinating very little or your urine turns dark (this can also indicate hepatitis), increase your fluid intake. When you sweat you lose salt, so make sure your intake covers this: add some extra to your food or take oral rehydration salts. The home-made equivalent is made by mixing three teaspoons of sugar and one of salt to a litre of water – this gives you roughly the correct mineral balance. A more serious result of the heat is **heatstroke**, indicated by high temperature, dry red skin and a fast erratic pulse. As an emergency measure, try to cool the patient off by covering them in sheets or sarongs soaked in cold water and turn the fan on them; they may need to go to hospital, though. **Heat rashes**, **prickly heat** and **fungal infections** are also common: wear loose cotton clothing, dry yourself carefully after bathing and use medicated talcum powder or anti-fungal powder if you fall victim.

INFORMATION AND MAPS

For information before you go, the Indonesian government maintains a number of tourist promotion offices abroad, where a variety of pamphlets are available. These offer general information on the islands, an outline of inter-island transport, and listings for upmarket accommodation and restaurants.

You'll find a better range of information about Indonesia on the **Internet**, from sites sponsored

> ### INDONESIA TOURIST PROMOTION OFFICES ABROAD
>
> **Australia and New Zealand**: contact the Indonesian Consulate General, 236–238 Maroubra Rd, Maroubra, NSW 2035, Australia (☎02/9344 9933).
>
> **Canada**: Contact the information divisions of the consulates in Toronto (see p.18).
>
> **Singapore**: 10 Collyer Quay, 15-07, Ocean Building, Singapore 0104 (☎534 2837 or 534 1795).
>
> **UK and Ireland**: 41 Whitehall, London SW1A 2BY (☎0171/493 0030; brochures ☎0891/600 180).
>
> **USA**: contact the information division of the consulate in Los Angeles (see p.18).

by commercial businesses to travellers' bulletin boards and newsgroups. The latter can be particularly useful if you want to canvass opinions on a particular destination or guest house, or if you want other travellers' advice on your proposed itinerary. A selection of the best Web sites is given in the box on p.32.

MAP OUTLETS

LONDON

Daunt Books, 83 Marylebone High St, W1M 3DE (☎0171/224 2295); 193 Haverstock Hill, NW3 4QL (☎0171/794 4006).

National Map Centre, 22–24 Caxton St, SW1H 0QU (☎0171/222 2466).

Stanfords, 12–14 Long Acre, WC2E 9LP (☎0171/836 1321); maps by mail or phone order are available on this number. Other branches in London are located within Campus Travel at 52 Grosvenor Gardens, SW1W 0AG (☎0171/730 1314), and within the British Airways offices at 156 Regent St, W1R 5TA (☎0171/434 4744).

The Travel Bookshop, 13–15 Blenheim Crescent, W11 2EE (☎0171/229 5260).

ENGLAND AND WALES

Austick's City Bookshop, 91 The Headrow, Leeds LS1 6OJ (☎0113/243 3099).

Blackwell's, 156–160 West St, Sheffield S1 3ST (☎0114/273 8906). General bookshop selling a wide range of foreign maps; mail-order service. Also 13–17 Royal Arcade, Cardiff CF1 2PR (☎01222/395036); 32 Stonegate, York YO1 2AP (☎01904/624531); Blackwell's University Bookshop, Alsop Building, Brownlow Hill, Liverpool L3 5TX (☎0151/709 8146).

Blackwell's Map and Travel Shop, 53 Broad St, Oxford OX1 3BQ (☎01865/792792). Specialist outlet.

Heffers Map Shop, 3rd Floor, in Heffers' stationery department, 19 Sidney St, Cambridge CB2 3HL (☎01223/568467).

The Map Shop, 30a Belvoir St, Leicester LE1 6QH (☎0116/2471400).

Newcastle Map Centre, 55 Grey St, Newcastle upon Tyne NE1 6EF (☎0191/261 5622).

Stanfords, 29 Corn St, Bristol BS1 1HT
(☎0117/929 9966).

Waterstone's, 91 Deansgate, Manchester M3
2BW (☎0161/832 1992).

SCOTLAND

Aberdeen Map Shop, 74 Skene St, Aberdeen
AB10 1QE (☎01224/637999).

James Thin Melven's Bookshop, 29 Union St,
Inverness IV1 1QA (☎01463/233500).

John Smith and Sons, 57–61 St Vincent St,
Glasgow G2 5TB (☎0141/221 7472).

IRELAND

Easons Bookshop, 40 O'Connell St, Dublin 1
(☎01/873 3811).

Fred Hanna's Bookshop, 27–29 Nassau St,
Dublin 2 (☎01/677 1255).

Hodges Figgis Bookshop, 56–58 Dawson St,
Dublin 2 (☎01/677 4754).

Waterstone's, Queens Building, 8 Royal Ave,
Belfast BT1 1DA (☎01232/247 355); 7 Dawson
St, Dublin 2 (☎01/679 1415); 69 Patrick St, Cork
(☎021/276 522).

USA

Book Passage, 51 Tamal Vista Blvd, Corte
Madera, CA 94925 (☎415/927-0960).

The Complete Traveler Bookstore,
3207 Fillmore St, San Francisco, CA 94123
(☎415/923-1511).

The Complete Traveler Bookstore,
199 Madison Ave, New York, NY 10016
(☎212/685-9007).

Elliot Bay Book Company, 101 S Main St,
Seattle, WA 98104 (☎206/624-6600).

Forsyth Travel Library, 226 Westchester Ave,
White Plains, NY 10604 (☎800/367-7984).

Map Link Inc., 30 S La Patera Lane, Unit 5,
Santa Barbara, CA 93117 (☎805/692-6777).

The Map Store Inc., 1636 1st NW, Washington,
DC 20006 (☎202/628-2608).

Phileas Fogg's Books, Maps and More,
#87 Stanford Shopping Center, Palo Alto, CA
94304 (☎800/533-FOGG).

Rand McNally, 444 N Michigan Ave, Chicago,
IL 60611 (☎312/321-1751); 150 E 52nd St, New
York, NY 10022 (☎212/758-7488); 595 Market
St, San Francisco, CA 94105 (☎415/777-3131).
Rand McNally now has more than twenty stores

across the US; call (☎800/333-0136 ext 2111)
for the address of your nearest store, or for
direct mail maps.

Sierra Club Bookstore, 6014 College Ave,
Oakland, CA 94618 (☎510/658-7470).

Travel Books & Language Center,
4437 Wisconsin Ave, Washington, DC 20016
(☎800/220-2665).

Traveler's Bookstore, 22 W 52nd St, New York,
NY 10019 (☎212/664-0995).

CANADA

Curious Traveller Travel Bookstore,
101 Yorkville Ave, Toronto, ON M5R 1C1
(☎800/268-4395).

International Travel Maps, 555 Seymour St,
Vancouver, BC V6B 3J5 (☎604/879-3621).

Open Air Books and Maps, 25 Toronto St,
Toronto, ON M5C 2R1 (☎416/363-0719).

World Wide Books and Maps, 1247 Granville
St, Vancouver, BC V6Z 1G3 (☎604/687-3320).

AUSTRALIA AND NEW ZEALAND

Bowyangs, 372 Little Bourke St, Melbourne, VIC
(☎03/9670 4383).

The Map Shop, 16a Peel St, Adelaide, SA
(☎08/8231 2033).

Perth Map Centre,
891 Hay St, WA (☎08/9322 5733).

Specialty Maps,
58 Albert St, Auckland (☎09/307 2217).

Travel Bookshop, Shop 3, 175 Liverpool St,
Sydney, NSW (☎02/9261 8200).

Worldwide Maps and Guides,
187 George St, Brisbane (☎07/3221 4330).

ONLINE TRAVEL BOOKSTORES

Adventurous Traveler
www.AdventurousTraveler.com

Amazon *www.amazon.com*

Bookpages *www.bookpages.com*

Literate Traveller *www.literatetraveller.com*

Rumah Bookstore
members.tripod.com/~minkx2/. An online
bookstore that deals only in books about
Indonesia; it's especially strong on titles about
Bali.

INFORMATION

There's a range of **tourist offices** in Indonesia, including **government-run organizations**, such as Kanwil Depparpostel offices, operated by the Jakarta-based directorate general of tourism, and the province-oriented **Dinas Pariwisata** (Diparda). You'll find their offices in larger urban areas and major tourist sites, and, though they often lack hard information, staff often speak some English, and may be able to provide useful maps and lists of services, advise about local transport options or arrange guides. **Opening hours** are roughly Monday to Thursday 8am to 2pm, Friday 8am to 11am and Saturday 8am to 12.30pm.

An increasingly common alternative to government services, **private operators** range from roving freelancers operating out of tourist hotels or restaurants, to established organizations with their own offices. Many are excellent and offer free advice, though they make money through steering you towards their friends and business associates, from whom they receive a commission. Word of mouth and your own judgement is the best way to avoid con artists.

While getting involved with the local **police** is sometimes more trouble than it's worth, in remote locations where there are no other sources of information they may have knowledge, and possibly even maps, of the surrounding region. Don't expect any English to be spoken, but if you're willing to spend some time in pleasantries they can go out of their way to help you out – just remember that they're not obliged to do so.

INDONESIA ONLINE

GENERAL TRAVEL

Access Indonesia www.accessindo.com
Detailed outline of Indonesia's travel potential from Sumatra through to Irian Jaya, with forums, regularly updated bulletin boards, and travel tips.

Batavia Net www.batavianet.com/links General Indonesia browser with links to over 4000 URLs about the archipelago – a great place for a random trawl.

Cybercaptive www.cybercaptive.com
Details of known cybercafés in Indonesia (and the rest of the world), plus links.

Rec. Travel Library www.travel-library.com
Highly recommended site, which has lively pieces on dozens of travel topics, from the budget travellers' guide to sleeping in airports to how to travel light. Good links too.

NEWSGROUPS AND BULLETIN BOARDS
Lonely Planet Thorn Tree
www.lonelyplanet.com/thorn/thorn.htm
Popular travellers' bulletin boards, divided into regions (such as Southeast Asia). Ideal for exchanging information with other travellers and for starting a debate. Also a good place to look for travel companions and up-to-the-minute firsthand advice.

Rec. Travel Asia news:rec.travel.asia
This Usenet forum deals specifically with travel in Asia and gets a lot of traffic, but it takes a long time to browse, as all Asian destinations are lumped under the single category.

Rough Guides Journal
www.roughguides.com/journal/
Newly designed site where you can read others' travel experiences, answer their questions and post your own.

SPORT

Action Asia www.actionasia.com
Net version of the lively adventure travel magazine, with bulletin boards, features and links on everything from hang-gliding to surfing and trekking in Southeast Asia.

AsianDiver
www.asiandiver.com/themagazine/index.html
Online version of the divers' magazine, with good coverage of Indonesia's diving sites including recommendations and firsthand diving stories.

Three Routes Scuba www.3routes.com
Worldwide scuba-diving directory, with scores of links to Indonesian operators.

ONLINE PUBLICATIONS

Asiaweek www.asiaweek.com
Good range of articles taken from the weekly print magazine that specializes in Asian affairs, plus headline snippets from the archive. Accessible without subscription.

Far Eastern Economic Review www.feer.com/
Condensed articles taken from the print version of this Asia-oriented news magazine. Registration is necessary but free.

MAPS

While there is no shortage of **maps** of Indonesia available abroad, none are absolutely accurate. Good all-rounders, suitable for general travel or for navigation in your own transport, include GeoCentre's 1:2,000,000 series, which covers Indonesia in two sections and fine detail, with clearly defined topography and road surfaces. Another longtime standby, the Nelles Indonesia series includes a more convenient single-sheet spread of the country, as well as larger-scale maps of individual regions and provinces, sometimes including basic plans of major cities. In the same league is Periplus' growing range of user-friendly city and provincial maps. All of the above mark locations of major tourist sights and services.

In Indonesia, bookshops and tourist organizations stock home-produced maps of provinces and localities, some listing every road, village, river tributary and mountain; others being more useful for wallpaper than for orienteering. A blend of both, Travel Treasure Maps have annotated sketches of popular regions such as Bali and Tanah Toraja, and make a good supplement to a decent road map.

GETTING AROUND

Comprising well over 10,000 widely scattered islands, it's likely that, unless you concentrate on a single region, simply getting around Indonesia will occupy a fair amount of your time here. At first, things look simple, with plenty of flights, boats, buses, and even trains waiting to ferry you across the archipelago. But, in practice, getting a ticket – which can be hard enough in itself – is no guarantee that the vehicle or vessel will even leave, at least at the advertised time or on any particular day.

While travel isn't always difficult, you'll save yourself a good deal of stress if you keep your schedule as flexible as possible, and are prepared for an inevitable number of frustrations. Delays are common to all forms of transport – including major flights – caused by weather, mechanical failure, or simply not enough passengers turning up. While this won't be a problem with destinations which are covered by multiple transport options, in some places there may be no choice except to travel in discomfort, or to spend days waiting for a plane or boat to materialize.

BUSES AND MINIBUSES

Although there are few regions of Indonesia where roads have yet to reach, **bus travel** is the most frequently used way of getting about the archipelago's islands. On the plus side, buses are cheap and easy to book, leave roughly on time, and give you a good look at the country. The down side is that they're slow, cramped and often plain terrifying: drivers manage incredibly well given the state of the roads and their vehicles, but, as they leave no margin for error, **accidents** can be devastating. In this regard, you'll find that, where there's a choice of operators on any particular route, it pays to ask local people which bus company they recommend.

Tickets are sold a day or more in advance from the point of departure or bus company offices – which are not necessarily near the relevant **bus station** (*terminal* in Indonesian). Where services are infrequent it's a good idea to buy tickets as early as possible, though on other routes it's seldom necessary to turn up more than an hour in advance. Buses might stop along the way to pick up passengers, though usually they don't leave until they're full. Tell the driver your exact destination, as it may be possible to get delivered right to the door of your hotel, though just as many buses terminate at their company offices, again leaving you some distance from the nearest terminal or city centre.

The average **long-distance bus** has padded seats but little leg- or headroom. Indonesians dislike draughts, so don't expect open windows, however hot or smoky conditions inside become. **Luggage** gets stored on the roof (where you can't keep an eye on it), in the aisle or on your lap. Sometimes films are shown, and there's always a sound system blasting out *dangdut* or Western pop. You'll probably get a **snack** of some sort as you board, and regular **meal stops** at roadhouses along the way. **Air-conditioning** alone is not worth paying any extra for – vents are often disconnected or blocked – but on long journeys it's worth forking out for a **luxury bus**, if available, which will have reclining, comfortable seats. These cost twice as much as the standard buses.

On shorter routes you'll use **minibuses**, widely known by their Balinese tag, **bemo**, along with **Kijang**, a jeep lookalike with only two-wheel-drive capability. Though cramped and annoyingly prone to circle their starting points endlessly, looking for customers and fuel, once on their way they are faster than buses and, if you use a series of them to hop long distances, cheaper. Fares are handed over on board, and rarely advertised – keep an eye on what others are paying to avoid being overcharged. You may also have to pay for any space your luggage occupies. In resort areas such as Bali, a more pleasant option are **tourist shuttle buses** specifically for Westerners – though far more expensive than local services, these will take you between points as quickly and smoothly as possible.

PLANES

In some areas, **flying** may be the only practical way to get around. The **cost** of air travel may seem high compared with your living expenses in Indonesia, but tickets are reasonably priced considering the distances involved, and the alternative to a three-hour flight may well be a hellish, forty-hour bus ride, or a ten-day sea voyage.

The main airlines are State-operated **Garuda**, which handles international flights (though you might use them for transport within Indonesia), and **Merpati**, the domestic operator. Provincial services are supplemented by smaller outfits such as **Mandala** and **Bouraq**, and you'll even find remote communities serviced by **missionary aircraft**. The quantity and quality of services is very

uncertain at present, however. The rupiah's devaluation means that most Indonesians can't afford to fly, leading to the closure of marginal routes for want of passengers, and spare parts for maintaining aircraft are becoming too expensive to import. Garuda's fleet is decent enough, but don't expect much from other airlines.

As long as you do so in advance, **buying a ticket** is usually straightforward on main routes, with airline offices and agents in any town with an airport – whether the flight actually eventuates is another matter. **Agents** may even offer discounts, and are often more conveniently located than airline offices. Avoid having to change international air tickets in Indonesia – usually there's no trouble, but you may find yourself stung for unofficial fees.

It's essential to **reconfirm** your seat, as waiting lists can be huge and the temptation for airline staff to bump you off at the slightest pretext in favour of a benefactor is enormous; get a computer printout of the reconfirmation if possible. **Check-in times** are an hour before departure for domestic flights, two hours for international, but you need to get to the airport **early**, as seats on overbooked flights are allocated on a first-come, first-served basis. At other times, "fully booked" planes are almost empty, the result of customers not appearing at the last minute, and if you really have to get somewhere it's always worth going to the airport to check. **Baggage allowance** is 20kg, though smaller aircraft may have a ten-kilo limit, with heavy excesses. On remoter routes, small craft and a lack of radar means weather conditions can cancel flights at short notice. **Departure taxes** are currently around Rp30,000 for internal flights and Rp100,000 for international ones.

BOATS AND FERRIES

Indonesia is a land of water, and **boats** are how most of the population – and an increasing number of foreigners – choose to travel between islands, either on the state shipping line, **Pelni**, or on anything from cargo freighters to tiny fishing vessels. Some regions also have extensive **river networks**, with local ferries and speedboats connecting coastal cities with the villages of the interior; see individual chapters for details of these. Slow, occasionally relaxing, but often as fraught as other forms of transport, going by water at least offers a complete change of style from buses or planes, and there's an unparalleled level of contact with local people.

PELNI

Pelni currently operates about twenty **passenger liners**, which run on two-week or monthly circuits and link Java with ports on all the main island groups between Sumatra and Irian Jaya, one service even extending beyond Indonesia to the Philippines; see pp.36–37 for a chart of the Pelni routes. The vessels are European built, carry 500 to 1600 passengers each, are well maintained, as safe and punctual as any form of transport in Indonesia can be, and the only widespread form of public transport that offers any luxury.

Booking a ticket can take some planning, especially if you're hoping to link up with specific services. Comprehensive **timetables** for the whole country are hard to find; though they won't have anything to give away, Pelni offices should have company wall calendars with complete timetables attached which you can copy, and they will at least know local schedules. **Tickets** are available from Pelni offices three days before departure, but as there's a big demand for cabin berths it's best to pay an **agent** to reserve you these as early as possible. Note that you can only buy tickets for services which depart locally – you can't, for instance, book passage in Ujung Pandang for a vessel that leaves from Bitung.

There are several levels of comfort to choose from, not all of them available on every vessel; it's always possible to **upgrade** after boarding, assuming that berths are available. **First class** consists of a private cabin with a double bed, washroom, TV and air-conditioning– about US$15 a day is standard. **Second class** is similar, but with four bunks and no TV (US$10); **third class** is a six-bunk cabin without the washroom (US$7.50); and **fourth class** is just a bed in a dormitory (US$5). All are good value for money, and include **meals**, eaten in a dining room, which tend to be plentiful rather than interesting; cabins also have large **lockers** to store your luggage.

The alternative is to travel **ekonomi class** (US$1); the experience is noisy, cramped and thick with cigarette smoke, though it's bearable for short trips and not always awful on long ones. You need to buy a rattan mat to sit on, get to the port early (timetables give expected arrival times as well as departures), get aboard and get down into the ekonomi decks to stake out your spot on the floor – all of which you'll be doing with hundreds of others. Don't leave luggage unattended in ekonomi: lock it shut and chain it to something immovable, or lose it. Food is doled out from a hatch and is edible at best, so stock up in advance with instant noodles and biscuits.

PERENTIS AND OTHERS

Where Pelni don't venture, you'll find that **Perentis** (Pioneer) **freighters** do, along with numerous local craft. While these are always willing to rent **deck space** to passengers for next to nothing – say US$1 for 24 hours – comfort and privacy aboard will be nonexistent. Boats are typically in poor condition and jammed to the gunwales with people, their possessions and livestock; if you're lucky there will be an awning to protect you from the elements. On larger vessels, you may find that the crew will rent their beds at about US$5 a person a day, but otherwise you'll need your own sleeping mat, drinking water and snacks, though on Perentis vessels there's usually a galley where you can buy rice and fish heads for a few thousand rupiah. Guard your gear and don't flash anything around, especially when the boat pulls in to ports en route. **Schedules** for these services will be posted at ports, and while you may be able to buy tickets in advance through local agents you can always **pay** for your passage on board.

TRAINS

Inevitably slow, not always cheap or comfortable, and restricted to Java and Sumatra, Indonesia's **railways** are nonetheless worth trying out for relief from the rigours of bus travel, though you'll find a range of service and comfort between different routes.

Java has a pretty comprehensive rail network stretching right across the island, and linking many important ports and bigger cities. Conditions range from fairly dire **ekonomi** class, horrendously overcrowded open carriages with bare wooden benches as the only furnishings, to comfortable **eksecutif** compartments complete with air-conditioning and karaoke, and even sleeper berths. **Tickets** for ekonomi can be bought at the time of travel, but anything more upmarket is best booked through an agent a few days in advance.

Sumatra's railways are pretty fragmentary, limited to disconnected services at either end of the island. In southern Sumatra a limited but useful service links Palembang, Bandar Lampung and Lubuklinggau.

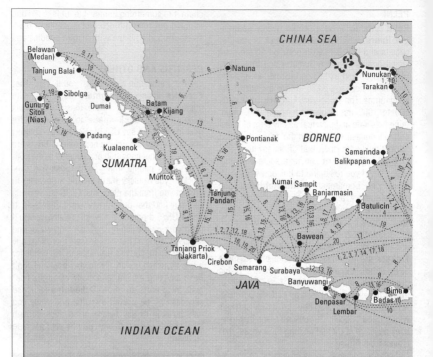

PELNI FERRIES

All **Pelni ferries**, with a couple of minor exceptions, follow the same routes on their outward and return legs, calling in at the same ports on both journeys. The exceptions are *KM Lawit* and *KM Tidar*, nos. 15 and 17 in the list below, which sail between northern Java and Kalimantan without doubling back on themselves, and *KM Kelud* and *KM Sinabung* (nos. 9 and 11), which both follow a circular route between Belawan, near Medan, and Jakarta's Tanjung Priok harbour.

The following table gives the departure and destination ports for each ship, along with a broad summary of the islands visited en route (the chart shows the exact route of each ferry).

Name of ship	Departure port	Destination	Via
1. *KM Kerinci*	Dumai	Nunukan	Kijang, Jakarta, Java, Balikpapan, W. Sulawesi
2. *KM Kambuna*	Gunung Sitoli (Nias)	Bitung	Padang, Jakarta, Balikpapan, W. Sulawesi
3. *KM Rinjani*	Surabaya	Jayapura	S. Sulawesi, Ambon, Tual, N. Irian Jaya
4. *KM Binaiya*	Surabaya	Samarinda	Bawean, Semarang, S. Kalimantan
5. *KM Kelimutu*	Surabaya/Semarang	Banjarmasin	–
6. *KM Bukit Raya*	Surabaya	Natuna	S. Kalimantan, Tanjung Priok, Kijang, West Sulawesi
7. *KM Bukit Siguntang*	Dumai	Kaimana	Kijang, Jakarta, Java, Sulawesi, Banda, Ambon, Tual

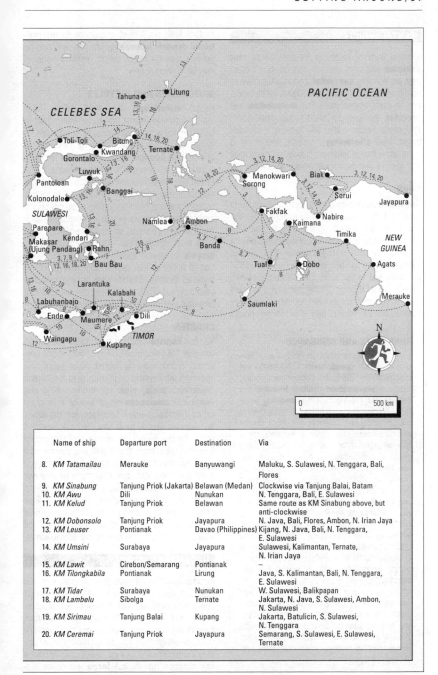

Name of ship	Departure port	Destination	Via
8. *KM Tatamailau*	Merauke	Banyuwangi	Maluku, S. Sulawesi, N. Tenggara, Bali, Flores
9. *KM Sinabung*	Tanjung Priok (Jakarta)	Belawan (Medan)	Clockwise via Tanjung Balai, Batam
10. *KM Awu*	Dili	Nunukan	N. Tenggara, Bali, E. Sulawesi
11. *KM Kelud*	Tanjung Priok	Belawan	Same route as KM Sinabung above, but anti-clockwise
12. *KM Dobonsolo*	Tanjung Priok	Jayapura	N. Java, Bali, Flores, Ambon, N. Irian Jaya
13. *KM Leuser*	Pontianak	Davao (Philippines)	Kijang, N. Java, Bali, N. Tenggara, E. Sulawesi
14. *KM Umsini*	Surabaya	Jayapura	Sulawesi, Kalimantan, Ternate, N. Irian Jaya
15. *KM Lawit*	Cirebon/Semarang	Pontianak	–
16. *KM Tilongkabila*	Pontianak	Lirung	Java, S. Kalimantan, Bali, N. Tenggara, E. Sulawesi
17. *KM Tidar*	Surabaya	Nunukan	W. Sulawesi, Balikpapan
18. *KM Lambelu*	Sibolga	Ternate	Jakarta, N. Java, S. Sulawesi, Ambon, N. Sulawesi
19. *KM Sirimau*	Tanjung Balai	Kupang	Jakarta, Batulicin, S. Sulawesi, N. Tenggara
20. *KM Ceremai*	Tanjung Priok	Jayapura	Semarang, S. Sulawesi, E. Sulawesi, Ternate

RENTAL VEHICLES

In some parts of Indonesia it's possible to **rent vehicles** and drive yourself around. Bali's compact scale makes **car rental** a good alternative to public transport for touring the island, for instance, and in many places you'll find **motorbikes** and **bicycles** available for short-range exploration. Bad roads, hectic traffic and bizarre road rules might make **chartering** a vehicle and driver a more attractive proposition, however – one that Indonesians themselves often take advantage of.

CARS

Car-rental agencies abound in tourist hot spots such as Bali, though at the time of writing the multinational operators, Avis and Hertz, had temporarily ceased operation. Local operators offer a range of vehicles, most frequently 800cc Suzuki Jimneys, which can seat about six (around US$30 per day), and larger, more comfortable jeep-like 1600cc Toyota Kijangs (US$50 per day). The rates drop if you rent for a week or more; one day means twelve hours, and the above prices

---

ROAD RULES AND INSURANCE

Traffic in Indonesia drives on the left and there is a maximum **speed limit** of 70kmph. **Fuel** costs Rp1000–1500 a litre. Drivers must always carry an **international driving licence** and the **vehicle registration documents**. Some cars are fitted with **seat belts** but using them is not obligatory. All motorcyclists, both drivers and passengers, must wear a **helmet**, which will be provided by the rental outlet. Some places have strange traffic rules, including certain roads that change from two-way to one-way during the day, which won't be publicized in any way that is comprehensible to foreigners. The **police** carry out regular spot checks and you'll be **fined** for any infringements.

A few rental outfits offer **insurance** for an added fee of around US$5 a day for a car and US$3 for a motorbike. Read policies carefully to establish exactly what you're covered for before signing. Some fix a maximum payment of perhaps US$25, even if you write the vehicle off; others don't cover you for more than minor damage. Before you take a vehicle, check it thoroughly, and get something in writing about any existing damage or you'll end up being blamed for it. Most vehicle rental agencies keep your passport as security, so you don't have a lot of bargaining power.

---

exclude fuel. You'll need to produce an **international drivers' licence** before you rent, and be warned that on major public holidays vehicles may be in short supply.

MOTORBIKES AND BICYCLES

Rental **motorbikes** vary from small 100cc Yamahas to more robust trail bikes. Prices start at US$5 per day without insurance, with discounts for longer rentals. If you don't have a valid international motorbike **licence**, it may be possible to obtain a local one by taking a test and paying a fee of Rp100,000. Conditions are not suitable for inexperienced drivers, with heavy traffic on major routes, steep hills and difficult driving once you get off the beaten track. There are increasing numbers of accidents involving tourists, so don't take risks.

In most tourist areas, it's possible to rent a **bicycle** for around US$2 a day; check the condition of it before you set off and carry plenty of water as it's hot and thirsty work. Bear in mind that bemos are extremely reluctant to pick you and your bike up if you get tired or stranded somewhere.

CHARTER

You can **charter** cars and motorbikes – meaning you rent the vehicle and driver – just about anywhere in Indonesia. In tourist areas you'll find operators who specialize in renting to foreigners; elsewhere, **taxis**, **ojek** (motorbike taxis) and even public **minibuses** are all available for charter by the hour or day – just approach the driver and bargain directly for a rate. You are expected to pay for the driver's meals and accommodation if the trip takes more than a day, and you must be very clear about who is paying for fuel, where you want to go and stop, and how many people will be travelling. With somebody else taking care of the roads, you've got plenty of time to look around, but it's impossible to predict the quality of the driving. Count on up to US$5 per day for the driver, in addition to the cost of the vehicle rental.

URBAN TRANSPORT

Indonesian cities all have comprehensive public transport, most of it congregating around transit points and marketplaces. Colour-coded or numbered, and bulging with passengers, minibus **bemos** are ubiquitous; they might run fixed circuits, or adapt their routes according to where their customers want to go. Rides usually cost a few hundred rupiah, but **fares** are never displayed, and you'll get overcharged at first – watch what others are paying and hand over the exact amount.

Taxis range from clapped-out rattletraps to shiny new Toyota Kijangs, and can usually be found at airports and outside bigger hotels. Airport taxis are very expensive, and you have to buy a fixed-price ticket from a booth in the terminal building. Elsewhere, make sure the **meter** is on and insist on its use, or **fix a fare** for your trip before setting off.

Other standbys include **ojek** (single-passenger motorbikes) and, in villages, towns and city suburbs, **becak** (cycle-rickshaws), which take two passengers in a covered seat in front of the driver. Jakarta and Banjarmasin also have motorized becak, called **bajaj**. Negotiating **fares** for these vehicles requires a balance of firmness and tact

that can only be picked up with practice; try for around US$1 for ojek and 50c a kilometre for bajaj or becak, though you'll have to pay more for the latter if there are any hills along the way. Other drawbacks to becak are that drivers are often not locals and may have no idea of your where your destination is. They are also notoriously tough customers – never lose your temper with one unless you want a serious fight.

In a few places – particularly on Lombok and parts of northern Sulawesi – you'll also find **horse-drawn traps** known variously as **dokar**, **bendi**, **andong** or **cidomo**. These are often nicely decorated, complete with jingling bells, which you'll hear long before the cart trundles into view, and are used to carry both goods and people. As always, negotiate the fare before getting aboard – US$1 would be about the minimum fare.

ACCOMMODATION

Indonesia boasts an enormous range of places to stay, most of which offer extremely good value, and finding a bed for the night to suit your budget is rarely a problem. In cities and larger towns, along with popular tourist locations, the choice includes basic hostels, family homestays and topnotch hotels, while even in the wilder reaches of the country you'll find villagers willing to put you up for the night.

Finding a room often begins immediately on reaching a new place, when **touts** who hang around the transport terminals approach new arrivals. It's worth listening to them, especially

during peak season in resort areas, when vacancies can be scarce; sometimes touts charge for their services, but the place they'll take you to may give them a commission instead (and often add it to your bill). **Prices** for the simplest double room start at around US$1, with luxury resort hotels topping US$300, and even up to US$1000 for a presidential suite. There's a good deal of **seasonal price variation** in resort areas, however: while in the **peak season** (mid-June through to August, and from December to January) you'll find room rates in these places at a premium, during the **low season** (February through to May, and September through to November) you can do some serious **bargaining**, saving up to forty percent of the published rate in hotels, or at the very least getting the service tax deducted. **Single rooms** (*kamar untuk satu orang*) are a rarity, so lone travellers will get put in a double at about 75 percent of the full price. **Check-out time** is usually noon. Many places are also happy to rent out rooms **long term** at monthly rates, with more salubrious long-term rental properties available in areas well patronized by foreigners.

The cheapest accommodation has shared **bathrooms**, where you wash using a scoop-and-slosh **mandi**. This entails dipping a scoop into a huge basin of water (often built into the bathroom

ACCOMMODATION PRICE CODES

All the **accommodation** listed in this book has been given one of the following price codes. The rates quoted here are for the **cheapest double room** in high season, except for places with dorms, where the code represents the price of a single bed. Where there's a significant spread of prices indicated (④–⑦, for example), the text will explain what extra facilities you get for more money. The 11–21 percent tax charged by most hotels is not included in these price codes.

Because of the current instability of the rupiah, accommodation prices are given throughout in their more stable **US dollar equivalents**, even for places which accept payment in rupiah.

① under $1	③ $2–5	⑤ $10–15	⑦ $35–60	⑨ $100
② $1–2	④ $5–10	⑥ $15–35	⑧ $60–100	and over

wall) and then sloshing the water over yourself. The basin functions as a water supply only and not a bath, so never get in it; all washing is done outside it and the basin should not be contaminated by soap or shampoo. **Toilets** in these places will be Indonesian-style squat affairs, flushed manually with water scooped from the pail that stands alongside, so you'll have to provide **toilet paper** yourself. More upmarket places will have en-suite rooms, with Western-style facilities such as sit-down toilets, showers, hot water, and bathtubs.

HOTELS

Almost any place calling itself a **hotel** in Indonesia will include at least a basic breakfast in the price of a room. All but the cheapest add a service-and-tax **surcharge** of up to 22 percent to your bill, and upmarket establishments quote **prices** – and prefer foreigners to pay – in dollars, though they accept plastic or a rupiah equivalent. In popular areas such as Bali or Tanah Toraja, it's

BARGAIN HOTEL ROOMS

With the vast drop in the number of tourists visiting Indonesia over the last couple of years, and the instability of the rupiah, there are now some terrific **bargains** to be had at the more luxurious end of the accommodation market. Many four- and five-star hotels (⑧–⑨) are now offering rooms for as little as US$12 per night. These sort of bargains are most prevalent in the low season (Sept–March), and in some cases may require bargaining to get the lowest possible price. For the sake of consistency, however, these unusually low prices are not indicated in any of the accommodation listings in the book, which gives the basic, standard room prices only, with no discounts.

worth **booking ahead** during the peak seasons; some hotels will also provide transport to and from transit points if requested in advance.

Bland and anonymous, **cheap urban hotels** (①–④) are perhaps the least attractive lodgings in Indonesia, designed for local businesspeople rather than tourists. Rooms will be tiny, and facilities limited to desk fans and shared, Indonesian-style toilets and mandi. Nonetheless, they are clean enough for short stays and tend to be conveniently located near transport terminals.

Moderately priced hotels (⑤–⑦) are larger and more formal operations. There may be a choice of fan or air-conditioned rooms, almost certainly with hot water. Fridges, phones and TVs feature in the more costly ones, along with swimming pools and "cottage" or "bungalow" style accommodation.

Expensive hotels (⑧–⑨) can be very stylish indeed – Bali has some beauties, complete with spacious ornamental gardens. Facilities are top-class, probably incorporating tennis courts and a gym, as well as several restaurants and a stage for nightly culture shows. The rooms themselves, however, though luxuriously equipped, often lack any local colour or flair. **Super-luxury category hotels** (⑨) are places where you'll certainly be treated to indulgent and tasteful accommodation, the furnishings occasionally inspired by traditional palace designs.

HOMESTAYS AND HOSTELS

The bottom end of Indonesia's accommodation market is provided by **homestays and hostels**, which come in several forms, with an emphasis on friendly service and simple, inexpensive lodgings. Breakfast is usually included, and **meals** are generally available for an extra charge and with advance warning.

Penginapan, or homestays, are most often simply spare bedrooms that a family rents out to supplement their income, though there's often not much difference between these and **losmen**, **pondok** and **wisma**, which are also family-run operations, though organized more along hostel lines. Rooms vary from whitewashed concrete cubes to artful rattan and bamboo structures built to resemble traditional buildings – some are even embellished with woodcarvings and set in their own walled gardens. Furnishings tend to be fairly stark: hard beds and bolsters are the norm, and you may or may not be provided with a light blanket. Most losmen rooms come with netted windows and fans, and nearly all have cold-water bathrooms.

STAYING IN VILLAGES AND CAMPING

If you spend much time roaming rural Indonesia, it's possible at some point that you'll end up staying overnight in **villages** without formal lodgings, where your only option is to seek a bed in a family house. It's certainly an experience to sleep over in a Dayak longhouse in Kalimantan, a Torajan tongkonan in Sulawesi, or a village hut in the Irian highlands, but even in more prosaic regions you're guaranteed close contact with local people – and where foreigners are rare come prepared to be the centre of attention.

In all events, first seek out the nearest person in authority, either the local police in larger villages, or the **kepala desa** (village head), to ask permission to stay. While this is seldom a problem, don't take people's hospitality for granted; some communities may be hardly able to spare what they feed you, and your presence may well disturb village life. In exchange for accommodation and meals, you should offer cash or useful **gifts**, such as rice, salt, cigarettes or food, to the value of about US$2. The only bathroom might be the nearest river, with all bodily functions performed in the open – avoid onlookers by waiting until after dark in these circumstances. Standard rations of rice and fish always become monotonous on extended stays, but it's sometimes possible to buy fresh food and ask your hosts to prepare it for you, giving you the opportunity to try some local delicacies.

With such readily available and inexpensive alternatives, **camping** is something you'll only need to do if you undertake extensive trekking through Indonesia's wilderness areas. Some national parks don't allow camping at all, while in others it's common practice, so always check first. In well-established hiking areas, such as Lombok's Gunung Rinjani, all camping gear, from tents to sleeping bags and cooking equipment, may be available from local villages; in other places you'll have to be entirely self-sufficient.

EATING AND DRINKING

If you come to Indonesia expecting the depth and exuberance of cooking elsewhere in Southeast Asia, you'll be disappointed. It's not that Indonesian food is bad – far from it – just that meals lack variety. Coconut milk and aromatic spices at first add intriguing tastes to the meats, vegetables and fruits, but after a while everything starts to taste the same – spiced, fried and served with rice. There are a number of regional cooking styles and local specialities in Indonesia, however, and with a little determination you'll be able to track them down amongst the higher-profile Chinese food, pizzas, hamburgers and French fries on offer.

INGREDIENTS

Particularly in the current economic climate, the **availability** of food varies greatly throughout Indonesia. Busy rural markets can be seasonally well stocked, but in poorer areas – including urban centres – the pickings can be slim and prices high for even basic necessities. If you're planning to spend time in Indonesia's **remoter places**, you may find yourself living off boiled rice and chillies unless you bring in your own supplies.

Rice (*nasi*) is the favoured **staple** across much of the country, an essential, three-times-a-day fuel. A few places, however, are either unable to afford this luxury or have yet to grow tired of local alternatives. Many regions with poor soil or low rainfall grow **cassava** (manioc), a tuber native to South America which was introduced during colonial times, in the highlands of Irian Jaya they favour **yams** (sweet potatoes), and in rural Maluku the crop is **sago** (tapioca), the starchy pith of a spiky, swamp-dwelling palm. **Noodles**, a Chinese import, are also widely popular, though they tend to supplement, rather than replace, rice.

As you would expect of an island nation, the **seafood** is often superb, and some markets regularly display excellent tuna, mackerel, reef fish, octopus, squid, lobster and shellfish. **Chicken**, **goat** and **beef** are the main meats in this predominantly Muslim country, but non-Islamic areas offer the chance to try other **game** – deer and pig are favourites, but you may also find dog, rat and even cassowary and fruit bat on local menus.

VEGETABLES AND FRUIT

Vegetarians can eat well in Indonesia: bitter starfruit leaves, aubergines, water spinach (*kangkung*), plus various beans, green peppers, assorted kales, cabbages, Oriental lettuces, carrots, tomatoes and pumpkins are all available in markets, though restaurant selections can be limited to **cap cay** – fried mixed vegetables. There's also plenty of **tofu** and the popular **tempeh**, a fermented soya-bean cake, thought to have originated in Java about a century ago.

There's an wide assortment of **fruit** available across the country. You'll see banana, coconut and papaya growing in back gardens, with markets often loaded with pineapple, watermelon, citrus fruit including **pomelo** (a sweet, thick-skinned grapefruit), guava, avocado, passion fruit, mango, soursop and its close relative, the custard apple. Then there are the seasonal, purple-skinned **mangosteen**, whose sweet white flesh is one of the best of all tropical fruits; hairy, perfumed **rambutan**, closely related to the lychee; dry **salak** or snakefruit, named after its brown scaly skin; and the **starfruit** (*carambola*), whose taste and texture resembles a watery, crunchy apple. **Jackfruit**, which can weigh 20kg, has bobbly skin and flesh, and can be eaten ripe as a fruit or cooked green in curries as a vegetable. Venerated by connoisseurs, you won't forget an encounter with **durian**: oval, football-sized, encased in a spiky armour, and emitting a stench which has seen it banned from airlines and hotels. Ripening towards the end of the year, the durian splits into segments, each revealing a seed surrounded by pasty yellow pulp, the taste of which is acrid, rich, acidic and savoury all at once. Indonesians adore durian and pay high prices for quality fruit, but many Westerners find the smell, let alone the taste, utterly foul.

INDONESIAN FOOD

The backbone of all Indonesian cooking, **spices** are ground and chopped together, then fried in copious oil to form a **paste**, which is either used as the flavour base for **curries**, or rubbed over ingredients prior to **frying** or **grilling**. While all pastes are broadly similar, their composition varies from place to place, and with which every meat or vegetable is being cooked. **Chillies** always feature, along with **terasi** (also known as *belacan*), a fermented shrimp paste whose raw odour is mitigated by cooking. Ginger, onion and garlic add background flavour; more subtle scents derive from lime leaves, lemon grass, pandanus leaves, lime juice, cinnamon and turmeric. Another vital ingredient is *gulah merah*, a dark **palm sugar** sold in cakes. Some regions also use **cloves** and **nutmegs**, two spices native to Maluku which have been exported overseas for two thousand years.

Cooking methods tend to be uncomplicated. **Chargrilling** adds a nicely smoky flavour to sate, chicken, and especially seafood, but **frying** is by far the most common way of preparing food – deep-fried chicken is so popular it could claim to be Indonesia's national dish. Vegetables may be plain boiled, but the other main cooking method is **stewing**, often in coconut milk. This results in either a soupy, **wet curry** (*gulai*), or continues until all the liquid is evaporated, producing a **dry curry** (rendang), with the ingredients left in a rich, spicy coat.

Meals are served with a number of **relishes** such as **soy sauce** – available in thick and sweet (*kecap manis*) or thin and salty (*kecap asin*) forms – and **sambal**, a blisteringly hot blend of chillies and spices, to be used with caution until your taste buds adjust.

COOKING AND STYLES

Light meals and **snacks** include various rice dishes such as **nasi goreng**, a plate of fried rice with shreds of meat and vegetables and topped with a fried egg, and **nasi campur**, boiled rice served with a small range of side dishes. **Noodle** equivalents are also commonly available, as are **gado-gado**, steamed vegetables dressed in a peanut sauce, and **sate**, small kebabs of meat or fish, barbecued over a fire and again served with spicy peanut sauce. Indonesian **soups** tend to be watery but filling affairs, stacked with noodles, vegetables, meatballs, or unidentifiable bits and pieces. Indonesian **bread** (*roti*) is made from sweetened dough, and usually accompanies a morning cup of coffee. **Cakes** (*kueh*) are a big afternoon institution in parts of the country; the Muslim city of Banjarmasin in Kalimantan is renowned for the special evening selection prepared during Ramadan for the faithful to break their daytime fast. Indonesians actually have a notoriously **sweet tooth**, relishing snacks such as **es kacang**, a mound of shaved ice piled over cooked soya beans, lovingly drenched in brightly coloured syrup and condensed milk – surprisingly refreshing. You'll also come across all sorts of fruit-flavoured **ice cream**, including durian.

Regional cooking tends to differ most in emphasis and ingredients used rather than the method of cooking. **Balinese** cuisine is one of the most accomplished, sweet and not overly hot, well worth tracking down if you visit the island. Sumatran **Padang restaurants** are found right across Indonesia, the typically fiery food precooked – not the healthiest way to eat – and displayed cold on platters piled up in a pyramid shape inside a glass-fronted cabinet. There are no menus; you either select your composite meal by pointing to the dishes on display, or just sit down, the staff bring you a selection, and you pay for what you consume. The range of options is variable. You may encounter boiled *kangkung* (water spinach); *tempeh*; egg, vegetable, meat or seafood curry; fried whole fish; potato cakes; and fried cow's lung.

ASIAN AND WESTERN FOOD

Indonesia's substantial ethnic Chinese population means that **Chinese food** is widely available, and you'll probably be familiar already with the range of southern- and Straits- style dishes. In the biggest cities and tourist spots you'll also find other **Asian and Western restaurants**, offering everything from Indian through to Mexican and Italian cuisine – sometimes very good, but often mediocre. Multinational **fast-food** chains have really taken the country by storm over the past few years, with *McDonald's, Burger King, KFC* and *Dunkin' Donuts* all well established in towns and cities.

PLACES TO EAT, ETIQUETTE AND PRICES

The cheapest places to eat in Indonesia are at the **mobile stalls** which ply their wares around the streets and bus stations during the day, and congregate at night markets after dark. Known as **kaki lima** – five legs – individual carts specialize in one or two dishes, and have their own cooking apparatus, ingredients and even plates, cutlery and stools for their customers. Vendors call out their selection, you simply place your order and they cook it up on the spot. In big cities you could spend weeks eating out at these carts and never be served the same thing twice; those in Sulawesi's Ujung Pandang are famous, forming a kilometre-long string along the seafront in the afternoon.

Slightly more upmarket – often only in that the fixtures and location are more permanent – **warung** are the bottom line in Indonesian restaurants, usually just a few tables and chairs in a kitchen offering much the same food as *kaki lima*. **Rumah makan** – literally "eating house" – are bigger, offer a wider range of dishes and comfort, and may even have a menu. Anything labelled as a **restaurant** will probably be catering to foreigners, with fully fledged service and possibly international food. Don't count on everyone's meal arriving together in smaller establishments, as there may be just one gas burner in the kitchen.

Indonesian **meal times** are vague, with many people snacking throughout the day rather than sitting down at fixed times for a major feed – if they do, it will most likely be in the evening. Coffee shops and market and transit-station snack stalls are open from dawn until after dark, but more substantial places generally open mid-morning and close by 8 or 9pm at night, possibly shutting down through the afternoon as well.

A FOOD GLOSSARY

GENERAL TERMS

Asam manis	Sweet and sour	*Makan*	To eat	*Piring*	Plate
Daftar makanan	Menu	*Makan malam*	Dinner	*Pisau*	Knife
Dingin	Cold	*Makan pagi*	Breakfast	*Saya injin bayar*	I want to pay
Enak	Delicious	*Makan siang*	Lunch	*Saya seorang*	I am
Garpu	Fork	*Minum*	Drink	*vegetaris*	vegetarian
Gelas	Glass	*Panas*	Hot (temperature)	*Saya tidak*	I don't eat
Goreng	Fried	*Pedas*	Hot (spicy)	*makan daging*	meat
				Sendok	Spoon

MEAT, FISH AND BASIC FOODS

Anjing	Dog	*Itik*	Duck	*Paniki*	Fruit bat
Ayam	Chicken	*Jaja*	Rice cakes	*Petis*	Fish paste
Babi	Pork	*Kambing*	Goat	*Sambal*	Hot chilli sauce
Bakmi	Noodles	*Kare*	Curry	*Sapi*	Beef
Buah	Fruit	*Kecap asam*	Sour soy sauce	*Soto*	Soup
Es	Ice	*Kecap manis*	Sweet soy sauce	*Tikkus*	Rat
Garam	Salt			*Telur*	Egg
Gula	Sugar	*Kepiting*	Crab	*Udang*	Prawn
Ikan	Fish	*Nasi*	Rice	*Udang karang*	Lobster

EVERYDAY DISHES

Ayam bakar	Fried chicken
Ayam goreng	Grilled chicken
Babi gulin	Balinese pork
Bakmi goreng	Fried noodles mixed with vegetables and meat
Bakso	Soup containing meatballs
Botok daging sapi	Spicy minced beef with tofu, tempeh and coconut milk
Cap cay	Mixed fried vegetables
Es campur	Fruit salad and shredded ice
Fu yung hai	Seafood omelette
Gado-gado	Steamed vegetables served with a spicy peanut sauce
Ikan bakar	Grilled fish
Ikan mas	Carp
Kangkung	Water convolvulus
Krupuk	Rice or cassava crackers, usually flavoured with prawn
Kue tiaw	Singaporean stir-fry of flat rice noodles and meat
Lalapan	Raw vegetables and sambal
Lawar	Balinese raw meat paste; also refers to a sea worm eaten in parts of Maluku
Lontong	Steamed rice in a banana-leaf packet
Lumpia	Spring rolls
Murtabak	Thick, dough pancake, often filled with meat
Nasi ayam	Boiled rice with chicken
Nasi campur	Boiled rice served with small amounts of vegetable, meat, fish and sometimes egg
Nasi goreng	Fried rice
Nasi gudeg	Rice with jackfruit and coconut milk curry
Nasi putih	Plain boiled rice
Nasi rames	Rice with vegetable and meat side dishes
Nasi rawon	Rice with soya-braised meat
Nasi soto ayam	Chicken-and-rice soup
Pisang goreng	Fried bananas
Rendang	Dry-fried beef and coconut-milk curry
Rijstaffel	Dutch/Indonesian dish made up of six to ten different meat, fish and vegetable dishes with rice
Rujak	Hot spiced fruit salad
Rujak petis	Vegetable and fruit in spicy peanut and shrimp sauce
Tahu goreng telur	Tofu omelette
Sate	Meat or fish kebabs served with a spicy peanut sauce

Soto ayam	Chicken soup			Sayur lodeh	Vegetable and coconut-milk soup
Soto daging	Beef soup				
Soto makassar	Buffalo offal soup			Urap-urap/	Vegetables with coconut
Sayur bening	Soup with spinach and corn			urap timum	and chilli

FRUIT

Apel	Apple	Kelapa	Coconut	Pisang	Banana
Belimbing	Starfruit	Mangga	Mango	Salak	Snakefruit
Buah anggur	Grapes	Manggis	Mangosteen	Semangkha air	Watermelon
Jeruk manis	Orange	Nanas	Pineapple	Sirsak	Soursop
Jeruk nipis	Lemon	Nangka	Jackfruit		

DRINKS

Air jeruk	Orange juice	Brem	Local rice beer	Tolong tanpa es	Without ice, please
Air jeruk nipis	Lemon juice	Kopi	Coffee		
Air minum	Drinking water	Kopi susu	White coffee	Tolong tanpa gula	Without sugar, please
Arak	Palm or rice spirit	Sopi	Palm spirit		
		Susu	Milk	Tuak	Palm wine
Bir	Beer	Teh	Tea		

Eating out, it's usual to order and eat individual dishes, though each diner may receive a bowl of rice and a range of smaller dishes which everyone shares – the origin of the **rijstaffel** (rice-table), a Dutch version of this style of serving food. **Food etiquette** is pretty much the same as in the West, though in cheaper places and at home Indonesians generally eat with their right hands instead of using cutlery, mashing a ball of rice in their fingers and using it to scoop up a mouthful of food. Most warung and restaurants will have a basin in a corner so you can wash before and after eating.

Prices vary dramatically depending on the location rather than the quality of the meals. Stalls or warung serve dishes for as little as 50c, while tourist restaurants will charge from three times as much for the same dish. For non-Indonesian food such as pizza, pasta and steak, prices start at around US$3.50. Where restaurants are reviewed in the Guide, **inexpensive** means you will get a satisfying main dish for less than US$2, **moderate** means it'll be US$2.50–5, and **expensive** is US$5.50 and over. In addition, many of the moderate and all of the expensive establishments will add up to 21 percent **service tax** to the bill.

DRINKS

Alcohol can be a touchy subject in parts of Indonesia, where public drunkenness is, on the whole, at least frowned upon, and in Muslim areas it may incur serious trouble. There's no need to be overly paranoid about this in cities, however, and the locally produced **beers**, Anker and Bintang Pilsners, are good, and widely available in 320ml and 620ml bottles at Chinese restaurants and bigger hotels. In non-Islamic regions, even small warung sell beer.

Spirits are less publicly consumed, and, depending on local rules, may be technically **illegal**, so indulge with caution. Nonetheless, home-produced brews are often sold openly in villages, discreetly supplied by local sources, or specially prepared for festivals. **Tuak** (also known as **balok**) or **palm wine** is made by tapping a suitable tree for its alcoholic sap, comes in plain milky-white or pale red varieties, and varies in strength depending

BETEL

One habit that you're bound to notice in rural Indonesia is the chewing of *pinang*, or **betel**. These small pellets are made up of three essential ingredients – sliced **areca palm nut**, wrapped in a **pepper leaf** smeared with chalky **lime** – lodged inside the cheek. The resultant juice works as a mild stimulant, also producing bright-red saliva which eventually stains the lips and teeth red. Other ingredients can be added according to taste, including tobacco, cloves, cinnamon, cardamom, turmeric and nutmeg. You'll see mainly the older folk indulging in this pastime, and may come across decorated **sireh boxes**, used to store the ingredients, in museums.

on how long it has been left to ferment – you can either walk away from a litre of the stuff, or else need two days to recover. Far more potent are rice wine (variously known as **arak** or **brem**), and **sopi**, a distillation of *tuak*, either of which can leave you incapacitated after a heavy session. **Imported spirits** are only available in major tourist areas and at expensive hotels.

Indonesian **coffee** is amongst the best in the world, and Indonesians are great coffee and **tea** drinkers. Coffee is prepared by putting ground coffee in a glass, adding boiling water, and waiting for the grounds to settle before drinking. Indonesians then ladle in copious amounts of

sugar, or occasionally condensed milk, and gape in disbelieving horror at Westerners who dare to drink their coffee unsweetened. Instant coffee is available in tourist restaurants.

Don't drink **tap water** in Indonesia. **Boiled water** (*air putih*) can be requested at accommodation and restaurants, and dozens of brands of **bottled water** (*air minum*) are sold throughout the islands, as are imported **soft drinks**. It's also tempting to try the masses of delicious, freshly made **fruit drinks** available, but be cautious, as in many places you can't be sure of the purity of the water or ice used in their manufacture (see "Health", p.25).

COMMUNICATIONS

Although the communications network in Indonesia is improving all the time, and the phone and postal services in the big cities are often very efficient, in smaller towns and villages you may still find the whole process very time-consuming and frustrating.

POSTAL SERVICES

The **postal system** in Indonesia is reasonably reliable, at least in the cities. Most **post offices** (*Kantor pos*) in Indonesia follow standard government office hours (Mon–Thurs 8am–2pm, Fri 8–11am, Sat 8am–1pm), though those in the larger cities often stay open longer, and some even open on Sunday. Stamps (*perangko*) and aerogrammes (*surat udara*) can be bought, letters

(*surat*) and parcels (*paket*) can be sent, and in some cases, email, fax and poste restante facilities are available at these offices. Supplementing the government offices are the privately owned **warpostels**, which are a little more expensive but often more conveniently located, and stay open longer.

LETTERS

Domestic mail (mail sent within Indonesia) can be sent either in a blue *kilat* envelope (Rp700), which is for regular airmail, or in a yellow *kilat khusus* envelope (Rp1200) for airmail express.

Overseas letters to Western Europe and America take between seven and ten days to arrive. International airmail rates for letters up to 20g are: Rp3500 to Australia, Rp4500 to Europe, Rp5000 to the USA and Rp3500 to Canada. Aerogrammes in Indonesia cost Rp1500 and can be bought from most post offices, while postcards cost Rp2500–3500 to send.

PARCELS

In the larger cities in Indonesia, the **parcels** section is usually in a separate part of the building to the rest of the post office (and sometimes even in a separate building altogether). Sending parcels overseas from Indonesia is expensive and time-consuming. From Indonesia, parcels can be sent by surface mail (under 10kg only) – the cheapest way of sending mail home – or airmail, and you can register (*tercatat*) and insure the contents too. Don't seal the parcel before staff at the post office have checked what's inside it; in the larger towns and cities there's usually somebody outside the post office who offers a parcel-wrapping service. A parcel weighing up to 3kg airmailed to Europe takes about three weeks and costs around Rp110,000; a 5–10kg parcel costs Rp375,000 (by sea it will cost Rp120,000 and takes three months). *Kantor pos* won't handle anything over 10kg, so if you want to send anything particularly large you're better off using the services offered by the major galleries and craft shops, who pack everything carefully and also insure it.

POSTE RESTANTE

Mail can be sent to Indonesia via **poste restante**. The system in Indonesia is fairly efficient, though stick to the cities – post offices in small towns and villages often don't have a poste restante service. Most post offices hold letters for a maximum of one month. To ensure that your mail doesn't get filed under your first name, ask the sender to write your surname in block capitals and underline it. The address should consist of: poste restante (preferably also in capitals), Kantor pos, city, province, Indonesia. When picking up mail, be sure that the staff check under your first name too, as misfilings are common.

EMAIL AND THE INTERNET

Internet access is becoming increasingly widespread in Indonesia, and there are now tourist-friendly Internet offices and cybercafés in many towns and cities. All these places offer Internet access as well as email services, and most charge around Rp6000 per fifteen minutes online. There's usually an extra charge for printing out emails, and a small charge for receiving emails at the cybercafé's email address.

If you're going to be passing through cyber-friendly tourist centres on a fairly regular basis, **email** can make a good alternative to post office postes restantes – even if you're not on the Internet at home. There are three different ways of doing this. Unfortunately, the most unreliable option is to use your existing, **home-based email account**. Though international Internet service providers (such as Globalnetwork and Uunet) and online service providers (such as AOL and Compuserve) pride themselves on having local connection numbers all over the world, the reality is that in Indonesia these local numbers (when they do exist) are nearly always confined to Jakarta – not at all useful if you're sitting in a cybercafé on Bali. Lines are so oversubscribed that it is almost impossible to get a line to major Jakarta ISPs at any time of day or. Do not be duped by ISP staff in your home country who assure you that connecting to the local number is no problem – it's unlikely they've tried it out for themselves.

If you have one of these international or online ISP accounts you would be much better off subscribing to a **free email account**, such as **Hotmail**, for the duration of the trip and relying on that instead. It's relatively cheap and easy to set up a forwarding system from your existing home-based email account to a new account. Even if you don't already have one, you can establish a free, private and personal email account either before you leave home (using someone else's system or through a local cybercafé) or in a cybercafé in Indonesia. Several companies offer this service, but by far the most popular is Hotmail which is completely free to join as it's financed by advertising. Any cybercafé will have Hotmail bookmarked for easy access and will help you set up a new account. All you need to do is access *www.hotmail.com* and follow the instructions. Give friends and family your new Hotmail address and they can send you email any time – it will stack up in a nice pile in your in-box, ready for you to access whenever you can. You can of course use your Hotmail account to send out email as well. Other free email accounts include those at *www.yahoo.com* and *www.mailcity.com* and one run by *tnt magazine* (*www.tntmag.co.uk*), for which you need to pay a small registration fee.

The third option is to use **local cybercafé addresses** as email postes restantes. This obviously involves getting the cybercafé's email address and giving it to your correspondents, so it's only really viable when you're staying near a cybercafé for a few days. Many cybercafés have an efficient system whereby they print out the day's emails and keep them in a file for a few weeks, much as a post office would; others just let you scroll through their in-box. The important thing to remember when using cybercafé addresses is that your correspondent should write your name in the subject field box. These cafés let you use their accounts to send email as well, so it doesn't matter that you haven't got your own. To find a list of cybercafés in Indonesia, check out *cybercaptive.com*.

For details on Indonesia Web sites, see "Indonesia online" box on p.32.

TELEPHONES

There are two types of telephone office in Indonesia: the government-run **Telkom** (and, occasionally, **wartel Telkom**) offices, which you'll find in every town and city, and privately owned **wartels**, which, like the warpostels above, tend to be slightly more expensive, but are often conveniently located. Both offer similar services, including fax, telex and telegraph services, though the wartels rarely have a **collect-call service** and if they do they tend to charge a premium for you to use it.

The government telephone offices are often open all the time; some of the wartels are also 24 hours a day, though most close at midnight and open again at 7am. In addition to these offices, large towns and cities also have public **payphones**, which are useful for local calls and which take Rp100 and Rp500 coins. Put the coins in only after the person you're calling has picked up the phone and started speaking. These phones are slowly being phased out in favour of phones that take telephone cards (*kartu telefon*). The cards come in denominations of 20 units (Rp2000), 60 units (Rp6000), 80 units (Rp8000), 100 units (Rp10,000), 280 units (Rp28,000), 400 units (Rp40,000) and 680 units (Rp68,000).

For dialling to and from the region, see the box below for all the relevant **dialling code** information.

LOCAL AND LONG-DISTANCE CALLS

A **local call** (*panggilan lokal*) is a call to any destination that shares the same area code. These calls can be made from coin-operated phones, card phones, or at Telkom and wartel offices.

Long-distance domestic calls (*panggilan inter-lokal*) – to anywhere in Indonesia with a different area code – are charged according to a zone system. For example, if you're ringing from Jakarta, Sumatra, Java and Bali are in Zone 1, Kalimantan in Zone 2 and so on, to Irian Jaya in Zone 5.

The rates per minute are: Zone 1, Rp900; Zone 2, Rp1000; Zone 3, Rp1200; Zone 4, Rp1500 and Zone 5, Rp2000. These rates are subject to a discount for calls made between 9pm and 6am. To confuse matters further, in addition to the zone system there is also a two-tier system of charges depending on whether you want to make a normal (*biasa*) call or an express (*segara*) call that connects you much faster, but costs twice as much.

INTERNATIONAL CALLS

A similar zonal system operates for **international calls** using **IDD** (International Direct Dialling) phones. The rates are fixed, though the premium charged by the private wartels varies. Most places quote their rates without the obligatory ten percent tax. The zones are:

Zone 1: Brunei, Malaysia and Singapore; Rp3650 per minute.

USEFUL CODES AND NUMBERS

For the time difference, see p.65.

PHONING ABROAD

From the UK: dial ☎0062 + area code minus the first 0 + number.

From the USA: dial ☎01162 + area code minus the first 0 + number.

From Australia; dial ☎001162 + area code minus the first 0 + number.

From Ireland; dial ☎01062 + area code minus the first 0 + number.

From Canada; dial ☎01162 + area code minus the first 0 + number.

From New Zealand; dial ☎0062 + area code minus the first 0 + number.

FROM INDONESIA

Dial ☎00 + IDD country code (see below) + area code (minus the first 0) + number.

DD CODES

Australia ☎61	UK ☎44	Canada ☎1	New Zealand ☎64	USA ☎1

USEFUL NUMBERS

International director enquiries ☎102
Local and long-distance directory enquiries ☎106

Local and long-distance operator ☎100
International operator ☎101

Zone 2: Philippines and Thailand; Rp4000 per minute.

Zone 3: Australia, Hong Kong, India, Japan, New Zealand, South Korea and the USA; Rp4900 per minute.

Zone 4: Canada and the UK; Rp5400 per minute.

Zone 5: Africa, Alaska, South America and Western Europe; Rp5650 per minute.

Zone 6: Israel; Rp6250 per minute.

These rates are subject to a 25 percent discount at night (usually between midnight and 6am) and at weekends.

In addition to IDD, a few of the big hotels, Telkom offices and airports also have **home-country direct** phones. With these, you simply press the appropriate button for the country you're ringing, and you'll be put through to the international switchboard of that country. With these phones you can **call collect** (reverse-charge calls), or the operator will debit you and you can settle with the cashier after the call. Home-country direct phones are also useful if you have a BT or AT&T chargecard. They do, however, cost more than IDD phones. To reach your home-country operator on an IDD phone, dial ☎001-801 – and then the special HCD country code: Australia ☎61, Canada ☎16, New Zealand ☎64, UK ☎44, USA ☎10.

THE MEDIA

Since Suharto was toppled in May 1998, Indonesia's newspapers, after years of suppression and enforced self-censorship, have become increasingly bold in their criticism of the government and their coverage of Indonesia's politics in general. It appears that these days newspapers are allowed to voice their own political opinions and, unsurprisingly, nearly all have sided with the pro-reform movement in its attempt to introduce democracy to the country. The pages of Indonesia's daily newspapers are filled with anti-government article and letters, and don't shy away from criticizing the government in their editorials. Occasionally the newspapers go too far and slip from reporting into polemic. But even this is a welcome change after thirty years of turgid, criticism-free reporting of the Suharto regime.

Europe, America and Australia. The *Bali Echo*, a glossy but informative English-language magazine, comes out every two months and can be found in the larger bookshops on Bali.

For a truly balanced and thought-provoking account of Indonesian current affairs, *Inside Indonesia* magazine, published six times a year from offices in Australia, is superb. Subscriptions can be taken out by writing to them at PO Box 190, Northcote, VIC 3070, Australia.

The foreign news section in the *Jakarta Post* is fairly slight, and for in-depth coverage of international events you're better off buying the Western weeklies like *Time*, *Newsweek* or the *Economist* – though the latter is hard to find in Indonesia. The much-respected *Far Eastern Economic Review* provides a more in-depth coverage of events in Indonesia, though outside the big cities it is almost impossible to find.

NEWSPAPERS AND MAGAZINES

Indonesia has a number of large-circulation dailies, including the Catholic mouthpiece, *Kompas*, the Denpasar-based *Bali Post*, the Jakartan *Sianr Harapan*, and *Suara Karya*, the newspaper of Golkar. There is currently just one **English-language** newspaper, the broadsheet *Jakarta Post*, which is published daily except Sundays. Most of the stuff they publish is pretty dull, though they do print international newsagency pieces and sports results from

TELEVISION AND RADIO

Thanks to the introduction of **satellite television**, almost everywhere in Indonesia can receive a TV signal, and even the smallest villages in the most remote corners of the archipelago have a satellite dish. **Televisi Republik Indonesia** is the national TV station, showing a mixture of soaps, sports and news bulletins. English-language news is given at around 6.30pm daily. The satellite dishes can also pick up CNN, MTV and other English-language channels.

Radio Republik Indonesia is the national radio station, broadcasting round the clock from every provincial capital in the country. Most of the programmes are in Indonesian, though they occasionally have English-language news bulletins. You can watch some of the programmes being recorded, such as the wayang performances in Central Java (see p.204 for details). Tickets are free, and details of forthcoming programmes can be found in the reception or lobby areas of radio stations. There are plenty of other, smaller stations in Indonesia that broadcast to the local area only. If you have a shortwave radio, you should be able to pick up English-language stations such as the BBC World Service and the Voice of America. Times and wavelengths can change every three months, so check a recent schedule before you travel.

OPENING HOURS, HOLIDAYS AND FESTIVALS

– including **government offices** – may also close at 11.30am on Fridays, the main day of prayer, and **national public holidays** see all commerce compulsorily curtailed for the duration of the event.

In addition to national public holidays, there are frequent **religious festivals** throughout Indonesia's Muslim, Hindu, Chinese and indigenous communities. Each of Bali's 20,000 **temples** has an anniversary celebration, for instance, and other ethnic groups may host elaborate **marriages** or **funerals**, along with more secular holidays. Your visit is almost bound to coincide with a festival of one kind or another, and possibly several.

Opening hours are complicated in Indonesia, with government offices, post offices, businesses and shops setting their own timetables.

As a rough outline, **businesses** such as airline offices open Monday to Friday 8am to 4pm and Saturday 8am to noon, with variable arrangements at lunchtime. **Banking hours** are Monday to Friday 8am to 3pm, Saturday 8am to 1pm, but may not handle foreign exchange in the afternoons or at weekends. Moneychangers usually keep shop rather than bank hours. **Post offices** operate roughly Monday to Thursday 8am to 2pm, Friday 8 to 11am, Saturday 8am to 12.30pm. **Markets** start soon after dawn and the freshest produce will be gone by 10am, though trading will continue through the day, firing up again after dark at **night markets**. Be aware, however, that all these times are **flexible**: opening times for **museums** or **temples** are also very fickle, and sometimes boil down to whenever staff or caretakers manage to turn up – advice for these places is given throughout the Guide.

Whatever they actually are, all opening hours also tend to be relatively longer in tourist areas, and much shorter in rural regions. **Muslim businesses**

NATIONAL PUBLIC HOLIDAYS

Most of the **public holidays** fall on different dates of the Western calendar each year, as they are calculated according to Muslim or local calendars.

December/January *Idul Fitri*, the celebration of the end of Ramadan.

January 1 New Year's Day (*Tahun Baru*).

March/April *Nyepi*, Balinese *saka* New Year.

March/April Good Friday and Easter Sunday.

May *Idul Adha* (*Hajh*) Muslim Day of Sacrifice.

May *Waisak* Day, anniversary of the birth, death and enlightenment of Buddha.

May/June Ascension Day.

June/July *Muharam*, Muslim New Year.

July/August *Maulud Nabi Muhammad*, the anniversary of the birth of Mohammed.

August 17 Independence Day (*Hari Proklamasi Kemerdekaan*) celebrates the proclamation of Indonesian Independence in 1945 by Dr Sukarno.

December Ascension Day of Mohammed.

December 25 Christmas Day.

MUSLIM FESTIVALS

Ramadan, a month of fasting during daylight hours, falls during the ninth Muslim month (starting in November/December/January). Followers of the Wetu Telu branch of Islam on Lombok observe their own three-day festival of *Puasa* rather than the full month, however. Even in non-Islamic areas, Muslim restaurants and businesses shut down during the day, and in staunchly Islamic parts of the country, such as rural Lombok, Sumatra or Kalimantan's Banjarmasin, you should not eat, drink or smoke in public at this time. **Idul Fitri**, also called *Hari Raya* or *Lebaran*, the first day of the tenth month of the Muslim calendar, marks the end of Ramadan and is a two-day national holiday of noisy celebrations.

Al Miraj (February), celebrates Mohammed's visit to God led through the seven heavens by the archangel and his return to earth with instructions for the faithful, which included observance of the Muslim five-times-a-day prayers. In May or June, the festival of sacrifice, **Idul Adha**, commemorates Abraham's willingness to sacrifice Isaac at God's command, and is marked by the cleaning and tidying of cemeteries and by animal sacrifice. **Muslim New Year**, *Muharram*, usually falls in June or July, followed by the celebration of the **birthday of Mohammed**, *Maulud Nabi Muhammed*, in August, with festivities lasting throughout the following month.

FORTHCOMING FESTIVAL DATES

Ramadan begins December 9, 1999; December 1, 2000; November 21, 2001.
Galungun June 9, 1999; Jan 5, 2000.
Idul Fitri January 8, 2000; December 21, 2001.
Kuningan June 19, 1999; Jan 15, 2000.
Maulud Nabi June 18, 2000; June 8, 2001.

LOCAL FESTIVALS

Many of these festivals change annually against the Western calendar. The *Calendar of Events* booklet, produced annually by the Directorate General of Tourism, should be available in tourist offices in Indonesia and overseas, and is vital if you are planning an itinerary to include a festival anywhere in the archipelago.

Erau Festival, Tenggarong, Kalimantan Timor. September. A big display of indigenous Dayak skills and dancing.

Tabut, Pariaman, west Sumatra and **Tabot**, Bengkulu, south Sumatra (the same festival by different names). An annual ceremony held in the tenth Muslim month to commemorate the martyrdom of Mohammed's grandchildren, Hassan and Hussein. The festivals involve huge models of the *bouraq*, a winged horse with a woman's head, believed to have rescued the souls of the heroes and carried them to heaven.

Funerals, Tanah Toraja, Sulawesi. Mostly May to September. With buffalo slaughter, bullfights, and *sisemba* kick-boxing tournaments punctuating days of eating and drinking.

Galungun, Bali. An annual event in the *wuku* calendar (just one of Bali's calendars), which means it takes place every 210 days. The elaborate, ten-day family festival celebrates the victory of good over evil, and all the ancestral gods are thought to come down to earth to take part.

Horse-racing, Takengon, Central Aceh. This annual seven-day horse-racing festival begins on August 18, the day after Indonesia's Independence Day. The jockeys, usually 12 or 13-year-old boys from the local area, ride bareback, while spectators gamble on the outcome.

Kasada, Bromo, East Java. Annual festival at Gunung Bromo in which offerings are made to the gods, thrown into the crater following the instructions of the gods to Jaker Serger, from who the Tenggenese people of the area are descended.

Nyepi, throughout Bali. End of March or beginning of April. The major festival of the *saka* year, another of the Balinese calendars, and the major purification ritual of the year. The days before *nyepi* are full of activity – religious objects are taken in procession from temples to sacred springs or to the sea for purification. Sacrifices are made and displayed at crossroads where evil sprits are thought to linger, to lure them into the open. The night before *nyepi*, the spirits are frightened away with drums, gongs, cymbals, firecrackers and huge papier-mâché monsters. On the day itself, everyone sits quietly at home to persuade any remaining evil spirits that Bali is completely deserted.

Sekaten, Central Java. The celebration of the birthday of the prophet Mohammed, held in the royal courts of Central Java, combined with more ancient, mystic rituals that predate Islam. The festivities kick off with a month-long festival of fairs, gamelan recitals, wayang kulit and wayang orang performances, before culminating in a procession around the royal courts, at the end of which food is offered to Java's fertility god. The date of Sekatan varies from year to year, being linked to the lunar Javanese and Islamic calendars.

BUYING ARTS AND CRAFTS

Indonesians have a strong artistic heritage, and separate regions of the country are renowned for their textiles, woodcarving, jewellery or general craftsmanship. Some pieces are only available in the provinces, towns or villages where they are created; others are on sale in tourist shops and marketplaces across the land. Although the export trade has dulled the initial impact a little, the sheer volume – and price – of all these things makes shopping in Indonesia a delight, and something which could easily become an all-consuming pastime.

There are various ways of learning about local styles and artistic quality. A trip around the nearest market stalls or shops will furnish a good idea of what's on offer, and perhaps the opportunity to meet artists or craftsmen. Major art galleries and **regional museums** are also a good starting point, illustrating more traditional pieces and quality. In hard-core tourist hot spots such as Bali, you'll find streets crammed with all manner of outlets, from makeshift stalls to sophisticated glass-fronted boutiques, liberally sprinkled with a persistent gang of **hawkers** who will try to flog you local handicrafts at prices that drop in seconds. Traditional covered **markets**, or **pasar**, tend to be much more rewarding places to hone your bargaining skills, and, while necessities are generally their mainstay, many also have sections selling locally crafted trinkets, or even gems and the odd antique coin. Often you'll find areas set aside as the *pasar seni*, or *art market*, which sell everything from sarongs and lengths of printed batik to gold bracelets and rings, all aimed at local consumers.

Remember that any touts, guides and drivers you may engage to help you often get as much as fifty percent **commission** on any item sold – not only at the customer's expense but also the vendor's.

WOODCARVING

There's a fine range of **woodwork** in Indonesia. Javanese factories turn out beautifully crafted teak **furniture** of mostly Dutch-inspired design. **Bali** offers an endless range of ornamental wooden fruit and animals as well as superb classical and modern designs from Ubud and the surrounding villages, while Kalimantan's Dayaks and the Asmat of Irian Jaya produce renowned **carvings**. You do need to be particularly careful with wood, however; a material which travels badly and whose exact provenance can have a major effect on the price. **Sandalwood** (*cenana*), for instance, is extremely valuable, but its pungent aroma can be faked by packing lesser timber in sandalwood sawdust for several days, or by scenting the impostor with sandalwood oil – both difficult tricks to detect. **Ebony**, originating from Kalimantan and Sulawesi, is another commonly faked wood – dyed mango wood is similarly heavy, but the genuine article has a pearly lustre rather than being boot-polish black.

Most tropical woods **crack** when taken to a drier climate, or as they lose sap after carving; check any potential purchase carefully for putty-filled flaws. Some places try to minimize the problem by treating finished pieces in polyethylene glycol (PEG), which can prevent cracking in certain circumstances. Conversely, newly carved pieces might deliberately be aged by exposure to the elements for a few months, so that they can be sold as "antiques" – Indonesia has been well combed by collectors over the years, and it's very unlikely that wooden artefacts are particularly old. Check all weathered pieces for rot and termite damage, as well as for shoddy restoration work.

TEXTILES

Javanese cotton **batik** is the best-known Indonesian **textile**, and you'll find a big selection at any city market. Stylish and boldly patterned, batik is used for everything from sarongs and formal shirts, to tablecloths and surfers' board-bags. Some pieces are **screen-printed**, but more authentic designs still involve a complex process of **waxing**, **dyeing** and **boiling**. Prices will reflect the method used, and check whether the colour has authentically percolated through to the reverse side of the cloth.

Weaving is also practised, both for commercial and private use – in villages across Indonesia you'll see women using hand looms. Cotton is the most widespread fabric employed, though **silk** is often preferred for important pieces, and artificial materials are replacing heavier, home-made plant fibres. Important ceremonial dress may incorporate luxurious materials such as gold-and-silver brocade. The most distinctive weaving style is **ikat**, a demanding technique that involves dying the weft threads with the finished pattern before weaving begins, creating a fuzzy edge to the bold designs. Some areas are famed for their distinctive *ikat*: the islands of **Flores** and **Sumba** in Nusa Tenggara produce marvellous patterns incorporating human and animal motifs, while **geringsing** double *ikat* from Bali's Tenganan village uses a painstakingly intricate process to produce stunning designs, and the island's **songket** weave is also renowned.

With such lovely fabrics to work with, it's hardly surprising that Indonesia also produces some great **clothes**. Aside from inexpensive wear available in markets countrywide, tourist centres such as Bali's Kuta swarm with classy and original boutiques, as well as the highest proliferation of stalls selling baggy *ikat* trousers, skimpy batik dresses, and even fine **leather clothing**. Local designers keep an astute eye on **Western fashions** and come up with stylish but unusual collections, many of which are geared as much to Western winters as they are to Asian climes.

JEWELLERY

Influenced by India and the Arab world, there is some exquisite **jewellery** available in Indonesia. Local smiths produce the ornamental kris and heavy wedding arrays worn by many ethnic groups, and turn out the day-to-day jewellery coveted by wealthier Indonesians. Men prefer heavy rings, sometimes set with semi-precious stones; women sport earrings, bracelets and necklaces. Most island groups have metalworking centres, such as Celuk in Bali, and Java's Yogyakarta.

Some things, such as Balinese imitation brand-name **watches**, are obviously fake, but look good anyway; at other times you'll want to make sure you're buying the real thing. Gold colour can be applied to other metals, or intensified on poor gold, by heating the artefact in nitric acid. Hailing from Maluku, Indonesian **pearls** – black, yellow or white – are reasonably priced because most are **seeded**, the growing process initiated by inserting a tiny plastic bead into the oyster, around which the pearl forms. Beware if someone starts justifying steep prices by claiming a pearl is natural, something you can't prove without an x-ray.

ETHNIC ART AND ANTIQUES

Some of Indonesia's myriad **ethnic groups** have discovered that Westerners will pay money for everything from their bows and baby carriers to their kitchen utensils, and have started to produce these trinkets for the tourist market. For the average tourist, it's best to stick to obviously genuine articles which would be pointless to fake: Lombok **pottery**, or **stone adze blades** or **penis gourds** from Irian Jaya make unusual and inexpensive mementos of your trip.

Other pieces, such as antique **Chinese porcelain** (often looted from tombs), gold heirlooms, clothing and carvings, are another story altogether. Apart from the likelihood of being ripped off – even experienced dealers have been duped by Indonesian forgers – export of old artefacts without a permit is illegal, and the practice of alienating such items from their cultural context is morally hard to justify.

Painting has a long history on Bali and is now a subject for serious study and collection, with exhibitions and sales overseas as well as on the island. For more on this, see p.514.

ENTERTAINMENT AND SPORT

Despite the new distractions of discos, cinemas and TV, religious festivals and ceremonies are a major form of entertainment. Encompassing all kinds of events, from Balinese dances and temple festivals to Javanese puppet shows and the traditional funerals of Sulawesi and Kalimantan, these events are still enthusiastically performed across the archipelago. Tourists, as exotic guests, are generally welcome to attend.

Traditional secular entertainment revolved around **gambling**, a practice which consumed so many people's fortunes that the Indonesian government banned it in 1981, though you'll often encounter discreet betting accompanying card games, cockfighting or bullfights.

TRADITIONAL AND NATIONAL SPORTS

Illegal unless performed for religious ceremonies, **cockfighting** can still be seen in Bali and, to a lesser extent, in parts of Kalimantan and Sulawesi, where certain rituals require the shedding of blood. Where it's practised, you'll see men of all ages and incomes caressing their birds in public, often gathering in groups to show them off and weigh up their rivals. When not being pampered, the birds spend their days in individual bell-shaped bamboo baskets, often placed in quite noisy public places, so that the bird won't be scared when it finally makes it to the ring. Prize cocks can earn their owners sizable sums of money, and a certain status too, but despite all this the men are unsentimental about their animals – a dead bird is a financial rather than an emotional loss. Traditional **buffalo races** are also held in Bali and Madura, and **bullfights** – bloodless battles of strength between two animals, rather than along the Spanish model – are an integral part of Torajan funeral ceremonies.

As far as competitive sports go, **takrau** is a popular backyard game, where players pass a rattan ball between them using any part of the body except the hands. Indonesia does well on the international **badminton** scene, with **soccer**, and an indigenous **martial arts** style called **pancak silat**, also enjoying nationwide popularity.

DANCE AND MUSIC

Given the enormous cultural and ethnic mix that makes up Indonesia, it's hardly surprising that the range of traditional **music** and **dance** across the archipelago is so vast. Each group of people has its own traditional forms, and in many cases these are highly accessible to visitors, although for many the most memorable moments will be the unplanned occasions when they stumble across a dance practice or an orchestra rehearsal.

Best known are the highly stylized and mannered **classical performances** in Java and Bali, accompanied by the **gamelan orchestra** (see p.966 and the box opposite). Every step of these classical dances is minutely orchestrated, and the merest wink of an eye, arch of an eyebrow and angle of a finger has meaning and significance. The tradition remains vibrant, passed down by experts to often very young pupils. Ubud on Bali and Yogyakarta on Java are the centres for these dances, with shortened performances staged to cater to the shorter attention spans of Western visitors. Other performances are much more geared to local audiences – the *Ramayana* and *Mahabharata* dance-dramas tend to fall into this category.

It's best to respect local **dress code** if you go to performances in the palaces in Java – avoid sleeveless tops and shorts. In Bali a temple sash must be worn if you visit a temple.

For more on individual dance forms, see pp.520–522 of the Bali chapter, and to find out about Indonesia shadow puppet plays, **wayang kulit** and **wayang golek**, see p.173 of the Central Java chapter.

GAMELAN PERFORMANCES

YOGYAKARTA (YOGYA)

There is lots going on in **Yogya**, much of it geared to the large number of tourists who visit the town each year, so if you're not staying long you'll find performances more easily than in Solo.

Daily **gamelan** and **dance** performances for tourists are held at the Kraton, and nightly two-hour wayang performances at the Agastiya Institute. Other central venues include the Kepatihan, Taman Budaya, and Pujukusuman, the dance school where the late Romo Sas (one of Yogya's top dance teachers) taught until recently. There are regular tourist performances of dance and gamelan in the hotels; the performers are often students from ISI (Institut Seni Indonesia), the Institute of Indonesian Arts. A live RRI (Radio Republic Indonesia) broadcast takes place at the Pura Pukualaman each month. Further out of town are the Lembaga Studi Jawa, a foundation set up recently for the study and performance of Javanese arts; Bagong Kussiardja's dance foundation, where you may be able to watch rehearsals; and ISI, where exam recitals and performances of new dance and gamelan music are held at certain times of year.

Annual **festivals** to look out for are the Festival Kesenian Yogyakarta (gamelan, dance and wayang), the International Gamelan Festival (including new compositions and groups from abroad), and the Sekaten and Kraton festivals. Sekaten is held each year in both Solo and Yogya. Performances of the **Ramayana** ballet are held regularly at Prambanan Temple (outside Yogya) – pricey, but worth seeing.

SURAKARTA (SOLO)

There are regular live RRI broadcasts of **gamelan** music from the two palaces in **Solo**: the Kraton Hadiningrat and the Mangkunagaran. Listeners are welcome – it's a great opportunity to see the palace gamelans being played. Broadcasts take place at lunchtimes and late evenings (10pm–midnight). Dates are determined by the 35-day month of the Javanese calendar. Go to the RRI and check the noticeboard for details of all live broadcasts. STSI (Sekolah Tinggi Seni Indonesia), the "High School of Indonesian Arts", is a bus ride from the centre of town. Exam recitals and performances take place at the end of each semester. **Dance rehearsals** take place at the Mangkungaran every Wednesday morning. There are all-night **wayang** performances each month at STSI (see p.204), Taman Budaya Surakarta (on the campus of STSI) and the RRI. Nightly **wayang orang** (dance-drama) performances take place at the Sriwedari Amusement Park and there are regular tourist performances at the larger hotels, such as *Hotel Kusuma Sahid*.

BALI

There is always plenty of activity in **Bali** – the easiest performances to find are those arranged for tourists. The best way to find out what's happening where is to go to the tourist board in Denpasar, buy a Balinese calendar, and get a list of the major **odalan** (village temple ceremonies). The major temple festivals Galungan and Kuningan are held every 210 days. *Odalan* are held more frequently. **Gamelan** and **dance** is a big feature in Ubud, Peliatan and Teges. Other places to visit if you have more time are Sabah (where there is a *legong* troupe), Sukawati (*gender wayang*), Batur (*gong gede*) and the villages of Sawan and Jagaraga in north Bali.

In Denpasar, the **Bali Arts Festival** is held in July/August each year, and performances are held at STSI throughout the year.

OUTDOOR PURSUITS

Indonesia is a dream location for those with a passion for the great outdoors. Its seas are home to coral reefs, there are scaleable mountains and volcanoes, wide rivers, rainforest, and endless stretches of beach.

In Java, Bali, Lombok and Sumatra you'll have little trouble finding companies who will set you up with anything from a mountain bike to a mask and snorkel. But it's the remote areas which are often more interesting, and there you'll need a little more imagination. Be aware that your **travel insurance** may not cover you for accidents incurred while participating in high-risk activities, or may require a higher premium.

SCUBA DIVING

The wealth of life beneath Indonesia's seas is beyond comprehension: many of the world's best **diving sites** are here. The Banda Islands in Maluku, Alor in Nusa Tenggara and Pulau Bunaken off Sulawesi have all been regularly rated in the world's top five and continue to impress, but a lot of diving in more accessible places is exceptional. The vast diversity of tropical fish and coral is complemented by visibility that can reach over 30m. During the wet season, particularly the monsoon, visibility can be reduced, so the best time for diving is between April and October.

PRACTICALITIES

The diversity and number of Indonesia's diving sites is pretty much unparalleled, but places where you can hire scuba equipment by the day are pretty limited. Most major beach resorts have dive centres, often in the smarter hotels, but once you get further afield you'll probably have to rely on liveaboard cruises or even on having your own gear.

Generally speaking, a day's diving with two tanks, lunch and basic equipment costs $30–100, subject to bargaining. Be aware that it is down to you to **check your equipment**, and that the purity of an air tank can be suspect, and could cause serious injury. Also check your guide's credentials carefully, and bear in mind that you may be a long way from a decompression chamber. Some intrepid divers have managed to hire equipment from pearling operations; again, remember that the equipment may not be safe.

Bali has many good sites including the famous *Liberty* wreck off the north coast, and lots of good tour operators; Lombok's operators are limited to Sengigi and the Gili Islands. There have been reports of dodgy equipment being used by some of the dive boats, so it's best to stick to the bigger, more established companies. Several large dive companies have offices in Jakarta, and there are dive opportunities in Ujong Kulong national park, Krakatau, and several (average to poor) sites along the south coast of Java.

Nusa Tenggara is alive with astounding reefs, but dive operators are very scarce apart from in Lombok. To get into the Komodo national park you will need to take the inexpensive liveaboard, the *Komodo Plus*, out of Sape Sumbawa. The park has some quite breathtaking diving, being particularly noted for the abundance of gargantuan pelagics. Out of **Lahubanbajo Flores**, you can take day-trips to reasonable sites with the Bajo Beach Diving Club at the hotel of the same name. Elsewhere on Flores, **Maumere** was once an important dive site, but after a massive earthquake in 1992 many sites are silted over. There are two good dive operators at Waiara, a short trip east of town. To get to other sites in Nusa Tenggara, you will have to rely on the rickety boats of Kupang's Donovan Whitford (☎0380/31154, fax 24833). No luxury here, but very reasonable tours to some of the most exciting destinations imaginable, including Sumba, Alor, Roti and Timor. There are also several expensive **live-aboards** out of Bali, such as Baruna (☎0361/751223) and Indonesia Diving in Kuta, (☎0361/751381), Dive and Dives in Sanur, (☎0361/288051) and Grand Komodo based in Denpasar, (☎0361/87166 fax 87165). These operators all run trips into Nusa Tenggara and further afield, though to count on such a trip you will need to round up your own group of passengers.

Sumatra is not well-known for its diving, though Pulau Weh off the north coast has dive facilities and some fantastic sites. The 99 islands of Pulau Banyak are also awash with potential, having burgeoning populations of turtles and stingrays and a couple of relatively new dive setups. The scene off Padang is enticing, as the Indian Ocean laps the coast there – there is one operator in Padang (see p.360).

Kalimantan has just one dive site, northeasterly Pulau Derawan, but it gets consistently good reports from those who've visted – manta rays and turtle rookeries, rather than coral, are the draw here. **Sulawesi**, on the other hand, pulls in divers from all over the world, most of whom home in on the vertigo-inducing walls at Bunaken Marine Reserve out from the northern city of Manado. Lesser-known sites include crystal-clear water around the Togian Islands in central Sulawesi, while virtually unexplored reefs of the Tukangbesi group off southeastern Sulawesi are attracting more adventurous divers.

Maluku is one of Indonesia's most underrated regions for scuba diving. The central group of islands around Ambon have everything from underwater hot springs to shipwrecks and patchy coral, while the Banda Islands provide some of the best sites in the country, with sponge-clad coral walls inhabited by staggering quantities of marine life. Those with initiative might also be able to get out to World War II wreckage off northerly Morotai, or some almost virgin territory off the Aru Islands in the region's far southeast.

SURFING

Indonesia is one of the world's premier **surfing** destinations, with an enormous variety of class waves, and destinations spreading from the tip of Sumatra right down to Timor and beyond. The prime attraction is surfing perfect, uncrowded breaks, with paradisal coastlines laid out before you. The price you'll have to pay for this is that, unless you take expensive all-in surf cruises, you'll have to drag your board hundreds of kilometres on rickety, crowded public transport in sweltering heat. The best-known waves are found on Bali, G' Land (Grajagan) on Java, and Nias off Sumatra. Sumbawa and Pulau Roti have been hot spots for a few years now, and Sumba, Savu and the Mentawi Islands are the destinations of the future. In June and July, during the best and most consistent surf, you can expect waves to be crowded, especially in Java and Bali. For all-in **surf safaris** on luxury yachts, try STC (*surftrav@ozemail.com.au*), who have boat trips around all major destinations.

EQUIPMENT

On Bali and in some of the larger surf centres you can rent **boards**, though they may not be up to much; you should try to bring your own board. A padded board-bag is essential, as your pride and joy is going to take a lot of pounding as it gets chucked up onto bus roofs with the trussed-up goats. Most public transport will want to charge your board as an extra seat, and there's not much point arguing, especially in Balinese bemo terminals where things can turn a little ugly if you refuse to pay. Kuta has some great surf shops, but if you're heading further afield you'll need your own kit, plus high-strength sun block and medical supplies (with plenty of iodine for coral cuts). A helmet and thin suit is advisable if you plan to be surfing over some of Indonesia's scalpel-sharp reefs.

THE WAVES

At its best, **Desert Point** is the best of Indonesia's waves. Situated on Lombok's southwest tip, it's also known for being very unpredictable, and many surfers do little else here than sit around in battered beach huts. It's a long barrelling left-hander, and when it's good it's very good – some say the best in the world.

The next big one is Grajagan in the Alas Purwo national park on Java's southeastern tip. **G' Land** as it's known, is one of the world's better left-handers and a stopoff for the pro tour. It has four sections, of which Speedies is the most consistent, with a perfect, long ride, promising endless tubes and walls. Unless you fancy trekking out there alone and camping, then the only way to hit G' Land is via an organized tour from Kuta Bali. Java's other "surfers-only" spot is **Pulau Panaitan** in the Ujong Kulon national park. One Palm Point is a perfect barrelling left, doable in a large swell, and there are more around to ensure you have a little breathing space. Other popular spots on Java include **Batu Keras** near Pangandaran, **Cimaja** near Pelabuhan Ratu and the turtle-breeding grounds of **Genteng**.

Nias off Sumatra is quite the surfing mecca, remote and primitive but playing host to the pro tour. You don't need to take expensive charter yachts to get to its cheap losmen, although you will to get out to the **Mentawai** and **Hinakos** islands (awesome empty waves with endless barrels). The outer reef at Nias offers the best rides here, but needs a hefty swell to take off. There is, however, a short right-hander to play around on while you wait. There are good sites all down the west coast including Meulaboh, Tapaktuan and nearby Pulau Simeulue.

Nusa Tenggara is the fastest growing of surfing locations, partially because of the short flight from Darwin to Kupang, and also because of the plentiful, empty waves and minimal cost of living. T' Land at Nembrala beach on **Pulau Roti** is legendary, a long consistent left that's not quite as hollow as its near-namesake on Java. You can often see surf legends supping coconut milk with the locals in Nembrala's laid-back beach bungalows. Rua, Pero and Tarimbang on **Sumba** offer everything from hollow to mellow, and even the remote **Savu** and **Raijua** islands are being explored, particularly as stops on cruising surf safaris. Sumba is becoming particularly popular with surfers and with big-game fishers. Cruises around Nusa Tenggara are likely to stop off at **Sumbawa's Hu'u**, with its multiple breaks, including the long-respected Lakey Peak and Periscopes. The more gnarled surfers could trudge down to Sumbawa's **west coast** and live it rough near the excellent breaks of Supersuck, Scar Reef and Yo Yos; don't expect four-star facilities, though. Lombok's south coast offers many reasonable rides for most of the year; **Kuta Beach** is as good a place as any to start looking.

Surf culture and **Bali** have become utterly inseparable. **Kuta** and **Legian** beach breaks are great for beginners, with boards for rent just about everywhere. You can also rent a boat out to the Kuta Reef which is pretty good between mid and high tide. Other sites on the west coast include **Padang**, which can be genuinely huge and pretty formidable. **Ulu Watu** is another that routinely leaves surfers in intensive care; don't be tempted unless you're totally up to it. On the east coast, **Nusa Dua** is a fast right-hander with long rides, and **Sanur** offers more of the same but over reef. In the western monsoon from October to March, Nusa Dua and Sanur are excellent, while the other side of the peninsula is better from April to September. Whenever Bali's waves are at their best, they are guaranteed to be jam-packed.

RAFTING

Indonesia's best established location for **white-water rafting** is on **Bali**, many tour companies in Kuta and Ubud offering tours to shoot the rapids in the rivers in the east of the island, There are also well-established operations in **West Java** near Pangandaran and Pelabuhan Ratu. Outfits offering white-water tours in new locations are gradually springing up in pockets around the archipelago; inquire at local tourist offices.

Some of the best whitewater is to be found in Sumatra's **Gunung Leuser national park**, where extended tours through the jungle offer occasional Grade VIs, and even the odd small waterfall to tumble down. Most tours start from Muarasitulan, but the most intense begin further upriver near Blankergeran. Three-day tours cost $150, with all meals included. Elsewhere in Sumatra, there are some relatively tame single-day tours out of Bukit Lawang, and popular tubing rides are organized by many of the losmen there.

At most locations around Indonesia, single days on the river generally cost $25–60, extended tours (around $50 per day) including camping out at the riverside, all meals, and a guide to cook them for you.

TREKKING

Indonesia offers endless **trekking** opportunities of various degrees of difficulty, with terrain ranging from broad, easily followed paths, to exhausting, near-invisible jungle trails which traverse steep mountain ridges and fast-flowing rivers. The reasons for trekking, where you decide to go, and – most of all – the rewards, are essentially personal. Some areas take you into the domain of remote tribes, while others are worth the effort for the experience and satisfaction that comes from simply completing the distance. You'll find that hardcore point-to-point hiking is not generally a good way to see **wildlife**, however, and for this you're better off thoroughly exploring a smaller region.

Whatever your motivation and wherever you go, it's worth knowing what you're up against. Thick forest can be a magical environment, especially when animals and birds start up their chorus at dawn and dusk; but weighed down with a pack, covered in leeches and soaked to the skin from sweat and rain it can also be exhausting and claustrophobic. More open country and wider trails means thicker vegetation to plough through, plus exposure to the sun, and you need to come properly prepared. **Boots** with a firm grip are essential; beware of poor stitching, which can rot within days. For longer treks you'll need a **tent** (or a guide who can build a shelter), and also some warm clothing and a **sleeping bag** for chilly evenings in high country. **Backpacks** leak, so put all your gear in plastic bags. Make sure you carry a knife, butane lighter, torch with spare bulb and batteries, hat, a water canteen, a compass and a first-aid kit. The first-aid kit should contain: anthistamines (for insect bites, or irritating plants); a crepe bandage; two compress bandages; a whistle; a good canteen; a strip of Band-Aid; scissors; antibiotic powder (more effective in the tropics than cream); fungicide cream; eyewash; fine tweezers; needles; candles; and a good penknife. Insect repellent is not much use while you're walking – it washes off within minutes – but you can use it to get rid of leeches at rest stops. You'll obviously have to take your own **food** when trekking, and it's also polite to have something to give to people who might provide meals elsewhere, as villagers may be short of supplies themselves. The standard village rations become monotonous on extended stays, but it's sometimes possible to buy fresh meat, and guides might carry spears or guns in case of an encounter with game along the way.

One way or another, you'll definitely need **guides**, and not just to find the paths: turning up at a remote village unannounced can cause trouble, as people may mistrust outsiders, let alone Westerners. If you have no time, experience or language skills, **tours** (arranged either overseas or within Indonesia) are the most convenient way to organize everything, though they suffer from high expense, a tendency to shield you, and the fact that, bound to a schedule, the experience can feel rushed. Far better options are either to track down an experienced, English-speaking guide in the nearest city, or – with adequate Indonesian – travel as far as possible on your own, and then engage local help, bearing in mind that locals may have neither the time nor the inclination to assist you. In some regions Indonesian may not be enough, so make sure your guides speak the local dialects. National-park officers will often know suitable people to act as guides.

While the possibilities for mountain trekking and volcano scaling are practically limitless in Indonesia, there is little or no structure for **sport climbing**, though you can bring all your own equipment. The only **mountains** of any serious note are Trikora and Puncak Jaya in Irian Jaya. The latter is the highest mountain between the Himalayas and the Andes, and can be climbed only on extended and expensive tours out of Jayapura or the Baliem Valley. To climb Trikora, special permits are required from government authorities in Jakarta. Gunung Rinjani on Lombok is a popular hike, possible without a guide in two days and one night. Kerinci on Sumatra and Semeru on Java are both serious endeavours for fit trekkers, while easier undertakings are Batur on Bali and Bromo on Java – both hugely rewarding, involving less effort. Straddling the border between North Sumatra and Aceh, the Gunung Leuser national park is Southeast Asia's largest, and offers some of the best trekking opportunities on the archipelago, from simple one-day walks around the Bukit Lawang orang-utan sanctuary near Medan, to two-week hikes to the summit of Gunung Leuser. Sumatra, Kalimantan and Irian Jaya contain some of the largest stands of **tropical forest** left on the planet, despite continued summer fires, clearance for farming and ferocious logging.

CULTURAL HINTS

The Indonesian people are extremely generous about opening up their homes, places of worship and festivals to the ever-growing crowd of interested tourists; but, though they are long-suffering and rarely show obvious displeasure, they can take great offence at certain aspects of Western behaviour. The most sensitive issues involve Westerners' clothing – or lack of it – and the code of practice that's required for formal situations.

It's worth noting, however, that the degree to which Indonesian etiquette is observed varies from place to place and in certain situations. Overall, Java and Bali have the strongest cultural codes, but this doesn't mean you should automatically drop your standards elsewhere, and it's best to be overly polite until you have assessed the local situation.

SOCIAL CONVENTIONS

Indonesians are generally very sociable people, and dislike doing anything alone. When forced to, it's normal for complete strangers engaged in some common enterprise – catching a bus, for instance – to introduce themselves and start up a friendship. **Sharing cigarettes** between men is in these circumstances a way of establishing a bond, and Westerners who don't smoke should be genuinely apologetic about refusing; it's well worth carrying a packet to share around even if you save your own "for later".

Conversations in Indonesia often open with "dari mana?". Though literally meaning "where are you from?", it's often intended as less of a question than simply a greeting – your nationality is a good response. Next will be inquiries into your marital status and whether you have children; negative answers often evoke expressions of sympathy as they are seen as essential stages in most Indonesians' lives.

As Indonesians find it difficult to understand the Western obsession with **privacy**, or the need for some Westerners to simply have a few minutes' to themselves from time to time, the constant attention – not to mention inevitable cries of "Hello mister" yelled out by children whenever a foreign face appears in less cosmopolitan regions of the country – means that Western tempers tend to fray after a while. Another major source of irritation for foreigners is the vague notion of **timekeeping** that pervades almost every aspect of Indonesian life. Lack of punctuality is such a national institution that there is even a term for it – *jam karet* (rubber time) – and you'll save yourself a lot of stress if you remember this when visiting a bank, or having to wait hours for transport to depart.

However bad things become, keep your temper: as elsewhere in Asia, Indonesians dislike **confrontational behaviour**, and will rarely show anger or irritation of any kind. Tourists who lose their cool and get visibly rattled for whatever reason – and you can add persistent souvenir sellers or becak drivers to the above list – will be derided, and even baited further, rather than feared.

Displays of affection are also subdued. Indonesians of the same sex often hold hands or hug in public, but heterosexual couples should avoid overt physical contact, which can cause trouble in conservative areas. **Critical opinions** of the State are likewise best kept to oneself, and the same goes for attitudes towards religious beliefs and conventions – people do discuss these things, but seldom with new aquaintances.

THE BODY

For various religious and practical reasons, Indonesians view parts of the body in specific ways. Broadly speaking, a person's **head** is seen as sacred, and should never be touched casually by another – not even to pat a child or to ruffle

someone's hair in affection. Conversely, the **feet** are held to be unclean, so never use them to indicate anything, or point them at a person or sacred object. The **left hand** is used for washing after defecating, and Indonesians never eat with it – avoid using it to pass or receive things.

Despite what you'll see around the biggest beach resorts, most Indonesians are extremely offended by topless and nude **bathing**. True, rural Indonesians bathe publicly in rivers and pools, but there's an unspoken rule of invisibility under these circumstances and women generally wear sarongs, and men shorts or underwear, often using segregated areas. If you bathe alongside them, do as they do.

SOCIAL ETIQUETTE

Dressing neatly is akin to showing **respect** in Indonesia, and away from the biggest resort areas it's best to avoid scruffy clothing or articles which are seen as immodest: these include thongs, shorts, vests, or anything which leaves you with bare shoulders.

When dealing with people in authority – police or government officials, for instance – wearing something formal shows that you take their position seriously, and they will be that much more willing to help you. While you should always do your best, this is obviously one area where local standards apply: visiting an immigration department for a visa extension will require more dress sense than greeting a village head (who may himself only be wearing shorts and thongs) after a day's hiking in the jungle.

Language (see Contexts, pp.984–988) is also used to express respect in Indonesia. Many Indonesian dialects include a "higher" language for use in formal situations, but even in everyday encounters, an older man than yourself (or even an obviously younger man if he's in a position of authority) should be addressed as *Bapak* or *Pak*, a woman as *Ibu* or *Bu*. **Body language** also comes in to play: when walking between people who are talking together, Indonesians apologize for the intrusion by dropping their shoulders in a characteristic stoop; until you pick up this gesture, saying *ma'af* will suffice.

RELIGIOUS ETIQUETTE

In a country where a belief in God is compulsory, Indonesians take their religions very seriously, and anyone entering a **place of worship** should be aware of the necessary etiquette. **Mosques** are generally open to the public, though everyone is required to take their shoes off before entering, and to wear long sleeves and long trousers; women should definitely cover their shoulders and may also be asked to cover their heads as well (bring a scarf or shawl, as there probably won't be any provided). Men and women pray in separate parts of the mosque, though there are unlikely to be signs telling you where to go. Dress regulations also apply when visiting **Balinese temples** and many religions also prohibit **women** from engaging in certain activities – or even entering a place of worship – during menstruation. If attending a **religious festival**, find out beforehand whether a dress code applies; guests at Torajan funerals, for example, should wear dark clothing.

POLICE, TROUBLE AND EMERGENCIES

Foreign fatalities resulting from the suppression of independence movements in Irian and Timor, and the urban violence which surrounded the political upheavals of 1998, all undermine the idea that Indonesia is a safe place to travel. However, while it would be misleading to play down these events, it's also true that serious incidents involving Westerners are rare and most tourists have trouble-free visits to Indonesia.

Petty theft, however, is a fact of life in the country, and without becoming overly paranoid, it's sensible to minimize any risks. Although as a Westerner you're obviously richer than the average Indonesian, most crime is opportunistic: the fewer opportunities you present, the less likely you are to be targeted. Don't flash signs of wealth around, such as expensive jewellery or watches. Carry travellers' cheques, the bulk of your cash and important documents – especially airline tickets, credit cards and passport – under your clothing in a **money belt**. While these can be irritating to wear, the major hassles incurred by losing vital items are considerably worse. Money belts are basically invisible, unlike all-too-obvious **bumbags**, which, besides signalling the location of your valuables, are easy to cut off in a crowd. Ensure that **luggage** is lockable (gadgets to lock backpacks exist), and never keep anything important in outer pockets, which deft fingers can swiftly open without your knowledge. Don't hesitate to check that doors and windows – including those in the bathroom – are secure before accepting **accommodation**; if the management seems offended by this, you probably don't want to stay there anyway. Some guest houses and hotels have **safe-deposit boxes** which solve the problem of what to do with your valuables while you go swimming; a surprising number of tourists leave their possessions unattended on beaches and are amazed to find them gone when they return.

Along with a list of travellers' cheque numbers, keep separate **photocopies of your passport** so you can prove who you are if the original goes missing. In many places the availability of exchange services makes carrying large amounts of cash unnecessary. If you have to do it, keep enough hidden away from your main stash so that if your money is stolen you can still get to the police, get in touch with a consulate and pay for phone calls while you sort everything out – US dollar notes are very useful in these circumstances.

If you're unlucky enough to get **mugged**, never resist and, if you disturb a thief, raise the alarm rather than try to take them on – they're after your valuables and are unlikely to harm you if you don't get in their way. More often, however, things will go missing by stealth, either from accommodation or the top of a bus, or from your pocket in a crowd. Be especially aware of **pickpockets** on buses or bemos, who usually operate in pairs: one will distract you while another does the job. Afterwards, you'll need a **police report** for insurance purposes. Police stations are marked on the maps in the Guide; in smaller villages where police are absent, ask for assistance from the headman. Unless your Indonesian is sound, try to take along someone to translate, though police will generally do their best to find an English speaker. Allow plenty of time for any involvement with the police, whose offices wallow in bureaucracy; you may also be charged "administration fees" for enlisting their help, the cost of which is open to sensitive negotiations. If you are **driving**, the chance of entanglement with

the police increases; spot checks are common, and by law drivers must carry their licence and the vehicle registration papers.

Finally, have nothing to do with **drugs** in Indonesia. The penalties are tough, and you won't get any sympathy from consular officials. If you are arrested, or end up on the wrong side of the law for whatever reason, you should ring the consular officer at your embassy immediately.

WOMEN TRAVELLERS

Indonesia does not, overall, present huge difficulties for women travellers, either travelling alone or with friends of either sex. However, an image of Western women as promiscuous and on holiday in search of sex is current across the archipelago, having spread outwards from Bali where the gigolo scene is well established. In tourist areas throughout the country – Bukittinggi and the Gili Islands being examples – there are plenty of young men hanging around hoping to strike lucky, although they are more likely to be a nuisance rather than anything more sinister.

Reactions to foreign women vary widely across the country, and in the particularly devout Muslim areas, most obviously Sumatra, it pays to be especially careful about **dress**. Even then, considerable verbal harassment of solo women travellers is not unknown. Observe how local women dress both on the streets and on the beach. While topless sunbathing has become very popular in major tourist areas on Bali and Lombok, and it is unlikely that local people will say anything directly to you when you are there, it's worth being aware how far outside the local dress code such behaviour is. Whatever you do on the beach, you should cover up when you head inshore, and visits to temples, mosques or festivals carry their own obligations regarding dress (see p.60).

There is a large population of young men on Bali and Lombok, and increasingly elsewhere, known variously as Kuta cowboys, guides, mosquitoes (they flit from person to person) or gigolos, whose aim is to secure a **Western girlfriend** for the night, week, month or however long it lasts. They vary considerably in subtlety, and while the transaction is not overtly financial the woman will be expected to pay for everything. You'll see these couples particularly in Bali and Lombok, where local outrage is not as overt as elsewhere in the country. If a Western woman and a local man are seen together, this is the first assumption made about their relationship. Local reaction on Bali and Lombok is variable, from hostility through acceptance to amusement, although outside these areas most Indonesian people are frankly appalled by such goings-on. **Sex** outside marriage is taboo in both the Hindu and Muslim religions, and young girls throughout Indonesia are expected to conform to a strict code of morality.

However Indonesian women are much freer with regard to dress, movement and employment than in many other Muslim countries, and you'll encounter women in public and in employment in the tourist industry pretty much everywhere you go. Many are keen to practise their English, especially if they are students, but as a woman travelling through the islands a bit of Indonesian is especially useful for talking to local women of all ages, who generally want to find out as much about life in the West as visitors want to learn about life in Indonesia.

TRAVELLING WITH CHILDREN

Indonesians love children, make a great fuss of their own and other people's, and permit them to go pretty much anywhere. The country has a great deal to offer children: plenty of beaches and outdoor activities, the colour and dynamism of traditional dance and music, and even a few theme parks in Java and Bali.

Travel itself is particularly exhausting for children, however, and at first it may be best to concentrate on a relatively small part of the country until you gauge how much they can take. You might choose to opt for the comfort and convenience of a **package deal**, where you can rely on having organized transport, air-conditioning, hot water and a swimming pool to hand, plus the use of babysitters if required. If you make your own arrangements, some **upmarket hotels** make significant concessions to couples with children, perhaps offering extra beds for one or two under-12s sharing a room with their parents, but in other accommodation you may need to rent three- or four-bed rooms if your child is too big to share a bed with you. On the whole, children who occupy their own seat on **buses and bemos** are expected to pay full fare. Most **domestic flight** operators charge two-thirds of the adult fare for children under 14, and ten percent for infants.

Although you can buy disposable **nappies** (diapers) in city supermarkets, prices are somewhat inflated. Bring a **changing mat**, as few public toilets have special baby facilities. Also consider investing in a **child-carrier backpack** for lugging around your smallest offspring (prices start at around US$45/£30 for ones that weigh less than 2kg), as pavements and road surfaces are invariably too bumpy for a comfortable pushchair ride. **Buggies**, however, can come in handy for feeding and even bedding small children, as highchairs and cots/cribs are only provided in a few of the most upmarket hotels; car-rental companies never provide baby seats. A child-sized **mosquito net** might be useful as well. **Powdered milk** is available in major centres, but is otherwise hard to find; sterilizing bottles is also a far more laborious process in Indonesian hotels and restaurants than it is back home.

As long as you avoid the spicier items, **Indonesian food** is quite palatable to children, though, as with adults, you should be careful about unwashed fruit and salads and about dishes that have been left uncovered for a long time (see p.25). The other main hazards are dogs (keep your distance), thundering traffic, huge waves and strong currents, and the **sun** – sunhats, sun block and waterproof suntan lotions are essential, and can be bought in the major resorts.

You might also want to canvas other travellers' opinions, which you can do by posting your queries on the "Travelling with Children" bulletin board *www.lonelyplanet.com/thorntree/kiddies /topics.htm*). For specific **advice** about kids' **health issues**, either contact your doctor, or consult one of the travellers' medical services listed on p.26 or (in the UK), call the Nomad Medical Centre (☎0181/889 7014), which publishes a special information sheet on keeping kids healthy when abroad.

GAY INDONESIA

Surprisingly for a society that places so much emphasis on parenthood, homosexuality is broadly accepted in Indonesia, and there is even a place in some of the archipelago's traditional societies for transvestites, who were formerly attached as retainers and dancers at royal courts. Today, the legal age of consent for both gay and heterosexual sex is 16, though homosexuals are often forced through social pressures eventually to marry and become parents. As it's more acceptable in Indonesia to show a modest amount of physical affection to friends of the same sex than to friends or lovers of the opposite sex, however, gay couples generally encounter less hassle about being seen together in public than they might in the West.

Jakarta and Bali are Indonesia's two main **gay centres**, with the younger scene gravitating towards Kuta, where there are renowned, unproblematic cruising areas and a mixed gay crowd of Indonesians and foreigners. A lot of gay visitors and expatriates do have affairs with Indonesian men, and these liaisons tend to fall somewhere between holiday romances and paid sex. Few gay Indonesians in these circumstances would classify themselves as rent boys – they wouldn't sleep with someone they didn't like and most don't have sex for money – but they usually expect to be financially cared for by the richer man (food, drinks and entertainment expenses, for example), and some do make their living this way. Outside Java and Bali, you won't find anything resembling a gay scene, and the most visible homosexuals are transvestite prostitutes (sometimes known as "waria") who hang out in locally known public spaces.

Bali's **gay support group**, Yayasam Usada Bhakti, which is based at Jalan Blimbing in Denpasar, runs AIDS awareness campaigns and distributes condoms in the main cruising areas. They also have a resident doctor at their headquarters and hold regular meetings and counselling sessions. For more information on the AIDS situation in Indonesia, see p.27.

DIRECTORY

ADDRESSES A recent law banning the use of foreign words for business names, including those for accommodation and restaurants, has caused a few problems. Some hotels have circumvented the new rule by just adding the word "Hotel" in front of their name (this is an Indonesian as well as an English word), but others have had to start over. Street names are another cause of confusion, many having been renamed as historical or political figures fall in and out of fashion. Where relevant, we have included both new and old names for hotels and streets, as many people still refer to them by the old name, though the sign will show the new version.

AIRPORT DEPARTURE TAXES Rp100,000 on international flights, and Rp30,000 for domestic flights.

CONTRACEPTIVES Birth control is a major issue in Indonesia, the government "Dua Anak-anak Cukup" (Two Children are Enough) campaign promoting restraint to a disbelieving population. Condoms (*kondom*) are available from pharmacists, but don't rely on local suppliers for other contraceptives.

CREDIT-CARD LOSS Contact your bank before departure for a list of credit-card agents in Indonesia.

ELECTRICITY Usually 220–240 volts AC, but outlying areas may still use 110 volts. Most outlets take plugs with two rounded pins.

LAUNDRY SERVICES There are no public laundries, but most hotels and losmen have a laundry service, and tourist centres have plenty of services outside the hotels as well.

LEFT LUGGAGE Informal services are offered by most losmen and all hotels. Major airports also have left-luggage facilities, charging around Rp3300 per item per day. It's expensive, but there's no time limit.

TIME The Indonesian archipelago is divided into three time zones. Sumatra, Java, Kalimantan Barat and Kalimantan Tengah are on Western Indonesian Time (7hr ahead of GMT, 15hr ahead of US Pacific Standard, 12hr ahead of US Eastern Standard, and 3hr behind Sydney); Bali, Lombok, the Nusa Tenggara islands, Sulawesi and South and East Kalimantan are on Central Indonesian Time (8hr ahead of GMT, 16hr ahead of US Pacific Standard Time, 13hr ahead of Eastern Standard Time, and 2hr behind Sydney); and Irian Jaya and Maluku are on Eastern Indonesian Time (9hr ahead of GMT, 17hr ahead of US Pacific Standard, 14hr ahead of US Eastern Standard, and 1hr behind Sydney).

TIPPING Tipping is not generally expected even in tourist resorts, where up to 22 percent service and goods tax is added to accommodation and restaurant bills in any case. If someone in authority has gone out of their way to help you, however, a gratuity may be appreciated, though expect some sort of hint to be made first or you may end up causing offence.

TOILETS *WC*, pronounced "wey sey" in Indonesian. Classier accommodation may have Western-style plumbing, but most Indonesian toilets are squatting affairs: a hole in the ground with somewhere to place your feet either side. Toilet paper is seldom provided, though paper or tissues are easy to buy across the country; instead, you clean yourself afterwards with your left hand, using the pail and scoop alongside, which are also used to flush the toilet. They tend to be very wet places, so avoid bringing in anything you'll have to place on the floor.

WORKING Working is forbidden on an Indonesian tourist visa, and cash-in-hand jobs are not exactly thick on the ground. A few tourists manage to set themselves up in Bali or Jakarta as foreign-language teachers; otherwise the most common moneymaking ploy is the exporting of Indonesian goods (fabric, clothes, jewellery and other artefacts). Divemasters have also been known to find short-term work, though sometimes in exchange for food and lodgings instead of wages. On Bali, the fortnightly *Bali Advertiser* carries a "situations vacant" column and is a good place to look for office and hotel jobs. It's available free from some hotels and tourist offices.

PART TWO

THE
GUIDE

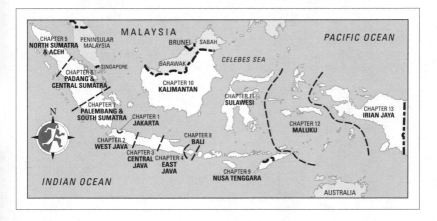

CHAPTER ONE

JAKARTA AND AROUND

Bounded to the north by the Java Sea and the south by the low Bogor Hills, Indonesia's overwhelming capital, **JAKARTA**, is one of the fastest growing cities in the world. From a mere 900,000 inhabitants in 1945, the current population is well over 10 million and – despite a 1971 moratorium that declared the city closed to immigrants – continues to grow at a rate of 200,000 every year. The capital currently sprawls over 656 square kilometres of northern Java, and its inexorable

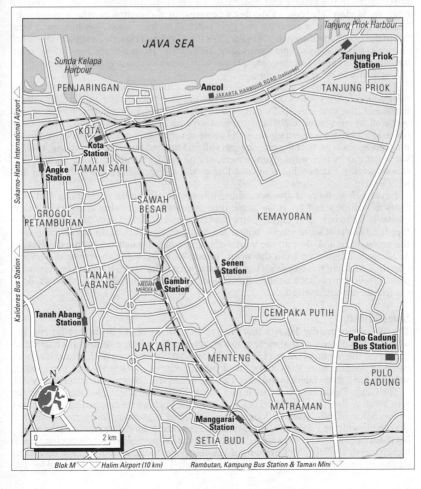

expansion continues both east to Tangerang and west towards Bekasi, districts with which it now almost imperceptibly blends.

Unfortunately, few foreign visitors find the city as alluring as the local population, and down the years Jakarta has been much derided. Yet those prepared to spend some time in the capital will find that the city, for all its faults, has a certain brash, go-getting charm all of its own. Indeed, once you've adjusted to its frenetic pace and mastered the bus system (the city is too hot and polluted to walk very far in), you'll discover a number of little pockets of interest dotted here and there. The endearing suburb of **Kota** in the north, for instance, the former heart of the old Dutch city, still retains a number of beautiful historic buildings, as does the neighbouring port of **Sunda Kelapa**. The capital also has some of the country's finest museums, including the **Maritime Museum** in Sunda Kelapa, the **Wayang Museum** in Kota and, best of all, the **National Museum** in the centre of the city. This museum, having raided many of Indonesia's most famous archeological sights for its exhibits, provides an excellent introduction to the culture and history of the entire archipelago. It's on the western edge of **Medan Merdeka** (Merdeka Square), in the centre of which stands the **Monas Monument**, a concrete and gold pillar 132m high which has become a symbol of the city. Immediately to the south lies the **Golden Triangle**, a square-kilometre cluster of glorious skyscrapers, muscular, 1960s-style "Heroes of the Revolution" monuments and multi-storey shopping plazas, with plenty of markets to trawl through by day and bars to hit in the evening.

To say that these attractions outweigh the capital's faults, however, would be misleading. Large chunks of Jakarta remain unconscionably ugly and breathtakingly inefficient, the vast metropolis ringed by endless crumbling suburbs, traversed and vectored by congested eight-lane expressways and malodorous canals, huge shiny office blocks sharing the roadside with rubble-strewn wasteland and slums. Even in the most prosperous parts of the city one can still find tiny but numerous kampung, twilight worlds of murky alleyways, open sewers, crying children and scurrying vermin. It is this stupefying juxtaposition of outstanding wealth and appalling poverty that many find so offensive.

Nevertheless, there is also something inherently fascinating about a city that both leads the country and yet at the same time appears to be growing apart from it. The capital is far richer (over eighty percent of foreign investment into the country flows through Jakarta at some stage), bigger and more cosmopolitan than anywhere else on the archipelago and, despite the waves of immigrants, the native citizens, the **Betawi** (a Malaysian derivation from the word "Batavia"), still cling to their own dialect and customs. As such, it is worth giving Jakarta at least a day or so, if only to experience a part of the country that's unique, in terms of wealth, size and flavour, in the whole of the Indonesian archipelago.

Some history

The site of modern-day Jakarta first entered the history books in the twelfth century, when the **Pajajarans**, a Sundanese kingdom based in West Java, established a major trading port at the mouth of Sungai Cilikung. Before that, this swampy area of land had been home to nothing more than a few small fishing villages, albeit ones that had existed, according to a stone tablet found near Tanjung Priok, since at least the fifth century AD.

The Hindu Pajajarans named their port Sunda Kelapa and maintained control over the area for more than three hundred years. In 1522, the Portuguese dropped by on their way to the Spice Islands, pausing long enough to erect a godown and sign a Treaty of Friendship with the Pajajarans. At that time the port was a flourishing trading post receiving ships from all over Southeast Asia, but when the Portuguese returned circumstances had changed. The Islamic **Sultanate of Banten**, 50km to the west of Jakarta, had invaded the city under orders from the sultans at Demak. The Portuguese had arrived too late and the Bantenese, under their leader Fatahillah, were able to beat off their attack and keep control of the port. Sunda Kelapa was renamed **Jayakarta**, "City of Victory", and the date of their invasion, June 22, 1527, is still celebrated as the city's birthday today. The Bantenese enjoyed only a short reign, however, before the **Dutch** arrived. In 1610, the Dutch were allowed by the ruling prince, Fatahillah, to move from Banten, their previous capital in the archipelago, to Jayakarta. Once there they built a large godown, which by 1618 – much to Prince Fatahillah's annoyance – they had converted into a fortress. They were now beginning to look ominously powerful. Fatahillah, in order to counteract this rise in Dutch power, made an alliance with the British, and together they attempted to oust the Dutch from the city. The Dutch barricaded themselves into their fortress and survived the onslaught until, in 1619, reinforcements led by **General Jan Pieterszoon Coen** arrived to raze the city and liberate the Dutch held there. The city was rebuilt, renamed **Batavia** after an obscure Germanic tribe of the Netherlands, and became the property of the East India Trading Company, the VOC.

For the rest of the seventeenth century, the Dutch, for whom Batavia had become the administrative centre of a vast trading empire, attempted to transform the city into a tropical version of their beloved Amsterdam. Twice, in 1628 and 1629, they came under attack from the powerful Mataram empire of Central Java (see p.950). Yet both times they were victorious in the face of enormous odds, and by the end of the century, Batavia, with its network of canals and imposing civic buildings, did indeed resemble the Dutch capital. It was soon dubbed the "Queen of the East".

The eighteenth century witnessed a decline in the city's fortunes. The canals silted in the swampy soil of Java and the stagnant water became an ideal breeding ground for diseases such as cholera and malaria. The situation became so bad that the city was nicknamed the **White Man's Graveyard**; according to contemporary statistics, every soldier who had been sent out to Batavia perished there. In an attempt to address the issue, the city gradually gravitated south to higher ground, where the air was less fetid and the water purer. Then, in 1740, the Chinese, who formed the backbone of the manual workforce in the city, rebelled against the harsh treatment by the Dutch. The Dutch and Indonesian populations responded by massacring the Chinese and destroying the Chinese enclave of Glodok, to the south of Batavia. While this prevented any further trouble, it also seriously depleted the city's workforce and the economy collapsed as a result.

Fortunes changed once more in the eighteenth century. After a brief tenure by the **British** between 1811 and 1816 under Governor Raffles, the city reverted to Dutch rule and began to flourish once more, earning the name, "The Pearl of the Orient". A new harbour, Tanjung Priok, was built to cope with the rapid increase in trade, and the city became a hub of enterprise and profit. Unfortunately, these profits were divided unequally between the city's population, with the native Betawi seeing little of the spoils. This naturally led to resentment, which eventually grew and flourished into the nationalist movement of the twentieth century.

On March 5, 1942, the **Japanese** invaded Batavia during their lightning tour of Southeast Asia. The city was once again retitled, with the old Bantenese name "Jayakarta" being shortened to "Jakarta". Dutch power was similarly reduced, and many of their imposing buildings were pulled down. The Dutch returned in 1946, one year after **Sukarno** and **Hatta** had declared Indonesia a republic. The Dutch hold on the city was now decidedly shaky, and after three years they were forced to admit defeat and leave the country. In 1949, Sukarno entered Jakarta, amid scenes of wild jubilation, to become the first president of the Republic of Indonesia.

Though few would begrudge Sukarno this success, his plans for a new Jakarta had town planners and architects alike shaking their heads in despair. Many of the Dutch civic buildings not destroyed during the Japanese occupation were pulled down by the new administration. In the following two decades, ugly, Soviet-style monuments sprouted like warts on the face of the city. Huge **shantytowns** emerged on the fringes of

THE PRO-REFORM RIOTS IN JAKARTA

As the seat of government, with a huge, disaffected underclass living in shantytowns on the outskirts of the city and a considerable number of universities which, with their high populations of politically literate students, are the traditional breeding grounds of protest and revolution in Indonesia, Jakarta was always likely to be at the forefront of any **anti-government demonstrations**. Open displays of resentment towards Suharto's regime first surfaced in 1997, following the economic turmoil of that year and the resulting collapse of the rupiah. Those charged with the task of quelling these protests — the police and armed forces — initially had little trouble confining these demonstrations to the university campuses. On May 12, however, they were caught unawares by one particular demonstration that had managed to elude the security cordon, and they began to march on the People's Consultative Assembly, or MPR (Indonesia's Parliament), in the west of the city near Grogol station. Hurrying to the scene, soldiers were greeted by demonstrators bearing flowers as a sign of their peaceable intentions, and for the first few hours the demonstration passed off without incident. But violence erupted later in the day when, according to eyewitness accounts, students unmasked what they believed were undercover military personnel in their ranks, and turned on them. In the mayhem that followed, six students were killed and ten injured as the security forces fired rubber bullets in their attempts to disperse the crowd.

The ruling Golkar Party, with Suharto at its head, hoped that this brutal show of strength would deter any other protesters from voicing their discontent; in fact, it only succeeded in increasing the resentment, anger and frustration felt by the ordinary citizens of Jakarta towards Suharto's corrupt regime. Over the next nine days, and despite the presence of over 15,000 troops deployed by the armed forces chief, General Wiranto, the situation in Jakarta deteriorated to a state of near anarchy. Huge columns of smoke rose all over the capital as banks, supermarkets, shopping plazas and cars were set alight by angry mobs. Looters passed from shop to shop, taking freely from the shelves, dragging their stolen booty out with them, while the security forces, unpopular and outnumbered, looked on helplessly. This temporary state of **lawlessness** also gave a few citizens the chance to vent age-old prejudices. In particular, the **Chinese community** in Jakarta, long resented for their business acumen and prosperity, became the target of some particularly savage attacks. Glodok, just south of Kota in the north of the city, has been Jakarta's unofficial Chinatown since before the days of the VOC, and the Glodok Mall, a large indoor electronics and clothes market that occupied two multi-storey blocks on either side of Jalan Gajah Mada, was always the most recognizable landmark of this quarter. At the time of writing, all that remains of the shopping centre are two charred, gutted concrete shells and a couple of large pillars standing in the middle of the road, the remnants of a pedestrian bridge that ran between the shopping centres.

As the violence and lawlessness increased, so did the death toll. In one incident, over one hundred people were burnt to death when yet another shopping centre, the Yogya Plaza in Klender in east Jakarta, was torched by demonstrators. According to eyewitnesses, most of the victims were looters trapped inside the shopping centre as it caught fire. The students, meanwhile, the organizers and participants of the original demonstration, tried to distance themselves from the anarchy that they had indirectly brought about, and called off a second planned march on Parliament, opting instead to join opposition leaders in handing over a **petition** calling for Suharto's removal. The tactic worked: on May 21, Suharto stepped down, and within a few days law and order had begun to return to the streets of the capital. The authorities have since estimated that nearly five thousand buildings and over a thousand vehicles were burnt and destroyed within the city, and mass burials were ordered for the two hundred charred and unclaimed bodies, most of which were found under the rubble of shopping centres burnt down during the riots.

NOVEMBER/DECEMBER 1998
Jakarta once again became the focus of anti-government protest in November 1998, following the convening of a special **session of parliament** called by the new president, B.J. Habibie. In the weeks leading up to the assembly, thousands of extra troops were drafted into the city, major arteries into the capital were policed and monitored, and armed volunteers were recruited by the police to try to prevent a repeat of the riots of May. Yet even these measures proved inadequate. The protesters, unhappy that pro-democracy reforms promised by Habibie's government weren't progressing fast enough, and worried that many of their demands – including the removal of the army from parliament and the prosecution of Suharto for corruption – would not be met, once again took to the streets to demonstrate. On what became known as **Black Friday**, November 13, 1998, an attempted march on parliament by a large crowd of pro-reform demonstrators ended in bloodshed when the security forces began firing on protesters at the Semanggi Cloverleaf Flyover, killing fourteen and injuring dozens. President Habibie further aroused anti-government passions by calling on General Wiranto to take "stern action" to restore order to the city, in a speech that was widely condemned as both insensitive and inflammatory by opposition leaders.

Further protests followed throughout the five-day parliamentary session, mainly in the Pasar Senen and Grogol districts, though there was little of the lawlessness and anti-Chinese violence that characterized the troubles in May. However, in an unusual and worrying twist, on November 22, just nine days after Black Friday, a group of Muslims attacked and destroyed over twenty churches in the city and hacked thirteen Christians to death. Though most experts don't see this incident as directly related to the current political turmoil, many concede that this attack could be a sign that the current political and economic upheaval is beginning to unravel the fragile and much-praised religious tolerance practised in the archipelago. At the time of writing, protests were continuing on an almost daily basis.

Jakarta during the 1950s, housing people drawn to the city by the irresistible lure of money. What they found when they got here was not their fortune, but abject poverty. Following social unrest in 1965, the newly installed president, Suharto, attempted to address the problem by implementing **welfare programmes** for the city's poorer inhabitants, and other measures designed to secure the long-term economic future of the capital. Though these programmes had some effect, they also led to even further migration to the city. The recession of the 1980s saw oil exports plummet and the government, in an attempt to stave off economic disaster, switched to a programme of rapid industrialization which only drew more workers to the city, where they joined the disaffected masses on the outskirts of Jakarta. The migrants' squalid living conditions contrasted sharply with the air-con lifestyles of the elite in the city, generating enormous resentment against the rich, the successful and the Chinese, who some saw as having benefited unfairly from the government's economic policies.

Despite Suharto's attempts to keep the city's burgeoning middle class happy, they were becoming tired of a government riven with corruption, and of a nepotistic leader who ensured that his own family got all the most lucrative business contracts. In May 1998, students took to the streets to protest against the old regime and its policies. Many were killed in the **violence** that followed as the city descended into anarchy until, on May 21, 1998, Suharto stepped down, to be replaced by his vice president, Habibie.

Few believe that Habibie's appointment will bring about the end of civil unrest. Jakarta still suffers from chronic overpopulation, and, as the gap between the have and have-nots increases, so too does the resentment of the dispossessed in their shanty-towns. As Indonesia's vibrant, booming capital strides towards the new millennium with a population approaching eleven million, it is this problem above all others that shadows its every step.

Orientation, arrival and information

To head from north to south through the centre of Jakarta is to go forward in time, from the old Dutch city of Batavia and the Chinese quarter of Glodok in the north to the modern golf courses and amusement parks in the south. **Medan Merdeka**, the giant, threadbare patch of grass crowned by the dizzying National Monument, is the spiritual centre of Jakarta, if not exactly its geographical one. The presidential palace lies on the northern rim of the square, and the main commercial district is just a short distance to the south. The major north–south thoroughfare which passes along the western edge of Merdeka forms the central artery of the capital, changing its name a number of times along its route, from **Jalan Gajah Mada** in the north to **Jalan Merdeka Barat** as it passes along the square, then **Jalan Thamrin** and finally, in the south of the city, **Jalan Jend Sudirman**.

Arrival

As you would expect for one of the world's largest cities, Jakarta has a wealth of international and domestic transport connections. Apart from the impressive **Sukarno-Hatta airport** to the west of the city, and the tiny Halim airport to the south (which, following the drop-off in domestic flights following the riots in 1998, currently does not serve commercial airlines and is being used as a base by the Indonesian air force), there are also four central **train stations** (and dozens of minor suburban ones) and three major **bus stations**, most of which are tucked away in the suburbs, a lengthy bus ride away from the city centre.

The main area for budget accommodation, **Jalan Jaksa**, lies to the south of Medan Merdeka (for detailed reviews of the city's accommodation, see p.78). Running south from the southwestern corner of Medan Merdeka, **Jalan M.H. Thamrin** (hereafter just called Jalan Thamrin) provides Jakarta with its main north–south thoroughfare and is lined with a number of world-class hotels.

By air

Both international and domestic flights into Jakarta land at **Sukarno-Hatta airport**, 13km west of the city centre. Beyond the huge queues at passport control, the baggage reclamation area has a number of exchange booths, one or two hotel booking companies and a small **yellow board** with details of how to get from the airport to the city centre, including approximate taxi fares and details of the DAMRI bus service. Through customs, there's a small and not over-helpful **tourist office** and more exchange booths, most of which close at 10pm. Try to change as little money here as possible: the rates are 25 percent lower than those on offer in the banks in the centre of town. There's a hotel, the *Aspac* (☎021/5590008, fax 5590018; ⑨), at terminal 2E, for those who can't face the trip into town immediately.

At Rp5000 per person, the **DAMRI bus** remains the cheapest way to get to the city centre. These single-decker white buses with a navy-blue stripe along the side leave regularly between 3am and 10pm, taking 45 minutes to reach Gambir station in the heart of the city (15min walk from Jalan Jaksa and 20min to Jalan Thamrin). From there they then head south towards Blok M, Rawamangun and Kemayoram.

With **taxis**, in addition to the metered fare, passengers must also pay the **toll fees** (approximately Rp7000 in total) plus another Rp2500 **guaranteed service fee**. In return for this last charge you are given a comment form, which not only gives you the chance to vent your spleen at the driver's hair-raising antics en route, but also greatly reduces the risk of you being ripped off. Adding all these charges together, the total cost of a taxi ride to Jalan Jaksa is approximately Rp33,500. Recommended taxi firms include Steady Safe, Kosti, Blue Bird and President.

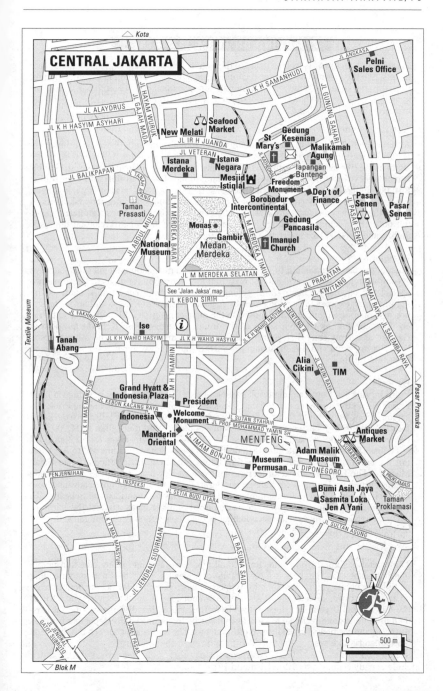

CENTRAL JAKARTA

Kota

JL ANGKASA

Pelni
Sales Office

JL K H SAMANHUDI

JL ALAYDRUS

JL K H HASYIM ASYHARI

JL HAXAM WURUK

JL GAJAH MADA

JL GUNUNG SAHARI

Seafood
Market

New Melati

St
Mary's

Gedung
Kesenian

Malikamah
Agung

JL IR H JUANDA

JL VETERAN

Istana
Merdeka

Istana
Negara

JL KATHEDRAL

Lapangan
Banteng

JL BALIKPAPAN

JL TANAH ABANG

Mesjid
Istiqlal

Freedom
Monument

JL ABDUL MUIS

Borobudur
Intercontinental

Dep't of
Finance

Pasar
Senen

Pasar
Senen

JL PASAR SENEN

Taman
Prasasti

Monas

Gambir

Gedung
Pancasila

National
Museum

JL M MERDEKA BARAT

Medan
Merdeka

JL M MERDEKA TIMUR

Imanuel
Church

JL M MERDEKA SELATAN

JL PRAPATAN

JL KWITANG

See 'Jalan Jaksa' map

JL KEBON SIRIH

JL KRAMAT RAYA

JL SALEMBA RAYA

Textile Museum

JL FAKHRUDIN

Ise

ⓘ

JL K H WAHID HASYIM

MENTENG R

Tanah
Abang

JL K H WAHID HASYIM

JL K H WAHID HASYIM

Alia
Cikini

JL CIKINI RAYA

TIM

Pasar Pramuka

JL M H THAMRIN

JL K H MAS MANSYUR

Grand Hyatt &
Indonesia Plaza

JL KEBON KACANG RAYA

President

Indonesia

Welcome
Monument

JL SUTAN SYAHRIR

JL PROF MOHAMMAD YAMIN SH

MENTENG

Antiques
Market

JL SURABAYA

Mandarin
Oriental

JL IMAM BONJOL

Adam Malik
Museum

Museum
Permusan

JL DIPONEGORO

JL PROKLAMASI

JL PENJERNIHAN

JL INSPEKSI

JL SETIA BUDI UTARA

Bumi Asih Jaya

Sasmita Loka
Jen A Yani

Taman
Proklamasi

JL K H MAS MANSYUR

JL JENDRAL SUDIRMAN

JL RASUNA SAID

JL SULTAN AGUNG

N

0   500 m

JL GATOT SUBROTO

Blok M

MOVING ON FROM JAKARTA

Travel agents in town, as well as many of the hotels, sell bus, ferry and discounted plane tickets. See the Listings on p.99 for recommended agencies. Train tickets can be bought from the special tourist window at Gambir station (see opposite). Though bus tickets are sometimes still available on the day of departure, plane, train and ferry tickets should be brought a week beforehand.

By plane
All scheduled **flights**, both domestic and international, currently leave from Sukarno-Hatta airport, though Merpati plan to operate a few services from Halim airport, in the south of the city, in the near future. DAMRI buses depart for Sukarno-Hatta from Gambir station every thirty minutes between 3am and 10pm (45–90min depending on traffic; Rp4000). Ignore the taxi drivers who will insist that the last bus has already left. **Check in** one hour before departure for domestic flights, two hours for international flights. A taxi to the airport can cost as little as Rp14,000, though this figure rises significantly after the buses have stopped running. There is a **departure tax** of Rp11,000 on domestic flights, and Rp30,000 for international departures.

By train
Most of the **trains** travelling to West and Central Java destinations begin their journeys at Gambir station; see "Travel details" on p.102) for destinations and times. There are two special offices (daily 7.30am–7pm) selling tickets for the luxury trains, such as the Parahiyangan express to Bandung and the Argolawu express to Yogya and Solo. The station also operates a tourist-only window on the main concourse. Although Kota station is on the same line as Gambir, some of the trains departing from Kota do not stop at Gambir, and many start their journey at Gambir and miss out Kota. The other two stations, Pasar Senen and Tanah Abang, are further out of town, have fewer services and rarely see tourists.

By ferry
Pelni ferries sail from Tanjung Priok harbour. Bus #14 runs from Tanah Abang via Jalan Kebon Siri, at the northern end of Jalan Jaksa, before continuing on to Tanjung Priok bus station, 500m from the harbour. Allow at least 75 minutes for your journey from Jalan Jaksa. A taxi from Jalan Jaksa to the harbour should cost no more than Rp11,000. The Pelni booking office is at Jalan Angkasa 18 (Mon–Thurs 8am–noon & 1–2.30pm, Fri 8–11.30am & 1–2.30pm); catch bus #15 or #P15 to Pasar Senen then bus #10 to Angkasa. For the latest timetable, call in at the fifth floor of the Pelni head office at Jalan Gajah Mada 14. The **Kapuas Express ferry** runs twice weekly from Godown 2 at the Sunda Kelapa harbour to Pontianak in Kalimantan Barat. Tickets can be bought in advance from PT Egel Tripelti, Rajawali Condominium Edelweiss Tower, Jalan Rajawali Selatan 1/1b (☎021/6409288). For details of other ferries from Sunda Kelapa, contact the harbourmaster, Pipit, in his office on the second floor of the Departemen Perhubungan at the end of Baruna III in Sunda Kelapa.

By bus
The capital has good **bus** connections to all points in Java, and many cities on neighbouring islands too. There is usually a range of prices for every destination, depending on the type of bus you're travelling in. While you pay a premium for tickets bought from an agency in town, some of the buses leave from outside the agency, saving you a trip to the bus station. If your bus does depart from the station, leave plenty of time (at least 90min) to get from downtown to your terminal, whichever one you're departing from, as traffic is always heavy in Jakarta. Note that bus #78 is the most direct bus between Sarinah and Kalideres.

By train

Gambir station is the most popular and convenient of all the major transport terminals, being just a fifteen-minute walk away from the travellers' centre of Jalan Jaksa. A bajaj between the two costs approximately Rp1500 – an unavoidable but extortionate fee for such a small distance.

Of the other stations, **Kota**, near old Batavia, is the busiest. To reach Jalan Jaksa from Kota, catch bus #P1, #P10, #P11 or #AC01 which will drop you by the Sarinah department store, about a ten-minute walk away. From there the buses continue south to the Welcome Monument and the international hotels. A third train station, **Tanah Abang**, serving Merak (for Sumatra), lies to the west of Jalan Thamrin (bus #P16 to Sarinah and Gambir), and a fourth station, **Pasar Senen**, is situated 1km east of Gambir (bus #15 or #P15 to Jalan Jaksa), though you are unlikely to arrive at either of these.

By bus

Jakarta's **bus stations** are uniformly noisy, bewildering and inconveniently situated; it's no wonder so many people choose to enter and leave the capital by train instead. Each of the bus stations serves different destinations, although there are overlaps: buses to and from Sumatra, for example, arrive at both Kalideres and Pulo Gadung stations.

The **Pulo Gadung** station, 12km to the east of the city, is probably the noisiest and least bearable of the lot. If you're travelling from Central or East Java or Bali you'll probably arrive here. To get to the centre of town, catch bus #507, which passes the south-western corner of Medan Merdeka by the fountain.

Buses from West Java pull in at the **Rambutan Kampung** station, 18km south of the city centre near Taman Mini. Buses #P10, #P11, #P16 and #AC70 all ply the route from Rambutan to the Sarinah department store (and vice versa), taking ninety minutes. The third station, **Kalideres**, serving destinations to the west of Sumatra, rarely sees tourists. Bus #64 provides a means of escape to Sarinah for those few poor souls who end up at this rat-infested dump, 15km to the west of the city centre.

By ship

All Pelni boats arrive at **Tanjung Priok harbour**, 500m from the bus station of the same name. For Jalan Jaksa, catch bus #P14 from the station and alight at the junction of Jalan Siri Timur and Jalan H.A. Salim. Travelling by ferry from Borneo, the chances are you'll arrive at the Sunda Kelapa harbour, near the Kota district. Walk to the Kota bus station and catch bus #P1, #P10, #P11 or #AC01.

Information

Jakarta's **tourist office** (Mon–Fri 9.30am–5pm, Sat 9.30am–noon; ☎021/3142067) – the "Pelayanan Informasi Parawisata Jakarta" to give it its full title – is tucked away in the Jakarta Theatre building, opposite the Sarinah department store on Jalan Wahid Hasyim. Though their knowledge of specifics (such as bus numbers) is a little sketchy, and they don't yet have a hotel booking facility, they do provide a good free map of the city along with a number of glossy brochures. If you're after something a little more detailed, consider buying a copy of the Periplus map of Jakarta, the most accurate and user-friendly available. A second, smaller tourist office dealing mainly with train inquiries can be found by the southern entrance of Gambir station.

The main tourist office stocks *The Visitor*, a free monthly guide to the city which includes brief listings of events and entertainments, and the free *Welcome to Indonesia* brochure, a bimonthly guide to the whole archipelago. Occasionally they have copies of the useful annual Jakarta *Shopping Mall Guide*.

City transport

Jakarta is too hot, smoggy and vast to walk in, and visitors should really try to grasp the basics of its extensive **public transport** options. The bus network is comprehensive, convenient and cheap. That said, the vast profusion of buses that thunder around the city can be a little bewildering, and many people prefer to pay a little more and catch a bajaj or taxi instead. Whatever mode of transport you choose, remember that the volume of traffic in Jakarta is such that jams are inevitable: for a bus journey of 10km, allow at least an hour.

Buses

Where possible, **bus numbers** have been included in the relevant sections of the chapter to help you find your way around the city. Sometimes the tourist office can also help with bus routes; the busiest bus stop in Jakarta lies just a few metres away from the tourist office, outside the Sarinah department store.

Buses operate a set-fare system, where the same fare is charged regardless of how far you travel. This fare changes, however, according to the type of bus you are travelling on. The cheapest are the small, pale blue minivans which operate out of Kota bus station (the numbers of which are always preceded by the letter "M"), which charge just Rp400–500, and the **large** coaches that can be found all over the city and which charge the same fare. However, if the bus number on these large coaches is preceded by the letter "P", the fare rises to Rp700. The small, battered orange **micro-minibuses** charge Rp500, regardless of whether there is a "P" in front of the number or not. The large, fume-belching **double-deckers** charge Rp750, and, at the top of the scale, **air-con buses** (easily recognizable because the doors are kept shut while in motion) cost Rp1800–2300. On the air-con buses you pay the driver as you board; for all the others a conductor comes round and collects the fare. The fare is usually posted on the inside of the bus so you should never be overcharged.

Bajaj

Now that the traditional cycle-rickshaws, or becak, have been banned from Jakarta for being too slow (although a small population survives in the theme park at Ancol), the two-stroke motorized rickshaws, or **bajaj** (pronounced "ba-jais"), have now monopolized Jakarta's backstreets. Before hopping in the back of one, however, be sure to bargain very, very hard and remember that bajaj are banned from major thoroughfares such as Jalan Thamrin, so you may well end up being dropped off a long way from your destination. As a guide to fares, Jalan Jaksa to the post office should cost no more than Rp2000.

Taxis

Jakarta's **taxis** are numerous and, providing you know your way around the city and aren't at the mercy of unscrupulous drivers, inexpensive. Rates are usually around Rp1000 per kilometre, with a standard flag-fall of Rp1500, and most cars are equipped with meters. Drivers generally expect a tip from foreigners and may be very reluctant to hand back all of your change.

Accommodation

There is an oversupply of business and tourist-class **hotels** scattered throughout Jakarta, the best of which are listed below. Budget hotels, however, are fewer in number and are all situated, with one exception, on and around the traveller's sanctuary of Jalan Jaksa to the south of Medan Merdeka in the heart of the city. Jakarta's **budget accommodation** is more expensive than elsewhere in the archipelago, with no

ACCOMMODATION PRICE CODES

All the **accommodation** listed in this book has been given one of the following price codes. The rates quoted here are for the **cheapest double room** in high season, except for places with dorms, where the code represents the price of a single bed. Where there's a significant spread of prices indicated (④–⑦, for example), the text will explain what extra facilities you get for more money. The 11–21 percent tax charged by most hotels is not included in these price codes.

Because of the current instability of the rupiah, accommodation prices are given throughout in their more stable **US dollar equivalents**, even for places which accept payment in rupiah.

For more on accommodation, see p.40.

① under $1	③ $2–5	⑤ $10–15	⑦ $35–60	⑨ $100
② $1–2	④ $5–10	⑥ $15–35	⑧ $60–100	and over

commensurate increase in quality: prices start at Rp7000 for a dormitory bed in the cheapest hostel. In spite of this, most places are constantly full, so try to ring ahead to book a space.

Jalan Jaksa and around

Jalan Jaksa is where you'll find the usual collection of restaurants, bookshops, travel agents and batik stores – everything, in fact, that travellers could want to make their sojourn in Jakarta as convenient as possible. All the places below are marked on the map of Jalan Jaksa on p.80.

Hotels

Arcadia, Jl Wahid Hasyim 114 (☎021/2300050, fax 2300995). An interior designer's dream, this unique, state-of-the-art hotel is characterized by clean lines, natural light and conversation-piece furniture. Quite a fun place, and it's worth looking around and having a drink in the bar (with happy hour between 5pm and 7pm), even if you're not staying here. ⑧.

Cipta, Jl Wahid Hasyim 53 (☎021/3904701, fax 326531). Unexceptional mid-priced hotel. Rooms are fairly standard, but do come with individually controlled air-con and a TV. ⑨.

Djody Hotel, Jl Jaksa 35 (☎021/3151404, fax 3142368). Pricier version of the *Djody Hostel*, though with no real difference in quality. ④.

Ibis Tamarin, Jl Wahid Hasyim 77 (☎021/3157706, fax 3157707). Large and rather ugly hotel with 130 reasonably pleasant rooms, an outdoor swimming pool, a health centre and 24hr room service. ⑨.

Indra Internasional, Jl Wahid Hasyim 63 (☎021/3152858, fax 323465). The oldest of the hotels on Jl Wahid Hasyim, the light and airy *Indra* has for over thirty years provided guests with clean air-con rooms (all with TV and mini-bar) and a friendly, helpful service. ⑥.

Karya, Jl Jaksa 32–34 (☎021/3150519, fax 3142781). One of a growing number of mid-priced hotels on budget-minded Jl Jaksa. All rooms are complete with air-con, TV and hot-water showers. ⑦.

Kresna, Jl Kebon Siri Timur I/175 (☎021/325403). Acceptable budget hotel with tiny and dank downstairs rooms but brighter ones upstairs – the showers are powerful and clean. Free tea on offer throughout the day. ③.

Le Margot, Jl Jaksa 15 (☎021/3913830, fax 324641). Average mid-priced hotel with some rather poky attached rooms. The basement air-con dorm is a recent addition. ③–⑥.

Sari San Pacific, Jl Thamrin (☎021/323707, fax 323650). Located to the north of the Sarinah junction, this is a standard international-class hotel with a nightclub (occasional live music), Japanese and Indonesian restaurants and a delicatessen. ⑨.

Tator, Jl Jaksa 37 (☎021/323940, fax 325124) Many people's favourite on Jl Jaksa, this spotless mid-priced hotel has friendly staff, and hot water – *and* the price includes breakfast. ⑤.

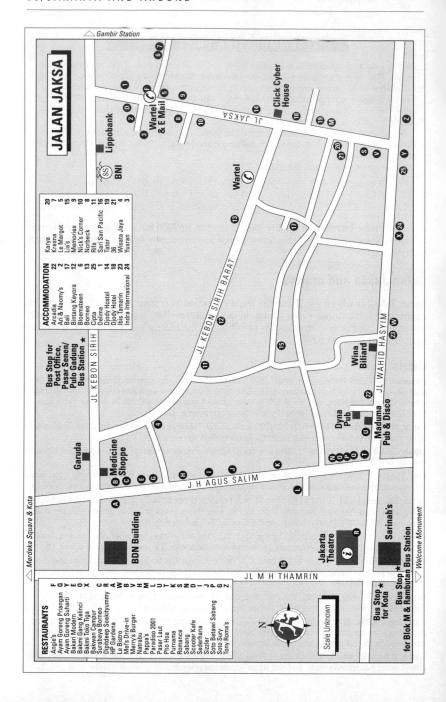

JALAN JAKSA

△ Gambir Station

ACCOMMODATION

Arcadia	22	Karya	20
Ari & Naomy's	2	Kresna	7
Bali	17	Le Margot	5
Bintang Keyora	12	Lia's	15
Bloemsteen	6	Memories	9
Borneo	13	Nick's Corner	10
Cipta	25	Norbeck	8
Delima	1	Rifa	11
Djody Hostel	18	Sari San Pacific	16
Djody Hotel	23	Tator	19
Ibis Tamarin	24	36	21
Indra Internasional		Wisata Jaya	4
		Yusran	3

RESTAURANTS

Angie's	F
Ayam Goreng Priangan	Q
Ayam Goreng Suharti	Y
Bakeri Modern	E
Bakmi Gang Kelinci	O
Bakmi Toko Tiga	X
Bakwan Campur	C
Surabaya Borneo	R
Dipitdeep Soakityummy	A
HP Gardena	W
Le Bistro	B
Mel's Drive-in	V
Merry's Burger	H
Natrabu	M
Pappa's	L
Paradiso 2001	U
Pasar Laut	T
Pho Hoa	K
Purnama	S
Romance	N
Sabang	D
Scooter Kafe	I
Sederhana	J
Sizzler	P
Soto Betawi Sabang	G
Soto Sury	N
Tony Roma's	Z

Bus Stop for
Post Office,
Pasar Senen/
Pulo Gadung
Bus Station ★

Garuda

Medicine
Shoppe

Click Cyber
House

Lippobank

BNI

Wartel
& E Mail

Wartel

JL KEBON SIRIH

JL KEBON SIRIH BARAT

JL WAHID HASYIM

Wina
Biliard

Dyna
Pub

Maduna
Pub & Disco

BDN Building

J H AGUS SALIM

Jakarta
Theatre

Sarinah's

JL M H THAMRIN

Bus Stop ★
for Kota

Bus Stop ★
for Blok M & Rambutan Bus Station

Welcome Monument

Merdeka Square & Kota

Scale Unknown

N

Yusran, Jl Kebon Siri Barat Dalam VI/9 (☎021/3140373). Surprisingly pleasant budget hotel tucked away at the end of Gang 6 to the west of Jaksa. The single is cramped, airless and full of mosquitoes, but the doubles are spotless and comfortable. Bargaining is possible. ④.

Hostels and losmen

Ari & Naomy's, Jl Kebon Siri Barat VII/3 (☎021/31904347). New and friendly little losmen just a few metres west of Jl Jaksa. Rooms are a little poky, though clean enough, and the room rate includes a reasonable breakfast. ③.

Bali, Jl Kebon Siri Barat Dalam GgX/7 (☎021/390069). Small, anonymous hostel tucked down an alley to the west of Jl Jaksa. Rooms are a little cramped and the walls are paper-thin – a big disadvantage considering there are at least three mosques within call-to-prayer distance. ③.

Bintang Keyora, Jl Kebon Siri Barat 52 (☎021/323878). A medium-sized hostel that's one of the better-value places in this price range, with clean, well-maintained rooms and cheap rates that include breakfast. ④.

Bloemsteen, Jl Kebon Siri Timur I/174 (☎021/323002). Perfectly acceptable hostel, managed by the irrepressible and helpful Budi, with spacious rooms and a pleasant, sunny balcony. The bathrooms are the cleanest and best in Jl Jaksa, and the showers even dribble hot water occasionally. ④.

Borneo, Jl Kebon Siri Barat 35–37 (☎021/3140095). Large, ramshackle hostel-cum-brothel with the cheapest dormitories in town. The east wing is a little sleazy, though bearable, while the west wing is filthy and should be avoided. The restaurant next to reception is popular and does good burgers. ①–④.

Delima, Jl Jaksa 5 (☎021/337026). The oldest and one of the best value of the city's hostels. Established in 1969, the *Delima* is beginning to rest on its laurels a little: some of the rooms could do with a good spring-clean, and the staff could be friendlier too. Nevertheless, it's still a good spot, especially by Jakartan standards, and nearly always full in the high season. ②–③.

Djody Hostel, Jl Jaksa 27 (☎021/3151404, fax 3142368). Not to be confused with its slightly more expensive sister down the road, the rather gloomy *Djody Hostel* comprises 24 rooms, all watched over by a 24hr security guard. ④.

Lia's, Jl Kebon Siri Barat Gg VIII/47 (☎021/3162708). Recommended little hostel with a pleasant front garden, located in an ideal spot behind high fences in a quiet alleyway 200m to the west of Jl Jaksa. The clean and basic rooms are reasonable value by Jakarta's standards, and there's free tea and coffee throughout the day. ③.

Memories Café, Jl Jaksa 17 (no phone). Secreted away behind the *Memories Café*, and reached via the toilets and a spiralling metal staircase, are two beautiful double rooms. Great value. ④.

Nick's Corner (aka **Wisma Niki**), Jl Jaksa 16 (☎021/336754, fax 3107814). Large and popular hostel offering a variety of budget and not-so-budget rooms. The two mixed-sex, air-con dormitories are reasonable, though they both lack windows and are a little dark. ①–④.

Norbeck, Jl Jaksa 14 (☎021/330392). From the barbed wire that surrounds it to the lists of rules plastered everywhere, this large hostel oozes inhospitality. The cell-like rooms are cramped and dark, each lit by a single, naked bulb. Such is the shortage of budget options in the capital, however, that many poor souls still end up here. ④.

Rifa, Jl Kebon Siri Barat Dalam 36a (☎021/3145523). Small hostel offering just two doubles and three singles. Not a bad alternative if the others are full. ③.

36, Jl Jaksa 36b. Small hostel with claustrophobic rooms located down Gang 12, at the southern end of Jl Jaksa. Rates are reasonable, however, and include breakfast. ④.

Wisata Jaya, Jl Kebon Siri Barat Dalam I/45 (☎021/3145853). Dilapidated hostel with grimy rooms and noisy staff. Not a pleasant place to stay at the best of times, and particularly during the monsoon with the noise of the rain clattering against the corrugated-iron roof. ④.

The rest of the city

Although there are plenty of mid-priced and rather bland hotels all over the city, mainly catering to businesspeople and with boardrooms and conference centres the norm, a couple of areas in the centre of town have a particularly high concentration. **Jalan**

Wahid Hasyim, at the southern end of Jalan Jaksa, plays host to a number of moderately priced places, while the best and most expensive hotels in the city huddle around the Welcome Monument on **Jalan Thamrin**, to the southwest of Gambir station. Be warned that most of the rates below are subject to a two percent tax and, although payment in rupiah is acceptable, the exchange rates they offer are often very poor.

Alia Cikini, Jl Cikini Raya 32 (☎021/3924444, fax 3928640). Blancmange-pink, newly opened hotel opposite the Indonesian Cultural Centre at Taman Ismael Marzuki, that at the time of writing was suffering from a few bureaucratic teething troubles – lost or incorrect bookings and double bookings. ⑥.

Aspac, Terminal 2e, Bandara Sukarno-Hatta (☎021/5590008, fax 5590018). Hotel situated in one of the terminals of Jakarta's international airport. Fairly basic and lacking atmosphere, but clean and satisfactory. Rooms can be hired out for 3hr or 6hr during the day, for those who fancy a little comfort and privacy when waiting for their flight. ⑧.

Borobudur Intercontinental, Jl Lapangan Banteng Selatan (☎021/3805555, fax 3809595). Once the best in the city, this grand hotel has struggled to regain its supremacy after closing briefly in 1998 for refurbishment. The gardens are beautiful, however, and contain an open-air swimming pool, tennis courts and a jogging track. The rooms themselves are equally sumptuous, and come with satellite TV, air-con and a mini-bar. ⑨.

Bumi Asih Jaya, Jl Solo 4 (☎021/3860839, fax 3900355). Small and relaxing fifteen-room hotel set in a leafy suburb to the south of Jl Diponegoro. The highlight is the carefully tended garden, a small smog-free haven in the heart of Jakarta. ⑤.

Grand Hyatt, Jl Thamrin (☎021/3901234, fax 334321). Massive complex in the centre of town with luxurious rooms and an entire shopping centre in the basement. Other features include a pool, restaurants, pubs and live entertainment. ⑨.

Indonesia, Jl Thamrin (☎021/2301008, fax 3141508). The cheapest of the hotels which huddle around the Welcome Monument roundabout, housing Japanese and Indonesian restaurants, a bar (hosting regular cultural evenings) and some pretty plush rooms. ⑨.

Ise, Jl Thamrin 168 (☎021/333463). The only budget option not on or near JL Jaksa, this family-run, foreigners-only hostel lies on the third floor and has a pleasant balcony overlooking the city. The rooms are nice, but be warned: you should check your bill carefully. ④.

Mandarin Oriental, Jl Thamrin (☎021/3141307, fax 3148680). Huge, superior-class hotel with swimming pool, Italian and Chinese restaurants and a nightclub. ⑨.

New Melati, Jl Hayam Wuruk 1 (☎021/3841943, fax 3813526). Indonesian-owned hotel which is struggling to compete with its international rivals. All rooms are fitted with TV, air-con, telephone, mini-bar and bath. Rates include breakfast. ⑥.

Omni Batavia, Jl Kali Besar Barat 46 (☎021/6904118, fax 6904092). Beautiful place located by a canal in the Kota district. The spectacular stained-glass facade conceals a plush hotel with the full set of facilities, including a swimming pool, cake shop and a number of restaurants. ⑨.

President, Jl Thamrin 59 (☎021/2301122, fax 3143631). Four-star, Japanese-owned hotel with 315 rooms, Japanese and Chinese restaurants and an outdoor pool. ⑨.

The City

Jakarta's prettiest quarter, and the home of some of its better tourist attractions, lies at the northern end of the city. The quaint old Dutch suburb of **Kota** and the adjoining port of **Sunda Kelapa** contain a number of handsome period buildings, many of which, such the former **Dutch Town Hall** (now the home of the **Jakarta Museum**) and the highly rated **Museum Wayang**, surround the old **Town Square of Batavia**. Photogenic schooners still dock at the port, which also features the extremely well-presented **Maritime Museum**.

Back in the centre of town, the **National Museum** is worth visiting for its vast and often dazzling collection of Indonesian antiquities, and a trip here can be combined with a climb to the top of **Monas**, for an overview of the city and its ever-present smog.

Some of the suburbs in the immediate vicinity of Monas are surprisingly quiet and leafy (though these are relative terms in Jakarta), including the **Lapangan Banteng** – featuring yet more Dutch architecture – and the embassy enclave of **Menteng**. Both have a number of buildings and sights that are mildly diverting, and are worth a stroll.

Kota (Old Batavia)

Located in the north of the city, the quaint old district of **Batavia** used to serve as the administrative centre of a great trading empire, stretching from South Africa all the way to Japan. The Dutch filled their tropical capital with glorious and imposing examples of colonial architecture, both civic and private, and enclosed the whole within a huge defensive wall. These walls, built in the 1620s by General Coen, the first governor of Batavia, have long since disappeared, and many of the old buildings have suffered a similar fate. A few classic examples of Dutch architecture have survived, however, and give a good idea of how this district must have looked during its heyday. Today, Kota, the district that encompasses Batavia, ranks as Jakarta's prettiest quarter, though it has to be said this is partly because of a lack of any real competition.

There are plenty of buses heading north from Thamrin to Kota: look out for #P1, #P11 or the air-con #P17. All these buses drive north along Jalan Gajah Mada past the impressive facade of the dazzling white **Kota train station** which stands to the right of the road. This is a good place to jump out and begin a tour of the city.

About 400m along Jalan Jembatan Batu, the road that runs east along the southern side of the station, stands the oldest surviving church on Java, the red-brick **Gereja Sion**. Built in 1695, it was originally constructed by the Dutch for the "Black Portuguese", Eurasian slaves brought over from Melaka to build the city. These slaves were later given their freedom as long as they converted from their Catholic faith to the Dutch Reformed Church, and the Gereja Sion, built outside the city walls, became their centre of worship. Sadly, the church is often locked these days, but, if you get a chance to peek in, check out the Baroque pulpit and organ, as well as the rather ornate chandeliers that hang low from the high vaulted ceiling.

To view the rest of Batavia's sights, head north from Kota station along Jalan Lada, past the Politeknik Swadharma, and enter the boundaries of what was once the walled city of Batavia. The centre of Batavia, **Taman Fatahillah**, lies 300m to the north of the train station, an attractive cobbled square hemmed in on all four sides by a number of museums and historical monuments. On the south side is the largely disappointing **Jakarta History Museum** (Tues–Thurs & Sun 9am–3pm, Fri 9am–2pm, Sat 9am–1pm; Rp1000). Housed in the seventeenth-century town hall, this museum sets out to describe (in Indonesian only) the history of the city from the Stone Age to the present day, although unfortunately it never finishes the job. The exhibits gradually peter out until, by the time the exhibition has reached the seventeenth century, only a couple of maps and a few stony-faced portraits of Dutch generals are used to illustrate the entire colonial period. Upstairs is more interesting, with many of the rooms furnished as they would have been two hundred years ago.

A more entertaining and informative museum stands to the west of the square. The **Museum Wayang** (Tues–Thurs & Sun 9am–3pm, Fri 9am–2.30pm, Sat 9am–12.30pm; Rp1000) is a four-storey mansion dedicated to the Javanese art of puppetry. The mansion is one of the oldest buildings in the city, and stands over the site of what was once the most important Dutch church in Batavia, the Oude Holandsche Kerk. In the central courtyard there's a small cemetery where important seventeenth-century Dutch officials were interred, including Jan Pieterzoon Coen, the leader of the Dutch forces during the capture of Batavia in 1619. Today the mansion houses a vast range of puppets from all over the archipelago, and a few donated by overseas dignitaries down the years – including a Punch and Judy set presented to the museum in the 1970s by the

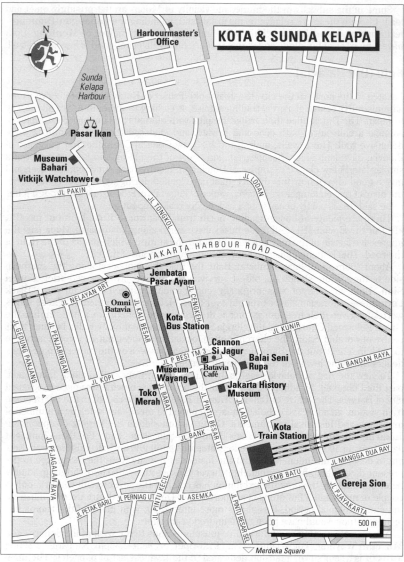

KOTA & SUNDA KELAPA

Merdeka Square

British ambassador. Every Sunday between 10am and 2pm some of the puppets are removed from their glass cases to appear in a free **wayang show**, after which the museum occasionally gives a demonstration of how the puppets are made. The final room in the museum displays a collection of puppets that depict the nationalist struggle, given to the museum on the fiftieth anniversary of Independence by the people of Rotterdam.

Continuing clockwise around the square, on the northern side – just next to the exquisite *Café Batavia* (see p.94) – stands the ornate **Cannon Si Jagur**, a cannon built by the Portuguese to defend the city of Melaka and taken by the Dutch as booty in 1641. On the side of the cannon is the Latin inscription *Ex me ipsa renata sum* – "Out of myself I was reborn" – and the whole thing is emblazoned with sexual imagery, from the clenched fist (a suggestive gesture in Southeast Asia, particularly when the thumb, as in this instance, pokes between the second and third fingers) to the barrel itself, a potent phallic symbol in Indonesia.

To the east of the square, the **Balai Seni Rupa** (Tues–Thurs & Sun 9am–3pm, Fri 9am–2pm, Sat 9am–1pm; Rp1000), Jakarta's fine arts museum, and accompanying **Ceramics Museum** are both undergoing extensive renovation, with large sections of both currently closed. Housed within the former are some works by Indonesia's most illustrious artists, including portraits by Affandi and sketches of the capital by Raden Saleh.

Sunda Kelapa

North of Taman Fatahillah lies the historic harbour of **Sunda Kelapa** (entry fee Rp250) which, established during Pajajaran times, grew to become the most important in the Dutch empire. Although the bulk of the sea traffic docks at Tanjung Priok today, a few of the smaller vessels, particularly some picturesque wooden schooners, still call in at this 800-year-old port.

Sunda Kelapa lies approximately 1km due north of Taman Fatahillah. You can either walk (about 20min) or, if you're lucky, you may be able to hail one of the ojek operating in the area. If you do catch one of these, ask the pedaller to drop you off by the entrance to the port itself, where, after paying the entry fee, you can wander amongst the beautiful schooners that dock in the harbour. Excellent photo opportunities abound, and rowing boats are available for rent.

From the port, cross over the bridge to the west of the harbour and turn right at the nineteenth-century watchtower, the **Uitkijk**, originally built to direct shipping traffic to the port. Here, buried in the chaotic **Pasar Ikan** (fish market) that occupies this promontory, you'll find the entrance to the excellent **Museum Bahari**, or Maritime Museum (Tues–Thurs & Sun 9am–3pm, Fri 9am–2.30pm, Sat 9am–12.30pm; Rp1000). This huge, cat-infested place, built in 1652, was once an old warehouse which housed such valuable eighteenth-century merchandise as spice, pepper, tea, coffee and cotton. The museum it houses today is neatly arranged in chronological order, and charts the relationship between the Indonesian archipelago and the sea that both divides and surrounds it, beginning with the simple early fishing vessels and continuing through the colonial years to the modern age. All kinds of sea craft, from the Buginese *phinisi*, the *kora-kora* war boat from the Moluccas and the tiny *alut pasa* boat from Kalimantan, can be seen here. The exhibits are thoughtfully displayed and the English-language labels are packed with information. Even though most of the exhibits are unspectacular, this place still ranks as one of the best and most enjoyable museums in Jakarta, and possibly in the whole archipelago.

After you've pottered around the fish market, head south, keeping the Kali Besar canal on your left. On the way you'll pass a number of old VOC shipyards and rather dilapidated warehouses before you come to an ornate wooden drawbridge. This is the 200-year-old **Jembatan Pasar Ayam** (Chicken Market Bridge), the only drawbridge left of the many that traversed the canals of this once-busy commercial district. The streets that flank the canal to the south of here were once the smartest addresses in Batavia, and the grand Dutch terrace houses still stand, the most famous being the Chinese-style **Toko Merah** (Red Shop) at no. 11 Jalan Kali Besar Barat – the former home of the Dutch governor general Van Imhoff. The Batavia bus station lies on the eastern side of the canal, from where you can catch a bus back to Jalan Thamrin (bus #938) or on to Ancol (minivan #M15).

Medan Merdeka and around

The heart and lungs of Jakarta, **Medan Mederka** (Freedom Square) is a square kilometre of sun-scorched grass in the centre of the city. Once a mere cattle field and later a Dutch military training ground, today the square is the symbolic and administrative centre of independent Indonesia. It has also become something of a revolutionary hot spot too: it was here in the 1940s that Sukarno whipped his supporters up into a revolutionary frenzy with impassioned anti-imperialist speeches, and the biggest demonstration of the riots in May 1997 took place here, as students confronted the soldiers assigned to protect the presidential palace, on the northern side of the square.

It seems fitting, therefore, that standing at the centre of the square today is the most recognizable of all of Jakarta's Independence monuments, the **Monas** (short for "Monumen Nasional"), a soaring 137-metre marble, bronze and gold torch, commissioned by Sukarno in 1962 to symbolize the indomitable spirit of the Indonesian people. Today, it also stands as a potent expression of Sukarno's hubris and extravagance. A lift has been incorporated into "Sukarno's last erection" (as it's commonly known amongst expats), allowing sightseers to survey the sprawling capital from the top (daily 8am–5pm; Rp3100, plus Rp1000 camera fee); avoid weekends when the queues are at their longest. The ticket includes entry into the **National History Museum** (daily 8am–5pm; Rp600) in Monas's basement, a series of 48 dioramas that depict the history of Jakarta. Unfortunately, Indonesia's early history has been rather glossed over, while the twentieth century, which takes up over half of the dioramas, has been given a pro-Suharto reworking. All in all, it's not particularly enlightening.

Looking north from the top of Monas, two neighbouring white buildings on the northern side of the square catch the eye. The one on the right is the back of the **Istana Negara** (National Palace), the front of which faces north onto Jalan Veteran. Formerly the rather sumptuous home of a Dutch businessman, and at one time used as a residence for the Dutch governors general, it is now used solely for important State functions. The Dutch governor general moved out of the Istana Negara in 1879, when the more splendid **Istana Merdeka** (Freedom Palace), formerly known as the Koningsplein Palace, was completed next door. President Sukarno made this palace his official residence during his term in office, but Suharto seldom used the place, preferring a more modest residence in Menteng.

The **Taman Prasasti** (Museum of Inscriptions; daily 9am–2pm; Rp1000), on Jalan Tanah Abang I, lies about 500m west of Medan Merdeka. This "museum" is actually the Kebon Jahe Cemetery, a peaceful, tree-shaded, eighteenth-century graveyard that is the last resting place of a number of notable people, including Olivia Raffles (who died in 1814), the first wife of Sir Stamford, and the nineteenth-century Dutch historian Dr F. Stutterheim. To get here from Monas, take the wide road heading northwest towards the Istana Merdeka, and from there continue west to Jalan Majapahit. About 50m north along Majapahit, a small canal runs west; walk along the path by the side of this canal, then turn left at the end of the path and head south for 300m.

The National Museum

The **National Museum** (Tues–Sun 8.30–11.30am; Rp200), on the western side of Medan Merdeka, is a fabulous place and the best introduction to Indonesia that central Jakarta can offer. Unfortunately, many of the exhibits, particularly on the ground floor, are unlabelled, though the Indonesian Heritage Society conducts **tours** in English (Wed–Fri 9.30am). The museum, established in 1778, is the country's oldest and largest, and houses a wide and eclectic range of items from all over the archipelago, grouped together into categories such as musical instruments, costumes and so on. Many of the country's top ruins have been plundered for their statues, which now sit, unmarked, in the courtyard in the centre of the museum. Highlights on the ground floor are a batik made by Raden Kartini, the huge Dongson **kettledrums** and, best of all, the skull and thighbone of **Java Man**, found by Eugene Dubois in 1936 at Sangiran, near Solo (see p.208).

The museum's most precious artefacts lie **upstairs**, however, in two high-security rooms. They include the cache of **treasures** found at the foot of Central Java's Mount Merapi in 1990 by workmen excavating volcanic gravel; the collection is held in the room on the left-hand side at the top of the stairs. Over 16kg of ancient golden artefacts were discovered there, including a beautifully wrought golden water scoop, a gold wallet (decorated with an unusual winged conch motif and fitted with a gold wire strap, so that it resembles a little handbag), and a tiny and exquisite gold bowl, probably used to hold flower petals during religious ceremonies. The second room, opposite, houses a small collection of daggers and necklaces from the fifth-century Hindu Kutai Kingdom of Tenggarong in Kalimantan, possibly Indonesia's first recognized kingdom.

Incidentally, the small bronze statue of an elephant that sits outside the museum was a gift from the king of Thailand in 1871. Thanks to this statue, the museum is often called Gedung Gajah, the "Elephant Building".

East of Medan Merdeka – the Lapangan Banteng

East of and opposite the Gambir station is the circular, pillared **Imanuel Church**, or Willemskerk as it was christened by the Dutch Protestants who built it in 1835. The church stands on the corner of Jalan Medan Merdeka Timur and Jalan Taman Pejambon, the latter leading, via the **Gedung Pancasila** (Pancasila Building) – a pretty, lawn-fronted mansion dating from 1830 and named after the famous Pancasila Speech, delivered from here by Sukarno in 1945 – to a tree-fringed square marked out with football pitches. This 300-square-metre expanse of grass and mud is **Lapangan Banteng** (Buffalo Field), or Waterlooplein as the Dutch, who designed the square as a centrepiece of their new Weltevreden district in the nineteenth century, used to call it. If you're coming here from Jalan Jaksa, catch bus #15 or #P15 from Jalan Kebon Siri.

From the centre of the park a huge, grimacing statue of a man looms up, his face contorted by the strain of breaking free from the chains that bind his arms. This is the **Freedom Monument**, erected by Sukarno in 1963 to celebrate the "liberation" of Irian Jaya from the Dutch. Like the majority of Sukarno's monuments, size is everything (it's over 80m tall), while aesthetic considerations take a back seat.

A number of buildings of note surround the square. The enormous white edifice to the east of the *Borobodur Intercontinental* is the **Department of Finance Building**. It was originally designed to be the residence of the French Governor Daendals, but was not completed by the time he had to leave the country in 1811; it has been used as a government office almost continuously since then. The **Mahkamah Agung**, Jakarta's Supreme Court, dominates the square's eastern end, and the Catholic **St Mary's Cathedral**, a Neo-Gothic structure on the square's northwestern corner dating from 1830, stands over the western end. With its black-topped spires and large circular window above the front entrance, the church looks rather like Notre Dame.

Directly opposite the Cathedral is the largest mosque in Southeast Asia, the dazzling white **Mesjid Istiqlal**, opened in 1978 on the site of the former Dutch fort of Noordwijk. The mosque and its grounds are so huge that it actually connects the northwestern corner of the Lapangan Banteng with the northeastern corner of the Medan Merdeka, about 350m away. The sheer scale of the mosque is impressive: it can hold up to 250,000 people, although it's only on the Muslim holy days of Idul Fitri and Idul Adha that it is likely to reach this capacity. It's not very prepossessing and, approaching from the east, the mosque resembles a giant multi-storey car park, with its five open-sided floors visible through the dull-grey concrete exterior framework. For a small donation, and providing you're not too skimpily dressed (don't wear shorts), the security guards will take you on a brief, informal tour. The main *qibla* room inside the mosque is the most interesting part, its floors decked with carpets from Arabia and Persia, while the twelve pillars that support the dome are made of steel imported from Germany. Heading back towards the main courtyard, in one corner the minaret towers, at its foot a 2.5-tonne wooden drum from east Kalimantan – the only traditional feature in this otherwise state-of-the-art mosque.

Menteng

Menteng is a prosperous and leafy suburb to the east of Jalan Thamrin which, originally just farmland, was bought and developed by the city council in 1908 and quickly became an exclusive enclave for ambassadors, politicians and top government officials. It's a pleasant area to walk through, although the sights are few and far between, so you should be prepared for a fair bit of walking.

From the Welcome Monument on Jalan Thamrin, catch one of the buses heading southeast along Jalan Imam Bonjol. Fifteen hundred metres along the road (buses #38 and #68 runs along the entire length of Jalan Imam Bonjol), on the right-hand side is the **Museum Permusan** (Mon–Thurs 8.30am–2.30pm, Fri 8.30–11am, Sat 8.30am–1.30pm; free). Once the home of Tadashi Maeda, a Japanese naval commander who was sympathetic to the Indonesian struggle for Independence, it was here that Sukarno and Hatta were brought following their kidnapping by the hardline Menteng 31 Asrama, a youth group dedicated to fighting for Independence. In the boardroom at the back the two leaders were forced to write their Proclamation of Pancasila speech, aided by Admiral Maeda.

Two hundred metres east beyond the museum, Jalan Thamrin becomes Jalan Diponegoro, and a further 300m after this is the **Adam Malik Museum** (Tues–Sat 9am–3pm, Sun 9am–4pm; Rp2000). Malik, a journalist-turned-ambassador for Indonesia, was something of a magpie, and throughout his life built up a number of impressive and occasionally bizarre collections. Following his death in 1984, his house was converted into a museum. Most of the main building – an impressive Dutch villa – is taken up with Malik's large acquisitions of ceramics, Chinese pottery vases and cameras, and one of the rooms upstairs has been given over to a dazzling display of sixteenth- to twentieth-century Russian icons. An extension to the villa houses Malik's collection of mainly Indonesian paintings; look for the image of the child flying a kite – the kite string is actually made up of a series of tiny Chinese characters.

Malik's house lies just to the east of the Jalan Diponegoro and Jalan Cikini Ditiro junction. Students of modern Indonesian politics may wish to head south down Jalan Ditiro to the canal, then west for two blocks to the **Sasmita Loka Jen A. Yani** (The House of General A. Yani, Tues–Sun 8am–3pm; free). Jen A. Yani, a man whose name lives on in a million street names throughout the country, was Chief of Staff during the latter years of the Sukarno era, and was responsible for the Irian campaign in 1961. This house, parts of which have been left virtually untouched since Yani's murder during the Communist coup of 1965, contains a hagiographic exhibition about his life and works, mainly told through old black-and-white photographs.

Like the Museum Permusan, this is just one of many museums dedicated to Indonesia's military heroes and its fight for Independence that lie scattered throughout the city, all of which are of minimal interest to the average tourist. Most sightseers would probably find it more worthwhile continuing east along Jalan Diponegoro to the **antiques market** of Jalan Surabaya (see p.96 for details). This is one of the best places to buy souvenirs in the capital, most of which, providing your bargaining skills are up to scratch, can be had fairly cheaply.

There are a couple of sights further east of here under the train tracks, though again they are of minority interest only. South along Jalan Panataran is the **Taman**

Proklamasi. As the name suggests, it was on this spot – the former site of Sukarno's house – that the Independent Republic of Indonesia was proclaimed on August 17, 1945. The house has now disappeared, to be replaced by a pleasant and very neat garden, in the middle of which are statues of Sukarno and Hatta. It's another 1.5km east of here, a very hot and dusty walk along the very busy Jalan Diponegoro, to **Pasar Pramuka**, Jakarta's large bird market where – as is typical with markets of this kind in Indonesia – birds, reptiles and rodents are kept in cruel, cramped conditions. Bus #P132 runs from Pasar Pramuka back to the Welcome Monument.

The Textile Museum

Jakarta's **Textile Museum** (Tues–Thurs & Sun 9am–4pm, Fri 9am–3pm; Rp1000) stands to the west of the Tanah Abang train station at Jalan Aipda K.S. Tubun 4. Catch bus #P16 heading north from Thamrin to the Tanah Abang market, then walk west for five minutes over the bridge. Housed in a spacious old Dutch villa, once owned by a Turkish consul, the collection displays over three hundred **indigenous textiles** from every part of the archipelago. The exhibits are well presented and the house is cool and spacious, though it's really only for those with a special interest in the subject. Exhibits include a rare set of **rattan armour** from Irian Jaya, an explanation of the batik-making process and examples of the different types of traditional batik patterns.

The outskirts

The **funfairs** at **Ancol** and **Taman Mini** – the extraordinary "Disney-esque" theme park in the southern suburbs – provide both locals and visitors with a perfect escape from the noise and smog of Jakarta's city centre. A trip to Taman Mini can be combined with a visit to the neighbouring **Museum Purna Bhakti Pertiwi**, a breathtaking collection of gifts presented to Suharto and his wife that really has to be seen to be believed.

Taman Impian Jaya Ancol

The oldest and nearest of Jakarta's two theme parks, **Taman Impian Jaya Ancol** (daily 8am–midnight; Rp2500, Rp3000 on Sun) lies 10km to the north of Medan Merdeka, 3km east of Kota. To get here from Thamrin, catch bus #P1, #P11 or #P17 heading north to Kota station, then minibus #M15 from Kota to Ancol — or you can wait for bus #125, which passes along Jalan Merdeka Barat on its way to Ancol. The entry fee gets you into the park, although many of the main attractions have a separate entrance charge. The centrepiece of Ancol is the **Dumia Fantasi** (Fantasy World, Mon–Fri Rp11,000, Sat & Sun Rp12,000), an Indonesian take on Disneyland featuring a fairly extensive collection of roller coasters and waterchutes (Rp5000–6000 per ride). If you're going to try more than a couple of them, it's worth buying the **all-inclusive ticket**, which covers the cost of all the rides (Mon–Fri Rp21,000, Sat Rp23,000, Sun Rp25,000).

Other attractions include **Seaworld** (Rp10,000 per show) where freshwater dolphins and sea lions perform, an excellent aquarium, the Gelanggang Samudra (Rp10,000), a **golf course**, souvenir market (Pasar Seni) and a rather busy **swimming pool complex** (Mon–Sat 8am–8pm, Sun & hols 7am–8pm; Mon–Fri Rp7000, Sat, Sun & hols Rp11,000), which includes a wave pool, waterslides and a river run. At night, and especially at the weekends, the park plays host to local bands, and there's also a drive-in cinema. All in all, it's a rather expensive day out, but the best place to come in Jakarta if you have kids to entertain.

Taman Mini Indonesia Indah

The **Taman Mini Indonesia Indah** (daily 8am–5pm; Rp2500), a huge theme park celebrating the rich ethnic and cultural diversity of the archipelago, was the brainchild and obsession of the late Madame Suharto. The park lies 18km south of Medan Merdeka: catch bus #P10, #P11 or #P16 to Rambutan bus station, then minibus #T19 or #M55 to the entrance, and allow an hour for the journey. Alternatively, a taxi from Jalan Jaksa to TMII costs Rp22,000. There is so much to see and do at Taman Mini that it's possible to spend all day here, although most of it can be seen in a frenetic three or four hours if you're really pushed for time.

The exorbitant cost of building the park (US$27million), and the enforced removal of the villagers on whose land it was built, drew stinging criticism from both home and abroad. Yet, ever since it opened in 1975 the park has been a roaring success, and visitors tend to be pleasantly surprised that it isn't as tacky as could be expected.

At the centre of the park is a huge man-made lake, around which are 27 houses, each representing one of the 27 provinces of Indonesia, built in the traditional style of that region: cultural performances often take place outside these houses. It is possible to rent a motorized **"swan-boat"** from the western side of the lake (Rp1500) to take you to the scale model of the archipelago that has been sculpted in the centre.

The park also contains a number of **museums**, all of which charge an entry fee of around Rp500. The best of these is the **Science Museum**, on the eastern side of the lake, which features plenty of interactive exhibits. The Asmat Museum, housing woodcarvings from the Asmat tribe of Irian Jaya, and the Museum Indonesia, with displays on the county's people, geography, flora and fauna, are also worth visiting. Other attractions include the **Sports Museum** – if you want to see photos of President Suharto in a tracksuit doing aerobics, this is the place to come – a **Telecommunications Museum**, the **Komodo Museum** (a natural history museum housed within a giant replica of a Komodo dragon), and an **insectarium**. Add to this two **aviaries** (Rp3000), a large **aquarium** (closed Mon; Rp3000) an **orchid garden** (Rp500), a **swimming pool** (Rp2000) and a **children's park**, and you have the makings of a fun day out. There's also a **cinema** (Rp4000, Rp8000 for "VIP seats"), built in the shape of a giant snail and housing what is said to be the world's largest cinema screen (29.3m by 21.5m) on which a whirlwind travelogue of the archipelago is shown daily (noon & 3pm).

There are plenty of ways of getting around the park. Next to the swan-boat port is the main station for the **sky-train** (Rp2000), which circles the lake and provides excellent views over it. There's also a **minitrain** (Rp1000) which rings the park at ground level, a **cable car** (Rp5000 for the 10min trip) which runs east–west above the lake, and a **car and open trailer** that ferries passengers around the park for free. These last three modes of transport can be picked up at the western end of the lake, near the **information kiosk** and the Pancasila Monument.

Museum Purna Bhakti Pertiwi

Although it's easily possible to spend all day at Taman Mini, try and put aside a little time to visit the neighbouring **Museum Purna Bhakti Pertiwi** (daily 9am–4pm; Rp2500) – you'll be amazed at what you find here. The luxurious marble building, spacious and deliciously air-con, has four floors, each containing a jaw-dropping array of treasures. This collection is, in the main, made up of gifts presented to President Suharto and his wife by foreign ambassadors, fellow heads of state and local dignitaries. While many of the exhibits are rather kitsch, and the very idea of such an outrageous display of opulence may seem obscene in one of Asia's poorest countries, nevertheless the artistry involved in some of the exhibits cannot fail to impress. Intricately carved elephant tusks, welcoming statues (*pembrana*), and even an entire gamelan orchestra made entirely of old Balinese coins threaded together, plus enough gold and jewellery to wipe out the national debt, are all gathering dust here. But it is the huge and intricately detailed woodcarvings that are astounding; a series of panels depicts the life story of Suharto on the walls of the lobby, in the centre of which stands a ten-metre tree trunk carved with the story of the *Rama Tambak*, an episode of the *Ramayana* tales where the force of good, represented by Sri Rama Wijaya, successfully builds a dam to reach his wife, Dewi Shinta, who is being held captive on Alengka by Rahwana, king of Alengka. Also on the ground floor, look out for the enormous rubber-tree root decorated with the gods of the *langlang buana*, the nine gods of Balinese Hinduism who control the nine points of the Balinese compass; it took fifteen craftsmen sixteen months to complete. The artistry displayed throughout the museum is amongst the best in Indonesia, and, when combined with the fierce air-con and the clear and concise English-language labels, more than justifies the effort it takes to get here.

Eating

Food is more expensive in the capital than anywhere else in Indonesia. It can come as a bit of a shock to find that staples such as *cap cay* and nasi goreng cost twice as much as they do elsewhere in the archipelago. That said, there is twice as much choice here too, and the number of different types of **cuisine** that can be found in the city centre, from French to Mexican to Japanese to Italian, lend Jakarta a truly international flavour. Over the last decade the capital has been swamped by **fast-food** restaurants, with all the big names from the West appearing, as well as their home-grown imitators. The *McDonald's* in the Sarinah store is the one most frequented by travellers, mainly because it's open 24hr and thus catches the post-nightclub crowd. There's also a *Pizza Hut* in the Jakarta Theatre building on Jalan Wahid Hasyim, and branches of *Dunkin' Donuts*, *Sizzler* and *Baskin Robbins* on Jalan H.A. Salim (aka Jalan Sabang).

Jalan Jaksa

The budget restaurants on **Jalan Jaksa** have become havens of peace and comfort; it's not surprising that travellers can spend much of their time in the capital sheltering inside one of them. These places look fairly similar: a bamboo-wall facade facing the street, with a map of Indonesia on the wall alongside pictures of Western rock stars. Ornate aquariums also feature prominently. For a map of eating places in and around Jalan Jaksa, see p.80.

STREET FOOD

Local street food still thrives as much in Jakarta as it does in other parts of the archipelago. **Jalan H.A. Salim**, more commonly known by its former name of **Jalan Sabang**, features a wide variety of warung that line the pavements in the evening, selling some delicious snacks including *murtabak* (deep-fried pancakes), both sweet and spicy, *bakso*, terrific sate, and a number of other tasty treats.

Other places to look for street food include **Jalan Kendal**, which runs east from Jalan Thamrin, 800m south of the Welcome Monument, which is known for its goat's-head soups; **Jalan Pecenongan**, running north directly opposite the Istana Negara, 1km due north of Monas, which specializes in seafood dishes; and the western end of **Jalan Kebon Siri Barat**, which offers some of the cheapest food in the capital. For sanitized versions of street food, consider the basement of the **Pasaraya** department store in Blok M, and the basement of **Sarinah's**.

Angie's, Jl Jaksa 15. One of the better-value places in Jaksa, this budget restaurant with a bicycle theme (there are even bicycles hanging from the roof) serves the usual combination of Indonesian staples and standard Western fare. *Angie's* is at its busiest during the early evening, as people come to eat before decamping to one of the livelier places on Jaksa. Their *tahu telor*, a pancake filled with peanut sauce and beanshoots (Rp2500), is one of the best-value meals on Jaksa.

Borneo, Jl Kebon Siri Barat 35–37. This budget restaurant, part of the *Borneo Hostel*, is popular with both travellers and local gigolos alike. It serves some of the best Western food in Jaksa – try their burgers (Rp5000) – and the local dishes aren't bad either, especially the Borneo fried rice (which is just nasi goreng with pineapple) at Rp4500.

Karya, Jl Jaksa 32–34. A surprisingly inexpensive café in the courtyard of the distinctly non-budget *Hotel Karya*. The (rather bland) all-you-can-eat breakfast (Rp6000) is reasonable value, and it's also one of the few places on Jaksa to serve draught beers (Rp4000 per glass).

Le Margot, Jl Jaksa 15. One of the newest and most popular places on Jaksa (possibly because it has MTV), this open-sided bar does some tasty but overpriced meals, including a very good ginger beef (Rp7000). The service can be somewhat slow.

Memories, Jl Jaksa 17. Recently renovated restaurant on two floors with a small bookshop built into one corner of the ground floor. The large menu of Western and local dishes is somewhat overpriced – though some of the dishes, including the Szechwan chicken (Rp9000), are terrific – but this place remains one of the most popular on the street.

Merry's Burger, Jl Jaksa 40. The cheapest and grimiest place on the street, no-frills *Merry's* offers burgers starting at Rp4000; inexpensive, but not especially good value.

Pappa's, Jl Jaksa 41. Another quality budget restaurant that is, inexplicably, not as popular as the nearby *Margot*, though its position at the quieter southern end of Jaksa may account for this. *Pappa's* specializes in Indian curries (Rp5000–7000), with "paper dums" (Rp500) optional. A good place for lunch.

Romance, Jl Jaksa 40. The most expensive place on the street – although still budget – this naffly named restaurant rustles up some particularly good quasi-Mexican food for around Rp7000. Try their Mexican pizzas.

Scooter Kafe, Jl Jaksa 2. A tiny café and bar serving mainly drinks, but with a small menu of Indonesian staples too. Seldom visited by tourists, but very popular with the local scooter gangs, who gather here in their hundreds on Friday and Saturday nights, parking their customized machines outside.

Jalan H.A. Salim (Jalan Sabang)

More commonly known as **Jalan Sabang**, Jalan H.A. Salim, running parallel with and west of Jalan Jaksa, plays host to a string of decent restaurants catering for every budget and taste. The restaurants in this area are marked on the map on p.80.

Ayam Goreng Priangan, Jl Sabang 55a. Fairly inexpensive Indonesian fried-chicken restaurant. A display of chicken pieces, marinated and cooked a variety of different shades, stands at the back of the restaurant for you to examine and make your selection from. Try their version of *ayam bakar* – chicken cooked in coconut milk and grilled in a sweet soya sauce – for Rp3300.

Bakeri Modern Sakura Anpan, Jl Sabang 25a. Western-style cake shop with a fine display of multi-tiered wedding cakes in the window. Luxurious and distinctly non-budget fare, but if you feel like treating yourself try their chocolate cake (Rp4000 per slice).

Bakmi Gang Kelinci, Jl Sabang 53. Small food mall which includes a *Baskin & Robbins* ice-cream parlour as well as the *Khong Guan* biscuit-and-cake shop.

Bakwan Campur Surabaya, Jl Sabang 23. Unpretentious and reasonably cheap Surabayan restaurant serving good-value East Javan food. Their *tahu isi* (tofu and vegetables in batter) is particularly delicious.

HP Gardena, Jl Sabang 1. Unusual "hot pot" restaurant, where you choose the ingredients – they are on display in a fridge at the back, and range from fish cakes (Rp4500) to meatballs (Rp4500) along with various salad items – which are then baked and served up with spicy sauce dips.

Mel's Drive-in, Jl Sabang 21. This inexpensive American-style fast-food shack serves some pretty decent low-price food. Their Rp5000 breakfast, including free tea and coffee, is superb value, and the happy hour (3–8pm) offers two glasses of beer (including Guinness) for the price of one – one of the best deals in Jakarta. *Mel's* stays open until midnight, and occasionally later if there's a big football match on TV.

Natrabu, Jl Sabang 29a. Flashy but excellent mid-priced Minang restaurant (Padang-style food from West Sumatra) with red-liveried waiters serving such delicacies as buffalo lungs and kidneys. There's also traditional live Minang music every evening (7–9.30pm).

Paradiso 2001, Jl Sabang 30. Excellent, cheapish little vegetarian joint, hidden down an alley next to the *Alfabet Restaurant*, serving a wide selection of tofu- and gluten-based meals accompanied by a vast array of fruit juices. Try their *tofu pepes* (spiced tofu cooked in banana leaf). The *Paradiso* closes on Friday at 5pm, opening again on Sunday at 6pm.

Purnama, Jl Sabang 41. Run-of-the-mill Padang restaurant serving some of the least expensive food on the street.

Sabang, Jl Sabang 51a. Mid-priced restaurant serving an unusual combination of Indonesian and Western dishes alongside a large but unimpressive bakery.

Sederhana, Jl Sabang 33. Clean, superior-quality Padang restaurant much patronized by locals. Expect to pay Rp2000–3000 per dish, but be warned: the bananas on the table are Rp500 each.

Sizzler, Jl Sabang 39. Western-style mid-priced restaurant, a cross between a fast-food shack and a steak-house, with all-you-can-eat salad bar and sundae bar. Much patronized by expats and wealthier locals.

Soto Betawi Sabang, Jl Sabang 55. Linoleum-floored budget cafeteria serving mainly soups. Check out their *Soto Betawi* special – fish soup – or the rather overpriced but tasty *soto ayam*.

Soto Sury, Jl Sabang 27b. As the name suggests, a no-nonsense soup kitchen, which has recently expanded its menu to include *nasi rawon*, gado-gado and nasi campur.

Jalan Wahid Hasyim

Running by the southern end of Jalan Jaksa, **Jalan Wahid Hasyim** has a selection of large restaurants at the moderate to expensive end of the market. The restaurants in this area are marked on the map on p.80.

Ayam Goreng Suharti, Jl Wahid Hasyim 51. Fried-chicken restaurant chain dedicated to serving up our feathered friends in as many different ways as possible. Clean, and with friendly staff, but both the decor and the menu are rather uninspiring and the food is not very good value (Rp15,000 for a whole chicken).

Bakmi Toko Tiga, Jl Wahid Hasyim 65. The latest branch of a chain of Indonesian/Chinese restaurants founded in Semarang. Noodles are the speciality here, but on the whole the food tastes a little mass-produced.

Dipitdeep Soakityummy, Jakarta Theatre, Jl Wahid Hasyim. Those who've visited a Mongolian barbecue will be familiar with the all-you-can-eat concept behind *Dipitdeep*, where you choose the raw ingredients from the display in the centre of the restaurant, and a chef comes over to your table and cooks them for you. As many courses as you like for Rp25,000 at weekends, Rp22,000 during the week, or Rp19,000 for vegetarians at any time.

Green Pub, Jakarta Theatre, Jl Wahid Hasyim. Tex-Mex food, country and western music, tequila slammers and margueritas: pricey, but popular with expats.

Le Bistro, Jl Wahid Hasyim 71. Classy French restaurant hidden behind a wealth of foliage and looking totally out of place on this busy road. Vintage wagons parked in the courtyard give a clue to the decor inside: a wealth of old pots and pans, gramophones and other antique ironmongery. The food (French, of course), although not cheap (main courses are in the region of Rp30,000) is terrific.

Pasar Laut, Jl Wahid Hasyim 125. Mid-priced seafood restaurant where most of the main ingredients are kept alive and on display by the door for you to select as you walk in. The *kepiting*, or crabs, at Rp4000 per 100g (approximately Rp16,000 per crab), are particularly good.

Pho Hoa, Jl Wahid Hasyim 135. Vietnamese fast food on the corner of Jl Sabang and Jl Wahid Hasyim. As you might expect, rice and noodles feature prominently, including excellent vermicelli with spicy chicken and lemon grass (Rp9000), which you can order with extra tripe (Rp1000) if you feel so inclined.

Tony Roma's – A Place for Ribs, Jl Wahid Hasyim 49. The name says it all: an expensive restaurant with a lengthy Western menu, the bulk of which is made up of ribs served in a variety of mouth-watering ways (Rp25,000–35,000 for a rack).

Elsewhere

Amongst the many restaurants in the rest of the city, there are a few that really stand out, either for the quality of their food, their excellent service, their ambience – or a combination of all three.

Akbar Palace, Wijaya Grand Centre, Kebayoran. Excellent Indian restaurant specializing in food from the north of the subcontinent, including some wonderful tandoori dishes.

Arts and Curios, Jl Kebun Bintang IV (off Jl Cikini). A favourite spot for the Boho set, this mid-priced old curiosity shop serves tasty snacks and meals, but the real reason to come here is to soak up the "olde-worlde" atmosphere and gawp at the knick-knacks on the walls.

Café Batavia, Taman Fatahillah, Kota. One of the best and most popular establishments in Jakarta, the 24hr *Café Batavia* is decorated with photos of Hollywood stars, who look down on you as you tuck into the beautifully cooked food: a mixture of Chinese, Indonesian and Western dishes. This café is the best place to come for cocktails in the city, with over sixty to choose from. An added attraction is the nightly live jazz and soul music. It's pricey, but if you have any reason to celebrate in Jakarta, this is the place to do it.

Oasis, Jl Raden Saleh 47 (☎021/3150646). Jakarta's finest, this historic restaurant, housed in a large, 1920s Dutch villa in Cikini, is expensive but worth it. The decor, with its huge teak-beamed ceilings, crystal chandeliers and enormous stained-glass window, is suitably opulent. To the strains of the house band, diners can tuck into Western delicacies such as steak tartare and duckling *bigarade*. For something a little different, try the *rijsttafel*.

Venezia Café, Taman Ismail Marzuki (TIM), Jl Cikini Raya 73. Western fast food and Korean barbecued dishes are on offer at this attractive bamboo-walled, mid-priced restaurant, part of the TIM centre in Cikini. The complex menu has pictures of every meal to help you decipher it.

Nightlife and entertainment

Most travellers don't even leave **Jalan Jaksa** in the evening, preferring to hang out in one of the many bars that are strung along the road: *Le Margot* at no. 15, which has MTV, and the newly revamped *Memories Café*, are currently the most popular. Occasionally a couple of adventurous souls venture a little further, to the Wina Biliard **pool hall** round the corner on Jalan Wahid Hasyim (Rp1000 a game) or the Jakarta Theatre **cinema**, opposite Sarinah's, which shows the latest Hollywood blockbusters, heavily censored (see "Listings" on p.98 for details of other cinemas in Jakarta).

However, those prepared to venture further than the end of Jalan Wahid Hasyim will be rewarded with the choice of highly professional cultural performances, some of the sleaziest, wildest nightclubs in Southeast Asia, plus excellent bars. You need to have a destination in mind before you leave your hotel, though – Jakarta is not a city where you can just wander around looking for somewhere to spend the evening.

Cultural shows

Jakarta isn't great for indigenous **cultural performances**, and if you're heading off to Central Java – and in particular Yogya and Solo – you're better off waiting. If you're not, however, don't despair: you shouldn't have to search for too long to find something going on somewhere in the capital. The big international hotels are a good place to begin looking, as they usually hold some form of traditional dancing or musical performance in the evening – though you'll almost certainly have to eat there in order to watch.

The **Gedung Kesenian**, at Jalan Kesenian 1 (☎021/3808283), just north of the general post office, is the oldest **theatre** in Jakarta – it was originally the Schouwberg Playhouse and dates back to 1821 – and following its reopening in 1987 has become regarded as the main venue in Jakarta for renditions of **classical music**, **ballet**, **wayang orang** and **choral concerts**. The Bharata Theatre at Jalan Kalilio 15, Pasar Senen (bus

#15 from Jalan Kebon Siri), is another venerable old venue in Jakarta, and holds traditional wayang orang and **ketoprak** performances every night at 8pm. If you're in Jakarta on a Sunday, check out the Wayang Museum on Fatahillah Square in Kota (see p.83), which holds a free four-hour **wayang kulit** performance at 10am.

The **TIM** (Taman Ismail Marzuki), at Jalan Cikini Raya 73 (☎021/322606), is the main arts centre in the capital, featuring musical performances, plays, dance, art exhibitions and films – there's even a small planetarium here, although this is currently closed to the public. Pick up a timetable of forthcoming events from the TIM or the tourist office in the Jakarta Theatre. The RRI (Radio Republik Indonesia), the national radio station whose headquarters are on Jalan Medan Merdeka, just to the north of the National Museum, occasionally records **gamelan** performances and wayang shows in the studios there. It's worth calling in to see when the next public performance is and whether there are any tickets available. Other venues that hold occasional cultural performances include the grounds of Ancol, near the Pasar Seni art market (see p.89) and the Taman Mini on Jalan Pondok Gede Raya (see p.90).

Nightclubs

Jakarta's **nightclubs** fall into three broad categories. The first category includes clubs that are part of one of the big international hotels, such as the *Music Room* at the *Borobudur Intercontinental*, and the *Pitstop* at the *Sari San Pacific*. These tend to be rather glitzy, expensive and exclusive establishments, though Westerners are seldom turned away, providing they obey the dress code of no sandals, shorts or T-shirts.

The second and largest group is the innumerable small, sleazy joints that can be found throughout the city. These are usually inexpensive (around Rp5000 entry), but a little dull unless you're into **karaoke**, which often takes place during the early part of the evening. The *Maduma Bar* on Jalan Wahid Hasyim, just to the west of the southern end of Jalan Jaksa, is typical of the genre.

And finally, in a class all by itself, there's the **Tanamur Disco** (Rp15,000), at Jalan Tanah Abang Timur 14. What separates this place from the rest is not the music, which is a danceable but fairly mainstream mix of European and American house, nor indeed the decor – a reasonably unexciting combination of neon strip lights and stained wood – but the clientele it attracts: expats, pimps, prostitutes, ladyboys, junkies and the occasional traveller, all gathered together on two floors under one roof to dance the night away. During the week you can expect about five hundred revellers every night, and on Friday and Saturday there can be three times that number. Next door is *JJ's*, a smaller and quieter disco which survives on the overspill from the *Tanamur*. Entry is free here after 2am, and the place stays open until 5am.

Bars and live music

The *Hard Rock Café*, part of the Sarinah building, is by far and away the most popular **live-music venue**, particularly with Jakarta's teenyboppers. In amongst the various bits of minor rock memorabilia, the stained-glass window of Elvis Presley is an unexpected delight. The drinks are very expensive (with a coffee at US$3 the cheapest item on the menu), but the place is usually packed, the atmosphere is always lively, and it's within crawling distance of Jalan Jaksa.

The most salubrious live-music venue in Jakarta, however, remains the *Café Batavia* on Fatahillah Square in Kota, a mix of Indonesian charm combined with colonial standards of cleanliness and comfort (see p.94 for more details). Jazz and soul groups perform here most evenings.

The *Jaya* pub, opposite the *Sari San Pacific* hotel at Jalan Thamrin 12, is now in its 22nd year and has become one of Jakarta's oldest and best-loved watering holes.

Early in the evening the *Jaya* can be depressingly quiet, with only the occasional expat dropping by, but after 10.30pm the place starts filling up as locals and Westerners alike come to listen to the jazz and soft-rock sounds of the resident band. In the same complex, and part of the same chain, *Pete's Tavern*, in the basement of the shiny ATD Plaza immediately north of the *Jaya*, offers a similar diet of live easy-listening music and waitress-served ice-cold beer. As with the *Jaya*, *Pete's* is at its busiest on Thursday and Friday nights.

The *Hard Rock* corporation is not the only Western company to have branches of their restaurants/cafés/bars in Jakarta: *Planet Hollywood*, on Jalan Jend Gatot Subroto, just southeast of the Semanggi Interchange, *TGI Fridays*, part of the Ascott Centre, west of the Welcome Monument along Jalan Kebon Kacang Raya, and the *Fashion Café*, behind the BNI Tower on Jalan Sudirman, have all been introduced to Jakarta recently. All of these are very popular with expats, as is the small *Dyna Bar*, down an alley just off Jalan Wahid Hasyim to the west of Jalan Jaksa, which has a happy hour in the early evening.

If you're after a huge night out, head for **Blok M**, which has a wealth of bars and Irish- and English-style pubs. A good place to start a crawl is the *Sportsman Bar & Grill*, Jalan Palatehan 6–8, which offers beers from around the world as well as pub food and a huge screen that shows all the big sporting events. There are plenty of bars nearby, including the *King's Head*, Jalan Iskadarasyah I 9, and the *Top Gun Bar*, just opposite the *Sportsman*. Having drunk those places dry, round off your evening by heading off to the *Prambors Café* in Basement II of the Blok Mshopping centre, which holds regular live-music evenings.

Shopping

Jakarta may be a little short on sights, but nobody could complain about the lack of **shops, bazaars, markets** and **shopping centres** in the capital. They range from the extremely downmarket (the Pasar Senen is the place to come for secondhand clothes and army surplus gear) to the exclusive (the air-con Indonesia Plaza under the *Grand Hyatt Hotel*, for example, plays host to all the top Western designer labels, for which you pay top Western prices). Many of the plazas and arcades are concentrated around Blok M in the south of the city, where you'll find a huge variety of stores and stalls to sift through. Best buys in Jakarta include **compact discs** and **batik clothing**.

Crafts and antiques

While the city has no particular indigenous craft of its own, in the way that Yogya, for example, has puppets and batik and Jepara has teak furniture, the capital isn't a bad place to go souvenir shopping. There are a couple of markets where artefacts from all over the archipelago can be found, and prices are reasonable. The **antiques market** on Jalan Surabaya, one block west of Cikini station in Jakarta's Menteng district, is a good place to begin your trawl. Much of the stuff cannot really be classified as antique, though there's some fine silver jewellery, and traditional Javanese wooden trunks and other pieces of furniture. Collectors of old records, particularly 1970s disco albums, will also find plenty of bargains, and the odd collector's item too.

The entire third floor of the **Sarinah** department store is given over to souvenirs, with wayang kulit and wayang goleng puppets, leather bags and woodcarvings a speciality. A similar selection of souvenirs can be found at Ancol's **Pasar Seni**, alongside galleries displaying work from a variety of local artists, most of whom produce paintings of stereotypical Indonesian landscapes and chaotic city scenes in an attempt to cater for tourists. There is also a bewildering array of rather gauche woodcarvings, from full-size models of eagles to scale models of Javanese houses. These carvings may not appeal to everyone, but the obvious skill and patience that goes into producing them is quite impressive. **Hadi Handicraft** in the Indonesia Plaza specializes in good-quality, reasonably priced, brightly painted wooden statues and ornaments, mainly from Central Java. Finally, there are three reasonable souvenir shops on Jalan Pasar Baru, north of the GPO: Toko Bandung at no. 16b, the Ramayana Art Shop at no. 17, and the Irian Art Shop at 16a. Despite their names, each sells souvenirs gleaned from all over the archipelago.

Records, compact discs and other bargains

Recorded music, both indigenous and Western, is particularly good value in Indonesia, and in Jakarta you get a wider and more up-to-date selection than anywhere else. Compact discs and tapes are thirty to fifty percent cheaper than in Europe. The ground floor of Sarinah's has a reasonable selection, as has Delta Disk at Jalan Sabang 27; Duta Disk nearby; Bulletin Records on the top floor of the Gajah Mada Plaza, 150m north of the Pelni head office on Jalan Gajah Mada; Duta Suara on Jalan Pasar Baru at no. 26, north of the GPO; and a number of neon-lit boutiques in theshopping centres around Blok M.

Clothes, **bags** and **watches** are also very cheap in Jakarta, although the quality is often suspect. The **Pasar Senen** (bus #15 or #P15 from Jalan Kebon Siri, at the northern end of Jalan Jaksa) is a good place to browse around for these articles. The stalls here also stock a wide selection of Indonesian army-surplus gear, including a lot of useful camping and trekking equipment. The fourth floor of Sarinah's is devoted to good-quality **batik** clothes, though not everyone will find the exuberant shirts and full-length skirts to their taste. A similar selection can be found at the branch of Batik Kris in the Indonesia Plaza, the most exclusive store of its kind in the capital. For batik clothes that are a little less pricey, and perhaps more tailored to the tourist market, the batik shop Yan's, on Jalan Jaksa, has a wide selection of patterned sarongs and shirts.

Listings

Ambulance ☎118.

Airlines International: Aeroflot, *Hotel Sahid Jaya*, Jl Jend Sudirman, Kav 24 (☎021/5702184); Air China, ADD Building, Tamara Centre, Suite 802, Jl Jend Sudirman (☎021/5206467); Air France, Summitmas Tower, 9th floor, Jl Jend Sudirman (☎021/5202262); Air Lanka, Wisma Bank Dharmala, 14th floor, Jl Jend Sudirman (☎021/5202101); Balkan Air, Jl K.H. Hasyim Ashari 33b (☎021/373341); Bouraq, Jl Angkasa 1–3, Kemayoran (☎021/6288815); British Airways, World Trade Centre, Jl Jend Sudirman Kav 29–31 (☎021/5703747); Cathay Pacific, Gedung Bursa Efek, Jl Jend Sudirman Kav 52–53 (☎021/5151747); China Airlines, Wisma Dharmala Sakti, Jl Jend Sudirman 32 (☎021/2510788); Emirates, *Hotel Sahid Jaya*, 2nd floor, Jl Jend Sudirman 86 (☎021/5205363); Eva Air, Price Waterhouse Centre, 10th floor, Jl Rasuna Said Kav C3 (☎021/5205828); Garuda, Jl Merdeka Selatan 13 (☎021/2311801), includes city check-in, with a second office at the BDN Building, Jl Thamrin 5; Japan Airlines, MID Plaza, ground floor, Jl Jend Sudirman Kav 28 (☎021/5212177); Kuwait Airways, behind the BNI building, Jl Sudirman; Lufthansa, Panin Centre Building, 2nd floor, Jl Jend Sudirman 1 (☎021/5702005); Malaysian Airlines, World Trade Centre, Jl Jend Sudirman Kav 29 (☎021/5229682); Myanmar Airways, Jl Melawai Raya 7, 3rd floor (☎021/7394042); KLM, New Summitmas, 17th floor, Jl Jend Sudirman Kav 61–62 (☎021/5212176 or 5212177); Korean Air, Wisma Bank Dharmala, 7th floor, Jl Jend Sudirman Kav 28 (☎021/5782036); Mandala, Jl Garuda 76 (☎021/4246100), also Jl Veteran I 34

(☎021/4246100); Merpati, Jl Angkasa 7, Blok B15 Kav 2 & 3 (☎021/6548888) and 24hr city check-in at Gambir station; Philippine Airlines, Plaza Mashil, 11th floor suite 1105, Jl Jend Sudirman Kav 25 (☎021/3810949, 3810950 or 5267780); Qantas Airways, BDN Building, Jl Thamrin (☎021/327707); Royal Brunei Airlines, World Trade Centre, 11th floor, Jl Jend Sudirman Kav 29–31 (☎021/2300277); Sabena, ground floor, Wisma Bank Dharmala, Jl Jend Sudirman Kav 28; Saudi Arabian Airlines, Wisma Bumiputera, 7th floor, Jl Jend Sudirman Kav 75 (☎021/5710615); Silk Air, Chase Plaza, 4th floor, Jl Jend Sudirman Kav 21 (☎021/5208018); Singapore Airlines, Chase Plaza, 2nd floor, Jl Jend Sudirman Kav 21 (☎021/5206881/5206933); Swissair, Plaza Mashil, 6th floor, Jl Jend Sudirman Kav 29 (☎021/5229912); Thai International, BDN Building, ground floor, Jl Thamrin (☎021/330816 or 3140607).

Airport inquiries ☎021/5505000.

Banks and exchange Offering a better rate than any bank or moneychanger, the numerous ATMs dotting the city are by far and away the best and most convenient places to buy Indonesian rupiah. Many of the banks, Sarinahs, the post office and Gambir all have their own ATM machines. Most banks open 8am to 3.30pm, with an hour for lunch. The majority of the big international banks in Jakarta line the main north–south thoroughfare through the city, Jl Thamrin. The Bank BNI and Lippobank, however, just west of the northern end of Jl Jaksa on Jl Kebon Siri, offer the best rates in town, with the latter also offering credit-card advances. The exchange counters of both open at 10am. The Bank Rama on the ground floor of the Sarinah department store has a reasonable rate for US dollars. The AMEX office is now located at Graha Aktiva, Jl Rasuna Said, Kuningan; catch bus #11 heading south from Sarinah. Currently, this is the only place that accepts Australian dollar travellers' cheques (AMEX travellers' cheques only). The rates of exchange at the moneychanging booths around Jl Jaksa offer a worse rate than the banks, but remain open until fairly late in the evening and over the weekend too, when the banks are closed.

Bookshops For new titles, the Times Bookshop in the Indonesia Plaza (under the *Hyatt*) has the widest selection, including a good collection of tomes on Indonesia. The fourth floor of the Sarinah department store is also worth a browse. For secondhand books, visit Cynthia's or Wan's bookshops on Jl Jaksa, or the small bookshop in the corner of *Memories Café*.

Car rental Avis, Jl Diponegoro 25 (☎021/3142900 or 3150853), is currently the only car-rental organization operating in Jakarta.

Cinemas The Jakarta Theatre, opposite the Sarinah department store, shows reasonably up-to-date films for Rp10,500. There's also the GM21 cinema north of the Gaja Mada Plaza on Jl Gajah Mada, and every Thursday and Saturday afternoon (3.30pm) on the eleventh floor of the British Council, there's a screening of a recent British film.

Cultural centres The foreign cultural centres, of which there are many in Jakarta, often organize movie screenings and art exhibitions to show off artistic talent from their country. Programmes change regularly, so phone for details: the American Cultural Centre, Wisma Metropolitan II, Jl Jend Sudirman (☎021/5711503), has a good library and occasionally screens movies; Australian Cultural Centre, Jl H. Rasuna Said Kav C 15–16 (☎021/5227111); British Council, Jl Jend Sudirman 71 (☎021/5223311), with an excellent library and regular Thursday-afternoon movie screenings; Centre Culturel Française, Jl Salemba Raya 25 (☎021/4218585); Erasmus Huis, Jl H. Rasuna Said, Kav 5–3 (☎021/5252321), is the Dutch arts centre, one of the oldest cultural institutes in the city; Goethe Institute, Jl Mataram Raya 23 (☎021/8509719), German cultural centre renowned for its photographic exhibitions; Italian Cultural Centre, Jl Diponegoro 45 (☎021/337445); Japanese Cultural Centre, Summitmas Building, Jl Jend Sudirman (☎021/5255201); Jawharlal Indian Cultural Centre, Jl Diponegoro 25 (no phone), which often organizes meditation courses.

Email The GPO is the largest (over 25 terminals), cheapest (Rp2000 for 15min, Rp9500 for 65min), and most efficient place to collect and receive email in Jakarta (Mon–Sat 8am–9pm, Sun 9am–3pm). Catch bus #15 or #P15 from Jl Kebon Siri. The Wartel at Jl Jaksa 17 has a small email centre on the first floor (daily 8am—9pm; Rp10,000 for 30min), while just a few metres south at no. 29 is the slightly more expensive Click Cyber House (Rp15,000 for 30min). A second branch, Click International, can be found at departure terminals D and E at Sukarno Hatta International.

Embassies and consulates Australia, Jl H. Rasuna Said Kav 10–11 (☎021/5227111); Britain, Jl H. Agus Salim 128 (☎021/3907448); Canada, Metropolitan Building 1, Jl Jend Sudirman Kav 29 (☎021/5250709); China, Jl Jend Sudirman Kav 69 Kebayoran Baru (☎021/7243400); Germany, Jl

Thamrin 1 (☎021/3901750); India, Jl Rasuna Said S-1, Kuningan (☎021/5204150); Japan, Jl Thamrin 24 (☎021/5212177); Malaysia, Jl Rasuna Said 1–3, Kuningan (☎021/5224947); Netherlands, Jl Rasuna Said S-3, Kuningan (☎021/5251515); New Zealand, Jl Diponegoro 41 (☎021/330680); Singapore, Jl Rasuna Said 2, Kuningan (☎021/5201489); South Africa, Wisma GKBI Jl Sudirman (☎021/7193304); Thailand, Jl Imam Bonjol 74 (☎021/3904055); US, Jl Medan Mereka Selatan 5 (☎021/360360).

Hospitals and clinics The MMC hospital on Jl Rasuna Said in Kuningan is widely regarded as the best in town (☎021/5203435). There is also the private SMI (Sentra Medika International) clinic at Jl Cokroaminoto 16 in Menteng (☎021/3157747), run by Australian and Indonesian doctors.

Immigration office The central immigration office is at Jl Teuku Umar 1, just 5min east of the southern end of Jl Wahid Hasyim (Mon–Thurs 8am–3pm, Fri 8am–noon).

Laundry Try the Angel Laundry service on Jl Jaksa Gg 7; clothes are hand-washed and ready in one day for a reasonable charge (approx Rp6000 for a small rucksack full).

Libraries Most of the cultural centres listed on p.98 have libraries which you are allowed to browse in.

Pharmacies The Medicine Shoppe, Jl Kebon Siri 2 (Mon–Sat 8am–9pm, is the best pharmacy near Jl Jaksa, and the staff are very helpful. Titimurni, Jl Kramat Raya 28 (catch the #P2 bus from Pasar Senen), is the only 24hr pharmacy in the centre of Jakarta.

Photographic shops There are plenty of good stores on Jl Agus Salim, or you can try the MM Photo Studio in Sarinah.

Post office Jakarta's huge main post office lies to the north of Lapangan Benteng (Mon–Sat 8am–8pm, Sun 9am–5pm), northeast of Medan Merdeka (catch bus #15 or #P15 from Jl Kebon Siri, to the north of Jl Jaksa). Poste restante is currently at counter no. 55; although this counter is officially closed on Sunday, you can usually find someone who'll check your mail for you. There are also plenty of warpostels dotted around, including a number on Jl Jaksa and Jl Thamrin, and all the big international hotels have mail services.

Swimming The *Hotel Indonesia* by the Welcome Monument allows non-residents to use their pool for Rp7000 during the week, rising to a hefty Rp15,000 at weekends. The price includes a soft drink. Or visit the Ancol Centre (see p.89).

Teaching English It's currently relatively easy and profitable to earn money teaching English in Jakarta, and more and more expats are turning their backs on the more traditional centres – such as Japan and Singapore – to teach in Indonesia's capital. Although a TEFL certificate opens a few more doors, there are plenty of opportunities for those who do not possess this qualification. A good place to start looking for jobs is the English-language *Jakarta Post*. If you can't find anything in there, try ringing around the language schools, most of which are based in the south of the city. They include the American Language Centre, Blok M, Jl Barito 2, Jakarta Selatan (☎021/7226449); the English Education Centre, Jl S Parman 68, Slipi (☎021/5323176); English First, Tamara Bank Building, 4th floor, Jl Sudirman, Jakarta Pusat (☎021/5203655); and the Korean Institute, Jl Bina Mirga 56, Jakarta Timur (☎021/8444958). These institutes, while they pay well (typically Rp3.2 million per month plus other perks), usually require a commitment of at least one school year (Sept–June). Part-time work, both at schools and in private homes, is also fairly easy to come by.

Telephone and fax With the closure of the 24hr Pelayanan Telekomunikasi Untuk Umum, which used to lie across the gangway from the tourist office in the Jakarta Theatre building, there is now no main government-run communications centre in the city. The Indosat building, however, at the southern end of Jl Medan Merdeka Barat (no. 21), has a small international phone office (including IDD and HCD) on its ground floor (payment by cash only), and the two wartels near Jl Jaksa – the RTQ warpostel at Jl Jaksa 17 (8am–midnight), and the wartel on Jl Kebon Siri Barat – offer a similar service, though the prices are a shade higher in these.

Travel agents and city tours There are a few good travel agencies on Jl Jaksa, including RQ Tours and Travel at no. 25 (☎021/3904501), PT Robertur Kencana at no. 20b, Jaksa Holiday at no. 11 (☎021/3140431), and Flamboyan Prima Wisata at no. 35 (☎021/3151404). The latter also runs tours around Jakarta for US$14 or US$19, taking in the National Museum, Batavia and Sunda Kelapa. Another good tour company is Gray Line, Jl Tanjung Selor 17a (☎021/6308105), which runs tours around Jakarta for US$15–20. Most of the international hotels have a Gray Line representative, who can book tours for you.

Around Jakarta

Most excursions from Jakarta are dealt with in Chapter Two, on West Java, but the paradise islands of **Pulau Seribu** are included here as they come under the administrative boundary of Jakarta. The islands make for one of the most popular day-trips from the capital, particularly with expats working in the city.

Pulau Seribu

Called the **Pulau Seribu** (Thousand Islands), the string of coral atolls running south–north off the shores of Jakarta actually number no more than two hundred, and the figure is nearer one hundred at certain times, depending on tidal changes. The Pulau Seribu chain is in fact a **marine park**, although development has been allowed on 37 of the islands, where some fairly high-class resorts have sprung up.

There is no doubt that the islands are beautiful: the sand is white and fine, palm trees stretch all the way from the lush green interior to the water's edge, and the seas surrounding the northernmost islands are a delicious shade of blue. They are not, however, perfect; their proximity to Jakarta ensures that they are swamped by day-trippers every weekend, and the effects this has on the islands and their surrounding coral is, alas, only too manifest. But if your visit to Indonesia is confined to its capital, and if you want a brief taste of what you're missing by not travelling further afield, then a trip to Pulau Seribu is highly recommended, particularly on a weekday, when the chances are you'll have an island all to yourself.

The islands

Some of the Pulau Seribu are of historic interest, especially those nearest to Jakarta. **Pulau Onrust** was the last stop for General Coen in 1619, where he mustered his troops and prepared them for the onslaught on Jayakarta. The remains of a nineteenth-century shipyard and fort can still be seen here, once the most magnificent in Southeast Asia, according to James Cook, who stopped by in 1770. The foundations of another old Dutch fort, this time dating from the nineteenth century, can be found on nearby **Pulau Kelor**, and a third on **Pulau Bidadari**, once the home of a large leper colony and today the most popular destination for day-trippers from Jakarta. Even though it is just 15km away, Pulau Bidadari is so peaceful during the week that it feels a million miles from the capital – that is, until the raw sewage from Jakarta laps against your shins as you paddle in the sea. For this reason it's a lot more pleasant and hygienic to head to one of the northern islands, which can be reached by boat from Bidadari.

The waters around **Pulau Ayer**, another popular day-trip from the capital, are marginally better, but it's only when you get to **Pulau Panggang Besar**, 40km due north of Jakarta's Sukarno-Hatta international airport, that they really start to improve. **Pulau Kelapa**, another 10km further north, is the liveliest of the islands, and home to almost half of the atoll's 16,500 population, most of whom have yet to share in the benefits of tourism and continue to eke out a living from the ocean. A little further north of Kelapa is **Pulau Panjang**, home to the only airstrip in the area, which is handy for people who wish to go snorkelling around the reefs of **Pulau Kotok**, play golf on **Pulau Bira**, or stay at the most exclusive resort in the atoll, the *Pulau Seribu Marine Resort* on the islands of **Pulau Antuk Timur** and **Pulau Antuk Barat**. North of Bira are some of the most picturesque parts of Seribu: **Pulau Putri**, with some of the best restaurants in the atoll, as well as a transparent underwater tunnel where you can observe the marine life without getting your hair wet; **Pulau Pelangi**, home to some of the best beaches and the *Pelangi Resort*, which has tennis courts; and finally **Pulau Papa Theo**, an exquisite divers' island with simple but well-maintained huts powered by a temperamental generator.

Practicalities

There is one daily public **ferry** to Pulau Seribu, leaving from the Ancol Marina (part of the Ancol fun park) and calling in at the islands of Tidung (Rp4000) and Kelapa (Rp6000). However, neither of these islands are "resorts", and you'll need to charter or rent a second boat to take you to the other islands. To rent a speedboat from Ancol for one day costs at least one million rupiah, but as the outermost islands are only a couple of hours away it is possible to cover a lot of the atoll in that time.

The resorts also operate their own private speedboats to whisk you to their islands: most boats depart from the Ancol Marina at about 10am. Only return tickets are available, with the costs varying from island to island. The resorts, such as those on Pulau Pelangi and Pulau Putri, generally include lunch on their trips, while others, such as the Pulau Seribu and Bidadari resorts, charge an entry fee. The rates are also a little cheaper (and sometimes free) if you are staying overnight in the resort. Return fares include: Pulau Bidadari (Rp25,000, plus Rp6000 entry fee), Pulau Ayer (Rp51,000), Pulau Putri (US$55), Pulau Pelangi (US$55) and Pulau Papa Theo (US$50).

ACCOMMODATION

Accommodation on all of the islands, though expensive, is not luxurious. Rooms can be booked before you arrive by visiting the resort representatives in Jakarta. Be warned that rates can rise by up to a third at most of these places during the weekends, and be certain to find out exactly what is included in the package – whether there are any trips to the neighbouring islands and so on. Make sure meals are included in the package too, as the resort restaurants are often the only option on the island and tend to be expensive. The following is a selection of the best and most popular resorts, along with their agents in Jakarta, listed by island, not by the name of the establishment.

Pulau Ayer, PT Sarotama Prima Perkasa, Jl Ir. H. Juanda III/6, Jakarta (☎021/342031). Resort consisting of 42 land and floating cottages plus three larger bungalows, along with tennis, volleyball and badminton courts, swimming pools, and a dive shop with diving equipment and jet skis for rent. ⑦.

Pulau Bidadari, PT Seabreez Indonesia, Terminal Pulau Bidadari, Marina Jaya Ancol, Jakarta (☎021/680048). Resort positioned at the southern end of the atoll with bar, disco, and both land and floating cottages. ⑨.

Pulau Kotok, Duta Merlin Shopping Arcade, Jakarta (☎021/362948). Excellent surfing and diving is available just offshore at this beautiful resort, much favoured by Japanese tourists. ⑦.

Pulau Papa Theo, PT Batemuri Tours, *Wisata International Hotel*, Jl Thamrin, PO Box 2313 (☎021/320807). The sparsest accommodation of all the Pulau Seribu resorts, where the simple thatched bungalows are situated right on the beach. ⑥.

Pulau Pelangi, PT Pulau Seribu Paradise, Jl Wahid Hasyim 69, Jakarta (☎021/335535). All rooms on beautiful Pelangi come with air-con, fridge and an outdoor shower. ⑨.

Pulau Putri, PT Pulau Seribu Paradise, Jl Wahid Hasyim 69, Jakarta (☎021/335535). Balinese cottages with traditional thatched roofs are the main feature of this exquisite resort in the north of the atoll. ⑨.

Pulau Seribu Marine Resort, PT Pantara Wisata Jaya, Jakarta (☎021/3805017). The most exclusive of the resorts, divided between the islands of Pulau Antuk Timur and Barat, which attracts Japanese tourists by the shipload. Facilities are fairly luxurious, and the diving shop is one of the best in the archipelago. ⑨.

travel details

Trains

Jakarta Gambir to: Bandung (hourly; 2hr 20min); Bogor (every 30min; 1hr); Cilacap (1 daily; 7hr 20min); Cirebon (18 daily; 5hr); Malang (1 daily; 18hr 5min); Merak (2 daily; 4hr); Purworketo (9 daily; 4hr 20min–6hr 10min); Semarang (7 daily; 5hr 35min–9hr 15min); Solobapan, Solo (4 daily; 7hr–10hr 25min); Surabaya (5 daily; 9hr–14hr 30min); Yogyakarta (6 daily; 6hr 50min–8hr 40min).

Buses

It is impossible to give the **frequency** with which bemos and buses run, as timetables change all the time, and are never strictly adhered to at the best of times. Nevertheless, on the most popular and shorter routes you should be able to count on getting a ride within the hour, especially before noon.

Jakarta (Pulo Gadung station unless stated) to: Balaraja (1hr); Banda Aceh (60hr); Bandung (from Kampung Rambutan station; 4hr 30min); Bogor (from Kampung Rambutan station; 45min); Bukittinggi (30hr); Cileungi (1hr); Denpasar (24hr); Garut (5hr); Jonggol (1hr 30min); Kotabumi (2hr); Medan (from Pulo Gadung or Kalideres; 2days); Merak (from Kalideres; 3hr); Padang (from Pulo Gadung or Kalideres; 32hr); Puworketo (8hr); Semarang (8hr 30min); Solo (13hr); Surabaya (15hr); Tegal (6hr); Yogyakarta (12hr).

Pelni ferries

All Pelni ferries leave from Tanjung Priok. For a chart of the Pelni routes, see pp.36–37 of Basics.

Jakarta to: Batam (*KM Kelud* every 4 days; 24hr); Belawan, Medan (*KM Kelud* every 4 days; 2 days);

Denpasar (*KM Dobonsolo* 2 monthly; 39hr); Kijang (*KM Bukit Raya* 2 monthly; 39hr/*KM Kerinci* 2 monthly; 24hr/*KM Sirimau* 2 monthly; 41hr); Kumai (*KM Lawit* 2 monthly; 3–4 days); Nias (*KM Kambuna* 2 monthly; 52hr; *KM Lambelu* 2 monthly; 2 days); Padang (*KM Kambuna* 2 monthly; 29hr); Pontianak (*KM Lawit* 4 monthly; 31hr/*KM Ambulu* 3 weekly; 37hr/*KM Tilongkabila* monthly; 31hr); Sampit (*KM Tilongkabila* monthly; 44hr); Ujung Pandang (*KM Lambelu* 2 monthly; 2 days/*KM Kambuna* 2 monthly; 2 days/*KM Sirimau* 2 monthly; 3 days/*KM Bukit Siguntang* 2 monthly; 2 days).

Other ferries

Jakarta Sunda Kelapa to: Pontianak (*Kapuas Expres* 2 weekly; 19hr).

Flights

Jakarta to: Ambon (10 weekly; 7hr 45min); Balikpapan (7 daily; 2hr 10min); Banda Aceh (daily; 3hr 45min); Bandung (10 daily; 40min); Banjarmasin (5 daily; 1hr 40min); Batam (8 daily; 1hr 35min); Bengkulu (2 daily; 1hr 15min); Denpasar (16 daily; 1hr 50min); Dili (4 weekly; 4hr 40min); Jambi (3 daily; 1hr 20min); Jayapura; (2 daily; 8hr); Manado (4 daily; 4hr 45min); Mataram (6 weekly; 3hr 15min); Medan (16 daily; 2hr 10min); Merauke (3 weekly; 10hr 20min); Padang (7 daily; 1hr 40min); Palangkaraya (daily; 1hr 45min); Palembang (14 daily; 1hr 5min); Palu (daily; 3hr 15min); Pangkalpinang (3 daily; 1hr 5min); Pekanbaru (7 daily; 1hr 40min); Pontianak (9 daily; 1hr 30min); Semarang (17 daily; 55min); Surabaya (33 daily; 1hr 20min); Surakarta (4 daily; 1hr 5min); Tanjungpandan (daily; 1hr); Ujung Padang (12 daily; 2hr 20min); Yogyakarta (14 daily; 1hr 5min).

RECOMMENDED TRAINS FROM JAKARTA

To	From	Name	Departs	Time
Bandung	Gambir	*Argogede*	10am	2hr 20min
			6pm	2hr 20min
	Gambir	*Parahiyangan*	hourly	3hr 30min
Cirebon	Kota	*Cirebon Eksp*	6.45am	2hr 50min
	Kota		10.10am	5hr 21min
	Gambir		4.55pm	3hr 4min
Semarang	Gambir	*Argobromo*	8.35pm	5hr 35min
	Gambir	*Senja Ekseku*	10.50am	6hr 52min
	Gambir	*Fajar Bis*	7.40am	6hr 27min
Solobapan (Solo)	Gambir	*Senja Utama II*	7.40pm	9hr 42min
Surabaya	Gambir	*Argobromo*	8.35pm	9hr
	Kota	*Bima*	6pm	13hr 50min
	Pasar Senen	*Kertajaya*	5pm	11hr 38min
	Gambir	*Jayabaya*	1.45pm	11hr 48min
	Pasar Senen	*GBM Selatan*	noon	14hr 30min
	Pasar Senen	*GBM Utama*	3.40pm	12hr 21min
	Kota	*Parcel Eksp*	6.05pm	12hr 48min
Yogyakarta	Gambir	*Fajar Utama*	6.10am	7hr 50min
	Gambir	*Fajar Utama II*	6.20am	7hr 45min
	Gambir	*Senja Utama*	7.20pm	8hr 21min
	Gambir	*Senja Utama II*	7.40pm	8hr 41min

CHAPTER TWO

WEST JAVA

O ne of the most populous places in all of Asia, **West Java** is still characterized by great natural beauty. Its central spine, the most mountainous region in Java – here, and towards the southern coast, the land is dominated by hundreds of tightly clustered volcanoes, many of which are still very evidently active. The fertile slopes of these peaks and craters are often claimed by mammoth tea plantations, which thrive on the province's plentiful rainfall. The northern coastal plain of West Java is, by contrast, a flat and fairly drab sweep that was mostly reclaimed from malarial swamps in the nineteenth century.

The travellers' route from Jakarta to Central Java passing through Bogor, Bandung and Pangandaran is well worn, but there are plenty of interesting destinations only slightly off the trail. **Krakatau**, one of the world's most famous and destructive volcanoes, is sandwiched between the Javan west coast and Sumatra; still extremely active, it offers a taste of the unpredictable power of nature. The **Ujong Kulon national park** on the southwest peninsula gives a glimpse of the island's wild inhabitants such as leopards, monkeys, crocodiles, turtles and the Banteng ox. Its most famous occupant, though, is the world's rarest large land mammal, the **Javan rhinoceros** – only an estimated seventy animals exist here and in Vietnam. Inland and east of the west coast beaches, the playground of Jakarta's wealthy, is an insular cluster of tiny villages whose inhabitants are known as the **Badui**. These isolated tribes are thought to be the descendants of the original Sundanese people, who inhabited the highlands before the advent of Islam. Their traditional society has resisted the Indonesian government's attempts to envelop them and erode their way of life, and visitors require a permit to visit the outer villages – the inner villages are completely off limits to outsiders.

South of Jakarta is the city of **Bogor**, with its famous botanical gardens and presidential palace. The gardens have a spectacular extension on the edge of the Gede Pangrango national park at **Cibodas**, which is surrounded by tropical jungle at high altitude between Bogor and West Java's capital city of **Bandung**. Colonial Dutch architecture, modern shopping centres and the gaudy appeal of "Jeans Street" are the main attractions here, though there is a profusion of waterfalls, hot springs, tea plantations and volcanic craters worth visiting around the city. Probably the most popular stop for visitors to West Java lies right at its boundary with Central Java – **Pangandaran**, a seaside town with superb seafood, crashing surf and endless expanses of sand. The variety of possible excursions around the town and the friendly atmosphere of some of its travellers' enclaves are a great draw, and some visitors end up staying for weeks. On the north coast near the boundary with Central Java is the seaport of **Cirebon**, with its ancient kratons and museums, rarely visited but rich in historical interest.

Java's rainy season lasts from January to March, during which time you can be guaranteed heavy rain every day and spectacular electrical storms, generally in the afternoons. West Java's tourist attractions are completely flooded with domestic visitors on all national holidays, and at weekends can be crowded. However, transport around West Java is easier than anywhere in Indonesia. Train lines join most of the major cities, and buses and luxury coaches regularly connect destinations within and without the region.

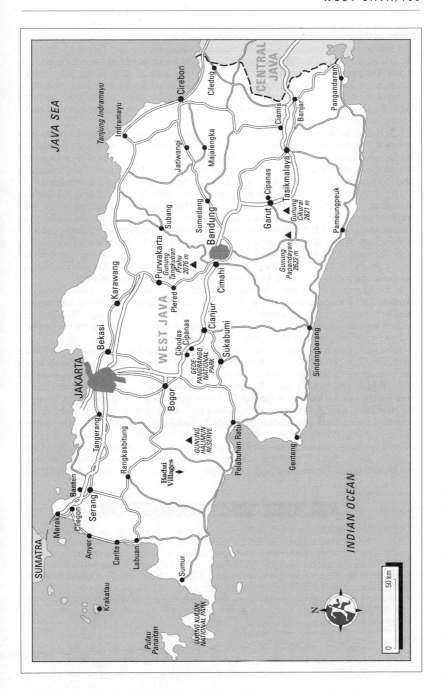

Some history

The Sundanese who continue to inhabit West Java today, and are Java's second largest ethnic group, are also its indigenous people. The first major power in the region was the Hindu **Tarumanegara empire**, which governed the area as early as the fifth century, whose most famous king, Purnavaraman, has his footprint immortalized in a rock at Ciampea near Bogor. It is thought that Hinduism probably came to Java from southern India; the Hindus came into Java from southern India to trade and passed on to the native Sundanese the legacy of their religion.

Much later, in the fourteenth century, the **Pajajaran empire** was formed, with its base as Bogor. The comparatively short period of Pajajaran's existence is seen as the Sundanese heyday, providing the source of most of the popular heroes and legends of West Javan culture, and constituting the last and pre-eminent period of Sundanese power and autonomy. The Pajajaran people are thought to have been the first to settle what is now Jakarta.

The history of the Hindu Sundanese came to an end with the defeat of king **Sri Baduga Maharaja** in around the fifteenth century. In the 1500s, the Muslim state of Demak sent prophets from Mecca into Southeast Asia in an attempt to convert the people to Islam; the Muslim army based itself in Banten, extending its influence to conquer Pajajaran and most of West Java. The most important of the prophets sent into Java was Syarif Hidayatullah, who managed to convert the most important harbour towns of Banten, Cirebon and Kelapa Sunda (modern Jakarta) before his death in 1568. Banten was thereafter to become the most vital port in Southeast Asia, taking over from Portuguese Malacca.

In the late sixteenth century, Western colonial powers first began to take interest in **Banten**. The Portuguese and British had the first trade interests here but they were to be utterly superseded by the Dutch. Under the Dutch, the towns of Bogor, Bandung and Batavia expanded into bustling cities with a European feel, and much of the countryside and its people was put to work growing tea and coffee.

The Dutch East India Company was dissolved in 1799, but Java remained under Dutch protection. This period was remarkable for the creation of the **Great Post Road**, which ran from Anyer on the west coast to Panarukan on the east. However, Java was soon lost to the British, and by 1811 was governed by Thomas Stamford Raffles, who was later to earn his fame as the founder of Singapore. There was little or no attempt made by any of the colonialists to bring European education or civilization to West Java; instead they concentrated their efforts on pacifying the public by disinheriting their leaders. This neglect had far-reaching effects: law and order degenerated until towns such as Banten were considered too dangerous for Westerners to venture into, and the Cirebon area suffered from a terrible famine that left hundreds of thousands dead. As a response to these hardships, the Muslim prince Diponegoro began the "Java War", which lasted from 1825 until 1830,

---

ACCOMMODATION PRICE CODES

All the **accommodation** listed in this book has been given one of the following price codes. The rates quoted here are for the **cheapest double room** in high season, except for places with dorms, where the code represents the price of a single bed. Where there's a significant spread of prices indicated (④–⑦, for example), the text will explain what extra facilities you get for more money. The 11–21 percent tax charged by most hotels is not included in these price codes.

Because of the current instability of the rupiah, accommodation prices are given throughout in their more stable **US dollar equivalents**, even for places which accept payment in rupiah.

For more on accommodation, see p.40.

| ① under $1 | ③ $2–5 | ⑤ $10–15 | ⑦ $35–60 | ⑨ $100 |
| ② $1–2 | ④ $5–10 | ⑥ $15–35 | ⑧ $60–100 | and over |

SUNDANESE CULTURE

The lush valleys of the province were the first places to be settled, in around the fifth century. The first inhabitants and their descendants are known as the **Sundanese**, who even today make up 75 percent of the province's population. They maintain their own language, although really only as a supplement to Bahasa Indonesian, and distinct forms of dance, theatre and cuisine. The language is similar to Javanese and Balinese in that it has three basic levels, depending on the social rank of the speaker and the addressee.

Apart from the tiny enclaves of the Badui in the Kendeng mountains and Kampung Naga near Tasikmilaya, **Sundanese religions** have dissolved into mainstream Islam, and most of the people are now staunch Muslim. Followers of the archaic Sundanese religions worshipped the spirits of their ancestors. Villages were probably arranged, as today's Badui villages, with the elders of sacred and protected inner villages acting as holy priests, dictating customs to the peasantry who inhabited the outer villages.

The original Sundanese art form is **pantun sunda**. A *pantun* is a story, recited by a solo, often blind, male performer with supposed supernatural powers, using narration, dialogue and songs to tell stories of ancestor heroes, the storyteller accompanying himself with a *kacapi* (zither). Performances are marathon affairs, beginning at 8pm, directly after the Islamic evening prayer, and finishing at 4am, before the morning prayer. These shows are usually commissioned by a family for a *hajat* (ritual feast), circumcision, wedding or rice harvest ceremony, the primary reason being that the storyteller is not just an entertainer but a shaman; the teller is believed to be able to contact the spirits and receive blessings for the *hajat*. Now the performances concentrate far more on entertainment than spirituality, and are likely to poke fun at modern preoccupations such as materialism. Shows are much shorter and often include a bowed-lute player, a female singer and a full gamelan orchestra.

Most Sundanese art forms have evolved within the strict social divide of the class system, and all of the different styles of dance and music were designed either for the elite or the masses. **Jaipongan**, for example, is a form of popular dance originally performed by prostitutes that can be quite bawdy and erotic. The style also acquired certain nuances of Indonesia's martial art form, **pencak silat**, when Dutch plantation owners tried to ban its practice. Jaipongan is now danced with the accompaniment of a drummer and a few gamelan players, and members of the audience are often asked up on stage to take part. An art form that developed almost entirely for the court and the elite was **gamelan degung**, an ensemble of gongs, metallophones and a flute, the instruments themselves becoming sacred possessions for the Priangan, West Java's hereditary rulers.

Wayang golek is the Sundanese puppet drama, and is in many ways closely related to *pantun sunda*. In contrast to the shadow plays of the rest of Java that use flat leather puppets, wayang golek uses three-dimensional wooden rod puppets. The stories are traditionally taken loosely from the *Mahabharata* and *Ramayana*, and can be a potent satirical weapon. Modern puppeteers often use the wooden characters to make caustic political comment and crude, near-the-knuckle humour that human performers would never get away with. The orchestrator of the wayang golek is the *dalang*, who operates all the characters while singing and reproducing the voices – a very similar figure to the storyteller of *pantun sunda*. He is also considered to be a sort of shaman, and someone with a divine gift. Certainly if you watch a good performance, the *dalang*'s craft is truly extraordinary. The play lasts from 9pm until 5am or 6am, with hundreds of different voices and songs, the *dalang* manipulating and vocalizing all of the puppets, while giving sound effects and emphasis by tapping on the wooden puppet's chest and playing a type of xylophone with his feet. It's an exhausting task, even for the spectator, perhaps made even more arduous by the constant noise of the accompanying nine-man gamelan orchestra. A good *dalang* commands an immense salary, and the profession, far from dying out, is flourishing.

Wayang topeng, or the mask dance, is a similar show that is found almost exclusively in Cirebon. It's generally accepted that the wayang forms were developed to convey Islamic teachings, used to mould audience opinion on political matters and provide information. Wayang was certainly commandeered in the 1960s to publicize government programmes.

and at the beginning of the twentieth century a new nationalist movement began to grow. One branch of the movement was to intensify the passion of its peasant members in their Islamic identity; the other branch went on to become the Indonesian Communist Party.

Krakatau and the west coast

The west coast of Java is not generally included in tourist itineraries, despite the two exceptional attractions of **Krakatau** and the **Ujong Kulon national park**; permits to both are required, as is a lot of planning if you're travelling independently. Between Jakarta and Merak is the old pepper port of **Banten**, a minor pilgrimage point for Muslims and a major historical site. Much of the west Javan coastline is taken up by the exclusive beach resorts of **Anyer**, **Carita** and **Labuan**, easy weekend escapes from the pollution of Jakarta and almost entirely the haven of the city's rich.

Banten and Pulau Dua

In the fifteenth century, the port of **BANTEN** was probably the largest and most important in all of Southeast Asia. Today Banten is a tiny cluster of Islamic buildings and ruins and has been forgotten by all but Javanese Muslims, who recognize its importance in the history of Indonesian Islam. It's very much a day-trip destination, with no accommodation and lots of tourist tat, but has some interesting buildings and a good deal of past glory. If you're coming to Banten from Jakarta, take a bus from the Kalideres bus station, getting off at **Serang**, a grotty nowhere town that lies about 90km to the west. From there it's a ten-kilometre minibus ride (20min) to Banten. There is no accommodation in town but there are lots of warung near the square selling soups and rice dishes.

In its heyday, Banten was a huge, bustling city where Ming porcelain was traded with the exotic spices of Maluku, and the Chinese set up trading posts and lived in communities alongside Vietnamese, Thais, Japanese, Arabs and seafarers from Sulawesi. In 1527, Sultan Hasanudin's Muslim army seized Banten and proclaimed him its king, after which Banten became a gateway into Indonesia for Islam, which very quickly took root in West Java and has remained the most powerful religion. The port was thriving: the most important commodity was pepper, with over 1500 tonnes exported each year, but silk, velvet, paper, gold, Chinese fans, ivory, rubies, medicine, olive oil, carpets and perfumes, honey, fruit and rice were also all traded here. In ancient Javanese, *banten* means "rebellion" or "refusal", and accordingly Banten's natives resisted Dutch occupation with frequent uprisings, until 1808, when the Dutch tired of this resistance and destroyed most of Banten, blockading the harbour and forcing traders to use their port of Sunda Kelapa in Batavia (Jakarta). After this, Banten was utterly bypassed by trade and fell into ruin, pretty much the state that it is in now.

The Town

As you come into Banten, the first sight of note is the **Istana Kaibon**, the palace of Queen Aisayah. It's now a crumbling ruin with an impressive main gateway and thick stone walls and archways, and is undergoing a long-running restoration programme, with limited results. Continuing towards the fortified alun-alun, the town's centre, the roadsides become crowded with gaudy vending carts. On the western side of the square is the **mosque**, the Mesjid Agung, built in 1566 by Sultan Hasanuddin (whose name adorns streets all over Indonesia). It's a large building with a five-tiered roof and is the main attraction for domestic tourists. At the north of the mosque is the royal cemetery, where four former sultans of Banten are buried, and nearby a squat **minaret** with a spiral staircase inside and two circular balconies offering limited views of the surrounding old town. In one corner of the square sits an engraved bronze cannon, and in another are two stone thrones dating from the fifteenth century. Close to the eastern side of the square, the **archeological museum** (Tues–Sat 9am–4pm; Rp1000) contains stacks of weapons, bronze and brass kris blades, ironwork, coins, pieces of terracotta and Ming porcelain. There are also a few examples of iron spikes once used by Banten's **Debus players**, Islamic ascetics who have for centuries specialized in self-mutilation, the effects of which are rendered harmless by meditation. In Banten there are still regular Debus performances on Saturday nights at Jalan Kebonjati 34 (Rp5000).

Pulau Dua

In Banten Bay lies **Pulau Dua**, a small island with a big reputation for birdlife. Since 1937 it's been a protected national park for migratory birds, but also has a burgeoning population of egrets, cormorants, pelicans, herons and sea eagles. It lies only 1km to the east of Banten and can easily be accessed at low tide, when you can walk all the way over to it across mud flats, although you should be careful not to get cut off by the water. At all other times you will have to charter a boat to reach the island.

Merak

At the extreme northwestern tip of Java, **MERAK** is the port for ferries across the Sunda straits to Bakauheni on **Sumatra**. The port is extremely busy and there is no reason to stay here, though if you should get stuck the *Hotel Anda* at Jalan Florida 4 has basic rooms with fan and mandi (☎0254/71041; ②). **Ferries** to Sumatra from Merak leave about every thirty minutes and take ninety minutes; crowds of buses connect with the ferries to take you on to Bandar Lampung, Palembang or destinations further north in Sumatra.

Anyer

The most prominent building in **ANYER**, which lies 15km south of Merak, is a delightful forty-metre **lighthouse** built by Queen Wilhelmina of Holland in 1885 as a memorial to the townspeople killed by the eruption of Krakatau. Its gleaming white plaster walls and classic shape offer a rare touch of elegance down this overdeveloped coast, and the views from the top are quite beautiful (although you may have problems finding the caretaker to let you in). Anyer is also credited with being the starting point for the **Great Post Road**, begun by the Dutch in the nineteenth century, that ran 1000km from here to the eastern tip of Java. Off the coast of Anyer lies Pulau Sangeang, an uninhabited island with vast areas of untouched jungle. Diving companies in town offer tours to the reefs that surround Sangeang, which boasts a sunken wreck and perfect coral formations swarming with tropical fish.

Accommodation

There are no road numbers or exact addresses for any of the buildings along the main coast road, so all **accommodation** is described in the order in which it appears as you head south from the market.

Pondok Sanghiang, close to Anyer village (☎0254/602910). Reasonable rooms with air-con and attached mandi. The restaurant provides decent fried-chicken, squid or prawn dishes for around Rp7500 per person, and breakfast is included. ⑥.

Kalimaya resort, tours and travel (☎0254/601266). Eleven rooms and cottages, each one different, from simple double or triple rooms to detached bungalows with kitchen and living room for up to eight people; most have air-con and all have bathrooms. The tour office specializes in diving tours for certified divers, at around US$60 a day. The restaurant serves European, Chinese and Indonesian food, from nasi goreng (Rp5000) to lobster (Rp60,000). ⑦–⑨.

Ryugu Hotel Putri Duyung (☎0254/601239). A Japanese-style resort, built to cater for the small number of Japanese expatriates working in Jakarta. Each room has its own Japanese name, a garden, telephone, fax, hot water, air-con and TV and, as you would expect, there is a profusion of karaoke facilities and Japanese food. ⑧–⑨.

Hotel Sangyang Indah (☎ & fax 0254/601299). This luxury hotel specializes in sports, with tennis, volleyball, badminton, billiards, swimming and watersports available. All rooms have satellite TV, air-con, hot water and telephone. ⑧–⑨.

Eating

The vast majority of people staying in Anyer opt for the hotel restaurants, which almost without exception serve a variety of Chinese dishes, steaks, hamburgers and seafood. There are several small warung opposite the *Pisita Anyer* beach resort, mostly frequented by staff from the local hotels, selling basic, inexpensive food such as nasi campur and nasi goreng. Opposite the *Hotel Sanghiang Indah* is the *Warung Ikan Bakar*, the building with the thatched roof and the wartel adjoining its restaurant. They have an excellent range of fresh seafood: shrimps, squid and whatever fish has been caught that day, served as a complete meal with rice and vegetables for under Rp10,000.

Carita

CARITA's resort strip starts about 20km south of Anyer market and 7km north of Labuan. It has a profusion of quality hotels lining the main road that runs parallel to the beach, but unlike Anyer has a few places in the inexpensive and moderate range. It can be quite an easy and welcome escape from the city; a bus from Kalideres bus station in Jakarta, usually changing to a colt at Labuan, will take just over three hours. If you do have to change at Labuan terminal, don't get conned into taking transport round to the stop for colts to Carita, just walk two minutes towards the seafront and round to the right.

Though Carita boasts one of the most sheltered stretches of sea in Java, at weekends the bay reverberates with the constant brain-numbing roar of jet skis and powerboats, and is not a particularly relaxing place for a swim. Carita is the best spot to arrange **tours** to Krakatau and Ujong Kulon: the Black Rhino tour company (☎0253/81072) on the opposite side of the road from the marina is recommended. A full four-day and three-night tour to Ujong Kulon costs US\$170 per person for a minimum of four people, a day tour to Krakatau costs US\$30–50. Guides who approach you at your hotel or on the street often quote ludicrous prices and can be totally unqualified. If **watersports** are your thing, the Marina Lippo Carita (☎0253/81525) offers everything from jet-skiing to parasailing, as well as tours to Krakatau and Putri Gundul for snorkelling. Sample prices include Rp12,000 for fifteen minutes in a speedboat, or Rp80,000 for thirty minutes' water-skiing. Between Carita and Anyer is the small beach of **Karang Bolong** – a massive boulder was dumped here by the tidal waves that followed the eruption of Krakatau, and it's now a popular attraction for Indonesian tourists. There is a Rp2000 charge to use the beach.

Accommodation

All **accommodation** is on or close to the main seaside road, known as Jalan Carita Raya or Jalan Pantai Carita. There are no building numbers, so all are listed here in the order they appear along this road heading north from Labuan town. All hotels and guest houses increase their prices dramatically at weekends and as much as triple them during national holidays, when it's advisable to book as much as a month in advance.

Cinde Wulung (☎0253/83307). Cheap rooms are available here at off-peak times, and bargaining is advisable. All rooms have either fan or air-con and come with en-suite mandi. Additional services include massage and a seafood restaurant – the spicy grilled fish is recommended. ④.

Pondok Karang Sari, (no phone). Has large family rooms for four to eight people inside huge, spotless wooden cottages with thatched roofs. ⑥.

Pondok Bakkara (☎0253/81260). One of the cheapest places here, though not especially clean and often full. All rooms have mandi inside but, unusually, no fan. ②.

Sunset View (☎0253/81075). Friendly staff, clean rooms and interesting decor make this one of the best-value places on the west coast. They are in the process of building a café, but until it's finished your "full breakfast" will be just a cup of tea. ③.

Yussi Penginapan (☎0253/81074). The cheapest rooms have shared facilities and are rather dingy, but (accordingly) cost less. Upstairs rooms with air-con and mandi are a little better. ③–④.

Carita Krakatau (☎0253/83027). Out back of the restaurant of the same name, these spotless tile-floored rooms with mandi, fan and breakfast included offer the best deal in town. ③.

New Gogona (☎0253/81122). The brand-new block of rooms with air-con are pristine, the older ones with fan are grotty and best avoided. ③–④.

Naida Beak, (no phone). Has a variety of family bungalows and is designed to take large budget-conscious groups, cramming up to ten people into each room. Single and double rooms are also available. ④–⑥.

Penginapan Joe (☎0253/82887). The rooms here are a little dark, but the proprietors are keen to bargain midweek. ④.

Krakatau Seaside (☎0253/81081). Utterly stunning houses on a private stretch of beach, all faithful reproductions of Indonesian *rumah adat*. The buildings' facades are beautiful two-storey copies of Acehnese, Torajan, Minahasan and Badui houses – inside they have air-con, TV and even billiard tables. ⑧–⑨.

Lucia Cottages (☎0253/81262). One of the few places in Indonesia that actually offers lower prices for tourists, with detached bungalows or single/double rooms around a swimming pool and some of the comfiest beds in Carita. ④–⑥.

Eating

The public parts of the beach are lined with food carts selling *murtabak*, sate and soto. The main road has many **warung** selling cold drinks, and some basic food such as *ikan bakar* and nasi goreng.

Café de Paris, at the 14km Anyer market. A plush air-con place with a variety of European and Chinese dishes and seafood. It's comparatively pricey, at around Rp15,000 for a hamburger.

Carita Krakatau, 30m towards Anyer from the marina, on the inland side of the road. The menu offers a limited seafood selection; a good fish or prawn steak will cost around Rp7500.

Diminati, opposite the entrance to the marina. Boasts the cheapest cold beer in town at Rp4500, and does an excellent *kakap* fish steak complete with vegetables and chips for Rp8000.

Marina Lippo Carita, on the beach in the prominent marina complex that is about halfway along Carita's resort strip (☎0253/81525). Great food but wildly overpriced. Thai spring rolls are only Rp7500, but fish and seafood dishes start at Rp25,000.

Pasundan Kusing, 100m short of the *Lucia Cottages* on the inland side of the road. A small Sundanese smorgasbord with fried chicken or beef, sweet-and-sour corn soup, fried *tempe* and *tahu*, rice and vegetables costs just Rp3500. A mixed hotplate with beef, prawns, squid and quails' eggs is Rp15,000.

Labuan

LABUAN is a dull and dirty port town serving as a transport crossroads for the glitzy coastal resorts further north. Regular buses come directly here from Jakarta's Kalideres terminal (3hr). A slow and smoky steam train chugs once a day between Labuan and Merak, taking about twice as long as the bus. The PHPA office in Labuan claims that the trains that run this route are the oldest still in service worldwide, one having been built in Germany in 1899, one in the Netherlands in 1909, and another in Switzerland in 1916.

Although not especially appealing in itself, Labuan does have some cheap (though poor value) accommodation which is useful at weekends, when everywhere from here to Anyer will be crowded and very expensive. It's also the best place to arrange **independent tours** to Krakatau and the Ujong Kulon national park, and the place to get the essential park **permits** (Rp5000). There is a small information centre inside with photographs, charts and commentary in English to give you a taster of what the parks offer; the people who work here are very friendly and helpful, though they don't speak much English. The **BRI** bank on the south side of the bus terminal will change cash and travellers' cheques, the **post office** is on Jalan Perintis Kemerdekaan heading towards Carita, as is the **PHPA parks office** which is further out, almost opposite the *Rawayan* hotel. There are a few nondescript **warung** around the town, but no restaurants.

Accommodation

Hotel Caringi, Jl Perintis Kemerdekaan 20 (☎0253/81388). All of the rooms here have mandi attached (but none have fans), and they are pretty dingy. ②–③.

Hotel Citra Ayu, Jl Perintis Kemerdekaan 27 (☎0253/81229). Basic but clean, and all the rooms have fans. ②.

Rawayan, Jl Raya Carita 41 (☎0253/81386). The nicest place in Labuan, out on the road towards Carita and away from the noise and grime of town, with quaint bungalows and private rooms, all with mandi and some with air-con. ④–⑤.

Telaga Biru, just off Jl Raya Carita, about 2km from Labuan and on the opposite side of the road from the sea (no phone). The best budget option in and around Labuan; all the quiet rooms have mandi inside. ②.

Krakatau

The makers of the disaster movie *Krakatoa, East of Java* were obviously too busy to get a map out before entitling their film. Clearly visible west of the beaches near Merak and Carita is **Krakatau volcano**, the crumbled caldera of Pulau Rakata and the epicentre of the 1883 explosion whose force was equivalent to 10,000 Hiroshima atomic bombs. Today, **Anak Krakatau**, the child of Krakatau volcano, is a growing infant island surrounded by what remains of the older peaks. Having first reared its head from the seas in 1930, Anak Krakatau's glassy black cone sits angrily smoking amongst a collection of elder relatives, and is the tangible legacy of one of the most destructive events in recorded history.

As you approach Krakatau from Java, you round the northeastern point of Pulau Rakata, its sheer northern cliff face soaring straight out of the sea to nearly 800m. Several small, jagged spurs of black lava jut out of the water and are thought to predate the 1883 eruption. The outer islands are all that remain of Krakatau's original cone, and are now forested and filled with birds, snakes and monitor lizards. Anak Krakatau, however, is the place most visitors want to see – it's a barren wasteland and still very much active. To get here requires a **motorboat trip** (4–6hr) from Labuan or Carita, which on a calm day is delightful, but at all other times should be avoided as the water can be too much for small boats to handle. From the landing point it takes about thirty minutes to walk up to the crater, from where you can see black lava flows, sulphurous fumaroles and smoke, with occasional expulsions of ash and rock.

The easiest way to visit Krakatau is with the Black Rhino tour company in Carita (p.110). They try to assemble tour groups and split the boat cost, and are pretty reliable. Depending on how many people can be gathered, it could cost Rp100,000 per person. If you have your own group, inquire at the PHPA parks office in Labuan (see above) and see if they can fix you up with a boat, which should cost around Rp500,000 for the day. Don't forget to bring lots of water and some food (include emergency supplies).

The volcano

Krakatau sits right on the brim of the Sunda shelf, a colossal continental plate underlying much of Asia, whose boundary runs just kilometres off the southern coast of Sumatra and Java. The shelf runs alongside one of the most volcanic regions of the world, with Krakatau its most infamous progeny.

In the middle of the nineteenth century, Krakatau was uninhabited, except for the hordes of tropical birds, monkeys and reptiles that filled its thick jungles. The island was dominated by three peaks, Danan, Perbuatan and Rakata (which means "crab" in ancient Javanese), and stood 813m above sea level. In 1620, the Dutch East India Company had set up a small naval station here to harvest timber and sulphur from the island's plentiful stocks. However, people didn't settle, and when Krakatau awoke the island was mercifully free of people.

In May 1883, the first **tremors** were reported in Sumatra and also in First Point Lighthouse, in Ujong Kulon national park. On May 19, after 200 years sleeping, Krakatau's northern volcano of Perbuatan **erupted**, explosions being heard along the coasts lining the Sunda straits up to 230km away. The air-pressure waves stopped clocks and smashed windows in Batavia (Jakarta) and Bogor, and pumice began to fall into the Sunda straits.

However, it was the *tsunamis* or **pressure waves** that caused the majority of deaths in the region. The first huge wave followed an explosion at 5.45am on August 27, 1883, which was heard in central Australia. This huge wave crashed into Anyer town on the west coast of Java and completely razed it, but was still only a ripple compared with what was to come. At 10am an explosion of unimaginable proportions rent Krakatau island; the boom was heard as far away as Sri Lanka. As the eruption column towered 40km into the atmosphere, a thick mud rain began to fall over the area, and the temperature plunged by 5°C. Tremors were detected as far away as the English Channel and off the coast of Alaska. One single *tsunami* as tall as a seven-storey building, raced outwards, demolishing everything in its wake. Three hundred towns and villages were simply erased, and 36,417 people killed as it rushed kilometres inland. The government gunboat *Berouw* was lifted from the middle of Teluk Betung's Chinese quarter, where an earlier wave had stranded it, and carried 3km inland, before being deposited up a hill 10m above sea level. Once into the open sea, the waves travelled at up to 700kph, reaching South Africa and scuttling ships in Auckland harbour.

The **aftermath** of Krakatau's eruption was to circle the globe for the next two years in the form of fine ash particles. These lowered global temperatures, created psychedelic sunsets and seemed to tinge the moon and the sun blue or green. In July 1884, well over a year after the eruption, bones and skulls were washed ashore in Zanzibar in East Africa; they had been borne across the Indian Ocean on pumice-stone rafts. Two-thirds of Krakatau had vanished for good, and on those parts that remained not so much as a seed or an insect survived.

The Ujong Kulon national park

At the extreme southwestern tip of Java is a small forested peninsula that the modern world seems to have overlooked. In the **Ujong Kulon national park** you can glide in a dugout canoe on abundant rivers overhung with dense jungle, and experience the Java that captured the imagination of explorers hundreds of years ago.

Practicalities

The first step of any journey into the park is to obtain a PHPA **permit** and book accommodation, both of which can be done at the PHPA office in Labuan (see opposite). One option is then to charter a boat for up to fifteen people from Labuan to one of the islands inside the park (5hr; around US$175). A cheaper alternative is to take a minibus from

Labuan to **SAMUR** (3hr; Rp5000), about 20km short of the park. In Samur there are hordes of ojek or motorcycle taxis waiting to ferry trekkers on to **TAMANJAYA** (45min; Rp5000), on the mainland before the isthmus that forms the gateway to the main body of the park. Tamanjaya is a small village with a few basic supply shops, a PHPA office where (at the time of writing) it was possible to obtain your **permit**, and a losmen. There are guest houses within the park on **Pulau Handeuleum** and **Pulau Peucang**; the latter also has a restaurant and rather swanky **accommodation** (⑥–⑦). This accommodation can either be booked at the PHPA office in Labuan, or through organized tour companies in Jakarta or Carita. If you intend staying in the park, you're much better off buying supplies in Labuan, as they're very limited here. A **guide** is required by park law for anyone entering Ujong Kulon. They can be hired most cheaply at Tamanjaya PHPA office, where there is a flat charge of Rp10,000 a day.

The park

The main body of Ujong Kulon is a bulbous peninsula joined to the mainland by a narrow land bridge. Also part of the park is large Pulau Panaitan, which lies about 5km off the northwestern shore, and a host of tiny islands, including Pulau Handeleum and Pulau Peucang, nestling in bays close to the mainland. The whole park covers around two hundred square kilometres, just over half being land, and the rest coral reef and sea, stocked with turtles, sharks and rays.

Ujong Kulon's most famous and dramatic inhabitant is unfortunately also the most elusive. The park was set up by the Dutch in the early twentieth century to protect the single-horned **Javan rhinoceros**, which has been on the verge of extinction for a century, killed by poachers who exported the horn to the Chinese, who value its qualities as an aphrodisiac. The famously myopic rhino has hide with four definite plates like body armour, its mouth hooked into a beak. The rhino's horn is actually a lump of solid hair and has no bone or connection to the animal's skull. Nowadays, although the rhino is the attraction that brings most visitors to the park, some of the guides who have worked here for years have never seen one.

What you are most likely to see are scores of **snakes** and sizable monitor lizards, monkeys, wild pigs and a cornucopia of **birds** in an environment of swamps, grassy fields, jungle and white-sand beaches. Some of the river mouths and swampy areas are home to the estuarine crocodile and false gharial, both shy of contact with humans. The **panther**, another notoriously timid and rare beast, dwells here in small numbers, and the **hawksbill turtle** comes annually to the beaches to breed and lay its eggs. The park is also famed for its **primate colonies**, the rare Javan silver leaf-monkey, crab-eating macaques and gibbons joining the hornbills and myna birds in making their presence noisily evident. The thieving macaques can be a real menace, so leave your possessions unguarded at your peril.

TREKKING

There are limitless possibilities for **trekking** inside the park. The best thing to do is consult your guide and decide what best suits your budget and what you most want to see. **Peucang** and **Handeleum islands** are good places to start from. They are both reachable by boat directly from Carita or Labuan, and have bungalow accommodation. Peucang also has its own restaurant, and the waves off the south coast have begun to attract a steady trickle of surfers.

It's possible to walk around the entire north edge of the peninsula in four days to a week. There are observation towers, where you can watch the wildlife without your scent and presence scaring them, at Cigenter, Nyiur near Cape Alang-Alang and also near Mount Bayung at Cibunar in the south. About fourteen rough wooden shelters are dotted around the park, where five or six people can sleep; bear in mind that you'll have to bring all your own provisions.

One of the most rewarding but well-worn trails starts at the guest house on Pulau Handeleum. Just across the water from here at the mouth of **Sungai Cigenter** is the feeding centre of the same name. It's an open meadow which is a grazing ground for Banteng ox and home to a huge colony of psychedelic bee-eaters. From the feeding grounds there's a rough walking trail all the way round the coast back to the Tamanjaya park headquarters, through knotted mangroves and rainforest. The first shelter for trekkers is just past Sungai Cikarang, about a nine-kilometre walk from Cigenter. You could either overnight here, or continue for 6–7km to Tanjung Alang-Alang where there's another shelter. This is a marshy area full of birds and, less enticingly, hordes of mosquitoes. From here it's a twenty-kilometre trek to Ciujungkulon feeding ground, which lies across the Peucang straits from Pulau Peucang. From Ciujungkulon you can either continue around the coast or take a short cut over the headland. Either way it will take you at least a couple of days to get back to Tamanjaya; there are five shelters at roughly ten-kilometre intervals along the trail.

The Badui villages

When Islam conquered Java, very few vestiges of the island's **animist** past were left. One of the few places left untouched was a group of isolated communities in the Kendeng mountains, right in the centre of the most Western area of Java. Today, around three thousand of their descendants still live in protected villages about 50km south of the town of Rankasbitung, and are known as the **Badui**. It's possible that one reason they managed to maintain their independence during the spread of Islam was because the new Muslim sultans may have feared tampering with the power of the Badui priests on their "magic mountain". Certainly, the Badui's tenacious retention of tradition in the face of 400 years of pressure is quite remarkable, and after the Indonesian government had consumately failed to force them to adopt their language, religion and methods of schooling, the villages were made a sort of national park.

Visitors now require a **permit** to enter and, even with a permit, can only visit the "outer villages". Badui magic and law are centred on three "inner villages" that are closed to visitors. The elders and high priests of Badui religion never leave here, and make the rules that govern all the other villages. Every year in April and May, during the *seba* ceremony, the Badui bring offerings to the *puun*, the high priest of the inner Badui, a sacred talismanic leader who possesses hereditary "magical" powers.

Practicalities

Unless you take an organized trek all the way from Jalan Jaksa or Carita, visiting the Badui is quite an undertaking. It will take you several days out of any of the major tourist centres and a fair bit of organizing. Whether you go alone or in a tour, you'll be staying in makeshift accommodation and walking pretty strenuously between villages.

The first stop for independent travellers intending to visit the Badui **Rankasbitung**, a large, dull town about 80km west and slightly south of Jakarta. To get there take a bus either from Labuan (1hr 30min; Rp2000), or from Kalideres in Jakarta (3hr; Rp3500). To visit the outer villages you must first get a **permit** from the PHPA office (Mon–Sat 7.30am–1.30pm) in Rankasbitung, which can be found at the Kantor Dinas Parawisata, Jalan Pahlawan 31a. The permit costs Rp8000 and lasts for three days. Pak Mardo at the PHPA office is the best source of information for the area, though he doesn't speak much English. Another option is to take a tour from a company such as Black Rhino tours in Carita (see p.110) or one of those that set up along Jalan Jaksa in Jakarta (see p.99). From Rankasbitung there are three minibuses a day to **Cibolger**, a small village just outside the Badui districts; the last minibus leaves at midday. To charter a minibus there and back will cost about Rp150,000. In Cibolger, Pak Hussein has a small souvenir shop and warung, and he also takes paying guests, though his house is not a losmen and should not be treated as such. From Cibolger it's about a one-kilometre walk to **Katu Ketek**, the first outer Badui village.

The villages

KATU KETEK has several traditional houses and the people all wear the blue garb, black sarong and batik headscarves of the outer villages. Priests from the inner villages wear white and do not cut their hair; they are also forbidden from keeping large domestic animals, getting drunk and eating at night. The villagers grow *tangkil*, a variety of nut, on the mountainsides: these are then processed into *emping* crackers. They also grow fruits such as sawo, soursop and durian. From Katu Ketek it's a two-hour walk to **KATU JANGKUNG**, through mountainous territory. The next village is **CIGULA**, three hours' walk away, passing **Dangdong Ageng**, a small lake that marks the gateway to the protected inner villages. Cigula is another charming village: its traditional houses have thatched roofs and open porches where people work shaded from the sun. If you're lucky you might see them making and playing the bamboo *angklung* instrument or weaving baskets out of rattan.

From Cigula it's another two hours' walk to **GAJEBOK**, probably the nicest village to stay, with exceptionally friendly people and a nearby river that's good for a cooling mandi. The people of Gajebok are known for their traditional textiles and for making bags from beaten tree bark. Ask for Pak Ailin if you are in need of food or shelter, as he often provides for visitors. If you don't want to stay, it's a hard four-hour trek back to Katu Ketek, passing through a few tiny kampung.

Bogor

Just an hour's train journey south of Jakarta and perhaps destined to become one of its suburbs, **BOGOR** is still tremendously different from the capital. Its cool, wet climate contrasts with Jakarta's stifling sweatiness, and Bogor's famous botanical gardens provide more greenery than can be found in the whole of the polluted capital. However, Bogor is no longer a serene colonial hill station; its streets are chaotic, crowded with smoke-chugging bemos, and Western-style shopping centres are springing up along the tree-lined avenues. The best relief from the increasing frenzy of the city is to be found right at its heart: the **Kebun Raya Botanical Gardens**, which have been Bogor's greatest asset since 1817. The plants are kept healthy by Bogor's ever eager rainstorms, averaging very nearly one a day – the city has well earned its nickname, "the city of rains".

Some history

Several engraved rocks in the vicinity of Bogor suggest its history dates back to long before the well-documented times of colonial occupation. These stones are known as *batu tulis* (rock writings). One such stone at Ciampea has several footprints and an inscription, said to have been left by the Hindu king Purnavaraman, who ruled Java in the fifth century, possibly centring his kingdom here in Bogor. Bogor was certainly the capital of the **Pajararan empire** from the twelfth to the sixteenth centuries. During **colonial** times, the wealthy Dutch grew tired of the swelter of Batavia (Jakarta) and sought residences in the cooler highlands. Although it stands not quite 300m above sea level, Bogor's climate is appreciably cooler, and was the obvious choice. In 1745, governor general Willem van Imhoff passed through Bogor region on a fact-finding mission and decided to make his home here. He started on a large estate named Buitenzorg, roughly translated as "free of worries", which was the site of many wild parties, the elite of Batavia flocking to hunt in the grounds. In 1811, Sir Stamford Raffles took up residence and renovated the buildings. It was he who made the first start on

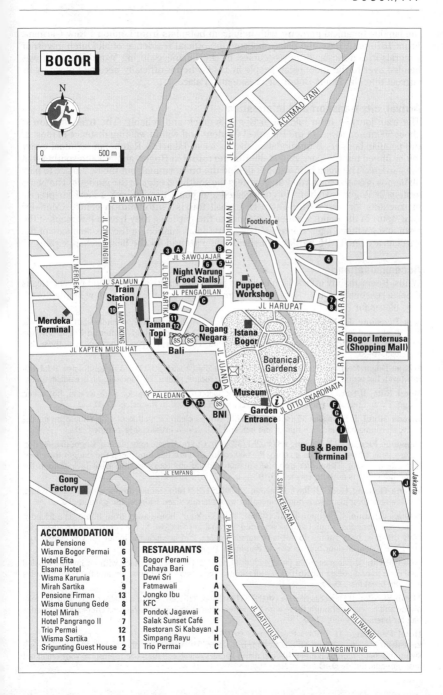

BOGOR

N

0   500 m

JL ACHMAD YANI

JL PEMUDA

JL MARTADINATA

JL CIWARINGIN

JL MERDEKA

Footbridge

JL JEND SUDIRMAN

JL SAWOJAJAR

JL DEWI SARTIKA

Night Warung
(Food Stalls)

JL SALMUN

Train
Station

Merdeka
Terminal

JL MAY OKING

JL PENGADILAN

Puppet
Workshop

JL HARUPAT

Taman
Topi

Dagang
Negara

Istana
Bogor

Bali

JL KAPTEN MUSILHAT

JL JUNDA

Botanical
Gardens

JL RAYA PAJAJARAN

Bogor Internusa
(Shopping Mall)

Museum

JL PALEDANG

BNI

Garden
Entrance

JL OTTO ISKARDINATA

Bus & Bemo
Terminal

Jakarta

JL EMPANG

JL SURYAKENCANA

Gong
Factory

JL PAHLAWAN

ACCOMMODATION

Abu Pensione	10
Wisma Bogor Permai	6
Hotel Efita	3
Elsana Hotel	5
Wisma Karunia	1
Mirah Sartika	9
Pensione Firman	13
Wisma Gunung Gede	8
Hotel Mirah	4
Hotel Pangrango II	7
Trio Permai	12
Wisma Sartika	11
Srigunting Guest House	2

RESTAURANTS

Bogor Perami	B
Cahaya Bari	G
Dewi Sri	I
Fatmawali	A
Jongko Ibu	D
KFC	F
Pondok Jagawai	K
Salak Sunset Café	E
Restoran Si Kabayan	J
Simpang Rayu	H
Trio Permai	C

JL BATUTULIS

JL SILIWANGI

JL LAWANGGINTUNG

the famous botanical gardens, with help from botanists from London's Kew Gardens. From 1870 until 1942, the palace became the official residence of all Dutch governor generals in Indonesia. Briefly occupied by the Japanese during World War II, it was handed over to the Indonesian people in 1949, when it officially became known by its current title: the Istana Bogor, or Presidential Palace.

Arrival, city transport and information

The train journey from Jakarta to Bogor is quick and reliable. The **train station** is about 500m northwest of the Botanical Gardens and within walking distance of most of the popular budget accommodation. Buses leave Jakarta's Rambutan terminal every ten or fifteen minutes, arriving at the **bus terminal** in Bogor, about 500m southeast of the gardens. The main bemo stop is behind the bus terminal, but the best place to pick up bemos is on the main road that borders the southern edge of the gardens. The bemo system in Bogor is extremely complicated and you'll need to ask a local for precise instructions for every trip. There is a small **tourist information** centre (Mon–Fri 9am–4pm) at the main, southern entrance to the gardens; they have a few maps of the town and gardens. Jalan Kapten Musilhat and Jalan Juanda on the western side of the gardens are lined with **banks**; you should shop around for the best exchange rates.

Accommodation

Whilst Bogor mainly offers flash business hotels, its status as a weekend retreat means it has a reasonably wide range of **accommodation**, and there are a few family hostel-type places for budget travellers.

Abu Pensione, Jl Mayur Oking 15 (☎0251/322893). With excessively friendly staff, river views, free drinks and excellent breakfasts, *Abu* is probably the best budget losmen in Bogor. The top rooms have hot water and air-con or fan as an option. The cheapest rooms have none of these, but are clean. ③–④.

Wisma Bogor Permai, Jl Sawajajar/Jend Sudirman 23a (☎0251/321115). A delightful new establishment with hot water, large beds and fridges in all the rooms, plus a good Indonesian breakfast. ⑤–⑥.

Hotel Efita, Jl Sawajajar 5 (☎0251/333400, fax 333600). Rather swanky, with air-con, hot water, fridge, TV and telephone in every room. Breakfast is included in the price. ⑤–⑥.

Elsana Hotel, Jl Sawajajar 36 (☎0251/322522). Not as clean or well kept as it should be for the price; all rooms have en-suite mandi and fan, and Indonesian breakfast is included. ④.

Pensione Firman, Jl Palendang 48 (☎0251/323246). Currently the only place in Bogor to offer dormitory beds (three people to a room; Rp9000 each), *Firman* has long been the budget travellers' favourite in Bogor. They offer good information and various tours around West Java, though the accommodation is nothing special. ②–③.

Wisma Gedung Gede, Jl Raya Pajaran 36 (☎0251/324148). Situated opposite the Bank Niaga, this is a sparkling place with huge suites, hot water, family-sized fridges, and gardens. ⑤.

Wisma Karunia, Jl Serupur 35–37 (☎0251/323411). Your "home away from home" is a friendly, family-run place that's quiet and as secluded as you'll get so close to the centre of a Javanese city. Only the most basic rooms do not have mandi and fan, and breakfast is included. The owners run an efficient door-to-door bus service to Bandung. ③–④.

Hotel Mirah, Jl Pangrango 9a (☎0251/328044, fax 329423). A new place with an inviting shaded pool open to non-guests for Rp10,000 – all rooms have air-con and hot water, and the price includes a decent breakfast. ④–⑥.

Mirah Sartika, Jl Dewi Sartika 6a (☎0251/312343, fax 315188). Quite a flashy place, with TV, telephone and air-con, although there's no hot water, even in its top-class rooms. There's a conference hall for business rental. ④–⑤.

Hotel Pangrango II, Jl Raya Pajajaran 32 (☎0251/312375, fax 377750). All the rooms here have knee-deep carpets, TV and video, air-con, hot water, fridge and telephone. In addition, there's a swimming pool, moneychanger, ballroom and laundry service. The basic rooms are very small but have good facilities. ④–⑥.

Trio Permai, Dewi Sartika 2 (☎0251/329672). The basic rooms here are a little dark and grotty but have fan and mandi; the more expensive ones are much better with good spring beds. The price includes tea, coffee and breakfast. ③–⑤.

Wisma Sartika, Jl Gedung Sawa III 19 (☎0251/323747). Run by a charming, English-speaking Indonesian woman, *Sartika* is spotlessly clean, and provides endless hot drinks and an American breakfast. Classier rooms have mandi inside; all the rooms have fans. ③–④.

Sriguning Guest House, Jl Heulang 11a (☎0251/311243), Jl Merak 14 (☎0251/323080) and Jl Bincarung 12 (☎0251/333296). This family-run group of guest houses sport absolutely over-the-top palatial architecture, with crystal chandeliers, gold leaf over everything and cavernous suite rooms with hot water, fridge, TV and air-con. Midweek, prices are subject to huge reductions and you can try additional bargaining. ⑥.

The City

The pathways of the **Botanical Gardens** (daily 8am–5pm; Rp1600) wind between towering bamboo stands, climbing bougainvillea, a small tropical rainforest, and ponds full of water lilies and fountains. Perhaps the garden's best-known occupants are the giant rafflesia and *bungu bangkai*, two of the world's hugest (and smelliest) flowers. About 15,000 endemic species have been collected here, as well as thousands of tropical varieties from around the world. Unfortunately, many of these are kept in the private greenhouses that are closed to the public.

Near the main entrance to the park is a memorial to Olivia Raffles, wife of the governor general Sir Stamford Raffles, who died in Bogor in 1814. Also near the entrance to the park is the **zoological museum** (daily 8am–4pm; Rp700), housing a collection of 30,000 specimens, one of the foremost botanical research centres in Asia. There is an immense collection of Asian insects and reptiles, as well as the complete skeleton of a blue whale, a stuffed Javan rhino, a giant Japanese crab, a mammoth Flores rat, a Komodo dragon and a selection of Indonesian mammals. It's a badly organized and dilapidated, but nonetheless fascinating, collection.

The **Bogor Presidential Palace** (Istana Bogor) is in the northern corner of the gardens; you can get within a stone's throw of it (across a pond) if you head directly north as soon as you enter the park. To actually enter the palace you'll need to get a **permit** about a week in advance from the tourist office at Jalan Merak 1 (☎0251/325705), and will probably have to join a tour. The grounds are patrolled by herds of roe deer; sources differ on whether the deer were introduced from mainland Asia or all the way from Holland, but either way it seems certain they were brought here to grace the governor general's dinner table. The palace was built in a mainly European style, the exterior having a distinctly Ionian facade, with pillars and a triangular pediment. It contains President Sukarno's immense art collection, as well as his library and film room. Though Sukarno loved the palace, his successor Suharto scorned it; some say this was because Sukarno's ghost still wanders the buildings. **Wayang golek puppets** are made at a workshop found to the northeast of the gardens; ask for Pak Dase's place. If you're interested in **gamelan** and **Javanese gongs**, visit Pak Sukarna's factory on Jalan Pancasan to the southwest of the gardens. Here the instruments are forged using traditional methods, and are also for sale.

There is one **batu tulis** in Bogor town, 2km southwest of the entrance to the gardens at Jalan Batu Tulis – make sure you remove your shoes before entering the shrine that houses the stone. The inscription dates from 1533 and was written in Sundanese Sanskrit, dedicated to King Surawisesa of the Hindu Pajajaran empire. What are said to be the king's footprints are also visible in the stone. Sukarno made his home close to the small shrine that now houses the stone, believing it to possess great magical power. He also asked to be buried near here, but Suharto refused permission. The other *batu tulis* in this area is to be found at **Ciampea**, northwest of Bogor. It's actually quite impressive, a sizable, shiny black boulder with the footprint of King Purnavaraman and an extremely clear inscription dating back 1500 years. To get there, take a bemo from the train station to Ciampea (30min; Rp1000) and then ask for a colt (20min; Rp600) on to Batutulis.

Eating

The growing market in Bogor is for **fast food**: the Bogor Plaza has *KFC* and *Dunkin' Donuts*; the Internusa Mall has *CFC* and *Dunkin' Donuts*; and the Hero Mall has *McDonald's* and more *Dunkin' Donuts*. The green minibus #7 (5min; Rp300) from outside the Bogor Permai food court takes you to the Plaza Jambu Dua, a huge shopping centre with ten-pin bowling and many fast-food joints. Along Jalan Pengadillan, near the Telkom and train station, are bunches of **night stalls**, which set up after 6pm and sell excellent seafood and Chinese snacks. You can get a terrific meal for under Rp8000, but these stalls sometimes shut very early. Near the gates to the gardens there is a profusion of **gorengan**, street vendors who look like Dutch milkmaids, with their wares dangling from poles across their shoulders. *Gorengan* means "frying" and, true to form, these vendors will wrap pretty much anything up in batter and deep-fry it. Favourites here are fried banana, yam and cassava.

Bogor Permai, on the corner of Jl Jend Sudirman and Jl Sawojajar. A small food complex housing a fine delicatessen, the best bakery in Bogor and a stand selling tasty pizza slices (Rp2000) as well as hot dogs and sandwiches. The *Bogor Permai* restaurant in the back of the building is one of the highest-quality places in Bogor, selling excellent seafood and steaks. Most courses start at around Rp15,000.

Cahaya Bari, Simpang Rayu, Trio Permai, all near the bus station on Jl Raya Pajararan. Three of the flashiest, cleanest Padang restaurants you will ever see. An excellent assortment of meats and seafoods cooked in a variety of sauces.

Dewi Sri, Jl Pajajaran 3. A clean establishment serving Indonesian food; ayam goreng is recommended, at Rp5000.

Fatmawali, Jl Sawajajar 7. A canteen-style self-service place with cold meats and veggies and excellent fried chicken. A very reasonable full meal will cost under Rp5000.

Jongko Ibu, Jl Juanda 36. Serves good, cheap Sundanese food and you can eat outside watching the world go by. *Karedok* – salad with chilli sauce – is good and fiery, while steamed carp in banana leaf is a local favourite.

Pondok Jagawai, Jl Raya Pajajaran 3. A variety of food from around the world is served here; *shabu shabu* (Japanese meat fondue) costs Rp25,000 for three people, Wiener schnitzel is Rp10,500. Chicken steak and Australian lamb chops are also recommended.

Salak Sunset Café, Jl Paledang 38. Serves a variety of Indonesian and European dishes and has views over the river and valley. Spaghetti costs Rp5000; a hamburger, Rp3200.

Restoran Si Kabayan, Jl Bina Marga I 2. One of the best places to try genuine Sundanese dishes. Tables are arranged under thatched parasols around a small garden and the food is quite exquisite. *Ikan mas* is a speciality and they also do several complete meals if you are a little blinded by the choice.

Selabintana and Sukabumi

SELABINTANA, a quiet hill resort sitting near to the foot of Gunung Gede, is dominated less by the volcanoes that surround it than by two-star *Hotel Selabintana*. It's a quiet, peaceful place, with some good walking, and is also an alternative gateway to the Gede Pangrano national park, with a path leading from nearby to the summits of the two mountains. The road uphill to the *Selabintana* is lined with guest houses, hotels and restaurants, but even so you will probably have trouble finding a place to stay at the weekends. To get here, first take a bus to nearby **SUKABUMI** from Bogor (3hr; Rp3000) or Bandung (3hr 30min; Rp4000). Sukabumi is a large town 8km south of Selabintana, with lots of hotels, banks and places to eat, but it's noisy and busy with none of the charm of its neighbour. Sukabumi is the transit town for those wishing to reach **Pelabuhan Ratu** (see below); otherwise its one claim to fame is that it has had more recorded tremors than any other town in Indonesia, and in 1972 was razed to the ground by a huge quake that killed 2500 people.

To get to Selabintana, catch *angkot* #10 heading up the mountainside from the Yogya department store in Sukabumi. At the six-kilometre marker is a turning off to the left. Occasionally bemos will run down here to the *Pondok Halimua* campsite (3km; Rp300, or Rp5000 for a charter). This riverside field amongst the tea plantations is used at the weekends for guide and scout jamborees, there are no facilities and you are allowed to pitch your tent (free). From the campsite there's a well-trodden path to the main tourist site in the area, the **Ciborum waterfalls**. Here the icy cold water falls 30m or so and you can take an invigorating mandi underneath, although at the weekend you will have a very large audience. From here it is a ten-kilometre walk to the Gede and Pangrango volcanoes – a much harder walk than from the Puncak Pass side.

Accommodation

Most of the **hotels** are along the road from Sukabumi to the *Hotel Selabintana* and the small bemo terminal at its entrance. There are no street numbers so they are listed here in the order they appear, proceeding uphill from the six-kilometre marker. It gets cool here in the evenings, so accommodation places do not have fans or air-con.

Pondok Asri (☎0266/225408). Guests have access to all of the *Hotel Selabintana's* facilities. The *Asri* has large bungalows and clean private rooms. ⑤–⑦.

Wisma Melati, Jl Selabintana Wetar 8 (☎0266/227905). Down the sideroad opposite the small bemo terminal, this is a friendly family-run place among the rice paddies. ④.

Hotel Melinda (☎0266/224444). Architecturally, the *Melinda* most resembles a multi-storey car park, but it has good clean rooms; only the more expensive ones have hot water. ④–⑤.

Hotel Pangrango (☎0266/211532, fax 221520). Most of the rooms are in private cottages; classier rooms have hot water and TV. Other facilities include tennis courts, a swimming pool and a Saturday-night disco. ④–⑥.

Hotel Selabintana (☎0266/221501 fax 223383). If you want to stay here at the weekend then you'll need to book over a month in advance. The hotel is looking a little worn and is in need of refurbishment, but is still the last word in country-club style. Facilities include tennis courts, volleyball, a swimming pool, golf course and conference centre. Both rooms and bungalows have hot water, TV, spring beds and a central video system. ④–⑧.

Sukabumi Indah (☎0266/224818). Boasts a pool and tennis courts; the basic rooms are very good value, with hot water and TV, and are clean, while the cottages are just palatial. ④–⑥.

Eating

All the hotels have their own **restaurants**, offering Indonesian, Chinese and European foods. However, midweek you will probably have to settle for nasi goreng. Around the terminal there are several cheap warung and a couple of rumah makan selling standard Indonesian fare such as mie goreng and nasi ayam.

Café Pondok Mendiri, slightly further downhill after the *Sukabumi Indah*. Serves European food such as hamburgers for Rp7500, as well as a few Chinese and Indonesian dishes.

Rumah Makan Sate Kelinci, 100m down the hill from the Pangrango on the opposite side of the road. As the name suggests, it specializes in sate, but also serves other Indonesian food. There are good views over the surrounding country. Figure on Rp5000 for ten sticks of goat, chicken or beef sate.

Pelabuhan Ratu and around

PELABUHAN RATU, "The Queen's Harbour", is a fishing village on the south coast of the Sukabumi district and has become a thriving weekend retreat. Its bay is filled with colourful fishing platforms and boats, and the nearby coves and stretches of clean, dark sand make this by far the most pleasant quick-fix escape from Jakarta. The queen who gave the harbour its name is the goddess of the South Seas, an unstable female deity who, according to the legend, threw herself into the waves at **Karang Hawu** to the west of here. On April 6 every year, local fishermen sacrifice buffalo and shower flower petals on the surface of the sea to please the goddess and secure themselves a good catch. Feasting, racing in brightly decorated boats and dancing follow the ceremonies. During the week, Pelabuhan Ratu is an idyllic, peaceful, sleepy village that practically siphons stress out of you. At the weekends and on public holidays it's extremely crowded, with rich domestic tourists from all the major cities in West Java – you have to book everything weeks in advance. There's a host of activities to enjoy around Pelabuhan Ratu, with several waterfalls, caves and rivers to explore, watersports and, of course, lots and lots of beaches.

The Town

From November 25 to 27 each year, Pelabuhan Ratu hosts the Indonesian big-game fishing tournament, and one look around the **fish market** to the east of the bus terminal will show you why. Huge black-striped and blue marlin, swordfish, sailfish and tuna are all on display, as well as shark and barracuda. The **tourist information centre** (daily except Fri 9am–4pm) is one of the best in all of West Java. They have a good selection of maps, brochures and pamphlets, and run diving, fishing and white-water rafting tours in the vicinity. **Diving** usually takes place near Karang Hantu and Sorong Parat down the southeastern peninsula, where there's some decent coral and lots of brightly coloured fish, though not any of the more exciting pelagic (open sea) species. A day's diving with two tanks runs to US$75, snorkelling costs US$48 and a PADI open water course US$285. To book, call Moray Diving (☎0268/41686). White-water rafting on the nearby grade III Sungai Citakik is Rp75,000 for a half-day or Rp120,000 for a full day. They give a student discount but all rates go up at the weekends; to book in advance call PT Linten Jeram Nusantara (☎0811/103397; *harsa@rad.net.id*).

Buses from Bandung and Bogor come via Sukabumi; once the trans-south coast highway is completed, traffic will be able to come direct from Carita on the west coast. All of these buses will arrive at the bus terminal just inland from the port, in front of which is the tourist information centre and **warpostel**. The majority of hotels are to the west of town and on the coastal road that runs all the way to Cilangkon.

ACCOMMODATION

The village to the west of Pelabuhan Ratu town is called **Citepus** and is a better place to stay, quieter and with a nicer beach, where practically every house offers rooms for rent. Most are well equipped and cost upwards of Rp30,000, but there are a few really cheap places. There are no road numbers here, so accommodation is listed in the order you'll find it along the coastal road heading west from Pelabauhan Ratu.

Gunung Mulia (☎0268/41129). On the main coastal road above the restaurant of the same name. Has a few rooms with fan and mandi and is a little noisy. ③.

Handayani Guest House, Jl Sirnagalik. Signposted from the main road, this is down a side street opposite the *Kebyar* disco. The *Handayani*'s rooms are rather dark, but all of them have en-suite mandi. ③.

Pondok Dewata, Jl Sirnagalik (☎0268/41022). Perhaps slightly overpriced but has en-suite mandi and fan; breakfast included. ④.

Simpang Pojok, Jl Sirnagalik (☎0268/41468). Very reasonable prices for quiet and clean rooms, the only drawback being that the lights are situated directly above the ceiling fan. ③.

Karang Sari, on the right-hand side of the road up the hill as you head out of Pelabuhan Ratu (☎0268/41078). The basic rooms here are good value, with fan and mandi, while the posher rooms have air-con. ④–⑤.

Buana Ayu (☎0268/41111). Well-appointed rooms by a good restaurant, all of them sporting mandi and fan. ④.

Bayu Amrta (☎0268/41031, fax 41344). All rooms have satellite TV, air-con and a water heater, probably a little surplus to requirements in this sweltering town. ⑤.

Bukit Indah, at the highest elevation of the hotels on the hill west of town (☎0268/41331). The restaurant specializes in Japanese food – *shabu shabu* and *sukiyaki* – and Korean *yaki niku*. Great views over the coast, and clean rooms with fan and en-suite mandi. ④–⑤.

Penginapan Makessa Indah, in Citepus village. Excellent setting amongst the rice paddies. Clean, well-kept rooms with air-con. ④.

Padi Padi, about 2.5km west of Pelabauhan Ratu in Citepus (☎0268/42124, fax 42125). A very well-equipped hotel, with swimming pool, book and film library, tennis courts (pending), games, rafting and fishing. All the beautifully designed rooms have air-con and TV with laser disc. ⑥.

Samudra Beach Hotel, about 5km from Pelabuhan Ratu (☎0268/41200, fax 41203). Boasts gardens with insipid sculptures of whimsical nude females. Superb rates for groups and midweek – rooms have air-con, phone, TV and hot water, and many sports are catered for. ⑥–⑦.

EATING

The **food** is Pelabuhan Ratu is generally first-rate, fresh seafood being the order of the day. In Citepus, the beach is lined with literally hundreds of identical seaview *warung* selling *ikan bakar*, squid and prawns. Most shut midweek, but the larger places such as the *Sederhana*, *Mulia* and *Ikan Bakar* always have a full menu. The restaurants below are listed as they appear heading west from the bus station.

Martini, opposite the tourist information centre. This restaurant, with its stripy awning and glass fronting, has a slightly fast-food feel about it, but sells decent seafood.

Sederhana, opposite the police station. Slightly more rough-and-ready than the majority of its counterparts, but with real quality cooking. The tofu special with shrimps, chicken, veggies and chillies is wonderful.

Gunung Mulia/Varia Sari. These identical places serve good seafood with a few Chinese and Indonesian dishes; you can ask what's fresh in that day. The frog fried in chilli is worth a try, if perhaps a little bony.

Ratu (Queen). The best place in Pelabuhan Ratu town, set apart by its huge fish tank containing a pair of black-tip reef sharks. They do an American breakfast for Rp6000, lobster for Rp17,000, and take a lot of care in the presentation of the food.

Periangan. The standard seafood menu is supplemented with several set menus for two people, usually fish, fried rice and gado-gado for Rp10,000.

Wantilan, the first place on the left as the road starts up the hill at the western end of town. The most expensive place here, with excellent seafood and European dishes. Figure on about Rp30,000 for a meal with fish, salad and a beer.

Around Pelabuhan Ratu

There are quite a number of things to do in the immediate vicinity of Pelabuhan Ratu. Heading west from town, over the first hill that cuts off Pelabuhan Ratu's cove, the next beach and village is **CITEPUS**. It has a long stretch of beach with mild surf and a profusion of cheap seafood restaurants and homestays. Another 3km along the coastal road is the *Samudra* hotel (⑥–⑧), a four-star establishment with every conceivable beach activity catered for. At **KARANG HAWU**, 10km from Pelabuhan Ratu, there's an interesting natural bridge and blowhole cave in the volcanic black rock at the water's edge, as well as a reasonable beach, perhaps a little too crowded with hawkers' stalls to be picturesque. This is the legendary beach where the goddess of the South Seas hurled herself into the waves, and is something of a pilgrimage site; there is a small shrine to her on top of a nearby rock. Angkots from town usually terminate 14km away at **Cisolok Kota**, from where you can catch an ojek to **CIPANAS**, where four geysers spurt sulphurous jets as high as 7m into the sky. The wind-borne spray provides a pleasant hot shower and you can bathe where two hot and cold streams meet. It's a three- to four-kilometre drive to Cipanas, which shouldn't cost more than Rp1000. From Cipanas there's a hot, steep three-kilometre trail up to a **waterfall**.

Also from Cisolok, you can take an ojek an extra 5km to **Cibangban beach**, probably the best along this stretch of coast. At the extreme west end of the long flat strand are some rocky caves, one filled with bats. At the eastern end of the beach, paths lead up over the clifftops to give spectacular panoramas of the coast and secluded coves.

At Rawakalang, 3km to the east of Pelabuhan Ratu, is Goa Lalay, a large smelly **bat cave**. It's not much to see during the day, but at dusk it's the exit point for tens of thousands of bats, off for a feed. They leave en masse in a huge flock and it can be quite a sight.

About 60km to the southeast of town lies **Ujung Genteng** beach, a good surfing spot but better known as the breeding ground for hundreds of giant leatherback, hawksbill and green turtles. You're particularly likely to see them coming ashore to lay their eggs during a full moon in October and November. From Pelabuhan Ratu, take a bus to Ciwaru (2hr; Rp3000) and then a minibus for the hour-long trip to Ujung Genteng.

Ciawi to Cipanas

The main road that heads east from Bogor through the **Puncak Pass** to Bandung goes first through the suburb of **Ciawi** and on through assorted hill resorts to **Cipanas**, where the tourist strip peters out. This road is for the most part thronged with holiday villas, bungalows, expensive restaurants and hotels that are a favourite retreat of rich Jakartans. Occasionally, a genuinely attractive panorama appears between the hoardings and dilapidated motels, most famously from the **mountain road** between Cisuara and Cipanas as it winds its way up through the tea plantations into the Puncak Pass.

Ciawi is not particularly attractive, and the profusion of accommodation is generally fairly empty. **CISUARA**, just before the pass, is slightly better. A favourite side-trip from here is to the **Cilember waterfalls**, seven small falls separated by forest and expanses of rice paddies. To see the first five is a fairly simple tour that can be managed without a guide and takes around five hours, allowing for a brief stop to cool off at some of the falls. If you want to see all seven, you will need a guide and a full day. To get to the first fall, hire an ojek from Cisuara (3km; Rp1500). This waterfall is overvisited, strewn with litter and full of picnicking families, but they get better the further up you go. The *Kopo Hostel* in Cisuara handles tours around here and to destinations in the Cibodas area (see opposite). The hostel is at Jalan Raya Puncak 557 (☎0251/254296; ②), near to the Telkom office, and has dormitory beds as well as a variety of private rooms. To get to Cisuara, either get on a Bandung bus and ask to be let off, or get green bemo #02 from Bogor to Suk Halte and then blue bemo #02 to Cisuara.

Slightly further towards the Puncak Pass from Cisuara is a public **swimming pool**, which is a cheap but often busy place to cool down. East of Cisuara is a turn-off for the **Taman Safari Indonesia**, a wildlife park with species from all around the world. Any transport plying the Bogor–Bandung route can drop you off at the turning, then you will have to flag down an angkot to get to the park. Some of the better **restaurants** in the Cisuara area are the *Ibu Cirebon*, on the right-hand side of the road about 2km towards the pass from the *Kopo Hostel*, which serves Sundanese and Indonesian food, and the *Frog Leg Jatiwangi* restaurant, worth a stop for its frog dishes and excellent *ikan mas*. Two novelty rumah makan a lot further towards the pass can be found next to the conspicuous *KFC*. The *Pinisi Rumah Makan* is a huge galleon in the style of a Makassar schooner, stuck in a pond and serving limited and pricey Indonesian food; they also have a tiny (pathetic) amusement park and at weekends there's a nightclub in the "hold". Across the road, the *Aero Rumah Makan* is utterly unmissable, mainly due to the entire, genuine, rapidly rusting DC6 suspended on tree trunks above the restaurant. Unfortunately it's now too dangerous to eat in the plane, but it still makes for an interesting setting for a meal – if you're willing to risk the fuselage crashing down through the roof halfway through your fried chicken, that is.

Almost at the top of the pass, the *Rindu Alam* restaurant has some of the best views money can buy. It's a perfect place to sit with a cup of tea that could have been picked a stone's throw away, looking over the endless undulating carpet formed by the meeting crowns of the tea bushes. From here, you can hike downhill 1km or so to the massive **Gunung Mas tea plantation**, which allows visitors to tour some of the site, and you may even get to try some of their tea.

On the Bandung side of the pass, **CIPANAS** is the first stop, a rather grotty town whose natural hot water is piped into baths in some of its hotels. It's still quite popular with domestic tourists and has a little nightlife, but is pretty sleazy, with none of the natural beauty of nearby Cibodas. If you're wondering why all the town's names here are prefixed with "*Ci*", it means "water", and refers to the area's abundant supplies of natural volcanic hot water, or *cipanas*.

Cibodas

Just before Jalan Raya Puncak enters Cipanas (coming from Bogor), a road heads south, uphill to the botanical gardens of **Cibodas**. The road is one huge nursery, lined with flowers, bonsai trees and shrubs, all for sale. The gardens are absolutely beautiful, filled with exotic plants and surrounded by the majestic, soaring mountains and thick forests of the **Gede Pangrango national park**.

There is a row of Padang **restaurants** at the turn-off up to Cibodas, all selling good cheap chicken and vegetable curries with rice. In Cibodas itself there is a profusion of snack food stalls but very little in the way of warung. The only one of note is *Rizkys*, which is on the left-hand side about 60m before the park gates. They are renowned for making a terrific fresh sambal to go with their basic rice dishes. The **Cibodas Golf Course**, 300m up the path to the right as the road splits, sells expensive Indonesian food and drinks. The course itself is beautifully manicured and green fees cost Rp40,000–150,000, the weekends being significantly more expensive.

Accommodation

Jalan Raya Cibodas, the side road from the main road, Jalan Raya Puncak, rises about 2km up to the main gates of the Cibodas park and is where most of the **accommodation** is to be found: the usual problems with weekend overcrowding apply.

Cibodas Guest House and Valleyview Restaurant, Jl Raya Cibodas 13–15a (☎0255/512051). A quality Balinese-style hotel with views of the surrounding valley and a swimming pool under construction. All rooms have TV and en-suite mandi. ⑤–⑦.

Freddy's Homestay, on the right-hand side of Jl Raya Cibodas as you head towards the main gate (☎0255/515473). Provides information about the park and has reasonably appointed rooms with shared mandi. ③.

Pondok 145, Jl Raya Cibodas 145 (☎0255/511512). A friendly place with very basic and inexpensive rooms. Has a basic rumah makan next door that provides breakfast for all the guests. ④.

Pondok Pemuda Cibodas, directly after the first gate into the gardens, the road splits right to this youth hostel (no phone). Dormitories here are best avoided – prison-camp-like rows of mattresses and with a booming rodent population. Private rooms are better, but may also suffer from the rat problem. ②–③.

Pondok Wisata Rulmsran, signposted to the left just before *Pondok 145* (no phone). Bungalows sleeping up to six people cost Rp175,000 and have fantastic views of the cultivated valley. ⑥.

The park

Established in 1889, **Cibodas** is one of the oldest tropical forest reserves in the world and is twinned with the Botanical Gardens of Bogor, which also owes its existence to Sir Stamford Raffles. **The Gede Pangrango park**, backing onto the gardens, was only declared a conservation area in 1980, and covers some 125 square kilometres. It is particularly well-known for its **primate population**: the Javan gibbon, ebony-leaf and rare Javan leaf-monkeys and the common long-tailed macaque all breed here. The Javan gibbon is the rarest gibbon in the world, with only around 100 animals here in the park and fewer than 1000 in total. Also rare, but known to still inhabit the park, are the blue leopard, leopard wild cat and even some wild dogs. A **permit** (Rp1000) is required for everyone entering the park, and can be obtained at the Cibodas gate (daylight hours only; Rp1000). Information on walks can be obtained from the excellent information centre near the gate. They show films on environmental work within the park, and on its flora and fauna.

Two **volcanoes** dominate the park: Gede is the more easterly of the two peaks and stands 2958m above sea level. Its first recorded eruption was in 1747, but the biggest was in the 1840s – though it has now been silent since a small event in 1957, many experts think it is due for a big blast. Pangrango is the taller and older peak that grew on top of the colossal Mandalawangi crater, standing at 3019m and considered to be long extinct. The two peaks are connected by an extended ridge running at around 2400m above sea level. It's possible to walk (2hr) across this saddle between the two summits, along a path tangled with lichen-covered branches.

It's a three-kilometre walk from the main gate up to the Cibeureum, Cidendeng and Cikundul **waterfalls**, which should take around an hour. Cibeureum is the largest, falling for an impressive 53m. There are several shelters and the (occasionally) aptly named **Telaga Biru** – Blue Lake – on the way. Sometimes the water is a wonderfully pure deep blue, and at other times soluble volcanic nitrates in the water encourage algae to grow, forming a green slime across the surface. The lower submontane zone is dominated by large oaks, rattans, chestnuts and laurels, with many of the impressive buttressed trees and lianas typical of lowerland rainforest.

After the waterfalls, 5km from Cibodas, is a **hot-water stream** where temperatures can reach 75°C but are lower after rainfall. From here it's a long hard slog to the **summit of Gede**: in total it's a ten-kilometre (5hr) walk from Cibodas. It's essential to be very well prepared for any walk to the summits: you should bring lots of water, food, warm clothes and strong walking boots. The summit of Gede offers spectacular views, particularly if you camp nearby the night before and can get here before the clouds roll in, but be warned that temperatures up here are about 9°C lower than in the village, and at night can fall close to 0°C. Near the top of Gede is an amazing **alpine meadow** named Suryakancana, presumably cleared long ago as a site for hunting, strewn with edelweiss flowers. It's possible to follow trails over the mountainside to Selabintana in Sukabumi province, a nine-kilometre (5hr) walk. Pangrango is more forested at the summit and views are limited.

The **birdlife** in the park attracts ornithologists from all over the world, with several species of eagle and owl as well as a multitude of colourful racket-tails, drongos and scarlet minivets.

Bandung and around

Nestling in a deep bowl 190km southeast of Bandung and protected by a fortress of sullen volcanoes, **BANDUNG** is the third largest city in Indonesia and the capital of West Java, its population exceeding 2.5 million. High above sea level, Bandung has one of the most **pleasant climates** in the country, enjoying cooler days and slightly fewer rainstorms than Bogor to the west. However, the city's few interesting **Art Deco** buildings are now lost in an ocean of smog-blackened plaster, crumbling pavements and chugging bemos, and the old alun-alun that was a tree-lined, refined social focus in colonial days is hemmed in by gaudy shopping centres and cinemas. It's a reasonably lively city, with a lot of restaurants, shops, bars and regular cultural performances, as well as a few good nightclubs.

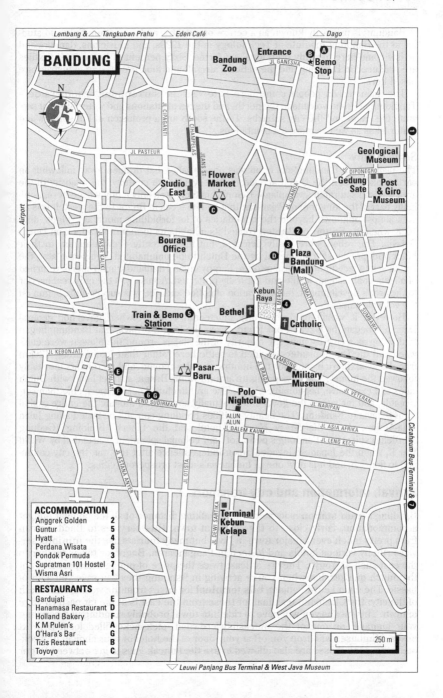

Lembang & △ *Tangkuban Prahu* △ *Eden Café* △ *Dago*

BANDUNG

N

Bandung Zoo

Entrance
Ⓑ ★ Ⓐ **Bemo Stop**

JL GANESHA

△ Airport

JL CIPAGANTI

JL PASTEUR

JEANS ST

JL CHAMPELAS

Studio East

Flower Market ⚖

Ⓒ

Bouraq Office

Geological Museum

DIPONEGORO

Gedung Sate

Post & Giro Museum

JL JUANDA

❷

❸

Ⓓ **Plaza Bandung (Mall)**

JL MARTADINATA

JL SUMATRA

JL SUMATRA

Kebun Raya

❹

Train & Bemo Station ❺

Bethel †

† **Catholic**

JL MERDEKA

JL KEBONJATI

JL GARDUJATI

Ⓔ

Ⓕ

❻ Ⓖ

JL JEND SUDIRMAN

⚖ **Pasar Baru**

JL BRAGA

JL LEMBONG

Military Museum

JL VETERAN

Polo Nightclub

ALUN ALUN

JL DALEM KAUM

JL NARIPAN

JL ASIA AFRIKA

JL LENG KECIL

JL DTISU

JL ASTANA ANYAR

JL DEWI SARTIKA

Terminal Kebun Kelapa

❶ ▷

▷ Cicaheum Bus Terminal & ❶

ACCOMMODATION

Anggrek Golden	2
Guntur	5
Hyatt	4
Perdana Wisata	6
Pondok Permuda	3
Supratman 101 Hostel	7
Wisma Asri	1

RESTAURANTS

Gardujati	E
Hanamasa Restaurant	D
Holland Bakery	F
K M Pulen's	A
O'Hara's Bar	G
Tizis Restaurant	B
Toyoyo	C

0 ———— 250 m

▽ *Leuwi Panjang Bus Terminal & West Java Museum*

Bandung is primarily known as a centre of industry and education: Sukarno studied at the Bandung Institute of Technology in the 1920s, and musicians, dancers and artists come here to study traditional art forms. Sixty percent of Indonesia's textiles are produced in Bandung and the nation's aircraft and food-processing industries are based here.

The main reason people come here is to visit the **surrounding countryside** – Tangkbuhan Prahu volcano to the north, and the tea plantations and waterfalls that separate the crater and the city suburbs. To the south are a profusion of hot springs and crater lakes as well as more tea plantations.

Some history

The plain which Bandung sits upon was once a lake, that drained away following an earthquake. When the Dutch arrived in the seventeenth century, the majority of the area was still saturated swampland. Before this there was only a tiny village here, nominally part of the kingdom of Pajararan that had its focus in Bogor to the west. It was an area almost unknown beyond the boundaries of its forbidding mountain ridges, until 1628, when the **Sultan of Banten** roused its inhabitants to mount an attack on Dutch Batavia. The rebels were easily defeated, but inadvertently drew attention to their homeland, previously considered by the Dutch to be uninhabited. Ten years later, the Dutch sent a fact-finding mission to the Parahyangan Highlands, and reports returned of a lush, cool plateau, fertile and naturally protected. Access was the only real barrier to the area's development, but cultivation of coffee and rice was successfully begun on the volcanic slopes.

However, it wasn't until the early nineteenth century, when governor general Daendels began the **Great Post Road** across the length of Java, that Bandung began to develop as a city. By now, the majority of the slopes around the plateau were cultivated and the Dutch planters decided to settle here rather than "commuting" 190km from Batavia; the rich came for the hunting and the climate, and merchants inevitably followed the money. The city sprang up around **Jalan Braga**, a street lined with Dutch cafés and expensive, fashionable shops. The architecture became more chic than serviceable, and for a time the government actually considered moving the entire capital from Batavia to Bandung. The beauty of 1920s Bandung can still be tasted along Jalan Asia-Afrika, where the *Savoy Homann* hotel and the Liberty Building (Gedung Merdeka) still stand. Bandung's period of hazy colonial splendour was ended by World War II, when the Japanese invaded; upon Independence after the war, the city continued to flourish, and it is now one of Indonesia's most prosperous cities.

Arrival, information and city transport

Bandung's **train station** is located within walking distance of all the popular budget accommodation, fairly close to the centre of town. **Bus** services to Bandung run from pretty much every major town in Java, but many tourists use the **minibus** services run by various hotels and losmen in Pangandaran, Bogor, or towns further to the east such as Yogya. They're at least twice the price of public transport and not that much quicker, but when you're arriving in Bandung they can save you a lot of hassle. The main Leuwi Panjang **bus terminal** for buses from the west is 5km south of the city; the Cicaheum terminal for those from the east is at the far eastern edge of town. This means you will have to ride into town, probably standing and carrying your luggage, on one of the unfeasibly crowded, pickpocket-filled local DAMRI buses. Minibuses will drop you off at your door of the hotel of your choice. At weekends, these minibuses are also allowed to use the Puncak Pass to get between Bogor

BANDUNG CENTRE

ACCOMMODATION			RESTAURANTS			
Hotel Astia Graha	10		Ahong	D	London Bakery	J
By Moritz	6		Amsterdam Café	G	Mandarin	C
Hotel Citra	5		Bakmi Ayam	R	Myukebra	E
FBI	4		Braga Permai	H	North Sea Café	G
Le Yossie	3		Canary Bakery	K	Queen	Q
Hotel Panghegar	2		Dunia Baru	M	Sumber Hidangan Bakery	I
Preanger Aerowisata	8		Fung Ling	N	Sindang Raret	L
Losmen Sakardana	1		Happy Seafood	B	Sari Sari	O
Savoy Homann	9		Hoo Reng	A	Sari Sunda	P
Hotel Trio	7		Kantin Jepang 88	F		

0 — 200 m

N

and Bandung, while buses are diverted via Sukabumi to avoid the traffic. The **airport** is 5km to the northwest of town, and plenty of taxis wait outside the terminal to ferry passengers into town.

If you're planning a tour around Bandung, it's best to start at the alun-alun. The helpful **tourist information** office is here (Mon–Sat 9am–5pm; ☎022/4206644), where you can pick up an assortment of maps and brochures; the staff are all excellent English speakers and can give you a rundown on imminent cultural performances and other events. They also keep copies of the free magazine, *Bandung Kini*, published monthly by the Indonesian Tourist Board. While you should definitely not believe all the hype, it has good practical information on restaurants, clubs and bars, and offers a bonanza of adverts for all of the class hotels in Bandung. The square itself is surrounded by shopping centres, several cinemas, banks and towering tinted-glass high-rises.

Bandung has a comprehensive but esoteric **public transport system**. White and blue DAMRI buses are supercheap, at Rp250 a journey, and ply routes between the bus terminals through the centre of town. Red angkots also run a useful circular route, around and past the train station and square, to the Kebun Kelapa bus terminal, which services Cicaheum bus terminal, Dago and Ledeng. Other angkots are usually named, but rarely with anything related to a destination you might need; it's best to ask a local.

Accommodation

Coming into town from the airport or bus terminals, it's usually best to get dropped off at the train station. The cheap **hostels** are all a stone's throw away, as are a few good mid-range places. If it's quality you're after, then head for the *Savoy Homann* or *Preanger Aerowista*, two of the most **elegant hotels** in the whole of Indonesia.

Anggrek Golden Hotel, Jl Martadinata 15 (☎022/4205537). All rooms have air-con, phone and hot water; the prices are quite reasonable for the immaculate rooms. ⑥.

Wisma Asri, Jl Merak 5. Near to the Post and Giro Museum, this is a charming, quiet place with comfortable, clean rooms. The large rooms with shared mandi are a little overpriced, but those with air-con, TV, fridge and hot water are very reasonable. ④–⑤.

Hotel Astia Graha, Jl Dalam Kaum 130 (☎022/435202). Although very central, this is a quiet place with a TV in every room and Indonesian breakfast included in the price. ④–⑤.

By Moritz, Jl Kebonjati/Luxor Permai 35 (☎022/4205788, fax 4207495). A popular travellers' hangout, with dormitory beds from Rp8500 a night, as well as singles and doubles with the choice of en-suite or shared mandi. Serves one of the best breakfasts around. ②.

Hotel Citra, Jl Gadujati 93 (☎022/6005061). Close to the train station, and one of the best bargains in Bandung. Sparkling new rooms with mandi, TV, fan and air-con, although no breakfast. ③.

Hotel Diana, Jl Cih 227 (no phopnes). Right at the top end of Jeans Street, the *Diana* suffers from a lack of natural light, but has reasonably clean rooms with en-suite mandi and air-con. ④.

FBI, Jl Kebonjati 81 (☎022/436053). Currently the best of Bandung's hostels, its dormitories (Rp8500) are spotless, beds comfortable and, best of all, a hot-water shower has been installed in the shared bathroom. ②.

Hotel Guntur, Jl Otto Iskandardinata 20 (☎022/4203763). An ageing hotel with pleasant, well-kept gardens. Double rooms have hot water and en-suite mandi as standard. ④.

Hyatt, Jl Sumatra 51 (☎022/4211234, fax 4204090). Probably the flashiest five-star hotel in Bandung. Facilities include a health and fitness centre, Cantonese restaurant, gardens and a pub. ⑧–⑨.

Le Yossie, Jl Kebonjati 53 (☎022/4204543). The downstairs café is popular for breakfast, but the hostel itself is not quite as well kept as some of the others here. ②.

Hotel Panghegar, Jl Merdeka 2 (☎022/432286, fax 431583). Well-known for its rooftop revolving restaurant, the *Panghegar* has all you would expect from a three-star hotel, with air-con, hot water, swimming pool and health club; it also stages classical dance on Wednesday and Saturday evenings. ⑧–⑨.

Pondok Permuda, Jl Merdeka 64 (☎022/4203155). Feels a bit like military barracks, but the prices reflect this. It's also much vaunted for its public music studios where you can pay by the hour to record a masterpiece. ②.

Preanger Aerowista, Jl Asia-Afrika 181 (☎022/431631, fax 430034). It hasn't quite got the charm of the *Savoy*, but is now more luxurious: the top rooms cost US$2000 a night, and come complete with your own butler (see opposite). The foyer shops sell Western newspapers and books. ⑧–⑨.

Losmen Sakardana, Jl Kebonjati 50/7b (☎022/439897). Rooms do not have a fan or breakfast included, but are very cheap; some travellers stay away because of the mournful-looking ebony leaf-monkey kept in a tiny cage by the foyer. ②.

Hotel Sartika, Jl Sumatera 52–54 (☎022/4203009). Lofty internal architecture makes this place look much like a modern shopping centre, but the rooms are much more appealing – pool, bar, coffee shop, restaurant and function rooms are all available. ⑧–⑨.

Savoy Homann, Jl Asia-Afrika 112 (☎022/432244, fax 436187). If you want colonial flavour then this is the place (see opposite). Sizable rooms, some with views of the courtyard gardens. The excellent restaurant offers a full *rijsttaffel* for a minimum of six people (Rp20,000). ⑨.

Supratman 102 Youth Hostel, Jl Supratman 102 (☎022/473204). Cheap and cheerful youth hostel that's a good place to hook up with Indonesian travellers. Dorm rooms are adequate. ②.

Hotel Trio, Jl Gardujati 55 (☎022/615755). Rooms range from basic ones with fan and en-suite mandi through to those with hot water and air-con. The restaurant serves European and Japanese food, and every Wednesday they have a draw for a lucky couple to stay free. ④–⑤.

The City

Heading east down Jalan Asia-Afrika, along the northern edge of the alun-alun, you come to the **Gedung Merdeka building** on the opposite side of the road from the square. It was built in 1895 as a union building for Dutch associations, but achieved a degree of fame in 1955 as the site of the first Asia-Afrika Conference, where delegates from 29 countries met to discuss issues of concern to the two continents. Today the building is known as the Asia-Afrika or Liberty building, and has a small **museum** inside commemorating the conference. The auditorium is arranged as it was then, and is decorated with documents and photographs of the delegates.

Another building of interest on Asia-Afrika is the **Savoy Homann** hotel (see opposite). The first hotel on this site was a rickety bamboo affair raised on stilts, opened in 1871 by the Homann family just before the first rail link from Batavia. The present Art Deco structure with its curved facade was not opened until 1939, just in time for the invading Japanese to take it over as a hospital and residence for their officers. During the Asia-Afrika conference, such dignitaries as Nasser, Sukarno and Ho Chi Minh all stayed here, and it's said that Sukarno employed call girls to garner information from prostrate diplomats. Another historic hotel on Jalan Asia-Afrika is the **Preanger Aerowista** (see opposite). Originally erected in 1889 and completely redesigned in 1928, the hotel continues to rival the *Savoy Homann* for elegant luxury. The facelift of the *Preanger* was headed by an architect named Wolf-Schoemaker, but it's thought that Sukarno himself worked on the project as a junior architect. The hotel is now under the management of Garuda Aerowista and has a five-star ranking. Slightly west of here is the beginning of **Jalan Braga**, the chic shopping boulevard of 1920s Bandung. There's still one **bakery** here that's tried to hang on to its history, and a few of the facades maintain their stylish designs above the Japanese fast-food and camera shops. The side streets that run off Jalan Braga were notorious for their raucous bars and brothels – at night a lot of the seediness remains without the liveliness. However, during the day it's an essential trip for the many quality bakeries fighting for your custom, with extravagant neon-decorated cakes, and sweet-looking but curry-filled pastries to choke the unwary.

Jalan Braga is bisected at its northernmost point by the train tracks, and a little further north is Bandung's biggest park, **Kebun Raya**, with the city hall and two large churches around it. Just east of here – off Jalan Sumatera – is the bizarre Taman Lalu Lintas, the "**Traffic Park**". Designed to educate kids in the way of the highway, it has a system of miniature cars, roads and street signs to introduce youngsters to road rage. A twenty-minute walk to the northeast of here, heading along streets with a few period buildings, is the **Gedung Sate** building at Jalan Diponegoro 22, known as the Sate Building because the regular globules on its gold-leaf spire resemble meat on a skewer. Built in the 1920s by a Dutch architect with Thai influences, it's one of the most impressive buildings in Bandung. Once the governor's office, it now houses local government offices. Next door to The Gedung Sate building is the **Post and Giro Museum** (Mon–Sat 9am–2pm; free), with stamps from around the world and assorted postal paraphernalia.

The excellent **Geographical Museum** (Mon–Thurs 9am–2pm, Fri 9–11am, Sat 9–1pm; free) is near to the Gedung Sate at Jalan Diponegoro 57. Inside are mountains of fossils, rock and mineral samples, as well as several full dinosaur skeletons, a four-metre mammoth skeleton and a replica of the skull of the famous Java man. It's a huge building, which also houses Indonesia's geological survey offices. At Jalan Lembong 38 is the **Military Museum** or Museum Wangsit Siliwangi (Mon–Fri 8am–2pm; free), which contains various weapons and artefacts from World War II. Even today, the Siliwangi regiment, the Green Berets of Indonesia, are based in Bandung, and this museum is also a celebration of their achievements. There is also the **Museum of**

West Java Province or Museum Negeri Jawa Barat (Tues–Sun 9am–2pm; free) south-east of the Kebon Kelapa terminal at Jalan Otto Iskandardinata 638. This contains a collection of mock-ups, reconstructing West Java's cultural history, including gamelan and angklung, as well as reconstructions of the *batu tulis* (inscribed stone) of Bogor.

Jeans Street

One of the foremost attractions of modern Bandung, Jalan Cihampelas, known to Westerners as **Jeans Street**, situated 1km to the north of the centre of town, is a kitsch kaleidoscope that demands to be seen. For a stretch of a couple of hundred metres, the street is flanked by shopping centres, fast-food palaces and stacks of shops selling cheap T-shirts, bags, shoes and jeans. To attract the floating punter, shopfronts are adorned with colossal plaster giants straddling spaceships and fluffy stucco clouds – a wide-eyed five-metre Rambo with chipped curls and fading headband glowers down onto cavorting aliens in Makkasar schooners. The full quotient of superheroes in glorious mortar soar above signs for supercheap Levis (complete with instantly detaching buttons), the whole show played to a soundtrack of the worst bubblegum pop. The jeans that gave the street its name are no longer a bargain, but there are some excellent cheap T-shirts, bags and trainers to be had, and no shortage of choice.

Eating

Bandung offers a varied range of cuisine, with Japanese, Sundanese and Chinese food, plus European-style bakeries and fast food. Most of the huge shopping centres have one of the multinational grease merchants represented, and some have excellent **food courts** as well. The Plaza Bandung is the city's best; they have *McDonald's, Churches Texas Fried Chicken, CFC* and *Dunkin' Donuts*. On the top floor is the Emerald Plaza, which serves a mixture of Indonesian, Japanese and Western fast food such as *teppanyaki, nasi rames, ayam bakar,* sandwiches and burgers, as well as a bewilderment of brightly coloured drinks. Yogya, near the square, is Bandung's top department store and has a top-floor food court. Here there's an *A&W* with Sundanese fast food, steaks, sandwiches and *abra kebabra,* and it costs Rp5000 for palatable lamb, chicken or beef kebabs.

Chinese

Ahong, Jl Kebon Kawang. Kangkung and *sapi* hotplate is popular here (Rp9500). The *Ahong* serves similar food to its neighbours the *Mandarin* and *Hoo Reng,* but at cheaper prices.

Dunia Baru, Jl Gardujati 39. Has a long menu including chicken in oyster sauce for Rp12,000 and pork hotplate for Rp11,500.

Fung Ling, Jl Gardujati 9. One of the best places in Bandung, specializing in dim sum. Takes all major credit cards and has a genuinely classy feel, with prices to match.

Gardujati, Jl Gardujati 52. Serves Mandarin food but specializes in frog and hotplate dishes, most of which cost Rp6000–12,000.

Hong Kong, Jl Sudirman 153. One of the most expensive Chinese restaurants in town but with excellent service and an extensive menu. Around Rp25,000 for a full meal.

Hoo Reng, Jl Kebun Kawang 64. The house speciality is *ayam kulayoak,* chicken fried in a kind of sweet-and-sour sauce at Rp11,000 – *ayam ca jamur* with corn is the same price and also delicious.

Mandarin, Jl Kebun Kawang. A little overpriced but popular for its Chinese-style seafood; figure on around Rp20,000 a head. Beer is cheap at Rp4000 for a large bottle.

Queen, Jl Dalam Kaum 79. Superb Cantonese food and an extremely popular place. The set menu is a great deal: for Rp15,000 you get crab and corn soup, sweet-and-sour pork, chicken soy, shrimps in a nut sauce, veggies, rice and fruit.

Indonesian

There are **Indonesian warung** all over Bandung; Jalan Gardujati manages to combine some of the most enticing and nauseating odours in Asia. Side streets near the square serve some of the best warung food, with excellent seafood, soto and sate, while the nearby Ramayana department store's ground-floor food hall serves the same food in more sanitized surroundings. Jalan Dalam Kaum has some good **Indonesian restaurants**: *Bu Jin* at no. 124 and *Sari Bundo* at no. 75 are two of the better Padang restaurants in town. *Aneka Sari* at no. 60 specializes in *kangkung* at Rp8500.

Bakmi Ayam, Jl Cibadak 52. Serves Indonesian staples such as nasi campur and ayam goreng at reasonable prices.

Happy Seafood, Jl Kebon Kawang 26. Dirt-cheap seafood: simply sift through the polystyrene buckets until you find the fish you fancy and they'll barbecue it in front of you.

Toyoyo, Jl Pasir Kartiki 32. An Indonesian barbecue with excellent sate and baked chicken, mostly at under Rp5000 a head.

Japanese

Eden Café, Jl Setiabudi 29a. Best known for its Korean *yaki niku*, but also serves tempura and noodles.

Hanamasa, Jl Merdeka 39–41. A selection of Japanese *izakaya* favourites such as *ebi furae* and *yaki tori* – a little on the expensive side.

Hoka Hoka Bento, Jl Setiabudi/Jl Merdeka. Opposite the Bandung Plaza, this fast-food, lunch-box chain does surprisingly good *bento*.

Kantin Jepang 88, Jl Braga 88. The location is a bit of a nightmare in Formica, but the food is fine: *ebi tempura* costs Rp5000; beef *yakiniku*, Rp4500; and *teriyaki*, Rp4500.

Sundanese

Ayam Goreng Indrawati, Jl Lengkong Besar 3c. Not a great deal of choice, but very cheap and tasty. You could buy virtually the entire menu for under Rp5000.

Dago Tea House, at the very end of Jl Juanda. A landmark that is the welcome finishing point for the Lembang to Bandung walk (see p.138). The fine views of Bandung valley and the outside tables are the primary attraction; diners sit on the floor on rattan mats looking down on the city. They also do good, reasonably priced Sundanese food, plus Western dishes such as steaks and omelettes.

Penineungan Indah, Jl Tubagus Ismail Raya 60. One of the best Sundanese restaurants there is; each table is in a private room around gardens and ponds from which your dinner is fished. The *ikan mas* steamed in banana leaves is a speciality.

RM Pulen 3, Jl Juanda 260. Up towards the *Dago Tea House* and the Bandung Zoo. Serves inexpensive, typical Sundanese food in a setting crammed with bamboo. Chicken *cizzadin herbs* is a delicious piece of chicken with a tasty coating and costs Rp1500; *ikan masis* Rp15,000.

Sari Sunda, Jl Sukarno Hatta 479/Jl Jenderal Sudirman 103–107. Two separate places run by the same management, both serving superb Sundanese food in pleasant surroundings. The croquette potatoes and tofu baked with chilli in banana leaves is excellent.

Sindang Raret, Jl Naripan 9. More often a destination for its Saturday-evening wayang golek performances than for its slightly overpriced food and gaudy interior. Gurame fish is a speciality at Rp12,000, and a large *bintang* costs Rp6000.

Thai

Coka Suki, Jalan Juanda 122. Pricey but tasty delicacies with top spring rolls and flaming coconut curries.

Royal Siam, Jalan Braga 121. A new place serving expensive but delectable Thai food: chilli prawn soup and Padang chicken are particular favourites.

Western

Western food is available from food courts in the big shopping centres and department stores, as well as in most of the hotel restaurants.

Amsterdam Café, Jl Braga. Popular with expats, this place serves outrageously small beers at large-bottle prices along with steaks and burgers.

Myukebra, Jl Kebon Kawang 9. At the bemo terminal on the north side of the train station. Has live music on Saturday nights. Most of the meals are based on package deals, such as steak, French fries and a drink for Rp9500.

North Sea Café, Jl Braga. The *North Sea* serves expensive European fare such as Wiener schnitzel and steak (Rp30,000). A long-established place, it's a little sleazy.

Tizis, Jl Kidang Pananjung 3 off Jl Juanda, just north of the large bemo stop. A real find and an expat haven, *Tizis* home-cook possibly the best bread, sausages and pastries in Java. There's a sit-down restaurant where you can have steaks, pizzas and ice cream, and the glazed apple pie (Rp2800) is sensational.

Bakeries

Due to the European influence in Bandung, the town is particularly rich in **bakeries**, with Jalan Braga having a particularly high concentration. See *Tizis* above for some of the best bread and cakes in Java.

Braga Permai, Jl Braga 58. Flashy and expensive bakery out the back of the even flashier restaurant (complete with grand piano). They have thirty kinds of ice cream and very elaborate cakes.

Canary Bakery, corner of Jl Braga and Jl Naripan. Serves paltry hamburgers and hot dogs alongside gaudy wedding cakes; prices are quite reasonable.

Holland Bakery, Jl Gardujati. There are a number of these bakeries around Bandung, serving Indonesian-style cakes.

London Bakery, Jl Braga. Specializing in a range of coffees and teas, this is a modern European-type place with newspapers and books in English.

Sari Sari, Jl Sudirman 90. An excellent delicatessen and bakery serving takeaway curries, soups and vegetarian fare as well as imported crisps and snacks.

Sumber Hidangan, Jl Braga. Apparently the same as it was in the 1930s, it certainly hasn't been painted since. Serves pastries, ice cream and Western snacks among yellowing black-and-white photos of the café's heyday.

Nightlife

For such a large city, Saturday nights are surprisingly unpredictable and you can't necessarily count on your bar or nightclub of choice being lively. On weekdays, you're best off heading for the **bars**. Most **clubs** start late on Fridays and Saturdays, with places like *Fame Station*, *Polo* and *Studio East* not really kicking off until midnight.

Caesars Palace, Jl Braga 129. Prepare to be stung at the bar – a small beer retails at Rp25,000. Door staff are fussy but unspecific about their dress code, so don't come looking messy – this aspires to being the most upmarket place in Bandung. 8pm–3am; Rp25,000.

Enhaii, Jl Setiabudi 186. A real student hangout, with pool tables and darts. Live bands have a tendency towards wailing Beatles numbers.

Fame Station, 11th floor, Lipo Building, Jl Gatot Subroto. This place has a generally lively, young crowd and often features live music. Terrific views of the city and Western food. 11am–2am; Rp15,000.

Laga Pub, Jl Junjungan 164. With food and live music every night, this is an expat favourite. A beer costs a reasonable Rp7000 and there's a Rp5000 cover charge.

North Sea Bar, Jl Braga 82. An unashamed pick-up joint for the elder expat male – others may be a little put off by the seedy atmosphere and the hefty prices.

O'Hara's, *Hotel Perdana Wisata*, Jl Jenderal Sudirman 66–68. Looks more like a Boston tavern than an Irish pub, featuring lots of polished dark wood and American pictures everywhere. The live music is generally covers of mainstream pop music. Rp5000.

Polo, 15th floor, BRI building, Jl Asia-Afrika. The expensive nightclub for Bandung's young elite; the music is mainly imported, from house music through to Euro-techno, which makes it the place for serious partying. 10pm–3am; Rp20,000.

Studio East, Jl Cihampelas 129. Draws a very young, mostly student crowd to the packed, sizable dance floors; they play a variety of dance music. You're likely to get completely mobbed by friendly Bandung students. 10pm–2am; Rp10,000.

Cultural performances

Bandung is the capital of Sundanese culture, with a high percentage of West Java's artists choosing to live and study here. Pick up a copy of *Bandung Kini* magazine from the tourist information office to find out about special performances. Sang Angklung Mang Ujo is a workshop where children study **angklung** and will perform for visitors. To get there, take a Cicaheum colt and ask to be let off at Padsuka near the Cicaheum terminal; from there, it's a five-minute walk north up on the right-hand side of the road.

Most regular cultural performances are held at hotels or restaurants. The *Sindang Raret* restaurant at Jalan Naripan 9 has Saturday-evening **wayang golek** performances at 8pm, which can be enjoyed with a traditional Sundanese meal. At Jalan Merdeka 2, the *Panghegar* hotel has Wednesday- and Saturday-evening cultural performances in its restaurant, generally Sundanese dance and classical singing; you don't have to pay for the show but you do have to have a meal. The *Sakadarna* homestay has Saturday-evening shows by Banten's **debus players**, who perform feats of self-mutilation, such as eating glass and setting red-hot coals upon their heads. On Sunday mornings there are often shows at Bandung Zoo in the north of town, usually either the Indonesian martial art **pencak silat**, or **puppet shows**.

In addition, many of the small villages around Bandung have wayang golek performances on Saturday evenings which can go on all night, the puppets often commenting on village gossip in rough, crude dialogue. Not something the tourist information can help you out with, you'll have to find yourself a contact in one of the kampung, and make sure a camera-wielding tourist will be welcome. Probably the most spectacular event to be seen in Bandung area is the local sport of **ram fighting**. To the sound of Sundanese flutes and drums, the rams are set 10m apart and then released. They sprint together, before making a huge rearing lunge till their horns clatter together with a bone-shuddering crack. There's no blood; just flying wool and clouds of dust as the locals wildly speculate on which ram will fade first. These fights begin at 10am every other Sunday near the Ledung terminal on Jalan Setiabudi. It's a 500-metre walk up Jalan Serson Bajuri; ask directions to the *adu domba*.

Shopping

Bandung's biggest **market** is the *pasar baru*, which is between the train station and the square. It's a bit of a fleapit and offers little to tempt tourists to part with their rupiah. The *pasar bunga* is the **flower market**, a much more aesthetically pleasing place just northeast of Jeans Street by the river. Kings **department store** near the square has cloths and sarongs on nearly every floor. The Sarinah department store at the southern end of Jalan Braga is not as extensive as the one in Jakarta, but has a range of souvenirs from all over the archipelago. Jalan Sulawangi features a cooperative called Just For You, an organization that employs handicapped people to make simple **batik and crafts** for tourist souvenirs. Just north of the train station on Jalan Kebon Kawang is the Cupu Manik wayang golek **puppet-making factory**, where you can buy puppets for upwards of Rp30,000. Jalan Cibaduyut in southwest Bandung has a variety of shops selling bags, leather shoes, sandals and T-shirts at reasonable prices.

Listings

Airline offices Garuda has its main offices in the *Hotel Preangher Aerowista* at Jl Asia-Afrika 181. Merpati is also on Jl Asia-Afrika at no. 73, and the Bouraq office can be found at Jl Cihampelas 27 on the way to Jeans Street.

Banks and exchange There are plenty of banks in Bandung, including the BRI on the alun-alun. The two Golden Megacorp moneychangers on JL Lembong opposite the 24hr Telkom building and at Jalan Otista 180, have excellent rates but often long queues.

Bookshops Several places on Jl Braga sell English-language books and newspapers. There is a good bookshop in the foyer of the *Aerowista*.

Hospital There is a 24hr clinic with English-speaking doctors at Jl Cihampelas 161.

Post office The main branch is on Jl Asia-Afrika at the corner of Jl Banceuy (Mon–Sat 8am–9pm).

Telkom For international telephone, telex and fax, the main Telkom office is on Jl Lembong and is open 24hr. There are also several wartels around town.

North of Bandung

The mountainous region to the north of Bandung is the heart of the **Parahyangan Highlands** – the "Home of the Gods" – a highly volcanic area considered by the Sundanese to be the nucleus of their spiritual world. The sights of this area can just about all be done in a day if you get out early and are feeling energetic. Public transport runs right to the summit of **Tangkuban Prahu volcano**, where you can walk around the craters for a few hours and catch a colt to **Ciater** to soak away the aches in the **hot springs** there. Then head back towards Bandung, stopping at **Maribaya**, site of some more hot springs and a set of **waterfalls**. From Maribaya, there's an established walk down through the monkey-filled forest to the **Dago Tea House**, where you can enjoy Sundanese food and – of course – a cup of locally grown tea, while looking down on Bandung city.

Tangkuban Prahu

The most famous and most visited volcano in West Java, 1830-metre **Tangkuban Prahu** lies 29km to the north of Bandung and has an asphalt road running right to its summit. The volcano's name translates as "the upturned boat", a tag whose origin is obvious if you get a day clear enough to see the volcano at a distance from Bandung. To get there from Bandung, take a Subang minibus from the train station (30min; Rp1500) and ask to be put down at the turn-off for the volcano. At the turn-off there's a guard post, where you must pay Rp1250 to visit the volcano. From here you can either charter an ojek or minibus to the summit (10min; Rp5000) or wait until a number of people arrive and share a minibus. Alternatively you could walk up – it's about 4km up the main road, or there's a good detour via the Domas Crater. Simply walk just over 1km up the road from the guard post, then take the footpath to the right by the first car park.

The **volcano** has not had a serious eruption for many years, though in 1969 there were a series of explosions and expulsions of mud, ash and smoke. Today the volcano still spews out vast quantities of sulphurous gases and at least one of its **ten craters** is still considered to be active. The main crater is called Kawah Ratu (Queen's Crater) and is the one you can see down into from the end of the main road. The car park at the summit is usually filled with vendors come to take advantage of the hundreds of people who come to see the volcano every day. There is also a small **information booth** here, where you can get details about walking around the main crater and down to some of the smaller ones. Kawah Ratu is a huge cauldron of dull greys, with occasional

THE LEGEND OF TANGKUBAN PRAHU

The Sundanese naturally have a **fable** to explain the distinctive shape of **Tangkuban Prahu**. Sunda was once ruled by a king and queen with a beautiful but petulant daughter. One day as she sat weaving she dropped her shuttle and vowed she would marry whoever returned it to her. Unfortunately the family's faithful dog came back with the shuttle in his mouth. When the princess married the dog and they had a son, **Sangkuriang**, the princess decided to keep his father's identity secret from her new offspring. One day the young prince and the dog were out hunting but failed to find a mark. Ashamed to return home empty-handed, Sangkuriang killed the dog and served it up to his mother. When eventually the dog was missed, the prince confessed that he had been supper. The princess was so distraught that she hit Sangkuriang a fierce blow on the head and then disappeared, to wander around the kingdom alone. Some years later she met a man and fell in love with him. On their wedding day, however, she discovered a mark on his head and realized it was the scar that he bore from her own blow and that he could only be her son. Desperate to put off the wedding, she set the condition that before sunrise Sangkuriang would have to build a huge dam across Sungai Citarum and build a boat for the two of them to sail away in, or they could not be married. He laboured through the night with the help of friendly spirits and his mother soon saw that he would accomplish the task. In desperation she called on the gods to save her and they broke the walls of the mighty lake. As the waters rushed away, Sangkuriang's boat was overthrown and he was crushed beneath it. The mother then took her own life. The capsized hull of Sangkuriang's boat is seen in silhouette, should you see Tangkuban Prahu from a distance.

splashes of yellow and black, and sometimes a small coloured crater lake. If you walk around the crater for about 500m, the other craters soon become visible. You can trek right down into these hissing, smelly pits and see pools of bubbling mud and clouds of rotten egg gas. From the summit you can also trek down to **Domas Crater**, which has fine views and, still, a small working sulphur mine. There are lots of guides offering their services to aid people on tours around and into the volcanoes, but they're not really necessary as it's pretty obvious where you should and shouldn't go. Just be sure to take some strong hiking boots and your common sense.

Ciater hot springs

Catch any minibus heading northeast from the gates of Tangkuban Prahu, and 6km further on you will be in **CIATER**, a small village nestling among the tea fields. The hot springs are kept from public use, having been tapped into a set of hot falls, showers and pools by the *Sari Ater Hot Spring Resort* (☎264/470894; ⑧–⑨). They have an extensive range of facilities, with electrotherapy, hydrotherapy, acupuncture, restaurants, tennis courts, horse-riding and, of course, loads of natural hot water. All of their rooms have TV, video, fridge, telephone and most have heaters. For those not staying at the resort, you can use the springs – for a price. It costs Rp2500 to enter the complex and then Rp7000 to use the pools, which is well beyond the pockets of Ciater locals. The pools are, however, some of the best around; you can sit under the steaming waterfalls at night, when the outside air is decidedly chilly – on a good clear night it's a sensational place for stargazing. There are plenty of cheap losmen and a few warung on the main road in Ciater, with prices starting at about Rp15,000.

From Ciater, you can take a minibus further north to the **Ciater tea factory**. The road ascends into the mountains until it seems you're sailing on a sea of tea: everywhere you look the bushes roll into the distance. The factory itself has a tour for visitors, where you can see the tea being processed, taste some of the product and climb their lookout tower for simply awesome views.

Maribaya to Dago

On the return journey from Tangkuban Prahu to Bandung you'll pass through Lembang, a hill town mainly known for its fruit and vegetable market but with a few quality hotels. From Lembang terminal near the market, take a minibus to **MARIBAYA** (4km; Rp500) a resort that at weekends is jam-packed with people. The **waterfalls** near to the entrance gate are so surrounded by landscaped paths that it seems even the falls are man-made. Nearby are the **hot springs**, which have been tapped into a public pool. Further down from the main melee of people and vendors is the largest waterfall, which you have to pay an additional fee to see. In a sublime piece of Asian tourist site planning, a huge iron bridge has been built right across the lip of the falls. From the bridge you can only see the river as the falls are too close and, from below, the metal monstrosity with its chipped red paint completely obscures the view of what is clearly a spectacular waterfall. However, the bridge is the starting point for a wonderful walk down to the **Dago Tea House** (see p.133) on the edge of Bandung. The path winds downhill through a gorge and forests – just before the teahouse are tunnels used by the Japanese in World War II and the **Dago waterfall**, which lies amongst bamboo thickets. The walk is about 6km and will take under two hours, all of it downhill. At the end of your walk is the teahouse, with private tables under their own thatched roofs, the diners kneeling on rush mats and looking out on superb views of Bandung city, which are especially impressive at night. From here there are plenty of minibuses heading back into the centre of town (15min; Rp500).

Garut, Cipanas and around

Surrounded on all sides by volcanic mountains, **GARUT** was the original Javan spa town. Since the 1920s it has been a retreat for those coming to laze in natural hot water and wander in the surrounding countryside to waterfalls, rivers and steaming volcano craters. These days, Garut is not popular, the majority of visitors choosing instead to head right to the foot of Gunung Guntur and **CIPANAS**, a quiet village with guest houses and hotels where you can enjoy the waters without the noise and grime of the large modern town Garut has become. There are many towns in West Java called Cipanas – it means "hot water" – but this is by far the most appealing. Garut is easily accessible by bus from Bandung (2hr; Rp2000) and Tasikmilaya (2hr; Rp2000). From Garut bus station, walk round to the next-door bemo terminal and take the brown bemo #4 to Cipanas (15min; Rp500).

Cipanas is just 6km away from Garut and is a delightful place to stay, the main attraction being the abundant clear, clean, hot water that is piped into tiled baths in all the hotels, losmen and private houses, but Cipanas and its surrounding villages are also a picture-postcard idyll of Javanese rural life. The plentiful rice paddies are punctuated by large, shallow, glassy ponds making perfect reflections of the palm trees and flowering bushes that surround them. Often you can see the remarkable sight of scores of villagers, waist deep in the water, herding tens of thousands of tiny fish into pens made out of moss and pondweed. Other villagers sort the fish into rattan baskets to be sold in town. A permanent, looming background to the affairs of the village are the sulky volcanic peaks of Gunung Guntur, Galunggung, Papandayan and the perfect cone of Cikurai. There are walks to nearby waterfalls and you can climb Gunung Guntur – a hard five-hour trek.

Accommodation and eating

All **accommodation** here is along the road that runs into Cipanas from the main Bandung–Garut road; every place features piped-in hot-water baths. The larger hotels all have **restaurants**, the *Tirta Merta* probably being the most reasonable. Otherwise, there are a few **warung** on the main street and a group of sate stalls around the terminal at the end of Jalan Raya Cipanas, though the food here is seriously basic.

Pondok Asri, Jl Raya Cipanas 184 (☎0262/231209). The rooms here are nothing special, but have the largest baths in town. ③–④.

Cipanas Indah, Jl Raya Cipanas 113 (☎0262/233736). Prices at this plush place double during holidays and weekends. Otherwise the pristine bungalows and rooms are a good bargain, and have all amenities. The restaurant is not bad, with a few European dishes to supplement the Sundanese cooking. ⑥–⑧.

Cipta Bela, Jl Raya Cipanas 111 (☎0262/231494). A very standard place: there are at least ten others around it which are practically identical. All have clean, white-tiled bedrooms and bathrooms whose plaster is in an advanced state of steam decay. ③.

Kurina, Jl Raya Cipanas 131. Quite possibly the best deal in Cipanas, this place has rooms made from rattan and bamboo and is very cheap. ③.

Pondok Melati, Jl Raya Cipanas 133. Pleasant place with rooms made from rattan and nice, deep baths. They claim not to raise their prices at weekends. ③.

Putra Lugina, Jl Raya Cipanas 711 (☎0262/237767). Behind the *Cipta Bela*, a quiet establishment with large rooms and wholesale midweek reductions. ④.

Tirta Merta, the first hotel on the left as you pass through the gateway into Cipanas. Reasonably upmarket rooms; the restaurant's speciality is ginseng coffee with a long list of its restorative qualities to supplement the healing waters. ⑤–⑥.

Tirtagganga Hot Springs, Jl Raya Cipanas 130 (☎0262/231811). The most expensive, and easily the best place, here – Suharto stayed here in the past. Has a large, clean outdoor swimming pool with the novel addition of a poolside bar, where you can order a beer waist deep in steaming water. ⑥–⑧.

Tirta Sari, Jl Raya Cipanas 120. Rooms lack natural light, but the place is cheap and has good views across the ponds towards Gunung Cikurai. ③.

Pondok Wulandari, Jl Raya Cipanas 99 (☎0262/234675). Unusually for this area, all rooms come with fan and TV, and are well kept and a good bargain at the price. ④.

Around Garut

On lily-covered **Situ Cangkuang** is a small island with the only Hindu shrine left in West Java, which possibly dates to the ninth century, older than both Borobudur and Prambanan. It's not particularly big or impressive, but boatmen will take you over to the island on punted bamboo rafts across the flower-tangled waters – an experience which makes the trip worthwhile. Take any bemo or bus heading to Bandung and ask to be let off at Leles; from here it's a fifteen-minute walk to the lake.

The most impressive sight in the area is the active volcano, **Gunung Papandayan**, 25km southwest of Garut town. Catch a minibus to Cisurupan, the turn-off for the volcano road, a small village with a cluster of houses and a few warung. Here hordes of ojek riders wait to ferry tourists the 8km to the summit car park. From the car park, it's a fifteen-minute uphill walk to the centre of the crater, and all around you pools of bubbling mud and enthusiastic steam geysers spew out sulphurous clouds, the vents marked by sparkling yellow deposits, a continual roar and a poisonous stench. Papandayan's biggest eruption was in 1772, but it is still distinctly alive. Trek upwards from the crater for superb views down into the valley and of the surrounding, forested peaks; the path leads upwards to a saddle at the crater rim, between twin summits. From here you can choose to walk upwards to either of the summits, or you can take the path right over the top of the mountain to descend into the valley on the other side. The path heads through beautiful forests full of skinny eucalyptus and fan palms, before suddenly breaking out into an endless unnaturally perfect expanse of tea plantations. Be warned that this is a very isolated area: you will be more than welcome in the villages, but when you need to return to civilization there is only one truck a day, which circles the area for Bandung at 8am. Otherwise it's a five-hour return trek over the mountain and back to Cisurupan.

From Garut, a road winds through tea plantations and pine forests to the **south coast**. **Pameungpeuk** is the main town, and has a couple of losmen. All the way from here to Pelabuhan Ratu is a coastal road with small villages that see very few visitors. The beaches are stunning and usually empty of people, but due to the strong currents you're best advised to stay close to shore when swimming.

KAMPUNG NAGA

About halfway between Garut and Tasikmilaya, lies **KAMPUNG NAGA**, a tiny village in a steep-sided valley. The village was constructed to ancient Sundanese dictates, with bamboo walls and thatched roofs, arranged facing the rising sun in neat rows. Kampung Naga is extremely picturesque, snug amongst the stepped rice paddies and shaded by abundant palm trees, with the river flowing past. There are a few souvenir stalls and a mosque, and though there's not really much to see or do and locals have learnt to pay scant attention to tourists zapping through on whistle-stop photo opportunity tours, they are extremely welcoming to (and curious about) those who take the trouble to stop and have a chat. To get to Naga, take any bus between Garut and Tasikmalaya and ask to get off at Kampung Naga – you will probably have to pay the fare (Rp5000–15,000) for the full journey. It takes about fifteen minutes to walk to the village down steep concrete steps. There is no accommodation here, but a handful of warung line the main road.

Tasikmalaya

Lying 120km southeast of Bandung is the town of **TASIKMALAYA**, famous for its batik cloth and woven rattan goods. There's not a tremendous amount to do in Tasik, but it's a good base if you want to climb **Gunung Galunggung**, which last erupted in the early 1980s. The crater has a large green and bubbling lake, most of the surrounding area is thick with ash and there are occasional expulsions of ash, smoke and even rocks from numerous vents around the area. The best way to reach the summit is to take a minibus to Pasar Indihiang (30 min; Rp700) and then change to another minibus or ojek to get you to Cipanas (45min; Rp2500). From the village it's a two-hour walk to the summit and there's only one trail, so you don't really need a guide. There are some **hot springs** at the beginning of the trail – a good spot to relax after the climb.

The last part of the road into Tasik from Bandung, about 10km before you reach the town, is lined with innumerable stalls, selling rattan, wooden and **bamboo handicrafts**: baskets, carvings, lampshades, floor-mats and furniture, as well as beautiful painted umbrellas.

Practicalities

The **train station** is fairly central, 800m northeast of the square, on the main line from Yogya to Jakarta, while the **bus station** is about 3km southwest of town so you'll need to catch a bemo or becak to get between the two. The *Hotel Yudanegara*, at Jalan Yudanegara 19 (☎0265/324906; ⑤–⑥), is the plushest in town: all its rooms have hot water, TV and air-con. For a more basic option, try the *Tasik* at Jalan Komala Sari 29 (②), a friendly family-run hotel, where the rooms come with en-suite mandi but no fan. Most of the other **accommodation** is on the central Jalan Yudanegara, where the mosque and police station are situated; there are also a lot of luxury hotels out on Jalan Martadinata, the road to Bandung. Jalan Mesjid Agung behind the mosque has a line of excellent, flashy Padang **restaurants**, and the *Top Bakery*, on Jalan Yudanegara opposite the *Wisma Gall*, has pastries and good fried chicken.

The Pangandaran peninsula

Pangandaran is a bulbous peninsula dripping down into the Indian Ocean, its beaches lashed by huge, impressive waves that have rolled unabated from Antarctica. Kilometres of sands back onto massive coconut plantations, and the surrounding countryside offers a dizzying wealth of trips. The **town** itself runs either side of the narrow isthmus that connects Pangandaran with the mainland, and then abruptly halts, most of the base of the bauble-shaped peninsula being taken up by a forested **national park**. The beach to the west is rent by powerful wind and waves, the eastern cove sheltered and quiet, and both are littered with idle, brightly painted blue prahus – sporadically the seafront comes alive, when nearly the whole town comes down to the waterfront to pull in nets full of writhing fish. Far less easy on the eye are the souvenir stalls that border the seafront. Amongst tacky beachwear, shells and coral are countless carcasses and shells from the once-abundant turtle and monitor lizard population of Pangandaran, with some stalls displaying as many as twenty turtles, their shells up to 1m across. Pangandaran has one of the best **fish markets** you'll ever see, surrounded by warung where they'll cook up pretty much anything they can catch.

The beaches

The **beaches** to the west are particularly famed for their **sunsets**, providing memorable images of silhouetted locals, cycling along the seafront with baskets and fruit on their heads, in front of crashing swell with the whole horizon stained scarlet. At dusk, the skies fill with incredible flocks of mammoth fruit bats, which have the wingspan of a young condor. The locals traditionally farm this natural flying-food extravaganza in a resourceful manner; boys stand on the seafront at dusk with kites, whose lines are intermittently strung with fish hooks. The bats catch their wing membrane on these snags and are drawn in like fishes. It's quite a rare sight now, which is not a bad thing for unsuspecting onlookers, as the high-pitched incessant wail of the bats as their wings rip like cling film is truly disturbing. The bat's flesh is said to be an excellent treatment for asthma and has a gamey flavour much like venison.

The national park

At present you can only walk in the **national park** on limited routes with guided tours from one of the many operators around town (see p.143). The park was once used by local people for farming, until 1921 when a wealthy landowner introduced Banteng cattle and Indian deer to the peninsula as a source of fresh meat for nearby farms. Just

---

PANGANDARAN FESTIVALS

Kites remain important in Pangandaran; every July and August, with the arrival of the east winds, there is a **kite-flying festival** held at the beach. Competitors come from all over the world for exhibitions and, more importantly, for kite-fighting. The strings of the kites are treated with glue and ground glass so that they become potent weapons: when a flier's string comes in contact with that of an opponent, they pull and release the kite in a swinging motion to try and sever the other's line. The fun is supplemented with beauty pageants and sports competitions, dancing and art exhibitions, and is pretty unmissable. Another festival is that of the **Sea Queen**, held in August, with decorated prahus putting out to sea and offerings made to the goddess to improve the year's fish crop.

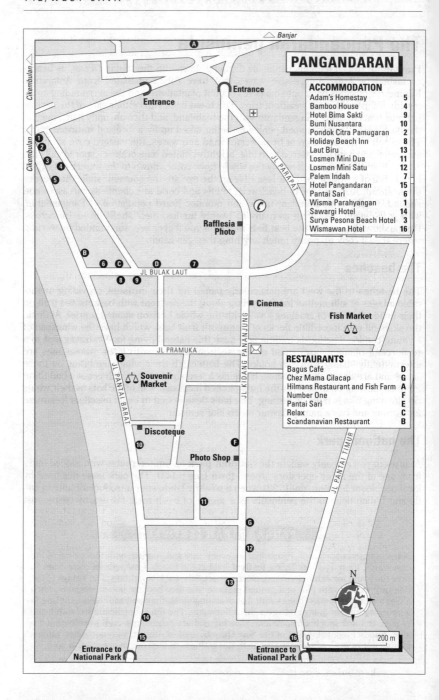

△ *Banjar*

PANGANDARAN

ACCOMMODATION

Adam's Homestay	5
Bamboo House	4
Hotel Bima Sakti	9
Bumi Nusantara	10
Pondok Citra Pamugaran	2
Holiday Beach Inn	8
Laut Biru	13
Losmen Mini Dua	11
Losmen Mini Satu	12
Palem Indah	7
Hotel Pangandaran	15
Pantai Sari	6
Wisma Parahyangan	1
Sawargi Hotel	14
Surya Pesona Beach Hotel	3
Wismawan Hotel	16

RESTAURANTS

Bagus Café	D
Chez Mama Cilacap	G
Hilmans Restaurant and Fish Farm	A
Number One	F
Pantai Sari	E
Relax	C
Scandanavian Restaurant	B

Entrance

Entrance

Entrance

Cikembulan

Cikembulan

JL PARAPAT

Rafflesia ■ Photo

JL BULAK LAUT

■ Cinema

Fish Market ⚖

JL KIDANG PANANJUNG

JL PRAMUKA

✉

JL PANTAI BARAT

⚕ Souvenir Market

■ Discoteque

Photo Shop ■

JL PANTAI TIMUR

N

0   200 m

Entrance to National Park

Entrance to National Park

fifteen years later the area was declared a wildlife reserve, and one reason it remains so is the presence of the **Javanese rafflesia**, a huge reeking flower that reaches the diameter of a car tyre. It's actually a parasite, flowering during the rainy season, and is pollinated not by bees but by a fly. Its relative, the Sumatran rafflesia, is the largest flower in the world and can grow up to 1m in diameter.

About eighty percent of the national park is secondary **rainforest**, with small stands of primary forest and open grasslands. Occupants include Banteng oxen, mouse- and barking deer, armadillos, civets, flying lemurs, several species of primates and horn-bills, and the beaches are good places to spot turtles, coming ashore both to lay their eggs and bask in the sun. You can get to some wonderful beaches and sheltered areas where the **snorkelling** is reasonable. Get your guide to take you to the magnificent limestone caves and the fifty-metre waterfall that tumbles straight into the sea; there's a good pool for swimming at the top. **Surfing** off the park is good to exceptional – there's a reef break on the Western border, though you are not, strictly speaking, sup-posed to be there. The coral the waves break over is razor-sharp, so bring a helmet and plenty of iodine.

Practicalities

Buses into Pangandaran town stop at the terminal just beyond the isthmus on the main-land, and outside the town gates. The nearest train station on the main line is at **Banjar**; regular trains to and from Bandung (4hr) and Yogya (4–5hr) call here. Banjar is two hours away by bus and, depending on whether you get a flash air-con-and-video-num-ber or a standard local one, you pay between Rp2000 and Rp15,000. With the expansion of Pangandaran town, most travellers tend to stay out to the beach enclave of **Cikembulan**, a small village 4km to the west. Most buses into Pangandaran continue past Cikembulan; alternatively, catch an ojek from the bus terminal.

The tourist information office is out by the main gates into the town and always seems to be closed. Tourist information booths in town are everywhere but are only interested in selling tours. The **information service** between the *Mini Satu Homestay* and *Chez Mama Cilacap* restaurant is an exception, with a friendly and accommodating owner who has maps of the town and some good advice about trips out of Pangandaran and into the national park.

Pangandaran has most essentials for tourists, but is short of a bank. The BRI in town has lousy rates for exchanging foreign currency and is only open until lunchtime. Many of the restaurants, hotels and tourist bureaus have exchanges, but their rates are also poor; at the time of writing, the best rates were to be found at the *Chez Mama Cilacap*. The **Telkom office** is open 24hr and very efficient, situated on Jalan Kidang Panunjang as you head from town towards the gates. The **post office** is also on Jalan Kidang Panunjang, closer to the centre of town (Mon–Sat 8am–2pm, Fri & Sun 8am–11am). Right by the post office is the local **cinema** (five showings daily), where a few relatively new English-language films are shown with Indonesian subtitles – and terrible picture quality.

Accommodation

The Pangandaran peninsula is now dripping with **losmen** and **hotels**, having very few residential buildings at all. Prices can as much as triple at weekends and holidays, and you'll need to book in advance. You may well find that you are expected to pay more for your first night in a place, or that you are required to stay more than one night. This is because the ojek/becak mafia have organized a system where losmen have to pay them as much as Rp10,000 commission for each guest. The best budget places are to be found at **Cikembulan**, 4km to the west of town; see p.144.

THE TOWN

Adam's Homestay, Jl Pamugaran Bulak Laut (☎0265/639164). A kind of traveller's guest house for those with a little extra cash, *Adam's* has quite an intimate atmosphere and amenities such as a library, a small swimming pool and bike and car rental. With its dark wooden beams and white walls, it has a very European feel, and the accommodation is pristine, ranging from basic rooms with fan to fully appointed family bungalows. ⑤.

Bamboo House, Jl Bulak Laut 8 (☎0265/679419). Probably the best budget place in town, it's quiet and well kept, with rooms with en-suite mandi and fan. There are also a couple of detached bungalows. ②–③.

Hotel Bima Sakti, Jl Bulak Laut 12 (☎0265/639194, fax 639640). Has a small swimming pool, and the rooms have air-con, TV and hot water – breakfast is toast with a boiled egg. ⑤–⑥.

Bumi Nusantara, Jl Pantai Barat (☎0265/379032). A variety of rooms, some of which have delightful balconies with swing chairs. Top rooms feature air-con and hot water, and the proprietors are very quick to offer a forty percent discount when things are quiet. Another attraction is their buffet meals – Rp20,000 for huge swaths of seafood. ⑤–⑧.

Pondok Citra Pamugaran, Jl Pamugaran 142 (no phone). Largish rooms designed for families – clean enough and a good bargain if there are three or four of you. ④.

Holiday Beach Inn, Jl Bulak Laut 50 (no phone). One of the cheapest places, though they don't offer breakfast. There is a choice of rooms with or without fan and mandi. ②.

Laut Biru, Jl Kidang Panang 228 (☎0265/639046). Reasonable rooms with fan and mandi can sleep up to four and include free coffee and breakfast. ③.

Losmen Mini Dua, Jl Kayen Buhaya (no phone). Quite similar to its sister losmen, rooms aren't that spacious but come with mandi, breakfast and fan, and offer some of the best value at the bottom end of the market. ②.

Losmen Mini Satu, Jl Kidang Pananjung (no phone). Basic but clean, and a long-standing favourite of budget travellers. Rooms come with fan and breakfast and a choice of en-suite or shared mandi. ②.

Palem Indah, Jl Bulak Laut (☎0265/639374). Quite well appointed for the price; rooms have satellite TV, en-suite bathrooms and air-con. ⑤.

Hotel Pangandaran, Jl Pantai Barat 95 (☎0265/639062). A very stylishly designed, faintly Mediterranean set of buildings with lots of climbing plants and flowers. All rooms come with breakfast, and range from simple ones with fan through to those with air-con and TV. ④–⑤.

Pantai Sari, Jl Bulak Laut 80 (☎0265/639175). Offering banana pancakes for breakfast and rooms with both fan and mandi; there's a huge range to suit every budget. ②–⑤.

Wisma Parahyangan, Jl Pamugaran 144 (☎0265/639324). A very clean and well-looked-after place, but considering the price they really need better fan and air-con facilities. Rooms can house up to five people for the same price. ④.

Sawargi Hotel, Jl Pantai Barat 47 (☎0265/639042). Airy, light and clean rooms – the cheapest only have fan and not air-con, but are really good value. ④.

Surya Pesona Beach Hotel, Jl Pamugaran (☎0265/639428). With a large swimming pool, massage parlour and beachside gardens, this is probably the best-appointed hotel in Pangandaran. It has three stars and the top-range rooms have all the luxuries you would expect, plus there are some rooms at the cheaper end of the scale. ⑤–⑦.

Wismawan Hotel, Jl Pantai Timur 262 (☎0265/379376). Right on the edge of the national park, the price doesn't include breakfast, but the good-value rooms are superclean, well laid out, have en-suite mandi and a choice of fan or air-con. ④.

CIKEMBULAN

Most travellers are now choosing to head 4km west of Pangandaran, to **Cikembulan**, a small village with several **beachside losmen** nearby. The beachfront road runs all the way from town to the back doors of these losmen, or a parallel road inland leads there from the bus station – most public buses will carry on down this road past the village.

Delta Gecko Village (☎0265/630286). Run by an Aussie character and her artist husband, this is probably the best losmen in West Java, with everything a traveller could require. The dormitories and bungalows are beautifully designed around well-kept gardens, a central meeting area and restaurant, and it's a top place to meet people and have a few cold beers. There's a lavish seafood buffet every Wednesday evening with Jaipongan dancing and *pencak silat* displays, vegetarian buffets every night, volleyball, free bike rental, coffee, tea, coconuts and breakfast, motorbike hire, a library, stacks of good information and a generally lively crowd. ②.

Kelapa Nunggal (no phone). Another excellent beach place, marked out by the interesting "bunch of plastic bottles in a tree" sculpture on its beach fronting. Does good home-cooked Indonesian-style meals; there is no dormitory, but private rooms are fairly priced, well kept and clean. ②.

Tono Homestay near to the roundabout on the beach road into town (no phone). A quiet, friendly and family-run establishment; all rooms have en-suite mandi and fan. ③.

Eating

The assorted restaurants near the **fish market** off Jalan Pantai Timur should not be missed. The small square is surrounded by warung; none are very plush but they all sell the cheapest, freshest seafood to be found for kilometres. Simply wander around the near-identical warung, looking through the polystyrene iceboxes outside until you find what you want and then barter for the price, cooked and with accoutrements; you can obtain a meal with enough fish to sink a battleship for around Rp5000. As for the rest, Pangandaran has a surfeit of places, usually constructed out of bamboo, offering hamburgers, omelettes, nasi goreng and seafood. To try and list them all would be futile.

Bagus Café, Jl Bulak Laut 66. This café's speciality is roasted rice and garlic with seafood (Rp5500), but they also serve a few European dishes. Inexpensive and popular.

Chez Mama Cilacap, Jl Kidang Pananjung 187. Quite a popular and well-established place – specialities include Asian and European desserts such as black-rice pudding, lychees, longon and crêpes suzettes.

Franco's Pizzeria, Cikembulan next to *Delta Gecko*. An Italian-run joint serving magnificent, oven-fired pizza. Considerably more expensive than the pizzerias in town, but well worth it. A large pizza with a few extra toppings will cost about Rp11,000.

Hilmans Restaurant and Fish Farm, Jl Merdeka 312. Outside the gates to Pangandaran town, but worth the trip if you fancy splashing out. The open verandah looks out over fish ponds where your lunch has probably been farmed. They have live music every night and the menu includes lobster tails (Rp40,000), club sandwiches (Rp5000) and a cold bottle of Bintang beer (Rp5000).

Holiday Beach Inn, Jl Bulak Laut 50. Has a cheap restaurant serving great Chinese food such as tofu, beef and shrimps for Rp5000 – their pizzas are pretty good too, at around Rp5000.

Number One, Jl Kidang Pananjung. Has a few Sundanese dishes such as *nasi timbel* for Rp3500 as well as pizzas for Rp5000; the *arak* cocktails are also an attraction.

Padang Jaya, Jl Pamugaran 37, right on the corner with Jl Pantai Barat. A typical Padang restaurant which serves very hot and spicy fish curries; you'll have a job to spend more than Rp5000.

Pantai Sari, Jl Bulak Laut 80. Has a menu of mainly European dishes and does pretty good pizzas for only Rp5000.

Relax, Jl Bulak Laut 74. Probably the swishest café/restaurant in town, *Relax* is well-known for its home-baked bread, milkshakes and ice cream, all of which are excellent but expensive. A mixed sandwich with chicken, cheese and salad will cost Rp8000.

Scandanavian Restaurant, Jl Pantai Barat near the junction with Jl Bulak Laut. Serves a good selection of European food, including meatballs, hot dogs and burgers – a full meal costs around Rp10,000.

Around Pangandaran

Although Pangandaran is the most popular beach resort in Java, it's beaches are for the most part too rough for swimming, the most potent attraction of the resort being the surrounding countryside. The area's particularly prevalent geological feature is raised coral beds and huge tracts of limestone that, when infused with the relatively high rainfall and number of rivers, leads to the formation of **gorges**, **caverns** and **waterfalls** of staggering beauty. Draped with moss and overhanging forest, these features are run through with emerald rivers and deep blue pools.

The most famous site in Pangandaran area is the unmissable **Green Canyon**. Groups of tourists take boats up Sungai Cijulang, either noisy motorboats, or rowing boats – slower and harder work but infinitely more appealing. Upriver, the banks steepen and close in around you until finally they are cliffs towering above in a narrow grotto. Finally the boats can go no further and moor at the entrance to a gorge so narrow it looks like a tunnel; the walls are draped with stalactites and water drips constantly from tree roots high above you. From here, you have to depend on sure-footing, swimming and care to take you over the rocks and through the pools upriver into the canyon. Essentials for the trip include a bathing costume and sun block; footwear is optional and you can hire a rubber ring for the up-canyon trek if you're unsure in the water. Boats takes about six people and can be haggled down to about Rp20,000. To get to the jetty, take a bus west from Pangandaran and ask to be let off at Green Canyon or Cukang Taneuh, which is right by the turn-off for Batu Keras. Alternatively, losmen and travel agents in town offer packages for upwards of Rp20,000 per person.

The **Cituman Dam** is a place of stunning beauty that is (as yet) still quiet even on weekends. The river here falls over several sets of broad, but low waterfalls with distinctive limestone shapes and caves, surrounded by thick forest. The only means of getting all the way to Cituman is by foot or by motorcycle, as the road is appalling. Either hire a motorbike, or take a minibus 8km west of town to the easily missed signpost, at the turn-off for Cituman Dam (on the right-hand side of the road), then hire an ojek to take you the remaining 3km (15min; Rp1500).

Quite difficult to find, but very attractive, is **Gunung Tiga**, a park near the Cituman Dam with great views, a few bat caves and another beautiful river and cavern system. To get there, take the same route as for Cituman, but ask for an ojek to Gunung Tiga. For the waterfalls, walk up the hill at the end of the rough road, and continue for about 500m. Just before the peak of the hill, there's a tiny path to the right down through the coconut palms – follow this all the way downhill to the river. The water has several glorious blue pools and, if you follow it upstream, there is a magnificent cave you can swim into, a vertical slash in the cliff-face.

Another extraordinary trip down the coast to the west of Pangandaran is to **Sindang Kerta**. In front of the beach of Sindang Kerta village is a flat rock bed that is usually above sea level, all except for a deep channel like a river through the rock. Fish swimming into the channel are inevitably trapped and, at the right time of day, **sea turtles** come in to feed. Standing on the rock bed, you can be almost within touching distance of giant-green, hawksbill, loggerhead and brown turtles, their massive heads popping up like bobbing coconuts before they dive in with a splash of flippers and shell. Unfortunately, this extraordinary site will probably not remain in existence for much longer. The piles of dead turtles in the stalls along Pangandaran's seafront have all come from these seas, and locals see them more as a menace to their fish stocks than as beautiful and rare creatures. The PHPA post in Sindang Kerta is recognizable by the sign outside advertising "Telur Penyu" ("Turtle Eggs"), which the guards will cheerfully dig up and sell to anyone who's interested. They also keep two adult turtles in minute tanks for tourists to photograph. To get to Sindang Kerta by public transport you will need to catch a minibus to Cijulang (30min; Rp750), then another bus to Cikalong (1hr 30min–2hr; Rp2000), before catching an ojek for the seven-kilometre ride to Sindang Kerta (Rp1500).

Batu Keras

BATU KERAS (Hard Rock) is a popular beach spot and **surfers enclave** 35km west of Pangandaran. From September to February there's a good right-handed reef break here; the unreliable right-handed point break at the west end of the beach often warms up in the early mornings and late afternoons and is good for beginners. Sharks are very regular visitors to this bay and it's not uncommon to see groups of mussel-collecting locals yelling and hurling rocks at a long black fin as it cruises around the point. There are several **places to stay** at Batu Keras. The *Dadang* **homestay** on Jalan Genteng Parakan (②) is a lovely, clean place, run by a young surfie couple who expect guests to be part of the household, sharing fish barbecues and evening singalongs. *Alanas* losmen is at Jalan Legok Pari 336 (☎0811/230442; ③) – it's the one at the beachfront with the funky surfboard as its signpost and is an unashamed surfers' hangout. They rent out **surfboards** at Rp15,000 a day, but it's a pretty casual arrangement. The *Teretai Cottages* (④) on the same road are the most expensive accommodation here, but are no longer good value, being desperately in need of a paint job.

On to Central Java

The journey between Central and West Java is either solely by bus, or can include a memorable riverboat trip through some of the quietest and most picturesque lowland scenery in Java. From Pangandaran, take a bus to the town of **KALIPUCANG** (45min; Rp700), 15km to the east of the main bus terminal. From this small village there's a regular ferry trip (4hr; Rp1300) through to Cilacap in Central Java, from where there are buses on to Yogya and beyond. The ferry takes you past mangrove swamps and fishing villages, across the Segara Anakan Lagoon. Boats leave at 7am, 9am and 1pm; if you intend making it all the way to Yogya or Wonosobo in one day, you'll need to try and make the first boat. There are many buses advertised in Pangandaran that sell the whole trip as a package. Otherwise, when the ferry stops at Cilacap harbour you'll need to catch a becak, bemo or ojek to the terminal, and then catch a bus on from there.

Cirebon and around

On the northern coast, right on the boundaries of Central and West Java, lies **CIREBON**, a port town with a long Islamic history that, due to being a good way off the tourist trail, receives very few Western visitors. In contrast with the large elevated towns of West Java, its coastal position makes it a sweaty place to tour around. The great Sang Cipta Rasa **mosque** is one of the oldest Islamic structures in Java, completed in 1480, with a two-tier roof similar to those found in Bali and Banten. The **kratons** are interesting and their museums filled with fascinating objects, but they're not as fine as those of Yogya. The old harbour of Cirebon is usually filled with beautiful **Makkasar schooners**, plying routes between here and Kalimantan with timber, concrete and rice.

Some history
Cirebon has always been a melting pot of Sundanese and Javanese culture, due to its situation right on the border between West and Central Java. It was only a tiny harbour settlement until the fourteenth century, when Hinduism began to spread over Southeast Asia; traders from India came upon the tiny outpost and began to use it as a port. However, when the Hindu Majapahit empire disintegrated, **Islam** began to take root in Java. Its first ambassador to Cirebon was the preacher Hidayatullah, who came here from Mecca and was to become the pre-eminent missionary for Islam in Western Java. As Hidayatullah was based in Cirebon, the town became the centre for West Java's Muslims, and as Banten, Sunda Kelapa, Karawang and Indramayu – Sunda's major towns – converted to Islam, so Cirebon's stature increased. Hidayatullah died in 1568, and was buried on the nearby mountain Gunung Jati, a name that became synonymous with his own and is an oft-used Indonesian street name in his honour. The mountain itself is a site of pilgrimage for Javanese Muslims.

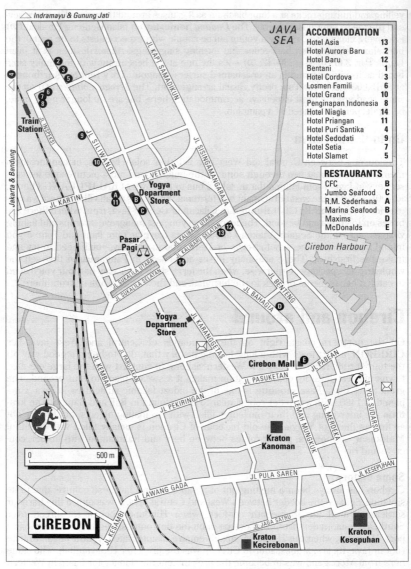

△ Indramayu & Gunung Jati

JAVA
SEA

ACCOMMODATION

Hotel Asia	13
Hotel Aurora Baru	2
Hotel Baru	12
Bentani	1
Hotel Cordova	3
Losmen Famili	6
Hotel Grand	10
Penginapan Indonesia	8
Hotel Niagia	14
Hotel Priangan	11
Hotel Puri Santika	4
Hotel Sedodati	9
Hotel Setia	7
Hotel Slamet	5

RESTAURANTS

CFC	B
Jumbo Seafood	C
R.M. Sederhana	A
Marina Seafood	B
Maxims	D
McDonalds	E

Train Station

Cirebon Harbour

Yogya Department Store

Pasar Pagi

Yogya Department Store

Cirebon Mall

Kraton Kanoman

Kraton Kecirebonan

Kraton Kesepuhan

N

0   500 m

CIREBON

JL KAPT SAMADIKUN · JL INSPEKSI · JL SILIWANGI · JL KARTINI · JL VETERAN · JL SISINGAMANGARAJA · JL KALIBARU UTARA · JL KALIBARU SELATAN · JL SUKALILA UTARA · JL SUKALILA SELATAN · JL KEMBAR · JL PARUJAAN · JL PEKIRINGAN · JL LAWANG GADA · JL KESAMBI · JL JAGA SATRU · JL PULA SAREN · JL KESEPUHAN · JL LEMAH MUNGKUK · JL PASUKETAN · JL PABEAN · JL MERDEKA · JL YOS SUDARSO · JL BAHAGIA · JL BENTENG · JL KARANGGETAS · Jakarta & Bandung

In the seventeenth century, Cirebon's power declined and it became a vassal state of Mataram. In 1678, the opulent Muslim sultans of Cirebon signed contracts with the Dutch East India Company, ceding them sole rights over the area's imports and exports in return for Dutch recognition of the sultan's control and agreements that would secure his wealth. However, the Dutch monopoly of trade was greatly abused and led to immense poverty and famine in the Cirebon area. Many of the peasants were sold into slavery and the colonists also brought with them the terrors of smallpox and venereal disease.

Later on, in the nineteenth century, the Dutch divided the kingdom of Cirebon into five royal households, before finally paying the sultans off and effectively removing them from power. The sultans kept their palaces and lifestyles but were to have no further part in the political affairs of the region. Today, the majority of Cirebon's 250,000 inhabitants are Muslim, totalling about eighty percent of the populace, and the rest are Hindu and Christian. Cirebon now prospers, as an important industrial link on the northern coast road and main Bandung road, connecting the first and third largest towns in Indonesia with the rest of Java.

Arrival and orientation

Cirebon town is strung northwest to southeast along the coast, with Teluk Penyu (Turtle Bay) off to the east. The main street is Jalan Siliwangi, which runs parallel to the coast; the **train station** is towards the north of town and just off Jalan Siliwangi, with the long-distance **bus station** lying on the outskirts of town in the southeast. When you arrive here you will be assaulted by the cab- and becak-driver mafia who will tell you categorically that there is no public transport in Cirebon. Ignore their rather aggressive demands, and just walk outside the terminal gates and catch a blue minibus into town, asking for *"dekat ke stasiun kereta api"* if you want to get close to the budget hotels near the train station. The real budget places are right outside the station gates, and the majority of **restaurants** and **accommodation** in all categories are within walking distance, most strung along Jalan Siliwangi. There are plenty of **banks** in Cirebon, many of which can be found on Jalan Yos Sudarso down by the old harbour. Bank Danamon at no. 12 is good for credit-card advances and has an ATM, while the BNI at no. 3, Bank Bali at no. 1 and Bank Lippo at no. 26 all have good rates for foreign exchange. The main **post office** is also on Jalan Yos Sudarso, as is the 24hr **Telkom office** for international phone and fax.

Accommodation

If you're arriving in Cirebon by train, you won't have to go far to find a place to stay; there's **accommodation** for all pockets within walking distance. The few **budget** places to be found in Cirebon tend to be fairly poor quality and many are brothels, though they probably won't cause you any hassle, while **moderate** hotels tend to be much more competitively priced here than in other places in West Java.

Hotel Asia, Jl Kali Baru Selatan 15 (☎0231/202183). A quiet and simple place that's kept relatively clean, offering a breakfast of bread, egg and coffee; cheaper rooms have shared mandi, while more expensive ones have en-suite bathrooms and fans. ③.

Hotel Aurora Baru, Jl Siliwangi 62 (☎0231/233145). Rooms here all come with air-con, hot water and TV and are actually quite plush, offering good value for money. ④.

Hotel Baru, Jl Kali Baru Selatan 3 (☎0231/201728). The ekonomi rooms here are clean and actually have some natural light, which is a rarity in Cirebon. They come with a shower, a decent fan and a breakfast of fried rice and bread, and are probably the budget traveller's best option. ③–⑤.

Bentani, Jl Siliwangi 69 (☎0231/203246). Probably the last word in luxury in Cirebon, with three stars, a swimming pool, tennis courts, sauna, Japanese, Chinese, Indonesian and European restaurants, plus all facilities in the rooms. ⑨.

Hotel Cordova, Jl Siliwangi 87 (☎0231/204677). Essentially a good mid-range hotel with air-con, en-suite rooms, the *Cordova* also has a few very cheap rooms out the back without the amenities. ②–⑤.

Losmen Famili, Jl Siliwangi 66 (☎0231/207935). The most basic rooms have shared mandi and no fan, while others are large and airy, with fan and mandi, but are a little dilapidated. ②–③.

Hotel Grand, Jl Siliwangi 98 (☎0231/208867). Quite a charming if faded old place – the sizable rooms have air-con, TV and hot water. ④–⑤.

Penginapan Indonesia, Jl Inspeksi 11. On the track outside the train station, this place has grotty boxrooms through to brand-new rooms with en-suite mandi; the latter are twice the price and three times the value. ②.

Hotel Niagia, Jl Kali Baru Selatan 47 (☎0231/206718). Despite its decrepit facade, this hotel is quite well kept inside, and its rooms have air-con, hot water and TV. ④–⑤.

Hotel Priangan, Jl Siliwangi 108 (☎0231/202929). A very clean place set around nice internal rock gardens; basic rooms come with mandi and fan and the top-class ones have air-con, TV and a mini-bar, and a breakfast of eggs and coffee is included. ④–⑤.

Hotel Puri Santika, Jl Dr Wahidin 32 (☎0231/200570). A top-class establishment with a pool, tennis courts and health club. The rooms are large, with hot water, fridge, mini-bar and air-con. ⑧.

Hotel Sedodati, Jl Siliwangi 72 (☎0231/202305). A two-star hotel with air-con, TV and hot water in all the rooms. They have a Chinese restaurant with reasonable prices, parking space for all their guests and offer a fried-rice breakfast free of charge. ⑥.

Hotel Setia, Jl Inspeksi 1222/31 (☎0231/207270). Has a good variety of rooms, from basic with fan through excellent-value rooms with air-con and TV, to those with hot-water showers and prices still only in the moderate category. ③–④.

Hotel Slamet, Jl Siliwangi 95 (☎0231/203296). An average place, its cheapest rooms have fan and TV, while for twice the price you get air-con, hot water and a fridge. ③–④.

The kratons

The three kratons (walled city palaces) that remain in Cirebon are today the city's only real attraction, and even so they are very much overshadowed by those of Yogya and Solo. The two kratons that are open to public viewing are **Kraton Kanoman** and **Kraton Kesapuhan**. **Kraton Kecirebon** is closed to the public, as it remains the residence of the royal family, though you can get a reasonable look at it through the fence. It is smaller and more modern than the other two, having only been built in the early nineteenth century; the other two date back to the sixteenth century.

Kraton Kesapuhan

The first building at the site of this most important **kraton** (daily 8am–4pm; Rp1000), about a twenty-minute walk from the centre of town at southern end of Jalan Lemah Wungkuk, was constructed on the orders of the preacher Hidayatullah in around 1552. It was completely rebuilt at least once before its major restoration in 1928. Though an Islamic building, the gate and main pavilions have the form of a Hindu *candi*, with the split gate commonly seen in Balinese shrines. While they are definitely older than the majority of the kraton's buildings, these features were probably only influenced by the thirteenth- and fourteenth-century Hindu styles (that predated the spread of Islam), rather than actually having been built by Hindus. The buildings are quite a mishmash, having clear Dutch, Chinese, Javanese and Sundanese influences. The kraton has a **museum**, containing artefacts such as gamelan instruments and kris, but it's not as good as the museum in the Kraton Kanoman.

Kraton Kanoman

The **Kraton Kanoman** is situated close to the centre of town on Jalan Kanoman (daily 8am–4pm; Rp1000), and features crystal chandeliers from France, tiles from Holland and Ming porcelain, alongside more conventional Sundanese and Islamic embellishments. The **museum** contains such oddities as a Portuguese suit of armour weighing 45kg found at Sunda Kelapa, wooden boxes from Egypt and China that are over 500 years old, and a bamboo cage used for keeping unruly children in. Other novelties include evil-looking spikes used for body piercing during trance by the Debus players from Banten, while the star exhibit is a very similar **chariot** to one found in the Kraton Kesapuhan – one of the two is original and one a copy, and both museums inevitably claim that theirs is the real thing. Hindu influence is evident in the chariot's elephant face, Chinese-dragon body and Egyptian wings, and the whole vehicle has an efficient suspension, the wings hinged so that, as it drove over rough roads, the bumping would make the wings flap. All in all it's about as strange a contraption as you'll ever see.

Eating

Cirebon's speciality is **nasi lengko**: rice with sambal, meat, tofu, *tempe*, bean sprouts and fried onions. Handcarts also sell delicious fried spring rolls with green chillies, and fried chicken. The Yogya department store to the north of Jalan Siliwangi has a ground-level Indonesian restaurant, which is perhaps a little overgenerous with the Formica. The Yogya further south on the same road features the *Marina* restaurant and a much more varied food court, with Sundanese, Padang, Madura and Yogyakartan food all served by different outlets. The Cirebon Mall Hero has *McDonald's, Dunkin' Donuts, KFC, Pizza Hut* and an Indonesian fast-food court with simple, quick nasi goreng for Rp1000. The Pasar Pagi off Jalan Siliwangi has some pretty cramped little warung where you can get a fantastic, cheap feed. Some places offer quarters of chicken, barbecued in a spicy marinade, for under Rp3000.

Jumbo Seafood, Jl Siliwangi 191. Does fantastic seafood barbecues at reasonable prices.

Marina Seafood, Yogya department store, Jl Siliwangi. A very flashy and expensive seafood restaurant that takes all major credit cards and serves up lobster tails, assorted seafood and fish soups. Expect meals to start at Rp40,000 a head.

Maxims, Jl Bahagia 45. Cirebon's best-known restaurant is, as you will see from the huge fish tanks as you enter, another seafood affair. Crab and prawns are the speciality but they have a pretty comprehensive and reasonably priced menu.

R.M. Sederhana, Jl Siliwangi 124. Serves up mainly Sundanese food; specialities include goldfish steamed in banana leaves.

Listings

Banks There are plenty of banks along Jl Yos Sudarso down by the old harbour; Bank Danamon at no. 12 is good for credit-card advances and has an ATM. BNI at no. 3, Bank Bali at no. 1 and Bank Lippo at no. 26 all have good rates for foreign exchange.

Bookshops There is a great bookshop/stationers in the Cirebon shopping centre at the southern end of Jl Bahagia, with lots of English-language books and maps from around the archipelago.

Post office Jl Yos Sudarso, near the harbour.

Telkom Jl Yos Sudarso; 24hr international phone and fax.

Around Cirebon

The foremost site of interest in the Cirebon area is **TRUSMI**, a **batik-making centre** 6km to the west of town. Other nearby villages such as Weru, Kalitengah and Kaliwuru are also known for their batik, but Trusmi is definitely the best place to go if you want to see the process and buy the finished article. Cirebon's batik is very different from that of Central Java, with its own distinctive designs, influences and colours. Chinese- and Arabic-style designs are commonplace, their use in local batik dating back at least five centuries. Colours are not generally as gaudy and bright as you might see in Yogya, tending towards indigos, dark browns, background whites and muted yellows, but the designs are generally very striking. Ibu Masina's workshop in Trusmi is the best place to start if you want to get a feel for Batik. Take angkot GP from Gunungsari terminal, 400m to the west of the Yogya department store, to Plered (15min; Rp500), and then ask for the Pabrik Batik.

travel details

Buses

It's almost impossible to give the **frequency** with which bemos and buses run, as they only depart when they have enough passengers to make the journey worthwhile. **Journey times** also vary a great deal. The times below are the minimum you can expect these journeys to take. Privately run shuttle, or **door-to-door**, buses run between the major tourist centres on Java.

Bandung to: Bogor (frequent; 3hr); Jakarta (from Leuwi Panjang terminal, frequent; 4hr 30min–5hr 30min); Pangandaran (twice daily; 5hr); Sukabumi (frequent; 3hr).

Bogor to: Bandung (frequent; 3hr); Jakarta (frequent; 1–2hr); Pelabuhan Ratu (frequent; 2hr 30min); Sukabumi (frequent; 1hr 30min).

Cirebon to: Bandung (frequent; 3hr 30min); Jakarta (frequent; 5hr); Yogya (frequent; 9hr).

Pangandaran to: Bandung (frequent; 5hr); Jakarta (frequent; 12hr); Tasikmilaya (frequent; 3hr).

Trains

Bandung to: Jakarta (hourly; 2hr 20min); Yogya (8 daily; takes from 9hr).

Bogor to: Jakarta (every 20min; 1hr 30min).

Cirebon to: Jakarta (four *ekspres* trains daily; 3hr).

Ferries

The only real option for sea travel is the ferry from **Merak** to Sumatra, which leaves about every 30min (90min).

Flights

Bandung airport is the only one in West Java that presently runs flights for tourists, with Merpati, Bouraq and Garuda all operating out of its Hussein Sastranegara terminal.

Bandung to: Mataram (daily; 8hr 25min); Palembang (daily; 2hr); Singapore (daily; 3hr); Solo (3 weekly; 1hr 30min); Surabaya (3 daily; 1hr 20min); Ujung Pandang (daily; 4hr 20min); Yogyakarta (4 weekly; 1hr 20min).

CHAPTER THREE

CENTRAL JAVA

Central Java is the breadbasket of Indonesia, a wide swath of farmland covering almost a third of the island. It's one of the most densely populated rural areas in the world: a 1990 census estimated the population to be nearly 32 million, crammed into an area of some 34,505 square kilometres. Despite this over-crowding, the scenery is remarkably pastoral, the volcanic soil and tropical climate con-spiring to produce a landscape of glimmering ricelands spotted here and there with the occasional classical ruin, a few large towns, countless small villages and, running from east to west across the province, a spine of temperamental volcanoes.

This mountainous backbone splits the province into two distinct regions. To the south is the **Kejawen**, homeland of the ethnic Javanese and the epicentre of their arts, culture and language. The Kejawen's boundaries extend well into both West and East Java, but its heart is undoubtedly within Java's two royal cities, **Yogyakarta** and **Solo**. Once the rival capitals of the disintegrating Mataram empire, today the two cities, steeped in culture and history and with first-rate facilities for travellers, are the main-stay of Java's tourist industry. They also provide excellent bases from which to explore the remains which dot the surrounding countryside. A little to the west of Yogyakarta is the world-famous **Borobudur**, a giant Buddhist temple built in the ninth century by the Saliendra dynasty. Midway between Yogya and Solo is the equally fascinating **Prambanan complex**, a series of soaring Shivaite temples constructed by the Saliendras's Hindu contemporaries, the Sanjayas. And continuing east, just before the border with East Java, are a couple of enigmatic fifteenth-century Hindu temples, **Sukuh** and **Ceto**, set on a glorious mountainside. Finally, high up in the centre of the chain of volcanoes, there's **Dieng**, a windswept plateau with some of the oldest classi-cal temples in Java, a chilly alternative to the sunbaked ruins of the plain.

North of the volcanoes the landscape gently melts into a narrow, fertile plain which separates the foothills from the sea. This is the coastal, or **Pasisir** (fringe) region of Central Java. Isolated from the court culture of the interior, the coastline has tradition-ally been influenced by foreign traders who docked in the port on their way to and from the Spice Islands, and thus has a more cosmopolitan, mercantile atmosphere. It was through these ports that Islam first entered Java, via Arabian and Indian sailors. Indeed, the island's first Islamic empire was founded around the twin ports of **Demak** and **Jepara**, and it is still one of the most emphatically Muslim parts of Indonesia. Today, the Pasisir region is home to some sacred **Islamic sites** (the revered mosques of Demak and Kudus and three of the graves of the Wali Songo), a number of big indus-tries (clove cigarettes in **Kudus** and batik in **Pekalongan**) and a smattering of crum-bling colonial buildings. Though it's frequently visited by devout Indonesian Muslims and foreign businesspeople, the lack of major tourist attractions and the inhospitable **climate** – the Pasisir is prone to flooding in the rainy season and searingly hot for the rest of the year – puts most tourists off.

In general, **getting around** Central Java is not a problem; the region is fairly small and is well served by both road and rail. Travelling between the north and the Kejawen is slightly tricky, though, as only three highways (between Purworketo and Tegal, Semarang and Salatiga, and Purwodadi and Solo), and one train track (Semarang to Solo), link the two regions. There are, nevertheless, a number of smaller, stomach-churning roads that wind their way through, up or around the volcanoes.

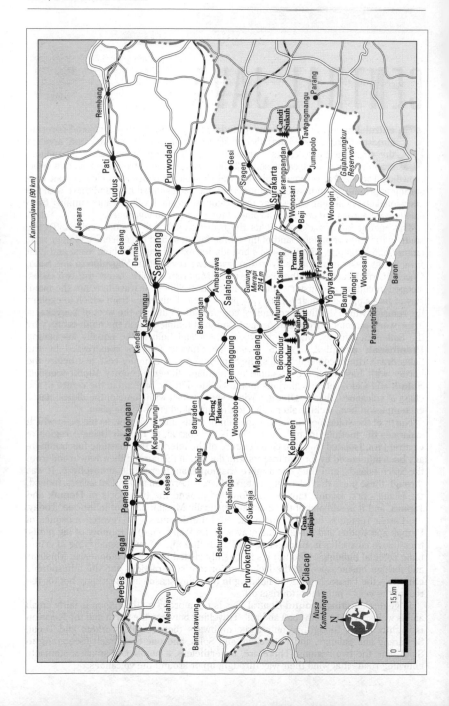

ACCOMMODATION PRICE CODES

All the **accommodation** listed in this book has been given one of the following price codes. The rates quoted here are for the **cheapest double room** in high season, except for places with dorms, where the code represents the price of a single bed. Where there's a significant spread of prices indicated (④–⑦, for example), the text will explain what extra facilities you get for more money. The 11–21 percent tax charged by most hotels is not included in these price codes.

Because of the current instability of the rupiah, accommodation prices are given throughout in their more stable **US dollar equivalents**, even for places which accept payment in rupiah.

For more on accommodation, see p.40.

① under $1	③ $2–5	⑤ $10–15	⑦ $35–60	⑨ $100
② $1–2	④ $5–10	⑥ $15–35	⑧ $60–100	and over

Moving on from Central Java should be fairly straightforward. From Yogya and Solo there are road and rail links with Jakarta, Bogor, Bandung and Surabaya, and direct buses to Bali; along the coast, the road and railway between Jakarta and Surabaya run through all the major towns in the Pasisir. The Pelni ferry company connects Semarang with Banjarmasin (Kalimantan), and there are airports in Cilacap, Semarang, Yogya and Solo.

Yogyakarta and around

Halfway between volatile Gunung Merapi and the treacherous Southern Seas, **YOGYAKARTA** (pronounced "Jogjakarta" and often just shortened to "Jogja"), a prosperous city of 500,000 inhabitants, stands proudly at the very heart of Javanese culture. Thanks largely to sponsorship from the city's two royal households, the Hamengkubuwonos and the Paku Alam family, the classical **Javanese arts** – batik, ballet, drama, music, poetry and puppet shows – all thrive in Yogya as nowhere else on the island. Even the city's name is a literary reference, being derived from Ayodya, the peaceful kingdom of King Rama in the *Ramayana* tales. Small wonder, then, that this is the best place to enjoy Javanese performances and exhibitions.

Yogyakarta also ranks as one of the best preserved and most attractive cities in Java. At its heart is the residence of Yogya's first family, the illustrious and revered **Hamengkubuwonos**, whose elegant, graceful palace lies at the centre of Yogya's quaint old city, the **Kraton**, itself concealed behind high castellated walls. These fortifications, while they have not always been successful in keeping out enemies, have certainly managed to ward off the ravages of time. Wander through at dawn, and the Kraton seems to have been totally forgotten by this century, its meandering alleyways and spacious, high-walled boulevards imbued with a sense of calm.

Yogya, however, is not just a museum piece, but a thriving modern metropolis, as well acquainted with email and MTV as it is with golek and gamelan. The city's forward-looking **Gajah Mada University** stands at the cutting edge of technology, and draws students from all over the archipelago. Tourists, too, flock to Yogya, attracted not only by the city's courtly splendour but also by the nearby temples of **Prambanan** and **Borobudur**. As a consequence, there are more hotels and tourist facilities here than anywhere else in Java and, unfortunately, a correspondingly high number of touts, pickpockets, con artists and other unsavoury characters. Nevertheless, with its handy transport connections, good food and accommodation options and easy-going, friendly nature, Yogya is the perfect base from which to become acquainted with the Javanese people, their history and their culture.

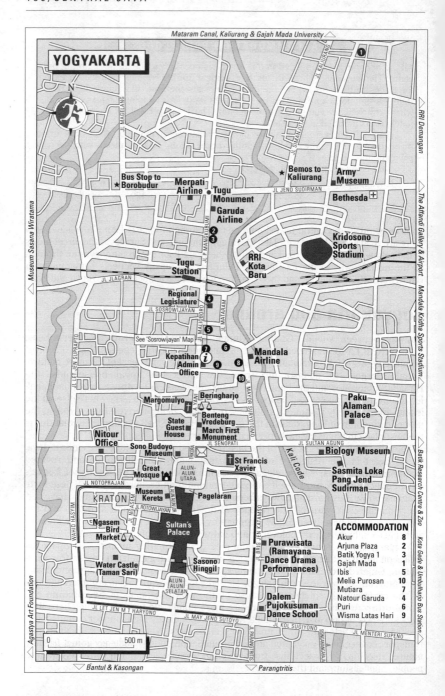

YOGYAKARTA

Mataram Canal, Kaliurang & Gajah Mada University

RRI Demangan

The Affandi Gallery & Airport

Mandala Kridha Sports Stadium

Batik Research Centre & Zoo

Kota Gede & Umbulharjo Bus Station

★ Bus Stop to Borobudur

Merpati Airline

Tugu Monument

Garuda Airline

★ Bemos to Kaliurang

Army Museum

Bethesda

Kridosono Sports Stadium

RRI Kota Baru

Tugu Station

Regional Legislature

See 'Sosrowijayan' Map

Kepatihan Admin Office

Mandala Airline

Paku Alaman Palace

Margomulyo

Beringharjo

State Guest House

Benteng Vredeburg March First Monument

Nitour Office

Sono Budoyo Museum

Biology Museum

Great Mosque

ALUN-ALUN UTARA

St Francis Xavier

Sasmita Loka Pang Jend Sudirman

Museum Kereta

Pagelaran

KRATON

Ngasem Bird Market

Sultan's Palace

Purawisata (Ramayana Dance Drama Performances)

Water Castle (Taman Sari)

Sasono Hinggil

ALUN-ALUN SELATAN

Dalem Pujokusuman Dance School

JL MAGELANG

Museum Sasana Wiratama

JL JEND SUDIRMAN

JL P MANGKUBUMI

JL JLAGRAN

JL SOSROWIJAYAN

JL MALIOBORO

JL MATARAM

JL LET JEN SUPRAPTO

JL KHA DAHLAN

JL AHMAD YANI

JL MAYOR SURYOTOMO

JL SENOPATI

JL SULTAN AGUNG

Kali Code

JL NOTOPRAJAN

JL NGASEM

JL ROTOWIJAYAN

JL BRIG JEN KATAMSO

JL WAHID HASYIM

Agastya Art Foundation

JL LET JEN M T HARYONO

JL MAY JEND SUTOYO

JL KOL SUGIYONO

JL MENTERI SUPENO

0   500 m

Bantul & Kasongan

Parangtritis

ACCOMMODATION

Akur	8
Arjuna Plaza	2
Batik Yogya 1	3
Gajah Mada	1
Ibis	5
Melia Purosan	10
Mutiara	7
Natour Garuda	4
Puri	6
Wisma Latas Hari	9

Some history

Yogyakarta grew out of the dying embers of the once-great Mataram dynasty. In 1752, the Mataram empire, then based in Solo, was in the throes of the **Third Javanese War of Succession**. The reigning susuhunan, **Pakubuwono II**, had been steadily losing his grasp on power for the past decade in the face of a rebellion by his brothers, **Singasari** and **Mangkubumi**, and the sultan's nephew, **Mas Said**. To try to turn the tide, Pakubuwono persuaded Mangkubumi to swap sides and defend the court, offering him control over three thousand households within the city in return. Mangkubumi agreed, but the sultan, backed by the Dutch (who were worried about Mangkubumi's growing popularity) later reneged on the deal. In fury, Mangkubumi headed off to establish his own court. He chose his spot carefully, one that was both in the shadow of the sacred mountain, Merapi, and also near to the previous Mataram capitals at **Kota Gede**, **Karta** and **Plered** (the royal towns of sultans Senopati, Agung and Amangkurat I, respectively). Thus Yogyakarta was born. Mangkubumi's new court was granted official recognition in the 1755 **Treaty of Giyanti**, with Mangkubumi bestowing on himself the title of **Sultan Hamengkubuwono I** (He Who Holds the World in His Lap).

Hamengkubuwono and his followers spent the next 37 years building the new capital, with the Kraton as the centrepiece and the court at Solo as the blueprint. Hamengkubuwono also set about capturing more land until, by the time he died in 1792, his territory exceeded Solo's. After his death, however, the Yogya sultanate went into freefall. Hamengkubuwono II fell out so badly with the newly arrived British that the latter stormed the palace in 1812, aided by the sultan's brother, **Prince Notokusumo**. It was the last time any of the courts were sacked by a European power. For his part, Notokusumo was rewarded with his own court in the centre of Yogya, with control over four thousand households. A second major altercation occurred in 1825, when a member of the royal house, **Prince Diponegoro**, led the Javanese into a bloody five-year battle against the Dutch, who by this time held most of Java: over ten percent of the population was killed as a result of the fighting. From this moment on, the Dutch were firmly in control and even had the power of veto when appointing sultans.

Drained of power and resources, the palace spent the rest of the nineteenth century convalescing, concentrating less on warmongering and more on its artistic side. **Sultan Hamengkubuwono VIII**, in particular, was a great sponsor of the arts, occasionally putting on epic, four-day spectacles of dance and drama at the Kraton.

Nationalist feeling, however, continued to grow throughout this period. In 1946, the capital of the newly declared Republic of Indonesia was moved to Yogya from Jakarta, and the Kraton became the unofficial headquarters for the republican movement. With the financial and military support of **Sultan Hamengkubuwono IX**, Yogya became the nerve centre for the native forces. The town was rewarded for its efforts by being granted its own province, the **Daerah Istimewa Yogyakarta** (Special Territory of Yogya). Today, fifty years on from the War of Independence, the royal household of Yogya continues to enjoy almost slavish devotion from its subjects. Indeed, during the May 1997 riots, it was only through the intervention of the current sultan, Hamengkubuwono X, who addressed an angry crowd of students demonstrating against the regime of President Suharto, that Yogya was saved from the looting and burning that afflicted so many other cities in Java. As one of the most influential politicians in the government, the sultan has received countrywide praise and respect for his position at the forefront of the democratic reform movement.

Orientation, information and arrival

There is no public transport running directly between Yogyakarta's **Adisucipto Airport**, 10km to the east of the city on the way to Prambanan, and the city centre. If you head 200m south out of the airport and on to Jalan Adisucipto, you can flag down a passing bus (Rp500) heading west to Yogya. Alternatively, a taxi from the airport to Yogya costs around Rp8000.

The **train station** lies just one block north of (and an easy 5min walk away from) Jalan Sosro, on Jalan Pasar Kembang. A becak from the station to Jalan Prawirotaman should cost no more than Rp2000; a taxi, Rp3000; or catch southbound bus #2 (Rp500) from Jalan Mataram, one block east of Jalan Malioboro.

All inter-city buses arrive at the **Umbulharjo bus station**, 3km east of the city centre. From the adjacent **local bus station** there are regular services into town, including bus #2 (Rp500), which travels via Jalan Prawirotaman. Bus #5 (Rp500) drives past the western end of Jalan Sosro, although it can take up to an hour. If you're arriving in Yogya from Borobudur, Magelang, Ambarawa or elsewhere in the north, and you plan to stay in Sosro, you can alight at the southern end of Jalan Magelang and walk (or take a becak) 600m south to Sosro.

Yogya is trisected by three parallel rivers – the **Winongo**, **Code** and **Gaja Wong** – running north to south through the city. Most of the interest for visitors is focused on the two-kilometre-wide strip of land between the two westernmost rivers, Kali Winongo and Kali Code – this is site of the **Kraton**, the historic heart of the city. Though most of Yogya follows a more or less orderly grid pattern, the Kraton is a welcome oasis of jumbled streets and capillary alleyways.

Although it clearly lies outside of the walled city, according to official definition the Kraton also includes **Jalan Malioboro**, the main street heading from the old city's northern gates into the heart of Yogya's noisy business district. A kilometre north of the Kraton walls, the budget travellers' mecca of **Jalan Sosrowijayan** (known as Jalan Sosro) runs west off Malioboro to the south of the train station. There's a second, more upmarket cluster of tourist hotels and restaurants on **Jalan Prawirotaman**, in the prosperous southern suburbs to the southeast of the Kraton.

Yogya's English-speaking **tourist office**, the most efficient and informative in Central Java, is located at Jalan Malioboro 175 (Mon–Thurs & Sat 8am–7pm, Fri 8am–1pm & 3–6pm; ☎0274/66000). This is the best place to come if you're interested in finding out about local events and entertainments, language and meditation courses.

City transport

Most of Yogya's major attractions can be visited on foot from either Jalan Sosro or Jalan Prawirotaman. However, for many of the city's lesser-known sights away from the city centre you'll need to use the comprehensive public transport system. The extensive bus network and the city's taxis are ideal for longer journeys, while becak are handy for trips within the city centre.

All **buses** begin and end their journeys at the Umbulharjo bus station. Always allow plenty of time for your journey, as the routes are circuitous and the traffic heavy. The fare, payable on the bus, is a set Rp500 regardless of the distance travelled. Most buses stop running at about 6pm, although the #15 runs to the GPO until 8pm (see box opposite). The most useful bus for travellers is the #4, which runs south down Jalan Malioboro before heading to Kota Gede and the Umbulharjo bus station

There are literally thousands of **becak** in Yogya, mainly hanging around the transport and tourist centres. Though the constant hassle from the drivers is annoying, they are the most convenient form of transport, especially as they can take the narrow back roads and bicycle lanes to bypass the circuitous one-way system. It should cost no more than Rp500 to travel from Jalan Sosro to the GPO (Rp1200 from Jalan Prawirotaman), although hard bargaining is required. The horse-drawn carriages, known as **andong**, which tend to queue up along Jalan Malioboro, are a little cheaper. **Taxis** are good value (Rp800, plus Rp400 per km). You can usually find them hanging around the GPO, or ring either Jas (☎0274/373388), Setia Kawan (☎0274/522333) or Sumber Rejo (☎0274/514786).

USEFUL BUS ROUTES

#2 Umbulharjo bus station–Jalan Sisingamangaraja (for Prawirotaman)–Jalan Brig Jen Katamso (along the eastern wall of the Kraton)– Jalan Mataram–Kridono sports centre– Gajah Mada University–Jalan Simanjutak (for minibuses to Prambanan)–Jalan Mataram–Jalan Sisingamangaraja– Umbulharjo.

#4 Umbulharjo–Jalan Sultan Agung–Jalan Mataram–Prambanan minibus station on Jalan Simanjutak–Jalan Malioboro–Jalan Ngeksigondo (Kota Gede)–Umbulharjo.

#5 Umbulharjo–Jalan Parangtritis (western end of Jalan Prawirotaman)–Jalan Wahid Hasyim (along the western wall of the Kraton)–Jalan Sosro (western end)– train station–Jalan Magelang (for buses to Borobudur)–Jalan Pringgokusuman (west of Sosro)–Jalan Let Jen Suprapto–Jalan Ngasem (bird market)–Jalan Parangtritis–Umbulharjo.

#15 Umbulharjo–Jalan Sisingamangaraja (for Prawirotaman)–Jalan Brigjen Katamso–GPO–Gaja Mada University–Umbulharjo.

(Bus #15 is often the only service running after 6pm, when it only runs as far as the GPO before heading straight back to Umbulharjo.)

Yogya is a flat city with fairly well-maintained roads, and as such is an enjoyable (if a touch hair-raising) city to **cycle** in. If your accommodation doesn't rent out bikes, try Bike 33 in Jalan Sosro Gang I: charges are a standard Rp3000 per day. Orange-suited parking attendants throughout the city will look after your bike for Rp100.

Accommodation

There are well over 150 **hotels** and **losmen** in Yogya, ninety percent of them concentrated around just two roads: Jalan Sosrowijayan and Jalan Prawirotaman. **Jalan Sosro**, in the heart of the business district, is a busy, downmarket location whose tempo is dictated by the thump of rock music emanating from the restaurants. **Jalan Prawirotaman** on the other hand, is a lazier, leafier and more affluent street, its pace set by the somnolent tap of the *bakso* seller who plods up and down the pavement every afternoon. The facilities at Jalan Prawirotaman are far superior, with most hotels boasting a swimming pool and air-con as standard. By and large, both streets offer excellent-value accommodation.

Jalan Sosro and around

BUDGET

Arjuna, Jl Sosro GT1/82 (☎0274/583104). Small and poky hotel with no atmosphere and forbidding iron bars on the windows. Functional, but nothing more. ③.

Atiep, Jl Sosro GT1/121 (☎0274/582641). Clean, quiet and amiable losmen, with a 4am wake-up call courtesy of the local mosque. ③.

Aziatic, Jl Sosro 6 (no phone). Asylum-like hotel with grandeur, so faded it is hard to discern. Ancient steel four-poster beds furnish the otherwise spartan rooms. ③.

Bagus, Jl Sosro Wetan GT1/57 (☎0274/515087). Small but adequate rooms, free tea and coffee, and bathrooms that are cleaned daily. Inexpensive and very good value. ③.

Beta, Jl Sosro GT1/28 (☎0274/512756). Losmen consisting of eleven reasonably comfortable though slightly cramped rooms, and four mandi. Guests are often subjected to batik hard sell from the owner. ③.

Bladok, Jl Sosro 76 (☎0274/560452). Friendly, efficient and impeccably clean hotel built round a central courtyard, with a fish pond in the centre and plans for a swimming pool in the back yard. All rooms come with mandi, and breakfast is included. ④.

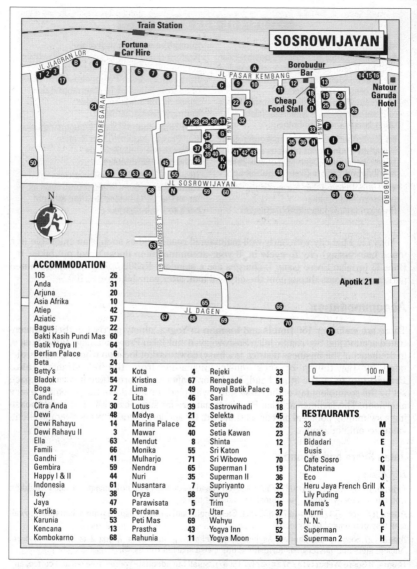

SOSROWIJAYAN

ACCOMMODATION

105	26				
Anda	31				
Arjuna	20				
Asia Afrika	10				
Atiep	42				
Aziatic	57				
Bagus	22				
Bakti Kasih Pundi Mas	60				
Batik Yogya II	64				
Berlian Palace	6				
Beta	24				
Betty's	34	Kota	4	Rejeki	33
Bladok	54	Kristina	67	Renegade	51
Boga	27	Lima	49	Royal Batik Palace	9
Candi	2	Lita	46	Sari	25
Citra Anda	30	Lotus	39	Sastrowihadi	18
Dewi	48	Madya	21	Selekta	45
Dewi Rahayu	14	Marina Palace	62	Setia	28
Dewi Rahayu II	3	Mawar	40	Setia Kawan	23
Ella	63	Mendut	8	Shinta	12
Famili	66	Monika	55	Sri Katon	1
Gandhi	41	Mulharjo	71	Sri Wibowo	70
Gembira	59	Nendra	65	Superman I	19
Happy I & II	44	Nuri	35	Superman II	36
Indonesia	61	Nusantara	7	Supriyanto	32
Isty	38	Oryza	58	Suryo	29
Jaya	47	Parawisata	5	Trim	16
Kartika	56	Perdana	17	Utar	37
Karunia	53	Peti Mas	69	Wahyu	15
Kencana	13	Prastha	43	Yogya Inn	52
Kombokarno	68	Rahunia	11	Yogya Moon	50

RESTAURANTS	
33	M
Anna's	G
Bidadari	E
Busis	I
Cafe Sosro	C
Chaterina	N
Eco	J
Heru Jaya French Grill	K
Lily Puding	B
Mama's	A
Murni	L
N. N.	D
Superman	F
Superman 2	H

0   100 m

Citra Anda, Jl Sosro Wetan GT1/144 (no phone). While the exterior resembles a maximum-security jail, the interior is thankfully much more homely. Recommended. ③.

Dewi I, Jl Sosro (no phone). Largish losmen offering decent-sized, spotless rooms at reasonable prices. Good value, despite the moody manager. ③.

Ella, Jl Sosrodipuran GT1/487 (☎0274/582219). Clean fan-cooled rooms, warm showers, free tea and coffee, wonderfully friendly staff and good information on local sights and events. Rates (which offer a small discount for students) include a decent-sized breakfast. One of the best. ③.

Gembira, Jl Sosro 35 (☎0274/512605). Sister of *Oryza*, with a high standard of rooms. Free tea and coffee included. ④.

Jaya, Jl Sosro GT1/79 (☎0274/515055). Inexpensive losmen with free tea and coffee. Resembles a junk shop, with furniture and assorted artefacts scattered everywhere, but not bad value. ③.

Karunia, Jl Sosro 78 (☎ & fax 0274/565057). Overdecorated hotel crammed with antiques and souvenirs. Most of the rooms are perfectly acceptable, though some have no windows and are a little gloomy, and the noise from the nearby church can be intrusive. ④.

Lita, Jl Sosro Wetan GT1 (no phone). Decorated with paintings and sculptures by local artists, this losmen offers large, spotless rooms at reasonable prices. Very good value indeed. ③.

Lotus, Jl Sosro Wetan GT1/167 (☎0274/515090). Light, airy and clean losmen, popular with Yogya's adolescents, who congregate in the lounge to watch the TV. Fine rooftop balcony. ③.

Monica, Jl Sosro GT1/192 (☎0274/580602). Formerly the *Losmen Wisma Wijaya*, this shimmeringly clean hotel, built round a fish pond, is one of the most handsome on Sosro. Unfortunately, it is let down by overzealous staff, harassing you to look at the batik shop. ④.

Oryza, Jl Sosro 49–51 (☎0274/512004). A less expensive version of the *Gembira*. Similar decor with huge pictures on the walls. Doubles only, with the economy rooms being particularly good value. ④.

Sari, Jl Sosro GT1 (no phone). Surprisingly clean rooms, given the state of both the courtyard and the owner. Reasonable, but not terrific value. ③.

Selekta, Jl Sosro (☎0274/566467). Rivalling *Ella* as the best of the budget bunch. On the whole a very welcoming losmen with a good atmosphere; the rooms are capacious, clean and cooled by ceiling fans. Rates include breakfast. ③.

Sri Katon, Jl Jlagran Lor 21 (☎0274/561559). Spartan hotel with friendly management and a menagerie of caged and uncaged birds fluttering and squawking in the central courtyard. ③.

Sri Wibowo, Jl Dagen 23 (☎ & fax 0274/563084). Javanese-style hotel, with lots of parking space, a souvenir shop and even a massage parlour. Rooms, however, are a little soulless. ④.

Superman I and II, Jl Sosro Gang I (no phone). *Superman I* was once the travellers' favourite, but is clearly being wound down now in favour of the newly built *Superman II*. The latter is in pristine condition and offers good-value accommodation, with fine rooms. ③.

Supriyanto Inn, Jl Sosro Wetan GT1/59 (no phone). Another very popular choice. Good location in central Sosro, away from the mosque and hubbub of the *gang*. Often full, though. ③.

Suryo, Jl Sosro Wetan GT1/145 (no phone). Jauntily decorated little homestay run by an energetic octogenarian. Free tea and coffee. ③.

Utar, Jl Sosro Wetan GT1/161 (☎0274/560405). A fairly popular losmen, but lacking in atmosphere. A little too much pressure is applied by the managers in trying to persuade residents to visit their batik shop, but otherwise it's not a bad place. ③.

Yossie, Jl Sosrodipuran GT1/384 (no phone). Long-haired, laid-back version of *Ella*. Friendly enough, but lacking in atmosphere. ③.

MODERATE

Most of these hotels are on **Jalan Pasar Kembang**, one block north of Jalan Sosro opposite the train station.

Asia-Afrika, Jl Pasar Kembang 21 (☎0274/514489). All the rooms here are en suite, and come with hot water. Attractive lounge/lobby area and an open-air pool complete the picture. ⑤.

Bakti Kasih Pundi Mas, Jl Sosro 33 (☎0274/514890). All the rooms in this large hotel, save for the economy ones, have air-con and hot water. Rates include a tasty breakfast. Caters mainly to Indonesian tourists. ⑤.

Batik Yogya II, Taman Yuwono complex, Dagen (☎0274/561828, fax 561823). Cottage-style accommodation in a quiet but convenient location, with a good swimming pool and restaurant attached. ⑥.

Berlian Palace, Jl Pasar Kembang 61 (☎0274/560312). Eighteen rooms with air-con, hot shower, TV and in-house video. ⑦.

Kencana, Jl Pasar Kembang 15 (☎0274/513352). Hotel with double rooms only, either with air-con or fan. Breakfast and tax included. ②–⑤.

Kota, Jl Jlagran Lor 1 (☎0274/515844). A real colonial feel pervades this lovely hotel, even though it was only established in the 1950s. Fifteen beautiful en-suite rooms, each complete with mini-bar and hot and cold running water. The best on the street. ⑤.

Marina Palace, Jl Sosro 3–5 (☎0274/588490). Good-value hotel, if only because a lack of custom has forced the owner to reduce the rates. Odd, overelaborate decor in reception, but plain, good-looking rooms, each with their own en-suite shower and toilet. No hot water, though. ⑤.

Mendut, Jl Pasar Kembang 49 (☎0274/563435). Large, clean rooms with air-con, hot water and telephone, built round a large outdoor pool. ⑥.

Peti Mas, Jl Dagen 27 (☎0274/560163, fax 561938). Fine hotel with excellent pool and clean, comfortable rooms. ⑥.

Royal Batik Palace, Jl Pasar Kembang 29 (☎0274/89849). Good outdoor swimming pool, bar and restaurant, and salubrious, en-suite, air-con rooms. ⑥.

Yogya Moon, Jl Kemetiran 21 (☎0274/582465). Sparkling hotel in a rather run-down area to the west of Sosro. The rooms (all en suite) are equipped with air-con, phone and TV. Economy singles are terrific value. ④–⑦.

Jalan Prawirotaman and around

Agung, Jl Prawirotaman 68 (☎0274/375512). Very likable staff, clean accommodation and a decent, if small, swimming pool. ④.

Asli, Jl Prawirotaman MGIII/510 (no phone, fax ☎0274/371175). Less a hotel than an acid flashback. Psychedelic pictures on the walls and music courtesy of Jimi Hendrix. Laid-back and friendly. ③.

Ayodya, Jl Sisingamangaraja 74 (☎0274/372475). Large, plush and elegant hotel with Javanese furniture and decor in reception. The rooms are depressingly bland, though. ⑦.

Duta, Jl Prawirotaman I 26 (☎ & fax 0274/372064). Big hotel that comes highly recommended by all who stay here; it has a good pool and does huge breakfasts. ④.

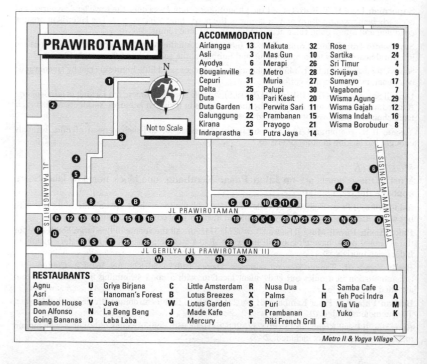

PRAWIROTAMAN

Not to Scale

ACCOMMODATION

Airlangga	13	Makuta	32	Rose	19
Asli	3	Mas Gun	10	Sartika	24
Ayodya	6	Merapi	26	Sri Timur	4
Bougainville	2	Metro	28	Srivijaya	9
Cepuri	31	Muria	27	Sumaryo	17
Delta	25	Palupi	30	Vagabond	7
Duta	18	Pari Kesit	20	Wisma Agung	29
Duta Garden	1	Perwita Sari	11	Wisma Gajah	12
Galunggung	22	Prambanan	15	Wisma Indah	16
Kirana	23	Prayogo	21	Wisma Borobudur	8
Indraprastha	5	Putra Jaya	14		

JL PRAWIROTAMAN

JL GERILYA (JL PRAWIROTAMAN II)

RESTAURANTS

Agnu	U	Griya Birjana	C	Little Amsterdam	R	Nusa Dua	L	Samba Cafe	Q
Asri	E	Hanoman's Forest	B	Lotus Breezes	X	Palms	H	Teh Poci Indra	A
Bamboo House	V	Java	W	Lotus Garden	S	Puri	D	Via Via	M
Don Alfonso	N	La Beng Beng	J	Made Kafe	P	Prambanan	I	Yuko	K
Going Bananas	O	Laba Laba	G	Mercury	T	Riki French Grill	F		

Metro II & Yogya Village ▽

Duta Garden, Jl Timuran MGIII/103 (☎0274/373482, fax 372064). Exceptionally beautiful cottage-style hotel smothered in a thick blanket of bougainvillea and roses. Rooms are equally exquisite; bargain hard in the low season for a discount. ⑦.

Galunggung, Jl Prawirotaman I 36 (☎0274/376915). Reasonable little hotel let down by some very uncomfortable beds. ⑤.

Indraprastha, Jl Prawirotaman MGIII/169 (☎0274/374087, fax 371175). Spotless rooms with ceiling fan, shower and toilet. Good value anywhere else, but a little overpriced for Yogya, especially as there is no pool. ⑤.

Metro, Jl Prawirotaman I 71 (☎0274/372364, fax 372004). A big hotel favoured by tour groups. Has a pool and restaurant, with a fairly grotty economy section in a different building at the end of the street. ④.

Metro II, Jl Sisingamangaraja 21 (☎0274/376993). Despite its central location, the *Metro II*, which has a huge stained-glass facade, still grabs most of its custom by employing touts at the bus station. Most of the rooms are very homely, but avoid the rodent-infested basement. ④.

Prambanan, Jl Prawirotaman I 14 (☎0274/376167). A new hotel with bamboo-walled rooms, swimming pool and eager-to-please staff. ⑥.

Rose, Jl Prawirotaman I 28 (☎0274/377991, fax 380011). The best value in Prawirotaman. Hearty breakfasts, a swimming pool and very cheap rooms. Bargain in the low season for an even better deal. ④.

Sumaryo, Jl Prawirotaman 22 (☎0274/377552, fax 373507). Perfectly adequate mid-priced hotel. Handy if the *Rose* next door is full. ④.

Vagabonds (aka **Kelana**), Jl Sisingamangaraja 28b (☎0274/371207). A budget hostel to rival the best of Sosro, this is Yogya's International Youth Hostel. Very cheap, excellent information, small library, laser-disc screening every night, and you can use the pool at the *Yogya Village Inn* (see below). ③.

Yogya Village Inn, Jl Menukan 5 (☎ & fax 0274/373031). Excellent, stylish little place combining homely hospitality with classy accommodation. Includes a library and games pavilion. ⑦.

Elsewhere

Akur Hotel, Jl Mataram 8 (☎0274/520527). Half-hotel, half-opticians, this modern, largish and rather bizarre hotel has comfortable rooms but is a little lacking in atmosphere. ⑥.

Ambarrukmo Palace, Jl Adisucipto 66 (☎0274/566488, fax 563283). Four-star international hotel on the way to the airport, comprising 265 air-con, en-suite rooms with TV and mini-bar. Good restaurant with nightly wayang and *Ramayana* shows. ⑧.

Aquila Prambanan, Jl Adiscipto 48 (☎0274/565005, fax 565009). Hotel with 191 rooms, many affording views over Prambanan. Japanese, Chinese and Javanese restaurants, and a pub with billiards and darts. ⑨.

Arjuna Plaza, Jl Mangkubumi 44 (☎0274/513063, fax 561862). Describes itself as a "hotel with a smile", but actually has quite a formal, businesslike atmosphere. Rooms are smart but not exceptional. ⑥.

Batik Yogya I, Jl Mangkubumi 46 (☎0274/562510, fax 561823). Sister of Sosro's *Batik Yogya II*, this place is less attractive, but with similar facilities. ⑦.

Gajah Mada, Bulaksumur, Gajah Mada University campus (☎0274/563461). Best of the accommodation options near the university. Nothing special, but perfectly acceptable for a short-term stay. ⑥.

Ibis, Jl Malioboro 52–58 (☎0274/516974, fax 516977). New, pastel-pink hotel ideally located behind the Malioboro Mall. Rooms are equipped with all the usual facilities (mini-bar, air-con and TV), and other features include a pool, sauna and gym. The room rates are exceptionally good value. ④–⑨.

Wisma Laras Hati, Jl Sosrokusuman DNI/182 (☎0274/514513). One of the better options on this small alley to the east of Malioboro, and one of the few to accept foreigners along this *gang*. ③.

Melia Purosani, Jl Suryotomo 31 (☎0274/589521, fax 588070). Imposing, peach-coloured monstrosity in a good location east of Malioboro. Yogya's only five-star hotel, with all the amenities you would expect. ⑨.

Mutiara, Jl Malioboro 16 (☎0274/563814, fax 561201). Central hotel split into two locations along Malioboro. Rooms have individual air-con, fridge, phones with IDD, and colour TV with in-house videos. ⑧.

Natour Garuda, Jl Malioboro 60 (☎0274/566353, fax 563074). Established in 1911, this is Yogya's oldest hotel, which has 235 standard and suite rooms, with tennis courts, two swimming pools and a shopping arcade. They also host gamelan recitals; see p.173. ⑨.
Puri, Jl Sosrokusuman DNI/22 (☎0274/514047). A little gloomy, with no windows, but the rooms have fans and are clean enough. ④.

The Kraton

The layout of Yogya reflects its character: modern and brash on the outside, but with a very ancient and traditional heart in the **Kraton**, the walled city designed by Yogya's first sultan, Mangkubumi. Derived from the Indonesian word for "king" (*ratu*), *kraton* means "royal residence" and originally referred just to the sultan's palace. Today, however, *kraton* usually denotes the whole of the walled city (plus Jalan Malioboro), which includes not only the palace but also an entire town of some ten thousand people.

The Kraton has changed little in the two hundred years since Mangkubumi's time; both the palace, and the 5km of crenellated icing-sugar walls that surround the Kraton, date from his reign. Essentially the Kraton is little more than a charming, close-knit town overlaid with a veneer of quiet aristocratic pride. Its character changes from one area to the next. Immediately around the palace there's a reverential hush in the high-walled, silent streets, which are lined with quaint whitewashed cottages. Further west, however, the atmosphere is as chaotic and intimate as of any other Javanese kampung: front doors are left open, laundry drips from lines strung between buildings, grandmothers sit gossiping on the doorsteps and children splash around in the mud in the alleyways.

With plenty of time you could wander through the Kraton for hours, but for those in a hurry, the main sights – the **Sultan's Palace**, **Sono Budoyo Museum** and the **Taman Sari** – can be visited on foot in a day.

Alun-alun Utara

Most people enter the Kraton through the northern gates by the GPO, beyond which lies the busy town square, **Alun-alun Utara**, a large field of threadbare, yellowing grass. The alun-alun has always been the venue for public entertainments. In the nineteenth century, by far the most popular of these were the fights staged between a tiger, of which there was once a ready supply in the region, and a buffalo. In typically Javanese fashion, these uneven contests took on symbolic meaning: the savage and cruel tiger was naturally identified with the Dutch, while the Javanese were represented by the buffalo, a steadfast, determined and proud beast. Almost invariably the tiger started off the strongest, only to be defeated in the end by the obduracy of the buffalo. The anti-colonial Yogyans would be doubly delighted at this result if a visiting Dutch dignitary was watching too. The tiger, however, was not always the victim of this entertainment:

> *The emperors sometimes make criminals, condemned to death, fight with tigers. In such cases, the man is rubbed with borri, or tumeric. The tiger, who has for a long time been kept fasting, falls upon the man with the greatest fury, and generally strikes him down at once with his paw. Even if he (the criminal) ultimately succeeds in killing his ferocious antagonist, he must suffer death, by command of the emperor.*
>
> *Island of Java*, John Joseph Stockdale (1811)

Of all the banyan trees growing on and around the alun-alun, the two at the centre are considered the most sacred. It was here, during the eighteenth and nineteenth centuries, that the opposing sides of a dispute would congregate – one at each tree – and put their arguments to the sultan. After deliberating for a while the sultan would issue his verdict, which was, of course, irrevocable.

As is traditional in Java, the city's grand mosque, or **Mesjid Agung** (visit outside of prayer times), built in 1773 by Mangkubumi, stands on the western side of the alun-alun. The mesjid is built along traditional Javanese lines, with a multi-tiered roof on top of an airy, open-sided prayer hall. The building is rather tatty, however, with a corrugated-iron roof and chipped paintwork sorely in need of repair.

A little to the north of the mosque, just by the main gates, stands the **Sono Budoyo Museum** (Tues–Thurs 8am–1.30pm, Fri 8–11.15am, Sat & Sun 8am–noon; Rp750). Opened in 1933 by Hamengkubuwono VIII, the museum houses a fine exhibition of the arts of Java, Madura and Bali. From the outside, the building, with a gamelan pendopo before the entrance, is a mini version of the sultan's palace that faces it. Of the exhibits inside, the intricate, damascene-style wooden partitions from Northern Java are particularly eye-catching, as are the many classical gold and stone statues dating back to the eighth century. Just outside the entrance, a shed houses a small puppet workshop that supplies the characters for the museum's evening wayang kulit performances (see p.173).

The Sultan's Palace

On the southern side of the alun-alun lies a masterpiece of understated Javanese architecture, an elegant collection of ornate kiosks and graceful pendopos housed within a series of spacious, interconnecting courtyards. This is the **Sultan's Palace**, or Karaton Ngayogyakarta Hadiningrat (Palace of the Town of Yogyakarta), to give it its full title. Distinctly unostentatious, and in places quite spartan, this single-storey palace is nevertheless rich in symbolism; it was designed as a scale model of the Hindu cosmos. Every plant, building and courtyard in the palace represents some element of this mystical universe. The sultans, though professing the Islamic faith, still held on to many of the Hindu and animist superstitions of their forefathers and believed that this particular design would ensure the prosperity of the royal house.

The palace is split into two parts, with two separate entrances (and, unfortunately, two sets of entrance fees too). The first section, the **Pagelaran** (Mon–Thurs, Sat & Sun 8am–1pm, Fri 8–11.30am; Rp1000, plus Rp500 camera fee, Rp1000 for video), lies immediately to the south of the alun-alun. It is bypassed by most tourists, as there is little to see save for two large, drab pendopos and an extremely mediocre display of regal costumes. The first and biggest pendopo functioned as the palace's reception, where foreign dignitaries and public officials would await an audience with the sultan. It was also the first home of the Gajah Mada University, founded in the 1940s by Hamengkubuwono IX, and is used today for theatrical and musical performances, particularly during the Sekatan festival (see p.51). The stairs at the back of the pendopo lead up to the **Siti Inggil** (High Ground), a platform on which the sultans of Yogya are crowned.

Forming a backdrop to the Siti Ingill, the massive wooden **Bronjonolo Gate** leads through to the rest of the palace. But, as it's now permanently closed, you have to walk down Jalan Alun-alun Lor, the road running alongside the western walls of the palace, to gain entrance. On the way you'll pass the small **Museum Kereta** (Mon–Thurs, Sat & Sun 8am–4pm, Fri 8.30am–1pm; Rp1000, plus Rp500 camera fee), housing a dusty collection of ten tatty royal chariots. Most impressive is the Kanjeng Kyai Cekatak, the diamond-studded saddle and harness of Hamengkubuwono I.

A hundred metres beyond the museum stands the entrance to the main body of the **palace** (Mon–Thurs, Sat & Sun 8.30am–2pm, Fri 8.30am–1pm; Rp3000 including optional guided tour, Rp500 camera fee, Rp1000 for video). Shorts and revealing clothes are frowned upon in this part of the palace; you will seldom be refused entry, but you may be required to rent a batik shirt from the ticket office (Rp1000). The palace has been the home of the sultans ever since Mangkubumi arrived here from Solo in 1755, and little has changed. The hushed courtyards, the faint stirrings of the gamelan drifting on the breeze and the elderly palace retainers, still dressed in the traditional style with a kris tucked by the small of their back, all contribute to a remarkable sense of timelessness.

You enter the complex through the palace's outer courtyard or **Keben** (after the keben trees that grow here), where the sultan used to sit on the stone throne which still stands in the centre of the large pendopo, and pass sentence on lawbreakers. The palace itself lies through the **Sriminganti Gate** to the south of the Keben. Throughout the palace you'll notice that most gates have a wall immediately behind them, to prevent evil spirits from entering further into the building – it is believed that they can only walk in straight lines.

Two pendopos stand on either side of a central path in the next courtyard – known as the **Sriminganti** (To Wait For the King) courtyard – each sheltering an antique gamelan orchestra under a timber roof. The eastern pendopo, the **Bangsal Trajumas**, also houses a number of royal curios including an early royal playpen, which looks like an oversized birdcage.

Two silver-painted *raksasa* (temple guardian statues) guard the **Donapratopo Gate** to the south and the entrance to the next courtyard, the **Pelataran Kedaton**. Once through, you find yourself in the largest and most important courtyard in the palace. On your left stands a small **Dutch Kiosk**, resembling a stained-glass bandstand. On your right, and forming the northwestern corner of the courtyard, is the yellow-painted **Gedung Kuning** (Yellow Building), the offices and living quarters of the sultan. This part of the palace is out of bounds to tourists, as the current sultan (Hamengkubuwono X), his wife and five daughters still spend much of their time here.

A covered corridor joins the Gedung Kuning with the so-called Golden Throne Pavilion, or **Bangsal Kencono**, the centrepiece of the Pelataran Kedaton. In the imagery of the Hindu cosmos, the pavilion represents Mount Meru, the sacred mountain at the very centre of the universe. It's an impressive pendopo, with an intricately carved roof held aloft by some hefty teak pillars, whose carvings neatly sum up the syncretism of the three main religions of Indonesia, with the lotus leaf of Buddhism supporting a red-and-gold diamond pattern of Hindu origin, while around the pillar's circumference runs the opening lines of the Koran: "There is no God but Allah and Mohammed is his prophet."

LORO KIDUL

The curious relationship between the Sultan of Yogya and the Goddess of the South Seas, **Ratu Loro Kidul**, is one of the most intriguing and enduring themes of court folklore. The tradition began with the founder of the Mataram dynasty, Senopati. Just before his assault on the kingdoms of the north coast, an attack that laid the foundations for the Mataram empire, Senopati withdrew to the south coast for a few days to gather his thoughts and contemplate a plan of action. Meditating on the cliffs, he was spotted by the goddess, whose underwater palace lies offshore at Parangtritis. Senopati followed Loro Kidul to the palace, where for three days she instructed him in the arts of war and love-making. Thanks to her tuition, Senopati went on to conquer the north coast with ease, and soon most of Java came under his control (whether the lovemaking classes were equally fruitful is not recorded).

All the subsequent leaders of Mataram have continued to pay tribute to Loro. In Solo, a tower in the centre of the royal palace has a floor reserved solely for the use of the susuhunan and the goddess, and Mangkubumi's Taman Sari (see opposite) was apparently modelled on Loro's water palace. The superstitious fixation with Loro Kidul continues to this day. Annual offerings are presented to the goddess at Parangkusumo (see p.179), where Senopati emerged after his crash course in love and war. In Solo, on the anniversary of the coronation of the susuhunan, the sacred *bedoyo ketaweng* dance is performed in tribute to the goddess (who, it is believed, sometimes joins in with the dancing). And many of the congregation who attended the coronation of Sultan Hamengkubuwono X of Yogya in 1989 noted a strong fragrance borne along by a sudden breath of wind halfway through the ceremony – a sure indication that Loro Kidul had come to witness the crowning of her next devotee.

Adjoining the Bangsal Kencono to the south is a large marble-floored ceremonial dining hall, the **Bangsal Manis**.

The only other rooms open to the public in the Pelataran Kedaton are the small **utility rooms** lining the courtyard's southern wall, which house a collection of tea sets as well as the odd regal spittoon. The royal tea-makers, a group of three elderly ladies, still make the tea three times a day and carry it forth, with all due ceremony, to the sultan's office in the Gedung Kuning.

Running north–south beyond the Pelataran Kedaton's eastern wall is a series of three more courtyards, once the quarters of the sultans' sons. A large, arched gateway flanked by two huge drums connects the Pelataran Kedaton with the middle of these three courtyards, the **Kesatrian**, home to both another gamelan orchestra and, in galleries along the east and southern wall, a collection of **royal portraits**, with some by the esteemed nineteenth-century artist Raden Saleh. Most of the buildings in the **southern courtyard**, including the central glass pavilion, are filled with the photographs and personal effects of the Independence hero Hamengkubuwono IX (whose face today adorns the back of the Rp10,000 note). The **Gedung Kopo**, the buildings lining the **northern courtyard**, was once the palace hospital and now houses a small palace museum. The exhibits here include replicas of the royal thrones, and gifts given to the sultans by various heads of state.

The Taman Sari and Pasar Ngasem

A five-minute walk to the west of the palace, along Jalan Rotowijayan and down Jalan Ngasem and Jalan Taman, is the unspectacular **Taman Sari** (Water Garden) of Mangkubumi (daily 9am–3pm; Rp1000, plus Rp500 camera fee). This giant complex was designed in the eighteenth century as an amusement park for the royal house, a convenient and luxurious escape from the everyday chores of being sultan. Incorporated into this paradise were a series of swimming pools and fountains, an underground mosque, a large boating lake and a few small groves of coconuts and cloves. A tower was also built, from which the sultan could watch his harem splashing around in the pools below. Having made his selection from the bathers, Mangkubumi would then retire to the tower's bedroom.

Unfortunately the Taman Sari fell into disrepair soon after the death of Mangkubumi. The elaborate design and multi-storey buildings required an enormous amount of maintenance, which the cash-strapped sultans simply could not afford. The British invasion in 1812 damaged many of the Taman's buildings and a serious earthquake in 1867 accelerated its decline, so most of what you see today is a concrete reconstruction. The main entrance gate is about the most complete and attractive part of the ruins; you can still wander through the cobwebbed underground passages, where the shell of the sultan's underground mosque is visible. Above ground, however, most of the complex has been lost to the advance of the kampung, which encroaches from every side and which has derived much of its building material from the Taman's rubble.

Also within the former grounds of the Taman Sari, Yogya's bird market, the **Pasar Ngasem**, has been established on a dusty half-acre lot on what was once part of the boating lake. The market is at its busiest on Sundays, although whatever day you arrive you should see all manner of birds, plus dogs, lizards and rodents, for sale.

Jalan Malioboro

The two-kilometre stretch of road heading north from the alun-alun is as replete with history as it is with batik shops and becak. Originally this panoply of souvenir stalls and batik outlets was designed as a **ceremonial boulevard** by Mangkubumi, along which the royal cavalcade would proceed on its way to Mount Merapi. The road changes name three times along its length, beginning as Jalan J.A. Yani in the south before continuing as Jalan Malioboro, and then finally Jalan Mangkubumi. It is one long unbroken stream of diesel-belching traffic heading south – the pavement is where the real action happens. In the very early morning, and especially on Sundays, it becomes an outdoor gymnasium with many Yogyans congragating to perform t'ai chi. During the day, these same pavements reach bursting point as the souvenir market gets into full swing. And then in the evening the food sellers wheel in to set up their stalls and create a great long alfresco diner.

At the southern end of the street, at the junction of Jalan J.A. Yani and Jalan Senopati, a number of historical buildings stand facing each other. On the northeast corner, opposite the imposing, colonial-style GPO, the **March First Monument** is a statue of four soldiers on a plinth marching purposefully behind their commander, flag-waving Colonel Suharto. The statue is also known as the *Six Hours in Yogyakarta* monument, as it commemorates the six-hour recapture of Yogya from the Dutch in 1949.

Behind it are the orderly hedgerows and flowerbeds of the **Benteng Vredeburg** (Tues–Thurs 8.30am–1.30pm, Fri 8.30–11am; Rp750). The Dutch, who, thanks to their successful divide-and-rule policies in the mid-eighteenth century, had acquired a stranglehold on Central Java, ordered Mangkubumi to build the fort in 1756. It took over twenty years to complete, however, mainly because Mangkubumi was unwilling to spare men and materials from his own ongoing pet project, the Taman Sari. This relic of Dutch imperialism has been restored to its former glory, and the solid, whitewashed walls form an impressive and austere facade on Jalan J. A. Yani. Inside, the fort houses a series of dioramas split between three barrack rooms which recount, ironically enough considering their setting, the end of colonialism in Indonesia. The dioramas, particularly of the battles that took place in Yogya itself, are well made and informative, and the air-con in the fort must be the best in Yogya.

Another imposing old colonial building lies over the road. The **Gedung Negara** (State Guest House) was built in 1823 for the Dutch Resident and became the presidential palace in the 1940s, when Yogya was made the capital of the republic during the Revolution. Just across the narrow road that runs along the northern wall of the Gedung Negara stands the small and peaceful Norman-style **Gereja Margomulyo** (1830), Yogya's oldest church.

Opposite, by way of contrast, the **Pasar Beringharjo** buzzes noisily throughout the day. Established during the reign of Mangkubumi and named after the bering-tree forest that once grew here, the current building was commissioned by Hamengkubuwono IX in 1925. A multi-level, dimly lit complex dominated by mass-produced batik (with a small, quality selection in the southeastern corner on the ground floor), the market is raucous, disorganized and great fun.

Three hundred metres north, on the right behind the tourist office, is a grand collection of pavilions known as the **Kepatihan Administration Office**, formerly the residence of the Patih, or minister of Yogya. Another 300km north, on the same side of the street, are the large lawns of the **Regional Legislature**; a statue of the Independence hero General Sudirman overlooks the road from the front of the lawn.

Malioboro continues for another kilometre north. The end of Mangkubumi's original path is marked by the **Tugu Monument**, a curious obelisk that commemorates the founding of Yogya in 1755; it replaced an earlier obelisk on the same spot, which once marked the official northern limit of the Kraton.

The rest of the city

Outside the Kraton walls, Yogya develops a split personality. To the **north** the city is permanently constipated with traffic and appears as rowdy and polluted as most Javan cities. The tourist attractions here are numerous, but cannot compare with what the Kraton has to offer. To the **south** of the Kraton the city is far calmer and more prepossessing, as well as more affluent. There are no sights as such, but a number of local artists have set up shops and galleries here that merit a look.

Jalan Senopati and Jalan Agung

The busy road heading east from the GPO, which initially goes by the name of **Jalan Senopati**, plays host to a number of sights. Three hundred metres east of the GPO, at the junction where Jalan Senopati transforms into Jalan Agung, your eye will probably be caught by Yogya's foremost Buddhist temple, the **Cetiya Buddha Prabha**, its vivid red paintwork flecked with gold; occasional wayang performances are held here. Four hundred metres further on, on the same side of the road at no. 22, is the **Biology Museum** (Mon–Thurs 7.30am–1.30pm, Fri 7.30–11am, Sat 7.30am–12.30pm, Sun 7.30am–noon; Rp200), a collection of long-dead animals, some pickled and some stuffed, the star attraction being a rather sorry-looking orang-utan. Just round the corner to the east of here, on Jalan Bintaran Wetan, is the **Sasmitaluka Jen Sudirman** (The House of General Sudirman) which has been preserved and turned into an unenthralling museum displaying photos and memorabilia associated with the Independence hero (Mon–Fri & Sun 8am–2pm; free).

Yogyakarta's second court, **Paku Alam** (Tues, Thurs & Sun 9.30am–1.30pm; free), lies 50m to the east of the museum on the north side of Jalan Agung. As is traditional, the minor court of the city faces south as a mark of subservience to the main palace. The royal household of Paku Alam was created in 1812 by the British for Notokusumo (Paku Alam I), the brother of Sultan Hamengkubuwono II and the Brits' most important ally in the sacking of the Kraton that year. By dividing Yogya between two courts, the British were deliberately duplicating the divide-and-rule tactic used so successfully by the Dutch in Solo fifty years earlier.

The current prince, the octogenarian Paku Alam VIII, is by far the longest-reigning ruler of all Central Java's royal courts, having been in place for over sixty years. His quarters are concealed from public gaze at the back of the palace. The part that is open to general view – by the southeastern corner of the courtyard – houses a motley collection of royal artefacts, including a huge family tree and a room filled with the prince's chariots, which unfortunately appear to be permanently shrouded in white dust cloths.

Two kilometres further east along Jalan Sultan Agung (which soon after Paku Alam changes its name to Jalan Kusumanegara), on the eastern banks of the Kali Gajah Wong, lies the **Gembira Loka Zoo** (daily 8am–4pm; Rp1500), home to a large selection of African and Asian animals kept in rather cramped conditions.

Jalan Sudirman

Jalan Sudirman, which heads east from the Tugu monument towards the airport, and its continuation, **Jalan Adisucipto**, are flanked by a number of minor tourist attractions. These sights are very spread out, so the road is probably best tackled by taxi or, if you can stand the traffic, bicycle. If you just want to see the Affandi Gallery – the biggest attraction on this road – catch bus #8 (from Umbulharjo) which stops outside.

The **Army Museum** (Mon–Fri 8am–1.30pm; free) is 1km east of Tugu, on the corner of Jalan Sudirman and Jalan Cik Ditiro. Housed in the former offices of revolutionary hero **General Sudirman**, the museum traces his rise through the ranks, as well as housing a wide collection of uniforms, medals and other paraphernalia, including Sudirman's old car. Some of the captions are in English, but not enough, unfortunately, to make sense of many of the exhibits.

Thanks to Yogya's one-way system, it is impossible to drive or cycle east for the next kilometre. To bypass this, head north for 400m along Jalan Cik Ditiro, then east for 1km along Jalan Terban, before heading south back along Jalan Gejayan to Jalan Sudirman, which by this time has reverted to a two-way road once more. Jalan Sudirman changes its name at this point to Jalan Adisucipto.

Two kilometres east along Jalan Adisucipto, on the west bank of the Kali Gajah Wong, you'll find the **Affandi Gallery** (Mon–Fri & Sun 8.30am–4pm, Sat 8.30am–1pm; Rp1250, Rp2500 camera fee). Heralded by the *New Statesman* in 1952 as the most important post-war painter in the world, Affandi, the son of a clerk at a Dutch sugar plantation, was born in Cirebon in 1907, but spent most of his life and did most of his paintings in Yogya, in the unusual house-cum-studio that still stands on stilts above the river near the galleries. After dropping out of high school, Affandi spent much of the 1920s and 1930s painting cinema hoardings in order to survive, scraping up the paint remnants at the end of the day to indulge in his own creative passion after work. It was during these formative years that Affandi developed his idiosyncratic style, discarding the paintbrush and palette because they denied him spontaneity, preferring instead to apply the paint to the canvas directly from the tube, forming thick swirls of colour into a style that Sukarno once described simply as "crazy". Many of the paintings were completed in just one hour. The galleries were built after his death in 1990 and contain over a hundred of his greatest works, including several self-portraits and a number of landscapes and streetscapes painted in America and Holland. His eldest child, Kartika, has since followed in her father's footsteps and become a painter, and a few of her works now hang in the gallery alongside those of her father. Affandi's unusual car – a fish-shaped Colt Galant hot rod – stands in the forecourt by the entrance.

The **Ambarrukmo Palace Hotel** is situated 1km further east, on the same side of the road. Its grounds once belonged to a pleasure palace built for Hamengkubuwono III. There's little to see now of the palace, save for the main pendopo and a floating pavilion (Bale Kambang), which has been converted into a top-class restaurant (see p.172). There's also the odd chariot, and a couple of mannequins looking rather awkward in court dress. From here, cross over the road to the **Ambar Budaya Craft Centre**, a government-owned souvenir superstore specializing in wayang puppets, woodcarvings and earthenware pottery. The goods aren't exceptional, and similar items can be found in town, although the prices are fixed and reasonable.

Continuing east for 1.5km, a major road – Jalan Janti – appears on the right. Head down here for a further kilometre, then turn left to the **Di Museum Pusat Tni-Au Dirgantara Mandala** (Mon, Tues & Sun 8am–1pm; Rp500), dedicated to Indonesia's glorious tradition of aviation. Officially, you are meant to tell the authorities – via the tourist office – at least one day in advance that you wish to visit this museum; in practice, however, if you just turn up and hand over some form of ID they will often let you through. The museum is an unexpected pleasure, with plenty of aircraft on show, from early biplanes to modern jet engines.

Kota Gede and the Museum Wayang Kekayon

The small, wealthy suburb of **Kota Gede** lies 5km southeast of the town centre. To get here, catch bus #4 from Jalan Malioboro and jump off at Tom's Silver, a journey of about forty minutes. The suburb is famous today as the centre of the silver industry (see the shopping section on p.174 for details). For 39 years, however, this was the capital of the Mataram empire. Founded by Senopati in 1575, the court at Kota Gede lasted until Senopati's grandson, Sultan Agung, re-established the court at Karta during the early years of the seventeenth century. The graves of Senopati and his son and heir, Krapyak, form the centrepiece of the **Kota Gede Cemetery** (Mon & Tues 10am–noon, Fri 1–3pm) which lies to the rear of the suburb's **Grand Mosque**. The body of Yogya's second sultan, Hamengkubuwono II (1810–11 & 1812–14), the bane of both the Dutch and British colonialists, also rests here. Traditional court dress must be worn, and can be rented at the ticket office.

One of Yogya's best museums lies 7km east of town on Jalan Raya Yogya (take a Wonosari-bound bus from the bus station for 10min; Rp300). The excellent **Museum Wayang Kekayon** (Wayang Museum; daily except Mon 8am–3pm; Rp1000) takes visitors on a journey through the development of puppeteering and explores the many different forms of wayang today. Fronted by a large pendopo, the displays inside the surrounding buildings include such seldom-seen treasures as a *wayang beber* set, where the action is drawn onto a large scroll of paper which is slowly unfurled as events unfold; a set of wooden puppets from a *wayang wahyu* set, used to tell the story of the Nativity; and a *sejati wayang* set, which employs the puppets as an educational tool to re-enact various twentieth-century events. If you didn't catch the Wayang Museum in Jakarta, this is the next best thing.

Eating

Yogya's specialities are ayam goreng and *nasi gudeg* (rice and jackfruit) and many food-stalls serve nothing else. Every evening on Jalan Malioboro, the noise of traffic is replaced by the equally clamorous night-time **food market**. Hundreds of warung set up at about 4pm, and by 8pm the entire street is thronged with diners. Wherever you choose to eat along this street, make sure you know how much everything costs: stall-holders are not averse to raising their prices to extortionate levels, and in many of the larger **lesehan** places (where you sit on the floor by low tables), particularly those by the end of Jalan Sosro, diners pay restaurant prices. The stalls by the train station and on the top floor of the Malioboro Mall are cheaper. If all this frenzy is a little too taxing on the nerves, head to the **warung** at the end of Gang I, a regular travellers' haunt serving a wonderfully spicy curry for around Rp1000.

Jalan Sosro and Jalan Prawirotaman are chock-full of good-quality restaurants dishing up pretty close approximations of Western dishes alongside standard Indonesian fare. Prices are usually very reasonable, too: about Rp2000 for nasi goreng. Most of these restaurants open at about midday, and remain open until the last customer has left – usually at about 10pm, although in some cases much later. The restaurants on Prawirotaman are a shade more expensive than those on Sosro, but their cooking is usually superior.

Jalan Sosro

Anna, Gang II. Popular little family-run restaurant proffering some wonderful, genuinely Indonesian food. If you don't like their *nasi gudeg* (Rp4250), they promise to refund your money.

Bladok, Jl Sosro 76. Part of a hotel, this open-air mid-priced restaurant serving mainly Indonesian dishes is a little more expensive than the Sosro norm, but definitely worth it.

Budarti, Gang II/125. Excellent-value restaurant, especially good for breakfasts and snacks. The pancakes are superb, the fruit juices very cheap, and the ginseng coffee (Rp1500) addictive.

Busis, Gang I. Small restaurant with an unimaginative Western and Indonesian menu. The food itself, however, is inexpensive and tasty.

Café Sosro, Gang II. Another family-run place, serving good, filling and reasonably priced Indonesian and Western food; try the chicken sandwiches or spaghetti bolognese. Come here for lunch rather than in the evenings (they close at 9pm), when the service can be very slow and many of the dishes are unavailable.

Chaterina, Jl Sosro. Very reasonably priced restaurant with *lesehan* seating at the rear, serving some of the best food in Sosro. Let down a little by hassle from the batik touts.

Eko, Gang I. Unpretentious little place serving hearty breakfasts and run-of-the-mill Indonesian dishes at reasonable prices.

Heru Jaya French Grill, Moderately priced restaurant serving tasty Western food of varying degrees of authenticity.

Lily Pudding, Jl Jlagran Lor. This place, 50m to the west of the train station on the opposite side of the road, turns out a treasure trove of treacle treats. Try their nine-inch caramel pudding for Rp4500.

Mamas, Jl Pasar Kembang. Most popular of all the cheap eateries by the train station, serving huge portions of tasty Indonesian food.

Murni, Gang I. Busy little alcohol-free budget restaurant serving huge portions of delicious food. Probably the best value in Sosro. Closed in the evenings.

N.N., Gang II. A family-owned place with hearty food (particularly the delicious soups), and good service. Very cheap too.

Prada, Jl Malioboro 145. Built above the tasteful souvenir shop, this medium-priced café serves some very authentic Western dishes and screens movies in the evening. Try their mouthwatering calzone (Rp8000).

Superman I and **II**, JL Sosro Gang I. Whilst *Superman I* is left to slip into disrepair, *II* continues to be the most popular restaurant in Sosro, with ice-cold beer, regular screenings of European football, and Internet facilities (it has one terminal that's reputed to be the fastest in Yogya) compensating for the rather bland, overpriced food and the gruff demeanour of the manager.

33, Gang I. A cross between a restaurant and a warung, this tiny two-tabled restaurant serving Indonesian standards and pancakes ranks as the cheapest in Sosro. Unpredictable opening hours.

Jalan Prawirotaman

Going Bananas, Jl Prawirotaman 48. Café/souvenir shop at the eastern end of the street. Good coffees and sandwiches.

Griya Birjana, Jl Prawirotaman. Hugely popular restaurant on the main drag, serving Indonesian and Western fare and ice-cold beer. Lively atmosphere in the evenings, and good value all the time.

Hanoman's Forest, Jl Prawirotaman 9. The main reason to come here is to watch the nightly (8pm) cultural entertainments – wayang puppet shows, Javanese ballet and live bands. The food is nothing special.

Little Amsterdam, Jl Prawirotaman II. Large menu of Western dishes with the emphasis on steaks and freshly baked bread. Medium-priced.

Lotus Breezes, Jl Prawirotaman I. The younger and better-looking of the two *Lotus* restaurants, with delicious if slightly overpriced food served by occasionally stroppy waiters.

Lotus Garden, Jl Prawirotaman MG3/593a. A partner of the *Lotus Breezes*, this mid-priced restaurant specializes in producing high-quality, healthy local dishes. Good vegetarian selection. Classical and modern dance and puppet performances throughout the week (8pm; Rp3000).

Mercury, Jl Parawirotaman II MG3/595. Beautiful, colonial-style restaurant serving surprisingly affordable mid-priced Indonesian and Western dishes.

Nusa Dua, Jl Prawirotaman. Highly recommended inexpensive restaurant with a large menu of Indonesian, Chinese and Western dishes served by very professional, friendly staff.

Prambanan, Jl Prawirotaman 14. This gloomy restaurant is one of the quietest on the street, serving filling Indonesian staples at fair prices.

Riki French Grill and **Harrys's** (sic) **Pancakes**, Jl Prawirotaman. Two noisy, popular restaurants in one location, with satisfactory food. Mid-priced.

Samba, Jl Parangtritis. Smallish café specializing in Western sandwiches and snacks. Open daytime only.

Via Via, Jl Prawirotaman 24b. Serves a different menu of inventive and excellent dishes every day. The staff are friendly and there are a couple of good "travellers' tips" books, along with current editions of *Time* and *Newsweek*.

Yuko, Jl Prawirotaman 22. Mid-priced restaurant in the *Rose Hotel*, serving mainly Indonesian dishes. The food is of a high quality, with particularly good chicken dishes; their *cap cai* (Rp3500) is tasty too.

Elsewhere

Ambarrukmo, Jl Adisucipto. This former palace (see p.170) has a marvellous floating restaurant where you can sit and watch traditional Javanese dancing or puppet shows. At over US$20 for the Indonesian buffet it's not cheap, but if you have a few loose rupiah in your pocket you won't regret spending them here.

Cirebon, Jl Malioboro. Large, high-ceilinged establishment full of caged birds and fish tanks. The food, in particular the noodle dishes, is tasty (although portions are small) and the drinks are ice-cold. Perfect for afternoon snacks.

Legian, Jl Perwakilan 9. Upmarket restaurant overlooking Malioboro. Serves scrumptious Indonesian fare – including some wonderful grilled fish and chops – and less-inspired Western dishes.

Lesehan Pojok, Jl Perwakilan. Inexpensive *lesehan* establishment just along from the *Legian*, serving *nasi gudeg* and other local dishes. A good alternative to the eateries of Sosro.

Sinar Budi Jl Mangkubumi 41. Mid-priced Padang food and a popular local hangout.

Street vendor, Jakarta

Cyclist, Jalan M.H. Thamrin, Jakarta

Gamelan, Yogyakarta, Central Java

Wayang Museum, Jakarta

Hindu temple, Gedung Songo and Gunung Merapi, Central Java

Borobudur, Central Java

Fishing boats, West Java

· Fruit juice vendor, Jakarta

Sultan's Palace, Yogyakarta, Central Java

Sulphur miners, Ijen plateau, East Java

Prambanan complex, Central Java

Gunung Bromo, East Java

Nightlife and cultural entertainment

Yogya's **nightlife** is really an early-evening life; very few places stay open beyond midnight, and most of the action happens between 7pm and 10pm, when the city's **cultural entertainment** is in full swing.

If you're not going to a show, your options for a night out are limited, though a couple of the **bars** are worth checking out. The *Laba Laba* on Jalan Prawirotaman is an overpriced restaurant and bar, with weird cocktails a speciality: try the "Laba Laba Special", a potent mixture of Guinness, whisky and shandy. The *Borobudur Bar*, on Jalan Pasar Kembang by the northern end of Sosro Gang I, is one of the few places that stays open beyond midnight. With its carefully cultivated downmarket image attracting locals, expats and tourists alike, this place continues to be a roaring success. Live bands, usually performing unintentionally hilarious covers of Western rock classics, feature most nights. After *Borobudur*, you could continue to the *Rumah Musik* **disco**, part of the *Hotel Mendut*, just 100m to the west. Popular with locals, this place has live music every evening (Indonesian *dangdut* usually) and doesn't charge an entrance fee. It's not a scintillating place, but if you want to keep on drinking this is one of the cheapest and most convenient places to come. A second disco, with a dress code (which is usually dropped for Westerners), operates under the *Mutiara* hotel at Jalan Malioboro 16. Once these two have closed (at around 3am), the only place left open will be the *Takashimura* karaoke bar in the east of the city at Jalan Solo 35. A taxi here should cost no more than Rp5000.

Wayang kulit and wayang golek

Wayang kulit is the epitome of Javanese culture, and visitors should really try to catch at least a part of one of these shows, although **wayang golek**, where wooden puppets are used, tends to be easier to follow, as the figures are more dynamic and expressive. For a preview of both forms, head to the Sultan's Palace. On Saturday mornings (9am–1pm) there's a practice-cum-performance of wayang kulit in the Sriminganti courtyard, and every Wednesday (9am–noon) a free wayang golek show. On Monday and Tuesday mornings between 10.30am and noon, free **gamelan** performances are given. The *Natour Garuda Hotel* also holds regular gamelan recitals every evening at 8pm.

With one honourable exception, all of the wayang performances listed below are designed with tourists' attention span in mind, being only two hours long. Hard-core wayang kulit fans, however, may wish to check out the all-nighter at the Alun-alun Selatan (see Sasana Hinggil below). For the latest timings and schedules, ask at the tourist office or your hotel.

Agastya, Jl Gedongkiwo 996. Tucked away on the banks of the Kali Winongo in the city's southwestern suburbs, this institute was founded to train *dalang* and prevent wayang kulit from dying out in Central Java. Wayang kulit performances are held every day at 3pm except Saturday – when a wayang golek performance is staged (Rp4000).

Ambar Budaya (aka **Dewi Sri**), Jl Adisucipto 66. This government craft centre opposite the *Ambarrukmo Palace Hotel* hosts a daily wayang kulit performance (8pm; Rp2500).

Ambarrukmo Palace, Jl Adisucipto 66. A free wayang golek show in the restaurant is put on as an accompaniment to the food (Mon 8pm).

Hanoman's Forest, Jl Prawirotaman 9 (☎0274/372528). Every Wednesday at 7pm this restaurant presents a 2hr wayang kulit show (Rp3000).

Nitour, Jl K.H.A. Dalan 71 (☎0274/376450). This centre, outside of the northern walls of the Kraton, puts on a wayang golek performance of the *Ramayana* tales. Daily except holidays 11am–1pm; Rp3000.

Sasana Hinggil, Alun-alun Selatan. Yogya's only full-length wayang kulit performance runs from 9pm to 5.30am on the second Saturday of every month, and on alternate fourth Saturdays (Rp3000).

Sonobudoyo Museum, Jl Trikora 1. The most professional and popular wayang kulit show, performed daily for 2hr (8pm; Rp4000).

Javanese dancing

The **Ramayana** dance drama is a modern extension of the court dances of the nineteenth century, which tended to use that other Indian epic, the *Mahabharata*, as the source of their story lines. These dramas can still be seen in many theatres throughout Yogya today. The biggest crowd-pulling spectacle around Yogya has to be the moonlit performance of the *Ramayana* ballet, which takes place every summer in the open-air theatre at Prambanan temple, and can be booked in Yogya (see p.186 for details). The city also hosts a number of other dance productions based on the *Ramayana* tales.

Ambarrukmo Palace, Jl Adisucipto 66. Javanese dance shows are held every evening at 8pm in the *Borobudur Restaurant*, on the seventh floor of the *Ambarrukmo Palace Hotel*, with the *Ramayana* ballet performed three times a week (Mon, Wed & Sat).

Hanoman's Forest, Jl Prawirotaman 9. Performances by Hanomans' dancers, combining elements of classical and modern dance (Rp3000).

Lotus Garden Restaurant, Jl Prawirotaman II. Selection of dance styles from the archipelago (Tues, Thurs & Sat, 8pm; Rp3000).

Melati Garden, Jl Prawirotaman II. Dance shows from Java, Sumatra and Bali (Mon, Wed & Fri 8pm–9.30pm; free).

Ndalem Pujokusirman, Jl Brig Jen Katamso 45. A two-hour performance of classical Javanese dance at this, one of the most illustrious dance schools in Yogya (Mon, Wed & Fri 8pm; Rp10,000).

Purawisata Theatre, Jl Brig Jen Katamso (☎0274/374089). Every night for the last eighteen years, the Puriwisata Theatre has put on a 90min performance of the *Ramayana*. The story is split into two episodes, with each episode performed on alternate nights. On the last day of every month the whole story is performed. Free transport from your hotel is also provided by the theatre (8pm; Rp20,000 or Rp32,000).

Sultan's Palace. Every Sunday and Thursday, the Kraton Classical Dance School holds public rehearsals (10am–noon). No cover fee once you've paid to get into the palace.

Shopping

Yogya is Java's souvenir centre, with keepsakes and mementos from all over the archipelago finding their way into the city's shops and street stalls. **Jalan Malioboro** is the main shopping area; you won't unearth any real treasures in the makeshift markets that hog Malioboro's pavements, but for inexpensive souvenirs (batik pictures, leather bags, woodcarvings and silver rings) this the place to come.

A recent development on the shopping scene is the establishment of a number of upmarket **souvenir emporiums** which steer clear of the usual mass-produced offerings, selling tasteful, individual local craft items instead: Sosro's Going Bananas and Something Different in Prawirotaman are two such places. Another excellent starting point, although a little way out of town, is the Desa Kerajinan, the government's craft centre opposite the *Ambarrukmo Palace Hotel* at Jalan Adisucipto 66 (see p.163).

Silver

The suburb of Kota Gede is the home of the **silver industry** in Central Java. It's famous for its fine **filigree** work, although the sort of products created are varied; if you've been hankering after a replica of Borobudur temple in solid silver, or even a scale model of an aircraft carrier, then Kota Gede is the place to come. If you can't find exactly what you want, it's possible to commission the workshops to produce it for you. Some workshops, such as the huge Tom's Silver at Jalan Ngeksigondo 60 (daily 8.30am–7.30pm), allow you to wander around and watch the smiths at work. A few, such as Borobudur Silver on the way to Kota Gede at Jalan Menteri Supeno 41 (daily 8am–8pm), also give discounts to HI and ISIC card-holders.

If your budget is limited, then the many stallholders along *Malioboro* sell perfectly reasonable silver jewellery, much of it from East Java or Bali. Expect to pay Rp2500 for a ring, and Rp4000 for earrings.

Batik

With the huge influx of tourists over the last twenty years, Yogya has evolved a **batik** style that increasingly panders to Western tastes. There is still plenty of the traditional indigo-and-brown batik clothing – sarongs, shirts and dresses – for sale, especially on Jalan Malioboro and the Beringharjo market. But recently Yogya has come to specialize in batik painting, much of it based around psychedelic swirls or chocolate-box Javanese landscapes designed to appeal to tourists. There are batik galleries everywhere, and touts hang around the tourist centres trying to persuade you to visit their gallery.

If your knowledge of batik is a little shaky, then it might be a good idea to begin your quest at the **Balai Penelitian Kerajinan dan Batik** (Batik and Handicraft Research Centre) at Jalan Kusumanegara 2 (Mon–Thurs 9–11.30am, Fri 9–10.30am). This government-run centre researches ways of improving production techniques; you can tour the building, and by the entrance there's a small shop selling fixed-price batik paintings from about Rp25,000.

From the research centre, head west to the gaggle of **galleries** in the Kraton, most of them tucked away in the kampung that occupies the grounds of the old Taman Sari. Ninety-nine percent of the paintings on offer here are mass-produced, but a thorough search should unearth that elusive one percent of original work. For the best-quality – and most expensive – batiks in town, head to **Jalan Tirtodipuran**, west of Jalan Prawirotaman, home of the renowned artists Tulus Warsito (at 19a) and Slamet Riyanto (61a), as well as a galaxy of good-quality galleries. If you still haven't found a piece of batik that you like, you could try and make one yourself by signing up for one of the many batik courses held in Yogya; see p.176 for details.

Leather and pottery

All around Yogya, and particularly in the markets along Jalan Malioboro, hand-stitched, good-quality **leather** bags, suitcases, belts and shoes can be bought extremely cheaply. A number of Maliobro's shops also sell leather goods; check out Kerajinan Indonesia at no. 193 and the Fancy Art Shop at no. 189a. Prices start at Rp20,000 for the simplest satchel – check the strength of the stitching and the quality of the leather before buying. Many of these leather products originate from the village of **Manding**, 12km south of Yogya. To get there, catch a white Jahayu bus from Jalan Parangtritis (25min; Rp300). The widest selection of leather goods and the best bargains are found here, and it is also possible, by visiting one of the workshops, to have something made to your own design.

Javanese pottery is widely available throughout Yogya. Again, the markets along Malioboro – and particularly in Pasar Beringharjo – are good sources, as are the souvenir shops along Jalan Tirtodipuran. Bargain hard, and expect to pay about Rp8000 for a thirty-centimetre-high pot.

Much of the pottery comes from tiny **Kasongan** village, 7km south of Yogya, 1km to the west of the main road to Bantul (Rp300 by Jahayu bus from Yogya bus station, or from Jalan Haryono). The town is a riot of ochre pottery, with huge Chinese urns, decorative bowls, erotic statues, whistles, flutes and other pottery instruments – and you can see the potters in action.

Antiques, puppets and curios

In the vicinity of Jalan Prawirotaman there are a number of cavernous antique shops dealing mainly in **teak furniture** from Jepara and the north. Much of it is very fine quality, but the cost of sending these bulky items home may be prohibitive. **Antique shops** include Ancient Arts at Jalan Tirtodipuran 50 and Dieng at no. 30. Many of these outlets sell traditional Javanese wooden trunks, the exteriors beautifully carved with detailed patterns, for which you can expect to pay at least US$50. Fancy Javanese chairs and desks are also very popular, though the prices are high.

Harto is a large company with a number of outlets around Jalan Tirtodipuran, each specializing in a particular sort of souvenir. One shop sells **woodcarvings**, for instance, and another deals in **wayang kulit puppets**; expect to pay at least Rp75,000 for a reasonable-quality thiry-centimetre puppet. There are also a couple of puppet shops on Jalan Prawirotaman, and two at the northern end of Malioboro.

Other popular souvenirs include personalized **rubber stamps**, made while you wait on the pavements of Jalan Malioboro, and the traditional Yogyan batik **headscarf** (*iket*), distinguishable from the Solo variety by the large pre-tied knot at the back, costing about Rp2500. A new shop, Samudra Raya at Jalan Sosro GT1/32, specializes in selling good-quality models of traditional Indonesian ships. Prices start at about Rp150,000.

Listings

Airlines Bouraq, Jl Mataram 60 (☎0274/562664); Garuda, *Ambarrukmo Palace Hotel* (☎0274/565835), and at the airport (☎0274/563706); Merpati, Jl Diponegoro 31 (☎0274/514272); Mandala, Jl Mayor Suryotomo 573 (☎0274/520603). All have the same opening hours: Mon–Fri 7.30am–5pm, Sat & Sun 9am–1pm.

Banks and exchange Yogya is one of the few places where the moneychangers offer a better deal than the banks, at least for cash. In particular, PT Gajahmas Mulyosakti, Jl A. Yani 86a, and PT Dua Sisi Jogya Indah, at the southern corner of the Malioboro shopping centre, offer very competitive rates. Baruman Abadi in the *Natour Garuda Hotel* offers only slightly inferior rates and stays open longer (Mon–Fri 7am–7pm, Sat 7am–3pm). In Prawirotaman, the Agung moneychanger at Jl Prawirotaman 68 and Kresna at no. 18 offer the best rates. Of the banks, go for the BNI, opposite the post office at the southern end of Jl Malioboro.

Batik courses Lucy's (no phone) in JL Sosro Gang I runs a very popular one-day course (9am–3pm; Rp10,000–25,000 depending on the size of the finished batik). The *Via Via Café* on Jl Prawirotaman runs a similar course for Rp15,000, and a one-week course for US$150. Right by the entrance to the Taman Sari is the workshop of Dr Hadjir (☎0274/377835), who runs a three- to five-day course (US$25 for three days, plus US$5 for materials). His course is one of the most extensive and includes tutoring on the history of batik and the preparation of both chemical and natural dyes. The Puriwisata school, at the northern end of Jl Brig Jen Katamso, runs a rather expensive but comprehensive batik course (Rp50,000 per session). Finally, the Batik Research Centre at Jl Kusumanegara 2 (no phone), runs intensive three-day courses for US$55. For the truly committed, they also run a three-month course.

Bookshops The Lucky Boomerang at Jl Sosro Gang I/67 has the best selection of English-language novels, guidebooks and other books on Indonesia. In Prawirotaman, both Bima Books (GangII) and Kakadu Books (Gang I) have the odd secondhand gem on their shelves, though neither is particularly cheap. The Gramedia Bookshop in the Malioboro shopping centre also has a fair selection of English-language books on Indonesia.

Bus tickets Most of the travel agencies and homestays sell bus tickets.

Car and motorbike rental Fortuna 1 and 2 are two branches of the same company near the train station at Jl Jlagran Lor 20–21 and Jl Pasar Kembang 60 (☎0274/564680 or 589550). A Honda Astrea motorbike can be rented for Rp25,000 per day. Jeeps cost Rp75,000, or double that if you wish to hire a driver too. Just down the road, Kurnia Rental at no. 63 (☎0274/520027) offers a similar deal, as does Star Rental at Jl Adisucipto 22 (☎0274/519603) near the *Ambarrukmo Palace Hotel*.

Cinema The Indra Cinema, behind the Cirebon Restaurant on Jl J. A. Yani, is the most central, mainly screening kung fu films. For the biggest choice of Hollywood films, visit Ratih 21, north of the train tracks on Jl Mangkubumi.

Cookery courses The *Via Via Café* on Jl Prawirotaman runs afternoon courses (Rp15,000), where they teach you how to make their wonderful version of gado-gado as well as other Indonesian staples. They also hold one-week courses for US$150.

Dance and gamelan courses Mrs Tia of the Ndalem Pujokusirman school at Jl Brig Jen Katamso 45 (☎0274/371271) is a former pupil-turned-teacher who invites foreigners to join her 2hr group lessons beginning at 4pm. At the northern end of the same street is the Puriwisata (☎0274/374089), an open-air theatre and mini-theme park which holds Javanese dance courses for Rp50,000 per 3hr session. They also run a school for gamelan (Rp50,000 per session). The *Via Via Café* on Jl Prawirotaman runs intensive one-week courses for US$150.

Email A proliferation of Internet places have recently opened in Yogya. Wasantara-Net (Mon–Sat 8am–9pm, Sun 9am–8pm) at the GPO charges Rp3000 for 30min, Rp5000 for 1hr. The *Pujayo Internet Café* at Jl C. Simanjutak 73, east of the Tugu monument, is open longer and charges just Rp1500 for 15min (daily 8am–10pm). Jl Sosro Gang I also has a number of places, including CMC at GT1/70 next to *Superman II* (Rp3000 for 15min), Whizzkids at GT1/96, opposite *Superman II* (Rp3000 for 15min) – this one is reputedly very slow – and *Superman II* itself (Rp3000 for 15min). Also around Sosro are Warung Internet (Rp1000 for 5min), at the northern end of Gang II, and Internet Rental (Rp1250 for 5min), a few metres north of *Ella's Homestay* on Jl Sosrodipuran Gang 1. In Prawirotaman, the *Metro Hotel* has recently installed an email terminal (Rp3000 for 15min), and there's the new *Café Internet* at Jl Prawirotaman 11.

Language courses Puri (☎ & fax 0274/583789), just to the east of the RRI auditorium at the Kompleks Kolombo 4 on Jl Cendrawasih, offers a two-week intensive course for US$390 (payable in dollars only), or a 10hr version for US$30. Puri Bahasa Indonesia (☎0274/588192) at Jl Bausasran 59, two blocks east of Jl Malioboro, runs similar language courses (Rp15,000–25,000). For a brief introduction, the *Via Via Café* on Jl Prawirotaman holds a 3hr course for Rp15,000. The Wisma Bahasa, Jl Rajawali Gang. Nuri 6 (☎0274/520341), is a new school that has already earned a good reputation for its teaching techniques, where conversation and role playing forms a large part of the curriculum. As well as their standard Bahasa Indonesian courses (90hr over three weeks for US$450), they also run a 30hr "travellers" course over five days (US$100).

Hospitals and clinics The Gading Clinic, south of the Alun-alun Selatan at Jl Maj Jen Panjaitan 25, has English-speaking doctors (☎0274/375396). The main hospital in Yogya is the Bethes Da, Jl Sudirman 81 (☎0274/81774).

Immigration office Jl Adisucipto Km10, on the way to the airport near the *Ambarrukmo Palace* hotel (Mon–Thurs 8am–2pm, Fri 8–11am, Sat 8am–1pm; ☎0274/514948).

Laundry Most hotels offer some sort of laundry service, or visit Bike 33 on Jl Sosro GangI, or the AGM laundry near the *Rose Hotel* on Jl Prawirotaman.

Massage and relaxation Gabriel, a fluent English speaker who works at *Anna's Restaurant* in Sosro Gang II, does a full-body massage for Rp10,000 (90min). The Lotus Moon, at the back of the *Lotus Garden Restaurant*, offers a traditional Javanese massage as well as herbal treatments in totally private rooms.

Pharmacies Kimia Farma 20, Jl Malioboro 179, is open 24hr. The Apotek Ratna, Jl Parangtritis 44, is open daily 8am–10pm.

Photographic shops There are two reputable stores: Kodak Expres and Fuji Film Plaza, near the eastern end of Sosro on Jl Malioboro. Fuji and Kodak also have branches near Prawirotaman at Foto Duta (Fuji), Jl Parangtritis 54, and nearby Foto Super (Kodak). The prices are about the same in all of them: Rp1500 for developing, Rp325 per photo for printing.

Post office Jl Senopati 2, at the southern end of Jl Malioboro (Mon–Sat 6am–10pm, Sun 6am–8pm). The parcel office is on Jl Maj Jen Suryotomo (Mon–Sat 8am–3pm, Sun 9am–2pm). Parcel-wrappers loiter outside the office during these times.

Swimming The *Batik Palas Hotel* south of Jl Sosro allows non-guests to use their pool for Rp2500 (daily 9am–9pm), as does the *Mutiara* (Rp4000). The *Ibis* allows non-residents to use its health centre including pool, sauna and gym for Rp20,000.

Telephone The main Telkom office at Jl Yos Sudarso 9 is open 24hr and has Home Direct phones too. There's a wartel office at no. 30 Jl Sosro and another on Jl Parangtritis, south of Jl Prawirotaman Gang II.

Tour operators Yogya is full of tour companies offering trips to the nearby temples (Rp25,000 for a tour of both Prambanan and Borobudur), as well as further afield. The price generally doesn't include entrance fees, and the only advantage of taking a tour is convenience. Kresna, based on Jl Prawirotaman at no. 18 (☎0274/375502) but with agents all over the city, is one of the largest and most experienced. However, a couple of companies offer something a little different. *Via Via*, the travellers' café on Jl Prawirotaman, organizes bicycle and hiking tours around the local area, while Moyasi Alternative Tours at Jl Prawirotaman 20 (☎0274/382863) organizes treks around the major temples. Neither is particularly cheap, however, with an 8hr Borobudur tour costing Rp47,500.

Travel agents Probably the most respected of Yogya's travel agents, and certainly one of the more reliable, is Indras Tours and Travel at Jl Malioboro 131 (☎0274/561972), just a few metres south of the eastern end of Jl Sosro. Or try Cendana Harum, Jl Prawirotaman Gang II 838 (☎0274/374760); Hanoman, Jl Prawirotaman 9 (☎0274/372528); Intan Pelangi, Jl Malioboro 18 (☎0274/562895); Jaya, Jl Sosro 23 (☎0274/586735); Kresna Tours, Jl Prawirotaman 18 (☎0274/375502); Panin Tour, Jl Sosro 28 (☎0274/515021); and Utama (Jl Dagen 17; ☎0274/518117).

South of Yogya

Yogya lies just 28km from the south coast of Java. Its nearest resort, **Parangtritis**, like most of the beaches on this southern coast, is a rather bleak, melancholy place. The people of Yogya have always associated the south coast with death. Loro Kidul, the Goddess of the South Seas who regularly drags unwary swimmers to their doom (see p.166 and opposite), is reputed to live off the coast of Parangtritis, the royal palace in Yogya was deliberately built with its back to the south, and the sultan was forbidden to exit through the palace's southern gate until after his death, when his body would be carried to the royal cemetery at Imogiri. This cemetery lies in the **Gunung Sewu** (Thousand Mountains), a line of limestone cliffs that rises up unexpectedly from the southern plain, separating Yogya from the coast. The cliffs also play host to the cave complex of **Goa Cerme**. All of these sights, whilst not essential, are mildly diverting and worth visiting if you plan to be in Yogya for a while. Buses run regularly, although, thanks largely to the Gunung Sewu, the road is not straight and journey times are lengthy considering the short distances involved.

Most of the other beaches on the south coast, such as **Krakal**, **Kukup** and **Baron**, lie in a chain 60km to the southeast of Yogya. Once again they are somewhat bleak, and

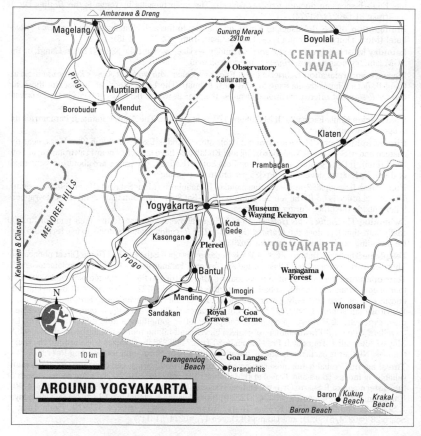

– with one exception – dangerous for swimming. Buses between Yogya and these beaches are at best infrequent and involve a change at Wonosari. After 3pm the bus service to this part of the coast stops altogether. Whilst these beaches are, admittedly, not very enticing, on the way to Wonosari you pass the tranquil **Wanagama Forest**, established by the Gaja Mada University on the side of once-barren Gunung Kidul.

South to Parangtritis
Right in the heart of the Gunung Sewu range lies the most important **royal cemetery** in Java (Mon 10am–1pm, Fri 1.30–4pm; Rp500, Rp200 camera fee, plus Rp1000 to rent the compulsory costume), 17km from Yogyakarta and 346 steps up a wooded hill in the village of **Imogiri** (Mountain of Mist). Regular minibuses from Yogya bus station take 45 minutes (Rp500). The cemetery, a terraced, walled-in compound hidden in the hilltop forest, is a delightfully peaceful spot. The deceased of three of Central Java's four royal houses are buried here (only the Mangkunegoros of Solo are excluded), with the Pakubuwonos of Solo on the left-hand side of the entrance and the Hamengkubuwonos of Yogya on the right. Most of these graves are rather simple and plain, although the tomb of Mataram's greatest leader, Sultan Agung, the founder of the cemetery, is a touch more lavish. A small brick shelter has been built around Agung's grave, which lies at the top of the hill, where worshippers – usually elderly palace retainers from Yogya – congregate to burn incense, sprinkle rose petals over the coffin and offer prayers to the sultan.

The **Goa Cerme** cave complex lies 9km southeast of Imogiri. From Imogiri, catch a bus to the small junction village of **Silok**, 5km to the south (Rp200 from Imogiri, Rp500 by Jahayu bus from Yogya), where it's easy to pick up an ojek (Rp1000) for the six-kilometre journey to Goa Cerme (daily dawn–dusk; Rp500), an elaborate cave system in the upper reaches of Gunung Sewu. From the point where you'll be dropped off there's a twenty-minute clamber up to the entrance. The caves are over 1km long, and to walk through them you'll need to bring a torch and clothes suitable for wading, as in some places the water is up to 1m deep. The caves are dark, dank and eerie, with stalactites and stalagmites and the odd bat and swift fluttering overhead. A local guide (around Rp5000 for 2hr), available from the entrance, is essential, and both the *Ella* homestay and *Vagabonds* in Yogya organize tours (see pp.160 and 163).

White Jahayu buses drive through Silok on their way to **Parangtritis**, 12km away, a vast four-kilometre windswept stretch of black sand which, no matter how many people are visiting, always seems a lonely and desolate place. This is the home of Loro Kidul, the Goddess of the Southern Seas; Senopati, the father of the Mataram dynasty, emerged from her palace at **Parangkusumo**, 1km east along the beach. Don't be tempted to go for a swim to look for her, however, as a vicious undertow will pull even the strongest swimmer under. The white Jahayu buses terminate here (Rp500 from Silok, Rp1000 from Jalan Parangtritis or the bus station in Yogya). The bus pulls in at the small village that separates the main road from the beach, consisting of a number of warung, the odd tired souvenir shop and a few wind-battered losmen. The spartan *Losmen Sriwidjaya* (②), in the heart of the village, is one of the best of these.

Wanagama Park and the southeastern beaches
Just thirty years ago, the lush forested hills of **Gunung Kidul**, 34km to the east of Yogya, were a barren desertscape: a combination of deforestation and soil degradation had left the area bare and infertile. In 1967, two members of Gajah Mada University's Faculty of Forestry attempted to reforest the hills, sowing only the hardiest plants and watering them using intensive irrigation techniques. The result is a sixty-square-kilometre marvel of rejuvenation that has attracted the attention of ecologists and scientists the world over. Even royalty, in the shape of Prince Charles, has paid a visit. More a curiosity than a tourist attraction, **Wanagama Park** is nice for a stroll, and

provides a breath of fresh air from Yogya. There's some accommodation behind the reception area, which can be used if there are no tour groups staying (ring Professor Oemi Susemo at Gajah Mada to check availability; ☎0274/515480; ②). It's possible to camp in the forest, though you will have to bring your own equipment. Wanagama lies 9km to the south of the Wonosari road, fifty minutes from Yogya; catch a bus from Yogya's Umbulharjo bus station (Rp700), then an ojek (Rp1000) from the junction.

The bleak, isolated **beaches** to the southeast of Yogya lie 40km further on from Wanagama. On one side is a churning, raging sea driven by a vicious undertow which has dragged many an unwary swimmer to their death; on the other are the snagging, sharp limestone cliffs, which plunge vertically down from 50m or more into the rough surf. Beyond these cliffs lies one of the poorest, most barren areas in the whole of Java, where people eke out a living growing peanuts on the poor soil. Even the beaches themselves are gritty, windswept and unwelcoming, far removed from the golden sands of Bali. Nevertheless, there's a sort of melancholy beauty about these beaches, and, if you just want to get away from the crowds, the south coast is the place to come. There are also a few secluded spots where swimming is possible, and even one or two stretches of white sand.

Unfortunately **Baron**, the most accessible of the beaches, is not pleasant. Baron's beach is a grotty, seedy alcove populated largely by fishermen, gum-chewing malcontents and snarling feral dogs. It is, however, a base for exploring the coast, and there is some accommodation. To get to Baron, catch a bus to Wonosari (75min; Rp800), then a colt for one hour south (Rp1000); if this colt is not running, catch one to Bintaos, 8km from Baron, and hitch from there. The last bus back from Baron leaves at 4pm, and 1pm on Fridays; if you are unfortunate enough to miss it, you can find basic rooms at *Bintang Beach* (③), a few of which boast hot water and TV.

A ten-minute walk west of Baron lies a small beach where it's safe to swim. On the eastern cliff, and clearly visible from the beach, a stairway leads over the hill to **Kukup**, a less busy and fractionally less ugly version of Baron. Six kilometres further east (Rp7500 by ojek from Baron) lies the similar-looking **Krakal**. Further east still is **Pantai Sundak**, possibly the bleakest, most isolated and, perversely, the most pleasant of the lot, with only a few fishing pagodas on the overshadowing hills to keep you company.

Gunung Merapi and Kaliurang

Marking the northern limit of the Daerah Istimewa Yogyakarta, symmetrical, smoke-plumed **Gunung Merapi** (Giving Fire) is an awesome 2911-metre presence in the centre of Java, visible from Yogyakarta, 25km away. This is Indonesia's most volatile volcano, and the sixth most active in the world. The Javanese worship the mountain as a life-giver, its lava enriching the soil and providing Central Java with its agricultural fecundity. Down the centuries its ability to annihilate has frequently been demonstrated. Thirteen hundred people died following a particularly vicious eruption in 1930, and as recently as 1994 an entire mountain village was incinerated by lava, which killed 64 people. If the nineteenth-century Solonese poet Ronggo Warsito is to be believed, this devastation is set to continue. Among his predictions, many of which have turned out to be uncannily accurate, he claims there will be a huge eruption just before the end of the millennium, which will cleave Java entirely in two. It's a prophecy the locals take seriously; every year at the anniversary of the sultan's coronation, an offering is brought from the Sultan's Palace in Yogya, and placed on the rim of the crater in an attempt to placate the mountain god.

Nearly a kilometre up on Merapi's southern slopes is the village of **KALIURANG**, a tatty, downmarket but tranquil hill station and an extremely popular weekend retreat for Yogyakartans. A bus from Yogya's Umbulharjo station costs Rp700; it's Rp1000 by bemo from behind the Terban terminal on Jalan Simanjutak. In Kaliurang, you can join

> For details of climbing the northern side of **Gunung Merapi**, see p.208.

a trekking group to the summit, a fairly arduous five-hour scramble through the snake- and spider-infested forest that beards Merapi's lower slopes. The tigers, which terrorized this forest as recently as the 1960s, have now all been killed off. During Merapi's dormant months (usually March to October) it is possible to climb all the way to the top, but at other times, when the volcano is active, you may have to settle for a distant view from the observation platform. All treks begin in the dark at 3am, when the lava, spilling over the top and tracing a searing path down the mountainside, can be seen most clearly. Bring warm clothes, a torch and sturdy boots (not sandals, which offer little protection against poisonous snakes).

Treks, which cost Rp7500 including breakfast, are organized by *Vogel's Hostel* in Kaliurang, Jalan Astya Mulya 76 (☎0274/895208; ③), which also happens to be one of the best budget **hostels** in Java. The hostel is split into two parts: the rooms in the new extension are beautiful and good value, while those in the old building (a former holiday home for one of Yogya's lesser nobility) are spartan but inexpensive. The **food**, including Indonesian staples and Western snacks, is truly delicious and there's a large travellers' library. The owner is a veritable encyclopedia of volcano knowledge, and is the head of the rescue team in Kaliurang. If you're looking for somewhere plusher, try the *Village Taman Eden*, Jalan Astya Mulya also (☎0274/895442; ⑤–⑧), a collection of reasonably luxurious villas of varying quality and price built round a central swimming pool.

Borobudur and around

Forty kilometres west of Yogya on the fertile Kedu Plain, surrounded on three sides by volcanoes and on the fourth by a series of jagged limestone cliffs, is the largest monument in the southern hemisphere. This is **Borobudur**, the number one tourist attraction in Java and the greatest single piece of classical architecture in the entire archipelago.

The temple is actually a colossal multi-tiered Buddhist stupa lying at the western end of a four-kilometre-long chain of temples (two of which, **Candi Mendut** and **Candi Pawon**, have been restored and stand by the road to Borobudur), built in the ninth century by the Saliendra dynasty. At 34.5m tall, however, and covering an area of some 200 square metres, Borobudur is of a different scale altogether, dwarfing all the other *candi* in the chain.

Despite its size, your first impressions of Borobudur may leave you feeling a little underwhelmed. It is rather squat – like a collapsed pyramid – and the sheer horizontal massiveness of the structure is somewhat obscured by the trees of the tidy park which surround it. Indeed, the Hindu temples at Prambanan (see p.187), with their soaring vertical lines uncluttered by surrounding foliage, seem more impressive when viewed from a distance. Nevertheless, Borobudur's greater fame is merited. It's bigger than Prambanan, older (by about forty years) and, if you turn up during the silent hours of dawn and dusk, more enchanting too.

NAMING BOROBUDUR

One of the greatest mysteries surrounding **Borobudur** is the origin of its name. One school of thought suggests that it's derived from the Sanskrit *Vihara Buddha Uhr* (Buddhist Monastery on a Hill). Others believe that *Budur* is actually a place name, and that *Borobudur* means "Monastery of Budur". The most likely explanation, however, comes from a stone tablet of 842 AD on which is inscribed the word *Bhumisambharabhudara* (Mountain of Virtues of the Ten Stages of the Boddhisattva). It's believed that the name *Borobudur* is derived from *bharabhudara*, the last part of this tongue twister.

Some history

The world's largest Buddhist stupa was actually built on **Hindu** foundations. In 775 AD, the Hindu Sanjaya dynasty built a large step pyramid – probably the beginnings of a Shivaite temple – on the plain of Kedu. The Sanjayas would have considered this site propitious; not only does the plain of Kedu stand by the confluence of two rivers, the **Elo** and the **Progo**, which to the Sanjayas would have evoked the most sacred confluence of all – the Ganges and the Yamuna in northern India – but also, to the northeast towards Magelang, stands **Gunung Tidar**, the so-called "Head of the Nail" that the Javanese believe fixes the island, preventing it from drifting on the sea.

Just fifteen years later, however, the construction was abandoned: the Buddhist **Saliendras**, having swept down through the Malay Peninsula and into Java, gradually drove the Sanjayas eastwards, forcing them to leave their building work behind. The Saliendras then appropriated the pyramid as the foundation for their own temple, beginning in around 790 AD and completing the work approximately seventy years later. Over 1.6 million blocks of andesite, a volcanic rock washed down by, and mined from, the nearby rivers, were used in Borobudur's construction, cut and joined together in such a way that no mortar was used. Sculptors then adorned the lower galleries with reliefs, before the whole lot was covered with stucco and painted.

Unfortunately, the pyramid foundation inherited from the Hindus proved to be inherently unstable, and throughout Borobudur's infancy the structure required constant attention. Though the classical architects had designed an ingenious **drainage system**, where water was channelled through gullies and collected in a gutter via the mouths of gargoyles, it proved insufficient and the temple began to **subside**. To try to remedy this, a "hidden foot" was added at the base of the temple as a buttress to prevent the whole lot sliding down the hill. (Interestingly, this base is adorned with reliefs which are every bit as detailed as the rest of the temple, even though it lay buried in the earth and out of view.)

But not even the hidden foot could solve the problem of drainage. As the temple lurched on its unsteady foundations, cracks appeared in the walls and floors, through which rainwater seeped until the hill became totally waterlogged. After about a century, the Saliendras abandoned the site. The return of the Hindu Sanjayas as the dominating force in the region, along with earthquakes, and the mysterious migration of the Javanese from Central to East Java, all contributed further to the temple's subsequent decline.

For almost a thousand years Borobudur lay neglected. Then in 1815 the English "rediscovered" it. Plans to restore Borobudur, however, didn't leave the drawing board for the rest of the century. A Dutchman, Theo Van Earp, made cosmetic improvements to the temple's exterior during a five-year project beginning in 1907, but the foundations, which by this time required urgent attention, remained untouched. Then in 1973, as Borobudur's condition became critical, **UNESCO** began to take the temple apart, block by block, and the waterlogged hill was replaced with a concrete substitute. The project took eleven years and cost US$21million, but at the end of it all Borobudur had, for the first time in its history, foundations worthy of its glorious exterior.

Practicalities

Most people choose to see the **site** (daily 6am–5.30pm; Rp10,000, Rp15,000 for optional guided tour) on a day-trip from Yogya. Plenty of agencies (see p.177) offer **all-inclusive tours**, or you can catch one of the regular buses from Yogya's Umbulharjo station, which calls in at the southern end of Jalan Magelang (handy for Jalan Sosro) before heading off to Borobudur bus station, ninety minutes away on the eastern edge of Borobudur village. The entrance to the temple lies 500m southwest of the bus stop, to the north of the temple.

RAFTING IN CENTRAL JAVA

With its wealth of navigable rivers and sumptuous scenery, **rafting** should be a well-established tourist activity in Central Java, but there are only two companies offering visitors the chance to ride the rapids. The best is the Lotus River Rafting Company (☎0293/88281), operating out of the *Lotus Guesthouse* in Borobudur, who arrange four-hour trips down the Progo and Elo (US$40–50). Some of the rapids have been classified as Class III, the highest level of difficulty allowed for untrained rafters. Both trips are exhilarating and, save for the occasional panicking buffalo (which might upset the boat), fairly safe. A slightly shorter trip through calmer water can be arranged through the *Puri Asri Hotel* in Magelang (☎0293/63695).

While waiting for your guide to arrive, there are two ways to pass the time: visit the free **museum** in the temple grounds, which has a detailed account of the UNESCO restoration, or ride on the **small train** (Rp1000) which circles the temple every ten minutes.

A number of **hotels** have sprouted up in the village in recent years. At the top of the range, *Hotel Manohara*, Komplek Taman Wisata Candi Borobudur (☎ & fax 0293/88131; ⑦), lies to the east of the temple within the actual grounds. All rooms have air-con, TV and hot water, and the temple fee is included in the price; each evening they put on a free lecture and slide show about Borobudur. The most popular budget choice is the *Lotus Guesthouse* at Jalan Medang Kamulan 2 (☎0293/88281; ③), opposite the entrance to Borobudur park. The awful rooms with their filthy beds are fit only for the hotel's burgeoning cockroach population, but they're partially compensated for by amiable staff and the opportunity to go rafting (see box). The unimaginatively titled *Losmen Borobudur* stands on the road that runs alongside the eastern edge of the temple grounds, at Jalan Balaputradewa 1 (☎0293/88258; ③); though scruffier on the outside, this losmen has better-value, cockroach-free rooms. Across the street to the north, at Jalan Balaputradewa 10, stands the *Saraswati* (☎0293/88283; ⑤), offering fairly smart though slightly overpriced rooms with ceiling fans. The large, shady tree-lined garden, however, is very pleasant.

Most people who stay in Borobudur overnight choose to eat in their hotel. There are a number of warung in the station, which all close at about 5pm, and one budget **restaurant** serving good, cheap meals that stays open until about 9pm; it has no name, but stands to the west of the station on the opposite side of the road.

The ruins

Borobudur is precisely orientated so that its four sides face the four points of the compass. The **entrance** to the grounds lies to the north, although the correct place to begin your tour of Borobudur is the **eastern side**. Buddhist pilgrims would have approached this side of the temple via the sacred path, which once connected Borobudur with Mendut and the other *candi*. Having reached the temple, they would then walk clockwise around its base, before ascending to the next tier via the eastern stairway. This process was repeated on every level, until eventually they arrived at the summit. In this way, not only would they be able to follow the stories of the reliefs which adorn each of the terraces, but they would also, by walking clockwise around the stupa, be performing *pradaksina*, a major ceremonial act in Buddhist worship.

Borobudur is pregnant with symbolism. Unlike most temples, it was not built as a dwelling for the gods, but rather as a representation of the Buddhist **cosmic mountain**, Meru. Accordingly, at the base is the real, earthly world, a world of desires and passions, and at the summit is **nirvana**. Thus, as you make your way around the temple passages and slowly spiral to the summit, you are symbolically following the path to enlightenment.

Every journey to enlightenment begins in the squalor of the real world, and at Borobudur the first five levels – the square terraces – are covered with three thousand **reliefs** representing man's earthly existence. As you might expect, the lowest level, the so-called **hidden foot**, has carvings depicting the basest desires and passions. In Buddhist teaching this level of existence is known as the *kamathadu*. For a taste of these ribald carvings, visit the **southeast corner** of the temple where UNESCO, during their restoration, left four panels uncovered.

The reliefs on the next four tiers – the first four levels above ground – cover the Rupadhatu, the beginning of man's path to enlightenment. On these levels there are ten series of carvings, four on the first tier – two, one above the other, on the inner or retaining wall and two on the outer – and two on each of the subsequent three tiers. Each one tells a story, beginning by the eastern stairway and continuing in a clockwise direction. Follow all ten stories, and you will have circled the temple ten times – a distance of almost 5km. Buddha's own path to enlightenment, the *Lalitavistara*, is told in the upper panels on the inner wall of the first gallery. The reliefs below this series, and indeed both series on the opposite wall, depict scenes from the *Jataka* tales, the stories of Buddha's former lives before his enlightenment. Climbing the stairs from this first tier, the second, third and fourth galleries recount the story of the *Gandavyuha*, about a merchant, **Sudhana**, who sets off on the path to enlightenment, encountering Bodhisattvas on the way. The story is concluded on the fourth level.

The high gallery walls, or **balustrades**, on these first four levels effectively reduce the light coming into the gallery and cut visitors off from the outside world – a symbol, perhaps, of the murky spiritual world inhabited by man on these lower terraces. As you enter the fifth level, however, the walls fall away to reveal a breathtaking view of the surrounding fields and volcanoes. You are now in the third and final section of Borobudur; just as levels two, three and four were the **Sphere of Forms**, so the upper levels – five, six, seven and eight – constitute the **Sphere of Formlessness**. Suddenly, all the busy reliefs that crowd the walls of the lower levels disappear. The visitor has reached enlightenment: below is the chaos of the world, above is nirvana, represented by a huge empty stupa almost 10m in diameter. Surrounding this stupa are 72 smaller ones, each occupied by a statue of Buddha. Including the Buddhas in the niches on the lower levels, there are in total 432 Buddhas at Borobudur. The stupa at the top, however, is empty. There was once a Buddha here, too, but it seems somehow appropriate that this has disappeared, nirvana signifying, after all, a state of non-being.

Candis Mendut and Pawon

Originally Borobudur was part of a chain of four temples joined by a sacred path. Two of the other three temples have been restored (the temple at the village of **Bajong** is, alas, beyond repair) and at least one, **Candi Mendut** (daily 6.15am–5.15pm; Rp100), 3km east of Borobudur, is worth visiting. Buses between Yogya and Borobudur drive right past Mendut (Rp800 from Yogya for the 80min journey, Rp300 for the 10min from Borobudur). Built in 800 AD, Mendut was rediscovered in 1834 and restored at the end of the nineteenth century. The exterior, while heavily decorated, is unremarkable. The three giant statues sitting inside, however, are exquisitely carved, marvellously preserved and startling. As Charles Walter Kinloch, the "Bengal Civilian", wrote in his travelogue, *Rambles in Java and the Straits in 1852*, "of the two ruins, the Boro-Bodor are by far the most extensive; but the figures of Mundoot are far more perfect". Originally there were seven statues here; those that remain are the great three-metre **Buddha** – who, unusually, sits on a throne with his legs in front of him rather than in the lotus position – flanked by the Bodhisattvas **Avalokitesvara** and **Vajrapani**. In the early evening the sun dips low enough to shine on all three: try and be here then.

One kilometre west of Mendut on the banks of the river is **Candi Pawon** (open 24hr; free). This small building is dedicated to the Buddhist god of fortune, Kuvera. Unlike both Mendut and Borobudur, the temple does not have Hindu foundations but is wholly Buddhist. From here, it is just 1.5km back to Borobudur bus station; it only takes about thirty minutes to walk, and passing bemos should charge Rp200.

The Prambanan Plain

The sixty-kilometre Yogya–Solo highway is one of the most dangerous routes in Java, with buses and lorries careering down the middle of the road, forcing pedestrians, becak and other traffic to scatter into the neighbouring paddy-fields. In contrast to all this mayhem, 18km outside of Yogya the highway passes through one of the most unhurried and verdant spots in Java. Nourished by the volcanic detritus of Mount Merapi and washed by innumerable small rivers and streams, this is the **Prambanan Plain**, a patchwork blanket of sun-spangled paddy-fields and vast plantations of wheat, maize and cane, sweeping down from the southern slopes of the volcano. As well as being one of the most fertile regions in Java, the plain is home to the largest concentration of ancient ruins on the island. Over thirty **temples** and **palaces**, dating mainly from the eighth and ninth centuries, lie scattered over a thirty-square-kilometre area.

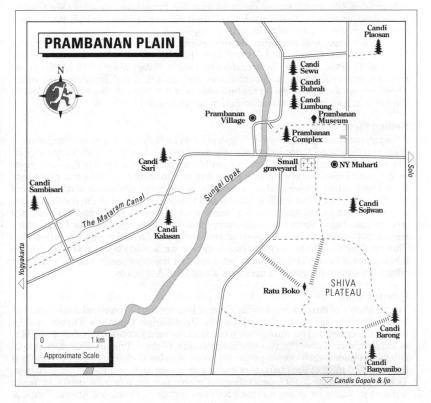

Though many of these are little more than heaps of rubble lying forgotten behind thick groves of sugar cane or amongst the lush forest of the hills, a number have been restored to something approaching their original state.

The temples were built at a time when two rival kingdoms, the Buddhist **Saliendra** and the Hindu **Sanjaya** dynasties, both occupied Central Java. Their relationship with each other is unclear, although it is widely believed that their rivalry was political rather than military. In 832 AD, the Hindu Sanjayas gained the upper hand, possibly after their king had married a Saliendran princess. It was soon after this that the greatest of the ruins, the Hindu Prambanan **temple complex**, was built, perhaps in commemoration of their return to power. It seems that some sort of truce followed, with temples of both faiths bring constructed on the plain in equal numbers.

Practicalities

Most people visit the Prambanan temples on a day-trip from Yogya, and, unless you're fanatical about ruins – or if you're too tired to cycle back – this is probably the best option. Although you could spend days looking at all the ruins on the plain, the majority of visitors come to examine only the three temples at the Prambanan complex, which takes no more than a couple of hours.

Prambanan village is little more than a small huddle of houses lining the southern side of Jalan Adisucipto, across the road from the Prambanan complex. Most public buses drop passengers off along this road, from where you'll have to walk for five minutes to reach the eastern entrance to the complex.

There are a couple of **accommodation** options in Prambanan: *Losmen NY Muharti*, Jalan Tampurnas Ngangkruk 2–3 (☎0274/496103; ④), offers rudimentary rooms and, to the north of the open-air theatre, the *Prambanan Village Hotel* (☎0274/496435; ⑤) provides more salubrious accommodation and houses a fine Japanese restaurant. There are also a couple of cheap **restaurants** near the *Muharti*, though these close in the evening, leaving visitors with no option but to dine in their hotel.

Getting there

Although many tour companies in Yogya offer all-inclusive packages to Prambanan, it is easy enough to get there independently by catching a local **bus** from Yogya or Solo. The only disadvantage is that there is no public transport to take you to the other ruins on the plain. This is one reason why many visitors choose to rent a bike and **cycle** here from Yogya. Fume-choked Jalan Adisucipto is the most straightforward route, but there's an alternative that's a little quieter and less polluted. Head to the north of Yogya along Jalan Simanjutak and Jalan Kaliurang until you reach the Mataram Canal, just past the main Gajah Mada University compound. Follow the canal east for 12km, which takes about an hour, and you'll come out eventually near Candi Sari on Jalan Adisucipto. This canal path is a little worn in places, and the surface has been seared by the sun into a series of bumps and potholes, but it is by far the most scenic route. Prambanan village lies 4km to the east of Candi Sari, along Jalan Adisucipto.

Entertainment

The highlights of the dancing year in Central Java are the phenomenal *Ramayana* ballets held during the summer months at the **Prambanan Open-Air Theatre**, to the west of the complex. The *Ramayana* story is performed just twice monthly from May to October, spread over the two weekends closest to the full moon. The story is split into four episodes, each evening from Friday to Monday (7–9pm). The second night is the best, with most of the characters making an appearance, and the action is intense. Tickets cost Rp5000–30,000, depending on where you sit; plenty of agents in Yogya organize packages including entrance fees and transport. Check out Kresna Tours, at

Jalan Prawirotaman 18 (☎0274/375502) or Jaya Tours in Sosro (☎0274/586735). Yogya's tourist office also organizes taxis to and from the theatre.

Throughout the year, Prambanan's **Trimurti Theatre**, an indoor venue to the north of the open-air arena, performs the *Ramayana* ballet (Tues–Thurs 7.30–9.30pm; Rp10,000–15,000). Tickets are available on the door or from the agencies mentioned above.

The Prambanan complex

As you drive east along Jalan Adisucipto from Yogya, your eye will be caught by three giant, rocket-shaped andesite temples, each smothered in intricate narrative carvings, that suddenly loom up by the side of the highway. This is the **Prambanan complex** (daily 6am–5pm; Rp10,000, Rp15,000 for optional guided tour), the largest Hindu complex in Java and a worthy rival to the Buddhist masterpiece at Borobudur.

The Sanjayas began work on the three giants around 832 AD, finishing them 24 years later in 856 AD. The choice of location for their masterpiece, just a few hundred metres south of the once mighty Buddhist **Candi Sewu**, is of considerable significance. Not only was it a reminder to the Saliendras that the Hindus were now in charge but, by leaving Sewu unharmed, it also gave a clear message to the Buddhists that the Sanjayas intended to be tolerant of their faith. Interestingly, the Sanjayas also built another three temples near Borobudur, called Candi Banon, presumably for the same reason; save for three statues in the Jakarta Museum, however, nothing of them has survived. The three Prambanan temples were in service for just fifty years before they were abandoned, following the mysterious migration of the Javanese from Central to East Java. Earthquakes in the seventeenth century compounded the temples' decline, and for centuries afterwards they were left in ruins. Restoration work finally began under the Dutch in the 1930s, but it was only in the last ten years that the restoration of the inner courtyard was completed.

There are two entrances into the complex: tour buses pull up at the eastern gate, where the souvenir sellers gather, while a second entrance stands by the northwest corner of the complex by the open-air theatre. A **tourist train** (Rp1000) has been added to Prambanan's attractions, which takes passengers on a ten-minute ride around the complex, beginning at the main entrance and continuing up to Sewu. It terminates by the **Prambanan Museum** (daily 7am–6pm), which houses a small cinema, where a thirty-minute **audiovisual** about the complex is screened (Rp2000).

The central courtyard

The temple complex itself consists of six temples in a raised **inner courtyard**, surrounded by **224 minor temples**, which now lie in ruins. The three biggest temples in the courtyard are dedicated to the three main Hindu deities: Shiva, whose 47-metre temple is the tallest of the three, Brahma (to the south of the Shiva temple) and Vishnu (north). Facing these are three smaller temples housing the animal statues – or "chariots" – that would always accompany the gods: Hamsa the swan, Nandi the bull and Garuda the sunbird. The only other buildings in the courtyard are two small kiosks, to the north and south, which were possibly once treasuries or storerooms.

A stone inscription dating from 856 AD, found at Prambanan and now in the National Museum in Jakarta, describes the **Shiva Temple** as a "beautiful dwelling for the God", and it's hard to disagree with this assessment. The base is decorated with the **Prambanan Motif**, a chaotic collection of creatures gathered around the so-called **Tree of Life**. The exceptional quality of the carving here is maintained on the balustrade of the first terrace, reached via one of the four stairways. A procession of singers and dancers parade on the outer side of the walkway of this first terrace, while the inner wall, beginning at the eastern steps and continuing clockwise around the temple, recounts the first half of the **Ramayana** epic in a series of gloriously intricate scenes.

LORO JONGGRANG AND THE UNWANTED SUITOR

According to local legend, the statue of Durga in the Shiva Temple is actually the petri-fied body of **Loro Jonggrang** (Slender Virgin), the daughter of King Ratu Boko. Indeed, it is not uncommon to hear the Javanese refer to the temple as "Candi Loro Jonggrang". The story goes that the princess was once pursued by a most unsuitable suitor. In her efforts to rid herself of his unwanted attention, one night she told him that she would marry him only if he built a temple for her before dawn.

Unfortunately for the princess, as the night progressed it became increasingly obvious that the man, aided by a troupe of gnomes, would complete the task. In desperation, the princess ran to the village and ordered the locals to pound the rice logs earlier than usual, this being the traditional way to announce the dawn. She also commanded them to set fire to the fields to the east of the village in the hope that the blaze would resemble, from a dis-tance, the sun rising. The unwanted suitor, however, recognized her deceit, and in a rage turned the princess to stone and placed her in his temple, where she remains to this day.

At the top of the steps is the inner sanctuary of the temple, divided into four chambers. The eastern chamber contains a statue of Shiva himself, the southern one houses a statue of the pot-bellied sage **Agastya**, while in the west is Shiva's elephant-headed son, **Ganesh**, and in the north Shiva's consort, **Durga**. Before heading off to view the other two temples, have a peek inside the temple of Shiva's chariot, **Nandi the Bull**. Inside you will find a large, beautiful sculpture of Nandi impassively facing the temple of his master.

Though smaller than the Shiva Temple, the other two temples are just as painstak-ingly decorated. The first terrace of the **Brahma Temple** takes up the *Ramayana* epic where the Shiva Temple left off, whilst the carvings on the terrace of Vishnu's temple recounts stories of **Krishna**. Statues of the relevant deities are housed in the chambers at the top of the stairways.

Other temples on the Prambanan Plain

The other **ancient sites** on the Prambanan Plain (dawn–dusk; free), although not as spectacular as the Shiva Temple, are nevertheless quite engaging. The fact that you are almost certain to be the only person on site, thanks to the poor transport facilities and a lack of interest amongst tourists, only adds to the attraction. Only the three temples immediately to the north of Prambanan are within easy walking distance of the Shiva Temple, although it's possible to reach most of the others by bicycle. A number are scattered on and around the **Shiva Plateau**, which rises sharply from the plain to the south of Prambanan village.

Temples near the complex

Three temples stand in a row to the north of Prambanan, reached via the children's park next to the museum. All three date from the late eighth century, just predating Borobudur. **Candi Lumbung** consists of sixteen small, crumbling temples surround-ing a larger, but equally dilapidated, central temple. The pile of stones to the north is **Candi Bubrah**. Both of these temples were merely subsidiary buildings to Candi Sewu (Thousand Temples), 200m to the north of Bubrah.

Buddhist **Sewu** once consisted of 240 small shrines surrounding a large, central tem-ple. Despite the presence of a number of Rakasa guards similar to those in the Sultan's Palace in Yogya, the temple has been severely vandalized and looted down the years. Yet the vast amount of building material, Buddhist stupas and some quite elaborately carved andesite stones scattered on the site are testimony to the scale of Sewu.

The two temples of **Candi Plaosan** are surrounded by a similar amount of building debris. These two temples are a ten-minute bike ride – or a thirty-minute walk – to the east of Candi Sewu. They are a bit of an oddity: two Buddhist structures built soon after the power had shifted back to the Hindu Sanjayas in 832 AD. The only temple at Plaosan currently open is a two-storey building which – thanks to an extra set of windows above the second floor – looks from the outside like three. Inside there are two stone Bodhisattvas sitting on either side of an empty lotus petal, which once held a bronze statue of Buddha. Circling the temple are the fragmented remains of 116 stupas and 58 smaller temples.

Temples west of Prambanan

The most westerly of all the temples on the plain, **Candi Sambisari**, lies 11km east of Yogya, 2.5km north of the highway and about 1km north of the Mataram Canal. Coming from Yogya, look for the turn-off to the left just past Yogya airport (the temple is not signposted from the Mataram Canal, so if you are travelling along this route be sure to ask directions frequently). Possibly the last of the Sanjayan temples, Sambisari is, like Prambanan, dedicated to Shiva. It was only discovered in 1966, having lain for centuries beneath layers of volcanic ash, and today is set in a large pit, 10m below ground level. The carvings on the exterior wall are of Durga (to the north), Ganesh (east) and Agastya (south). A lingga, a symbol of Shiva, stands to attention on the altar inside.

From Sambisari, return to the Mataram Canal and continue east once more. After thirty minutes the canal meets the highway at Kalasan village. **Candi Kalasan** lies on the other side of the road in a small copse of trees, just 200m south of the canal. This fourteen-square-metre Buddhist temple, dedicated to the cult of Tara, is the oldest ruin on the plain, and in fact the oldest Buddhist temple on Java, having been inaugurated in 778 AD. Despite restoration in the early 1920s, the building is in a far from perfect condition. The statues, some of which were solid bronze, have all disappeared, as has the central, crowning stupa and the decorative plasterwork that once shrouded the entire building. Nevertheless, what remains, especially the fierce *kala* carved above the doors and windows, is very fine. Two hundred metres along the highway north of Kalasan, across the road, is the turn-off for **Candi Sari**, an early ninth-century Buddhist temple. This seventeen-metre-high edifice originally had two storeys which, like Candi Plaosan, from the outside looked like three. The wooden second floor has long since rotted away. The exterior of the temple is finely chiselled and includes many portraits of the female Bodhisattva, Tara, to whom it is dedicated.

Temples south of Prambanan

This set of temples is best tackled by bicycle, as the paths are narrow and the distances fairly large. From Prambanan village, cycle down the path which begins by the small graveyard for ten minutes until you come across a small village school on the left-hand side. Turn left and cycle for a further five minutes: **Candi Sojiwan** is on the right-hand side of the path. This plain, square temple, sparingly decorated with *Jataka* scenes, was a Buddhist sanctuary and was contemporary with Candi Sewu.

From here, head back on to the main path and south towards the foot of the Shiva Plateau. The path to the summit of the plateau and **Kraton Ratu Boko** is too steep and bumpy for bicycles, so ask to leave them at the house at the bottom. Little is known about this kraton, which today is little more than widely dispersed set of ruins; some suggest it's a religious building; others that it was for a king, namely Ratu Boko (Eternal Lord). The ruins are in two parts: one section consists of a series of bathing pools, while the other, 400m to the west, includes the ceremonial gate that adorns many tourist posters and postcards.

The views from the kraton are wonderful, as they are from **Candi Barong**, a *candi* to the south of Kraton Ratu Boko. It is possible to walk between the two; the walk is over 1km each way and the path is very indistinct. If you are cycling, head west towards the main road, Jalan Raya Piyungan. From here turn left (south) and cycle for 1.5km until a signpost on your left points the way to Barong, a further 1km away to the east. This *candi* is actually two hillside Buddhist temples mounted on a raised platform on the southern slopes of the plateau. A little way back along this path and to the south is **Banyunibo**, a pretty Buddhist shrine dedicated to Tara. From there, head back onto the main road and turn right; Prambanan village lies 2km away.

Yogya to Dieng

The road between Yogya and the Dieng plateau, home of the oldest temples in Indonesia, is punctuated by dozens of small towns and surrounded by some beautiful, bucolic scenery. Most of these towns hold little of interest to the average tourist, though those interested in Indonesian history may wish to visit **Magelang**, where Diponegoro, leader of the Javanese during the five-year war against the Dutch, was arrested and sent into exile. If you don't want to tackle the fairly arduous journey from **Yogya to Dieng** in one day, you could stop at gorgeous **Wonosobo**, a hill-top retreat with a couple of minor tourist attractions in its immediate vicinity.

The main highway heading north from Yogya wriggles through the Kali Progo valley at the foot of Gunung Merapi. After 30km, the road bisects Muntilan, a medium-sized town which, thanks to its unfortunate position at the end of a lava channel which begins at Merapi's crater, suffers more than most whenever the volcano erupts. The town huddles around the Magelang–Yogya highway at the point where two minor roads branch away, one heading east to the mountain village of **Selo** (see p.208) and the other running southwest in the direction of **Purworejo** and Borobudur.

Magelang

Forty kilometres to the north of Yogya and set right in the heart of a huge amphitheatre of volcanoes, sprawling **MAGELANG**, a conglomeration of wide boulevards and grand colonial architecture, is the starting point for buses to Wonosobo village. Most people catch the next bus out, but it's worth venturing outside of the bus station to see Magelang's only attraction, the one-room **Diponegoro Museum** (open daily on request; free). The museum is located in a wing of what is now a teaching academy, once the home of the local Dutch Resident. It was in this house that Diponegoro was arrested by the Dutch on March 28, 1830 (see p.157), and amongst the Diponegoro memorabilia that makes up the museum's collection is the chair he sat on when negotiating with Governor De Kock, as well a set of his robes and a couple of paintings of the hero on horseback.

Wonosobo

Magelang is also the transit town between Yogya and **WONOSOBO**, an hour's drive from Magelang. Wonosobo is a sleepy hill-top village, 35km west of Magelang, along a slender mountain road with splendid panoramic views of Sumbing's grassy foothills. For most visitors, pretty Wonosobo is little more than a gateway to the Dieng plateau. A few travellers, however, prefer to stay in Wonosobo and commute to the plateau, a one-hour bus ride away, since the hotels and restaurants here are superior to those in Dieng and the climate is far more agreeable. There is little to do Wonosobo itself, although a couple of attractions are located nearby. At **Kalianget**, 3km north of Wonosobo, there's a hot spring and swimming pool (daily 6am–6pm; Rp600), where the waters are believed to be good for eczema. An angkuta (with "Garung" written on the side), leaves from behind the tourist office and takes just ten minutes to get there (Rp300). Seven kilometres along the same road is **Telaga Menjer**, a pretty little lake set in picturesque foothills where it's possible to swim; take a local bus from Menjer village (Rp500).

Practicalities

Wonosobo stretches languidly between the bus station in the south, up the hill to the alun-alun, where you'll find the helpful **tourist office** (Mon–Thurs 7am–2pm, Fri 7–11am, Sat 7am–12.30pm). **Buses** from the lowlands pull into the southern terminus. If you wish to travel straight on to Dieng, walk up the hill to the junction with Jalan Kyai Muntang: Dieng buses run past here before calling in at the Dieng terminus to the west of town. An **andong** between the two stations costs Rp1000.

There is **accommodation** to suit all budgets in Wonosobo. At the top end of the scale is the *Surya Asri Hotel* at Jalan A. Yani 137 (☎0286/22992, fax 23598; ⑦). All rooms are en suite, have hot and cold running water, TV and phone. The *Duta* at Jalan RSU 3 (☎0286/21674; ④), 200m south of the Dieng bus station, is the most popular with backpackers. It has a pleasant, family atmosphere, a couple of pet deer run around the garden, and the en-suite rooms are extremely comfortable. One block east of Jalan A. Yani is the *Citra Homestay*, Jalan Angkatan 45 (☎0286/21880; ④), a new place with very clean rooms (all with shared bathroom only). Like the *Duta*, they also offer a Rp5000 **tour** around the paddy-fields and local villages. Anybody who stays in Wonosobo for a night should pay a visit to the *Dieng Restaurant* on Jalan Angkatan 45 – the Chinese, Western and Indonesian **food** is terrific.

Dieng

A 26-kilometre bus ride north of Wonosobo, through, round and over the creases and folds of Gunung Sindoro, brings you to the damp and isolated **DIENG** village, nestling on a plateau of the same name. The landscape up here, four hours north of Yogya, represents a radical departure from the rest of Java. The vegetation is sparse, the largely denuded hills are terraced not with paddy-fields but with cabbage patches and flowerbeds, and the chilly plain is more windswept and misty than humid and sun-kissed.

The **Dieng plateau** lies in a volcanic **caldera** formed by the collapse of underground lava reservoirs. This unusual inception has led to some curious natural phenomena, such as multicoloured **sulphurous lakes** and craters where pungent gas hisses and billows out of crevices in the earth. Dotted among these features are a number of small **temples**, some of the oldest in Java. The name Dieng is a corruption of the Sanskrit *Di-Hyang* (Abode of the Gods), and it is thought that the plateau was considered sacred by the Hindu Sanjaya dynasty. The temples are largely unimpressive when compared to the giants at Prambanan and Borobudur, and indeed the scenery, though a pleasant change from the lowlands, becomes a little monotonous after a while. Nevertheless, the combination of the temples with the sheer strangeness of the landscape make Dieng a highly unusual and rewarding stop for tourists, and a must for geologists, hikers and temple lovers.

It is also possible to reach the plateau from the north coast. Buses leave from Pekalongan, taking four hours to cover the 107km to **Batur**, a tiny village on the western edge of the plateau. This journey often involves a change of buses in Kalibening. From Batur it takes 45 minutes by bus to Dieng (Rp700).

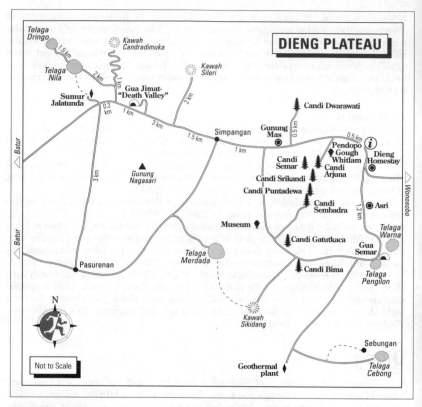

Practicalities

Dieng is at its best in the morning before the mists roll through and the damp sets in, so try to arrive at the temples early, and bring **warm clothes** and **waterproofs**. Although there are plenty of **tours** from Yogya, they're really not worth considering since it's a four-hour journey each way, with just one hour on the plateau. Instead, try to spend a night or two here, but be prepared to rough it a little: the weather is temperamental, the nights are cold and the food is bland.

Tiny **Dieng village** is just a string of buildings lining the eastern side of **Jalan Raya Dieng**, the road that runs along the plateau's eastern edge. Four hundred metres north of this village the road turns sharply left and heads west. The road to Wonosobo (1hr bus ride away) ends at Jalan Raya Dieng by the village's two main travellers' **hostels**. This junction also acts as Dieng's **bus stop**, for buses to Wonosobo as well as other villages on the plateau. The **tourist office** (which seldom sticks to the advertised opening times of 8am–4pm) lies 200m north of the junction. When it's closed, a small kiosk near the two hostels deals with new arrivals and sells tickets to the Arjuna complex, the main set of temples that lies across the road from the village.

One would expect the "Abode of the Gods" to offer **accommodation** a little more heavenly than Dieng's tawdry bunch of losmen. The best on the plateau is the *Gunung*

Mas Hotel (☎0286/92417; ④), at the northern end of town. The prices charged for this somewhat shabby accommodation are ludicrous, but the VIP rooms have both hot water and TV. The rooms at the *Dieng Homestay*, Jalan Raya Dieng 16 (☎0286/92623; ③), are basic and full of flies, and the mandi are excruciatingly cold; this is, however, the best of the budget bunch. *Bu Djono*, next door (☎0286/92814; ③), has shabbier rooms but superior food. Two hundred metres to the south at Jalan Telaga Warna 117–119 stands the *Asri Losmen* (③). The rooms are smarter than the *Dieng Homestay's* (those in the new wing are the best value), but the place lacks atmosphere.

Transport and tours

All of the temples are within easy walking distance of Dieng village. Five of them, comprising the **Arjuna complex**, are in a field immediately to the west of the village; a sixth, Candi Gatutkaca, stands 300m to the south; and the furthest temple from the village, **Candi Bima**, is just 1km south of here. The eighth temple, **Dwarawati**, overlooks Dieng village from behind the *Hotel Gunung Mas*.

Many of the plateau's other attractions, however, are a bus or car ride away, and the bus network on the plateau is limited. All **westbound buses** from Dieng pass through Simpangan village (Rp200), 2km distant, where the road splits. The buses all take the southern road to Batur, 11km away (Rp700 from Dieng), annoyingly for those who want to visit the sights, which are all on the northern road. The only way to reach these by public transport is to stay on the bus until **Pasurenan** (Rp500), 4km before Batur, then take an ojek (Rp1000) up the hill to the northern road and Sumur Jalatunda. Alternatively, hire an ojek from Dieng village to take you directly to the sights (Rp10,000 per day). Most of these tourist attractions are signposted from the main road, although you may still have trouble finding them as the paths are badly maintained. Place-name spellings change frequently on the signposts, but note that Dieng and Tieng are two different places.

The *Dieng Homestay* offers tours around Dieng: their sunrise tour (Rp5000) is very popular. They also run excursions to **Sembungan**, the highest village on Java, at an altitude of 2160m.

The temples

It is believed that the Dieng plateau was once a completely self-contained **retreat** for priests and pilgrims. The ominous rumblings of the volcano beneath their feet, combined with the mist that daily enveloped them, must have convinced the early Hindus that this plateau was indeed sacred. Unfortunately, it was also completely waterlogged, and the architects of the day had to devise a series of **tunnels** to drain the fields. The entire plateau, including the drainage system, was eventually abandoned in the thirteenth century during the unexplained evacuation of Central Java. Dieng sank into swampy obscurity until 1814, when the Dutchman **H.C. Cornelius** visited the area and discovered the ruins of over **two hundred temples** on the plateau. Forty years later, the basin was drained and the ruins fully catalogued.

The Arjuna complex

The eight temples left on Dieng today are a tiny fraction of what was once a huge complex built by the Sanjayas in the seventh and eighth centuries. Of these temples, the five that make up the **Arjuna complex** (daily 6.15am–5.15pm), standing in fields opposite Dieng village, are believed to be the oldest. The tourist office at Dieng have imposed a Rp3000 entrance fee, payable at the small kiosk in the village. Many visitors, however, manage to avoid paying – often unwittingly – by simply turning up outside of the official opening hours or by walking through the fields rather than along the entrance path.

Where once tunnels drained the plateau, wooden walkways today bridge the squelchier parts of the caldera. The temples have been named after heroes from the *Mahabharata* tales, although these are not the original names. Three of the five were built to the same blueprint: square, with two storeys and a fearsome kala head above the main entrance. The most northerly of these two-storey temples, the **Arjuna temple**, is the oldest on Java (cc680 AD). Dedicated to Shiva, the temple once held a giant **lingga** (a phallic-shaped stone) which was washed by worshippers several times a day; the water would then drain through a spout in temple's north wall. The ugly, dumpy construction opposite, appropriately called **Candi Semar** after Arjuna's ugly, dumpy servant in the *Mahabarata*, is thought to have held Shiva's carriage, **Nandi**. Next to Arjuna stands **Candi Srikandi**, the exterior of which is adorned with reliefs of Vishnu (on the north wall), Shiva (east) and Brahma (south). This configuration is unique in Java, suggesting that the Javanese Hindus had not yet established the standard pattern of gods that can be seen at Gedung Songo (see p.221) and Prambanan (see p.187). The next temple south, **Candi Puntadewa**, is (at 15m), the tallest of the five. It towers above neighbouring **Candi Sembadra**, the most southerly and smallest of the group.

Other temples

Candi Gatutkaca, a contemporary of Candi Arjuna, overlooks the Arjuna complex to the southwest. Nearby, a singularly unimpressive **museum** (no set opening hours; free), acts as a warehouse for the decorations and furnishings of Dieng's unrestored temples, which have been dumped here in a random fashion. The caretaker who has the key to unlock the museum is often absent, so you can't always get in – which is no great loss.

The most peculiar-looking temple on the plateau (and the only one to face east) is **Candi Bima**, named after the brother of Arjuna. The temple is a twenty-minute walk south of Gatutkaca along a rutted path. Rows of faces stare impassively back at passers-by from the temple walls, a design based on the temples of southern India.

The eighth and final restored temple on the plateau lies some way to the north of the rest, 500m beyond the village behind the *Hotel Gunung Mas*. This is **Candi Dvaravati**, a fairly plain, single-storey stone structure dating from the middle of the eighth century. The lingga found inside proves that it was once dedicated to Shiva. It's a peaceful place to sit and listen to the noises of the village below.

Natural attractions at Dieng

Dieng perches 2093m above sea level in the crater of a still-active volcano, which occasionally stirs to remind villagers of its presence, as in 1979 when over 150 people died after a cloud of poisonous gas bled into the atmosphere. For most of the time, however, these sulphurous emissions do little more than provide the plateau with a number of unusual natural phenomena. Amongst these are the **coloured lakes**, where sulphurous deposits shade the water blue, from turquoise to azure. **Telaga Warna** (Coloured Lake), 2km along the main road heading south from the village, contains the best example of these sulphur-tinted waters. The lake laps against the shore of a small peninsula which plays host to a number of meditational caves. It was in one of these caves, **Gua Semar**, that Suharto and Australian prime minister Gough Whitlam decided the future of Timor in 1974. A visit to the lakes and caves can be combined with a visit to the Arjuna complex and Candi Bima, which makes for an interesting day's hiking.

Of the other lakes on the plateau, **Telaga Nila** and **Telaga Dringo**, 12km west of Dieng village, are the prettiest (but don't be tempted to swim, as the waters are too sulphuric). A visit to these two can be combined with seeing **Sumur Jalatunda**, a vast, vine-clad well just off the main road. The small boys who hang around the well selling stones will, for a fee, show you a little-used path to the two lakes, although the route is too slippery to use after heavy rain.

Just 250m further along the road is the turn-off to **Kawah Candradimuka**, one of a number of *kawah* (mini-craters) dotted around the plateau. The crater is a twenty-minute walk up the hill from the road; five minutes along its length a small path on the left heads west to Telaga Nila. Take care, as there's no guard rail on the slippery slope to prevent you from sliding into the crater below. The sulphurous smell can be nauseating, and the steaming vents may obscure your view of the bubbling mud pools below. Further east along the road, an extremely overgrown path leads up to **Gua Jimat**, where the sulphurous emissions are fatal to anyone and anything who stands too close.

Tuk Bima Lukar is a small spring situated just a few hundred metres behind the *Dieng Homestay* on the road to Wonosobo. The spring water, which is said to keep bathers eternally young, trickles from stone spouts which are over a thousand years old.

Cilacap and around

Isolated from Yogya by the **Menoreh hills**, a slender, low-lying limestone ridge to the west of the city, and from the north coast, or Pasisir region, by Java's imposing row of volcanoes, the coastal region to the southwest of Yogya has a distinctive backwater feel. There are few attractions in the region, which comprises the regencies of Kulonprogo, Purworejo, Kebumen and Purworketo, but it's pleasant to travel through the landscape of gently undulating, forested hills. Most foreign travellers who stray down this far have joined the major west–east highway at **Cilacap**, a busy port at the southwestern corner of the province, and won't stop again until Yogya. Local holiday-makers venture here quite regularly, though, to enjoy the fresh mountain air of **Baturaden** or view the strange statuary at **Gua Jatijajar**.

Cilacap

The biggest city on Central Java's southern coast, friendly **CILACAP** sees plenty of tourists, many passing through on their way to and from Pangandaran. The port at Cilacap, 170km from Yogya, has the only deep-water berthing facilities on Java's south coast, a fact the Dutch were quick to recognize and exploit during their tenancy. They built a large fort overlooking the sea, **Benteng Pendem** (daily 8am–6pm; Rp500), and today this is Cilacap's main tourist attraction. Though neglected and overgrown, the husk of the fort is in quite a good state of repair compared to most on the island, with fortifications, barrack-rooms and even the former surgery intact.

The fort stands in the shadow of a huge **oil refinery**, the main source of Cilacap's wealth today. Both occupy the southeastern tip of town by **Pantai Teluk Penyu** (Turtle Bay), an ugly stretch of black sand used by the locals as a venue for early evening fifty-a-side soccer matches. If you have a little time to kill, consider renting a fishing boat (Rp3000 per hour) from **Seleko harbour**, to the west of the oil refineries, and ask the owner to take you to **Nusa Kampangan**, a small island lying a few kilometres off Cilacap's western coast. The island features a wildlife park, although the wildlife isn't much in evidence. There are no facilities of any kind here, but it's a pleasant place to amble around.

Practicalities

The **ferry** from Pangandaran disgorges passengers at **Lomanis port** in the northwest corner of the city; the **bus station** is 1km to the east. **Angkuta #C2** performs a complete loop around the city, beginning at the bus station, heading south to the town square then returning to the station via Lomanis port.

The **hotels** in Cilacap are very good value. The *Wijayakusuma*, Jalan J. A. Yani 12 (☎0282/34871, fax 31150; ⑧), opposite the tourist office and near the town square, is the best, with all rooms equipped with air-con, hot water and colour TV; catch angkuta #C2 from the station or ferry port. At the other end of the scale is the *Losmen Tiga*, Jalan Mayor Sutoyo 61 (③), where the cell-like rooms are basic and bare but the prices are extremely low. Across the road stands the *Rumah Makam Sari Murni*, an inexpensive Chinese **restaurant** serving excellent *ayam bakar*. There are a couple more reasonable, mid-price restaurants, the *Sien Hieng* and *Perapatan*, which share the same address at the end of the street at Jalan J. A. Yani 62.

Purworketo, Baturaden and Gua Jatijajar

PURWORKETO, one hour by bus from Cilacap and two from of Wonosobo, is the main transport junction for the southwestern corner of Central Java. It's a well-organized city that promotes itself with the acronym "BERSERI", the components of which are the Indonesian words for clean, healthy, neat and beautiful. It is all of these things, but this doesn't alter the fact that there is absolutely nothing here to persuade tourists to linger.

Nineteen kilometres to the north, however, and 670m up on the southern flanks of **Gunung Slamet**, sits the large mountain village of **BATURADEN**. Regarded by many as the prettiest hill station in Central Java, the village is easily accessible by taking a green bemo from the Puworketo terminus (Rp500). The slopes above Baturaden are shaggy with pine and provide the village with the most beautiful backdrop of any hill station in Central Java. It is possible to scale Gunung Slamet from Baturaden, a climb of seven hours, although it's easier and safer to begin the **ascent** from the northern slopes and the village of **Serang**. **Permits** (Rp5000) are required by all climbers, and are available from the permit office at the northern end of the village of Moga, near Serang. To get here, take a bus to Belik, on the eastern slopes of Slamet, from Purworketo (1hr), then a thirty-minute colt ride from there to Moga. A guide, which is essential, is also available from Moga. The sheer size of the climb necessitates a night out on the mountain, so bring the appropriate gear.

Baturaden itself comprises just one road, Jalan Parawisata, which splits into two at the bus station before reuniting further up the hill at the tawdry fun park **Taman Rekreasi** (daily 6am–6pm; Rp700). As with most hill stations in Java, the bottom end of the **accommodation** market is located at the bottom end of the village. The unfinished *Inti Sari* (④), opposite the *King Karaoke Singing House*, is one of the cheapest options in the village. Rooms are large, beds are clean and the manager is very pleasant. Losmen *Puji* (④) and *Kerta Rahayu* (④), even further down the hill towards the gates of the city, are of a similar standard and price to the *Inti Sari*. At the top of the hill, the *Hotel Rosenda* on Jalan Parawisata (☎0281/32570, fax 32571; ⑦), ranks as the best in town, with a swimming pool and tennis courts – as such, it's usually stuffed full of foreign tour groups. Down below the *Rosenda*, the *Pringsewu* **restaurant** serves some very tasty Indonesian dishes – try their *cap cay* – but beware that the prices are higher on the English-language menu.

Gua Jatijajar

The statue and stalactite monstrosity of **Gua Jatijajar** (daily 6am–5.30pm; Rp800) ranks as the number one tourist attraction in the tiny regency of **Kebumen**, attracting local sightseers by the thousands every day. The cave lies 35km to the south of Purworketo; if you're coming from that direction, ask the bus driver to drop you off at Ijo (Rp500), 13km from Jatijajar, then catch a minibus (Rp300) from there. There are four direct buses from Cilacap (Rp1300), with the last one returning to Cilacap at 4pm. If you're coming from the east, alight at Gombong (Rp3300 from Yogya), where you can pick up a direct bus to the cave (Rp400).

The cave, hollowed out of a series of limestone cliffs running parallel with the coast, was probably quite attractive until the authorities decided to cram the interior with ghastly statues recreating the history of the mythical **Pahaharan Kingdom**. It has since been defaced with centuries worth of graffiti, which is probably the most interesting thing about it. Outside, hundreds of hawkers try to flog all manner of tourist tat. There are two **accommodation** options nearby; the first, right by the entrance, is the adequate *Pondok Jati Diri* (④), a no-nonsense little family losmen with cramped rooms. A ten-minute walk back towards Ijo brings you to pristine *Hotel Puspita* on Jalan Raya Guajatijajar (⑤), a dazzlingly new establishment.

Surakarta (Solo)

Sixty-five kilometres northeast of Yogya, along the same terrifying, high-speed highway that bisects the Prambanan Plain, stands quiet, leafy low-rise **SURAKARTA**, or, as it's more commonly known, **SOLO**. This is the older of the two royal cities in Central Java, and its ruling family can lay claim to being the rightful heirs to the Mataram dynasty. For all Yogya's pomp and ceremony, its royal house is merely the younger, brasher sibling of Solo's ancient court.

Like Yogya, Solo has two **royal palaces** and a number of **museums**, evidence of a past and culture that's every bit as colourful as its rival's. Indeed, Solo's traditional court society is widely regarded as the most refined, or *halus*, on Java. The dancing performances are considered to be more graceful, the poetry more "highbrow", and the court language more polished and polite. Yet Solo's tourist industry is nowhere near as developed as Yogya's. Instead, the city's main source of income is from textiles, and a huge **textile market**, the biggest on Java, stands next to the larger of Solo's two royal houses, **Kasunanan Palace**, in the heart of the city. A number of cottage industries have also sprung up around town, producing everything from gamelan sets to tofu.

Because tourism takes a back seat in Solo, many visitors are fooled into believing that the city can be seen on a day-trip from Yogya. But it has enough attractions to keep sightseers occupied for a couple of days, and also makes an ideal base from which to visit the home of Java Man at **Sangiran**, as well as the intriguing **temples** of **Gunung Lawu**, **Candi Ceto** and **Candi Sukuh**.

Some history

Up until 1744, Solo was little more than a quiet backwater village, albeit one that lay just 10km east of Kartasura, then the capital of the Mataram kingdom. The Matarams had already had a rough start to the eighteenth century. Exhausted by two destructive **Wars of Succession**, the dynasty then suffered at the hands of the Dutch after the reigning susuhunan (king), **Pakubuwono II**, unwisely chose to back the Chinese in their attempt to avenge the Batavian massacre of 1740. The Dutch, supported by the Madurese, had little trouble overcoming the opposition, and the court at Kartasura was sacked as a result. Convinced that Kartasura was jinxed, Pakubuwono II (which translates as "Nail at the Centre of the Universe") consulted various soothsayers and advisers in his search for a more auspicious location for his capital. He soon found one, and in 1745 the entire court was dismantled and transported in a **great procession** to Surakarta, on the banks of the Kali Solo.

The Mataram's luck, however, did not change, and internecine squabbles within the royal house continued to weaken it. Pakubuwono II died just four years later, and his heir, Pakubuwono III, was powerless to stop his uncle, Mangkubumi, taking half the kingdom for his new court at Yogya following the **Third Javanese War of Succession**. Two years later, in 1757, the power of the Surakarta court was diminished

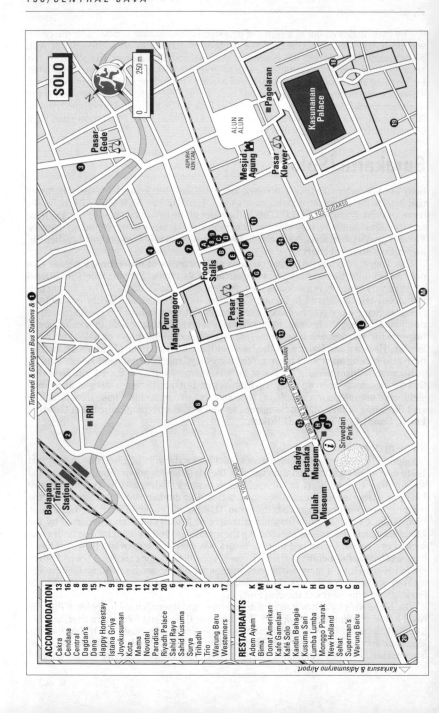

still further by the creation of the **royal house of Mangkunegoro**, right in the centre of Solo. Thereafter, Solo's royal houses wisely avoided fighting and instead threw their energies into the arts, developing a highly sophisticated and graceful court culture. The nobles of the city, particularly those who lived during the rule of the aesthete **Pakubuwono V**, laid down their weapons, and the gamelan pavilions became the new theatres of war, with each city competing to produce the more *halus* court culture.

This non-aggressive stance has continued into the twentieth century. Although a breeding ground for nationalist sentiment during the 1920s, the town took a back seat to Yogya in the **War of Independence**. With hindsight, this inertia seems to have been a poor choice; whilst Yogya was rewarded with its own province and is still fêted today as the epicentre of the Independence movement, Solo was denied any special privileges and was forced to merge with the rest of the Central Javan province.

Taking in the calm, unhurried atmosphere of the city today, it's hard to believe that Solo suffered more permanent damage than any other city on Java (with the possible exception of Jakarta) during the **riots** of May 1997. Yet in just five hours of protests and rioting on the evening of May 14, both of the city's shopping centres – the Singosaran and Gajah Mada plazas – were burnt down, and nineteen people were killed when a shoe shop near the Singosaran Plaza collapsed after looters started fires within the building. Fearful of further destruction at the hands of zealous protesters, most property owners in Solo have replaced their Suharto posters with banners and graffiti proclaiming their support of the pro-reform movement. Only time will tell whether this tactic has been successful.

Orientation, arrival, information and city transport

Solo sits on the western banks of the Kali Solo, Java's longest river. It doesn't take long to become acquainted with the layout of central Solo, as nearly all of the hotels, sights and facilities are either on, or within walking distance of, the main road through the city, **Jalan Brig Jen Slamet Riyadi** (hereafter called simply Jalan Riyadi), which stretches from **Kartasura** in the west to the **Adpura Kencan** monument near the kraton in the east. The centre of the travellers' scene is Jalan Dahlan, a smallish road heading north off Jalan Riyadi. Behind the shops on the south side of Jalan Riyadi are a series of traditional kampung: riddled with winding alleyways which are flanked by some of the oldest houses in the city, they're fascinating places to get lost in.

Adisumaryno Airport, Central Java's only international airport, occupies a square of former farmland 10km to the west of Solo and just 2km north of Kartasura. There is no public transport direct to Solo from the airport, although a half-hourly **minibus** to Kartasura (Rp300) drives along the main road alongside the runway, and from Kartasura you can catch a double-decker to Solo (Rp400). A **taxi** from the airport to Solo will cost approximately Rp10,000, slightly less in the opposite direction.

All buses to Solo terminate at the **Tirtonadi bus station** in the north of the city. Just across the crossroads by the northeastern corner of Tirtonadi is the **minibus terminal**, Gilingan. From the front of the *Hotel Surya*, overlooking Tirtonadi, orange angkuta #6 departs for the town centre, stopping at **Ngapeman**, the junction of Jalan Gajah Mada and Jalan Riyadi. Heading to the bus station from the town centre, catch a BERSERI bus (Rp400) from the bus stop on Jalan Riyadi, 100m east of Jalan Dahlan. A becak from the bus station to Jalan Dahlan costs approximately Rp1200. You'll pay the same fare from the **Balapan train station**, 300m south of Tirtonadi.

Solo boasts three **tourist offices**, located at the airport, at Tirtonadi bus station and behind the Radyo Pustoko museum at Jalan Riyadi 275. Only the latter (Mon–Sat 8am–4pm; ☎0271/711435) is of any real use, however, with a reasonable range of brochures and a couple of staff who speak a little English.

City transport

Solo's **double-decker buses** are unique in Central Java. Ignore the numbers on the front of them, as they all travel along the same route: from Kartasura in the west, down Jalan Riyadi, past the post office and on to Palur, where you can catch buses to Tawangmangu. Unable to return on the same route thanks to the one-way system of Slamet Riyadi, they head west along Jalan Veteran instead. The fare is a flat Rp200, whatever the distance.

The main **taxi** stand is situated by the Mata Hari department store; taxis are metered. The **becak** are more reasonable: unlike the ones in Yogya, Solo's becak do not charge a higher rate if there is more than one person in the carriage. As ever, remember to bargain hard. Being flat and, for a Javanese city, relatively free of traffic, **cycling** is an excellent way to get round the city. Bikes can be rented from many of the homestays for Rp5000 per day.

Accommodation

Solo is stuffed full of **hotels** and **losmen** catering to every pocket, with new ones going up all the time. Nearly all of them lie within 100m of the main road, Jalan Riyadi, or near the train station. Most of the **budget hotels** are hidden in the kampung to the south of Jalan Riyadi, and can be difficult to find. The simplest solution is to hire a becak driver to take you to the hostel of your choice, although, as is usual, the hostel owner pays a commission to the driver which comes out of your pocket via a higher room charge. **Breakfast** is included in the price in nearly every hotel.

Cakra, Jl Riyadi 201 (☎0271/45847, fax 48334). With its swimming pool, billiard room, batik shop, parking facilities and air-con rooms, this is one of the best-value hotels in this category, and in a great location too. ⑥.

Cendana, Gang Empu Panuluh III 4, Kemlayan Kidul (☎0271/52821). One of the newer places in town, aimed at the budget market. The owner, Bullet, is eccentric but harmless. His hotel contains some of the nicest rooms in this price range, featuring Javanese furniture and large fans. ③.

Central, Jl Dahlan (☎0271/42814). A big place that's seen better days. The green-tiled floor and cheap, wooden furniture are tatty, and the rooms aren't exactly cosy. Useful, however, as an over-spill option if the other places in the city centre are full. ③.

Dagdan's, Baluwerti Rt II/7 42 (☎0271/54538). The only hotel within the kraton walls, by the southeast corner of the palace. Attractive little place with roses growing up the walls of the central courtyard and smart rooms sharing a well-scrubbed bathroom. Highly recommended. ④.

Dana, Jl Riyadi 286 (☎0271/711976, fax 713880). Large hotel with 47 air-con rooms, conveniently situated opposite the tourist office and museum. ⑦.

Happy Homestay, Jl Honggowongso, Gang Karagan 12 (☎0271/712449). Also known as *Hotel Bahagia*. Basic rooms in the main house, with a mattress on the floor and a small fan often the only furniture, are supplemented by cleaner, more spacious rooms in the main floor annexe. One of the friendliest homestays around, however, and deservedly popular amongst backpackers and long-term residents. The upstairs rooms are bigger and better. ③.

Istana Griya, Jl Dahlan 22 (☎0271/634378, fax 632667). New and highly efficient homestay tucked away down a little *gang* behind the *Steak House*, with the smartest and best-value rooms in this price range. Quiet and highly recommended. ③.

Joyokusuman, Jl Gajahan 7 Rt II/3 (☎0271/54842). Large, beautiful, individually decorated rooms with net-covered four-poster beds and balconies. Most guests are long-term residents, many studying meditation. ⑤.

Kota, Jl Riyadi 125 (☎0271/632841). Unexceptional mid-priced hotel with all the usual facilities and a slightly seedy atmosphere, well situated in the centre of town near Jl Dahlan. ⑤.

Mama Kauman Gang III/49, Jl Yos Sudarso (☎0271/52248). One of the best places to come for a batik course. Also provides good local information and runs bicycle tours to nearby villages. The breakfasts (included in price), though sometimes bland, are occasionally excellent (their fruit salads are particularly good), and free tea and coffee is available throughout the day. Upstairs rooms are cheaper and noisier. ③.

Novotel, Jl Riyadi 272 (☎0271/724555, fax 724666). Brand-new, sparkling luxury hotel with its own pool, gym, Indonesian, Japanese and Chinese restaurants and plush, air-con rooms. ⑦.

Paradiso, Jl Kemlayan Kidul I/3 (☎0271/54111, fax 52960). A laudable attempt to recreate paradise down a back alley in Solo. Hidden behind huge white walls and tastefully festooned with statues and baubles, the reception rooms of the *Paradiso* look sumptuous. The 32 bedrooms can't quite maintain this standard, however, and the cheaper ones are a little grotty. ③.

Riyadh Palace, Jl Riyadi 335 (☎0271/717181, fax 721552). One of Solo's newest hotels, occupying a good central location, but otherwise fairly unexceptional. ⑦.

Sahid Kusuma, Jl Sugiopranoto 20 (☎0271/46356, fax 44788). Once the royal court of Susuhunan Pakubuwono X's son, this place is undoubtedly the most stylish in central Solo. Set in five landscaped acres with a swimming pool at the back and pendopo reception, complete with gamelan orchestra, at the front. Air-con, TV and fridge come as standard in all rooms. ⑧.

Sahid Raya, Jl Sahid Raya 82 (☎0271/44144, fax 44133). Four stars and 160 rooms. Facilities include a swimming pool, pub, café, and rooms with air-con, fridge and TV. ⑧.

Surya, Jl Tagore 125 (☎0271/721915). Right next to the bus terminal, which is hardly an ideal location. Reasonable rooms, but you'll find better-value accommodation in town. ⑤.

Trihadhi, Jl Monginsidi 97 (☎0271/637557). One of the better options by the train station, a sparkling-new place that is at once both professionally run and homely. Rooms are large and cool. ③.

Trio, Jl Urip Sumoharjo 25 (☎0271/632847). Forty-five years old and still looking good. The cool, tiled reception opens into a pleasant courtyard, a wonderful retreat from the bustle of the market outside. Rooms are a little dark, but clean. No breakfast, but tea and coffee served throughout the day. ④.

Warung Baru, contact the *Warung Baru Restaurant*, Jl Ahmad Dahlan 23 (☎0271/656369). Travellers' restaurant which now has a small hotel, just off Jl Ronggowarsito. Has a very homely atmosphere, probably because it's a converted house. Four rooms only. ④.

Westerners, Jl Kemlayan Kidul 11 (☎0271/633106). Cramped, plant-filled hangout that accepts foreign travellers only. Inexpensive rooms, with dormitory beds for only Rp5000. ③.

The City

Solo has grown horizontally rather than vertically down the years. There are no skyscrapers in the centre, and nearly all the twentieth-century constructions are just a few storeys high, merging seamlessly with the city's traditional architecture to form a pleasing harmony of ancient and modern.

The best examples of Solo's architectural heritage are the royal houses off Jalan Riyadi, namely **Puro Mangkunegoro** to the north of the street and the **Kasunanan Palace** to the south. The latter lies within Solo's **walled city**, an area every bit as pretty as Yogyakarta's Kraton. Unlike Yogya's old quarter, however, Solo's kraton does not dominate the city centre; it's tucked away to the east of the city.

The kraton

The kraton at Solo provided Yogya's first sultan, Mangkubumi, with many ideas for the layout and design of his new city. Anyone who has been to Yogya will doubtless see many similarities, starting with the **alun-alun**, a large grassy square lying immediately behind the city gates on Jalan Riyadi. (Incidentally, the two huge banyan trees that grow in the centre of the alun-alun headed the procession of 1745 that transferred the royal court from Kartasura to Solo.) Further exploration reveals still more similarities: to the west of the square stands the **royal mosque**, or **Mesjid Agung**, built to a traditional Javanese design by Pakubuwono III in 1750, with a multi-tiered (*joglo*) roof surmounting an enclosed pendopo, and to the south of the alun-alun a giant open-sided pendopo announces the austere presence of the city's royal residence, the **Kasunanan Palace**.

KASUNANAN PALACE

Brought from Kartasura by Pakubuwono II in one huge day-long procession in 1745, the **Kasunanan Palace** (daily except Fri 9am–2pm; Rp2000) is Solo's largest and most important royal house. Guides are available free of charge and are definitely worth taking, as the charms of the place lie not in spectacular construction or ostentatious furnishings, but in the tiny architectural and ornamental details, many imbued with symbolism, which are easy to overlook.

Behind the *pagelaran* stands a second pendopo, the **Siti Inggil**. This provides shelter for a **sacred cannon**, yet another relic of Kartasura brought here in the 1745 procession. Traditionally the susuhunan would give speeches from this pendopo, taking advantage of the structure's excellent acoustics.

Continuing south, you pass through one gate and come to a second, which leads through to the main body of the kraton. This gate is saved for ceremonial use only. A smaller gate to the right remains the sole preserve of members of the royal family, and plebeians must turn left and enter the main body of the palace by the eastern entrance. This opens out into a large courtyard whose surrounding buildings house the palace's fairly disorganized **kris collection**, as well as a number of chariots, silver ornaments and other royal knick-knacks. Highlights include three Dutch chariots dating from the last century and a huge ceremonial kris, used to protect the palace from evil spirits.

An archway to the west of the courtyard leads into the susuhunan's living quarters; shoes must be removed before you enter this section. The current sultan, the septuagenarian Pakubuwono XII, is still in residence, along with a few of his 35 children and two of his six wives. Many of the buildings in this courtyard are modern copies, the originals having burnt down in a fire in 1985 caused by an electrical fault. The octagonal **watchtower** to the north, however, is original. One of its floors is the sole preserve of the susuhunan for his meetings with Loro Kidul, the Goddess of the South Seas (see p.166). Every year, on the anniversary of his coronation, the susuhunan, in a private ceremony, enters the room to renew his acquaintance with the sea goddess.

Outside the kraton

The rest of Solo's major sights lie to the west of the kraton, on or around Jalan Riyadi. The second royal house in Solo, the **Puro Mangkunegoro** (guided tours only Mon–Thurs 8.30am–2pm, Sun 8.30–1pm; Rp2500) stands 1km west of the kraton and, like Yogya's court of Paku Alam, faces south towards the Kasunanan Palace as a mark of respect. With its fine collection of antiques and curios, in many ways the Puro Mangkunegoro is more interesting than the Kasunanan palace to which it is subservient.

The palace was built in 1757 to placate the rebellious **Prince Mas Said** (Mangkunegoro I), a nephew of Pakubuwono II, who had originally joined forces with Mangkubumi against the king during the Third Javanese War of Succession. Relations with Mangkubumi deteriorated, however, after the latter founded Yogya and was recognized as its sultan, and at one stage Mas Said was regarded as an enemy of both royal courts as well as the VOC (Dutch East India Company). Exhausted by fighting wars on three fronts, Mas Said eventually accepted a VOC-brokered peace deal which gave him a royal title, a court in Solo and rulership over four thousand of Solo's households. In return, Mas Said promised peace.

The palace hides behind a high white wall, entered through the gateway to the south. The vast **pendopo** (the largest in Indonesia) which fronts the palace, shields four gamelan orchestras underneath its rafters. Three of these are sacred and only to be played on very special occasions. Be sure to look up at the vibrantly painted roof of the pendopo, with Javanese zodiac figures forming the main centrepiece.

The main body of the palace lies behind the pendopo. A portrait of the current resident, Mangkunegoro IX, hangs in the **Paringgitan** – an area reserved specifically reserved for wayang kulit performances – by the entrance to the **Dalam Agung**, or living quarters. The reception room of the Dalam Agung has been turned into a museum, and an extremely good one at that. The displays of ancient coins, ballet masks and chastity preservers are particularly interesting.

Another kilometre west along Jalan Riyadi brings you to the **Radya Pustaka Museum** (Mon–Thurs & Sun 8am–1pm, Fri & Sat 8–11am; Rp500). Built by the Dutch in 1890, this is one of the oldest and largest museums in Java, and houses a large Dutch and Javanese library as well as collections of wayang kulit puppets, kris, and scale models of the mosque at Demak and the cemetery at Imogiri. Just a few metres west is the **Sriwedari Park** (daily 2–8pm), an amusement park which holds nightly wayang orang performances (see p.204). Another 200m further west, at Jalan Dr Cipto 15, is the **Dullah Museum**, a gallery holding paintings and sculptures by Pak Dullah, a prolific artist whose work was collected by, amongst others, President Suharto. Currently the museum is closed for restoration.

Eating and drinking

Solo has some good-value restaurants, including a couple of very good budget places around Jalan Dahlan, but nothing like the number or variety that can be found in Yogya. Its warung, however, are renowned throughout the island. Local specialities include *nasi liwet* – chicken or vegetables and rice drenched in coconut milk and served on a banana leaf – and *nasi gudeg*, a variation on Yogya's recipe. For dessert, try *kue putu* (coconut cakes) or *srabi*, a combination of pancake and sweet rice served with a variety of fruit toppings. Most of these delicacies can be purchased along Jalan Teuku Umar, one block west of Jalan Dahlan, and on the roads around the Sriwedari Park in the evening.

Solo's sweets and cakes are also irresistible. The *Donat Amerikan*, just round the corner from Jalan Dahlan on Jalan Riyadi, sells a plenty of tasty cream-topped, jam-filled goodies. The *New Holland Bakery*, further up Jalan Riyadi, has a similarly saccharine selection, with a pub and restaurant upstairs.

Restaurants

Adem Ayam, Jl Riyadi 342. Large, slightly overpriced restaurant split into two sections, serving Javanese and Chinese food.

Bima, Jl Riyadi 128. Large and swish new ice-cream parlour serving a reasonable selection of Indonesian and European dishes at surprisingly low prices, backed up by a decent selection of ice creams. Open 11am–9.30pm.

Kafe Gamelan, Jl Dahlan. Quiet place serving adequate, medium-priced travellers' fare.

Kafe Solo, Jl Secoyadan 201. Stylish mid-priced restaurant with an excellent selection of beef and chicken steaks, salads and other Western dishes. Great if you fancy a change from rice.

Kantin Bahagia, Pujosari Market, Jl Riyadi 275. Highly recommended tiny bar and restaurant just to the south of Jl Riyadi in the Pujosari Market, serving good-value Indonesian staples and cheap beer. Stays open till 1am to catch the post-cinema crowd.

Kusuma Sari, Jl Riyadi. An ice-cream and fast-food restaurant, with, unusually for Indonesia, a no-smoking policy. Popular local hangout.

Lumba Lumba, Pujosari Market, Jl Riyadi 275. One of a large number of restaurants/warung to the west of Sriwedari Park, most of which offer a similar, small menu. A shady, welcoming retreat offering standard Indonesian snacks and lunches.

Monggo Pinarak, Jl Dahlan 22. This mid-priced restaurant/book and batik shop is owned by a well-travelled, woolly-hatted Bangladeshi, and most of its menu is made up of dishes from the subcontinent. The food, apart from the excellent chicken *dopiaza*, is adequate rather than exceptional, but the dishes make a refreshing change from Indonesian food and the service is very good. There's an Internet connection at the rear of the restaurant and a good-quality souvenir shop at the front.

Sehat, Pujosari Market, Jl Riyadi 275. A snake restaurant/warung near Sriwedari. You choose your meal whilst it's still hissing and tell the chef how you want it done. Rp10,000 for the whole snake, Rp3000 for sate or, if you just want a snack, Rp1000 for the penis.

Supermans, Jl Dahlan. Another mid-price travellers' place, this time specializing in steaks. Their nasi goreng special, with the rice is wrapped inside an omelette, is a tasty twist on an Indonesian staple.

Warung Baru, Jl Dahlan. The most popular travellers' restaurant in Solo. Good, inexpensive food, with delicious home-made bread. Also organizes tours, batik courses, and often a little old lady calls round offering massages (from 7pm).

Nightlife and entertainment

The Solonese will try to convince you that this is the "city that never sleeps", but, in spite of the best efforts of the muezzin at 4am, this simply isn't true. There are four **nightclubs** in Solo: the rather dingy *Nirwana* in the central market district; *Legends*, a slightly better place catering for a youngish crowd on Jalan Honggowongso; *Freedom*, to the northwest of the city centre in the Manohan district; and *Solo Bilyar & Disco Dangdut* above the Pasar Gede, a disco specializing in *dangdut* music (see p.970) with an attached pool hall. Only the latter is worth staying up for. All charge a Rp10,000 entrance fee, for which you receive one free beer (except on Saturday). If you just want a drink, head to the *New Holland Pub and Restaurant*, where a live band performs every evening after 10pm.

As with all big Indonesian cities, Solo has plenty of **cinemas** and **pool halls**. The Sriwedari Park has a four-screen cinema – Solo 1234 – showing recent Hollywood blockbusters alongside the mandatory kung-fu flicks, with tickets only Rp4000. A similar diet is offered by the huge cinema, Fajar 123, on Jalan Sudirman near the post office.

Performing arts

For the last two centuries, the royal houses of Solo have directed their energies away from the battlefield and towards the stage, with each developing a highly individual style for the traditional Javanese arts of gamelan and wayang. The Puro Mangkunegoro's performances of **wayang orang** (daily 10am–noon) are more rumbustuous and aggressive than the graceful, fluid style of the Kasunanan Palace (Sun 10am–noon). Another option is the three-hour performance at Sriwedari Park (Mon–Sat 8pm). Radio Republik Indonesia (RRI) records wayang orang performances every first and third Tuesday of the month (9.30pm–midnight); inquire at the RRI, just to the south of the Balapan train station, for tickets to the show.

Both court styles were, until recently, fiercely protected from impersonation. It was forbidden to stage a performance of the sacred *bedoyo* (where a troupe of female dancers move in exact unison with each other) and *srimpi* (four dancers moving in two pairs) dances outside of the two courts. Now, however, a third player has come onto the scene. The STSI – Indonesia's Academy of Performing Arts – in the suburb of Kentingan to the northeast of the city, has invented new, non-traditional forms of wayang. Visit the **academy** (Mon–Thurs & Sat 9–5pm; free) and you can see a variety of dances, diluting traditional Solonese movements with Balinese and other styles.

Gamelan is also something of a Solonese speciality. The small gamelan orchestra at the *Sahid Kusuma Hotel* plays every afternoon and evening in the reception hall. Radio RRI records a gamelan performance every second and fourth Thursday of the month (9pm). Inquire at the RRI building (see above) for tickets and performance times. The Kasunanan Palace also gets in on the act, holding a gamelan performance every fifth Monday (on the Javanese day of Malam Selasa Legi), while the Puro Mangkunegoro puts on a ninety-minute performance on Saturday evening (9pm).

Wayang kulit fans are also well catered for. The finest *dalang* in Java, Ki Anom Suroto, lives down a small *gang*, Kampung Kusumodining, off Jalan Riyadi near the *Cakra Hotel*; when he's not touring the world, Suroto plays for private functions in Solo. Inquire at the tourist office for details of his next performance and you may be fortunate enough to be invited along. Every 35 days (on the Javanese day of Rebo Legi) Suroto invites a *dalang* to perform at his house. The Kasunanan Palace also organizes a performance of wayang kulit in the evening of the fourth Saturday of every month, which is then broadcast on radio. On the third Saturday of every month, RRI (the radio station) allows the public in to watch the recording of their wayang kulit performance.

Shopping

There are some excellent markets in Solo, two of which are of particular interest to foreign visitors. The three-storey **Pasar Klewer** (daily 9am–4pm), by the southwest corner of the alun-alun, lays claim to being Java's largest **batik** market. It's certainly confusingly huge; trying to locate a particular stall can take forever, especially as so many of them look alike and sell similar products. Designs from all over Java can be found here, although (naturally) brown and indigo, the traditional colours of Solo's batik, predominate. Most of the batik is *cap*, although *tulis* and *lurik* homespun are also available. It's possible to have an item of clothing made to measure for you in just one day, although unless your Indonesian is very good you may have trouble explaining exactly what you want.

The **Pasar Triwindu** (daily 8am–4pm), just to the south of the Puro Mangkunegoro, is supposedly an antiques market, but you'd have to be very lucky to find anything of value among the piles of cheap souvenirs. Another "antique" merchant is the **Bali Art Shop** at Jalan K.H. Hasyim Asyari 51, between the kraton and Jalan Yos Sudarso. This boutique is crammed to the rafters with all kinds of souvenirs and junk – and possibly the odd antique – making it the most enjoyable place for rummaging around in.

There are two other markets in Solo. The large and buzzy **Pasar Gede**, or Central Market, is a mainly Chinese affair 300m north of the post and telephone offices, selling fruit and vegetables. It is not, however, the biggest market in Solo. That award goes to the intoxicating **Pasar Legi**, which sells food and household goods – come here for the vegetables and the chaos. It's on the way to the bus station; catch a BERSERI bus heading east along Jalan Riyadi.

Listings

Airlines Garuda, *Cakra Hotel*, Jl Riyadi 201 (☎0271/630082); Silk Air, 3rd floor, Grup BCA Building (☎0271/41374).

Banks and exchange The Bank BCA, in the vast BCA building at the eastern end of Jl Riyadi, currently offers the best rates in town. The exchange offices are on the second floor, and are open 10am–noon only. The Golden Money Changer at the northern end of Jl Yos Sudarso, and PT Desmonda, next to the *Bima Restaurant* at Jl Riyadi 128, are both open throughout the day, though their rates are inferior to the banks. Most of the banks, which can be found at and around the eastern end of Jl Riyadi, have ATMs, as does the *Novotel* hotel at Jl Riyadi 272.

Batik courses For all the hype of Yogya, the best place to try your hand at batik is Solo. The homestays and restaurants organize a number of courses costing Rp10,000–20,000 depending on whether you are making a small wall-hanging or designing a T-shirt: the *Warung Baru* restaurant on Jl Dahlan runs an extremely popular course taught by the amiable Ecoh. His workshop is 2km from the restaurant, but transport is provided. *Mama's Homestay*, Kauman Gang III/49, Jl Yos Sudarso (☎0271/52248), was once a batik factory, and a few high-quality cloths are still produced there. Those who sign up for the course will be working alongside the local artists.

Bookshops There is no English-language bookshop in Solo. The *Monggo Pinarak* restaurant has a small selection of books for sale, although it keeps the best ones for itself and its diners.

Bus Tickets Most homestays and travellers' restaurants sell door-to-door bus tickets to popular tourist destinations, as does Niki Tours on Jl Yos Sudarso. For the complete selection of bus and minibus companies, however, head to the Gilingan minibus terminal, east of the main Tirtonadi bus terminal.

Car rental Star Car Rental, Jl Laksda Adiscupto 22 (☎0271/562403). Their in-town agent is Niki Tours on Jl Yos Sudarso. Jeeps cost Rp80,000 per day, rising to Rp175,000 for a Honda Grand. Weekly and monthly rates are also available.

Email Currently only the *Monggo Pinarak Restaurant*, Jl Dahlan 22, has an Internet connection (Rp7500 for 30min).

Ferries On Jl Veteran there are a couple of tiny kiosks which have details of the Pelni ferries.

Hospital Rumah Sakit Panti Kosala (aka Rumah Sakit Dr Oen), Jl Brig Jen Katamso 55.

Immigration office Jl Adisucipto, on the way to the airport (☎0271/48479).

Meditation courses Solo has become the centre of meditation in Java. The staff at the *Joyokusuman Hotel*, Jl Gajahan 7 Rt II/3 (☎0271/54842), will be able to advise you on the courses available. Some of the most popular teachers are: Pak Soewondo, at the green-doored Jl Madukoro 21, a few hundred metres west of the kraton walls, who holds a free, 2hr Javanese relaxation session every Wednesday evening at 6pm; Pak Ananda Suyono, of Shanti Loka at Jl Ronggowarsito 88 (☎0271/42348), to the north of Jl Dahlan, who offers New Age meditation five days per week; Pak Hardjanto, who teaches yoga at the statue-encrusted Global Hinduism centre, opposite the eastern entrance to the Kraton at Jl Sidikoro 10a; and Pak Suprapto Surjodarmo, the most popular teacher with European students, whose dance/meditation courses (approximately US$700 for a month) are held out of town to the north of Solo in Mojosongo.

Photographic shops There are two reasonable photo stores in Solo: Foto Citi, just a few metres east of Jl Dahlan on Jl Riyadi, and Foto Sampurna, further east on Jl Riyadi at no. 24.

Post office Jl Jend Sudirman (daily 6am–10pm). The poste restante closes in the evening.

Swimming The pool at the *Sahid Kusuma* hotel is open to non-residents for a hefty Rp7500 (daily 7am–8pm), while that at the *Cakra* (7am–7pm) charges a more reasonable Rp4000.

Telephones Just behind the Telkom offices on Jl Sumoharjo, at Jl Mayor Kusmanto 3, there's a 24hr wartel office. There's also a wartel on Jl Riyadi to the west of Jl Yos Sudarso.

Tours Niki Tours, Jl Sutowijoyo 45 (☎ & fax 0271/717733), offers a number of trips to nearby attractions, such as Sukuh and the Tawangmangu waterfall, for US$22. Most travellers use them for their bus to Bali, which includes a night's accommodation at Mount Bromo (US$39). They also have an office at Jl Yos Sudarso 17. Inta Tours & Travel, Jl Riyadi 96 (☎0271/51142, fax 56128), offers a similar deal. Better value, and more rewarding, are the cycling tours organized by many of the homestays and travellers' restaurants – for example, *Mama's*, *Relax*, *Bahagia* and *Warung Baru*. The cost is around Rp10,000 and usually includes a visit to a gamelan factory, bakery, tofu factory and even an arak manufacturer.

Travel agents Try Sahid Gema Wisata, Jl Riyadi 380 (☎0271/42105 or 41916) or Niki Tours, Jl Sutowijoyo 45 (☎ & fax 0271/717733).

Around Solo

You could happily spend a week making day-trips from Solo, though there's nothing in the vicinity of the city quite as impressive as Yogya's two most famous excursions, Prambanan and Borobudur. Nevertheless, all of the following attractions are accessible by public transport and some, particularly the *candi* on **Gunung Lawu**, **Sukuh** and **Ceto**, 40km due east of Solo, are well worth visiting. Kartasura, the first capital of the Mataram, lies just to the west of downtown Solo and is the nearest of the attractions, though there's little actually to see. The discoveries of the remains of one of mankind's oldest ancestors at **Sangiran**, 18km to the north of Solo, are now housed in a small archeological museum; although of vital importance to paleontologists, they are unlikely to captivate the average visitor. Forty-eight kilometres west of Solo, the village of **Selo**

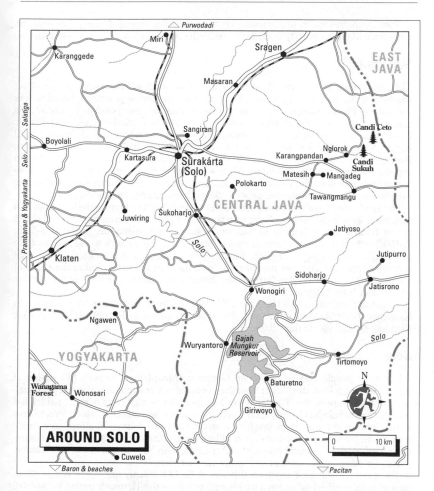

provides climbers with an alternative base to overcrowded Kaliurang from which to tack-le **Gunung Merapi**, and 16km to the south of Solo is the regency of **Wonogiri** which, as with most of the south coast regencies, remains largely undisturbed by tourists.

Kartasura

Ten kilometres to the west of Solo lies the ancient city of **Kartasura**, the former capital of the Mataram kingdom, founded by Amangkurat II in 1677 after his uncle, **Puger**, had appropriated the old court at Plered for himself. Thanks to the complete removal of the court to Solo by Pakubuwono II, there is little to see here except the former kraton's massive old **brick walls** which today encircle a graveyard. Double-decker buses from the junction of Jalan Wahidin and Jalan Riyadi in central Solo head west to Kartasura every ten minutes. The walls are about 1km to the south of the main Kartasura–Solo road; jump off at the "Kraton" road sign and walk or take a becak the rest of the way.

Two kilometres south of Kartasura lay an even older capital, **Pajang**, home of the embryonic Mataram dynasty in the early sixteenth century, but nothing of it now remains.

Sangiran

The unassuming little village of **SANGIRAN**, 18km north of Solo, ranks as one of the most important archeological sites in Central Java. One million years ago, Sangiran was the home of **Pithecantropus Erectus**, or **Java man** as he's more commonly known. His remains – a few fragments of jawbone – were discovered by Berlin-born paleontologist Dr G.H.R. von Koenigswald in 1936, following excavations by Eugene Dubois in 1891. Until human bones over 2.5 million years old were discovered in the Rift Valley in Kenya, Koenigswald's discoveries were the oldest hominid remains ever found, and the first to support Darwin's theory of evolution. Many scientists of the day even suggested that Java man might have been the so-called "missing link", the creature that is supposed to provide the evolutionary connection between the anthropoid apes and modern man.

Plenty of other fossils were unearthed here, including the four-metre-long tusk of a mastodon. These discoveries, along with replicas of Java man's cranium (the real skulls are in Bandung), are housed in Sangiran's single-room **museum** (daily 8am–5pm; Rp1000), where a life-size diorama tries to bring to life Java man's world. None of the museum's captions is in English, though you can buy a pricey English-language brochure (Rp5000). Another prehistoric site in the area is **Miri**, 10km to the north of Sangiran off the main road to Purwodadi, although the museum is fairly uninformative and smaller than Sangiran's.

To get to Sangiran, take a Damri or BERSERI bus from Solo's Jalan Slamet Riyadi to Kalijambe (Rp500), then either wait for a yellow angkuta (Rp200) or hire an ojek (Rp1500) to take you to the village.

Selo

While most people choose to ascend **Gunung Merapi** from Yogya's hill station at Kaliurang (see p.180), the ascent from the north side offers a rather different yet equally enthralling experience. The lip of the Merapi crater is higher its northern side, and for this reason Selo has been largely unaffected by the lava streams, which tend to flow south. Scaling the mountain involves a straightforward four-hour **climb** to a small plateau, followed by a one-hour slog uphill on loose shingle to the summit. The continuous patchwork of volcanic hills and paddy-fields, with Yogyakarta in the far distance, makes for possibly the most breathtaking view on Java.

The most popular base camp on this side is **SELO**, a dusty one-horse village 43km west of Solo, reached by taking a westbound bus from the Tirtonadi station to Boyolali (Rp600), then a minibus from outside Boyolali station to Selo (Rp600). There is also a very infrequent direct bus from Solo (Rp1500).

Selo village is not so much of a tourist trap as Kaliurang, but there are three places where tourists can stay, all of which will be able to arrange a **guide** (three people per guide maximum, Rp10,000) to take you to the summit. The biggest **hotel**, patronized by all the tour groups, is the *Agung Merapi* (③), 200m up the road from where the minibuses disgorge their passengers. Its pleasant bamboo lounge/reception area is let down by some substandard, dingy rooms and surly staff, though it does have a dormitory (Rp5000). The decrepit and basic *Jaya Losmen* (③) lies just 100m further down the hill, and at the end of the village, just round the corner from the bus stop, hides the mar-

For details of climbing the southern side of **Gunung Merapi**, see p.180.

vellous 25-year-old *Melati Homestay* (③). It is owned by a former mountain guide, Pak Arto, whose son leads tours up the mountain. Though the facilities in the losmen are basic, the price includes a nasi goreng breakfast.

Wonogiri

The regency of **Wonogiri**, 16km to the south of Solo, comprises an area of placid lakes, limestone caves and, right in the centre, a huge man-made reservoir. It was originally part of the territory given to Mangkunegoro in 1757 as part of the peace deal with the VOC (see p.202). **WONOGIRI TOWN** is the capital, an undulating, tree-lined place with little to tickle the average tourist's fancy, though there is an imposing black-stone **heirloom tower** on the road to Solo, 6km west of Wonogiri. The tower was built during Mangkunegoro's reign and holds sacred relics from his court; every year, in the Javanese month of Suro, they are taken out and washed in the **Gajah Mungkur Reservoir** (daily 7am–6pm; Rp600), an 83-square-kilometre freshwater lake formed when the Kali Solo was dammed near its source. To get there, catch one of the very frequent minibuses from Wonogiri station (Rp300). A lot of controversy surrounded the building of this dam, as an estimated sixty thousand villagers were moved to accommodate the project. Today the reservoir serves as a water **fun park** for locals, with jet skis (Rp20,000 for 15min) and motorboats (Rp15,000 for 1hr) for rent. This region is also popular with local hikers and trekkers, who can take advantage of one of the few wilderness spots in Java. A small information booth by the park's entrance has details of these.

Gunung Lawu

Pine-crowned **Gunung Lawu** (3265m), a two-hour drive due east of Solo, is one of the largest volcanoes on Java. It is also one of the least active, and its placid nature has

---

WALKING ON LAWU

Always start your **treks on Lawu** as early as you can before the sun gets really fierce. There are more workers in the fields in the morning too, who can help you if you get lost. It is possible to walk all the way from Candi Ceto to Candi Sukuh, and from there to the waterfall at Tawangmangu in around five hours. There is not enough time to do this as a day-trip from Solo, however, as it can take up to four hours just to get to Ceto, and the last bus back to Solo leaves Tawangmangu at 5pm. Day-trippers should thus consider missing out Candi Ceto and joining the trail at Candi Sukuh for the final leg to the waterfall.

The walk **between Ceto and Sukuh** is a pleasant three-hour ramble, passing first through large fields of vegetables and summer fruits, then under the branches of the pine forest shrouding the summit of Gunung Lawu. The path begins 200m below Ceto, where a small track branches left from the road towards the fields. This path is very difficult to follow, and you will probably need to ask the workers in the field for directions (*Di mana Candi Sukuh?*). After about an hour you arrive at the **forest**, where again you will probably need help in finding the correct path. Once you have, following the trail is straightforward.

The two-hour stroll **from Sukuh to the waterfall** at Tawangmangu, over gently undulating fields and foothills, is the easiest and most rewarding walk on Lawu. The trail is fairly easy to follow, although 1km from Sukuh the road splits; a signpost points the way to **Candi Palanggatan**. The fifteenth-century *candi* itself is nothing more than a collection of mossy boulders under a tree, but the village is pretty and the inhabitants can point out a short cut through fields that leads back onto the main path. After skirting a few hills, crossing the occasional stream and passing through the villages of **Plalar** and neighbouring **Goyong**, you eventually reach the waterfall.

tempted a few religions down the years to build temples on the forested slopes. Over ten such sites stand on the mountain's upper reaches, of which two, **Sukuh** and **Ceto**, have been restored to their former glory.

The temples are usually visited on a day-trip from Solo, but the area deserves more time if you can afford it. In particular, the mountain provides perfect conditions for **hikers**. The gradients are mainly gentle and the air, particularly on the upper slopes, is cool and refreshing. And, despite the whine of the cicadas, the chatter of tea-pickers and the distant din of isolated villages, the whole mountain is imbued with a soothing sense of peace and stillness.

Tawangmangu, a hill resort on Lawu's southwestern slopes, is the best place to stay. The main transport hub in the area is **Karangpandan**, 12km back towards Solo from Tawangmangu, and 45 minutes by bus from Solo on a twisting mountain road, past a large stone statue of Semar, Indonesia's favourite *Mahabharata* character. From Karangpandan there are frequent buses towards the temples and the other nearby attractions. Ojek are available to all the sites too, but their prices are often ridiculously high.

Tawangmangu

The fairly large mountain village of **TAWANGMANGU** has a pleasant climate and features a busy fruit market and a forty-metre waterfall, **Grojogan Sewu** (8am–4.30pm; Rp1500), at the northern end of the village. Tawangmangu spreads over one square kilometre, from the bus station in the south up to the waterfall. An **angkuta** (Rp200) from the bus station describes a loop around the town, driving right past the waterfall.

Accommodation tends to be unexceptional, but is fine for hikers who just require a base around Lawu: note that room prices double at weekends at most of the hotels. Below Tawangmangu's bus station, at the bottom of the hill, hides the *Balaistirahat Dana* at Jalan Lawa 47 (②), the cheapest losmen in the village. The stone-floor rooms are depressingly rudimentary, but the enclosed balcony is a small compensation. Fifty metres up from the bus station stands *Pak Amat*, Jalan Raya Tawangmangu 117 (☎0271/97022; ③), a losmen, restaurant and billiard hall in one. The rooms are fine, though the attached bathrooms are rather dingy. Their restaurant is the best place in Tawangmangu for cheap, filling **food**. At the other end of the scale, at the top of the hill, *Pondok Garuda* on Jalan Raya Tawangmangu (☎0271/97239, fax 97294; ⑤), is the sister of the *Berlian Palace* in Yogya. All rooms come with bathroom and MTV, and breakfast is included in the price.

Candi Sukuh

Situated 910m up the forested western slopes of Gunung Lawu, **Candi Sukuh** (daily 6.15am–4.30pm; Rp300) is one of the most interesting of Java's classical temples. Catch a bus from Karangpandan bound for Kubening and hop off at **Nglorok** village (Rp300), where you buy your ticket for the temple. From here you can hire an ojek (Rp2500) for the steep two-kilometre journey.

Sukuh was built in around 1430, though nobody knows exactly who constructed it, to whom it was dedicated, or why. About a hundred years later the great Islamic conversion of Java occurred, and it is thought that the temple was abandoned at this time. It was discovered in 1815 and a little restoration was done in 1917, but it wasn't until 1989 that the temple was returned to something approaching its previous splendour.

From the statuary and reliefs it would appear that Sukuh was linked to some sort of **fertility cult**. It is a west-facing temple built on three low terraces and fronted by the remains of a small ceremonial gateway; three large turtles, their backs flattened to form three circular dais, stand on the third terrace, guarding the entrance to the temple proper. A grey stone pyramid with its top lopped off, it bears a remarkable resemblance to the Mayan temples of Central America. A set of steps leads up from the western side of the temple to the **roof**, from where you can enjoy marvellous views over the valley below.

The Sukuh is unadorned, but lying all around is a veritable orgy of semi-explicit statuary, with a few displaying fairly impressive genitalia. There are also plenty of grotesque **bas reliefs** that appear to have been lifted straight from a comic book. Most of the reliefs depict scenes from the life of **Bima**, an incarnation of Shiva in the *Mahabharata*, who became the centre of a religious cult in the fifteenth century.

Candi Ceto

Candi Ceto, the youngest classical temple on Java, was built 1400m up on the northern flanks of Gunung Lawu in around 1470, during the death throes of the Majapahit empire. Catch a bus from Karangpandan to **Kalbening** (Rp500), from where it's a steep two-hour climb (5km) up the mountainside. There is rumoured to be a very occasional bus from Kalbening to Ceto, but recent sightings have been few and far between.

It might just be the isolated location, or perhaps it's the mist that frequently shrouds the terraces, but there can be no doubt that Candi Ceto has a mystical, almost eerie atmosphere, an effect that's heightened when Hindu worshippers from Bali pay a visit and perform their chanting in the main temple.

Ceto was built on ten narrow terraces stretching up the mountainside, beyond a large monumental gateway, similar in style to those found on Bali. The first few terraces beyond the gate are bereft of decoration, though look out for the paving on the fourth level on which a **giant bat** has been carved. The bat carries on its back a **large turtle**, which in turn carries crabs, lizards and frogs on its shell. The upper levels have been filled with a few open-sided wooden pendopos. On the top three terraces there are also a number of small kiosks sheltering a variety of icons, including one of Bima, as well as yet another large lingga. The main temple, with the same pyramidal shape as Sukuh, stands on the very top terrace.

Mangadeg hill

Mangadeg hill, 8km southeast of Karangpandan, is home to two **royal grave** sites, rarely visited by tourists. Catch a bus from Karangpandan to Matesih (ask for Makam Suharto; Rp300), then an ojek (Rp1500) or very infrequent bemo (Rp300) from there. The drive up affords some stunning views over the rice fields below, with Lawu dominating the background, and on the way souvenir sellers line the road offering visitors the chance to stock up on Suharto memorabilia.

The first set of graves you come to is the Suharto family mausoleum, **Astana Giribangun** (daily 7am–5pm; free), a large wooden pendopo modelled on the royal graveyard at Imogiri (see p.179); the plots for every member of the family have already been marked out. Crowds still gather round the grave of Mme Suharto, who died in 1995, to pay homage with rose petals and prayers to the genius behind Jakarta's Taman Mini (see p.90). Just a few hundred metres above the Suhartos, reached by a spiralling path, is the final resting place of the members of the **Mangkunegoro dynasty** (daily 7am–5pm; donations compulsory), of which Mme Suharto was a part. The Mangkunegoros are the only royal family of Yogya or Solo not buried at Imogiri. The tombs of the first eight sultans are here, and attract their own set of devotees.

Semarang and around

SEMARANG is the capital of Central Java and, with a population approaching 1.5 million, the country's fifth largest city. It's a typically big and bustling Indonesian metropolis, a **commercial centre** rather than a tourist town. Visually, the city resembles a scaled-down version of Jakarta, with its wide, tree-lined streets and muddy canals, between which a surfeit of ugly shopping centres, unlovely office blocks, imposing

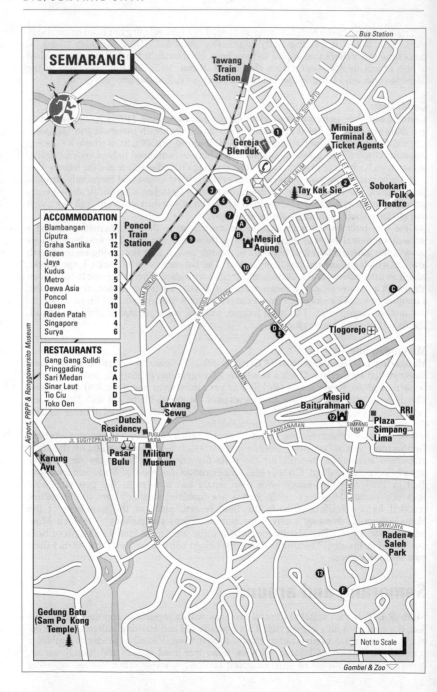

SEMARANG

Bus Station

Tawang
Train
Station

Gereja
Blenduk

Minibus
Terminal &
Ticket Agents

Tay Kak Sie

Sobokarti
Folk
Theatre

Poncol
Train
Station

Mesjid
Agung

ACCOMMODATION
Blambangan   7
Ciputra   11
Graha Santika   12
Green   13
Jaya   2
Kudus   8
Metro   5
Oewa Asia   3
Poncol   9
Queen   10
Raden Patah   1
Singapore   4
Surya   6

RESTAURANTS
Gang Gang Sulldi F
Pringgading   C
Sari Medan   A
Sinar Laut   E
Tio Ciu   D
Toko Oen   B

Airport, PRPP & Ronggowarsito Museum

Tlogorejo

Lawang
Sewu

Dutch
Residency

JL SUGIYOPRANOTO

Mesjid
Baiturahman

Plaza
Simpang
Lima

RRI

SIMPANG
LIMA

JL PANDANARAN

TUGU
MUDA

Karung
Ayu

Pasar
Bulu

Military
Museum

JL DR SUTOMO

JL PAHLAWAN

JL SRIVIJAYA

Raden
Saleh
Park

JL IMAM BONJOL

JL PEMUDA

JL DEPOK

JL GAJAH MADA

JL THAMRIN

Gedung Batu
(Sam Po Kong
Temple)

Not to Scale

Gombel & Zoo

international hotels and tacky fast-food shacks have been hastily erected. But the buildings and roads are neither as huge nor as numerous as Jakarta's, the levels of noise and pollution are similarly reduced, and on the whole the city is a good deal more attractive and unhurried than the capital.

Manuscripts from the ninth century refer to a small port called **Pergota**, which seems to correspond to the location of present-day Semarang, and suggest that the city was originally an entrepôt harbour for the Hindu kingdoms of the interior. For centuries the port remained relatively insignificant while the neighbouring harbours at Jepara and Kudus grew into the centres of the island's first Islamic empire. But in the seventeenth century these ports to the east of Semarang began to slowly clog up with silt washed down from the volcanoes, and Semarang soon became the biggest on the north coast. It continued to grow under the Dutch after it was given to the **VOC** in lieu of debts by the Mataram sultan **Amangkurat I** in 1677. The decision by the Dutch to install the **governor** of Java's Northeast Province here was further evidence that the city now enjoyed a pre-eminent status on the north coast.

Today Semarang stretches all the way from the silted coastline in the north right across the flat coastal plain and up into the foothills of **Gunung Ungaran** in the south. As with Jakarta, the city's charms lie not in the modern parts of the town but in the small pockets that have thus far evaded the attentions of the developers. These include the **Chinese quarter**, the largest in Java, which provides the city with some much-needed colour and vibrancy, and the eerily quiet former **Dutch commercial district**. There is also the **Gedung Batu**, one of the most important and intriguing Chinese temples on Java, in the southwestern suburbs of the city.

Though you can see pretty much all the city has to offer in a day or two, Semarang is the best base for exploring northern Central Java, with excellent train and bus connections to the rest of the Pasisir (the northern coastal region of Java), as well as south to Yogya. The batik town of **Pekalongan**, along with the ancient ports of **Demak**, **Kudus** and **Jepara**, once the most important harbours on Java and still amongst the wealthiest cities on the island, are all within a two-hour bus ride from Semarang, while the countryside to the south of the city holds a number of sights worth exploring, including the delightful Hindu temples of **Gedung Songo** in the foothills of Mount Ungaran.

Orientation, arrival, information and city transport

For the most part, Semarang is a flat city, which only begins to curl up towards the south as it climbs the first, shallow inclines of Gunung Ungaran. Two canals, the **Banjer Kanal Barat** and **Timur**, demarcate the western and eastern limits respectively of the city centre. Most of the action takes place in a triangular area formed by three major hubs: **Simpang Lima**, the heart of the modern part of Semarang in the south of the city; the **Tugu Muda roundabout**, in the west; and, on the edge of the Chinese quarter in the northeast of downtown, **Johar market** and the nearby **post office**. Once you have grasped the relative positions of these three hubs and the three roads that link them – **Jalan Pemuda**, which links Tugu Muda with Pasar Johar, **Jalan Pandanaran**, which runs between Simpang Lima and Tugu Muda, and **Gajah Mada**, which heads north from Simpang Lima and bisects Jalan Pemuda a few hundred metres to the west of the post office – finding your way around the city should present few problems.

Arrival

All of Indonesia's major national airlines operate flights into Semarang's **Jend A. Yani Airport**, 5km to the west of central Semarang. There is no direct bus service into town, although if you walk 1km south from the airport you can catch bus #2 which travels east via Tugu Muda and Jalan Imam Bonjol to the bus station. Alternatively, a taxi will set you back about Rp7000.

Semarang has two **train** stations. Most trains stop at the **Tawang station** in the heart of the old Dutch quarter on Jalan Merak, from where a becak to Jalan Pemuda should cost no more than Rp1000. The *Tawang Mas* and *Tawang Jaya* from Jakarta terminate at the **Poncol station** on Imam Bonjol, which is within walking distance of many inexpensive hotels. A few trains – including the *Bangunkarta*, (which travels from Jombang via Solo and Semarang to Jakarta), and the *Pandanaran* from Solo – call at both stations.

Arrive in Semarang by public bus and you'll be deposited at the **Terboyo bus terminal**, about 3km to the east of the town centre. Bus #2 (Rp250) travels from the station past Pasar Johar and down Jalan Pemuda. Travelling in the opposite direction, catch one of the buses that pass by the *Hotel Oewa Asia*. **Private minibuses** usually drop passengers off by the junction of Jalan Let Jend Haryono and Jalan H. Agus Salim, about 1km east of Pasar Johar. Walk or take a becak (Rp800) from there.

Finally, those who arrive by Pelni **ferry** from Banjarmasin, Pontianak or Kumai on Kalimantan, or possibly from Jakarta's Tanjung Priok harbour, should hire a becak to take them from the port into town, a distance of 2km (Rp1000).

Information

There are no fewer than four **tourist offices** in Semarang. By far the most useful is the provincial tourist office, **Dinas Parawisata** (Mon–Thurs 7am–2pm, Fri 7–11am, Sat 7am–1pm; ☎024/607184), in what is known as the PRPP zone, an industrial area to the northwest of the city centre; it has the most knowledgeable staff, as well as the widest collection of maps and brochures, covering the whole of the Central Javan province. Catch one of the many PRPP-bound buses from Pasar Bulu, then walk east to the first set of traffic lights; the office is 100m to the south of the junction in Blok BB, Jalan Maduroko.

The most central tourist office in the city is the desk on the ground floor of the **Plaza Simpang Lima**. Often deserted, it can be useful for finding out city bus numbers. The third tourist office hides in the former reception of the old zoo at **Raden Saleh Park**, Jalan Srivijaya 29 (☎024/311220); nobody here speaks English. Finally, there's a small office at the **airport**. These three have approximately the same opening times as the Dinas Parawisata.

City transport

With the searing heat and the city's points of interest so widely dispersed, Semarang is not really a place for aimless wandering. Fortunately, the **public transport** network is fairly comprehensive, though the city's one-way system means buses and angkuta often alter their routes on the return journey.

Fares on the big blue-and-white **city buses** are a flat Rp250; bus #2 is the most useful route, running from the bus station to the Kalibenting roundabout via Jalan Pemuda. For most of your time in the city you'll probably be using the orange **angkuta** vans, which buzz around the city beeping their horns at bystanders. Like the city buses, they charge a flat Rp250. Nearly all Semarang's angkuta begin and end their journeys at Simpang Lima. **Becak** are as common in Semarang as they are in the rest of Central Java. They aren't allowed to use many of the major roads and have to take more circuitous routes, so it may be quicker to walk. **Taxis** are a rare species in Semarang. A few congregate around the big hotels on Simpang Lima, and outside the post office; alternatively, call Atlas (☎024/315833) or Puri Kencana (☎024/288291).

Accommodation

Semarang's **hotels**, like the city itself, are not geared towards tourists but cater more for businesspeople. Most of the hotels tend to be in the medium or expensive price bracket, although there are a number of cheaper options on Jalan Imam Bonjol, the street to the north of Jalan Pemuda near the train station. A fan is fairly essential in this sweaty city, and it's worth paying a little extra to have one in your room. Free tea and coffee, usually left outside your room in a plastic jug, come as standard in virtually every hotel.

Blambangan, Jl Pemuda 23 (☎024/541649). A clean hotel, if a little threadbare in places, 300m west of Pasar Johar. Less expensive rooms have fans, the rest have air-con; the suites also have TV. Parking facilities and a free photocopied map of central Semarang are two of the advantages. A step up from the other budget hotels – but then so is the price. ④.

Ciputra, Simpang Lima (☎024/449888, fax 447888). One of the best and newest in town, overlooking the main square, with all the facilities you would expect from a four-star hotel. ⑨.

Graha Santika, Jl Pandanaran 116–120 (☎024/413115, fax 413113). Four-star hotel just off Simpang Lima and probably the best in town. All rooms have mini-bar, TV and in-house films. There is also a gymnasium, swimming pool and a very good 24hr café. ⑨.

Green, Jl Kesambi 7 (☎024/312642). Another excellent mid-range hotel in the foothills of Candi, 2km south of Simpang Lima. The hotel is shaped like a traditional Javanese house from the last century, but with a 1920s Art Deco interior, a terrace in the garden affording beautiful views of the valley below. The bungalows, with TV and fridge, are especially good value. ⑤.

Jaya, Jl M.T. Haryono 27 (☎024/543604). Cavernous, rather neglected hotel, convenient for the minibus station. The rooms are airy with high ceilings, and most have en-suite bathrooms. ③.

Kudus, Jl Imam Bonjol 89 (no phone). A very basic and fairly sleazy losmen. No air-con, no fan, and often no window either. It's cheap, however, convenient for the Poncol station, and stays open for late arrivals. ③.

Metro, Jl H. Agus Salim 2–4 (☎024/547371, fax 510863). Long-established three-star hotel, once the best in town, opposite Johar market. The Health and Hair Studio in the basement includes a sauna, whirlpool, exercise room and barber, and there's even a department store. ⑦.

Oewa Asia, Jl Kol Soegiono 12 (☎024/542547). A traditional favourite with Western travellers, sited near the post office. The rooms are a little basic for the price, although breakfast is included. Rooms with fan or air-con; for Rp5000 more you can have a TV too. All rooms have an intercom for room service. ④.

Poncol, Jl Imam Bonjol 60 (no phone). Inexpensive, large hotel named after the train station it faces. Try to grab one of the quieter rooms at the back. ③.

Queen (aka **Quirin** or **Quirien**), Jl Gajah Mada 44–52 (☎024/547063, fax 547341). Rather a trendy hotel, with designer lampshades in the lobby and local modern art hanging from the walls of the café. Pleasant, relaxed atmosphere, and the rooms come with TV, air-con and hot water. ⑥.

Raden Patah, Jl Jend Suprapto 48 (☎024/511328). A very good budget choice, east of the Gereja Blenduk. The fully renovated building is over fifty years old and has a dignified atmosphere. Rooms are light and airy; those in the west wing are newer, more attractive and very good value. ③.

Singapore, Jl Imam Bonjol 12 (☎024/543757). Reasonable budget option near the *Oewa Asia*. The staff at this large hotel are very friendly, and there are plenty of sofas and chairs in the sociable lobby area. Unfortunately, the rooms are rudimentary and graffiti-strewn, and the wooden shuttered windows offer little protection against the noise outside. ③.

Surya, Jl Imam Bonjol 28 (☎024/540355, fax 544250). Attractive marble-tiled hotel just 100m down from the *Singapore*. Air-con, hot water and TV come as standard. ⑥.

The City

Semarang's sights are grouped around the three major hubs of the town centre: Tugu Muda, Pasar Johar and Simpang Lima. **Tugu Muda** has been the administrative centre of Semarang since the eighteenth century, and is still surrounded by some important government buildings from the Dutch era. The area around **Pasar Johar** was the main commercial district and remains one of the liveliest parts. This is also the home of the city's huge Chinese population, and a stroll through the alleyways of the vibrant **Chinese quarter** is one of the most rewarding ways to spend an afternoon here. **Simpang Lima** is the modern centre of town, a large grassy square surrounded by big hotels, shopping centres and, in the northwest corner, the city's biggest mosque, the **Mesjid Baiturahman**.

Travelling by **public transport** between these three hubs is not a problem, though the one-way system dictates that it's far easier to travel clockwise around the centre of town. Bus #2 travels east along Jalan Pemuda from Tugu Muda to Pasar Johar. To get from Pasar Johar to Simpang Lima, listen for the cry of "Peterongan" or "Tegalwareng" from the angkuta queuing from the northwest corner of the market. (For the return trip, catch angkuta #7 or #16 from outside the Mesjid Baiturahman, which travels straight up Gajah Mada to Jalan Pemuda.) Finally, around the corner to the south of the mesjid, on Jalan Pandanaran, angkuta #8 pulls in to pick up customers wishing to travel west to Tugu Muda and on to Karung Ayu.

Tugu Muda and Jalan Pemuda

The major transport hub of **Tugu Muda** is surrounded by well-preserved, austere Dutch buildings, relics from a time when this was the administrative centre of Semarang. At its centre stands a giant stone **candle-shaped sculpture** dedicated to the memory of the two thousand local youths who perished fighting the Japanese in 1945. Locals often refer to this roundabout as **Pasar Bulu** after the market that stands to the west. This ramshackle, rather dingy two-tier bazaar deals mainly in food and household goods, is always lively, and offers a welcome retreat from the sun. Moving clockwise around the roundabout from here, to the north, facing Pasar Bulu, is the white-painted home of the **Dutch Resident** Nicolaas Hartingh, a gleaming eighteenth-century construction that has now been converted into a teachers' academy. To the north of the roundabout is **Lawang Sewu** (Thousand Doors), named for its many doors and windows. Constructed in 1913, it was once the offices of the Dutch train company and was later appropriated by the Japanese army during the war. Opposite, to the southwest of the roundabout, stands the former Dutch law court. Today the building houses the **Museum Perjuangan Mandala Bhakti**, Semarang's military museum, which appears to be permanently closed.

From Tugu Muda, heading northeast, is **Jalan Pemuda**, the colonial city's main boulevard. At over 2km long, Jalan Pemuda remains a wide and handsome thoroughfare, with huge government buildings and imposing steel-and-glass offices dominating the western end, while the eastern stretch is flanked by small terraced shops and restaurants. At the very eastern end of Jalan Pemuda stands the impressive **post office**, another colonial building, dating from the beginning of the twentieth century.

The old city and Chinatown

Just across the road from the post office is **Pasar Johar**, the most atmospheric and boisterous part of Semarang. The **market**, a tangle of claustrophobic covered alleyways punctured by several wide dirt tracks running north–south, stands over the site of the former alun-alun. The nearby **Mesjid Agung**, occupying the traditional position to the west of the square, was once the city's major mosque; it's still called the Grand Mosque today, even though it has now been eclipsed in size and importance by the modern **Mesjid Baiturahman** on **Simpang Lima**. Non-Muslims are forbidden to enter either mosque.

Sandwiched between two of the city's many canals to the northeast of Pasar Johar, the former **Dutch commercial district**, once the throbbing heart of the city, has long since disintegrated into a dusty, deserted area of crumbling offices and dilapidated warehouses. These canals were once the major arteries transporting goods to the warehouses from the **harbour** – a good place to begin a tour of this quarter; you will probably need to catch a becak to get there.

One kilometre due south of the harbour is the solid, white-walled **Gereja Blenduk** (Domed Church), now known as the Gereja Immanuel, on Jalan Jend Suprapto, the only building in this quarter that really shouldn't be missed. Built in 1753, it is the second oldest church on Java (after Jakarta's Gereja Sion), and inside there's a wonderful Baroque **organ**, now defunct – a modern organ hides behind the facade.

The large and busy Jalan Let Jend Haryono runs north–south a few metres east of Gereja Blenduk. Walking south down the road, past the junction with Jalan H. Agus Salim, you can duck down one of the narrow entrances on the west (left-hand) side. This is the **Chinese quarter**, a suffocating kampung of twisting paths and terraced multi-level shacks festooned with drying laundry and caged songbirds. The most striking building in this area, the eighteenth-century **Tay Kak Sie Temple**, lies tucked away on Gang Lombok on the east bank of the canal. The temple, garish red amongst the dull, grey shantytown buildings of the rest of the area, was built in 1772 and is dedicated to both the goddess of mercy, **Kuan Yin**, and Confucius, and contains many bronze and gilt figures, scattered apparently at random.

Out from the centre

Within a five-kilometre radius of the town centre are a number of attractions, many of which are very popular with local tourists. **Gedung Batu**, perhaps the most famous Chinese temple on Java, is the most interesting of these, although the **Nyona Meneer jamu factory** provides visitors with a fascinating insight into Javanese herbal medicine. The **PRPP** complex in the north of the city plays host to an **amusement park**, a **beach** (of sorts), the **Puri Maerokoco** (a version of Jakarta's Taman Mini), and a **Marine Recreation Park**. On the way to the PRPP is the highly recommended **Ronggowarsito Museum**, one of the best in the province.

Gedung Batu

Gedung Batu (Stone Building; daily dawn–dusk; free) lies 5km southwest of the city centre on the west bank of the BANJER KANAL BARAT. The deep-red Gedung Batu temple is dedicated to **Zhenghe**, a fifteenth-century envoy of the Chinese Ming dynasty, whose work took him to most of Southeast Asia, India and the East African coast. It consists of four shrines standing roughly shoulder to shoulder at the foot of a steep, wooded hill, and is built around a cave in which Zhenghe supposedly meditated after landing on Java for the first time in 1406. A number of building projects partially obscure the temple as you approach from the north, including the ongoing construction of a substantial wayang theatre right outside the main gates, and a large platform nearby for the annual Jaran Sam Po festival. Zhenghe's **cave** lies at the rear of the third shrine from the left as you face the temple. Next door, in the westernmost shrine, a monk offers to read your fortune (in Mandarin only).

Unusually, Muslims also worship at this site. Zhenghe was a follower of Islam, as was his helmsman **Kyai Juru Mudi Dampoawang**, whose grave lies a little to the left of Zhenghe's cave. As two of the first Muslims to visit Java, their trip probably paved the way for the conversion of Java to Islam, over a century later. The easternmost shrine, to the left of Kyai's grave, combines elements of both faiths: a red anchor to symbolize the seaborne arrival of the Islamic faith (although the anchor is actually from a Dutch VOC ship), neatly juxtaposed with a statue of Confuscius.

To get to the temple, catch city bus #2 from Jalan Pemuda to Karung Ayu, then take one of the dilapidated Daihatsus (Rp300) that journey south along the canal.

The Nyona Meneer jamu factory

The **Nyona Meneer jamu factory** at Jalan Kaligawe 4 (Mon–Fri 8am–5pm; free), 500m west of the bus station, provides an excellent introduction to **jamu**, the Javanese version of **herbal medicine**. The Nyoma Meneer Jamu Corporation is one of the biggest manufacturers in Indonesia. What started off as a one-woman operation at the beginning of the century is now a vast international concern employing over two thousand people, with shops in every high street in Java, sending remedies to New Zealand, Holland, Saudi Arabia and Japan. A factory guide will take you upstairs to a **museum** recounting the life and times of Nyona Meneer, using old photographs and a number of her personal effects (including the mixing bowl she used to conjure up many of her potions), as well as large displays of herbs and Nyona Meneer goods. If you ask nicely, you may also be given a tour of the **factory** itself, which is back downstairs on the ground floor. This is where many of the company's 250 lotions and potions are produced. For men there are virility pills and impotence cures, while women can choose from a range of remedies designed to counteract the ravages of time, such as *tresanih*, which, apparently, "keeps wife attractive to husband, to maintain husband and wife intimacy". Whatever your ailment, it is not uncommon for the guide to present visitors with a little box of assorted products at the end of the tour.

Catch the station-bound bus from outside the *Oewa Asia* hotel to get here, and jump out when you see the large portrait of Nyona Meneer stuck above the entrance on the front of the factory.

Pekan Raya Promosi Pembangunan (PRPP)

Lying right on the coast to the northwest of Semarang, the **PRPP** is a government-planned commercial district and the site of Semarang's huge annual trade fair, a fairly soulless place. If you do want to see it, catch one of the frequent buses (Rp250) from Pasar Bulu.

The biggest attraction at the PRPP is probably the **Puri Maerokoco** (daily 7am–6pm; Sun & hols Rp1500, all other times Rp1000), which lies 500m to the west of the PRPP bus stop. This is Semarang's version of Jakarta's Taman Mini, a brief introduction to the cultures and crafts of Central Java. The 35 full-size houses, one for each regency in Central Java, have been designed and built using the traditional methods of that regency. Each has been placed at the appropriate position on an island shaped to resemble Central Java, in the middle of a small lake. A bridge on the northern side of the lake connects the island to the "mainland".

Signposted to the northeast of the bus stop is the overpriced **Marina Recreation Park** (daily 8am–5pm; Rp5000), boasting a large swimming pool. Another kilometre to the east lies the awful **Tanjung Mas Beach** (dawn–dusk; Rp400), a wasteland of mud flats, food shacks and coarse heathland by the sea, popular with Sunday day-trippers from the city.

On the way back from the PRPP, it's worth hopping off the bus as it re-joins Jalan Sugiyopranoto and catching a #2 bus west to Kalibanteng and the **Ronggowarsito Museum** (Mon–Thurs 8am–2pm, Fri 8–11am, Sat 8am–12.30pm, Sun 8am–1pm; Rp200). This well-organized museum is the largest in Central Java, and presents a chronological history of the province, including a detailed section on the Hindu-Buddhist empires – illustrated with a few stone statues and icons – as well as the usual overkill on the Independence struggle. There are only a few captions in English, but guides are on hand (for a fee).

Eating, drinking and entertainment

Evenings in Semarang are considerably enlivened by the presence of **warung**, which set up at dusk around Simpang Lima and Pasar Johar. Semarang has a couple of culinary specialities, including *lumpiah*, a tasty vegetarian spring roll usually dripping with grease. Pasar Johar abounds with stalls where you can get them for around Rp100 each. *Murtabak* are also popular here, as they are on much of the north coast. At the southern end of Gajah Mada, right by Simpang Lima, are a number of stalls selling these savoury pancakes for Rp1500–10,000, depending on size and choice of filling. There's another stall in Pasar Johar.

For such a big town, **nightlife** in Semarang is pretty sleepy. The *Metro Hotel*, Jalan J.H. Agus Salim 2–4, houses the *Xanadu* disco, but it's often rather empty and dull. The

MM disco on Jalan Gajah Mada is livelier – especially at weekends – and attracts a younger crowd. The *Ritzeky Pub* on Jalan Sinabung Buntu is the place to meet expats and play pool or darts. It also serves some good, filling Western food. Finally, there's the *Restaurant Odrowino* on Jalan J. A. Yani, which has a live band from 9pm to midnight. Other than these options, there's little to do except go to the **movies** (see "Listings") or play **billiards** (check out the hall above Pasar Johar).

Though Semarang isn't exactly a cultural hotbed, there are a couple of options if you want to see traditional **Javanese entertainment**. The Raden Saleh Park at Jalan Srivijaya 29 (☎024/311220) hosts a special outdoor **wayang kulit** performance every 35 days, on each Thursday Wage night of the Javanese calendar. The Sobokarti Folk Theatre, next to the Yogya Plaza on Jalan Dr Cipto 31–33, also stages a wayang kulit performance, every Saturday night (8–11pm). If you're in the vicinity on Saturday morning, pop in to see the local children being taught the basics of puppeteering. A third venue for wayang kulit is the RRI at Jalan J. A. Yani 134–136 (☎024/316330), which holds a lengthy (8pm–4am) performance on the first Saturday of every month. If you'd rather see live action rather than puppets, there's a free performance (8pm–1am) of the popular folk melodrama **ketoprak** every Monday night in the fields of the Raden Saleh Park.

Restaurants

The choice of good-quality restaurants is disappointingly limited, although, as you'd expect from a city with such a large Chinese population, there are some decent **Chinese restaurants** in the centre of Semarang. Those who hunger for a fix of Western **fast food** should head to the Simpang Lima, where there's a *Californian Fried Chicken* and a *McDonald's* at the Ciputra Mall and a *Pizza Hut* at the Plaza Simpang Lima. There's also a *Kentucky Fried Chicken* 500m west of the Simpang Lima, at the junction of Jalan Pandanaran and Jalan M.H. Thamrin.

Gang Gang Sulldi, Jl Sudiharto. Glamorous Korean restaurant by the driveway to the *Green Guesthouse*. Expensive and delicious.

Pringgading, Jl Pringgading 54. Tasty Chinese food – a little pricey, but with very good service.

Queen Coffee Shop, *Queen Hotel*, Jl Gajah Mada 44–52. An excellent, mid-priced air-con retreat from the midday sun serving a good range of Western fast food, ice-cold drinks and ice creams. Closes at 4pm.

Sari Medan Jl Pemuda. At the eastern end of Jl Pemuda. The best Padang food in Semarang, and reasonably priced too.

Sinar Laut, Jl Gajah Mada. Medium-priced Chinese restaurant next door to the marginally superior *Tio Ciu* (see below), with an extensive menu, including a wide range of seafood.

Tio Ciu, Jl Gajah Mada. A huge menu of Chinese food – much of it exotic – is the main attraction at this large medium-priced restaurant, although dishes are often unavailable.

Toko Oen Jl Pemuda 52. Almost a tourist attraction in its own right, this fifty-year-old Dutch restaurant serves some tasty Western food, including excellent cakes. Trophies from the Cannes food festival – pertinent reminders of its heyday of linen tablecloths and uniformed waiters – are proudly displayed. Mid-priced.

Listings

Airline Inquiries ☎024/608735.

Airlines Bouraq, Jl Gajah Mada 16 (☎024/515921); Deraya Air, Semarang airport; Garuda, *Graha Santika* hotel, 2nd floor, Jl Pandanaran 116–120 (☎024/413217); Mandala, Jl Gajah Mada (☎024/543021); Merpati, Jl Gajah Mada 11 (☎024/20178) and Jl Pandanaran, close to Tugu Muda.

Banks and exchange BCA (Mon–Fri 8am–3.30pm, Sat 8am–noon) at Jl Pemuda offers reasonable rates and will give cash advances on Visa and Mastercard. The BDN, further down Jl Pemuda, offers a very competitive rate, but only accepts Citicorps US dollar travellers' cheques.

Bookshops There is a small English-language section at the back of Merbabu, a large stationers in the basement of the Plaza Simpang Lima. A small bookshop near the Garuda office in the *Graha Santika* hotel mainly sells books on Indonesia.

Buses Most door-to-door bus companies are gathered around the north end of Jl Let Jend Haryono, including Patas Tours, Jl Let Jend Haryono 47(☎024/544654), and Fortuna, Jl Let Jend Haryono 76 (☎024/544848).

Cinema Studio 21, on the southwest corner of Simpang Lima, and the Admiral 21 on Jl Kimangun, 200m north of Jl J. A. Yani, both show current Hollywood movies.

Email The GPO has planned to install email for a long time now; until they finally do, the only place where you may be able to connect is Stmik Aki (Mon–Fri 8am–9.30pm; ☎024/552555; email *techsmg@indosat.net.id*). They currently have small offices next to the Gajah Mada Conference Centre at Jl Gajah Mada 74–76, but will soon be moving to Jl Pemuda 49–51.

Ferries The Pelni office is at Jl Mpu Tantular 25, just over the canal from the GPO.

Hospital Tlogorejo Hospital, Jl Ahmad Dahlan (☎024/446000).

Permits Research permits for the islands of Karimunjawa are available from the fourth floor of the Office of Nature Conservation (KSDA), Jl Menteri Supeno, at the end of Gang 1 (Mon–Thurs 7am–2pm, Fri 7–11am; ☎024/414750).

Photographic shop The Fuji Image Plaza, Jl Gajah Mada 3, is one of the biggest and, for processing films, probably the most reliable film store in Semarang.

Post office Jl Pemuda 4. The poste restante counter is a hole in the wall on the eastern side of the building (daily 8am–4pm).

Swimming The best pool is probably the Marina Recreation Park (daily 8am–5pm; Rp5000). Alternatively, try asking at one of the big hotels; the *Graha Santika* is usually amenable if it's quiet, and they don't charge either.

Telephones The 24hr Telkom office is at Jl Jendro Suprapto 7, east of the GPO.

Travel agents Nitour, Jl Indraprastha 97; Nusantara, Simpang Lima Plaza.

South of Semarang

The northern slopes of Gunung Ungaran play host to a number of seldom-visited (yet charming) sights, which can be seen either on a day-trip from Semarang or as stopovers on the way to Yogya and the Kejawen region. Thirty kilometres south of the city reposes the attractive little hill station of **Bandungan**. Just a few kilometres east of Bandungan, the Hindu temple complex of **Gedung Songo** provides a peaceful alternative to the overcrowded ruins at Prambanan. And 10km further south lies **Ambarawa**, a bustling little market village and the home of Java's train museum.

Bandungan

The small village of **BANDUNGAN**, 1000m up on the northern slopes of Gunung Ungaran, is the closest **hill-top retreat** to Semarang (Rp1000 for the 75min trip from the Terboyo terminal). City folk head to the hills in their hundreds at weekends to escape Semarang's heat (although even in Bandungan the afternoon temperature is hot enough to melt the village's only tarmac road), so the village tends to cater more for the tastes of Indonesian holiday-makers than Western visitors. A few foreigners do make it here, as the village, with its green-carpeted hills, is one of the prettiest hill retreats in Central Java, and also makes a convenient base for visiting the nearby Gedung Songo temples.

Bandungan is little more than a number of hotels built round a fairly large daily agricultural market. It lies at the junction of three roads: one leads to Semarang, a second plummets down to Ambarawa, while a third heads off to the medium-sized town of Temanggung via the Gedung Songo. All the facilities (save for a place to change money) are clustered around this junction where the buses drop you off. Despite its small size, the town still manages to cram in a recreation park (Rp1000, plus extra for swimming or tennis), massage parlour, tofu factory and flower market.

The best-value **hotel** in town is the *Girimulyo* at Jalan Gitungan 79a (☎0298/711175; ④), a fifteen-minute hike up the very steep hill at the top of the town. The comfortable doubles have stained-glass windows, the singles are adequate but less pleasant. Also in the budget range are the *Trisukamaju* (③) on Jalan Widosari, with very basic, no-frills rooms, and the *Riana III* (③), 100m back up the hill from Trisukamaju, where you'll probably have to share your en-suite accommodation with ants and cockroaches. The best of the hotels in the upper-price bracket, the colonial *Rawa Pening Pratama* on Desa Kenteng (☎0298/711134; ⑤) is a few hundred metres west of Bandungan on the way to Gedung Songo. Rooms are large, cool and uncluttered, prices very reasonable and the well-trimmed gardens (with pool and tennis courts) are perfect for relaxing in after a day's hiking. There's even a free breakfast on Sunday.

Gedung Songo

One of many archeological gems in Central Java, **Gedung Songo** (daily 6.15am–5.15pm; Rp850) is a series of eighth-century **Hindu temples** ranged up the slopes of **Gunung Ungaran**. To get here from Bandungan, catch a westbound bus (Rp250) to the turn-off, 4km away, then an ojek for the final, steep 6km (Rp1200 up, Rp800 on the downhill run). The temples are arranged around the sides of a ravine; it takes about two hours to walk around the entire site, or you can hire a **horse** from behind the ticket office (Rp4000–5000). Turn up very early, bring a picnic (officially forbidden, but unpunished as long as you clear up after yourself) and make a day of it. Bring your swimsuit and a towel too, as it is possible to bathe in the hot **sulphurous spring** at the bottom of the ravine. Avoid weekends and you'll have the place pretty much to yourself.

The location of Gedung Songo is stunning. To the west loom the twin mountains Sumbing and Sundoro; to the south, perfectly symmetrical Gunung Merbabu, with the smoke-plumed summit of Gunung Merapi over its left shoulder. In the distance to the southeast, completing the volcanic crescent, towers slate-blue Gunung Lawu.

The name Gedung Songo (Nine Buildings) is a strange one – there are a lot more than nine buildings here. But the Javanese consider nine to be a propitious number, and have divided the temple groups accordingly. Of these nine groups, only five have been restored (groups I, II, III, VI and VII). The other four are still in ruins, and are usually passed unnoticed by sightseers. All bar one of the temples were built between 730 and 780 AD, the exception being the **first temple** on the route, which was constructed in the early years of the ninth century. It's also the only temple to stand alone, unaccompanied by any subsidiary buildings. From here, a path, part of the original eighth-century walkway, heads up the hill to temple groups II and III.

Gedung Songo provides a neat link between the first Hindu temples in Java – the seventh-century temples at Dieng (see p.193) – and the magnificent Hindu *candi* that were to follow a few years later. They share scale, simplicity of design and dramatic scenery with Dieng, and also provide the prototype for the temples of Prambanan and Sambisari. This is best illustrated at **temple group III**, the last complex before the ravine. The layout of the main temple is, like Dieng's, very simple; it even has a small building facing the main temple similar to Dieng's Candi Semar. However, the layout of the temple and the carvings on the walls follow a pattern that was to be repeated on the Prambanan Plain a few years later. The walls are adorned with pilasters, and have icons of **Ganesh**, **Agastya** and **Durga** carved into the rear, south and north walls respectively. Nearby is a small shrine to **Nandi** and, on the left, a shrine to **Vishnu**.

From here, head down into the ravine and up the other side for the last two restored temple groups, VI and VII. Both of these share many of the same architectural features as group III. At **group VI**, for example, as with temple group III, a small stairway on the western side leads up to a small portico and into a small empty *cella*. The exterior of the temple is once again decorated by pilasters, and a central niche has been carved in each wall, each of which once housed a statue of a Hindu god.

Ambarawa

The busy market town of **AMBARAWA**, in the southern foothills of Ungaran, lies 32km south of Semarang on the main Yogya–Semarang highway. Home to a major prison camp during the Japanese occupation, today, with the prison walls long since demolished, the city is known for its rather fine train museum, **Museum Kereta Api** (daily 8am–midnight; Rp500). Here you'll find 21 turn-of-the-century steam locomotives, built mainly in Germany and Switzerland. The museum is also the starting point of Java's only **cog railway**. The line runs for just 9.5km, between Ambarawa and **Bedono** via Jambu. For Rp850,000, you and up to 79 others can travel along the line to Bedono and back in a sumptuously restored train dating from 1905, a three-hour journey including a one-hour stop at Bedono for lunch; contact the PJKA, Jalan Thamrin 3, Semarang (☎024/524500). Those on a smaller budget will have to content themselves with the **toy train**, the *Lori Wisata*, which runs as far as **Jambu** (10km trip; Rp10,000), via **Ngampin** (5km return trip; Rp5000).

There is no reason to stay in Ambarawa, and the hotels at Bandungan, 7km away, are better value. However, if you do need to spend a night here, the *Hotel Aman* at Jalan Pemuda 13 (☎0298/91791; ③), halfway between the museum and the bus station, has some perfectly adequate rooms, and there are a couple of Padang restaurants in the town centre.

The Pasisir

The **Pasisir region** of Central Java provides an interesting alternative, or indeed supplement, to the usual Yogya–Solo route through Central Java; the word *pasisir* is the Javanese word for "fringe", and is used to refer to the northern coastal region of Java. Most of the towns of the Pasisir are connected by a single train line which runs alongside the great **Coastal Road** stretching between Anjar and Banyuwangi, a highway commissioned by the Dutch Governor Daendals in 1805 using local labour – 20,000 Javanese perished during its construction. As a result of their efforts, no north-coast town in Central Java is more than a couple of hours' drive from Semarang, and all the most interesting places can be visited as day-trips from the provincial capital.

With one exception – the batik town of **Pekalongan** – the coastal region **west of Semarang** holds little for the average sightseer and sees few tourists. There are a number of sights to the east, however, which are of particular interest if you want to learn more about Javanese history and the spread of Islam on the island. East of Semarang is a large promontory that was once a separate island, formed by the volcanic thrust of **Gunung Mariah** at its centre and severed from the mainland by a navigable channel. Some of the towns which today lie inland were once major ports serving this channel. These ports were the first to convert to Islam, and **Demak** and **Jepara** even became the centre of a short-lived Islamic empire in the early 1500s. As the silt from the volcanic hills flowed to the coast, however, these harbours suffocated and the channel separating Gunung Muriah from Java disappeared. Today these cities retain a rather strict and, by Java's standards at least, orthodox atmosphere. Some of the former ports have found new ways of making money – **Kudus**, for example, has a thriving *kretek* industry – while others have slipped into an undisturbed sunbaked torpor.

Most people who travel to the Pasisir from the Kejawen do so by taking the Yogya–Semarang route via Magelang and Ambarawa. There is, however, a far more scenic route from Yogya via Dieng to Pekalongan. Be warned that this journey takes well over eight hours to complete – the roads are terrible – and it is advisable to spend at least one night in Dieng (p.191) or Wonosobo (p.190) to break the journey.

Pekalongan and around

Eighty-three kilometres west of Semarang is **PEKALONGAN**, a compulsory stop for anyone who's been bitten by the **batik** bug. Everywhere you go in this pretty, relaxing old colonial town, the words *Kota Batik* (Batik City) seem to follow you, painted on public buildings, slapped on the sides of buses and even printed on litter bins. It's an apt description, for Pekalongan runs on batik: babies are swathed in it, kids march to school in it, government officials perspire in it, couples get married in it and the dead are buried in it.

The batik produced in Pekalongan is in marked contrast to that of Yogya and Solo. Unrestricted by tradition and the whims of a sultan, Pekalongan's batik is far more innovative, the colours more celebratory: a violent clash of vivid reds, creams and yellows. The town was one of the first to embrace the new dyeing technology in the eighteenth century, and with so many more colours at its disposal, and a disproportionately large number of master craftsmen setting up in the town, the Pekalongan repertoire expanded to include ever more outrageous, vibrant designs. Despite a serious decline in the traditional batik industry in recent years, as techniques for mass-producing printed cloth improve, Pekalongan's reputation as *Kota Batik* remains firmly rooted.

The **Batik Museum** (Mon–Thurs & Sat 7.30am–3.30pm, Fri 7am–noon; free) in the south of the city (Rp500 by becak west from the alun-alun) displays a small selection of different batik styles from all over Java. The few accompanying captions are, unfortunately, all in Indonesian, and many find the museum a little dull, although you can combine a visit here with the squawking bedlam that is Pekalongan's **bird market**, which you pass on the way.

Pasar Banjarsari, the large and muddy market on Jalan Sultan Agung, 500m north of the alun-alun, is an excellent place to shop for batik, with cheap, ready-to-wear items such as the exuberant shirts so beloved by Javanese males. If you're after something a little more exclusive, head to one of the boutiques that hide away in the **Arab Quarter** to the east of Jalan Sultan Agung; try Jacky's Batik on Jalan Surabaya VA/1, or Ridaka at Jalan H.A. Salim Gang VI/4. Jalan Hayam Wuruk, the main east–west road at the southern end of Jalan Sultan Agung, also plays host to a string of batik purveyors, including Ayu Batik, Larissa, Aneka and, best of all, Achmad Yana Batik, down a little *gang* to the west of the bridge on Hayam Wuruk.

Kedungwungi

The finest batik factory on the north coast – if not the whole of Java – is the **Oey Soe Tjoen factory** (daily except Fri 8am–3.30pm) in **KEDUNGWUNGI**, a small village 9km to the south of Pekalongan. To get here, catch a bemo from the junction of Jalan Mansyur and Jalan Siamet (Rp300). The workshop is on the main street, Jalan Raya 104 (☎285/85268); look out for a tiny "Batik Art" sign above the door.

The workshop was established in 1923 by the eponymous Oey Soe Tjoen, grandfather of the present owner, Muljadi Widjaya. The latter's wife, Istiyana, is the shop-floor supervisor and will guide you around the workshop, where you can see the painstaking skill of the artists as they carefully apply each dot of wax to the cloth. Only three or four pieces are produced per month, with a top-quality batik taking nine months to complete and costing in the region of Rp800,000. Those who are tempted to splash out will have to order and pay in full now, then wait nine months for their purchase to arrive (delivery within Indonesia only).

Practicalities

Pekalongan's **train station** hides in the southwest corner of the town, about 1km to the west of the alun-alun; the **minibus** companies congregate to the north of the alun-alun, while the main **bus station** lies to the southeast of the city. To reach the bus station, catch an angkuta from the junction to the north of the unhelpful **tourist office** on Jalan Angkatan 1945 (Mon–Sat 7am–2pm), 1km east of the train station.

The main focus of the town is the large square to the north of Pasar Banjarsari, about 1km north of the alun-alun. Here, housed in a couple of attractive old colonial buildings, are the **GPO** and **Telkom** office. A becak from the train station should cost no more than Rp1000, and most bemos drive by the square too.

Pekalongan has some fairly good **accommodation** options. The *Asia*, Jalan Wahid Hasyim 49 (☎0285/22125; ③), an extremely friendly hotel conveniently close to the minibus station, offers the best-value rooms in town. However, tatty *Gajah Mada*, Jalan Gajah Mada 11 (☎0285/22185; ③), remains the most popular of the budget hotels, if only because it's opposite the train station and stays open to receive late arrivals. The *Hayam Wuruk*, Jalan Hayam Wuruk 152–154 (☎0285/22823 or 24322; ⑥), is the best in the mid-range price bracket, a clean hotel with a kindly manager and comfy rooms. The plushest and largest place in town is the *Istana* at Jalan Gajah Mada 23–25 (☎0285/23581; ⑦), opposite the train station, with a billiard room and karaoke club (beginning at 8pm), which converts into a nightclub at 10.30pm.

Most of Pekalongan's **eating places** tend to be concentrated around the train station along both sides of Jalan Gajah Mada. Look out for the Pekalongan speciality, *soto kerbau* (water-buffalo soup). The *Purimas Bakery*, Jalan Hayam Wuruk 191, sells excellent fresh bread as well as cold drinks and snacks.

Demak

Lying halfway between Semarang and Kudus at the southwestern corner of the Gunung Muriah peninsula, **DEMAK** was once both a major port and the capital of the first Islamic kingdom on Java. The town is only a thirty-minute bus ride east of Semarang's Terboyo terminal (Rp500), and is best visited either as a stop on the way to Kudus, or as a day-trip from Semarang. Demak's bus station is located on the southern side of the alun-alun.

Details of Demak's glory days are very sketchy, but it is widely believed that the city was founded in around 1500 by either a Chinese Muslim called **Cek Ko-po**, or by his son, **Raden Patah**. The town then went on to defeat the last remnants of the ailing Hindu Majapahit empire, although there are few details as to when this occurred. The most popular theory is that Raden Patah's son, **Trenggana** (c 1505–47), led Demak to a final victory against the Majapahits in around 1527. After expanding the kingdom of Demak to most of north and eastern Java, Trenggana was killed in battle in 1547; his kingdom collapsed soon after.

Whilst Trenggana used his sword to spread the word of Mohammed, one of the members of his court, **Sunan Kalijaga**, enticed the Javanese population to Islam by hosting gamelan and wayang kulit performances in the fifteenth-century **Mesjid Agung** (Grand Mosque). This mosque, the oldest in Central Java and the holiest on the whole island, stands to the west of Demak's alun-alun and is the centrepiece of the town. Legend tells that the mosque was built by the Wali Songos; Sunan Kalijaga himself was said to have fashioned the central pillars in the pendopo by squashing together pieces of chipboard. Indonesia's Muslims attach such importance to the mosque that seven visits here are believed to be equivalent to a haj to Mecca. Despite this, the mosque holds little of interest, except for its combination of incongruous architectural styles: the three-tiered roof is typically Javanese, the **minaret** is a Hindu–Muslim hybrid, and the fairy lights at night are reminiscent of a British seaside resort.

Sharing the mosque's courtyard is a small **museum** (daily 8am–5pm; donation), which traces the fortunes of the building through the centuries, with photos and scale models. The large, overcrowded **cemetery** at the back houses the graves of the first three sultans of Demak, including Trenggana and Raden Patah.

Kudus and around

If Pekalongan rejoices in the name Kota Batik, then **KUDUS**, a fairly quiet industrial city built around Sungai Serang, can justifiably claim to be Kota Kretek. **Kretek**, ubiquitous sweet-smelling clove cigarettes, were mass-produced for the first time here in the 1920s, and today over 25 *kretek* manufacturers are based in and around the city, mostly to the east of Sungai Serang in the newest part of Kudus. This is also where most hotels, restaurants and shopping plazas can be found, many of them around the alun-alun in the north of town.

The western part of the city is quieter and prettier, and here you can find traces of Kudus's past, including the **Mesjid Al-Aqsa**, the city's most important **mosque**, one of the most venerated on Java; the city is renowned as a centre for Islamic study, its name being derived from the Arabic for "holy", *al-Kuds*. The mosque was founded in 1549 by **Jafar Shodiq**, who later joined the ranks of the Wali Songo as Sunan Kudus. The building you see today is a twentieth-century construction, though the dumpy-looking **minaret** is an original seventeenth-century design and resembles contemporary Hindu towers found on Bali. It's possible to climb the tower to study the old drum at the top,

---

KRETEK AND KUDUS

Many people in **Kudus** will try to convince you that *kretek* was a Kudus invention and the brainchild of a local man, **Almarhum Nitisemito**. In fact, people had been smoking cloves in Java for centuries, wrapping the tobacco and clove compound in dried corn husks. Mr Nitisemito, however, was the first to use cigarette paper rather than corn husks, and this simple innovation led to the establishment of Java's first *kretek* factory, built right in the heart of Kudus. The **Bal Tiga** (Three Balls) brand he founded in the 1920s brought great prosperity to his home town. It also made Mr Nitisemito, who always insisted that he smoked *kretek* as a way of alleviating the symptoms of asthma, a very wealthy man indeed. He became famous for his tireless promotional work, which included sponsoring sporting occasions, starting up his own radio station and even producing a full-length feature film. But ferocious competition and incompetent management brought his company to its knees. When Mr Nitisemito gasped his last, wheezy breath in 1953, he was already bankrupt. *Kretek* cigarettes, however, continue to go from strength to strength. Today *kretek* is the preferred choice of over ninety percent of Indonesia's smoking population. Over 138 billion cigarettes were smoked in 1992, and the industry now employs over four million people, two percent of the population of Indonesia. Most of the cigarettes are still hand-rolled in the traditional way in order to avoid the higher taxes (16 percent as opposed to 34 percent) placed on machine-rolled cigarettes. Despite this avoidance, taxes on *kretek* are still worth about five percent of the national budget to the government – only oil revenue contributes more.

But are *kretek* cigarettes as good for asthma sufferers, and the smoking population in general, as Nitisemito claimed? Unfortunately, the answer is a resounding "no". Tar and nicotine levels in *kretek* are up to four times higher than those of conventional cigarettes, and they are even banned in several countries. Estimates vary, but it is thought that between 50 and 85 percent of the population smoke – something confirmed by casual observation anywhere in the country. The other problem is that eugenol, the clove oil produced in the cigarette, also produces damage to the lungs. The World Health Organisation estimates that 57,000 Indonesians die annually because of smoking, and the Indonesian Health Department estimates 200,000 new cancer cases annually – it is not known how many are smoking-related.

The name "*kretek*" is onomatopoeic: *kretek* means "to crackle", and describes the sound of the cigarette as it burns. The cigarettes also frequently make a popping sound, and occasionally a husk of clove will fizz out and burn the smoker's clothes; more than one person has gone up in flames in this way.

which is still used today to call the faithful to prayer. Sunan Kudus's body lies to the rear of the mosque, in a tomb embellished with intricate latticework.

The minaret (menara) of Al-Aqsa was used as a model for the 27-metre **Tugu Identitas**, the ungainly tower opposite the Mata Hari department store. Visitors can climb the tower (daily 8am–5pm; Rp500), which affords reasonable views over the rather unprepossessing city.

The oldest and largest *kretek* manufacturer in town is **Djarum**, which, with 25,000 workers located in sixteen factories throughout the town and nearby villages, is also the city's biggest employer. The strong perfume of cloves emanating from their main factory off Jalan J. A. Yani, which runs south from the alun-alun, is likely to be one of your lasting impressions of the north coast. It is possible to have a **guided tour** around this factory; simply take your passport to their head offices on Jalan J. A. Yani, 1km south of Kudus's alun-alun. You'll be shown around the **blending and rolling room**, where 800 women (all the workers are female, and the supervisors nearly all male) produce, on average, 2,400,000 cigarettes per eight-hour day, six days a week. You should also be able to visit the **packing room**, where another 300 women work feverishly in teams of six, producing 300,000 packs per day.

To find out more about the origins and development of *kretek*, visit the **Kretek Museum** (Mon 8am–2pm, Tues & Thurs 9am–2pm, Sat 9am–1pm; donation), set in a field on the southeastern fringes of town; a becak from the Mata Hari department store in the centre of town should cost no more than Rp750. As well as recounting, in Indonesian only, Mr Nitisemito's life (see. box p.225), the museum also houses a display of the machinery used in *kretek* production. A collection of promotional merchandise and cigarette packets takes up almost half of the museum.

Practicalities

The **bus station** lies an inconvenient 4km from the **Mata Hari department store** at the centre of Kudus. Yellow angkuta travel between the bus station and the Mata Hari junction, costing a standard Rp250. Kudus' main thoroughfare, Jalan J. A. Yani, runs north from Mata Hari to the alun-alun.

The **tourist office** is situated in a children's park to the east of town. There is an entry fee of Rp500 to the park, although this will be waived if you explain you want to visit the tourist office only. The **BCA** bank on Jalan J. A. Yani has a foreign-exchange counter, but will change no more than US$200.

The **accommodation** options are pretty paltry. The cheapest, the *Losmen Amin* at Jalan Menur 51 (☎0291/38301; ③), stands one block south of the Pasar Kliwon, an ugly concrete shopping centre to the east of the alun-alun. The *Amin* is less of a hotel than a zoo, with mice in the courtyard, mosquitoes in the bedrooms and even fish in the mandi. The hotel's genial manager does provide free tea and a mosquito coil, however. For something a little more upmarket, yet equally bizarre, head to the *Hotel Air Mancur* at Jalan Pemuda 70 (☎0291/32514; ④), east from the southeastern corner of the alun-alun. This is one of these surreal hotels that the Chinese seem to specialize in, bursting at the seams with caged birds, monkeys, mini-waterfalls and lily ponds. The rooms seem positively bland by comparison, though they're very comfortable and reasonable value.

There are some decent **eating** options in Kudus. The local speciality is *lenthog Kudus*, sticky rice wrapped in banana leaf, which you'll find being sold on the streets in the evening. A couple of roads leading east off Jalan J. A. Yani come alive at night with food stalls: Jalan Kepodang specializes in *murtabak* sellers, while those on Jalan Kutilang proffer the usual Indonesian fodder. Also on Jalan Kutilang is the *Rilek's Café*, which serves tasty toasted sandwiches; it's a good place to come for lunch. The *Garuda Restaurant* at the junction of Jalan Jend Sudirman and the alun-alun is one of the top places in town, and their prices are reasonable – check out the *nasi rames*.

Colo

Eighteen kilometres to the north of Kudus lies the small village of **COLO**, the starting point for the one-kilometre hike up the side of Gunung Muriah to the **grave of Sunan Muriah**. Sunan Muriah was another member of the Wali Songo, and his grave has become a place of pilgrimage for devout Javanese. Yellow-and-brown angkuta from behind the Mata Hari shop in Kudus terminate in Colo (Rp1000). The grave lies at the top of a set of steps, in the shade of a mosque reputedly built by the Sunan himself. Most of what you see today was built in the last 150 years, and few of the features are original. The view over the valley below, however, is quite breathtaking.

Jepara

The affluent coastal town of **JEPARA** basks on the western side of the Gunung Muria promontory, 41km northeast of Semarang. Clues as to the source of Jepara's wealth line all the roads into the city, where carpenters and **woodcarvers** can be seen sitting outside their shops producing furniture, reliefs and souvenirs of occasionally stunning quality. So renowned are the craftsmen of Jepara that their town is nicknamed **Kota Ukir** (The City of Woodcarvers).

In contrast to the serene and unassuming little port of today, Jepara was once one of the most powerful towns in the region. Following the death of Demak's Sultan Trenggana in 1546, Jepara rose to become the most important port on the north coast, first under Trenggana's brother-in-law, **King Yunus**, and then under the leadership of the notorious **Queen Kalinyamat**. Together these two organized three raids on the Portuguese stronghold of Melaka. The Portuguese successfully repelled the attacks every time, but not before an enormous amount of damage had been caused to the city's defences.

Jepara's strategic position and excellent deep-water berthing facilities also caught the eye of the early Dutch arrivals. In the early 1600s, Jepara became the coastal headquarters of the **VOC**, whose tenure proved to be an awkward period in the town's history. In 1614 the fragile relationship between the Mataram ruler **Sultan Agung** and the VOC disintegrated, after the former refused to give the latter rice for their troops. In retaliation the Dutch urinated against Jepara's mosque and insulted the sultan,

RADEN KARTINI

As the daughter of the Regent of Jepara, **Raden Kartini** had, by Javanese standards, a very privileged upbringing. Born in 1879 in Mayong, a small village to the south of Jepara, Kartini was one of the very few Indonesian women allowed to attend the Dutch school in the town. The education she received there led her to question certain fundamental mores of Javanese society: in letters to Dutch friends, written after she left school, she attacked polygamy, which at the time was still widely practised on the island. She also opposed the role of the Dutch colonialists, whom she felt had deliberately deprived the Javanese people of a proper education. After marrying the Regent of Rembang, Kartini published a powerful article entitled "Educate the Javanese!", and went on to put her theories into practice, founding a school with her husband in their home. Both the classroom and the house have been preserved, and can be visited by applying to the Kabupaten in Rembang, a small town 30km east of Kudus. Tragically, Kartini died at the age of 24 giving the birth to her first child. Her letters and articles were collected and in 1911 published under the title *From Darkness to Light*. Her pioneering efforts at social restructuring are still celebrated throughout Indonesia on April 21 every year, a date that is now known in Java as Kartini Day.

comparing him to a dog. The Javanese took their revenge by killing three soldiers, and the Dutch in turn responded by setting fire to all the Javanese ships in the port. Thereafter, the two sides played out a cold war, until eventually, in 1799, the VOC was wound up by the Dutch government and the coastal headquarters were moved to Semarang. Jepara's importance dwindled as a result.

Today, Jepara is a fairly small town centred around the alun-alun, and everything, save for the port from where you catch the boats to Karimunjawa, and the woodcarving villages of Tahunan and Senenan (see box), is within walking distance of this square. Surrounding the alun-alun are a number of historical sights, which survive as testimony of the town's colourful past. The former residence of the regent of Jepara, now a faceless collection of government offices, stands on the eastern side of the alun-alun. This was the childhood home of **Raden Kartini**, the social reformer and campaigner for Javanese rights (see box p.227). A **museum** dedicated to her life and work lies on the north side of the square (Mon–Fri 7am–4pm, Sat & Sun 9am–5pm; Rp300). A guide from the neighbouring tourist office will take you around this reasonably diverting museum, pointing out the **Kartini family tree** and quotes from her book, *From Darkness to Light*, both of which are carved out of teak. Up the hill behind the museum are the remains of the **VOC fort**, now little more than a few foundations set amidst an abandoned graveyard.

Practicalities

Jepara is a very compact little town. The **bus station** is no more than 400m west of the alun-alun, where you'll find the **tourist office** (Mon–Thurs 7am–1.30pm, Fri 7–11am, Sat 7am–12.30pm). **Ferries** to and from Karimunjawa dock at Kartini beach, a rather dismal fun park 1.5km southwest of the bus station; a becak from the town centre to the port will set you back Rp1500.

For **accommodation**, the firm favourite with budget travellers is *Losmen Menno Jaya*, behind Menno Photo at Jalan Diponegoro 40b (☎0291/91143; ③), 200m east of the bus station. The old Lancaster car in the courtyard hints at the state of the rooms surrounding it: old and dilapidated, but comfy. At the other end of the scale, the *Hotel Jepara Indah* at Jalan Cokroaminto 12 (☎0291/93348; ⑥), two blocks south of the alun-alun, is the newest and best in town. All the rooms have TV, air-con and fridge.

Of the numerous **eating** options, *Bulyo*, at the junction of Jalan Kartini and Jalan Dr Sutono, is a good-value restaurant/souvenir shop serving passable Indonesian food and ice-cold drinks. Further west down Jalan Sutomo, the mid-priced *Milyo*, a bamboo-and-wood construction, serves very tasty Indonesian food. Finally, the *Bakmi Bandung* is a spotless eatery on Jalan Diponegoro turning out Western dishes: this is the place to come for crinkle-cut chips and MTV.

JEPARAN WOODCARVINGS

Though the souvenirs and furniture of Jepara can sometimes veer towards the kitsch, there is no denying the skill and patience of the craftsmen who produce them. Genuine antiques, reproductions and modern designs, carved mainly out of locally grown **teak**, can all be purchased here. Before buying, however, remember to include the cost of shipping in any calculations, which often far exceeds the purchase price. A trawl of the wood shops should begin at **Tahunan**, 4km south of Jepara (take a brown angkuta; Rp300), a tiny village with a high concentration of furniture and souvenir stores. About 1km back towards Jepara a turn-off leads to the village of **Senenan**, where craftsmen specialize in carving exquisitely intricate reliefs, many of which end up as table tops or wall-hangings in Jepara's sitting rooms. Most of the craftsmen here are only too willing to show you around their workshops.

The Karimunjawa national park

The coral-ringed islands of the **Karimunjawa national park** are a sleepy, sun-drenched haven where life is conducted in perpetual slow motion. An approximate translation of *Karimunjawa* is "Not clearly visible from Java", and although they lie just 90km off the mainland coast, the islands might as well be a million kilometres away, such is the contrast they provide with the mainland. There is so little traffic on the biggest island, **Pulau Karimunjawa**, that the local cats take their afternoon naps on the sunbaked tarmac of the only road. Karimunjawa doesn't suffer from Java's population problem, either – of the 27 islands, only five are inhabited.

All of which, sadly, may be about to change. While most of Karimunjawa has been declared a **nature reserve**, the parts which haven't have been bought up by developers keen to cash in on the islands' undoubted beauty, their golden beaches and the excellent snorkelling and diving opportunities. A casino has already been planned for Pulau Tengah, and every second Monday a boat laden with wealthy sunseeking day-trippers arrives from Jakarta at gorgeous Pulau Menjangan Kecil. But the development boom is still in its infancy and, for the time being, Karimunjawa remains an isolated idyll.

Practicalities

The most comfortable way of getting to Karimunjawa is to catch one of the twice-weekly **flights** from Semarang. A very irregular bemo service runs between the airport and the village (Rp2000). The alternative method is to take one of two **ferries** from Jepara, both of which sail twice a week. The larger, modern *KMP Muria* docks at the pier at the eastern end of Karimunjawa village, while the smaller *Kota Ukir* arrives at the western end.

The only way to travel between the islands is to **rent a fishing boat**. A day-trip around pulaus Geleang, Burung, Menjangan Kecil and Menjangan Besar should cost no more than Rp40,000 per boat.

There are eight **homestays** in Karimunjawa village, and the deal is much the same in all for them. The *Arie* homestay (③), run by an ex-Jeparan woodsmith-turned-prawn-farmer, Ipong, ranks as the best. His immaculate homestay serves excellent food (largely fish, of course); they also run tours, rent snorkelling gear and can arrange fishing boats to the other islands. *Arie's* lies 400m west of the eastern pier. The *Kelapa Desa* (③), 150m west of *Arie's*, offers the best accommodation option for large groups. Two other islands offer accommodation: **Pulau Menjangan Besar**'s only inhabitants have a couple of rooms above their outdoor aquarium (③), and there are also some "luxury" (a relative term here) cottages on **Pulau Tengah** (⑥), one of the less attractive islands lying to the east of Pulau Karimunjawa. These need to be booked in advance: contact PT Satura Tours, at Jalan Cendrawasih 4, Semarang (☎0297/555555).

There is a **GPO** and **Telkom** office in Karimunjawa village, and even a couple of souvenir shops, but no bank. There are a couple of tiny warung, both at the western end of the village near the small pier, which only open for a couple of hours (5–7pm).

The islands

The main settlement on Karimunjawa lies on the southern tip of **Pulau Karimunjawa**, one of the largest islands in the group. A road from the village heads north along the west side of the island and continues north through adjoining **Pulau Kemujan** via the airport, which serves planes coming from Semarang. About 11km along this road from the village, a set of 616 steps leads off up the hill to the **grave of Nyumpungan**, the islands' only man-made tourist attraction. Nyumpungan, the wayward son of Sunan Muriah (see p.227), introduced Islam to the island after his father had banished him from court and sent him into exile. As with so many other graves on the north coast, the tomb appears to have been made from bathroom tiles.

In attempting to balance the islands' potential earnings with the need to preserve their unquestionable beauty, the authorities have divided the Karimunjawa islands into several zones. In the first of these, the **utilization zones**, developers are allowed to do pretty much what they want. The most westerly of the Karimunjawa islands (15km from Pulau Karimunjawa) and the cluster of islands to the south of Pulau Karimunjawa have both been placed in this category. Most of the other islands, plus the central hills of Pulau Karimunjawa, have been declared **wilderness zones**, where limited tourist activities, such as snorkelling and hiking, are allowed. Finally, there is the **core sanctuary zone**, consisting of **Pulau Geleang** and neighbouring **Pulau Burung**. Officially, these islands and their splendid coral are off limits to anybody who doesn't have a research permit (available from the KSDA in Semarang – see p.220). However, the authorities have yet to devise a way of policing the zone properly. Though this is good news for snorkellers, who can paddle away unhindered here, it is tragic for the fauna of these islands; fishing and turtle-egg collecting still continue unhampered on both.

The best **beaches** in Karimunjawa are undoubtedly on **Pulau Menjangan Kecil**, southwest of Karimunjawa. The sand is white, and a paddle around the western side of the island attracts hundreds of small fishes, crabs and rays. If and when Menjangan Kecil is spoiled, the award for best beach will go to **Pulau Cemara Kecil**, west of Pulau Karimunjawa.

travel details

Buses and bemos

It's almost impossible to give the **frequency** with which bemos and buses run, as they only depart when they have enough passengers to make the journey worthwhile. **Journey times** also vary a great deal. The times below are the minimum you can expect these journeys to take. Privately run shuttle, or **door-to-door**, buses run between the major tourist centres on Java.

Borobudur to: Magelang (45min); Yogyakarta (1hr 30min).

Cilacap to: Purworketo (1hr); Wonosobo (4hr); Yogyakarta (5hr).

Dieng to: Pekalongan (4hr, via Kalibening); Wonosobo (1hr).

Semarang to: Cirebon (5hr 30min); Demak (30min); Jakarta (9hr 30min); Jepara (1hr 30min); Kudus (1hr); Magelang (2hr); Pekalongan (2hr 30min); Surabaya (8hr); Yogyakarta (3hr 30min).

Solo to: Bogor (11hr); Jakarta (13hr); Malang (7hr); Purwodadi (1hr 30min); Surabaya (6hr); Yogyakarta(2hr).

Wonosobo to: Dieng (1hr); Magelang (1hr) Purworketo (2hr 30min).

Yogyakarta to: Bandung (9hr 30min); Bogor (10hr 30min); Borobudur (2hr); Cilacap (5hr); Denpasar (15hr); Jakarta (11hr 30min); Magelang (1hr 30min); Prambanan (45min); Probolinggo (9hr); Semarang (3hr 30min); Solo (2hr); Surabaya (7hr 30min).

Trains

The estimated journey times listed below are for the fastest scheduled trains.

Cilacap to: Jakarta (2 daily; 8hr 10min); Surabaya (daily; 11hr 15min).

Pekalongan to: Cirebon (13 daily; 1hr 50min); Jakarta (13 daily; 4hr 20min); Semarang (14 daily; 1hr 20min); Surabaya (6 daily; 4hr 45min).

Semarang to: Cirebon (13 daily; 3hr 5min); Jakarta (13 daily; 5hr 40min); Pekalongan (14 daily; 1hr 20min); Solo (2 daily; 3hr 20min); Surabaya (6 daily; 4hr).

Solo to: Bandung (5 daily; 8hr 50min); Jakarta (6 daily; 10hr 30min); Malang (1 daily; 6hr 25min); Purworketo (6 daily; 3hr 15min); Semarang (2 daily; 3hr 20min); Surabaya (6 daily; 3hr 20min); Yogyakarta (14 daily; 1hr 30min).

Yogyakarta to: Bandung (6 daily; 6hr 30min); Jakarta (14 daily; 8hr 45min); Malang (daily; 7hr 30min); Purworketo (7 daily; 4hr 15min); Solo (14 daily; 1hr 30min); Surabaya (11 daily; 4hr 50min).

Pelni ferries

For a chart of the Pelni routes, see pp.36–37 of Basics.

Semarang to: Banjarmarsin (*KM Kelimutu* weekly; 24hr); Kumai (*KM Lawit* 2 monthly; 21hr/*KM Binaiya* 2 monthly; 21hr); Pontianak (*KM Lawit* 2 monthly; 33hr/*KM Tilongkabila* 2 monthly; 2–3 days); Sampit (*KM Tilongkabila* monthly; 24hr); Ujung Pandang (*KM Ceremai* 2 monthly; 30hr/*KM Sirimau* 2 monthly; 50hr).

Other ferries

Cilacap to: Pangandaran (4 daily, last at 1pm; 3hr 30min).

Jepara to: Karimunjawa (*KMP Muria* 2 weekly; 4hr; *Kota Ukir*, 1 weekly; 7hr).

Karimunjawa to: Jepara (*KMP Muria*, 2 weekly; 4hr *Kota Ukir*, 1 weekly; 7hr).

Semarang to: Banjarmasin (1weekly; 26hr); Kumai (1 weekly; 24hr); Pontianak (2 monthly; 33hr); Sampit (2 monthly; 24hr); Tanjung Priok (2 monthly; 20hr).

Flights

Cilacap to: Jakarta (1 daily; 1hr 15min).

Semarang to: Jakarta (17 daily; 55min); Surabaya (4 daily; 50min); Karimunjawa (2 weekly; 1hr); Ujung Pandang (1 daily; 2hr 20min).

Solo to: Jakarta (6 daily; 1hr 5min); Singapore (2 weekly; 2hr 20min); Surabaya (2 daily; 1hr 5min).

Yogyakarta to: Bandung (4 weekly; 1hr 15min); Denpasar (6 daily; 2hr 15min); Jakarta (13 daily; 1hr 5min); Surabaya (6 daily; 1hr).

CHAPTER FOUR

EAST JAVA

The province of **East Java** (Java Timur) stretches over 350km, from near Solo in the west to the port town of Banyuwangi in the east. The main settlement is **Surabaya**, the second largest city in Indonesia, with a population of around 2.5 million, which most visitors will at least pass through. It is a huge, often over-

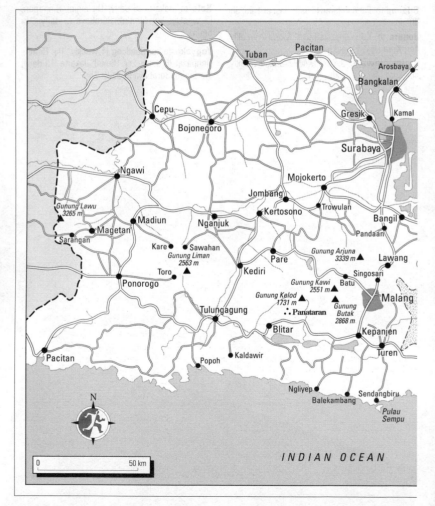

whelming metropolis with a few sights of interest, but is a useful base from which to explore the extensive remains of the Majapahit kingdom at Trowulan to the southwest.

The people of the region are predominantly Javan, but around ten percent are from **Pulau Madura**, located just a few kilometres across the water from Surabaya, and have a different ethnic, linguistic and cultural background to the mainland. Known for its fast, furious and colourful annual ox races, the island is a peaceful backwater peppered with interesting historic remains.

The **mountains** that form the spine of Java spread right through the province, from Gunung Lawu (3265m) in the west, with the attractive hill resort of **Sarangan** nestling on its lower slopes, to the more dramatic peaks further east: for most visitors the major draw is the huge volcanic massif and national park around **Gunung Bromo**. The views from **Gunung Penanjakan** and **Cemoro Lawang** and a dawn trip to the summit of Bromo

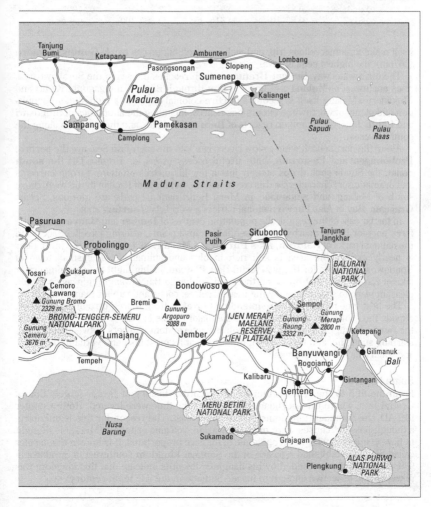

itself make for a marvellous trip, and well-prepared hikers can tackle **Gunung Semeru** (3676m), the highest peak in Java.

The main waterway, **Sungai Brantas**, which reaches the sea in the Surabaya area, rises northwest of **Malang** and flows 314km through Blitar, Tulungagung, Kediri and Mojokjerto. Malang itself is a cool, attractive colonial city, with a high student population and plenty of worthwhile excursions nearby, including the antiquities of **Singosari** and **Candi Jawi**, the mountain resorts of **Batu** and **Selecta**, and the **beaches** along the southern coast.

Along the north coast, where slow rivers run into the calm Java Sea, are the ports of **Probolinggo** and **Pasuruan**, both useful access towns for Bromo. Off the **south coast**, the Sunda shelf drops steeply just a few kilometres offshore. Strong currents and dramatic surf characterize this coast, and the **beaches** of Pacitan in the west, those south of Malang, and Sukamade in Meru Betiri national park, are glorious. Scenic **Grajagan Bay** in Alas Purwo national park is a world-class **surfing** spot.

In the far east of the region, the population centres of **Jember** and **Banyuwangi** (the ferry port for Bali is nearby) are essentially transit points, offering excellent access to the national parks of **Baluran**, **Alas Purwo** and **Meru Betiri**. Although the Javan tiger is nearly extinct, the area is still rich in bird and animal life. The small town of Bondowoso is a base for the wonderful **Ijen Plateau**, its highlight the stunning crater lake of Kawah Ijen. **Kalibaru**, on the main Jember to Banyuwangi highway, is a cool, pleasant place to stay and enjoy the nearby coffee, cocoa and rubber plantations.

The best time to visit if you're intending to **trek** is from March through to October, outside the **monsoon** period. Many of the major climbs in East Java are impossible in the rains, although the monsoon does bring intermittent showers between periods of startling sunshine, and this is when the area is at its most lush and verdant, the rivers and waterfalls full and dramatic.

Some history

From the fifth to the tenth centuries, the recorded history of Java is largely that of Central Java, where the ascendant kingdoms of the time were located. However, after 919 AD, the dominant kingdoms shifted to the east. The reason for this is unknown, although possible causes were outside invasion, volcanic eruption (Merapi is thought to have erupted in 928) or an epidemic of massive proportions. It is known that a ruler called Sindok established a palace of the **Sanjaya kingdom** southwest of Surabaya in 929, and was later succeeded by his daughter. Records indicate that this kingdom was powerful and assertive enough to invade Sumatra in the late tenth century.

The most famous early ruler of the region was **Airlangga**, who ruled the Sanjaya kingdom in the eleventh century. He came to power following the defeat of King Dharmawangsa in 1016; such was the ferocity of the battle that accounts of the time describe Java as a "sea of fire". Airlangga was the previous king's son-in-law, and only 16 years old at the time. He retreated to the forest for four years, from where he emerged to claim first a small kingdom near Surabaya, and then gradually to reconquer the entire region over several decades until his death in 1049, by which time he had united large areas of Java and Bali under one throne. On Airlangga's death he divided his kingdom between his two sons, Kediri in the west and Janggala in the east. Against his wishes these kingdoms became bitter enemies, with first one and then the other gaining ascendancy for almost two centuries, from 1050 to 1222. The final ruler of the Kediri kingdom was Kertajaya, defeated in 1222 by Ken Angrok, who went on to defeat the Janggala kingdom and found the Singosari dynasty, based just north of present-day Malang, with his beautiful queen, Ken Dedes.

The area around Malang is rich in the remains of the **Singosari kingdom**, which lasted just seventy years until the death of the final ruler, Kertanagara, in 1292; during this period, parts of the Malay peninsula and Sumatra, as well as Java, were ruled by it. Following Kertanagara's death, various claimants to the throne were defeated by Kertanagara's son-in-law, Vijaya, who established the mightiest and greatest Hindu/Javanese kingdom, the **Majapahit** (the name means "bitter gourd"). At its height in the mid-fourteenth century, the kingdom controlled most of what is now Indonesia, as well as parts of mainland Southeast Asia. Much of this is due to its renowned prime minister and commander in chief, Gajah Made, who served from 1331 to 1364, and King Hayam Wuruk who ruled from 1350 to 1389.

Following the fall of the Majapahit kingdom after Hayam Wuruk's death, the **Islamic kingdoms** of the region rose to prominence, initially Demak in the early fifteenth century, based around the port of the same name on the north coast, and then the Central Javanese **Mataram** kingdom. Although the rulers and army of Surabaya challenged Mataram's attack on the north coast in an attempt to control all trade in the area, they could do little against Sultan Agung who, from 1620 to 1625, laid siege to the city and defeated it by starvation.

In the early seventeenth century, the **Dutch** established themselves in Java via the Dutch East Indies Company (VOC), and became embroiled in local politics in their efforts to subdue the population. From 1767 to 1777, their efforts were turned against East Java and in particular **Blambangan**, which was the last remaining Hindu kingdom on Java. Its defeat resulted in large areas of the east being deserted. However, with the colonial development of the port of Surabaya, East Java's fertile agricultural heartland became the destination for many Central Javanese, as well as settlers from the north coast and Madurese. Today, Surabaya is the main port and manufacturing centre in the region, and is ringed by industrial complexes, their growth accelerating year by year. However, away from the metropolis extensive rice terraces dominate the valleys between the volcanoes, and fruit orchards, vegetable fields and coffee, rubber and cocoa plantations are the mainstay of the upland economies.

Surabaya and around

Polluted, noisy and sprawling, **SURABAYA** is the second largest city in Indonesia, and the major port of East Java. With time and effort the city is comprehensible and even somewhat enjoyable, but for most tourists Surabaya is somewhere to head through as fast as possible on the way to more interesting destinations. If you do want to linger, the **Chinese** and **Arab quarters** to the north of the city centre and the **zoo** and **museum**

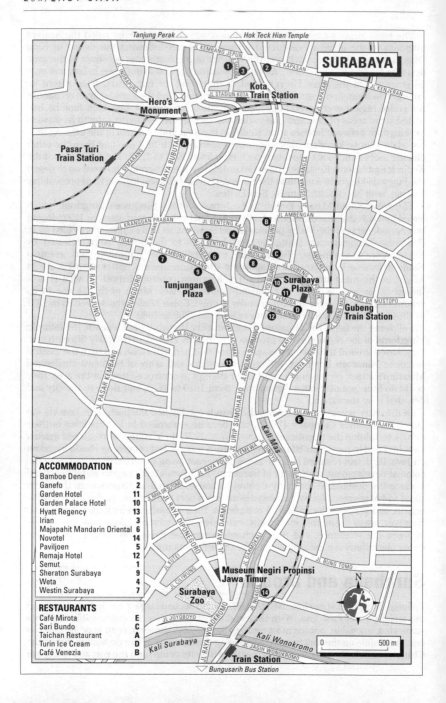

Tanjung Perak △   △ Hok Teck Hian Temple

JL KEMBANG JEPUN

SURABAYA

**Kota
Train Station**

JL STASIUN KOTA

**Hero's
Monument**

JL DUPAK

**Pasar Turi
Train Station**

JL SEMARANG

JL RAYA BUBUTAN

JL KRANGGAN PRABAN

JL GENTENG KALI

JL TIDAR

JL EMBONG MALANG

JL GENTENG BESAR

**Tunjungan
Plaza**

JL AMBENGAN

JL KUSUMA BANGSA

JL WALIKOTA
MUSTAJAR

JL GUBENG
POJOK

**Surabaya
Plaza**

JL PEMUDA

JL EMBONG KENONGO

JL PROF DR MUSTOPO

**Gubeng
Train Station**

JL POL M DURIYAT

JL PANGLIMA SUDIRMAN

JL RAYA GUBENG

JL KAYUN

JL URIP SUMOHARJO

JL SULAWESI

JL RAYA KERTAJAYA

JL DINOYO

JL RAYA POLISI ISTEMEWA

JL NGAGEL

JL RAYA DIPONEGORO

JL RAYA DARMO

JL BUNG TOMO

**Museum Negiri Propinsi
Jawa Timur**

**Surabaya
Zoo**

JL JOYOBOYO

Kali Surabaya

JL RAYA WONOKROMO

Kali Wonokromo

JL JAGIH WONOKROMO

Train Station

▽ Bungusarih Bus Station

N

0   500 m

ACCOMMODATION

Bamboe Denn	8
Ganefo	2
Garden Hotel	11
Garden Palace Hotel	10
Hyatt Regency	13
Irian	3
Majapahit Mandarin Oriental	6
Novotel	14
Paviljoen	5
Remaja Hotel	12
Semut	1
Sheraton Surabaya	9
Weta	4
Westin Surabaya	7

RESTAURANTS

Café Mirota	E
Sari Bundo	C
Taichan Restaurant	A
Turin Ice Cream	D
Café Venezia	B

to the south are the most interesting sights, and a trip to one of the monster shopping centres is a great insight into how more and more local people are spending their leisure time. Outside the city, **Trowulan**, a couple of hours' bus ride to the southeast, features impressive Majapahit remains in a peaceful, rural setting.

Some history

It isn't certain when Surabaya was actually founded, although May 31, 1293 has been designated for that honour, the supposed date of the founding of the mighty **Majapahit** kingdom. During the era of the Majapahit, the city was less important than the other north-coast ports such as Tuban and Gresik, and it was not until the early nineteenth century that Surabaya overtook Pasuruan in size. Although it was small, it gradually became more influential, and by 1622 had control of Gresik, much of the Brantas valley and even parts of Kalimantan. The kingdom of Mataram was in the ascendant in Central Java, and by the seventeenth century the two kingdoms were at loggerheads. In 1610, Mataram started what would be a long-running **war** against the kingdom of Surabaya, and in 1620 Sultan Agung attacked the town with 80,000 troops, devastating the hinterland and even poisoning the city's water supply. By 1625 Surabaya was on its knees; records of the time indicate that not more than 500 of its 50,000–60,000 people were left. But the **VOC** established a post in the city at the end of the seventeenth century, and trade in all sorts of products, including rice, salt and sugar, flourished. In 1717 the inhabitants rebelled against the colonizers, although after six years the city was again defeated by the Dutch, who developed it into the largest and most important port in Java. By 1900, Surabaya, with its avenues, large imposing bungalows and civic buildings, was the biggest town in the Dutch East Indies, even bigger than Batavia, and until the 1950s, when Tanjung Priok took over, the most important port in Indonesia.

The Dutch development of the nineteenth and early twentieth centuries meant that whole communities were displaced. Conditions in the kampung outside the showcase colonial areas were appalling and a huge police presence protected the Dutch from increasing local dissatisfaction. Following the declaration of Indonesian **Independence** on August 17, 1945, the people of Surabaya were hopeful that colonial rule was over. However, by early September, Dutch officials released from their wartime internment had returned to Surabaya as though nothing had happened. On September 16 in the *Oranje Hotel* on Jalan Tunjungan (now the *Hotel Majapahit Mandarin Oriental*), the Dutch flag was raised on the roof and a group of young local people stormed the hotel and tore part of it down, an event now known as the **Flag Incident**.

In the following months, groups of Indonesian youths went on the rampage against foreigners, and the situation became increasingly tense when a British infantry brigade landed in October. At Jembatan Merah, a three-day battle was waged between the British and thousands of Indonesian youths armed only with bamboo spears. Eventually the British as well as resident foreigners were overwhelmed by the **Indonesian People's Security Army** (Tentara Keamanan Rakyat), and thousands of attached supporters; the death toll on both sides was high. British reinforcements eventually arrived and the **Battle of Surabaya** lasted for three weeks before the eventual defeat of the Indonesians by Allied and Dutch land, sea and air assaults. Thousands of Indonesians died and most of the population fled the city. The beginning of the battle on November 10 is celebrated throughout Indonesia as **Heroes Day** (Hari Pahlawan), for although the Indonesians lost the battle it marked a significant point in the fight for Independence.

Arrival

All **flights** arrive at Juanda International Airport, 18km south of the city. No public bus service connects with the town centre, but there's a rank for fixed-price **taxis** (Rp12,500). There is a **tourist office** at the airport (Mon–Sat 8am–9pm; ☎031/8667513 ext 538).

MOVING ON FROM SURABAYA

Surabaya is the main air, sea, rail and road hub for East Java and has excellent **connections** across Indonesia and internationally. It is a visa-free entry point for arrivals by air (see Basics p.16). Some **international flight** destinations are reached direct, whilst others have connections via Jakarta or Denpasar; see "Listings" p.245 for airline offices in Surabaya, and p.288 for flight details. **Domestic flights**, through Bouraq, Garuda and Merpati, are numerous. Taxis from Gubeng station taxi rank to the airport are fixed at Rp20,000.

From **Bungusarih bus station**, there are frequent departures to destinations on Java, and as far east as Flores and up to Banda Aceh on Sumatra. Buses to local destinations operate several times hourly during daylight hours and hourly through the night. For departure within East Java, just buy your ticket on the bus. You will pay Rp100 for a ticket to get into the departure area – the bays are clearly labelled and porters will point you in the right direction for your bus. Be wary, though: the lists detailing fares are not easy to find, and overcharging has been known.

Express **air-con buses** are considerably more expensive than the standard variety. Long-distance journeys are completed by night buses (departing 2–6pm) from Bay 8 – the ticket offices for all the night-bus companies are in the bus station. Booking is advisable at least the day before, but outside holiday time you'll probably get be able to buy your ticket on the spot. If you can't bear the slog out to the bus station, central **minibus** companies run more expensive daily trips to the main Javan destinations, leaving from outside their offices. Try Tirta Jaya, Jalan Jend Basuki Rachmat 64 (☎031/5468687) for Yogyakarta, Solo and Semarang.

Tanjung Perak, Surabaya's port, is the major port in East Java, and no fewer than thirteen of the fleet of twenty **Pelni ferries** call here on their routes through the archipelago, making it an excellent place to leave by sea. Staff speak some English and have information about the Pelni services throughout Indonesia. There is also an office at Gedung Gapura Surya, Jalan Zamrut Utara 5 (☎031/3293197, fax 3293195) at Tanjung Perak.

Trains depart from all three Surabaya stations; see below for departure details.

If you arrive by **sea**, probably by Pelni ferry, you'll dock at Tanjung Perak port in the far north of the city, which is served by C, P and PAC buses (see opposite).

Surabaya has three main **train stations**. **Gubeng station** is in the east of town: there are entrances on Jalan Gubeng Mesjid and Jalan Sumatera. A hotel reservation desk is located here (daily 8am–8pm), but they only deal with the most expensive places. Gubeng serves Banyuwangi, Malang, Blitar, Yogyakarta, Solo and Jakarta via the southern route across Java – some but not all of these trains also pass through **Kota station**, which is towards the north of the city centre. The entrance to Kota is at the junction of Jalan Semut Kali and Jalan Stasiun. **Pasarturi station**, in the west of the city centre on Jalan Semarang, serves destinations along the northern route across the island to Jakarta via Semarang.

The main **bus terminal** is Bungusarih (also known as Purabaya), 6km south of the city, reputed to be the biggest in Indonesia. All long-distance and inter-island buses start and finish here, plus many of the city buses and bemos. Local buses into the city leave from the far end of the terminal: follow the signs for "Kota". Many of the C, P and both PAC buses serve Bungusarih. There's also a huge taxi rank here, but you'll almost never get a driver to agree to use the meter or fix a reasonable price to the city, and you should expect to pay about Rp10,000, even with hard bargaining, to anywhere in town.

Orientation, information and city transport

The city centres on a triangle of major roads: **Jalan Jend Basuki Rachmat, Jalan Raya P. Sudirman** and **Jalan Pemuda**. Government buildings, major shopping centres and facilities such as exchange and tourist offices are here or nearby. Jalan Jend

Basuki Rachmat turns into Jalan Tunjungan to the north and leads eventually, via several more name changes, to the port of Tanjung Perak on the coast. To the south of the centre, Jalan Urip Sumoharjo changes its name equally often and leads eventually to Bungusarih via the zoo and museum. Just to the east of the central area, Sungai Kali Mas winds roughly north–south through the city, although its frequent twists and turns make it a rather unreliable orientation point. A word of warning: **crossing the road** in Surabaya is hair-raising. Roads are often four or five lanes wide, traffic is fast, traffic lights are regarded as mere suggestions by drivers, and footbridges very few. Look out for long poles with red dots on them at some traffic lights – you hold them high towards the traffic to let drivers know you're there.

Information
There are **tourist offices** at Jalan Pemuda 118 (Mon–Fri 7am–5pm, Sat 7am–3pm; ☎031/5478853), which is across the road and east of the Surabaya Plaza, almost at the junction with Jalan Kayun, and at Jalan Darmokali (Mon–Thurs 7am–3pm, Fri 7am–2pm; ☎031/575448). They have sketch maps of Surabaya and will try to answer general and specific questions. The main office is at Jalan Wisata Menanggal (Mon–Thurs 7am–3pm, Fri 7am–2pm; ☎031/8531814, fax 8531822), but is very hard to find, out towards the bus station, and probably most useful for telephone inquiries. The Surabaya Municipality Tourism Service, Jalan Jend Basuki Rachmat 119–121 (Mon–Fri 7am–2pm; ☎031/5344710, fax 5468717), opposite the *Hyatt Regency Hotel*, has a few leaflets.

One of the best places to get **information** is *Bamboe Denn* (see p.240). They give their guests up-to-date details of bus, train and air connections, have a useful sketch map, and are great on local bus and bemo connections in the city.

The free monthly **magazine** *Surabaya Kini* is an excellent resource for visitors, stocked by most of the upmarket hotels; otherwise, you can collect one from the magazine office, Indo Multi Media at the *Hyatt Regency*, Jalan Jend Basuki Rachmat 106–128c; ☎ & fax 5326299; Mon–Fri 8.30am–5pm). The company has offices throughout Indonesia, and you can also collect the current issues of *Bali Kini, Jakarta Kini* and *Solo/Yogya Kini*, plus maps of Jakarta, Sulawesi, Bandung and Bali, from the Surabaya branch.

If you're staying in Surabaya for any time, a detailed **city map** is useful; both Gramedia and Toko Gunung Agung stock them. The Karya Pembina Swajaya map (Rp7000) is the best, but you need to buy the pack labelled *Pariwisata Surabaya* to get a street index as well. Periplus's *Surabaya and East Java* is available overseas as well as locally and is very clear, but doesn't cover the whole of the city: it doesn't reach as far south as Bungusarih.

City transport
City transport in Surabaya is provided by a vast fleet of **buses** and **bemos**. There are also plenty of **metered taxis**; meters start at Rp1300 and a trip within the city centre will cost Rp2000–3000. These are supplemented by huge numbers of becak, which cover the back roads not served by the main motorized transport.

Three types of public buses operate in the city, with routes indicated by letters. They stop only at designated places, which are often signified by blue bus-stop signs. Signal to them to stop, and pay the conductor once you are seated. **Ordinary buses** cost Rp300 per trip; one useful service is the "C" route, which runs from Bungusarih past Tunjungan Plaza, in through the centre of the city and up to Tanjung Perak, passing conveniently close to the post office on the way. Slightly more luxurious buses cost Rp500–700, depending on the route, and are designated by "P"; both P1 and P2 complete the same route as the ordinary-service C. Top of the range are the extremely comfortable **air-con buses** – they cost Rp1000 and are designated PAC1 and PAC2, operating the same routes as P1 and P2.

Accommodation

The range of **accommodation** in Surabaya isn't great: many of the places in the centre is aimed at top-flight business travellers, although with a couple of excellent exceptions for budget travellers. The less expensive places are slightly further from the centre, in the area north of Kota station, which isn't good either for buses (you'll need to figure out the bemos around here) or the central sights, but better for exploring the older parts of the city and convenient for Kota station.

Bamboe Denn, Jl Ketabangkali 6a (☎031/5340333). This is the main backpacker accommodation in the city. It isn't easy to find, about 30min walk from Gubeng station (Rp2500 by becak), but local people will point you in the right direction. Accommodation is very basic in tiny singles, doubles and dorms, all with shared bathrooms, but there's a pleasant sitting room and simple, inexpensive meals and snacks are available. The real plus is the excellent information available – everyone gets a sketch map of the city and staff are always keen to help. ②.

Hotel Ganefo, Jl Kapasan 169–171 (☎031/311169, fax 361390). This is a large, unrenovated colonial bungalow down an alleyway opposite Bank Umum. There are plenty of high ceilings and original features although the rooms are fairly basic. Cheaper ones have fan and outside bathroom; pricier ones, air-con and bathroom. ③–④.

Garden Hotel, Jl Pemuda 21 (☎031/5321001, fax 5316111). Showing its age, but comfortable and convenient. Guests can use the *Garden Palace Hotel* facilities, including the pool, to which it is linked by a corridor. ⑤.

Garden Palace Hotel, Jl Yos Sudarso 11 (☎031/5321001, fax 5316111). Whilst not in the luxury class of some of the newer city-centre hotels, this place, and the attached *Garden Hotel*, is very popular with Indonesian businesspeople. It has an attractive lobby area with a bustling atmosphere, a business centre, 24hr coffee shop and small pool. The rooms are comfortable without being outstanding. ⑤–⑥.

Hyatt Regency, Jl Jend Basuki Rachmat 106–128 (☎031/5311234, fax 5321508). The grandest centrally located hotel. The rooms are plush and comfortable and the communal areas extremely grand. There are six restaurants and bars, two pools, squash and tennis courts plus a health and fitness centre. ⑨.

Hotel Irian, Jl Samudra 16 (☎031/334937). A pleasant old-style bungalow, cool and with a choice of rooms. There are shared bathrooms and fan at the lower end and attached bathrooms in the more expensive rooms. ③–④.

Hotel Majapahit Mandarin Oriental, Jl Tunjungan 65 (☎031/5454333, fax 5454111). The outside is pretty unprepossessing, but there's a brilliant Art Deco lobby area and great facilities, including a business centre, health centre (Rp45,000 for a day's membership) and 25m outdoor pool. ⑨.

Novotel, Jl Ngagel 173–175 (☎031/5682301, fax 5676317). The chain is usually reliable and this hotel lives up to expectations, although it is a long way to the south of the city centre. The lounge and entrance areas are relaxed but stylish, with plenty of wood and bamboo, and the rooms all have hot water and air-con. There's an attractive pool, tennis courts and fitness centre, and apartments for monthly rental. ⑨.

Hotel Paviljoen, Jl Genteng Besar 94–98 (☎031/5343449). Spotlessly clean rooms in an old colonial bungalow; the ones at the back have excellent verandahs around a courtyard and all have attached cold-water mandi, while top-end rooms have air-con. This is an excellent choice if you want to be fairly central and have a bit of comfort. Southbound buses P1 and P2 stop just at the end of the street on Jl Tunjungan, and guests get a small sketch map of the city. ③.

Remaja Hotel, Jl Embong Kenongo 12 (☎031/5341359, fax 5310009). In a quiet but central location, this place is adequate and utilitarian without much character, but a good bet in this price range as all rooms have air-con and hot showers. ④.

Hotel Semut, Jl Samudra 9–15 (☎031/24578, fax 332601). In the area north of Kota station. All rooms have air-con and attached bathroom: cold-water in the less expensive rooms and hot-water in the pricier ones. There are deep, cool verandahs looking into the garden, a coffee shop and restaurant. ④.

Sheraton Surabaya, Jl Embong Malang 25–31 (☎031/5468000, fax 5467000). Centrally located, with all the luxury and facilities that you'd expect at this end of the market, with a small outside pool surrounded by foliage, a health club, business centre and excellent restaurants and bars. Highly recommended. ⑨.

Westin Surabaya, Jl Embong Malang 85–89 (☎031/5458888, fax 5193034). The only Indonesian *Westin* is centrally located, with a great lobby area two storeys high, an interior waterfall feature, plenty of opulence and comfort plus a rooftop pool and fitness centre. Prices range up to US$2000 for the presidential suite. ⑨.

Hotel Weta, Jl Genteng Kali 3–11 (☎031/5319494, fax 5345512). With a small but attractive lobby area, friendly and helpful staff, clean, attractive rooms with air-con and hot-water bathrooms, this is a central, good-value choice in this price range. Staff will always discuss discounts. ⑧.

The City

There are enough **sights** in Surabaya to keep most visitors occupied for a day or two: imposing colonial architecture, a lively Chinese quarter, and the harbour, where traditional schooners dock. However, unless your natural habitat is the Asian metropolis, there is little to keep you here long.

The centre

In the **centre** of Surabaya, the main sights are grand, colonial era buildings. On Jalan Tunjungan, the *Hotel Majapahit Mandarin Oriental*, previously the **Oranje Hotel**, was the site of the "Flag Incident" (see p.237), in which a blow was struck for Indonesian Independence. It doesn't look much from the outside, although the refurbished interior has some attractive Art Deco features. Nearby on Jalan Pemuda, **Grahadi** is the graceful and elegant official residence of the governor of East Java. Built in the late eighteenth century, it is much modified and renovated. The statue across the road depicts **R.T. Soerjo**, the first Indonesian governor to live in Grahadi after Independence. In a small garden nearby, the most famous statue in Surabaya, **Joko Dolog** (1289), depicts King Kertanagara, the last ruler of the Singosari kingdom, in the form of Buddha. Originally erected in the area of Malang, it was brought to Surabaya about three hundred years ago and remains highly revered by local people, as the floral offerings all around testify. At the end of Jalan Pemuda by the river is the **submarine** *Pasopati*, which was originally Russian but served in the Indonesian navy from 1962 to 1994.

SURABAYA SUE

Christened **Surabaya Sue** by the Australian press during the Indonesian War for Independence, the woman also known as K'tut Tantri, Vannine Walker and Muriel Pearson, remains a controversial figure. Born of Manx parents in Scotland in 1908, she moved to Hollywood and worked as a journalist. She travelled to Bali in the 1930s, inspired by the film that persuaded many foreigners to travel there, *Bali: The Lost Paradise*. She told her own story in *Revolt in Paradise* (see p.979), which, although it's a pretty gripping read, many have argued strays from the facts. By her own account she initially lived as a guest of the Raja of Bangli and then established one of the first hotels on Kuta Beach. However, she gained fame as a fighter for **Indonesian Independence**. Imprisoned by the Japanese for two years during their occupation of Surabaya, placed in solitary confinement and tortured, on her release she joined the Independence movement and had plenty of hair-raising adventures. She is best known for her broadcasts about the Indonesian cause which, as a foreign woman reporting from the scene of the conflict, attracted much-needed international attention. After Independence was won she lived for many years in a hotel in Jakarta courtesy of the Indonesian government, but eventually died on August 5, 1997 in an old people's home in Australia. Her last wish was for her ashes to be taken to Bali for a full *ngaben* ceremony, the Hindu cremation rite. As a non-Hindu, this wish caused considerable disturbance among the religious authorities on Bali – she was as controversial in death as she was in life.

North of the centre

Surabaya's **Chinese quarter** hums with activity, an abundance of traditional two-storey shophouses lining narrow streets and alleyways, and minuscule red-and-gold altars glinting in shops and houses – it's an evocative contrast to the highways and massive malls of the city centre. The area centres on Jalan Slompretan, Jalan Bongkaran and the part of Jalan Samudra southwest of the 300-year-old **Hok Teck Hian temple** on Jalan Dukuh. The temple itself is a brilliant and vibrant place with several tiny shrines spread over two floors, and Buddhist, Confucian and Hindu effigies. Four splendidly fierce statues guard the main entrance, just inside the door. The main altar downstairs is the largest in the complex, dedicated to Kong Cow Kong Ting Cun Ong, the "Son of the Angels". Also downstairs, Macho, the "Angel of the Sea" is the focus of prayers for those involved in export and import. Upstairs, at the altar to Kwan Im Poosat, the "Valentine Angel", pregnant women come to pray for the sex of their child.

The oldest and most famous mosque in Surabaya is **Mesjid Ampel**, located in the Arab area, the **kampung Arab** or **Qubah**, to the north of the Chinese quarter. The whole kampung, bounded by Jalan Nyanplungan, Jalan K.H. Mas Mansur, Jalan Sultan Iskandar Muda and Jalan Pabean Pasar, was originally settled by Arab traders and sailors who arrived in Kali Mas harbour: their descendants still live here. It's a maze of tidy, well-kept alleyways crammed with flowers, beggars and shops selling Muslim hats, perfumes, dates and souvenirs. Mesjid Ampel, built in 1421, is the site of the grave of Sunan Ampel, one of the nine *wali* (see p.949) credited with bringing Islam to Java in the sixteenth century, and as such, a site of pilgrimage and reverence. Sunan Ampel is regarded as one of the most important *wali*, guiding and advising the others, two of whom (Sunan Bonang and Sunan Drajat) were his sons. Sunan Ampel's own origins are uncertain: it is thought his father was from Central Asia or the Middle East. He married a princess of Campa, came to East Java in the early fifteenth century and died in 1479. The area isn't particularly tourist-friendly, and women will have to dress extremely conservatively and take a scarf to cover their heads to stand any chance of being allowed in the mosque.

The **Heroes Monument** (Tugu Pahlawan), between Jalan Bubutan and Jalan Pahlawan and to the south of the Arab quarter, is a tall pointed pillar built in the 1950s to celebrate the heroes of the Battle of Surabaya, located in a plain open space surrounded by wide, traffic-clogged roads. Further north, the **Jembatan Merah** (Red Bridge) is so called because of blood spilt during a legendary fight between the shark (*sura*) and crocodile (*baya*), which now form Surabaya's coat of arms and are the possible origin of the city's name. It was the site of some serious fighting during the Battle of Surabaya (see p.237); the flaming gold monument in nearby Jembatan Merah Plaza commemorates that battle.

In the far north of the city, timeless **Kalimas harbour** (the name means "river of gold"), a two-kilometre length of wharves and warehouses at the eastern end of the main port, lies just north of the Arab Quarter on Jalan Kalimas Baru; take bus C, P1 or P2 or either PAC bus to Tanjung Perak and walk around to the east. It's fantastically atmospheric, the traditional Sulawesi schooners (*pinisi*) loading and unloading cargoes which are either unsuitable for containerization, or destined for locations too remote for bigger ships. You need permission to take photographs; ask at the police post by the harbour entrance.

South of the centre

One of the best places to visit in the city, **Surabaya Zoo** (Kebun Binatang Surabaya), Jalan Setail 1 (daily 7am–6pm; Rp1500), lies 3km south of the city centre; take buses C, P1, P2 or either PAC bus pass on their way between the city centre and Bungusarih. Spacious, and with over 3500 animals, it's surprisingly pleasant and, at least in parts, less distressing for animal-lovers than many Indonesian zoos. The enclosures of the orang-utans, Komodo dragon and giraffes are large and separated from the public by moats, but the big cats, bears and horses are kept in cramped conditions, the birds have piti-fully small cages and there's even a bad-taste display of stuffed animals. Still, it's a ver-dant, peaceful spot, popular with families and groups of young people, a pleasant escape from the lunacy of the city and a good place to take a picnic and relax for a few hours.

A few minutes' walk from the zoo is the **Museum Negiri Propinsi Jawa Timur**, MPU Tantular, Jalan Taman Mayangkara 6 (Tues–Thurs 8am–2.30pm, Fri 8am–2pm, Sat 8am–12.30pm, Sun 8am–1.30pm; Rp200). The entrance features a *thuk-thuk*, an ornately carved wooden drum from Madura, while the galleries are crammed with arts and crafts and assorted archeological objects. There is an especially fine collection of shadow pup-pets and *topeng* masks, and some of the more outlandish items include a penny-farthing bicycle, a Daimler motorcycle and an ancient gramophone and records. Some attempts have been made to label items in English, although there's little explanation.

Eating and drinking

From the central night market on Jalan Genteng Besar through the popular food courts in the shopping centres to luxurious dining in the top-flight hotels, the city has a wealth of **eating** options.

Kafé Bromo, *Sheraton Surabaya Hotel*. Probably the best of the top-class hotel restaurants, although it's fairly informal and comfortable rather than grand. The attraction is the Rp30,000 lunchtime buffet and Rp37,500 dinner buffet. The food is fabulous, with Indonesian, Western, Chinese and Japanese options, excellent salads and bread and a whole counter of desserts. Pasta, sandwiches and Indonesian meals are also available à la carte for around Rp20,000, and imported T-bone steak for Rp43,000.

Kafé Excelso. This Indonesian chain has branches on the ground floor of Surabaya Plaza and a cou-ple in Tunjungan Plaza, and is very popular with well-heeled Indonesians and expatriates. They have an excellent choice of expensive Indonesian coffees (choose between Bali, Toraja, Sumatra or Java blends), plus iced coffee, salads, snacks, cakes and ice creams.

Lobby Lounge, *Westin Surabaya*, Jl Embong Malang 85–89. The *Lobby Lounge* has deep-pile car-pets, huge windows, plenty of greenery and expensive cafetières of coffee, plus cakes, pastries and shakes. Dress up and lounge the afternoon away in real style.

Café Mirota, Jl Sulawesi 24. Attached to the souvenir shop of the same name, this café serves snacks and light meals of soup, rice and noodles.

Pizza Pasta. On the ground floor of Surabaya Plaza and the top floor of Tunjungan Plaza. One of a chain of local places, with a big choice of moderately priced pizza, pasta and salads, none of it par-ticularly authentic, but pleasant enough.

Sari Bundo, Jl Walikota Mustajab 70. A popular place serving reasonably priced Padang food.

Taichan Restaurant, Jl Kramat Gantung 203. On the south side of the Heroes Monument square. An upmarket Japanese restaurant with great air-con, ordinary tables or a low-seating area, and a large menu of noodle, teriyaki, fish, tempura and plenty of set meals available. Staff are friendly and there is a small menu of drinks including sake.

Toko Deli, *Hotel Majapahit Mandarin Oriental*, Jl Tunjungan 65. Just off the lobby of the central hotel, this small coffee shop has stunning cakes and pastries, plus a range of coffees and teas. It is expensive and you should dress up, but well worth the money and effort.

Tunjungan Plaza Food Court. On the seventh floor of the biggest and brashest of the city's shop-ping plazas. There is a vast array of fast food available here in the largest food court in Surabaya: *McDonald's*, Singaporean noodles, Cajun grills, New Zealand ice cream, crêpes and kebabs.

Turin Ice Cream, Jl Kayun 10a. The address is a bit misleading: the entrance is at the east end of Jl Embong Kenongo. They have a small menu of inexpensive and moderately priced Indonesian and Chinese food, but the speciality is their own ice cream, which ranges from vanilla through durian to concoctions such as "Avocado Dream", "Blue Italiano" and "Lady in Black".

Café Venezia, Jl Ambengan 16. Located on a busy and noisy corner; you can eat outside or in the high-ceilinged cool interior. There's a comprehensive menu of Indonesian, Chinese, Japanese, Korean and Western food, plus plenty of ice creams and sundaes. Prices are in the moderate to expensive range.

Entertainment

There is no shortage of **entertainment** in Surabaya, although it's a lot easier to find a disco or cinema in the city than a wayang kulit show. The **discos** (daily 10pm–3am) are generally fairly pricey: admission is from Rp7000, and drinks are expensive, with beer around Rp12,500 a glass. Popular discos include *Studio East*, *Top Ten*, *Qemi* at the *Elmi Hotel* and *Atum*. With a large student population in the city there are plenty of **live-music** venues. Try *Tequila Willies*, Jalan Kayon 62 (daily 6pm–5am), *News Café*, Jalan Raya P. Sudirman 47–49 (daily 11pm–1am), and hotel venues where bands come for a few weeks at a time: the *Tavern* at the *Hyatt Regency* (☎031/5311234) has live music every evening at 9pm (except Sun), and *Bongo's* at the *Sheraton* also gets going at 9pm (daily except Mon).

Traditional music, dance and drama

More traditional entertainment is available at RRI Surabaya, Jalan Pemuda, where every Saturday evening there are free **wayang kulit** shows (10pm). At Taman Hiburan Rakyat (locally called Tee Ha Air) on Jalan Kusuma Bangsa, regular folk **comedy** performances are held (contact the tourist office for more information). Slightly further afield, performances of traditional **dance** and **drama** are given during the dry season (July–Nov) at Pandaan (see p.264); many people travel from Surabaya for the shows. Contact Surabaya travel agents for all-inclusive trips, or the tourist offices for information.

Shopping

Monster **shopping centres** have hit Surabaya with a vengeance: the most modern and popular are the Surabaya Plaza (daily 10am–9.30pm) on Jalan Pemuda, and Tunjungan Plaza, Jalan Jend Basuki Rachmat 8–12 (daily 10am–10pm), which has seven storeys and an indoor ice-skating rink on the lower ground floor. In the **Tunjungan Plaza** you'll find all the top-class clothes stores including Boss, Emporio, Versace, Escada and Guess plus Marks & Spencer and Louis Vuitton, as well as a couple of department stores, food courts, a supermarket and a cinema on the top floor. **Surabaya Plaza** is smaller and it's easier to find your way around. There's a Galeria department store, and stalls on the top and bottom floors which add some character; a dentist's surgery is located on the top floor. Further afield, **Jembatan Merah Plaza** is to the north, near the famous bridge (see p.242), and has four storeys including a Ramayana department store and supermarket, as well as plenty of stalls and tiny shops; it resembles an indoor market and is full of local people hunting out the excellent bargains in textiles, shoes, bags and clothes. Inevitably there's a *McDonald's* and *KFC*, but also a local food court. More central, **Siola department store and supermarket**, Jalan Tunjungan 1, also attracts a large local clientele. For a more traditional shopping experience, try **Pasar Atum**, a two-storey concrete local market, packed with stalls selling pretty much everything. It's very popular, and Bemo M will get you here from the east end of Jalan Genteng Kali in the city centre.

Books, magazines and newspapers

There's a reasonable range of English-language **books** available in the city, but don't expect bargain prices, as there are only a few secondhand places.

Gramedia, Jl Jend Basuki Rachmat 95. A range of English-language titles plus some maps and guidebooks. The *Jakarta Post* usually gets here by the afternoon and there are some international magazines.

Mirota, Jalan Sulawesi 24. Secondhand books start from Rp8000, and they buy back at half the price.

Sheraton Surabaya Hotel and **Hyatt Regency** (near the reception at the back). The best selection of English-language titles in town, with a good choice of paperback fiction, Oxford in Asia books, magazines and newspapers (Rp26,000–77,000).

Toko Gunung Agung, Tunjungan Plaza (the biggest branch) and Surabaya Plaza. A reasonable range of imported novels in English, both contemporary and classic, plus a selection of Periplus guidebooks and maps, as well as cookery, health, business and self-improvement titles.

Souvenirs

Shopping for **souvenirs** in Surabaya doesn't give you the number or range of shops or choice of goods that you'll get in Bali or Yogyakarta, but don't despair if you arrive here with things still to buy – there are a few places well worth checking out.

Batik Keris, Tunjungan Plaza. This is a well-known chain of textile and souvenir shops that has an extensive range, from tiny batik purses (Rp2000) to pure-silk sarong and scarf sets (Rp500,000). They have a good choice of sarongs in all styles of Javan batik, plenty of shirts and other ready-made clothing, plus carvings, puppets and pictures.

Mirota, Jl Sulawesi 24 (daily 9am–9pm). A brilliant souvenir shop with plenty of items from across the islands: carvings in modern and classical style, basketware, leatherwork, furniture, paintings, ready-made batik items and material (from Rp7000 a metre), T-shirts, silk textiles and silver. There is also a good secondhand book selection (see opposite), one of very few in the city.

Sarinah, Jl Tunjungan 7. Has a souvenir and craft department on the second floor with a huge range of textiles, woodcarvings and assorted craft items. The range also includes penis sheaths from Irian Jaya. Fitting rooms are available.

Listings

Airline offices The following airlines are found in the Skyline Office Building, *Hyatt Regency*, Jl Jend Basuki Rachmat 106–128: British Airways, 5th floor (☎031/5326383); Cathay Pacific, 1st floor (☎031/5317421, fax 5321582); China Southern, 2nd floor (☎031/5326319, fax 5311734); Eva Air, 5th floor (☎031/5465123, fax 5455083); Garuda (☎031/5457747, fax 5326322); Lufthansa, 5th floor (☎031/5316355, fax 5322290); Malaysia, 1st floor (☎ & fax 031/5318632); Northwest, 5th floor (☎031/5317086, fax 5684843); Qantas, 5th floor (☎031/5452322, fax 5452569); Saudia, 2nd floor (☎031/5325802); Thai, 5th floor (☎031/5340861, fax 532638). Elsewhere are: Bouraq, Jl P. Sudirman 70–72 (☎031/5452918, fax 5321621), and Jl Genteng Kali 63 (☎031/5344940); Emirates, Lt Dasar, *Hyatt Regency*, Jl Jend Basuki Rachmat 106–128 (☎031/5460000, fax 5479520); KLM, World Trade Centre, Jl Pemuda 27–31 (☎031/5315096, fax 5315097); Mandala, Jl Diponegoro 73 (☎031/5687157); Merpati, Jl Raya Darmo 111 (☎031/5688111, fax 5685400); Singapore Airlines, 10th floor, Menara BBD Tower, Jl Jend Basuki Rachmat 2–6 (☎031/5319217, fax 5319214); Trans Asia Airways Regency, Jl Jend Basuki Rachmat 106–128 (☎031/5463181, fax 5467675).

Airport information ☎031/8667642.

Banks and exchange All of the main Indonesian banks have huge branches in Surabaya, with exchange facilities. Bank Duta, Jalan Pemuda 12 (Mon–Fri 8.30am–2pm), is fast, central and efficient and, offers Visa and Mastercard advances; the BNI is at Jalan Pemuda 36.

Car rental Avis, Jl Darmo Indah Timur II Blok G32 (☎ & fax 031/711319) and *Westin Surabaya* (☎031/5508130), charge from Rp120,000 for 8hr in the city in a Kijang, to Rp450,000 for a BMW. Outside the city the range is Rp120,000–400,000 for 5hr, including the driver; charges vary and some include petrol. Self-drive is available from Rp150,000 per day for a Kijang, plus Rp15,000 collision-damage waiver and a ten percent service charge. Globe, Jl Jend Basuki Rachmat 147 (☎031/548111), has many types of car available, from Kijang, saloon cars and limousines. Rates start at Rp80,000 for 5hr in the city including driver and fuel, and Rp147,000 for 7hr outside the city area. Self-drive is available at Rp100,000 per day including insurance; payment is by credit card only and a there's a minimum rental period of three days. You must book two to three days in advance.

Consulates Australia, World Trade Centre, Jl Pemuda 27–31 (☎031/5319123); Belgium, Jl Raya Kupang Indah III/24 (☎031/716423); CIS (Commonwealth of Independent States – the former Soviet Union), Jl Sumatra 116 (☎031/5342091); Denmark, Jl Sambas 7 (☎031/5675047); France, Jl Darmokali 10–12 (☎031/5678639); Germany, Jl TAIS Nasution 15 (☎031/5343735); Great Britain, c/o Hong Kong and Shanghai Bank, 3rd floor, Skyline Office Building, *Hyatt Regency*, Jl Jend Basuki

Rachmat 106–128 (☎031/5326381, fax 5326380); India, Jl Pahlawan 17 (☎031/5341565); Japan, Jl Sumatra 93 (☎031/5344677); Netherlands, Jl Pemuda 54 (☎031/5311612 ext 558); Sri Lanka (☎031/715732); USA, Jl Dr Sutomo 33 (☎031/5676880).

Ferries The Pelni office is at Jl Pahlawan 112 (Mon–Thurs 9am–noon & 1–3pm, Fri–Sat 9am–noon; ☎031/339048, fax 338958).

Hospitals The following have doctors who speak English, Dutch and German: RS St Vincentius A Paula, Jl Diponegoro 51 (☎031/5677562), and RSUD Dr Soetomo, Jl Dharamahusada 7–9 (☎031/5501111). Otherwise, contact your hotel for recommended hospitals or doctors.

Immigration office Jl Jend S. Parman 58a (☎031/8531785).

Post office The main post office (Mon–Thurs 8am–3pm, Fri & Sat 8am–1pm), is at Jl Kebonrojo 10. To get there from the city centre take a C, P1, P2, PAC1 or PAC2 bus from outside Tunjungan Plaza to the junction of Jl Kebonrojo and Jl Bubutan; to get back to the city go along to the other end of Jl Kebonrojo and pick up the same buses on Jl Pahlawan. Poste restante is at the philatelic counter in the centre of the post office; get mail addressed to you at Poste Restante, Post Office, Jl Kebonrojo 10, Surabaya 60175, Java Timur. The parcel office (Mon–Thurs 8am–3pm, Fri 8–11am & 12.30–3pm, Sat 8am–1pm) is to the right of the main building. There are four public Internet terminals in the main post office (Mon–Thurs 8am–8pm, Fri & Sat 8am–3pm; Rp1500 for the first 15min and Rp100 per minute after that). If you are just sending letters, a more central post office is at Jl Taman Apsaril 1 (Mon–Thurs 8am–12.30pm, Fri 8–11am, Sat 8am–noon), just off Jl Pemuda in the city centre.

Swimming If you want to swim in some luxury, the pool at the *Elmi Hotel* charges Rp10,000 for non-residents. The ultimate in pampering comes at the *Sheraton Surabaya* (☎031/5468000), where a day's use of the gym, sauna and pool, a treatment, traditional massage and lunch or dinner will set you back Rp110,000.

Taxis Citra (☎031/592555); Merpati (☎031/5315050); Star (☎031/8280228).

Telephone and fax The warpostel at Jl Genteng Besar 49 (daily 5am–11pm) has telephone, fax and letter services. One of the most convenient wartels (daily 24hr) is the one on the ground floor of Tunjungan Plaza. It's a bit tucked away, under the main steps leading down into Tunjungan 2, just behind *Kafé Excelso*. There's another 24hr wartel at Jl Walikota Mustajab 2–4.

Travel agents Many agents in Surabaya offer all-inclusive tours to the sights of the region, either day-trips or longer. The following is a selection of the largest, best-established set-ups. Dwidaya, *Hyatt Regency*, Lt Dasar, Jl Jend Basuki Rachmat 106–128 (☎031/5471009, fax 5471114): various options are available starting at Rp350,000 per person (minimum two people) for a two-day/one-night package to Bromo staying at the *Grand Bromo*. Orient Travel, Jl P. Sudirman 62 (☎031/5456666, fax 5454666; Web site *www.orientexpress.co.id*): a wide variety, from Surabaya city tours (3hr; US$20), Tretes (US$45), Malang (US$50) and trips to Bromo from two day/one night (US$95 per person) to seven days including Bromo plus Ubud and Lovina on Bali (from US$395 per person). Pacto Tours, Lt Dasar, *Hyatt Regency*, Jl Jend Basuki Rachmat 106–128 (☎031/5460628, fax 5326385) have a range of trips: Surabaya City (US$15), Bromo (midnight–10am; US$35), Trowulan (US$30), Malang and Singosari temples (US$45) and many longer options, including four days/three nights in Bromo and Kalibaru (US$326), and four days/three nights in Bromo and Ijen (US$352). There is a two-person minimum for all tours.

Trowulan and around

Almost certainly the capital of the glorious Majapahit kingdom from the late thirteenth century, **TROWULAN** is situated 35km southwest of Surabaya, en route to Jombang. Trowulan itself is a small sleepy village, with archeological remains spread across an area of about a hundred square kilometres around it. The number and impressive size and design of the buildings, plus the range of artefacts found, give a sense of the might and majesty of the kingdom that had such influence on the region and beyond, into Bali. This historical significance, combined with the peaceful setting – a lovely maze of small, quiet lanes leading between cornfields and through small hamlets with tiny house compounds and thatched barns – make it well worth seeing.

While some of the sites are really too far flung from Trowulan unless you have a rental car or motorcycle, the best way to visit most of the places of interest is to get a bus heading for Jombang and ask to be put off in Trowulan; you'll know you're there as all the pillars and gateposts on the main road are painted red. The turning you want is Jalan A. Yani: it's through two large red pillars, a few metres after a small wartel sign, on the left if you are coming from Surabaya. Crowds of **becak** can take you around the sights (Rp20,000–25,000 for about 3hr), or you can do the whole lot on foot, but you'll need the entire day. There is no accommodation in the village but **Mojokerto** (see below) makes a good base if you want to stay in the area.

The site

The **Trowulan Museum** (daily except Fri 8am–2pm; Rp200) on Jalan A. Yani is a useful and enlightening adjunct to visiting the sites, and is perhaps the best introduction to it: labels are in English. The most famous artefact is an enormous stone statue of Airlangga as the god Wishnu perched atop a *garuda*. But the range of items is huge, including stone statuary, terracotta, earthenware and Chinese porcelain. Nearby, the artificial lake of **Kolam Segaran** provides an illustration of the huge disposable wealth of the Majapahit kingdom: it's said that at the end of opulent feasts laid on to impress outsiders, crockery and cutlery from the meal would be thrown into the lake.

Turning right out of the museum, it's almost 1km to the **Pendopo Agung**, the totally rebuilt Grand Reception Hall: only the stone foundations under the pillars supporting the roof are original. There are vivid modern statues of Gajah Made, the famous fourteenth-century commander in chief and prime minister of the Majapahit kingdom, and Raden Wijaya 1, the founder and first ruler of the Majapahit, whose 1293 coronation is depicted in a relief on the back wall of the hall.

Around 200m north of the Pendopo Agung, a turning to the right leads for 2km to one of the most imposing Trowulan sites, **Candi Bajang Ratu**. It's a dramatic red-brick gateway on the left of the road, thought to date from the mid-fourteenth century – originally there were walls running to the left and right of the gateway. Continuing on the same road, which bends around to the right, after 500m you'll come to the village of Dinuk, just beyond which is **Candi Tikus** (Rat Temple), which has been sympathetically renovated and lies in attractive and well-maintained grounds. It is so named because it was discovered (in 1914) by farmers who were looking for a nest of rats that was plaguing the area. The ancient ritual-bathing area, now dry, is sunk deep into the ground: it has a central platform, on which are the remains of what were the highest structures in the complex, representing the mythical and holy Mount Mahameru, from which Hindus believe the elixir of immortality springs.

Retrace your steps up Jalan A. Yani to the main road: several of the most impressive remains lie to the north of here, including the hugely impressive **Candi Brahu**, a solid, imposing, tower-like rectangular temple, the largest of all the remaining structures from the Majapahit kingdom. Another 500m along the same road, a sign points to **Candi Siti Inggill**, a shady burial ground in a high, walled compound. Turning right out of here it's another 500m back to the main road: you'll then be about a kilometre beyond the main Jalan A. Yani junction towards Jombang. Heading back towards Surabaya, **Gapura Wringin Lawang**, another great red-brick gateway, lies about 200m to the right off the road, 1.5km from the junction.

Mojokerto

The small town of **MOJOKERTO**, 8km north of Trowulan, provides the closest accommodation to the ruins. There are regular buses to Mojokerto from Surabaya, terminating at Terminal Kertojoyo. To get to the town centre, pick up a bemo (most are yellow) to the centre of town, locally called "pasar". These bemos also head out to Trowulan and end their journey about 200m beyond the Jalan A. Yani junction in Trowulan that leads down to the museum.

Mojokerto's station is centrally located on Jalan Bhayangkara, and the post office is a kilometre north of the town centre on Jalan A. Yani, next to the 24hr telephone office. There are just a couple of **accommodation** options. *Hotel Slamet*, Jalan P.B. Sudirman 51 (☎0321/321400; ②–④), offers a huge variety of rooms, with air-con in the more expensive ones. To get there, turn right out of the station, take a left at the next junction and the hotel is 200m down the road on the right – about a ten-minute walk. A budget alternative is *Wisma Tenara*, Jalan H.O.S. Cokroaminoto 3 (☎0321/322904; ②–③). Go past the *Hotel Slamet* to the next junction, turn right and *Wisma Tenara* is on the left just before the BCA building; they are used to tourists here and staff are friendly and welcoming. Two standards of room are available – cheaper ones with fan or newer ones with air-con – and they all have attached bathrooms. There is a pleasant garden in the back and attractive verandahs. Mojokerto currently has no **exchange facilities**, so be sure to bring enough local currency with you.

Pulau Madura

Located just 3km across the Madura Strait, **Pulau Madura** could hardly be more different from Surabaya: it's a restful and totally rural place, where village and small town life continue in timeless fashion. Although a quiet backwater for much of the year, the island bursts into activity during the exciting **kerapan sapi** (ox races), held every August and September. There is plenty of accommodation and public transport, although the driving is notoriously fast and dangerous.

Stretching 160km from west to east and around 35km from north to south, Madura is mostly flat, although there is a low range of hills across the centre. The main towns are **Bangkalan** in the west, **Pamekasan** and **Sampang** in the centre and **Sumenep** in the east. The main road on the island links the major settlements along the south coast, and there is a narrower, quieter and well-surfaced road along the north coast; Sumenep is more visitor-friendly than the other larger towns.

Some history

Previously made up of several warring states, Pulau Madura was first unified in the fifteenth century by the prince of Arosbaya. **Islam** was brought to the island in the fifteenth and sixteenth centuries by the Wali Songo and their disciples: Sunan Giri from Gresik is considered to have been most involved in Madura's conversion. Arosbaya's son converted to Islam in 1528 and eventually established the whole island as Muslim.

Relations between Java and its much smaller neighbour have always been volatile. In 1624, the Central Javanese kingdom of Mataram conquered Madura as part of the siege of Surabaya; it was recorded as a long and hard battle, the Madurese women fighting beside their men to try to repel the invaders. In 1670, the famous and much-fêted **Prince Tronojoyo** began his takeover of the whole of Madura with the help of Makasar pirates, and then led a revolt against the Mataram and drove them off the island. By 1671 he had control of the island, in 1675 he took Surabaya back from Mataram, and within a couple of years much of East Java was in his hands. However, that same year, the Dutch sided with the Mataram against Trunojoyo, and he was eventually defeated. In the first half of the eighteenth century, Mataram ceded Madura to the Dutch, who installed princes at Bangkalan, Pamekasan and Sumenep, and, in exchange for the Dutch accepting and supporting them as rulers, the **Madurese princes** provided goods, workers and soldiers for the Dutch colonial government. Gradually, in the course of the nineteenth century, their power was reduced and by the beginning of the twentieth century they were effectively figureheads.

During World War II, the Japanese occupation was very harsh and, since Independence, conditions on the island have continued to be very difficult. Farming is tough, the soil is stony and the climate dry, the result being that throughout Indonesia and beyond there are many Madurese who have left the island to make a living elsewhere. Those who remain behind are mostly involved in **agriculture** – tobacco is a major cash crop – and fishing.

Arrival, information and island transport

Ferries operate from **Tanjung Perak** in Surabaya across the Madura Strait to Kamal in the west of Madura around the clock (every 30min; 30min; Rp500). There are plans for a bridge to span the strait, but it remains to be seen whether it will ever be built. An alternative route to Madura is the daily ferry (4hr) from **Tanjung Jangkhar** in the far east of Java, 60km north of Banyuwangi, to **Kalianget** in the east of Madura. At Kalianget, there is one losmen, *Baitul Kamal* (①–②), if you get stranded.

Madura has no tourist offices, as it is covered by the offices in Surabaya – you can expect little in the way of hard facts but you may get some colour brochures. The PT *Karya Pembina Swajaya* **map** of Madura available from Surabaya bookshops (see p.244) is the most detailed available, and is very useful if you are planning on getting off the beaten track with your own transport.

Minibuses operate on the routes between the major towns on the island – Kamal to Sumenep (3hr 30min–4hr), Kamal to Sampang (1hr 30min–2hr) and Kamal to Pamekasan (2hr 30min) – and these are supplemented by smaller, local routes within and around the larger towns. From Kalianget, local minibuses operate to Sumenep.

There are no official **car or motorcycle rental** outlets, but it is easy to make unofficial arrangements: inquire at your accommodation. Car rental will always include the driver (Rp40,000 per day and Rp20,000 for the driver, plus you'll pay for petrol), but if you leave your passport as security you may get a self-drive motorcycle for Rp15,000–20,000 per day.

Bangkalan and the west

The town of **BANGKALAN**, 16km north of the port of Kamal, is the main population centre in the west of the island and a busy commercial and administrative hub, though there is little to persuade visitors to linger. The **museum** (Mon–Fri 7.30am–5pm, Sat & Sun 8am–4pm; Rp300) looking onto the main square has some old carriages, cannons, musical instruments and lovely carvings, but only justifies a short visit. The main sight of the west is **Air Mata**, 11km northeast of Bangkalan and 5km southeast of the village of Arosbaya, the cemetery of the Cakraningrat family, who once ruled Sumenep. It's an extensive area, with a vast number of graves, most of which have been attractively restored. The furthest and highest grave and a favourite pilgrimage spot is that of Srifar Ambami Tjakraningrat I, popularly known as Ibu Ratu, who ruled from 1545 until 1569. A short walk down the hillside, there's a **spring** whose waters are reputed to guarantee eternal youth – most visitors leave with a bottleful of it. To get there, take public transport to Arosbaya and then change for Air Mata.

Practicalities

The only decent **accommodation** in town is at the *Hotel Ningrat*, Jalan K.H. Moh Kholil 113 (☎031/3095388; ③–④). The open-sided lobby area is fabulously attractive, with high ceilings and lots of intricately carved wooden decoration. However the rooms, unless you are prepared to pay for VIP luxury at the top end, with air-con, hot water and lots of traditionally carved furniture, are nothing special. If this is outside your price range and you get stranded, you could try the *Melati Hotel*, Jalan Maygen Sungkono 48 (☎031/3096457; ②), or *Hotel Surya Purnama* at Jalan Kartini 19 (☎031/3096449; ②), but there is little to recommend either. *Depot Wirasa*, Jalan Trunojoyo 75a, has a good selection of Indonesian and Chinese **food** and is inexpensive and clean. The **post office** is at Jalan Trunojoyo 2, the **telephone office** nearby at Jalan Trunojoyo 11, and, for **changing money**, BCA is further along at Jalan Trunojoyo 15a.

The centre of the island

The next large town to the east is **SAMPANG**, a small commercial centre built around an alun-alun, with a notable absence of sights. Should you wish to stay, try *Hotel Rahmat*, Jalan Hagussalim 31 (☎0323/21302; ②–④), 2km from the town centre on the road to Camplong; it's new, clean and good value, with a variety of rooms. The post office can be found on Jalan Pahlawan, the wartel at Jalan Trunojoyo 91, and the bus terminal west of the town centre, with long-distance bus offices along Jalan Jaksa Agung Suprapto. The main market, Pasar Kota, lies on the road in from Bangkalan to the west of the town centre.

The small market town and beach resort of **CAMPLONG**, 35km east of Sampang, is situated on an attractive river estuary. You'll find one of the best **accommodation** places on Madura here: *Pondok Wisata Camplong* (☎0323/21586; ③–④), comprising attractive bungalows and two-storey cottages, all with verandahs, set in pleasant, well-maintained grounds. There's a good beach, a fair-sized pool, and an inexpensive restaurant serves Indonesian and Chinese food. Cheaper rooms have fans, more expensive ones air-con, and all have attached bathroom. All public transport between Pamekasan and Bangkalan passes the entrance.

The capital of Madura and its largest town, **PAMEKASAN** lies in the middle of the island. Centred on the large, shady alun-alun, with the bold new central mosque on the northern side, the town has little charm and not much to interest visitors. The main shopping area, Pasar Kampung Arab, can be found just off Jalan Diponegoro, west of the alun-alun. The only thing that can be described as a sight is the **Api Alam** (Rp100 on foot, Rp1000 with a car), 4km south of the town on the road to Sampang. Supposedly a supernatural fire, it re-lights spontaneously when extinguished by rain. You'll see a small dirt circle surrounded by a fence, inside which the flames slowly consume assorted items of rubbish. The area, lined with warung, is a favourite weekend excursion for locals.

The main **bus terminal**, just east of the town centre, provides regular direct services to Surabaya, Bandung, Jakarta, Semarang, Cirebon, Jember and Banyuwangi. The long-distance buses (beyond Surabaya) leave at around midday, others operating throughout the day. Amongst the town's limited **accommodation**, try *Hotel Garuda*, Jalan Masgit 1 (☎0324/22589; ①–③), a rambling high-ceilinged place on the alun-alun, with very basic rooms without fan and with shared bathroom that are often full up, and more luxurious ones with air-con and attached bathroom. *Hotel Madura Inda*, Jalan Joko Tole 4c (☎0324/21258; ②–③), is down an alleyway between BCA and the church on a road that leads off the alun-alun; there are rooms with shared or attached bathroom. Further from the town centre, *Hotel Ramayana*, Jalan Niaga 55–57 (☎0324/22406; ②–③), has various standard rooms; more expensive ones have air-con and TV, and the middle-range ones attached bathroom and fan.

Bima Wartel, Jalan Segara 19, has a 24hr **telephone** and fax service and there are plans to set up public Internet access. Alternatively, the wartel, Seba Dadi II, is at Jalan Joko Tole 38 (7am–11pm). BCA at Jalan Joko Tole 4 **change money** and travellers' cheques, and the main **post office** is at Jalan Mesigit 3.

The village of **KARDULUK**, 28km east of Pamekasan, has several furniture workshops where the craftsmen use **jati wood** from the Kangean Islands. It's unlikely that you'll be carrying a four-poster bed or a huge chest home, but it's fun to look at the intricately carved designs. Also on show are the high Bekisar cages, built for the famed local cocks. At Meubel Ricky in the village you can see the **workshop** as well as the product.

Sumenep and the east

SUMENEP in the far east of the island is the most attractive town, with worthwhile sights – an old palace, museum, mosque and beaches – and the best choice of accommodation. Hugely prosperous in the eighteenth century, the Dutch claimed that this was due to local trading outside the VOC monopoly, which was illegal at the time. It is now a quiet, peaceful backwater, with its past glory still in evidence for visitors to enjoy.

The Town

The centrepiece of the town is the eighteenth-century **Mesjid Agung** (also known as Mesjid Jam'q), a large, cool and white-tiled edifice with a lovely and imposing tiered gateway. The mosque is carefully tended and there are wonderfully carved wooden doors and an attractive interior, with rich gold decoration and blue-and-white Chinese tiles. The two grandfather clocks on the verandah add to the colonial feel of the place, which is well worth a visit; women should cover arms and legs, but a scarf isn't necessary. Opposite Mesjid Agung, the **Taman Adipura Kota Sumenep** are attractive, well-laid-out gardens.

Museum Daerah and the neighbouring kraton (Mon–Fri 7.30am–5pm, Sat & Sun 8am–4pm; Rp300) are two intriguing sights, located at Jalan Dr Sutomo 8, which leads from the east side of Taman Adipura Kota Sumenep directly opposite the mosque. The museum is in two parts: an old carriage house and another building across the road. Together they house an enormous and eclectic collection of old photographs of the Madurese royal family, carriages, textiles, furniture, porcelain, masks, weapons, wooden shoes, a tiger skin and a whale skeleton. There are no labels in English and everything is incredibly jumbled up: the museum staff will show you round and explain things as far as possible, but it is very frustrating that such a potentially fascinating collection is lying around in disrepair.

KERAPAN SAPI

Each year in August and September, when the season's ploughing is over, early knockout heats of **kerapan sapi** (ox races) start throughout Madura to find the fastest pair of oxen on the island. In the rural economy, dependent on the strength and expertise of the animals, the races originated as a way of toughening up the oxen – and having some fun. Individual and village pride can be boosted considerably by having a prizewinning pair of these enormous beasts. Each weighing up to 600kg, they are yoked together and adorned with highly decorated bridles, while the rider half-stands and half-sits very precariously on a flimsy-looking long pole that is dragged behind. Charging over a course just over 100m long and reaching speeds up to 50km per hour, the stakes are high. The overall island-wide winner can usually count on a motorcycle and/or a TV as their prize, while local loss of face and misery results from a defeat. The owner of a good racing ox will be able to sell it for Rp20 million; a promising two- or three-year-old with racing potential changes hands for Rp5–7 million.

The oxen are carefully looked after by their owners, exempted from heavy work, fed herbal potions and vast quantities of raw eggs, and it is said they are even massaged and sung to to lull them to sleep at night. It isn't surprising that a favourite Madurese saying tells how local farmers treat their cattle better than their wives. The finals take place in September or October in Pamekasan, accompanied by ceremonies, parades, dancing and gamelan orchestras. Check in tourist offices in Surabaya for exact dates (see p.239).

Far better is the **kraton**, the old palace, which dates from 1762, was designed by a Chinese architect and is the only remaining palace in East Java. The Pendopo Agung (Grand Hall) is an open-sided and especially fine building, with lovely gold-painted woodcarving, old lanterns and a cool tiled floor. Visitors can look into but not enter the other rooms, which include bedrooms with carved Madurese four-poster wooden beds and dressing tables. The entrance to the palace compound is called the "Smiling Gate", apparently because the rajah used to sit up there and smile as he watched the princesses bathing and relaxing in the **Taman Sari** (Water Garden) next door. The pools are now dry, painted in modern colours and poorly maintained, but it is easy to imagine how it must have looked. Every year on the anniversary of the founding of Sumenep, October 31, a procession through the town starts from the palace.

The local market, **Pasar Anom**, just north of the bus terminal, is wonderfully lively, with textiles, clothes, household goods and food and drink stalls: it bustles with people every day, although the main market days are Monday and Thursday. There is also a small market complex at the top of Jalan Trunojoyo just north of Mesjid Agung, with a couple of shops selling batik, but the choice is very limited. Other options for **souvenir shopping** are Primitif Antique, Jalan Wahid Hasyim 12a, which stocks furniture, carvings and attractive small boxes (from Rp10,000; Prima, at Jalan A. Yani 88, which sells boxes and small wooden boats alongside bulkier items; and Madura Art Shop, Jalan Brig Jend Abdullah 34, which is worth a browse.

Practicalities

The main **bus terminal**, Wiraraja, is 1.5km south of the town centre. Jalan Trunojoyo leads from the terminal into the town centre, which is just north of Mesjid Agung. All long-distance buses, as well as buses from Pamekasan and points west, arrive at Wiraraja; take a becak or local bemo into the town centre from here. There are two other, smaller, terminals in Sumenep: Giling is the one for bemos to Lombang, and Kegongagong for bemos to Kalianget. Leaving Madura, there are direct buses from Sumenep back to Surabaya, departing from Wiraraja and going via Kamal. Get tickets on the bus or at the ticket offices along Jalan Trunojoyo just north of the terminal.

Sumenep offers several **accommodation** options. *Hotel Wijaya 1*, Jalan Trunojoyo 45–47 (☎0328/21433; ①–④), is a good central choice with rooms with shared bathroom through to VIP en-suites with air-con. *Hotel Wijaya 2*, Jalan Wahid Hasyim 3 (☎0328/21532; ①–③), about 200m away from its namesake, sits in a quieter road and has rooms of a similar standard. *Wisma Sumekar*, Jalan Trunojoyo 53 (☎0328/21502; ①–③), a block south of *Hotel Wijaya 1* towards the bus station, offers rooms with no fan and outside bathroom up to those with air-con and TV.

Maduran **food** long ago entered the mainstream Indonesian diet: sate, soto and *rujak* (hot spiced fruit salad) all hail from here. Whilst the local specialities of Maduran sate and soto seem very similar to the varieties found on the mainland, local people will tell you firmly they are vastly superior, owing to the inclusion of high-quality fish stock in the ingredients. In the evening on the Jalan Trunojoyo side of Taman Adipura Kota Sumenep, a small **night market** mushrooms, with a range of stalls selling plenty of tasty meals. If you prefer to eat inside, there are several pleasant **Padang** places on Jalan Trunojoyo: *Do'a Bundo* at 10a is clean and good value, as is *Megajus* next door. Slightly further away, *Rumah Makan 17 Agustus*, Jalan Raya P. Sudirman 34, has a limited rice and noodle menu, with some sate and plenty of good-value drinks. To get there, turn right at the crossroads just north of the Mesjid Agung.

The **post office** is at Jalan Urip Sumoharjo 5 (Mon–Thurs 8am–2pm, Fri 8–11am, Sat 8am–noon), 1km east of the town centre. The most convenient wartel is at Jalan Raya P. Sudirman 55 (daily 24hr) and the 24hr **telephone office** is 1km beyond the post office at Jalan Urip Sumoharjo 41. You can **exchange** cash and travellers' cheques at BCA, Jalan Trunojoyo 196.

AROUND SUMENEP
High on a hill near Sumenep lies the royal burial ground of **Asta Tinggi**. Get a becak to the bottom of the final hill, and you'll then have a thirty-minute walk to the top. The major royals are in the central walled area, with the minor relatives off to the sides. The most venerated graves belong to the second and third rajahs, and it's here that the faithful come to recite the Koran.

Whilst August and September are the months to visit Madura to see *kerapan sapi* (see box p.251), every Monday throughout the year in the late afternoon at **BLUTO**, 12km southwest of Sumenep, there is a practice session when farmers try out their cattle. It's all very informal and without the pomp and ceremony of the big races, but it's a good chance to get a flavour of what it's all about.

Lombang

The beach at **LOMBANG**, 43km northeast of Sumenep, is long and lovely, with white sand in all directions and a few warung located in the trees behind. There have been attempts to prettify the area – a red-tiled promenade with fancy lamp has been constructed – but it doesn't detract from the spot too badly. There are some direct minibuses from Sumenep at the weekends and on public holidays, when the beach is a favourite excursion spot for local people, but otherwise you'll have to get a minibus from Giling terminal in Sumenep to Legung; it goes through attractive, rolling countryside via the small villages of Gapura, Antulung and Batang Batang. From Legung it's 3km to the gate, where the beach track leaves the road, and then another kilometre to the beach – it may be possible to pick up a becak to the beach or you can negotiate with minibus drivers, although they'll still drop you at the gate. It's a pleasant walk down to the beach on a track lined with *cemara udang*, the elegant, feathery bush for which the area is famous.

On the track down to the beach, *Lombang Homestay* (①) offers very simple **accommodation** in the family house, with outside shared mandi. The owners will prepare simple local food by arrangement.

The islands to the east

Administratively attached to Sumenep, the 66 islands that spread east from here are well off the beaten track: it's over 240km from the mainland to **Sekala**, the furthest island. The islands are hugely varied: some have fabulous white-sand beaches, others thick vegetation right to the water's edge. The largest group is the **Kangean Islands**, a group of thirty, the smallest of which, Bungin, is a mere 50m by 35m. There are twice-weekly ferries from Kalianget to the Kangean Islands, which take cargo and passengers. The ferry docks at Batu Guluk, 10km from the main town of Arjasa, where the only official accommodation on the islands is at the *Pasanggrahan*, the government rest house which also takes travellers.

The north coast

The roads along the **north coast** have a few more bends than those along the south, but are well maintained and surfaced and present vehicles with few problems. There are no towns, just small villages beside the river estuaries that dot the coastline. With the dry climate and poor soil, the majority of people here earn their living from fishing. From Sumenep to Kamal along the north coast is 163km (along the south it is 170km, but along much faster roads). There is no direct public transport between these two towns along the north coast, but you can village-hop between them, changing at Pasongsongan, Ketapang, Tanjung Bumi and Bangkalan to get to Kamal.

Located 20km northwest of Sumenep, the pretty beach at **SLOPENG**, several kilometres long and backed by big dunes, spreads away from the small village. The most attractive part lies to the west of the village, where the bays are more sweeping and visitors and inhabitants fewer. The village specializes in *topeng* mask production: there are about ten makers in the area and buyers come from craft shops in Jakarta, Bali and Surabaya. Some are sold as new, while others are "antique" in the usual Indonesian sense of being made to look old. If you have your own transport and want to see the masks being made from local *bintaos* wood (it takes three days from start to finish and the skill is passed from father to son), then visit the hamlet of Tenggina, 4km south of Slopeng – you'll have to ask for the workshops and will probably be able to buy a mask for Rp30,000 if your bargaining skills are good.

The village of **PASONGSONGAN**, 10km west of Slopeng, has market day on Tuesday, when things get very packed and lively. It's an attractive village with red-roofed houses, and there's a good place to stay: the *Coconut Rest House* (①; ask for Pak Taufik) on the road down from the village to the new fish auction building on the coast. Accommodation is in the family house, which has two bedrooms with a shared bathroom, and a small verandah at the front where you can watch the world go by. There's a 24hr wartel and a post office in the village. Minibuses operate direct to Pasongsongan from Sumenep.

The largest north-coast settlement is **KETAPANG**, where the road from Sampang on the south coast meets the north coast. The only accommodation in the village is at *Pasanggrahan* (①), on the opposite side of the football field from the police station, in the centre of the village. It is very basic, and more used to government officials than tourists. The only "sight" is Air Terjun, a waterfall on the east side of the village, where you can swim.

One of the island centres of batik is **TANJUNG BUMI**, 25km west of Ketapang, where all the families are involved in the work, the skills passed from mother to daughter. The most time-consuming part of the enterprise is the waxing of cloth using tiny fine-tipped pourers, and you are more likely to see this than the more colourful dyeing operations. They don't get many visitors up here and people are generally happy to show you what they do. If you are interested in buying, you should be able to negotiate a sarong for around Rp40,000, which, given that it will have taken a month to make, is pretty fair.

From here it is 60km to Kamal via Bangkalan (see p.249); there are many prawn farms along the coast and a number of distinctive and opulent mosques under construction in the area.

West of Surabaya

The area to the **west of Surabaya** looks fairly enticing on the map: the volcanic masses of Gunung Lawu and Gunung Liman in the middle bounded by the northern plains and the low southern hills leading to the sparsely populated southern coastline. Although it has some spots of interest, most particularly **Sarangan**, **Pacitan** and **Candi Penataran**, in fact the area is dominated by large towns such as Madiun and Kediri, which are really only useful as transit points.

Sarangan and around

Located 40km west of Madiun in the Gunung Lawu area beyond the village of Magetan, the hill resort of **SARANGAN** is a popular destination, attracting visitors from all over Java to enjoy the pretty views of the lake, the upland climate and the clear air. Most local people come up for a weekend, and a couple of days is probably long enough for most visitors. It is easily accessible on public transport: take a bus from Madiun to Magetan and then a microlet to Sarangan. West from Magetan, the road begins to climb fairly steeply, with good views of the mountains ahead. As the road climbs it passes through small villages surrounded by vegetable fields, which begin to appear alongside the paddy. At Plaosan the hills get higher and more dramatic, beginning to tower on each side of the road as the village blends into Ngerang, with brilliant views back to the plains, Sarangan suddenly appearing on the hillside ahead. Alternative access is from Tawangmangu in Central Java (see p.210): regular minibuses ply this route. There is a **payment gate** at the entrance to the resort area (Rp1000 per person, Rp1500 per car, Rp1000 per motorbike).

Sarangan itself covers quite a small area, concentrated on the north and east shores of the small **crater lake**, Telaga Pasir, with a cluster of accommodation, restaurants and market stalls. It is at its liveliest at weekends and holidays: there are motorboats and peddle-boats for rental (Rp7500 per hour), you can take a horse ride (notice the little bags under their tails to collect the manure for local fields), walk around the lake and visit the local waterfalls of Tirtosari, Sarang Sari and Mojoseni – ask for directions locally.

There is a huge amount of **accommodation** in Sarangan, although there are fewer budget options than at Tawangmangu. *Telaga Mas Internasional Hotel* (☎ & fax 0351/98761; ④–⑥) is a gleaming red-roofed place on the lakeside at the luxury end of the market. *Hotel Abadi* (☎0351/98018; ④–⑥) is set up above the northern end of Telaga Pasir; all the rooms are large and there are pleasant views to the lake. *Sarangang Hotel* (☎0351/98022, fax 98203; ④–⑤), high on the hill overlooking the lake, is a well-established place, popular with tour groups, offering pleasant terraces and good views. *Nusa Indah*, Jalan Raya Telaga 171 (☎0351/98021, fax 98333; ③–④), in the centre of town, has a huge number of options and is close to the lake, with some rooms with terraces and views. It is white-tiled, functional and all rooms have hot water. A simpler alternative is the *Mayang Sari*, Jalan Raya 85 (☎0351/98068; ③); there are seats on the roof and hot water is available.

The 24hr **wartel** is at Jalan Telaga 65, the **post office** is on Jalan Cemoro Sewu (the main road that heads through the resort and on to Tawangmangu), as is the **tourist office** (☎0351/98401). Sarangan has no shortage of **places to eat**, one of the simplest and most pleasant being the *Rumah Makan Rejeki*, with a limited menu of inexpensive local food and a small verandah: it is just opposite the *Telaga Mas Internasional Hotel* on the road to the lake.

Pacitan

The small coastal town of **PACITAN**, with its wonderful nearby beaches, is located 119km southeast of Solo. There are some direct buses from Solo; otherwise change at Wonogiri. Alternatively, access is from Ponorogo, which typically takes two to three hours on the invariably packed buses.

Pacitan is a small, quiet, pleasant little town, with an attractive, good-sized alun-alun, with animal statues, well laid-out flowerbeds and pretty shrubs. Jalan A. Yani runs along the south side, with the bus terminal 1km to the south along Jalan Gatot Subroto, which leads southwest from the eastern end of Jalan A. Yani. If you want **accommodation** in town rather than by the beach, then by far the best option is *Srikandi*, Jalan A. Yani 67 (☎0357/81252; ③–④), a new, gleaming place with good rooms, located in two buildings: all have TV, attached mandi, either fan or air-con, and fine views in all directions. The attached restaurant, set back from the main road to avoid the traffic noise, has a substantial menu of chicken, seafood, Indonesian, Chinese and Western dishes, and plenty of vegetarian options.

The **tourist office** is at Jalan Letjen Suprapto 4 (Mon–Thurs 7am–3pm, Fri 7am–noon, Sat 7am–1pm; ☎0357/884535), the 24hr **Telkom** office at Jalan A. Yani 65 and there's a 24hr wartel attached to *Hotel Pacitan*. You can **exchange** money at: BRI, Jalan A. Yani 12; Bank Danamon, Jalan Raya P. Sudirman 143a; and BNI, Jalan Raya P. Sudirman 142. The **post office** is at Jalan Ronggowarsito 11.

The main **beach**, Pantai Teleng Ria (admission Rp300, car Rp500, motorbike Rp300), lies 4km southwest of town. Either hire a becak directly from town or one of the microlets that ply the route at weekends and on holidays, or take a westbound bus and get off where the beach road joins the main road, about 3km west of the town: it's 1km down to the beach from here. The long and curving white-sand bay has forested headlands at either end and attractive hills rising up behind. It's a lovely spot, but not always safe for swimming: take local advice and be careful. *Happy Bay Beach Bungalows* (☎0357/81474; ③), the only **accommodation** on the coast, just on the left at the end of the road to the beach, provides rooms or bungalows with a small verandah attached and a great upstairs balcony. The attached restaurant provides a limited menu of Western, Indonesian and seafood options. The beach can be very busy at weekends and during holidays when the warung open up for business, but the rest of the time it is totally peaceful. There is a swimming pool on the road down to the beach (8am–5pm; Rp500), plus a small children's play area.

Blitar and around

Probably founded in the ninth century and with a current population around 120,000, **BLITAR**, southwest of the Arjuna mountains, is rather ignored by Western tourists – it's a small, busy town and **Candi Panataran** is a significant draw, but there's little else to lure tourists. It is, however, much visited by Indonesians, who come to visit the mausoleum of President Sukarno, the country's first president.

The town centres on the **alun-alun**, where the government offices and Mesjid Agung are located. Jalan Merdeka runs along the south side of the square and continues west for about 1km as the main shopping street, until it makes a sharp left and becomes Jalan Mawar. Another smaller turning, Jalan Kerantil, continues straight on at this bend to the market area, Pasar Legi, and then a couple of hundred metres further to the bus terminal. There are no metered taxis, but plenty of becak and ojek; a trip across town will cost Rp1500–2000.

Situated on Jalan Slamet Riyadi, a couple of kilometres northeast of the centre of town on the way to Candi Panataran, **Sukarno's Mausoleum**, *Makam Bung Karno* (daily 8am–5pm; free), is a huge and imposing monument. The entrance is through a large, dark grey split gate, the graves inside a glass building with a three-tiered roof. Sukarno is in the centre with his parents on either side. Inside it's a very Indonesian scene, with elderly people intoning prayers and young visitors posing for photographs. Following his overthrow in May 1967, Sukarno retired to Bogor, where he remained until he died in 1970. He was buried on this site, next to his mother, in the (clearly misplaced) hope of the government of the time that such an obscure location would not become a pilgrimage site.

Not easy to find even when you are on top of it, **Sukarno's Museum**, Jalan Sultan Agung 59 (daily 6.30am–6pm), has no sign and is not obviously open: you need to ring for admission. Clearly a political embarrassment to the present government – the opposition leader Megawati Sukarnoputri is Sukarno's daughter – the house was the home of Sukarno's parents and is full of family pictures, photographs of world leaders (including JFK), as well as personal mementos.

Candi Panataran

Situated 10km north of Blitar, **Candi Panataran** (daily 7am–5pm; admission by contribution) sits on the lower slopes of Gunung Kelod (1731m); bright-yellow bemos ply directly from town. Dedicated to Shiva, it's famous as the largest temple complex in East Java, but is a pleasant rather than grand historical site, the grounds dotted with attractive statues. Nothing in the complex is complete and, although with a bit of imagination you can get some idea of the original 300m by 100m site, it has nothing to rival great Central Javan monuments, in scale or interest.

Dating back to the end of the twelfth century, the temple was continuously expanded, and much of what is visible today was built during the Majapahit times, when it was very prominent, visited several times by King Hayam Wuruk and Gajah Made. The area is divided into three major courtyards. The outer courtyard has the bases of what would have been large and imposing assembly halls (pendopo), one carved and the other not. At the back of this courtyard, discernible by red marks on the ground, is the Dated Temple, with the inscription "1369", a worn Ganesh inside and a very eroded Bhoma over the door. The middle courtyard houses the roofless Naga Temple, named because of the snakes carved around it: it is thought that originally this would have supported a Balinese-style multi-tiered, wood-and-thatch *meru*. The main temple (built in 1347) would have been in the third and inner courtyard, although all that now remains are the lower terraces of what must once have been a very impressive building. There are some very well-carved reliefs, including circular tablets with animal carvings and images from the *Ramayana* epic. The highly eroded stone to the side of the main structure carries the earliest inscription on the site, "1197". At the back right-hand corner of the complex, a short path leads about 200m down to an attractive pool dating from 1415.

Practicalities

The best **accommodation** in Blitar is at *Sri Lestari*, Jalan Merdeka 87 (☎0342/81766, fax 81763; ②–⑥). The garden is pleasant, there's a high-ceilinged lounge at the rear, and a range of rooms to suit all budgets. To get there, exit the bus terminal to Jalan Kerantil and walk up Jalan Merdeka: the hotel is on the right. Less expensive, *Penginapan Aman*, Jalan Merdeka 130 (no phone; ①), has very basic rooms with unattached bathroom and no fans – it stretches back from the road so some rooms are fairly quiet.

There is a choice of **places to eat** in town, from a pleasant night market at the northern end of Jalan Mawar just near the Jalan Kerantil junction to the more formal *Ramayana*, Jalan Merdeka 63–65, with a huge range of Chinese meals and a smaller choice of Indonesian ones. The restaurant at *Sri Lestari* is moderate to expensive with Indonesian, Chinese and Western dishes; portions are large and attractively presented. *Roti Orion*, Jalan Merdeka 113, sells sweet breads and muffins.

For **foreign exchange**, BNI, Jalan Kenanga 9, can change only cash, not travellers' cheques. The **post office** is at Jalan Mastrip 87 (Mon–Thurs 8am–2pm, Fri 8–11am, Sat 8am–1pm), the **Telkom** office at Jalan Jend A. Yani 10.

Moving on, in addition to services from the terminal, you can take the luxurious **minibus** services provided by Rosalia Indah, Jalan Mayang 45 (☎0342/82149), or Ranta, Jalan Mayang 47 (☎0342/82583), which are close to the terminal, include a hotel pick-up in the price and have daily services to Surabaya, Solo and Jogyakarta. They also sell long-distance bus tickets but these may well not be direct. The **train station** is directly south of *Sri Lestari Hotel*: go down Jalan Kenanga, which leads from Jalan Merdeka in the middle of the south side of the alun-alun (*Rendy's* is on the corner), and at the bottom turn right and then left at the post office. There are frequent trains to Surabaya, via Kediri and Kertosono and via Malang and Bangil.

Malang and around

The second largest city in East Java, **MALANG**, 90km south of Surabaya, is a busy city with a population in excess of 600,000. Situated at an altitude of 450m and circled by attractive volcanoes, it is cool, tree-lined and much more tourist-friendly in all respects than Surabaya. The city has a reputation similar to Bandung in West Java (see pp.126–136) as a centre for higher education and learning, with an enormous number of schools and colleges attracting students from all over Indonesia; it is said that up to half the population is made up of students. Though there are no real rock-bottom places to stay, value for money is far better than in Surabaya.

Outside the city, the temple remains of **Candi Singosari** and **Candi Jawi** offer an insight into the ancient kingdoms of the area, **Taman Candra Wilwatika** at Pandaan stages regular dance performances in the dry season, and the **Bogor Botanic Gardens** at Purwodadi, spreading onto the lower slopes of Gunung Arjuna, are a peaceful escape. Further afield, the **hill resorts** of Batu and Selecta are great escapes from the lowland heat, while the **beaches** along the south coast make for a long trip from Malang, but provide stunning scenery, idyllic offshore islands and a sense of being well off the tourist trail.

Some history

Stone inscriptions found at Dinoyo, a suburb of Malang, suggest the area has been inhabited for over 1200 years. A king called Gajayana ruled the **Kanjuruhan kingdom** from Malang, which is believed to have been founded on November 28, 760. It was also the centre of the thirteenth-century **Singosari kingdom**, whose legacy is visible in the temples at Singosari (see p.263) and Prigen (see p.264). It remained significant in Majapahit times, and important ministers were always stationed in the area, a prominence that continued into the time of the Mataram kingdom. Used as a refuge by the defeated Surapati following the Third Javanese War (1746–1757), the area around the city suited the rebel purposes as it was inaccessible and difficult to search. Various VOC campaigns finally led to the defeat of the final Surapati threat in 1777, but by that time the successive campaigns against the rebels had caused pretty much the entire population to flee the area.

Malang reached its current prominence only in the last 130 years, following the European enthusiasm to establish rubber, coffee and cocoa **plantations** in the area as well as the government sugar ones. As the European population grew, Malang developed, with fine, distinctive bungalows on tree-lined avenues and vacation houses in attractive resorts further afield. Merdeka Square, on the south side of Sungai Brantas, was built in 1882, and circular Tugu Park on the north side developed as an administrative centre in 1914, when a big colonial residential area was also developed to the northwest. Since World War II and Independence, cigarettes have been a major local employer (Bentoel are based here), with education the other main focus of activity.

Arrival, city transport, orientation and information

The Arjosari **bus terminal**, 7km northeast of the city centre on Jalan Ratu Intan, connects with frequent bemos to the city; the **city bemos** (4am–11pm; flat fare Rp350) are blue. City routes run between two of the three Malang bus terminals and are labelled by the two letters of the relevant terminals. "A" refers to Arjosari, "G" is Gadang, 5km south of the city centre on Jalan Kolonel Soegiono, and "L" is for Landung Sari on Jalan Majen Haryono, 6km northwest of the city centre. So, for example, LA operates between Landung Sari and Arjosari. It is worth noting that route GA and AG are not the same route – this is not a problem if you are going to the terminals, but it can be if you're heading to an intermediate point.

The city's **commercial centre** is the alun-alun to the south of Sungai Brantas, with the main shopping and market area along or near Jalan Agus Salim, which runs off the south side. Jalan Mojopahit runs across Sungai Brantas and links this commercial sector with the Tugu area to the north, in which most government offices are located; the **train station** is a short walk from here. Also heading north from the alun-alun is Jalan Jend Basuki Rachmat, which, changing its name several times on the way, eventually leads to the Arjosari terminal.

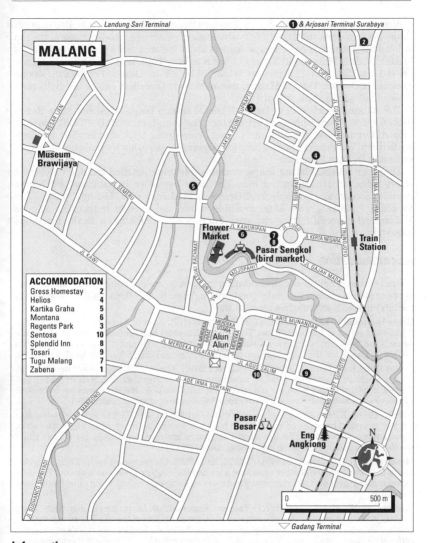

Information

There are several **tourist offices** in Malang. The best is a bit tucked away at Jalan Semeru 4 (Mon–Sat 9am–5pm, Sun 9am–1pm; ☎0341/366852, fax 367637) in a small shop next to *Dunkin' Donuts*, operated by the local members of the Indonesian Guides Association. They have plenty of leaflets and reference books on the whole region, and the knowledgeable staff book minibus tickets, operate tours (see "Listings" p.263), advise on hotels and restaurants, rent out bicycles (Rp5000 a day), motorcycles (Rp15,000) and cars (Rp150,000 including driver and petrol), and can find you a **licensed guide** (Rp50,000 per day). They can also book white-water rafting (see p.263 for more details).

Also convenient is the East Java Tourist Office, Jalan Jend Basuki Rachmat 6h (Mon–Fri 8am–2pm; ☎0341/323966), which operates out of a wooden kiosk at the top of Jalan Mojopahit and has a few pamphlets about the area and a photocopied map of Malang. Malang Municipality Tourist Office is at Jalan Tugu 1a (Mon–Thurs 9am–1pm, Fri 9–11am, Sat 9am–12.30pm; ☎0341/327661); it's in Dewan Perwakilan Rakyat Kotamadya Daerah, Tigat II Malang, the municipal offices just east of the Balai Kota (Town Hall) on the south side of Tugu.

The **national park office**, Taman Nasional Bromo-Tengger-Semeru, Jalan Raden Intan 6 (Mon–Thurs 8am–2pm, Fri 8–11am, Sat 8am–1pm; ☎0341/491828), close to Arjosari terminal, has general leaflets about Bromo and a booklet in English on climbing Semeru. You can get a permit here for climbing Semeru, but it's probably more convenient to buy it in Ranu Pane (see p.270).

There are several Malang **maps** available. Most are detailed but don't include a street index, so are of limited use. The most extensive is published by Kariya Pembina Swijaya and available from Gramedia in Malang (see "Listings" p.262). The *Surabaya Periplus Travel Map*, available inside and outside Indonesia, includes Malang and is useful for the city area, but it doesn't reach as far as the three bus terminals.

Accommodation

There is some excellent **accommodation** in Malang, and, although there are no really cheap places, value is generally good, which (allied to the climate and atmosphere of the city) makes it an attractive place to stay.

Gress Homestay, Jl Kahayan 6 (☎0341/491386, fax 474407). A GA or AL bemo will drop you off at Jl Mahakan; get off at Apotik Mahakan. This is a real homestay with spotless rooms, attached bathroom (some hot-water) and fan in an attractive family house with plenty of greenery. There's a kitchen for guests, and the lady owner can help you arrange trekking, fishing and local tours. ③–④.

Helios Hotel, Jl Pattimura 37 (☎0341/362741, fax 353797). The best budget choice in the city: clean rooms, all with large verandahs, lead off an attractive, lush courtyard garden. Staff are knowledgeable and helpful; there are tours, car and motorcycle rental available; and bus tickets can be booked. Cheaper rooms have shared mandi; more expensive ones have attached mandi. ②–③.

Kartika Graha, Jl Jaksa Agung Suprapto 17 (☎0341/361900, fax 361911). The light, airy lobby area has four storeys of balconies on one side and huge windows on the other, and a 24hr coffee shop. There are two pools (Rp3000 for non-guests) and rooms are very comfortable. If you can't afford the *Hotel Tugu Malang*, this is the next best option. ④–⑤.

Montana Hotel, Jl Kahuripan 9 (☎0341/362751, fax 327620). Conveniently close to Tugu. All rooms have a hot-water bath; the cheaper ones have a fan and the more expensive ones air-con. The communal areas are light with lots of greenery and there's a lobby coffee shop. Good value for this location. ④–⑤.

Regents Park Hotel (aka **Hotel Taman Regents**), Jl Jaksa Agung Suprapto 12–16 (☎0341/363388, fax 362966). A multi-storey hotel on the north side of the city. The rooms are very comfortable, with hot tub, air-con and good views. The lobby is a bit dark, but there's an attractive coffee shop plus a pleasant pool (non-guests can use this for Rp7500). Occasional special discounts make it a good deal at this end of the market. ⑧–⑨.

Hotel Sentosa, Jl K.H. Agus Salim 24 (☎0341/366889, fax 367098). In the middle of the main shopping area, but surprisingly quiet. The plain but spotless lower-end rooms have outside bathrooms while the top ones have hot water and air-con. ③–④.

Hotel Splendid Inn, Jl Mojopahit 4 (☎0341/366860, fax 363618). All rooms have hot-water bathrooms and there is a small pool; this is an old-fashioned, pleasant maze of a place. Lower-end rooms have fans; upper-end ones, air-con. ④.

Hotel Tosari, Jl K.H. Ahmad Dahlan 31 (☎0341/326945, fax 367098). In a central location with clean, tiled rooms and seats in the corridors outside the rooms. Cheaper rooms have shared bathroom while the most expensive ones have an attached bathroom and hot water. ②–④.

Hotel Tugu Malang, Jl Tugu 3 (☎0341/363891, fax 362747; email *malang@tuguhotels.com*). This is the most luxurious hotel in Malang, with a lovely atmosphere; it has won awards and features regularly in the travel pages of newspapers. Attractive, individually furnished rooms (those facing inwards are quieter), a pool in a lush courtyard, antiques and art displays everywhere and a business centre. ⑨.

Zabena Hotel, Jl Jaksa Agung Suprato 60a (☎0341/361772, fax 324560). A bit tucked away behind Apotik Raja Bally Farma: if you're coming from Arjosari on bemo GA, ask to be put off at Istana Buah, the fruit shop nearby (if you get to *Dunkin' Donuts* you've gone too far). This is a new, spotless place – all rooms have private shower and the more expensive ones have hot water and TV. When the planned roof garden is complete, it will feel more homely. They organize tours, car and motorcycle rental, and bus tickets can be booked. ③.

The City

There's no shortage of things to look at in Malang. The most attractive and evocative **colonial area** is Jalan Ijen, with renovated bungalows in wide, palm-lined boulevards. It's a rich and refined area, with fabulous iron railings that guard the privacy of the wealthy of the city. To get there, take bemo GL (which goes along Jalan Ijen), or MM (along Jalan Kawi nearby). **Museum Brawijaya**, Jalan Ijen 25a (daily 8am–2pm; donation), is a military museum fronted by tanks, guns and amphibious vehicles. Only the enthusiast will find much of interest inside, though it's full of paintings and photographs of military events and past commanders, cases of guns of every type, memorabilia and old maps of Malang. Altogether the museum is a rather chilling celebration of Indonesian military might, including artefacts connected with the suppression of Irian Jaya. In the courtyard at the back is a Dutch colonial train and the canoe with which the famous local hero Joko Tole attacked the Dutch in Madura in 1847.

The circular park at Jalan Tugu, fifteen minutes' walk from the city centre on Medan Mereka, was also laid out by the Dutch, with the Balai Kota (Town Hall) on one side; the **Independence monument** in the centre has replaced the original fountain. It's a ten-minute walk from here along Jalan Mojopahit, across Sungai Brantas (a rather narrow, uninspiring waterway at this point) up to the alun-alun. A fascinating **bird market** can be found in the Pasar Sengkol/Jalan Brawijaya area; head down towards the river from Jalan Mojopahit on the south side of the river. The number and variety of birds is amazing and there are brilliantly carved wooden cages on sale too. Birds change hands for Rp2–3 million for good singers, and up to Rp7 million for exceptional ones – the black grasshoppers on sale are for feeding them. Local bird-singing competitions are held every two to three months; inquire at the tourist office if you're interested. The **flower market** is slightly further north of the bird market – you can walk to it from Jalan Brawijaya. It ranges down the riverbank of Sungai Brantas and is more like a nursery, with huge amounts of shrubs and garden plants on offer, and some cut flowers in the sheds at the bottom.

A Chinese temple, **Eng Ankiong**, Jalan Laksamana Martadinata 3, is at the junction of that road with Jalan Zainel Zakse, Jalan Pasar Baru and Jalan Jend Gatot Suproto. It's an imposing, new temple with a marble-tiled floor and a splendid gateway, some lovely gold altar-fronts, plenty of detailed and dramatic sculpted dragons curling around columns and a lily pond to the right of the main temple with a dramatic rock island in the centre. Don't miss the temple behind the main shrine, where there are two rows of beautifully and evocatively carved modern wooden statues of ancient Chinese sages.

Eating, drinking and entertainment

Performances of **traditional dance** and **gamelan** are held at Senaputra (Sun 11am except during Ramadan; Rp1100). During the week it's possible to see the students practising and you may be lucky to see the traditional dances – *basakalan*, a welcoming dance, and the Malangan masked dance, which tells the *Panji* stories. The only **disco** in Malang is at the *Kartika Graha Hotel* (daily 10pm–2am; Rp10,000); on some evenings women get in free.

Eating

There is an excellent **night market** on Medan Merdeka on Saturday evenings and every night during Ramadan, which turns the whole of the square into a bustling tent city with a terrific range of food. For more formal dining there are plenty of choices.

Amsterdam Restaurant, Jl Terusan Kawi 2. On a busy corner with tables inside and out, there is a huge menu with steak as the speciality but also many Indonesian staples. Also sandwiches, hot dogs, salads, French fries, seafood and Chinese food. Moderate to expensive.

Asri Dua, Jl Brig Jen Slamet Riadi 14. Has a small menu of good-value Indonesian and Chinese food plus steak and sandwiches in clean, attractive surroundings.

Dunkin' Donuts, at Ramayana Centre, Jl Merdeka Timur. The usual sweet and savoury choices in this air-con chain.

Hemat Lezat, Jl Trunojoyo 19a. Serving traditional Indonesian food, with a big menu of rice, soup and noodle options. This is one of a trio of good-value inexpensive places, convenient if you are staying in *Helios Hotel*. *Soto Madura* at no. 20 is nearby and serves sate and soup, whilst *Disiko Jaya* at no. 14 has Padang food.

Kole Kole, Jl Jend Basuki Rachmat 97a. Air-con, attractive and clean with pleasant music and no TV, this is a good place for a quiet meal in the moderate to expensive range, with Indonesian, Western and Chinese options.

Melati Pavilion, *Hotel Tugu Malang*, Jl Tugu 3. Probably the most luxurious dining in Malang: the restaurant is beside the pool in a leafy courtyard. There is a huge menu of expensive steaks, with plenty of other Western, Indonesian, Chinese, Japanese and Dutch dishes. It's a lovely, evocative place, part of an excellent hotel, and well worth a splurge if your budget runs to it.

Rindu, Jl K.H. Agus Salim 29. Centrally located Padang restaurant with a big selection of attractively prepared and displayed food.

Toko Oen, Jl Jend Basuki Rachmat 5. This has been a restaurant and ice-cream parlour since 1930 and is a Malang institution, particularly favoured by Dutch visitors, many coming to see where their ancestors ate. The menu is substantial, with sandwiches, salads, steaks, seafood and Chinese food, all at moderate prices. The room has high ceilings, net curtains, plenty of dark-wood and cane chairs, a bay window looking across to *McDonald's* across the road and some stained glass. The grandeur is decided faded, however, and whilst the waiters do tog up in uniforms in the evenings, during the day they look pretty ordinary.

Tugu Kafé Dan Roti, Jl Kahuripan 3. Attached to *Hotel Tugu Malang*. The café is well decorated and furnished and has an excellent range of moderately priced sweet breads, cakes and savouries, and customers can order anything from the *Melati Pavilion* menu (see above). The downside is that the road is very noisy – this place looks idyllic, but certainly doesn't sound it.

Listings

Airline offices Garuda, Jl Merdeka Timur 4 (☎0341/369494, fax 369656); Merpati, *Kartika Graha*, Jl Jaksa Agung Suprapto 17 (☎0341/361909, fax 354745).

Banks All the big banks have large branches in Malang. The following are convenient for foreign exchange: Bank Bumi Daya, Jl Merdeka Barat 1; BNI, Jl Jend Basuki Rachmat 75–77; and BCA, Jl Jend Basuki Rachmat 70–74 (on the corner of Jl Kahuripan).

Bookshops Gramedia, Jl Jend Basuki Rachmat 3, has the best choice, with a good range of imported English books, travel guides and maps. An alternative is Toko Sari Agung, Jl Jend Basuki Rachmat 2a, which has three floors but a smaller choice of English books. Jl Mojopahit, just south of the bridge across Sungai Brantas, is lined with secondhand bookshops. Most are Indonesian and cater for the large local student population, but there are quite a few English books and ageing periodicals if you rummage.

Buses Minibuses are available between Malang and Surabaya, Solo, Jogyakarta, and Semarang; expect to pay around three times the express bus price. Several places also sell night-bus tickets which include a hotel pick-up – you'll pay slightly more than if you book directly, but if you have piles of luggage it can be helpful. Agents are: *Helios Hotel*, Jl Pattimura 37 (☎0341/362741, fax 353797); Haryono, Jl Kahuripan 22 (☎0341/367500), who can book Pelni and flight tickets; Tuju Transport, Jl Kertanegara 5 (☎0341/368363), who also book Pelni and flight tickets; Toko Oen

Travel Service, Jl Jend Basuki Rachmat 5 (☎0341/364052, fax 369497), which is next to the restaurant; Juwita, Jl K.H. Agus Salim 11 (☎0341/362008); and Harapan Transport, Jl Surapati 42 (☎0341/353089), close to *Helios Hotel*.

Car and motorbike rental There are no official agencies, so inquire at your accommodation. *Helios Hotel* has motorcycles for Rp15,000 without insurance. Guests leave a photocopy of their passport as security and people not staying at the hotel must leave their actual passport. Car rental from *Helios Hotel* is Rp120,000 per day inclusive of driver and petrol.

Hospital Rumah Sakit Umum Daerah Dr Saifal Anwar, Jl Jaksa Agung Suprapto 2 (☎0341/366242); Rumah Sakit Umum Lavalette, Jl W.R. Supratman 10 (☎0341/362960).

Immigration office Jl Jend A. Yani Utara (☎0341/491039).

National park office, Taman Nasional Bromo Tengger Semeru, Jl Raden Intan 6 (Mon–Thurs 8am–2pm, Fri 8–11am, Sat 8am–1pm; ☎0341/491828).

Pharmacy Kima Farma 53, Jl Kawi 22a (☎0341/326665), is large, well-stocked and open 24hr.

Post office Jalan Merdeka Selatan 5. Public Internet access via eight terminals (Rp1500 for the first 15min, then Rp100 per min). More public Internet terminals can be found at Auka Warung Internet at Jalan Surapati 40 (daily 9am–9pm; ☎0341/32652; Rp1800 for the first 15min, Rp600 for the next 5min and Rp7000 per hour). There's a postal and bus-ticket agent at Jalan Surapati 42 (daily 6.30am–8.30pm).

Shopping There are several modern shopping centres in Malang, most of them along Jl K.H. Agus Salim – they're not as glossy as the Surabaya ones, but are well stocked. If you are looking for souvenirs, Sarinah Department Store & Hero Supermarket, Jl Jend Basuki Rachmat, has a second-floor gift shop selling craft items from both Bali and Java. There's an excellent range of goods, from Rp2000 for small batik items and Rp20,000 for batik cotton sarongs, up to Rp500,000 for silk. There are also woodcarvings in both traditional and modern styles, baskets, boxes, dolls and puppets. Batik Keris, Komplek Pertokoan Ria, Jl Merdeka Timur 2d/e is just opposite the Mitra Shopping Centre and comprises five floors of brilliant textiles and gift items, with sarongs from Rp20,000 to more than Rp500,000 for pure silk sarong and scarf sets, a huge range of textiles sold by the metre and many ready-made items of clothing. There are also some wood and leather gift items. Pasar Besar, Jl Kyai Tamin, occupies a whole city block and contains all the stalls, range of goods and excitement usual in excellent Indonesia market areas. Attached to this is the Matahari department store, the best in town, with a food court, supermarket and *KFC*.

Tours There are several places in Malang that can arrange tours. Typically, day tours will include some sights in Malang and the local temples of Jago, Kidal, Singosari or the southern beaches. *Helios Hotel* offers a large range aimed at backpackers with a considerable reduction in the per-person price if more than five people go on the same trip. The tourist office run by local members of the Indonesian Guides Association, Jl Semeru 4 (☎0341/366852, fax 367637), has a huge range of guided tours, from a 3hr Malang city tour (Rp40,000 per person for two people, Rp20,000 per person for five or six people), through day tours to Balekambang, Batu, Kawi, Blitar or Bromo (Rp50,000–90,000 per person for two people, Rp30,000–60,000 if there are five or six people), up to a two-day trip to Bromo and the Ijen Plateau (Rp175,000 per person for two people, Rp120,000 per person for five or six people).

White-water rafting PT Alfaria Romea, Jl Kawi 23 (☎0341/369642, fax 369643); you have to get yourself to Lumajang: buses run hourly from Gadang terminal in Malang 6am–9pm (2–3hr; US$60 per-person). You can also book through the tourist office at Jl Semeru 4 (☎0341/366852, fax 367637).

Between Malang and Surabaya

There are plenty of local sights that are on or very close to the main Malang–Surabaya road, most of them easily reached from either place. **Candi Singosari** (sometimes known as Ken Dedes Temple after the wife of Ken Angrok, the founder of the Singosari kingdom) is on Jalan Kertanegara, just 300m to the west of the main road in **SINGOSARI**, 12km north of Malang. The bright-green bemo (LA) operates from Arjosari to Lawang via Singosari. The turning to the temple is just on the Malang side of BCA bank in Singosari and is marked by a large black gate – plenty of becak wait here to ferry visitors.

It is almost certain that the area was the capital of the powerful Singosari kingdom from 1222 until 1292. The **temple** was built in the early 1300s in memory of Kertanegara, the last king of Singosari, who died in 1292. His kingdom flourished while Kublai Khan ruled over China; Kublai Khan demanded tribute from all the rulers in Asia and sent a messenger to Kertanagara's court. The king sent his reply back to China, carved in the forehead of the messenger. Just as Kublai Khan was getting ready to send armed retaliation, Kertanagara and much of the court was ambushed and murdered by soldiers of neighbouring kingdoms.

The temple itself is tall and grand, built on a central platform with a soaring roof. It seems that it was never completed: the carving was carried out from the top down and the bottom parts are bare. Niches are carved in the sides of the temple but most are empty, apart from the statue in the south side thought to represent Agastya, who was also known as Bhatara Guru, an ancient sage said to have arrived in Java walking on water. There are plenty of assorted figures in the grounds but they are very eroded, the really fascinating statues being the ferocious **Arca Dwarapala**, a pair of four-metre-high rotund and goggle-eyed guardians who possibly guarded the entrance to the long-vanished palace of Singosari; they are on either side of the road 200m further west from the crossroads, just beyond the temple entrance.

At **PURWODADI**, 21km north of Malang, **Kebun Raya Purwodadi** (daily 7am–4pm; Rp1000, car Rp400, motorcycle Rp200) has an entrance right beside the road. It's an outpost of the Bogor Botanic Gardens (see p.119) and is a lovely spot: peaceful, quiet and well maintained, spreading across the lower slopes of Gunung Arjuna.

At **PANDAAN**, midway between Surabaya and Malang, about 45km from each, the open-air amphitheatre, **Taman Candra Wilwatika**, is 2km from the town centre towards Tretes and hosts fortnightly dance-dramas in the dry season (July–Nov). Admission is free; inquire at the tourist offices in Surabaya for a schedule, or at the travel agents there if you want to arrange an all-inclusive tour.

Built in the thirteenth century to commemorate Kertanagara, **Candi Jawi** is located in the village of **PRIGEN**, 4km west of Pandaan on the road to Tretes. It is one of the most complete of the local temples and has been well restored. It soars 17m high; the brick moat surrounding it is still visible; and the backdrop of the mountains, especially Gunung Penanggungan, is lovely. It's thought that the temple once housed statues of both Shiva and Buddha, as the king believed there to be a strong connection between Shivaism and Buddhism. Next to the temple, the Candi Art Shop, Jalan Raya Candi Jawi 25, has loads of stuff to browse through, including old money, ceramics, kris, textiles and pictures.

The Batu area

The twin hill resorts of Batu and Selecta are close together on the southern slopes of Gunung Welirang and Gunung Arjuna, just over 20km west of Malang. Previously favoured **hill resorts** of the Dutch, they are now extremely popular with visitors from Malang and Surabaya, the most wealthy of whom own villas in and around the villages; for a few cool days up in the mountains, out of the noise and heat of the cities, they are well worth a trip. The area is easily accessible on public transport as pale-purple bemos ply from Landung Sari terminal in Malang to Batu, and plenty of buses pass through the resort.

The centre of **BATU** is the large alun-alun with an incongruous central statue of a glossy apple perched on top of a cabbage – all facilities for visitors are close by. The local shopping centre, Plaza Batu, is on the north side opposite Mesjid Besar An Nuur. The post office can be found at Jalan Raya P. Sudirman 87, the BCA bank and Telkom office on Jalan A. Yani, and there's a 24hr wartel to the right of Plaza Batu. *Pelangi*

Restaurant, Jalan Raya P. Sudirman 7, is a good, clean, inexpensive **eating place**, with an Indonesian, Chinese and East Javan menu and tables and chairs at the front or low sitting areas behind. The more exotic *Warung Bethania* on Jalan Diponegoro has a woodland theme.

The small and delightful village of **SONGGORITI** is down in the valley off the main road west from Batu; lime-green bemo route B operates from Batu terminal to Songgoriti. There's a pleasant public swimming pool in the village, Tirta Nirwana (daily 7am–5pm; Rp2000), and non-residents can pay to use the pool at *Hotel Air Panas Alam Songgoriti* (Rp2500). Jalan Arumdalu has plenty of warung offering inexpensive local food.

Six kilometres north of Batu, **SELECTA** is higher (at 1150m) and slightly quieter than Batu, but has little character. The main attraction in Selecta is the **Taman Rekreasi** (7am–5pm; Rp3150), which has accommodation (see p.266), and was established by the Dutch in 1930, burnt to the ground in 1947 during the fighting for Independence, and since restored. There's a lovely swimming pool here, with an attractive garden. The **wartel** in Selecta is open from 7am until 10pm.

Heading **west from Batu**, the road climbs up, finally through countryside, to a large plain and the neighbouring villages of Pandesari and Pujon, where vegetable fields and nurseries line the road. All of the roads beyond Batu have fine views of the whole area. The small village of Sepalu is marked by a cow monument on the road; take the turning here for the one-kilometre road to the gateway to **Coban Rondo waterfall** (daily 7am–5pm; Rp2000, car Rp1000, motorcycle Rp500), but beware that it's another 4km to the waterfall itself; it's an attractive road with bamboo stands and some good views of the surrounding countryside across Songgoriti, Batu and Arjuna. There's a **campsite** about 2km from the gate (Rp2500 per tent per night; inquire at the ticket office) and the **Arena Gajah** (Elephant Arena), where three Sumatran elephants (from the elephant training school at Way Kambas national park in Sumatra; see p.457) give displays on Sundays. From the parking area it's 200m on a tiled pathway to the impressive waterfall, a thirty-metre drop down a horseshoe-shaped cliff. There is also a small children's swimming pool (Rp500).

Accommodation

Much of the **accommodation** in the area is aimed at well-heeled Indonesians who come up to the hills for a cool weekend or holiday – the value isn't brilliant, but on quiet weekdays a discount is often a possibility. If you're in a group, you could consider renting a **villa**, one of the many grand houses that dot the hillside. Local touts will approach you as soon as you arrive, and you should bargain hard.

BATU

Hotel Kartika Wijaya, Jl Panglima Sudirman 127 (☎0341/592600, fax 591004). Acknowledged as one of the best in the area. Although it looks grand from the outside, the rooms are ordinary and the whole lot is due for renovation. However, any problems are made up for by the excellent pool and its attractive surroundings and the nearby coffee shop. ⑥–⑦.

Hotel Kawi, Jl Panglima Sudirman 19 (☎0341/591139). Decent travellers' losmen – rooms are very basic and there are small verandahs facing across a small garden area. It isn't easy to find; look out for Depot Kawi and Salon Kawi about 200m to the north of the town centre. ②.

Hotel Metropole, Jl Panglima Sudirman 93 (☎0341/591758, fax 595456). One of the better-value places towards the top of the market: the rooms are comfortable and there's an attractive lobby, coffee shop, pool and children's play area. ⑤–⑥.

Perdana Hotel, Jl Panglima Sudirman 101 (☎0341/591104, fax 591727). Block-built and with no outstanding features, but better value than many similar places in town. ③.

Permata Hijau, Jl Panglima Sudirman 104 (☎0341/594856). On the right heading north from town, opposite the *Hotel Metropole*; the spotless tiled rooms have big verandahs looking out onto a large rather unkempt garden. In this area of inflated prices it's good value. ③–④.

SONGGORITI

Hotel Air Panas Alam Songgoriti, Jl Raya Songgoriti 51 (☎&fax 0341/593553). This is the most upmarket option in the village, spread over two sites several hundred metres apart. The hotel is well maintained and attractive, and all rooms have water supplied by the local hot spring believed to have curative value; those at the main site are adobe-style, and there are cottages at the upper site, where the swimming pool (admission Rp2500 for non-guests) is located. Significant discounts are available outside weekends and holidays. ⑥–⑦.

Hotel Arumdalu, Jl Arumdalu 4 (☎ & fax 0341/591266). This is a large setup with a small pool and garden and plenty of accommodation options; the cheaper rooms are very basic and can be noisy as they are close to the restaurant. It isn't luxurious, but the location is pleasant. ②–④.

Pondok Rahayu, Jl Arumdalu 8 (☎0341/593814). A good budget alternative that has basic rooms with cold-water mandi. This is a family house and there's a small garden. ③.

SELECTA

Hotel Santosa, Jl Hotel Santosa 1 (☎0341/591066). Signed off the road to the left just below the *Hotel Victory*, several hundred metres through back alleyways, this place is well worth considering at the budget end. The rooms are pleasant, have cold-water mandi, verandahs and good views across town. ③.

Hotel Selecta, Taman Rekreasi (☎0341/591025, fax 592369). The accommodation here is expensive for what you get and rather shabby. The big advantage is proximity to the excellent pool and the attractive grounds, overrun with people on holidays and at weekends. ⑤–⑥.

Hotel Victory, Jl Raya Junggo 107 (☎0341/592985, fax 593012). Located 200m beyond the turning to the Taman Rekreasi, the cheaper rooms are nothing special but the big plus is the two-storey-high upper lounge with huge windows. The coffee shop overlooking the pool is particularly pleasant. ④–⑥.

Southern beaches

The road **south of Malang** heads along the course of Sungai Brantas for 18km to the small town of **Kepanjen**, where it divides – east to Lumajang around the southern flanks of the Bromo area, and west around the southern side of Gunung Butak and its nearby peaks to Blitar. Due south again, the rolling southern hills are nowhere near as dramatic as the volcanoes around Malang, but the area is peaceful and rural and the coast has three fine **beaches** (entrance charge for all three: Rp2100 per adult, Rp500 per car and Rp300 per motorbike). All are popular weekend excursions for local people, and very quiet during the week. With your own transport any or all are a very easy day-trip from Malang. If you are using public transport, the busy village of Sendangbiru is easily accessible, with Balekambang and Ngliep easiest to get to at weekends. There is basic accommodation at all of the beaches.

Road access to **Sendangbiru**, the furthest east of the three beaches, is via Turen, 16km east of Kepanjen. The junction to the beach is south of Turen: turn left at the main junction, then right after about 1km and the turn is signed. Using public transport, there are a few direct microlets from the Gadang terminal in Malang to Sendangbiru. Alternatively, take a Lumajang-bound bus from Gadang terminal, get off in Turen and pick up a minibus to Sendangbiru. The busy 43-kilometre road to Sendangbiru from Turen twists and turns through the rolling coastal hills via the small, cool market town of Sumbermajung Wetan. The beach itself is gorgeous, very sheltered, with colourful boats pulled up onto the sand and a jetty 500m to the west. There are lovely views along the coast, especially to the east, where great cliffs line the shore, surf pounding against them. Just 500m off the beach, forested, hilly **Pulau Sempu** is clearly visible, with some enticing beaches and rocks just off the coast. A charter to the island is Rp40,000–50,000 if you bargain well. The **losmen** (no phone; ③) at the western end of Sendangbiru beach has no name, and rooms are basic; it's in a good location overlooking the water, though surrounded by an unattractive fence.

The next beach west is **Balekambang**, accessed via Gondanglegi, 6km west of Turen on the road from Kapanjen. There are bemos and buses from Gadang terminal in Malang via Gondanglegi to Bantur, 13km before the beach. From Bantur there may be minibuses to the beach at the weekends; otherwise you'll need an ojek (Rp2500). The beach is about 500m long and is incredibly picturesque, with three small offshore islands. Pulau Wusanggeni has a small *bale* and is joined to the beach by a walkway. Next west is Pulau Ismoyo, with the Balinese-style Pura Sagara Amritajati overlooking the ocean. Then, another 400m west, forested Pulau Anoman is joined to land by another walkway. Next to the *Depot Asri* warung, near the bridge to Pulau Ismoyo, is a small **losmen** (no phone; ③) with basic bamboo-and-tile rooms with attached mandi. They are set close to the beach and have small verandahs. If you want something a bit smarter, walk further east, to Depot Barokah, where there's a new losmen (③), also nameless, with white-tiled, red-roofed rooms.

Access to **Ngliep**, 35km from Gondanglegi, the most westerly of the three beaches, is also via Bantur; there are some bemos from Gadang terminal in Malang to Ngliep, and more frequent ones from Kepanjen, but during the week it's very quiet. With your own transport you can take a back road from Balekambang to Ngliep, but it isn't a straightforward route; check directions on the way. Ngliep beach is actually two small beaches enclosed by rocky headlands covered by forest with a few enticing paths to explore. The scenery is impressive, with some attractive offshore islands, the closest one, Gunung Kombang, being linked to the most easterly bay by a dodgy-looking bridge; massive surf pounds the rocks here. There are plenty of warung and two places to stay: the *Pasanggrahan* (③), on the beach, with small rooms and shared bathroom, and another small place (③) at right angles behind it.

The Bromo region

The **Bromo region** is best known for its awesome scenery; at its heart is a vast, ancient volcanic crater with sheer walls over 300m high. Within this crater, a host of picturesque mountains, including the dramatic, still-smoking Gunung Bromo (2392m), rises up from the "Sea of Sand", the sandy plain at the crater's base. Hundreds of thousands of visitors come to the area each year to climb Bromo for the sunrise – a stunning sight, and far less strenuous than many other Indonesian peaks.

THE TENGGER

The Tengger area is home to the **Tengger** people, who are ethnically, culturally and linguistically different to the Javanese. Legend tells that the Tengger people are descended from Rara Anteng, daughter of the last king of Majapahit, and Jaker Serger, a descendant of the god Brahamana. They could not have children and prayed to the gods, promising to sacrifice a child if they were made fertile. Their wish was granted and they went to on to produce 25 children, but did not keep their promise. The gods were angered and the area was devastated by disease and death, and eventually the youngest child of the couple, Raden Kusuma, was taken by his father to the Sea of Sand where a huge eruption took the child and created Gunung Bromo. Jaker Serger was also ordered to donate half the harvest to the Bromo crater every Kasada month (last month) of the Tengger calendar. Today, the **Kasada festival** (movable against the Western calendar, so inquire at tourist offices for the exact date) is the most important in the area; at midnight priests begin their prayers on the Sea of Sand to call the gods down to earth and bless the people, who then climb to the Bromo crater at dawn and throw their offerings of vegetables, flowers and money into the caldera.

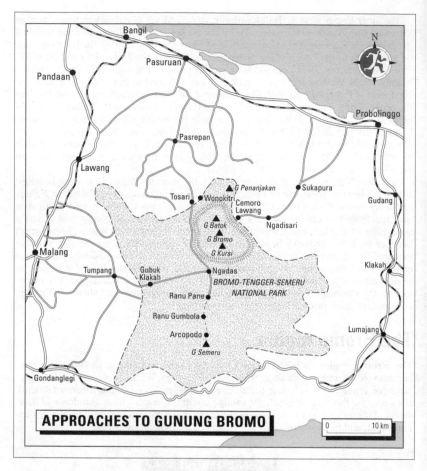

APPROACHES TO GUNUNG BROMO

0   10 km

One hypothesis for the formation of the area is that Gunung Tengger, then the highest mountain in Java at over 4000m, erupted to form a caldera of between 8km and 10km in diameter and crater walls between 200m and 700m high. This is now the main outer crater rim with the Sea of Sand in the bottom. However, eruptions continued to occur, forming the smaller inner peaks such as Bromo, Batok and Widodoren that rise up from the Sea of Sand.

This unique landscape now comprises the **Bromo-Tengger-Semeru national park**, which ranges in altitude from 750m to 3676m, with mountainous rainforest, casuarina forest and grasslands. It is estimated that around 600 species of flora survive in the park, including 157 species of orchid in the southern areas. The fauna includes monkey, macaque, barking deer, leopard, panther, porcupine and pangolin. The park's boundaries encompass **Gunung Penanjakan** which is a favourite viewing point in the area, and soaring **Gunung Semeru**, the highest peak in Java and a reasonable objective for trekkers who are fit and prepared.

There are two main **approaches** to the Bromo region. The most popular is to head inland from Probolinggo on the north coast via the villages of Sukapura, Wonkerto and Ngadisari, to the crater's edge at Cemoro Lawang. There is accommodation in all of the villages, although most people stay at **Cemoro Lawang**, on order to make the dawn trip to Gunung Bromo as easy as possible. Alternative access is from Pasuruan, also on the north coast, inland to the villages of Tosari and Wonokitri. These villages are further west from Cemoro Lawang, but linked by road to Gunung Penanjakan, so they offer an excellent approach for the sunrise from there. For more detail on these access points, see p.274.

It is best to visit in the **dry season** when the clouds are fewer, views better, and the walking more pleasant. However, whatever time of year you visit, take warm clothes – it gets chilly at night. All the accommodation places will provide you with a blanket.

Bromo and the other peaks

The highlights of the area are **Gunung Bromo**, with its dramatic smoking crater; **Gunung Penanjakan**, on the outside crater's edge and one of the favourite sunrise spots; and **Cemoro Lawang**, with its brilliant panoramic view of the crater, where most visitors stay (see p.272). The park also contains the highest mountain in Java, **Gunung Semeru**, and, while most visitors will be content with admiring its dramatic profile from a distance, it is also possible to climb to the summit. The Bromo area attracts more than 250,000 tourists each year, peak seasons being June to September and again at Christmas and New Year.

Gunung Bromo

There are a variety of excursions possible from Cemoro Lawang (see p.272), the most popular being the wonderfully atmospheric climb to the top of **Gunung Bromo** (2392m). If you are lucky with the clouds, there may be an absolutely spellbinding sunrise. You can walk, get a horse or take a vehicle down the crater's edge and across the Sea of Sand to the base of Gunung Bromo. To walk, either follow the cobbled road or the path from near the *Hotel Bromo Permai* to the Sea of Sand and follow the main track across to the mountain. Allow about an hour to get to the base of the mountain and, if you're going for the sunrise, a torch is useful as you'll be walking in the dark. If you want a **horse**, the fixed prices are posted on notice boards in the centre of Cemoro Lawang (Rp6500 one way between Cemoro Lawang and Bromo, Rp12,500 return; you can also rent horses by the hour). It is possible to do it by vehicle, either in a hired car or by ojek; there is a steep, cobbled but motorable three-kilometre road down to the Sea of Sand from Cemoro Lawang and then the main road is marked across the Sea of Sand by white stones. Vehicles go to just beyond the temple at the bottom of Gunung Bromo while horses can continue the steepish 500m or so to the base of the steps up the mountain itself. However you get there, you'll still have to manage the 249 concrete stairs (30min) up to the crater rim, from where there are great views down into the smoking crater and back across the Sea of Sand. Just at the top of the steps there are some protective railings, but these don't extend far; you can walk further around to get away from the crowds, but it is very narrow with long drops on either side.

For a longer trip, you can charter a jeep from Cemoro Lawang to take you to **Penanjakan** for the sunrise, back to Bromo for the climb and then return to Cemoro Lawang. All prices are negotiable and it's much cheaper if you arrange it yourself with a driver rather than through a hotel, but you'll be looking at around Rp50,000 for the return trip to Bromo and Rp80,000 or more for the longer trip described above. All prices are per jeep, which will hold two or three people.

Gunung Penanjakan

There are three choices for excursions which include **Gunung Penanjakan** (2770m), the best spot for the sunrise across the entire Bromo area; you'll need to charter local transport for any of them. The most straightforward is to go to Gunung Penanjakan for the sunrise and return to Wonokitri or Tosari (Rp40,000 per jeep, Rp15,000 motorcycle). Alternatively, you can go to Penanjakan for the sunrise, cross the Sea of Sand to Bromo and then return to Wonokitri or Tosari after you've climbed to the top. The longest option is to go to Penanjakan and Bromo and then on to Cemoro Lawang (Rp60,000 per jeep, Rp25,000 per motorcycle for either of the final two). This last option doesn't seem very popular, but is a good choice if you want to visit both the Tosari/Wonokitri and Cemoro Lawang areas, avoiding a trip via the north coast. There is no motorable road that links Penanjakan, Tosari or Wonokitri directly with Cemoro Lawang.

The road from Wonokitri and Tosari up to Penanjakan (11km) is steep and attractive with some excellent views, but very twisty. There's a lookout at Dingklik, 6km beyond Wonokitri and 5km before Penanjakan, where one road goes down the crater wall to the Sea of Sand and the other up to Penanjakan. Leave Tosari or Wonokitri at around 4.30am to get to the lookout spot for sunrise; it's about 200m from the car park to the usually crowded lookout itself. The whole crater area lies below, Bromo smoking and Semeru puffing up regular plumes while the sun rises dramatically in the east. This is a national park, so you can **camp** up here if you wish, but be aware that unless you select your spot carefully you'll be invaded before dawn by the hordes.

Gunung Semeru

Essentially a dry-season expedition (from June to September or possibly October), the climb up **Gunung Semeru**(3676m), Java's highest mountain, is for fit, experienced trekkers only and requires good preparation and equipment. It takes at least three full days. The volcano is still active, with over 20,000 seismic events recorded in a typical year; the last major eruption was in 1909 when 200 people died, and since 1967 it has been constantly active. It is vital to take a local guide and listen to advice about the safety of the area. Even the approaches to the main climb can be confusing, as the farmland and forest are extensive. In fact, there are two main routes up the mountain, a newer, more popular trail and an old trail called "Ajek-Ajek", which is shorter but steeper.

The path starts at the village of **RANU PANE**, to the north of the mountain, accessible by microlet and chartered jeep from Malang or Tumpang, or – if you are in the Bromo area – via a path across the Sea of Sand. In the village you need to check in at the **PHPA office** and get your **permit** (Rp2100; for an extra charge you can also get a certificate if you complete the climb), unless you already have it from Malang (see p.260). The PHPA office will also recommend porters – one porter is needed for each person climbing (Rp30,000 per porter). It's best to bring your own sleeping bag and tent, and rent a cooking stove in Ranu Pane. In the village, trekkers can stay in the *Forest Guest House* (②), where you'll need to cook for yourself, or there's a **campsite** near the PHPA office.

The first part of the trek is the three hours from Ranu Pane to **Ranu Gumbolo** (2400m), a wide path leading gently uphill through the forest. There is lake here; you can camp or find a place to stay in the village but most people carry on, through the small upland village of Oro Oro Ombo to **Cemoro Kandang**. Near this path is Sumber Manis, the last water source before the summit, so make sure you get directions to it. At Cemoro Kandang it's possible to camp among the *cemoro* trees, or a few of the shelters may be useable. Alternatively, continue for a further thirty minutes or so to **Kalimati** (2700m), two to three hours from Ranu Gumbolo, along a much steeper path. If you still have time and are fit, you could continue for another one to two hours to the last camping point at **Arcopodo** (3000m). It's through the forest and is tough going, but will make the following day shorter and easier. From here you'll feel the earth shudder every twenty or thirty minutes as the volcano erupts.

If you camp at Arcopodo and are fairly fit, allow three hours to the **summit** and leave at about 3am to get there for the sunrise. It means you climb in the pitch dark for much of the time. There are very few trees above Arcopodo, and this is the really tough part, extremely steep, and covered in fine, slippery sand up to ankle height which gets more slippery as the day progresses and it warms up; carry only water and plenty of high-energy food. From the crater's edge on a clear day, you can see as far as Bali. The regular explosions of gas and ash throw debris 100m into the air, and it's especially dangerous if the wind changes direction as the gas is poisonous. In 1997, two climbers were killed by a big eruption which sent boulders flying out of the crater. On the way back, stay the night at Cemoro Kandang and descend the next day to Ranu Pane; don't forget to report back to the PHPA office.

If you don't want to make your own arrangements, a **package trip** for two to four people will run to about Rp500,000 excluding transport and porters from Ranu Pane, but including a guide and equipment. To arrange this, contact the *Helios Hotel* in Malang (see p.260).

Approaches to Bromo

There are several **approaches to the Bromo area,** the most popular routes being via **Probolinggo** to **Cemoro Lawang** and via **Pasuruan** to **Wonokitri** or **Tosari**. Both Pasuruan and Probolinggo are pleasant, bustling north-coast towns, although most people pass through quickly. The road from Probolinggo heads south from the coast via Sukapura, Wonokerto and Ngadisari to Cemoro Lawang. The route from Pasuruan passes through Pasrepan.

Probolinggo

Visited by King Hayam Wuruk of the Majapahit dynasty in 1359, the area delighted the king so much that it was named Prabu Linggah (The Place the King Was Pleased to Stay), which these days has become **PROBOLINGGO**, a town of around 200,000 people 38km east of Pasuruan. The alun-alun in the centre of town isn't particularly impressive, although the **Mesjid Agung** on the western side is low and elegant. The area around the alun-alun and down Jalan Dr Suroyo is the government and administration centre, whilst Jalan Sutomo and Jalan Raya P. Sudirman form the commercial and shopping hub. From **Bentar Indah**, the local harbour, there are regular public ferries to **Gili Ketapang**, a small rural island 8km off the coast to the north, which provides an attractive, relaxing getaway from the bustle of the mainland. Five kilometres to the east is **Pantai Bendah Indah**, a popular local beach.

The **station** is on the northern side of the alun-alun, while the **bus terminal** is 6km southwest of town; yellow microlets run to the town centre. There are good road and rail connections from throughout East Java, Bali, Yogyakarta and Jakarta. Minibuses for Cemoro Lawang leave from the terminal, and there are two buses daily – they are labelled "Sukapura" and "Ngadisari" on the front but also serve Cemoro Lawang.

The best **accommodation** is *Hotel Bromo Permai*, Jalan Raya P. Sudirman 237 (☎0335/427451, fax 22256; ①–③), with six standards of room ranged around a small garden with a little restaurant attached. Prices include a nasi goreng breakfast. They have a map of the town to consult, and staff are helpful and used to travellers. They can arrange chartered transport to Cemoro Lawang and have train information; a warpostel is attached to the hotel. To get here from the bus station take a G or F yellow microlet and, from here to the terminal or station, a G. For **eating**, *Rumah Makan Sumber Hidup*, Jalan Dr Moch Saleh 2, is a big airy place at the junction with Jalan Raya P. Sudirman; you can eat inside or outside from an extensive menu of rice, sate, soup, juices and ices. *Restaurant Malang*, Jalan P Sudirman 48, has an extensive menu of well-cooked Indonesian and Chinese dishes in the inexpensive to moderate range, plus plenty of drinks.

The banks on Jalan Suroyo do **foreign exchange**: Bank Bumi Daya at no. 23, BCA at no. 28, BRI at no. 30, or BNI at no. 46. The **post office**, Jalan Suroyo 33 (daily 7am–8pm), will soon have public Internet access. The **wartel** (7am–11pm), next to the main Telkom administration office, is at Jalan Suroyo 37. For everyday **shopping**, the Sinar supermarket, Jalan Raya P. Sudirman 102, will meet most needs, or try the Sinar Terang department store, Jalan Dr Sutomo 125. Gajah Made (or GM), Jalan Dr Sutomo 42, is the newest shopping centre, with a department store and supermarket plus some food places.

Cemoro Lawang

The small village of **CEMORO LAWANG**, 46km from Probolinggo, is perched on the crater's edge and has grown up largely to service the tourists who visit the Bromo region; it's the easiest place from which to set off on the pre-dawn excursion to Gunung Bromo itself.

From the crater's edge in Cemoro Lawang there are brilliant **views** of the entire area. Gunung Penanjakan is over to the far right; you can identify it by the radio and telecommunications masts at the summit. The chopped-off cone in the foreground is Gunung Batok (2440m); looking left, the two pointed peaks are Gunung Widodoren (2614m) and Watangah; then there is huge smoking Gunung Bromo in the foreground. Gunung Semeru is in the far distance behind and to the left of Bromo. The best look-out spots are at the end of the road from the north coast in Cemoro Lawang and in front of *Lava View Lodge*. Access to Cemoro Lawang is from Probolinggo, minibuses run up to the crater rim from 6am to 5.30pm via the villages of Sukapura, Wonokerto and Ngadisari, all of which also have accommodation.

There is a **national park post** on the Probolinggo–Cemoro Lawang road where you pay admission to the park at Ngadisari (Rp2100, Rp6000 per jeep, Rp2500 per motorcycle); you'll be issued with a ticket. The **national park office** (Kantor Taman Nasional Bromo Tengger Semeru; daily 7.30am–4pm) in Cemoro Lawang has displays about the area, but little printed material either about the park or local treks. *Hotel Yoschi* (see opposite) is the best place for local information, especially if you want to trek.

The **postal agent** at the *Hotel Bromo Permai* charges Rp1100 for a Rp1000 stamp and doesn't know postal rates to anywhere, so it's probably best to bring stamps with you. There's a **wartel** (daily 3am–10pm) on the left as you reach the top of the road and you can call worldwide; the lines from here are less reliable than from more accessible areas. If you want **souvenirs**, the shop attached to the wartel in Cemoro Lawang has some good T-shirts. There's a **health centre** in Ngadisari, Jalan Raya Bromo 6, just by the checkpost.

Moving on, minibuses (8am–4pm) and buses (two daily) operate from Cemoro Lawang to Probolinggo. Several places advertise minibus and express-bus tickets, which are more expensive but more convenient than organizing them yourself in Probolinggo. Make sure you know what standard of bus ticket you are buying and whether you are paying for a minibus for the whole journey or just to Probolinggo.

ACCOMMODATION IN AND AROUND CEMORO LAWANG

There is plenty of **accommodation** in Cemoro Lawang, Ngadisari, Wonokerto and Sukapura: Ngadisari is 3km, Wonokerto is 5km and Sukapura is about 18km from the rim. **Camping** is no problem, as this is a national park; Penanjakan is popular, although you will get disturbed by the sunrise hordes, and there's a good site 200m further along the rim from the *Lava View Lodge* in Cemoro Lawang.

Hotel Bromo, Jl Wonokerto 5, Wonokerto (☎0335/23484). If you're on a very tight budget, this place is worth considering. Small rooms, with cold-water mandi, around a small garden area. There's an attached restaurant. ①–②.

Hotel Bromo Permai (☎ & fax 0335/23459). Just on the left at the end of the road as it reaches the crater's edge at Cemoro Lawang. There's a wide choice of rooms and, whilst top-end ones are big and comfortable, at the bottom end there's little to recommend: they are small with shared cold-water mandi. ②–⑤.

Café Lava Hostel (aka **Puri Lava**) (☎0335/23458). A justly popular travellers' choice, close to the crater rim, on the main road into Cemoro Lawang. There are two standards of room, the less expensive ones being basic with shared cold-water mandi (often a long walk away) and the more expensive ones, which are spotless, with lovely sitting areas in an attractive garden. ②–③.

Cemoro Indah (☎0335/23457). On the crater's rim around to the right from the *Hotel Bromo Permai*. The main road into Cemoro Lawang forks about 200m before it reaches the crater rim. The left fork goes to the centre of the village, and the right fork to the *Cemoro Indah*. There's a big choice of rooms, from basic ones with cold-water shared mandi to stunningly positioned bungalows with hot water. The attached restaurant is equally well located. ②–⑥.

Hotel Cik Arto (☎0335/21618, fax 22103). Just below the terminal in Ngadisari. This is a new place, with smart rooms at the front and less expensive rooms at the back, in a pleasant garden setting. All rooms have attached cold-water mandi. ③.

Grand Bromo Hostel (☎0335/581103 ext 571). In the grounds of the *Hotel Raya Bromo* (see below for location), this budget option has three beds in each room, with shared hot-water bathrooms and small sitting areas outside. Guests can use the *Hotel Raya Bromo* pool. ①.

Lava View Lodge (☎0335/20272). About 500m left along the crater's edge from the centre of Cemoro Lawang; go through the concrete area between the row of shops and *Hotel Bromo Permai* and follow the main track. It doesn't look too great from the outside, but rooms are comfortable – all have attached bathrooms and the views are brilliant, especially from the top-end rooms and the attached restaurant. ③–④.

Hotel Raya Bromo (ex *Grand Hotel Bromo*) (☎0335/581103, fax 581142). Located 2km south of Sukapura, a long way from the crater, this is the most upmarket place in the area, with comfortable rooms, all with hot-water bathrooms, and staff who speak excellent English. More expensive rooms have stunning views north to the coast. There are tennis courts and three pools (non-guests can use the pool for Rp5000). ⑦–⑨.

Hotel Yoschi, Jl Wonokerto 1, Wonokerto (☎0335/23387, fax 432107). A great place with many options: the cheaper rooms have shared bathroom, while the top-priced ones are actually cottages. The decor is attractive and the garden is a delight. Staff provide plenty of good information on the area and sell maps of local hikes. You can also use the book exchange, book bus tickets, arrange local guides, charter transport and rent warm jackets. ③–⑥.

EATING AND DRINKING

Well used to catering to Western tastes, there are plenty of **places to eat** in the vicinity of Cemoro Lawang. All those listed below offer Western and Indonesian food or, if you fancy cheaper eats, you'll see mobile food stalls selling basic soups and noodles throughout the day and evening on the main roads in Cemoro Lawang.

Café Lava, attached to the *Café Lava Hostel*. Moderately priced with plenty of travellers' favourites, including steaks, pancakes, sandwiches and drinks.

Cemoro Indah Restaurant. Attached to the *Cemoro Indah Hotel* and located near the crater rim; the views are brilliant and the moderately priced food is varied.

Hotel Yoschi Restaurant, attached to *Hotel Yoschi* in Wonokerto. Delightful place with lots of wood, bamboo, batik, fresh flowers and a pleasant atmosphere, plus an excellent range of inexpensive to moderately priced food.

Kafé Venus, at the Cemoro Lawang terminal. Has attractive bamboo decor; this is a clean place with inexpensive to moderately priced food, and is excellently located if you've just arrived and are starving or waiting for transport.

Lava View Lodge Restaurant. Offering the same menu as *Café Lava* in the village (see above), but quieter, set in a great position not far from the crater's edge with spectacular views.

Pasuruan

Located 60km southeast of Surabaya, the port town of **PASURUAN** is a convenient stopping-off spot close to Bromo on the way to or from Tosari and Wonokitri; buses run every few minutes throughout the day between Surabaya and Pasuruan (1–2hr), and there are daily trains (1hr 30min) from Gubeng station in Surabaya.

The town's only notable feature is the recently restored **Mesjid Agung Ali-Anwar**, on the west side of the main square, a gleaming delight with white-and-green patterning, lovely arches, gleaming domes and a towering minaret. The main north-coast road is Jalan Raya, which runs west–east along the northern edge of the town parallel to the coast. The town centre, the alun-alun, lies several hundred metres south and is reached via Jalan Niaga, which turns into Jalan Nusantara further south. The **bus terminal** is at the eastern end of Jalan Raya, about 1.5km from the alun-alun, and the **train station** just north of Jalan Raya, on Jalan Stasiun. The **tourist office**, Jalan Hayam Wuruk 14 (☎0343/429075), is situated in the district government offices, Kantor Kapeputan Pasuran.

For **accommodation**, *Hotel Pasuruan*, Jalan Nusantara 46 (☎0343/424494, fax 421075; ③–④), has three standards of room, from cold-water bathroom and fan rooms up to those with air-con and hot-water bathrooms. *Wisma Karya*, Jalan Raya 160 (☎0343/426655; ②–③), has a range of rooms behind an old colonial bungalow, although the cheaper ones are often full. The top-end rooms have air-con, but the cheaper ones with fan and attached cold-water mandi are adequate.

There are plenty of **places to eat** in Pasuruan, from the small night market around the alun-alun to *Rumah Makan Savera*, on Jalan Raya 92a, a clean and welcoming place with a huge, inexpensive menu of Indonesian and Chinese food.

The **post office** (Mon–Thurs 7.30am–2pm & 3–8pm, Fri 7.30–11.30am & 1–8pm, Sat 7.30am–1pm & 2–8pm), Jalan Alun-alun Utara 1, provides public Internet access (Rp2500 for 15min). There's a 24hr **wartel** at Jalan Stasiun 11 and **exchange facilities** at BNI, Jalan A. Yani 21 and BCA, Jalan Periwa 200, 200m west of the terminal.

There are good **bus and rail services** throughout East Java, as well as east to Bali and west to Yogyakarta. Microlets run direct to Tosari, although there is no sign at the terminal.

Tosari and Wonokitri

Just over 40km south from Pasuruan, the small villages of Tosari and Wonokitri sit 2km apart on neighbouring ridges of the Bromo massif foothills. These are excellent choices for early access to **Gunung Penanjakan** and are less tourist-orientated than Cemoro Lawang. Both villages are quiet, upland communities with a peaceful atmosphere, and a day or so here can easily be combined with a stay at Cemoro Lawang to get the most out of the area. Microlets that go to one also go to the other, and both villages have accommodation. Coming from Pasuruan, the road divides about 500m before Tosari: the right fork leads up to the market area of that village, and the left fork twists up to the next ridge and Wonokitri. Wonokitri is a compact, shabby town with good views, while Tosari is more spread out, with an attractive ridge to the northeast that leads to the *Hotel Bromo Tosari*. Although there is no sign at the bemo station in Pasuruan, there are direct minibuses from there to Tosari, better than getting a minibus to **Pasrepan** and having to change there. There are bemos from Pasrepan to Tosari and Wonokitri, and ojek also ply the route – they tend to inflate the price for tourists (Rp5000 is fair).

In **TOSARI**, the *Hotel Bromo Tosari* (☎343/571222, fax 571333; ⑧–⑨) provides luxurious accommodation in attractively furnished cottages, with hot water, bathtubs and stunning views. In the main building there is a comfortable lounge, and the *Dahlia Restaurant* offers moderate to expensive Chinese, Indonesian and Western meals. They can arrange local trips, have karaoke and traditional dance shows and the shop rents out warm jackets. There are often discounts available. If you are coming via Surabaya, it's worth checking Orient Travel (see p.246), as they quote competitive prices at the hotel either for accommodation only or as part of a package deal to Bromo. On the same ridge, about 300m before *Hotel Bromo Tosari, Penginapan Wulun Aya*, Jalan Bromo Cottage 25 (☎0343/57011; ③), is small and clean with good views from the balconies. *Mekar Sari*, Jalan Raya 1 (no phone; ③), is a small rumah makan selling inexpensive Indonesian food, and has a few simple rooms with shared cold-water mandi and a good roof terrace.

WONOKITRI features several places to stay. At the time of writing, the only place that was signed was *Pondok Wisata Surya Nuta* (③), a concrete, charmless building with little going for it. Far better choices are *Kartiki Sari* (no phone; ③) with simple rooms, and *Bromo Surya Indah* (☎0343/571049; ③), which is just before the *pendopo agung*, the Balinese-style village meeting hall, about 300m before the national park checkpost at the far end of the village; rooms have attached bathroom, clean bedding and good views. A new hotel is under construction 6km north of Tosari and Wonokitri near the village of Baledono. It will be towards the top end of the market and, although further from Gunung Penanjakan, may be an attractive option if you have your own transport.

At the **national park checkpost** and information centre at the southern end of Wonokitri there are some maps and charts to consult, though their main role is collecting the **admission fee** to the park (Rp2100, Rp6000 per car, Rp2500 per motorcycle).

The far east

The **far east** of Java, between Bromo and Bali, is often overlooked by visitors, who simply want to transit it as quickly as possible. This is unfortunate, as the area not only contains some excellent and accessible **national parks** – Baluran, Alas Purwo and Meru Betiri – but also some lovely **coastline** on the southern side, plus the largely neglected but stunning **Ijen Plateau**, with its rolling upland areas of coffee plantations, dramatic soaring peaks and the spectacular crater lake of **Kawah Ijen**. The east remains largely rural, although communications are good and there is sufficient accommodation.

Jember

The city of **JEMBER** is large, busy and invariably clogged with traffic. However it has good facilities for travellers and is a useful place to get information about the Meru Betiri national park and to book accommodation there.

Buses from the north arrive at the Arjasa terminal 6km north of Jember; others, including long-distance services, drive in at the Tawang Alun terminal 6km west of the city centre on Jalan Darmawangsa. From both terminals there are Damri buses or yellow microlets into the town centre: A or B buses marked "Tawang Alun-Arjasa" travel via the alun-alun, a useful orientation point. From Tawang Alun it is also possible to pick up metered Argo taxis. There's a third bus station at Pakusari, 8km southeast of the city, served by Banyuwangi buses, which also use Tawang Alun.

The **train station** is on Jalan Wijaya Kusuma, which runs north from the northwest corner of the alun-alun. Jember is on the main line across Java as well as the branch line to Panarukan on the north coast and there are plenty of services throughout East Java. Longer-distance services between Jember and Jakarta or Bandung involve a change in Yogyakarta or Surabaya.

There is a 24hr **Telkom office** at Jalan Kartini 4–6, at the southwest corner of the alun-alun. For **exchange** there's BCA, Jalan Gajah Made 14–18, BNI Jalan Raya P. Sudirman 9, or Bank Bali, Jalan Trunojoyo 35. The **post office** (Mon–Fri 8am–9pm, Sat 8–11am, Sun 8am–1pm) is on the north side of the alun-alun, at Jalan Raya P. Sudirman 5, and offers public access to the Internet (Mon–Sat 8am–5pm, Sun 8–11am; Rp6000 per hour), or try Warung Internet, Jalan Kalimantan 77, near the university – microlet D passes the door. For **shopping**, the Johor Plaza on Jalan Diponegoro has a three-storey Matahari department store.

Information

The **tourist office**, Jalan Gajah Made 345 (Mon–Thurs 7am–2pm, Fri 7–11am, Sat 7am–12.30pm; ☎ & fax 0331/425471), produces a brochure about the area but is otherwise not particularly useful. It's possible to book tours and accommodation on the **Ijen Plateau** at PT Perkebunan Nusantara XII (known as PTP 12), Jalan Gajah Made 249 (☎0331/86861, fax 85550). The KSDA office, Jalan Jawa 36, has responsibility for Pulau Sempu. The **national park office** for **Meru Betiri**, Jalan Sriwijaya 40 (Mon–Thurs 7am–2pm, Fri 7–11am, Sat 7am–1pm; ☎0331/435535), is 3km southeast of the alun-alun; staff are knowledgeable and keen to help and have literature in English. Some Meru Betiri accommodation needs to be booked here; otherwise, book at Ledokombak, Jalan Gajah Made 224 (Mon–Fri 7.30am–noon & 12.30–3pm, Sat 7.30am–12.30pm; ☎0331/84814), which is 200m east of the Bank Indonesia building.

Accommodation

Catering largely for business travellers, there are several good **accommodation** choices in the city.

Hotel Anda, Jl Kartini 40 (☎0331/89475). A 10min walk west of the alun-alun but not easy to find, so take a becak. Very popular with visiting Indonesians, the rooms are clean, tiled, and have balconies and attached mandi – more expensive rooms have air-con and hot water. ②–③.

Hotel Lestari, Jl Gajah Made 347 (☎0331/87920). Just off Jl Gajah Made, there's a sign 3km west of town, next to the tourist office, but it's easy to miss. Rooms, in a multi-storey block, are clean and tiled, and all have balconies. Cheaper rooms have shared bathrooms. ②–④.

Hotel Safari, Jl K.H.A. Dahlan 7 (☎0331/81882, fax 81887). A central option, off a small road south of Jl Trunojoyo, with Bank Bali on the corner. It's quiet, and has a huge variety of rooms. Look at several: the nicest overlook the small garden. ②–④.

Hotel Seroja, Jl Raya P. Sudirman 2 (☎0331/83905, fax 85580). About 2km north of the alun-alun on the way to Arjasa terminal. It's set back from the road and fairly quiet, with simple rooms and a pleasant atmosphere. ②–④.

Hotel Sulawesi, Jl Letjen Suprapto 48 (☎0331/433555, fax 431343). About 1km south of the alun-alun, the most luxurious hotel in Jember is new, attractive and popular, so book ahead. All rooms have air-con, hot water and TV, and there's a 24hr coffee shop in the lobby area. ④–⑤.

The Meru Betiri national park

Declared a national park in 1982 to protect the habitat of the fast-declining Javan tiger, **Meru Betiri** lies on the south coast to the east of Jember, and contains some of the last remaining lowland rainforest in Java. The chances of seeing the **Javan tiger** are virtually nil: in two recent censuses only faeces, marks on trees and footprints were found, and staff reckon there are no more than four of the animals left. Far more common are two varieties of leopard, wild pig, banteng, birds (the hornbill, peacock and kingfisher are the most dramatic, but there are also yellownapes, woodpeckers, pigeons, bulbuls and eleven species of cuckoo) and – the main reason visitors go to the park – the **turtles** that nest on Sukamade beach. Four varieties of turtle have been seen on the beach: green, hawksbill, snapping and leatherback. The best season for spotting them is November to March, although some observers note that, for leatherbacks, April to July and September to December is better. The park is also home to the **Rafflesia** plant (*Rafflesia zollingeriana*), which is visible at the beginning of the rainy season.

Practicalities

Access is much easier with your own transport or on an organized tour – Jember, Kalibaru and Banyuwangi are possible places to arrange this. On public transport, head to Jagag by bus (2hr from Jember or Banyuwangi), take a microlet or microlet to Pasangrahan (1hr), and another microlet to Sarangan via the park post at Rajekwesi (1hr). From Rajekwesi, it's another 10km to Sukamade beach – engage an ojek or charter a microlet, and you'll need to bargain hard. There is access to the park from both the west and the east, although the eastern entry point is most popular.

During the rainy season – December and January are the most difficult – the park is very often inaccessible, as the rivers that rise in the coastal hills and flow to the south coast tend to flood. **Permits** (Rp1500) are available in the park office in Jember, or at the park posts at Rajekwesi or Curahnangko.

To get into the park from the east, head for **Jagag**, a small village 10km south of the Banyuwangi–Jember road two hours' drive from either town. If you want to break the journey, *Hotel Baru Indah*, Jalan A. Yani 3 and Jalan Genteng 79 (☎0333/36515; ②–④), has two entrances; it's 200m from the bus station and is a big utilitarian setup with clean rooms, all with attached bathroom.

From Jagag it's 22km to Pasangrahan and then another 22km to the park post at **Rajekwesi**; there's a government guest house here if you get stranded (③), and you can hire a trekking guide at the park post if you want to get off the beaten track (Rp20,000–25,000 per day). There's a **beach** near Rajekwesi, called Teluk Hijau (green water), which has white sand and, as the name suggests, green water.

From Rajekwesi it's a further 18km to **Sukamade beach**. There is a camping area near the beach and national park **accommodation** (①), but as there are only four rooms you need to book at the office in Jember (see opposite); you can either take food to cook in the kitchen or the staff will supply simple meals. The other accommodation is at the plantation guest house about 5km from the beach, run by Ledokombak, Jalan Gajah Made 224, Jember (Mon–Fri 7.30am–noon & 12.30–3pm, Sat 7.30am–12.30pm; ☎0331/84814; ③), which must be booked in advance at their office. Accommodation is in basic rooms with fan and attached cold-water mandi, and breakfast is included in the price. Simple meals can be cooked by the staff.

There are even fewer visitors to the **west** of the park; access is from Jember to Ambulu (from Ajung terminal), 25km south of Jember, and from there to **Pasarat Curahnangko**. From the market there, arrange an ojek to travel the further 19km to the beach at **Bandialit** via the **park post** at Curahnangko. The campsite at Bandialit is pretty scruffy, and at the time of writing the plantation guest house was closed, but check in Jember.

Bondowoso

Attractively situated between Gunung Argopuro to the southwest and Gunung Beser to the north, **BONDOWOSO**, 33km north of Jember, is a small, relaxed town, useful for access to the Ijen Plateau. There's good **access** by road or rail; the **train station** is 2km southeast of the alun-alun and there are regular trains from Panarukan on the north coast via Situbondo, and from Jember. The **bus station** is 500m beyond the train station and served by direct buses from throughout East Java. Coming from Banyuwangi (see p.280), you'll need to change at Situbondo if you come around the north coast, or Jember if you come on the southern route. **Becak** wait at the bus terminal and station to ferry arrivals around town.

The centre of town is the **alun-alun**, less manicured than many but still attractive, and surrounded by the main administration buildings. The main shopping street, Jalan Raya P. Sudirman, runs from the northeast corner of the square.

There is good **accommodation**: the place most used to travellers is *Hotel Anugerah*, Jalan Mayjen Sutoyo 12 (☎0332/21870; ③), with lots of options including top-end rooms with air-con – all have attached mandi and outside sitting areas overlooking a small garden. The owner speaks good English and can advise on things to see and help with chartering transport (Rp120,000 including fuel and driver to Ijen) and there is a small restaurant attached. The plushest place is *Hotel Palm*, Jalan A. Yani 32 (☎0332/21505, fax 22953; ②–⑥), with nine standards of room from very small, basic ones with shared bathroom to huge rooms with air-con, TV and hot-water bathrooms. The lounge/coffee bar overlooks the attractive garden and there's a swimming pool (daily 5am–6pm; non-residents weekdays Rp1500, Sat & Sun Rp2000).

The most atmospheric **place to eat** is the extensive night market along Jalan Martadinata, which heads east off the southeast corner of the alun-alun. The restaurant attached to *Hotel Anugerah* is a good bet for simple Indonesian and Chinese meals, as is *Rumah Makan Lezat*, Jalan Raya P. Sudirman 95, which is clean, airy, good value and popular – see the food glossary on pp.44–45 as they only have an Indonesian menu.

The **post office** is at Jalan Jaksa Agung Suprapto 9 (Mon–Thurs 7.30am–noon & 1–4pm, Fri 7.30–11.30am, Sat 7.30am–1pm, Sun & hols 8–11am). There's a 24hr **Telkom office** at Jalan Mayjen Panjaitan 6; the road is left off Jalan A. Yani about 500m south of the alun-alun. You can only **exchange** cash, not travellers' cheques, at BNI, Jalan A. Yani 26.

Moving on from Bondowoso, there are direct buses throughout East Java and to Denpasar. There are no direct buses to Banyuwangi, so change at Jember or Situbondo. Bondowoso is on the branch rail line between Panarukan on the north coast 8km west of Situbondo and Jember – change here onto the main east–west railway line from Banyuwangi through to Surabaya and points west.

The Ijen Plateau

The **Ijen Plateau** is a large upland area southeast of Bondowoso, which includes the peaks and foothills of Gunung Ijen, Gunung Raung (3332m), Gunung Suket (2950m) and Gunung Merapi (2800m), plus several smaller peaks. The entire area is rural, coffee plantations and vegetable gardens blending into the forested uplands, with a few widely dispersed villages. The highlight is the dramatic lake, **Kawah Ijen**, in the crater of the dormant volcano from which dozens of miners dig sulphur by hand.

Access and accommodation

From Bondowoso, head for the small village of Wonosari 11km to the northeast; the turning to Ijen is signposted 2km north of here. The road winds through the village of Sukosari and then begins to rise more steeply, the rice giving way to pine forest as the air gets cooler and habitation peters out. At the checkpost onto the plateau, Pos Malabar, the small *Warung Ijen* sells noodles, coffee, soft drinks and cigarettes. The road then descends 7km to the small village of **SEMPOL**, a total of 55km from Wonosari. It's a tiny upland village, the main population centre in the area, superbly located amongst coffee plantations and forested mountains. One kilometre from the main road in the hamlet of **Kalisat** are the guest houses, *Jampit II* and *III* (no phone; ③–④), which are signposted "Penginapan Kaliasat" from the centre of Sempol. Located on the edge of a small valley, the accommodation is set in pleasant grounds: cheaper rooms have cold-water attached mandi, whilst the more expensive ones have hot water. Staff here can arrange riding, fishing, coffee-plantation walks, coffee-factory tours, excursions to Kawah Ijen, local guides, transport and inexpensive food.

There's a fourteen-kilometre rough road from Sempol via the hamlet of Kepekan to **JAMPIT**, where you'll find *Jampit I* (no phone; ②–⑤), in an attractive colonial house set in manicured grounds. Cheaper rooms have nearby hot-water bathrooms, and more expensive ones have attached hot-water bathrooms with bathtubs. They get few visitors and even fewer vehicles: the local people get around on horseback. Book at *Jampit II* and *III* (see opposite), where they will help you arrange transport.

Two kilometres beyond Sempol is another checkpost, Pos Plalangan. There is a junction here with the poorly surfaced, five-kilometre road to **BLAWAN**; ojek run from Sempol (Rp5000 one way). The village is attractively located in a sheltered valley, with hot springs nearby as well as a waterfall. The only accommodation is at the *Catimore Homestay* (③), next to the coffee-processing factory behind an old colonial bungalow. The rooms are clean although basic, with attached hot-water bathrooms and pleasant grounds at the front. Staff prepare simple meals on request.

From Bondowoso there are four **buses** daily to the plateau and irregular buses between Sempol and Jampit and Blawan and Pal Tuding (see below). Buses tend to leave the Ijen area early in the morning for Bondowoso and then head back up from about 10am onwards, but it is worth checking at the terminal in Bondowoso. From Sempol to Pal Tuding, it's necessary to hitch or use an ojek (Rp10,000 one way).

The **alternative access** to the plateau is from Banyuwangi (see p.280), with a fifteen-kilometre climb initially to Licin, then another 18km to Pal Tuding via Pos Pengamatan at the village of Jambu (4km from Licin) and the villages of Ampel Gading and Sodang (8km from Licin). Without your own transport, take a Lin 3 microlet to Sasak Perot in Banyuwangi, a small microlet terminal in the west of the city. There are microlets to Licin and the 4km on to Jambu, then you can charter an ojek to Sodang but only occasionally all the way to Pal Tuding (Rp30,000 return). If not, it's a ten-kilometre walk from Sodang to Pal Tuding.

Kawah Ijen

The main road from Pos Plalangan continues another 10km to **Pal Tuding**, the starting point for the three-kilometre (90min) hike to the highlight of the area, **Kawah Ijen**, the crater lake. There is a campsite at Pal Tuding, next to the **national park office**, where you must register and pay the entrance fee (Rp1000, car Rp2000, motorcycle Rp1000). There is also dormitory accommodation at the national park office (①); you'll be more comfortable with your own sleeping bag. At the tiny *Café Edelwys* attached to the office you can buy snacks, drinks and basic meals. From Pal Tuding, the path heads steeply uphill northeast through the forest and is wide and easy to follow. After 45 minutes it passes a building, and the climb steepens. Just above here the path splits; the right fork, the best route, leads to the crater rim and the left fork to the dam at the end of the lake. After a while the path to the crater rim levels out, continues around the mountain and suddenly arrives on the bare, exposed rock of the mountainside, 200m above the lake in the crater below. It's a dramatic, austere landscape with folds of almost bare rock sloping down into the crater and stunted lichen the only sign of life. You can walk along the top of the crater for a fair distance in both directions, or descend to the edge of the lake along the narrow path that the sulphur miners use – allow 30 to 45 minutes to get down, and twice that to get back up.

The **sulphur miners** come up to Kawah Ijen daily; they set off from the Banyuwangi area before dawn, walk up to the lake from Licin, hack out a full load of sulphur (50–70kg) by hand, which they bring up to the crater rim and back down to Licin where they receive around Rp125 per kilo. It's dangerous work, and sudden eruptions and sulphur fumes have been known to kill miners.

Situbondo

Located 34km north of Bondowoso, the not-quite-coastal town of **SITUBONDO** is spacious, clean and convenient for access to and from Bondowoso and the Ijen Plateau. The town is quite spread out, with the central commercial and administrative area around the bus terminal. Five hundred metres west is the alun-alun, with **Mesjid At-Abror** on the west side, a low, modern mosque with a tall minaret. The train station is 500m southwest from the alun-alun. The main west–east road through town runs along the north side of the alun-alun and north of the bus station/market area: it is named Jalan A. Yani to the west of the town centre and Jalan Basuki Rachmat to the east. The junction with the road south to Bondowoso is on the eastern outskirts of town.

If you want to **stay**, *Hotel Ramayana* at Jalan Sepudi 11a (☎0338/61663; ②–③) is central; turn right out of the bus terminal and you'll find it 20m along the road. There's a big choice of rooms so look at several before you choose. There are plenty of **places to eat** in the market area near the bus station, and also *Rumah Makan Malang*, Jalan Basuki Rachmat 207, which is a clean, cool, Chinese place with a huge menu of inexpensive and moderately priced food.

There are a couple of banks which **exchange** cash, but not travellers' cheques: BNI, Jalan Basuki Rachmat 235, and BCA, Jalan Diponegoro 68. The **post office** is at Jalan A. Yani 131 on the north side of the alun-alun, with the 24hr **Telkom office** next door. Alternatively, there's a wartel at Jalan Sepudi 7 (8am–11pm), close to the bus station. Situbondo is on the **rail** branch line between Panarukan on the north coast and Jember, and there are regular **buses** from throughout East Java.

The Baluran national park

Located in the far northeast corner of Java, the **Baluran national park** is one of the driest parts of the island, forty percent of it comprising savannah grassland, which surrounds the central mountain, the extinct volcano of **Gunung Baluran** (1275m), although there is also mangrove, coastal forest, swamp forest and monsoon forest.

The park is particularly good for **birds**: over 150 species have been spotted here, including weavers, woodpeckers, kingfishers, peafowl, jungle fowl and the increasingly rare Java sparrow. Monitor lizards up to 2m long also inhabit the park, and larger mammals are common, including banteng, deer, wild pig, monkeys, macaque and leopard. For serious nature-spotting, avoid the weekends, when the park is very crowded.

The **national park post** where you buy tickets (Rp2000, car Rp2000, motorcycle Rp1000) and can book accommodation at Bekol and Bama is at **Wonorejo**, 30km north of Banyuwangi on the main road around the north coast. A couple of hundred metres into the park from the post there's a **visitor centre** with maps, photographs and other information. From here, a twelve-kilometre poor-quality road leads through forest and grassland to **BEKOL**, a fairly built-up spot with concrete accommodation (no food available; ①) and offices and several observation towers. One observation tower overlooks the nearby waterhole, whilst the one on the top of the hill gives great views of the broken crater rim of Gunung Baluran, inland up to Gunung Merapi and across the Bali Strait. There are plenty of well-marked walking trails in the park, most of them around 3km long. If you want to explore the more remote areas, arrange a park guide. Without your own transport, ojek (Rp5000) or taxis (Rp20,000) are available from the park entrance to Bekol.

On the coast at **Bama**, 3km along a rough but motorable track from Bekol, there's a two-hundred-metre beach with mangrove stands at either end and basic accommodation (no food available; ①) in wooden cottages on stilts, which have verandahs looking seawards and bathrooms nearby. From the beach there are views across to Bali, as well as various local walks.

Banyuwangi

The town of **BANYUWANGI** (Fragrant Water) is often bypassed by visitors, as the port giving access to **Bali** and **Java** is actually in **Ketapang**, 8km to the north. However it's a manageable, lively place, built against the stunning backdrop of the Ijen Plateau

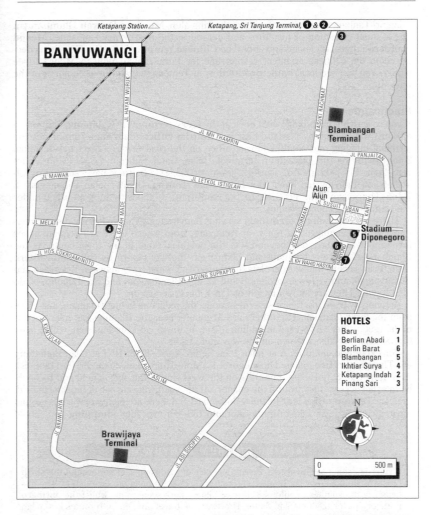

to the west and with fine views across to Bali to the east. It's a useful base for excursions to the **Alas Purwo** and **Baluran national parks** and, with good-quality accommodation in all price brackets, is a great place to draw breath and plan your route through East Java, or through Bali if you are travelling eastwards – the town has excellent transport links throughout the region.

Historically, Banyuwangi was the capital of Blambangan, the sixteenth-century Hindu kingdom that ruled the eastern tip of Java. Although the rapidly expanding Muslim kingdom of Mataram attacked Blambangan during the early seventeenth century, it managed to survive as the last Hindu kingdom on Java and was mostly ignored by the Dutch until the eighteenth century, when they took it over.

The main market area is on Jalan Susuit Tuban, which links the alun-alun with the sports stadium, Stadium Diponegoro, 500m to the southeast. In a modern building at

Jalan Sri Tanjung 3 on the north side of the alun-alun, **Museum Daerah Blambangan** has a small collection of furniture and ceramics; the nearby main mosque, **Mesjid Baiturrachman**, is elegant and cool. The **Chinese temple**, Vihara Tan Tin Jin, is dedicated to the Chinese architect responsible for Pura Taman Ayun in Mengwi (see p.581). You can see local **batik production** in Temenggungan, the area north of the museum.

Practicalities

If you're arriving from Bali, you'll dock at the **ferry terminal** at **Ketapang**, 8km north of Banyuwangi; there is a helpful East Java **Tourist Office** (daily 8am–7pm) inside the terminal building and another tourist office on the road towards the truck terminal 200m south of the passenger terminal, Jalan Gatot Subroto LCM (Mon–Thurs 7am–2pm, Fri 7–11am, Sat 7am–12.30pm; ☎0333/41172); they have some English leaflets. In Banyuwangi itself, the **East Java Tourist Office**, Jalan Diponegoro 2 (Mon–Thurs 8am–2pm, Fri 8–11am, Sat 8am–1pm), is opposite the post office under the stands of the sports ground.

There are several **bus terminals** serving Banyuwangi. The main long-distance terminal is Sri Tanjung, 2km north of Ketapang, from where there are regular buses throughout East Java and beyond. On the northern edge of the town centre is the Blambangan microlet terminal and, 3km from the city centre on the southwestern edge, Brawijaya terminal. Microlets numbered 1, 2, 4 and 5 ply between Brawijaya and Blambangan, and yellow microlets 6 and 12 link Blambangan and Sri Tanjung, as do blue Kijang. They are known locally as Lin 1, Lin 2, and so on.

Arriving by **train**, there are several stations, the main one being Ketapang, just 500m from the ferry terminal. The others are Argopura, near the Blambangan microlet terminal (get off here if you are intending to stay in town), and Karangasem, which is on the western outskirts of town on the way up to Licin.

For **exchange**, go to BCA at Jalan Jend Sudirman 85–87 or BNI at Jalan Banetrang 46. The **post office**, Jalan Diponegoro 1 (Mon–Thurs 8am–3pm, Fri 8–11am, Sat 8am–1pm, Sun & hols 8am–noon), is on the west side of the sports field and has public Internet access. Just around the corner, off the southwest corner of the sports field, the 24hr **Telkom office** is at Jalan Dr Sutomo 63 and there are plenty of wartels around town, including Jalan Jaksa Agung Suprapto 130. For everyday **shopping** you should

---

MOVING ON FROM BANYUWANGI

If you're heading **to Surabaya**, there's a choice of road routes, either around the north coast via Situbondo or via Jember; the routes meet at Probolinggo (see p.271). The distance via the southern route is 311km, a hillier, more scenic way, whilst the northern route is shorter (280km) and flatter. However, the travel time on both routes is similar, at five to seven hours.

If you are travelling by **rail**, book at Ketapang station (9.30am–3pm).

There is a convenient **Pelni** agent on the main road opposite the Ketapang ferry terminal: Hariyono NPPS, Jalan Gatot Suproto 165 (☎ & fax 0333/22523). The Pelni office is at Jalan Raya Situbondo (☎0333/510325, fax 510326). Pelni ship *KM Tatamailou* calls at Banyuwangi every two weeks (see p.287). You can also book tickets for the *KM Dibonsolo*, which calls at Benoa on Bali.

To Bali from Banyuwangi

Two ferry terminals serve the traffic between Java and **Bali**. The truck terminal is about 200m south of the main passenger terminal. Passenger ferries (24hr) cross every thirty minutes (30min; passengers Rp1000, bicycles Rp1700, motorcycles Rp2700, cars Rp12,500 including driver).

be able to meet most of your needs at Pioner Swalayan or Wijaya Department Store, both on Jalan M.H. Thamrin. In the market area along Jl Susuit Tuban, Borobodur at Jalan Susuit Tuban 37 has a good range of batik. For **vehicle rental**, Koko Rental, Jalan Ikan Pesut 34 (☎0333/411371), has Suzukis at Rp70,000 and Kijang at Rp90,000 for 24hr (including the driver but excluding petrol).

There are two **national park offices** in Banyuwangi: Kantor Balai Taman Nasional Baluran, Jalan K.H. Agus Salim 132 (☎0333/24119), and Kantor Balai Taman Nasional Alas Purwo, Jalan A. Yani 108 (☎0333/411587, fax 411857), both are open Monday to Thursday 7am to 2pm, Friday 7am to 11am, Saturday 7am to 1pm. They have some brochures in English about the parks and try to answer queries. Accommodation in the parks can be booked at the park posts close to the entrances.

ACCOMMODATION

There are plenty of **places to stay** in Banyuwangi and on the way to Ketapang in all price brackets; most are used to tourists and can help with vehicle charter.

Hotel Baru, Jl M.T. Hariyono 82–84 (☎0333/21369). Popular with travellers, in a quiet central location 10min walk from the post office. All rooms have attached mandi, and the more expensive ones have air-con. ②–③.

Hotel Berlian Abadi, Jl Yos Sudarso 165 (☎0333/27688). 4km north of Blambangan terminal on the way to Ketapang, this is an excellent new addition to the top end of the market, although it can be a bit noisy as the road is so busy. All rooms are tiled and the pool is excellent, although not included in the room charge at the lower end; admission is Rp2500. There is an attached restaurant. ③–⑥.

Hotel Berlin Barat, Jl M.T. Hariyono 93 (☎0333/21323). With the same owners as *Hotel Baru*, this place is more spacious; rooms are of a similar standard and all have attached mandi. ②–③.

Hotel Blambangan, Jl Dr Wahidin 4 (☎0333/21598). On the south side of the sports field about 100m from the post office, accommodation is in an old colonial bungalow and a two-storey building behind. All rooms are large with high ceilings, and those upstairs have balconies. ②–③.

Hotel Ikhtiar Surya, Jl Gajah Made 9 (☎0333/21063). About 1.5km west of the town centre, reached by Lin 8 from Brawijaya terminal or Lin 4 or 7 from Blambangan. This is a large setup with rooms around a garden, and there are many standards of accommodation on offer. ②–④.

Hotel Ketapang Indah, Jl Gatot Suproto Km6 (☎0333/22280, fax 23597). The best of the top-end hotels in the area – accommodation is spread throughout attractive grounds, 6km north of Blambangan terminal on the way to Ketapang. All rooms have partially open-air bathrooms, hot-water showers and air-con, and there is a pleasant lounge area and restaurant with great views across to Bali, plus a good-sized swimming pool. Special discounts are often available. ⑥.

Hotel Pinang Sari, Jl Basuki Rachmat 116–122 (☎0333/23266, fax 26173). In a garden setting, 500m north of Blambangan terminal, the grounds are attractive and some rooms are furnished in traditional bamboo and wood. ②–⑥.

EATING AND DRINKING

Many of the hotels have attached **restaurants** and there is a **night market** along Jalan Pattimura.

CFC, Jl Sudirman 170. The usual fast-food fried options and blissful air-con.

Rumah Makan Hotel Baru, Jl M.T. Hariyono 82–84. Just opposite *Hotel Baru*, this place serves up inexpensive rice and noodle dishes in cool, relaxed surroundings.

Watu Bodol, Pantai Tepi. The beach is nothing special, but this place has a great location in an open *bale* looking across to Bali, serving moderate and expensive Indonesian, Chinese and seafood dishes. For less formal dining, head a few hundred metres north along the road to simpler warung. From here you can charter boats (bargain hard) just offshore to enticing Pulau Tabuan, with its white beaches.

Wina Restaurant, Jl Basuki Rachmat 62. On the street side of Blambangan terminal; they serve inexpensive fried chicken, *nasi ramen*, *nasi rawon*, juice and ices. It's an excellent place if you're passing through the terminal.

South of Banyuwangi

There are several spots worth a visit to the **south of Banyuwangi**. Gintangan offers an excellent chance to view rural Javanese life firsthand, whilst the **Alas Purwo national park** is a terrific draw for surfers, and great for wildlife-spotting.

The small, attractive village of **GINTANGAN** is located 30km south of Banyuwangi. There's plenty to see in the locality: it's just 3km to the local beach and 7km to Muncur, the second largest natural harbour in Indonesia. Bamboo items are produced here, including hats, baskets and boxes. To access Gintangan, get off the Banyuwangi–Jember bus at the village of Gladag, a few kilometres south of the large junction town of Rogojampi. Gintangan is 3km east of Gladag: ojek, becak, andong and the occasional microlet ply the route. There is a **homestay** in the village, *Victria's English Course* (☎0333/632166; ②–③); the owner, Amanu, was previously a guide in Bali and now teaches English, and he can arrange for you to visit the local traditional bone-setter who uses massage to heal. Simple warung provide basic meals.

On the northwestern side of Grajagan Bay, **GRAJAGAN** is a bustling fishing village; the **surfing** in its bay is world-class. The **beach**, Pantai Coko, is signed from the village: it's 300m to the gate (admission Rp1050, car Rp300, motorcycle Rp100) and then another 2km through the forest to the beach. This is a favourite local excursion spot, but during the week is pleasantly quiet. Due to the surf, take local advice (there's a forestry office) about safe swimming spots, be very careful and never swim near the rocks. The black-sand beach is fairly small, with a wooded headland to the south and brilliant views around the bay – to the east it's possible to see across to Cape Purwo, south of Plengkung. There is **accommodation** at *Wisma Perhutani* (no phone; ②) in basic rooms (bring your own sheet sleeping bag) with deep verandahs, attached mandi and electricity supplied by a generator in the evening. To get to **Plengkung**, where a surf camp caters for the visitors who flock here from April to October, it's possible to charter boats from Grajagan – you'll start bargaining at US$200 for a boat for ten people, so there is little advantage in going from Grajagan rather than overland through Alas Purwo (see below). **Access to Grajagan** is through Srono, a village 11km south of Rogojampi. By public transport there are minibuses from Brawijaya terminal in Banyuwangi to Purwoharjo, 10km south of Srono, and then microlets for the final 14km to Grajagan.

The Alas Purwo national park

Occupying a densely forested peninsula at the far southeastern extremity of Java, the **Alas Purwo national park** offers a good chance to see the Asiatic wild dog, banteng, deer and monkeys. There is plenty for birdwatchers, including peafowl, jungle fowl, pitta, kingfishers, waders, and several varieties of migrant birds such as plovers, redshanks, whimbrels, samerlings and pelicans.

To get to Alas Purwo, buses from Brawijaya in Banyuwangi marked for Kalipait actually terminate 1km further on at **Dam Bunting**, a small village with a few shops where you can stock up on food, although you'll get a better choice if you bring supplies from further afield. From here the road to the beach passes through **Pasar Anyar** where there's a **visitor centre** with maps, displays and information about the park. Then it's 14km to the beach at Triangulasi via the park post at **Rowobendo**, where you pay for **admission** (Rp2000, car Rp2000, motorcycle Rp1000) and can arrange accommodation. Without your own transport you'll need to charter an ojek from Dam Bunting to Triangulasi (Rp7000–8000 one way if you bargain).

The beach at **Triangulasi** is stunning: a curving white arc several kilometres long, with huge surf pounding as far as the eye can see across to Plengkung in the distance, and Grajagan and Grajagan Bay to the west with the coastal hills rising behind. It's a fabulous spot, although far too dangerous for swimming. At Triangulasi, there is basic **accommodation** (②) 200m from the beach, in simple wooden rooms on stilts with a bathroom at the back, a kitchen with a wood fire and a few simple utensils. There are no warung on the beach; you need to take food with you and be prepared to cook it. Two kilometres from Rowobendo at **Sadengan** there's a tower from which to observe the wildlife. At **Ngagelan**, accessed by a motorable road 6km from Rowobendo, turtles (green, leatherback, hawksbill and Oliver Ridley) come to the beach to lay eggs (November to March is the best time), and there is a hatchery where the eggs are protected. From Triangulasi it's 3km to **Pancur**, on the coast towards Plengkung – you can walk or the road is passable – where there's a **campsite**. From Pancur it's about 3km to Goa Istana, an ancient meditation spot, and 13km from Triangulasi to Plengkung. The only accommodation at Plengkung beach can be booked through PT Wadasari Wisata Surf, Jalan Pantai Kuta 8b, Denpasar, Bali (☎0361/7555588, fax 755690) or Plengkung Indah Wisata, Andika Plaza Blok A 22/23, Jalan Simpang Dutah 38–40, Surabaya (☎031/5315320).

Kalibaru

Located 50km west of Banyuwangi, along twisting roads with dramatic views north to the Ijen area and south to Meru Betiri national park, **KALIBARU** is a cool and pleasant village and a good base from which to explore the surrounding coffee, cocoa and rubber plantations. If you want to see the **plantations** at their best, the coffee season is from April to September; cocoa is dependent on the water supply but the crop is most prolific from June to August, and rubber is produced all year and is most spectacular in the rainy season when the trees produce most latex. PTP Nusantara XII is a substantial plantation (closed Sun), located 12km south of Glenmore, 10km east of Kalibaru; there is public transport but it's much easier with your own vehicle. If you go on Friday you'll also be able to enjoy the large weekly cattle market in Glenmore.

Other local **excursions** include **Tirto Argo**, a natural spring surrounded by a pool 10km from Kalibaru, and the waterfall, **Air Terjun**, at Wonorejo, 5km north of Kalibaru, which is a popular Sunday excursion for local people and accessible by ojek (Rp10,000 return if you bargain well). **Rafting** is available from *Margo Utomo* (see below) and a small **train** runs to Dresin from Kalibaru (minimum of six people); there's nothing much in Dresin, the pleasure being the leisurely journey through the countryside. If you want to explore further afield, Meru Betiri national park (see p.276) is accessible from Kalibaru, either on an organized tour or with your own transport.

The best place to stay in Kalibaru is the *Margo Utomo Homestay* (sometimes called *Margo Utomo I*), Jalan Lapangan 10 (☎0333/97700, fax 97124; ⑥), which is behind the station; cross to the north side of the tracks on foot and the homestay is up a small sideroad. **Accommodation** is in attractive bungalows with high ceilings, verandahs and hot-water bathrooms set in pleasant grounds. They can organize transport to anywhere in East Java and Bali (Rp195,000 to Surabaya, Rp214,500 to Denpasar on Bali) and have a range of local tours available to plantations and villages, or further afield to Baluran, Sukamade, Alas Purwo and Kawah Ijen. They also arrange local guides (Rp25,000 per day) and jungle trekking, from the area south of Glenmore through to Rajekwesi beach, where you are collected by car. There are minimum numbers, mostly two people, for all trips. Next door to *Margo Utomo Homestay*, *Wisma Susan*, Jalan Lapangan 12 (☎0333/97289; ③), has clean, neat, tiled rooms in the garden of a family house. All rooms have attached mandi and there is warm water in the evening. The price includes breakfast.

The **wartel** is about 50m west of the station in Kalibaru, Jalan Raya Jember 168 (5am–midnight). Next door is the **post office**, Jalan Raya Jember 15 (Mon–Thurs 7.30am–3pm, Fri 7.30–11.30am, Sat 7.30am–1pm). **Access** to Kalibaru is straightforward: all **buses** between Banyuwangi and Jember pass through (every 10min during the day). For long-distance destinations, change in Banyuwangi. Kalibaru is on the main east–west **rail** line between Banyuwangi and Surabaya, Malang and Yogyakarta.

travel details

Buses

It's almost impossible to give the **frequency** with which **bemos and buses** run, as they only depart when they have enough passengers to make the journey worthwhile. **Journey times** also vary a great deal. The times below are the minimum you can expect these journeys to take. Privately run shuttle, or **door-to-door**, buses run between the major tourist centres on Java.

Banyuwangi to: Bandung (daily; 24hr); Jakarta (daily; 20–24hr); Jember (every 20min; 3–4hr); Kalibaru (every 20min; 2hr 30min); Madura (Sumenep; hourly; 12hr); Malang (hourly; 7hr); Pasuruan (5 hourly; 6hr); Probolinggo (5 hourly; 5hr); Semarang (2 daily; 15–17hr); Situbondo (every 20min; 2–3hr); Solo (hourly; 11–13hr); Surabaya via the southern route (every 20min; 5–7hr); Surabaya via the northern route (every 10min; 5–7hr) Yogyakarta (hourly; 12–14hr).

Batu to: Jombang (hourly; 3hr); Kediri (hourly; 3hr); Malang (hourly; 30min).

Blitar to: Banyuwangi (hourly; 12hr); Denpasar (8 daily; 18hr); Jakarta (6 daily; 19hr); Kediri (4 hourly; 2–3hr); Malang (every 10min 3am–11pm; 3hr); Solo (5 daily; 6hr); Surabaya (2–6 hourly 2am–7.15pm; 4hr); Yogyakarta (hourly; 7hr).

Bondowoso to: Besuki (every 30min; 1hr); Blawan (4 daily; 3hr); Denpasar (daily; 8–9hr); Jember (every 20min; 1–2hr); Madura (Sumenep; 7 daily; 9hr); Malang (2 daily; 5–6hr); Situbondo (every 20min; 1hr); Surabaya (hourly; 4hr).

Jember to: Banyuwangi (7–12 hourly; 3–4hr); Blitar (2–4 hourly; 6–7hr); Denpasar (1–5 hourly; 7–8hr); Kalibaru (7–12 hourly; 1hr); Madura (Sumenep; every 30min; 9–10hr); Malang (4–6 hourly; 5–7hr); Probolinggo (every 5min; 3–4hr); Surabaya (every 5min; 6–8hr); Yogyakarta (hourly; 12–14hr).

Kalibaru to: Banyuwangi (7–12 hourly; 2hr 30min); Jember (7–12 hourly; 1hr).

Kediri to: Blitar (4 hourly; 2–3hr); Denpasar (daily; 18hr); Jakarta (daily; 18hr); Malang (4 hourly; 3hr); Nganjuk (6 hourly; 1hr); Surabaya via Pare and Malang (5 hourly; 5hr); Surabaya via Kertosono (5 hourly; 4hr); Yogyakarta via Solo (5 daily; 6hr).

Madiun to: Jakarta (daily; 16hr); Solo (hourly; 4hr); Surabaya (every 20min; 3–4hr); Yogyakarta (hourly; 6hr).

Malang to: Bandung (daily; 16hr); Banyuwangi (hourly; 7hr); Bengkulu (daily; 36hr); Blitar (hourly; 3hr); Denpasar (daily; 15hr); Jakarta (daily; 15hr); Jambi (daily; 48hr); Jember (hourly; 4–5hr); Kediri (hourly; 3hr); Medan (daily; 3 days); Palembang (daily; 36hr); Pasuruan (hourly; 1–2hr); Pekanbaru (daily; 48hr); Probolinggo (hourly; 2–3hr); Situbondo (hourly; 4hr); Surabaya (every 20min; 1hr 30min–2hr 30min); Yogyakarta (hourly; 7–9hr).

Mojokerto to: Surabaya (every 20min; 1hr 30min–2hr).

Pacitan to: Blitar (hourly; 4–5hr); Jakarta (18 daily; 13–15hr); Solo (4 hourly; 4–5hr); Surabaya (daily; 7–8hr).

Pasuruan to: Banyuwangi (5 hourly; 6hr); Denpasar (daily; 12hr); Jember (hourly; 3hr); Malang (hourly; 2–3hr); Mojokerto (hourly; 2hr); Probolinggo (5 hourly; 1hr); Surabaya (5 hourly; 1–2 hr).

Probolinggo to: Banyuwangi (5 hourly; 5hr); Bondowoso (1–2 hourly; 2–3hr); Denpasar (hourly; 11hr); Jakarta (hourly; 24hr); Jember (4 hourly; 2–3hr); Malang (hourly; 2–3hr); Mataram (Lombok; hourly; 16hr); Pasuruan (5 hourly; 1hr); Situbondo (5 hourly; 2–3hr); Solo (hourly; 7hr) Yogyakarta (hourly; 8–9hr).

Situbondo to: Banyuwangi (every 20min; 2–3hr); Bondowoso (every 20min; 1hr); Jember (every 20min; 2hr); Malang (hourly; 5–6hr); Pasuruan (every 20min; 3–4hr); Probolinggo (every 20min; 2–3hr); Surabaya (every 20min; 5–6hr).

Surabaya to: Banyuwangi (every 30min; 5–7hr); Bondowoso (hourly; 4hr); Bukitinggi (daily; 48hr); Denpasar (5 daily; 11hr); Jakarta (20 daily; 14hr); Jember (every 30min; 4hr); Madura (Sumenep; hourly; 5hr); Malang (every 30min; 2hr 30min); Mataram (2 daily; 20hr); Medan (daily; 3 days); Mojokerto (every 20min; 1hr20min); Padang (daily; 48hr); Palembang (daily; 36hr); Pekanbaru (daily; 48hr); Probolinggo (every 30min; 2hr); Semarang (every 30min; 6hr); Solo (every 30min; 5hr); Sumbawa Besar (daily; 26hr); Yogyakarta (every 30min; 7hr).

Trains

Banyuwangi to: Jember (daily; 3–4hr); Kalibaru (daily; 2hr 30min); Malang (daily; 5–6hr); Probolinggo (daily; 5–6hr) Surabaya (3 daily; 7hr); Yogyakarta (daily; 15hr).

Blitar to: Bangil (5 daily; 3hr 20min); Kediri (3 daily; 1hr 30min); Kertosono (3 daily; 2hr 30min); Malang (5 daily; 1hr 50min); Surabaya (8 daily; 4–5hr).

Bondowoso to: Jember (2 daily; 2hr); Kalisat (2 daily; 1hr); Panarukan (2 daily; 2hr); Situbondo (2 daily; 1hr 30min).

Jember to: Banyuwangi (6 daily; 3–4hr); Malang (daily; 4hr); Panarukan (2 daily; 4hr); Probolinggo (3 daily; 1–2hr); Surabaya (2 daily; 3hr); Yogyakarta (daily; 12hr).

Kalibaru to: Banyuwangi (7 daily; 1–2hr); Jember (2 daily; 2hr); Malang (daily; 6hr); Probolinggo (daily; 4hr); Surabaya (2 daily; 5hr); Yogyakarta (daily; 14hr).

Madiun to: Bandung (3 daily; 9–11hr); Banyuwangi (daily; 11hr); Jakarta (5 daily; 8–12hr); Jombang (daily; 1hr 30min); Kediri (daily; 2hr); Malang (daily; 5hr); Purwokerto (daily; 5hr); Solo (5 daily; 1hr 20min); Surabaya (8 daily; 2hr 30min–3hr 30min); Yogyakarta (5 daily; 3hr 30min).

Malang to: Banyuwangi (daily; 5–6hr); Blitar (5 daily; 1hr 50min); Jakarta (daily; 12hr 30min–18hr); Surabaya (8 daily; 3hr).

Mojokerto to: Bandung (daily; 18hr); Blitar (3 daily; 3hr); Jakarta (2 daily; 15hr); Madiun (2 daily; 1hr 45min); Malang (3 daily; 4hr 15min); Surabaya (7 daily; 1–2 hr); Yogyakarta (2 daily; 4hr).

Pasuruan to: Banyuwangi (4 daily; 5hr); Blitar (daily; 3hr 30min); Denpasar (daily; 12hr); Kediri (daily; 4hr 40min); Malang (daily; 1hr 40min); Surabaya (daily; 1hr 30min); Yogyakarta (daily; 10hr).

Probolinggo to: Banyuwangi via Jember and Kalibaru (4 daily; 5–6hr); Kediri via Malang and Blitar (daily; 5–6hr); Surabaya (3 daily; 2–4 hr).

Situbondo to: Bondowoso (2 daily; 1hr 30min); Jember (2 daily; 2–3hr); Kalisat (2 daily; 1–2hr); Panarukan (2 daily; 30min).

Surabaya Kota station to: Bandung (2 daily; 16–18hr); Banyuwangi (3 daily; 6–7hr); Blitar via Malang (5 daily; 4–5hr) or Kertosomo (4 daily; 4–5hr); Malang (7 daily; 3hr); Jakarta (3 daily; 14–16hr); Kertosomo (6 daily); Yogyakarta (2 daily; 5–6hr). Pasar Turi station to: Jakarta (6 daily; 12–16hr). Gubeng station to: Bandung (3 daily; 16–18hr); Banyuwangi (2 daily; 6–7hr); Jakarta (3 daily; 14hr); Mojokerto (7daily 1–2hr); Pasuruan (daily; 1hr 30min); Probolinggo (3 daily; 2–4 hr); Purwokerto (daily; 7hr 50min); Yogyakarta (daily; 5hr 10min).

Pelni ferries

For a chart of the Pelni routes, see pp.36–37 of Basics. Surabaya is the busiest port for Pelni boats; ferries from Surabaya sail to their destination ports every two weeks, unless stated below. The following is a summary of the more popular routes and not a complete listing.

Banyuwangi The *KM Tatamailou* calls in at Banyuwangi every 2 weeks, destination Merauke (5 days). Ports visited include: Amahai (4 days); Ambon (4 days); Badas (22hr); Bau Bau (3 days); Bima (28hr); Dili (3 days); Denpasar (7hr); Dobo (5 days); Fak-Fak (5 days); Kaimana (6 days); Labuanbajo (35hr); Larantuka (2 days); Makasar (46hr); Merauke (5 days); Saumlaki (4 days); Tual (5 days); Timika (2 times fortnightly 6–8hr).

Surabaya: Ambon (*KM Bukit Siguntang, KM Dibonsolo, KM Lambelu, KM Rinjani*; 2–3 days); Badas (*KM Pangrango*; 21hr); Balikpapan (*KM Tidar*, 3 times fortnightly; 22hr); Banda (*KM Bukit Siguntang, KM Rinjani*; 3 days); Banjarmasin (*KM Kelimutu*, 5 times fortnightly; 24hr); Batulicin (*KM Binaiya, KM Leuser*; 23hr); Bau-Bau (*KM Bukit Siguntang, KM Lambelu, KM Rinjani*; 2 days); Bawean (*KM Pangrango*; 7hr); Biak (*KM Dibonsolo*; 5 days); Bitung (*KM Kambuna, KM Lambelu, KM Umsini*; 3 days); Blinyu (*KM Bukit Raya*; 5 days); Denpasar (*KM Dibonsolo*; 16hr); Dili (*KM Dibonsolo*; 53hr); Dobo (*KM Bukit Siguntang*; monthly; 4 days); Dumai (*KM Bukit Siguntang, KM Kerinci*; 3 days); Ende (*KM Pangrango*; 3 days); Fak-Fak (*KM Rinjani*; 4 days); Jayapura (*KM Dibonsolo, KM Rinjani, KM Umsini*; 6–7 days); Kaimana (*KM Bukit Siguntang*; monthly; 4 days); Ketapang (*KM Pangrango*; 3 days); Kijang (*KM Bukit Siguntang, KM Kerinci*; 2 days); Kumai (*KM Leuser*, 22hr); Kupang (*KM Dibonsolo*; 44hr); Kwandang (*KM Umsini*; 3 days); Labuanbajo (*KM Pangrango*; 2 days); Letung (*KM Bukit Raya*; 4 days); Makasar (*KM Bukit Siguntang, KM Kambuna, KM Kerinci, KM Lambelu, KM Rinjani, KM Tidar, KM Umsini*; 24hr); Manokwari (*KM Dibonsolo, KM Rinjani, KM Umsini*; 4–5 days); Midai (*KM Bukit Raya*; 3 days); Nabire (*KM Rinjani, KM Umsini*; 5 days); Namlea (*KM Lambelu*; 3 days); Natuna (*KM Bukit Raya*; 3 days); Nias (*KM Kambuna, KM Lambelu*; 3 days); Nunukan (*KM Tidar*, 3 days); Padang (*KM Kambuna, KM Lambelu*; 30–42hr); Pantoloan (*KM Tidar*, 43hr); Pare-Pare (*KM Tidar*, 26hr); Pontianak (*KM Bukit Raya*; 39hr); Rote (*KM Pangrango*; 3 days); Sabu (*KM Pangrango*; 3 days); Samarinda (*KM Binaiya, KM Leuser*; 3 days); Sampit (*KM Binaiya, KM Bukit Raya, KM Pangrango*; 21–24hr);

Semarang (*KM Binaiya, KM Kelimutu*; weekly; *KM Leuser, KM Pangrango*; 44–50hr); Serasan (*KM Bukit Raya*; 3 days); Serui (*KM Rinjani, KM Umsini*; 6 days); Sibolga (*KM Kambuna, KM Lambelu*; 3 days); Sorong (*KM Dibonsolo, KM Rinjani, KM Umsini*; 4 days); Tambelan (*KM Bukit Raya*; 3 days); Tanjung Priok (*KM Bukit Siguntang, KM Dibonsolo, KM Kambuna, KM Kerinci, KM Lambelu*; 16–21hr); Tarakan (*KM Tidar*; weekly; 3 days); Tarempa (*KM Bukit Raya*; 3 days); Ternate (*KM Lambelu, KM Umsini*; 4 days); Toli-Toli (*KM Binaiya, KM Kambuna, KM Kerinci, KM Leuser*; 3–4 days); Tual (*KM Bukit Siguntang, KM Rinjani*; 4 days); Waingapu (*KM Pangrango*; 48hr).

Other ferries

Banyuwangi to: Gilimanuk (Bali; every 30min; 30min).

Kalianget (Madura) to: Tanjung Jangkhar (daily; 4hr).

Kamal (Madura) to: Surabaya (every 30min; 30min).

Surabaya to: Kamal (Madura; every 30min; 30min).

Tanjung Jangkhar to: Kalianget (Madura; daily; 4hr).

Flights

Surabaya to: Ambon (18 weekly; 4hr); Balikpapan (3 daily; 2hr); Banda Aceh (daily; 10hr); Bandung (4 daily; 1hr–2hr 30min); Banjarmasin (2 daily; 2hr); Batam (3 daily; 3hr 25min); Denpasar (12 daily; 1hr 10min); Dili (10 weekly; 4hr 30min); Gorontalo (4 weekly; 5hr); Jakarta (22 daily; 1hr 20min); Jayapura (5 daily; 9hr); Kendari (2 daily; 5hr); Kupang (3 daily; 6hr 35min); Manado (daily; 4hr); Mataram (5 daily; 1hr 30min); Medan (5 daily; 7hr); Palangkarya (daily; 5hr); Palu (2 daily; 6hr); Pekanbaru (daily; 6hr); Pontianak, via Jakarta (4 daily; 6hr); Samarinda (daily; 7hr); Semarang (6 daily; 50min); Solo (daily; 1hr 10min); Ternate (daily; 8hr 15min); Timika (2 daily; 11hr 40min); Ujung Pandan (11 daily; 1hr 30min); Waingapu (3 weekly; 3hr 20min–5hr 35min); Yogyakarta (8 daily; 50min).

CHAPTER FIVE

NORTH SUMATRA AND ACEH

The landscape of Indonesia's two westernmost provinces, **North Sumatra** and **Aceh**, is defined by the Bukit Barisan, a volcanic mountain range that runs along the whole of the western side of Sumatra. In Aceh and North Sumatra, the mountains rear almost vertically from the Indian Ocean in the west, before sloping gradually away towards the Malacca Straits in the east. The rivers that run from these central highlands to the plains of the east coast carry vast deposits of extremely fertile volcanic silt, and since colonial times the eastern deltas have featured huge coffee, tea and tobacco plantations. This agricultural richness, combined with some considerable offshore oil reserves, has helped to ensure the prosperity of this far-flung corner of the Indonesian archipelago.

For tourists, however, the main interest of these two provinces lies not on the east coast, but in the rugged central highlands. The inhabitants of the formidable highlands – descendants of a wave of immigrants who arrived in the North Sumatran hinterland over four thousand years ago – evolved almost completely in isolation from the rest of the island, developing languages and cultures that owe little to any outside influences. There are a number of these highland tribes scattered throughout the two provinces, but the most famous are the **Batak** of North Sumatra.

When Europeans first discovered the Batak at the end of the eighteenth century, their tales of cannibals engrossed the Western world. The fascination obviously still holds: every year visitors flock in their thousands to the Batak homelands. The chilly hill station of **Berastagi**, part of the Karo Batak territory, and the many waterside resorts around beautiful **Danau Toba** – Southeast Asia's largest lake and the spiritual home of the Toba Batak – throng with tourists every summer. Indeed, North Sumatra now receives more tourists than any other Indonesian province except Bali and Yogyakarta.

The province also features the hugely popular Orang Utan Rehabilitation Centre at **Bukit Lawang**, just a couple of hours' drive from the bustling provincial capital of **Medan**, an entry point from Malaysia, as well as the surfer's mecca of **Pulau Nias**, home to another indigenous group of ex-cannibals.

Bukit Lawang, Berastagi, Danau Toba and Nias form such a perfect diagonal route across the centre of Sumatra that most tourists bypass the province to the north. But Aceh has almost everything you could hope for in an Indonesian province: dense primary jungle and exotic wildlife in the **Gunung Leuser national park**, the largest reserve in Indonesia; picture-perfect beaches on **Pulau Weh** and the deserted **west coast**; a colourful mix of indigenous cultures in the isolated **Gayo** and **Alas highlands** in the centre of the island; and good food and breathtaking scenery almost everywhere you go.

Due in part to the lack of tourists who venture this far north, very little English is spoken in Aceh and an ability to speak some Indonesian is helpful. In North Sumatra, save for the remote outpost of Nias and the seldom-visited southern Batak lands, English is widely understood. With such a diverse terrain in Northern Sumatra, **weather** is fairly localized, though in general the highlands are much less humid than the sweltering eastern plains, and can occasionally be bitterly cold at night.

Some history

The coastal towns of North Sumatra and Aceh were amongst the first in Indonesia to convert to **Islam**, brought over by seafaring traders from India and Arabia as early as the eighth century AD. These towns, located at the mouths of the numerous small rivers that empty into the Malacca Straits from the highlands, thrived as trading ports, eventually coalescing into a number of small kingdoms. A visit by the Chinese eunuch and envoy **Cheng Ho** in the fifteenth century persuaded these coastal kingdoms that there was a fortune to be made by fulfilling China's demand for **pepper**, and for the next four hundred years North Sumatra and Aceh were amongst the world's biggest pepper producers: it constituted the region's most lucrative export. As a result, some of the small kingdoms, particularly in Aceh, enjoyed a degree of power that was out of all proportion to their tiny size.

This wealth attracted the attention of outsiders, keen to appropriate some of the spoils for themselves. The **Portuguese**, following their capture of Malacca in 1511, began to raid the east coast, which by this time had already fallen under the sway of the Sriwijayan empire of southern Sumatra. The Sriwijayan tenure in the Sumatran east coast was brief, thanks in part to the rise in power of the Acehnese sultanate based on the northern tip of Sumatra at Banda Aceh. This sultanate enjoyed supremacy over much of northern Sumatra, and even, under the leadership of **Iskandar Muda** (1607–36), over the Malaysian peninsula. Their hold over the straits was finally relaxed with the arrival of the **Dutch** in the mid-nineteenth century. Though the colonizers never fully subsumed the region, and their stay in Sumatra was characterized by numerous protests and occasional pitched battles fought against Acehnese freedom fighters, the people of North Sumatra and Aceh were never to acheive the level of autonomy they'd enjoyed prior to the Dutch invasion.

The Dutch were quick to exploit the natural riches of the island, and by the end of the nineteenth century the eastern slopes of the Bukit Barisan were covered by vast **plantations** of coffee, tea, pepper and palm oil. These products continued to form the backbone of North Sumatra's prosperous economy long after the Dutch had finally conceded their Sumatran territories in 1946.

While all this was happening on the coast, life in the **interior** continued much as it had done since the first settlers arrived from the Malaysian peninsula over three thousand years ago. Until Europeans first ventured into the Sumatran interior in the latter part of the eighteenth century, the Batak people of North Sumatra and the Gayo and Alas highlanders of Aceh had lived in virtual isolation from the outside world, only occasionally visiting their coastal cousins in order to trade or, occasionally, raid the villages there. These highland tribes were hostile both to outsiders and to each other, with villages often existing in a state of perpetual war with their neighbours. The way of life revolved around **agriculture**, **animism** and **cannibalism**. Eventually, however, the outside world began to exert an ever stronger influence over the highlands: the Alas and Gayo people and a couple of the Batak tribes converted to Islam in the first half of the nineteenth century, following the fundamentalist **Paderi movement** of the 1830s (see p.951), and though a few Batak villages continued to practise their animistic rituals until well into the twentieth century, most had succumbed to the teachings of the **Dutch missionaries** – by the early 1900s the majority professed the Christian faith.

NORTH SUMATRA

Sumatra's third largest province, **North Sumatra** plays host to a disproportionately large number of the island's big attractions. These include the orang-utans at **Bukit Lawang**, the Batak lands, with such geographical wonders as Danau Toba and the smoking volcanic peaks of Sinabung and Sibayak at Berestagi – and **Pulau Nias**, off the west coast. Curious Westerners have been visiting these and other attractions for well over a century, with most arriving at the island's capital, **Medan**, on the east coast. The tourist infrastructure in the province is good, with an excellent transport network (most points of interest are near the Trans-Sumatra Highway), and some first-class hotels, homestays and restaurants.

Medan

MEDAN, Indonesia's fourth largest city, has acquired a reputation for being a filthy and chaotic metropolis with few charms. This is somewhat unjust: although it's true that Medan is as addicted as any other big Indonesian city to shopping centres and fast-food culture, the capital of North Sumatra also has some glorious examples of turn-of-the-century **colonial architecture** and a couple of vivid **temples** from the same period. To the south and west of the city there are pleasant leafy suburbs and neat parks, where the roar of traffic is reduced to a barely audible hum.

During the nineteenth century, these tranquil **suburbs** were the home of the Dutch gentry, who grew rich on the back of the vast plantations that stretch up the slopes of the Bukit Barisan to the west of the city: prior to the plantation boom, **Medan Putri** was a small village at the confluence of the Deli and Babura rivers. *Medan* is Indonesian for "battlefield", and for most of the sixteenth century the fields surrounding the village were the venue for pitched battles between the rival sultanates of Deli Tua, near the modern-day port of Belawan, and Aceh. The Acehnese eventually prevailed and, as peace returned to the region, Medan slipped back into obscurity until an itinerant Dutch entrepreneur, **Jacob Nienhuys**, arrived in 1862. Recognizing the potential of the rich volcanic soil of the Bukit Barisan, Nienhuys began to grow tobacco on a small plot of land granted to him by the Sultan of Deli. Soon European entrepreneurs were flocking to North Sumatra to ask for similar concessions from the sultan, and the rapid transformation of the region began.

Modern Medan is largely a product of these prosperous colonial times. From a sleepy backwater village of fewer than two hundred people in 1823, the city has blossomed into a huge metropolis with a population of 1.2 million. The European entrepreneurs who built sumptuous **mansions** and grand offices brought with them thousands of immigrant labourers from China and India, who in their turn established quarters in the booming city, constructing an array of **temples**. Even the local royalty migrated to the city to be nearer the action, and the Sultan of Deli's official residence, **Maimoon Palace**, and the nearby **Mesjid Raya**, were added to the cityscape. Though none of these buildings are unmissable, if you fancy the comforts of a large and modern metropolis combined with some faded colonial grandeur, then Medan deserves a day of your time at least.

Arrival, orientation, information and city transport

Thanks to a local superstition that noise drives away evil spirits, Medan's **Polonia Airport** lies near the town centre at the southern end of Jalan Imam Bonjol. A taxi from the airport to the main square, Lapangan Merdeka, shouldn't cost more than Rp4000.

Belawan Harbour is 25km to the north of the city. A complimentary bus service to the town centre is laid on to meet the hydrofoil ferries from Penang; the yellow "Morina" angkutas #811 or #122 (Rp1500) also ply the route.

Medan has two main **bus stations**. The huge Amplas terminal, 5km south of the city centre, serves buses arriving from points south of Medan, including Java, Bukittinggi and Danau Toba. White "Medan Raya" minibuses (Rp750) leave from the hectic bemo station next door to Amplas, travel past Mesjid Raya and on to Lapangan Merdeka via Jalan Brig Jend A. Yani. The Pinang Baris bus station, 10km west of the city centre, serves buses travelling between Medan and destinations to the north or west of the city, including Bukit Lawang, Berastagi and Aceh. A DAMRI bus leaves from Pinang Baris to Lapangan Merdeka every twenty minutes (Rp300).

In the highly unlikely event that you arrive in Medan by **train** (Medan is connected by train to just a couple of minor towns in North Sumatra), you'll alight at the station on the eastern side of Lapangan Merdeka, in the very centre of town.

MOVING ON FROM MEDAN

Medan's Belawan Harbour serves both passenger **ferries** to Malaysia and local Pelni ferries to other parts of Indonesia. There are currently two ferries sailing to Penang: the *Perdana Expres* and the *Bahagia Expres*. With both, transfer to the port from the agency is free, and the cost for both is the same: Rp115,000 one way and Rp195,000 return, including the departure tax from Indonesia. The **Pelni** ship *KM Bukit Siguntang* calls in every four days at Belawan on its way to Jakarta. Pelni does not offer a complimentary lift from central Medan to Belawan, so you'll have to make your own way; the cheapest method is to catch the yellow angkuta "Morina" #811 or #122. See p.300 for ferry agents.

When leaving Medan by **bus**, remember that buses to points north and west of Medan depart from Pinang Baris (DAMRI bus #2 from the tourist office, or angkuta "Koperasi" #64 from Jalan Katamso), while the Amplas terminal (angkuta "Soedarko" #3 or #4 from the tourist office) serves all other destinations. There are two exceptions to this rule: travellers to **Berastagi** will find it much quicker to catch an angkuta to Padang Bulan (#60 from the Istana Plaza on Jalan R.H. Juanda, or #1 from the tourist office), in the southwestern corner of the city, from where buses leave every ten minutes; while those heading to **Singkil** (for Pulau Banyak) have their own direct minibus service, leaving daily at 1pm (Rp17,000) from the *Singkil Raya Café* at Jalan Tobing 81 (aka Jalan Bintang), a few blocks east of the Medan Mall in the heart of the bird market.

Medan can initially be quite confusing, though it shouldn't take you long to become acquainted with the basic **layout** of the city. The main south–north artery alters its name regularly along its length, beginning with Jalan Brig Jend Katamso as it passes the Maimoon Palace, before changing to Jalan Pemuda, Jalan Brig Jend A. Yani, Jalan Balai Kota, and finally Jalan Putri Hijau. A second major road, Jalan Sisingamangaraja (Jalan S.M. Raja for short) runs from the centre of town all the way to the Amplas bus terminal.

Medan's very friendly and knowledgeable **tourist office** is at Jalan Brig Jend A. Yani 107 (Mon–Thurs 7.30am–4pm, Fri 7.30am–noon; ☎061/538101), just a couple of hundred metres south of Lapangan Merdeka near the *Tip Top Kafé*.

The **transport system** is fairly comprehensive, so it's rarely necessary to walk too far in the hot and polluted city centre. **Angkuta** mini-vans are the mainstay of the transport network; they are numbered, and many have names too, according to the route they are travelling on. The relevant angkuta names and numbers are given in the text. The main angkuta station is at **Sambu**, west of the Olympia Plaza and the Central Market on Jalan Sutomo.

Accommodation

Most of the city's hotels have been built with the business traveller in mind, and those looking for mid-range or upmarket **accommodation** have plenty of choice. Medan has no distinct travellers' centre, although a number of cheap hotels have recently opened near the Mesjid Raya.

Danau Toba, Jl Imam Bonjol 17 (☎061/557000, fax 530553). The liveliest of the luxury hotels, with first-class facilities including a health centre and an excellent outdoor pool, as well as the *Tavern Pub* and *Ari Kink Kink* disco in the grounds – two of the busiest nightspots in town. Currently undergoing a much-needed restoration, the *Danau Toba* has dropped its prices drastically and now offers the best-value accommodation in town, persuading even backpackers to splash out and stay here. ③.

Garuda Plaza, Jl S.M. Raja 18 (☎ & fax 061/711411). The best of a fairly uninspiring bunch strung out along Jl S.M. Raja, the 151-room *Garuda Plaza* can boast a coffee shop, a decent-sized swimming pool and some of the fiercest air-con in Sumatra. ⑦.

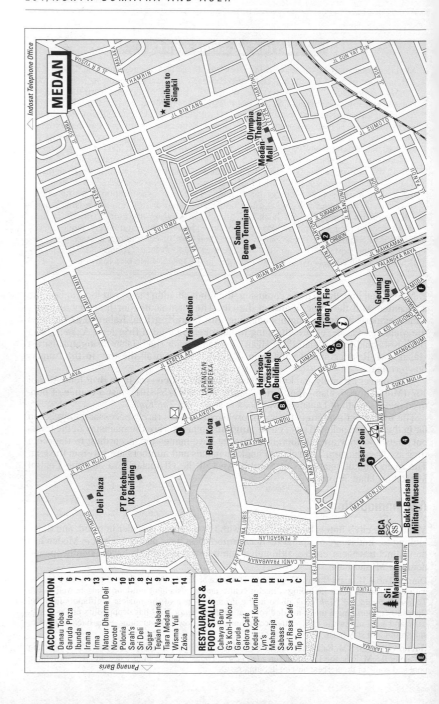

◁ Indosat Telephone Office

MEDAN

★ Minibus to Singkil

JL BINTANG

JL G H YUSUF
JL THAMRIN
JL MALAKA

JL SUN YAT SEN
JL ASIA

Olympia
Medan Theatre
Mall

JL SUMOTO

JL SEI KERA

JL SUBRA

Sambu
Bemo Terminal

JL SUTOMO

JL VETERAN

JL H. M. MUHAMID YAKIN

JL SURABAYA
JL CIREBON

JL BANDUNG
JL HARYONO

JL BOGOR
JL BANDU

JL IRIAN BARAT

JL LEJEN M T HARYONO ❷

JL MAHKAMAH

JL PALANGKA RAYA

Train Station

JL JAVA

JL KERETA API

Mansion of
Tjong A Fie

JL PEMUDA

Gedung
Juang ❻

JL KOL SUGIONO

JL A YANI V

JL A YANI VIII

JL AHMAD YANI

JL MANGKUBUMI

JL SUKA MULIA

Harrison-
Crossfield
Building

JL A YANI VII

LAPANGAN
MERDEKA

BALAIKOTA

JL A YANI

❶

JL MESJID

ⓘ
Ⓓ
Ⓒ

Ⓑ

Ⓐ

JL HINDU

Balai Kota ■

JL RADEN SALEH

JL H.M.A SYINAB

JL PALANG MERAH

Pasar Seni

❸

❹

PT Perkebunan
IX Building

Deli Plaza ■

JL PUTRI HIJAU

JL GURU PATIMPUS

JL MAY JEND SUTOYO

JL IMAM BONJOL

Bukit Barisan
Military Museum

BCA
$

JL PENGADILAN

JL KAP MAULANA LUBIS

JL CANDI PRAMBANAN

JL KEJAKSAAN

Sri
Mariamman ★

JL H ZAINUL ARIFIN

JL TEUKU UMAR

JL AIRLANGGA

JL KALINGGA

JL TRUMA

JL ARHUMA

Ⓔ

◁ Panang Baris

ACCOMMODATION

Danau Toba	4
Garuda Plaza	6
Ibunda	7
Irama	3
Irma	13
Natour Dharma Deli	1
Novotel	2
Polonia	10
Sarah's	15
Sri Deli	8
Sugar	12
Tepian Nabana	9
Tiara Medan	5
Wisma Yuli	11
Zakia	14

**RESTAURANTS &
FOOD STALLS**

Cahaya Baru	G
G's Koh-I-Noor	A
Garuda	F
Gelora Café	I
Kedai Kopi Kurnia	B
Lyn's	D
Maharaja	H
Sabass	J
Sari Rasa Café	C
Tip Top	C

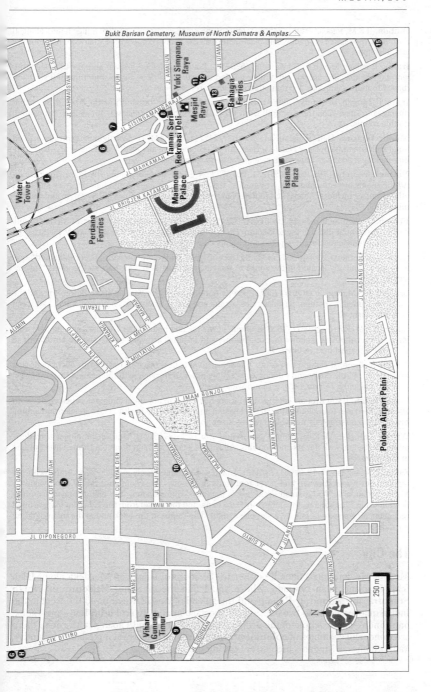

Bukit Barisan Cemetery, Museum of North Sumatra & Amplas

JL SUHRISNO
JL SUHRISNO
JL RAHMADSYAH
JL PURI
JL AMALUN
JL SISINGAMANGARAJA
JL UTAMA
Yuki Simpang Raya
Mesjid Raya
Bahagia Ferries
Taman Seri Rekreasi Deli
JL MAHKAMAH
Water Tower
Istana Plaza
Maimoon Palace
JL BRIGJEN KATAMSO
Perdana Ferries
JL PADANG GOLF
ALIMIN
JL TERATAI
JL KEMANA
JL MELATI
JL MULTATULI
JL LET JEN SUPRAPTO
JL IMAM BONJOL
JL K H A DAHLAN
JL AMIR HAMZAH
JL R H JUANDA
Polonia Airport Pelni
JL TENGKU DAUD
JL CUT MEUTIAH
JL R A KARTINI
JL CUT NYAK DIEN
JL HAJI AGUS SALIM
JL JENDERAL SUDIRMAN
JL MANGKUBUMI
JL RIVAI
JL DIPONEGORO
JL SOKHO
JL R H JUANDA
JL HANG TUAH
JL MONGINSIDI
Vihara Gunung Timur
JL CIK DITIRO
JL SUDIRMAN
JL URIP
N
0   250 m

Ibunda, Jl S.M. Raja 33 (☎061/745555). One of the smaller, cheaper and friendlier hotels along Jl S.M. Raja, the *Ibunda* is a family-run place where all the rooms come with TV, air-con, hot showers and telephone. ⑥.

Irama, Jl Palang Merah 112–115 (☎061/579118). Long-established losmen and one-time favourite with the backpacking crowd – until they got fed up with the airless dorms and unhelpful staff and moved to more salubrious accommodation elsewhere. ③.

Irma Jl Tengah 1b (☎061/758954). Basic, clean losmen to the south of the Mesjid Raya that manages to survive on the overspill from the *Zakia*, with twenty sparsely furnished, fan-cooled, double rooms. ②.

Natour Dharma Deli, Jl Balai Kota 2 (☎061/547744, fax 544477). Prestigious, centrally located hotel built round the former *Hotel De Boer*. All 180 rooms have air-con, TV and mini-bar; other facilities include a pool, bar, expensive café and a good cake shop. ⑦.

Novotel, Jl Cirebon 76a (☎061/561234, fax 572222). Large hotel adjoining the Plaza Hong Kong. All the rooms are equipped with air-con, TV, IDD telephone, mini-bar and hair dryer as standard; other features include Chinese and Indonesian restaurants, a pub, tennis courts, a gym and a swimming pool. ⑨.

Polonia, Jl Jend Sudirman 14 (☎061/542222, fax 538870). Located in the heart of Medan's well-heeled residential district, the 200-room *Polonia* boasts, amongst the usual luxury features, an excellent Chinese restaurant, squash and tennis courts and a small pool. ⑦.

Sarah's, Jl Pertama 10/4 (☎061/743783). Decent, quiet budget option with clean rooms and good food, inconveniently located in the south of the city, just west of Jl S.M. Raja by the large "Toyota" signboard. ③.

Sri Deli, Jl S.M. Raja 30 (☎061/713571). Pretty hotel where every window has a flower-box and the walls are painted in soothing pastel shades of pink and green. Rooms are adequate, but the staff can be a little surly. ⑥.

Sugar, Jl S.M. Raja 59 (☎061/743507). Small, newly opened hotel under German management aiming to corner the backpacker's market. Rooms and facilities are very basic, but the bar claims to serve the cheapest beer in town. ③.

Tepian Nabana, Jl Hang Tuah 6 (no phone). The cheapest place in town (with dorm beds just Rp3000), it's a little dingy and difficult to reach by public transport, with the nearest bus or angkuta stop outside the *Danau Toba*, a 15min walk away. ③.

Tiara Medan, Jl Cut Mutiah (☎061/519414, fax 510176). Luxury hotel and conference centre with 204 air-con rooms (complete with IDD, television and mini-bar), a health centre, restaurant, a number of bars but (strangely for a hotel of this size) no pool. ⑨.

Wisma Yuli, Jl S.M. Raja, Gang Pagaruyung 79b (☎061/719704). One of the oldest travellers' places in Medan, with dorms and doubles. All rooms have a fan, and there's a Home Direct phone in reception. ③.

Zakia, Jl Sipisopiso 10–12 (☎061/722413). Unexceptional but hugely popular guest house with the most numerous, aggressive and persistent touts in the city. The rooms are pretty good value by Medan's standards, and a small breakfast is included. Unfortunately, the call to prayer from the neighbouring Mesjid Raya, the uniformly hard beds, and the racket from the lads who hang around reception, all conspire to ensure a sleepless night. The rooms at the back and in the main building are quieter. ④.

The City

Most of Medan's attractions lie either to the south of Lapangan Merdeka along Jalan S.M. Raja and Jalan Pemuda, where you'll find the diverting **Museum of North Sumatra**, the **Maimoon Palace** and the splendid **Mesjid Raya** or, to the west in the Indian quarter, home to two of the most spectacular and atypical **temples** – one Taoist, one Hindu – in the whole of the archipelago. And all around Lapangan Merdeka there are wonderful examples of **colonial architecture**, particularly along Jalan Brig Jend A. Yani, which was Medan's high street during the Dutch era.

The Museum of North Sumatra, Mesjid Raya and Maimoon Palace

If you plan to spend only one day in Medan you should restrict your sightseeing to the city's three main attractions, all of which lie in the south of the city on or near Jalan S.M. Raja (named after a Batak king killed by the Dutch in 1907). The first of these is the **Museum of North Sumatra** (Tues–Sun 8.30am–noon & 1.30–5pm; Rp200), at Jalan Joni 51, 500m east of Jalan S.M. Raja on the southern side of the Bukit Barisan cemetery. Like most provincial museums in Indonesia, this a large, informative, well-laid-out and inexplicably deserted place. The concrete reliefs on the museum's facade depict a couple dressed in traditional costume from each of the different ethnic groups of the province (the various Batak tribes, the Niha people of Nias and the Malayu of the east coast). Inside the museum, the story of North Sumatra is told, from prehistory to the present day, with the inevitable emphasis on Indonesia's struggle for Independence. Highlights include a couple of Arabic gravestones from 8 AD – proof that Islam arrived on Sumatra more than a thousand years ago – and a number of ancient stone Buddhist sculptures found buried under Medan's Chinatown district. Most of the exhibits are labelled in English.

Eight hundred metres north of the museum on Jalan S.M. Raja, the black-domed **Mesjid Raya** (9am–5pm, except prayer times; donation) is, along with the mosque in Aceh, probably the most recognizable building in Sumatra. Built in 1906, the mosque, with its arched windows and blue-tiled walls, seems to have a Turkish or Moroccan influence, though it was actually designed by a Dutch architect in 1906. While obeying the iconoclastic restrictions of Islam in its refusal to depict living creatures, Mesjid Raya manages to be both ornate and colourful, with vivid stained-glass windows (from China) and intricate, flowing patterns painted on the interior walls and carved into the doors.

The mosque was commissioned by Sultan Makmun Al-Rasyid of the royal house of Deli. The family graveyard lies at the back of the mosque, while, just 200m further west, opposite the end of Jalan Mesjid Raya, stands their royal house, **Maimoon Palace** (daily 8am–5pm; Rp1000), built in 1888. With its yellow-painted walls (yellow is the traditional Malay colour of royalty), black crescent-surmounted roofs, Moorish archways and grassy lawns (which, like the mosque's, are the venue for impromptu thirty-a-side football matches every evening), the palace has many features in common with the mosque, and the two complement each other fairly well. The interior of the palace, however, is rather disappointing: the brother of the current sultan still lives in one wing, and only two rooms are open to the public, neither of which justify the entrance fee. The first room is the **reception hall**, complete with the royal throne (yellow, of course) and pictures of the sultans and their wives. The second room is a showcase for bad batik paintings and souvenirs.

Maimoon Palace lies at the southern end of **Jalan Pemuda**, a busy six-lane highway with few other attractions apart from, perhaps, the **Gedung Juang '45** (closed Fri 9am–2pm). This is yet another museum devoted to Indonesia's fight for Independence. If you've been to one of these sort of museums before then you'll know what to expect, though this one is slightly different in that it uses oil paintings and storyboards (rather than the usual dioramas) to recount Indonesia's glorious struggle of fifty years ago. It isn't really worth visiting, though one bizarre inclusion is a Molotov cocktail, for which the museum thoughtfully provides the full list of ingredients.

Jalan Brig Jend A. Yani and Lapangan Merdeka

At the northern end of Jalan Pemuda, **Jalan Brig Jend A. Yani** was the centre of colonial Medan and, amongst the modern sports and souvenir shops, there are a couple of early twentieth-century buildings. Of these, the most impressive is the weathered **Mansion of Tjong A Fie** at no. 105. This beautiful, green-shuttered, two-storey house was built for the head of the Chinese community in Medan, who made and lost a fortune investing in the plantations during the turbulent 1920s and 1930s. The mansion is closed to the public, but there's plenty to admire about the exterior – the dragon-topped gateway is magnificent, with the inner walls featuring some (very faded) portraits of Chinese gods and mythological characters.

The mansion stands almost directly opposite one of Medan's oldest and finest eateries, the *Tip Top Kafé* (see opposite), one of a number of handsome anonymous European buildings along this street. The most impressive, the 1920s **Harrison-Crossfield Building**, at Jl Brig Jend A. Yani's northern end, was the former headquarters of a rubber exporter and is now the home of the British Consulate and the British Council library.

Beyond this building, the road, as it passes along the western side of Lapangan Merdeka, changes its name to **Jalan Balai Kota** after the gleaming white **Balai Kota** (Town Hall). The **Natour** *Dharma Deli Hotel* – formerly the *Hotel De Boer*, the setting for the Ladislao Szekely novel *Tropic Fever* – is next door, while the **Kantor Wali Kota Madya**, the city post office that dates back to 1911, stands nearby on the northwestern corner of the square. In front of the post office is a (now defunct) **fountain** dedicated to the man who brought prosperity to the city, Jacob Nienhuys.

There's little of interest on the rest of Jalan Balai Kota, though the grand headquarters of **PT Perkebunan IX** (a government-run tobacco company) lie just to the west along narrow Jalan Tembakau Deli, 200m north of the **Natour** *Dharma Deli Hotel*. This dazzlingly white building, the first two storeys of which are faced by a series of small, attached pilasters, was commissioned by Nienhuys in 1869 as the offices of the VDM (Vereenigde Deli Maatschappij), the organization of Dutch plantation owners. It was the first European building in Medan and remains one of its most impressive and lavish examples of colonial architecture.

The Military Museum and the Indian quarter

Running west from the southern end of Jalan Brig Jend A. Yani, Jalan Palang Merah crosses Sungai Deli before continuing west as Jalan H. Zainul Arifin. The sights along this strip are really of minor interest and include the former **Dutch Assistant Resident's Office**, now a branch of the Standard Chartered Bank, which stands in the grounds of the *Hotel Danau Toba* on the southeastern corner of the junction with Jalan Imam Bonjol. Four hundred metres further on, past the incredibly dull **Bukit Barisan Military Museum** (Mon–Fri 8am–3pm; donation) – home to a few tatty old uniforms and amateurish paintings of Indonesia's struggle for Independence – is the **Sri Marriamman Temple**. Built in 1884 and devoted to the goddess Kali, this typically colourful and elaborate temple is Medan's oldest and most venerated Hindu shrine. Visitors are asked to remove their shoes before entering, and remain silent inside the temple grounds.

The Sri Marriamman temple marks the beginning of the **Indian quarter**, the **Kampung Keling**, the largest of its kind in Indonesia. Curiously, this quarter also houses the largest Chinese temple in Sumatra, the Taoist **Vihara Gunung Timur** (Temple of the Eastern Mountain), which, with its multitude of dragons, wizards, warriors and lotus petals, is tucked away on tiny Jalan Hang Tuah, 500m south of Sri Marriamman.

Eating and drinking

Medan has a cosmopolitan mix of **eating places**. Chinese food tends to dominate the warung, while there are some fine Indian restaurants in and around Kampung Keling. Medan also has its own style of alfresco eating, where a bunch of stall-owners gather in one place, chairs are put out, and a waitress brings a menu listing the food available from each of the stalls. The best of these is the *Taman Rekreasi Seri Deli*, which encircles the small pond to the north of Mesjid Raya.

The expat community's contribution to Medan's cusine is pastries and cakes. Amongst the many Western-style **bakers** in town are the *French Baker* at Jalan Pemuda 24c, *Medan Bakers* at Jalan-Zainul Arifin 150, and three on Jalan Tuama opposite the northern end of Jalan Cik Ditiro: the *Tahiti*, *Suans* (which does good ice cream) and the *Royal Holland*. **Fast-food** junkies are also well catered for, with a branch of *McDonald's* recently opened opposite the Mesjid Raya, a *Wendy's*, *Jolibee*, *Dunkin' Donuts* and *KFC* in the Deli Plaza on Jalan Balai Kota, and a *McDonald's* and *Dunkin' Donuts* in the Medan shopping centre.

Restaurants and warung

Cahaya Baru, Jl Cik Ditiro 8l. Newest and best of Medan's Indian restaurants, the service at this small place in the heart of the Indian quarter is fast and friendly, the prices very reasonable and the food excellent (including some delicious *masala thosas*).

G's Koh-I-Noor, Jl Mesjid 21 (☎061/513953). A long-established travellers' favourite, this Indian restaurant, run by the chatty Singh family, serves a delicious mutton korma; their comment books are filled with gushing praise.

Garuda, Jl Pemuda 201c–d. Good, cheap, 24hr Padang restaurant with superb fruit juices and a wide selection of Padang dishes.

Gelora Café, Jl S.M. Raja 4. An indoor version of the *Taman Rekreasi Seri Deli* (see opposite), where you sit at a table and a waitress brings you a menu with all the food on offer from the budget-priced stalls: the *murtabak* are particularly fine.

Kedai Kopi Kurnia, Jl Maj Jend Sutoyo 22. One of the most popular Chinese eateries in Medan, the open-sided *Kedai Kopi Kurnia* serves hearty portions of no-nonsense noodle dishes at very reasonable prices. Try their *kue tiawgoreng* – possibly the best of its kind in Sumatra.

Lyn's, Jl Jend A. Yani 98. Overpriced, dimly lit, wood-panelled restaurant, often deserted during the day but considerably rowdier in the evening when the Hash House Harriers (see below) call in.

Maharaja, Jl Cik Ditiro 8c. The *Koh-I-Noor's* only serious rival, this budget Indian restaurant's menu is small, unimaginative and rather overpriced, but the food is tasty and the staff welcoming.

Sabass, Jl Cik Ditiro 42. Cheap and cheerful Indian café selling scrumptious *murtabak* and – rare in Indonesia – spicy *roti canai* (Rp750).

Sari Rasa Café, Jl Brig Jend Katamso 38. Ideal budget place for those who hanker after Western food and are staying near the Maimoon Palace. The owner, the irrepressible Sylvia Tatty, serves tasty (though overpriced) Western meals, including a decent attempt at spaghetti bolognese.

Tip Top Kafé, Jl Jend A. Yani 92. One of the oldest restaurants in Sumatra and a tourist attraction in its own right, the mid-priced *Tip Top's* vast menu contains page after page of mouthwatering Western food. Beef sandwiches, frogs legs and, best of all, a wide selection of ice cream, alongside more traditional Indonesian and Chinese dishes. Try and get a seat on the verandah – the perfect place to sit and watch the world go by.

Nightlife and entertainment

For such a big city, Medan's **nightlife** is surprisingly subdued. *Lyn's*, at Jalan Jend A. Yani 98 is one of the few karaoke-free joints in town. With a dartboard, a piano, a well-stocked bar and a well-stained carpet, it's the closest you'll come to a British pub in Medan, and has become the favourite watering hole for that most British of establishments, the Hash House Harriers, an expat club founded Malaysia in the nineteenth century which dedicates itself to drinking and raising money for charity. The *Tavern Pub*, part of the *Danau Toba* complex, also aims for a pub atmosphere, and its combination of draught beer and live music (usually local rock bands performing Western covers) is currently a hit with well-heeled locals and expats alike. The *Equator Pub*, upstairs in the Hong Kong Plaza, is pretty soulless, though it does have occasional live music (usually local soft-rock bands).

Disco devotees are restricted to just a few choices. The *Ari Kink Kinh Disco*, next to the Standard and Chartered Bank in the grounds of the *Hotel Danau Toba*, has an excellent sound system and is, by quite some distance, the trendiest and most popular in town. You need to buy a drink at the door (beers cost Rp12500), though there is no extra entry charge. The same entrance policy is enforced by the *Haus Musik Nightclub* on Jalan Sutoyo, just 50m east of the bridge, which draws a younger crowd, with a mix of Western dance classics and Asian bubblegum pop: this is also the club of choice for Medan's **gay** community. The third, and by far and away the sleaziest option, is the cavernous *Horas Theatr*, opposite the water tower at the northern end of Jalan S.M. Raja, which does have a certain seedy glamour.

Medan isn't a hotbed of culture, but there is usually some sort of **dance** or **music display** happening somewhere. The tourist office will be able to advise you on what's going on and where. The small stage at the back of the Pasar Seni on Jalan Palang Merah holds regular performances by traditional dance troupes and bands; look on the board by the entrance on Jalan Listrik for details of forthcoming events. The North Sumatra Cultural Centre (also known as the Taman Budaya), on Jalan Perintis Kemerdekaan near the PT Indosat building, also holds music and drama performances.

Listings

Airline offices Bouraq, Jl Brig Jend Katamso 411 (☎061/552333); Cathay, Tiara Building, Jl Cut Mutiah (☎061/537008); Garuda, Jl Suprapto 2 (☎061/516066; includes city check-in), also at the *Hotel Dharma Deli*, Jl Balai Kota (☎061/516400), and the Tiara building, Jl Cut Mutiah (☎061/538527); Mandala, Jl Brig Jend Katamso 37e (☎061/513309); MAS, *Hotel Danau Toba*, Jl Imam Bonjol 17 (☎061/519333); Merpati, Jl Brig Jend Katamso 71d (☎061/321888); Silk Air, 6th floor, Bank Umum Servitas Building, Jl Imam Bonjol (☎061/537744); SMAC, Jl Imam Bonjol 59 (☎061/564760); Thai, *Hotel Dharma Deli*, Jl Balai Kota (☎061/510541).

Banks The BCA, at the corner of Jl Pangeran Diponegoro and Jl H. Zainul Arifin, offers by far the best rates in town, though it is only open for changing money between 10am and noon.

Bowling Taman Ria (Mon–Fri 5pm–midnight, Sat & Sun 2pm–midnight) Rp2500 per game, Rp1500 students 5–7pm only, shoe rental Rp1000. Catch any Pinang Baris-bound bus or bemo and jump off when you see the Taman Ria (on your right as you come from the town centre).

Cinemas The President Theatre on Jl Balai Kota, 100m north of the GPO near the Deli Plaza, shows the latest Hollywood releases.

Consulates Australia, Jl Kartini 32 (☎061/557810); Denmark, Jl Hang Jebat 2 (☎061/323020); Germany, Jl Karim MS (☎061/537108); Japan, Jl Suryo 12 (☎061/510033); Malaysia, Jl Pangeran Diponegoro 11 (☎061/25315); Netherlands, Jl A. Rivai 22 (☎061/519025); UK, Jl Brig Jend A. Yani 2 (☎061/518699).

Email Indonet, Jl Brig Jend Katamso 32l, is currently the cheapest in town (Rp4000 per hour), though it's usually very busy and can be slow. The *Novonet Café*, on the third floor of the Hong Kong Plaza (9am–midnight), and the new Infosinet, Jl Brig Jend Katamso 45J, on the corner opposite the palace, are a little quicker. The Warposnet at the GPO (Mon–Sat 8am–11pm, Sun 8am–7pm) charges Rp6000 per hour.

Ferries Pelni is at Jl Sugiono 5 (☎061/518899), opposite the blue BNI building (Mon–Fri 9am–3pm, Sat 8–10.30am). For ferries to Penang, visit the Perdana agent at Jl B.I. Katamso 35 (☎061/545803, fax 549325), or the Bahagia agent, Sukma Tours and Travel, at Jl S.M. Raja 92 (☎061/706500), one block south of the Mesjid Raya.

Hospital Dewi Maya Hospital, Jl Surakarta 2 (☎061/519291).

Pharmacy Apotik Kimia Farma, Jl Palang Merah 32, is open 24hr.

Post office Jl Balai Kota, on the northwest corner of Lapangan Merdeka (Mon–Fri 7.30am–8pm, Sat 7.30am–3pm). The Internet centre here is inefficient and expensive. The poste restante is currently at counter 11, while the Paket Pos office is round the north side of the building.

Shopping Medan's main shopping centre lies to the east of Lapangan Merdeka on Jl Letjen M.T. Haryono. Here you'll find dozens of small street stalls selling everything from fake Rolex watches to clockwork drumming monkeys, and two gigantic shopping centres: the swish Medan Mall, crammed with flashy boutiques and fast-food shacks, and the more downmarket Mata Hari Plaza. Jl Brig Jend A. Yani is the centre of Medan's souvenir and antiques trade: the Rufino Art Shop at no. 56, Asli Souvenirs at no. 62 and the Indonesian Art Shop at no. 30 are all worth investigating. Pasar Seni, the open-air market on Jl Palang Merah, also has a large selection of souvenir kiosks, though there's little in the way of antiques and the overall quality is not very good. The Yuki Simpang Raya is a new department store opposite the mosque.

Swimming The *Danau Toba* allows non-residents to use their pool for Rp8000 per day, for which you also get a free soft drink. The public swimming baths, Renang Kolam, at Jl S.M. Raja 6, charge only Rp2000 (6am–6pm).

Telephone offices Overseas calls can be made from the futuristic Indosat office (7am–midnight), on Jl Jati at the intersection with Jl Thamrin (Rp500 by becak from the GPO). The *Tip Top Kafé*, *Wisma Yuli* and the *Losmen Irama* all have Home Country Direct telephones.

Travel agents Chinderella, Jl Palang Merah 44; Lagundri Tours, Jl Pabrik Tenun 54 (☎061/553891, fax 547508); Trophy Tours, Jl Brig Jend Katamso 33 (☎061/555666); Valentine Tours and Travel, Jl Palang Merah 1, Komplek Pasar Seni (☎061/560530, fax 568427).

Work The Grand Education Centre, Jl Kapten Muslim (☎061/852872), invites tourists and travellers to come and teach English to their pupils in exchange for food and accommodation.

Bukit Lawang

Tucked away on the easternmost fringes of the Bukit Barisan range, 78km north of Medan, the **Orang-Utan Rehabilitation Centre** at **BUKIT LAWANG** is one of the most enjoyable places in North Sumatra. The centre has enjoyed great success in the 25 years since its inception, and has become a major tourist attraction, with travellers and day-trippers turning up in droves to watch the orang-utans during their twice-daily feeding sessions.

Whilst the orang-utans never cease to be entertaining, they aren't the only attraction of Bukit Lawang. The setting for the village, on the eastern banks of the roaring Sungai Bohorok opposite the steep, forest-clad slopes of the Gunung Leuser national park, is idyllic. The village also contains some of the most charming and inexpensive losmen in Sumatra, with balconies overlooking the river and macaques on the roof looking for food. In between the feeding times there are a number of other activities to choose from, ranging from the life-threatening (rafting down the Bohorok in an inner tube) to the leisurely (sitting in one of the many riverside restaurants writing postcards). Bukit Lawang does have its faults: at weekends it's often insufferably clogged with day-trippers from Medan, and during the rainy season some of the low-lying losmen can become flooded. But don't let this put you off – most of the time Bukit Lawang is rarely less than enchanting.

Practicalities

Bukit Lawang village is little more than a kilometre-long, hotel-lined path running along the eastern side of Sungai Bohorok (though recently a number of newer hotels have sprung up on the western side too). The village charges a one-off Rp1000 **entrance fee**, which will probably be extracted before you even alight from the bus. The bus stops at the southern end of the path in a square dominated by a multitude of identical souvenir stalls, as well as a small **wartel** (closed at the time of writing) and an uninformative **tourist office** (Mon–Sat 7am–2pm). There is no bank in Bukit Lawang, but the travel agencies all **change money**; the PT Pura Buana International, right on the southern end of the path just before the square, offers reasonable rates, though not as good as those in Medan.

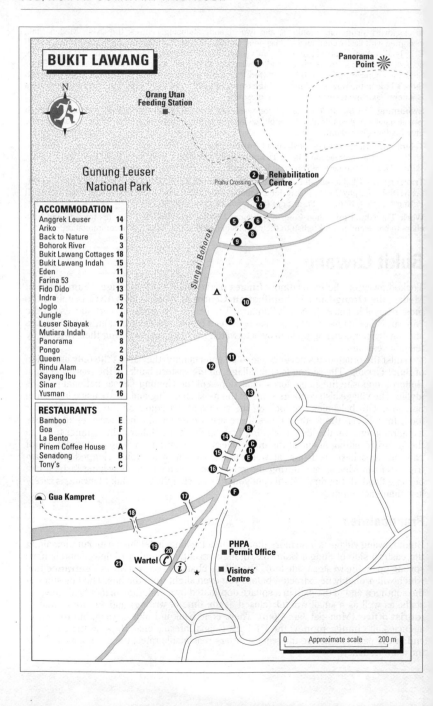

BUKIT LAWANG

N

Panorama Point

Orang Utan Feeding Station

Gunung Leuser National Park

Rehabilitation Centre

Prahu Crossing

Sungai Bohorok

ACCOMMODATION

Anggrek Leuser	14
Ariko	1
Back to Nature	6
Bohorok River	3
Bukit Lawang Cottages	18
Bukit Lawang Indah	15
Eden	11
Farina 53	10
Fido Dido	13
Indra	5
Joglo	12
Jungle	4
Leuser Sibayak	17
Mutiara Indah	19
Panorama	8
Pongo	2
Queen	9
Rindu Alam	21
Sayang Ibu	20
Sinar	7
Yusman	16

RESTAURANTS

Bamboo	E
Goa	F
La Bento	D
Pinem Coffee House	A
Senadong	B
Tony's	C

Gua Kampret

Wartel

PHPA Permit Office

Visitors' Centre

0   Approximate scale   200 m

You'll need a **permit** to watch the feeding sessions at the rehab centre, costing Rp4500 per day and available from the **PHPA Permit Office** (daily 7am–5pm) that overlooks the square to the east. Trekking permits (Rp3500 per day) are also available here; officially they do not include a visit to the feeding station. The permit office is part of the excellent **WWF Bohorok Visitor Centre** (daily 8am–3pm), which is packed with information about the park and the animals which live there, with particular emphasis given, inevitably, to the success of the orang-utan rehabilitation programme. Every Monday, Wednesday and Friday at 8pm the centre screens an excellent (but now rather scratched) British documentary about the work of the Rehabilitation Centre which is well worth catching.

Accommodation

Most of the larger **hotels** lie at the southern end of the path near the bus stop, whilst the **losmen** line the path up to the crossing by the Rehabilitation Centre. Virtually none of the losmen have phones, but if you're desperate to book ahead (unnecessary, unless you are in a very large group) you can always send a fax to the village wartel (☎061/575349). There's also a campsite halfway along the path, though, at Rp750 per person per night, it's only a fraction cheaper than a room in a losmen.

Anggrek Leuser (☎061/545559). Large, quiet hotel on the western side of the Bohorok with some good-value rooms, those set back from the river being slightly cheaper than the ones on the waterfront. The restaurant, standing on stilts in a fish pond, is recommended. ②.

Ariko Inn. Set in a lovely forest clearing a 30min walk from the bus stop, the *Ariko's* 24 bungalows are clean and pleasant, the restaurant (complete with pool table) serves some hearty meals, the staff are very helpful and there's a good atmosphere. Remember to bring a torch if you head out at night. ④.

Back to Nature (aka **Kembali ke Alam**). Scruffy but friendly losmen near the boat crossing to the Rehabilitation Centre. ②.

Bukit Lawang Cottages. Huge hotel to the north of the Bohorok at the southern end of the village. Each room comes with a shower and fan, and the restaurant is one of the best in Bukit Lawang. ⑤.

Bukit Lawang Indah (☎061/575219). Large hotel built on similar lines to the neighbouring *Leuser Sibayak*, with nicer rooms but less friendly staff. ②.

Eden Inn (☎061/575341). Don't be put off by the *Eden's* ugly facade – this is one of the best-value places in Bukit Lawang. The rooms are spacious and clean and have pleasant balconies overlooking the river, plus the staff are friendly and the food is excellent. ②.

Farina 53. Impressive guest house up on the slopes away from the river. The rooms are good value, though the disco (Wed & Sat 10pm) can be a nuisance if you don't want to join in. ③.

Jungle Inn, about 100m down from the canoe crossing. Popular losmen with some of the most spacious and comfortable rooms in the budget price range; the "honeymoon suite", where the bed has been partitioned off behind curtains, is particularly attractive. The popular restaurants serves some good curries and cakes. ②–④.

Leuser Sibayak. Large, attractive and long-established wisma situated at the bend of Sungai Bohorok opposite the bus station. Prices start at less than US$1 in the low season for a big double room with attached bathroom, while the new luxury rooms by the river have shower and TV. ①–④.

Pongo Resort (☎061/542574). Attractive resort with an unattractive name situated right next to the Rehabilitation Centre. The 21 smart but unexceptional villas are quite expensive by Bukit Lawang's standards, though a permit to watch the feeding sessions is included in the price. ⑥.

Queen Resort (☎061/579159). Large losmen set away from the river with adequate rooms and a big restaurant serving cheap Western food and, in their own words, "bloody cold beer". ②.

Rindu Alam (☎061/545015, fax 575370). Vastly overpriced, impersonal hotel to the west of the bus station that's popular with tour groups, though the gardens are pleasant and the rooms are large and comfortable. ⑥.

Eating

Most of the losmen have their own **restaurants**, and many travellers choose to eat in them rather than venturing out. The menus are similar in all of them, but down the years a few have come to specialize in a certain type of food. The *Jungle Inn*, for instance, is famous for its curries, while the *Eden* is renowned for its cheap Western food. Away from the losmen, the budget *Bamboo* does a good pizza, the mid-priced *Senadong* specializes in fish, and the newly opened *La Bento* claims to be Bukit Lawang's first vegetarian restaurant. But, for the best-value food in Bukit Lawang, pay a visit to the excellent *Goa Restaurant*, just 50m north of the bus stop: superb curries and Indonesian staples start at just Rp1500, and the beer is always cold.

The Orang-Utan Rehabilitation Centre

The **Bukit Lawang Orang-Utan Rehabilitation Centre** was founded in 1973 by two Swiss women, Monica Borner and Regina Frey, with the aim of returning captive and orphaned orang-utans back into the wild. The wild orang-utan population had been pushed to the verge of extinction by the destruction of their natural habitat, and the apes themselves had become extremely popular as pets, particularly in Singapore, where a baby orang-utan can fetch up to US$40,000. The centre's aim was to reintroduce domesticated orang-utan back into the wild, and transfer those apes whose habitat was under threat from the logging companies to the Gunung Leuser national park.

Upon arrival, new inmates are kept in cages for up to six months at the **quarantine station** behind the centre. Here, those who have spent most or all of their life in captivity are retaught the basics of being a wild orang-utan, such as the art of tree climbing and nest building. Once they've mastered these techniques, the orang-utans are freed into the forest near the centre to gain experience of living in the wild. These feral apes are still offered food twice a day at the centre's feeding platform, though the menu – bananas and milk – is deliberately monotonous to encourage the apes to forage for their own food in the forest. Once they have proved that they can successfully fend for themselves, the orang-utans are taken far off into the park and released to begin a new life.

Though the Rehabilitation Centre is normally closed to the public, visitors are allowed to watch the twice-daily (8am & 3pm), hour-long **feeding sessions** that take place on the hill behind the centre. All visitors must have a **permit** from the PHPA office (see p.303), which should be handed in at the Rehabilitation Centre on arrival. The centre is reached by a small pulley-powered canoe that begins operating approximately thirty minutes before feeding begins. A member of staff leads people past the quarantine station and up the hill to the feeding station – a wooden platform in the forest on the side of the hill. All being well, you should see at least one orang-utan during the hour-long session, and to witness their gymnastics, swooping over the heads of the crowd on their way to the platform, is to enjoy one of the most memorable experiences in Indonesia.

Trekking and tubing around Bukit Lawang

Bukit Lawang is the most popular base for organizing **treks** into the Gunung Leuser national park (see p.344), with plenty of guides based here, including a number who work part time at the rehabilitation centre. The park around Bukit Lawang is actually a little over-trekked, and most serious walkers now prefer to base themselves in Ketambe in southern Aceh (see p.344). But if you only want a short day-trek, a walk in the forest around Bukit Lawang is fine, and your chance of seeing monkeys, gibbons, macaques and, of course, orang-utans is very high. If you do decide to do a **long trek** from Bukit Lawang, the five- to seven-day walk to Ketambe is pleasant and passes through some excellent tracts of primary forest. The three-day hike to Berastagi is also very popular.

Most of the information about trekking in the Gunung Leuser national park is given in the Ketambe section, but it's worth mentioning a few points here. First, you must to have a **permit** (see opposite) for every day that you plan to spend in the park. You should also be careful when choosing your **guide**. The PHPA office at Bukit Lawang recommends three local guides: Pak Nasib, Pak Mahadi and Pak Arifin. Their fees are higher than average, at approximately US$15 including lunch and permit for a one-day trek, but you can be certain that they know the forest well. Most of the other guides charge about Rp20,000 per day. Whoever you decide to hire, they shouldn't feed the orang-utans.

There are a couple of **minor walks** around Bukit Lawang that don't actually cross into the park, so permits and guides are unnecessary. The short, forty-minute walk to the **Gua Kampret** (Black Cave) is the simplest. It begins behind the Bukit Lawang cottages and heads west through the rubber plantations and, though it's easy, you'll still need good walking shoes and a torch if you're going to scramble over the rocks and explore the single-chamber cave. Officially the cave has an Rp1000 entrance fee, though there's often nobody around to collect it.

By contrast, the path to the **Panorama Point**, in the hills to the east of Bukit Lawang, is difficult to follow. Most people take the path that begins behind the *Back to Nature Guesthouse*, though this heads off through secondary forest and it's very easy to lose your way. A slightly easier route to follow – though much longer – is the path behind the Poliklinik near the visitor centre. It passes through cocoa and rubber plantations and, if you're successful, ninety minutes after setting out you should be able to gaze upon the valley of Bohorok, with only the chatter of monkeys and birds to keep you company.

Tubing

Despite the risks involved, at some stage during your stay in Bukit Lawang you might be tempted to have a go at **tubing** – the art of sitting in the inflated inner tube of a tyre as it hurtles downstream, battered by the wild currents of the Bohorok. The tubes can be rented from almost anywhere for about Rp2000 per day, or your losmen may supply them for free. There is a bridge 12km downstream of the village, where you can get out, dry off and catch a bus back. If you're not a strong swimmer, consider tubing on a Sunday, when lifeguards are dotted along the more dangerous stretches of the river around Bukit Lawang, to cope with the influx of day-trippers from Medan.

The Karo Highlands

Covering an area of almost five thousand square kilometres, from the northern tip of Danau Toba to the border of Aceh, the **Karo Highlands** comprise an extremely fertile volcanic plateau at the heart of the Bukit Barisan mountains. The plateau is home to over two hundred small farming villages and two main towns: the regional capital, Kabanjahe, and the popular market town and tourist resort of **Berastagi**.

According to local legend, the Karo people were the first of the Batak groups to settle in the highlands of North Sumatra – indeed, the name means "first arrivals". As with all Batak groups, the strongly patrilineal Karo have their own language, customs and rituals, most of which have survived, at least in a modified form, to this day. These include the **reburial ceremony**, held every few years, where deceased relatives are exhumed and their bones are washed with a mixture of water and orange juice, and convoluted **wedding** and **funeral ceremonies**, both of which can go on for days.

When the Dutch arrived at the beginning of this century they assumed, mistakenly, that the Karo were cannibals. The now-defunct Karonese tradition of filing teeth, combined with a fondness for chewing betel nut that stained their mouths a deep red, gave the Karo a truly fearsome and bloodthirsty appearance. In fact, the Karo, alone amongst

THE BATAK

Despite two hundred years of fairly intensive study by ethnologists, anthropologists and linguists, the **Batak** people of the North Sumatran highlands remain something of a mystery. Nobody is sure exactly when they arrived (it was probably three to four thousand years ago), where they came from (north Thailand, Burma and Borneo all being possibilities), or why they chose to settle in the remote Sumatran hinterland rather than on the fertile plains of the east coast where they presumably first landed.

The Batak have never ceased to fascinate Western observers since European missionaries encountered them in the latter years of the eighteenth century. Part of their appeal lies in their uniqueness: with a homeland that was almost inaccessible until this century, and a reputation for belligerence and cannibalism that served to deter would-be explorers from venturing too far onto their territory, the Batak lived and evolved in almost total isolation. Batak hostility towards outsiders extended to their neighbours. Early Batak villages, though traditionally very small, were completely self-contained; communication between one settlement and its neighbour was virtually nonexistent, with no paths or roads running between them, and inter-village feuding was commonplace. Inevitably, this eventually led to more permanent divisions, and today the Batak are divided into six distinctive ethnolinguistic groups: the **Pakpak**, whose homeland lies to the northwest of Danau Toba; the **Karo** of Berastagi and Kabanjahe; the **Simalungun** who live in the region around Pematangsiantar; the **Toba** Batak of Danau Toba; and the southern **Mandailing** and **Angkola** groups. Each of these groups has its own language, rituals, architectural style, mode of dress and religious beliefs.

Some history

Apart from a brief mention by the Greek historian Herodotus, Marco Polo's claim that the Batak ate their parents when they were too old to work in the fields, and an account by the fifteenth-century Venetian merchant, Nicolo di Conto, who talked of a "Batech" tribe that practiced cannibalism regularly (and used the skulls as a form of currency), there is almost no pre-eighteenth-century record of the existence of the Batak. The first detailed account was written by a botanist, **Charles Miller**, in 1772. According to Miller, these highland people were skilled farmers who lived in heavily fortified villages, worshipped the spirits of their ancestors, and spent most of their spare time waging war with their neighbours.

Following from Miller's reports, in 1783 the British explorer, **William Marsden**, set off for the Batak lands to carry out the first detailed study of its people: work that eventually resulted in his seminal book, *The History of Sumatra*. Marsden was fascinated by the dichotomous nature of the Batak: though they practised cannibalism, their culture, complete with its own distinctive languages and a unique system of writing, was one of the most advanced on the island. What was even more amazing was just how unique this culture was, though Marsden did notice traces of a southern Indian influence in the various calendars and languages and he cited over 150 Toba Batak words which have their origins in Sanskrit.

By the mid-nineteenth century, however, outside influences – particularly religious ones – had begun to make incursions into the Batak way of life. The two southernmost Batak groups, the Angkola and Mandailing people, had both converted to Islam following their defeat in the Paderi Wars of 1829–31 (see p.951). Following the "discovery" of Danau Toba by the eccentric Dutch linguist **H.N. Van der Tuuk** in 1853, the Dutch campaign to convert the Batak people to Protestantism began in earnest. When the **Dutch army** arrived in 1907, the Batak, riven by petty internal disputes, failed to present a united force and were quickly subjugated. The last Batak king, Sisingamangaraja, died in battle in 1907, and thereafter the highlands of North Sumatra were added to the growing list of territories under Dutch control.

Batak religion

As with most of Indonesia, the traditional beliefs of the various Batak groups have a veneer of Islam or Christianity. However, with the Batak, that veneer is thinner than elsewhere in the archipelago, and the various animist religions are still widely practised, particularly in the Karo and Pakpak homelands. Every Batak religion maintains that there is one **supreme god** who created the earth, although the exact method he used (in Batak mythology the supreme god is always male) varies from one Batak group to the next. This deity, whilst all-powerful, is also a remote figure who meddles little in petty human affairs, preferring instead to spend his time at home with his wife (which, according to the Toba Batak, is a giant blue chicken).

The Batak people contact their late ancestors when they require a little spiritual assistance, and to help them in this they hire the **village shaman**, known as the *guru* in Batak (or *dukun* in Toba), whose job it is to communicate with the deceased. As the Batak traditionally ascribe the onset of sickness as a sign that the soul (*tondi*) has temporarily left the body, so the guru also acts as the local doctor, healing the body by calling back the soul. The village guru is a vital part of village life even today, ranking second only to the village head in the local hierarchy.

Contacting the spirit world, however, is no easy matter. For starters, the *dukun* is all but impotent without his or her (*dukun* are just as likely to be female as male) trusty staff, known as the *tunggal* in Toba Batak. This staff – exquisitely carved from dark wood – was useless unless it had first taken possession of a **magic spirit** and, as with most Batak ceremonies, the method of obtaining this spirit was fairly gruesome. The first step was to catch a child from a nearby hostile village, which would then have molten lead poured down his or her throat. Cutting the body open, the guru would take the deceased child's entrails and, having added a few secret ingredients, mash them into a magic pulp which would then be poured into a hollow in the centre of the staff.

Cannibalism and the Batak

It is unknown what significance, if any, the Batak attached to the eating of human flesh. For five of the six groups, however (the Karo are the exception), cannibalism was an established – if infrequent – pastime. Marco Polo, during his time on the island in 1492, was one of the first Europeans to hear about cannibalism in Sumatra. His tales were added to and exaggerated by a number of Portuguese explorers who followed in his wake, though as neither they nor Marco Polo ever set foot in Batak territory their stories were always secondhand and usually exaggerated. The first European to give an eyewitness account of cannibalism was the nineteenth-century German geographer Franz Junghun, who reported just three instances during his eighteen-month stay with the Toba Batak in 1840–41. Whilst this would indicate that the frequency with which the Batak practised cannibalism was greatly exaggerated by the early Europeans, Junghun's account of one such feast shows that the rumoured savagery of such events was most certainly not:

> *The captive is bound to a stake in an upright position . . . the chief draws his knife, and explains that the victim is an utter scoundrel and not a human being at all. The Raja* [chief] *then cuts off the first piece, being either a slice of the forearm or the cheek, if this be fat enough. He holds up the flesh and drinks with gusto the blood streaming from it . . . Now all the men fall upon the bloody sacrifice . . . some eat the meat raw . . . the cries of the victim do not spoil their appetites. It is usually eight or ten minutes before the wounded man becomes unconscious, and a quarter of an hour before he dies.*

The nineteenth-century Batak positively advertised the love of human flesh; not only was this an effective deterrent against would-be invaders, but also helped them to gain employment as mercenary soldiers with the coastal Sumatrans. As in other parts of Indonesia, the practice died out earlier this century.

Islam and Christianity

The first major change to the religious make-up of the Batak occurred in the early nineteenth century with the **Paderi movement**. Formed in the Minangkabau Highlands and led by **Imam Bonjol** (who lives in street names all over the country today), the Paderi were a fundamental Islamic force whose "convert or die" approach to proselytizing met with remarkable success in the southern Batak lands, particularly in the Tapanuli region inhabited by the Angkola and Mandailing Batak. The Dutch, distracted by the Diponegoro-led uprising in Java (see p.951), suffered some heavy defeats at the hands of the Paderi before winning a comprehensive and lasting victory at Daludalu in 1838.

THE BATAK (continued)

Surprisingly however, though flanked to the north (by the Acehnese) and south by Muslims, the four remaining Batak groups – the Toba, Pakpak, Karo and Simalungun tribes – resisted all attempts to convert them to Islam. Even more surprisingly, where Islam failed, Dutch missionaries succeeded, and soon the majority of the Toba, Pakpak and Simalungun Batak had converted to Protestantism. The Karo continued to resist, however, and by 1940 there were only five thousand Karo Christians. They were eventually persuaded to convert in 1965 following the suppression of the Communist coup when, in a state of McCarthyite paranoia, the Sukarno government considered any member of a minority faith – including animists and atheists – to be communists.

Although the nineteenth-century Dutch missionaries met with a lot of resentment in the early days – due in part to their policies of banning un-Christian festivals, and prohibiting the use of Batak musical instruments – they did expose the Batak to Western **education**. Dutch missionary schools were founded in the Batak lands during the early 1800s, particularly around Danau Toba, and as a result the Toba Batak people are amongst the most educated, powerful and richest minorities in the country today, with senior figures in government, commerce and the military. The Toba Church has also grown to become the largest in Indonesia, with over three million members.

the Batak tribes, abhorred cannibalism, though their traditional **animist religion** was as rich and complex as any of the other Batak faiths. Today the Karo are a religiously pluralist society, over seventy percent of the people being Christian, fifteen percent Muslim and the rest adhering to the traditional Karo religion.

Asserting an even stronger influence than their religious beliefs, however, are their **family ties**. The Karonese society is ordered along strong patrilineal lines, with each member of society belonging to one of five the Karonese clans. Marriage within a clan is forbidden, and every member of Karonese society is bound by obligations to their clan, which are seen as more important than any religious duties. Failure to obey these ties, so the Karo believe, can result in severe misfortune, from drought to disease and even death.

Berastagi

Lying 1330m above sea level, 70km southwest of Medan and 25km due north of the shores of Toba, **BERASTAGI** is a cold and compact little hill station in the centre of the Karo Highlands. It was founded by the Dutch in the early 1920s as a temperate retreat from the sweltering heat of Medan, and has been popular with tourists ever since. Though there's little to do in Berastagi apart from savouring the three different **markets** or challenging the locals to game of chess, the town provides a perfect base for **trekking** and exploring the surrounding highlands. Berastagi is encircled by neatly ploughed fields and tiny, thatched Karo villages, a gorgeous bucolic landscape bookended by two huge but climbable volcanoes, **Gunung Sibayak** and **Gunung Sinabung**. Throw in the town's plentiful supply of cheap restaurants and hotels, and you begin to see why Berastagi has blossomed into North Sumatra's favourite hill station.

The Town

Berastagi – the town, incidentally, with perhaps the greatest number of alternative spellings in the entire archipelago, with Brastagi and Berestagi being the two most common variants – is little more than an overgrown, one-street village. That street is Jalan Veteran, at the northern end of which stands the **Tugu Perjuangan**, a memorial to those who fell in 1945 against the Dutch. Continue north and you'll find a number of luxurious

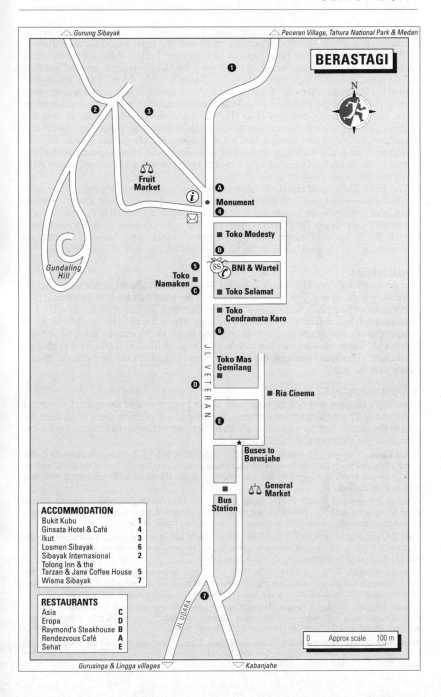

△ Gunung Sibayak

△ Peceren Village, Tahura National Park & Medan

BERASTAGI

❶

N

❷ **❸**

⚖ **Fruit Market**

ⓘ

Ⓐ **Monument**
❹

Gundaling Hill

■ **Toko Modesty**
Ⓑ

💰 🏛 **BNI & Wartel**

❺
Toko Namaken ■
Ⓒ ■ **Toko Selamat**

■ **Toko Cendramata Karo**
❻

J L   V E T E R A N

Toko Mas Gemilang
■

Ⓓ

■ **Ria Cinema**

Ⓔ

★ **Buses to Barusjahe**

⚖ **General Market**
■
Bus Station

ACCOMMODATION

Bukit Kubu	1
Ginsata Hotel & Café	4
Ikut	3
Losmen Sibayak	6
Sibayak Internasional	2
Tolong Inn & the	
Tarzan & Jane Coffee House	5
Wisma Sibayak	7

RESTAURANTS

Asia	C
Eropa	D
Raymond's Steakhouse	B
Rendezvous Café	A
Sehat	E

❼

J L   U D A R A

0	Approx scale	100 m

Gurusinga & Lingga villages ▽

▽ Kabanjahe

hotels and, in the far distance, Gunung Sibayak. Overlooking Berastagi to the west is Gundaling Hill, which provides an excellent view over the town, especially at sunrise.

Though most people use Berastagi just as a base for hiking, there are a number of attractions in the town itself, including three markets: the photogenic **general market**, selling meat, fish and fruit, takes place five times a week (Mon, Tues, Thurs–Sat) behind the bus station; the daily **fruit market**, which seems to sell more souvenirs than fruit, to the west of the roundabout, and the **Sunday market**, which takes place every other week on top of Gundaling Hill. This market attracts traders from all over the province, including such novelty acts as the teeth-pulling man (Rp200 per tooth) and the snake charmer. There are also half a dozen **souvenir shops** along Jalan Veteran, selling traditional woodcarvings, sculptures, instruments and knick-knacks from every corner of the Batak lands, including the highly recommended Toko Cendramata Karo at no. 89b and Toko Modesty at no. 33.

The *Bukit Kubu's* **golf course** is open to non-residents, though it's rather expensive (Rp20,000 green fees plus Rp25,000 club rental) and poorly maintained. There's a **swimming pool** at the *Sibayak Internasional* (10am–8pm; Rp4000), which is also the venue of Berastagi's only **disco** (Rp15,000). Other evening entertainment includes catching a kung-fu flick at the **Ria Cinema** (Rp1500), watching a **video** at the *Losmen Sibayak* (7pm onwards), or playing **pool** in one of the halls on the western side of Jalan Veteran.

Practicalities

The **post office** (Mon–Thurs 8am–2pm, Fri 8–11am) and **Telkom office** stand together by the war memorial, just off Jalan Veteran on the road that leads to Gundaling Hill. The **tourist office** (daily 8am–7pm) is just over the road; seldom visited, this office has been made all but redundant by the local losmen, whose information tends to be more comprehensive and practical. There is only one **bank** in Berastagi – the BNI at Jalan Veteran 53. Their rates are fair, but well below those in Medan. If you want to change US dollars, Toko Mas Gemilang, the jeweller at no. 139, offers the best rates in town – better than the bank.

ACCOMMODATION

Berastagi's **losmen** and **hotels**, especially at the budget end of the market, are great value and offer a wide range of facilities. Because of the altitude there is no need for fans in the rooms, but thick blankets are vital. Hot water is important too, and most losmen offer hot showers at Rp1000 a time.

Bukit Kubu, Jl Sempurna 2 (☎0628/91533). The best-looking hotel in Berastagi, built by the Dutch in the 1930s and set in the middle of its own nine-hole golf course. The old part of the hotel, with its polished-wood floors and open fireplaces, is a delight. Book ahead, as it fills up quickly with tour groups from Holland. ⑥.

Ginsata, Jl Veteran 27 (☎0628/91441). Quiet, unfussy hotel overlooking the main roundabout that's good if you want solitude. The rooms are basic but adequate and inexpensive, and there's even cheaper accommodation available in the cottage behind the hotel. ②–③.

Ikut, Jl Gundaling 24 (☎0628/91171). Housed in a dreamy old Dutch cottage in a garden just to the north of Jl Veteran, this budget losmen's rooms are a little scruffy and nothing special, though the beds in the draughty dorm are the cheapest in town. ③.

Losmen Sibayak, Jl Veteran 119 (☎0628/91122). Younger sister of the *Wisma Sibayak*, under the same management but with a slightly higher standard of rooms and a few added features such as a book exchange, Pelni ticket office and a pizza restaurant that shows videos every evening. ③.

Wisma Sibayak, Jl Udara 1 (☎0628/91104). One of Sumatra's best and longest-established hostels: the walls are smothered with good information (some a little dated), the travellers' comments books are very useful, and the beds are clean and very cheap. ③–④.

Megaview, Jl Raya Medan (☎0628/91650, fax 91652). Huge, luxurious hotel on the road to Medan with a decent-sized swimming pool, bar and karaoke lounge. Rooms have IDD telephones, hot water, satellite TV and a balcony. ⑥.

Mutiara, Jl Peceren 168 (☎0628/91555). Another enormous luxury hotel to the north of Berastagi with a Chinese restaurant, cocktail lounge and a swimming pool that has its own floating bar. Buffet breakfast is included in the rates. ⑦.

Sibayak Internasional, Jl Merdeka (☎0628/91301, fax 91307). The oldest of Berastagi's luxury hotels, with 73 rooms and 30 cottages. Facilities include squash and tennis courts, a heated swimming pool, billiards and even a small cinema. ⑧.

Sibayak Multinational Guest House, Jl Pendidikan 93 (☎0628/51031). Yet another branch of the Sibayak chain, set in its own gardens to the north of town on the way to Sibayak. Even the cheapest rooms come with their own terrace and a hot shower; rooms in the old 1930s Dutch section of the house are larger but cost more. ③–⑤.

Torong Inn, Jl Veteran 9 (☎0628/19966). Friendly but overpriced budget option with a good travellers' restaurant. ④.

EATING

For such a small town, Berastagi has a surprisingly wide range of **restaurants**. *Raymond's Steakhouse*, Jalan Veteran 49, is one of the best in town: prices compare with the losmen restaurants, yet it provides better service, music and food – New Zealand lamb, T-bone and rump steaks (Rp8000–12,000). The *Tarzan and Jane Restaurant*, part of the *Torong Inn*, is another decent budget eatery with an interesting collection of home-brewed drinks, including arak and papaya wine – best sipped whilst admiring the views of Gunung Sibayak. The *Ginsata Café*, below the hotel of the same name, serves up bitter tamarillo juice, which complements their fiery curries pretty well. The *Asia*, Jalan Veteran 10, is a very busy mid-range Chinese restaurant with an extensive menu, as is the *Eropa*, at no. 48g, which does an excellent plate of steaming *kue tiaw* for just Rp2500. Another good option, the *Rumah Makan Sehat* at no. 315, is a no-nonsense, family café selling cheap Indonesian and Chinese food.

The Karo villages

During the Dutch invasion of 1904, most of the larger **villages** and towns in the Karo Highlands were razed to the ground by the Karonese themselves to prevent the Dutch

from appropriating them. If you're interested in seeing traditional Karo architecture (see p.312), it's worth making a visit to the few small outlying villages that survived the Dutch period.

The most accessible of these traditional villages is **PECEREN** (Rp400 entrance fee), just 2km northeast of Berastagi. Coming from the town, take the road to Medan and turn down the lane on your right after the *Rose Garden* hotel. There are six traditional houses here, but although some are in good condition – the colourful gables on the first house in the village look as if they were made yesterday – the village itself is probably the least picturesque in the region, with modern housing encroaching on every side.

There are three more villages to the south of Berastagi that, when combined, make a pleasant day-trek from town: it takes about three hours to cover all three. The villages tend to be extremely muddy in places, so don't wear sandals, and many of the villagers, especially the women, are very shy, so always ask before pointing your camera at them.

The first village, **GURUSINGA**, lies about an hour due south of Berastagi. From the southern end of Jalan Veteran, take the road running southwest alongside the *Wisma Sibayak*. After about twenty minutes you'll come to a path signposted "Jl ke Koppas", which heads off through neatly sown cabbage and potato fields, many of which are dotted with bathroom-tiled family graves. Gurusinga, home to a number of huge traditional thatched longhouses sandwiched between more modern concrete homes, stands at the far end of these fields. The path continues along the western edge of the Gurusinga to the village of **LINGGA TULU** (which has a few unspectacular longhouses by the pathway), before passing through a bamboo forest. At the end of the path, turn left and head down the well-signposted road to **LINGGA**, the main tourist village in the Karo.

Three hundred metres before Lingga village itself, is the one-room **Karo Lingga Museum** (7am–5pm; donation), home to a few wooden cooking utensils, the odd totem and other obsolete Karonese implements. There are English labels, though they can be difficult to decipher. An attendant is usually on hand to provide further explanations.

Lingga has some of the best *rumah adat* in the area, many of which are over 150 years old. Unfortunately, the village has also become something of a tourist trap: you have to pay Rp300 just to enter and, if you want a guide – necessary if you want to go inside one of the houses – it's another Rp500. None of this money seems to have gone on restoring the buildings, some of which are in a terrible state of repair.

Once you've finished wandering around the village, head back to the main road and catch a minibus to Kabanjahe (last bus 5pm; Rp250), from where you can catch a bemo back to Berastagi (last bus 7pm; Rp300).

There are another couple of villages to the east of Berastagi – **Barus Jahe** and **Desa Serdang** – within a couple of kilometres of each other. The best thing about these two villages is that very few tourists make it here, so there's not the mercenary atmosphere evident at Lingga. Because there are so few tourists, though, there's little incentive to restore the houses, most of which date from the 1930s and are in a terrible state. Buses to Barus Jahe leave from the north side of the market; from Barus Jahe it's a stiff thirty-minute walk to Desa Serdang.

KARO ARCHITECTURE

There are only a few examples of the Karo *rumah adat* (traditional houses) left on the plateau today. Each house takes an entire village up to six months to build and, following the destruction wreaked during the Dutch invasion of 1904, most villagers turned their back on this sort of communal dwelling in favour of simpler, one-family concrete units. As a result, not one of the traditional houses on the plateau today is less than fifty years old.

Rumah adat were made of wood from the local forests, with braided bamboo for the gables and palm for the roofs; nails were never used. The houses are extremely tall and stand on thick, metre-high stilts, but nevertheless look fairly dumpy. The most impressive part of the exterior are the gables, the palm triangles at either end of the house that are usually woven into intricate and attractive patterns. At the gables' apex, at either end of the roof ridge (which, unlike the concave ridges of the Toba Batak houses, is straight), are a set of buffalo horns, and beneath each gable a bamboo ladder leads up to a verandah and into the house. Inside, a central corridor runs between the entrances, dividing the ground floor in half. There are no partitions on this floor, save for the sleeping quarters, and family life is carried out in full view of the neighbours. Eight to ten families live inside each of these houses, though once a member of the family turned 17 – assuming they were still single – he or she would then have to sleep outside, either in a room attached to the rice barn or in the local *los*, the open-sided meeting hall in the centre of the village.

Volcanoes around Berastagi

There are two active **volcanoes** more than 2000m high in the immediate vicinity around Berastagi: **Sibayak**, to the north of town, is possibly the most accessible volcano in the whole of Indonesia, and takes just four hours to climb up and down, while the hike up **Sinabung**, to the southwest of town, is longer and tougher. The lists of missing trekkers plastered all around Berastagi prove that these climbs are not as straightforward as they may at first seem. The tourist office urges climbers always to take a guide, which you can hire from them or from your losmen, though for Sibayak a guide is really unnecessary providing you're climbing with someone. For both volcanoes, set off early in the morning. It's a good idea to take some food too, particularly bananas and chocolate for energy, and warm clothing.

Gunung Sibayak and the Taman Hutan Raya Bukit Barisan

Before attempting your assault of **Sibayak** (2094m), pick up one of the *Wisma Sibayak*'s free maps, and read their information books too. The path begins fifteen minutes' walk beyond the *Sibayak Multinational Guest House* at the northern end of town. A wide, muddy track branches off from the road and up the mountain; having registered your name with the booth at the bottom and donated Rp500, follow the path for over ninety minutes until you come to a set of concrete steps heading straight up to the summit on your left. At the top are a number of sulphuric fissures and an attractive turquoise lake.

The most difficult part about this trek is trying to find the path back down. Having reached the rim of the crater, walk around the path in an anticlockwise direction until the stone hut in the crater stands between you and the lake. From this point, scramble up and over the top of the crater and with any luck you should see the first few broken steps of the path down. The steps are in a terrible condition and eventually peter out altogether, but the path that continues through the forest to the Sibayak Geothermal plant at the bottom is clear enough. Behind the plant are some **hot springs** (Rp500), where you can soak your tired calf muscles (take off any silver jewellery before entering the pool, or the sulphurous water will turn it black). From the spring you can catch a bemo back to Berastagi (Rp800), passing on the way the **Taman Hutan Raya Bukit Barisan** (Rp1100), a small arboretum that keeps a few wild animals in filthy and cramped conditions.

Gunung Sinabung

At 2452m, **Gunung Sinabung** is only slightly higher than Sibayak, but the ascent takes longer – at least three hours in total – and is a lot harder. A guide is recommended for this trek, as the trail is difficult to follow. Once again, the *Wisma Sibayak* have a good photocopied map of the climb.

The path begins by the side of a restaurant to the north of tiny Danau Kawar, and continues through cabbage fields for approximately an hour, before entering fairly thick jungle. The walk becomes relentlessly tough soon after; having left the jungle you soon find yourself scrambling up some steep and treacherous rocky gullies. All being well, a couple of hours later you'll be standing on the edge of a cliff looking down into Sinabung's two craters. Take care when walking around up here, as the paths are crumbling and it's a long way down.

Danau Toba

Lying right in the middle of the province, jewel-like **Danau Toba** is Southeast Asia's largest freshwater lake, and (at 525m) possibly the world's deepest too. It was formed about eighty thousand years ago by a colossal volcanic eruption: the caldera which was created eventually buckled under the pressure and collapsed in on itself, the high-sided basin that remained filling with water to form the lake.

A second, smaller volcanic eruption, 50,000 years after the first, created an island the size of Singapore in the middle of the lake. This island, **Samosir**, is the cultural and spiritual heartland of the **Toba Batak** and the favoured destination for foreign travellers. Ferries leave regularly from **Parapat** – the largest and most convenient gateway for Samosir – and other lakeside towns to the tiny east-coast peninsula of **Tuk Tuk** and neighbouring **Ambarita**, the most popular resorts on Samosir. From these resorts you can go trekking in the deforested hills in the centre of Samosir, or cycle around the coastline, calling in at the **tiny Batak villages** with their flamboyant tombs, distinctive concave-roofed houses and pretty wooden churches on the way.

If you're not into hiking or biking, however, there's very little to do on the island except relax. Luckily, the **resorts**, with their bookshops, bars and magic mushroom omelettes (illegal but ubiquitous), are well equipped to help you do just this, and all in all Danau Toba is the perfect spot to chill out after the rigours of travel in Sumatra.

Getting there

There are five main gateways to Samosir – details of ferry schedules are given on p.350. Most tourists catch a ferry from the Tigaraja Harbour in the resort of **Parapat** (see opposite); it's certainly the most convenient jumping-off point, with ferries every

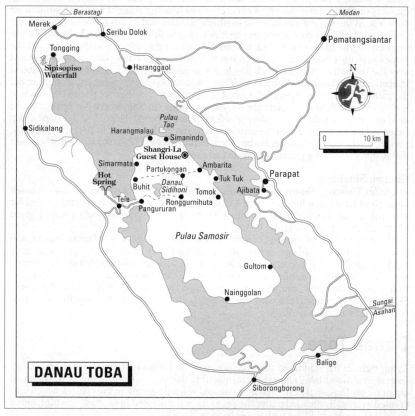

MOVING ON

Most travel agents on Tuk Tuk can sell through-tickets to your next destination, with the ferry crossing to Parapat included in the price. Ferries leave every hour from Ambarita (6.45am–4.45pm; Rp800) and Tuk Tuk (7am–2pm; Rp1000) to Parapat, calling in at all the ferry ports on the peninsula before they do so. If your bus leaves early in the morning (for example, the popular 6am bus to Bukittinggi; see p.350), you may have to spend a night in Parapat. There's also the occasional ferry to Tongging (from Ambarita and Tuk Tuk) and Haranggaol (from Ambarita); details are given on p.350.

The trip to **Berastagi** (see p.308) is a complex one, involving two bus changes and a total journey time of four to six hours. Firstly, you'll have to catch a bus to Pematangsiantar from Parapat (1hr; Rp1000), and from there a bus to Kabanjahe (3hr; Rp1700) and then a bemo to Berastagi (15min; Rp300). An alternative is to catch the daily tourist bus (Rp15,000), a four-hour ride that takes in the Sipisopiso Waterfall and the small Pematangpurba King's Palace on the way. Tickets can be bought from any travel agent.

If you are heading to the **west coast of Aceh** or **Singkil**, there are buses from Pangururan to Sidikalang, from where you can catch a bus to your destination. The journey time is only marginally quicker than if you went via Parapat, but at least this gives you the opportunity to see the western side of the lake. The first bus to Pangururan from Tomok (via the Tuk Tuk turn-off and Ambarita) leaves Tomok at 8am. From Pangururan buses leave every hour up to 2pm for Sidikalang, two hours away.

---

hour during the day to Tuk Tuk and Ambarita. If you have your own transport, **Ajibata**, the next cove south of Parapat, operates five car ferries per day to Tomok, the main town on Samosir's east coast.

Though the other two towns with ferry connections to Samosir are more charming than Parapat, frequent bus changes are necessary to get to either of them, and the ferries are far less frequent: the market town of **Haranggaol**, 40km north of Parapat, has just two weekly ferries to Samosir, while **Tongging** has just one (Mon 9am). Tongging is ideally located on Toba's northern shore near the 120-metre **Sipisopiso** (Like a Knife) **Waterfall**, a fairly spectacular local landmark that plunges from the side of the Toba basin to a small stream near the lake. Tongging's *Wisma Sibayak Guesthouse* (②) is a well-run place with some smart rooms – it's best to check that it's open before you arrive by contacting the *Losmen Sibayak* in Berastagi (☎0628/91122), which is run by the same family.

Finally, there is a way of getting to Samosir overland: buses from the Pakpak Batak town of Sidikalang travel to the east coast of Samosir via the **bridge** that connects the western shores of the island with the mainland. Travellers coming from the west coast of Aceh pass through Sidikalang and may want to take advantage of these buses.

Parapat

Situated at the point where the Trans-Sumatran Highway touches the eastern shore of Toba, **PARAPAT** is a town split in two. There's the rather tawdry **resort**, crammed with hotels, restaurants, karaoke bars and souvenir shops and, set on the hills away from the lake, a fairly humdrum area where you'll find the bus station, bank and telephone office. Buses arriving in Parapat drive through the resort to the ferry terminal before heading back to the bus station.

Nearly all the hotels in Parapat are geared towards Southeast Asian tourists rather than Westerners, who tend to head straight for the resorts on Samosir instead. Parapat does, however, have one or two advantages over Samosir's resorts: the rates at Parapat's **Bank BNI**, for example, on Jalan Sisingamangaraja, are far superior to anything offered on Samosir, and the cost of calling home from Parapat's **Telkom office**, on the back road between the bus station and the quay, is fifty percent cheaper than from Samosir. The twice-weekly (Wed & Sat) **food markets** by the Samosir jetty are lively and diverting.

With over sixty hotels in town, there's plenty of **accommodation** to choose from, though there are only a few at the budget end of the market. Of these, *Charley's*, right by the ferry terminal and next to the market at Jalan Pekan Tiga Raja 7 (☎0625/41277; ③), is by far the best. The hotel has some comfortable and spotless en-suite doubles, and Charley is one of the most helpful and entertaining hotel managers in Sumatra. In the mid-price bracket, the *Wisma Danau Toba* (☎0625/41302; ⑤), on Jalan Pulau Samosir near the highway, is the best of a pretty average bunch, while at the upper end of the market the three-star *Natour Parapat*, Jalan Marihat 1 (☎0625/41012, fax 41019; ⑨), stands head and shoulders above everything else. Each of the *Natour*'s 97 rooms come equipped with a TV, video and hot water, and the residents can make use of the hotel's private beach.

Pulau Samosir

Pulau Samosir is the spiritual heartland of the Toba Batak people, and one of the most fascinating, pleasant and laid-back holiday resorts in Indonesia. Until 1906, Samosir was not an island at all but a peninsula, connected to the lake's western shore by a narrow sliver of land running between Pangururan, the capital of Samosir, and the mainland hot spring resort of Tele. Then, in 1904, the Dutch carved a hole through this 250-metre-long isthmus to create a canal, simultaneously converting Samosir into an island. A bridge was built over the canal to connect the island with the mainland once more.

Few tourists get to see this side of the island, preferring instead to stay on the touristy eastern shores of Toba, where there's a string of enjoyable resorts, from **Tomok** in the south, to **Tuk Tuk**, **Ambarita** and the island's cultural centre, **Simanindo**, on Samosir's northern shore.

Despite the vast number of hotels and restaurants, the tourist infrastructure on Samosir is actually fairly poor. There is no official **tourist office**, for example (though the Gokhon Library, a small bookshop on Tuk Tuk, has some good maps of the island, and will also refill your water bottle with filtered water for Rp500), none of the **banks** is willing to change money, the only **telephone office** on the east coast, in Tomok, is not equipped to make international calls, and the only place with an **Internet** connection, the *Tabo Guesthouse*, charges up to Rp100,000 per hour. The travel agents and international hotels in Tuk Tuk do allow you to make international calls, though at inflated prices, and will also change your cash at dreadful rates. The *Anju Hotel* claims to charge the cheapest phone rates on the island, though they're still not as good as the rates in the Telkom office in Parapat.

Though sunbathing, reading, shopping and drinking are the most popular activities on Tuk Tuk, there are alternative recreational activities on the peninsula if you look hard enough. The waters that laps the shores of Tuk Tuk are safe for **swimming** in, for example; the roped-off section of the lake by *Carolina's*, complete with pontoons, canoes and a diving board, is the most popular place. One or two of the big hotels plan to buy and rent out jet skis. Many of the larger homestays and hotels have **sports equipment**, which they often allow non-residents to use. *Bagus Bay*, for example, provides facilities for badminton, volleyball, basketball and even a pool table – though the condition of the equipment is uniformly poor. *Roy's Pub* features a table tennis table, which they allow patrons to use during the day.

TRADITIONAL CRAFTS AND PERFORMING ARTS ON TOBA

Step inside any souvenir shop in Toba, and it won't take you long to realize that the Batak are skilled **woodcarvers**. The *tunggal*, the guru's magic staff, is traditionally carved with the faces of ancestors, as well as lizards, geckos and other creatures. Seldom used today, *tunggal* are still produced for the tourist market, cut into three segments to make them easier to fit into a rucksack. The Toba Batak also make the *pustaha*, a concertina-style book made of bark (or sometimes bamboo) and used to record spells and rituals. Another souvenir-shop favourite is the *porhalaan*, bamboo cylinders covered with Batak script that the villagers would use to determine the most propitious time to harvest crops or get married.

The Batak are skilled **weavers**, and on special occasions such as weddings or funerals the women of Toba still wear the traditional full-length woven shawl over their shoulders (Karo women tend to wear the woven cloth as a head covering). These days most of the weaving is done by machine with chemically produced dyes, though there are a couple of shops in Parapat where you can pick up a used, hand-woven shawl for as little as Rp15,000, depending on quality and condition.

Toba Batak pride themselves on their musical prowess: you'll notice that all the men on Toba seem to be able to play the guitar, which Western women are serenaded with ad nauseum. Amongst the indigenous **musical instruments** are sets of cloth-covered metal gongs, called the *gondang*, and the two-stringed violin. These instruments accompany the traditional dances. Batak **dances** tend to be slow and repetitive, with minimum movement. They aren't very spectacular, though sometimes, during weddings and funerals, the dance can go on all night and the stamina of the performers is incredible. The unique *sigale gale* **funeral dance**, where a life-size wooden puppet, its face painted to resemble the deceased, is wheeled around the room to offer comfort to the relatives, is perhaps the most famous – and certainly the strangest – of the Toba Batak dance forms. Some of the more advanced *sigale gale* puppets even have sponges built in behind the eyes, so that the puppet can cry at the whim of the puppeteer (who operates the mannequin by strings). You can see performances of *sigale gale* at Simanindo on Samosir.

Accommodation

In general, the **accommodation** on Samosir is excellent value, and it can be even better if you're good at bargaining, especially in the low season when the hotels are desperate for custom. You'll usually be set upon by touts way before you even reach the island, such is the fierce competition between the losmen, but it's important that you choose your accommodation carefully, as in most cases the hotel owner will insist that you eat in their restaurant every evening. Accommodation in the homestays often takes the form of quasi-Batak bungalows, which resemble traditional bungalows on the outside, but are often made of concrete rather than wood, and are usually a tad more comfortably furnished. If you're in Tuk Tuk in the high season and the hotels are full, try asking in the restaurants, many of which have a couple of rooms for rent out the back.

TUK TUK

Over thirty losmen and hotels, numerous restaurants, bars, bookshops, travel agents and souvenir stalls stand cheek by jowl on the **Tuk Tuk** peninsula. If you plan to stay here, tell the ferryman which hotel you plan to go to and he'll drop you off on the nearest quay. In general, the cheapest accommodation is on the northern side of the peninsula; the more luxurious hotels, on the long eastern shoreline.

Bagus Bay Homestay (☎0625/41481). Clean and basic bungalows set in large grounds, with excellent facilities including a pool table, badminton court, board games, bar, videos three times a night and a twice-weekly Batak dancing display. The food is variable. ②.

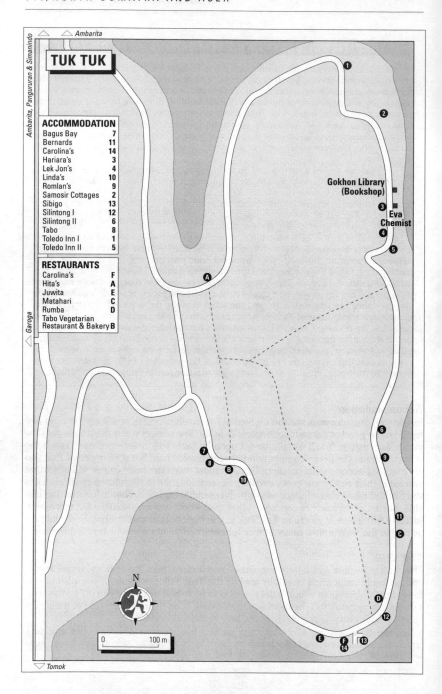

△ △ Ambarita

Ambarita, Pangururan & Simanindo

TUK TUK

Garoga ◁

Gokhon Library
(Bookshop) ■

■ Eva
Chemist

ACCOMMODATION

Bagus Bay	7
Bernards	11
Carolina's	14
Hariara's	3
Lek Jon's	4
Linda's	10
Romlan's	9
Samosir Cottages	2
Sibigo	13
Silintong I	12
Silintong II	6
Tabo	8
Toledo Inn I	1
Toledo Inn II	5

RESTAURANTS

Carolina's	F
Hita's	A
Juwita	E
Matahari	C
Rumba	D
Tabo Vegetarian Restaurant & Bakery	B

N

0   100 m

▽ Tomok

Carolina's (☎0625/41520). One of the classiest complexes on the peninsula: accommodation comes in the form of huge, Batak-style bungalows, each with a lakeside view and its own little section of beach. The Rp120,000 luxury rooms with fridge, hot water and TV are the best on the island. ⑥–⑦.

Hariara's. One of the most charming spots on Tuk Tuk: four spacious, tastefully decorated rooms situated in wonderful, carefully tended gardens. Rooms come with a walk-in wardrobe and Western bathroom; ask at the *Boruna*, 100m along the road, for the key. ③.

Lek Jon's (☎0625/41578). Budget, 38-room losmen with possibly the pushiest touts in Parapat. The rooms are plain but pleasant, and the staff are a lot of fun (Roberto will even serenade you with his guitar) – until, that is, you decide to eat elsewhere. ②.

Linda's. Long-established travellers' favourite, run by the indefatigable Linda and family. *Linda's* old and rather spartan accommodation has recently been augmented by a set of four luxury rooms with hot running water. This is one of the few places that doesn't mind if you eat elsewhere, though the cooking is a revelation and the portions are always huge. ②.

Mas (☎0625/451051). A combination of draughty, old cottages (over 100 years old in some cases) and newer, more comfortable, concrete homes, located halfway between Tuk Tuk and Ambarita next to an allotment of banana and papaya fruit. Once again, the management gets extremely cross if you don't eat at their restaurant. ③.

Romlan's. This exquisite little guest house has been hugely popular for many years now, despite its unfavourable location behind a rubbish dump. The traditional-style bungalows, with their freshly painted exteriors adorned with hanging baskets, are probably the best of their kind on the island. ③.

Samosir Cottages (☎0625/41050). Possibly the best mid-range accommodation on the peninsula, with prices ranging from basic rooms above the reception to luxury bungalows (complete with hot water and a bathtub) overlooking the lake. ④–⑤.

Sibigo (☎0625/451074). Small but expanding guest house down a small track near *Carolina's*. *Sibigo's* clean, quiet and comfortable rooms, particularly those on the beach overlooking the water, are a bargain. ②.

Silintong I (☎0625/41345) and **II** (☎0625/41439). Yet another oversized and overpriced hotel along the eastern stretch of the peninsula. The rooms are pleasant enough, and the hotel's orchid collection in the garden is gorgeous – but the rates, by the standards of Tuk Tuk, are absurdly high. ⑦.

Tabo Guesthouse (☎0625/41614). Mid-range hotel run by Anto and his German wife Annette. The rooms are most comfortable, though the garish pink decor in some could give you a migraine. However, the food conjured up in the restaurant and bakery is above reproach. ④.

Toledo Inn I and **II** (☎0625/41181). *Toledo I* is a massive, characterless complex that would be more at home in Torremolinos than Tuk Tuk. For all its amenities – hot water, fans, air-con in the more expensive rooms – it still feels like a prison camp. The *Toledo II*, down the road near the *Brando's Blues Bar*, is marginally better, but still cramped and overpriced for Tuk Tuk. ⑥.

AMBARITA

The **Ambarita resort** actually lies 2km north of Ambarita town. Unfortunately, boats have stopped calling at the resort, and now terminate in the town harbour before returning back to Parapat. Buses heading north often call in at the harbour to see if there's a ferry arriving, though you may have to wait a while for one. You could also try booking your accommodation in advance, as many hotels lay on a free transfer service from the harbour to the hotel.

Barbara's (☎0625/41230). The most popular hotel in Ambarita, thanks to its excellent and well-deserved reputation for friendly service and comfortable rooms. ②.

Kings I and **II** (☎0625/41421). Formerly known as *Gordon's*, *Kings I* and *II* are a long-established and popular pair of inexpensive homestays. *Kings II* has some smart Batak bungalows (all complete with hot showers), and is generally a more upmarket version of the busier, budget-orientated *Kings I*, a fairly nondescript place redeemed by its restaurant which serves some great vegetarian dishes. ①.

Sopo Toba (☎0625/41616). Large and long-established package-holiday resort, built on a steep hill to the south of the Ambarita resort. The supremely comfortable rooms come with hot water and a bathtub and are some of the most luxurious on the island. ⑥.

Shangri-La. Lying an awkward 6km to the north of the main Ambarita resort, this excellent home-stay has for years acted as a hideaway for travellers who want to avoid the travelling hordes on Tuk Tuk. The rooms are smart and comfortable, the restaurant serves large portions of standard Indonesian dishes, but what really sets this place above all others is the owner, Pami, whose generosity, helpfulness and encyclopedic knowledge of Sumatra distinguishes him from almost all the other hotel owners on Samosir. ③.

Thyesza (☎0625/41443). One of a string of fairly similar-looking places on Ambarita, with rooms ranging from the simple neo-Batak bungalows to the pricier rooms in the main building that come with hot water. ①.

Around the island

Though it would appear on most maps that there is a decent coastal road ringing Samosir, in reality this highway is in good condition only between Tomok and Simanindo. On the western side of the island the road is in a terrible state but navigable, while in the southern half of the island it has almost completely disintegrated and is off limits to all but the hardiest vehicles. This is a pity because the best **white-sand beaches**, including Gultom and Nainggolan, fringe the south coast. If you're adept at handling off-road **motorbikes**, available to rent from most homestays for Rp15,000–20,000 per day, you may be able to fight your way around. Stories have circulated recently about extortionate repair bills charged to travellers by the rental companies, so make sure you take care of the machines. **Bicycles** are a cheaper option, at Rp4000–5000 per day. It's possible to cycle all the way to Simanindo from Tuk Tuk, though set out early if you want to be back before dark.

Samosir does have a **public bus service**, too, though none of the buses drive through Tuk Tuk, instead sticking to the highway that runs to the west of the peninsula. Public buses run throughout the day from Pangururan to Tomok (5.30am–5.30pm) and vice versa (8am–9pm), a ninety-minute journey (Rp1500) round the north coast via Ambarita and Simanindo.

TREKKING ACROSS SAMOSIR

The hills in the centre of Samosir tower 700m above the lake and, on a clear day, afford arresting views over the water and beyond. At the heart of the island is a large plateau and **Danau Sidihoni**, a body of water about the size of a large village pond. It is possible, just, to walk from one side of the island to the other in one day – it takes ten hours or more – but a stopover in one of the villages on the plateau is usually necessary, so take overnight gear and a torch.

The climb from the eastern shore is very steep, but from the western shore the incline is far more gradual, so many trekkers start by catching the first bus to Pangururan (leaving at 8am from Tomok), arriving at about 9.30am. This account, however, begins in Ambarita on the eastern shore, and more specifically on the uphill path that starts to the north of the Ambarita petrol station. It's a stiff climb, but if you don't lose your way you should, two hours later, find yourself in the tiny hilltop village of **Partukongan** – aka Dolok or "summit" – the highest point on Samosir. There are two hostels here, *John's* and *Jenny's*, in fierce competition not only with each other, but also with the three losmen in the next village on the trail, **Ronggurnihuta**. The villagers can be a bit vague when giving directions, so take care and check frequently with passers-by that you're on the right trail. All being well, you'll find Ronggurnihuta is a three- or four-hour walk away, with **Pangururan** three to fours hours further on at the end of a torturously long downhill track (18km) that passes **Danau Sidihoni** on the way. Arrive in Pangururan before 5pm and you should be in time to catch the last bus back to the eastern shore; otherwise, you'll have to stay in one of Pangururan's rather soulless hostels, such as the *Wartel Wisata* (☎0626/20558, fax 20559; ④) at Jalan Dr T.B. Simatupang 42 by the bus stop.

TOBA ARCHITECTURE

As with all Batak houses, the cottages of the Toba are made of wooden planks bound together with palm fibre, and stand on two-metre-high pillars (these days made of stone to prevent them rotting away). They have two distinguishing features. The first is the **saddle-shaped roof** that slopes down towards the centre of the house, but rises at either end above the front and back entrances. Originally this roof would have been thatched with palm fibres, but corrugated metal is far more common these days. The second feature is the highly decorated wooden **gable**, intricately carved into a number of geometric patterns and cosmological designs and painted with the traditional Toba colours of black, white and red. One of the best examples of this kind of work stands by the highway in Ambarita, just north of the Tuk Tuk turn-off. As is customary, the smiling, mythical elephant–buffalo hybrid, Singa, features prominently, looking out above the front entrance that's deliberately small, so visitors are forced to bow in respect when entering. Though much smaller than the *rumah adat* of Berastagi, Toba houses could still hold up to four families; today, however, there are very few communal houses left.

Between Tomok and Pangururan

TOMOK, 2km south of Tuk Tuk, is the most southerly of the resorts on the east coast and a good place to begin a tour of this side of the island. The original town has been engulfed somewhat in recent years by the tourist boom, with dozens of virtually identical souvenir stalls lining the main street. This chain of stalls leads all the way up the hill to Tomok's most famous sight, the early nineteenth-century stone **sarcophagus of Raja Sidabutar**, the chief of the first tribe to migrate to the island. The coffin has a Singa face – a part-elephant, part-buffalo creature of Toban legend – carved into one end, and a small stone effigy of the king's wife on top of the lid, sitting with a bowl by her knees and a coconut shell on her head. It's an unusual coffin, and the best surviving example of the ornate stone sarcophagi that once dotted the landscape of Samosir. On the way to the tomb, halfway up the hill on the right, is the small **Museum of King Soribunto Sidabutar** (Mon–Sat 9am–5pm; Rp500), a small collection of tribal artefacts, stuffed animals and fading photographs relating to Tomok's turn-of-the-century king, housed in a one of a row of traditional Batak cottages.

On the way to Ambarita from Tomok, due west of Tuk Tuk, is the tiny village of **Garoga**, from where you can hike to the waterfall of the same name. The falls are only really worth seeing after a heavy downpour, being little more than a dribble at other times, though it's possible to go swimming in the pools at the bottom; ask the locals for directions.

In **AMBARITA** itself there is a curious collection of stone chairs (dawn to dusk; Rp1000), one of which is mysteriously occupied by a stone statue. Most of the villagers will tell you that these chairs acted as the local law courts two hundred years ago, where defendants were tried and the guilty executed. Others say that the chairs are actually less than fifty years old, and the work of a local mason who copied drawings of the original.

SIMANINDO lies at the northern end of the island, 15km beyond the town of Ambarita and 9km beyond the *Shangri-La Hotel*. The **Simanindo Museum** (daily 12.30–5pm; Rp1000) is housed in the former house of Raja Simalungun, the last Batak king, who was assassinated in 1946 for colluding with the Dutch. The museum has some mildly diverting household implements, including spears, magical charms and a wooden *guri guri* (ashes urn). The large *adat* houses in the **traditional village**, through the stone archway, are unexceptional save for their thatched roofs – a rarity on Samosir. The museum and village also hold traditional Batak dancing performances every morning (10.30–11.10am at the museum, 11.45am–12.30pm in the village), though the performances at the **Gokasi cultural centre** (10–11am & 11.15am–12.15pm; Rp3000), 1.5km further along the highway, are said to be better.

Continuing round to the western side of the island, **Simarmata**, halfway between Simanindo and Pangururan, is one of the best-preserved Batak villages on Samosir, though sadly all of the houses have lost their thatched roofs. There's little to see in **Pangururan** itself, though there's a **hot spring** (Rp1500) across the bridge in the village of **Tele**. The springs are at their busiest at the weekends and are cleaned out on Mondays, so Tuesday and Wednesday are the best and most hygienic days.

Eating

While many of the hotels try to prohibit their guests from eating anywhere else except their own restaurants, there are plenty of eateries dotted around Tuk Tuk should you manage to escape. Many of the restaurants try to cook Western food – burgers, pancakes and so on – and down the years they've become quite good at it. Local delicacies include *babi guling* (roast suckling pig) and *anjing* (dog, though the restaurants on Tuk Tuk tend not to advertise this).

Berastagi Juice House. Positioned on the small road running between the north and southern sides of Tuk Tuk, this Dutch-owned budget café is the perfect place to stop after a hard day's walking or cycling. As its name suggests, it serves nothing but delicious freshly squeezed juices: try their exquisite *marquisa* juice (Rp2000).

Carolina's. Widely recognized as the best-quality restaurant on the island, the expensive *Carolina's* – part of the hotel of the same name – has an extensive menu of Indonesian and Chinese food and hosts cultural performances most evenings.

Hita's, on the north side of the "neck" of the peninsula, opposite the footpath. The best-value budget restaurant on the whole of Tuk Tuk, a no-nonsense travellers' place that isn't half as popular as it deserves to be. The menu consists mainly of excellent tacos and curries, all of which, as the signboard says outside, are "good and cheap". If you're on this side of the peninsula, don't miss out.

Juwita, on the southern tip of peninsula, at the top of the hill, 100m to the west of *Carolina's*. Plain, unpretentious budget café serving dishes that are a little overpriced but occasionally delicious – for example, the *kanghung* (a kind of spinach) with *teras* (fermented shrimp paste).

Matahari, on the east side of the island, 200m south of *Romlan's* guest house. Unexceptional midprice restaurant notable only because they serve roast suckling pig, as long as there are at least ten of you willing to pay Rp8000 each.

Rumba. Swiss-owned budget to mid-priced restaurant with two branches on Tuk Tuk. Most the food at *Rumba's* is of a very high standard, particularly the pizzas, and if you order a day in advance you can try such local delicacies as *ikan mas*.

Tabo Vegetarian Restaurant and Bakery, next door to *Bagus Bay Homestay* on the southern side of the peninsula. Part of the guest house of the same name, this mid-priced restaurant has the most imaginative menu on Samosir. Try the *tempe* with lemon for starters, then move on to the vegetable curry before rounding it all off with a milkshake. Their freshly baked bread is the best in North Sumatra.

Nightlife

Toban **nightlife** revolves around videos, rock music and alcohol. In Ambarita you're pretty much confined to your hotel, such is the paucity of restaurants and bars there, but in **Tuk Tuk** you have some choice. Many of the hotels and bars on the peninsula offer free videos, including the *Bagus Bay* (three videos per night) and *Leo's* (two). A couple of bars shun videos in favour of loud music, such as the *Brando's Blues Bar*, which has a large selection of CDs, and *Roy's Pub*, which has its own disco and sometimes hosts live bands. *Saza's*, near *Leo's* and *Brando's*, has a number of pool tables that have only recently been installed and are still in a fairly good condition – a rarity in Indonesia.

For those who prefer something a bit more cultural, the *Bagus Bay Homestay* has traditional **Batak dancing** (Wed & Sat 8pm); they even promise to drop you off back at your hotel at the end of the performance. The dancers are a lacklustre bunch who look like they'd rather be elsewhere, but the band are enthusiastic and good fun. *Anju's* has live bands playing traditional Batak tunes (Tues, Thurs & Sat), and most of the big hotels on the peninsula (*Carolina's, Silintong, Toledo*) put on some sort of cultural entertainment – though you may have to eat in their restaurants if you want to catch the show.

Pulau Nias

Through the journey is long and arduous, and involves passing through the unlovely town of **Sibolga**, most visitors agree that any effort expended to get to Nias is worth it. An island the size of Bali, with a rich tribal culture, wonderful beaches and some of the best surfing in the country, **Pulau Nias** is a microcosm of almost everything that's exciting about Indonesia. Lying 125km southwest of Sibolga, the islands' reputation as a land of malarial swamps and bloodthirsty natives succeeded in keeping visitors at bay for centuries, leading to the development of a culture free from the influences of India, Arabia, Europe and, indeed, the rest of Indonesia. The 600,000 Niasans speak a distinct language, one that has more in common with Polynesian than any Indonesian tongue.

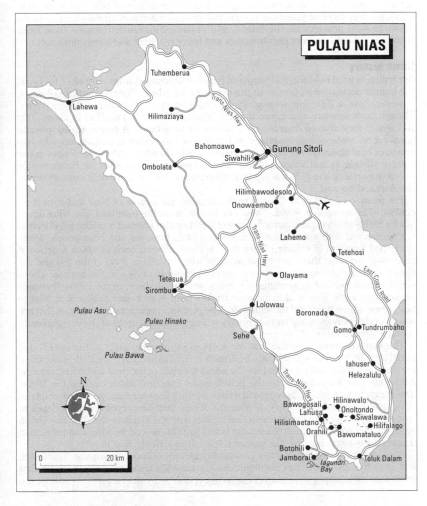

Pulau Nias is, culturally at least, split into two distinct regions – north and south. The north of Nias is largely swampland and, save for the capital, **Gunung Sitoli**, contains little that would appeal to the average tourist. The south, however, plays host to a number of fascinating **hill-top villages**, such as **Orahili**, **Bawomataluo** and the spiritual heartland of **Gomo**, where the last few remnants of Nias's famed megalithic culture survive. The south also has the best and most popular beaches, such as the **surfer's paradise** at **Lagundri Bay**, invaded every year by hordes of sun-bleached boarders eager to catch some of the best right-handers in the world.

Nias can be a difficult place to travel around. The landscape is rugged and there are very few roads, with only two major highways on the whole island: the **Trans-Nias Highway** between Gunung Sitoli in the northeast and Lagundri in the southwest, and a smaller track running along the island's eastern shore. The Nihas also have a reputation for being unfriendly and over-aggressive – a reputation that isn't entirely undeserved. Nevertheless, most visitors agree that the hardships of Nias are more than outweighed by its beauty, and the unique nature of its culture. **Malaria** (see p.28) continues to be a problem on the island, and chloroquine-resistant strains have been reported. Take the correct prophylactics and bring repellent and a mosquito net.

Some history

According to local folklore, the people of Nias are descended from six gods who begat the human population of Gomo, in the centre of the island. Western anthropologists, however, have a different view of early Niha history – or, rather, different views. Though most scholars now agree that the Niha people arrived on Nias in about 3000 BC, where they arrived *from* is still a matter for conjecture. A **proto-Malay people** speaking an Austronesian language with traces of Polynesian and Malagasy (the language of Madagascar), whose sculptures resemble closely those of the Nagas in the eastern Himalayas and whose physiognomy shows similarities with the Batak people of North Sumatra, the Nihas seem to have evidence linking them with most of southern Asia and beyond.

For many centuries after their arrival/inception, the people of Nias had almost no contact with the outside world. Thus, like the Batak on the mainland, the Niha developed a highly idiosyncratic, agrarian way of life; they also showed a similar predilection for waging war with each other. (Unlike the Batak, however, the Niha people never developed a system of writing.) They lived in small villages, each of which functioned according to a strict three-tier **class system**, with the village chief at the top and the slaves – usually people captured from nearby villages in raids – at the bottom. These slaves were important as symbols of prestige and wealth; later, in the 1600s, they also became a valuable source of income, as traders from Aceh began calling in at Nias to buy slaves, which they paid for with gold. The precious necklaces and bangles that are worn during festivals today were probably wrought from the gold of these eighteenth-century slave-runners.

The **slave-traders** were the first outsiders to pay regular visits to the island, and paved the way for others to follow. The **Dutch** arrived in 1665 to exploit the slave trade for their own ends, and remained on the island for most of the next 250 years, save for a brief five-year interregnum by the British under Stamford Raffles during the 1820s. The Dutch tenure was largely characterized by their increasingly violent attempts to subjugate the island completely. During the 1860s, they destroyed several villages in southern Nias – an act of aggression that rankles with the locals to this day. The Dutch finally gained complete control over the island in 1914, only to be forced to relinquish it again thirty years later by the Japanese army during World War II.

Attempts to convert the Niha to Christianity met with similar resistance. The Dutch and British both failed, and although the German Rhenish missionaries, who first arrived in 1865, managed to convert most of north Nias by the end of the century, the southern half remained resistant. This resilience led to some pretty heavy-handed tactics by the missionaries, culminating in a campaign to rid the island of all traces of animism. Nearly all of the Niha's animistic totems were either destroyed or shipped to Europe, where they still reside in the museums of western Germany and Holland, and many of the island's oldest megaliths disappeared at this time. Indeed, so complete was the eradication of the old religion that, of the few stone megaliths that are left, nobody knows who created them, why, or what all their hieroglyphics mean. Today, over 95 per cent of Nias is now, nominally at least, Christian, and the last recorded instance of head-hunting, an essential component of Niha animism, occurred way back in 1935.

Approaching Pulau Nias: Sibolga

With its series of pitch-black tunnels cut into the jungle-clad cliffs, its roadside waterfalls and heart-stopping hairpin bends, the last, vertiginous five-kilometre drive down to **SIBOLGA** from Parapat is breathtakingly dramatic. Even the town itself looks pretty from this distance, resembling the sort of quaint and quiet little seaside settlement that you find all the way along this western coastline. Unfortunately, the reality is somewhat different: Sibolga is a small drab place with a chronic lack of anything worth seeing, and with little to recommend it other than one or two good hotels and a couple of decent Chinese restaurants. It is, however, the main port for ferries to Nias, and, as such, sees its fair share of travellers.

The most interesting thing about Sibolga is its **racial mix**: though not officially Toba Batak territory, there has been a huge influx of people from the Toba region who came looking for work. Indeed, they now outnumber the original coastal Muslim inhabitants, and, when you add to this the significant ethnic Chinese population who've been here for centuries, you end up not only with a highly cosmopolitan town, but also one that's filled to bursting with mosques, churches and Buddhist temples.

Although there's almost nothing to do in town – except, maybe, visit the Tagor Cinema in the evening – there are a couple of reasonable **beaches** nearby: the white-sand **Pantai Pandan**, 10km south of Sibolga, is quiet and pretty, while **Pantai Kalangan**, 300m further on, is popular with locals and charges an R250 entry fee. Oplets (the local term for "bemo") to both run from Sibolga bus terminus on Jalan Sisingamangaraja.

Practicalities

All **buses** and bemos call in at the terminus on Jalan Sisingamangaraja, at the back of the town away from the coast. The **port** for ferries to Nias – as well as the occasional Pelni boat from Padang – is about 1.5km south of here at the end of Jalan Horas. For full details of passenger ferries to Nias, which run every day except Sunday, see "Travel details" on p.350. **Tickets** for the daily fast ferry to Nias, the *Jambo Jet*, can be bought from the small counter by the harbour gate (☎0631/22370); for tickets for either of the slow ferries, visit PT Simeulue at Jalan S. Bustami Alamsyah 9 (☎0631/21497), near the Bank BNI. The **Pelni agent**, PT Sarana Bandar Nasional, is near the market by the bus terminus at Jalan Patuan Anggi 39 (☎0631/22291).

If you're going to Nias, it's important to **change money** before you go, and the BNI bank on Jalan Parman 3 (Mon–Fri 8am–4.15pm) is your last chance; the rates are slightly lower than those in Medan, but far superior to anything on Nias.

Budget travellers forced to stay in Sibolga overnight should head to one of the Chinese-run **hotels**, such as the friendly and efficient *Pasar Baru*, on the junction of Jalan Raja Djunjungan and Jalan Imam Bonjol (no phone; ④) or the *Indah Sari* at Jalan Jend A. Yani 29 (☎0631/21208; ③) which is a tad scruffier but still acceptable. The best hotel is the upmarket *Wisata Indah* at Jalan Brig Jend Katamso 51 (☎0631/23688, fax 23988; ⑤), with air-con rooms and a sea view.

The best **restaurants** are on Imam Bonjol. The *Hebat Baru* at no. 79 and the slightly cheaper *Restoran Restu* opposite at no. 58c both serve excellent Chinese food and are very popular with the locals. If Chinese food isn't your thing, the surgically clean *Hidangan Saudara Kita* at Jalan Raja Djunjungan 55 serves some excellent Padang food.

Gunung Sitoli

The capital of Nias, **GUNUNG SITOLI**, is a fairly charming little seaside town. There's nothing exceptional about the place, however, and if it wasn't for the fact that the people here are about 30cm smaller than their mainland neighbours, you could be anywhere on the west coast of Sumatra. As the island's administrative centre, Gunung Sitoli has the best facilities on Nias, and if you want to send a letter, make a phone call or change money, this is the best place to do it.

If you do decide to stay in Gunung Sitoli for a day, consider paying a visit to the **Nias museum** (daily 8.30am–5pm; free), halfway between the town and the harbour. This tiny building houses the most complete set of Niha antiquities in Indonesia, most of which are labelled in English. The small armoury by the front entrance contains some of the most impressive items, including leather shields and tunics from the last century. The centre also offers visitors the chance to watch videos of the traditional dances of Nias: unless you're very fortunate, this is probably the only chance you'll get.

Practicalities

Gunung Sitoli is little more than two streets – Jalan Gomo and Jalan Sirao – running parallel to the shore, with a number of roads running off them up the hills that overshadow the town. Until the ferries to Teluk Dalam begin sailing again, almost everybody's first sight of Nias will be Gunung Sitoli's **harbour**, approximately 2km north of the town; bemos (until 6pm; Rp500) and becak (Rp2000) connect the two, terminating at the **bus station** at the southern end of town. Those who take advantage of SMAC airlines' reasonably priced flights from Medan to Gunung Sitoli, arrive at the tiny **airstrip** to the southeast of town; the fifteen-kilometre jeep ride to the town centre is included in the flight price.

Two of the ferries to Sibolga – the *Poncan Mo'ale* and *KM Cucut* – share a **ticket office** on the main road by the port, while PT Simeulue, Jalan Sirao 23, and *Jambo Jet*, Jalan Gomo 41, are right in the centre of town. A fourth ticket office, for the **Pelni ferries**, lies tucked away to the east of Jalan Sirao, one block back from the coast at Jalan Lagundri 38 (☎0639/21846). Nias's only **tourist office** is located behind the green square on Jalan Gomo, at Jalan Sukarno 6 (☎0639/21545); they're open during the week (Mon–Thurs 8am–4pm, Fri 8am–noon) but have little information and no maps. The **post office** stands on the opposite corner of the green at Jalan Hatta 1, next to the **Telkom office**. One block further south, at Jalan Imam Bonjol 40, is the **Bank BNI**; the rates (US dollar cash and travellers' cheques only) are pretty poor.

One of the reasons why so many travellers hurry through Gunung Sitoli is its paucity of decent **accommodation**. The better-value places are on the southern side of town, near the bus station and across the river bisecting Gunung Sitoli. These include the *Marja* (☎0639/22812; ②), at Jalan Diponegoro 128, and the slightly grimier *Laraga* (☎0639 /21760; ②), at no. 135, both of which offer acceptable but poky rooms. On the other side of the river the quality deteriorates: *Losmen Beringin*, at Jalan Surdirman 1 (☎0639/21990; ③), is one of the cheaper options, offering rooms with fans and clean sheets, while the *Hawaii Hotel*, one block east of the green on Jalan Sirau (☎0639/21021; ④), has doubles with mandi and fan; both places are overpriced, but then so is everywhere else in town.

Sitoli's most popular **restaurant**, the excellent Padang food specialist *Rumah Makan Nasional*, is just 100m further down Jalan Gomo at no. 87. Back near the *Hawaii*, at

Jalan Sirao 10, is the Chinese restaurant *Bintang Terang*, which serves that rarest of north Nias luxuries: ice-cold beer.

Gomo and the villages of the central highlands

Both north and south Nias look upon the **central highlands** as the cradle of their culture, where, according to local mythology, the six Niha gods descended to earth and begat the island's human population. The main village in the central highlands, the rather unprepossessing **GOMO**, is, thanks to its location 8km west of the east-coast road on a rutted mud track, virtually inaccessible. There is one bus, at 6am, from Teluk Dalam to Gomo; otherwise, you'll have to catch a bus to Lahuser, halfway between Teluk Dalam and Gunung Sitoli on the coastal road, and hope that you can hitch a lift from there.

Gomo has just six **rumah adat** left (the others burnt down in a fire some years ago), built in the style of southern Nias with a rectangular rather than an oval floor plan. The most important is the **Chief's House** which, though nothing like as elaborately decorated as the one in Bawomataluo (see p.330), is still reasonably ornate and has a wealth of lizards and monkeys carved into the woodwork below the rafters. A set of stone tables and chairs, remnants of a much greater collection of stone furniture, stands outside.

Though there's little to do in Gomo itself, the people are quite friendly– certainly when compared to the inhabitants of the villages further south – and, with its one unnamed **losmen** (①), Gomo is the best base for exploring in the central highlands. When trekking to any of the villages hereabouts, it's a good idea to hire a guide, available in Gomo, as the paths are often extremely difficult to follow and you may have to ford rivers. Good boots, warm waterproof clothing and a torch are essential.

Of the villages, **TUNDRUMBAHO**, 4km northeast of Gomo, is perhaps the most interesting and contains the best examples of Nias's megalithic art, including a number of menhirs (oblong or rectangular standing stones) and stone chairs carved with the heads of Naga (a mythical, snake-like creature).

Boronada, the hill where the gods were supposed to have arrived on earth, has little in the way of sights, but the atmosphere here is really quite eerie, as befits the most sacred spot on the island. Boronada is a two-hour, six-kilometre walk northwest of

THE ARCHITECTURE OF NIAS

Although the **rumah adat** of north and south Nias look very different, they do share some important design features. As with Batak houses, no nails were used in their construction, the Nihas instead binding the planks together with palm leaves. Both styles of houses are **earthquake-proof** too: the stilts on which the houses stand are placed both vertically and obliquely, giving the foundations greater flexibility and allowing them to ride the tremors rather than collapse altogether. Indeed, the number of stilts used to support the house were an indication of how important the resident was in the village hierarchy. A chief would usually own a house that was at least six supporting posts wide, whilst a commoner's would measure only four posts across.

The most obvious difference between the two types of house is the floor plan, which in north Nias is an oval shape and, in the south, a rectangle. The houses of the north are also squatter and tend to stand alone, whilst those of the south are much taller, have soaring, two-sided roofs and stand shoulder to shoulder with each other along the village street.

There is plenty of the traditional housing of southern Nias left in the hill-top villages (see p.328 for details), though only a few examples of the houses of northern Nias remain, and no new ones are being built. There is one house built in the traditional northern Nias style on the Trans-Nias Highway, about 30km outside Gunung Sitoli. The village of **Siwahili**, 6km uphill from Sitoli, also has a couple of good examples, though there are no buses and little in the way of traffic, so be prepared to walk the whole way.

Gomo along a very slippery and difficult-to-follow path, beginning on the asphalt road heading down to the river. On the way, after 45 minutes or so, you should pass a small path by a shop that winds its way down for 200m to a deep pool, once the entrance to a nineteenth-century **gold mine**. At the end of the main track, which quickly dwindles into a slippery and indistinct path, is Boronada. There's little here now save for a curious two-metre-tall stone pyramid, which the locals will tell you was once filled with gold, and a couple of unimpressive small statues.

South Nias

South Nias is the home of the island's greatest tourist attractions, including the **surfer's paradise** of Lagundri and the **hill-top villages** around Bawomataluo. At the moment all travellers are forced to travel down from Gunung Sitoli, though there are hopes that the direct ferry from Sibolga to **TELUK DALAM**, the largest town in southern Nias, will begin sailing again soon. There is little to do in undistinguished Teluk Dalam, though you can change money (at a painfully bad rate) in the shops, and there is a small post office.

The horseshoe bay of **Lagundri** lies 12km west of Teluk Dalam; buses run regularly between the two (Rp500), stopping by the small bridge at the Jamborai/Botohili junction, where the Trans-Nias highway starts. (This is also the place to wait for buses out of Lagundri.) Lagundri has been famous amongst surfers since the 1970s, though it's at neighbouring **Jamborai**, on the western edge of the bay, that the waves actually break. In July and August the waves are over 4m high and travel for up to 150m – fantastic for experienced surfers. Because of the size of the waves and the coral reefs that lie hidden underneath the water, this is not a good place for beginners. If you're not a surfer and don't fancy trekking in the highlands, there's little to keep you occupied in Jamborai, though in the centre of the bay the water is calm enough to **swim** in, and **Botohili**, the nearest traditional village, is just a twenty-minute walk away in the hills behind Jamborai.

The **accommodation** at Lagundri Bay consists almost entirely of simple wooden beachside bungalows. There are over fifty of them stretching out all along the bay, with a particularly high concentration at Jamborai. These losmen are virtually identical, and recommending one above the other is impossible. Most have electricity now, cost next to nothing (usually Rp1000 per night, or free if you stay for a fortnight or more), though you'll be expected to eat there too. Watch out for your stuff in Lagundri too, as tales of pickpockets and robbers are numerous.

The local authorities plan to tear these cheap losmen down eventually and replace them with more upmarket places, such as the *Cantana Inn* (☎0630/21048; ⑤) in the very centre of the bay, and the luxurious air-con *Sorake Beach Resort* (☎0630/21195; ⑧) at the western end of Jamborai. Things are progressing at a snail's pace, however, and it looks as if the cheaper losmen will be here for a few years yet.

The **food** in Lagundri is slightly more expensive than elsewhere in Sumatra and, though it has improved recently, can be a little bland and unvarying. To pep up mealtimes, consider buying the lobster, crayfish and other seafood from the fishermen who stroll up and down the bay. If you do manage to escape from your losmen, the *Zita Restaurant*, on the road running along the back of Jamborai, has an extensive menu of Western food and some ice-cold beer.

Bawomataluo and the south Nias villages

The **villages of south Nias** are fairly small, being little more than two neat rows of rectangular thatched houses separated by a wide paved street lined with stone tables, chairs and sculptures. For defensive purposes, the villages were always built on hilltops and surrounded by a large stone wall, though, almost without exception, these walls have now disappeared. In the centre of every village you'll find a two-metre tall **jumping stone** (*fahombe*), which once would have been topped by sharp sticks and thorns. The custom was for teenage boys to jump over this stone to show their bravery and agility (or, if they didn't jump high enough, their innards); you can see a picture of a *fahombe* ceremony on the back of a Rp1000 note.

BAWOMATALUO (Sun Hill) is the most impressive of these villages. It's an hour's walk uphill from the turn-off on the Teluk Dalam–Lagundri road; taxis from Lagundri to the turn-off charge Rp1000, and ojek cost Rp2000 (or Rp3000 all the way to Bawomataluo). If it's Saturday morning you may be able to catch one of the buses returning from Teluk Dalam market at the turn-off.

Bawomataluo has been exposed to tourism for too many years now, and touts don't leave you at any time here. The old village consists of just two roads: the main one runs east–west, while a shorter but equally wide cul-de-sac branches off due south from opposite the Chief's House. As you'll notice with almost every village, the primary function of these streets seems to be to dry laundry, and Bawomataluo's famous **stone carvings** are usually strewn with various undergarments during daylight hours. This is a pity, as the stonework, particularly on the tables and chairs outside the Chief's House, is exceptional. These chairs once held the corpses of the recently deceased, who were simply left to decay in the street before being buried. The jumping stone here is the largest on Nias; boys charge tourists upwards of Rp10,000 for the privilege of watching them jump over it.

TREKKING AROUND BAWOMATALUO

Bawomataluo can be seen as part of a larger **trek** around the southern hills; the map on p.323 is designed to help you plan a route around the nearby villages. When trekking, always take waterproof clothing, plenty of food (there aren't many shops en route) and a torch, and aim to reach a main road by mid-afternoon at the latest in order to catch a bus back. Buses from Teluk Dalam to Lagundri along the south coast road cease running at about 4pm, and along the Trans-Nias Highway to Lagundri they stop at about 5pm.

The following account describes a longer walk around all the villages in the immediate vicinity of Bawomataluo, a fifteen-kilometre loop that a fairly fast walker should be able to complete in five hours. The trek begins one hour uphill from the Bawomataluo turn-off at the pleasant but plain village of **Orahili**, home to a couple of small and unimpressive stone carvings and a number of traditional houses, most of which have swapped the thatch on their roofs for more practical corrugated metal. At the far end of Orahili, at the end of the cul-de-sac on your left, a series of steps heads uphill to **Bawomataluo** (see above).

Behind the Chief's House in Bawomataluo, a scenic path leads to **Siwalawa**, one hour away. The village stretches along the path for at least 500m, though the oldest part actually lies at the very end, up some steps to the left of the main path. At the end of this old quarter a path heads downhill and divides: turn right and you eventually arrive at Hilifalago; turn left and you pass through the rather unexciting villages of Onoltondo and, twenty minutes further on, the large village of **Hilinawalo**. The old part of the village has some good examples of traditional housing, though the introduction of a huge satellite dish to the main street does somewhat ruin the look of the town. The former Chief's House has been converted into a guest house, the *Ormoda*, though this was closed at the time of writing.

After Onoltondo the path descends to a large stream (which can be waist-high in the rainy season) and continues for an hour, via Hilinawalo, to **Bawogosali**, a small village with some recent stone carvings lining the path. The village is dominated by the large church, behind which a path leads up to the crest of a hill and along to **Lahuna**. This village lies at an important crossroads: continue past the end of the village and you'll reach, 45 minutes later, Bawomataluo, or turn right, and after a steep descent you arrive at **Hilisimaetano**. For many visitors, Hilisimaetano is their favourite spot on Nias: the village is an excellent state of preservation, the people seem to be a little friendlier than in other places on Nias and, unusually, many of the paving stones have been carved with reliefs of lizards, ships and signs of the zodiac. At the very end of the path, twenty minutes beyond Hilisimaetano, the Trans-Nias Highway thunders by, from where you can catch an ojek back to Lagundri (Rp2500–3000).

This quality of craftsmanship is continued inside the nineteenth-century **Chief's House** (9am–5pm; donation), where the walls are decorated with carvings of lizards, monkeys, and, in the top right-hand corner of the eastern wall, a depiction of an early European ship – a reference, perhaps, to the arrival of the Dutch in 1665. A pair of carved royal seats for the chief and his wife share the same wall. Other notable features of the house are the plethora of pig's jaws hanging from the rafters, and the huge hearth at the back of the room.

ACEH

With vast reserves of oil and natural gas off its northern coastline, huge seams of gold, copper, silver and coal in the interior, and enormous plantations of pepper, palm oil, tobacco and other cash crops stretched along the eastern hills of the Bukit Barisan, it's hardly surprising that **Aceh** has become the fourth wealthiest province in Indonesia. Tourism, as yet, contributes the merest fraction towards this total wealth, probably because many travellers are put off by the region's undeserved reputation for religious fanaticism. Although it's true that bare legs and arms are frowned upon in Aceh, and outside of the posh hotels and Chinese restaurants it's difficult to find alcohol, the locals are no less friendly than anywhere else in the archipelago and, refreshingly, they are more likely to leave you alone too.

Most of Aceh's attractions lie along the stunning west coast, where you'll find kilometre after kilometre of deserted, palm-fringed **beaches** and a number of delightful **fishing villages** such as **Tapaktuan** and **Lhoknga**. A sprinkling of exquisite islands lies offshore too, including picture-perfect **Pulau Weh**, to the north of Banda, and the 99 islands of **Pulau Banyak**, off the west coast near **Singkil**. The **Gayo** and **Alas highlands** in the centre of the province, home to serene **Danau Takengon** in the **Gunung Leuser national park**, the largest nature reserve in Indonesia, are also worth exploring. The following account describes two routes through the province: south from **Banda Aceh** to Tapaktuan down the west coast, and north from **Kutacane** to Takengon through the centre of Aceh.

One word of warning: Aceh supplies most of Indonesia's marijuana; while it's easy enough to get hold of, it's still illegal and there are regular police checkpoints on the road where your bag is likely to be thoroughly searched.

THE ACEHNESE

The term **"Acehnese"** refers to those people who live on the province's coastline, an ethnically separate group from the Gayo and Alas people of the highlands. The Acehnese are a far more cosmopolitan bunch than the highlanders, having had contact with merchants from Arabia, China, Turkey and India for centuries, and this is reflected in their appearance: the variety of skin tones, eye colours and physiques. Despite the province's strong Islamic flavour, animism continues to play an important part in the day-to-day life of the Acehnese. The spirits of trees, rocks and rivers and the ghosts of deceased ancestors are still worshipped, and the village *dukun* (witch doctor) is still one of the most important people in the village.

The Acehnese are fiercely proud of their culture. Many of the region's traditional crafts are still widely practised today, including *pandamus* weaving and embroidery, which they use to decorate everything from wall-hangings to trouser cuffs. The most common style of embroidery, where brightly coloured thread is sewn onto black cloth, is known as *mendjot bebongo*, and was traditionally done by men, though nowadays it is more likely to be practised by women. The Acehnese are also renowned for their swords, daggers and knives, which fill the souvenir shops of Banda today. The most instantly recognizable of these weapons is the *rencong* dagger, whose Arabian influences are evident in the highly decorated handle and curved blade.

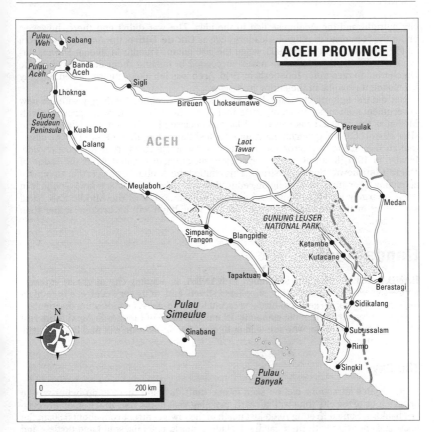

Some history

The Acehnese were the first people in Indonesia to embrace Islam, brought over by Arab sailors as early as the eighth century. Indeed **Pasai**, the **first Islamic sultanate** in the archipelago, was founded on Aceh's northeastern coast, just to the south of modern-day Lhokseumawe, in the thirteenth century.

Other sultanates – Pidie, Lingga and Perlak – soon emerged on the same stretch of coastline until, in the early sixteenth century, they were consolidated under one all-powerful sultanate, with the capital at **Kuta Raja** (now Banda Aceh). The town grew to become a major commercial centre with control over the Malacca Straits, one of the busiest shipping lanes in the world. Under the rule of **Iskandar Muda** (1607–36), Aceh also became one of the foremost military powers in the region, with peninsular Malaysia and most of North Sumatra under its control. Further prosperity arrived with the burgeoning pepper and spice trade: by 1820, Aceh was producing over half of the world's supply of pepper.

The Dutch eventually broke Aceh's grip on the Malacca Straits in the mid-nineteenth century, an action that signalled the beginning of over fifty years of hostility. Fearful that the Acehnese had grown too powerful, the Dutch launched an all-out attack on Banda Aceh in March 1873, destroying the mosque in the first days of battle. After a bitter and bloody struggle that claimed over 100,000 lives, the Dutch eventually took the city outright and the Acehnese fled to the hills. The war didn't end there, however: under the command of religious leaders such as **Cik de Ditiro**, the Acehnese waged a jihad (holy war) right up to 1903, when the last sultan, Tuanku Muhamat Dawot, surrendered. Whilst the Acehnese never succeeded in ousting them directly, when the Dutch tried to reconquer Indonesia in 1946, Aceh was left alone and remained the only independent republic in the entire archipelago.

Nor did the fighting stop after Independence. The Acehnese, unhappy with the new government's attempts to incorporate them into the North Sumatran province with Medan as the capital, broke away in 1953 and declared itself part of the Islamic World (Dar Islam). Central government troops quelled the rioting that followed in the cities, though the Acehnese terrorists continued to launch attacks from the countryside. Finally, in 1967, in an attempt at appeasement, Suharto granted Aceh the status of **Daerah Istimewa** (Special District). This entitled the Acehnese to a certain amount of autonomy over matters of religion, education and *adat* (customary law) – which in Aceh is largely a watered-down version of the Islamic law of the Middle East: steal something in the province, for example, and your hand will be broken, rather than amputated.

Banda Aceh

BANDA ACEH, often just shortened to **BANDA**, is a sunny city of grassy squares, impressive white mansions, tidy, shop-lined streets and, at its very centre, a breathtaking series of minarets and coal-black, crescent-topped domes, an indication that you are now in the capital of the most staunchly Islamic province of Indonesia. As with the rest of Aceh, however, those who are willing to obey the dress code will find Banda a laid-back and pleasant city.

The City

Banda Aceh's attractions can be seen in one (full) day, and there is no better way to begin a tour of the city than with an early-morning visit to the **fish market**, on the eastern banks of Sungai Kreung Aceh just north of the town centre. From about 5.30am the boats start arriving with their catch – including shark, octopus, squid and turtle – and gory photo opportunities abound.

The market lies 500m north of the geographical and spiritual heart of Banda, the onion-domed **Mesjid Raya Baiturrahman**. The city's previous mosque, which had stood on this site since the thirteenth century, was burnt down during the first Dutch attack in 1873. General Kohler, leader of the Dutch operations in Aceh, was killed during the attack; a plaque by the current mosque's northern gates marks the spot where he fell. Six years later, in an attempt at reconciliation, the Dutch financed the construction of a new mosque, for which they hired the services of an Italian architect. His original design was influenced by a range of styles from India and North Africa, though it has been augmented considerably down the years: the Dutch added two more domes in 1936, and the Indonesian government contributed another two in 1957, bringing the total number to seven. There are also three minarets, two attached to the mosque itself and one that stands by itself at the eastern end of the grounds, and which just pips the nearby transmission tower as the city's tallest building. The **tower** is occasionally open to tourists (daily 3–5pm; Rp1000). This mosque is vast, but still cannot contain the congregation that gathers for Friday prayers; latecomers are forced to sit out on the steps and lawns and listen to the service via loudspeakers. Throughout the day hundreds of locals gather to splash in the fountains or just sit in the sun: there is nothing to stop you from joining them, though you'll have to ask the guards for permission to go into the mosque itself.

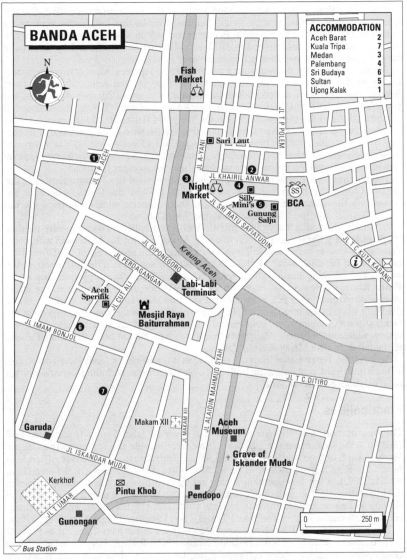

BANDA ACEH

ACCOMMODATION	
Aceh Barat	2
Kuala Tripa	7
Medan	3
Palembang	4
Sri Budaya	6
Sultan	5
Ujong Kalak	1

Fish Market

Sari Laut

JL KHAIRIL ANWAR

Night Market

Silly Mini's

Gunung Salju

BCA

JL DIPONEGORO

JL PERDAGANGAN

Kreung Aceh

Labi-Labi Terminus

Aceh Sperifik

JL CUT ALI

Mesjid Raya Baiturrahman

JL IMAM BONJOL

JL T C DITIRO

Garuda

Makam XII

JL MAKAM XII

Aceh Museum

Grave of Iskander Muda

JL ISKANDAR MUDA

Kerkhof

JL T UMAR

Pintu Khob

Pendopo

Gunongan

0   250 m

Bus Station

Banda's other major sight, the **Aceh Museum** (Tues–Thurs, Sat & Sun 8am–6pm, Fri 8–11am & 2.30–6pm; Rp200) lies on the eastern banks of Sungai Assyiqi, 300m southeast of the mosque along Jalan Sultan Alauddin Mahmudsyah. Right by the gateway is a **bell** presented to Sultan Pasai in 1469 by the renowned Chinese adventurer, ambassador, Muslim and eunuch, Cheng Hoe. When the Acehnese conquered Pasai in 1524, the founder of Aceh, Sultan Ali Mughayat Syah (1514–30) took the bell as war booty. Opposite is the **Rumah Aceh**, a traditional

Acehnese longhouse that once housed much of the museum's collection, though this has moved to the nearby brick buildings while the longhouse undergoes extensive renovation. The museum is one of the oldest, smallest and dullest of the provincial museums, established in 1915, its collection only enlivened by the freaky presence of a stuffed two-headed Siamese deer.

Dotted all around the museum are a number of **royal graves**. Most of them lie immediately to the south, including the green-and-yellow-painted tomb of Aceh's most famous and successful sultan, **Iskandar Muda**, who presided over Aceh's golden years between 1607 and 1636. Iskandar's son-in-law, Iskandar Thani, who succeeded Iskandar Muda to the throne and ruled for five years (Iskandar Muda's own son was murdered at his father's behest), lies – possibly – 200m west of the museum in a separate royal plot called, rather prosaically, **Makam XII** (Twelve Graves). Only three of these twelve graves have been positively identified, although a few years ago excavators unearthed a golden coffin that may have held the younger Iskandar.

The plot lies by the side of a dirt path in an area called the **Taman Kraton** – the "Palace Gardens". The palace itself was razed in 1878 by the Dutch, who built the Governor's House, or **pendopo**, in its place. The residence, which is not open to the public, lies just over the bridge from Iskandar Muda's tomb.

As with the Kraton at Yogya (see p.164), Aceh's kraton had its own pleasure garden, the **Taman Sari Gunongan**, which Iskandar Muda built for his Malaysian wife, Putri Pahang. The taman today is a children's park lying to the southwest of the Governor's House along Jalan Iskandar Muda. There is little to see here, although amongst the swings and climbing frames you'll notice a small, white, stone archway. This is the **Pintu Khob**, a gateway that once connected the palace to the **Gunongan**, the large, whitewashed, man-made hill, resembling a giant wedding cake, which stands south of the Pintu Khob in the middle of a field. Nobody knows exactly what the purpose of the Gunongan was, though some believe that it is some sort of seventeenth-century observatory, while another theory suggests that it was built for the homesick Putri Pahang to remind her of the Malaysian highlands.

Across Jalan Teuku Umar from the Gunongan is the **Kerkhof** (daily 8am–5pm; free), a Dutch graveyard containing the bodies of over 2500 troops, including General Kohler, most of whom died of cholera.

Practicalities

The **bus station** is in the southern part of town on Jalan Teuku Umar. **Labi-labi** (Rp350) – the local name for a bemo – leave from outside the station to the Central Market, south of the river by the Mesjid Raya Baiturrahman. The **tourist office** is at Jalan Chik Kuta Karang 3 (Mon–Thurs 7.30am–2pm, Fri 7.30am–noon, Sat 8am–2pm; ☎0651/23692). A few bus companies have set up their own unofficial tourist offices at the bus station: their knowledge is scant but they do have some useful brochures. The Garuda **airline** office is in the *Sultan Hotel* (☎0651/31811, fax 23474) and the Pelangi agent is Indomatha Wisata Tours and Travel, Jalan Panglima Polem 3 (☎0651/23706).

The **post office** on Jalan Nyak Arief (Mon–Thurs & Sat 8am–7pm, Fri 8–11am & 2–7pm) also has email and poste restante counters. **Bank BCA**, Jalan Panglima Polem (10am–noon only), has rates comparable to the BCA in Medan, though it accepts Malaysian and US dollar travellers' cheques only.

Accommodation

The city has little in the way of budget **accommodation**, with many of the cheapest places refusing to take foreigners. A small knot of hotels lies to the north of the river along Jalan Khairil Anwar, where most visitors stay.

Aceh Barat, Jl Khairil Anwar 16 (☎0651/23250). The prettiest budget losmen, comprising basic fan-cooled rooms with shared bathrooms. ④.

Kuala Tripa, Jl Tgk Abdullah Ujong Rimba 24 (☎0651/24535). Long established as the best hotel in Banda (though now that boast is seriously threatened with the arrival of the *Sultan*) and the home of the only disco in town. Other features include a coffee shop, billiard room and pool. All 45 rooms have TV and air-con. ⑧.

Medan, Jl Jend A. Yani 15 (☎0651/21501, fax 32256). Friendly establishment that from the outside resembles an international-class hotel, but is really just a glorified losmen. The cheapest doubles are reasonable value. ⑤.

Palembang, Jl Khairil Anwar 51 (☎0651/22044). One of the more bizarre of budget places, this multicoloured bungalow plastered with Disney characters has surprisingly plain rooms, with the cheapest not even boasting a fan. The highlight is the giant Swiss-style TV cabinet in reception; the lowlight is the monkey chained up in the back yard. ④.

Sri Budaya, Jl Prof A. Majid Ibrahim-III 25e (☎0651/21751). Large, cavernous and welcoming losmen housing twenty simple fan-cooled rooms. ④.

Sultan, Jl Hotel Sultan 1 (☎0651/22469, fax 31770). Banda's newest and flashiest hotel, where each of the ninety rooms is furnished with a TV, phone, air-con and hot and cold running water. ⑦.

Ujong Kalak, Jl St. Johan 7 (☎0651/31146). Small and cramped losmen with the cheapest rooms in town, tucked down an alley to the west of Jl T.P. Aceh. The rooms are fairly smart, but bargaining is necessary to get the cheapest price possible; some come with bath and fan. ②–③.

Eating

Aceh actually has its own style of **cuisine**, though unless you're a connoisseur you probably won't notice any difference between Acehnese and Padang food. The best Acehnese restaurant, the mid-priced *Aceh Spesifik*, is behind the mosque on Jalan Cut Ali. At the western end of Jalan Khairil Anwar is Banda's excellent **night market**, home to dozens of stalls that serve a variety of different fried rice, noodle and *murtabak* dishes. There are a number of ice-cream parlours near the *Hotel Sultan*, such as *Gunung Salju*, at Jalan Polem 45, or *Silly Mini's Ice Cream Parlour* at Jalan Hotel Sultan 32, which does some delicious cream cakes. For something more substantial, visit the *Sari Laut* at Jalan Yani 84, a cheap and reasonably cheerful Chinese restaurant that serves the best *kiew tiaw* in town.

Pulau Weh

A mountainous outcrop of dark green rising sharply from the azure waters of the Indian Ocean north of Banda Aceh, **Pulau Weh** is yet another gorgeous Indonesian paradise. Its history, however, thanks to its highly strategic location at the northern end of the Malacca Straits, is a shade more interesting than that of your average tropical hideaway. The island was once a major gateway into Indonesia and, up to the end of World War II, its capital, **Sabang**, outranked Singapore in size and importance. Indeed Sir Stamford Raffles, the founder of Singapore, once said of Weh:

There is a fine harbour on the northern side of Pulau Weh, the best in the Acehnese dominions and until this period unknown to Europeans.

The fortunes of the island have fluctuated since 1945. The port lost most of its trade to Singapore while the War of Independence in Sumatra raged, then enjoyed a twenty-year renaissance, beginning in 1965, when it was declared a tax-free port by Sukarno. But after losing this status to Batam in 1985, Weh slipped into the backwaters once more, where it has remained ever since.

Today Sabang has a population of less than 10,000; the population of the whole island is less than 25,000. This figure is supplemented by a considerable number of soldiers and sailors from the Indonesian armed forces, garrisoned here to protect this strategic outpost, as well as a few lucky travellers who've heard about the island's excellent diving and snorkelling possibilities, its white sandy beaches and untouched forest.

Weh's airport has been closed since 1985, though currently the runway is being extended and it is hoped that flights to the island should begin soon. Until they do, the twice-daily **ferry** crossing from Kreung Raya harbour, 35km west of Banda Aceh, is the only connection from the mainland (2hr 30min; Rp4250). Labi-labi from Banda Aceh to Kreung Raya leave regularly during the morning from outside the Pasar Ikan (fish market), and also from Jalan Diponegoro (Rp1500). The ferries dock on Weh at **Balohan**, on the southeastern corner of the island, from where it's a fifteen-minute bemo ride to Sabang (Rp1500).

Sabang

SABANG is a compact and pretty little town with plenty of quaint colonial architecture. On the main street, Jalan Perdagangan, there's a small **post office**, a **Telkom office** next door (with Home Dialling Direct phones), a branch of the **BRI bank** (which will change both US dollar cash and travellers' cheques, though both at a dreadful rate), four losmen, a hotel and a number of surprisingly good restaurants. There's also Weh's only **diving shop**, the Stingray Dive Centre, Jalan Teuku Umar 3 (☎0652/21265), which not only organizes diving courses but runs an underwater photography workshop (US$100). The manager, Pak Dodent, acts as the local tourist information officer and has a selection of secondhand books for sale. He also rents out **motorbikes** for approximately Rp20,000 per day.

Of the **losmen**, the *Irma* (☎0652/21148; ③) and *Pulau Jaya* (☎0652/21344; ③), which stand just 50m apart at Jalan Teuku Umar nos. 3 and 17 respectively, are the two most popular choices with travellers, though they are both basic and the rooms overlooking the road are extremely noisy. The *Sabang Marauke* (☎0652/21928; ③), which stands down Jalan Seulawah, a sideroad opposite the *Irma*, is cheaper, friendlier, quieter and, although not used to dealing with tourists, a much better option. The fourth losmen, the *Holiday*, Jalan Perdagangan (☎0652/21131; ②–⑤), 200m east of the *Irma*, is actually more of a hotel, with some air-con en-suite doubles. The rooms at the *Holiday* are bettered only by the *Hotel Samudera*, by the park at the top of Jalan Teuku Umar at Jalan Diponegoro 21 (☎0652/21503; ⑤), a beautiful little **colonial house** featuring rooms with air-con and bathroom. All of these losmen and hotels lie within 200m of the bus stop in Sabang, which stands opposite the *Irma* losmen.

When it comes to **restaurants**, visitors to Sabang are spoilt for choice. The *Dynasty*, Jalan Perdagangan 54, serves the best food – try their *cumi goreng* (fried squid) for Rp6500. *Harry's*, the café below the *Irma*, is the main travellers' café in Sabang and serves excellent pancakes, which you can eat while watching satellite TV. There are a couple of excellent waterfront places, too. The *Kantin*, next to the rattan factory on Jalan Malahayati, is the best place to sit, drink tea and watch harbour life floating by, whilst the *Ujung Asam*, a fifteen-minute walk north of Sabang towards Pantai Paradise, was once a gay bar and the liveliest place in town. Now under new management, it to be seen whether it's will recapture its former flavour.

Weh resorts

For most visitors, Sabang is just a temporary stop on the way to the **beaches** on Weh's northwestern promontory. The most popular of these is **IBIOH**, 45 minutes by bemo from Sabang, which runs three times a day from Sabang (10am, 1pm & 6pm, returning at 6am, noon & 4pm). Ibioh is a tiny fishing village, at the end of which lies the tourist resort (Rp1000 one-off entry fee). The resort is actually little more than a collection of

WALKS AROUND WEH

Aneuk Laot (Child of the Sea) is Weh's largest lake and supplies Sabang with much of its fresh water. The lake is just a forty-minute **walk** from Sabang. Simply follow the main road, Jalan Perdagangan, south; after twenty minutes you'll pass, on your right, the **Zwembad** – an old Dutch swimming pool – after which the road climbs to the PTT power station, where you take the left fork then the first right. The lake is only five minutes from here. It's a picturesque and peaceful spot surrounded on three sides by coconut palms and ramshackle cottages, and on its western side by a large and sheer bank of pristine forest, with herons swooping majestically above the water and snakes gliding across its surface.

It is possible to visit the lake as part of a much bigger tour around Weh's northeastern shoreline. It will take approximately five hours, so remember to bring plenty of water. From the lake, head up the hill to the airport. Take the road on the left that runs along the near end of the airstrip, then follow it until you reach a tin-roofed mosque standing opposite a field of electricity pylons. Turn to the right here, and after 45 minutes you'll reach the east coast of Weh. Turn and you'll reach a large black-sand beach, turn left and you'll eventually come to **Pantai Sumur Tiga** (Three Wells Beach), about 1.5km away. This is undoubtedly one of the most beautiful beaches on Weh, though between December and May it is reclaimed by the sea and disappears completely.

Twenty minutes north of here is the Sabang suburb of **Meulee**, where you can stop for a coffee at the Warung Kopi Pantai Jaya. From Meulee you have a choice: follow Jalan Teuku Cik Ditiro for the more direct inland route back to Sabang, or take the coastal path that runs via **Pantai Tapak Gajah** (Elephant's Footprint Beach) and, just before Sabang, **Pantai Kasai** (Lover's Beach). Sabang is only twenty minutes from here.

Walks from Ibioh

The most rewarding **trek** on the island follows the main road from Ibioh (see p.336) to the very northern tip of Weh. This road passes through the **Ujung Ba'U Forest**, a substantial region of primary rainforest that's home to monkeys, lizards, wild boars, civet cats, birds (including the endangered common drongo and the nicobar pigeon) and whole clouds of butterflies that flutter up from the path as you approach. It's a pleasant and shady two-hour walk each way that's best done in the morning before the sun gets too fierce. At the end of the path is the newly erected **Kilometre Zero Monument**, a curious blue-and-white-tiled affair that marks the northwestern end of Indonesia (though there are actually couple of smaller, uninhabited islands further north). Keep on heading northwest from here and you'll eventually hit Saudi Arabia, which is why Weh is sometimes known as Mecca's Porch.

Another pleasant walk from Ibioh takes in the beaches of the northwestern promontory. Gapang lies forty minutes to the south of Ibioh; ten minutes before you arrive you come to a road that branches west over the hills to Lhong Angen, about thirty minutes away. The **Gua Sarong**, a huge bat cave, lies 3km south of Lhong Angen, but is accessible by boat only – ask at the *Flamboyan Bungalows* (see p.338) if you wish to rent a boat.

simple tourist bungalows and restaurants stretched along a rocky and forested hillside running down to the shore.

The main attraction in Ibioh is the excellent **snorkelling**. Snorkelling gear can be rented from Stingray's office in Ibioh (Rp2000, or Rp5000 with flippers). The coral starts just a few metres from Ibioh beach and continues all the way to **Pulau Rubiah**, 200m away. Once a quarantine post for pilgrims returning from Mecca, this tiny islet has some picture-perfect beaches and forms the focus of the **Pulau Rubiah Underwater Garden**, a large nature reserve founded to protect the coral. If you don't fancy swimming, you can rent a boat for a few hours instead (Rp10,000), which will take you out into the ocean to see the **dolphins**.

Accommodation in Ibioh is in simple A-frame bungalows, although more sophisticated accommodation is currently under construction. At the moment guests have to wash at the well in the middle of the resort. There are over fifty bungalows in the resort now, though from June to August it can still be very difficult finding a room. Try to ensure that your bungalow has a mosquito net, if you're not travelling with one, as malaria is a problem on Weh. Most of the bungalows are pretty similar, though *Patimah's* (①) and *Oong's* (①–②) are recommended.

The island features two other beaches with accommodation. **Gapang** is an attractive, horseshoe-shaped beach 2km south of Ibioh, with its own family of five hawksbill turtles. There is a small selection of bungalows here, with prices similar to those at Ibioh. Unfortunately, in the off season most of them close down, and those that stay open often turn their electricity off. The best bungalows (③) are owned by the *Barracuda Restaurant*, though a rather plush hotel is currently under construction on the road down to the beach which, when completed, will be the best on the island.

The third beach, **Lhong Angen**, lies on the western side of the island. This is the place to come for spectacular sunsets, and the beach is one of the best too, although for six months of the year it completely disappears – swept away by the sea in November, returning again in May. The *Flamboyan Bungalows* (②) at the northern end of the beach provide possibly the best-value accommodation on the island, and during the high season the owners hold weekly barbecues. The *Manta Ray Bungalows* (②), 500m away, offer some healthy competition: contact the *Losmen Irma* in Sabang if you wish to stay here (see p.336).

The west coast

Until recently, Aceh's **west coast** was one of Sumatra's best kept secrets, a gorgeous strip of golden beaches and roaring surf backed by steep, forested hills. The coastal road used to be one of Sumatra's worst, a potholed series of chicanes, corkscrews and hairpin bends. Today, however, the road is much improved, and a steady stream of travellers is now journeying through, stopping at one of the beachside bungalows or village losmen on the way to make the most of the splendid scenery and isolation.

Before heading off along this road, however, there are a few things to consider. First, there are **no banks** along the route, so make sure you have enough cash before you head off. Second, **malaria** is a problem on Aceh's west coast, so bring a decent mosquito net and keep taking the tablets. And finally, though **public transport**, in the form of Mitsubishi Colt mini-vans, passes up and down the coastal road every ten minutes in the mornings, by the afternoons they are much less frequent, so always try to set off to your next destination before noon. And finally, all along Aceh's west coast there are **dangerous undercurrents**; every year a number of unwary swimmers are dragged out to sea. Always ask a local if it's safe to swim before taking the plunge.

Lampu'uk Beach and Lhoknga

Just 13km west of Banda, **Lampu'uk Beach** is a glorious sandy arc that's both a popular day-trip for the citizens of Banda and a perfect first stopover for travellers heading down the west coast. The beach is clean and, despite the strong surf, it's safe to swim here. To get to Lampu'uk from Banda, catch labi-labi #4 from Jalan Diponegoro and ask the driver to stop at MNS Balee, a small school and council office that's a fifteen-minute walk from the bungalows.

The best thing about Lampu'uk is the **accommodation**. The *Aceh Bungalows* (③) at the northern end of the beach are a set of six newly opened wooden chalets run by an Englishman and his Indonesian wife. All the bungalows have electricity, the reception hall has satellite TV and the food is excellent. The place opened only recently, but already many travellers are choosing to stay here and commute into Banda Aceh rather than staying in the city itself.

During the week Lampu'uk is usually deserted, but at weekends the beach is packed with locals, most of whom stay at the *Taman Tepi Laut Resort* (☎0651/32029; ⑨) in the town of **LHOKNGA** at the southern end of Lampu'uk Beach. The resort has its own mini-zoo (open only to guests) and golf course (☎0651/42981; Rp35,000 club rental plus Rp20,000 course fee). The only budget travellers in Lhoknga tend to be surfers, who reckon the waves that break around here are the best on the west coast. The *Darlian* (③), in front of the entrance to the golf course, and the *Pondok Indah* (③) next door, are the homestays of choice for surfers, and boards can be rented from both places.

To continue south from Lampu'uk, catch a labi-labi to Simpang Golf, the junction by the entrance to the Lhoknga golf course, and take a Mitsubishi mini-van from there. The road south passes through a string of prawn farms and picturesque fishing villages where traditional Acehnese houses, constructed on stilts to avoid floods, are very much in evidence. After an hour the road begins to climb over the coastal mountains which mark the border between Aceh Besar and Aceh Barat. At the top of the hill is the **Geurutee View**, affording a spectacular vista out over the **Ujung Seudeun Peninsula**, a finger of sand-fringed land pointing southwest into the Indian Ocean.

From Geurutee View the road descends again, passing through **Lamno**, where a number of the locals have blond hair and blue eyes; legend has it that they are the descendants of a Portuguese crew whose ship sunk just off the coast. Lamno is an easy-going little place with a small market every Sunday. Those wishing to stop over can stay at the basic *Losmen Singgahan*, just 50m off the main road at Jalan Pasar 45 (☎0651/95045; ②).

Fifty kilometres south of Lamno, and about a two-and-a-half-hour drive from Lampu'uk, is the busy little seaside village of **Patek**. Minibus drivers often stop here for a break, which gives you time to wander along the shore and take photos of the many dried-fish shops that line one side of the street, their wares hanging up on strings.

Kuala Dho

KUALA DHO, a village of just seventeen houses, a restaurant and two fiercely competitive bungalow operators, lies twenty minutes south of Patek. It's a very popular stop with travellers, who come here to enjoy the kilometres of deserted beaches. Be warned, however, that there are some extremely dangerous undertows, and locals advise bathers not to go far into the sea.

Of the two **accommodation** options, *Camp Europa* (no phone; ④) is the oldest, comprising simple but very pleasant beachside bungalows, with variable food. However, an orang-utan is incarcerated on the premises, which many visitors find upsetting. There is now an alternative: the *Pantai Wisata Sunset Beach Flower*, aka *Hassan's* (②) is just next to *Camp Europa*. The eponymous Hassan is a likable fellow, and his bungalows, whilst they have no electricity, are clean and come with mosquito nets, and the food is always excellent; the price covers your accommodation and three meals.

Meulaboh and Pulau Simeleue

MEULABOH, the capital of Aceh Barat and the largest and ugliest town on Aceh's west coast, lies 95km south of Kuala Dho. The onion-domed **Mesjid Nurul Huda** on Jalan Teuku Umar constitutes the town's only tourist attraction, though some of the beaches nearby are worth a short trip. The best is the **Pantai Ujong Kareung**, 2km north of town, where you'll find the **Hat of Teuku Umar**. Teuku Umar, a district chief and former Dutch ally who defected to the Independence movement in 1896, was killed by the Dutch on this beach in 1899, and this monument, in the shape of a traditional Acehnese hat, marks the spot where he fell. There are a number of decent hotels, such as the friendly *Tiara* by the main roundabout at Jalan Teuku Umar 157 (☎0655/21531;

③)). Amongst the losmen are poky *Simeleue* (☎0655/21401; ③)) and *Erna* (☎0655/21729; ②), at Jalan Singgah Mata nos. 120 and 78a respectively.

Overall, however, there's little reason to spend a night in Meulaboh unless you're waiting to catch the thrice-weekly boat to **SINABANG** on **Pulau Simeleue**. Simeleue is one of the bigger islands off the west coast of Aceh, seldom visited by tourists and covered by clove and coconut groves. The surfing on the west coast of Simeleue is excellent, however, and you can reach it by bemo from Sinabang, the capital of Simeleue and the only place with accommodation: the *Losmen Simeleue* at Jalan Nasional 134 (☎0650/21037; ③)) has doubles only.

To Tapaktuan

After Meulaboh, the road veers away from the coast and doesn't re-join it again until Sawang, almost four hours away, passing through innumerable small villages and a chain of photogenic plank and tin-roofed houses. Two hours' drive south of Meulaboh is **Simpang Trangon** (Trangon Junction), a tiny village that lies at the junction of the coast road and a smaller jungle track through the Leuser national park to the village of Trangon, in the heart of the Gayo Highlands (see p.347 for details). Forty minutes further south is **BLANGPIDIE**, a fairly sweet little inland town with a number of losmen: friendly *Losmen Yusri*, Jalan Irian 6 (☎0659/91061; ③)), has budget rooms with no fan and more expensive ones with fan and bath. It's another 75 minutes from Blangpidie to the nondescript village of Sawang, and from there another thirty minutes to Tapaktuan, the most popular stop with travellers on Aceh's west coast.

Hemmed in between the lower reaches of the Gunung Leuser national park and the Indian Ocean, **TAPAKTUAN** is fast becoming western Aceh's number one tourist town. Like the rest of this stretch of coastline, Tapaktuan has little in the way of historical sights and other attractions, but the town is one of the prettiest in Aceh and there's plenty to see and do in the immediate vicinity. You'll find nearly everything of interest along the main street, Jalan Merdeka, which runs along the seafront. There is no official tourist office, though the **HPI tourist information**, a non-profit-making organization, uses the *Restoran Flamboyan* at Jalan Merdeka 273 as a base. If there are no HPI representatives around, ask the restaurant staff to get the informative HPI folders on attractions in the area. A number of the local lads have also started guiding tourists around the local attractions; some are very knowledgeable, and their rates are minimal.

Currently the only place to **change money** is the Bank BRI, 400m back from the shore on Jalan Nyak Adam Kamil; the rates are very poor and they accept US dollar cash only. Both the **GPO** and the **Telkom** office stand at the southern end of town on Jalan Angkasah, the continuation of Jalan Merdeka. The GPO is within walking distance and there's a wartel nearby, though the Telkom office is over 2km away.

There are a number of cheap **losmen** along the seafront by the harbour. The *Pondok Wisata Kanada*, Jalan Merdeka 52 (☎0656/21145; ②), is a poky and dilapidated old losmen with little to recommend it save for cheapness and the excellent view from the verandah at the back overlooking the harbour. The *Bukit Barisan* (☎0656/21145; ③)), at Jalan Merdeka 37, is another travellers' favourite and offers excellent-value accommodation, especially if you can get a room in the Dutch section of the building. Next door at no. 33 is the *Hotel Panorama* (☎0656/21004; ③)–⑤) – it's good value, although the rooms are a little musty. The *Panorama* is only bettered by the weird-looking, decagonal *Dian Rana* (☎0656/21444; ④), 1km south of the centre, past the GPO on Jalan TR Angkasah. Though it overlooks the only unattractive stretch of shoreline in the area, the *Dian Rana* is good value, and every room comes with a TV and fan.

Unless you're a big fan of Padang food you'll be disappointed with the restaurants in Tapaktuan, though the small **night market** by the quay opposite the *Bukit Barisan* hotel offers some respite, serving Chinese-style fried rice and noodle dishes instead.

Around Tapaktuan

The fifty-metre long **Gua Kelam** (Dark Cave) lies 3km west of Tapaktuan in the foothills of the Bukit Barisan. The walk here takes about ninety minutes, following a path that heads off from behind the PLN Electricity Company in Tapaktuan. At one point the path splits in half; take the high road that hugs the hillside. On the way you should see troops of gibbons and macaques crashing through the trees and, if you're very lucky, a family of sedate siamang gibbons. The cave itself, by a fast-flowing river, is fairly spectacular, and it's possible to wade through the water or clamber over the rocks to get right inside it.

Tingkat Tujuh (Seven Steps) is a picturesque waterfall stretching up the hills, 7km to the south of Tapaktuan; labi-labi from the main drag of Tapaktuan to the Tingkat Tujuh charge Rp250. The fall is divided, as its name suggests, into seven levels, each with its own natural pool where it's possible to swim. The upper three pools, however, are an important local source of drinking water, so don't swim here. Concrete steps head up the side of the waterfall to the first and second stream; after that you'll have to find your own way. If you're quiet, and come in the morning, you should have a chance of seeing lots of wildlife, including snakes, monkeys and even freshwater turtles basking on a rocks in the middle of the stream.

Of the many beaches around Tapaktuan, **Pantai Air Dingin** (Cold Water Beach) is reckoned by many to be the best. It's certainly the most scenic, with a pleasant sandy strip on one side of the road and a huge waterfall on the other, at the bottom of which is a small pool of refreshing cold water. The *Kasa Tiga Homestay* (②), owned by the amiable If, is a new place right near the beach.

Singkil and Pulau Banyak

Aceh's west-coast highway continues south for approximately 100km beyond Tapaktuan, before turning inland towards the busy transport hub of Subussalam. This main road then continues east towards Medan, and a hazardous, uncovered eighty-kilometre track heads southwest from Subussalam towards **SINGKIL**, an unassuming little port town constructed almost entirely of wood in the delta of Sungai Alas. Though it's set back a little from the coast, Singkil acts as the main port for boats to **Pulau Banyak** (Many Islands), which leave from the bridge in the centre of town three times every week, taking around four hours.

Singkil is quite a pleasant place, though unless you're planning to go to Pulau Banyak there is absolutely no reason to come here. The attention foreigners receive from the local schoolkids can be overwhelming; the best place to hide away is in one of the coffee houses by the bridge, where you can sit and watch the river life drift by. The food in Singkil is expensive, but accommodation is very cheap and excellent value. The *Rumah Makan Indah* on Jalan Jend A. Yani (☎0658/21107; ②) has some very large, tidy rooms with a fan, and the daughter of the owner speaks excellent English (a rarity in Singkil). If they're full, the *Favorit*, at Jalan Jend A. Yani 19 (☎0658/21066; ②), and the *Indra* (☎0658/21047; ②), on Jalan Perdagangan, are acceptable alternatives. Your minibus driver should drop you off at the losmen of your choice.

Pulau Banyak has all the features necessary to be a top holiday destination. The atoll is made up of 99 fabulous **tropical islands**, each ringed by coral and fringed with white, powdery sand beaches. Currently the islands receive few visitors, save for the occasional adventurous traveller and the population of leatherback, hawksbill and green turtles who return to lay their eggs on Banyak's westernmost islands each year. It is idyllic, providing that you don't mind the almost complete lack of creature comforts: there's nowhere to change money, international phone calls are all but impossible and only the most heavily populated of the islands, Pulau Balai, has electricity – and even then only from dusk to dawn.

Ferries from Singkil arrive twice-weekly at **Pulau Balai**, the administrative centre of Banyak. There are a couple of basic losmen in Desa Balai, the largest village on Banyak, including the *Jasa Baru Indah* (③) on the waterfront by the harbour and the *Lei Kombih* (②) at Jalan Iskandar Muda 1. Balai can boast a little bit of coral at its southern end near the lighthouse, but the island's main role is as a transport hub for boats to the outer islands. For some reason, the people on Balai are fond of telling visitors that there are no more boats to the other islands that day. Take this information with a pinch of salt and sit and wait in the *Rumah Makan Indah's* by the harbour – you'll often find a boat to your destination if you hang around long enough.

Of the other islands, the most popular destination for foreigners is **Pulau Palambak Besar**, a four-kilometre long strip of paradise 8km to the south of Balai. Palambak Besar is made up of an awful lot of sand, a wealth of coconut trees, a swamp forest in the centre of the island and twelve huts belonging to the Nias families who've settled there. There are also three sets of tourist bungalows, of which the *Point* (①), on the western edge of the island, is the most comfortable (a relative term in Banyak); it even has electricity. The bungalows are excellent value, though the food can get a little monotonous at times, a criticism that can be levelled at the two other options – the *Bina Jaya Bungalows* (①–②), next to the best swimming beach on the southwestern side of the island, and the *Pondok Asmara Palambak*, or *PAP* (①) on the northern side. Sunbathing is the main occupation on Palambak Besar, though, if you fancy a spot of diving, nearby **Pulau Palambak Kecil** and **Pulau Gosong Sianji** are better venues.

From Palambak Besar you can hire a boat to take you to one of the other islands. The cost varies according to distance and whether an overnight stay is involved, though for nearby islands you shouldn't pay more than Rp5000. The islands range in size from tiny one-tree hillocks sticking out of the ocean to the huge **Pulau Tuangku** in the centre of the atoll, which is bigger than all the other islands put together. Tuangku, with its heavily forested interior and diverse range of wildlife, is the best island for hiking, though a guide is essential, and there is no accommodation on the island.

The *Point Bungalows* on Pulau Palambak Besar are currently organizing trips via Tuangku to the island of **Bangkaru** in the southwest of the atoll. The trip is not cheap – prices begin at Rp275,000 per person (minimum eight people) for a minimum three-day excursion – but this is one of the prime spots for turtle-watching and makes a worthwhile trip. Bangkaru is a national park and the **turtles** which come to lay their eggs every year are supposedly left undisturbed; though, unfortunately, as Bangkaru is so remote, the policing of the island is very difficult. The trip to Bangkaru takes up to five days, depending on the length of the hike around Tuangku, and often has to be aborted due to rough seas (a very common problem around Banyak). Sharks are another danger, so make sure you keep your limbs within the boat.

Kutacane to Takengon

The road through the Gayo and Alas Highlands, between **Kutacane** in southern Aceh and the northern highland town of **Takengon**, passes through some awesome mountain scenery and one or two areas of thick, pristine rainforest. It's one of the most spectacular roads in Sumatra, and also one of the most ragged, both terrifying and exhilarating to travel along.

Straddling the border between the provinces of Aceh and North Sumatra, the **Gunung Leuser national park**, at over eight thousand square kilometres, is the largest wildlife reserve in Indonesia. Over 300 bird species and 132 different mammals have made their home in the Leuser ecosystem (see the box on p.345 for details). Part of the reason why there are so many different creatures in Leuser is that the park covers such a diverse range of climates and habitats, from sea level, on the west coast near Tapaktuan, to an altitude of 3404m at the top of the park's highest mountain, the eponymous Gunung Leuser.

Travellers to the highlands should prepare themselves for some pretty rough conditions: nights can be extremely cold, there's usually a lot of rain and the losmen tend to be very basic. The people of the highlands are also very conservative, so it's important to keep your arms and legs covered. Make sure you change enough money too, as there's only one bank en route (at **Takengon**), and a couple of moneychangers at Kutacane.

Kutacane

Coming from the south, the first major town on the highland road is **KUTACANE**, the capital of Aceh Tenggah and the centre of the Alas people. Kutacane sits in a fertile volcanic basin, once covered by a huge lake, and on either side huge volcanic hills loom up from behind the town's rooftops. It's a typical Acehnese one-street town: a little grimy, a little smelly, fairly laid-back and always welcoming. A few years ago tourists had to stop here to collect their permit for the Gunung Leuser national park, available from the **PHPA office**, 2km north of town. But, now that permits are also available at the entrance to the park, most tourists only stop in Kutacane for as long as it takes to change buses.

However, those who are interested in the **crafts** of the Alas people are advised to stick around Kutacane for a day or so. The villages around Kutacane are home to many local craftspeople making everything from *pandamus* mats and baskets to hunting knives and betel-nut packages. A **bicycle tour** around the villages is a wonderful way to spend a day, and bikes (Rp10,000 per day) can be rented from Alas River Tours and Travel opposite the town mosque. Staff here can also advise on which are the best villages to visit.

There are several **places to stay** in Kutacane. The smartest is the *Wisma Marron* (③) at Jalan Jend A. Yani II 15–17. Nearby *Rindu Alam*, Jalan Jend A. Yani 7 (☎0629/21289; ③), is an old travellers' favourite, though the rooms could definitely do with a spring-clean. Many of the bedroom walls have peepholes drilled into them, which you may well want to cover up with band-aids or tissues. The *Rindu Alam* has a sister hotel in Ketambe, and will arrange free transport if you decide to stay there. A hundred metres further up the road, at no. 93, is the *Wisma Wisata* (⑤), a recent addition; the rooms are cleaner than the *Rindu Alam*'s, but they charge double the rates.

RAFTING ON SUNGAI ALAS

Sungai Alas is Aceh's longest waterway, with its headwaters in the Central Aceh Highlands near Gunung Leuser and its mouth at Gelombang near Singkil, Aceh Selatan. The river wends its way through some of the most unspoilt jungle scenery in Sumatra, including large tracts of the Gunung Leuser national park, and as such it's perfect for **rafting**. All the travel agencies in **Kutacane** and **Ketambe** now organize trips down Sungai Alas, lasting between one and five days, with the cost working out at about US$100 per day including food and permit. It's a very good idea to inspect your raft before you go to make sure it's riverworthy; traditional rafts have been known to disintegrate midstream. Life jackets are a must too, so make sure that they are included in the price. Finally, remember to bring sun lotion, insect repellent, a torch, a camera and a change of clothes, which will be stashed under waterproof sheeting in the boat.

The most popular rafting trip is the **three-day** jaunt from **Muarasitulam**, just south of Ketambe, to **Gelombang**. This is a pleasant (if slightly dull) river trip on very placid waters through sheer-walled canyons. A more exciting expedition begins at **Rumahbundar**, 5km north of Ketambe, and finishes at **Natam**, 7km north of Kutacane. The 33-kilometre trip takes six hours, even less if the water level is high, and its pretty exhilarating all the way down. The most thrilling section of all is the fifteen-kilometre stretch between **Miluak** and Rumahbundar, a white-knuckle two- or three-hour journey through some pretty rough waters. Adrenalin junkies may want to tackle just this section as a one-day trip.

A number of agencies on Jalan Jend A. II Yani, including Alas River Tour and Travels
(☎0629/21709), can arrange **trekking** and **rafting** trips in the Gunung Leuser national
park, though you're probably better off sorting everything out when you get to
Ketambe. These agencies are useful, however, if you want to **change money** (both
cash and US dollar travellers' cheques).

Ketambe

KETAMBE (aka Gurah) is little more than six hotels and a sprinkling of houses at the
very edge of the Gunung Leuser national park, a ninety-minute bus ride north of
Kutacane. There's nothing to do here except plan a trek in the forest, or recover from
one. At the northern end of Ketambe is a small kiosk, where you can pick up a **permit**
(Rp2000) for the park.

Two of Ketambe's **homestays**, the *PHPA Guest House* (③) and the *Gurah Bungalows*
(⑥), are actually inside the park beyond the entrance gates. The *Gurah Bungalows* have
the best accommodation in the area, with spotless and salubrious doubles. Of the
homestays to the south of the gates, the *Sadar Wisata* (☎0629/21406; ③) is the newest
and best looking, with attractive wooden bungalows overlooking lily ponds on the
banks of the Alas. The *Pondok Wisata Ketambe* (☎0629/21289; ②) is the largest place
in town, and has some charming little bungalows, all with attached shower.
Unfortunately, the food here, especially when the manager is away, can be dreadful,
and the restaurant is a little noisy at night. The *Pondok Cinta Alam* (②), nearest the
park entrance, is older and scruffier than the others but has the cheapest rooms; the
manager is a sweet old boy and he's currently building some more luxurious bungalows away from the road by the river. The *Cinta Alam Family*, just down the road, is
owned by the same family but was closed at the time of writing.

The Gunung Leuser national park

All visitors to the **Gunung Leuser national park** must be accompanied by a registered guide and buy a **park permit**, available at the entrance (Rp2000 per day). **Guides**
cost upwards of Rp20,000 per day, the price increasing the longer you stay in the park.
Choosing the right one is very important: there are over two hundred licensed guides
operating out of Bukit Lawang (see p.301) alone, and, whilst many are knowledgeable,
there are a number who are not. There are also some who, in an attempt to impress
tourists, feed the orang-utans. Not only does this ruin the work of the rehabilitation centre, which is to teach the apes to fend for themselves, but it also increases the apes'
chances of catching a virus or disease to which they have no immunity. Before choosing a guide, therefore, read the comments books at the hostels in Ketambe and Bukit
Lawang, and ask other travellers for their recommendations. In Ketambe, Daniel and
Syamsul of the PT Intan Leuser Tour and Travel Agency are two very experienced
guides, and their knowledge of the park is excellent.

One of the keys to an enjoyable trek is to take as little as possible; see p.58 of Basics
for the essentials. **Tents** are usually provided by the guides – ensure that this is so
before setting off. There is no one best time of the year to go trekking, although it is
probably best if you avoid the rainy seasons (April, May & Oct–Dec), when some rivers
are impassable and fewer animals come to the rivers and watering holes to drink. Late
July and August are good months, as the fruit is ripe then and you'll see lots of primates.

There are two main **entrance points** into the Gunung Leuser national park:
Ketambe and Bukit Lawang (see p.304). Those interested in trekking around Leuser
for a few days should use Ketambe as their base; there are a greater variety of treks to
make from here, and the jungle is wilder and less explored. If you just want to spend a
day in Leuser, you should consider trekking from Bukit Lawang, which has superior

facilities, is much easier to get to from Medan and offers the greatest chance of spotting some of the jungle wildlife.

Treks in the park
There are a number of established **treks** through the park, which you can either follow or adapt to suit your own requirements. A popular choice is the six-day trek between the two entrances, Ketambe and Bukit Lawang. If you just want to make a one-day trail from Ketambe, consider the walk to the nearby **sulphurous springs**. These springs are popular with the local wildlife as a source of important minerals, and though the

FAUNA AND FLORA IN THE GUNUNG LEUSER NATIONAL PARK

Tigers are found everywhere in Sumatra and are very numerous in some districts. On the whole they are useful animals, as they keep down the number of boars, which are harmful to cultivated fields. But when the tiger is old and no longer fleet enough to catch wild pigs, deer, and apes, it has to be satisfied with poorly armed human beings. Such a man-eater spreads terror in the neighbourhood and is a hindrance to social intercourse.

Sumatra, Its History and People, Edwin M. Loeb (1935)

The **Sumatran tiger** is no longer the "hindrance to social intercourse" that it once was. There are only about five hundred left in the whole of Sumatra, and about sixty of these live within the Gunung Leuser national park – one of the largest populations left on the island. Your chance of seeing one of these magnificent creatures is extremely slim, and, sadly, they are not the only endangered creature in the park. The **Asian elephant**, **clouded leopard**, **marbled cat** and its cousin the **golden cat**, plus **crocodile** and **sun bear**, live within the confines of the park, and all have dwindled alarmingly in number over the last fifty years. The park also plays host to possibly the most endangered animal in the whole of Indonesia: the **Sumatran rhinoceros**. About forty of these shy creatures are believed to still live in Leuser, mainly near Sungai Mamas in the southwestern corner of the park in an area that is out of bounds to trekkers.

Of all the endangered species in Leuser, the only one that visitors have a reasonable chance of encountering is the **orang-utan**; thanks largely to the rehabilitation centre at Bukit Lawang, over five thousand now live in the park. Other primates that you should see include the white-breasted **Thomas leaf monkey** – easy to spot as it crashes through the forest canopy – **long- and pig-tailed macaques**, the **white-handed gibbon** and the cuddly **black siamang**, looking like an elongated teddy bear as it hangs from the uppermost branches of the tallest trees.

Back on the ground, Leuser also has four species of **deer** (the muntjac, barking deer and two types of mouse deer), the **ajak** (a wild dog) and, in the upper reaches of the park, a fairly large **mountain goat** population. Flying squirrels, flying foxes, bats, tortoises, turtles, and a number of species of snake are also present in the park, including the **king cobra** and the magnificent **python** – the biggest snake in Indonesia, at over 10m long.

Of Leuser's 325 different bird species, the **hornbills** are probably the most recognizable. There are eight different types in Leuser, including the rhinoceros and helmeted hornbill. Sightings of both types are common. Other species of birds include the **kingfisher, babbler, argus pheasant** (a dull-brown cousin of the peacock) and the **common drongo**.

There are estimated to be over 8500 plant species in Leuser, and new ones are still being discovered. **Orchids** are common in the park, particularly at the higher altitudes, and they can provide some much-needed colour amongst the muted greens and browns of the forest floor. Indeed, the higher you climb, the more colourful Leuser becomes, with meadows of primrose and wild strawberries dominating the hillsides. The most spectacular flower of all, however, is the lowland **rafflesia**. There are two different types in the park, the *Rafflesia acehensis* and the *Rafflesia zippelni*, and, although neither are as sizable as the *Rafflesia arnoldi*, the flower can still be as big as a large cabbage. Late October, when the plant is in bloom, is the time to see them.

spring water is scalding, when combined with the fast-flowing Gurah River water in the nearby pools, it is wonderfully warm. On the way back you can take a short detour to the foot of a beautiful waterfall, in the hills behind the Wisata Ketambe.

To really experience the park, however, it's much better to spend at least one night out in the jungle. The four-day trek to **Danau Marpunga** (aka Danau Tiga Sagi) is a newly established trail to a small lake near a flat sulphurous gully, where many animals – including elephants – come to feed, extracting minerals from the rocks. There are also a number of treks up various volcanoes that feature a variety of different types of flora, from lowland jungle to the mosses and lichen of the highland slopes. The most accessible peak is **Gunung Bendahara** (3012m), a six-day hike there and back from the village of Seldok, near Ketambe. The trek to the top of **Gunung Perkison**, to the northeast of Kutacane, takes seven days, with spectacular views from the top overlooking the Alas Valley and a lot of wildlife to see on the way.

The mother of all trekking routes in Gunung Leuser national park, however, is the walk to **Gunung Leuser** (3404m) itself, a draining twelve- to fourteen-day hike through untouched forest and mountain meadows to Sumatra's highest peak. At the top there's a small monument, and you're rewarded with some marvellous vistas.

Ketambe to Blangkejeren

This 72-kilometre stretch of worn tarmac and potholes is possibly the most spectacular road in Indonesia. Many travellers prefer to travel on the roof of the bus on this section; this can be a little hair-raising, though without a doubt it's one of the best ways to appreciate the awesome scenery. For the first two hours the road follows closely the course of the Alas as it winds its way through the Gunung Leuser national park. Apart from the orderly squares of paddy-fields that hug the river, the landscape is fairly wild and rugged along this stretch, with only a few tiny villages along the way. After an hour the road passes through **Gumpang**, an important market town, before beginning the climb up the slopes to the east of the valley. Thirty minutes outside of Blangkejeren the road passes above **Agusan**, a small town in the Alas Valley and the starting point for expeditions to the summit of Gunung Leuser. The *Green Agusan Bungalows* (②), built on two sites – the first on the hill just down from the road, the second on the other side of Sungai Alas in the Agusan Forest – provide an excellent base for trekkers. There are restaurants in both sections and, though the food is rather bland, the accommodation is perfectly acceptable and the setting wonderful.

Soon after Agusan the scenery changes dramatically. Lush jungle now gives way to rolling hills of pasture and tree stumps, an indication that you have left the unspoilt wilderness of the national park.

The busy rural town of **BLANGKEJEREN** stands at an important crossroads; as well as being on the main Kutacane–Takengon highway, Blangkejeren also has connections with both the west and east coasts. An appalling road from the tiny Blangkejeren suburb of Trangon heads to Simpang Trangon, north of Blangpidie on Aceh's west coast, and a similarly hazardous road from the village of Pinding, 15km east of Blangkejeren, connects the town with Pereulak on the east coast. Blangkejeren itself is peaceful and pleasant, and it's hard to believe that at the beginning of this century the villages in this rugged part of the Gayo homeland suffered some of the worst massacres of the colonial era. Entire villages were razed and their inhabitants slaughtered in the years 1903–04, as the Dutch attempted to expand into the highlands from their base in Banda Aceh. Their actions caused an outcry back in the Netherlands, and fermented anti-colonial feeling in Sumatra.

Blangkejeren also lies at the heart of a marijuana-growing region; the locals use it in their cooking. Tobacco is also grown locally, and an entrepreneurial soul in nearby hillside village of **Kedah** has converted the tobacco huts into isolated bungalows for tourists (see opposite).

Blangkejeren practicalities

As most buses leave Blangkejeren in the morning, it is probable that you'll have to spend a night in town. The *Rahmat*, Jalan Besar, Gang Tengah 200 (☎0642/21023; ②), 250m south of the bus station, is the best and cheapest **accommodation** place here, with huge clean rooms. The *Juli*, Jalan Kong Bur 53 (☎0642/21036; ②), with simple but smart doubles, is another popular option.

Those seeking even more peace and seclusion, however, should consider the *Green Sinebuk Bungalows* (②) and tobacco huts above the village of Kedah. The owner, Mr Jali, has built thirteen simple wooden bungalows – each with mosquito nets – and three mandis in a picturesque hillside setting on the edge of a forest by a stream. It really is a wonderful – if chilly – retreat, and Mr Jali is a warm and sincere host. He organizes **treks** into the neighbouring Sinebuk Forest, which, though not part of the Leuser park (so no permits are required), is alive with troops of monkeys, orang-utan and other primates.

The bungalows themselves are rather difficult to get to, and are not really recommended for those who are only stopping over for one night. From Blangkejeren, catch a bemo to Kota Panjang (Rp500), 12km away. From there you'll have to rent a becak (Rp2000) for the 4km uphill to Kedah, though if you arrive on market days (Mon & Thurs am) you may be able to catch a second bemo all the way to Kedah. The *Sinebuk Grin Coffee Shop* is a twenty-minute climb above the village, then it's another fifteen minutes down into the gorge and the bungalows.

If even these bungalows aren't isolated enough, ask Mr Jali to take you to his **tobacco huts** (② including meals), a further hour uphill in the heart of the forest. The accommodation is very rudimentary, with no toilet or shower facilities save for a stream.

Takengon and around

The highway north from Blangkejeren is a throwback to the early days of travel in Aceh, when breakdowns were the norm rather than the exception. Mud slides, rock falls and potholes are just some of the hazards encountered on this stretch, and in some places large sections of the road have just collapsed and remain unfixed. The scenery remains superb as the road winds its way round up and over the northern slopes of the Bukit Barisan, but it's not uncommon for the six-hour journey to stretch to double that length due to hazards en route.

THE GAYO HIGHLANDERS

Numbering about 250,000, the **Gayo** are one of the smaller ethnic groups in Sumatra. Their ancestors first arrived from South Vietnam about four thousand years ago, settling in the remote northern tip of the Bukit Barisan mountain range immediately to the south of Banda Aceh. The Gayonese language is related to the Batak tongues of North Sumatra, suggesting that there has been significant contact between the two down the centuries. The highlands of the Gayonese became part of the kingdom of Aceh during the reign of Iskandar Muda, at which time most of their number converted to Islam.

The Gayos' reputation for belligerence is largely undeserved, and probably stems from the struggle of 1965 when Aceh attempted to break from the rest of Indonesia. They are in fact a sociable people who value education highly, are proud of their ability to adapt to changes in technology and whose inter-village rivalry traditionally manifests itself in nothing more violent than *didong* contests, where teams from each village attempt to out-perform each other in dancing, singing and **poetry-reciting** competitions. They are also famed for their dazzlingly bright *kerawang* embroidery, which uses brightly coloured threads (the valuable golden thread that was once used has largely been phased out now) to describe the swirling arabesque patterns found on everything from tablecloths to prayer mats.

At the end of the journey the road drops into a volcanic caldera divided into neat paddy squares, in the centre of which is **TAKENGON**, the delightful capital of the Gayo people. Takengon sits perched on the edge of placid **Laot Tawar**, a fifty-metre-deep lake flanked to the north and south by sheer volcanic hills. Like other lakeside resorts in Sumatra – Toba and Maningau, for example – there isn't actually that much to do in Takengon, although the coffee company in nearby **Pondok Gajah** makes for a surprisingly enjoyable day-trip. Even sunbathing is not really an option in chilly Takengon, where temperatures are well below the Indonesian norm and blankets are essential at night.

Indeed, in some respects, Takengon doesn't seem like a part of Indonesia at all. There are no becak in town, and out of town the fields are ploughed not by buffaloes but by **horses**. For one week of every year, just after Independence Day, these horses are taken out of the fields and raced by local youths in a week-long festival. If you're in the province at this time, a visit to the races is a must.

One way to pass the time in Takengon is to go **shopping**; there are a number of vendors in town dedicated to the Gayo art of *kerawang* embroidery (see the box on p.347). Prayer mats, tablecloths, handbags, racket holders and traditional Gayo shawls and hats, all made from black cloth and embroidered with bright cotton, form a dazzling display in the shop windows. The best quality *kerawang* can be found at Keramat Mupakat Bintang Timur Kerawang Gayo, Jalan Lebe Kadir 24; the two old ladies who run the shop also make the wares. There are three more shops on Jalan Sudirman, including Toko Souvenir Rezeki at no. 86 and the Toko Souvenir Ida Kerawang Gayo Asli at no. 68.

Practicalities

As with most of Aceh, the tourist industry in Takengon is still in its fledgling stages. The **tourist office** on Jalan Senggeda has never opened, and the **BRI bank** at Jalan Yos Sudarso 89 (Mon–Fri 8am–noon), on the road to Blangkejeren, is the only place to change money. Only US dollars cash and travellers' cheques are acceptable, and the rates are fairly poor.

There are nine **hotels** and **losmen** in Takengon, though they're not particularly good value and there are no singles. A cluster of cheap hotels lies to the south of the mosque. These include the popular *Batang Ruang*, just down from the cinema at Jalan Mahkamah 7 (☎0643/21524; ③), which has some reasonably comfortable wooden rooms (though the walls are punctuated with peepholes, which can very be unnerving). The slightly cheaper *Fajar*, next door at no. 8 (no phone; ③), and the cheapest of the lot, the *Penginapan Umah Beroker* (☎0643/21941; ②), just round the corner at Jalan Kampung Baru 55, are acceptable alternatives. At the other end of the scale, the *Hotel Renggali*, about 2km away on the southern side of the lake on Jalan Bintang (☎0643/21144; ⑥), is Takengon's finest. Features here include tennis and badminton courts, a small pool and hot water in all the rooms. This is also the place to come for some alcohol.

Takengon's **restaurants** are disappointing, particularly considering the abundance of fresh fish and fruit available in the market. As ever, Padang food is the mainstay of most of the eateries, though the *Mega Bakso* at Jalan Malem Dewa 40 does a fair *mie bakso*. There's a whole string of warung kopi near the roundabout on Jalan Lebe Kadir, including the *Yusra Bara* at no. 9 and the *Baorena* at no. 40, both of which cook up some pretty delicious *murtabak* in the evening.

Around Takengon

The most enjoyable way to explore **Laot Tawar** and its environs is by boat. The owners of the Loyang Koro caves (see opposite) rent out paddle **boats** for the day for Rp2000, slightly more if you have somebody to row for you. There also have a few motorboats, with the rental rate, depending on the size of the motor, beginning at Rp15,000 for a small 5-HP motor.

It's possible to travel all the way round the lake, 56km in total, by public transport in one day. Labi-labi to Bintang, on the eastern side of the lake, leave from the station to the north of the roundabout on Jalan Lebe Kadir. On the way, 4km past the *Hotel Renggali* on the southern side of the lake, are the **Loyang Koro** (Buffalo Caves; Rp1000) a series of dank tunnels that once ran from the village of Isak all the way to Toweran, 20km away. In the days when the jungle was still full of wild and dangerous animals, the villagers would use these caves to transport their buffalo from one village to another. Since then the caves have fallen into disuse, stalactites and stalagmites have formed, and it is now impossible to penetrate more than 100m inside. Bring a torch (the electric lighting is temperamental) and some sturdy boots, as it's quite muddy and slippery in the caves. Many tourists combine a visit to the caves with an afternoon on the **Ujung Nunan** beach, near the village of Toweran, 4km further on. A labi-labi from Takengon costs Rp500 to the beach.

The best day-trip in the region actually lies away from the lake, 21km northeast of Takengon on the way to Lhokseumawe. The village of **Pondok Gajah** is home to the **PD Genap Mupakat Coffee Company**, who throw open their doors to tourists wishing to see the various processes involved in producing fine quality coffee. At the end of the tour around the factory there's a free tasting session and a chance to buy some packets of coffee at greatly discounted prices. Take a minibus to Pondok Gajah (Rp1000); the factory is at the beginning of the village on the left-hand side of the road.

travel details

North Sumatra and Aceh both have a reasonably large and efficient transport network. Don't despair if the bus times given here don't tie in with your plans: there are dozens of minibuses, bemos and labi-labi also plying the routes. On the west coast of Aceh, for instance, you will probably be relying on the Mitsubishi Colts that zoom up and down the coastal road (every 20min).

Buses

Where the bus frequency is not given, buses depart at least once an hour.

Banda Aceh to: Bireuen (4hr); Medan (10hr); Jakarta (60hr); Lhokseumawe (7hr); Meulaboh (5hr); Padang (24hr); Takengon (8hr); Tapaktuan (9hr).

Berastagi to: Kutacane (daily 9am; 6hr); Medan (2hr); Parapat (via Kabanjahe and Pematangsiantar; 6hr).

Blangkejeren to: Blangpidie (daily 9am from Trangon; 6hr); Kutacane (hourly; 3hr); Langsa (daily from Pinding; 8hr); Takengon (3 daily at 9am, 10am & 1pm; 7hr).

Bukit Lawang to: Berestagi (tourist bus, daily; 5hr); Medan (every 20min, last at 6pm; 3hr).

Gunung Sitoli to: Teluk Dalam (every 30min, last at 4pm; 4hr).

Ibioh to: Sabang (3 daily at 6am, noon & 4pm; 1hr).

Kabanjahe to: Pematangsiantar (every 30min 8am–3pm; 3hr).

Kutacane to: Berastagi (3 hourly; 6hr); Blangkejeren (10 daily; 3hr); Ketambe (10 daily; 1hr); Takengon (daily at 9am; 10hr).

Medan (Amplas terminal) to: Bukittinggi (18hr); Jakarta (48hr); Padang (20hr); Parapat (hourly, last at 6pm; 3hr); Sibolga (daily at 6pm; 12hr).

Medan (Jalan Tobing 81) to: Singkil (daily at 1pm; 10hr).

Medan (Padang Bulan) to: Berastagi (every 20min; 2hr).

Medan (Pinang Baris terminal) to: Banda Aceh (hourly; 10–12hr); Bukit Lawang (every 20min until 6pm; 3hr); Kutacane (12 daily; 8hr); Tapaktuan (3 daily; 12hr).

Parapat to: Berastagi (via Kabanjahe and Pematangsiantar; 6hr); Bukittinggi (6 daily; 14hr); Jakarta (3 daily; 43hr); Medan (10 daily, last at 11am; 3hr); Padang (3 daily; 16hr); Sibolga (daily at 10am; 6hr).

Sabang to: Ibioh (3 daily at 10am, 1pm & 6pm; 1hr).

Sibolga to: Bukittinggi (12hr); Medan (8hr); Parapat (4hr).

Singkil to: Banda Aceh (2 daily at 9am & 11am; 15hr); Berastagi (daily at 11am; 8hr); Medan (daily at 11am; 10hr); Sibolga (Mon, Thurs & Sat 8am; 10hr).

Takengon to: Banda Aceh (3 daily; 7hr); Blangkejeren (3 daily at 10am, noon & 1pm; 7hr).

Trains

Medan to: Balai (3 daily; 4hr); Binjai (3 daily; 30min); Pematangsiantar (3 daily; 3hr 30min).

Pelni ferries

For a chart of the Pelni routes, see pp.36–37 of Basics.

Gunung Sitoli to: Padang (*KM Kambuna*, fortnightly, Sat 3pm; 13hr); Sibolga (*KM Lambelu*, fortnightly, Sat 9am; 4hr/*Sumber Rezeki*, daily except Sun, 10am; 10hr).

Medan (Belawan harbour) to: Jakarta (*KM Sinabung*, every 4 days; 42hr); Penang (*KM Bahagia*, Mon & Tues 2.30pm, Thurs noon, Sat 10am; 4hr/*KM Perdana*, Wed, Fri & Sun 10am; 4hr).

Sibolga to: Gunung Sitoli (*KM Kambuna*, fortnightly, Sat 10am; 4hr); Padang (*KM Lambelu*, fortnightly, Sat 4pm; 12hr).

Other ferries

Ajibata to: Tomok (5 daily; 45min).

Ambarita to: Haranggaol (Mon 6.30am; 3hr); Parapat (hourly 6.45am–4.45pm; 45min); Tongging (Tues 9am; 3hr 30min).

Banda Aceh (Kreung Raya) to: Pulau Weh (daily 10am & 2.30pm; 2hr 30min).

Gunung Sitoli to: Sibolga (*KM Cucit/Poncan Moale*, daily except Sun 8pm; 8hr/*Jambo Jet*, daily except Sun 2pm; 4hr).

Haranggaol to: Ambarita (Mon 1pm; 3hr); Simanindo (Mon 1pm, Thurs 7pm; 1hr 10min).

Meulaboh to: Pulau Simeleue (Mon, Wed & Fri 6pm; 12hr).

Parapat to: Ambarita (hourly 8.45am–6.45pm; 45min); Tuk Tuk (hourly 9.30am–7.30pm; 30min).

Pulau Banyak (Pulau Balai) to: Singkil (Wed & Sun 8am; 4hr 30min).

Pulau Simeleue (Sinabang) to: Meulaboh (Tues, Thurs & Sat 6pm; 12hr).

Pulau Weh (Balohan) to: Banda Aceh (2 daily 10am & 2.30pm; 2hr 30min).

Sibolga to: Gunung Sitoli (*KM Cucit/Poncan Moale*, daily except Sun 8pm; 8hr/*Jambo Jet*, daily except Sun 8.30am; 4hr/*Sumber Rezeki*, daily except Sun 6pm; 10hr).

Simanindo to: Haranggaol (Mon 9am; 1hr 10min).

Singkil to: Pulau Banyak (Mon, Thurs & Fri 8am; 4hr 30min).

Tongging to: Ambarita (Mon 9am; 3hr 30min); Tuk Tuk (Mon 9am; 3hr 45min).

Tuk Tuk to: Parapat (hourly 7am–2pm; 30min); Tongging (Tues 10am; 3hr 45min).

Flights

Banda Aceh to: Kuala Lumpur (3 weekly; 2hr); Medan (2 daily; 55min).

Gunung Sitoli to: Medan (6 weekly; 1hr 10min); Padang (weekly; 1hr).

Medan to: Banda Aceh (2 daily; 55min); Batam (3 daily; 1hr 15min); Dumai (weekly; 1hr 25min); Gunung Sitoli (7 weekly; 1hr 10min); Jakarta (15 daily; 2hr 15min); Kuala Lumpur (17 daily; 1hr); Padang (3 daily; 1hr 10min); Pekanbaru (daily; 2hr); Penang (11 weekly; 40min); Sibolga (6 weekly; 1hr); Sinabang (3 weekly; 1hr 20min); Singapore (2 daily; 1hr 30min).

Meulaboh to: Medan (SMAC, 3 weekly; 1hr 45min); Sinabang (SMAC, 3 weekly; 45min).

Sibolga to: Medan (6 weekly; 1hr).

Sinabang to: Medan (3 weekly; 1hr); Meulaboh (3 weekly; 45min).

CHAPTER SIX

PADANG AND CENTRAL SUMATRA

C entral Sumatra is dominated by the soaring Bukit Barisan mountain range, and characterized by cool upland valleys, mountain lakes and innumerable jungle-covered peaks. The range drops steeply to the Indian Ocean on the west coast and slopes more gently to the eastern plains, providing the source of the huge river systems – the Siak, Kampar, Indragiri and Batanghari – that cross the eastern plains on their meandering way to the Malacca Straits and the South China Sea.

Major **gateways** into Indonesia are provided by the west coast port of **Padang** and the islands of **Batam** and **Bintan** in the Riau Archipelago, between the Sumatran mainland and Singapore: the islands have excellent transport connections to the rest of the country. Travellers entering Sumatra through the Riau Islands can transit in the prosperous city of **Pekanbaru** before heading north to Medan and Danau Toba, south to Bandar Lampung, perhaps via the little-visited city of **Jambi**, or west to Bukittinggi, the main tourist destination in the region.

The heartland of Minang culture, **Bukittinggi** is a cool and relaxed town with a thriving travellers' scene, perched picturesquely on the edge of the Ngarai Sianok Canyon, within sight of Gunung Merapi and Gunung Singgalang. Nearby, **Danau Maninjau** is developing plenty of low-key lakeside guest houses: what it lacks in scale compared to Danau Toba, it makes up for in atmosphere and tranquillity. Further south lies the **Kerinci-Seblat national park**, one of the largest and most diverse parks in Indonesia, with a rich plant and animal life and a huge number of ecosystems, home to the (possibly mythological) *orang pendek*, the local equivalent of the Himalayan yeti. The second highest peak in Indonesia, Gunung Kerinci (3805m) is, with care and preparation, a feasible summit for fit trekkers, but the park also offers less demanding treks. The **Mentawai Islands** lie 100km off the west coast of Sumatra, separated by the 2000-metre-deep Mentawai Strait and are inhabited by groups of people who have long been isolated from the Sumatran mainland and who manage to maintain a traditional way of life.

For those with the time and inclination, it's possible to meander through the back roads of central Sumatra, not only to avoid a lengthy haul on major roads, but to visit some pleasant villages and towns and see the glorious scenery on the coastal route **south to Bengkulu**.

Getting around the area on public transport can be gruelling. Whilst long-distance buses are regular and frequent, the distances involved are great. The roads, like those on the rest of Sumatra, are tortuous, and the driving can be hair-raising in the extreme. There are plenty of road connections on to Java from even the smallest towns, but if you intend to use sea or air to make your trip less stressful then you'll need to plan carefully, as only the large cities have airports, and ferry connections are generally irregular, especially on the west coast.

The **climate** of the area is far from temperate. The city of Padang, on the western side of the Bukit Barisan range where the precipitation of the Indian Ocean is dumped as the moisture-laden winds rise over the mountains, is extremely hot and humid and

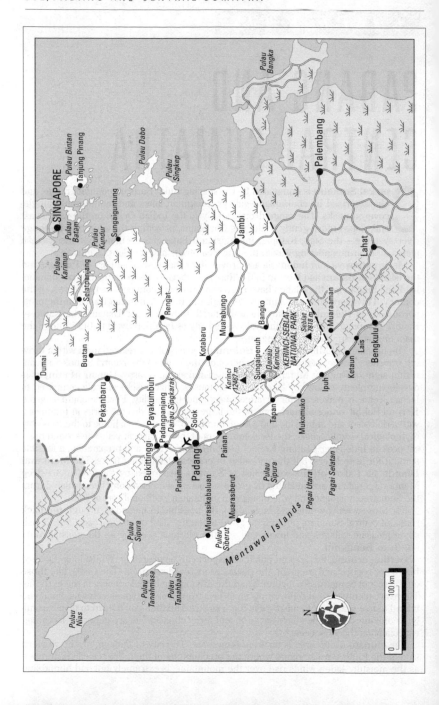

an awful sweaty shock if you're flying in from cooler climes. It has the highest rainfall in Indonesia, with a yearly average of 4508mm – putting it in the top ten of rainiest inhabited spots in the world. Pekanbaru and Jambi on the eastern side of the island can be just as hot, but as they are in the rain shadow they have a drier, more tolerable climate. Throughout the region, the mountains offer a pleasant relief from the heat, and up on the summit of Gunung Kerinci temperatures as low as 5°C are common.

Some history

The history of the Padang hinterland, the Minang highlands (see p.362), and the Kerinci area (see p.386) is traceable back to prehistoric times, but settlement of the west-coast areas took place rather later. Reefs off the west coast made it difficult for ships to negotiate, and until the sixteenth century all trade routes were along the Malacca Straits to the east of Sumatra. The most famous **ancient kingdom** in this area, the Malayu, based on Sungai Batang Hari near Jambi, flourished from the seventh to thirteenth centuries and was located in the east of the island, open to outside influences from that direction: remains at Muara Takus suggest Buddhism had reached the island as early as the ninth century.

Late in the seventeenth century, the **British**, driven from their major Indonesian stronghold at Banten in 1682, began to expand their interests in Sumatra; they controlled the port of Padang from 1781 to 1784, and again between 1795 and 1816, shipping coffee to America. However, life and trade was seriously interrupted by warfare in the Minang highlands, which broke out in 1803 between the traditional long-established Minangkabau rulers and the Paderi, fundamental Muslim reformers. In some valleys, the Paderi gained control without a fight, while in others fierce warfare raged for years. The British had operated as arbitrators to some extent, a role which the **Dutch** inherited when they took over the region. (The **conflict** between the colonial powers had been long and intense, and it was only at end of the Napoleonic Wars in 1816 that Britain was forced to return Holland's prewar holdings to them.) The Dutch signed a treaty with the Minangkabau nephew of the Raja Alam of Pagarruyung and built a fort at Bukittinggi. Eventually, after years of fierce resistance, the so-called **Paderi Wars**, the Dutch gained control of the entire area in the 1837 on the death of Imam Bonjol, the Paderi leader.

The Dutch victory united the Minang highlands and Padang under one administration. Enforced production of **coffee** in the highlands continued, increasingly with conditions that only benefited the Dutch. In 1868, the discovery of a **coalfield** along Sungai Umbilin began years of debate about the best method of exploitation of the resource, eventually resulting in the construction of a **railway** between the highlands and **Padang**, which was

---

ACCOMMODATION PRICE CODES

All the **accommodation** listed in this book has been given one of the following price codes. The rates quoted here are for the **cheapest double room** in high season, except for places with dorms, where the code represents the price of a single bed. Where there's a significant spread of prices indicated (④–⑦, for example), the text will explain what extra facilities you get for more money. The 11–21 percent tax charged by most hotels is not included in these price codes.

Because of the current instability of the rupiah, accommodation prices are given throughout in their more stable **US dollar equivalents**, even for places that accept payment in rupiah.

For more on accommodation, see p.40.

① under $1	③ $2–5	⑤ $10–15	⑦ $35–60	⑨ $100
② $1–2	④ $5–10	⑥ $15–35	⑧ $60–100	and over

completed in 1896. The city began to thrive: ships called at the port to stock up with coal, and Teluk Bayur, the port for Padang, was constructed to cope with the traffic.

Dutch rule was not without its problems, and local Minangkabau, well educated but unable to find jobs, took part in an armed uprising in 1926. When it was quashed by the Dutch, many of the participants ended up in the prison camp, Boven Digul, in what is now Irian Jaya. In modern times **Pekanbaru** has grown rich on the oil- and gas fields that have boomed throughout Central Sumatra, providing about sixty percent of the total Indonesian output. The **Riau Islands** are the site of huge tourist and industrial investment and Padang is gradually opening up, with improved international air connections.

Padang and around

A bustling port and university town, attractive **PADANG**, with a population of over 600,000, is the administrative capital of West Sumatra province and the business and transport hub for the entire region. Situated on the north bank of Sungai Arau and ranging north for 10km between the coast and the Bukit Barisan mountains, the city is famed throughout Indonesia as the home of *Makanan Padang* (Padang food), whose typically spicy dishes feature large amounts of chillies, served on individual small plates from which every diner takes their pick. The city's roads are broad and leafy, and many of the modern buildings show the influence of Minang architecture, usually in their impressive, soaring roofs. Public transport is easy to negotiate and there are excellent air, road and sea connections both throughout the region and on to other islands, with a number of worthwhile **excursions** possible to nearby beaches and islands. However, most tourists pause only briefly in Padang, the majority aiming for the nearby hill town of Bukittinggi, the Mentawai Islands, the Kerinci-Seblat national park, or more distant Bengkulu.

Padang has always been an **ethnically mixed** place, the largest group being the Minangkabau people from the nearby highlands, plus Javanese, Chinese, Tamils and Niasans. The Niasans, from the Nias Islands (see p.323), are descendants of slaves brought to the mainland by the Dutch, while the Javanese are descended from nineteenth-century soldiers sent to help the Dutch in the Paderi Wars and convicts sent as forced labourers, with more recent arrivals coming as workmen and civil servants. The earliest Chinese migrants came in the late seventeenth century, and the Tamils arrived with the British army during their periods in control of the area.

Arrival, orientation, information and city transport

Padang is a **visa-free entry point** to Indonesia (see p.16). All flights land at **Tabing Airport**, 9km north of the city centre. The bank and moneychangers are located at the front of the international arrivals building, and there's a taxi ticket office – collect the fixed-price ticket from the office and pay the driver on arrival at your destination (prices within the city are Rp7000–9000). Out on the main road (200m walk from the terminal), buses #14a and #14b (Rp250) stop just outside the airport gates: those heading to the left go into the city. Small white bemos also stop here and will take you to the bemo terminal in town (Rp500). Pelni **boats** arrive at the port of Teluk Bayur, 7km south of town, from where you can take a white bemo to the city centre.

Although it sprawls inland and along the coast for several kilometres, the **central area** of Padang is quite compact and easy to negotitate, while the efficient public transport system means that most areas are accessible, the exception being Batau Arau, where you'll end up walking several hundred metres for the Mentawai boats or grabbing a taxi. The main road in the central area of the city is Jalan Moh Yamin, which runs west–east for almost a kilometre from the junction in the west with Jalan Pemuda, to the large junction in the east with Jalan Bagindo Azizchan and Jalan Proklamasi. Within easy reach of Jalan

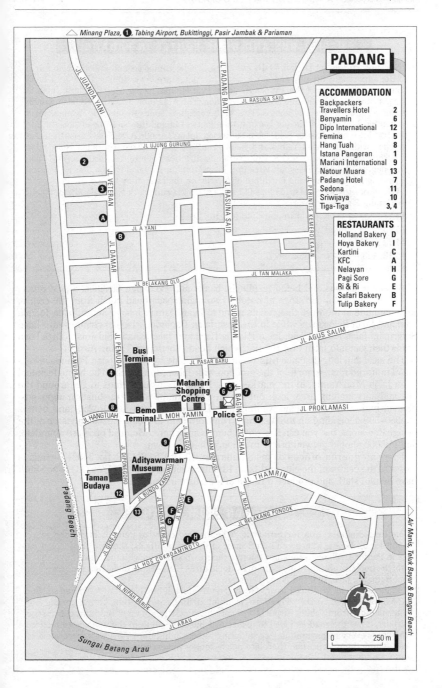

△ Minang Plaza, ❶, Tabing Airport, Bukittinggi, Pasir Jambak & Pariaman

PADANG

ACCOMMODATION

Backpackers Travellers Hotel	2
Benyamin	6
Dipo International	12
Femina	5
Hang Tuah	8
Istana Pangeran	1
Mariani International	9
Natour Muara	13
Padang Hotel	7
Sedona	11
Sriwijaya	10
Tiga-Tiga	3, 4

RESTAURANTS

Holland Bakery	D
Hoya Bakery	I
Kartini	C
KFC	A
Nelayan	H
Pagi Sore	G
Ri & Ri	E
Safari Bakery	B
Tulip Bakery	F

JL JUANDA YANI
JL PADANG BAJU
JL RASUNA SAID
JL UJUNG GURUNG
JL VETERAN
JL RASUNA SAID
JL PERINTIS KEMERDEKAAN
JL A YANI
JL DAMAR
JL TAN MALAKA
JL BELAKANG OLO
JL SUDIRMAN
JL AGUS SALIM
JL SAMUDRA
JL PEMUDA
Bus Terminal
JL PASAR BARU
Matahari Shopping Centre
JL HANGTUAH
Bemo Terminal JL MOH YAMIN
Police
JL BAGINDO AZIZCHAN
JL PROKLAMASI
JL DIPONEGORO
JL HI GOO
JL IMAM BONJOL
Adityawarman Museum
Taman Budaya
JL BINDO KANDUNG
JL BANDAR GEREJA
JL THAMRIN
JL NIAS
JL BELAKANG PONDOK
JL GEREJA
JL HOS COKROAMINOTO
JL NIPAH BEROK
JL ARAU

Padang Beach

△ *Air Manis, Teluk Bayur & Bungus Beach*

Sungai Batang Arau

N

0   250 m

USEFUL BUS AND BEMO ROUTES IN PADANG

Local **bus routes #14a** and **#14b** complete circular routes around Padang from north of the airport into the city and out again. The routes are very similar. They both head south into the city past the airport via Jalan Prof Hamka to the Minang Plaza, Jalan S. Parman and the Jalan Khatib Sulaiman junction. The #14a then heads along Jalan Khatib Sulaiman towards the city centre. The #14b continues south to Jalan S. Parman, Jalan Raden Saleh and Jalan Padang Baru; it then joins #14a and they both head straight into the city down Jalan Rasuna Said, Jalan Sudirman, Jalan Bagindo Azizchan, across the main junction with Jalan Moh Yamin and Jalan Proklamasi, Jalan Thamrin, Jalan Nias, Jalan Belakang Pondok, Jalan H.O.S. Cokroaminoto, the beach entrance, Jalan Gereja, Jalan Diponegoro, the Adityawarman Museum, Jalan Moh Yamin, Jalan Hilgoo, Jalan Thamrin, Jalan Bagindo Azizchan and north out of the city on the route they have come in.

White bemos #416, #419, #420, #422, #423 and #424 run north from Jalan Pemuda out to Minang Plaza and towards the airport.

#437, signed "TI Kabung Bungus", to Bungus Beach.

#423 Pasir Jambak.

#402 Air Manis.

#432, #433, #434 to Teluk Bayur.

Moh Yamin are bus and bemo terminals, banks and exchange facilities, a post office, police station, and a fair range of hotels. Two main roads head north from the centre: Jalan Pemuda in the west changes its name to Jalan Damar, Jalan Veteran, Jalan Juanda Yani and Jalan S. Parman, while in the east, Jalan Bagindo Azizchan changes into Jalan Sudirman, Jalan Rasuna Said, Jalan Padang Baru and Jalan Khatib Sulaiman. These two roads then join into Jalan Prof Hamka, which heads north past Tabing Airport.

The local and long-distance **bus terminals** are side by side on Jalan Pemuda, a couple of hundred metres north of the junction with Jalan Moh Yamin. The bemo terminal is on Jalan Moh Yamin, in the market area. If you are using bemos to get around the city and surrounding area, look out for the route number and destination signs suspended high above the bemo waiting area. Local buses (flat fare Rp250) and bemos (Rp250–500 depending on the distance) run from 6am to 10pm. Buses only stop at the designated stops, but you can flag down bemos anywhere. Metered taxis are abundant, and Rp5000 should get you pretty much anywhere in town.

There are **tourist offices** at Jalan Sudirman 43 (☎0751/34232, fax 34321), which is closer to the centre of the city, and Jalan Khatib Sulaiman 22 (☎0751/55711). They both have helpful staff, and produce a range of literature in English.

MOVING ON FROM PADANG

The **long-distance bus terminal** (Rp200 entrance) on Jalan Pemuda is the departure point for all buses, where you'll find most of the ticket offices; the rest are located on Jalan Pemuda. All bus companies operate their own schedule with their own fares so it's worth shopping around. There are daily departures (6am–7pm) to destinations throughout Sumatra, Java, Bali and Nusa Tenggara.

Pelni **boats** call at Teluk Bayur, which is on the fortnightly circuit of *KM Lambelu* and *KM Kambuna* (see p.419). There are plentiful **airline connections**, both domestic and international, from Tabing Airport. If you are heading straight up to Bukittinggi from the airport, cross the road and hail long-distance buses heading in the opposite direction: they pass every twenty minutes or so during the daylight hours. Although there's talk of reinstating them, at present there are no passenger rail services in the area.

Accommodation

As with most Sumatran cities, **accommodation** in Padang is aimed predominantly at domestic business travellers. Mid-range and luxury hotels predominate, with an emphasis on facilities such as air-con and satellite TV rather than ambience. However, with the increasing use of Padang as a gateway into Indonesia, the number of tourist hotels is growing. If you don't want to stay in the city itself, see p.360 for accommodation options within easy travelling distance, and remember that Bukittinggi (see p.362) is only two hours' drive away, with very frequent buses plying the route.

Backpackers Travellers Hotel, Jl Pursus 2, 13 (☎0751/34261, fax 34265). Sparkling-clean, welcome new addition to the budget accommodation in the city, offering dorms and rooms with and without attached mandi. The building is a multi-storey anomaly in the middle of a residential area and near a beach. It's signed off Jl Veteran a couple of hundred metres south of *Hotel Tiga-Tiga* and local people will direct you. Alternatively they will arrange transport for you at *Hotel Dipo International* on Jl Diponegoro near the city centre. There's an overly complex pricing structure, with prices quoted in dollars and plenty of discounts available. ①–⑥.

Benyamin, Jl Pasar Baru IV (☎0751/22324). In a small alleyway that runs along the side of the *Femina Hotel* on Jl Bagindo Azizchan, served by the #14a and #14b buses. Clean fan rooms with attached bathrooms are in two-storey buildings around a central courtyard. The only down side is the early-morning noise from the nearby market area. ②–③.

Hang Tuah, Jl Pemuda 1 (☎0751/26556). The best, and most popular, of the hotels near the bus terminal, this is on the corner of Jl Pemuda and Jl Hang Tuah. There's a range of basic but adequate rooms with fan and attached cold-water mandi, up to those with air-con and satellite TV. ③.

Istana Pangeran, Jl Veteran 79 (☎0751/51333, fax 54613). Between the city centre and airport, close to a rather unattractive local beach, this is one of the top Padang hotels, and is very popular with tour groups. There's a good-sized swimming pool (non-guests can use this for Rp5000) and tennis courts (rackets available at the hotel). Rooms are comfortably furnished, and communal areas are attractive and welcoming. ⑧–⑨.

Mariani International, Jl Bundo Kandung 35 (☎0751/25466). Centrally situated opposite the *Sedona*, this hotel offers comfortably furnished rooms with attached cold-water mandi and air-con as well as more expensive rooms with hot water. The communal areas are nothing special, but the location is convenient for the city centre. Motorbike rental is available. ④–⑤.

Natour Muara, Jl Gereja 34 (☎0751/35600, fax 31163). Located near the museum and beach, with a quiet atmosphere and an attractive outdoor dining area. The rooms are pleasant but not outstanding and the cheaper ones front onto the car park. There's no pool. ④–⑥.

Padang Hotel, Jl Bagindo Azizchan 28 (☎0751/22563). Accommodation is in very faded bungalows around an equally faded garden, conveniently located and due for a refit, when prices will undoubtedly rise. Served by the #14a and #14b buses in both directions. ③–④.

Sedona, Jl Bundo Kandung 20–28 (☎0751/37555, fax 37567). The most luxurious and most expensive hotel in Padang offers everything that a top-class hotel should, with pool, tennis courts, business centre and comfortable and tasteful communal areas in a central location. ⑨.

Sriwijaya, Jl Alanglawas (☎0751/23577). This budget option is tucked away in a quiet road that runs south from Jl Proklamasi. It's about 10min walk from the #14a and #14b bus routes. The compound is quiet and rooms are basic, but there are small sitting areas outside each. Staff speak little English. ②–③.

Tiga-Tiga, Jl Pemuda 31 (☎0751/22633). The older of the two hotels in town with this name is opposite the bus terminal, an unprepossessing downstairs giving way to a pleasant upstairs sitting area – the lighter, airier rooms are on the upper floors and a good choice of accommodation is on offer. The cheapest have no fan, and outside mandi, and the most expensive have attached bathroom and air-con. ②–③.

Tiga-Tiga, Jl Veteran 33 (☎0751/22173). The newer *Tiga-Tiga* is further out from the city centre than its namesake, about 3km north, and is pleasant and clean with slightly better and more expensive rooms. ③–④.

The City

With some shopping, a visit to the museum and trips to nearby beaches, it's possible to pass a pleasant couple of days in Padang; the climate is not particularly conducive to long **walking tours** of the city. The Chinatown area (Kampung Cina), roughly bounded by Jalan H.O.S. Cokroaminoto, Jalan Pondok and Jalan Dobo, features traditional shophouses and herbalists, as well as restaurants and coffee shops (see below) in which to cool off. Just south of here, between Jalan H.O.S. Cokroaminoto and Jalan Arau, is the Muara district – now very dilapidated, but still the commercial area serving the port, and with a couple of good examples of faded colonial architecture.

The **Adityawarman Museum** (Tues–Sun 9am–4pm; Rp200) is housed in a large *rumah gadang*, a traditional Minang house, with some great carved woodwork and an attractive red-tiled roof and traditional rice barns at the front, set in well-maintained grounds. It's one of the most pleasant museums in Sumatra: the rooms are light and airy and the grounds are a popular meeting and picnic place for local people, especially at weekends. There's some attempt to label the exhibits in English, although the usual range of farm implements, musical instruments, carpentry tools, textiles, old banknotes and weapons isn't exactly a revelation, but the displays relating to Minangkabau culture, plus the textiles, kris and finely worked basketware, all make a visit worthwhile.

For a good **local shopping** experience, ignore the large new shopping centres (see "Listings" p.360) and head instead for Pasar Raya in the city centre, a terrific **market**, awash with fruit and vegetables, cooking ingredients, household goods and clothes.

Padang beach (Rp500) is accessed from the southern end of Jalan Samudra near the junction with Jalan Gereja. Though many local people are quite dismissive of it – the sand is dark and the area is popular and decidedly scruffy – it's lively and sociable around sunset and at weekends, when the warung and the drink carts arrive.

Eating

It makes little sense to come to the homeland of **Padang food** without visiting at least one of the city's **restaurants**, distinguishable by dishes overflowing with curries piled up in their windows. There's no menu: you simply tell staff you want to eat and up to a dozen small plates are placed in front of you (see p.43 for details of the most common dishes on offer). However, it's a cuisine with problems for vegetarians – make sure there are some eggs or tofu on offer before you sit down – and it's usually extremely spicy. Generally, the redder the sauce, the more explosive it is to the taste buds: the yellow, creamy dishes are often less aggressive.

At the southern end of Jalan Pondok, due south of the market area towards the river, you'll find a small **night market** of sate stalls, and this street, and nearby Jalan Niaga, has a range of good places. Another night market operates on Jalan Imam Bonjol, a few hundred metres south of the junction with Jalan Moh Yamin.

California Fried Chicken, Minang Plaza. This pricey *KFC* lookalike sells fried chicken, fries and drinks (with a ten-percent sales tax on top of the listed prices) and the air-con is a life-saver on a hot day.

Es Teler 77, Minang Plaza. The stalwart Indonesian chain sells juices plus a good range of sickly sweet ice concoctions and a few soups, rice and noodle dishes.

Holland Bakery and Cake Shop, Jl Proklamasi 61b. With a good choice of cakes and sweet breads, this is especially popular at weekends with local people.

Hoya Bakery, Jl H.O.S. Cokroaminoto 48. A thriving bakery with a small coffee shop attached.

Kartini, Jl Pasar Baru 24. The most popular of the many Padang-style restaurants along this street. They are unfazed by tourists and the food is fresh and well cooked, with all the usual Padang specialities on offer.

KFC, Jl Bundo Kandung and Jl Veteran. Expensive and predictable, but a cool haven on a hot day.

Matahari Foodcourt, 2nd floor, Matahari Shopping Centre. Air-con, with a wide range of Indonesian options such as soup, gado-gado, sate, *murtabak*, drinks and juices.

Nelayan, Jl H.O.S. Cokroaminoto 44a–b. Expensive Chinese and seafood specialist, with an air-con first floor. The food is good, the menu vast (five types of fish alone, cooked in four different ways), but it's the place for an expensive blowout rather than everyday eating.

Pagi Sore, Jl Pondok 143. A popular and good-value Padang restaurant with plenty of choice, one of the nicest of the many restaurants on this road.

Ri & Ri, Jl Pondok. Pleasantly decorated, with a relaxed atmosphere, this is both a Padang place (10am–2pm) and a slightly more upmarket restaurant in the evening, when there's a menu offering frog, chicken, squid and goat dishes, as well as the basic rice and noodle options.

Safari Bakery, Jl Damar, at the corner with Jl A. Yani. Popular bakery and coffee shop, often crowded with students.

Tulip Bakery, Jl Pondok 139. Stretching back from the road, with high ceilings, this is a cool place to take a rest. Basic fried rice and noodles are on offer as well as the bakery items.

Entertainment

The Taman Budaya **cultural centre** is on Jalan Diponegoro, close to the museum. It hosts the occasional cultural show or concert, but appears to be largely underused, and during the day is almost totally deserted. Look out around town for posters advertising events, or inquire at the tourist offices. Currently popular **discos** are the *President*, in the cinema complex, and the *Luky* on Jalan Diponegoro, a few hundred metres south of the museum. Both operate daily (10pm–2am) and the Rp5000 cover charge includes a drink.

TABUT

Although there's little to attract visitors to the coastal town of **Pariaman**, 36km north of Padang, for much of the year, the annual **Tabut festival**, held from the first to the tenth of the Islamic month of Muharam (movable in the Western calendar, but around June to August), is the highlight of the West Sumatran cultural calendar, also celebrated in Bengkulu as the Tabot festival (see p.51). Access to Pariaman is by bus from either Padang or Bukittinggi.

The festival is staged in honour of Hassan and Hussein, Mohammed's grandsons, who were martyred at the Battle of Karbela defending their religion. A magical *bouraq*, a winged horse with the head of a woman, was believed to have rescued the souls of the heroes and carried them to heaven. Local villages compete to create the grandest *bouraq* effigies, and on the final day they are paraded through the streets accompanied by much music, dancing and festivity. Two *bouraq* meeting on the route indulge in a mock battle with much praise of their own *bouraq* and hurling of insults at others. The procession ends at the coast, where the effigies are flung into the sea followed closely by local people who want to grab mementos – the gold necklaces decorating the effigies are the most prized. Horse races, swimming contests and cultural performances accompany the event. Inquire at the tourist office if you are in the area at this time.

Listings

Airline offices Garuda, *Hotel Istana Pangeran*, Jl Veteran 79 (☎0751/58489, fax 58488); Mandala, Jl Pemuda 29a (☎0751/32773, fax 33184); Merpati, Jl Gereja 34 in the grounds of the *Natour Muara Hotel* (☎0751/32010); Pelangi, Jl Gereja 34, in the grounds of the *Natour Muara Hotel* (☎0751/38103, fax 38104); Silk Air, Jl Hyam Wuruk 16 (☎0751/38122, fax 38120).

American Express representatives Pacto Tours and Travel, Jl Tan Malaka 25 (☎0751/37678, fax 33335); red bemos heading north outside the post office on Jl Bagindo Azizchan pass the office. American Express customers can use this office to receive mail – it takes a day or two longer than at the post office but they also accept faxes.

Banks and exchange Bank of Central Asia, Jl H. Agus Salim 10a; Bank Dagang Negara, Jl Bagindo Azizchan 21; Bank Negara Indonesia, Jl Dobi 1. There are several moneychangers near the bus station offering slightly poorer rates but longer hours and less paperwork: PT Citra Setia Prima, Jl Diponegoro 5 (Mon–Sat 8am–noon & 1–4.30pm); PT Enzet Corindo Perkasa, Jl Pemuda 17c (Mon–Fri 8am–4pm, Sat 8am–2pm).

Courier DHL is at PT Birotika Semesta, Jl Damar 57a (☎0751/22769).

Diving Whilst still in its infancy, diving in the waters off Padang is enticing. This coast is the only part of Indonesia that touches the Indian Ocean and features some species particular to those waters. Other advantages are that the water is generally warm and visibility good. There are several sites within an hour or two by motorboat from Padang including Pulau Pandan, Pulau Sibuntar, Pulau Laut, and the Kapal Wreck, the remains of a cargo ship. However, the highlight of the area is Pulau Pieh, which features a submerged reef and a wreck. The only dive company in town is Padang Diving, Jl Batang Arau 88 B/6 (☎0751/25876, fax 28121); prices depend on the number of people in the group but are typically US$77 per person if there are three people, which includes transport, a diving guide, two full tanks, a weight belt and lunch. Other equipment is available for rental. An alternative is to access the area from a live-aboard charter from elsewhere.

Ferries The Pelni office is at Jl Tanjung Priok 32 (☎0751/33624) at Teluk Bayur, 7km south of Padang.

Hospitals Rumah Sakit Umum Padang, Jl Perentis Kemerdekan (☎0751/25181); Rumah Sakit Selasih, Jl Khatib Sulaiman 72 (☎0751/51405).

Immigration office Jl Khatib Sulaiman (☎0751/55113).

Post office The main post office is conveniently located at Jl Bagindo Azizchan 7, just north of the junction with Jl Moh Yamin. Poste restante here is reasonably efficient.

Shopping Whilst you are unlikely to head to Padang for your main souvenir shopping (Bukittinggi offers a far better choice), you'll find everyday necessities at the Matahari Shopping Centre on Jl Moh Yamin. The gleaming new Minang Plaza, 7km north of the city centre on Jl Prof Hamka, houses three floors of shops and fast-food outlets including the Suzuyu Department Store. Postcards are elusive: try Gramedia Bookstore on Jl Damar, but don't hold out too much hope for English-language novels – they are virtually nonexistent between the secondhand bookshops of Bukittinggi and Jakarta. For souvenirs, Sartika, Jl Sudirman 5, has a considerable range of stuff; modern handicrafts including purses and baskets start at the Rp5000 mark, and there are textiles plus a range of wooden carvings from the Batak and Nias areas of Sumatra as well as further afield from Lombok and Maluku (up to Rp500,000).

Telephone and fax The main Telkom office is several kilometres north of the city centre on Jl Khatib Sulaiman, at the junction with Jl K. Ahmad Dahlan. More convenient 24hr wartel are at Jl Imam Bonjol 17 and Jl Belakang Tangsi 3, which isn't far from the Matahari Shopping Centre and the bus terminal; it's signed south from Jl Moh Yamin. There's also a 24hr warpostel on the ground floor of the Minang Plaza.

Tour operators PT Bingkuang Mas Tours, Jl Veteran 32c (☎0751/36950), offers Minangkabau tours from US$175 for three days and two nights, Siberut for seven days and six nights (from US$379) and Kerinci (from US$329) – all prices are per person and minimum numbers of two or four are required. They also have charter cars at Rp150,000 per day. Pacto Tours and Travel, Jl Tan Malaka 25 (☎0751/37678, fax 33335), offers Minangkabau tours to the Bukittinggi area for three nights and four days (from US$230), and Siberut for five days and four nights (from US$414).

Nearby beaches and islands

The **beaches** and **islands** north and south of the city easily accessible. Although not outstanding, there are some attractive spots with pleasant accommodation; ideal if you need to recover from long-distance travel.

Bungus beach

If you inquire locally for a good beach, people will direct you unerringly to **Bungus beach**, 20km south of Padang, easily reachable on bemo #437 (40min; Rp700) from the city-centre terminal. The long curving white-sand bay enclosed by lush, jungle-covered headlands, with Pulau Kasik just offshore, is very enticing. But there's an oil depot at the southern end of the bay, tankers thunder up and down the road just behind the beach and, at the northern end, a plywood factory dominates. There's a range of economical beachside **accommodation**, a good choice being at km21, where the *Knokke Inn* (☎0751/30356; ②–⑥) comprises simple bamboo bungalows with attached bathrooms through to more spacious, substantial bungalows with air-con. All are on the beach, facing the ocean, and the large restaurant offers simple Indo-Chinese and travellers' fare. Further north, at *Pesona Restaurant*, a new set of tiled bungalows will soon be a welcome addition to the scene. *Carlos Coffee Shop and Losmen* (☎0751/30353; ②–③) is a loud, happening place with a lively coffee-shop scene and a range of basic bungalows. Trips to the nearby islands are available here, from Rp20,000 per person for the day.

The Bungus Islands

The scattered **Bungus Islands** are, as yet, little developed for tourism, and are best explored on a trip from Bungus beach (see above) – if one idyllic, unspoilt spot isn't quite to your liking, you can simply find another. If you want to stay on the islands, *Pusako Island Resort* (☎0751/61777, fax 61774, or contact Pusako Sikuai Wisata, Jalan Muara 38b, Padang ☎0751/37811, fax 22895; ⑨) is an upmarket resort with plenty of facilities on **Pulau Sikuai**, with accommodation in comfortable bungalows with air-con, hot water and TV. Further south, on larger, mountainous **Pulau Cubadak**, where there are opportunities for trekking and wildlife-spotting, *Paradiso Village* (contact INA Tours, *Hotel Dipo International*, Jalan Diponegoro 25, Padang ☎0751/34261, fax 34265; ⑧–⑨) is a similar development, with accommodation in two-storey wood-and-thatch bungalows. Canoe rental and boat trips are available.

Air Manis

Closer to Padang, **Air Manis** (Sweet Water) is a popular excursion for local people. Take bemo #402 from the bemo terminal in Padang (30min; Rp500) for a hilly ride along lanes that cut through the jungle. The dark grey beach is several kilometres long, with myriad paths up onto the headland at the southern end. There are plenty of warung but, whilst the area is pleasant enough, the litter is a real eyesore. If you want to stay you'll need to ask for *Papa Chili Chili's* (no sign, no phone and there may be nobody home when you arrive; ①).

Pasir Jambak

Pasir Jambak, 15km north of Padang, is a long, black-sand beach which you'll share only with local fisherfolk during the week. Take bemo #423 (30min; Rp500) to the entrance gate of the beach area (Sat & Sun Rp350). The sole **accommodation** place is *Uncle Jack's Homestay* (☎0751/39739; ③); either walk along the beach or head straight through the gateway and stay on the road for 2km or 3km – this is the shorter and easier route if you are lugging a pack. Accommodation is in basic rooms situated a few metres from the beach, some with mosquito nets and some without. Day-trips to nearby Pulau Sawo are possible, and you can rent snorkelling gear. It's definitely a very convenient beachside place for your last night if you're flying out from Padang, and staff can arrange a taxi to the airport.

Bukittinggi and the Minang highlands

As far as the eye could distinctly trace was one continued scene of cultivation interspersed with innumerable towns and villages, shaded by coconut and other fruit trees. I may safely say that this view equalled anything I ever saw in Java. The scenery is more majestic and grand, the population equally dense, and the cultivation equally rich.

Almost two hundred years later, Sir Stamford Raffles' description of the **Minang highlands** still rings at least partially true; whilst the area is densely populated and served by hectic roads, the gorgeous mountainous landscape, soaring rice terraces and easily accessible Minang culture make this a justly popular stop on any trip through Sumatra.

The Minang highlands consist of three large valleys. The **Agam Valley** runs north–south between the towering masses of Gunung Singgalang to the west and Gunung Merapi to the east, with **BUKITTINGGI**, a bustling hill town, the administrative and commercial centre of the whole district. The craft villages of Koto Gadang and Pandai Sikat are easily accessible in the Agam Valley, as is Batang Putuh, which features the famous rafflesia flower. The **Limapuluh Valley** lies east of Bukittinggi, and has its commercial centre in the town of **Payakumbuh**. The road between Bukittinggi and Pekanbaru passes through this valley, from where there's a detour for the beautiful **Harau Canyon**, popular with local people and tourists alike. Centred around the town of Batusangkar, southeast of both Bukittinggi and soaring Gunung Merapi, the **Tanah Datar Valley** was the site of the **Minang court** for five hundred years from the fourteenth century: the wonderful **palace** at Pagaruyung is the finest surviving example of Minang architecture.

Located to the west of the main highland area, **Danau Maninjau** is rapidly developing as an appealing travellers' destination, though there's little to do but enjoy the cool air and beautiful scenery.

Some history

The origins of the **Minangkabau** people are shrouded in myth. One legend tells that they are descended from Iskander Zulkarnain (in some stories said to be Alexander the Great) who was the product the union of Adam's youngest son with a fairy. Iskander's third son, Maharaj Diraja or Sri Maharajo Dirajo (Glorious King of Kings), reached Gunung Merapi at a time when the remainder of Sumatra was underwater, and he founded the first clan, which settled first in Pariangan on the southern slopes of the mountain.

The name "Minangkabau" has several possible origins. Some sources claim it comes from *"pinang kabhu"* which means "original home". Another legend tells of a fight between a Javanese and Minang buffalo; facing an attack by a massive Javanese army, the Minang suggested a fight between two buffaloes instead of a conflict between the two armies. The Javanese found a gigantic animal for the contest and the Minang a very small calf. However, the Minang had starved the calf for ten days and they tied an iron spike to its head. It mistook the Javanese buffalo for its mother, and savaged its opponent to death in its furious attempts to suckle, and thus became the *minang kerbau* (victorious buffalo).

The first historical records of the area date from the fourteenth-century stone inscriptions of the ruler **Adityavarman**, who ruled from 1356 to 1375 and who is thought to have created a unified kingdom in the area. There's little evidence of his successors, though, in the seventeenth century, Portuguese envoys reported that three Minang rulers controlled the three highland valleys. The wealth and importance of the area in the fourteenth and fifteenth centuries sprung from the gold which was mined there, and the power accompanying such resources meant that at their height the Minangkabau kingdoms covered most of Central Sumatra.

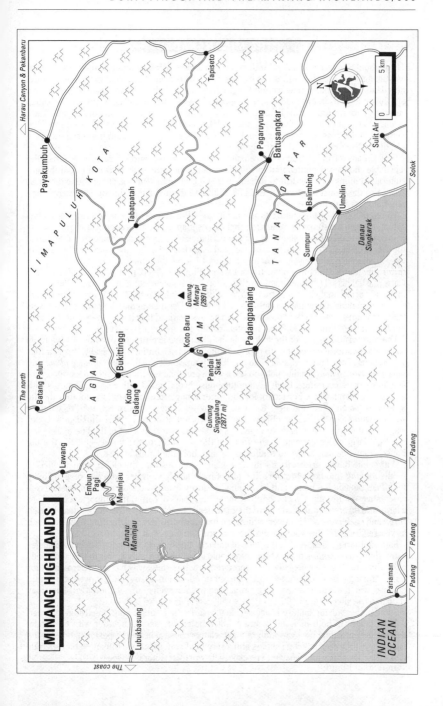

THE MINANGKABAU

Throughout Sumatra and indeed Indonesia, you'll meet **Minangkabau** people, also known as Minang, who proudly regard the highlands (*darek*), around Bukittinggi as their cultural heartland. It's estimated that around four million Minangkabau live in the Bukittinggi area, but that at least as many, if not more, live outside, examples of the ages-old Minangkabau custom of **merantau** – travelling to find one's fortune. Distinctive Minang architecture, colourful costumes and stylized, exuberant dances are easily accessible to visitors to West Sumatra, and across the entire archipelago the popular Padang restaurants serve the spicy and distinctive food of the Minang people.

While many of these traditions remain, especially in the rural area of the *darek*, the inevitable changes brought about by increased population, the shift away from a purely agricultural economy and the drift to urban centres has changed the society to the extent that, at least to the casual observer, there's often little to distinguish a Minang family from any other in West Sumatra.

The traditional Minang culture is staunchly **matrilineal**, one of the largest such societies extant. It's also Muslim, a combination that makes it appealing to academic anthropologists who have studied the people extensively. Inheritance of property, name and membership of the clan is through the female line, houses and fields passed on from a woman to her daughters. Traditionally, the males, often as young as 10, leave their mother's home to live in the *surau* (the men's religious prayer house) where they eat, sleep, pray, study the Koran and learn martial arts. Daughters stay in their mother's house up to and after marriage, their husbands occasional visitors to them in the *bilik* (sleeping room). As one writer described, "The Minangkabau man has no rights over his wife other than demanding that she remains faithful to him . . . she on the other hand, can always demand that her husband come to visit her from time to time and fulfil his marital obligations."

The most visible aspect of the culture is the distinctive **architecture**, with massive roofs soaring skywards at either end (to represent the horns of a buffalo). Typically, three or four generations of one family would live in one large house built on stilts, the *rumah gadang* (big house) or *rumah adat* (traditional house), a wood-and-thatch structure often decorated with fabulous wooden carvings. Each area of the house is decorated with a range of motifs with a particular significance. For example, one pattern may represent humility, another the difference between good and evil. Each has a row of separate bedrooms for the younger women who sleep with their children and are visited at night by their husbands. Older women and unmarried girls do not have separate bedrooms. In front of the line of sleeping rooms, a large meeting room is the focus of the social life of the house. Outside the big house, small rice barns, also of traditional design, hold the family stores.

Within one house, **authority** for internal matters resides with the oldest woman, advised by the *mamak* (mother's brother), the oldest male family member, who has responsibility for affairs outside the house and is the final authority over the children within it. Male representatives of the village meet together to decide affairs of communal importance, and are a large and diverse group made up of the male head of each clan, *penghulu*, the head of each *surau* and each *mamak*. However, while men have authority over matters in the village such as village land, only the women own the land and can pass it on.

Some authorities believe that this lack of important positions for young men in the villages drove them to *merantau*, from which they would ideally return with stories to tell, and goods with which to attract a wife. However, more recently this shift away has been permanent for many Minangkabau in search of employment or education, many taking wives and young children with them and some young, unmarried women even going on their own. They may return to the village rarely, although they will invariably regard it as home.

Some of the Minang culture is accessible to visitors via **pencak silat**, the traditional martial art, taught to both men and women. You'll be able to see it, together with traditional dances, accompanied by a variation of a gamelan orchestra, in tourist performances in the Bukittinggi area (see p.369). Textiles and a variety of craft items are Minangkabau specialities – their jewellery and weaving are especially worth seeking out (see p.370).

Minang authority began to decline after the eighteenth century, when the mines were exhausted, the alternative crops of coffee, salt, gambir and textiles being controlled largely by Muslim traders. A frontal assault on the Minangkabau was launched in the early nineteenth century by the **Paderi**, fundamentalist Muslims intent on forcing the matriarchal Minangkabau to adopt Islam, and abandon gambling, drinking, taking opium and betel (see box opposite). Violence was precipitated in 1803, and by 1815 the Paderi had control of much of the Minang highlands. In 1821 the Dutch became involved, signing an agreement with the nephew of the Raja Alam of Pagarruyung (who may or may not have had the right to sign it), whereby they were given the Tanah Datar Valley. They built Fort de Kock, in the area now called Bukittinggi, and joined with the remaining Minangkabau leaders to fight the Paderi. It was a long campaign and not until 1837, when they captured the renowned Paderi leader Imam Bonjol in his home in Bonjol, did the tide really turn. The fighting stopped the next year, with the Minang highlands under Dutch control. However the war had a long-term impact, and today devout Islamic ideas coexist alongside a large number of traditional beliefs and customs or *adat*.

Arrival, orientation, information and city transport

Whilst a few long-distance tourist services may drop you at your hotel of choice (check at the time of booking), other **long-distance buses** terminate at the Air Kuning terminal, 3km southeast of the town centre. Buses from Padang stop on the southern outskirts of town on Jalan Sudirman before turning off for the terminal; you can get a red #14 bemo into the town centre from this junction, and much of the accommodation is within an easy walk of the route.

Situated on the eastern edge of the Ngarai Sianok Canyon and with the mountains of Merapi and Singgalang rising to the south, Bukittinggi spreads for several kilometres in each direction into adjoining suburbs, before fading into open fields. However, the central part of town, which is of most interest to visitors, is relatively compact and easy to negotiate. The most useful landmark is the clock tower just south of the market area at the junction of Jalan A. Yani (the main thoroughfare) and Jalan Sudirman (the main road leading out of town to the south). Jalan A. Yani, 1km from north to south, is the tourist hub of Bukittinggi, and most of the sights, hotels, restaurants and shops that serve the tourist trade are on this street or close by.

The **tourist office**, Jalan Syech Bantam 1 (Mon–Thurs 8am–2pm, Fri 8–11am, Sat 8am–12.30pm; ☎0752/22403), close to the clock tower, has friendly staff and plenty of reference material. **Bemos** scurry around town in a circular route, with a flat fare of Rp300. To get to the bus terminal, stop any bemo heading north on Jalan A. Yani, which will circle to the east of town and pass the main post office before turning left to Air Kuning.

MOVING ON FROM BUKITTINGGI

All local and long-distance buses leave from the Air Kuning terminal to the southeast of the town centre, where you'll find the ticket offices. **Local buses** operate from 7am to 5pm although, as usual, frequency tails off in the afternoon. There are departures throughout the day to Padang, Solok, Batusangkar, Payakumbuh, Maninjau, Bukit Palupuh and Bonjol. For **long-distance** destinations, there are several companies (see pp.370–371), but it's worth booking two or three days ahead to get the departure and seat you want. Destinations include Aceh, Sibolga, Parapet, Medan, Jambi, Pekanbaru, Bengkulu, Palembang, Lubuklinggau (for the South Sumatra train service), Jakarta and Bandung.

Tourist buses to Danau Toba are also on offer, through the travel agents in town (see p.371). Travel agents in Bukittinggi can also arrange Pelni and airline tickets from Padang, which is the closest port and airport.

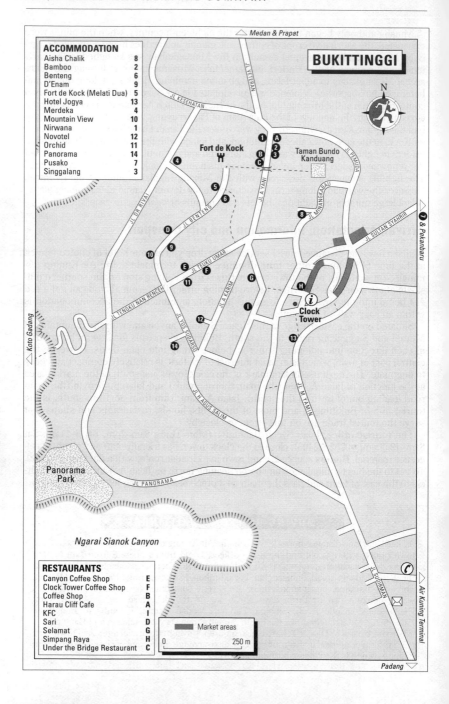

△ Medan & Prapat

BUKITTINGGI

N

ACCOMMODATION
Aisha Chalik	8
Bamboo	2
Benteng	6
D'Enam	9
Fort de Kock (Melati Dua)	5
Hotel Jogya	13
Merdeka	4
Mountain View	10
Nirwana	1
Novotel	12
Orchid	11
Panorama	14
Pusako	7
Singgalang	3

Fort de Kock

Taman Bundo Kanduang

△ & Pekanbaru

Clock Tower

△ Koto Gadang

Panorama Park

Ngarai Sianok Canyon

△ Air Kuning Terminal

RESTAURANTS
Canyon Coffee Shop	E
Clock Tower Coffee Shop	F
Coffee Shop	B
Harau Cliff Cafe	A
KFC	I
Sari	D
Selamat	G
Simpang Raya	H
Under the Bridge Restaurant	C

Market areas

0   250 m

Padang ▽

Accommodation

Now flourishing as a popular tourist destination, Bukittinggi is awash with **accommodation** at all prices and all levels of sophistication. At the budget end of the market, the places on Jalan A. Yani are an option, although many are decidedly grubby and noisy with distant mandi. Fortunately, some better-value places have sprung up nearby. The luxury hotel trade is gradually moving in, and the competition should produce good discounts.

Aisha Chalik, Jl Cinduo Mato 101 (☎0752/35260). Basic accommodation in a characterful old house with a quiet but central location. Rooms do not have attached bathrooms. ①–②.

Bamboo, Jl A. Yani 132 (☎0752/23388) The rooms are basic and dark without attached mandi, but there's a small sitting area which makes this better than the average Jl A. Yani place. ①–②.

D'Enam, Jl Yos Sudarso (☎0752/21333). Not far from the centre on a quiet road, with a variety of dorms and rooms in an airy bungalow. All are good value and there's a lounge for residents and a laundry service next door. ①–②.

Fort de Kock (Melati Dua), Jl Yos Sudarso 33 (☎0752/33005). Across the road from the more prominent *Benteng*, this is a small hotel with clean, pleasant rooms in a quiet, convenient location. All rooms have hot water. ③–④.

Merdeka, Jl Dr A. Rivai 20 (☎0752/22153). On the corner with Jl Benteng; the #14 bemo passes the door. A small guest house in and around a colonial bungalow set in a good-sized garden – the large, cool rooms have high ceilings. Hopefully the current remodelling will retain the character of the place without hiking prices too much. ②–③.

Mountain View, Jl Yos Sudarso (☎0752/21621). One of the few places to take advantage of the scenery. However, rooms are extremely basic, all with cold-water mandi. The road is quiet and the small garden has seats from which to admire the great views. ②.

Nirwana, Jl A. Yani 113. The most characterful of the rock-bottom places at the northern end of this road. Rooms without attached mandi are in a rambling old bungalow. If you don't fancy this one, it's easy to look at the other places nearby. ①.

Novotel, Jl Laras Datuk Bandaro (☎0752/35000, fax 23800, *novotelbkt@padang.wasantara. net.id*). Located in the middle of town, this is the newest addition at the luxury end of the market and has a balconied multi-storey foyer with fountain, heated swimming pool and classy ambience. ⑨.

Orchid, Jl Teuku Umar 11 (☎0752/32634). Gleaming new place with attractively furnished rooms, many with balconies. The price includes breakfast and the more expensive rooms have hot water. Excellent value. ③.

Panorama, Jl Dr Setia Budhi 16e (☎0752/21309). Centrally located on a quiet road, the rooms have attached bathroom with hot water. The accommodation is adequate for this price but the real bonus is the balcony with its stunning views. ③.

Pusako, Jl Sukarno-Hatta 7 (☎0752/32111, fax 32667). Recently knocked off its perch as Bukittinggi's premier establishment by the new *Novotel*, this Aerowisata hotel is located on a quiet hillside 7km east of the town centre in lush gardens with an attractive swimming pool. Rooms have balconies with swimming pool or mountain view. ⑨.

Singgalang, Jl A. Yani 130 (no phone). The rooms without mandi are adequate but very variable, so ask to see several. Those with attached mandi are grossly overpriced. However, there's a quiet sitting area towards the back of the hotel and for this reason it's probably the best place on Jl A. Yani. ①–③.

The Town

The most famous landmark in the town is the **Clock Tower** (*Jam Gadang*), which was built in 1827 by the Dutch when the town was their stronghold during the Paderi Wars. Situated in manicured gardens, it's attractive during the day, despite the traffic hurtling around it, but even more so at night, lit by strings of fairy lights.

A few hundred metres to the north, **Fort de Kock** (daily 8am–7pm; Rp1350, plus Rp350 for the museum) was built by the Dutch in 1825 and is linked to the park, **Taman Bundo Kanduang**, on the hill on the other side of Jalan A. Yani, by a footbridge high above the road; there's little left of the original fort but some old cannons and the obvious remnants of the protective moats. It's a popular place with local people and there are plenty of seats and quiet spots to enjoy the views. Looking south, Gunung Merapi, although the higher, is the less impressive mountain on the left, and Gunung Singgalang the much more dramatic and stereotypically cone-shaped volcano to the right.

The park's **museum** is housed in a traditional *rumah gadang*, and features clothing, musical instruments, textiles, household objects and models of traditional houses. Some of the exhibits have English descriptions and there are attempts to explain aspects of Minangkabau life. Unfortunately, the way to the museum passes through the **zoo** area which is sadly well stocked and is as inhumane an example of such a place as you'll find anywhere: crocodiles languish in a few centimetres of slimy water, an orang-utan gazes out mournfully from a bare and filthy cage, and delicate deer graze on dusty, litter-strewn earth. The building at the top of the hill provides a good explanation of why the Sumatran tiger is nearing extinction: several of them of them are dead, stuffed and on show here.

Much more pleasant is a trip to **Panorama Park** (daily 7am–7pm; Rp300), perched on a lip of land overlooking the sheer cliff walls down into Ngarai Sianok Canyon, the best Bukittinggi sight by far. Local people use Panorama Park as a picnic area and general strolling ground, especially in the late afternoon or at weekends. Beneath the park stretch 1400m of Japanese **tunnels** (Rp500) and rooms built with local slave labour during World War II as a potential fortress. You can venture down into these dank, miserable depths, although there's nothing really to see. The **Ngarai Sianok Canyon** is part of a rift valley that runs the full length of Sumatra – the canyon here is 15km long and around 100m deep with a glistening river wending its way along the bottom. The Dutch named the canyon "Buffalo Hole", as the sides are so steep that any animal grazing on the edge would inevitably plunge to its death hundreds of metres below.

Eating and drinking

There are plenty of **restaurants** in town – a good mix of travellers' places and local ones, and a small **night market** each evening near the junction of Jalan A. Yani and Jalan Teuku Umar, serving simple sate, noodles and rice dishes.

Canyon Coffee Shop, Jl Teuku Umar 18b. An inexpensive and popular travellers' place with a friendly atmosphere in a quiet street just off Jl A. Yani. They offer seventeen varieties of toast and eight variations on coffee, plus the usual shakes, juices, salads, omelettes, steaks and basic Indonesian dishes.

Clock Tower Coffee Shop, Jl Teuku Umar 7d. Pleasant furnishings and the option of sitting outside on this quiet road. The menu features a good range of Western and Indonesian favourites including steak, spaghetti with various sauces, and tacos. Inexpensive to moderate.

Coffee Shop, Jl A. Yani 105. A popular place with a small porch area right on the busy main street, which serves the usual travellers' fare at reasonable prices. Good for people-watching.

Harau Cliff Cafe, Jl A. Yani. Although situated on a particularly noisy section of road, this place is extremely good value (steak is Rp7000 and sate, gado-gado and cap cay under Rp2000) and has attractive furnishings and a relaxed atmosphere.

KFC, Jl A. Yani 1. Pricey Western fast food has invaded Bukittinggi, a combination meal for one costing about Rp7000. The listed prices don't include ten-percent tax.

Sari, Jl Yos Sudarso 31. Large establishment with an extensive and expensive menu (fried rice and noodles are over Rp3000, vegetable dishes Rp5000–6000), with an outside area giving good views of the canyon. The service is a bit erratic, but it's a pleasing place to relax for a while.

Selamat, Jl A. Yani 19. One of the best Padang restaurants in town, they usually have eggs in coconut sauce, which is especially good for vegetarians, and are used to Westerners.

Sianok Restaurant, *Novotel Hotel*, Jl Laras Datuk Bandaro. Offering the plushest, most expensive dining experience in town, with imported steaks, Western and Indo-Chinese meals, at a price. There are better-value buffets, Italian, Chinese, Indonesian, Minang and Western barbecue nights, special Minang lunches and daily afternoon tea.

Simpang Raya, Jl Muka Jam Gadang. This large, popular restaurant has good-quality Padang food plus a basic Indonesian menu with soup, rice or noodle dishes. The upstairs windows overlook the clock tower.

Under the Bridge Restaurant, Jl A. Yani. Situated under the footbridge across Jl A. Yani that joins the two parts of Fort de Kock, this is a slightly upmarket travellers' restaurant well decorated with textiles and carvings, which are for sale. Steaks, pasta, pizza, apple pie and chocolate cake are served, as well as sate, noodles and rice dishes.

Entertainment

Nightly **Minangkabau dance shows** (8.30pm; Rp7500) are put on by a variety of local dance troupes in a hall just behind *Hotel Jogya* on Jalan Moh Yamin; head up the small road on the left of the hotel and the hall is on the right. The venue is a bit spartan, and out of the tourist season the shows are poorly attended, but the energy and vibrancy of the music and performers makes it a must-see in Bukittinggi. The audience are welcome to take photographs, and if you're a shrinking violet sit near the back or you'll be hauled up to join in at the end.

Minang dancing is accompanied by *talempong pacik*, traditional Minang music performed by a **gamelan orchestra** similar to those of Java and Bali, with gongs (both on a stand and hand-held), drums and flutes. While the music clearly belongs to the same family as that of Sumatra's eastern neighbours, it's far more vibrant, energetic and catchy. The dances – although equally carefully choreographed and reliant upon stylized foot, hand and even eye movements – are much more exuberant, with expansive movements and even smiles of sheer pleasure on the faces of the performers, a sight rare in the classical Javanese and Balinese performances.

The show, a series of traditional dances, begins with a great **drumming** display on the *tabuah*, a huge drum which traditionally sent messages between villages and later signalled the times of attendance at the mosque, and continues with a welcome dance (*tari pasambahan*), where the male dancers begin with movements from the Minang martial art of *silek* and the female dancers offer betel leaf to the guests. The instruments include the *bansi*, a high-pitched wind instrument, and the *saluang*, a small, reedless bamboo flute, which uses a five-tone minor scale and hence produces a melancholy sound. Most shows include a demonstration of *silek*, the Minang martial art taught to both young men and women, and the *tari piriang*, a dance that originated in the rice fields after harvest time when young people danced with the plates they had just eaten from: piles of extremely sharp crockery shards are trodden, kicked and even rolled in by the dancers as part of the performance.

Shopping

Apart from the shops aimed particularly at tourists, Bukittinggi is a thriving **market town** for the surrounding area every day of the week, but with even more produce and energy on Wednesday and Saturday. Lively **Pasar Atas** (Upper Market) is just south of the clock tower and is an area of alleyways lined with stalls and shops selling everyday goods and souvenirs; the newspaper stalls at the clock tower end usually have the English-language *Jakarta Post* by the afternoon. Across the other side of Jalan Pemuda, **Pasar Bawah** (Lower Market) sells more foodstuffs and produce and is equally vibrant.

Bookshops

Anyone heading into central and southern Sumatra, an English-language book desert, is advised to take full advantage of the **bookshops** in Bukittinggi. Whilst the postcard situation isn't quite so dire, you won't encounter the choice that you'll get in Bukittinggi, so it pays to stock up. Javanese batik greetings cards are also on sale for Rp1000; they vary from gaudy to attractive.

Setia, corner of Jl Teuku Umar and Jl A. Yani. They have a reasonable choice of secondhand material.

Stylist, Jl A. Yani. Worth a quick look.

Tilas, Jl Teuku Umar 11a and Jl A. Yani 124. Bookshops that are also postal agents, they offer a good selection of new and secondhand books, including a range of titles about Indonesia and Sumatra.

Souvenirs

Bukittinggi is a good hunting ground for a range of **souvenirs** from across the archipelago, although prices of items from further afield are high. It's generally the case that the closer you get to the place of origin the cheaper the items will be, so bear your itinerary in mind. It's wise to read claims about the antiquity of items with scepticism. There are a couple of unnamed, new shops on Jalan Teuku Umar, with attractive boxes from Lombok, Batak calendars and Irian and Batak wood carvings.

Borobodur, Jl Teuku Umar 7b. Slightly upmarket shop with pricey ceramics, textiles, carvings and some kris, plus a good variety of local bamboo calendars (Rp10,000–15,000) – you'll get a written explanation if you buy one.

Minang Art Shop, Jl A. Yani 51. The range here is wide, even up to large wooden cupboards, but think about shipping before you indulge.

Pusaka, Jl A. Yani 88a. Selling a wide variety of items, they specialize in Asmat carvings from Irian Jaya at around Rp335,000, and a wide range of jewellery.

Sumatera, Jl Minangkabau 19. This place is worth searching out in the Pasar Atas market area – the range is extensive, including textiles from Sumba and Irian Jaya (around Rp150,000) and king sticks of various sizes and designs (Rp45,000) from North Sumatra.

Tanjung Raya Art, Jl A. Yani 85. Centrally located with affable staff, this place is a treasure trove of ancient and modern artefacts, all jammed into a few rooms. Javanese puppets rub shoulders with spooky bone figures from Kalimantan, textiles, rifles, cellos, ceramics, bows, old money, telescopes, Chinese compasses and fob watches.

Listings

Banks and exchange Bank Rakyat Indonesia, Jl A. Yani 3; Bank Negara Indonesia, Jl A. Yani. Several travel agents including Tigo Balai Indah, Jl A. Yani 100 (daily 8am–8pm; ☎0752/31996), change travellers' cheques and offer cash advances against Visa and Mastercard.

Car and motorbike rental Inquire at your accommodation or any of the travel agents in town. Typical prices are Rp100,000 for a 12hr car rental with or without driver, and Rp125,000 for 24hr, although these will be prices for local trips – if you are going further afield they will be higher. Expect to pay Rp15,000 for a 100cc motorbike or Rp20,000 for a 125cc one. All these prices are without insurance, which isn't available.

Hospital Rumah Sakit Dr Achmad Mochtar is on Jl Dr A. Rivai (☎0752/21013). The tourist information office will advise on English-speaking doctors in Bukittinggi.

Post office The main post office is inconveniently far from the town centre on Jl Sudirman. Poste restante here is reasonably secure and organized. However, there's a convenient postal agent near the clock tower, and Tilas bookshops on Jl Teuku Umar and Jl A. Yani are also postal agents.

Telephone The main telephone office is on Jl M. Syafei towards the southern end of town, around the corner from the post office. There's a wartel at Jl A. Yani 111 (8am–7.30pm) but a much better value 24hr one at Jl Yos Sudarso 1.

Tour operators There are a variety of one-day tours (Rp25,000 per person) available: inquire at your accommodation, in the tourist office or in the coffee shops. The Minangkabau tour goes by several names and takes in Baso, the lookout at Tabek Patek, the traditional water-driven coffee mill at Sungai Tarab, Batusangkar, the palace at Pagaruyung, Balimbing, Danau Singkarak and Pandai Sikat. The Maninjau tour includes Koto Gadang, Sungai Landir, Danau Maninjau, Lawang, Embun Pagi and the Ngarai Sianok Canyon. The Harau Valley tour first visits the caves at Ngalau Indah, followed by Payakumbuh and then Andaleh to see rattan crafts, the irrigation system at Payobasung, the traditional water mill at Batu Balang and the waterfalls in the Harau Valley. A wide range of longer tours are on offer from the travel agents in town. Typically these are three or more days involving trekking, camping and/or staying overnight in local villages. Average costs are US$20 or US$22.50 per person per day. Travina Tours and Travel Service, Jl A. Yani 107 (☎0752/21281) offers a three-day "Village, Jungle and River" trip taking in Sungai Hitan, Alahan, Laring Mountain, Jambak, Sungai Masang, Tapian and Maninjau. Puti Bungus, Jl Teuku Umar 7a (☎0752/23026) has something similar, but includes Bonjol and calls it an "Equator Trip". It also has a five-night/six-day trip to visit the Kubu people in Jambi district. Inquire at the *Harau Cliff Café* on Jl A. Yani for local rock-climbing trips. You can arrange kayaking or white-water rafting at Minangkabau Rafting, Jl Tengku Nan Renceh 20 (☎ & fax 0752/22913). All trips cost US$39 per person per day and have minimum requirements of two or three people. The most widely publicized tour is a trip to Siberut in the Mentawai chain of islands, accessed via Padang. Bukittinggi is the best place to arrange such a trip; see pp.379–380 for more details on Siberut and tips on arranging your tour.

Travel agents PT Tigo Balai Indah, Jl A. Yani 100 (☎0752/31996); Travina Tours and Travel Service, Jl A. Yani 107 (☎0752/21281); PT Batours Agung, Jl A. Yani 105 (☎0752/34346, fax 22306); Puti Bungus, Jl Teuku Umar 7a (☎0752/23026). Tourist buses are on offer to Danau Toba. Expect to be quoted Rp27,000 and 13hr or 14hr, although, as always, the reality may well be longer. Travel agents can also arrange Pelni and airline tickets from Padang.

Around Bukittinggi

Whilst Bukittinggi is a pleasant place to relax for a couple of days, it's also worth making the effort to get out into the surrounding countryside to get a closer glimpse of highland rural life, enjoy the scenery and visit some of the cultural sights. The Agam Valley area, with Bukittinggi at its centre, features **Koto Gadang** village, famous for silverwork; **Pandai Sikat**, a weaving and woodcarving centre; the Rafflesia Sanctuary at Batang Puluh, 13km of town (see the box below); as well as the sights in and around **Padangpanjang**. Further southeast, **Danau Singkarak** is an appealing mountain lake, and Gunung Singgalang to the west and Gunung Merapi to the east of the Agam Valley are enticing climbs for the fit and energetic. Located in the Limapuluh Valley, **Payakumbuh** is the main population centre of the area but is useful mostly as an access point to the Harau Canyon beyond. Southeast of Bukittinggi, in the Tanah Datar Valley, **Batusangkar** is probably the most rewarding of all the Minangkabau towns, with the palace at Pagaruyung the real gem.

RAFFLESIA

One of the most accessible places in Sumatra to see the rare **Rafflesia** flower is at Batang Paluh, 13km north of Bukittinggi; take a local bus (Rp900) and ask in the village. Inquire at the tourist office in Bukittinggi first as to whether it's worth making the journey: the blooms are irregular, but even in bud the plant is remarkable.

Rafflesia arnoldi is the largest flower in the world – up to 90cm across, named after Sir Stamford Raffles of Singapore fame and his botanist chum Dr Joseph Arnold, who discovered the plant in southern Sumatra whilst Raffles was based in Bengkulu. It grows in tropical, extremely humid conditions and is actually a parasite on a forest vine, without a stem, leaves or roots of its own. Whilst many writers extol its size and the remarkable red-and-white colouring, most do not wax nearly so lyrical about its appalling smell (resembling rotting meat), which attracts the insects that pollinate the flowers. It generally flowers for a couple of weeks between August to December.

Koto Gadang

KOTO GADANG is a small attractive village situated on the western edge of the Ngarai Sianok Canyon. Though you can get local transport to the village, many people try to find the route from Bukittinggi by foot that starts off down Jalan Tengku Nan Renceh, and then heads along a footpath to the footbridge across the river and up the steps on the other side of the canyon. Be aware that there's a well-orchestrated scam, with local people refusing to point the way and hapless tourists being helped by young lads who lead them for a two-hour rough trek through the canyon and then expect payment. The village itself is quiet and attractive with plenty of small **silver workshops** and shops selling various good-value pieces of silver jewellery – much is traditional filigree work, but many places have adapted to more Western tastes.

BUFFALO FIGHTS

Animal-lovers may balk at the idea of watching **buffalo fights** (*adu kerbau*), a popular local event in several of the villages near Bukittinggi, but the reality is rarely gory, usually good fun and occasionally hilarious. Fights draw huge crowds, and it can be as entertaining watching them as watching the bovine contestants.

There are usually three bouts, starting at around 4pm. The massive buffalo are led towards each other and enticed to lock horns. They are in fact not particularly aggressive beasts, so this can take a while. Once their horns are locked they then push and heave against one another, with spectators urging on their favourite – the loser is the buffalo which turns tail and runs away first. At this point the hilarity begins, the crowding spectators diving for cover.

Regular contests take place in villages near Bukittinggi: currently Pincuran Tujuh on Tuesday and Batagak on Wednesday, but check with the tourist information office in Bukittinggi. Either arrange a Rp5000 ticket through a travel agent or at the tourist office, who will include transport, or go independently and pay Rp500 at the gate. The most accessible location is Batagak, 9km south of Bukittinggi on the way to Panangpanjang; the entrance is through a set of white gates just above the road.

Gunung Merapi and Gunung Singgalang

Access to 2890-metre **Gunung Merapi** (Fire Mountain) is from Koto Baru, 12km south of Bukittinggi. Typically, the climb, which is strenuous rather than gruelling if you are reasonably fit, takes five hours up and four down; and most people climb at night to arrive at the top for the sunrise. The first four hours or so are through the forest on the lower slopes of the mountain and then across bare rocks leading to the summit. The top, although you can't tell this from below, is actually a plateau area with the still smoking crater in the middle. You may spot bats, gibbons and squirrels in the forest, but the main reason to go is the view across to Gunung Singgalang. Although easily accessible from Bukittinggi and a popular climb, bear in mind that the mountain did erupt in the 1980s and killed several people. You should engage a local guide (your losmen will find you one), who knows the mountain and has climbed before. Make sure you take enough water, food to keep up your energy, warm clothes for the top and sturdy footwear. Typical prices for the guide and transport are US$15 per person from Bukittinggi.

You'll need to be much fitter if you want to tackle the steeper, longer (allow 5–6 hr to get up and 4–5hr to get back down) and tougher climb up **Gunung Singgalang**. At 2880m it's almost as high as Merapi, and from Bukittinggi appears the more enticing of the two, with its almost perfect conical shape. It has a small crater lake, Telaga Dewi, at the summit, from where you'll be treated to fine views of the surrounding area. Access is from Pandai Sikat and the trail begins from the TV relay station 5km up the mountain at 1600m – vehicles can go this far. Take all the precautions advised above for Merapi; prices for a guide are similar.

Pandai Sikat, Padangpanjang and the Anai Valley

The small village of Koto Baru, 12km south from Bukittinggi, is the starting point for the climbs of Gunung Merapi and Gunung Singgalang, and also marks the turning to the village of **PANDAI SIKAT**, famed for **weaving** and **woodcarving**. Take the turning at the

Yus Djamal sign: Pandai Sikat is 2–3km up the road, and bemos ply the route if you don't want to walk. The village is full of craftspeople, based in small workshops with shops attached. Weaving is done on a simple foot loom to produce the traditional *songket* cloth for the scarf, *selendang*, and sarong sets; the amount of effort involved will depend on how fine the thread is, but typically it will take a woman, weaving for five hours each day, about three weeks to produce 3m of cloth. However, whilst pretty much everything else is done by hand and the patterns are largely traditional, new patterns based on old motifs can be computer-generated to make the task of fitting the pattern into the thread counts much easier. Whilst you'll see *songket* sets costing up to Rp1 million and huge items of furniture, the shops also sell attractive small souvenirs, with carved wooden boxes from Rp15,000 and purses from Rp12,500.

The junction town of **PADANGPANJANG** is situated at the junction of the roads west to Padang (72km), north to Bukittinggi (19km) and east to Batusangkar (20km). It's a long ribbon development that lines the road for several kilometres and has a laid-back atmosphere, an attractively bustling small market area and a couple of **accommodation** options as alternatives to the tourist enclave of Bukittinggi (though be aware that prices are far less competitive here). *Wisma Mutiara* (☎0752/83668; ③) is on the main road leading north from the town centre, and is adequate, with private, cold-water bathrooms.

The main attraction in town is the **Centre for Information and Documentation on Minangkabau Culture** (Pusat Dokumentasi and Informasi Kebudayan Minangkabau; daily 9am–1pm & 2–5pm; ☎0752/82852), which has a fine collection of Minang items housed in a fabulous *rumah gadang*, set in gorgeous grounds with a small cafeteria; for Rp10,000, you can get dressed up in traditional Minangkabau costume. A reproduction Minang village is under development, with different types of buildings, all full size, currently standing in somewhat sterile surroundings. The **tourist office** is also here, at Jalan A. Hamid Hakim 11 (Mon–Fri 8am–3pm, Sat 8am–1pm; ☎0752/82320), but they get very few foreign visitors and have no English material available.

Further southwest, towards Padang, the **Anai Valley** is 10km from Padangpanjang. A small **nature reserve** has been established here (the entrance is between the road markers "Padang 63km" and "Padang 64km") and is home to tapirs, monkeys, a good smattering of Sumatran birds and, at certain times of the year, the gigantic flower *Amorphophallus titanum*. It's a very popular weekend day-trip for Padang people, when it turns into a hubbub that anything wild steers very well clear of, but if you stay during the week you'll see more. There's simple **accommodation** at *Uncle Dede's* (no phone; ② per person including meals) in Kandung Empat, the village just south of the entrance to the reserve (towards Padang). Nearby, the *Anai Resort and Golf Course*, Jalan Kandang Ampek (☎0752/83224, fax 83404), has an excellent eighteen-hole golf course. Green fees are US$50 per round.

Batusangkar and Tanah Datar

Accessed via Padangpanjang, the largest town in the Tanah Datar Valley is **BATUSANGKAR**, 39km southeast of Bukittinggi. The **Minang court** of the fourteenth to nineteenth centuries was based in the valley, the gold and iron mines of ancient times the source of its riches. The entire area is awash with cultural relics, megaliths and places of interest, and to explore it fully takes more than the limited time available on the one-day Minangkabau tours from Bukittinggi (see p.370). Unfortunately, while the town itself is convenient as a base, it isn't particularly attractive.

The **tourist office** is at Jalan Pemuda 1 (☎0752/71300), and the **accommodation** all clustered fairly close together on the same street: *Pagaruyung*, Jalan Prof Hamka 4 (☎0752/71533; ①–③); *Yoherma*, Jalan Prof Hamka 15 (☎0752/71130; ①–③); and *Parma*, Jalan Hamka (☎0752/71330; ①–③), all have a range of basic but adequate rooms and restaurants attached. If you have time to stay longer, BIEC (Brotherly International English Course) at Jalan S. Parman 99 (☎0752/93268) offers accommodation to visitors in exchange for English tuition for their students.

The most worthwhile tourist destination in the area is **Pagaruyung** (daily 7am–6pm; Rp1000), the reconstructed palace of the last Raja Alam of the Minangkabau, Sultan Arifin Muning Alam Syah. The palace was reconstructed using traditional techniques just over twenty years ago following a devastating fire in 1864, the woodcarving alone taking two years to complete by Pandai Sikat carvers. The building comprises the traditional three storeys – the first for official visitors, the second for unmarried daughters and the third for meetings; the rice barn at the front would traditionally have held food to help the poor and the palace mosque is in the garden, with the kitchen at the back.

Danau Singkarak and beyond

Danau Singkarak, a spectacular crater lake about 20km long, is reached via a turning to the south, 5–6km along the Padangpanjang–Batusangkar road. Alternative access from Padang is via Solok. The lake doesn't have the grandeur of Maninjau (see opposite) and, with the main road hugging the eastern shore, the surroundings can be a bit noisy, but it's still an attractive area.

Buses heading south from Bukittinggi to the Kerinci area pass through here, and with seats on the right-hand side of the bus you'll get good views. There isn't much **accommodation** in the area: at the northern end of the lake the *Singkarak Sumpur Hotel* (☎0752/82529, fax 82103; ④–⑤) is signed from the road as it descends to the lakeside, and is located 6km along a country lane. The more expensive rooms are pleasant with balconies and fine views, the lower price ones poor value; meals are moderately priced. The lake at this end is rather dirty, although the hotel does have a pool.

On the main road at Batutebal there's a white gateway and road to the lakeside; enquire at *Mutiara*, a small warung, about **boat charter**: you'll start negotiating at Rp200,000 for the day for a boat holding five or six people. One kilometre further south the *Jayakarta* (☎0752/21279; ③), Jalan Raya Padang Panjang Solok Km 19, is the only other accommodation on the lakeside (it's 19km south of Padangpanjang and 44km from Solok) with adequate rooms, and a great terrace with chairs where you can relax in between swims in the lake.

Further south, **Umbilin** is a big transit village around the mouth of the river, which is crossed by a large iron bridge. This is the junction for the Batusangkar road via Balimbing, and bemos ply the route irregularly and on south to Singkarak and Solok. Just 14km south of Umbilin, *Tenbok Kachang* is a small restaurant area on the lakeside, from where you can also rent pedal boats (Rp6000 an hour) to explore the waters. From here, the road continues south towards the village of **Singkarak** at the southern edge of the lake and then turns away south from the lakeside to the large, busy market town of **SOLOK**.

While there's little to recommend the town in its own right – it's too spread out and busy to be attractive – if you need **accommodation**, head for *Sinar Timbulun*, Jalan K.H.A. Dahlan (no phone; ②), an old family house with simple rooms a few hundred metres from the centre. For more luxury, *Caredek*, Jalan Dr Paraptih Nan Sabatang (☎0755/20931; ③–④) is about 1km from the town centre. There's a **tourist office** at Jalan Lubuk Sikarah 40 (Mon–Thurs 7.30am–2.30pm, Fri 7.30–11.30am, Sat 7.30am–1pm; ☎0755/23640), but they look frankly terrified when foreigners walk through the door, and have little to offer.

It's another 27km south from Solok to the town of Lubuk Selasih, with Gunung Tabang rising 2599m behind, and then 10km to the two lakes, **Danau Dibawah** and **Danau Diatas** (Lower Lake and Upper Lake). They're far smaller than the other lakes in the area but still beautiful, and are renowned because they lie just 1m apart, but at different levels. If you want to explore the area, the nearby village of **ALAHANPAN-JAN** has **accommodation** at *Hillmaya Guest House*, Jalan Imam Bonjol 227 (☎0755/60151; ①–②), which is 2km beyond the village centre up a very steep road. Public transport plies the route on market days (Thurs & Sat); otherwise you'll have to walk or hitch a lift.

Payakumbuh and the Harau Canyon

PAYAKUMBUH is the main population centre in the **Limapuluh Kota Valley**, a stunningly fertile, densely populated area that's thought to have been the first part of the Minang highlands to be settled. The town lies 33km to the northeast of Bukittinggi, at the foot of Gunung Malitang (2262m). There's a small **tourist information office** at Jalan Olah Raga 1 (Mon–Thurs 8am–2.30pm, Fri 8–11.30am, Sat 8am–1pm; ☎0752/92907) and **accommodation** at *Rizal's Guest House*, Jalan Parit Rantang 71 (no phone; ①–②), or the slightly more upmarket *Wisma Flamboyant*, Jalan Ade Irma Suryani 11 (☎0752/92333; ②–③), both just off Jalan Sudirman, the main road into town from Bukittinggi.

Numerous **megalithic remains** pepper the area, most densely around Sungai Sinamar, Guguk (a village 13km from Payakumbuh) and the isolated valley of Mahat – a rough track leads north from Limbanang, 20km from Payakumbuh. Most are simple standing stones or mortars, only a few are inscribed and they lack the beauty of the Pasemah Plateau megaliths (see p.446), although the mystery of their existence is just as intriguing. Skeletons have been found underneath some of the stones, suggesting a role in burial, but local legend tells that they played a part in feasts or in the prediction of the weather.

The Harau Canyon

The most popular excursion in the area is to the **Harau Canyon**, a nature reserve in an area bounded by dramatic towering cliffs. It lies just off the main road 14km northeast of Payakumbuh. **Permits** (Rp1500) are available from the ticket office at the entrance. For rock-climbing expeditions, inquire at the *Harau Cliff Cafe* in Bukittinggi (see p.368). It's said that tigers, leopards, panthers, deer and honey bear inhabit the nature reserve, which consists of rainforest and has some spectacular waterfalls. But this is much-visited territory, especially at weekends, and realistically you can expect monkeys, butterflies, birds and *Homo sapiens*. Most of the tour operators in Bukittinggi offer a day-trip here, but these generally include the Harau Valley only briefly, and if you want to see the canyon properly you'll need to take two or three days, camping in the valley. Inquire in Bukittinggi for someone who will put a trip together for you, or ask at the tourist office there.

Danau Maninjau

Rapidly developing a reputation as a pleasant and hassle-free area for rest and relaxation on the way to or from Danau Toba, **Danau Maninjau** is situated 15km due west of Bukittinggi, although public transport on the road takes a long-winded 37km (90min) to get there, with the final descent to the lake along a great 44-bend road. At an altitude of 500m, the lake is 17km long and 8km wide and set 600m below the rim of an ancient volcanic crater, with jungle-covered crater walls, almost sheer in places, providing a picturesque backdrop. The area of interest for tourists, and all the facilities, centres on the village of **MANINJAU** (meaning "to look out across"), just where the road from Bukittinggi reaches the lakeside road, and, to a lesser extent, the village of **Bayur** 4km to the north.

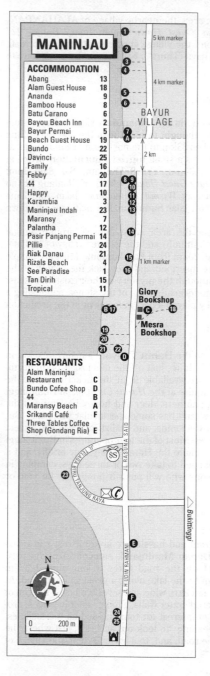

MANINJAU

ACCOMMODATION
Abang	13
Alam Guest House	18
Ananda	9
Bamboo House	8
Batu Carano	6
Bayou Beach Inn	2
Bayur Permai	5
Beach Guest House	19
Bundo	22
Davinci	25
Family	16
Febby	20
44	17
Happy	10
Karambia	3
Maninjau Indah	23
Maransy	7
Palantha	12
Pasir Panjang Permai	14
Pillie	24
Riak Danau	21
Rizals Beach	4
See Paradise	1
Tan Dirih	15
Tropical	11

RESTAURANTS
Alam Maninjau Restaurant	C
Bundo Cofee Shop	D
44	B
Maransy Beach	A
Srikandi Café	F
Three Tables Coffee Shop (Gondang Ria)	E

Many visitors spend all their time here swimming or chilling out, although a few places have canoes to rent and there are plenty of **excursions** in the area. If you get off the bus at the point where the road from Bukittinggi reaches the crater rim to the east of the lake, **Embun Pagi** (Morning Mist), at almost 1100m, offers stunning views of the lake. Alternatively, descend at the village of Matur, walk the 5km to the village of Lawang and then another 5km to the higher lookout point of **Puncak Lawang**. Halfway down the track from Lawang to Bayur village, the *Anas Homestay* (①) is a great place to relax. Accommodation is in log cabins in the forest, lit by oil lamps at night, and with monkeys scampering around outside.

Roads and tracks circle the lake, which is about 55km in circumference, and plenty of places rent out bicycles (Rp4000) and motorcycles (Rp20,000–25,000 per day). However, the track on the far side of the lake from Maninjau village has become extremely rough during the road "improvements", so check the current condition before you set off, and be sure to take plenty of water and food for the day. There's a **waterfall** in the forest above Maninjau village – the path goes up from just after the *Palantha* guesthouse – and it takes about 45 minutes to walk there.

After your exertions, **traditional massage** is available from an elderly Javanese lady for Rp10,000 per hour; inquire at the *Alam Maninjau Restaurant*. Most evenings on Danau Maninjau are given over to eating and then an early night, although the *Alam Guest House* hosts **traditional dance shows** twice a week (currently Tues & Fri 9pm; Rp6000 including a soft drink, or Rp8500 including beer).

Practicalities

The **tourist information office** is located at Jalan Rasuna Said 15 (daily 8am–5pm; ☎0752/61056, fax 61257), just north of the main junction, and the **post office** isn't far from the main junction on Jalan Telaga Biru Tanjung Raya; the

24hr **Telkom office** is on the main street, as is the **bank**. There are a couple of secondhand **bookshops**: the *Mesra Bookshop* gets the English-language *Jakarta Post*. **Moving on**, there are regular **buses** back to Bukittinggi. If you want to go to Padang, there are two direct buses daily (currently 7am & 2pm), which take about three hours and go via Lubukbasung and out to the coast road and Pariaman before coming into Padang past the airport – it's a popular route, so book at your guest house or the tourist office. Otherwise, the lakeside bemos go to Lubukbasung, where you can pick up Padang buses during the day. There's little time difference between going via Bukittinggi and via the coast. Inquire at the tourist office about other direct buses in Maninjau: daily direct buses run to Pekanbaru and you can also book through to Batam with a few hours halt in Pekanbaru – allow two days and a night.

ACCOMMODATION

Accommodation is ranged along the east side of the lake, from about 500m south of the junction of the lakeside road with the road from Bukittinggi, to just north of the five kilometre marker. There's a range of accommodation available, most in simple homestays or small guest houses, although a few places offer more luxurious options, a trend that looks set to increase. Not many rooms have attached mandi: reviews state if they do.

Alam Guest House (☎0752/61242). Up on the hillside away from the lake, the slog up the hill is worth it and this is the only place in the area to take advantage of the lake scenery. All construction is wooden, of good quality, and the views from the balcony are fantastic. A range of rooms are on offer, from those without attached mandi to more comfortable ones with. ①–③.

Bamboo House (no phone). This is the best of a small clutch of simple homestays just north of the *Pasir Pangang Permai*. They all offer basic, budget accommodation in simple rooms, but the *Bamboo House* is tucked away on the shore with some lovely views across the lake. ①.

Beach Guest House (☎0752/61082). Large, bustling and popular place in a great location on the lakeside, with a small beach and hammocks. Offers a wide range of rooms, up those with attached mandi and a small verandah. ①–②.

Bundo (no phone). A tiny, central homestay in the middle of the fields, this is a friendly, family-run place a short walk to the lakeside. ①.

Davinci (☎0752/61137). The most southerly option, just before the mosque if you head south from the junction with the Bukittinggi road. A small place on the lakeside with a bamboo sitting area. ①–②.

Febby (☎0752/61586). Smaller and quieter than the *Beach Guest House* nearby, this is right on the lakeside but still convenient for the facilities of Maninjau village. ①.

44 (no phone). New wooden shoreside bungalows with attached mandi and a small restaurant. Excellent value. ①.

Maninjau Indah (☎0752/61018, fax 61257). Rooms range from basic ones with cold-water bathroom attached to those with hot water overlooking the pool, which is large but not very attractive and in clinical surroundings. This operation is disappointing as one of the top Maninjau options, but hopefully will improve when the extension is complete. ③–④.

Pasir Panjang Permai (☎0752/61111, fax 61255). One of only two large setups on the lake, but the rooms are nothing special and the corridors dark and dingy. Look at several rooms, as they are very variable. ④–⑤.

Pillie (☎0752/61048). Towards the southern end of Maninjau village, this lakeside place is clean, cool and tiled, with simple rooms and huge mandi nearby plus a pleasant upstairs balcony. ①.

Rizals (no phone). Basic bamboo bungalows with mosquito nets, set back from their own white-sand beach in a coconut grove just over 4km north of Maninjau village. There are good views of the lake and a restaurant is attached. ①.

See Paradise (no phone). Over 5km north of Maninjau village, this is currently the most northerly development. Bamboo cottages with attached mandi are set in quiet grounds on the lakeside with a little white-sand beach and great views. A small restaurant is attached. ③.

Tan Dirih (☎0752/61263). Small, tiled, spotless place with sun loungers on a terrace overlooking the lake. All rooms have hot water. ④.

EATING AND DRINKING

A good variety of **restaurants** offers Indonesian dishes as well as fast food, and all are situated on or close to the lakeside road; much of the fun of a stay in Maninjau is trying them out.

Alam Maninjau Restaurant. Situated just off the road at the start of the track up to the *Alam Guest House*, this open-sided *bale* is well decorated, has a relaxed atmosphere with easy-listening music, magazines to read and a good range of meals. Main courses are around Rp7500 for chicken, sirloin and *teriyaki*, while baked potatoes with cauliflower cheese cost Rp3000 and basic Indonesian dishes Rp3000–4000. They offer an Indonesian set meal for four or more people at Rp10,000 a head if you order in advance.

Bundo Coffee Shop. Situated close to the road but with good views across the rooftops down to the lake. A vast inexpensive menu offering all the usual Western and Indo-Chinese favourites.

Maransy Beach. This is the place for a special meal or a sunset beer. The restaurant is set on stilts over the lake and offers an excellent range of drinks, including cocktails (Rp3000 upwards), beer and white wine. The food consists of soups and appetizers such as papaya cocktail and stuffed eggs, and main courses, including goulash and beef escalope as well as Indonesian, Chinese and Western options. To finish up, you can have Irish coffee (Rp5000). Moderate to expensive.

Srikandi Café. With a small shaded garden at the front containing a tiny waterfall, this place at the southern end of Maninjau village offers a slightly grander dining experience than most of the nearby options. The menu is large and varied: soups come in at Rp2000–3000 (pumpkin, curried apple, Thai tom yam), with main courses at Rp5500–9000 including stir-fries, sate, fish, steak, pizzas and burgers.

Three Tables Coffee Shop (Gondang Ria). Just across the road from the louder, more assertive *Bodo's* south of the main junction, this is a tiny place with a good upstairs balcony, serving inexpensive Padang food plus the usual travellers' fare.

The Mentawai Islands

The enticing **Mentawai Islands**, 100km off the west Sumatran coast and separated by waters around 2000m deep, are home to an ethnic group who are struggling to retain their identity in the modern world. There are over forty islands in the chain, four main ones plus a host of smaller dots of land. From north to south the main islands are Siberut, Sipora, North Pagi and South Pagi. Only **Siberut**, the largest island, at 110km long by 50km wide, is accessible to tourists, and all visitors must be registered by the authorities.

The breaks off the Mentawai chain are already popular; in Padang, the Mentawai Surf Sanctuary at Jalan Sumatera X5, Wisma Indah 1 (☎ & fax 0751/52335, *gbinet@iinet.net.au*), operates live-aboard ten-berth yachts from the city and has "full wave priority permits" in protected surf zones with more than forty breaks; a trip will set you back US$160 per person per night. Diving, snorkelling and river treks are also on offer and there are plans for accommodation in the isolated west-coast areas of the region.

The islands are covered in primary tropical rainforest, and their traditional **culture** was based on communal dwelling in longhouses (*uma*), shared by between five or ten related families and scattered along the river valleys with all transport on foot or by canoe and, more recently, speedboat. The ages-old culture had, until fairly recent times, been largely unaffected by events on the mainland, and the Hindu, Buddhist and Islamic waves of cultural change that swept Sumatra in the past left the Mentawai chain largely untouched, its people pursuing a lifestyle of subsistence agriculture, growing sago, yams and bananas as the staple crops, with husbandry of chickens and pigs supplemented by hunting and fishing. It's a largely egalitarian society without chiefs or servants, with **religious beliefs** centred on the importance of coexisting with the invisible spirits that inhabit the world and all the objects in it; even the personality and spirit of a person's possessions are important and they must not be used thoughtlessly. Many traditional ceremonies are carried out to appease the spirits in case the activities of humans accidentally distress them.

With the advent of Christian missionaries and the colonial administration at the beginning of this century, change was forced upon the people and many of their religious practices were banned. Following Independence, when the Indonesian government forbade all indigenous religions, the people were forced to ascribe to one of the state religions and most became nominal Christians. Although many traditional rituals were officially banned, ritual objects destroyed and the people moved away from the *uma* into single-family houses, many beliefs and practices have survived and some villages have built new *uma*.

However, there's no doubt that the islands themselves and the people on them remain under considerable **threat** from all sides. The culture is in danger as the Indonesian government seeks to integrate the people into what it perceives as mainstream life. The environment is under immediate threat from a planned 700-square-kilometre **palm-oil plantation** which would cover sixteen percent of the island of Siberut – an oil-palm nursery is already open in the village of Saumanuk. Work on the plantation seems likely to be offered to transmigrants from other parts of Indonesia rather than the islanders themselves, who would soon be outnumbered. At the same time, big business is also interested in the islands for exclusive tourist developments. Overall, the future for the traditional life of Mentawai looks bleak.

Siberut

The island of **Siberut** is the best-known, largest and most northerly of the Mentawai chain and the only one with anything approaching a tourist industry. Access to the island is by **overnight ferry** from Padang and, whilst it's possible, still, to visit the island independently, the vast majority of visitors go on trips arranged and starting from Bukittinggi, organized and guided by young men from West Sumatra rather than Mentawai people. The tours are loudly marketed in Bukittinggi as a trip to see the "primitive" people and "stone-age" culture, and photos will be shoved under your nose of tattooed people in loincloths. Generally, Mentawai people welcome tourism, although they get little financial benefit from it; they see it as a way of validating and preserving their own culture and raising awareness of their plight in the outside world.

The long separation from the mainland – Siberut was once joined to Sumatra – has meant that some primitive species of **flora and fauna** have survived on the island, while many species have evolved separately. Siberut is home to monkeys, squirrels, civets, frogs and reptiles as well as a range of birdlife. However, the rare primates are the most famous inhabitants, and the black gibbon, Mentawai macaque, Mentawai leaf-monkey and pig-tailed langur are endemic to the island.

If you go on a **tour**, it will probably centre on the southeast of the island. You'll typically bypass Muarasiberut on the way in and take in Maillepet beach, then the areas of Tateburu, Ugai, Madobag, Rogdog and Bat Rorogot with a speedboat back to Muarasiberut. You'll be able to watch and join in with people going about their everyday activities, such as farming, fishing and hunting. The ceremonies of Siberut are something of a draw for tourists, but many of those that tourists "happen" to see are actually staged for them with replica items; to wear the real clothing and use the real ritual items for such a purpose might well insult and distress the spirits.

TOUR TIPS FOR SIBERUT

You'll be inundated by guides in Bukittinggi touting **trips to Siberut**. The following tips may help you decide whether to go, who with and how to cope when you're there.

- You may spend some days hanging around in Bukittinggi waiting for the tour to be put together; there are usually minimum numbers required, so it makes sense to start making inquiries as soon as you get to Bukittinggi and spend the waiting days sightseeing while it all gets put together.

- Try to get a guide by personal recommendation.

- Listen carefully to the guide's attitude toward the Mentawai people.

- The people speak a language totally distinct from Indonesian on the mainland and you'll have a better time if you really try to communicate. See below for some phrases.

- Read and obey guidelines about behaviour that are given to you. The people have a complex system of taboo behaviour.

- Be aware that on a five-day trip Day One usually means a 3pm departure from Bukittinggi and two hours hanging around in Padang waiting for the boat. Similarly, the boat docks soon after dawn in Padang, so Day Five may well end at 10am when you get to Bukittinggi.

- Try to keep it small – four to six people is bearable. More than that and you'll inundate the places you visit.

- Meet the people on the trip before you leave and confirm what you've been told about numbers and itinerary.

- Trekking in the jungle will give you very poor views of anything but the jungle: it's muddy, slippery and you have to get across rivers and tackle leeches. Accommodation is extremely basic. Take as little with you as possible; most tours arrange for you to store stuff in Bukittinggi.

- Malaria is endemic on the island. Ideally take your own net or borrow one from the tour company. Follow the advice in Basics (p.28), for entering a malarial area.

Some language

Hello	*Ani loita*	I don't smoke	*Tak maubek aku*
Thank you	*Masura bagata*	Water	*Oinan*
You're welcome	*Sama makerek*	Today	*Gogoy nenek*
What's your name?	*Kai see onim?*	Tomorrow	*Mancheb/sobi*
My name is . . .	*Onningkku . . .*	Yesterday	*Sokat*
Are you married?	*Umu daley mo an ekeo?*	Slowly	*Moiley moiley*
Not yet	*Tabey*	I am hot	*Ma ro ket aku*
Already	*Aley pak an*	I am hungry	*Ma lajei aku*
How many children do you have?	*Peega togum?*	I am thirsty	*Ma ongo aku*
		I am tired	*Ma geyla aku*
Many	*Myget*	I am sick	*Ma bey si aku*
What is that?	*Ponia edah?*	Leech	*Alu matek*
Wait a minute	*Bola*	Mosquito	*See ngit ngit*
Go	*Mayeeta*	Pig	*Sakokok*
Come back	*Doilee*	Cat	*Mow*
Cigarette	*Oobey*	Dog	*Jojo*

Visiting independently

To visit Siberut **independently**, you'll need to get a **permit** in Padang from PT Mentawai Wisata Bahari, Jalan Sumatera X5, Wisma Indah 1 (Mon–Sat 8am–5pm; ☎ & fax 0751/52335, *gbinet@iinet.net.au*): you won't be sold a boat ticket without one. Go to the office at least a day in advance of when you want to travel (for travel on Monday, apply on Friday), with a photocopy of your passport, including the Indonesian entry stamp, and the immigration card you got on arrival in the country. The company has Indonesian government authority to issue permits but the future is uncertain; they may consider limiting tourist numbers, limiting and/or licensing tour operators from Bukittinggi or limiting the areas, times and group sizes of trips. Listen out in Bukittinggi for developments.

Two companies run **ferries** between Padang and the island: PT Rusco Lines, Jalan Bt Arau 88 D/11 (☎0751/21941) and PT Semeleue, Jalan Bt Arau 7h; tickets are Rp10,000, plus Rp1000 port tax for deck class or Rp15,000 plus tax for a cabin. Currently sailing days are Monday and Wednesday to Siberut with PT Rusco Lines and Saturday with PT Semeulue, with return trips on Tuesday, Thursday and Monday. Rusco also call at Sikabulan, the small coastal settlement on the east coast further north from Muarasiberut. Most ferries are 25-metre motorboats; the lower decks are close to the extremely noisy, exhaust-belching engine with little breeze from outside. In a cabin you'll get one of the four bunks on the next deck up; there's an open area in the back to sit, but the ship video operates until all hours just outside the door.

If you are travelling independently, you should approach the Siberut Guide Association (☎0759/21064) to find a **guide**. The cost depends largely on where you want to go. The major expense is speedboat transport to the start and from the end of the trek. One person in the southeast area will be looking at about Rp600,000 for five days, to include transport, accommodation, food, porters and a guide, whilst three people will pay about Rp350,000 each. If you want to go over to the west coast, for example, to Atabai or Sakuddei, trekking across the island to get there and trekking back via the coast, two weeks would cost about Rp850,000 per person for a party of three.

Muarasiberut and the beaches

The main town of **MUARASIBERUT** is the administrative and commercial centre of the island, although in reality it's a sleepy little shanty-style village along the coast and around the mouth of the river, with a population of under a thousand people. Many of the inhabitants are from other parts of Indonesia and are here for commercial or business reasons. There's a working beach: the entire population seems to turn out every couple of days to see the ships call in and local owners operate small "speedboats", most of them unstable large canoes with a powerful engine on the back, which ferry passengers and cargo around. The town has electricity and every couple of houses boasts a satellite dish. Whatever is happening to the traditional lifestyles in the interior, the Muarasiberut population is well tuned to CNN news and Hindi movies.

The only **accommodation** in Muarasiberut is the *Syahruddin Hotel* (☎0759/21014; ①–②) on the coast at the mouth of the river. The building is wooden, light and airy, but at low tide looks straight onto stinking mud flats which is where the toilets discharge. Rooms have no mosquito nets, and unattached mandi. There's an excellent coffee shop across the road serving inexpensive rice, noodles and barbecued fish, plus several other rumah makan and a few small shops with basic supplies. A good landmark is the town mosque with its corrugated iron dome, a couple of hundred metres back from the shore. The **post office** and **Telkom** offices are just behind, but there are no banking or exchange facilities on the island.

It's possible to visit the beaches independently, the main expense being transport from Muarasiberut – take your own snorkelling gear. A basic guest house at **Masilo beach**

(Rp18,000 per person including meals), provides accommodation in bamboo-and-thatch huts – mattresses and mosquito nets are not supplied. A charter boat will cost about Rp80,000 one way. The beach is white sand, but the offshore coral isn't brilliant; it's popular with tour groups and domestic tourists, so an idyllic getaway can't be guaranteed. Further away, **Pulau Sibiti** is far quieter and less popular. It's a great white-sand beach with good snorkelling; fishing is a possibility, but it's advisable to take food and a stove. It'll cost about Rp2000 to camp here for the night – pay the family who live on the beach.

The west-coast road

As an alternative to all or part of the Trans-Sumatran Highway thrash from the Padang/Bukittinggi area south to Lubuklinggau, about 149km east of Bengkulu, it's possible to travel **south to Bengkulu** on the far pleasanter, quiet coastal road. The great advantage of this is the spectacular scenery, the isolated rural villages and the slow pace of life: it could be a million kilometres away from the major cities at either end. Be warned, however, that although there's public transport the full length of this route, it's time-consuming, and much of the accommodation is very simple. Cyclists may find the route appealing as it's quiet and fairly flat, though shadeless for long stretches. There's also an interesting detour possible – east from **Tapan to Sungaipenuh**, into the Kerinci-Seblat national park (see opposite).

Padang to Bengkulu

The road from Padang to Painan, 77km south of Padang, runs inland through the foothills of the Bukit Barisan range. **PAINAN** is a small fishing town with a long, curving beach littered with fishing boats and their associated paraphernalia. Traces of the fort built in 1664, soon after the Dutch established their first west Sumatran base here, can be seen on Pulau Cingkruk, just offshore at Painan. There's basic accommodation in town; inquire at the **tourist office** at Jalan Ilya Yakub (Mon–Thurs 8am–2pm, Fri 8–11am, Sat 8am–12.30pm; ☎0756/21005).

South of Painan the road leaves the mountains and follows the coastal plain through to Tapan (136km), although from Air Haji it runs inland rather than following the coast as it juts out to Cape Indrapura. The junction market town of **Tapan** is a three-road town: north to Padang (213km), east to Sungaipenuh (64km) and south to Bengkulu. The route to **Sungaipenuh** in the heart of the Kerinci-Seblat national park is convenient; there are regular buses between Tapan and Sungaipenuh. The village of **Sungai Gambir** offers easy access to national park forests and is a good place to relax; you can swim in the nearby Batang Tapan and walk in the forest. Tigers roam the area during the durian season (October to December), and you can watch them safely from tree houses built by the villagers. You'll need to stay in family houses or with the kepala desa, but there's a warung that sells snack meals like *mie sop* and gado gado. Further east on this road, the village of **Sako** offers good birding – look out for the Argus pheasant, hornbills, bulbuls, leafbird, drongo and forktail. Ask at the local rumah makan about accommodation.

From Tapan, the road south heads out towards the coast again. Located 20km south of Tapan, and 1km south of **Lunang**, the restaurant/losmen *Kasihan Ombak* (no phone; ①) is the best place to stay along this stretch of road. Just west of the village, the **Lunung Silaut Reserve** is a freshwater swamp forest over which there have been fierce battles in recent years, with big-business interests campaigning to turn it into a palm-oil plantation, while environmentalists are concerned with the area's importance as a fish breeding ground where tapir, tiger, bear and crocodile thrive. The swamp is home to two sorts of parrot, and one of the rarest storks (Storm's stork), has been seen here, as well as the threatened white-winged wood duck. Inquire at the village of Tanjung Pondok, just south of Tapan, or at *Kasihan Ombak*, about finding a local boatman for a trip out into the area.

From here on south, the road surface is good and the whole area is pretty enticing, with plenty of glimpses of glittering ocean just a few hundred metres to the west. Beware though – these beaches have a savage undertow and not all are safe for swimming, so you must take local advice.

Although **Muko-Muko**, 40km south of *Kasihan Ombak*, is marked pretty boldly on maps, the reality is somewhat different. It has the only Telkom office between Sungaipenuh and Bengkulu, but apart from this boasts only a few remains of an English fort, Fortress Anne, where Sir Thomas Raffles had a garrison in the early nineteenth century. The town beach, lined with spruce trees rather than palms, is between the estuaries of the rivers Manjuto and Selagan, which flow into the Indian Ocean at Muko-Muko.

At the village of **Penarik**, about 30km south of Muko-Muko, there's basic accommodation in *Losmen Bayung* (①) in the centre of the village. Further south at **Ipuh** there's more of a choice, including *Wisma Damai* (①). Inquire here about the best local beaches – Air Hitam to the north is pretty good. Further south again, at **Seblat**, there are more local beaches and basic accommodation. The village of **Ketahun**, a few kilometres further on, is spread out along the two banks of a small river; there's a small losmen on the southern side. The larger, bustling town of **Lais** at the junction with the road east to Arga Makmur, lies just 95km north of Bengkulu.

The Kerinci-Seblat national park

Sumatra's largest national park, with elevations varying between sea level and 3800m, the **Kerinci-Seblat national park** is named after its two highest mountains, Gunung Kerinci (3805m), north of Sungaipenuh, and Gunung Seblat (2383m), much further south. It's a brilliant destination for nature-spotting and trekking, and the scenery is particularly lush.

The park was established in the 1990s and comprises a huge variety of ecosystems, including tropical lowland forest, hill forest and mountain forest. Thirty species of mammal roam here, including the Sumatran rhinoceros, Sumatran elephant, Sumatran tiger (there are perhaps seventy or eighty within the park, so a sighting is unlikely), tree leopard, clouded leopard (the least-known of all the cats in Asia), tapir, muntjac deer, Malaysian bear and gibbon. There are also records of 139 bird species and 4000 species of flora, and sporadic sightings of the perhaps mythological *orang pendek* (see the box on p.386).

Around the edges of the park, **encroachment** is a serious issue; local farmers cross park boundaries to clear forest and plant crops, as part of a shifting agriculture system that will move to another area the following year and destroy more. Many of the animals are under constant threat from **poaching**, both for food but also because of the continuing international trade which includes rhino horn and bear's gall bladder. Another threat is from **illegal logging**, which in Kerinci-Seblat is said to account for the loss of thousands of hardwood trees annually. There are several culprits: local pirate operators, the army, and large logging concerns which trespass in the park area. Don't assume that every logging operation you see is illegal: some selected areas are cut legally and then returned to the park, one advantage being that with regrowth the undergrowth gets denser and the leaf-eaters get fatter, attracting both them and their natural hunters into the area. There are also designated permanent logging areas where the trees are cut and reforestation takes place. The other major threat to the park is that the government simply gives whole areas over for use as rubber, tea, sugar cane, cocoa or palm-oil **plantations**, which support an extremely limited biodiversity. The message from all of this is to get to the park and enjoy it while you can, as there'll probably be less of it in coming years.

TREKKING IN KERINCI-SEBLAT NATIONAL PARK

Scores of treks are possible, ranging from easy one- and two-day walks along well-used trails between villages, to forest treks of a week or more. National park officers and rangers are happy to advise on the huge number of possibilities, and if you've a special interest in perhaps flowers or birds they will advise.

Trekking in the area isn't only for those with an interest in flora and fauna. **Traditional villages** and longhouses still survive in the heart of the oldest villages in Kerinci: look for them in Siulak Mudik, Lempur and Pondok Tinggi. Ask about traditional **Kerincinese dancing** and **magic ceremonies** in villages such as Seramphas, Lempur, Siulak, Kluru and even, on occasion, Sungaipenuh. These aren't advertised or put on for tourists, but are the real thing, including one, *tarik asiek*, where the spirit of a tiger supposedly enters the dancer.

Inquire at the national park office, *Mitra Kerja*, in Sungaipenuh for national park **guides**; they are often villagers already working as volunteer helpers for the park. Guide fees for non-English-speaking deep-forest village guides are around US$6.50 per day and for porters US$5 per day, but rates vary from area to area. Trekkers requiring guides who speak English or who have a particular speciality should expect to pay a higher daily rate.

Trekkers pay for their guide's food and transport, and it's traditional to also provide a daily packet of cigarettes.

Suggested itineraries

Talang Kemoning (or Lempur) – Sungai Ipuh (Bengkulu). Three days. There are fine views of Gunung Raya (2576m), and a possible detour via Gunung Beliarang for sulphur fountains, geysers and hot springs. Good birding, and you may spot tiger, tapir and siamang. Alternatively, rhino were spotted in the mid-1990s on a trail slightly to the north.

Talang Kemoning – Gunung Beliarang. Gunung Beliarang is immediately south of Gunung Raya and north of Gunung Kunyit, an active volcano. You can go there and back in a day, but it's better to make it a two-day trip.

Lempur to Seramphas–Dusun Tuo (Jambi). This is two or three days on easy and well-used trails between villages. There's little climbing, but the trail is muddy during the rainy season. Highlights are elephant, tapir and tiger, giant tortoises (which are occasionally seen between Lempur and Seramphas) plus caves and hot springs.

Pungut–Renapermatik–Pelompek. A three-day trek mainly through traditional farms and forest on well-used trails. There are excellent views of Gunung Tujuh and Gunung, with siamang, deer and tiger sometimes reported, good birdwatching – and look out for the Kerinci rabbit, which hasn't been spotted since 1933.

Pungut–Patah Tiga. This is three to four days of walking through beautiful hill forest, with very fine birding, many animals and superb cloud forest on Bukit Sunting and Gunung Danau. The trek can be extended (five days) to Air Liki, where you can take a raft to Banko.

Tanjung Genting–Gunung Mesjid–Sungaipenuh. A stiff walk from the village to the peak of Gunung Mesjid, followed by an easy walk along the peaks fringing the Kerinci valley, with hot springs, waterfalls and good moss forests. An extra day to Air Haji or Sungai Gambir is possible.

Tandai–Gunung Tujuh–Danau Tujuh–Palompek. This takes five days, initially on old logging trails in lowland hill forest (400m) with much wildlife and sensational birding, before entering primary hill forest and the climb up to just below Gunung Tujuh (2700m) and down to Danau Gunung Tujuh and then (one day) to Palompek. Take a local boat across the lake with fishermen.

Danau Tujuh circular. Three days' walking the lakeside and ridge trails with fantastic views and many rare orchids in season (September to November). Sampans can be borrowed from local fishermen.

Padang Aro–Kayu Aro. Deep-forest trekking in the hills behind Gunung Kerinci, with fantastic views of the volcano.

There are various **access points**, and it's possible to traverse a considerable length of Sumatra dipping in and out of the park. The most northerly parts are accessible from Painan just below Padang, the southern areas around Curup and Lubuklinggau are accessible from Bengkulu, whilst **Sungaipenuh** (see below) is the location of the park headquarters (you can obtain **permits** from here; Rp1500) and the place from which to tackle Gunung Kerinci and the trek to Danau Gunung Tujuh.

Sungaipenuh and Danau Kerinci

Situated in a high fertile valley close to Danau Kerinci and densely farmed with rice, tea, coffee and cloves, the small, attractive town of **SUNGAIPENUH**, 277km southwest of Padang, is the location of the Kerinci-Seblat national park headquarters and, as well as being well worth a couple of days in its own right, is an excellent base for the exploration of the park.

Mesjid Agung in the Pondok Tinggi area of town is a huge and highly unusual mosque, with Roman as well as Arabic features, built in 1874 on the site of an older mosque and constructed without the use of a single nail. The six-metre-long drum (*beduk*) is used to summon the worshippers to prayer, and the whole interior has a wonderfully graceful and devout atmosphere. You'll be asked to make a donation.

Nestling at more than 750m above sea level and surrounded by peaks of about 2000m, the glorious highland lake **Danau Kerinci** lies 5km southeast of Sungaipenuh. The whole area is a rift valley on a geological fault line: Danau Kerinci was the epicentre of an earthquake in October 1995 that registered 7.1 on the Richter scale. There are predictions of more problems, plus a possible eruption of Gunung Kerinci, in the near future. To get good views of the lake, which is invisible from Sungaipenuh, take public transport along the lakeside road to Jujun and then on along the road to Lempur. Alternatively, head up Bukit Tapan to the west of town.

The wealth of **megalithic remains** in the area point to the existence of an ancient civilization which vanished about a thousand years ago and whose disappearance may have been linked to an eruption of Gunung Raya to the southwest of the lake. There's even speculation that at one time the great Sriwijaya kingdom was based here. The most impressive stones are at Muak village, 30km south of Sungaipenuh at the southern end of Danau Kerinci; access is via Jujun and Lempur. The weirdest is **Batu Gong**, a three-metre-long spaceship shape – with circles supposedly representing portholes and stick figures visible. Also worth a look is **Batu Patah** (Broken Stone), a four-metrelong column which local legend says was part of a column that once reached almost to the moon – a child toppled it and it broke it in half, with one part falling to earth near Bukittinggi and one part here. For those who want to explore further, Benik, Lempur, Pendung, Pondok and Kunum, 6km south of Sungaipenuh, all have megaliths. Amateur archeologists may want to root around at Masego, south of Lempur beyond the southern end of the lake, where standing stones have been discovered: the area has been little investigated.

There are plenty of **waterfalls** – the most accessible being Letter W (pronounced "Way"), 10km north of Kersik Tua; the fifty-metre waterfall is 200m from the main road to the right. Birdwatchers should look out for spotted leafbirds and swifts here.

Several villages in the Danau Kerinci area produce distinctive **handicrafts**. At Pendung village, accessed from Semerup, the blades for traditional knives (*parang*) are manufactured; local blacksmiths mourn the demise of the British-made Land-Rover, as the worn-out springs were a good source of metal. The scabbard and handle are added at Jujun at the southern end of the lake. You can see the craftsmen and buy an example, for which you can expect to pay expect to pay Rp12,000–15,000 – the most expensive have a scabbard made from a single piece of surian root, while cheaper ones arc made from strips of wood. Rattan baskets are produced at Sungai Tutung.

ORANG PENDEK

The terrestrial primate **orang pendek** (short man), apparently a little over 1m high, is well-known to local people throughout the Bukit Barisan Mountain Range. Workers have seen, heard and found the footprint of this elusive creature, but so far it has eluded photographers – to the extent that many naturalists doubt its existence. Sceptics say it's a sun bear seen in unusual lighting conditions and others believe it to be a folk memory of the orang-utan, which once lived in the area. However, if this was the case, the animal would be arboreal, yet all the signs are that *orang pendek* is terrestrial. The search continues and has international support.

Practicalities

The **bus terminal** is in the market area between Jalan Prof J. Amin and Jalan H. Agus Salim; plenty of dokar wait to ferry arrivals around town. Sungaipenuh is easily accessible, although you may have to change buses in Bangko on the Trans-Sumatran Highway.

There are several **accommodation** options in town. The most luxurious place is *Aroma*, Jalan Imam Bonjol 14 (☎0748/21142; ②–④), conveniently central with well-decorated rooms, the most expensive with hot-water bathrooms. *Matahari* on Jalan Basuki Rahmet (☎0748/21061; ②–③) offers large rooms in a big old house, some with attached mandi, and a huge amount of information about the local area is available in the lobby. Slightly more centrally, *Yani*, Jalan Muradi 1 (no phone; ②), has a less spacious feel and is on a busier road, but offers similar accommodation.

For **eating**, *Soto Minang*, Jalan Muradi 4, serves good, inexpensive Padang food, as does *Sate Amir* next door. *Simpang Tiga*, on Jalan H. Agus Salim in the market area, dishes up excellent Padang food: the brains in coconut sauce are particularly good. Up the hill from the *Matahari*, *Dendeng Batokok Diatas* provides very simple local food.

The BNI bank, opposite *Matahari*, has **foreign exchange** facilities, the 24hr **Telkom office** is on Jalan Imam Bonjol, and the **post office** is at Jalan Sudirman 1a. The **national park office**, Jalan Basuki Rahmat 11 (Mon–Thurs 7am–2pm, Fri 7–11am, Sat 7am–12.30pm; ☎0748/22250, fax 22300), can be found on the edge of town: look for a white gateway with red lettering. They offer information and advice about the park and issue **permits** (Rp1500 for Gunung Kerinci or Danau Gunung Tujuh), although you can also get these at the park offices closer to each place. Inquire here for national park guides, who will charge Rp30,000–40,000 per day. The office has some printed material and excellent photographs of local wildlife on display. Look especially for the image of the black golden cat, a variety of the golden cat with an excess of the pigment melanin – this picture, taken in 1996, was the first ever taken of the creature.

If you stay in town for a day or two, particularly at the *Matahari*, local tour guides will probably find you and offer their services. Several **tours** are on offer, including visits to the Kubu people near Bangko (see p.417) from around US$100; trips to the Ladeh Panjang swamp area including Gunung Beliarang lasting two days and one night (from US$75); three-day/two-night trips to the Belibis and Kasah caves (US$75); a one-night/two-day guided climb up Gunung Kerinci (US$75); and a day-trip to the megalithic stones in the area (US$15). Alternatively, it is possible to charter a car and local driver for upwards of Rp50,000 a day and put together your own trip. Be very careful that both parties are clear about what is and isn't included, and clarify the time scale and exact itinerary.

Gunung Kerinci and around

The grandeur of **Gunung Kerinci** (3805m), the highest mountain in Sumatra, can be admired and (for the energetic) scaled from the attractively cool highland village of **KERSIK TUA**, 48km north of Sungaipenuh. The entire region is beautiful, with brilliant green-tea plantations on gently rolling hillsides as far as the eye can see.

To get to Kersik Tua, catch a local bus from Jalan H. Agus Salim in Sungaipenuh (the bus conductors yell "Kayuaro", which is the local name for the entire district); it takes between and hour and ninety minutes to get to Kersik Tua, via the attractive market village of Bendeng. If you are coming from Padang, the long-distance buses to Sungaipenuh pass through Kersik Tua. There are several homestays in the village, although at the time of writing the Eco-Rural Travel Co-operative office, the coordinating body for homestays and guides in the area, had been closed for some time. *Darmin Homestay* (no phone; ③) is on the main road, several hundred metres north of the sideroad to Gunung Kerinci and is clean and welcoming, with an upstairs sitting area and a balcony out the front with views straight towards Gunung Kerinci. The owners will cook basic meals. *Homestay Keluarga Subandi* (no phone; ③) is also at the southern end of the village, opposite the turning to Gunung Kerinci.

You can obtain local information and details of possible trips at any of the homestays. Expect to pay Rp20,000–25,000 per day for a porter and Rp25,000–40,000 for a guide. They will help you plan **excursions** in the area or arrange all-in tours including transport. Tours and per-person prices include: Kerinci (two days; US$54), Danau Gunung Tujuh (one day; US$17), Danau Belibis (one day; US$16), Ladeh Panjang (four days; US$99), Danau Kerinci (one or two days; US$29/44), tea estates (one day; US$9), and the Kasah cave and around (three days; US$60).

Climbing Gunung Kerinci

The highest active volcano in Sumatra, **Gunung Kerinci** (3805m) is a tough climb with uncertain rewards at the top. The views can be stunning early in the morning, but the weather is very changeable, and after a hard slog to get to the top you may be enveloped in fog. The crater, over 500m across, is still active and belches poisonous gases, so a great deal of care is necessary: there's no path around the crater's edge. The mountain is famous for the white-flowered Javanese edelweiss (*Anaphalis javanica*), which is found only on volcanoes, can grow to 4m and looks remarkably striking on the bare volcanic soil. It's also incredibly enticing for birdwatchers as scene of recent sightings of Schneider's pitta: the bird was first spotted on this trail in 1988, after forty years during which it was thought to be extinct. Salvador's pheasant is even more elusive, but, like the pitta, is generally seen on the lower slopes, while another rare bird, the red-billed partridge, prefers the higher elevations. Altogether, the Kerinci trail is one of the best birding areas in the park: expect babblers, thrushes, mesias and fantails as well as warblers, woodpeckers, minivets and the rare Sumatran cochea, plus several species of hornbill. You can also hope to spot gibbons, macaques, leaf-monkeys, and there are thought to be tigers in the area.

To tackle the summit you need to be properly prepared. Temperatures regularly plummet to 5°C and, although there are "shelters", they are open-sided and often roofless: you will definitely need a sleeping bag and a tent is highly desirable. Inquire at the homestays about rental, but it's far better to have your own. Regardless of the dubious environmental impact of using wood from the forests to cook, the wood is often wet, so it's advisable to take a stove, as well as appropriate rain gear. A spring above Shelter 2 provides fresh drinking water, but check this before you set off. Hiring a guide is very highly recommended, as a number of climbers have come to grief up here – whilst it's relatively straightforward to follow the path going up, it can be easy to miss on the descent.

The route goes from a sideroad in Kersik Tua, guarded by statue of a roaring lion, and you walk 5km, following the obviously main route, to the PHPA office, where you'll need to sign in and get a **permit** (Rp1500). From here it takes about two hours' climbing through cultivated fields and then into the forest to Shelter 1; you'll pass a small shelter on the way that has no number. From Shelter 1 it's a further two to three hours to Shelter 2, where most people aim to spend the night. You'll need to get up between 3am and 5am to get to the top for dawn. The slippery volcanic rock gets steeper and steeper as you go up above the treeline – in places steps have been cut, but it's very hard going. Most people make the descent back to Kersik Tua in one day.

Danau Gunung Tujuh

The trek to **Danau Gunung Tujuh** (Seven Mountains Lake), the highest volcanic lake in Southeast Asia at an altitude of 1996m, is a much less gruelling excursion than that to Gunung Kerinci. However, it's still extremely picturesque and rewarding: you can hope to spot pretty much the same variety of wildlife here as you would on the mountain, and the variety of birds is wonderful. Danau Gunung Tujuh is a freshwater lake in the ancient crater of an extinct volcano, 4.5km long and 3km wide. As long as you leave early it's a relatively straightforward day-trip from Kersik Tua, but really deserves more time and appreciation than this. Lone male travellers should be especially careful, as the lake is said to be home to *dewa*, beautiful female spirits who sing to entice men into a life of eternal slavery.

The walk starts from the village of Pelompek, 7km north of Kersik Tua, which is the last place to buy supplies for the trek, and there are a couple of rumah makan. The only major turning in the village to the right (east) leads 2km to the small village of Ulujernih; just under 1km beyond Ulujernih, the national park office is amongst a small huddle of concrete houses at the far end of the valley and you'll see the national park gateway. At the office you can book in, buy a **permit** if you don't already have one (Rp1500), get information, arrange **accommodation** at the PHPA guest house and, if necessary, arrange a **guide** (around Rp25,000 per day).

The track from the office is wide, cobbled and negotiable on a motorcycle for 1.5km to a clearing in the forest where the park **guest house**, consisting of several buildings, stands. The most attractive and comfortable is the large wooden one with big verandah at the front. It costs Rp6000 per night, which includes the use of a cooking stove and a water supply to the bathroom at the back, though there's no electricity. Beds and mattresses are supplied, but little else – you'll need to bring your own food and check whether there are pots and plates. And be warned: it gets very chilly at night. It's a great setting and good spot to start the walk from. The path to the lake passes to the left of the wooden building and on into the forest, where it climbs relentlessly to Shelter 2, between one and two hours' hike through the forest from the guest house, which is on the crater rim above the lakeside. From here, the steep descent to the lakeside takes about thirty minutes.

The lake is surrounded by mountains, the seven of the name, and dominated by Gunung Tujuh on the far side, with densely forested slopes right down to the water's edge. This scene is particularly lovely in the early morning, when wisps of mist rise off the surface and the siamang gibbons (one of the highest recorded sightings of the species) start to call as the sun comes up. Down on the lakeside there's a fairly sizable shelter, but you'll be more comfortable in a tent. The duration of your stay is really only determined by how much food you've brought: you should bring a stove. For those with time and inclination there are shelters further around the left-hand side of the lake called Pos Merah and Pos Maliki – you'll need a guide to help you find these.

The rest of the park

With time and determination, there are huge areas of the park to be explored. Situated in a side-cone of Gunung Kerinci on the southern flanks, **Danau Belibis** is a small crater lake set at 2050m above sea level. It's known for sightings of wild duck and is an easy day-trip from Kersik Tua. The start of the trail is two hours from Kersik Tua at the edge of the plantation land (you'll need a guide to locate it), and you'll have to make a two-kilometre leech-infested forest hike to the lake, which has some great views of Gunung Kerinci.

There are two **swamps** within reach of Kersik Tua. At 1950m, Ladeh Panjang is the highest peat-moss swamp in Sumatra, situated due west of Kerinci and caused by geological blocking of the valley forming two nearby lakes – Sati and Singkarak. The habitat is of dwarf peat-swamp woodland with tussocks of sedge and grass between the trees, which are hung with long lichens. Access is on foot (6hr) from Kebun Baru village, 18km from Kersik Tua. The track starts through cultivated land with most of it in the forest – you'll need camping gear as well as a guide. Danau Bento (Sangir Hulu) is a freshwater swamp forest at 1375m, named after a type of wild rice that used to dominate the swamp.

Pekanbaru and around

The administrative capital of Riau province, an amalgamation of mainland and island districts spreading from the edge of the Bukit Barisan mountains almost to the coast of Borneo, the booming oil town of **PEKANBARU** is a major gateway into Indonesia from Singapore. Most travellers head straight through and, whilst there are few specific sights to detain you, the town is easy to get around, has a relaxed atmosphere as long as you get away from the bus terminal, a reasonable range of accommodation options and some excellent restaurants. It's worth considering a journey break here – it's six hours west to Bukittinggi and another nine or ten hours east to Singapore.

The historical origins of Pekanbaru date back to a small village called Payung Sekaki which changed its name to Senepelan during the time of the Siak kingdom. Gradually, a commercial centre grew up at the site and a market (*pekan*) was established: in 1784 the name Pekanbaru was coined. Just before World War II, oil was discovered in the area and exploited first by the Japanese, and then by newly independent Indonesia, turning Pekanbaru into a boom city in the process.

Located 130km west of Pekanbaru, roughly equidistant between it and Bukittinggi, **Muara Takus** is home to the remains of a ninth- and tenth-century Buddhist kingdom, and **Siak Sri Indrapura**, 120km towards the coast from Pekanbaru, provides the most tangible evidence of the Siak kingdom, which dominated the area from 1725 to 1945. **Dumai**, around 190km north of Pekanbaru, is the major east-coast Sumatran port – there's no reason to come here except for ferries (see p.395).

Arrival, orientation, information and city transport

Flights land at the Simpang Tiga airport, 9km south of the city centre. The closest public transport is 1km away on the main highway, where you can catch public buses into the Pasar Pusat terminal in the city centre. Otherwise, fixed-price taxis charge Rp10,000 for the trip. **Long-distance buses** arrive at the terminal on Jalan Nangka about 5km south of the river, from where you can catch a blue bemo to the city centre. Most express **ferry services** from Batam or Bintan land at Buton, where you can take a bus either to the bus terminal at Jalan Nangka or the express-ferry office at the northern end of Jalan Sudirman. Slow boats arrive at the main port area at the northern end of Jalan Saleh Abbas in the Pasar Bawah market area, a couple of hundred metres west of Jalan Sudirman.

With only a few suburbs to the north, the bulk of Pekanbaru is situated on the south banks of Sungai Siak, extending for 8km out towards the airport. The main street is Jalan Sudirman, which runs north–south right from the river itself through the centre of town to the airport area. Most places of interest to tourists, including hotels, restaurants and shops, are within easy reach of this thoroughfare.

The **tourist information office**, Jalan Diponegoro 24 (Mon–Thurs 8am–2pm, Fri 8–11am, Sat 8am–12.30pm; ☎0761/31562, fax 31565) have plenty of English-language leaflets and will try to help with inquiries – it's a bit out of the way and probably not worth the trek unless you have very specific inquiries.

Public buses and bemos operate on roughly fixed routes around town. **Buses** (6am–9pm; Rp300) run the length of Jalan Sudirman and beyond, between the Pasar Pusat terminal near the Jalan Imam Bonjol junction with Jalan Sudirman and Kubang terminal, which is 3km beyond the turning to Simpang Tiga airport. **Bemos** (Rp250) operate to and from the main bemo terminal, Sekapelan, which is situated just west of

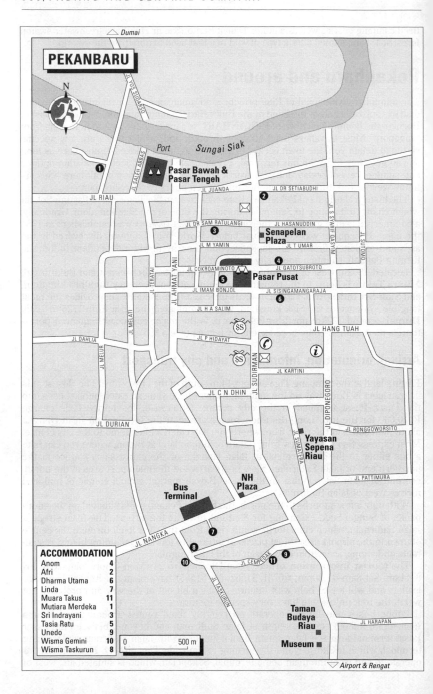

PEKANBARU

△ *Dumai*

Sungai Siak

Port

JL SALEH ABBAS

JL SUDIROSO SA IF

Pasar Bawah &
Pasar Tengeh

JL RIAU

JL JUANDA

JL DR SETIABUDHI

②

JL DR SAM RATULANGI

③

JL HASANUDDIN

Senapelan
Plaza

JL M YAMIN

JL T UMAR

JL S SYARIF QASYIM

JL SUTOMO

JL COKROAMINOTO

⑤

Pasar Pusat

④

JL GATOTSUBROTO

JL TERATAI

JL AHMAT YANI

JL IMAM BONJOL

JL SISINGAMANGARAJA

⑥

JL H A SALIM

JL MELATI

JL P HIDAYAT

JL HANG TUAH

JL DAHLIA

JL MELUR

ⓒ

ⓘ

JL SUDIRMAN

JL KARTINI

JL C N DHIN

JL DURIAN

JL DIPONEGORO

JL RONGGOWORSITO

Yayasan
Sepena
Riau

JL SUMATERA

JL PATTIMURA

NH
Plaza

Bus
Terminal

⑦

JL NANGKA

⑧

⑪

⑨

⑩

JL CEMPEDAK

JL TASKURIN

Taman
Budaya
Riau

JL HARAPAN

Museum ■

0   500 m

▽ *Airport & Rengat*

ACCOMMODATION

Anom	4
Afri	2
Dharma Utama	6
Linda	7
Muara Takus	11
Mutiara Merdeka	1
Sri Indrayani	3
Tasia Ratu	5
Unedo	9
Wisma Gemini	10
Wisma Taskurun	8

the main market area behind Jalan Sudirman. Bemos are colour-coded and marked with their destination. A couple of useful services are the **blue** bemo (6am–11pm) to Tangkerang, which is the museum area, south of town (they usually pass near the Jalan Nangka bus terminal on their way back into town), and the **yellow** service (6am–8pm), which goes to Rumbai, a northeast suburb, via Jalan Riau, passing close to the *Mutiara Merdeka* hotel. Other areas of town that are named on bemos are Sukajadi (the bemo terminal next to the bus terminal on Jalan Nangka) Panam in the southwest suburbs, and Pasar Limapuluh at the north end of Jalan Sutomo on the east side of town.

MOVING ON FROM PEKANBARU

Pekanbaru is a major transport hub for Sumatra, and sea, land and air **connections** are extremely good, both throughout the island and for the rest of the archipelago.

High-speed ferry services for Pulau Batam and Pulau Karimun leave from the ticket offices at the northern end of Jalan Sudirman. Although located near the river and with adverts conspicuously picturing speedboats, most services actually involve a three-hour bus trip to Buton, where you transfer to the high-speed ferry for the three- to four-hour trip to Batam. The exception to this is the *Garuda Express* (☎0761/42489), which leaves Pekanbaru by boat to Perawang, then takes the bus to Buton and the high-speed ferry from Buton to Pulau Batam and Pulau Karimun. Prices vary from Rp30,000 to Rp35,000, and ticket sellers make all sorts of dramatic claims for the length of the trip, typically from six to eight hours. However, this is the travelling time and doesn't include delays in leaving Pekanbaru or missing the ferry at Buton and the two-hour wait for the next one. If you're planning to go straight through to **Singapore**, it's best to take the earliest departure from Pekanbaru (they all leave within a couple of hours in any case). Some companies also sell tickets straight through to Tanjung Pinang, but check whether you have to change boats in Batam. PT Lestari Polajaya Sakti (see below) operate daily speedboats to Tanjung Pinang and Karimun from Buton.

Slow ferries leave from the port area at the northern end of Jalen Saleh Abbas, where the ticket offices are located, in the Pasar Bawah/Pasar Tengah area. Inquire at PT Lestari Polajaya Sakti, Jalan Saleh Abbas 8 (☎0761/37627, fax 35623), for daily sailings that leave at 9pm for the 25-hour trip to Pulau Batam via Selatpanjang, Tanjung Samak (on nearby Pulau Rangsang), Tanjung Batu (on Pulau Kundur south of Karimun), Moro (on Pulau Sugibawah), Tanjung Pinang and Tanjung Balai on Karimun.

Long-distance buses leave from the terminal on Jalan Nangka; many of the bus offices are in the terminal itself but others are spread along Jalan Nangka up to about 500m west of the terminal and also at the very start of Jalan Taskurun. There are a number of bus companies, all operating their own schedules with their own price lists so it is worth shopping around, and you should book a day or two in advance. There are regular buses to destinations throughout Sumatra and east to Java and beyond.

There's a good choice of domestic and international **flights** from Simpang Tiga airport. Merpati operate to Batam, Padang, Medan, Jakarta, Tanjung Pinang, and Mandala daily to Jakarta and Batam. Merpati and Silk Air fly to Singapore and Pelangi to Kuala Lumpur and Malacca. Departure tax is Rp10,300 for domestic and Rp20,000 for international departures. Fixed-price taxis to the airport cost Rp10,000, and the Pasar Pusat–Kubang public bus will drop you at the junction of the airport road and the main highway, a one-kilometre walk to the terminal.

The immigration situation at **Dumai**, the port for the massive ocean-going oil tankers and cargo carriers, 189km north of Pekanbaru, is somewhat ambiguous. Officially it is not a visa-free entry point, but many long-term expatriates in Sumatra report that **visas** are issued here and, with the daily high-speed crossing taking between two and three hours to Malacca, it's actually the cheapest and quickest way to exit and re-enter Indonesia by sea. Check the situation locally before you set off. If you get stranded in Dumai there's little accommodation to recommend, but check out the *City Hotel*, Jalan Sudirman (☎0765/21550).

Accommodation

Pekanbaru has a wide variety of **accommodation**, with an especially wide choice at the middle to top range; there isn't a great deal under Rp20,000 for a double. The essential choice is between the central area – most places are within a short distance of Jalan Sudirman – or the bus terminal area, about 5km south. If you decide on the bus terminal area, you are advised to steer clear of the basic, noisy and poor-value places on Jalan Nangka itself and aim for the quieter roads to the south. Jalan Taskurun and Jalan Cempaka are good hunting grounds.

Afri, Jl Dr Setiabudhi 5 (☎0761/33190). Conveniently located on the corner of Jl Sudirman about 200m south of the speedboat ferry dock, this is a clean, multi-storey setup with rooms with and without air-con and attached mandi. Extremely convenient if you arrive very late at this end of town. ③.

Anom, Jl Gatot Subroto 3 (☎0761/22636). Located centrally, about 100m from Jl Sudirman, this recently renovated place has spotlessly clean rooms opening off a central courtyard, some with hot water. Prices include a small breakfast and there's a popular Chinese restaurant attached to the hotel. ④.

Dharma Utama, Jl Sisingamangaraja 10 (☎0761/21171). Conveniently situated close to the junction with Jl Sudirman, this place looks grand from outside but this isn't reflected in the rooms, although there are some reasonably priced options. ③–④.

Wisma Gemini, Jl Taskurun 44 (☎0761/32916). Slightly more upmarket than the other places nearby, with a pleasant garden setting and a relaxed and quiet atmosphere. There are a range of rooms on offer, from those with fan and attached cold-water mandi to options with air-con and hot water. ③–④.

Hotel Linda, Jl Nangka 145 (☎0761/36915). A big white house with a pleasant atmosphere and character on a quiet alleyway that leads off Jl Nangka, opposite the bus terminal, about 50m west of *Penginapan Linda* – don't get these places confused. Offers a big range of rooms, all with bathrooms attached. This is a much better bet than any of the more obvious places on the main road. ②–④.

Muara Takus, Jl Cempaka 17 (☎0761/21045). Set back slightly from the road and convenient for the bus terminal, this place offers very good value, with rooms ranging from those with outside bathroom and no fan to those with attached bathroom and fan. ②–③.

Mutiara Merdeka, Jl Yos Sudarso 12a (☎0761/31272, fax 32959, *merdeka@indon.net.id*). The plushest and most expensive hotel in town, which offers excellent facilities including a travel agent, business centre and small pool (open to non-residents for Rp5000). This is still the most popular option at this end of the range and there's an efficiency and buzz missing in the imitators, but you pay for it, and it isn't particularly convenient for public transport. They offer occasional excellent weekend deals. ⑧–⑨.

Sri Indrayani, Jl Dr Sam Ratulangi (☎0761/35600, fax 31870). The most pleasant rooms have a small verandah leading out into a garden area. This is more spacious and classier than others in this price range and has an attractive, well-decorated lobby. It lacks the facilities of the *Mutiara Merdeka* but is good value. ⑦–⑧.

Tasia Ratu, Jl K.H. Hasyim Ashari 10 (☎0761/33431, fax 38912). A small, quiet and friendly place in this price range, centrally located just off Jl Sudirman. It's signed from Jl Sudirman and has air-con and hot water in all rooms, which are well furnished. ⑦–⑨.

Wisma Taskurun, Jl Taskurun 37 (☎0761/23555) Situated on Jl Taskurun, which runs south off Jl Nangka just opposite the bus terminal, this is 200m up on the left. All rooms have an attached mandi – with fans at the lower price range and air-con at the upper. The rooms are basic but it's a convenient location. ②–③.

Unedo, Jl Cempaka 1 (☎0761/223396). Rooms have fan, attached cold-water mandi and there's a small garden. It's about 50m from Jl Sudirman and is convenient for the bus terminal. ③.

The City

Pekanbaru is a bustling oil city, well maintained and featuring broad, spacious streets, with a mixture of Sumatran, Javanese, Chinese and expat inhabitants.

The city is rather low on sights, but one must-see is **Yayasan Sepena Riau**, Jalan Sumatera 7 (Mon–Sat 10am–4pm), a small private museum and souvenir shop. It's an absolute treasure trove that rivals most provincial museums, the artefacts collected by one family over many years. The centrepiece is a collection of artefacts connected with traditional Riau weddings – costumes, furnishings and crockery – surrounded by Chinese ceramics, weapons, European glass, photographs and jewellery; there are no labels but the owner will show you around and explain things. **Museum Negeri Propinsi Riau** (Mon–Sat 8am–4pm; Rp200) is a typical Sumatran museum with the prerequisite stuffed animals, traditional-wedding setup, model traditional houses, costumes, weapons, implements, Chinese ceramics and old money, displayed with very little explanation. There are some Western children's games: kites, spinning tops and hoops, and a local game called *pari* with counters and holes in a board. There's also a model of Muara Takus (see p.394), but overall it's a forlorn collection with little entertainment or educational value. Next door, the **Taman Budaya Riau**, the cultural centre, hosts occasional performances of dance and music: inquire at the tourist office.

The **markets** provide a fascinating kaleidoscope of local life: Pasar Pusat is the food and household-goods market, and Pasar Bawah and Pasar Tengeh in the port area have an excellent range of Chinese goods, including ceramics and carpets.

Eating, drinking and entertainment

Pekanbaru's nightlife scene isn't particularly thriving. The **bar** at the *Mutiara Merdeka* hotel is the liveliest and most popular with the well-heeled business travellers who abound in the city. The local **disco** scene is very variable: ask at your accommodation for the latest recommendation. Pekanbaru has an excellent range of **restaurants** serving Western, Chinese and Indonesian food as well as several small **night markets** – even if you stayed in the city for a month, you could have every meal at the brilliant Pasar Pusat night market (located in the market area near Jalan Bonjol) and not eat the same thing twice. Tables are laid out for diners, protected against the rain by awnings.

Anom, Jl Gatot Subroto 3. Attached to the *Anom Hotel*, this is a popular moderate/expensive Chinese restaurant with a range of seafood, chicken and pork dishes plus the usual Chinese delicacies.

Burger PLS, Jl Sumatera. Senapelan–Gobah bemos run along the street: this place is just outside the *Amie Art Shop*. It's a basic, good-value, fast-food stand and they do fine hot dogs and burgers with dill pickles. Tell them to go easy on the chilli sauce, which is extremely hot.

Es Teler 77, Jl Nangka 124b. The usual range of ices, juices and simple Indonesian snacks in the standard fast-food setting that this chain specializes in.

KFC, Senapelan Plaza, Jl Teuku Umar 1 (just off Jl Sudirman) and Jl Nangka 69–71. The same expensive menu as always, but the air-con is a dream come true on a hot day.

Kuantan Coffee Shop at the *Mutiara Merdeka* hotel. The prices here match the location in the plushest hotel in town, with a huge menu of Japanese, Chinese and Western food (up to imported T-bone steak at Rp26,000), but offering other options such as pizza, sandwiches and ice cream. They have special theme nights and a business lunch, which are good deals. Open 24hr.

New Holland, Jl Sudirman 153. A two-storey, very popular fast-food place which veers towards the upper end of the price range (steaks for Rp16,000), but also offers burgers, pizza, juices and drinks at moderate prices. With air-con, a relaxed atmosphere and a few tables looking out into the street, it's cool and comfortable.

Sederhana, Jl Nangka 121–123. One of many Padang-style restaurants that offer good value but spicy eating in the area near the bus terminal. This is one of the larger, more popular places.

Swensen's, Jl Teuku Umar 1. In the Senepelan Plaza just off Jl Sudirman, this international ice-cream-parlour chain offers a standard range of sundaes and soft drinks that are undoubtedly a taste of home, but pricey.

Listings

Airline offices Garuda, *Mutiara Merdeka* hotel, Jl Yos Sudarso 12a (☎0761/32526, fax 32959); Mandala, Jl Sudirman 308 (☎0761/28390, fax 23808); Merpati, Jl Sudirman 343 (☎0761/41555); Pelangi, Jl Pepaya 64c (☎0761/28896, fax 29435); Silk Air, *Mutiara Merdeka* hotel, Jl Yos Sudarso 12a (☎0761/28175, fax 28174).

Banks and exchange All the main banks have branches in the city, including BCA, Jl Sudirman 448, and BNI 1946, Jl Sudirman 63.

Car rental Inquire at PO Gelara Indah, Jl Sisingamangaraja 1 (☎0761/27754) and Rumpun Jaya Car Rental, Jl Arengka 57 (☎0761/62678, fax 37397). Expect to pay about Rp100,000 for a Kijang or similar for a day excluding petrol and driver; a driver would be a further Rp25,000 per day.

Ferries High-speed ferry service ticket offices for Batam are at the northern end of Jl Sudirman and include Marina Indah (☎0761/63540), Kubu Indah (☎0761/22365) and Garuda Express (☎0761/42489). Slow ferries leave from the port area at the northern end of Jl Saleh Abbas, where ticket offices are located, in the Pasar Bawah/Pasar Tengah area. PT Lestari Polajaya Sakti, Jl Saleh Abbas 8 (☎0761/37627, fax 35623).

Hospitals Rumah Sakit Santa Maria, Jl A. Yani 68 (☎0761/20235); Rumah Sakit Umum Pusat Pekanbaru, Jl Diponegoro 2 (☎0761/36118).

Immigration office Jl Singa (☎0761/21536).

Pharmacies Several are situated on Jl Sudirman and are generally well stocked; Kencana, Jl Sudirman 69; Djaya, Jl Sudirman 185, on the corner with Jl Gatot Subroto.

Post office The main post office is at Jl Sudirman 229 and poste restante should be sent here; it's reasonably efficient, but there's a more convenient post office for sending mail at Jl Sudirman 78, close to the northern end of Jl Sudirman.

Shopping There are a couple of multi-storey shopping centres – Senapelan Plaza, Jl Teuku Umar 1, just off Jl Sudirman, has five floors including a Suzuyu Department Store, *KFC, Swensen's* ice cream-parlour and the Gelael Supermarket, plus a variety of clothing, fabric, cassette and CD shops. The newer NH Plaza, Jl Husni Thamrin 2, is just off Jl Nangka east of the bus station, and houses a similar range of shops. The main Pekanbaru market is Pasar Pusat, around Jl Cokroaminoto to the east of Jl Sudirman. Pasar Bawah and Pasar Tengah, between Jl M. Yatim and Jl Saleh Abbas in the port area, is excellent for souvenirs, especially ceramic Chinese goods. Guci Indah, Jl M. Yatim 1a, has a very good selection ranging from tiny teapots to 2m vases. The Amie Art Shop, Jl Sumatera 178 (Senapelan–Gobah bemos go up this street), is one of the few souvenir shops in town and also offers some modern art by local painters.

Telephone and fax The Telkom office is at Jl Sudirman 117 and there are wartel all over town, including Jl Gatot Subroto 6.

Travel agents Mutiara Nusantara Travel at *Mutiara Merdeka* hotel, Jl Yos Sudarso 12a (☎0761/32495, fax 32959); Prima Travel, Jl Sudirman 25 (☎0761/21421); PT Kotapiring Kencana, Jl Sisingamangaraja 3–7 (☎0761/24009, fax 34970), are Pelangi agents and they offer day-tours to Muara Takus, Siak and Ma Lembu for Rp65,000 per person and a half-day city tour for Rp25,000, but you'll need a minimum of two people.

Around Pekanbaru

Further afield, a hefty 130km west of the city, is **Muara Takus**, the remains of an ancient Buddhist complex which is only part of a far larger collection of ruins spread over several square kilometres: it was probably built between the ninth and eleventh centuries during the time of the Sriwijayan empire. Whilst archeologists may find the rather desolate complex of interest, and there's enough mystery centred around the site to enable plenty of amateur theories, this isn't an unmissable sight in Sumatra. To get to Muara Takus by public transport, take a westbound bus to Muaramahat and then a bemo to the site via Kototengah. The *Arga Sonya* (①–②) is the government **guest house** in the area.

One local legend tells that the ancient city was so big it would take a cat three months to cross the roofs of the buildings, while another relates that it was the burial ground of an ancient Hindu ruler who was turned into an elephant upon his death – wild elephants are said to congregate here at the full moon to dance in his honour. It seems likely that the temples are royal graves, and the complex features a rare ancient brick stupa, **Candi Maligai**, which has been completely restored; this is a construction rarely seen in Indonesia, associated with the Mahayana Buddhist tradition. The entire complex is surrounded by walls over 70m long on each side, as well as earth ramparts.

Far more worthwhile, but almost as far from the city in the opposite direction, is **Siak Sri Indrapura**, the restored palace of the eleventh Sultan of Siak, Sultan Abdul Jalil Syafuddin, which lies 120km downriver from Pekanbaru. A bus (2–3hr) leaves from the northern end of Jalan Sudirman each morning, and from the terminal at Pasar Lima Puluh; inquire at the port area of Jalan Saleh Abbas if you fancy a river trip (ferry 4hr, speedboat 1–2hr).

The palace was built in 1889 at a time when the sultan controlled a huge area of eastern Sumatra as his ancestors had done since 1725. The palace was abandoned after Independence and soon began to deteriorate, until Caltex, the petroleum company, contributed to its renovation. It's now brilliant white, with a multitude of minarets, arches and colonnades contributing to the grand effect. There's a small **museum** in the palace with many historical objects and photographs linked to the royal family, especially the last sultan, though the best of them have been removed to the National Museum in Jakarta (see p.86). Royal burial grounds, a mosque and a court building lie in the palace grounds. Inquire locally for the basic **hotels** and **losmen** in town; there are several rumah makan and a small market.

The immigration situation at **Dumai**, the port for the massive ocean-going oil tankers and cargo carriers, 189km north of Pekanbaru, is somewhat ambiguous. Officially it isn't a visa-free gateway (see Basics p.16), but many long-term expatriates in Sumatra report that **visas** are issued here. Combined with the daily high-speed crossing (2–3hr) to Malacca, this is the cheapest and quickest way to exit and re-enter Indonesia by sea. Check the situation locally before you set off.

The Riau Islands

The original home of the *orang laut* (sea people), the descendants of pirates and nomadic traders, the **Riau Archipelago** consists of more than a thousand islands spread in a huge arc across the South China Sea between the east coast of Sumatra and the northwestern tip of Kalimantan. These islands can be a brief staging post on the sea journey from Singapore, but are interesting destinations in their own right, meriting at least a few days' exploration – perhaps on the way to further-flung destinations such as the Lingga Islands. Beware though: Singaporean influence is strong here, and prices are high. Some of the islands are off limits to visitors, as they house refugees from mainland Asia.

The largest and most accessible islands, **Karimun**, **Batam** and **Bintan**, are the best known, and are rapidly developing as the industrial and tourist hinterland for their close neighbour Singapore. Up until 1975 these were forest-covered islands, ringed by mangrove swamps and with a small population living in scattered coastal villages. In the 1980s, however, industrial and tourist development commenced. Batam has the most obvious industrial parks, alongside golf courses, high-quality holiday accommodation and expensive resort areas, while Karimun and Bintan are still managing to hang onto traditional life to some extent. On Bintan this is achieved by the massive tourist enclave in the north of the island, Bintan Resort, separating most of the tourist infrastructure from mainstream island life. For real adventurers, the islands to the east and north, the Anambas, Natuna and Tambelan islands have little infrastructure for visitors, and transport is infrequent.

LUXURY RIAU AT BARGAIN PRICES

The **luxury resorts** of Batam and Bintan are expensive compared with most Indonesian accommodation, although good value by Western standards. Whilst facilities are among the best in Sumatra, catering largely for the highly discerning Singaporean holiday market, the walk-in prices are high, anything from US$100 per night plus tax and service. However, you can book a hugely discounted stay through travel agents in Singapore – many trips booked in Singapore include return transport. Batam and Bintan are well advertised in Singapore in the English-language newspaper, the *Straits Times*, and the best current deals are featured there. Singaporeans gravitate to the islands at weekends, so weekday deals are even better value. The resorts are very variable in facilities, atmosphere and location – decide which suits you best and be especially careful in Batam – plenty of the advertised breaks are based in Nagoya rather than on the coast. If you miss the *Straits Times* adverts, try the following Singapore travel agents, who all do deals to the islands – you could expect to pay less than half the walk-in price – or contact the Singapore offices of the resorts to see what they have on offer. Typical offers are US$240 per person for a three-day/two-night stay during the week, including transport and meals.

For **golf** you'll be better off booking an all-in deal from Singapore than arranging accommodation and visitors' rates at the golf clubs separately. Many of the clubs arrange deals through offices in Singapore. Tering Bay Development (☎065/2718823, fax 2718851) offers an all-in deal including accommodation in Nagoya and green fees, from US$144 per person.

Channel Holidays PTE Ltd (☎065/2761332, fax 2769700).

Continental Travel and Tours PTE, 3 Coleman St, #02-14 Peninsula Shopping Centre (☎065/3388920).

Fascinating Holidays, 333 Orchard Rd, #03-47 Mandarin Shopping Arcade (☎ & fax 065/7355511).

Gunung Raya, #01-13 Golden Mile Complex (☎065/2947711).

Ken-Air, 35 Selegie Rd, #02-25, Parklane Shopping Mall (☎065/3367888).

SIME Travel, 100 Beach Road, #02-50/53 Shaw Leisure Gallery (☎065/2977922, fax 2977422).

Sinba Travel, #02-56 World Trade Centre (☎065/2707779)

Pulau Karimun

The most westerly of the accessible Riau Islands is **Pulau Karimun**, which is a smaller version of Batam: there's considerable industrial development, although most of it in quarrying rather than manufacturing, and an embryonic tourist industry that's trying to lure the cash-rich Singaporeans here for their weekend breaks. The main town of Tanjung Balai is about 60km west of Batam and easily reached from Pekanbaru (the boats going to Sekupang on Pulau Batam call here), Batam, Bintan or Singapore. The closest **tourist offices** are in Batam and Bintan but they have very little information about Karimun. The most detailed printed map of the island (which isn't saying much) are Periplus's *Batam* and *Bintan*.

Located at the far west of the Riau group, at the southern end of the Malacca Straits, Karimun was strategically important during the seafaring centuries, and from the seventh through to the sixteenth century the allegiance of the local *orang laut* was vital to control of the shipping routes through the strait. In more recent times, outsiders sought to take the island from various branches of the Riau sultanate, but in 1824 the Dutch took control and continued their occupation until Independence. Unfortunately, there are absolutely no discernible remains of what must have been a colourful and turbulent history.

Tanjung Balai

The main population centre, the town of **TANJUNG BALAI** on the south coast, is one of the draws of the island, an incredibly busy port that spreads for about 2km along the shore, with numerous wooden jetties where a huge variety of craft load and unload their wares to service the bustling market area behind. There are three main streets in the town: Jalan Nusantara runs parallel to the sea and about 100m inland, from close to the ferry terminal westwards for 2km, until it peters out into wasteland; further inland and parallel to this in the town centre is Jalan Trikora at the eastern (terminal) end which becomes Jalan Pramuka further west; and, parallel to these roads and further inland again, is Jalan Teuku Umar. The main shopping street is Jalan Nusantara, around 1km of shops selling pretty much anything you could want, from coffee through clothes to gold. To the north of Jalan Nusantara, in and around the three major roads described above, numerous smaller roads and alleyways comprise the commercial heart of the town; at the western end, off Jalan Setia, Pasar Baru is a typical Indonesian **market**, which is open daily from early morning until mid-afternoon, with stalls piled high with food of all varieties and household goods galore.

The **post office** can be found at Jalan Pramuka 43 (Mon–Thurs 7.30am–3pm, Fri 7.30–11.30am, Sat 7.30am–1pm) and, about 200m up the hill further east from the eastern end of Jalan Teuku Umar, the **telephone office** (daily 24hr) is at Jalan Teluk Air 2. There are numerous **wartel** around town, including a 24hr one in the ferry terminal area and others at Jalan Ampera 28 (daily 6am–midnight), Jalan Nusantara 6 (6.30am–midnight) and Jalan Trikora 25 (7am–midnight), all of which have fax facilities. To **change money**, head for BNI (Mon–Fri 7am–3pm, Sat 9am–noon), about 100m from the eastern end of Jalan Trikora. For most people the night market at Jalan Pelabuhan (see p.398) will be entertainment enough; otherwise, all of the plusher hotels have karaoke bars.

Both domestic and international departures leave from the **ferry terminal** at the eastern end of Tanjung Balai; all the ticket offices are located just inside the gates. The Pelni agent is CV Putra Karimun Jaya, Jalan Kesatria 1a (☎0777/22850). There are no commercial flights from Bandar Sei Bati, the airport 12km north of Tanjung Balai, although PT Bintan Panormama Tours and Travel, Jalan Trikora 10 (☎ & fax 0777/22060), and PT Pandu Siwi Sentosa, Jalan Trikora 22 (☎0777/22869), are agents for Merpati, Garuda and Bouraq, selling tickets for flights from Batam. SMAC have an office at *Wisma Gloria*, Komplek Gedung Putih (☎0777/21133).

ACCOMMODATION

Most of the **accommodation** caters for the Singaporean weekenders and tends to emphasize facilities rather than ambience or character. Independent Western travellers are extremely rare on the island and there are few places that cater specifically for them.

Wisma Gloria, Komplek Gedung Putih (☎0777/21133, fax 21033). Located at the far eastern end of Tanjung Balai; come out of the ferry terminal car park and turn right along the coast past *Wisma Karimun* – it's about 300m walk up on the hill at the end of the road. Though rather ramshackle and poorly maintained, this place has plenty of character, is convenient for both the port and the town and has some good views from the balconies. ③.

Harmoni, Jl Pelabuhan 55 (☎0777/21099). This street turns into the night market after dark, so if you stay here you'll be right in the thick of things; rooms are very basic with outside bathroom but they have fans and make for one of the few budget options in town. ②.

Wisma Indah, Jl Nusantara 27 (☎0777/21490) Rooms are unexciting, although they have air-con and hot water, but there's an open sitting area on stilts over the water at the back. Fair value in this price bracket. ③.

Wisma Karimun, Pantai Taman Wisata (☎0777/21088, fax 21488). The most economical of the three pricey seafront places, with discounts during the week. You pay for the convenient location, air-con and en-suite hot-water bathrooms rather than the ambience. ④.

Paragon Hotel, Jl Trikora and Jl Nusantara 38b (☎0777/21688, fax 31331). About 400m from the ferry terminal in the heart of the town, this large hotel is a block deep, so has entrances on two roads. It's the most professional place in town, with good-quality rooms, all with air-con and hot-water bathrooms; booking is recommended. ④–⑤.

Hotel Pelangi, Jl Teuku Umar (☎0777/23100, fax 23558). This large setup with reasonable-quality rooms is close to the ferry terminal; walk straight ahead (away from the sea) out of the terminal car park up the hill and the hotel is about 100m up on the left. All rooms have air-con and hot water and there's a moderately priced lobby coffee shop and restaurant. ④–⑥.

Hotel Taman Bunga, Pantai Taman Wisata (☎0777/324088, fax 324388). Right next to the ferry terminal and painted bright turquoise. It's a bustling, lively place catering for a young Singaporean crowd, and all rooms have air-con and hot-water bathrooms attached. ④.

Wisma Tanjung Balai, Jl Nusantara 127b (☎0777/21072). Despite an unpromising, tiny doorway, rooms are adequate and there's a restaurant on stilts over the water at the back. Jl Nusantara is a main shopping street and runs parallel to the water to the west of the terminal; come out of the terminal car park, turn left and left again to get down onto it. ③–④.

EATING

There's an excellent choice of **places to eat** in Tanjung Balai, and prices aren't unduly inflated to take advantage of Singaporean affluence, although if you are going for top-of-the-range seafood options you should find out the prices beforehand. The **night market** on Jalan Pelabuhan, between Jalan Nusantara (just west of BNI) and Jalan Teuku Umar, operates from early until late evening, is extremely popular and great for a whole range of inexpensive Indonesian dishes. If you fancy **Padang food**, head for Jalan Kesatria, which links the eastern end of Jalan Trikora with Jalan Nusantara. There are several places – wander along and see who has the best selection on show.

Do & Me, Jl Nusantara 48. One of the few air-con fast-food places in town. They serve moderately priced fried chicken, and Western options such as lamb chops, sausages, sirloin steak, French fries and baked beans plus a wide range of burgers, ice desserts and drinks.

Pujasera Food Centre, Jl Nusantara. A typical Indonesian food court consisting of several inexpensive food and drink stalls with a sitting area in the middle. The huge bonus here is that the tables at the back overlook the water, so catch the breeze – it's a great place to chill out in the day and watch harbour life.

Siang Malam, Jl Trikora 178. Extremely popular seafood place with tanks outside where you choose your meal – this is one of several seafood stops in this area, not far from the night market. The food is moderate to expensive.

Around the island

Pulau Karimun offers beaches, mountains and a waterfall, all relatively close together and, while none of these features are unmissable on their own, the island is pretty in parts and has largely managed to retain its rural character, despite development. With your own transport or relying on public transport, it's possible to visit Pantai Palawan on the west coast, the inscribed Batu Bersurat stone, and Gunung Jantan and the Pelambung waterfall in the northeast.

As the island is only just over 20km at its longest point, you can cover a fair chunk of it in a day, and the old-style **buses** are a fun way to get around. An alternative is to rent one of the unofficial taxis that hang around in the ferry terminal area; with your own transport and without climbing Gunung Jantan or lingering too long on the beaches, you'll be able to cover the entire island in three to four hours. Bargain hard and you should be able to get car, driver and petrol for Rp80,000–100,000.

There are three main roads from Tanjung Balai and the nearby town of **MERAL,** 10km to the west, to the other points of interest. Minibuses operate from 6am to 10pm between Tanjung Balai and Meral (Rp300), where they stop in or just outside the small but hectic bus terminal in the centre of town and from where you can catch buses north. The road between Tanjung Balai and Meral is busy and uninteresting – the south of the island is flat and built-up and there's little of interest to stop off for.

The attractive beach of **Pantai Palawan**, a 400-metre-long white-sand curving bay between rocky headlands, is located on the west coast, 20km from Tanjung Balai. The road there isn't particularly attractive: quarries start 5km north of Meral and the coast is dotted with industrial ports. However, from the beach itself the industrial hinterland is invisible and this is a favourite weekend picnic and excursion spot. There are several warung, some open during the week, and there's **accommodation** in one small, nameless, losmen (no phone; ③) which has wood-and-thatch bungalows with verandahs facing the beach, electricity supplied in the evenings by generator, mosquito wire at the windows and attached cold-water mandi. To get here by public transport, take a bus from Meral towards the west-coast settlement of Pangke (Rp1000). Tell the driver where you are heading and you'll be dropped off at the junction with the beach road, 2km before Pangke. From here it's a three-kilometre walk to the beach – you may be able to hitch at the weekends but during the week the road is totally deserted. The alternative is to get one of the unofficial taxis that wait outside the ferry terminal at Tanjung Balai; expect to pay about Rp25,000 per person each way if you bargain well. Be sure to make the pick-up arrangements when you get there, as there are no phones.

The road to the small settlement of **PASIR PANJANG** at the northern end of the island, 26km from Tanjung Balai, passes to the west of Gunung Jantan, the only real hill on the island. The foothills are attractively forested, and this part of the island feels very distant from the hustle and bustle of the south. The reason to visit the north is the beach, 2km beyond Pasir Panjang, where the **Batu Bersurat** stone bears an ancient Malay inscription. There are various interpretations of the inscription – one theory is that it is graffiti carved by a Buddhist monk. To one side of the inscription, the indentations in the rock are said to be the footsteps of Lord Buddha himself, making it something of a pilgrimage spot, adorned with white cloths and other offerings. The entire area is being quarried and you'll only be able to visit the beach and stone on Sundays, when there's no blasting in the area.

If you want to visit **Gunung Jantan**, the highest point on the island at 439m, and the waterfall, **Air Terjun Pelambung** (also known as Air Terjun Pongkar), you'll need to travel up the east-coast road. There's a bus from Tanjung Balai to Pongkar and a minibus from Tanjung Balai to Pasar PN (also known as Kota PN and Teluk Uma), 12km up the coast, and then another bus on north. About 1km before Pongkar, a small nondescript village, a wide asphalted road leads inland from a spot called Bukit Pongkar, up towards the mountain – this is the road that maintenance vehicles use to access the telecommunications tower at the top. It's 5km to the summit, from where there are good views to Singapore and Malaysia. Alternatively, there's a path to the top from the Air Terjun Pelambung waterfall; you'll need to take someone to show you the way, as it's pretty overgrown and very muddy. To reach Air Terjun Pelambung, follow the main road through Pongkar; it turns into a track after about 1km and there's a flooded tin quarry on the sea side and a small warung and parking spot on the left. The foreground isn't particularly attractive, but there are good views offshore to the northeast to the island of Karimun Kecil (Small Karimun), also known as Karimun Anak (Child of Karimun). From here it's a 700-metre walk along a mostly concreted path to the waterfall where water tumbles about 15m down a jumble of rocks into a concreted pool. There are several stalls, the rubbish is depressing and the humidity and mosquitoes unenticing.

Pulau Kundur

Situated just south of Karimun and southwest of both Singapore and Batam, **Pulau Kundur** is the furthest of the Riau Islands on the tourist trail, a laid-back spot where it's quite easy to get off the beaten track for a few restful days. It isn't a visa-free entry point, however, and arrivals from Singapore must clear immigration in Tanjung Balai.

Tanjung Batu

The main town, **TANJUNG BATU**, is situated on the southeast coast, separated from nearby Pulau Unggar by a narrow strait. Concentrated just behind the port area, it has wide streets, plenty of shops and a relaxed atmosphere. There's little specific to see apart from **Giri Shanti**, one of many Chinese temples, on the coast on the northeast side of town. It's a spectacular spot for catching the breeze, there are tables on the balcony outside, and the temple has fabulous doors, decorated with images of fierce guardian deities, and an intriguing grotto altar guarded by a tiger statue.

The town has several **accommodation** options, but prices here are inflated by the proximity of Singapore. At the top of the scale, *Hotel Gembira*, Jalan Usman Harun 18h (☎0779/21888, fax 21474; ④–⑤), is the largest and most professional setup; it's the blue-and-white multi-storey building close to the river, visible as the ferry approaches the dock. They accept credit cards and can arrange a taxi service (Rp15,000 per hour in town, Rp25,000 outside). More economical alternatives are *Wisma Tanjung Batu*, Jalan Usman Harun 22 (☎0779/21788, fax 21572; ③–④) and *Wisata Lipo*, Jalan Pemuda 3 (☎0779/21076; ③), in the same road as the ferry terminal. In both places all rooms have air-con and attached bathrooms, the pricier ones with hot water. The cheapest option in town is *Penginapan Indah*, Jalan Sudirman Blok C, 1–2 (☎0779/21267), which is central and has reasonably clean, tiny rooms but is rather noisy.

For informal **eating**, the night market at Jalan Merdeka near the clock tower at the junction with Jalan Sudirman operates from early evening until late. It's large, with a huge variety of food – you could put together a seven-course meal if you had the inclination. For something more formal, Jalan Besar, parallel to Jalan Sudirman towards the northeast side of town, is lined with Chinese restaurants, and Jalan Sudirman itself has plenty of *kedai kopi* for basic breakfasts and daytime snacks. *Gembira Restaurant*, attached to the hotel of the same name, is located right on the water's edge, some tables having good views of the bustle of the wharves and across to Pulau Unggar. You can eat here economically by sticking to fried rice and noodles – the chicken, prawns and seafood are in the moderate to expensive range.

There are no **exchange** facilities on the island, so make sure you bring enough cash. The **post office** (Mon–Thurs 8am–2pm, Fri 8–11am, Sat 8am–12.30pm) is at Jalan Kartini 44, a **wartel** (daily 7am–11pm) at Jalan Sudirman 43. There are no **vehicle rental** companies but inquire at your hotel if you want to rent a motorcycle, for which you can expect to pay around Rp25,000 a day. For car rental, either inquire at your hotel – the *Gembira* (see above) has fixed rates – or negotiate with the unofficial taxis that hang around on Jalan Pemuda, just up from the ferry terminal, bargain very hard. All **ferries** leave from the terminal at the end of Jalan Pemuda in Tanjung Batu and the ticket offices are here.

Around the island and nearby

The island sights are pretty much limited to **beaches**. Some are attractive with white sand, but much of the island is ringed by mangrove swamp. The other problem is that the tin-dredging platforms, clearly visible off most of the coast, churn up the sea bottom so that the water is essentially dark-brown sludge. Around 3km southwest of town, **Gading** can be reached by ojek (Rp3000): there's no public transport. It's a pleasant enough beach with a forest behind and a grave – a local pilgrimage spot – at the far end. The sweeping white-sand bay of **Lubuk**, 4km from town (Rp1000 by bus from Jalan Merdeka, Rp5000 by ojek) has a small village and a Chinese temple behind. Inland from the village, a short climb through the forest leads to **Siamban Hill**; you'll need to ask for directions. Take a picnic – there's a shelter at the top and a rock-pool for bathing on the way. Further up the west coast, 18km from Tanjung Batu, **Sawang** (Rp1000 by bus) is another small village with a beach. Further north from here, **Pantai Mata Air** is one of the more attractive beaches, with dramatic rocks in the water and onshore. Heading

towards the north of the island the land is increasingly devastated by the quarry work-
ings for granite and sand, and there's no major forest cover left.

Over on the east coast, the village of **URUNG** has an attractive market area and a
large Chinese temple, Vihara Maitri Segara. From here it's possible to get the local
ferry to **Pulau Belat** just across a small strait – you can take an ojek across the island
to another ferry on the northeast coast, over to Sungai Utan on Pulau Papan, which has
some sulphur springs. From Tanjung Batu there are plenty of small local ferries that
cross the Ungger Strait to Alai on **Pulau Ungger**, from where you can take an ojek or
bus across to the other coast to see a small arrangement of stones that are said to have
magical properties.

Pulau Batam

Apart from its proximity to Singapore, just 20km at the closest point, and usefulness as
a major staging post on to Indonesia, there's little to recommend **Pulau Batam** to travellers, and nothing to make staying here overnight a worthwhile experience, unless
you can afford top-class accommodation or can arrange one of the excellent deals available in Singapore.

For much of its **history**, Batam was a jungle-covered island, surrounded by mangrove swamp, its few inhabitants making a living from the sea. Things have changed
dramatically in the last decade, as Singapore's labour shortage has caused it to look to
the surrounding areas for manufacturing bases. There are now numerous joint ventures between the Singapore government and Indonesian companies, and people from
throughout Indonesia are flocking here for work – the population of 100,000 may well
increase twentyfold in the next few years.

Just as the thrust for industrial development has come from Singapore, so the tourist
industry is developing its facilities to cater for stressed Singaporeans seeking weekend
breaks in top-class accommodation, or the ministrations of Indonesian prostitutes, now
that the AIDS scare has frightened them away from the Thai border towns. The island
boasts several excellent **golf courses**, where visitors can play – for a price. **Getting
around** the island isn't easy or efficient on public transport. Regardless of what hotels

---

MOVING ON FROM PULAU BATAM BY SEA

There are several ferry terminals on Batam. The **domestic** and **international ferry** terminals at **Sekupang** are about 200m apart. The route to Nagoya is to the right from
either terminal. The international terminal features a bank and post office and departures are highly organized. An electronic board announces the time of the next
Singapore (World Trade Centre) departure – they operate every thirty minutes from
7.30am to 7pm, with an 8pm final departure in each direction Monday to Wednesday.

The **international ferry terminal at Nongsa** (☎0778/761777) operates six crossings
a day (8am–6pm) to and from Tanah Merah terminal in Singapore. The **Waterfront
ferry terminal**, Teluk Senimba, has fourteen daily ferries to the World Trade Centre in
Singapore, operating 7.40am to 7.40pm from Singapore and 8.45am–8.30pm from Batam.
There's also a ferry service from **Batu Ampar** to Singapore (World Trade Centre) with
nine crossings daily 8am to 8pm. This is the latest service on offer, 8.15pm Singapore
time to Batam and 8.20pm from Batam to Singapore. The **Pelni boat**, *KM Sirimau*, operates from Batam. Booking is through Pelni agent, Andalan Aksa Tour, Komplek New
Holiday, Block B, 9 (☎0778/454181, fax 456443).

The arrival and departure point for Tanjung Pinang on Pulau Bintan is **Telaga Punggur**
on the east coast. Ferries operate every fifteen minutes from 8am to 5pm. No bus service
operates to Telaga Punggur, so you'll need to use taxis: expect to pay Rp15,000 between
the terminal and Nongsa, Rp15,000–20,000 to Nagoya and Rp30,000 to Sekupang.

tell you, there are public buses between main centres from the bus terminal in Jodoh but they are irregular, and operate only in daylight hours. However, there are services between Batu Ampar and Nagoya and from Sekupang to Bengkong via Nagoya. Most local people use share taxis for local hops – they'll pull up if they see you by the road – but for longer trips you'll end up taking your own taxi. You'll have to bargain hard, as there are no meters. The **Batam Tourist Promotion office**, Jalan R.E. Martadinata (Mon–Thurs 8am–2pm, Fri 8–11am, Sat 8am–12.30pm; ☎0778/322852), is in a row of shops, that also features a travel agent, to the left across the car park as you exit the international terminal at Sekupang.

Nagoya

Situated on the northeast coast of the island, the main town on Batam is **NAGOYA**, also named Lubuk Baja (Pirate's Waterhole). Soulless, and inconvenient for all transport points, the town has little to recommend it, although you may find yourself spending an (expensive) night here if you miss ferry connections at some point. Designated for commercial and administrative development, **Batam Centre** is a few kilometres southeast of Nagoya. At present it comprises just a couple of shopping centres, not even good ones at that, so there's little reason to come.

ACCOMMODATION

Your choice of **accommodation** is between luxury hotels and resorts, lower-quality places catering for less affluent Indonesian businesspeople in Nagoya and the grossly overpriced basic losmen, many of which charge by the hour, also in Nagoya. Make sure you know what currency you are being quoted because Singapore dollars (S$) are widely used throughout the island, although you can pay in either currency to settle your bill. It's worth repeating that the best rates are available from Singapore (see the box on p.396) and if you do arrive on spec or book independently, especially midweek, then you should seek discounts of up to fifty percent of the walk-in price. At the time of writing, *Palm Beach*, the only resort up on the north coast above Sekupang, was undergoing extensive renovation but will be worth checking out when finished.

Batam View Beach Resort, Jl Hang Lekir, Nongsa (☎0778/761740, fax 761747). Accommodation is in a five-storey block, but the rooms are saved by attractive wooden floors and great views from floor-length glass windows and some have balconies. The pool is a good size but a bit shadeless and there are white-sand beaches nearby. This is a bustling place with plenty of activities on offer, including massage, fishing and special deals at nearby golf courses. ⑨.

Wisma Bougenville, Komplek Nagoya Business Centre, Block 11, 28/29 (☎0778/426682, fax 424909) One of the most economical places in town. The cheapest rooms have fan and cold-water bathroom attached and the more expensive have hot water and air-con. ③–④.

Wisma Garuda Mas, Komplek Jaya Putra Batam, Block D, 11–12 (☎0778/424130). With attached bathroom (cold-water), air-con and TV, many of the rooms are windowless but this place is convenient and clean. ④.

Hilltop Hotel, Jl Ir Sutami 8 (☎0778/322482, fax 322211). This is the closest development to Sekupang and boasts a great situation on a hill with excellent views. Rooms are simple but well furnished, the pool is a good size and surrounded by attractive gardens and this is one of the most relaxed options, although well away from other facilities. ⑧–⑨.

Mandarin Regency, Jl Imam Bonjol 1 (☎0778/458899, fax 458057). This is the classiest hotel in Nagoya, with a grand yet relaxed look and feel, extremely comfortable rooms, all the facilities and eating options to be expected at this end of the range, and a good-sized pool in the central courtyard. ⑨.

Hotel Nagoya Plaza, Jl Imam Bonjol (☎0778/459888, fax 456690). Without a swimming pool or fitness centre, this hotel has all the other luxury facilities, with an attractive lobby and a pleasant atmosphere. ⑧–⑨.

Hotel New Holiday, Jl Imam Bonjol (☎0778/459308, fax 459306). One of the best hotels in town with a third-floor swimming pool, several restaurants, a fitness centre, bar and karaoke lounge. There's a pleasant atmosphere and lots of shops in the huge reception area. ⑨.

Nongsa Beach (☎0778/761913). Attached to *Setia Budi* restaurant, which serves basic inexpensive food close to the beach; an unsigned track 500m west of *Sei Nongsa* runs about 500m to the beach. Accommodation is in extremely small basic rooms: there's a bed, fan and little else, in a block with mandi outside. However, it's right by the beach and is the cheapest place on the coast. ③.

Nongsa Point Marina (☎0778/761333, fax 761348). At the top end of the luxury market, catering for yacht owners who fancy a few days ashore. The hotel accommodation overlooks the marina and there are rooms and two- to three-bedroom chalets on offer – with wooden floors and comfortable furnishings. ⑨.

Pura Jaya Beach Resort, Jl Hang Lekir, Nongsa (☎0778/761435, fax 761438). This is a very classy addition to the island. Public areas are open, light and airy with high ceilings and an elegant wooden finish. There are several restaurants and bars and the pool is a well-designed landscape of small, intersecting pools complete with bridges and palm trees near the beach (the white sand is imported from Bintan). ⑨.

Puri Garden, Jl Teuku Umar (☎0778/458888, fax 456333). Comfortable, but without the flashiness or facilities (no pool) of the pricier places. The rooms are small but have good facilities. ⑧–⑨.

Sei Nongsa, Pantai Bahagia, Nongsa (☎0778/761909, fax 761914). Wood-and-thatch cottages with verandahs, air-con and attached bathrooms in a compound close to the beach. There's a small pool. ⑤–⑥.

Wisma Taman Sari, Complex Nagoya Centre, Block A, 6–8 (☎0778/423395, fax 427478). Small rooms with very thin partitions but attached bathrooms and air-con. ③.

Turi Beach Resort, Nongsa (☎0778/761080, fax 761042). Built on a hillside behind the beach, accommodation is in wood-and-thatch chalets, and there are large open-sided public areas on several levels. There's a large curved pool and a huge number of activities on offer. ⑨.

Waterfront City (☎0778/381067, fax 381059; booking also through 1 Maritime Square 02-13, Singapore, ☎065/2765179, fax 2765536). On the coast south of Sekupang, served by its own ferry terminal, this enormous site is set to develop as the premier activity resort on Batam. Water-skiing, jet skiing, paragliding, bungy-jumping, paintball, all-terrain vehicles and, most exotically, an inside ski slope, complete with artificial snow, are available – at a price. For example, ski lessons are Rp20,000–25,000 for 30min, bungy-jumping S$49. Special deals, which include some activities in the all-in price, are a possibility here. ⑦–⑨.

EATING

Staying in the resorts pretty much limits you to eating there unless you have your own transport or use taxis. If you are staying in Nagoya, there are plenty of authentic Indonesian **restaurants** and prices are fair – in the evening a good **night market** sets up at Pujasera Mira, next to the *Mandarin Regency Hotel* on Jalan Imam Bonjol, where good-priced sate, soup, noodles, rice and drinks are available in relaxed surroundings.

Es Teler, Komplex TG Pantun, Block X. Ever-popular Indonesian fast-food, juice and ice-cream chain with some Indonesian soups and snacks.

Food centre, Komplex New Holiday. With plenty of counters selling seafood, Chinese and Indonesian food, plus coffee and assorted drinks, this place is constantly busy and has a good, buzzy atmosphere.

Gardino, Komplex TG Pantun, Block N, 9. A small bakery with cakes and sweet breads and a few tables in case you want to eat in.

KFC, Komplex TG Pantun. Follow the unmissable signs if you want highly priced chicken and French fries served in savagely cool air-con. The prices displayed don't include tax.

Nusantara Coffee House, *Mandarin Regency Hotel*. Plush surroundings and seamless service with good but expensive food – curries and stir-fries for Rp12,000–15,000 up to pepper steak at Rp30,000. Tax and service aren't included in the price.

Saraso, Komplex New Holiday, Block E, 6. A small place, popular with local people and serving good-quality, inexpensive Padang food.

Simpang Tiga, Komplex TG Pantun, Block EE, 1. This large Padang place is popular and offers good-value food.

LISTINGS

Airline offices Bouraq, Jl Imam Bonjol, Komplek Bumi Ayu Lestari, Block A, 3, Nagoya (☎0778/421830, fax 452788); Garuda, Jl Imam Bonjol, Danagraha Building, Levels 1 & 3, Nagoya (☎0778/458620, fax 452515); Merpati, Komplek Jodoh Square, Block A, 1, Nagoya (☎0778/457288, fax 453187).

Banks and exchange BCA, Jl Raja Ali Haji 18; Bank Rakyat Indonesia, Jl Imam Bonjol 8/9. The gold shops on and behind Jl Imam Bonjol operate as moneychangers if you have cash; Tanjung, Komplek Bumi Indah, Block I, 9.

Golf Day membership is available at golf clubs, but is expensive. At the Indah Puri Golf Club, for example, green fees are S$90 for eighteen holes during weekdays, S$130 at weekends, plus caddy, trolley, clubs and shoe rental.

Hospitals Rumah Sakit Rita, Jl Sekupang (☎0778/323931), and Rumah Sakit Otorita Batam, Jl Dr Cipto Mangunkusumo (☎0778/322121).

Immigration office Jl Laki L.R.E. Maradinata (☎0778/322036).

Post office The main post office is at Jl Sudirman at Batam Centre. In Nagoya, the post office is on the second floor of the row of shops after the *Hotel Nagoya Plaza* – the sign points up to Mesjid Arafah.

Telephone Wartels (7.30am–midnight): PT Tandiguna Utama, Komplek TG Pantun, Block E, 5; Kelabang Sakti, Komplek New Holiday, Block B, 7/8; and Mahligai Sari, Komplek Nagoya Business Centre, Block IV, 34 (24hr).

Pulau Bintan and beyond

Situated less than 10km from Batam at the closest point, **Pulau Bintan** is about two and a half times the size of Singapore, which seems to have left plenty of room for **traditional culture** to survive alongside the plush tourist development. For this reason there's much to recommend it: not only is it more attractive than other nearby islands, but there's much more of an Indonesian feel about the place and things are reasonably priced. Visitor numbers look set to rocket: in 1995, around 30,000 tourists came, and this number more than tripled in 1996. However, for independent travellers, especially those on a budget, the delight of Bintan is that **Tanjung Pinang** the main town on Pulau Bintan has been largely untouched by the tourist influx and, with the most aggressive development confined to the massive Bintan Resort enclave on the north coast, the low-key guest houses of **Trikora** on the east coast continue to cater for those who want a few days of sun and sand.

Historically, Bintan was far more significant than Batam. In the sixteenth century the ruler of Malacca, defeated by the Portuguese, fled to Bintan with his court. Although the court then moved several times, to Johor and Lingga, a branch of the royal family settled on Pulau Penyengat, a tiny island within sight of Tanjung Pinang.

Tanjung Pinang

Lying on the southeast coast of the island, the traditional capital of the Riau Islands, **TANJUNG PINANG**, is an attractive bustling port town with an excellent market, good tourist facilities and brilliant transport links throughout Indonesia – rather better than those on the island itself – it's often quicker to get to Singapore than to cross the island on a public bus. However, there's plenty of accommodation in all price ranges in the town and many of the sea departures leave from the centrally located ferry port.

There are a few sights in the town itself although **Pasar Baru**, between Jalan Merdeka and the harbour, is undoubtedly the gem. This is a terrific traditional Indonesian market: tiny alleyways are lined with shops and stalls selling mountains of exotic food, household goods, textiles, tools and religious artefacts, all scrutinized by determined local shoppers. It's a colourful and invigorating scene.

MOVING ON FROM PULAU BINTAN

The **international and domestic ferry terminals** are on the coast at Tanjung Pinang, with the ticket offices ranged in the terminal area and along Jalan Merdeka. There are connections throughout southern Sumatra and on to Java. For **Pulau Batam**, ferries operate every fifteen minutes from 8am to 5pm between Tanjung Pinang and Telaga Punggur on the east coast of Batam. **Bandar Bentan Telani** is the ferry terminal in Bintan Resort, with connections only with Tanah Merah ferry terminal on Singapore.

There are several **Pelni sailings** to and from Pulau Bintan, which give access to the entire archipelago: they operate out of Kijang on the southeast corner of the island and all boats operate on a two-weekly cycle. The Pelni agent in Tanjung Pinang is Netra Service Jaya, Jalan Pos 1 (☎0771/21384, fax 22114).

Flights leave from Kijang airport, 15km southeast of Tanjung Pinang. The airlines don't have offices in town, so book through the agent, PT Pinang Jaya, Jalan Bintan 44 (☎0771/21267, fax 22046).

The town has a large Chinese trading population and there are plenty of red-and-gold **temples** with smoking incense, fierce dragons and serene statues of Chinese goddesses. One of the most attractively situated and atmospheric temples – with Kuan Yin, the goddess of mercy, in pride of place – is on the harbourfront looking across the water at the end of the most easterly jetty, Jalan Pelantar II, and Vihara Bahtra Sasana, at the top end of Jalan Merdeka. The **Riau Kandil Museum**, Jalan Bakar Batu, is currently closed; ask at the tourist office for the latest information.

The Tanjung Pinang **tourist office** is at Jalan H. Agus Salim (☎0771/25373) and the main post office is at Jalan Brigjenkatamso 122. All poste restante should be sent here; they don't get many tourists using the service, but staff are helpful and efficient. The **Telkom** office is at Jalan Hang Tuah 11 (7am–midnight). The **bus terminal** is Batu Tujuh (Stone Seven) on the outskirts of town; bemos ply between the town centre and the terminal (Rp300) from 6am to 10pm and public buses operate to Kijang (1hr), Trikora (1–2hr) and Tanjung Uban (2hr) during daylight hours, but are irregular and infrequent.

ACCOMMODATION

There's a good range of **accommodation** in Tanjung Pinang, from luxury operations to much more basic, budget places. The budget mainstays are the **homestays** on Jalan Lorong Bintan II, which connects Jalan Samudera and Jalan Bintan.

Bintan Beach Resort, Jl Pantai Impian 1 (☎0771/23661, fax 23661). This is the only resort conveniently close to Tanjung Pinang, 5km from the ferry terminal. There are great coastal views, a big pool and plenty of activities on offer including island tours. All rooms and public areas are comfortable, the deluxe rooms with verandahs being especially appealing. ⑦–⑧.

Bong's, Johnny's and **Rommel's**, Jl Lorong Bintan II (no phones). These are all very similar basic, budget homestays with rooms in family houses. They are close together but poorly signed – inquire when you get into the street. ②.

Furia, Jl Merdeka 6 (☎0771/29922, fax 29955). A clean, tiled, new option, just opposite the harbour exit. All rooms have hot water and air-con. ⑥.

Wisma Gunung Bintan Jaya, Jl Samudera 38 (☎0771/29288). A three-storey building just at the exit from the harbour area. It's clean, and although the rooms are small, they all have hot water and air-con, and couldn't be any closer to the ferry. ⑥.

Laut Jaya Hotel, Jl Pelantar II 98 (☎0771/311471, fax 311473). Clean new place overlooking the water right at the sea end of the market, a short walk on from *Riau Holidays Indah*. ⑥–⑦.

Riau Holidays Indah, Jl Pelantar II 53 (☎ & fax 0771/22715) The entrance in the new market, Pasar Baru, is unpromising, but this place extends far back in various courtyards. The rooms are adequate, but the real delight are the verandahs at the back and the upstairs terraces overlooking the harbour and across to Senggarang. ⑥.

Royal Palace Hotel, Jl Adi Sucipto km10 (☎0771/41234, fax 41111). With grand public rooms, a sweeping staircase, lots of dark wood and stained glass, the dated feel here is part of the charm. Rooms are comfortable without being showy, and there's a good-sized swimming pool. ⑦–⑧.

Surya, Jl Bintan (☎0771/21811). This is a good budget choice with just a few fan rooms, some with and some without attached mandi, set around a small garden. Get a room as far from the busy road as you can. ②–③.

Tanjung Pinang, Jl Pos 692 (☎0771/21236, fax 21379). One of the biggest, most-advertised, mid-range places, this is conveniently located in the middle of the market area and has a big range of rooms, all with air-con and TV but little personality. ⑤.

EATING, DRINKING AND ENTERTAINMENT

Stella is a popular **disco** opposite the *Paradise Hotel* on the outskirts of town, but other than this Tanjung Pinang doesn't exactly throb with excitement after dark.

There are several **night markets** in town: there's a convenient little one at the entrance to the harbour area on Jalan Hang Tuah, and another, Kedai Harapan Jaya, just outside the entrance to the *Laut Jaya Hotel* at the end of Jalan Pelantar II, but the biggest in town is at **Bintan Mall** (daily 5pm–2am), on the outskirts of town next to the *Paradise Hotel* and near the main post office. Most food here is inexpensive, but check prices of more exotic seafood before you commit yourself or you may get a surprise.

Ayam Goreng 88, Bintan Mall. Air-con, fast-food place offering fried chicken, fish and fries, plus basic Indonesian staples and drinks. The food is moderately priced and not outstanding, but the air-con can be appealing on a hot day.

Bintan Indah 99, Bintan Mall, Jl Pos. There are various stalls in this small, popular food centre at the entrance to Bintan Mall.

Damai Baru, Jl Merdeka 69. One of many open-fronted coffee shops that dot the town – great places to watch the world go by, although rather hot and noisy.

Roti Saiman Perancis, Bintan Mall Blok A-7. A branch of the Jambi bakery, they stock a well-presented, good-quality range of sweet breads, savouries and cakes at moderate prices, that you can eat in or take away.

Suka Ramai, Jl Merdeka 18. On the second floor above a shop, the menu is varied and moderately priced, with Indonesian favourites, fish and steaks, plus plenty of drinks.

LISTINGS

Banks and exchange BCA, Jl Temiang 27–29; BNI, Jl Teuku Umar 630; BDN, Jl Teuku Umar 23; Lippo Bank, Jl Merdeka 11. Jl Merdeka is lined with moneychangers, who will change Singapore and US dollars cash.

Bookshop Ganesha Bookshop, Jl Merdeka 76, gets the *Jakarta Post* daily.

Car rental Inquire at your accommodation, but you should be able to get a decent vehicle, such as a Kijang with or without driver, for Rp125,000 a day.

Hospitals Rumah Sakit Umum, Jl Sudirman 795 (☎077121733); Rumah Sakit Angkatan Laut, Jl Ciptadi (☎0771/25805)

Immigration Jl Jend A. Yani 31 (☎0771/21034); there's also an office on the ferry pier.

Souvenirs There isn't a great choice of souvenirs in town, but Sangga Budaya, Jl Teuku Umar 5 (opposite Bank Rakyat Indonesia), is an Aladdin's cave of items both new and old from across the archipelago. Embong Fatimah at the corner of Jl Samudera and Jl Merdeka, just at the exit to the ferry terminal area, also stocks a range of new wooden, basketware and textile items.

Supermarket Yupiter, Jl Merdeka 60.

Telephone office Jl Hang Tuah 11 (7am–midnight).

Travel agents PT Pinang Jaya, Jl Bintan 44 (☎0771/21267, fax 22046); Bintan Panorama, Jl Bakar Baru 50a (☎0771/21894, fax 22572); New Oriental, Jl Merdeka 61 (☎0771/521614, fax 24145) for ferry tickets to Singapore; Osaka, Jl Merdeka 43 (☎0771/21829), also for ferry tickets to Singapore.

The beaches

At **TRIKORA**, on the east coast of Pulau Bintan, the beach area covers around 30km of coastline comprising bay after palm-fringed bay. The disadvantage is that, when the tide goes out, it goes quite a long way, leaving dull-looking flats.

The accommodation begins 5km north of the small, attractive village of **KAWAL**, situated at the point where the main trans-island road reaches the east coast, and where many of the houses are built over the river on stilts. Heading north from Kawal, the first accommodation is at *Bukit Berbunga Cottages* (no phone; ③), where there's just a hand-painted sign on the road and a hundred metre track leads down to the wood-and-thatch cottages with attached mandi, mattresses on the floor and electricity at night. Just 200m north, *Yasin's Guest House* (☎0771/26770; ②–③) has three types of wood-and-thatch chalets on offer, all with verandahs, from small ones without attached mandi to large options with shower and toilet attached. There's a restaurant serving inexpensive Indonesian food, and a charter boat is available for snorkelling trips to nearby islands. Another kilometre north, *Trikora Beach Resort* (☎0771/24454, fax 24455; ⑥–⑧) is the most upmarket place on this coast, with attractive gardens, good views to offshore islands, and accommodation in comfortable bungalows with verandah, air-con and hot water. A moderately priced restaurant serves Indonesian and Chinese food, and bicycles are available for rental. In the next bay, *Restaurant Pantai II* is a series of wooden houses on stilts built over the water and joined by wooden walkways, whose extensive menu offers moderate to expensive prawn, chicken and fish dishes. Heading 2km north, *Shady Shack* (☎ & fax 0771/29734, or book in Singapore ☎065/5657207, fax 5602631; ⑤) caters largely for Singaporean visitors in wood-and-thatch cottages with outside mandi; you need to book so that food can be organized. Snorkelling gear and boats are available for rental. Currently, there's no development further north, although one of the best beaches on the coastline, Trikora Tiga, is 10km beyond *Shady Shack*. It consists of several kilometres of glorious white sand, gently lapped by turquoise waters. At the weekends, several warung open up to cater for day-trippers from around the island, but during the week it's pretty much deserted.

Around 16km off the east coast of Bintan, **Pulau Mapur** has long white beaches, rocky headlands and very few visitors. There's basic accommodation at *Ronny's Guesthouse* (no phone; ④) towards the northern tip of the island (ask at *Rommel's Homestay* in Tanjung Pinang for information), or inquire in the villages for homestays near the most popular beaches of Pantai Belakang on the north coast or Pantai Songsing on the east. It takes an hour to get to the island on one of the local boats that ply throughout the day from Kijang, the ferry port on the southeast corner of Bintan.

A huge section of the island, covering the entire northern coastline, an area half the size of Singapore, has been designated as the **Bintan Resort**, known as Lagoi locally, with over three hundred lots of land ready for development. It's a huge and grand concept, and a massive example of the type of tourist development that aims to separate tourists from local people as securely as possible – for whose protection is never entirely clear. Bintan Resort has its own **ferry terminal** at Bandar Bentan Telani serving Tanah Merah terminal on Singapore, and its own extremely good road and transport system. However, only one rutted and decaying nine-kilometre road links Bintan Resort to the rest of the island, along which there's no public transport, and it's watched over by several security checkposts, and anyone taking rental cars outside the resort area to the rest of the island pays a premium. Within the resort, **car rental** is available from *Indorent* (☎0771/91931); they have a counter at Bandar Bentan Telani and offer everything from two-hourly rental with or without driver to daily and longer rental of 59-seater coaches. A four-seater jeep costs US$100 per day excluding driver or petrol. If you don't want to rent transport, a **shuttle bus** service operates between the hotels and the ferry terminal (S$3–9) and is especially timed for getting to and from your accommodation as well as moving between the hotels for lunch and dinner.

BINTAN RESORT ACCOMMODATION

Banyan Tree (☎0771/26918, fax 81348, or book in Singapore ☎065/3254193, fax 2266128). This is the most tasteful, stylish and refined establishment, with accommodation in beautifully decorated private villas that have a private outside Jacuzzi or swimming pool. There are several top-class restaurants here, a private health spa, and a sailing boat for charter. Walk-in prices start from S$580 at weekends. ⑨.

Club Med (☎0771/92801, fax 92826). Part of the international hotel chain, there are almost three hundred rooms, two pools, a spa and a wide range of sports facilities, including a range of watersports. Good facilities for small children. ⑨.

Mana Mana (☎0771/20195, fax 20196). This bustling place is big on watersports and activities, and is the liveliest and least expensive of the resorts. Accommodation is in wood-and-tile cottages, which are comfortable without being plush, and there's a thriving watersports centre (jet skiing Rp136,000 per hour, windsurfing Rp25,000–34,000 per hour; dives for qualified divers from Rp59,500) and tennis courts. Surfing is possible in February and March, diving is best in April. ⑨.

Mayang Sari (☎ 0778/323088, fax 0778/323080, or book in Singapore ☎065/7328515, fax 7323959). The most westerly resort offers accommodation right on the beach, in fabulously high-ceilinged, simply but stylishly decorated cottages in cream and dark wood with a verandah overlooking the gardens. This is a quiet, elegant place, but there's no pool – visitors use the facilities at nearby *Mana Mana*. Meals in the restaurant cost S$15–25. ⑨.

Hotel Sedona (☎0771/91388, fax 91399, or book in Singapore ☎065/3373577, fax 3376668). The largest setup, at Bintan Lagoon, with over four hundred rooms in four-storey blocks. Public areas are huge and busy, there are six restaurants and snack bars, a large swimming pool, a health spa and leisure centre. Plenty of other activities are also on offer, including sea sports, table tennis, table football, and there are bicycles for rental. ⑨.

Sol Elite (☎0770/692505, fax 692516). With a gym, pool, tennis courts, watersports, sauna, traditional massage, business centre, coffee shop, two restaurants and karaoke, this place caters well for stressed executives. ⑨.

Senggarang

Just across the bay, **SENGGARANG** village was originally settled by Bugis people from Sulawesi, with traditional stilted houses over the water. Take a public ferry during daylight hours (10min; Rp500) from Pelantar II, the jetty leading out from the Pasar Baru market area in Tanjung Pinang. From the end of the Senggarang jetty you'll walk several hundred metres inland through the village before you get to dry land. It's pretty picturesque, although the humidity, rubbish smell and mosquitoes can be ghastly.

Once on land, turn left along the road and walk for 200m or so to the local volleyball court. The simple **warung** on the coast side are good places for refreshment, and a huge banyan tree nearby has overtaken a two-storey **Chinese temple**, whose walls are suspended in the roots, with a small shrine still at ground level. A further 200m brings you to the modern Chinese temple, Vihara Tirta Maitreya, at the foot of the shipping beacon. There's little reason to linger, because another couple of hundred metres around the coast is **Vihara Darma Sasana**, a complex of three temples facing seawards: the temple compound is very large and clearly affluent, featuring statues, fountains, ponds and artificial waterfalls galore – often gaudy but with an endearing exuberance. The right-hand temple has a 200-year-old dragon statue on the roof, and the central deity in the smallest temple is Toa Pek Kong, god of the earth – people intending to build a house make offerings here for good fortune in the enterprise.

Pulau Penyenget

Out in the bay, clearly visible from Tanjung Pinang, small **Pulau Penyenget** is well worth a trip for its pleasant and peaceful atmosphere, lovely old buildings and lingering sense of ancient glories. The name means "Wasp Island", and is thought to have come about because of the wasp stings inflicted on early sailors who came ashore for fresh water.

During the eighteenth century, the island was united under the Sultan of Johor. However, in 1804, Sultan Mahmud gave Penyenget to his wife, Raya Hamidah, an action that split the state of Johor into two rival factions: Penyenget and the surrounding islands went on to be ruled by Raya Hamidah's son, while his half-brother took over Lingga. In 1819, Sir Thomas Stamford Raffles persuaded Hamidah's son to give him Singapore in exchange for protection and a stipend from the British. With security and British funds Penyenget became a major centre for Muslim religion and literature – scholars from Mecca came to teach in the mosque and many works of Malay literature were written here. Many of the ruins date from that time, an era regarded as a "Golden Age" when around nine thousand people lived on the island. Many of the current population of around two thousand are descended from the ancient royal family.

Just 2500m long by 750m wide, the island is reached by small **ferry** (daylight hours; 15min; Rp500) from Pelantar I, at the end of Jalan Pos, just around the corner from the small post office in the centre of Tanjung Pinang. There are two jetties on Penyenget, both on the north coast and about 500m apart; boats call at both but it's easiest to orientate yourself if you get dropped at the most westerly near the mosque – you'll see the turrets and creamy paintwork from the water. Allow three or four hours to explore the island, and take plenty of water and some snacks as there are only a few shops. From the jetty, walk through the village built on stilts over the water to dry land. Prior to Dutch colonization, the centre of population was on the southern side of the island, looking away from Tanjung Pinang. However, the people were forced to move to the north, where they could be overseen by the Dutch in Tanjung Pinang.

From the jetty, the road leads straight to **Mesjid Raya Sultan Riau**, which was commissioned by Sultan Abdurrahman in 1832, although not completed until 1844, and is now restored to its turreted and domed glory. The floor is covered with richly patterned prayer mats, fabulously carved old cupboards hold an Islamic library, and in the glass case there's a stunning nineteenth-century Koran. Outside the mosque, a left turning along Jalan Y.D.M.R. Abdurrahman leads past a munitions store, **Gedung Mesiu**, up the hill to the **grave of Raja Abdurrahman**, who lies alongside other royal dignitaries. Follow the path up the left side of the graveyard enclosure, and at the top you'll see the moat walls and a few remaining cannons from the fort of **Bukit Kursi**, built in 1782 at the highest point of the island for defence against Dutch attack during the Riau Wars (1782–1832).

Back on Jalan Y.D.M.R. Abdurrahman, a right turn past the mosque takes you south across the island to **Istana Raja Ali**, the palace of the raja who ruled from 1844 to 1857. It isn't huge by palace standards and is undergoing renovation, but in the grounds there's a map of all the island sights: about a dozen sights are identified, many of them no more than a pile of stones. The path goes through the palace grounds and, continuing out the other side, leads across to the south side of the island. Off to the left of the road across the island are the **graves of Raja Ali** and **Raja Jaafur**, his father, who ruled from 1806 to 1832. Down on the south coast, turn left, and after a couple of hundred metres follow Jalan Nakhoda Ninggal to **Tungku Bilek** (Lady Room), the ruined two-storey house by the sea. It was once inhabited by the sister of one of the sultans and was so named because she was said never to leave her room. Nearby are the remains of other residences and a palace.

On the north side of the island, about 200m east of the mosque, is the **grave of Raja Hamidah**, also known as Engku Puteri, who died in 1844 and is revered as the original owner of the island. This is a place of pilgrimage for Muslims, who believe it to be *keramat*, able to bring about miracles. Of all the graves on the island it's the most lovely, set in a restored yellow-and-green compound with a central mausoleum.

Other ferry excursions

Plenty of other excursions are possible from Tanjung Pinang, if you're willing to char-ter a boat. On the Senggarang side of the inlet, take a boat from the Pelantar II jetty in Tanjung Pinang for an expedition along **Sungai Ular** (Snake River). The river winds inland through mangroves to a small Buddhist temple, with painted murals of the life of Buddha adorning the walls. Ask directions here for the walk to Senggarang, or nego-tiate the boat trip as a return.

Another possible excursion from Tanjung Pinang is to uninhabited **Pulau Sore**, which lies about 8km to the southwest of town. There are attractive white-sand beach-es where you can spend a pleasant day relaxing, but be sure to take all supplies. Negotiations for the return trip from Pelantar I will start at Rp30,000, and make sure you fix the time you want to be collected. **Pulau Terkulai**, about 20km to the north-west, is also attractive, but the Batam ferries pass very close by.

The Lingga Islands

Ranging about 120km either side of the equator, the **Lingga Islands** are a scattered group of hundreds of dots of land, which feature in few travel itineraries despite their great scenery, easy access from Tanjung Pinang or Jambi, quiet charm and the conve-nience of regular (if infrequent) ferry connections. The main islands of the group are **Pulau Lingga** and **Pulau Singkep**, both of which get a handful of visitors and have basic facilities. With a bit of Indonesian, though, you can hop off the boat at one of its ports of call throughout the islands and inquire about accommodation with the kepala desa. Wherever you are heading, and for however long, take enough cash, as there are no exchange facilities on the islands and no tourist offices.

Pulau Lingga and Pulau Penuba

With a torturous shape, few roads and a jungle-covered mountainous interior, **Pulau Lingga** is an enticing place for adventurous visitors. The central towering summit of Gunung Daik (1164m), the highest point in the Riau or Lingga islands, is said never to have been climbed; its shape gives the island its name – *linggam* is Sanskrit for "phal-lus". The island was the base of part of the Riau sultanate in the nineteenth century, when one faction established itself on Pulau Penyenget and the other removed itself here. Many of today's inhabitants are descended from royal families and there are some ancient remains to explore.

The main settlement on the island is **DAIK**, towards the south of the island, a small ramshackle development on the river banks. One route of access is from the north on the daily (except Sun) speedboat from Tanjung Pinang, which docks at Pancur on the east coast. From here it's thirty minutes by sampan (Rp5000 per boat, so the fare depends on the number of passengers) along the river to the end of the road at Resun, and then another thirty minutes (Rp5000) by ojek to Daik. Three times a week there's a speedboat direct to Tanjung Buton, on the coast south of Daik, and from here it's an ojek ride (Rp1500) into town. Small ferries from Pulau Penuba, between Pulau Lingga and Pulau Singkep, go directly up the small river to Daik.

There are a couple of basic **losmen** in Daik – inquire locally – some simple **warung**, a **post office**, but no telephones, no central electricity supply (some places have their own generators) and no exchange facilities. The only public transport on the island is by ojek, but the road system isn't extensive, heading around 20km southeast of Daik. Otherwise, small local boats circle around the coast.

There's little to do in Daik itself apart from enjoy the unhurried pace. Just to the north of town is the nineteenth-century **Mesjid Jamik**: according to local legend, the carver of the fine pulpit was executed after finishing the job so that no one else could ever own such a beautiful work of art. Outside town itself you can walk for an hour or so north to **Istana Damnah**, the palace of Sultan Mahmud, who is buried behind Mesjid Jamik; built a considerable distance inland for protection from pirate raids, the palace was taken by the Dutch in 1911. Much of the building was constructed from wood, which was destroyed when the Dutch attacked, or has rotted over time, but some foundations, remnants of a pavilion, a toilet and parts of a staircase are still discernible. Some of the path is very overgrown, so make sure you get clear directions or take a guide. The old fort, **Bukit Cengkeh**, just off the path to the palace, was built on a hill overlooking the river, but a few ancient cannons are all that remain.

Located in the strait between Pulau Lingga and Pulau Singkep, the small island of **Pulau Penuba**, which features great beaches on both its north and south coasts, is accessible either from Tanjung Buton on Pulau Lingga or Jago on Pulau Singkep: regular public boats run between both destinations during daylight hours. If you're in a rush you can charter, but bargain hard – negotiations will start at around Rp30,000 one way. There are two small, basic places to stay on Pulau Penuba: *The Mess* near the town square (①) and *Penginapan Penuba* (①).

Pulau Singkep

The most southerly of the Lingga chain, **Pulau Singkep** is a large island about 20km south of Pulau Lingga, roughly 35km at its longest and widest points, with the main population centre at **Dabo** in the middle of the east coast. Now a backwater, this once-flourishing island is a terrifically friendly place, great for seeing genuine island life, free from modern industry and the influence of Singapore. Ferry connections to Sumatra leave from here, but the main port for connections north, particularly from Tanjung Pinang, is at Jago, on the northern tip of the island, about 25km by road from Dabo (the bus takes 1hr; Rp3000).

Singkep lacks the ancient royal links of nearby Lingga, but has a history as a **tin** island akin to that of Bangka and Belitung. It was always a smaller player than the other islands but became a commercial producer in 1891 when world demand was at a height; production ceased in the 1980s, as demand and prices fell. These days the inhabitants earn a living from farming, rubber and timber, but many have moved elsewhere for work, particularly north to the new industrial and tourist enclaves of the Riau Islands. There's talk of Riau-style luxury tourism developing down here, but (as yet) no concrete plans.

Dabo

DABO is pretty much a ghost town since the tin company ceased operation, but evidence of its former glory is still apparent in wide, spacious streets and attractive bungalows, and it offers a pleasant, laid-back glimpse of ordinary Indonesian life. If you **arrive** from Jambi you'll dock at the main jetty in town from where it's a short walk to any of the accommodation places. Buses from the port of Jago will drop you at the accommodation of your choice, as will taxis from Bandar Udara Dabo airport (Rp5000), 2km outside town.

There isn't a great amount to do in town. **Cetiya Dharma Ratna** is a new, grand Chinese temple well worth a look for its fabulously colourful murals and statues, the wafting incense helping to create a rich atmosphere. The town jetty is a rather bizarre construction, heading 500m out to sea but obviously made from several sections, so there are some interesting sixty-degree bends part of the way along. Much of the population takes a stroll out here in the late afternoon and there are good views along the sweeping, white-sand, palm-fringed bay, which stretches for several kilometres in each direction.

The main **Telkom office** is about 1km outside town; more convenient is the Singkep Agung 24hr wartel on Jalan Penuba. The **post office** (Mon–Thurs 7.30am–3.15pm, Fri & Sat 7.30am–1.30pm) is on Jalan Pahlawan, about 100m west of the junction with Jalan Kartini and the grand Mesjid Azzulfa mosque. The only **airline** serving the island, SMAC, are on Jalan Pemandian (☎0776/21073). Ferry bookings can be made at Toko Subur Baru, Jalan Pelabuhan 4.

The town offers several **accommodation** options. *Gapura Singkep*, Jalan Perusahaan 41 (☎0776/21136; ②–③), is a two-storey building set back from the road, centrally located with a variety of rooms, all with attached bathroom. At Jalan Bukit Kapitan 1 (☎0776/21139; ②–③), *Sentosa* is a new single-storey place around a small courtyard. Rooms all have attached bathrooms and the most expensive have air-con; the small inexpensive restaurant next door is convenient for dinner. A ten-minute walk west of town, away from the coast, *Wisma Singkep*, Jalan Pemandian 36 (☎0776/21483; ③), is the most relaxing place if you don't mind a walk to town to get food: the rooms are large, all have air-con and bathroom, there are pleasant grounds and big verandahs. For a more personal experience, head for the homestay of Rudolfa Apituley (*Ibu Rein*), at Jalan Kartini 27 (③). She lives in a large old colonial bungalow and has one double room with attached bathroom and three singles with shared bathroom (③). She speaks good English as well as Dutch and her house is busy – she teaches English to local children and the waltz to Chinese ladies. Rudolfa is keen to promote tourism in the area and knows pretty much all there's to know about the island.

There are plenty of **places to eat** in town, including many nameless coffee shops and warung: head for Jalan Pramuka and Jalan Merdeka, north of Jalan Pasar Lama that runs across the centre of town. For a more formal meal, *Gongang Lidah* on Jalan Pelabuhan serves basic, inexpensive Indonesian and Chinese meals.

Around the island

A few buses ply the lanes **around the island**: the nondescript towns of Jago and Raya are the main destinations. If you want to explore independently, inquire at your accommodation or in shops in town; you should be able to pick up a bicycle for about Rp3000 a day, but motorcycle rental is pricey (around Rp4000 an hour).

If you travel outside Dabo, the beach of **Pantai Batu Berdaun**, 4km southwest of town (Rp2000 by ojek), is narrow but long and sweeping, with good views back to Dabo and across to Pulau Lalang off the coast to the south. It's a popular weekend excursion with local people but very quiet in the week, and big enough so that you can get away from the crowds at any time. Closer to town, 3km to the northeast, **Pantai Jodoh** is near enough to walk to fairly easily. Inland, the Batu Hampar **waterfall**, just off the Raya road about 11km from Dabo, is a pleasant spot – you can swim in the pool.

Jambi and around

Most travellers bypass the eastern city of **JAMBI**, the capital of the province of the same name, situated on the south bank of **Sungai Batang Hari**, the longest river in Sumatra. Although there's little to detain visitors to Jambi for long, there are some interesting archeological sites nearby and the city makes a pleasant halt for a couple of days if you're heading east through Sumatra, or are taking the ferry route from/to Pulau Singkep.

Arrival, orientation, information and city transport

The situation with **long-distance bus terminals** is confused, with some arriving and leaving from Simpang Karwat at the junction of Jalan Prof J.M. Yamin and Jalan H.O.S. Cokroaminoto or the bus offices in the roads nearby, and others from the newer

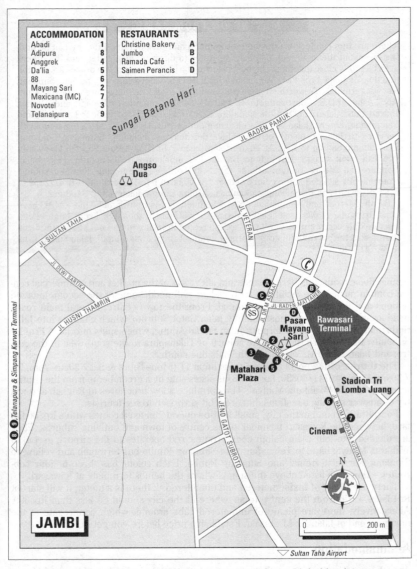

ACCOMMODATION
Abadi	1
Adipura	8
Anggrek	4
Da'lia	5
88	6
Mayang Sari	2
Mexicana (MC)	7
Novotel	3
Telanaipura	9

RESTAURANTS
Christine Bakery	A
Jumbo	B
Ramada Café	C
Saimen Perancis	D

Sungai Batang Hari

Angso Dua

JL RADEN PAMUK

JL VETERAN

JL SULTAN TAHA

JL DEWI SARTIKA

JL HUSNI THAMRIN

Telanaipura & Simpang Karwat Terminal

JL DR M ASSAAT

JL RADEN MATTAHER

Pasar Mayang Sari

Rawasari Terminal

JL ISKANDAR MUDA

Matahari Plaza

Stadion Tri Lomba Juang

JL JEND GATOT SUBROTO

JL HALIM PERDANA KUSUMA

Cinema

N

JAMBI

0   200 m

▽ Sultan Taha Airport

Simpang Rimbo terminal several kilometres west of there. Light-blue bemos run to Rawasari terminal in the centre of town from Simpang Karwat, and yellow bemos from Simpang Rimbo. **Flights** land at Sultan Taha airport, 6km south of the city centre; red bemos operate between the airport and Rawasari terminal in the town centre, and fixed-price taxis charge Rp5000.

The river and the area around the port is the main **orientation** point in Jambi, with Jalan Sultan Taha and Jalan Raden Pamuk running along the southern bank. Just

---

MOVING ON FROM JAMBI

There are **bus** connections throughout Sumatra and Java but the difficulty can be finding out about them, as each company operates to different destination and the offices aren't terribly close together. The best place to start inquiries is at the offices around the junction of Jalan Prof J.M. Yamin and Jalan H.O.S. Cokroaminoto opposite Simpang Karwat terminal. It's worth shopping around a bit to get the departure time you want. ANS, Jalan H.O.S. Cokroaminoto 42 (☎0741/64801), operate to Padang and Medan; Indrah Putri, Jalan H.O.S. Cokroaminoto 22 (☎0741/65502), to Bandar Lampung and Palembang; Lorena, Jalan H.O.S. Cokroaminoto 14 (☎0741/40620), are a big setup with services to Jakarta, plenty of other Java destinations including Surabaya, Solo and Probolinggo and on to Bali. At Toko Melan, Jalan Prof H.M. Yamin 56 (☎0741/60240), you can book straight through to Batam. For departures to Bengkulu, Pekanbaru, Bangko and Muara Bungo, ask at the ticket offices in Simpang Rimbo terminal. Conveniently situated in the centre of town, ACC, Jalan Dr M. Assaat 60 (☎0741/25593), offer departures to Palembang, Pekanbaru, Muara Bungo, Jakarta and Bandung.

By **air**, Merpati and Mandala operate scheduled flights from Jambi while SMAC have some irregular flights (see "Listings" p.416 for offices in the city). From Jambi, Pelni operate only cargo **ships**, but if you are interested in trying to find out about other sailings, ask at the port administration office, Kantor Administrator Jambi, Jalan Sultan Taha 4 (☎0741/22020).

---

behind these roads, the maze of lanes and alleyways of the market and commercial centre contain most of the facilities that travellers will need, some of the accommodation options and the Rawasari bemo terminal. From the town centre, several main roads head away from the river, most usefully Jalan Gatot Subroto, which changes into Jalan Sudirman on the way to the airport; Jalan Sultan Agung, which splits into Jalan Prof Dr Sumantri Brojonegoro through the suburb of Telanapura to the southwest of the centre; and Jalan Prof J.M. Yamin, which leads due south.

The **tourist office** on Jalan Basuki Rachmat 11 (Mon–Thurs & Sat 7.30am–2pm, Fri 7.30am–11am; ☎0741/40330, fax 41733) is accessible by a green bemo from the central terminal; ask for "Walikota Madya". They produce a few brochures in English and will try to answer specific questions, but are a bit surprised to see tourists.

For getting around in the city, small **bemos** operate on fixed routes with a Rp300 flat fare, between the Rawasari terminal in the centre of town and outlying suburbs. They are divided into four main colour-coded routes: red operates to the airport; green, to Walikota Madya; blue, to Telanapura and Simpang Rimbo bus terminal; and yellow, to Simpang Karwat terminal and Simpang Rimbo. Each colour has three or four subroutes – these are listed above the stands where the bemos terminate at Rawasari.

There are plenty of **taxis**, metered and unmetered. If there is a meter, it will start at Rp1350 – a trip from the centre to anywhere in the city should be less than Rp5000. Alternatively, there are plenty of unmetered cabs around, which congregate at the northern end of Jalan Dr M. Assaat. Establish a price before you get in.

Accommodation

As with most Sumatran cities, the **accommodation** scene is dominated by hotels catering for business travellers, although it's possible to find reasonable budget accommodation. Most hotels are located in the central area, either on and around Jalan Jend Gatot Subroto or up Jalan Halim Perdana Kusuma, with some alternatives in the southwestern suburb of Telanapura, where the exterior grandeur and character of some places is unfortunately not reflected in the rooms.

Abadi, Jl Jend Gatot Subroto 92–98 (☎0741/25600, fax 23065). Despite the access from the main road down an unprepossessing alleyway, this centrally located place is one of the most comfortable in town, although prices will probably rise when the new building is finished. Rooms have air-con, hot water and TV. ④–⑤.

Adipura, Jl Prof Dr Sumantri Brojonegoro 119 (☎0741/60200, fax 32869). The bemos running between Simpang Rimbo and Rawasari terminal pass the door; the partly traditional building and attractive entrance hall is alluring but rooms are utilitarian rather than luxurious. Rooms away from the road are quieter. ④.

Anggrek, Jl Iskander Muda, Lorong Camar III 94 (☎0741/25545, fax 33956). This central, clean place on a quiet alleyway directly behind the *Novotel*/Matahari Plaza complex is excellent value. Less expensive rooms have outside bathroom and fan and the more costly ones have bathroom and air-con. ③.

Da'lia, Jl Lorong Camar III 100 (☎0741/50863). Right in the middle of town on a quiet alleyway between the Matahari shopping centre and Rawasari terminal. Rooms are clean and tiled – budget ones have fan and outside mandi, whilst more expensive options have air-con and inside mandi. Ask to see several rooms, as they vary in size. ③–④.

88, Jl Halim Perdana Kusuma 8 (☎0741/33286). Close to the town centre, there are plenty of rooms on offer, from some with fans and unattached mandi to some with air-con and attached mandi. ②–③.

Mayang Sari, Jl Iskander Muda, Jl Lorong Camar III 88–90 (☎0741/20695, fax 20898) Close to the *Anggrek*, this is a large setup offering utilitarian rooms, all with air-con and bathroom. ③.

Mexicana (MC), Jl Halim Perdana Kusuma 10 (☎0741/22163). Featuring basic concrete-floored rooms with attached cold-water mandi, this is close to the centre and is reasonable value. ③.

Novotel, Jl Gatot Subroto 44 (☎0741/27208, fax 27209). The new, gleaming, central hotel offers the best and most expensive facilities in town, including swimming pool, fitness and business centres and tennis courts. Rooms are luxurious and there are good views across the city. ⑧–⑨.

Telanaipura, Jl Prof Dr Sumantri Brojonegoro 14 (☎0741/60827). One of the few hotels in the city with a garden, but the nearby roads are noisy. Rooms at the bottom end have fan and attached mandi, while more expensive ones have air-con and a small outside sitting area. Blue bemos pass the door. ③–④.

The City

Jambi is a combination of the old prewar seat of the Jambi sultanate on the banks of the river with the new administrative suburb, **Telanapura**, to the southwest. It's a bustling tidal river port, with exports of palm oil, plywood, timber and rubber (the mainstays of the thriving provincial economy) passing through; sad testimony to the destruction of much of Jambi's ancient forests by rubber and palm-oil plantations. The province was also very badly hit by the devastating forest fires of 1997–98. With its position close to the Malacca Straits and prominence as an ancient kingdom, the ethnic mix in the city includes Malays, Arabs, Chinese and Buginese as well as Javanese and Balinese from more recent transmigration initiatives and the mobile Minangkabau from nearby western Sumatra.

One of the best sights in the city, and a fascinating place to wander around, is the daily **Angso Dua market**, located between Jalan Sultan Taha and the river. It's an unmodernized maze of tiny alleyways lined with stalls selling fresh and dried fish, vegetables, fruit, spices and all kinds of meat. About 1km further east, a small public park on the banks of **Sungai Batang Hari** at the eastern end of Jalan Sultan Taha, where it turns into Jalan Raden Pamuk, gives views across the broad expanse of the river and west to the main port area. Towards dark, you may be lucky with a dramatic sunset, and plenty of food stalls cater for local people who come to enjoy the river breeze.

Jambi has its own textile tradition, believed to have been developed at the time of the ancient Malayu kingdom. In traditional **Jambi batik** designs you can see Sungai Batang Hari wending its way through the patterns, which often include old-style sailing ships and swans, although the traditional dark-blue, dark-red and yellow colour range is now being widened to fit modern tastes. At the Sanggar Batik dan Kerajinan **workshop**, Jalan

Prof Dr Sri Soedewi 18a (Mon–Sat 8am–3pm; ☎0741/62028), you can the tortuous process of batik production, where designs are sketched out followed by repeated waxing, dyeing and drying: a sarong typically takes twenty days to make. There's a good range of items for sale – cotton scarves are in the Rp10,000–15,000 range and you'll pay around Rp300,000 for a four-metre length of pure silk. An alternative destination to see Jambi batik is **Mudung Laut**, a small village across the Batang Hari – you can reach it by ferry (Rp300) from Jalan Sultan Taha, where Selaras Pinang Masak is also a workshop/showroom.

The **Museum Negeri Propinsi Jambi** (Tues–Thurs & Sun 8am–2pm, Fri 8am–11am, Sat 8am–1pm; Rp200), Jalan Prof Dr Sri Soedewi, at the junction with Jalan Jend Urip Sumoharjo, is about 4km from the city centre; take a green bemo from Rawasari. It contains a selection of old weapons, local costumes, stuffed animals, traditional wedding ceremony decorations and models of houses: labelling is mostly in Indonesian. There are some beautiful Chinese ceramics found in Sarko regency from the Tang, Sung and Han dynasties and many intricate fish-traps. The **Arca Bhairawa** is a fabulous four-metre, fourteenth-century statue of the half-Sumatran, half-Javanese nobleman Adityavarman who ruled over the area, decorated with human skulls at its base. He is depicted as a Tantric Buddhist deity, standing on a hapless baby – the statue here is a replica, the original being in the National Museum in Jakarta (see p.86).

Eating and drinking

Jambi is crammed with **eating places**, from the **warung** of the Jalan Camar area up to top-quality **restaurants** in the luxury hotels, and everything in between.

Christine Bakery, Jl Dr M. Assaat 40. One of several small bakeries in town serving a good range of sweet breads and cakes; there's some seating.

Jumbo, Jl Raden Mattaher 116. This is a simple local favourite with an extensive and inexpensive range of sate, *martabak, pempek, mie bakso*, ice desserts and juices.

Mayang Mangurai Kafé at the *Novotel*. Located on the balcony above the hotel lobby, with some good views onto the bustling road below, the atmosphere is plush and, although there are plenty of expensive options, including burgers, sandwiches, smoked salmon, steaks and lamb chop, there are also much more reasonable dishes such as gado-gado and nasi goreng. Drinks are pricey though, beer is Rp5400 a glass.

Ramada Café, Jl Raden Mattaher 48. The large inexpensive Indonesian menu, including *pemplek*, nasi goreng, sate and chicken dishes, is served in clean and pleasant surroundings with big fans creating an airy atmosphere.

Saimen Perancis, Jl Raden Mattaher 51. This large, clean, pleasant cafeteria and bakery serves a huge range of cakes and sweet breads and basic inexpensive Indonesian food.

Listings

Airline offices Mandala agent, PT Aquavita Jaya Travel Service, Jl Jend Gatot Subroto 86 (☎0741/26524); Merpati (also agents for Garuda), Jl Jend Gatot Subroto 92–98 (☎0741/21370, fax 20774, in the *Abadi* hotel; SMAC, Jl Orang Kayo Hitam 26 (☎0741/22269).

Banks and exchange BCA, Jl Raden Mattaher 15; BNI, Jl Dr Sutomo 20; BRI, Jl Dr Sutomo 42.

Bookshops Toko Buku Gloria, Jl Raden Mattaher 43–44, stocks the English-language *Jakarta Post* and *Observer* newspapers and a city map of Jambi, and they occasionally sell postcards. M. Media bookshop is located on the third floor of the Matahari Plaza. There are almost no English-language novels available apart from the occasional classic, so bring reading material with you.

Cinema Sumatera 2, Jl Halim Perdana Kusuma, is central and has showings on four screens.

Ferries The Pelni office is at Jl Sultan Taha 17 (☎0741/23649) – only cargo routes operate out of Jambi.

Golf Lapangan Golf Jambi, Jl Jend A. Thalip (☎0741/62854). Green fees for nine holes are Rp32,000 and Rp39,000 for eighteen holes. There are clubs for rent for additional fees.

Hospitals Rumah Sakit DKT (military hospital), Jl Raden Mattaher 33 (☎0741/32792); Rumah Sakit Santa Theresia, Jl Dr Sutomo 19 (☎0741/23119); Rumah Sakit Umum Jambi, Jl Letjen Suprapto 2 (☎0741/62364).

Immigration office Jl Dr Sam Ratulangi 2 (☎0741/23380).

Port administration office Contact the Kantor Administrator Jambi, Jl Sultan Taha 4 (☎0741/22020), for details of shipping out of Jambi.

Post office Jl Sultan Taha 5; they get few tourists here and it isn't recommended for poste restante.

Shopping Matahari Plaza, Jl Jend Gatot Subroto, is the newest and best shopping centre in town, with a fast-food plaza, bookstore, department store and supermarket.

Swimming Jl Slamet Riyadi (daily 7am–6pm; Rp1500).

Telephone and fax The main 24hr Telkom office is at Jl Raden Mattaher 2.

Around the city

The major archeological site within reach of Jambi is the **Muara Jambi** complex (daily 8am–4pm), 26km downstream from the city. If you go on Sunday, when most local people visit, boats ply Sungai Batang Hari (speedboats charge Rp25,000 for ten passengers) leaving from two spots, east of Boom Batu just in front of the governor's office and west of Boom Rakit. Make sure you fix the price before you embark. Alternatively, the taxi fare will cost Rp10,000 each way.

Thought to date from the seventh to the thirteenth century, the complex is testimony to the power of the Malayu kingdom. Chinese histories detail the visit of Malayu emissaries to the court of the Tang dynasty in 644–645 AD, and a Chinese monk, I-Tsing, visited the Malayu court around thirty years later. The site comprises the remains of the ancient port of Malayu, an extensive area of Hindu and Buddhist shrines set amongst canals and large water tanks on the north bank of Sungai Batang Hari. The city is said to have been destroyed in about 1377 by the son of Prince Telanai, the last ruler of the city. A fortune-teller predicted that the son of the prince would bring disaster to the kingdom, so the prince put him in a chest and threw it into the sea. It arrived in Siam, where the child was raised as a member of the royal court, eventually returning to Muara Jambi with a huge Siamese army to kill his father and destroy the city.

So far, three main structures have been restored – Candi Tinggi, Candi Gumpung and Candi Kedaton – and, whilst many of the finds in the area are in a small site **museum**, a lot of artefacts have been taken to Jakarta.

VISITING THE KUBU PEOPLE

Around 1000 remaining **Kubu** people, the original southern Sumatran inhabitants, still live in the Jambi forests. They traditionally lived as hunter-gatherers in the jungle, and have resisted government efforts to settle them, preferring to maintain their nomadic lifestyle. However, as their environment has been under threat from all sides, they have begun to settle to some extent, taking up agriculture but still resisting integration into mainstream Indonesian life – it remains to be seen what the future holds for them. Travel agents in Jambi (see below) may be able to put a tour together; otherwise, ask in Bukittinggi at Puti Bungus, Jalan Teuku Umar 7a (☎0752/23026); guides in Sungaipenuh (see p.385) also offer a trip. In Jambi, try:

Jambi Mayang Tour, Jalan Raden Mattaher 27 (☎0741/25450, fax 32869).

PT Maya Safera, Jalan Sudirman 8 (☎0741/20392, fax 32113).

PT Aquavita Jaya Travel Service, Jalan Jend Gatot Subroto 86 (☎0741/26524).

To go independently, you'll need fairly good Indonesian. From Bangko, take a local bus to Pauh village, where you'll need to report to the *kepala camat* (the district head), and then to Air Hitam, close to the areas where some Kubu people have settled and where you'll need to find a guide to take you on foot the rest of the way.

travel details

There are no longer any passenger train services in West Sumatra.

Buses

Bukittinggi to: Banda Aceh (3 daily; 25hr); Bandar Lampung (5 daily; 24hr); Bandung (5 daily; 34hr); Batam (daily; 24hr); Batang Palupuh (hourly 7am–5pm; 30min); Batusangkar (hourly 7am–5pm; 1hr 30min); Bengkulu (4 daily; 16hr); Bonjol (hourly 7am–5pm; 1hr); Jakarta (5 daily; 35hr); Jambi (5 daily; 15hr); Lubuk Basang (hourly 7am–5pm; 1hr 30min); Lubuklinggau (4 daily; 12hr); Medan (5 daily; 18hr); Maninjau (hourly 7am–5pm; 1hr 30min); Padang (every 20min 7am–5pm; 2hr 30min); Palembang (4 daily; 15hr); Payakumbuh (hourly 7am–5pm; 1hr); Pekanbaru (6 daily; 6hr); Prapat (5 daily; 14hr); Sibolga (daily; 12hr); Solok (hourly 7am–5pm; 1hr 30min–2hr).

Jambi to: Bandar Lampung (10 daily; 22hr); Bandung (daily; 34hr); Bangko (hourly; 5hr); Batam (daily; 24hr); Bengkulu (2 daily; 11hr); Denpasar (Bali, 2 daily; 48hr); Jakarta (daily; 30hr); Mataram (Lombok, daily; 3 days); Medan (10 daily; 36hr); Muara Bungo (hourly; 5hr); Padang (10 daily; 24hr); Palembang (10 daily; 5hr); Pekanbaru (2 daily; 11hr); Probolinggo (daily; 48hr); Solo (daily; 48hr); Surabaya (daily; 48hr); Yogyakarta (daily; 36hr).

Maninjau to: Batam (daily; 24hr); Bukittinggi (hourly 7am–5pm; 1hr 30min); Padang (2 daily; 2–3hr); Pekanbaru (daily; 8hr).

Padang to: Banda Aceh (4 daily; 28hr); Bandar Lampung (10 daily; 25hr); Bengkulu (4 daily; 18hr); Bukittinggi (every 20min 6am–7pm; 2hr 30min); Jakarta (10 daily; 30–35hr) Jambi (6 daily; 24hr); Medan (10 daily; 20hr); Palembang (4 daily; 18hr); Pekanbaru (10 daily; 8hr); Prapat (10 daily; 18hr); Sibolga (4 daily; 18hr); Solok (every 20min 6am–7pm; 1hr).

Pekanbaru to: Bandar Lampung (10 daily; 24hr); Bengkulu (2 daily; 30hr); Bukittinggi (10 daily; 6hr); Denpasar (daily; 4 days); Dumai (10 daily; 3hr); Jakarta (10 daily; 34hr); Jambi (6 daily; 9hr); Maninjau (daily; 8hr); Mataram (Lombok, daily; 4 days); Medan (daily; 25–35hr); Padang (10 daily; 8hr); Palembang (20 daily; 15–18hr); Prapat (daily; 22–30hr); Sungaipenuh (daily; 12hr) Yogyakarta (4 daily; 42hr).

Sungaipenuh to: Bangko, transit for Palembang, Bandar Lampung and Jakarta (10 daily; 5hr); Bengkulu (daily; 9hr); Dumai (daily; 14hr); Jambi (daily; 7hr); Muko-Muko (daily; 4hr); Padang (4 daily; 9hr); Painan (2 daily; 7hr); Pekanbaru (daily; 12hr).

Pelni ferries

For a chart of the Pelni routes, see pp.36–37 of *Basics*.

Batam to: Batulicin (*KM Sirimau*, fortnightly; 5 days); Kualaenok (*KM Sirimau*, fortnightly; 12hr); Kupang (*KM Sirimau*, fortnightly; 7 days); Larantuka (*KM Sirimau*, fortnightly; 7 days); Makasar (*KM Sirimau*, fortnightly; 5 days); Panjang (*KM Sirimau*, fortnightly; 3 days); Semarang (*KM Sirimau*, fortnightly; 3 days); Tanjung Priok (*KM Sirimau*, fortnightly; 2 days).

Pulau Bintan (Kijang) to: Ambon (*KM Bukit Siguntang*, fortnightly; 5 days); Balikpapan (*KM Kerinci*, fortnightly; 4 days); Banda (*KM Bukit Siguntang*, fortnightly; 5 days); Batam (*KM Sirimau*, fortnightly; 7hr); Batulicin (*KM Sirimau*, fortnightly; 5 days); Bau Bau (*KM Bukit Siguntang*, fortnightly; 4 days); Bawean (*KM Bukit Raya*, fortnightly; 4 days); Blinyu (*KM Bukit Raya*, fortnightly; 12hr); Dobo (*KM Bukit Siguntang*, monthly; 6 days); Dumai (*KM Bukit Siguntang*, fortnightly; 17hr/*KM Kerinci*, fortnightly; 14hr); Kaimana (*KM Bukit Siguntang*, monthly; 6 days); Kualaenok (*KM Sirimau*, fortnightly; 22hr); Kupang (*KM Sirimau*, fortnightly; 7 days); Larantuka (*KM Sirimau*, fortnightly; 7 days); Letung (*KM Bukit Raya*, fortnightly; 12hr); Makasar (*KM Bukit Siguntang*, fortnightly; 3 days/*KM Kerinci*, fortnightly; 3 days/*KM Sirimau*, fortnightly; 6 days); Midai (*KM Bukit Raya*, fortnightly; 33hr); Natuna (*KM Bukit Raya*, fortnightly; 27hr); Nunukan (*KM Kerinci*, fortnightly; 6 days); Panjang (*KM Sirimau*, fortnightly; 3 days); Pantoloan (*KM Kerinci*, fortnightly; 4 days); Pontianak (*KM Bukit Raya*, fortnightly; 3 days); Sampit (*KM Bukit Raya*, fortnightly; 5 days); Semarang (*KM Sirimau*, fortnightly; 4 days); Serasan (*KM Bukit Raya*, fortnightly; 38hr); Surabaya (*KM Bukit Raya*, fortnightly; 4 days/*KM Bukit Siguntang*, fortnightly; 3 days/*KM Kerinci*, fortnightly; 3 days); Tambelan (*KM Bukit Raya*, fortnightly; 48hr); Tanjung Priok (*KM Bukit Raya*, fortnightly; 38hr/*KM Bukit Siguntang*, fortnightly; 26hr/*KM Kerinci*, fortnightly; 26hr/*KM Sirimau*, fortnightly; 3 days); Tarakan (*KM Kerinci*, fortnightly; 6 days); Tarempa (*KM Bukit Raya*, fortnightly; 16hr); Toli Toli (*KM Kerinci*, fortnightly; 5 days); Tual (*KM Bukit Siguntang*, fortnightly; 6 days).

Padang to: Ambon (*KM Lambelu*, fortnightly; 5 days); Balikpapan (*KM Kambuna*, fortnightly; 4 days); Bau Bau (*KM Lambelu*, fortnightly; 4 days); Bitung (*KM Kambuna*, fortnightly; 6 days/*KM Lambelu*, fortnightly; 6 days); Makasar (*KM Kambuna*, fortnightly; 3 days/*KM Lambelu*, fortnightly; 3 days); Namlea (*KM Lambelu*, fortnightly; 5 days); Nias (*KM Kambuna*, fortnightly; 20hr/*KM Lambelu*, fortnightly; 11hr); Pantoloan (*KM Kambuna*, fortnightly; 5 days); Sibolga (*KM Kambuna*, fortnightly; 13hr/*KM Lambelu*, fortnightly; 18hr); Surabaya (*KM Kambuna*, fortnightly; 3 days/*KM Lambelu*, fortnightly; 3 days); Tanjung Priok (*KM Kambuna*, fortnightly; 30hr/*KM Lambelu*, fortnightly; 30hr); Ternate (*KM Lambelu*, fortnightly; 6 days); Toli Toli (*KM Kambuna*, fortnightly; 5 days).

Pulau Karimun (Tanjung Balai) to: Belawan (*KM Sinabung*, 6–8 monthly; 15hr); Mentok (*KM Sinabung*, 6–8 monthly; 9hr); Tanjung Priok (*KM Sinabung*, 6–8 monthly; 25hr).

Other ferries

Padang to: Siberut (3/4 weekly; 12hr).

Pekanbaru to: Sekupang (daily; 7–11hr); Selatpanjang (daily; 16hr); Tebingtinggi Island (daily; 6–10hr); Tanjung Balai (Pulau Karimun; daily; 5–9hr and 25hr); Tanjung Pinang (daily; 8–12hr and 22hr). Tanjung Samak (Pulau Rangsang; daily; 18hr); Tanjung Batu (Pulau Kundur; daily; 20hr); Moro (Pulau Sugibawah, daily; 21hr).

Pulau Batam to: Singapore: Batu Ampar (World Trade Centre; 9 daily; 1–2hr), Sekupang (World Trade Centre; 24 daily;1–2hr), Nongsa (Tanah Merah; 6 daily; 1–2hr), waterfront ferry terminal Teluk Senimba (World Trade Centre; 14 daily; 1–2hr); Tanjung Pinang (from Telaga Punggur) (Pulau Bintan; 36 daily; 45min).

Pulau Bintan (Tanjung Pinang) to: Batam (every 15min; 45min); Belitung (Tanjung Pandan; weekly; 12hr); Dabo (daily; 2hr 30min); Johor (daily; 6hr); Pangkal Balam (weekly; 8hr); Pekanbaru (daily; 12 hrs); Pulau Lingga (6 weekly; 4–6hr); Singapore (from Tanjung Pinang to Tanah Merah 3 daily; 1hr 30min; from Bandar Bentan Tanah Merah 3–7 daily; 45min); Tanjung Balai (2 daily; 2–3hr); Tanjung Batu (daily; 3–4hr); Tanjung Priok (daily; 24hr).

Pulau Karimun (Tanjung Balai) to: Dabo (via Tanjung Pinang; daily; 7hr); Johor (4 daily; 4–6hr); Pekanbaru (2 daily; 6–7hr); Selat Panjang (for connections to Pekanbaru or Jambi; 4 daily; 5hr); Sekupang on Pulau Batam (8 daily; 3hr);

Singapore (9 daily; 1hr 30min); Tanjung Batu (on Pulau Kundur; 5 daily; 1–2hr), Tanjung Pinang (4 daily; 3hr).

Pulau Kundur (Tanjung Batu) to: Dabo (via Tanjung Balai and Tanjung Pinang; daily; 7–8hr); Pekanbaru (daily; 5–6hr); Sekupang, (4 daily; 3hr); Singapore via Tanjung Balai (5 daily; 1–2hr); Sungai Guntung (for connections to Jambi 2 daily; 3–4hr).

Pulau Lingga to: Tanjung Pinang (from Pancur; 6 weekly; 4hr); (from Tanjung Buton; 3 weekly; 5hr).

Pulau Singkep (Jago) to: Tanjung Batu (daily; 7–8hr); Tanjung Balai (daily; 6hr); Tanjung Pinang (daily; 4hr).

Siberut to: Padang (4 weekly; 12hr).

Flights

Pulau Batam to: Ambon (daily; 9hr); Balikpapan (9 weekly; 4hr 25min); Bandung (2 daily; 3hr 20min); Banjarmasin (daily; 6hr); Denpasar (daily; 4hr 20min); Jakarta (5 daily; 1hr 35min); Jambi (2 weekly; 55min); Manado (daily; 7hr 40min); Mataram (2 weekly; 3hr 55min); Medan (daily; 1hr 20min); Padang (daily; 1hr); Palembang (daily; 1hr 15min); Pangkal Pinang (2 weekly; 40min); Pekanbaru (daily; 45min); Pontianak (5 weekly; 3–4hr); Semarang (daily; 3hr 10min); Surabaya (3 daily; 3hr 30min); Ujung Pandang (9 weekly; 6hr 30min); Yogyakarta (2 daily; 2hr 5min).

Pulau Bintan to: Jakarta (6 weekly; 1hr45min); Pekanbaru (6 weekly; 55min).

Dabo (Pulau Singkep) to: Batam (4 weekly; 45min); Jambi (2 weekly; 35min); Pangkal Pinang (2 weekly; 1hr).

Jambi to: Balikpapan (daily; 6hr 30min); Batam (4 weekly; 1hr 15min); Denpasar (4 daily; 5hr 10min–7hr 20min); Jakarta (6 daily; 1hr 20min); Medan (2 daily; 6hr 40min); Pontianak (daily; 4hr 25min); Semarang (2 daily; 4hr); Solo (daily; 4hr); Surabaya (3 daily; 4hr 20min); Yogyakarta (3 daily; 3hr 35min).

Padang to: Bandung (daily; 2hr–3hr 30min); Batam (daily; 1hr); Jakarta (4 daily; 45min); Medan (1–2 daily; 1hr 10min); Palembang (1–2 daily; 1hr 10min–2hr 40min); Pekanbaru (3 weekly; 50min).

Pekanbaru to: Batam (3–4 daily; 45min); Jakarta (6 daily; 1hr–1hr 40min); Kuala Lumpur (4 weekly; 1hr); Malacca (4 weekly; 40min); Medan (daily; 1hr 20min); Padang (3 weekly; 40min); Tanjung Pinang (4 weekly; 50min).

CHAPTER SEVEN

PALEMBANG AND SOUTH SUMATRA

D espite its soaring mountains, picturesque lakes, areas of historical interest, fascinating offshore islands and dramatic coastline, **South Sumatra** is often passed over as travellers rush between Bukittinggi and Java. In fact it has a great deal to offer those willing to get off the beaten track.

The geographical division between the western mountains of the Bukit Barisan range and the low-lying plains, swamps and river estuaries of the east continues right down to the south of the island. The huge city of **Palembang** straddles the mighty Sungai Musi 70km from the east coast and, though there's little to entice visitors, it's an important access point for the rarely visited islands of **Bangka** and **Belitung**, both now sleepy backwaters after the death of the lucrative tin trade that was the mainstay of their economies for centuries.

On the west coast, the old British colonial outpost of **Bengkulu** retains plenty of charm, has several sights worth visiting and is a useful stopping-off point if you're heading offshore to remote **Pulau Enggano**, inland to **Curup** and the mountainous Rejang Lebong area or, to the southeast, to explore the mysterious megaliths of the **Pasemah Plateau**.

Highland **Danau Ranau** doesn't have the scale or majesty of the more famous Sumatran lakes, but its tranquillity and situation off the main tourist drag make it an excellent alternative, while the nearby fishing village of **Krui** offers access to the full glory of the totally undeveloped southwest coastline.

In the far south of Sumatra, **Bandar Lampung** is an almost inevitable staging post on any journey between Sumatra and Java, and beautifully located on the shoreline and hills surrounding Lampung Bay. From here there are good routes to the rarely visited **Bukit Barisan Selatan national park** through the southern town of Kota Agung, and the better-known **Way Kambas national park**, which features a remarkable elephant training school.

This whole area is south of the equator, with average **temperatures** at sea level hovering around 26–27°C, and an October to May rainy season. However, the complex geographical features of the island mean that small microclimates exist, particularly in the mountains, where the weather is consistent only in its inconsistency. In the "dry" season you can still expect rain on about one day in four, while in the wet season torrential downpours are interspersed with hours of bright sunshine, although anyone planning a lot of trekking or travelling on back roads (the rain causes landslides and blockages) would be well advised to avoid this period.

Much of southern Sumatra is now developing basic **tourist facilities**, although it's perfectly possible to travel for weeks in the area without meeting more than a handful of other travellers. **Access** into and within the area is excellent: the larger towns have airports and there's a limited but useful passenger rail service between Palembang, Bandar Lampung and Lubuklinggau. Frequent and speedy bus services link Sumatran cities with Java, via a highly efficient 24hr ferry service between Bakauheni on Sumatra and Merak on Java. As in all of Sumatra, distances are huge, driving can be terrifying and, once you get onto smaller cross-country routes, patience and planning are needed.

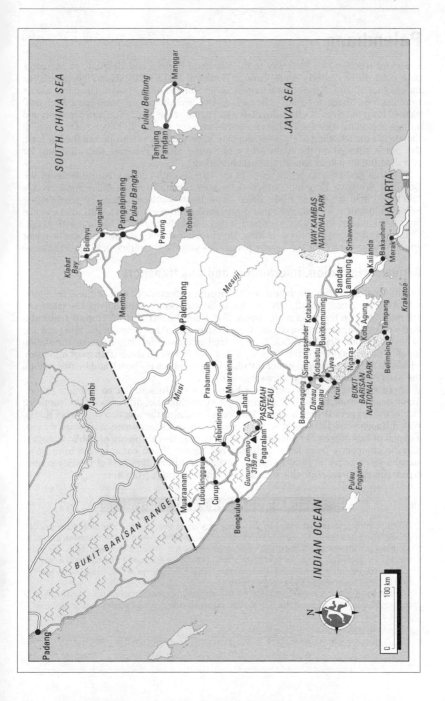

Palembang

Useful for travellers on their way to the islands of Bangka and Belitung, or as a stopping point on an easterly route through Sumatra, **PALEMBANG**, with a population nudging 1.2 million, is the second largest city in Sumatra after Medan. The name comes from *limbang*, "to pan for gold" – the early affluence of the city probably came from gold panned from the river. It's the administrative capital of the South Sumatra province, and a huge sprawling metropolis that has grown up over the last 1200 years. Once one of the world's main trading ports, near shipping lanes that linked Europe and the Far East, the city is situated on the main artery of Sungai Musi, with vast ships docking for access to the industrial and agricultural hinterland.

The area first rose to prominence in the late seventh century as the heart of the Buddhist Sriwijaya Kingdom, which dominated Sumatra for the following four centuries and had important trade links throughout Southeast Asia. Even when the Sriwijaya kingdom waned, Palembang remained an important port, with international links to China and the Malay mainland; it had a turbulent political history, with Malay, Chinese and Javanese rulers. During Dutch colonial rule, Palembang was a major administrative centre for the nearby plantations and the tin mines on Pulau Bangka.

Arrival, orientation, information and city transport

Flights land at **Sultan Badaruddin II airport**, 12km northwest of the city centre, with fixed-price taxis (Rp12,500) running to the city centre – the only public transport are red Kijang on the main road, almost 2km from the terminal. **Kertapati train station** is 4km southwest of the city centre on a spur of land between Sungai Musi and one of its main tributaries, the Ogan. Taxis, official and unofficial, linger outside the station for all arrivals and their drivers will try to tell you there's no public transport into town, which isn't true. Turn right out of the main station entrance – buses and bemos wait on the main road about 300m walk away.

There are several arrival points for **long-distance buses**, but no terminal proper. Many buses terminate at their offices – the main cluster of offices is on the southern side of the Ampera Bridge on Jalan Pangeran Ratu, near the junction with Jalan K.H.A. Wahid Hasyim and Jalan Jend A. Yani. Pekanbaru buses terminate at Kilometre Lima, a clutch of bus offices 5km north of the city centre; there's plenty of public transport into the city centre from here, including red Kijang. If you come by sea from Pulau Bangka you'll arrive at Bom Baru, the small **ferry port** 2km east of the city centre; cream Kijang operate into the area around Ampera Bridge from here.

ACCOMMODATION PRICE CODES

All the **accommodation** listed in this book has been given one of the following price codes. The rates quoted here are for the **cheapest double room** in high season, except for places with dorms, where the code represents the price of a single bed. Where there's a significant spread of prices indicated (④–⑦, for example), the text will explain what extra facilities you get for more money. The 11–21 percent tax charged by most hotels is not included in these price codes.

Because of the current instability of the rupiah, accommodation prices are given throughout in their more stable **US dollar equivalents**, even for places that accept payment in rupiah.

For more on accommodation, see p.40.

① under $1	③ $2–5	⑤ $10–15	⑦ $35–60	⑨ $100
② $1–2	④ $5–10	⑥ $15–35	⑧ $60–100	and over

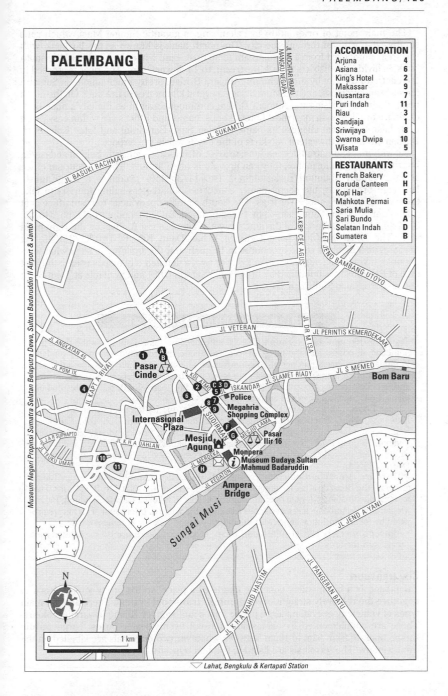

PALEMBANG

ACCOMMODATION

Arjuna	4
Asiana	6
King's Hotel	2
Makassar	9
Nusantara	7
Puri Indah	11
Riau	3
Sandjaja	1
Sriwijaya	8
Swarna Dwipa	10
Wisata	5

RESTAURANTS

French Bakery	C
Garuda Canteen	H
Kopi Har	F
Mahkota Permai	G
Saria Mulia	E
Sari Bundo	A
Selatan Indah	D
Sumatera	B

Museum Negeri Propinsi Sumatra Selatan Belaputra Dewa, Sultan Badaruddin II Airport & Jambi

JL MOCHTAR PRABU MANGKU NEGARA

JL SUKAMTO

JL BASUKI RACHMAT

JL AKBP CEK AGUS

JL LET JEND BAMBANG UTOYO

JL VETERAN

JL DR M ISA

JL PERINTIS KEMERDEKAAN

JL ANGKATAN 45

JL POM IX

Pasar Cinde

JL KAPT A RIVAI

JL KOL ATMO

ISKANDAR

JL SLAMET RIADY

JL S MEMED

Bom Baru

Police

Megahria Shopping Complex

Internasional Plaza

JL J AR SUPRAPTO

JL K H A DAHLAN

JL SUDIRMAN

MESJID LAMA

Pasar Ilir 16

TEUKU UMAR

Mesjid Agung

Monpera

Museum Budaya Sultan Mahmud Badaruddin

JL MERDEKA

JL KEDATON

Ampera Bridge

Sungai Musi

JL JEND A YANI

JL K H A WAHID HASYIM

JL PANGERAN BATU

N

0   1 km

The main point of **orientation** in Palembang is gigantic Sungai Musi, which runs southwest–northeast through the city. The north bank is known as the Ilir bank, with the areas numbered from 1 downstream to 36 upstream, while the Ulu bank, the south bank, is divided in districts from 1, upstream, to 14 downstream. The river is crossed in the centre of the city by the mammoth Ampera Bridge, pretty much unique in Sumatra for scale and ugliness, and the Musi Bridge, several kilometres to the west. On the north bank, the road crossing the Ampera Bridge continues straight as the city's main thoroughfare of Jalan Sudirman; most hotels, shops, banks and offices are within easy reach of it. Jalan Sudirman changes its name to Jalan Suka Bangkuni and Jalan Kolonel H. Burlian on the northwestern outskirts of the city towards the airport.

As with most Sumatran destinations, **tourist offices** are generally helpful and eager, but the quality of information they can provide is often limited. The city tourism office at Jalan Sultan Mahmud Badaruddin 1 (☎0711/358450) produces a few English-language brochures, but seem mainly concerned about persuading tourists to take them along as guides for river trips. The South Sumatra provincial tourism office is at Jalan Pom IX (Mon–Thurs 8am–2pm, Fri 8am–11am, Sat 8am–noon; ☎0711/357348, fax 373490), about 300m north of the junction with Jalan Kapten A. Rivai on the right-hand side. The Diparda office, Jalan Demang Lebar Daun Kav IX (☎0711/311345, fax 311544), also displays some brochures in English, but the building is somewhat inaccessible. If you're staying more than a day or two, a detailed city map is useful; the best map of Palembang is published by Indo Prima Sarana (IPS) and available at Toko Buku Diponegoro, Jalan Sudirman 27b.

MOVING ON FROM PALEMBANG

The **long-distance bus terminal** (Rp200 entrance) on Jalan Pemuda is the departure point for all buses, and the ticket offices are inside the terminal with a few on Jalan Pemuda. There are a number of bus companies, all operating their own schedules with their own price lists so it's worth shopping around to get the departure time you want and the best price. Departures throughout the day (6am–7pm) run to destinations throughout Sumatra, Java and eastwards.

Pelni **boats** call at Teluk Bayur, and Padang is on the fortnightly circuit of *KM Kambuna*, which starts from Bitung and then circuits through Toli Toli, Pantoloan, Balikpapan, Makasar (Ujung Pandang), Surabaya, Tanjung Priok, Padang, Sibolga, Nias, Padang, Tanjung Priok, Surabaya, Makasar, Balikpapan, Pantoloan, Toli Toli and back to Bitung. Get up-to-date sailing dates from the Pelni office at Jalan Tanjung Priok 32 (☎0751/33624).

There are plentiful **airline connections**, both domestic and international, from Tabing airport – the departure tax for domestic destinations is Rp10,300; it's Rp100,000 for international destinations. Merpati operate four times daily to Jakarta, daily to Bandung, Batam, Medan and Palembang, and three times weekly to Pekanbaru. International flights are provided by Pelangi to Johor Bahru and Kuala Lumpur and Silk Air to Singapore.

Although there is talk of reinstating them, at present there are no passenger train services in the area.

City transport

Palembang is a big bustling concrete jungle of a place, so it's pretty vital to learn to negotiate the relatively straightforward **public transport** system. There are two main types of vehicle in operation: large public buses and smaller Kijang in various colours. These are supplemented by old-fashioned small twenty-seater buses. Large **public buses** operate from 6am to 10pm between whatever two terminals are labelled on the front window. The terminals are listed in the box opposite.

PALEMBANG TRANSPORT

Bus terminals

KM12 (Kilometre Duabelas) is on the main road close to the airport.

Kertapati 4km southwest of the city centre on the south side of Sungai Musi.

Perumnas is at Terminal Sako, northeast of the city centre; buses head here along Jalan Sudirman, east along Jalan Basuki Rachmad and Jalan Sukamto and north along Jalan Mochtar Prabu Mangku Negara.

Plaju is at the Pertamina oil complex southeast of the city centre. Buses arrive via Ampera Bridge, east along Jalan Jend A. Yani and Jalan Di Panjaitan, and south along Jalan Kapten Abdullah.

Pusri is the Pusri industrial complex, east of the city on the north bank. Buses go north along Jalan Sudirman, east along Jalan Veteran and Jalan Perintis Kemerdekaan, north along Jalan Yos Sudarso and Jalan R.E. Martadinata, and terminate close to Jalan Mayor Zen.

Kijang routes

Red west on Jalan Tasik to Jalan Kapten A. Rivai, north at Jalan Sudirman to the airport turning, then back into town along Jalan Sudirman, down Jalan Kol Atmo into Jalan Mesjid Lama, across the top of Pasir 16, straight across the major roundabout at the north side of Ampera Bridge into Jalan Merdeka and into Jalan Tasik.

Blue Jalan Merdeka, Jalan Tasik, west across Jalan Kapten A. Rivai at Jalan Teuku Umar into Jalan J.A.R. Suprapto to UNSRI (University of Sriwijaya) on Jalan Srijaya Negara, out onto Jalan Demang Lebar Daun, and south along Jalan Sudirman to Jalan Merdeka.

Grey from Ampera, along Jalan Merdeka, north along Jalan Diponegoro, to Jalan Radial, across Jalan Kapten A. Rivai to Jalan Angkatan 45 to the Pakjo area; returns the same way.

Brown Ampera, Jalan Merdeka, south along Jalan Diponegoro, Jalan Wirosentiko and Jalan Pangeran Sidoing Laut to Pulau Palah (the area roughly opposite Kertapati station but on the north bank); returns the same way.

Yellow east on Jalan Merdeka and Jalan Sudirman, behind *Internasional Plaza* on Jalan Candiwalang, Jalan Sudirman, Jalan Veteran, then the area north of Jalan R. Sukamto (Sekip area) and back to Kantor Gubernor on Jalan Kapten A. Rivai, Jalan Tasik and Jalan Merdeka.

Green Ampera, Jalan K.H.A. Dahlan, Jalan Radial, Jalan Kapten A. Rivai, to the golf course via Jalan May Ruslan, to Jalan Let Jend Bambang Utoyo and the terminal at the northern end of Jalan Yos Sudarso.

Cream Ampera, Jalan Sayangan, Jalan Slamet Riady, Jalan Memed, to Bom Baru and along Jalan Yos Sudarso to the terminal at the top end.

Smaller buses operate circular routes: the **yellow** bus plies Kertapati, Ampera Bridge, Jalan Merdeka, Jalan Diponegoro, Jalan Letkol Iskander, Jalan Sudirman and back to Kertapati; and the **red** operates between Ampera Bridge and Plaju.

Old-fashioned **Kijang** are the other mainstay of the public transport system, operating on colour-coded routes throughout the city for a flat fare of Rp250; there's a bell push in the back when you want to get off. Times are variable: most operate from 4am to 10pm, but the Kertapati service runs 24hr. Many of them pass through the area known as Ampera, at the north end of the bridge around the junction with Jalan M. Lama. The main routes are shown in the box below.

There are plenty of meter **taxis** in the city, which you can simply flag down. If you want to charter one, expect to pay Rp7500 per hour in the city and Rp80,000–100,000 for day-trips out of town.

Accommodation

There's a huge amount of **accommodation** in Palembang and, although there's a preponderance at the middle and top end, you can find budget options. Much of the accommodation is either close to Jalan Sudirman or easily accessible by public transport.

Arjuna, Jl Kapten A. Rivai 219 (☎0711/356710, fax 358505). A newly tiled clean place offering a variety of rooms, with a small lobby coffee shop. Yellow Kijang heading west from the large Jl Sudirman/Jl Veteran junction pass the door, as do red Kijang from outside the post office, although they go a long way round. ⑤–⑦.

Asiana, Jl Sudirman 45e (☎0711/365016). Central but difficult to find; look out for a penginapan sign and blue-tiled stairway leading up from a small door just north of the junction with Jl Letkol Iskander/Diponegoro, with Internasional Plaza on the corner. All rooms have unattached mandi, but this place has recently been tiled throughout and is excellent value. There's a balcony where you can look down on the street below – rooms away from the street are quieter. ④.

King's Hotel, Jl Kol Atmo 623 (☎0711/362323, fax 363633). Heavily advertised luxury hotel in the centre of town, with grand communal areas and restaurants and plush rooms with individual safes, hair dryers, hot water and air-con. There's a small fitness club, business centre, karaoke bar and nightly live music in the fourth-floor bar until 2am, but no swimming pool. Rooms are variable so look at several. ⑦–⑨.

Makassar, Jl Letkol Iskander 17 (☎0711/359565). Next door to the *Nusantara*, this place is orientated towards budget travellers. Some rooms have attached mandi and some don't. ④.

Nusantara, Jl Letkol Iskander 17 (☎0711/351306). One of the most popular cheaper options in this street, it's down an alleyway right next to the Pasaraya JM department store. Rooms at the bottom end have fan and attached bathroom, while the pricier ones have air-con. There are alternatives nearby if it's full. ⑤–⑥.

Puri Indah, Jl Merdeka 38–40 (☎0711/356912). In a quiet location about 2km from the centre, reached by red Kijang. The rooms are adequate rather than luxurious, but even bottom-end ones have air-con. ⑤–⑦.

Riau, Jl Dempo Luar 409 (☎0711/352011). Good-value, popular budget place; all rooms have fan and outside bathroom. Situated on a quiet but central road with space out the front to sit and watch the world go by. ④.

Sandjaja, Jl Kapten A. Rivai 6193 (☎0711/310675, fax 313693). Central and well furnished, with all the luxury and facilities to be expected at this end of the range, including a pleasant swimming pool with shady sitting area nearby. ⑧–⑨.

Sriwijaya, Jl Letkol Iskander 31 (☎0711/355555, fax 364565). Just 50m from the junction with Jl Sudirman, the hotel is at the end of an alleyway in a central but quiet location; it's easy to miss the sign on the main road. Plenty of rooms with a variety of facilities, with fans at the lower price range and air-con at the top, and pleasant balconies. ④–⑥.

Swarna Dwipa, Jl Tasik 2 (☎0711/313322, fax 382992). Good-quality hotel located about 2km west of the city centre in a pleasant suburb opposite a park. It's on the route of the red Kijang that operates from the town centre. Features a small pool, restaurant and a bar with nightly live music. ⑦–⑨.

Wisata, Jl Letkol Iskander 105–7 (☎0711/313956, fax 352750). Centrally located, with a small and pleasant coffee shop on the ground floor, the rooms have all the comfort of the grander places with air-con, hot-water tub and colour TV. ⑥.

The City

Palembang's major landmark is the huge **Ampera Bridge** that straddles Sungai Musi. Built with war reparation money from the Japanese government, it was opened in 1964; the central section of the bridge originally lifted to allow larger ocean-going vessels to pass through, but this caused such traffic chaos that when the mechanism broke down in 1970 it wasn't repaired.

A trip on **Sungai Musi** is widely touted by the tourist office as a "must-do" in Palembang and, although it's interesting to see river life, an hour or so is more than enough, especially as the river itself is so polluted you can easily end up with itching skin and streaming eyes and nose. However, it's chastening to see the families living near the river doing their washing and other chores on the banks and it's also a good way to get a grip on the geography of the city, especially if you head west to the tributaries of the Musi: the Ogan is crossed by the Wilhelmina Bridge near the station and Sungai Kramasan slightly further west. On Independence Day (August 17), the *bidar* boat races take place on Sungai Musi, the long canoes shaped like animals, each holding forty rowers dressed in colourful costumes.

Heading east along the river, you'll spot leafy **Pulau Kemaro** just off the north bank. The island has a Buddhist temple on a spot also sacred to Muslims, so followers of both religions come to pray. Legend maintains that the temple is the burial spot of a Chinese princess who came to the area with her dowry to marry the king of the Sriwijaya kingdom. Her dowry was sent ashore in huge jars, and the king, expecting precious jewels, flung them into the river when he opened the first one only to find preserved vegetables. In despair the princess threw herself into the river and drowned as the other pots broke open, proving that they were indeed full of gold and precious stones.

The concrete monstrosity adorned with a huge black Garuda located at the junction of Jalan Sudirman and Jalan Merdeka is **MONPERA** (Monumen Perjuagan Rakyat Sumatera Bagian Selatan; Rp300), commemorating the "Battle of Five Days and Nights" in 1947, when the Dutch regained control of the oil- and coalfields around Palembang from the nationalist rebels. The modern ugliness is in stark contrast to the towering minarets and fine lines of the **Mesjid Agung** (Grand Mosque) across the road, which was built in 1740 by Sultan Mahmud Badaruddin I and recently and sympathetically renovated.

Just behind MONPERA in the town centre, **Museum Budaya Sultan Mahmud Badaruddin** (Mon–Sat 8am–2pm; donation), is on the first floor of a grand nineteenth-century building that is due to reopen soon, following renovation. The collection is not extensive and features rather predicable displays of textiles, weapons, traditional dress, crafts and money. However, the gardens of the museum, from which huge numbers of Sriwijayan artefacts were excavated, are pleasant, and there are a couple of attractive Ganesh and Buddha statues.

Far more worthwhile, in fact one of the best Sumatran museums, is **Museum Negeri Propinsi Sumatra Selatan; Belaputra Dewa**, the South Sumatra regional museum, Jalan Srijaya 1, Km5.5 (Mon–Thurs & Sat 8am–2pm, Fri 8–11am; Rp200), which lies 6km north of the city centre. Built about twenty years ago, it consists of several large, airy galleries with huge verandahs, set in pretty, well-kept gardens. The galleries hold geological exhibits, weapons, ceramics, textiles and traditional costumes, supplemented by a collection of *pallawa prasasti*, stones inscribed in the ancient Malay language. In the grounds are stone megaliths and troughs, many from the Lahat and Pagaralam area (see p.446), plus an attractive, traditional *limas* house, closed to the public.

Eating and drinking

There are plenty of places to eat in Palembang, from the **night markets** on Jalan Letkol Iskander and Jalan Sayangan via more formal rumah makan, up to top-class restaurants. The Palembang **specialities** are eel (*ikan belida*) served with various hot and spicy sauces (thankfully the eels no longer come from the polluted Musi), and *pempek*, which is available throughout Sumatra but originated in this area. They are balls made from sago, fish and seasoning, and fried or grilled before being served up with sauce.

French Bakery, Jl Kol Atmo 481. One of several small bakeries in town, where you can sit inside and enjoy the variety of sweet bread and cakes on offer. This one also has a small menu of Indonesian soups and basic foods, and is very popular.

Garuda canteen, in the same building as the Garuda supermarket/department store, about 400m west of the main post office. With inexpensive ice concoctions, juices, soups, noodles and local *pempek*, this is a good place for a filling meal.

KFC, next to Gelael supermarket at Internasional Plaza. Serves up the usual expensive chicken and French fries, but it's cool and the air-con is free, even if the food and drink has ten percent tax added to displayed prices.

Kopi Har. There are several of these great Muslim Indian coffee shops around town, one of the most central being at Jl Sudirman 23 at the corner of Jl T.P. Rustan Effendi. They are especially good for *murtabak* breakfasts; the pancake comes with an egg inside and served with potato curry. Splash out on a coffee as well and you'll still pay less than Rp3000.

Mahkota Permai, Jl Mesjid Lama 33. Inexpensive place serving Palembang food including eel.

Sari Bundo, Jl Sudirman 1301. Located on the corner with Jl Kapten A. Rivai, this bustling, popular, inexpensive Padang restaurant dishes up good food in utilitarian but pleasant surroundings.

Saria Mulia, Jl Sudirman 679. Just opposite Internasional Plaza, this is a cool and airy place to get inexpensive local soups, drinks and ice dishes.

Selatan Indah, Jl Letkol Iskander 434. A moderate to expensive priced place with an extensive Chinese menu and a good local reputation.

Sumatera, Jl Sudirman 906. A substantial menu offers traditional inexpensive Indonesian food plus burgers, sweet breads and juices.

Swenson's in *KFC* at Gelael. At Rp5000–8000 for your favourite sundae, the American ice-cream chain has great air-con and is a conveniently central place (though expensive) to rest from the sightseeing.

Shopping

From modern shopping centres to old-fashioned markets selling local textiles and lacquerware, Palembang has plenty of **shopping** options.

Shopping centres and markets

For a thoroughly modern shopping experience, the four-storey **Internasional Plaza** at the junction of Jalan Sudirman and Jalan Letkol Iskander, includes a Matahari department store, supermarket, food plaza and fast-food outlets. Some good textile shops are clustered on the ground floor: Safari Jaya sells batik from Java, Palembang *songket*, sets of sarong and *selendang* for Rp200,000, and silk lengths from Rp80,000. Far more traditional, although it's about to move into a concrete multi-storey block, is the famous **Pasir Ilir 16 market**, between Jalan Mesjid Lama and Sungai Musi just to the east of Ampera Bridge. Further north on Jalan Sudirman, between Jalan Cinde Welan and Jalan Letnam Jamais, the traditional **Pasar Cinde** market features a maze of alleyways lined with stalls selling food, clothes and household items galore. The **Megahria shopping complex** on Jalan T.P. Rustan Effendi, a covered market with alleyways of tiny shops, sells pretty much anything you could desire. If you're in the market for **gold**, try the western end, which is lined with jewellers.

Textiles

The **textile specialities** of Palembang are *songket* and *jumputan pelangi*, silk material with patterns created using tie-dye techniques; *pelangi* means "rainbow" in Indonesian. The centre for the **workshops** and **showrooms** is in 32 Ilir to the west of the city centre; a brown Kijang will get you there. On Jalan Ki Gede Ing Suro, you can watch *songket* weaving on backstrap looms. The cost depends partly on the fineness of the thread and the amount of effort needed to create a piece; typically a sarong and *selendang* set will take a weaver working eight-hour days a month to complete. Prices are from Rp200,000 to Rp900,000 for such sets, and from Rp150,000 for a batik set, skirt, jacket or four-metre silk dress length. Whilst the *songket* stuff is generally rather glittery and showy, much of the *jumputan pelangi* work is extremely attractive. Try **Serengam Sentai**, 32 Ilir Serengam, Jalan Ki Gede Ing Suro 264, RT 11 (Mon–Sat 9am–5pm) and **Cek Ipah**, Jalan Ki Gede Ing Suro 141, which has an excellent range of textiles and helpful staff. Their workshop produces *songket* sets up to Rp35 million, but these are usually not in stock – the Rp300,000 versions are available. *Jumputan pelangi* is available in four-metre lengths from Rp20,000to Rp50,000 per metre and both *ikat* and a very unusual *batik prada*, batik cloth with gold paint, is also for sale. *Prada* means "gilded", and the gold in this work is more subtle and less dense than that used in other parts of the archipelago.

Lacquerware
Another Palembang speciality is **lacquerware**, a technique probably introduced to the area by the Chinese, in which wood and basketware items are sealed, painted, decorated with black ink designs and covered in a layer of lacquer produced from ant's nests. Deep red and gold are the traditional colours. Each of the decorations has significance: flowers for beauty, a lion for strength, the golden phoenix for an end to problems, and butterflies to signify the pleasures of the night – good sleep, good dreams and love. Mekar Jaya, Jalan Slamat Riady 45a, has a variety of bowls and vases up to 1m tall in black and gold, with flowery, swirling patterns, priced from Rp15,000 to over Rp1 million. The Jalan Guru Guru and Serelo areas (see below) are also good hunting grounds.

Souvenirs
On **Jalan Faqih Jalahuddin**, a small road heading north of Jalan Merdeka just west of Mesjid Agung, you'll find woodcarving, lacquerware and a range of "antiques". Toko Antik at no.39 is great fun, a real treasure trove of ceramics, junk and antiques, where you can spend hours rooting around. At 103f, Karya Ukir Saria Agung sells lacquerware, with attractive small bowls at Rp15,000–20,000 and impressive larger plates for Rp30,000. The other main area is **Serelo**, at the far end of Jalan Guru Guru: turn left and first right (about 300m walk) and you'll be in Jalan A.K.B.P.H.M. Amin. Alternative access from the other end is 100m south of Internasional Plaza opposite the BNI bank. There are plenty of small shops and workshops; the most exclusive is Galleri Mir Senen at no.43, with a huge range of old and new arts and crafts from throughout Indonesia including furniture, carvings, ornaments and jewellery. Everything is displayed in attractive surroundings, and the owners can arrange shipping, and accept credit cards. Batik Palembang is next door at no.45 and has gorgeous old textiles, which cost from Rp750,000 to Rp1 million. However, there are plenty of less expensive shops around and it's a great area for browsing. Mahligan Art at no.442 and Toko Lukman at no.41a both sell attractive lacquerware.

Bookshops
The Gramedia **bookshop**, Jalan Kol Atmo 1301, close to *King's Hotel*, has postcards and even the occasional English classic novel; Toko Bulu Anggrek, Jalan Sudirman 138, is also worth a browse and Toko Buku Diponegoro, Jalan Sudirman 27b, sell the most detailed city map of Palembang, published by Indo Prima Sarana (IPS).

Entertainment and nightlife

There are several **cinemas** in town: try Studio on Jalan Sudirman, which is set back off the road just south of the prominent Bank Bumi Daya, or International 21, on the fifth floor of Internasional Plaza, and Megahria cinema in the shopping complex of the same name on Jalan T.P. Rustan Effendi. Much of the diet is sex or kung fu, but Western movies also make it here. The **bar** of the *King's Hotel* is something of a meeting place with the better-off, especially at the weekends, and the current happening **disco** is *Darma Agung* at km6, north of the city on Jalan Sudirman (11pm–2am; Rp20,000). Less expensive, but also popular, are nightly discos at the *Puri Indah* and *Princess* hotels.

Listings

Airline offices Bouraq, Jl Dempo Luar 31 (☎0711/313790); Deraya agent, PT Saung Mas, Jl Kapten A. Rivai 220a (☎0711/363421, fax 358350); Garuda, *Hotel Sandjaja*, Jl Kapten A. Rivai 6193 (☎0711/364404); Mandala, Jl Letkol Iskander Block D2/66 (☎0711/312168, fax 310424); Merpati, 24hr city check-in and ticketing office, Jl Sudirman 75 (☎ & fax 0711/360003).

Banks and exchange Bank Bumi Daya, Jl Sudirman 1779; BCA, Jl Kapten A. Rivai 22; BNI, Jl Sudirman 132; Bank Rakyat Indonesia, Jl Kapten A. Rivai 15.

Buses The main concentration of bus offices is just south of Ampera Bridge on Jl Pangeran Ratu, while the Pekanbaru offices and departures are at Kilometre Lima, near the 5km marker on Jl Sudirman, north of the city centre. There are also several bus offices on Jl Kol Atmo, just north of *King's Hotel*. Prices vary considerably but make sure you know what you're getting – there are large buses, small buses and minibuses on most routes. Benteng Jaya, Jl Kol Atmo 632a/1230 (☎0711/370730), have daily air-con services to Jakarta. Bintang Mas, Jl Kol Atmo 582 (☎0711/372452), depart three times daily, in air-con minibuses to Bandar Lampung and Jakarta. C.S.H. 88, Jl Kol Atmo 621/66 (☎0711/357107), operate daily to Bengkulu. Kramat Djati, Jl Kol Atmo 582c (☎0711/350774), do all Java destinations – in many cases transiting in Jakarta or Bandung. Lorena, Jl Kol Atmo 50 (☎0711/360441), is one of the largest operators, with huge numbers of destinations on Sumatra, Java and on to Bali. NPM, Jl Merdeka 317 (☎0711/363319), offer air-con and non-air-con buses to Bukittinggi, Padang, Medan and Jakarta.

Golf Lapangan golf course, Jl A.K.B. Cep Agus 23 (☎0711/352952) This eighteen-hole course is the largest in South Sumatra. Green fees are Rp25,000 (Mon–Thurs) and Rp40,000 (Fri–Sun & hols). There's a caddy fee of Rp7500. Equipment is available for rental: Rp35,000 for a full set of clubs for eighteen holes, and Rp10,000 for shoes.

Hospitals Charitas, Jl Sudirman 809 (☎0711/353375); Rumah Sakit A.K. Gani, Jl Benteng, near the main post office (☎0711/354691); Rumah Sakit Umum Palembang, Jl Sudirman 890 (☎0711/354008).

Immigration office Jl May Memet Sastrawiriya 1 (☎0711/710055).

Pharmacies There are plenty of pharmacies in the central areas of town: Apotik Rora, Jl Sudirman 200 (☎0711/350086), is open 24hr.

Post office The main post office is centrally located at Jl Merdeka 3 and has an efficient post restante system and a public email service (Rp2000 per email).

Swimming Lumban Kirta, Jl Pom IX, features an indoor Olympic-sized pool with separate diving area (daily 8am–7.30pm; Rp1500).

Telephone and fax The main 24hr Telkom office is at Jl Merdeka 5, and there are wartels at Jl Sudirman 1004b (daily 7am–midnight) and Jl Letkol Iskander 902a (24hr).

Travel agents Caremta Tours and Travel, Jl Dempo Luar 29–30 (☎0711/356653, fax 312589), is one of the largest and best-organized agencies and offers city tours for Rp36,000 (3hr) and Rp70,000 (7hr), Sungai Musi trips (Rp52,000 for 3hr) and tours further afield (Bangka: three nights/two days for Rp295,000). Try also Wisin Tours and Travel, Jl Taman Siswa 173h (☎0711/366811).

Pulau Bangka and Pulau Belitung

Usually mentioned in the same breath by locals and travellers alike, **Pulau Bangka** and **Pulau Belitung** are located in the South China Sea off the coast of east Sumatra, and have many historical and modern characteristics in common. The islands are pleasant and sleepy backwaters on the way to nowhere, although administratively attached to the South Sumatra province. The lucrative tin trade that fuelled the islands' economies for centuries has virtually died, the pepper trade brought plentiful but unpredictable rewards to Bangka, and the anticipated tourist boom on both islands has so far failed to materialize. Bangka and Belitung remain, for now, ideal destinations for those who want to get a bit – but not too far – off the beaten track.

Geologically the islands are similar, low-lying with no hint of the volcanic origins of mainland Sumatra, springing instead from the ancient, non-volcanic core of the Sunda

Shelf, like the Riau and Lingga islands to the north. A rich vein of tin runs through the islands and on northward to Pulau Singkep, Malaysia and Thailand. Originally covered in tropical jungle, mining and tin-smelting have decimated the primary habitat of the islands, which has been replaced by scrubland interspersed with countless *kolong*, most easily visible from the air, artificial lakes created by the open-cast tin-mining and since abandoned.

Some history

Tin was probably discovered on the islands about 1710. As well as Europeans, the Chinese had a huge demand for the metal, which they used for joss paper (very thin foil to be burnt in religious ceremonies), and to mix into alloys to make mirrors, teapots, candlesticks, vases and coins. The tin mined from mainland China could not meet demand, and from an early date the Chinese were interested in the deposits on Bangka and Belitung, as were the Dutch, who had failed in their attempt to get a monopoly on the tin trade in the Malacca area after they acquired the city in 1641. Over the following centuries, it was largely **Chinese coolie labour** that worked the mines, initially for the sultan of Palembang and later for the Dutch, and though the islands acquired a worldwide reputation for the tin itself they also gained notoriety for appalling working conditions, dubious recruiting methods and the poor health of the coolie labour. Generally, conditions on Bangka were worse than on Belitung – a writer earlier in the twentieth century described coolies cutting off their own thumbs so they could not work in the mines near Mentok and could return home. By the mid-nineteenth century, tin was third behind coffee and sugar in export earnings from the Dutch East Indies.

Throughout the history of the tin mines, many Chinese labourers did not return home after the end of their contracts and settled on the islands, raising families of their own. Local-born or *perinakan* Chinese now form about 25 percent of the population of Bangka, the largest settlement of *perinakan* Chinese outside Java, but rather less on Belitung (about ten percent).

Both islands suffered badly during World War II. Bangka was occupied by the Japanese two days after the surrender of Singapore on February 15, 1942, and Belitung was taken two months later. A thousand Japanese soldiers were based on the islands, and poor nutrition and disease were rife among the local population and the Chinese. Many young people were sent elsewhere as forced labour; in 1943, a thousand people from Belitung were shipped to Palembang to work in the petroleum fields. By the end of the war a hundred men from Bangka had vanished and many young women had been forced to work as prostitutes.

Pulau Bangka

Attractive scenery, good beaches, a peaceful and relaxed style of life and easy access from the mainland make **Pulau Bangka** an ideal place to rest up for a few days away from the crowds and noise of Palembang, or it can be a peaceful stop-off point on an island-hopping trip between Jakarta and the Riau Islands.

Separated from the Sumatran mainland by just 20km of the Bangka Strait at the closest point, the island of **Bangka**, with a population of around 650,000, describes the shape of a seahorse's head – a very large seahorse, 180km long from northwest to southeast, roughly a tenth of the size of Java. The origins of its name have produced several speculations: *vanga* (tin) in Sanskrit, sometimes spelt *wangka*, features on a Sriwijayan inscription from 686 AD found on the island, and the early settlers were said to have discovered *bangkai* (bodies) of previous inhabitants. Another interpretation is that the name comes from *wangkang*, which in Southeast Asia is the name for a Chinese junk. Whichever is true, they point to the two foundations of Bangka history – tin and seafaring.

GETTING TO BANGKA FROM PALEMBANG

High-speed ferry departures to **Pulau Bangka** are from Bom Baru, a couple of kilometres east of Palembang city centre; take a cream Kijang from Ampera and get off at the BNI bank – the terminal is 200m walk towards the river. A couple of companies operate and there are four departures daily (7–9.30am; 2–3hr) to Mentok. The fare one way is Rp25,000, plus Rp1500 port tax. You can also buy a Mentok–Pangalpinang bus ticket when you check in at the terminal – at Rp5000 it will get you taken to your hotel and it saves hassle when you arrive. There are plenty of agents in Palembang selling tickets but it's just as easy to buy your ticket at the terminal. The ship *Adiyasa* sails overnight (11hr) three times weekly (Rp9750–13,750) – check departures at Bom Baru.

By the turn of this century, with the local population increasing but only involved in the tin industry in secondary ways (such as supplying the workers), it became apparent that local income needed a boost. The Dutch encouraged **pepper** as an income crop, which has now largely taken over the Bangka economy. Travellers to Bangka will spot the vines in fields lining the road; they grow to about 3m and produce pepper for around five years. The main problem with pepper production, as with primary goods throughout the world, is the huge fluctuations in price on the world market; local initiatives are currently exploring fruit exports to Palembang and Jakarta, shrimp farming, timber production and the export of granite, in an attempt to create a stable local economy.

Islanders are hopeful that **tourism** is going to develop on Bangka to take the place of tin. The reality is that tourist development remains very low-key, catering largely for the domestic market. Until there's more big money invested to entice the Singaporean tourists who flock to Batam and Bintan to make a much longer trip, this is unlikely to change significantly. In fact, at the time of writing, the large investment was going into Belitung (see p.435) and, whilst the attractive beaches of Bangka make it unlikely the island will be overlooked altogether, it's safe to assume it will remain a quiet, little-known and rather charming destination in the foreseeable future.

The main reason to visit the island is the peaceful pace of beach life, where a few days of relaxation is possible, perhaps after a day or so in **Pangalpinang** and/or **Sungailiat**.

Mentok, Sungailiat and the northern beaches

Both the hydrofoil service from Palembang and Pelni ferries from elsewhere in Indonesia arrive at **MENTOK** harbour on the northwest coast. Two accommodation options are located near here: new and good-quality *Hotel Jati Menumbing* (☎0716/21388; ⑤–⑧) at Gunung Menumbing, 15km from Mentok; and basic *Losmen Mentok* (no phone; ②) on Jalan Sudirman.

There are also a couple of attractive strands, but the best **beaches**, which are indeed the main reason to come here, are located in the north of the island, one on Klabat Bay and the main concentration on the northeast coast. The easiest option for getting around is to charter **transport** – ask at your accommodation place – but there is public transport between the major towns and villages.

Romodong Seaview Cottages (book at Jalan Bukit Intan 1, 147, Pangalpinang; ☎ & fax 0717/21573 or make reservations in Jakarta ☎021/5604150, fax 5670469; ⑥–⑦) is 20km north of the small village of Belinyu along a road that's mostly asphalt but in poor condition. It's situated in a great position on a picturesque white-sand bay 4km long, with excellent views to the offshore island of Pulau Lampu and across Klabat Bay, which makes it one of the best places on the island. Accommodation is in wooden bungalows with air-con, cold-water bathrooms and good verandahs, and there's an inexpensive to moderately priced restaurant attached. Other beaches to explore lie nearby, and a ferry service runs across to the other side of the bay.

The beaches on the northeast coast of the island range north and south of **SUNGAILIAT**, a small town 32km from Pangalpinang, which is pleasant enough but really only useful for access to the beaches. The tourist office is at Jalan Jend Sudirman (Mon–Thurs & Sat 8am–2pm, Fri 8–11am; ☎0717/92496); staff are helpful and have English-language brochures. Amongst the **accommodation** options are *Wisma Flamboyant*, Jalan Dr Sam Ratulangi 1 (☎0717/92076; ③–④), which has some rooms with air-con and attached mandi and some without. *Pondok Wisata Moeliya Homestay*, Jalan Jend Sudirman 154–156 (☎0717/92157, fax 92111; ④) is a real homestay with accommodation in a family house with a spacious garden, set back from the busy road. There are a variety of rooms on offer, from those with fan to some with air-con and TV, and it's advisable to book. At the top end of the range, *Hotel Citria*, Jalan Jend Sudirman 343 (☎0717/92404, fax 92386; ⑥), is the smartest place in town, rooms featuring air-con and hot water. *Bangka Permai*, Jalan Jend Sudirman 173 (☎0717/92090; ④–⑦), has an attractive, quiet garden setting, and a wide range of rooms.

Heading south from the town, the first hotel on the beach is *Teluk Uber Hotel*, Jalan Pantai Teluk Uber 1 (☎0717/93138; reservations can be made in Palembang, Jalan Dr Wahidin 1; ☎0711/350388; ⑥–⑦). It's less heavily publicized and much simpler and cheaper than the other places on this coast, and is just 7km south of Sungailiat. Accommodation is in an attractive block with verandahs looking to the beach and there's a moderately priced restaurant set in the large grounds.

Two kilometres further south, *Tanjung Pesonna*, Jalan Pantai Rebo (☎0717/92794, fax 92796; ⑦–⑧), is situated on a headland 9km from Sungailiat, with bays on either side and fine views north to Teluk Uber and south to the Tikus and Rebo beaches. It's a huge establishment, with a large restaurant, coffee shop, disco, karaoke and billiard hall. During the weekend it's lively and busy but it's rather soulless during the week.

Twelve kilometres north of Sungailiat, the *Sahid Parai Indah* (☎0717/92335, fax 93001; reservations can be made in Jakarta ☎021/5655828, fax 5655458; ⑦–⑨), is the largest and most expensive operation on the coast, with a grand two-storey entrance lobby. The lower-priced accommodation is in a two-storey block, with more expensive rooms in cottages in the grounds. Meals are US$4 for breakfast, US$6 for lunch and US$8 for dinner, in an attractive open-sided restaurant near the beach, which is a pretty white-sand cove. There's a large swimming pool and tennis courts with rackets for rent, and the glorious Matras beach is only about 500m to the north.

Pangalpinang

The main town of Pulau Bangka, **PANGALPINANG** lies on the east coast, 138km away from Mentok (2–3hr), and is a small, pleasant town with wide streets and a laid-back atmosphere. There's an ethnically mixed population of around 120,000, including descendants of early Chinese, Arab and Indian settlers. The town has good tourist facilities but few sights: the Tin Museum was opened in 1932 but is now unfortunately closed (check on its current status with the tourist office).

Local bemos run from the **bus terminal** on the southern outskirts into the market area in the town centre. Pangkalan Baru **airport** is 6km south of town and served by fixed-price taxis (Rp5000); Belitung hydrofoils and Jakarta jetfoils arrive at **Pangkal Balam port**, 4km north of town, also served by taxis (Rp5000).

The main street in Pangalpinang is Jalan Sudirman, which runs roughly north–south for well over 1km; the centre of town is at the main crossroads with Jalan Mesjid Jamik, and the market area is a couple of hundred metres east of this. Most hotels, restaurants and offices are either on or close to Jalan Sudirman. The **tourist office**, Jalan Bukit Intan (Mon–Thurs & Sat 8am–2pm, Fri 8–11am; ☎0717/32546), has a good English brochure about the island but is a bit short on other information; it's probably better to make specific inquiries to hotels or travel agents in town.

The **post office** is at Jalan Sudirman 18, the 24hr **Telkom** office at Jalan Sudirman 6, and there are several **banks**: BNI at Jalan Sudirman 1, BCA at Jalan Mesjid Jamik 15, and Bank Dagang Negara at Jalan Sudirman 7. The **airlines** serving the island have offices here: Merpati, Jalan Sudirman 45 (☎0717/21132), and Mandala, Jalan Sudirman 36 (☎0717/22268), and the Deraya agent is PT Priaventure, Jalan Sudirman 10 (☎0717/21013). For Jakarta jetfoils, book at CV Gunawan Wisatajaya, Jalan Sudirman 69 (☎0717/22734) and Belitung for hydrofoils and ferries book at Carmeta, Jalan Sudirman 35a (☎0717/24333, fax 31785) – book at either place for Palembang hydrofoils. The Pelni office is at Jalan Depati Amir 67 (☎0717/22216).

For **souvenirs**, *Toko Timah TKF* has some attractive and unusual tin gifts ranging from keyrings at Rp5000, through vases and boxes (Rp19,000–35,000) up to large and intricate model ships (Rp650,000).

ACCOMMODATION

There are several **accommodation** choices in town in all price brackets and with all degrees of comfort. The closest **beach hotel** to Pangalpinang is at Pantai Pasir Padi, 10km away: the *Serrata Hotel* (☎0717/31574, fax 31573; ⑦–⑨), which has wooden cottages with tiled roofs – there's a good-sized pool, restaurant, boating lake, tennis courts and you can charter boats out to nearby Pulau Pinang.

Bukit Sofa Hotel, Jl Mesjid Jamik 43 (☎0717/21062). Justly popular and sometimes full, with several standards of room including some good-value singles. ④–⑥.

Hotel Griya Tirta, Jl Semabung Lama 272 (☎0717/33436, fax 23859). A new gleaming place 1.5km from Jl Sudirman towards the coast. Well-furnished rooms open off an attractive courtyard with a small coffee shop. ⑦.

Hotel Jati Wisata, Jl Kartini 3 (☎0717/31600, fax 31222). New and plush with clean, comfortable rooms with air-con and hot-water, and a restaurant and coffee shop. Jl Kartini is a side street off Jl Depati Amir, which itself branches off Jl Sudirman at the northern end of town. ⑥.

Wisma Jaya 1, Jl Depati Amir 8 (☎0717/21696). On the corner with Jl Sudirman, with clean and pleasant rooms with air-con and hot-water, and attractive deep verandahs around a courtyard at the back, which houses an open-air restaurant. ⑥.

Hotel Karya Bhakti, Jl Sudirman 11 (☎0717/22007, fax 32019). A large range of rooms with fan and cold-water mandi at the lower end, and hot-water and air-con at the top. There's a garden area surrounded by verandahs at the back. ④–⑤.

Melati, Jl Mesjid Jamik 51 (☎0717/24419). Clean, economical rooms, some with attached mandi. Rooms are varied so ask to see several; the upstairs ones are quieter. ④.

Hotel Sabrina, Jl Diponegoro 73 (☎0717/22424). In a quiet location a short walk from the main street, Jl Sudirman. All rooms have hot water, bathtub, colour TV and air-con. ⑤–⑦.

Sera Indah, Jl Imam Bonjol 18 (☎0717/21579). On the street opposite the *French Bakery* on Jl Sudirman. It's a small, family-run place with rooms leading off an overgrown garden with cold-water attached mandi and one grand marbled room with a mirrored ceiling. ④–⑥.

Srikandi, Jl Mesjid Jamik 42 (☎21884). A rambling, friendly, lively place featuring rooms with cold-water mandi attached. Unfortunately it's often full. ④.

EATING

The *French Bakery* at Jalan Sudirman 27 and *Holland Bakery*, nearby at no. 25, offer a good choice of sweet breads and cakes. *Bagadangraya*, Jalan Sudirman 30, and, across the road, *Saribundo*, Jalan Sudirman 77, both serve good-value **Padang food**, while *A Sui*, Jalan Kampung Bintang Dalam, is the locally recommended seafood restaurant, with excellent dishes at moderate prices in simple surroundings. *Pondok Kelapa* on Pantai Pasir Padi, close to *Serrata Hotel*, serves moderately priced meals and enjoys a sea breeze.

Pulau Belitung

Batam's larger neighbour, 80km to the southeast, is **Pulau Belitung**. Despite great beaches and enticing offshore islands, very few tourists make it this far and it remains, for now, an almost undiscovered gem. The island is turning to tourism for income, and development is already under way on the best **beach** on the island, **Tanjung Tinggi**.

According to one local story the name comes from "Bali potong" (a cut of Bali): supposedly Belitung was once part of Hindu Bali but was for some reason cut off and driven away to its present site. One intriguing aspect of Belitung history relates to the Dutch sailors captured by pirates that roamed the area. For centuries Belitung was at the furthest reaches of the powerful ancient Indonesian kingdoms, and the inlets and offshore islands close to one of the world's most lucrative shipping channels in the Malacca Straits made the island an ideal pirate hideaway. In 1822, pirates captured the Dutch ship *Anna Maria* and two members of the crew were sold as slaves to the chief of the village of Sijuk in the northwest, but were eventually freed when a Malay noble paid two balls of opium for their release. Other Dutchmen were known to have been kept as slaves on the east coast of the island in Burung Mandi; when they gained control over the island there was already a Dutch-style house in the area.

Tanjung Pandan

The main town on Belitung is **TANJUNG PANDAN**, a pleasant, laid-back port with just its personality and atmosphere to attract and detain visitors. The **museum** at Jalan Melati 41 (Sat, Sun & hols 8am–5pm) is pretty much the only sight in town; housed in a bungalow, it features a small collection of weapons, coins, textiles and craft items. The **beach** is tidal and quite grey, with the added disadvantage of being fairly close to the port. However, some warung here open at dusk, and it's a pleasant place to have a sunset drink looking across to Pulau Kalmoa and other distant islands.

Ferry services arrive at the **port** area of Tanjung Pandan, about 1km from the town centre, flights arrive at Buluhtumbang **airport**, 14km from town. Fixed-price taxis are Rp10,000 into the centre; there's a taxi counter at the front of the terminal. Otherwise it's a one-kilometre walk to the main road between Tanjung Pandan and Manggar, where you can pick up public transport into the bus terminal. Although the town is spread out, it's small enough to walk around; if you catch an **bemo** (they run from 7am to 5pm, as do buses around the island) it'll be Rp400 flat rate anywhere in town.

There's very little nightlife, and by far the best way to spend time after dark is at the friendly **night market** at the end of Jalan Endek, where plenty of stalls cook up the usual Indonesian specialities quickly, cheaply and well. If you want **restaurant** dining, *Pribumi*, Jalan M.T. Haryono 21, serves excellent Indonesian food in a neat, open-fronted restaurant with friendly staff.

The **post office** is at Jalan Merdeka 12; for **money exchange**, use Bank Rakyat Indonesia, Jalan Merdeka 11, or BNI at Jalan Gegedek. The **tourist office**, Jalan Sekolah 23 (☎0719/21398), publishes English-language brochures, provide general information and try to answer specific queries, and there's a **wartel** at Jalan Sriwijaya 41 (5am–11pm).

Moving on from Belitung, the options are plentiful. Pelni, Jalan Pabean 119 (☎0719/21719), operate the *KM Lawit,* which calls four times fortnightly, twice on its way to Tanjung Priok and twice en route to Pontianak (see p.641). The office in Tanjung Pandan will, for some reason, only sell ekonomi tickets. There are several flight options and the airlines have offices in Tanjung Pandan: Deraya, Jalan Merdeka 12 (☎0719/22333), and Merpati, Jalan Sudirman 2 (☎0719/21677, fax 21422).

ACCOMMODATION

Dewi Wisma, Jl Sriwijaya 122 (☎0719/21134). This small popular place is a bit out of the town centre in an old bungalow, with deep verandahs and high-ceilinged rooms opening out onto a small garden. A restaurant is attached and rooms have air-con and cold-water mandi. ⑤–⑥.

Hotel Makmur, Jl Endek 24 (☎0719/21320). Centrally located with a variety of rooms, from ekonomi with a fan and outside bathroom up to a suite, although there's no hot water. Ground-floor rooms open out onto a small garden at the back and have small sitting areas in front. ④–⑥.

Hotel Martini, Jl Yos Sudarso 17 (☎0719/21432, fax 21433). The grandest and most expensive set-up in town is centrally located and has pleasant, open-sided corridors with plenty of garden areas and fountains; staff are friendly and helpful and rooms are comfortable although not luxurious. ⑦.

Wisma Pantai Belitung Permai, Jl Pantai Pandan (☎0719/21659, fax 22310). The only beach accommodation in town has a huge variety of rooms in large bungalows close to the beach, but with the more luxurious accommodation in bungalows further away. The location is good but the places in town are better value. ⑤–⑦.

Hotel Surya, Jl Endek 808 (☎0719/21550). Just along the road from *Hotel Makmur*, on the second floor with a small entrance on the street. All rooms are basic but clean and have outside mandi, while more expensive rooms have air-con. ④.

Around the island

The main reason to come to Belitung is in search of that magical little white-sand **beach** that you can enjoy in isolation. While it isn't particularly easy to get around the island and the chances of somewhere being undiscovered are shrinking fast, there are still deserted little coves to explore. Getting around is much easier with your own **transport** (inquire at your accommodation) – there is public transport around the island but it is infrequent.

Ten kilometres north of Tanjung Pandan, the small village of **TANJUNG BINGA** lines the road just behind the pretty white beach, with a multitude of attractive wooden jetties protruding into the ocean as mooring for the local fishing boats. It's very pleasant, but foreign sunbathers soon draw a crowd of onlookers. However, there are four alluring offshore islands: Pulau Kera, Pulau Batu, Pulau Burung and Pulau Babi, all five to ten minutes away by chartered speedboat and excellent for a day-trip (take all your supplies). There are simple cottages on Pulau Burung; inquire in Tanjung Binga, at the shops on the main street or at the police station, for more information.

Another 17km north at **TANJUNG KELAYAN**, which has an attractive sandy beach, there are basic thatched cottages with concrete attached mandi at *Kelayan Indah* (no telephone; ④). The cottages have verandahs, with good views to Pulau Kelayan off the coast to the left, and Tanjung Tinggi off to the right. It gets busy here at the weekends when warung and drinks stalls open up to cater to day-trippers, but weekdays are totally peaceful. However, at the time of writing, a multi-storey upmarket hotel was under construction next door, so the peace may not last long.

At **TANJUNG TINGGI**, undoubtedly the most gorgeous beach on the island, 4km beyond Tanjung Kelayan, the beauty is due to the purity of the gleaming white sand and the brilliant clarity of the turquoise and azure waters. The big money has chosen well: the *Belitung Indah Resort* is due to open in 2001, with three hotels, an eighteen-hole golf course and a marina. At present a tiny, unnamed inexpensive rumah makan at the entrance to the construction site is situated next to a lovely little beach, a surprisingly peaceful spot in which to catch the gentle breeze.

Around on the **east coast** there are some large, isolated, pleasant beaches north of the small town of Manggar, but they have no facilities and access can be difficult. The best centre for exploring this coast is **MANGGAR**, a pleasant little town, although rather spread out; it's 3–4km from the terminal to the town centre, which has all basic amenities such as a post office and telephone office. There are several inexpensive places to stay, but the best is *Nusa Indah*, Jalan Pegadaian 87 (☎0719/91293; ④), a small, clean, friendly homestay near Pasar Sayur and the town centre with fan and air-con rooms with attached mandi. One of the most popular and attractive beaches is at the small village of **BURUNG MANDI**, a few kilometres north of Manga, a long, curving strand that attracts plenty of day-trippers at the weekends but is otherwise quiet. Further north, **Pulau Pring**, **Kelapa Kampit** and **Sengaran** are well off the beaten track, while **Malang Lepau** is a small working beach with a huge wooden jetty protruding into the sea with enticing views south to other distant and deserted coves.

Bengkulu and around

Located across the other side of the Bukit Barisan Mountain range from the Trans-Sumatran Highway, the ex-colonial city of **BENGKULU** has long been something of a backwater. The administrative capital of the small province of the same name, it boasts several attractive sights and is a pleasant stopping-off point on trips to remote **Pulau Enggano**, the lively town of **Curup** which is a good base for walkers, and the **Pasemah Plateau**.

The area around Bengkulu is home to several ethnically distinct peoples. The mountain-dwelling Rejang comprise the main groups: the highland Rejang and Rejang Pasisir

who inhabit the lower western land, with the remainder the Pasemah people of the Plateau (see p.444) and the Serawai people of the southern area. The people of Enggano (see p.443) are a different ethnic mix, more closely related to Mentawai dwellers than the people of the mainland.

With improved communications, Bengkulu is now relatively **accessible** from throughout Sumatra, although you need a bit of time as it's a hefty 149km from the Trans-Sumatran Highway at Lubuklinggau. However, access to the Pasemah Plateau is straightforward from the city and, with attractive beaches and mountain areas as well as sights to explore, there's plenty of reason to add Bengkulu to any itinerary.

It's worth bearing in mind that Bengkulu shares the geography and **climate** of Padang on the west side of the Bukit Barisan range, and the moisture-laden winds off the Indian Ocean dump their burden of water as they rise up over the mountains. Bengkulu is an attractive, but decidedly humid place.

Some history

The **British** first took Bengkulu (then called Bencoolen) as their Sumatran base in 1685, after they had been driven out of Banten by the Dutch; for 140 years it was Britain's only colony in Southeast Asia. Just as the Dutch had established themselves in Padang in 1663 to form part of their trade network, so the British founded Bengkulu in 1685, initially as an alternative source of pepper, although its importance soon declined and later reports tell of little trade, poor health and desperate boredom.

Bengkulu was way off the main trade routes and an extremely isolated outpost of empire, and British control was not unbroken; in 1719, local people regained control and held the city for several years, the French Admiral Comte d'Estaing took it for some months in 1760, and his compatriot Admiral Linois overran and pillaged Bengkulu in 1803. However, during their sojourn in the city, the British explored far and wide, and the earliest accounts of many parts of Sumatra date from that time. Thomas Stamford Raffles was governor from 1818 to 1824, visiting the Minang highlands in 1818 from his base in Bengkulu, from where he completed many of his naval excursions throughout the region. In 1825 the British exchanged Bengkulu with the Dutch for authority over the Malay Peninsula and Singapore. Whilst the British had only maintained control of the coastal area, the Dutch launched a series of military expeditions in the 1850s and gained control of the mountainous region inland where, at the end of the century, gold was discovered, and it soon became the major supplier of gold in the Dutch East Indies.

Arrival, orientation, information and city transport

Flights come into Padang Kemiling **airport**, 14km south of town and a 200-metre walk to the main road from the terminal (the city is to the left); **boats** dock at Pulau Baai harbour, 15km south of the city centre. From both of these, fixed-price **taxis** are Rp10,000, or take public transport either to Panorama terminal or Pasar Minggu in the city centre; you may need to change at Simpang Lingka Barat. The situation regarding **bus terminals** is confused. Panorama terminal, a few kilometres from the city centre, is the long-distance terminal and it remains in use for all arrivals and departures. Most of the bus offices are in the streets nearby. However, a new terminal has been built at Sebakul, around 12km southeast of the city, which has so far been ignored as being too distant and inconvenient, but eventually operations may shift there.

Situated on and behind the coast of the Indian Ocean between the estuaries of Sungai Air Bengkulu to the north and Sungai Jenggalu to the south, the oldest part of Bengkulu is on an attractive headland around Fort Marlborough overlooking the sea. The main bulk of the town spreads south behind and parallel to the coast for about 10km, with a main thoroughfare running the entire length of town. roughly northwest–southeast, but changing its name from Jalan A. Yani at the top near Fort Marlborough through Jalan Sudirman, Jalan Suprapto, Jalan S. Parman, Jalan Jend Sutoyo, Jalan Kapt Tendean and finally Jalan Pangeran Natadiraj out towards the airport.

The best **tourist office** is the central Kanwil Depparpostel, Jalan Bali 42 (Mon–Thurs 7.30am–2pm, Fri 7.30–11am, Sat 7.30am–1pm; ☎0736/21883, fax 24000).

City transport

Negotiating Bengkulu's **city transport** is difficult for locals and visitors alike. There are no local buses, but hundreds of yellow, dark-red and green **bemos**, known locally as "taxis", scurry around town. The trouble is that they pretty much go where they want when they want – neither the colour of the vehicle nor the destinations fading on the windscreen seem to bear any relationship to where they are heading. You simply flag one down and tell them your destination and the driver will nod or not. The trick is to know what the various areas of town are called – the area around Fort Marlborough is "Kampung", the Pasar Minggu area is known as "Minggu", the bus terminal is "Panorama" and the main roads through town known simply by name "Suprapto", "Sudirman" and so on. The Simpang Lima (Five Ways) junction is a convenient landmark, where Jalan Suprapto changes into Jalan S. Parman at the junction with Jalan Fatmawati and Jalan Sukarno Hatta. **Cycle rickshaws** and **horse-drawn carts** are also available to rent, mostly off the main streets, and any bemo will turn itself into a taxi in the wink of an eye. Be sure to establish the price before you get in.

Accommodation

The **accommodation** options in Bengkulu aren't brilliant: there are plenty of utilitarian noisy hotels catering for the Indonesian business market, but only a few that appeal to the budget traveller.

Asia Hotel, Jl A. Yani 922b (☎0736/21901). Rather scruffy but central, with a huge range of rooms on offer, from budget ones with cold-water attached mandi up to those with air-con and hot water. ④–⑦.

Balai Buntor, Jl Khadijah 122 (☎0736/21254). Inexpensive rooms with cold-water mandi, or more expensive ones with air-con which are good value. Near the landmark of the Bank Indonesia. ⑤–⑥.

Bumi Endah, Jl Fatmawati 29 (☎0736/21665). Conveniently close to Simpang Lima, although on a fairly quiet road – despite the same street number as the *Denai* this smaller, less expensive option is across the road. Cheaper rooms have fan and more expensive ones have air-con. ④–⑤.

Denai, Jl Fatmawati 29 (☎0736/21981, fax 22029). Busy and popular in a convenient location near Simpang Lima – all rooms have hot water and air-con. This is a good choice in this price range, but you need to book ahead. ⑥.

Horison, Jl Pantai Nala 142 (☎0736/21722, fax 22072). Situated on a small hill just behind the beach, this is the best hotel in town, with a pleasant swimming pool and good views of the ocean. Rooms all have hot water and air-con, but it feels rather cavernous if it isn't busy. ⑦–⑨.

Malabero, Jl Prof Dr Hazairin S.H. 23 (☎0736/21004). With a central location near the Governor's House, this is a large old bungalow with high ceilings. A pleasant option in this price range. ③–④.

Nala Seaside Cottages, Jl Pantai Nala 133 (☎0736/21855). The best of the seaside places, all of which are across the road from the beach. During the weekends and in the evenings the area is busy, but on weekdays you'll often end up with the beach to yourself. Accommodation is in basic wooden bungalows with air-con and cold-water mandi, good-sized verandahs and excellent views to the beach. ⑤.

Ragil Kuning, Jl Kenanga 99 (☎0736/22682). By far the best budget option in the city, situated in a great water garden complete with streams and sitting areas; the area is quiet and hard to locate, but well worth the effort. You need to get an bemo to "Skip Lewat Simpang Pantai", which will go up Jl Flamboyant, along Jl Rafflesia and stop at the top of Jl Kenanga if coming from the centre of town. Rooms have attached mandi and a small verandah; drinks are available and they can rustle up a couple of basic dishes. ③.

Rio Asri, Jl Veteran 63 (☎0736/21952, fax 25728). Situated down a quiet sideroad, this high-quality hotel is well located. The rooms are very variable so ask to see several; all have air-con and hot water, and there's a pool. ⑤–⑦.

Samudera Dwinka, Jl Sudirman 246 (☎0736/21604, fax 23234). Centrally located at the junction of Jl Sudirman and Jl Suprapto; the cheaper rooms with fan and cold water aren't good value, but the more expensive options with air-con and hot-water mandi are better. ⑥.

Vista, Jl Mt Haryono 67 (☎0736/20820). This simple and clean place is one of the best central budget places; any bemos going into Pasir Minggu pass along here. There's a range of rooms, and a pleasant garden area at the back. ③–④.

The City

The overriding impression of Bengkulu is of a garden city, especially in the area around Fort Marlborough and the Governor's House at the northern end of town. Here in particular, roads are wide and tree-lined, pavements and even trees are painted in gleaming white and blue, and the stately buildings and parks are bedecked with statues and monuments.

Built in 1715, **Fort Marlborough** (Benteng Marlborough; daily 8am–7pm; Rp500) was constructed to replace the original British fortification at Fort York, 2km away. It has been well restored and almost sparkles in the sunshine, set in pretty gardens and with excellent views out to sea and up the coast. It looks sturdy enough – there are cannons positioned to guard against attack from the ocean, solid walls, hefty doors and surrounding ramparts – but on the two occasions it came under serious attack, from local people in 1719 and the French in 1760, the British did not manage to defend it effectively. An English gunner writing at the time had little confidence: "It would moulder away every wet season and the Guns often fall down into the Ditches." The outer wall is surrounded by a further defence, a dry moat, its aim not only to keep the enemy out but to keep the sentries in, as they had a habit of wandering off duty in search of alcohol. It's an evocative spot; at the entrance you walk between old gravestones of soldiers who died in Bengkulu, and it's easy to imagine their sense of isolation if you look westwards from the walls across the ocean. The nearest land is thousands of kilometres distant, whilst behind the fort, in the days before roads, the soaring mountains were virtually impenetrable.

Close to Fort Marlborough, at the northern end of Jalan A. Yani, the **Thomas Parr Monument** is prominently marked on maps, but is a fairly insignificant, empty domed building. Parr was a very unpopular governor of the colony who was stabbed and beheaded, probably by Bugis mercenaries, in 1807. He had come to Bencoolen from Bengal and tried to reduce the power of the "Bugis Corps", which the British East Indies Company used in addition to their own forces.

To the west of the fort around Jalan Panjaitan, a recent fire destroyed some of the old **Chinese quarter** of town, with its characteristic two-storey shophouses; it remains to be seen what rebuilding will look like here. Further south, the **Governor's House** is not open to the public, but you can look through the iron railings at the grand Classical lines of the white-painted building and carefully manicured grounds, while in the park nearby the **Daerah Monument** is an elegantly soaring pinnacle in its own grounds, surrounded by railings.

The Christian **cemetery** behind the church on Jalan Veteran is a rather shadeless and sad place, which reflects the savage toll that life in the tropics took on the foreign occupiers. It's said that some of Raffles' family are buried here.

Two kilometres south, at the junction of Jalan Sudirman, Jalan Suprapto and Jalan Mount Haryono, **Mesjid Jamik** was designed by President Sukarno, an architect by profession, while he was exiled in Bengkulu. It has the clean, austere lines of most mosque architecture, but the speeding traffic on all sides is a somewhat distracting counterpoint to prayer. A couple of hundred metres south of the mosque, just to the east of Jalan Suprapto,

Pasar Minggu is a wonderful old-style Indonesian market that has not yet been transferred into a boring concrete box: wander the tiny alleyways crammed with local coffee, songbirds in cages, piles of fruit, rattan and basketware. Out on the back road leading into the market, stalls selling stainless steel for mosque domes are clustered.

A kilometre southwest of here and a short walk from the Simpang Lima junction, **Sukarno's House** (Rumah Kediaman Bung Karno; daily; 8am–5pm; Rp250), on Jalan Sukarno Hatta, is the house to which the first president of Indonesia Sukarno was exiled from 1938 to 1942 together with his family. It's a large, airy bungalow with high ceilings and deep verandahs, set back from the road in spacious grounds. The rooms have been left largely as they were at the time of his occupation, with mouldy books and faded clothes behind glass-fronted cupboards. There's even the bicycle that Sukarno used to visit his second wife, who lived locally. Old photographs on display suggest that, even in exile, Sukarno maintained a vigorous political and social life.

Three kilometres south of Simpang Lima, the **Museum Negeri Bengkulu**, Jalan Pembangunan (Mon–Thurs 8am–4.30pm, Fri 8–11am, Sat & Sun 8am–1pm; free), is housed in a grand and impressive traditionally designed building, but the inside offers the usual range of poorly labelled items that can be seen in provincial museums all over the island: faded textiles, baskets, models of traditional houses, ceramics, old money and weapons, and artefacts connected with traditional wedding ceremonies. Of slightly more interest is the colourful display of Tabot towers, drums and flags from the annual local Tabot festival (see p.51).

Eating and drinking

There's a good range of places to eat in Bengkulu, from simple roadside warung to more expensive and stylish restaurants. The best **night market** is near Pasar Minggu, on Jalan K.Z. Abidin, which leads from the market area out onto Jalan Suprapto. It doesn't cover a huge area but the stalls are varied and you could easily put together a four-course meal of soup or sate, followed by a main rice or noodle dish, moving onto *murtabak* and then *es campur* and/or coffee.

Gandhi, Jl Suprapto 6a. One of several good bakeries in this part of town – they all serve sweet breads and cakes and have a few tables and chairs if you want to sit and relax.

Sari Segara, Jl Sudirman 199a. The best of the clutch of seafood places on Jl Sudirman, opposite Mesjid Jamik at the junction with Jl Suprapto. The menu is huge, and includes crab, squid, fish and lobster in a choice of sauces. Moderately priced but good-value, well-cooked food in basic surroundings.

Sate Solo, Jl Suprapto 157. Offers similar fare to the nearby *Sri Soto* and is clean, popular and bustling.

Si Kabayan, Jl Sudirman 51. Pleasant place in a garden setting: meals are eaten a low tables in individual bamboo huts. There's a wide range of Indonesian food on offer, most of it reasonable value, although the juices are expensive.

Simpang Raya, Jl Suprapto 380a. Almost opposite the Telkom office, this large restaurant is the local branch of the popular chain of Padang restaurants.

Sri Soto, Jl Suprapto 118. Sells basic, inexpensive noodle, chicken, rice, soup, sate, ice and juices. Good value, and popular with locals.

Listings

Airline offices Mandala, Jl Sukarno Hatta 39 (☎0736/25437); Merpati, Jl Sudirman 246 (☎0736/27111, fax 23105).

Banks and exchange BCA, Jl Suprapto 150, is the only bank in town which will touch anything apart from American dollar travellers' cheques; they also offer advances on Visa and Mastercard. If you have the more convertible dollar travellers' cheques you'll be welcome at BNI, Jl S. Parman 34.

Buses PT Mawar Selatan, Jl Sudirman 1 (☎0736/22366), has departures to Banda Aceh, Bukittinggi, Medan and Parapet; next door, Giri Indah, Jl Sudirman 1 (☎0736/22366), offers Jakarta, Yogyakarta, Solo, Probolingo and Denpasar; Siliwangi Antar Nusa (San Travel), Jl Mt Haryono, has Jakarta, Bandar Lampung and Manna departures.

Car rental Inquire at your hotel or Yudi Rent A Car, Jl Khadijah 95 (☎0736/26726). Expect to pay around Rp150,000 per day with or without driver.

Cinema Bioskop Segar, Jl Sudirman.

Disco Long Beach, at the south end of Pasir Panjang Cempaka Gading just behind the new *Pasir Putih Cottages* (nightly 10pm–2am; Rp10,000).

Ferries There are currently no Pelni passenger services serving Bengkulu. Inquire at the Pelni office, Jl Khadijah 10 (☎0736/31013), to see if they get reinstated.

Golf Rafflesia Golf Club, Jl Jenggalu 73 (☎0736/25335). Visitors are welcome at this picturesque nine-hole course beside the ocean (green fees Mon–Fri Rp15,000, Sat & Sun Rp25,000). Rental of clubs and shoes costs Rp25,000 and caddy fees are Rp1500.

Hospital Rumah Sakit Umum, Jl Padang Harapan (☎0736/21118).

PHPA Jl Mahoni 11 (☎0736/21697) for local information about Rafflesia. The office for Bukit Barisan national park is at Kota Agung (see p.459).

Post office The central post office is located at Jl S. Parman 111. They get very few tourists and the poste restante service is not recommended. A more convenient office is near the Parr Monument at Jl R.A. Hadi 3.

Shopping Puncak, Jl Suprapto 28. Despite an unpromising entrance, this three-storey department store includes a small supermarket and will meet most everyday needs.

Telephone and fax The 24hr Telkom office is centrally located at Jl Suprapto 132. There's another 24hr office at Jl Kolonel Barlian 51, next to the post office near the Parr Monument.

Textiles The local speciality is *batik besurek*. Originally used as a wrap for the dead, it's now made in cotton or silk and consists of batik with hand-painted elements applied afterwards. The best place to see the workshops is Bem Collection, Jl Ciliwung Bawah 2 (☎0736/25420); they also have a showroom. Take any bemo heading south towards the airport. Beyond the Padang Harapan roundabout a sign points east to Billar Pasir Putih – it's a pleasant, rural stroll along a small lane for 1–2km to the small house and workshop.

The coast

Bengkulu's **beaches** are a terrific attraction. The main strand is 7km long and starts as Pasir Nala in the north, changing its name further south to **Pasir Panjang Gading Cempaka**; it runs along the west side of the city, reached by walking along the coastal road from the port. It was supposedly named after a princess of the same name who, legend tells, was as fragrant as frangipani (*cempaka*) and had skin like ivory (*gading*). Just 5km off the coast, **Pulau Tikus** (Rat Island) is an excellent option for a day-trip, despite its name. It's only about 100m long and is part of a much larger underwater coral reef which still contains some iron anchors from old sailing ships that sheltered in the lee of the reef from the huge Indian Ocean swells. It's rich in sea life, but you'll need to take your own snorkelling gear and supplies for the day. Arrange a boat charter from the beach from Rp50,000.

Curup and around

The 85-kilometre trip from Bengkulu to **CURUP** is attractive, with pleasant views and interesting pinnacle mountain formations; regular buses run the route throughout the day. At Bukit Daun there's a lookout point with views back to Bengkulu, before the road climbs through the forest up to the pass and gate at Puncak and descends to Kepatiang and the Penanjung area, where you'll spot coffee drying by the road.

Curup is a small bustling market town, in the centre of the region known as the Rejang Lebong, cooler than the scorching coastal heat of Bengkulu, and a useful base from which to explore the mountainous area around or to stop over on the trip between Bengkulu and the Trans-Sumatran Highway at Lubuklinggau.

There are a few **accommodation** options. *Griya Anggita*, Jalan Iskander Ong 24 (☎0732/23289; ③–④), offers a range of rooms and is clean, quiet and friendly, with a 24hr restaurant offering inexpensive Indonesian food such as nasi goreng, mie goreng and sate. Ask for "Gang Berlian" to get there by bemo from town. A few hundred metres from the junction with the Muaraaman road, the more central *Hotel Aman Jaya*, Jalan Dr A.K. Gani 10 (☎0732/21365; ④–⑤), is the biggest hotel in town, with poor-value rooms. Further from the town centre, *Hotel Mira*, Jalan Letjen Suprato 106 (☎0732/21506; ④–⑤), is family-run and in a quiet location (ask bemo drivers for "Talang Rimbo Lama") offering a range of clean rooms, all with attached cold-water mandi.

The main commercial street is Jalan Merdeka, and the BCA and Bank Rakyat Indonesia are located here along with several **restaurants**. Excellent Padang food is available at *Bundo Kandung*, Jalan Merdeka 175, with especially fine *otak* (brains), *ayam kalio* (chicken in coconut sauce) and *perkadel* (croquettes).

Around Curup

There are several excursions around town, one of the closest being to the **Suban hot springs** (daily 5am–7pm; Rp400, plus Rp1000 for swimming and Rp1000 for a hot shower-er), but don't expect natural surroundings: huge amounts of concrete were used to construct the pools, water channels, sitting areas and restaurants. The main swimming pool is large, clean and very cold, and there's a small hot pool nearby. Take a bemo for 5km from Curup to the signed gateway on the main road, and you'll then have 1.5km to walk along a leafy lane to the entrance.

Further afield, **Bukit Kaba** is about 30km from Curup and is an active volcanic area. If you're using public transport, take a local bus or bemo from the terminal along the Lubuklinggau road to Simpang Bukit Kaba and then a bemo to Sumber Urip. From there the path is wide and obvious and it takes two hours to walk to Puncak (a four-wheel drive vehicle can get this far) from where it's an hour's walk to Kawah, where you can look down into the smoking crater belching sulphurous fumes. The nearby landscape is volcanic and bleak with only lichens able to survive the chemical composition of the soil, although the distant forests and mountains are rather more picturesque. This part of the path needs care; although it's well-trodden and there are steps cut in the steep parts, it's narrow in places and can be windy. If you want a **guide** – you shouldn't go alone – negotiate in Sumber Urip. It's best to go early – leave Curup at 6–7am, as the views will be much better and it gets cloudy and rainy up here later in the day. Due north of Curup, the road to Muaraanam passes **Danau Tes**, a local beauty spot and the largest lake in Bengkulu province.

Pulau Enggano

Pulau Enggano, 29km long and 14km wide, is situated 114km from the coast of Sumatra and is surrounded by fantastic coral, great beaches, brilliantly coloured oceans and five other, smaller, islands. The name means "mistake" in Portuguese, and probably relates to the time of the Portuguese exploration of the archipelago. There are absolutely no tourist facilities so you'll need to walk or get the boat around the coast. **Accommodation** is only in local houses and you should go first to the **kepala desa** at Malakoni to let him know you're there, and to ask advice. The scenery, sea and the chance to get way off the beaten track are the main reasons to come here, with little specific in the way of sights, and you'll need a fair level of Indonesian to make the most of the chances to mingle with the local people.

The origins of the Engganese people are somewhat mysterious – they are thought to be a mix of the Veddoid people of South India and Sumatrans from the mainland, though they resemble the people of the Nicobar Islands in the Bay of Bengal. Other sources suggest they are descended from the original nomadic Sumatrans who fled across the ocean when the Malay people began to arrive, and they also share some characteristics with the inhabitants of the Mentawai Islands further north. Their language is related to the Austronesian family of languages, and is radically different from anything on the mainland. These days the indigenous Engganese are greatly outnumbered by Javanese, Sumatrans and Chinese. With swampy coasts and with no primary forest left, the island is mainly flat (the highest point is 281m), inhabited by wild pigs, cattle and buffalo. The local economy is based on fishing, copra and the cultivation of rice, coffee, pepper and cloves.

Reaching the island is an adventure in itself and **access** is difficult. PT Sumber Bahargia Semesta (☎0736/21640) operate a three-times-weekly **ferry** service between Bengkulu and Enggano, calling first at Tanjung Kaholbi in the north and then Malakoni, the main harbour, on the east coast. PT Angkutan Pertambangan, Jalan Kenanga 29 (☎0736/21640), operates an infrequent service between Jakarta, Enggano and Bengkulu. The tourist office on Jalan Bali in Bengkulu (see p.439) is the best place to go for information.

The Pasemah Plateau

Located in a cleft in the Bukit Barisan range of mountains, the seventy-kilometre-long **Pasemah Plateau** is an extensive fertile highland plain surrounded by mountains. The interest of the area for tourists centres on the ancient stone **megaliths** that are believed to be remnants of a Bronze Age culture and, for hikers, **Gunung Dempo**. Access to the area is straightforward and visitors can either base themselves in **Lahat**, close to the Trans-Sumatran Highway or, more pleasantly, the higher, smaller town of **Pagaralam**, 67km to the southwest, that is also accessible directly from Bengkulu on a highly picturesque bus trip.

Lahat

With good road and rail links to the rest of Sumatra the town of **LAHAT** is a useful jumping-off point to the Pasemah Plateau, although the town itself has little to detain tourists. Lahat centres around the roundabout at the crossroads of Jalan Mayor Ruslan and Jalan Inspektur Yazid; the Trans-Sumatra Highway runs to the north of town.

The **train station** is extremely central, about 100m off Jalan Mayor Ruslan I, with daily services to and from Lubuklinggau and Palembang. There's a small **bus terminal** in town on Jalan Mayor Ruslan II, but long-distance arrivals and departures are from the bus offices, either in town or on the Trans-Sumatran Highway on the outskirts; it's 500m into the centre from here. There are several ticket offices on the Trans-Sumatran Highway or try *Sinar Denpo*, Jalan Mayor Ruslan III 30 (☎0731/22051). For closer destinations such as Baturaja (for Danau Ranau), the best thing is to go down onto the highway and flag down a passing bus. The **tourist office**, Jalan Let Amir Hanzah 150 (Mon–Thurs 7.30am–1.30pm, Fri 7.30–11am, Sat 7.30am–12.30pm; ☎0731/22469) has little material in English and no information about how to reach any local sights except by "charter taxi". Just around the corner is the 24hr **Telkom** office, Jalan Serma Yamis 1, but the **wartel** at Jalan Mayor Ruslan III (daily 7am–11pm) is more convenient. You'll find the **post office** at Jalan Emil Salim 2.

Nusantara, Jalan Mayor Ruslan III 33 (☎0731/21336, fax 22666; ③–⑥), is the largest and most professional **accommodation** option in town, offering a wide choice of rooms. Nearby *Hotel Permata*, Jalan Mayor Ruslan III 32 (☎0731/21642; ③–⑤), offers adequate but basic rooms. Out on the Trans-Sumatran Highway, the *Hotel Cendrawasih*, Jalan Cemara 185 (☎0731/21981; ④–⑥), is a good choice and, although predictably noisy, does have a pleasant garden.

Lahat has plenty of **eating** places. *Metro*, Jalan Mayor Ruslan III 18, is one of several bakeries in town selling sweet and savoury bread and cakes with a few tables inside; *Singga Kudai*, Jalan Mayor Ruslan III 24, and *Pagi Sore*, Jalan Mayor Ruslan III 15, are popular, inexpensive Padang restaurants; while *Lantana*, Jalan Mayor Ruslan II 69, is the most upmarket and relaxing place, with good value and excellent-quality food. There's no menu here: you choose what you fancy from the display and should check out the prices of the more exotic stuff if you're on a tight budget.

Pagaralam and Gunung Dempo

Situated a cool 710m above sea level, the small upland town of **PAGARALAM** to the east of **Gunung Dempo**, which towers over the area, is an attractive base from which to explore the area, particularly the megaliths, for which it's best known. It's a busy market town serving the small villages dotted around the highland area and gets enough visitors for people to be unsurprised by Westerners.

Long-distance buses from Bengkulu, Lahat, Palembang, Bandar Lampung and Jakarta serve the **bus terminal**, 2–3km west of the town centre; take a red bemo (Rp200) to the central market area.

The best **accommodation** for travellers intending to either trek or visit the megaliths is *Hotel Mirasa*, Jalan May Ruslan 62 (☎0730/21484; ④), with simple rooms with verandahs and attached cold-water mandi in a garden setting; the cheaper rooms at the back look out across local paddy-fields and there's a restaurant attached serving good, inexpensive Indonesian food. Inquire here for details of the local megaliths or about local guides either for the megaliths or for the Gunung Dempo climb. To get to the *Mirasa*, take a blue bemo along Jalan May Ruslan from the market area.

As darkness falls, the market area turns into a **night market** and there are several **restaurants**. In the market, *Toko Tasdik*, Jalan Lettu Hamid 104, is a relaxed place serving plenty of Indonesian favourites and specializing in *murtabak* and *pempek*. *Singgah Kudai*, Jalan Lettnan Penalis 27, offers local and Padang food: try the *sayur nangkha* (jackfruit curry), *sambal tempe* (dry potatoes, nuts and chilli served in a fiery sambal sauce) or *pindang* (beef soup flavoured with saffron, ginger, chilli and onions).

The **post office** is at Jalan Kapten Senap 37 on the road south towards *Hotel Mirasa*, with the **Telkom office** (24hr) next door at Jalan Kapten Senap 36, and there's a more central wartel on Jalan Vandrik Karim 355 (6am–11pm). Pagaralam has no exchange facilities.

Climbing Gunung Dempo

Dominating the town and the entire Pasemah Plateau, 3159-metre **Gunung Dempo** is best climbed during the dry season, from May to August. It takes two full days to get up and down, if you leave Pagaralam at around 6am on the first morning; the summit comprises two peaks separated by a col. There are thought to be tigers and several species of monkeys and birds in the forest, but you're more likely to hear than see them. It's highly recommended that you take a **guide** from Pagaralam who is familiar with the mountain, as the trails are little-used, hard to find and it's very easy to get lost. Expect to pay US$30–40 for the two days; the guide can also provide all equipment except sleeping bags. Ask at the *Hotel Mirasa* about local guides.

The megaliths

Many of the best **megaliths** from the area have been removed to museums in Jakarta (the National Museum; p.86) and Palembang (the Museum Negeri Propinsi Sumatera Selatan; p.427), but many weird and ancient stonecarvings (1–500 AD), troughs and graves remain dotted around fields and villages close to Pagaralam. Some are solitary, others are in groups, and they depict humans and animals; although most are seriously eroded, they are strangely evocative. The local belief is that an angry magician called Lidah Pahit (Bitter Tongue) was responsible for the statues, and that anyone who displeased him was turned into stone. Most stones have some sort of caretaker and you'll be expected to sign the visitors' book and pay Rp1000 per person for a look.

There are megaliths in all directions from Pagaralam; either ask for directions locally or negotiate a guide for the day (about Rp25,000). The easiest to locate, in the grounds of **Mesjid Takwar**, 300m before *Hotel Mirasa* coming from town, is a small carving depicting a man subduing an elephant. Others which are further afield, but worth seeking out include: the group of statues known as Batu Beribu and the relief carving of a warrior (Batu Balai) in **Tegur Wangi**, about 6km from Pagaralam; the metre-tall Batu Gajah (Elephant Stone), also known as Batu Kerbau at **Belumai**, 3–4km from Pagaralam; Arca Manusia Debelit Ulas (Stone Megalith Fighting Snake) at **Tanjung Aro**; and Batu Gajah or Batu Orang, a mother with long hair and a baby on an elephant in a forest site at **Pulau Panggung**, 10km northeast of Pagaralam.

Danau Ranau and Krui

Nestling in the crater of Gunung Seminung, which rises to 1340m from the western shore, **Danau Ranau**, 16km long and 9km wide, is the most peaceful of all the Sumatran lakes. It offers the cool, mountain scenery of other popular lake destinations such as Toba and Maninjau, but, being a couple of hours off the Trans-Sumatran Highway, takes a bit of effort to reach – there are no real tourist facilities. However, it's a great place to chill out (literally – take a sweater) for a day or two, and is easily combined with a stop at the low-key coastal village of **Krui**, about 70km to the west, a brilliant place from which to explore the entire coastline.

Danau Ranau

Situated around 100km from the Trans-Sumatran Highway town of Baturaja and 70km from the west coast at Krui, **Danau Ranau** is surrounded by the attractive mountain scenery of the Bukit Barisan range, with forest-covered mountain slopes and settled areas planted with coffee, cloves, tobacco and fruit trees. Several small villages dot the lakeside: **Bandingagung** on the north side, **Simpangsender** on the northeast, the accommodation area on the eastern shoreside known locally as Pusri, and Kotabatu towards the south. With easy transportation between them, a variety of accommodation options and only a few other visitors, this is a pleasant place to relax, enjoy the lake and gain a view of small-town upland life.

It's possible to charter a boat for the hour-long trip across the lake to the **hot springs** on the western shore, where you can bathe in the hot water and then dip in the cold of the lake. Unfortunately, zealous use of wire and concrete has created a rather ugly setting for this. The wind gets up in the afternoon, making for a colder and choppier trip across, so it's advisable to go early and take a sweater.

This can be combined with a trip to the small island of **Pulau Marisa**, located a few hundred metres off the shore. Local people tell how the island appeared one night as a test in a love triangle. A princess, Puteri Aisah, was being courted by two undesirable men: Lidah Pahit (Bitter Tongue) – the rather fearsome fellow responsible for the

Pagaralam megaliths – and Simata Empat (Four Eyes). Desirous of neither, she nevertheless agreed to marry the one who could build a bridge from the hot springs to the village of Bandingagung in a single night. Both were thankfully rejected when small Pulau Marisa was all either of them could manage.

The most excursion from the lake is to scale **Gunung Seminung**, usually tackled as a very long day-trek. The path goes up from near the hot springs, so you start and finish with a boat trip across the lake then climb up, through the jungle, for about five hours to the summit, from where there are excellent views of the area. It's four or five hours' descent before the trip back across the lake from the hot springs. Inquire at your accommodation for a **guide** who is familiar with the path up the mountain, which is not much used, and likely to be overgrown.

Subik waterfall, 25m high and right by the edge of the lake, is an easy fifteen-minute walk along the path that heads across the top of *Wisma Putri Agung* at Pusri on the eastern side of the lake.

Practicalities

Access to the area from the north is via the Pasar Baru bus terminal in Baturaja, an otherwise uninteresting town on Sungai Ogan, and the Trans-Sumatra Highway, 272km north of Bandar Lampung. Large minibuses leave irregularly through the day for Danau Ranau and, unfortunately, one or two drivers hike the prices for tourists, secure bags in their vehicle and then vanish for three or four hours until they fancy making the trip, while other buses have come and gone. The trick is to hang onto your bag until you board a bus that is clearly about to depart; there are plenty of stalls selling tea and snacks in the bus station while you wait.

The road from Baturaja is via the bustling village of Muaradua, and arrives in the Ranau area at Simpangsender, at the northeast side of the lake; one branch turns west to Bandingagung on the north shore, while the other heads south along and above the east shore through the Pusri area and on to Kotabatu on the south shore. Coming from Krui or points south, buses pass through Liwa and then arrive at the lakeside at Kotabatu on the southern shore. Regular and frequent **bemos** scurry between Kotabatu, Simpangsender and Bandingagung, and there are long-distance bus connections from all three towns (see p.461). There's a **post office** (Mon–Thurs 7.30am–3pm, Fri 7.30–11.30am, Sat 7.30am–1pm) at Simpangsender, on the road from Muaradua, but currently no telephones in the area – Muaradua and Krui are the closest.

Moving on, there are plenty of bus offices in the area, the biggest range being in Simpangsender, where they line the main road out towards Pusri. Twice-daily services leave for Jakarta, Bengkulu and Bandar Lampung. In Bandingagung, PT Putri Sulung has an office in Jalan Batu Mega, the main street, offering daily departures to Jakarta, Bandar Lampung and Palembang. The same company has an office just as you enter Kotabatu from the north, offering the same departures. Buses to Liwa (change there for Krui) leave each morning from all three villages; check at your accommodation or the bus offices for current times.

ACCOMMODATION

The biggest choice of **accommodation** is in the small, quiet village of **Bandingagung** on the north shore, where the Saturday market is just about the only excitement, although at holiday time visitors arrive in droves to rent out boats for lake trips. The **Pusri** area on the sloping hillside overlooking the eastern shore offers the best views of the lake, although there's almost no habitation nearby so eating options are limited. For all the Pusri accommodation there's a steep walk of 1km or so down from the road marked by a gateway. At **Kotabatu** at the southern end of the lake you'll find two accommodation options, both situated in town; the town is far livelier than the other settlements around the lake, but there aren't really any lakeside walks.

Losmen Batu Mega, Jl Sugiwaras 269, Bandingagung. If you want to be outside the village, go straight on along a track and over a plank bridge from *Losmen Permata* and you'll reach this place, which has rooms with attached mandi, good views of the lake from the lounge and a small verandah out front. ③.

Losmen Danau Indah, Jl H. Faqih Usman 28, Bandingagung. Backs onto the lake road and has a large restaurant area and garden. The rooms are very small and basic, although they have an attached mandi and the lighter garden rooms have a small sitting area out front. ③.

Danau Ranau Cottages, Pusri. The most upmarket place in the area, with attractive, well-maintained grounds sloping down to the lake. There's a pleasant open-sided restaurant, and excursions can be arranged from here. A variety of accommodation is available, from simple rooms in a block away from the lake with attached cold-water mandi to lakeside wood-and-thatch cottages (no hot water). ④–⑦.

Losmen Pantai Indah, Jl Pembangunan II, Kotabatu. This is on the unpaved road down to the lakeside from town and has basic rooms. ④.

Losmen Permata, Jl Empu Sepadang 97, Bandingagung. Towards the far edge of town, about a 500m walk from the market; walk straight along the road at the top of the market. It's simple and pleasant in a quiet location. ③.

Wisma Pusri, Pusri. Just past *Danau Ranau Cottages* (it's hard to see where one establishment starts and the other ends, and indeed there's talk of a merger); the place was undergoing a refit at the time of writing, but is a large setup with a range of rooms but no cottages. ④–⑥.

Wisma Putri Agung, Pusri. A few hundred metres north of *Danau Ranau Cottages* (follow the sign to the right just before them), this place is run-down and neglected in a huge old house with a massive lounge and small beach down on the lakeside. ④.

Losmen Seminung Jaya, Jl Perintis Kemerdekaan 25, Kotabatu. The downstairs rooms are dark and unexciting – try to get the upstairs room, which is next to a sitting area overlooking the main street. At the time of writing there was no sign outside; it's 300m towards Liwa from the sharp bend in the middle of town and about 100m past the mosque on the right – you'll probably need to ask. ③.

Hotel Seminung Permai, Jl Akmal 89, Bandingagung. Central and near the shops and lake; the rooms are clean, without attached mandi. ④.

Hotel Surya Indah, Bandingagung. On the road into town close to the local school, offering good rooms, all with attached cold-water mandi. There's a small garden and a verandah and it's out of the bustle of town but therefore a good walk down to the lake. ④.

Hotel Wisata, Jl Pasar, Bandingagung. Situated opposite the market, offering rooms without attached mandi; they are variable, so ask to see several. ④.

Krui

The small west-coast fishing town of **KRUI** is well off the tourist track. It was once the site of a tiny British outpost during their occupation of Bengkulu between 1685 and 1824, although little evidence of this remains. These days it's simply a pleasant (although very hot) place to spend some time enjoying small-town life and the brilliant beaches along the deserted, unspoilt coastline that stretches north and south from the town. To reach the furthest of the beaches, you need to rely on the rather haphazard public transport of the area or charter your own transport, but even the beaches close to town are worth exploring. **Access** to Krui is either direct from Bandar Lampung (there are daily buses), from Danau Ranau via Liwa, or from Bukitkemuning on the Trans-Sumatran Highway, also via Liwa. Bemos from Krui leave from the Liwa bus terminal through the day. If you get stuck in Liwa, there's accommodation at, among others, *Permata Hotel*, Jalan Raden Intan 53 (④–⑤), which is adequate but has a variable water supply.

The two local **beaches** in Krui, separated by a high, tree-covered headland with a large warning lamp on the top, are great fun and both are several kilometres long. Adorned by fishing boats and nets, Salalau is the working beach to the north of town. To the south of town, Labuhan Jukung is a palm-fringed white-sand beach lapped by turquoise waters, darkening to azure and deep-blue further offshore. There are views of the coastline to the north as well as Pulau Pisang, and on a weekday you can have several kilometres of deserted sand all to yourself.

An interesting offshore excursion is to **Pulau Pisang** (Banana Island), just off the coast. You can either charter a boat from Krui (you'll pay about Rp10,000 one way) or take a bemo to the village of Tambakak, 14km north of Krui, and catch the local boat service that operates from there (Rp1500). There's no accommodation on the island and you should assume you'll have to walk everywhere, although there's an occasional bemo. The island is especially famous for *kain tapis,* and you should see local women weaving the age-old traditional designs of this intricate cloth.

Further afield up and down the coast from Krui, there are tiny villages and **beaches** to explore, to the north as far as Pugung Tanjung, 50km from Krui, and to Mandiri, 10km south of Krui. Local bemos reach both these spots, and in the south beyond this to Ngaras, but they are irregular, tail off early in the afternoon and you should take plenty of water in case you have a long wait for transport. The coves are all very varied and everyone will find a favourite, but **Pugung Penengahah**, 30km north of Krui, is particularly attractive, with large rocky outcrops set amongst the pale sand. Malaya, 5km further north, has lovely white sand and picturesque rocks rising from the ocean.

Practicalities

Krui offers several basic, good-value **accommodation** options. *Hotel Sempana Lima*, Jalan Kesuma 708 (☎0728/51040; ④), is central and the largest place in town, with a variety of rooms on offer. Although the Tourist Information Service downstairs seems largely defunct, staff can help with local information. Slightly further on through town across the road, *Losmen Stabas*, Jalan Kesuma 743 (☎0728/51056; ④), is a small family setup in an old bungalow with high ceilings and a small lounge at the front. Nearby *Losmen Gembira*, Jalan Kesuma 701 (☎0728/51009; ④), has rooms with and without attached mandi; the more expensive ones are better value and out the back there are a couple of pleasant garden areas. *Hotel Dwi Putri*, Jalan Merdeka 172 (☎0728/51069; ④), is about 500m before town on the road in from Liwa. It's a new, clean, tiled place and offers good value.

The usual range of Indonesian **food** is on offer in town with plenty of small rumah makan. Try *Abu Sutarno*, Jalan Kesuma 705, opposite *Hotel Sempana Lima* – it's a big friendly open-fronted place and the sate is especially fine.

Moving on, there are bus offices on Jalan Kesuma near the *Hotel Sempana Lima*, as well as on the edge of town on the Liwa road. PO Sumber Jaya Indah has daily departures to Bandar Lampung (everyone calls it "Rajabasa" after the bus terminal), and Krui Putri, Jalan Kesuma (☎0728/51633), offers daily departures to Bandar Lampung and Bengkulu via the coast road, plus a daily service to Ngaras. The **post office** is at Jalan Tanah Lapang, about 300m further south from the fork on a road parallel to Jalan Kesuma. You can make local and international calls from the **wartel** at Jalan Kesuma 526 (daily 7.30am–midnight).

The far south

The **far south** of Sumatra comprises bays and inlets, offshore islands, wild coastline, soaring mountains and extensive plains. As the island narrows towards its southern tip, just 27km from Java, there's easy access between the major sights. As the major transport hub of the region, the city of **Bandar Lampung** is beautifully situated, but lacks decent budget accommodation, though there are plenty of extremely good-quality moderately priced hotels. To the east, many visitors are attracted to the famous birdwatching haunts and elephant training school at the **Way Kambas national park**. Although the **Bukit Barisan Seletan national park** on the southwestern peninsula is much less visited, it's an enticing area with forests and coastline to explore, sustaining a wide range of flora and fauna. At the southern tip of Sumatra, south of Bandar Lampung, the inlets and coves of **Lampung Bay** are peaceful and attractive, and the offshore islands both in and beyond the bay offer exciting excursions. Access to Java is from the port of **Bakauheni**; most travellers between Java and Sumatra will pass through the area, although relatively few stop off.

Bandar Lampung and around

With the most stunning location of any Sumatran city, in the hills overlooking Lampung Bay from where you can see as far as Krakatau, **BANDAR LAMPUNG** is an amalgamation of the cities of Teluk Betung, the traditional port and trading area down on the shorefront, and Tanjung Karang, the administrative centre on the hills behind. Local people and bus drivers and conductors all continue to talk about Teluk Betung and Tanjung Karang, and when you're coming to the city from other parts of Sumatra your destination will usually be referred to as Rajabasa, the name of the bus terminal.

To the southeast of the city, **Pulau Condong** is accessible via Pasir Putih beach, and, also to the southeast, a day-trip to **Padang Cermin** is a pleasant excursion, with some wonderful coastal scenery along the way. East of the city are the ancient remains at **Pugung Raharjo**, with traces of a fortified village and megalithic stones.

Arrival and information

If you arrive by bus from anywhere north of Bandar Lampung, you'll arrive at the **Rajabasa terminal**, 7km north of the city, one of the busiest bus terminals in Sumatra which shifts thousands of people every day. Follow the signs towards the main road for "microlet" – the local name for bemos – and you can either get a light blue bemo into town, which terminates at Pasar Bawah, the market area just south of Jalan Kotoraja, or catch the bus that goes to Pasar Bawah but then continues its circular route down Jalan Raden Intan, along Jalan A. Yani and up Jalan Kartini before going out to Rajabasa again. If you stay on past Pasar Bawah it counts as two journeys, so you'll pay double.

Coming to the city from Bakauheni or Kalianda, buses arrive at **Panjang terminal**, about 1km east of Panjang market to the east of the city on the coast. Some terminate there, while others go on to Rajabasa. Orange bemos run between Panjang terminal

---

MOVING ON TO JAVA

There are regular **buses** to destinations in **Java** from Rajabasa terminal. Alternatively, buses to Bakauheni (the ferry terminal for departures to Merak on Java) leave from Rajabasa or, more conveniently, **Panjang terminal** on the southeast edge of the city – take an orange bemo from Sukaraja terminal.

Charter or **share-taxis** to Jakarta are available from Bandar Lampung taxi firms. Try Dynasty, Jalan K.H.A. Dahlan 53 (☎0721/485674), or Taxi 666, Jalan Kartini (☎0721/485769). Expect to pay Rp20,000–30,000 per person.

A high speed **jetfoil** operates five times daily (6am–4pm) from the ferry terminal just beside the Sukaraja bus terminal to Merak. The crossing takes about ninety minutes and costs Rp15,350.

Ferries from Bakauheni operate around the clock for the two-hour crossing to Merak, every twenty minutes during the day but less frequently at night. There are two classes: it costs Rp2500 in A (with air-con) and Rp1800 in B (no air-con). High-speed ferries also depart hourly from 7.40am to 5pm (40min; Rp6000).

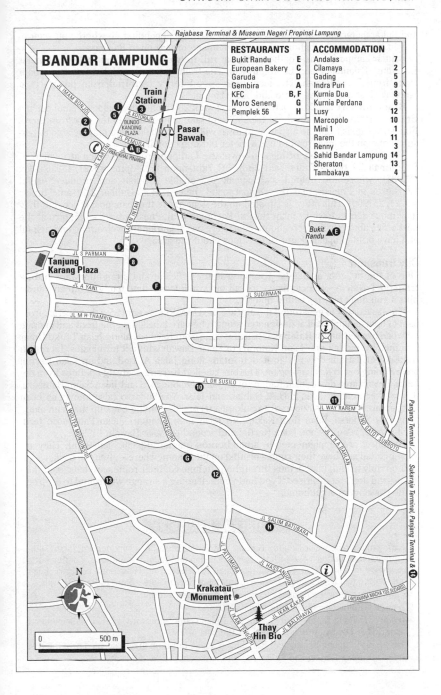

△ Rajabasa Terminal & Museum Negeri Propinsi Lampung

BANDAR LAMPUNG

RESTAURANTS		ACCOMMODATION	
Bukit Randu	E	Andalas	7
European Bakery	C	Cilamaya	2
Garuda	D	Gading	5
Gembira	A	Indra Puri	9
KFC	B, F	Kurnia Dua	8
Moro Seneng	G	Kurnia Perdana	6
Pemplek 56	H	Lusy	12
		Marcopolo	10
		Mini 1	1
		Rarem	11
		Renny	3
		Sahid Bandar Lampung	14
		Sheraton	13
		Tambakaya	4

Train Station

Pasar Bawah

Tanjung Karang Plaza

Bukit Randu ▲Ⓔ

JL IMAM BONJOL
JL KOTARAJA
BUNDO KANDING PLAZA
JL PEMUDA
JL LAMTIN
PANGKHAL PINANG
JL RADEN INTAN
JL S PARMAN
JL A YANI
JL M H THAMRIN
JL SUDIRMAN
JL DR SUSILO
JL WAY RAREM
JL JEND GATOT SUBROTO
JL WOLTER MONGINSIDI
JL DIPONEGORO
JL KH A DAHLAN
JL SALIM BATUBARA
JL PATTIMURA
JL HASSANUDIN
JL IKAN KAKAP
JL LAKSAMANA MADYA YOS SUDARSO

Krakatau Monument

Thay Hin Bio

Panjang Terminal ▷
Sukaraja Terminal, Panjang Terminal & ⑭ ▷

N

0   500 m

and Sukaraja terminal in the heart of Teluk Betung; depending on where you want to stay in town it may be better to get off at Panjang or stay on to Rajabasa.

Bandar Lampung is part of the triangular **rail network** that extends between Bandar Lampung, Palembang and Lubuklinggau. The train station is on Jalan Kotoraja, about 100m from Pasar Bawah. The local **high-speed ferry terminal** from Jakarta is at Sukaraja, just next to the bemo and bus terminal.

Branti airport is 25km north of the city; walk 200m onto the main road and catch a Branti–Rajabasa bus to Rajabasa (Rp250) and take connections to the city from there. Fixed-price taxis from the airport into town will cost Rp20,000; you may be able to persuade one on the main road to use a meter but don't count on it.

There are two **tourist offices** in town: the Lampung regional office at Jalan W.R. Supratman 39 (Mon–Thurs 7am–3pm, Fri 7am–noon & 1–3pm; ☎0721/482565, fax 482081), where the helpful staff speak reasonable English and produce useful brochures in English, and the Depparpostel, Jalan K.H.A. Dahlan 21 (same times; ☎0721/251900). This office is situated on the floor above the main post office, but they may move across town to Jalan Basuki Rachman in the near future, so inquire at the post office about their whereabouts. Staff here are also friendly, welcoming and helpful and have printed material and suggestions about the area.

City transport

One of the delights of Bandar Lampung is the efficient and straightforward **public transport** system – the city is so spread out you'll waste time trudging up and down hills if you don't to grips with it quickly.

The easiest way to get around the city are the DAMRI **bus services** that operate from 6am to 6pm and only call at designated stops. They are labelled on the front and operate between two terminals. **Rajabasa–Karang** runs from Rajabasa along Jalan Teuku Umar into the city and left into Jalan Kotoraja to Pasar Bawah where it terminates. Its return route to Rajabasa is down Jalan Raden Intan, along Jalan A. Yani and up Jalan Kartini before going out to Rajabasa again. The bus labelled **Karang–Betung** operates from the Pasar Bawah area down Jalan Raden Intan, Jalan Diponegoro and Jalan Salim Batubara, the southern end of Jalan K.H.A. Dahlan and Jalan Yos Sudarso (also known as Jalan Laksamana Madya Yos Sudarso) to Sukaraja terminal. Coming back up they run along Jalan Yos Sudarso, Jalan Ikan Kakap, up Jalan Ikan Tenggiri, Jalan Pattimura, Jalan Diponegoro, Jalan A. Yani, Jalan Kartini and around to Pasar Bawah.

The buses are supplemented by small **bemos** (flat fare Rp350; 5am–9pm). They are colour-coded and have their routes printed on them somewhere – often the back, which isn't terribly useful. Like bemos throughout Indonesia, their routes are less fixed than buses, and don't be surprised if you find yourself going a strange way round to drop one of the passengers off at home.

USEFUL BEMOS

Dark purple – between Tanjung Karang and Sukaraja via Jalan Diponegoro, Jalan Salim Batubara, the southern end of Jalan K.H.A. Dahlan and Jalan Yos Sudarso. Coming back up, they run along Jalan Yos Sudarso, Jalan Malahayat, up Jalan Ikan Tenggiri, Jalan Pattimura, Jalan Diponegoro, Jalan A. Yani, Jalan Kartini and around to Pasar Bawah.

Light blue – between Rajabasa terminal and Tanjung Karang.

Orange – Sukaraja and Panjang terminals.

Green – Tanjung Karang and Garuntang (Jalan Gatot Subroto) via Jalan Sudirman and Jalan K.H.A. Dahlan, which is useful for the post office.

Dark red – Tanjung Karang and Kemiling (Langka Pura) on the western edge of the city.

Grey – Tanjung Karang and Sukarame on the eastern edge of the city.

In addition, there are plenty of easily identified metered **taxis**; the meter starts at Rp1350 and a fare across the city will rarely run to more than Rp4000. Be firm with drivers about using the meter before you get in, as they prefer to try to negotiate a (high) price with you beforehand.

Accommodation

Whilst Bandar Lampung has a brilliant range of mid- to top-range hotels, offering extremely pleasant and good-value **accommodation**, if you're on a very tight budget there's plenty of choice but generally poor value. If you're strapped for cash, the best thing to do is to stay at Kalianda (see p.460) and come up to the city for day-trips or onward connections.

Andalas, Jl Raden Intan 89 (☎0721/263432, fax 261481). Good-value, centrally located place with a good range of pleasant rooms, from those with cold water and fan to ones with air-con and hot water. It's centrally located, just across the road from the *Kurnia Perdana*. ⑤–⑥.

Cilamaya, Jl Imam Bonjol 261 (☎0721/263504). Basic, centrally located place that's popular and unfortunately often full. ④.

Gading, Jl Kartini 72 (☎0721/255512). Offering a variety of rooms, conveniently located near the market area, it's a short walk from the bus route from Rajabasa and is a large setup on a quiet alleyway in a busy area. ④–⑥.

Indra Puri, Jl Wolter Moginsidi 70 (☎0721/258258, fax 262440). This is another luxury place, perched high on a hill, without the gloss of the *Sheraton*. Look out for the special deals that they offer from time to time. ⑧–⑨.

Kurnia Dua, Jl Raden Intan 75 (☎0721/252905, fax 262924). Accessible from Rajabasa terminal on the DAMRI bus, this utilitarian concrete place has little character, but is large and popular with Indonesian travellers, offering plenty of options, from basic rooms without mandi through to those with mandi and air-con. ④–⑥.

Kurnia Perdana, Jl Raden Intan 114 (☎0721/262030, fax 262924). A small, friendly and pleasant setup, close to *Kurnia Dua*, all rooms offering air-con and colour TV. More expensive rooms have hot water, all have bathroom and TV, and the price includes breakfast. ⑤–⑥.

Lusy, Jl Diponegoro 186 (☎0721/485895). Situated about 1km down Jl Diponegoro from the large Jl Dr Susilo junction; Karang–Betung buses pass the door. The accommodation is very basic, although all rooms have attached mandi. Some have fans and some air-con, and the ones at the front are noisy, but the generally poor quality of Bandar Lampung budget places make this a good option. ④.

Marcopolo, Jl Dr Susilo 4 (☎0721/262511, fax 254419). Whilst there's no public transport past the hotel, it's only 200m from the junction of Jl Dr Susilo and Jl Diponegoro, where Karang–Betung buses pass. All rooms have hot water, air-con and TV. The hotel has three swimming pools including an Olympic-sized main pool and a great terrace restaurant/bar with excellent views across Lampung Bay. The less expensive rooms are extremely good value. ⑤–⑦.

Mini 1, Jl Dwi Warna 71 (☎0721/2555928). This is a small setup in a quiet alley off Jl Kartini; it's opposite *Hotel Gading* and offers clean, basic rooms with no frills but attached mandi. ④.

Rarem, Jl Way Rarem 23 (☎261241, fax 262691). Tucked away behind Jl K.H.A. Dahlan and not far from the green bemo route (get off at the junction of Jl Dr Susilo and Jl K.H.A. Dahlan), this small place is super-clean: even the shared bathrooms are pristine, with rooms with shared mandi up to those with private bath and air-con. The small garden is a haven of peace in the bustling city. ④–⑥.

Renny, Jl Kotoraja 9 (☎0721/253974). This is an option if you're very short of cash and stranded, but that isn't saying much. The hotel is on a quiet alleyway off Jl Kotoraja but is signed from the main road. Rooms are very basic. ④.

Sahid Bandar Lampung, Jl Yos Sudarso 294 (☎0721/488888, fax 486589) One of the best hotels in town, the public areas are comfortable and relaxed and the rooms attractive. There's a 24hr coffee shop, with a range of moderate to expensive Western and Indonesian meals; the hotel has a small pool and is situated on a not-particularly-attractive beach 1km east of Sukaraja terminal. Seaview rooms have a good panorama of Lampung Bay. ⑧–⑨.

Sheraton, Jl Wolter Moginsidi 175 (☎0721/486666, fax 486690). The most luxurious and expensive hotel in town is inconveniently located on the western outskirts; public transport doesn't pass by. There's a small and attractive pool, fitness centre, business centre and tennis courts, while communal areas are luxurious but with a relaxed atmosphere. The rooms are at the standard you'd expect of this international chain. ⑨.

Tambakaya, Jl Imam Bonjol, Gang Beringin 60 (no phone). Tucked away behind Jl Imam Bonjol, follow the sign that is about 50m from *Cilamaya* towards the town centre, fork right at the nursery school just inside the alleyway, go over the stream and it's a small compound on the left. Basic but adequate. ④.

The City

Perhaps the most thought-provoking but apparently uninteresting thing to do in Bandar Lampung is to visit the **Krakatau monument**. This is positioned in a small park on Jalan Veteran, quite a steep climb up from the waterfront at Teluk Betung. It's a huge metal buoy which was washed up here from Lampung Bay in 1883 in the tidal waves that followed the eruption of Krakatau, killing over 35,000 people on both sides of the straits.

Due south of the monument on Jalan Ikan Kakap – head south along Jalan Ikan Tenggiri and Jalan Ikan Kakap goes off to the left – the lovely **Chinese temple**, Thay Hin Bio, is fabulously atmospheric; buses heading up to Tanjung Karang from Teluk Betung pass along here. Worshippers make offerings and pray here, and the ornate statues and red-and-gold decorations are enclosed in swirls of smoke from burning incense. You're welcome to buy a pack of incense and printed prayers for offerings, and local people will show you where to place each item.

Several kilometres north in Tanjung Karang, there are brilliant views of the whole city, one of the easiest vantage points being from the top of **Bukit Randu**. It's about 1km to the east of Jalan Raden Intan, and the scenery is worth the hike. If you don't want to use the pricey restaurant at the top, just keep walking up between the various buildings to the lookout spot on the top of the hill.

The museum, **Museum Negeri Propinsi Lampung**, Jalan Abdin Pagar Alam 64 (Tues–Thurs 8am–1.30pm, Fri 8–10.30am, Sat & Sun 8am–noon; Rp200), is 1km south of Rajabasa terminal, a huge traditional building set back from the road behind a car park. There's a good collection of artefacts, including drums, kris, statues, jewellery and masks, plus some megalithic figures, mostly reproductions of items found at Pugung Raharjo (see p.457). Some of the large traditional baskets, up to 1m tall, are very impressive. Only with the textiles is any attempt made at English labelling and that is very cursory. There are some good items here, but, given Lampung's rich textile heritage, it's not a significant or educational collection.

Eating

There's a great range of places to eat in Bandar Lampung, the highlight being a visit to Pasar Mambo, the **night market**, at the southern end of Jalan Hassanudin, which operates from dusk until about 11pm. The range of food on sale is huge and each stall has its own set of tables. Chinese and seafood stalls are a speciality, and the more exotic stuff such as prawns and crabs can be pricey. There are plenty of stalls selling sweets ices: *Es John Lenon* is one.

Bukit Randu, perched on top of the hill of the same name. This place transforms into a restaurant in the evenings, which is so extensive that there's an information booth at the entrance. The main options are a couple of large dining rooms or individual pavilions in the garden, with panoramic views of the city and Lampung Bay. It's about 1km off Jl Raden Intan, and you'll need transport to get here unless you want to work up a real appetite.

European Bakery, Jl Raden Intan 35a. This standard bakery offers an extremely good and attractive range of moderately priced sweet breads and cakes, which you can either eat in or take away.

Garuda, Jl Kartini 31. Just north of Tanjung Karang Plaza, this is a central and convenient branch of a popular chain, serving all the Indonesian staples at moderate prices in relaxed surroundings.

Gembira, Jl Pangkhal Pinang 20. Next door to *KFC* in a street with plenty of good *mie ayam* places, *Gembira* offers a huge range of local dishes including *pempek*, soups, chicken dishes and ice confections. It's inexpensive and popular.

Kebun Raya at the *Sheraton Hotel*. This is the place for a real splurge, with steaks at Rp39,000 and veal at Rp30,000, although you can get away with luxurious surroundings and seamless service with nasi goreng at Rp10,000, all plus 21 percent tax and service.

KFC, upstairs at Gelael, Jl Sudirman 11–15 and Jl Pangkhal Pinang 18. The air-con is a life-saver on a hot day, whilst the fries and chicken staples are expensive and the displayed prices will have ten percent tax added.

Marcopolo Restaurant at the *Marcopolo Hotel*. The room inside is plain and uninspiring but the outside terrace, with a fantastic view over the entire city and out into Lampung Bay, makes this a great place for a meal or just a drink. Western, Chinese and Indonesian food ranges from rice and noodle dishes at Rp6000, up to pepper steak at Rp20,000, all plus 21 percent.

Moro Seneng, Jl Diponegoro 38. Easy to get to on public transport. You can eat in basic style at the front or in the garden at the back; they offer good-value Indonesian and Chinese food such as nasi and mie dishes at Rp2500–3000, up to shrimp, *gurame* and squid at Rp8,000–10,000.

Pemplek 56, Jl Salim Batubara 56. Just one of a huge range of *pempek* places along this road; they are named by the number on the street and all serve inexpensive *pempek*, the grilled or fried Palembang speciality of balls made from sago, fish and flavourings, which are dished up with a variety of sauces.

Nightlife

If you want to join the jet-setters, the **bar** at the *Sheraton Hotel* is fairly lively. At Rp250,000 for a bottle of champagne (plus tax and service) you'll need to be fairly well heeled, although less exotic drinks come in at Rp9000–11,000. Get there between 4 and 7pm for happy hour. The **disco** area of town is Jalan Yos Sudarso. At the time of writing, *Oya* (9pm–late; Rp10,000–15,000), about 500m east of the Sukaraja terminal, was the favourite, but check locally for up-to-date information as the Indonesian disco scene changes fast.

Shopping

While it isn't a mecca for shoppers, Bandar Lampung is a good place to stock up on necessities if you're heading off the beaten track in Sumatra, and there are some good **textile shops** both for the local speciality, *kain tapis*, and for imports of batik from Java. If you need postcards, stock up here; the nearest ones to the north are in Bukittinggi.

For traditional shopping, **Pasar Bawah** is at the top end of Jalan Raden Intan just south of the train station, a maze of stalls piled high with fruit and vegetables as well as mountains of household goods. (A massive Matahari department store is being developed nearby, so the future of the market is uncertain.) At the northern end of Jalan Kartini, **Bundo Kanding Plaza** is a traditional market now housed in a concrete box: this is the place for clothing, bags, make-up, toys and household stuff.

The most extensive **bookshop** is **Gramedia**, Jalan Raden Intan 63, which sells postcards, a good range of dictionaries, and the English-language *Jakarta Post* newspaper.

SHOPPING CENTRES, DEPARTMENT STORES AND SUPERMARKETS
The **Gelael supermarket**, Jalan Sudirman 11–15, supplies extremely expensive fresh fish, meat, fruit and vegetables and all the items that the affluent Indonesian middle-classes require, such as cheeses, cornflakes, and canned soups. The **King's department stores** (Jalan Raden Intan 73, Jalan Let Jend Suprapto 138 and Jalan Ikan Hiu 1a) have supermarkets attached, selling a small range of souvenirs including *songket* purses and hangings and postcards. The newest **shopping centre** is Tanjung Karang Plaza, Jalan Kartini 21, with an Artomoro department store, supermarket, and several fast-food places plus a host of small shops – Batik Galeri sells a range of cotton sarong lengths at Rp50,000 and has some glorious, but pricey, silk.

TEXTILES AND SOUVENIRS

Batik Indonesia, Jl Dwi Warna 1 (opposite the main Telkom office). They stock an excellent range of *kain tapis*, but expect to start negotiating at Rp40,000–50,000 for a 100cm by 70cm hanging, and also the much more demure *tenung Lampung*, an *ikat* weave, at around Rp10,000 per metre. Smaller items such as purses and bags are also on sale from Rp10,000 upwards.

Mulya, Jl Pemuda 2. A good range of Javanese batik, with prices from Rp12,000.

Mulya Sari Lampung Collection, Jl M.H. Thamrin 79. At the Jl Wolter Moginsidi end of this road, this shop is top quality and asks top prices for old and new textiles. There's a great selection, but staff think little of quoting Rp10 million for a 4m by 50cm panel.

Odi Gallery, Jl S. Parman 4b. Not far from Jl Kartini, this gallery sells fabulous modern, locally made pottery in great contemporary shapes from Rp15,000, and ironwork stands to go with it.

Putra Indonesia, Jl S. Parman 37. Midway between Jl Kartini and Jl Raden Intan. They have an excellent and extensive selection of textiles and fabric items including cotton bags and *songket* at Rp20,000–25,000 and small panels of *kain tapis* from Rp20,000.

Ruwajurai, Jl Imam Bonjol 34. Opposite Bundo Kanding Plaza, Ruwajurai has a huge range of textiles including *kain tapis*, with negotiations for smaller items (20cm by 30cm) starting at Rp20,000, up to Rp500,000 for 1m-long panels.

Listings

Airline offices Merpati, Jl A. Yani 88b (☎0721/258046).

Banks and exchange BCA, Jl Yos Sudarso 100; BRI, Jl Raden Intan.

Car rental Inquire at your hotel or at the travel agents in town. Expect to pay Rp150,000 per day for an air-con Kijang with or without driver. If you rent a taxi by the day, you should be able to get a basic saloon without air-con for Rp80,000–90,000 per day.

Hospital Rumah Sakit Bumi Waras, Jl Wolter Moginsidi (☎0721/263851); Rumah Sakit Immanuel Way Halim, Jl Sukarno Hatta B (☎0721/704900); Rumah Sakit Abdul Muluk, Jl Kapten Rivai (☎0721/702455).

Immigration office Jl Diponegoro 24 (☎0721/482607).

Pharmacies There are plenty of pharmacies on Jl Raden Intan, one of the larger ones being Enggal, Jl Raden Intan 122, just south of the *Kurnia Perdana Hotel*.

Post Office Jl K. H. A. Dahlan 21.

Telephone and fax The main Telkom office is at Jl Kartini 1 and there's also a 24hr wartel at Jl Majapahit 14.

Tour operators Elendra, Jl Sultan Agung 32 (☎ & fax 0721/704737); Krakatoa Lampung Wisata, next to the *Sheraton Hotel* and at Jl Kartini 19–25 (☎ & fax 0721/263625); Primawahana Mandiri, Jl Ikan Tongkol, Block B/9 (☎0721/480091, fax 480092). They typically offer day-trips to Way Kambas (US$61), Way Kanan (US$99), Pugung Raharjo (US$40) and Merak Blantung (US$60), plus a two-day trip to Krakatau (US$150). All prices are per person and minimum numbers, usually two, will be required.

Around Bandar Lampung

About 8km from Panjang terminal on the southeast edge of Bandar Lampung, **Pasir Putih beach** is easily accessible from the city on any of the public transport plying from Panjang towards Bakauheni. It's not the most glorious beach in the world – it's within sight, and smell, of the nearby factories – but you can arrange a charter from here to some worthwhile offshore islands, and the *bagan* (floating fishing nets) just offshore are picturesque. **Pulau Condong**, about 3km from the beach, is actually three islands, including Pulau Bule (Albino Island, perhaps named after the sands or the foreigners who frolic here) which is the most attractive, with excellent white-sand beaches and some offshore coral. It's totally undeveloped, so you'll need to take all your food and water plus snorkelling gear. Bargain for around Rp20,000 for the return boat trip, fifteen minutes each way, and don't forget to tell the boatman your pick-up time.

An excursion along the western edge of Lampung Bay towards **Padang Cermin** makes for a good day out, with the road clinging to the rocky shoreline along tiny coves, through small villages and with great views of the bay itself across towards Kalianda and back to Bandar Lampung. Bemos and minibuses operate from Jalan Ikan Bawal, near the *Hotel Sriwijaya*. Seven kilometres from Bandar Lampung, the small village of Lampasing is the scene of daily fish auctions (4–5pm – catch those on the return journey). At Gunung Betung there's a forestry office and small **camping** ground with great views of the area, and at Ketapang, a small fishing village 32km from Bandar Lampung, you can charter a boat for a half- or full-day trip to the white beaches of **Pulau Legundi** out to the south on the way to Krakatau. It's a two-hour trip in each direction and you'll begin negotiating at Rp60,000–70,000 for the day. There's little to see once you arrive at Padang Cermin – it's a small town – but you catch return transport here.

The remains at **Pugung Raharjo**, 42km east of the city, are said to date from the twelfth to the seventeenth centuries, with megalithic standing stones, stepped temple mounds, and ramparts and ditches providing evidence of a fortified village. Local legend claims that water from the spring has magical properties and can restore youth. Set in amongst local crops and spread over quite a large area, there isn't much here for the casual visitor, although enthusiasts may appreciate the small **museum**, which houses inscribed stones and statues found on site. Explorations only began about forty years ago when transmigrants to the area began discovering remains and relics as they cleared their land. It's accessible by public transport from Panjang terminal; take a bus towards Sribawono, and the site is 2km to the north of the main road at Jabung. If you have your own transport, combine this trip with a visit to Way Kambas national park.

The Way Kambas national park

If the southern tip of Sumatra is famous for anything, it's for the **WAY KAMBAS NATIONAL PARK**, and in particular the **Elephant Training Centre** there. The park is entirely lowland, never rising more than 100m above sea level, but comprises a variety of ecosystems including freshwater swamp, forest, grassy plains and coastal and riverine systems. It has been designated as a protected area for over seventy years, but has unfortunately been extensively logged, so that only around a fifth of the original forest remains.

The park's inhabitants include Sumatran elephants (there are thought to be about 300 living in the park, including those at the training centre), rhinos, leopards and tapirs, several varieties of primate, honey bears, deer, tree cat and wild pig. Reptiles include monitor lizards and crocodiles, and 286 species of birds have been sighted. Serious birdwatchers visit the park as one of the best places to spot the **white-winged duck** and **Storm's stork**, both of which are endangered species and very rare. There are thought to be only about 250 white-winged duck throughout Southeast Asia, and thirty or so of them in Way Kambas national park; some have favourite spots close to the accommodation at Way Kanan. Storm's stork is very elusive and rare – its nest was only described in 1987 – but there are areas close to the Way Kanan accommodation as well as further afield where there's a chance of seeing the bird. The dry season, from June to November, is the most comfortable visiting time, and you're likely to see kingfishers, fish-eagles, adjutants, leafbirds, bulbuls and sunbirds.

Practicalities
The problem for visitors is that Way Kambas is rather difficult to get to and get around once you're there. No vehicles are allowed in the park, so you'll either need to have your own vehicle at your disposal (see "Listings" p.456) or rely on **ojek** that operate, for hefty fees, within the park. It'll depend to some extent on your negotiation skills, but expect to pay Rp7500–10,000 for the one-way trip from the park entrance to the elephant training centre and at least fifty percent more to Way Kanan – you'll need to arrange a time to be collected.

Many people choose to visit on a **day-trip** from Bandar Lampung that centres on the Elephant Training Centre and so omits the opportunity to see the wilder parts of the park. To appreciate the area properly you should stay in the park itself.

Access is at Tridatu, 10km north of Jepara; the access road leads off the main road at the small village of Rajahasa Lama – it's about 7km from the village to the gate. At the national park office you'll need to buy a **permit** (Rp1750). There are two main routes from the park entrance, one leading 9km to the Elephant Training Centre at Karang Sari, the other 13km to *Way Kanan Resort* for extremely basic **accommodation** (④); you need to take cooked food or food and a stove. From *Way Kanan* it's possible to arrange trips on Sungai Way Kanan (2hr; Rp25,000) and **jungle treks** (park guides cost about Rp15,000 per day). If you're using public transport, the best way is to take a bus to Sribawono from Panjang terminal in Bandar Lampung (90min) and then a local bus from Sribawono through Jepara to Rajahasa Lama (1hr).

The park

The **Elephant Training Centre** (daily 8am–4pm) opened in 1985 and is one of the largest of these operations in Southeast Asia. It was created as the solution to the wild elephant problem of the region. Since the 1960s, much of the forest had been cleared for plantations and settlements and the displaced elephants were a constant nuisance and danger to new settlers, attacking crops and, in some cases, homes. As protected species, the elephants were legally immune from retribution, so, with the help of Thai elephants and their trainers, a programme was set up to begin to train them to operate within the tourist industry rather than become prey to illegal poaching and revenge by angry villagers. You can see the elephants in **training** (Mon–Sat 8–10am & 3–4pm) or see the Sunday **display** that is put on for tourists (11.30am & 1.30pm), when the elephants demonstrate football, counting and other tricks. There are also short (Rp12,500 for 30min) and long (Rp20,000 per hour) elephant rides available.

Way Kambas is currently the site of a controversial and extremely expensive scheme to create a breeding and ecotourism reserve for the **Sumatran rhinoceros**. Currently under construction, when the sanctuary is complete, rhinos will be repatriated here from zoos around the world where they have failed to breed, in the hope that in larger numbers and in more natural surroundings they will reproduce successfully. Currently being financed by Indonesian and international funds, the plan is that the centre should become self-financing from tourist income generated by elephant-back safaris through part of the park; a series of lodges and cottages is being built on the edge of the area for the affluent tourists, mostly from Jakarta, who will be lured here. There's already controversy, as the local people say they have been inadequately consulted, and it's uncertain when the scheme will get underway.

Kota Agung and the Bukit Barisan Selatan national park

The deeply indented coastline to the west of Bandar Lampung is generally ignored by tourists. Yet the areas around Lampung Bay and the more westerly Semanka Bay are hugely attractive, as the Bukit Barisan Mountain range reaches its southern extremity at the Indian Ocean, with rolling, mist-covered hills and forests rising from glistening waters dotted with myriad tiny islands. Access to the **Bukit Barisan Selatan national park** is from **Kota Agung**, a small coastal town 80km west of Bandar Lampung (2–3hr by bus from Rajabasa terminal).

Kota Agung

The quiet, attractive town of **KOTA AGUNG** is a pleasant destination in its own right, even if you don't want to go to the national park. Streets are wide, life is slow and there's little to race around for, and the port area is busy and bustling with fishing boats and ships unloading. The town has all the facilities you need: the **post office** is at Jalan Bhayang Kara, the 24hr Telkom office is an inconvenient 3km outside town on the Bandar Lampung road, while the wartel Jalan Merdeka 86, (5.30am–11.30pm), is more central, opposite the bus terminal. The Bukit Barisan **national park office** (Mon–Fri 7am–3pm; ☎0722/21064) is at Jalan Raya Terbaya (also known as Jalan Juanda).

Setia Hotel, Jalan Samudra 294 (☎0722/21065; ③), is the best-value **accommodation** option, with basic but clean rooms, some with and some without attached mandi. From the bus terminal, walk down the road that runs along the left side of the wartel, and, after 200m, *Setia Hotel* will be facing you. Three hundred metres closer to the sea is *KS*, Jalan Samudra 90 (no phone; ④), whose rooms are similar although none have attached mandi.

The Bukit Barisan Selatan national park

Consisting of the entire southwest finger of land pointing into the Indian Ocean, the **Bukit Barisan Selatan national park** (South Bukit Barisan national park) stretches from Cape Rata and Cape Cina in the south to the area northwest of Danau Ranau. Covering 3568 square kilometres, it is home to elephants, tigers, bears, rhinos, crocodiles, the Sumatran mountain goat, the slow loris, hornbills and argus pheasants, among many other species. The floral highlights are orchids, rafflesia and the world's tallest flower, *Amorphophallus titanum*. **Permits** are available at the national park office in Kota Agung (see above).

Alternative access to the park is from **Sukaraja**, 20km west of Kota Agung, where there's a camping ground, cool at 560m above sea level, with some good views of Semanka Bay. Sukaraja is accessible by local bus to Sedatu and then ojek, and national park guides can advise on treks in that area. It's possible to see rafflesia in the area between June and October. The **Danau Suwoh** area is another possible destination, but access is difficult, four hours by ojek up an atrocious track to a camping ground in an area that is actually made up of four lakes: Asam Besak is the largest, and the others are Lebar, Minyak and Belibis. Access to the **northern areas** of the park is via the PHPA post at Liwa.

TREKKING IN THE PARK

There are various routes into the park, one of the most interesting being a **four-day trek** across the southern tip. You'll sleep in the national park "pos" on the trek and you'll need to contract a **guide** – inquire at the national park office in Kota Agung. Expect to pay a national park guide about Rp20,000 a day, plus expenses; you'll need to discuss with him the supplies to take. Day one involves a five-hour scheduled boat service from Kota Agung to Tampang on the southern edge of Semanka Bay. Day two is an eight- or nine-hour trek through the lowland tropical rainforest crossing the south-flowing Blambangan and Seleman rivers on the way, over to the west coast at the village of Belimbing, situated on a beautiful bay backed by beach forest including Australian pine. Day three is a walk back to Tampang via the coast. Wild buffalo roam between the mouths of the two rivers and it's possible to spot turtles here: green turtles, hawksbill turtles and leatherback turtles are all known in the area. You'll also pass Danau Menjukut, a naturally dammed lake of brackish water just behind the coast that is home to various water birds and waders such as wild ducks, egrets and kingfishers. Somewhat perversely, the water level is lower in the rainy season, as the hard rain breaks the natural dam between the lake and the ocean. The trek from Tampang to the lake takes four hours, so it's a possible destination for a shorter trek if you don't want to do the whole thing. Day four is back from Tampang to Kota Agung. An alternative return route from Belimbing is to head north to Ngaras (there are a lot of river crossings so this isn't a trip for the rainy season) and from there pick up public transport to Krui (see p.448).

Kalianda

Situated just under 60km south of Bandar Lampung, the small coastal town of **KALIAN-DA** is a great alternative to the hassles and expenses of the city, and an excellent stopping-off point whether you're entering or leaving Sumatra. It's served by public transport from the Bakauheni ferry terminal and from the Panjang and Rajabasa terminals in Bandar Lampung. Public transport in Kalianda arrives at Terminal Pasar Impress in front of the main market; wander the alleyways here to enjoy the sights, sounds and smells.

The best travellers' **accommodation** is in the *Beringin Hotel*, Jalan Kesuma Bangsa 75 (☎0727/2008; ③), in a large, colonial-style bungalow with big rooms, an airy lounge and a garden at the back. To get here from the terminal, go back onto the road, turn right for about 400m to a junction where a large road joins from the right; head down here past the local school and the hotel is at the far end on the left. Alternatively, engage one of the many ojek that hang around the terminal, and cruise around town.

The **post office** is at Jalan Pratu M. Yusuf and the **telephone office** on the main street is open 7am to midnight. The main shopping street is Jalan Serma Ibnu Hasyim, a short walk from the *Beringin Hotel*, where you'll find most necessities. There are several basic local restaurants in town.

There's little to do here, although the local **beach** is pleasant and there's a small **Chinese temple** near the post office. However, the *Beringin Hotel* will advise on and/or organize **excursions** further afield. One kilometre south of the village, Way Panas Cukuh is a hot-water spring near the ocean, while 2km inland are the hot sulphur springs of Way Belerang. Further afield, you can take a trip to Krakatau, overnighting on Pulau Sebesi, to Kahai and the nearby islands, to Bandar Lampung and to local Balinese villages, complete with traditional Balinese house compounds and temples; the people relocated here after the 1963 eruption of Gunung Agung (see p.538).

Around Kalianda

The small semicircular white-sand beach at **Merak Belantung**, 10km north of Kalianda, lies 2–3km from the main Bandar Lampung–Bakauheni road; there's a huge sign pointing the way and bus conductors and bemo drivers know it well. Plenty of ojek wait at the turning to take you down there. Entrance to the beach area costs Rp1500 at the weekend and Rp1000 on weekdays, when you'll pretty much have the place to yourself. The beach is a bit grubby, but there are good views back to Bandar Lampung and out to Sebesi and Sebuku, and Krakatau on a clear day. There's basic **accommodation** in brick-and-thatch cottages with a tiny verandah and small attached mandi at *Merak Blantung Cottages* (no phone; ⑤), with electricity from 5pm and no fans. During the week you'll need to make arrangements about food with the cottages, as there's nothing nearby, but at weekends the hosts of warung that set up near the beach for day-trippers will provide plenty of choice.

Around 30km south of Kalianda, the ferry terminal between Java and Sumatra is at **Bakauheni**. There's no reason to stay in Bakauheni; arriving at any time of the day or night there are buses to Rajabasa terminal and Panjang terminal in Bandar Lampung, bemos to Kalianda and other local villages, and taxis to Bandar Lampung. There's also a 24hr wartel and a couple of shops.

travel details

Buses

Bandar Lampung to: Bakauheni (every 30min; 2–3hr); Banda Aceh (3 daily; 3 days); Bengkulu (5 daily; 14hr); Bukittinggi (6 daily; 24hr); Denpasar (4 daily; 3 days); Dumai (4 daily; 48hr); Jakarta (20 daily; 8hr); Jambi (8 daily; 24hr); Kalianda (every 30min; 1–2hr); Kota Agung (every 30min; 2hr); Krui (4 daily; 8hr); Liwa (4 daily; 6hr); Medan (10 daily; 48hr); Padang (6 daily; 24hr); Palembang (10 daily; 8hr); Pekanbaru (6 daily; 24hr); Parapet (10 daily; 48hr); Yogyakarta (20 daily; 24hr).

Banding Agung (Danau Ranau) to: Bandar Lampung (daily; 6hr); Jakarta (daily; 14hr); Palembang (daily; 8–10hr).

Bengkulu to: Bandar Lampung (7 daily; 20hr); Curup (10 daily; 3hr); Denpasar (daily; 3 days); Dumai (5 daily; 20hr); Jakarta (daily; 24hr); Jambi (5 daily; 10hr); Krui (2 daily; 10hr); Lubuklinggau (10 daily; 6hr); Medan via Parapet and Danau Toba (2 daily; 48hr); Pagaralam (2 daily; 6hr); Palembang (5 daily; 18hr); Pekanbaru (5 daily; 20hr); Probolinggo (daily; 48hr); Solo (daily; 2 days); Yogyakarta (daily; 48hr).

Kotabatu (Danau Ranau) to: Bandar Lampung (daily; 6hr); Jakarta (daily; 14hr); Liwa (every 2hr; 1hr); Palembang (daily; 8–10hr).

Krui to: Bandar Lampung (4 daily; 8hr); Bengkulu (2 daily; 10hr); Bukit Kemuning (hourly; 2–3hr); Liwa (every 30min; 1hr–1hr30min); Ngaras (daily; 3hr).

Lahat to: Bandar Lampung (3 daily; 8hr); Bengkulu (3 daily; 7hr); Jakarta (3 daily; 14hr); Palembang (10 daily; 4hr).

Pagaralam to: Bandar Lampung (2 daily; 8hr); Bengkulu (2 daily; 6hr); Jakarta (2 daily; 20hr); Lahat (10 daily; 1hr 30min); Palembang (5 daily; 5hr).

Palembang to: Bandar Lampung (10 daily; 8hr); Bengkulu (5 daily; 12hr); Bukittinggi (10 daily; 18hr); Denpasar (10 daily; 48hr); Jakarta (10 daily; 18–20hr); Jambi (10 daily; 5hr); Medan (10 daily; 40–55hr); Padang (10 daily; 18hr); Pekanbaru (20 daily; 15–18hr); Yogyakarta (10 daily; 48hr).

Simpangsender (Danau Ranau) to: Bandar Lampung (2 daily; 6hr); Baturaja (hourly; 3–4hr); Bengkulu (2 daily; 8hr); Jakarta (2 daily; 14hr); Liwa (every 2hr; 1hr).

Trains

Bandar Lampung to: Palembang via Kotabumi, Martapura, Baturaja and Prabamulih (3 daily; 6–8hr).

Lahat to: Lubuklinggau (3 daily; 4hr); Palembang (2 daily; 5hr).

Lubuklinggau to: Palembang via Tebintinngi, Lahat, Muaraenam and Prabamulih (3 daily; 6–8hr).

Palembang to: Bandar Lampung, via Prabamulih, Baturaja, Martapura and Kotabumi (3 daily; 6–8hr); Lubuklinggau via Prabamulih, Muaraenam, Lahat and Tebintinngi (3 daily; 6–9hr).

Pelni ferries

For a chart of the Pelni routes, see pp.36–37 of Basics.

Mentok to: Belawan (*KM Sinabung*, 3–4 times fortnightly; 25–28hr); Tanjung Balai (*KM Sinabung*, 3–4 times fortnightly; 8–10hr); Tanjung Priok (*KM Sinabung*, 3–4 times fortnightly; 14hr).

Tanjung Pandan to: Cirebon (*KM Lawit*, fortnightly; 48hr); Kumai (*KM Lawit*, fortnightly; 3 days); Pontianak (*KM Lawit*, weekly; 15hr); Semarang (*KM Lawit*, fortnightly; 3 days); Tanjung Priok (*KM Lawit*, weekly; 17hr).

Other ferries

Bakauheni to: Merak (every 20min; 40min–2hr).

Bandar Lampung (Sukaraja) to: Merak (5 daily; 90min).

Bengkulu to: Enggano (3 weekly; 12hr).

Mentok (Pulau Bangka) to: Palembang (hydrofoil 4 daily; 2–3hr); (ferry 3 weekly; 11hr).

Palembang to: Mentok (Pulau Bangka) (hydrofoil 4 daily; 2–3hr, ferry 3 weekly; 11hr).

Pangkal Balam to: Tanjung Pandan (Pulau Belitung) (jet foil weekly; 3hr, ferry 2 weekly; 12hr); Jakarta (2 weekly; 8hr).

Tanjung Pandan (Pulau Belitung) to: Pangkal Balam (Pulau Bangka) (jet foil weekly; 3hr, ferry 2 weekly; 12hr).

Flights

Bandar Lampung to: Jakarta (6 daily; 55min); Palembang (weekly; 1hr 5min).

Bengkulu to: Jakarta (3 daily; 1hr 15min); Palembang (5 weekly; 1hr 15min).

Palembang to: Balikpapan via Jakarta (2 daily; 7hr 40min); Bandar Lampung (weekly; 1hr 5min); Bandung (3 weekly; 1hr 5min); Batam (10 weekly; 1hr 5min–1hr 35min); Bengkulu (5 weekly; 1hr 15min); Denpasar via Jakarta (5 daily; 4hr 30min); Jakarta (12 daily; 1hr 5min); Johor Bahru (4 weekly; 1hr 40min); Kuala Lumpur (4 weekly; 2hr 50min); Padang (daily; 1hr); Pangalpinang (2 daily; 50min); Semarang via Jakarta (daily; 4hr 5min); Singapore (3 weekly; 1hr 50min); Surabaya via Jakarta (4 daily; 5hr); Tanjung Pandan (daily; 1hr 20min); Ujung Pandang via Jakarta (3 daily; 8hr); Yogyakarta via Jakarta (daily; 2hr 45min).

Pangalpinang (Pulau Bangka) to: Batam (8 weekly; 1hr 30min); Jakarta (6 daily; 1hr); Palembang (2 daily; 50min).

Tanjung Pandan (Pulau Belitung): Jakarta (3 daily; 1hr 10min); Palembang (11 weekly; 1hr 20min); Pangalpinang (daily; 50min).

CHAPTER EIGHT

BALI

The island of **Bali** has long been the primary focus of Indonesia's flourishing tourist industry. The island is small (it extends less than 150km at its longest point), volcanic, and graced with swaths of extremely fertile land, much of it sculpted into terraced rice paddies. Sandy beaches punctuate the dramatically rugged coastline and world-class surf pounds the shoreline. Culturally, Bali is equally rewarding. It is the only Hindu society in Southeast Asia, and exuberant religious observance permeates every aspect of contemporary Balinese life.

The tiny island with a population of just three million draws in more than one and a half million foreign visitors every year, plus around a million domestic tourists. As a result, it has become very much a mainstream destination, offering all the comforts and facilities expected by better-off tourists, and suffering the predictable problems of congestion, commercialization and breakneck Westernization. However, Bali's original charm is still very much in evidence, its stunning temples and spectacular festivals set off by the gorgeously lush landscape of the interior.

Bali's most famous resort is **Kuta** beach, a six-kilometre sweep of golden sand, whose international reputation as a hangout for weekending Australian surfers is enhanced by its numerous attractions – restaurants, bars, clubs and shops. Travellers seeking more relaxed alternatives generally head across the southern peninsula to **Sanur** or, increasingly, to peaceful **Candi Dasa**, and further east, the black, volcanic sands of **Lovina** on the north coast or the rapidly developing villages in the **far east** beyond Culik. All these resorts make comfortable bases for **divers** and **snorkellers**, being within easy reach of the islands' fine reefs; Bali also boasts an unusually accessible wreck-dive. **Surfers** on Bali head for the famed south-coast swells, particularly around **Uluwatu**, and the offshore island breaks of **Nusa Lembongan**.

Despite the obvious attractions of the beach resorts, most visitors also venture inland to experience more traditional island life. On Bali, the once tiny village of **Ubud** has become something of a cultural centre, a still charming but undeniably commercialized place, where traditional dances are staged every night of the week and the streets are full of arts and crafts galleries. In general, the villages are far more appealing than the towns, but Bali's capital, **Denpasar**, the ancient capital of **Klungkung**, and the north coast city of **Singaraja**, are all worth a day-trip for their museums, markets and temples.

The island's other big draw is its proliferation of elegant Hindu **temples** – particularly the stunning island temple of Tanah Lot and the extensive Besakih complex on the slopes of Gunung Agung. Temple **festivals**, held throughout the island and at frequent intervals during the year, are also well worth attending; most are open to tourists. There are also a number of hiking possibilities – most of them up **volcanoes**. The ascent to the summit of Bali's **Gunung Batur** is extremely popular, while **Gunung Agung** is for the very fit. Bali's sole **national park**, Bali Barat, has relatively few interesting trails, but it is a rewarding place for **birdwatching**, as is the area around Danau Bratan in the centre of the island.

Visitors to Bali should be aware of the **peak tourist seasons**; resorts get packed out between mid-June and mid-September and again over the Christmas and New Year period, when prices rocket and rooms can be fully booked for days, if not weeks, in advance.

ACCOMMODATION PRICE CODES

All the **accommodation** listed in this book has been given one of the following price codes. The rates quoted here are for the **cheapest double room** in high season, except for places with dorms, where the code represents the price of a single bed. Where there's a significant spread of prices indicated (④–⑦, for example), the text will explain what extra facilities you get for more money. The 11–21 percent tax charged by most hotels is not included in these price codes.

Because of the current instability of the rupiah, accommodation prices are given throughout in their more stable **US dollar equivalents**, even for places that accept payment in rupiah.

For more on accommodation, see p.40.

① under $1	③ $2–5	⑤ $10–15	⑦ $35–60	⑨ $100
② $1–2	④ $5–10	⑥ $15–35	⑧ $60–100	and over

Some history

The earliest written records in Bali, metal inscriptions or *prasasti*, dating from the ninth century AD, reveal Buddhist and Hindu influence from the Indian subcontinent, visible also in the statues, bronzes and rock-cut caves at Gunung Kawi and Goa Gajah. The most famous event in early Balinese history occurred towards the end of the tenth century, when Princess **Mahendratta** of East Java married the Balinese King **Udayana**. Their son, **Erlangga**, born around 991 AD, later succeeded to the throne of the Javanese kingdom and sent his regent to rule over Bali, thus bringing the two realms together until his death in 1049.

In the following centuries, the ties between Bali and Java fluctuated as kingdoms gained and lost power. In 1343, the island was colonized by the powerful Hindu **Majapahit** kingdom of East Java. The Balinese who did not accept these changes established their own villages in remote areas. Their descendants, known as the **Bali Aga** or *Bali Mula*, the "original Balinese", still live in separate villages, such as Tenganan near Candi Dasa and Trunyan on the shores of Danau Batur. Throughout the fifteenth century, the power of the Majapahit empire on Java declined as the influence of Islam expanded. The empire finally fell in 1515 and the priests, craftsmen, soldiers, nobles and artists of the Hindu Majapahit fled east to Bali, flooding the island with **Javanese cultural ideas**.

The Balinese first came into contact with Europeans – Portuguese and Dutch – during the sixteenth century, though the island was largely ignored, as it produced little of interest to outsiders. The exception was **slaves**, who were shipped through the port of Kuta and had a reputation for being particularly strong and hard-working. However, by the mid-1830s the main Dutch concern was to gain control of the region before the British, and in 1840 the **Dutch envoy**, Huskus Koopman, began a series of visits with the aim of persuading the Balinese to agree to Dutch sovereignty over the island. This ultimately led to violent clashes with the rajahs, and in 1849 the **Third Dutch Military Expedition** of 7000 troops landed in Buleleng, attacked the fortress at Jagaraga and defeated the Balinese with the loss of only about thirty men to the Balinese thousands.

The Dutch then set up headquarters at Padang Bai and decided to attack Karangasem. On their arrival at the palace, the rajah of Karangasem, his family and followers, all committed **puputan** (ritual suicide). The Dutch troops then headed west towards Klungkung. However, an **agreement** was drawn up in Kuta on July 13, 1849, whereby the Balinese recognized Dutch sovereignty, and in return the Dutch agreed to leave the rajahs to administer their own kingdoms. From their administrative capital in **Singaraja**, the Dutch made some improvements on the island, particularly in irrigation and by planting coffee as a cash crop. They also brought in new regulations against

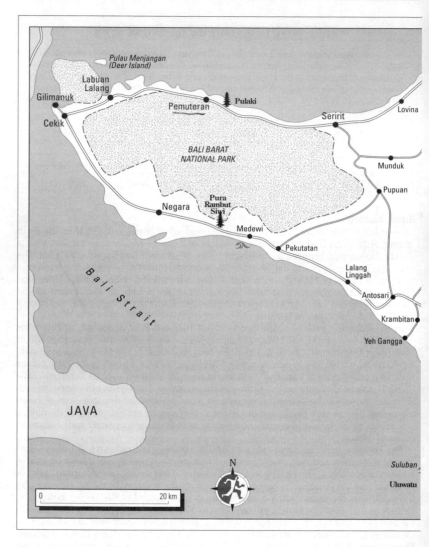

slavery and the tradition of suttee, when widows would throw themselves on the funeral pyres of their dead husbands.

Having taken control of the south of the island, the Dutch then decided to assert their monopoly over **opium trading**, traditionally carried on by Chinese and Buginese traders. On the announcement of this on April 1, 1908, there was **rioting in Klungkung** followed by clashes with Dutch troops. When more troops arrived in Klungkung on April 28, 1908, they witnessed another *puputan* in which two hundred members of the royal household committed suicide. In January 1909, the whole of the island of Bali came under **Dutch control**.

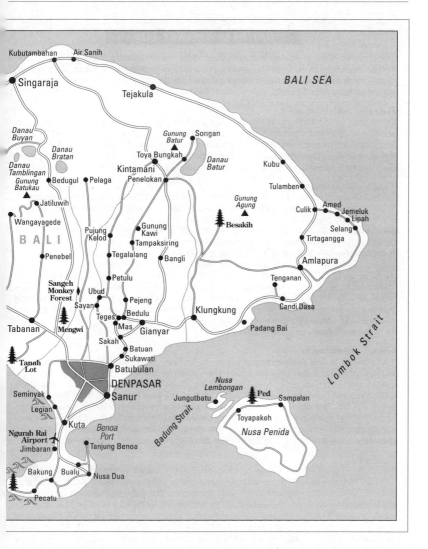

In December 1941, Japan entered **World War II**; their fleet arrived off Sanur on February 18 and landed 500 troops, which moved unopposed to Denpasar and then through the island, which they occupied without a fight. The **occupation** was short-lived, but it had profound political effects as it showed that the Dutch colonialists were vulnerable.

When Indonesia made its declaration of **Independence** on August 17, 1945, some Balinese were unhappy: Java was Muslim, and the traditional enmity between the two islands made many people uncertain about joining a republic dominated by Java. Returning to retake their colony in March 1946, the Dutch faced ferocious fighting on

BALINESE VILLAGE LIFE

The majority of the people on Bali earn their living from agriculture and live in **villages**. People employed in the cities or tourist resorts may well commute from their village homes each day, and even those whose villages are far away still identify with them and return on particular festivals.

Balinese village layout

Orientation in the Balinese world does not correspond to the compass points of north, south, east and west. Gunung Agung, dwelling place of the gods and the highest peak on Bali, is the reference point, and the main directions are **kaja**, towards the mountain, and **kelod**, away from the mountain, which in practice usually means towards the sea. The other directions are *kangin*, from where the sun rises, and its opposite, *kauh*, where the sun sets.

House compounds

Each Balinese household consists of several structures, all built within a confining wall. When a son of the family marries, his wife will usually move into his compound, so there are frequently several generations living within the same area. Most domestic activities take place outside or in the partial shelter of **bale**, raised platforms supported by wooden pillars, with a roof traditionally thatched with local grass (*alang-alang*). Outside the *kelod* wall, families have their garbage tip and pig pens. Prior to calling in the *undagi*, the master builder who understands the rules relating to buildings laid down in ancient texts, an expert in the Balinese calendar is consulted, as an auspicious day must be chosen. Before building starts, a **ceremony** takes place in which an offering, usually a brick wrapped in white cloth sprinkled with holy water, is placed in the foundation of each building so that work will proceed smoothly. When the building work is finished, a series of ceremonies must take place before the compound can be occupied. The final ceremony is the **melaspas**, an inauguration ritual which "brings the building to life".

Village organization

The smallest unit of social organization in each village is the **banjar**, or neighbourhood. Each adult male on Bali joins the local *banjar* when he marries. The size of *banjar* varies enormously – the largest ones in Denpasar may have five hundred heads of household, while the small rural ones may have as few as fifty. The *banjar* meets in the village meeting house, the **bale banjar**, to discuss land issues, plans for temple ceremonies, the local gamelan orchestra, government projects, and any problems. Although there is a head of the *banjar* (*kliang*), all decisions are reached by consensus. The *banjar* has considerable authority. If members neglect their duties they can be fined or even expelled from the village.

The subak

Much of the daily life of a village revolves around the *sawah*, or **rice-fields**, and numerous complex rituals accompany all the stages of rice cultivation encapsulated in the worship of Dewi Sri, the goddess of rice and prosperity. The local organization in charge of each irrigation system is the **subak**; these are known to have existed on Bali since the ninth century. The maintenance of the irrigation system, along with detailed planning to ensure that every farmer gets the water he needs, is coordinated by the *kliang subak*. Any *subak* with plans that may influence the irrigation system, such as changing dry fields to wet, has to consult the regional water temples, and ultimately, the **Jero Gede**, chief priest of Pura Ulun Danu Batur. The **Subak Museum** (see p.582) is well worth a visit for information on this unique aspect of Balinese life.

Balinese life-cycle celebrations

On **Bali**, rituals and ceremonies are carried out at important points in an individual's life to purify them, and make sure they have sufficient spiritual energy to remain healthy and calm. The first life-cycle ritual, **pegedong-gedongan**, takes place about six months after conception, and emphasizes the hope of a long healthy life for the child. Subsequent **birth rituals** focus on the placenta (*ari-ari*), which is washed and buried inside a coconut, wrapped in sacred white cloth, near the gateway of the parents' household. Following the birth of a baby, the parents and child are regarded as unclean (*sebel*). For the mother and baby this lasts 42 days; for the father it lasts until the baby's umbilical cord drops off, when the **kepus pungsed** ritual is carried out. The cord is wrapped in cloth, placed in an offering shaped like a dove and suspended over the baby's bed. Twelve days after birth, the ceremony of **ngelepas hawon** takes place, with offerings made for the baby in the kitchen, the well and the family temple, followed by the **tutug kambuhan**, 42 days after the birth, which marks the end of the *sebel* period for the mother. After 105 days, **telubulan** is a large ceremony at which the child is named, and may be given an amulet to guard against evil spirits. The child's **first birthday**, *oton*, occurs after 210 days (a Balinese year), and is the first occasion that it is allowed contact with the ground. The next ceremony, **maketus**, takes place when the child's milk teeth fall out; prayers are offered to the gods to ensure that the adult teeth will be strong. The child is now guarded by the family ancestors. The next life-cycle ceremonies occur at **puberty**, with *manggah daa* rituals for a girl and *manggah teruna* for a boy. The **tooth-filing ritual**, *mapandes*, takes place between six and eighteen years of age, and is a huge celebration with guests, music and lavish offerings. It is considered to be a vital ritual, and the elderly, and even the dead, have been known to have their teeth filed. The aim of the ritual is to remove any hint of coarse, uncontrolled behaviour from the person by filing down the upper canine teeth or fangs – *caling*, as the Balinese call them – and the four teeth in between: six in total. Rituals are also performed to rid the person of lust, greed, anger, drunkenness, confusion and jealousy, in order that they will lead a better life and be assured a more favourable reincarnation. There are two options for **marriage** (*pawiwahan* or *nganten*). The most correct is *mamadik*, when the marriage is agreed between the two sets of parents, and a huge financial outlay for ceremonies is involved. Much more common is *ngerorod* or *malaib*, elopement. The man and woman run off and spend the night together, with sufficient subterfuge that the girl's parents can pretend to be outraged. The following morning, a private ceremony (*makala-kalaan*) is carried out, and the couple are married. The girl's parents will not be invited as there is supposed to be bad feeling between the two sides. However, three days later the two sets of parents meet at the *ketipat bantal* ceremony and are reconciled.

Cremation

The ceremony that visitors to Bali are most likely to witness is **cremation** (*pengabenan* or *palebonan*). Following death, the body must be returned to the five elements of solid, liquid, energy, radiance and ether to become ready for reincarnation. The lengthy and complex rituals, the magnificent objects and the spectacular burning itself, make this the most picturesque manifestation of religious observance on the island. Following death, the body is usually buried, sometimes for years, while the elaborate **preparations** for the cremation are made. Poorer families will often share in the cremation ceremonies of wealthier families. The extended family and *banjar* is involved in building temporary shelters for shrines and preparing offerings. Animals must be slaughtered, holy water acquired, and gamelan, dancers and puppet shows organized. An animal-shaped sarcophagus is built from a solid tree trunk, covered with paper and cloth and decorated with mirrors, tassels and tinsel. The cremation tower has tiers similar to the roofs on the *meru* in temples; a small *bale* at the base of the tiers houses an effigy of the dead person and the body itself, or just the bones if burial has previously taken place. The event itself is joyful, accompanied by the soft music of the bamboo **gamelan angklung**. The sarcophagus and cremation tower are carried to the cemetery and twirled around many times to make sure the soul is completely confused and cannot find its way back home to cause mischief for the family. At the cremation ground, the body is transferred from the tower into the sarcophagus, which is anointed with holy water and set alight. After burning, the ashes are carried to the sea or to a stream which will carry them to the ocean. A further purification ceremony takes place three days after the cremation, and another at twelve days, finishing with the ritual of *nyagara-gunung*, when the family take offerings to important sea and mountain temples.

BALINESE VILLAGE LIFE (continued)

Caste and names

Balinese society is structured around a hereditary **caste system** which, while far more relaxed than its Indian counterpart, does nonetheless carry certain restrictions and rules of etiquette, as ordained in the Balinese Hindu scriptures. Of these, the one that travellers are most likely to encounter is the practice of **naming a person** according to their caste. At the top of the tree is the **Brahman** caste, whose men are honoured with the title **Ida Bagus** and whose women are generally named **Ida Ayu**, sometimes shortened to **Dayu**. Traditionally revered as the most scholarly members of society, only Brahmans are allowed to become high priests (*pedanda*). **Satriya** (sometimes spelt *Ksatriya*) form the second strata of Balinese society, and these families are descendants of warriors and rulers. The Balinese rajas were all *Satriya* and their offspring continue to bear the tell-tale names: **Cokorda**, **Anak Agung**, **Ratu** and **Prebagus** for men, and **Anak Agung Isti** or **Dewa Ayu** for women. The merchants or **Wesia** occupy the third most important rank, the men distinguished by the title **I Gusti** or **Pregusti**, the women by the name **I Gusti Ayu**. Finally, at the bottom of the heap, comes the **Sudra** caste, the caste of the common people, which accounts for over ninety percent of the population. *Sudra* children are named according to their position in the family order, with no distinction made between male and female offspring. Thus, a first-born Sudra is always known as **Wayan**, the second-born is **Made**, the third **Nyoman** and the fourth **Ketut**. Should a fifth child be born, then the naming system begins all over again with Wayan, and so it goes on. Unlike their counterparts in the far more rigid Indian caste system, the *Sudra* are not looked down upon or denied access to specific professions (except that of *pedanda*). It's not at all abnormal for a university professor to hail from the *Sudra* caste, for example, or for a waiter or a bemo driver to be a *Brahman* or a *Satriya*, and a high-caste background guarantees neither a high income nor a direct line to political power.

Java but initially little opposition on Bali. However, the **guerrilla forces**, led by **Gusti Ngurah Rai**, a young army officer, in a tactic known as the "Long March to Gunung Agung" attempted to ambush the Dutch, who eventually killed all 97 of the rebels; Ngurah Rai is now remembered as a hero. The status quo returned to the island, with local rulers overseen by Dutch administrators. The Dutch, having lost control of the islands to the west, created the Republic of East Indonesia, with the capital in Makassar in Sulawesi, and in 1948 declared Bali to be an autonomous state within that republic.

The early years of Independence were not kind to Bali; although Sukarno's mother was Balinese, the Balinese felt neglected by the government in Jakarta. Sukarno visited his palace at Tampaksiring regularly, with a massive entourage that demanded to be fed, entertained and then sent on their way with gifts. During the 1960s, a ground swell of resentment against the government grew in Bali. The Balinese began to believe that a state of spiritual disharmony had been reached, and preparations were made for a traditional island-wide **purification ceremony**, Eka Dasa Rudra, held in 1963 against the backdrop of a fiercely rumbling Gunung Agung that eventually erupted causing great devastation (see box on p.538).

Later events in Jakarta increased the disaster in Bali. Following the **Gestapu** affair during the night of September 30, 1965, a wave of **killings** spread across Indonesia from December 1965 until March 1966. Estimates suggest that 100,000 were killed on Bali, with actual or suspected members of the Communist Party, their sympathizers and the Chinese population the main targets.

Until recently it was difficult to know what most people in Bali felt about the **Suharto regime** – criticism was made in hushed voices. Over the past decade there has been growing concern about the extent to which the Balinese have lost control of the tourist industry to wealthy entrepreneurs from Jakarta. Many of the major resorts are owned by companies with Suharto family links, many built on ancestral Balinese lands, and many employ the Balinese only as menial workers. By mid-June 1998, students in Denpasar were marching three times each week in support of total political reform. It remains to be seen whether they will be successful.

THE SOUTH

The triangle of mainly flat land that makes up **the south** is some of the most fertile in Bali, and is also the most densely populated, with more than a thousand people to every square kilometre. Bali's administrative capital, Denpasar, is here, and so too are the island's major tourist resorts, which have sprung up along the spectacular white-sand beaches: at Kuta and Jimbaran in the west, and Sanur and Nusa Dua in the east. Furthermore, the combination of large offshore reefs and a peculiarly shaped coastline have made this region a genuine **surfers' paradise**, with some of the most sought-after breaks in the world.

Denpasar

Far removed from most people's image of a typical Asian capital, **DENPASAR** (formerly known as Badung, and still sometimes referred to as such) is a surprisingly calm city, centred on a grassy square and dominated by family compounds grouped into traditional *banjar* districts, with just a few major shopping streets crisscrossing the centre. It feels nowhere near as hectic as Kuta, but, as there's no nightlife (and no beach) – few tourists spend much time here.

Arrival, information and city transport

If you're arriving in Bali by air, you'll land at **Ngurah Rai Airport**, which is not in Denpasar as sometimes implied, but just beyond the southern outskirts of Kuta (all information on the airport is given in the box on p.478). Arriving in Denpasar by bemo or public bus from another part of the island, you'll almost certainly be dropped at one of the four main **bemo stations**, which lie on the edges of town (see "Bemo connections" plan on p.472). Getting from one to another is fairly easy, but connections can be quite time-consuming.

Denpasar's **tourist office** is just off Puputan Square, at Jalan Surapati 7 (Mon–Thurs 7am–2pm, Fri 7–11am, Sat 7am–noon; ☎ & fax 0361/223602).

MOVING ON FROM DENPASAR

Destinations south of Denpasar (including Kuta, Nusa Dua and Uluwatu) are served by **Tegal** bemo station; Sanur is served by **Kereneng**; Ubud and the east coast (including Candi Dasa and Tampaksiring) are served by **Batubulan** station in the village of Batubulan (see p.502); and the north and west of the island (including Tanah Lot, Gilimanuk for Java, Bedugul, and Singaraja for Lovina) are served by **Ubung** (see p.473). **Buses** to and from Java also use Ubung.

City transport

Denpasar's city transport system relies on the fleet of different coloured **public bemos** that shuttle between the city's bemo terminals. However, only certain routes are covered, and the complex one-way system often means that the bemos take different routes on each leg of their journey; see the "City bemo routes" box on p.473 for major

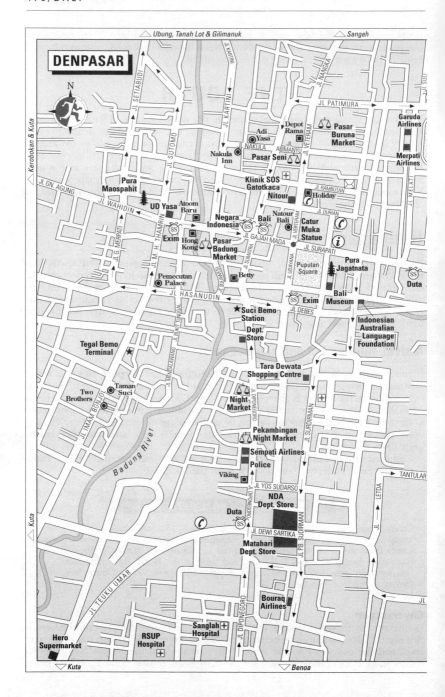

DENPASAR

N

Ubung, Tanah Lot & Gilimanuk

Sangeh

Kerobokan & Kuta

Kuta

JL SETIABUDI

JL GN. AGUNG

JL WAHIDIN

JL KARTINI

JL SUTOMO

JL MERPATI

JL G. MERPATI

JL H. THAMRIN

JL IMAM BONJOL

JL MANDAWANG

JL BUKIT TUNGGAL

JL TEUKU UMAR

Badung River

JL KARTINI

JL NAKULA

ABIMANYU

JL VETERAN

JL PATIMURA

JL MANGKA

JL SULIT

JL MELATI

JL RAMBUTAN

JL DURIAN

JL GAJAH MADA

JL SUMATRA

JL KERTEHAM

JL UDAYANA

JL SURAPATI

JL HASANUDIN

JL DEBES

JL DIPONEGORO

JL SURDIRMAN

JL YOS SUDARSO

JL LETDA

TANTULAR

JL PB. SUDIRMAN

JL DEWI SARTIKA

JL DIPONEGORO

Pura
Maospahit

UD Yasa

Atoom
Baru

Negara
Indonesia

Exim

Hong
Kong

Pasar
Badung
Market

Pemecutan
Palace

Tegal Bemo
Terminal

Two
Brothers

Taman
Suci

Adi
Yasa

Nakula
Inn

Pasar Seni

Klinik SOS
Gatotkaca

Nitour

Bali

Natour
Bali

Depot
Rama

Pasar
Buruna
Market

Garuda
Airlines

Merpati
Airlines

Holiday

Catur
Muka
Statue

Betty

Puputan
Square

Pura
Jagatnata

Bali
Museum

Exim

Duta

Suci Bemo
Station

Dept.
Store

Indonesian
Australian
Language
Foundation

Tara Dewata
Shopping Centre

Night
Market

Pekambingan
Night Market

Sempati Airlines

Police

Viking

NDA
Dept. Store

Duta

Matahari
Dept. Store

Bourag
Airlines

Sanglah
Hospital

Hero
Supermarket

RSUP
Hospital

Kuta

Benoa

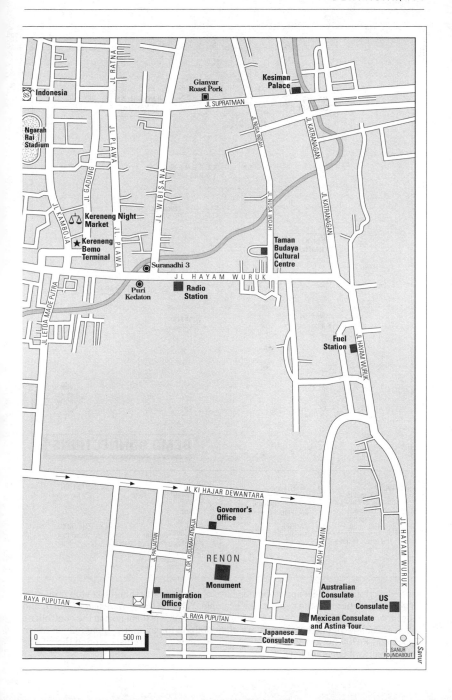

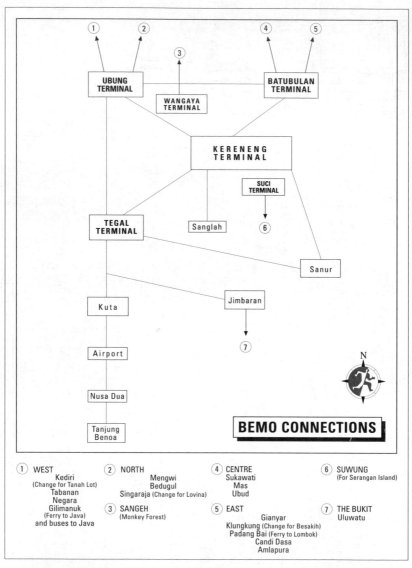

BEMO CONNECTIONS

N

1 WEST
Kediri
(Change for Tanah Lot)
Tabanan
Negara
Gilimanuk
(Ferry to Java)
and buses to Java

2 NORTH
Mengwi
Bedugul
Singaraja (Change for Lovina)

3 SANGEH
(Monkey Forest)

4 CENTRE
Sukawati
Mas
Ubud

5 EAST
Gianyar
Klungkung (Change for Besakih)
Padang Bai (Ferry to Lombok)
Candi Dasa
Amlapura

6 SUWUNG
(For Serangan Island)

7 THE BUKIT
Uluwatu

route descriptions. All Denpasar bemos have at least their first and last stop printed in large roman letters on the vehicle (for example, *"Tegal–Ubung–Kereneng–Tegal"*), and most are colour-coded. Prices are fixed, and a list of rates is displayed in the controller's office at each terminal, but tourists are often obliged to pay more – generally between Rp500 and Rp700 for a cross-city ride. Metered **taxis** also circulate around the city, as do horse-drawn carts (dokar).

CITY BEMO ROUTES

The following information describes the major cross-city routes between Denpasar's main bemo terminals. Some routes alter slightly in reverse.

Kereneng–Jalan Plawa–Jalan Supratman–Jalan Gianyar–corner Jalan Waribang (for *barong* dance)–Kesiman–Government Handicraft Centre–Tohpati–**Batubulan**.

The return Batubulan–Kereneng route is identical, except that bemos go down Jalan Kamboja instead of Jalan Plawa just before reaching Kereneng.

Ubung (grey-blue)–Jalan Cokroaminoto–Jalan Gatot Subroto–Jalan Gianyar–corner Jalan Waribang (for *barong* dance)–Government Handicraft Centre–Tohpati–**Batubulan**.

The return Batubulan–Ubung route is identical.

Kereneng (dark green)–Jalan Hayam Wuruk–corner Nusa Indah (for Taman Budaya Cultural Centre)–Sanur roundabout (for Renon consulates)–Jalan Raya Sanur–**Sanur**.

The return Sanur–Kereneng route is identical.

Kereneng (turquoise)–Jalan Surapati (for Tourist Information, Bali Museum and Pura Jagatnata)–Jalan Veteran (alight at the corner of Jalan Abimanyu for short walk to Jalan Nakula losmen)–Jalan Cokroaminoto–**Ubung**.

Tegal (yellow or turquoise)–Jalan Gn Merapi–Jalan Setiabudi–**Ubung**–Jalan Cokroaminoto–Jalan Subroto–Jalan Yani–Jalan Nakula (for budget hotels)–Jalan Veteran–Jalan Patimura–Jalan Melati–**Kereneng**–Jalan Hayam Wuruk–Jalan Surapati–Jalan Kapten Agung–Jalan Sudirman–Tiara Dewata Shopping Centre–Jalan Yos Sudarso–Jalan Diponegoro–Jalan Hasanudin–Jalan Bukit Tunggal–**Tegal**.

Tegal (dark blue)–Jalan Imam Bonjol–Jalan Teuku Umar–Hero Supermarket–junction with Jalan Diponegoro (alight for Matahari and NDA department stores)–Jalan Yos Sudarso–Jalan Sudirman–Jalan Letda Tantular–junction with Jalan Panjaitan (alight for 500m walk to Immigration and GPO)–Jalan Hajar Dewantara–Jalan Moh Yamin–Sanur roundabout–**Sanur**.

The return Sanur–Tegal route goes all the way along Jalan Raya Puputan after the round-about, passing the entrance gates of the immigration office and the GPO, then straight along Jalan Teuku Umar, past Hero Supermarket to the junction with Jalan Imam Bonjol (where you should alight to pick up Kuta-bound bemos) before heading north up Jalan Imam Bonjol to Tegal.

Accommodation

Accommodation in Denpasar is disappointingly shabby and overpriced, catering more for the quick-stop Indonesian business traveller than for fussier tourists.

Adi Yasa, Jl Nakula 23 (☎0361/222679). This friendly, family-run losmen is most backpackers' first choice. Rooms, however, are slightly run-down and not all that secure. From Kereneng, take an Ubung-bound bemo to the Pasar Seni market at the Jl Abimanyu/Jl Veteran junction. Yellow/turquoise Tegal–Kereneng bemos pass the front door. ③.

Nakula Inn, Jl Nakula 4 (☎0361/226446). Modern, clean rooms with bathroom. Not as popular as *Adi Yasa* across the road (see above for bemo access), but friendly and more comfortable. ③.

Natour Bali, Jl Veteran 3 (☎0361/225681, fax 235347). Central Denpasar's oldest and most upmarket hotel, with a certain quaint appeal in its colonial architecture and ambience. It offers well-equipped if rather characterless rooms, has a swimming pool, and is centrally located. ⑥.

Taman Suci, Jl Imam Bonjol 45 (☎0361/485254, fax 484724). Shiny new mid-range hotel, with air-con, hot water and TVs in every room, but not convenient for Denpasar's big sights. ⑦.

Two Brothers (Dua Saudara), Jl Imam Bonjol Gang V11, 5 (☎0361/484704). Rooms are spotless if a bit scruffy; none has its own bathroom. A 5min walk south of Tegal bemo station. ③.

The City

Denpasar's central and most convenient landmark is **Puputan Square**, marking the heart of the downtown area and the crossover point of the city's major north–south and east–west roads. A huge stone statue of **Catur Muka** stands on the traffic island here, the four-faced, eight-armed, Hindu guardian of the cardinal points indicating the exact location of the city centre. The other important district is **Renon**, Denpasar's leafy-green administrative centre on the southeastern edge of the city, very close to the resort of Sanur and served by Sanur-bound bemos.

Puputan Square

Right in the heart of Denpasar, the grassy park known as **Puputan Square** (Alun-alun Puputan, or Taman Puputan) commemorates the events of September 15, 1906, when the Rajah of Badung marched out of his palace, followed by hundreds of his subjects, and faced the invading Dutch head on. Dressed all in holy white, each man, woman and child clasping a golden kris, the people of Badung had psyched themselves up for a **puputan**, or ritual fight to the death, rather than submit to the Dutch colonialists' demands. Historical accounts vary, but it's thought that the mass suicide took place on this square and was incited by Badung's chief priest who, on a signal from the rajah, stabbed his king with the royal kris. Hundreds of citizens followed suit, and those that didn't were shot down by Dutch bullets; the final death toll was reported to be somewhere between 600 and 2000. The huge **bronze statue** on the northern edge of the park is a memorial to the Badung citizens who fought and died in the 1906 *puputan*.

The Bali Museum

Overlooking the eastern edge of Puputan Square on Jalan Mayor Wisnu, the **Bali Museum** (Tues–Thurs 8am–2pm, Fri 8–11am, Sat 8am–12.30pm; Rp200; turquoise Kereneng–Ubung bemo route) is Denpasar's most significant attraction and is prettily located in a series of traditional courtyards.

The downstairs hall of the **Main Building**, which stands at the back of the entrance courtyard, mostly houses items from Bali's prehistory, including stone axes, bronze jewellery and a massive stone sarcophagus from the second century BC. The four black-and-white photographs of the 1906 *puputan* are also well worth lingering over. Upstairs you'll find a fine exhibition of traditional household utensils, many of which are still in common use today. These include the **coconut grater** – here carved into an animal shape, complete with genitalia – and the bizarre, tiny bamboo cages for **fighting crickets**, designed to hold the male insects used in the popular local sport of cricket fighting.

The compact **First Pavilion** holds some fine examples of the four major styles of Balinese **textiles**: the ubiquitous *endek* (or *ikat*), the rarer *geringsing*, or double-*ikat*, which comes from Tenganan (see p.551), *songket* brocades, and gold screenprinted *per-ada* (or *prada*). For more on Balinese textiles, see p.550. Built to resemble the long, low structure of an eighteenth-century Karangasem-style palace, the **Second Pavilion** contains all manner of **religious paraphernalia**, including a curious bell-shaped **bamboo cage** that's still used by some villagers in a traditional ceremony to mark the first Balinese year of a baby's life (210 days). The Balinese **calendars** on the right-hand wall are complex compositions arrived at through astrological and religious permutations and are still used to determine auspicious dates for all sorts of events, from temple festivals to house-building. The **Third Pavilion** is given over to **theatrical masks, costumes and puppets**. Most impressive are the costumes for the shaggy-haired Barong Ket and his archenemy, the witch-like **Rangda** (see p.531 for more on their role in Balinese dance-dramas).

Pura Jagatnata

Just over the north wall of the Bali Museum stands the modern state temple of **Pura Jagatnata**, set in a fragrant garden of pomegranate and frangipani trees. As with nearly every temple in Bali, Pura Jagatnata is designed as three courtyards, though in this case the middle courtyard is so compressed as to be little more than a gallery encircled by a moat. **Carvings** of lotus flowers and frogs adorn the tiny stone bridge that spans the moat (access at festival times only) and there are reliefs illustrating scenes from the *Ramayana* and *Mahabharata* carved into the gallery's outer wall. Twice a month, on the occasion of the full moon and of the new moon, **festivals** are held here, with wayang kulit (shadow puppet) shows performed from around 9pm in the outer courtyard.

Pasar Badung

The biggest and best of Denpasar's traditional markets is the chaotic **Pasar Badung**, which stands at the heart of the downtown area, set slightly back off Jalan Gajah Made, in a three-storey covered stone and brick *pasar* beside Sungai Badung. Trading takes place here 24 hours a day, with buyers and sellers pouring in from all over the island. Despite first impressions, the market is laid out in very clear sections, with meat in the basement, fresh fruit and vegetables on the ground floor, spices and pulses on the first floor, and clothes, batik and ceremonial gear at the top. Be prepared to find yourself landed with a **guide**: local women hang out around the market entrance and are keen to accompany tourists round the market.

Taman Budaya Cultural Centre

In the eastern part of town, on Jalan Nusa Indah, fifteen minutes' walk from the Kereneng bemo station, or direct on a Sanur-bound bemo, the **Taman Budaya Cultural Centre** (daily 8am–4.30pm; Rp250) houses a moderately interesting art museum and stages spectacular nightly **kecak dance** performances (see "Entertainment" on p.476). From mid-June to mid-July it also hosts the annual **Arts Festival**, a huge programme of drama, dance and art exhibitions.

The main **exhibition hall** is housed in the long, two-storey building towards the back of the compound, and begins with an overview of Balinese **painting**, with a few examples in the classical wayang style, followed by works from several different schools, taking in the so-called Ubud, Batuan and Young Artists styles (see pp.514–515 for more on these). Religious and secular **woodcarvings** fill the next room, together with an assortment of *Ramayana* and *topeng* dance masks. There are more ambitious carvings downstairs, along with a collection of modern non-traditional paintings spanning a range of styles from batik through to Cubism.

Eating and drinking

Eating and **drinking** hardly rates as one of Denpasar's great pleasures, but you won't go hungry here. Most restaurants stop serving by 9pm, after which your best option is a visit to the Kereneng night market.

Betty, Jl Sumatra 56. Highly recommended café with a big, cheap menu that includes an imaginative and tasty vegetarian selection. Closes at 9pm.

Depot Rama, Jl Veteran 55. Inexpensive neighbourhood warung serving nasi campur, nasi goreng, *nasi soto ayam* and lots of noodle dishes. Very convenient for the Jl Nakula losmen.

Hong Kong, Jl Gajah Made 99. Classy, air-con Chinese restaurant offering a huge variety of moderately priced meals, including seafood. Karaoke at night.

Kereneng Night Market, just off Jl Hayam Wuruk, adjacent to Kereneng bemo station. Over fifty vendors convene here from dusk to dawn every night, serving up soups, noodle and rice dishes, fresh fruit juices and beers. Good for a snack after the *kecak* show at the Cultural Centre.

Puri Agung, inside the *Natour Bali Hotel* at Jl Veteran 3. The 1920s decor is of more interest than the menu, but their *rijsttaffel*, which includes six separate dishes, is recommended.

Entertainment

Denpasar holds little in the way of bars or clubs, but there's a five-screen Wisata 21 **cinema** complex at Jalan Thamrin 69, and a smaller one on nearby Jalan Kartini; soundtracks are usually in the original language, and tickets cost Rp6000. All tour agents can arrange transport and tickets for Balinese **dance performances** in the Denpasar, Kuta and Ubud areas; shows are staged daily in most places. Prices start at Rp20,000 through a tour agent, or about Rp6000 on the door. If you're going to a show independently, the nearest options are the nightly **kecak** (6.30–7.30pm) at the Taman Budaya Cultural Centre on Jalan Nusa Indah (see p.475); the daily **barong** (9.30–10.30am), at both the Catur Eka Budhi on Jalan Waribang on the eastern edge of town (Batubulan-bound bemo from either Ubung or Kereneng) and at the Pura Puseh in Batubulan (bemo from Ubung or Kereneng). For some background on Balinese dance, see the box on pp.520–522.

Listings

Airline offices and agents Garuda city check-in at Jl Melati 61 (☎0361/225245). Domestic Garuda and Merpati tickets from Nitour at Jl Veteran 5 (☎0361/234742); international flights from Astina at Jl Moh Yamin 1a (☎0361/223552) in Renon.

Banks and exchange There are exchange counters at most banks. Visa cash advances from Bank Bali, opposite Matahari department store, at Jl Dewi Sartika 88 (☎0361/261678), or at Jl Sulawesi 1 (☎0361/261684); and at Bank Duta, Jl Hayam Wuruk 165 (☎0361/226578).

Email and Internet access Bali's Internet HQ is Wasantara Net (Mon–Sat 8am–8pm), located at the back of the GPO compound in Renon (Sanur–Tegal bemo route); this is the cheapest and fastest place in Bali to access the Net.

Embassies and consulates Most foreign embassies are based in Jakarta (see p.98), but there are US and Australian consulates in Denpasar. Residents of Australia, Canada, Great Britain, Ireland and New Zealand should apply for help in the first instance to Bali's Australian consulate, which is at Jl Moh Yamin 51 in Renon (☎0361/235092). The US consulate is at Jl Hayam Wuruk 188 in Renon (☎0361/233605).

Hospitals and clinics Sanglah Public Hospital at Jl Kesehatan Selatan 1, Sanglah (five lines ☎0361/227911–5; bemos from Denpasar's Kereneng bemo station), is the main provincial public hospital, with the island's most efficient emergency ward and some English-speaking staff. It also has Bali's only divers' decompression chamber. Kasih Ibu at Jl Teuku Umar 120 (☎0361/223036), and Surya Husada at Jl Pulau Serangan 1–3 (☎0361/225249) are both private hospitals and fine for minor ailments, but not equipped for emergencies. Klinik SOS Gatotkaca at Jl Gatotkaca 21 (☎0361/223555) is open 24hr and staffed by English-speaking medics.

Immigration office At the corner of Jl Panjaitan and Jl Raya Puputan, Renon (Mon–Thurs 8am–3pm, Fri 8–11am, Sat 8am–2pm; ☎0361/227828; Sanur–Tegal bemo).

Language courses The Indonesian-Australian Language Foundation (IALF) at Jl Kapten Agung 17 (☎0361/221782) runs regular month-long Indonesian language courses (Rp400,000) both here and in Ubud, Sanur and Legian. International Language Programs (ILP) at Jl Kartini 83 (☎0361/245929) also runs courses in Bahasa Indonesia.

Left luggage At *Adi Yasa* hotel, Jl Nakula 23 (☎0361/222679).

Post offices Denpasar's poste restante (Mon–Sat 7.30am–9pm; Sanur–Tegal bemo) is at the GPO on Jl Raya Puputan in Renon. The Jl Rambutan PO, near Puputan Square, is more convenient.

Shopping English-language books, fashions and handicrafts at Matahari department store, Jl Teuku Umar (Tegal–Sanur bemo; 9am–9pm) and Tara Dewata Shopping Centre, Jl Sutoyo (Kereneng–Tegal bemo; 9am–9pm). For crafts, try the Sanggraha Kriya Asta Government Handicraft Centre (Mon–Fri 8.30am–5pm, Sat 8.30am–4.30pm) on Jl Gianyar; call ☎0361/222942 for a free ride, or get a Batubulan-bound bemo from Ubung or Kereneng.

Swimming Public pool at Tara Dewata Shopping Centre, or at the *Natour Bali* hotel for a small fee.

Telephone and fax Telkom offices at Jl Teuku Umar 6, and on Jl Durian. IDD phones in the Tiara Dewata Department Store on Jl Sutoyo; Home Country Direct phone at the Bali Museum.

Kuta-Legian-Seminyak

The biggest, brashest, least traditional beach resort in Bali, the **KUTA-LEGIAN-SEMINYAK** conurbation continues to expand from its epicentre on the southwest coast, just 10km southwest of Denpasar. Packed with hundreds of losmen, hotels, restaurants, bars, clubs, souvenir shops, fashion boutiques and tour agencies, the six-kilometre strip plays host to several hundred thousand visitors a year, many of them regulars and a lot of them Australian surfers – all here to party, to shop or, indeed, to surf. And yet, for all its hustle, it's a very good-humoured place, almost completely unsleazy, with no strip bars, and arguably the best beach on the island.

Orientation

Although Kuta, Legian and Seminyak all started out as separate villages, they've now merged together so completely that it's impossible to recognize the borders. In this guide, we've used the most common perception of the Kuta-Legian-Seminyak borders: **Kuta** stretches north from the *Patra Jasa* hotel to Jalan Melasti; **Legian** runs from Jalan Melasti as far as Jalan Arjuna (aka Jalan Double Six); and **Seminyak** goes from Jalan Arjuna/Double Six up to the *Bali Oberoi* hotel in the north. The resort's main road, **Jalan Legian**, runs north–south through all three districts, a total distance of 6km, and a lot of businesses give their address as nothing more than "Jalan Legian". Kuta's other main landmark is **Bemo Corner**, the tiny roundabout at the southern end of Kuta that stands at the Jalan Legian–Jalan Pantai Kuta intersection. The name's misleading, as the Denpasar bemos don't actually depart from this very spot, but it's a useful point of reference.

Arrival, information and getting around

All international and domestic flights land at **Ngurah Rai Airport** (☎0361/751011), in the district of Tuban, 3km south of Kuta. Once through customs, you'll find several 24hr **currency exchange** booths, and a **hotel reservations desk**, which deals in mid-range and expensive hotels only. The **domestic terminal** is in the adjacent building, and domestic airlines Garuda and Merpati have offices here.

Most mid- and top-priced hotels can arrange to pick you up at the airport. Otherwise, the easiest but most expensive transport from the airport is by **prepaid taxi**. The counter is located in the arrivals area beyond the customs exit doors. Current rates are fixed at Rp8000 to Kuta's Bemo Corner; Rp10,000 to anywhere along Jalan Pantai Kuta; Rp11,500 to Legian (as far as Jalan Arjuna/Double Six); and Rp12,500 to Seminyak. **Metered taxis** are usually the cheapest option, and they ply the road in front of the airport gates as they're not allowed to pick up within the airport compound.

Cheaper still are the dark-blue **public bemos** whose route takes in the big main road, Jalan Raya Tuban, about 700m beyond the airport gates. The northbound bemos (heading left up Jalan Raya Tuban) go via Kuta's Bemo Corner and Jalan Pantai Kuta as far as Jalan Melasti, then travel back down Jalan Legian, before continuing out to Denpasar's Tegal terminal. You should pay around Rp500 for a bemo ride to Kuta or Legian, or up to Rp1000 with luggage.

If you want to go straight from the airport to **Ubud**, **Candi Dasa** or **Lovina**, the cheapest way is to take the bemo to Denpasar's Tegal bemo station and then continue by bemo from there, though this is only feasible between 6am and 6pm; see the "Bemo connections" plan on p.472 for more information.

AIRLINE OFFICES IN BALI

International
Most airline offices open Monday to Friday 8.30am to 5pm, Saturday 8.30am to noon; some close for lunch at noon or 12.30pm. Garuda has offices in the *Grand Bali Beach Hotel* in Sanur (☎0361/288243), at the *Natour Kuta Beach* hotel in Kuta (☎0361/751179), and in the Galleria complex in Nusa Dua (☎0361/771864).

The following international airlines all have their offices inside the compound of the *Grand Bali Beach* hotel in Sanur: Air France (☎0361/288511 ext 1105, fax 287734); Ansett Australia (☎0361/289636, fax 289637); Cathay Pacific (☎0361/286001, fax 288576); Continental Micronesia (☎0361/287774, fax 287775); JAL (☎ & fax 0361/287576); Korean Air (☎0361/289402, fax 289403); Lufthansa (☎ & fax 0361/287069); Malaysia Airlines (☎0361/285071, fax 288716); Northwest Airlines (☎0361/287841, fax 287840); Qantas (☎0361/288331, fax 287331); Thai International (☎0361/288141, fax 288063).

Air New Zealand has offices in Ngurah Rai Airport (☎0361/756170, fax 754594) as does China Air (☎0361/754856); KLM (☎0361/756124, fax 753950) and Royal Brunei (☎0361/757292). Singapore Airlines/Silk Air is on the third floor of the Bank Bali building at Jalan Dewi Sartika 88 in Denpasar (☎0361/261666, fax 261653), and British Airways is in Jakarta (☎021/5211500).

Domestic
Bouraq: Jalan Sudirman 7a, Denpasar (☎0361/223564); Garuda: Jalan Melati 61, Denpasar (☎0361/263523); Mandala: Jalan Diponegoro 98, Blok D23 Komplek Pertokoan, Kerta Wijaya Plaza, Denpasar (☎0361/222751); Merpati: Jalan Melati 51, Denpasar (☎0361/263918); and Komplek Kuta Centre, Jalan Kartika Plaza, Blok A11 and A25 no. 8x, Kuta (☎021/758667).

Arriving in Kuta by **shuttle bus**, you'll probably be dropped at Perama Travel's office on Jalan Legian, about 100m north of Bemo Corner. This leaves you close to the largest concentration of cheaper hotels in Kuta, but a longish hike from Legian and Seminyak.

Public bemos have a number of drop-off points in the Kuta area. Coming from Denpasar's Tegal terminal, the most convenient option is the **dark-blue Tegal-Kuta-Legian service** that goes via Bemo Corner, west and then north along Jalan Pantai Kuta, east along Jalan Melasti before heading north up Jalan Legian only as far as Jalan Yudisthira (aka Jalan Padma) before turning round and continuing south down Jalan Legian as far as Bemo Corner. It's up to you to decide which point on this clockwise loop is the most convenient for your chosen losmen; for any destination north of Jalan Padma, you're probably better off getting a taxi.

Information
The most helpful government **tourist office** is the Bali and Java Tourist Information Centre at Jalan Buni Sari 36b (Mon–Sat 8am–8pm), but you could also try the Badung Tourist Offices at Jalan Raya Kuta 2 (Mon–Thurs 7am–2pm, Fri 7–11am, Sat 7am–12.30pm; ☎0361/751419) and beside the beach on Jalan Pantai Kuta (Mon–Sat 10am–5pm; ☎0361/755660). Amanda Tour in the Century Plaza complex at Jalan Buni Sari 7 (daily 9am–8pm; ☎0361/754090) has good long-distance travel information, and sells shuttle bus tickets, domestic flights and bus and train tickets to Java; they also store luggage and act as a postal agent. The North Sulawesi Tourist Office is also in this building. The West Nusa Tenggara Tourist Office is on the first floor, *Mastapha Garden Hotel*, Jalan Legian 139 (Mon–Sat 9am–4.30pm; ☎0361/751660 ext 204).

Getting around
Public transport in Kuta-Legian-Seminyak is less than ideal, as the dark-blue public **bemos** only cover a clockwise loop around Kuta, leaving out most of Legian and all

of Seminyak. Originating in Denpasar, they run up Jalan Raya Tuban, turn left at Bemo Corner along Jalan Pantai Kuta, proceed north up the beachfront Jalan Pantai Kuta, turn right along Jalan Melasti and then continue north up Jalan Legian for one

MOVING ON FROM KUTA

Flights

If you're flying Garuda, you might want to make use of the city check-in offices in Kuta, Denpasar and Sanur where you can offload your luggage the day before and get your boarding card and seat number. Most hotels in Kuta, Sanur, Nusa Dua and Jimbaran will provide **transport to the airport** for Rp10,000–20,000, though **metered taxis** are cheaper: around Rp2500 from south Kuta and Rp5000 from Seminyak. Perama **shuttle buses** from Kuta and Sanur to the airport cost Rp5000 and leave eleven times a day, and there are shuttle-bus services to the airport from all other major tourist centres on Bali; they should be booked the day before. During daylight hours, you can also take the dark-blue Tegal (Denpasar)–Kuta–Tuban **bemo** from Denpasar, Kuta or Jimbaran, which will drop you just beyond the airport gates for Rp500–1000. Airport **departure tax** is Rp100,000 for international departures and Rp30,000 for domestic flights.

Bemos

To get from Kuta to most other destinations in Bali by bemo almost always entails going via Denpasar, where you'll have to make at least one cross-city connection.

Bemos **to Denpasar** from Kuta run regularly throughout the day and terminate at Denpasar's Tegal terminal (25min; Rp600–1000) on the southwest edge of the city. The Tegal-bound bemos are dark blue, and the easiest place to catch them is at the Jalan Pantai Kuta/Jalan Raya Tuban intersection, about 15m east of Bemo Corner. If you're staying further north in the resort, you can also pick up the Tegal-bound bemos on their clockwise loop around Kuta, on Jalan Melasti for example, or anywhere on Jalan Legian between Jalan Padma and Bemo Corner. From Tegal, you can make direct connections to **Sanur**, or further across the island via the city's other bemo terminals. Full details on how to make these connections are given on p.473, and shown in the "Bemo connections" plan on p.472. If you're heading for **Ubud**, the quickest public transport option is to take the white Damri bus service that runs from Nusa Dua to Batubulan, but this means walking to the eastern edge of Kuta, to the Jalan Imam Bonjol/Jalan Setia Budi intersection at the fuel station, about ten minutes northeast of Bemo Corner. Alternatively, take the dark-blue bemo from central Kuta to Tegal and then make cross-city connections to Batubulan and on to Ubud.

To travel to **Nusa Dua**, **Tanjung Benoa** or **Jimbaran** by bemo from Kuta, you need to go out to the eastern edge of the resort, about ten minutes' walk from Bemo Corner, to the point where Jalan Setia Budi intersects with Jalan Imam Bonjol at the fuel station. The dark-blue Tegal–Nusa Dua bemos pass here and will pick you up from Jalan Setia Budi if you signal. Some of these Tegal–Nusa Dua bemos serve Jimbaran on the way, but there is also a dark-blue Tegal–Jimbaran service, which occasionally continues on through the Bukit, possibly as far as **Uluwatu**.

Shuttle buses and transport to other islands

If you're going anywhere beyond Denpasar, it's always quicker – although more expensive – to take a tourist **shuttle bus** from Kuta. Perama Travel (☎0361/751551), located 100m north of Bemo Corner on Jalan Legian, offer regular transport several times a day to Ubud, Candi Dasa and Lovina, and sometimes don't need to be booked ahead. Lots of other tour agents offer shuttle-bus services too, including Amanda Tour, in the Century Plaza complex at Jalan Benesari 7 (☎0361/754090).

Perama Travel, Amanda Tour, and others, also provide transport from Kuta to destinations on **Java** and **Lombok**, including Jakarta, Yogyakarta and the Gili Islands. Transport is by shuttle-bus and/or overnight bus or train.

For information on getting **to the airport**, see box on p.478.

block, as far as Jalan Yudisthira, where they do a U-turn and come all the way back down Jalan Legian as far as Bemo Corner, stopping to fill up with Denpasar-bound passengers at the Jalan Pantai Kuta/Jalan Raya Kuta intersection. You can flag them down at any point along this route; the standard fare for any distance within this area is Rp300, but tourists are sometimes obliged to pay Rp500. During the day, bemos usually circulate at five- or ten-minute intervals, but very few bemos run after night-fall and none at all after about 8.30pm. The alternative to bemos is either a **metered taxi** or the informal taxi service offered by the **transport touts** who hang around on every corner.

Most **car rental** places offer 800cc Suzuki Jimnys as well as larger, more comfort-able 1600cc Toyota Kijangs; try Santa Bali at Jalan Pantai Kuta 32a (☎0361/755271). The most reputable transport rental outlets offer **insurance** for an added fee. You can also rent **motorbikes** from many of the same outlets: the ABC Bookshop at Jalan Pantai Kuta 41e (☎0361/752745) has a good selection. **Bicycles** can also be rented at some car and motorbike rental places, or through your losmen.

Accommodation

Although the Kuta-Legian-Seminyak strip is continuous, it does take some time to get from end to end, so it's as well to decide where to stay before you arrive. The **inex-pensive** losmen are mainly concentrated in the Kuta area of the resort, particularly along Poppies 1 and the *gang* running off it, and along Poppies 2 and Jalan Benesari. Legian has a few ③ and ④ losmen and hotels. **Moderately priced** rooms are good value in both Kuta and Legian, and in the ⑤ and ⑦ brackets you're likely to get a pool and air-con. The **expensive** places that dominate Kuta's Jalan Kartika Plaza and north-ern Legian and Seminyak all offer international-standard facilities, generally with grounds right on the beach.

Kuta

Kuta is where the action is, the most congested and hectic part of the resort, where you'll find the bulk of the bars, restaurants, clubs and shops squashed into every avail-able square centimetre of land. The beach gets crowded, but it's a good stretch of clean, fine sand and deservedly popular; it's also the surfing centre of the resort. South of Jalan Pantai Kuta, Kuta beach officially becomes Tuban beach and things quieten down a great deal.

INEXPENSIVE

Arena, off Poppies Gang 1 (☎0361/752974). Good-value, fairly large, modern place about 5min from the beach, with hotel rooms, bungalows, traditional-style cottages, plus some air-con and a pool. Most bemos and taxis will only drop off at the *Maharani* hotel on Jl Pantai Kuta, from where you'll have to walk. ④–⑤.

Arthawan, Poppies 2 (☎0361/752913). Decent, inexpensive budget losmen. Rooms are quiet, if a bit faded, and breakfasts are huge. ③.

Bali Indah, between Poppies 2 and Jl Benesari (☎0361/752509). Slightly shabby rooms in a block and a bit of a trek from the beach, but rates are low. ②.

Bali Sandy Cottages, off Poppies 2 (☎0361/753344). Excellent-value, prettily furnished rooms set round a huge lawn. Quiet location, 3min from the beach and 5min from Poppies 2. ④.

Bamboo Inn, Gang Kresek 1, off Jl Singo Sari (aka Jl Bakung Sari; ☎0361/751935). Typical small and welcoming losmen set round a courtyard garden. Rooms are basic, but have character. ③.

Jus Edith, south off Poppies 2 (no phone). Basic rooms, but exceptionally cheap for the area. Extremely popular. ②.

Komala Indah 1, Poppies 1 (☎0361/751422). Compact square of terraced bungalows around central courtyard garden. Slightly claustrophobic but very reasonably priced. ②.

Komala Indah 2, Jl Benesari (☎0361/754258). No-frills rooms located just thirty seconds from the beach, which makes them good value and popular. ③.

Nagasari Beach Inn, Jl Singo Sari (aka Jl Bakung Sari) (☎0361/751960). Idiosyncratic two-storey bungalows with bedroom and balcony upstairs. Set in a garden compound, right in the heart of downtown Kuta and just 2min from the beach. Can get noisy at night. ④.

Puri Ayodia Inn, on the *gang* running parallel between Poppies 1 and Poppies 2 (☎0361/754245). Simple, inexpensive losmen rooms in a convenient but quiet location. Fills up fast. ②.

Rempen, off Poppies 1 (☎0361/753150). Well-kept rooms, some in a three-storey tower affording rooftop views of Kuta, others in terraced garden bungalows. Directions as for *Arena*, opposite. ③.

MODERATE

Adi Dharma, access from Jl Legian and Jl Benesari (☎0361/751527, fax 753803). Range of nicely furnished comfortable rooms, all with air-con and TV, plus pool. Good value and central. ⑦–⑧.

Bounty Hotel, Poppies 2 (☎0361/753030, fax 752121). Large, extremely good-value terraced bungalows set in a garden. Each room has air-con, TV and fridge; there are two pools and a games room. Permanent fifty-percent discount offered on published rates. ⑦.

Mastapha Garden Hotel, Jl Legian 139 (☎0361/751660, fax 755098). Lovely, secluded garden haven, with pool. Extremely central location, but quiet nonetheless, and popular with families. ⑦.

Old Poppies, Poppies 2 (☎0361/751059, fax 752364). Stylish and sizable Bali-style cottages with carved doors, thatched roofs, fridges and fans. Beautiful garden, and use of the pool at the sister operation, *Poppies Cottages*. ⑥.

Pendawa Bungalow, Gang Puspa Ayu, off Jl Kartika Plaza (☎0361/752387, fax 757777). Peacefully located on a residential street, with a choice of rooms, some in traditional-style cottages and some with air-con and hot water. Well-kept garden and a small pool. ⑥–⑦.

Sari Yasa Samudra Bungalows, Jl Pantai Kuta (☎0361/751562, fax 752948). Range of good-value bungalows just across the road from the beach; big beds, some air-con and a pool. ⑥–⑦.

Sorga Cottages, on the *gang* running parallel between Poppies 1 and Poppies 2 (☎0361/751897, fax 752417). Recommended, good-value rooms in a three-storey block set round a small pool. Comfortably furnished and efficiently run; some air-con. ⑤–⑦.

EXPENSIVE

Bali Garden Hotel, Jl Kartika Plaza (☎0361/752725, fax 753851). Huge, attractive low-rise hotel complex, with high-standard rooms and a lovely beachfront garden. ⑨.

Hotel Intan Legian, corner of Jl Pantai Kuta and Jl Melasti (☎0361/751770, fax 751891). Upmarket cottages set in terraced gardens, a hop across the road from the beach. Swimming pool. ⑧.

Kartika Plaza Beach, Jl Kartika Plaza (☎0361/751067, fax 752475). Enormous package-tour beachfront outfit. Check room location carefully, as some of the cheaper bungalows are crammed in close beside the road. Open-air theatre, fitness club and five restaurants. ⑨.

Kuta Jaya Cottages, Jl Pantai Kuta (☎0361/752308, fax 752309). Peaceful and pretty, the attractively furnished cottages here are dotted around a garden set back off the main road. Games room and pool on the premises, but a bit of a hike from most bars and restaurants. ⑧.

Natour Kuta Beach, Jl Pantai Kuta (☎0361/751361, fax 751362). The most central of all the resort's beachfront hotels, but the hotel rooms and garden cottages (all with fridge, TV, air-con) are disappointing for the price. Facilities include two pools and several restaurants. ⑨.

Poppies Cottages, Poppies 1 (☎0361/751059, fax 752364). Extremely popular traditional cottages built to the same elegant designs as the sister operation, *Old Poppies*, but with more upmarket facilities including air-con and a swimming pool. Reservations essential. ⑧.

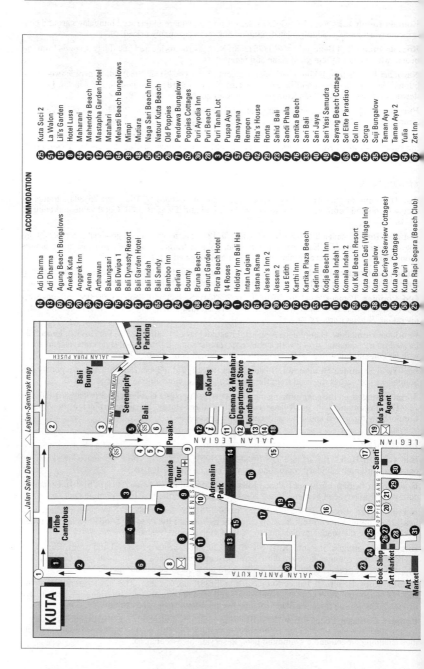

ACCOMMODATION

14	Adi Dharma
13	Adi Dharma
60	Agung Beach Bungalows
50	Aneka Kuta
20	Angrek Inn
34	Arena
27	Arthawan
19	Bakungsari
75	Bali Dwipa 1
72	Bali Dynasty Resort
21	Bali Garden Hotel
31	Bali Indah
65	Bali Sandy
41	Bamboo Inn
24	Berlian
4	Bounty
68	Bruna Beach
62	Bunut Garden
78	Flora Beach Hotel
1	Holiday Inn Bali Hai
22	Intan Legian
61	Istana Rama
70	Jesen's Inn 2
30	Jessen 2
66	Jus Edith
73	Karthi Inn
47	Kartika Plaza Beach
53	Kedin Inn
11	Kodja Beach Inn
51	Komala Indah 1
2	Komala Indah 2
59	Kul Kul Beach Resort
9	Kuta Aman Gati (Village Inn)
38	Kuta Bungalow
6	Kuta Ceriya (Seaview Cottages)
45	Kuta Jaya Cottages
58	Kuta Puri
25	Kuta Rapi Segara (Beach Club)

23	Kuta Suci 2
16	La Walon
15	Lili's Garden
8	Hotel Lusa
44	Maharani
12	Mahendra Beach
18	Mastapha Garden Hotel
64	Matahari
39	Melasti Beach Bungalows
49	Mimpi
40	Mutiara
55	Naga Sari Beach Inn
28	Natour Kuta Beach
77	Old Poppies
36	Pendawa Bungalow
33	Poppies Cottages
43	Puri Ayodia Inn
74	Puri Beach
7	Puri Tanah Lot
57	Puspa Ayu
46	Ramayana
42	Rempen
71	Rita's House
67	Ronta
35	Sahid Bali
37	Sandi Phala
76	Santika Beach
63	Sari Bali
48	Sari Jaya
5	Sari Yasi Samudra
7	Sayang Beach Cottage
63	Sol Elite Paradiso
32	Sol Inn
52	Sorga
56	Suji Bungalow
3	Taman Ayu
17	Taman Ayu 2
54	Yulia
67	Zet Inn

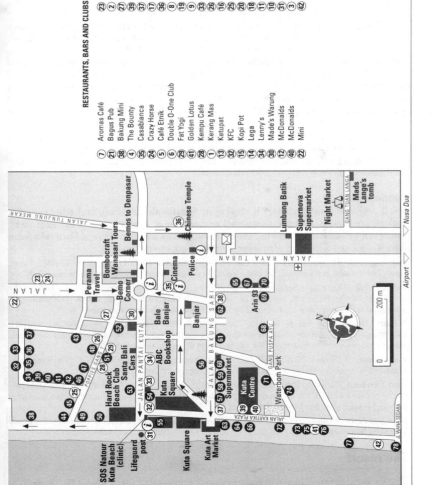

RESTAURANTS, BARS AND CLUBS

⑦ Aromas Café
㉑ Bagus Pub
㊳ Bakung Mini
④ The Bounty
㉟ Casablanca
㉔ Crazy Horse
⑤ Café Etnik
⑥ Double O-One Club
㉙ Fat Yogi
㊶ Golden Lotus
㉘ Kempu Café
① Kerang Mas
⑬ Ketupat
㉜ KFC
⑮ Kopi Pot
⑭ Lega
㉞ Lenny's
㉚ Made's Warung
⑫ McDonalds
㊵ McDonalds
㉒ Mini

㉓ Peanuts 1
② Peanuts Club
㉗ Poppies
㊴ Pizza Hut
㊲ Rama Bridge
⑰ Sari Club
㊱ Sinarifa
⑧ Southern Cross
⑲ Studebaker's
⑨ Subway Café
㉝ Suci
㉖ TJs
⑯ Tokyo Rose
㉕ Tree House
⑳ Tubes
⑱ Twice
⑪ Viva's (Gemini) Restaurant
⑩ Warung Brasil Bali
㉛ Warung PKK
③ Yanie's
㊷ Zero Six

Legian

Significantly calmer than Kuta, **Legian** has a reputation for attracting the resort's more laid-back travellers as well as long-stay surfers. It's also more spread out than Kuta, so you may have to walk further to eat and drink.

Ayodia Beach Inn, Gang Three Brothers (☎0361/752169). Shabby but inexpensive terraced rooms in a garden. ③.

Hotel Kumala, Jl Werk Udara (☎ & fax 0361/730407). Huge complex of nicely furnished rooms and cottages, all with air-con, some with fridge. Two pools. Good value. ⑦–⑧.

Legian Beach Bungalow, Jl Padma (☎0361/751087). Average but pleasant enough bungalows set in a garden close to the shops and near the beach. Friendly staff and relaxed eating area. ④.

Lumbung Sari, Gang Three Brothers (☎0361/752009). Huge, good-value two-storey bungalows, with kitchen, plus some cheaper rooms in a central block. Swimming pool on the premises. ⑥.

Puri Mangga Bungalows, Jl Arjuna (aka Jl Double Six) (☎0361/730447, fax 730307). Very good-value rice barn-style bungalows for two to four people, with kitchen and bathroom included. Discounts for weekly and monthly rental. 1min from the beach. ⑥–⑧.

Sri Ratu Cottages, Gang Three Brothers (☎0361/751722, fax 754468). Set in a pretty garden away from the main drag, with good-value bungalows for one to six people; swimming pool. ⑥.

Suri Wathi, Jl Sahadewa 12 (aka Jl Menuh) (☎0361/753162). Friendly, family-run losmen with good-value bungalows and some smaller rooms. Quiet but convenient, with a pool. ④–⑤.

Su's Cottages, Jl Bagus Taruna 532 (aka Jl Rum Jungle) (☎0361/730324). Spotless, nicely furnished rooms in a small, friendly, family-run losmen. Recommended. ④.

Taman Legian Hotel, Jl Arjuna (aka Jl Double Six) (☎0361/730876, fax 753405). Adequate bungalows, just 1min walk from the beach, with a swimming pool on the premises. ⑦.

Three Brothers Inn, Gang Three Brothers (☎0361/751566). Large cottages in a lush garden; some air-con. Efficiently run and good value. ⑥–⑦.

Seminyak

You'll probably need transport if staying in **Seminyak**, as eating and entertainment options are limited, and the shops and restaurants of Legian are at least 1km away. There are a couple of car and motorbike rental places on Jalan Dhyana Pura (aka Jalan Gado-Gado) and a handful of omnipresent transport touts too.

Bali Imperial, Jl Dhyana Pura (aka Jl Gado-Gado), Seminyak (☎0361/730730, fax 730545). Plush, classy hotel rooms and cottages set in a tropical beachfront garden; pool and tennis courts. ⑨.

Bali Oberoi, Jl Kayu Ayu, Seminyak (☎0361/751061, fax 752791). The most exclusive hotel in the resort, set beside the beach, several kilometres north of other Seminyak hotels. The traditional-style coral-rock bungalows are favoured by the rich and famous. Very expensive. ⑨.

Mesari Beach Inn, off Jl Dhyana Pura (aka Jl Gado-Gado), Seminyak (☎0361/730401). Exceptionally cheap accommodation for this area: small semi-detached cottages, plus some two-storey cottages with kitchen and living room. Direct access to the beach. ③–⑤.

Panca Jaya, Jl Dhyana Pura (aka Jl Gado-Gado), Seminyak (☎ & fax 0361/730458). Simple but comfortable enough losmen, offering some of the cheapest rooms in the area. ⑤.

Puri Cendana, Jl Dhyana Pura (aka Jl Gado-Gado), Seminyak (☎0361/730869). Balinese-style two-storey cottages with air-con in a gorgeous garden just 30m from the beach, but a longish hike from bars and restaurants; good value. Swimming pool. ⑦–⑧.

Raja Gardens, Jl Dhyana Pura (aka Jl Gado-Gado), Seminyak (☎ & fax 0361/730494). Six nicely furnished bungalows, a 2min walk from the beach. Family-run and good value; pool. ⑥.

The resort

There's nothing much to see in Kuta-Legian-Seminyak, but there's plenty to do, both in the resort and on day-trips out. The **beach** is quite possibly the most beautiful in Bali, with its gentle curve of golden sand stretching for 8km, its huge breakers, and the much-lauded Kuta sunsets. Though perpetually crowded with tourists, the beach stays amazingly clean, and also refreshingly clear of hawkers.

The waves that make Kuta such a great beach for surfers make it less pleasant for **swimming**, with a strong undertow as well as the breakers to contend with. You should always swim between the red- and yellow-striped flags, and take notice of any warning signs. **Lifeguards** are stationed all along the Kuta–Legian stretch and the central lifeguard post is on the beach at the corner of Jalan Pantai Kuta.

Surfing

Because the beach is sandy and there's no coral or rocks to wipe out on, Kuta is the best place in Bali to learn to surf. The resort's four main **breaks** – known as Kuta Beach, Legian Beach, Airport Lefts and Kuta Reef – all offer consistent, almost uniform waves, with lots of tubes, and are best surfed from April to October. Monthly **tide charts** are compiled by *Tubes* bar on Poppies 2 and are available there as well as at most surfwear shops in the resort. Poppies 2 is the centre of Kuta's surf scene, and the best place to buy **boards** or get them repaired; you can also rent boards on the beach (about Rp10,000).

A few tour agents in Kuta organize **surfing tours** to the mega-waves off Sumbawa, East Java (including the awesome G-Land; see p.284), West Java, Lombok and West Timor. Most of these "surfaris" last about a week, and cost from US\$250 to US\$1000. The longest-established surfari operator in Kuta is Wanasari Wisata at Jalan Pantai Kuta 8b (☎0361/755588, fax 755690); there are a couple of smaller surfari operators on Poppies 2, but these need to be contacted in person.

Watersports and organized tours

Surfing aside, Kuta is not a great centre for **watersports** and, although the resort is stuffed with tour agencies offering snorkelling, diving, sea-kayaking, whitewater rafting and fishing trips, they will all take you elsewhere to do these things – to either Sanur or Tanjung Benoa or further afield. Internationally certified **diving courses** (see p.499) can also be organized through agents in Kuta-Legian-Seminyak. If you want to go parasailing, jet-skiing, windsurfing or water-skiing, your best option is to make your own way to Tanjung Benoa (see p.496) or Sanur (see p.499). For watersports of a slightly different nature, check out Kuta's Waterbom Park on Jalan Kartika Plaza, south Kuta (daily 9am–6pm; Rp30,000), a kind of **aquatic adventure park** with water slides, helter-skelters, and a lazy river with inner tubes.

Many of Bali's most spectacular sights are easily visited from Kuta as part of a daytrip, and every tour agent offers ten or more fixed itinerary **organized tours**, designed to take in the maximum number of attractions in the shortest possible time. Tours generally travel in an air-con eight- to ten-person minibus, last from around 8.30am to 4.30pm, and cost Rp30,000–50,000 per person.

Eating

There are hundreds of **places to eat** in Kuta-Legian-Seminyak, and the range is phenomenal, from tiny streetside warung to the plush hotel restaurants. Kuta's main **night market** (*pasar senggol*) gets going after sundown on Gang Tuan Langa at the southern edge of Kuta. Hawkers gather here to brew up noodle soup, barbecued corn and *ayam goreng*, and the market warung barbecue fresh fish.

Kuta

Aromas Café, Jl Legian. Outstanding and imaginative vegetarian food served in large portions (if a bit slowly). Menu includes Lebanese, Italian, Indian and Indonesian dishes. Mid-priced.

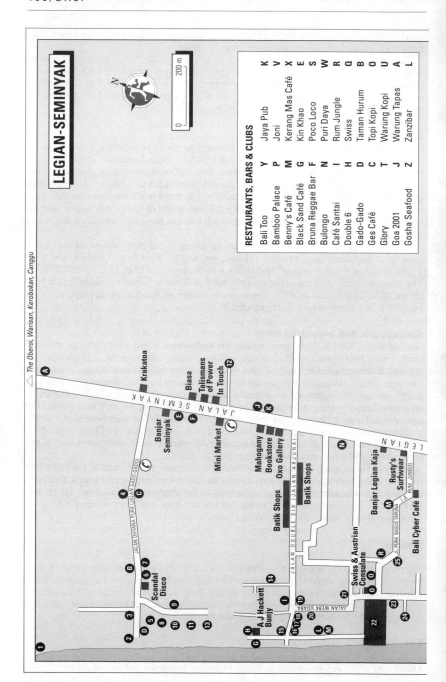

LEGIAN-SEMINYAK

N

0   200 m

△ The Oberoi, Warisan, Kerobokan, Cangu

RESTAURANTS, BARS & CLUBS

Bali Too	Y	Jaya Pub	K
Bamboo Palace	P	Joni	V
Benny's Café	M	Kerang Mas Café	X
Black Sand Café	G	Kin Khao	E
Bruna Reggae Bar	F	Poco Loco	S
Bulongo	N	Puri Daya	W
Café Santai	I	Rum Jungle	R
Double 6	H	Swiss	Q
Gado-Gado	D	Taman Hurum	B
Ges Café	C	Topi Kopi	O
Glory	T	Warung Kopi	U
Goa 2001	J	Warung Tapas	A
Gosha Seafood	Z	Zanzibar	L

Krakatoa

Biasa
Talismans
of Power
In Touch

JALAN SEMINYAK

Banjar
Seminyak

Mini Market

Mahogany
Bookstore
Oxo Gallery

Batik Shops

Batik Shops

JALAN DOUBLE SIX (JALAN ARJUNA)

JALAN DHYANA PURA (JALAN GADO-GADO)

Scandal
Disco

A J Hackett
Bunjy

JALAN WERK UDARA

Swiss & Austrian
Consulate

Banjar Legian Kaja

Rusty's
Surfwear

JL. PURA BAGUS TARUNA

JL. RUM JUNGLE

LEGIAN

Bali Cyber Café

ACCOMMODATION

Ayodia Beach Inn	36	Panorama Cottage 1	52
Baleka Beach	25	Puri Bunga	7
Bali Coconut House	26	Puri Cendana	3
Bali Holiday Resort	13	Puri Damai Cottage	44
Bali Imperial	2	Puri Duyung	4
Bali Malindra Cottage	45	Puri Mangga Bungalows	19
Bali Niksoma	27	Puri Naga Seaside Cottages	16
Bali Oberoi	1	Puri Tantra	24
Bali Padma	42	Raja Gardens	8
Balisani	10	Raja Legian Cottage	14
Bhuwana	31	Sari Bunga	18
Dhyana Pura	5	Sinar Beach Cottage	28
Hotel Kumala	20	Sinar Indah	33
Hotel Pantai Legian	50	Sing Ken Ken	17
Jayakarta (Kuta Palace)	22	Sorga Beach Inn	51
Ketty Club	48	Sri Ratu Cottages	39
Legian Beach Bungalow	46	Sri Ratu Cottages	37
Legian Garden View	40	Suri Wathi	49
Legian Village	43	Surya Dewata	32
Legian Village	47	Su's Cottages	21
Lumbung Sari	38	Taman Legian	15
Mabisa House	23	Three Brothers Inn	41
Maharta	29	Tjendana Paradise	6
Mesari Beach Inn	11	Tunjung Bali	30
Nusa di Nusa	10	Villa Lalu	12
Panca Jaya	9	Wisata Beach Inn	35

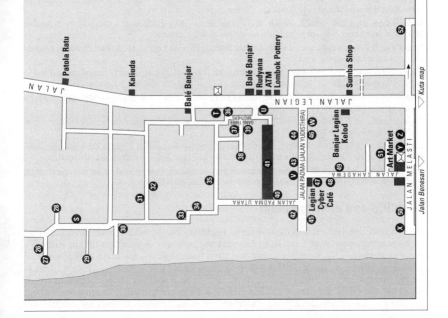

Bamboo Corner, Poppies 1. Small inexpensive restaurant that serves especially delicious *fu yung hai* (fluffy Chinese omelettes stuffed with seafood or vegetables).

Golden Lotus, inside the *Bali Dynasty Resort* on Jl Kartika Plaza. Recommended upmarket dim sum and à la carte Chinese restaurant; pricey but tasty. Dim sum not served after 2pm.

Kempu Café, Poppies 1. Tiny warung serving cheap, tasty travellers' food and veggie dishes.

Kerang Mas Café, corner of Jl Pantai Kuta and Jl Melasti. Great location right on the beach – ideal for beers at sunset. Average, inexpensive fare including pizzas, sandwiches and juices.

Ketupat, behind the Jonathan Gallery jewellery shop on Jl Legian. Superb menu of exquisite Indonesian dishes based around fish, goat and chicken, plus some vegetarian options. Upmarket in both style and quality, but not overpriced. Moderate to expensive.

Kopi Pot, Jl Legian. Café-restaurant serving several different coffee blends, plus some quality seafood, including lobster thermidor. Pleasant outdoor setting, with tables on a terrace.

Made's Warung, Jl Pantai Kuta. Long-standing Kuta favourite whose table-sharing policy encourages sociability. Mainly standard Indonesian fare, plus cappuccino and cakes.

Warung PKK, beachfront location in front of *Natour Kuta Beach* near the corner of Jl Pantai Kuta. Very standard menu, but a perfect beachside position, ideal for brunch. Inexpensive.

TJs, Poppies 1. Popular, efficiently run Mexican restaurant with tables set around a water garden. Moderately priced menu covering the full gamut of tacos, enchiladas and burritos.

Viva's (Gemini) Restaurant, Jl Legian 135. Excellent Chinese and seafood dishes, where specialities include crab and salted vegetables. Inexpensive to moderate.

Legian and Seminyak

Bali Too, Jl Melasti, Legian. Popular inexpensive place serving recommended spicy Thai soup and some less interesting Indonesian and Western standards.

Black Sand Café, beachfront off Jl Arjuna (aka Jl Double Six), Legian. Lovely spot for daytime chill-outs and 6pm sunset-watching. Inexpensive.

Bulongo, Jl Legian between Jl Bagus Taruna (aka Jl Rum Jungle) and Jl Arjuna (aka Jl Double Six), Legian. Slightly trendy version of a typical Masakan Padang café, where you assemble your own meal from the selection of cold Sumatran dishes displayed in the window.

Cafe Santai, Jl Arjuna (aka Jl Double Six). Wholesome soups, salads and sandwiches including tasty cold pumpkin soup and good blue-cheese salad. Inexpensive.

Ges Café, Jl Dhyana Pura (aka Jl Gado-Gado), Seminyak. Good range of seafood dishes at reasonable rates considering the area.

Glory, 200m north of Jl Yudisthira (aka Jl Padma) on Jl Legian, Legian. Hearty breakfasts and weekly Saturday-night Balinese home-cooking buffets. Call ☎0361/751091 for free transport.

Goa 2000, Jl Legian, Seminyak. Stylish, barn-like restaurant with a huge, moderately priced menu spanning several national cuisines plus a range of cocktails.

Gosha Seafood, Jl Melasti, Legian. The most popular seafood restaurant in Legian; lobster a speciality. Inexpensive to moderate.

Kin Khao, on Jl Legian, between Jl Arjuna (aka Jl Double Six) and Jl Dhyana Pura (aka Jl Gado-Gado), Seminyak. Upmarket, authentic Thai food served in stylish surroundings. Moderate.

Warung Kopi, Jl Legian 427, Legian. Delicious and imaginative mid-priced menu of experimental Indonesian and classic Western dishes, with the emphasis on wholefood.

Nightlife and entertainment

Kuta boasts the liveliest and most diverse **nightlife** on the island, with most bars and clubs staying open till at least 1am. As most of the action is concentrated in Kuta, it's quite possible to walk from bar to bar and then home again – the main streets are well lit and usually pretty lively till about 3am at least. There are occasional reports of muggings, though, so you might want to think twice about walking home unaccompanied. As a rule, the clubs and bars of Kuta-Legian-Seminyak are friendly enough towards lone drinkers – male or female. Although women are unlikely to get serious hassle, you will get seriously chatted up by the resident gaggle of **gigolos** who haunt the dance floors and bars in search of romance. Female prostitution is on the increase in Kuta, but is mainly confined to the beach, certain stretches of Jalan Legian, and a few well-known pick-up joints. There's also quite a public transvestite scene, which includes a group of "sucky sucky girls" who tout for custom outside *McDonald's* on Jalan Legian.

Kuta's **gay scene** is very understated and, to date, there's not a single exclusively gay bar or club in the resort. But after midnight there's nearly always a discernible gay crowd at *Goa 2001*, and then later at either *Gado-Gado* or *Double Six*.

Bars

Some of Kuta's bars have small dance floors, others have live bands, pool tables or videos to keep customers entertained. If you can't stand the prospect of drinking alone, you could join the twice-weekly **Peanuts Pub Crawl**, which starts at *Casablanca* and progresses north up Jalan Legian to the *Peanuts* disco-bar (☎0361/754149; every Tues & Sat, departs hotels from 6.30pm; Rp3000). With an upper limit of two hundred participants, this has become a Kuta institution – so much so that there are organized *Peanuts* reunions in several Australian cities.

Bagus Pub, Poppies 2, Kuta. Large and loud tourist restaurant and video bar, popular with Australians and surfers.

The Bounty, Jl Legian, Kuta. Novelty building, built to resemble Captain Bligh's eighteenth-century galleon, with a heaving dance floor after 10pm. Closes at 2am.

Casablanca, south of Bemo Corner on Jl Buni Sari, Kuta. Lively enough drinking spot, with live music at least twice weekly, when the Peanuts Pub Crawl rolls in.

Double O One Club, Jl Legian, Kuta. Popular mid-sized bar with pool table and small dance floor serving cheap beer till 1am and spinning 1980s dance hits. Closes at 1am.

Goa 2001, Jl Legian, Seminyak. Sophisticated restaurant that serves drinks after midnight and gets packed with the trendy pre-clubbing crowd. Closes around 3am.

Hard Rock Café, Jl Pantai, Kuta. Nightly cover band; expensive drinks.

Jaya Pub, Jl Legian, Seminyak. Fairly sedate live-music venue and watering-hole for older tourists and expats. Twenty or so tables; no real dance floor.

Tubes, Poppies 2, Kuta. *The* surfers' hangout in Kuta, with notice boards, surfing videos and signed champion boards, plus a bar and pool tables. No food or dancing. Closes around 1am.

Clubs

Kuta's **clubs** tend to keep well up with current mainstream dance sounds from around the world; few of them charge admission and they're always packed.

Bruna Reggae Bar, Jl Legian, between Jl Arjuna (aka Jl Double Six) and Jl Dhyana Pura (aka Jl Gado-Gado), Seminyak. Nightly sets from local reggae bands (starting around 10.30pm); free.

Double Six ("66"), off the beachfront end of Jl Arjuna (aka Jl Double Six), Seminyak (☎0361/731266). Current club hits from around the world, often spun by European DJs, attract a fashion-conscious local and expat crowd. Opens midnight to 6am every Mon, Thurs & Sat, but call first, as it's a long hike from Kuta. Admission costs Rp10,000–20,000, depending on the event.

Gado-Gado, Jl Dhyana Pura (aka Jl Gado-Gado), Seminyak (☎0361/730955). Huge, stylish beachfront club, with a trendy atmosphere very similar to *Double Six*. Admission costs Rp10,000–20,000, depending on event. Open midnight–6am, closed Mon & Thurs, but call to check.

Peanuts Club, just south of the Jl Melasti intersection on Jl Legian, Kuta. Large disco and bar with low-grade live music in the streetside section, and a classic rock sound system inside. Pool table, karaoke and reasonably priced drinks; closes around 2am.

Sari Club ("SC"), Jl Legian, Kuta. Hugely popular bar and club which attracts a hip young crowd of drinkers and clubbers plus a fair number of trendy young gigolos. Closes about 3am.

Studebakers, on Jl Legian opposite Poppies 2. Popular live-music venue and dance floor. Closes about 2am.

Entertainment

Kuta is not exactly renowned for its wealth of cultural entertainment, but most tour agencies organize trips to see **Balinese dancing** at venues outside the resort. In Kuta itself, both *Natour Kuta Beach* hotel and the *Lega Bar and Restoran* stage regular traditional dance shows. (See the box on pp.520–522 for more about Balinese dance.) Kuta's main **cinema** complex, the Legian 21, is on the top floor of the smaller of Kuta's two Matahari department stores, midway down Jalan Legian.

Shopping

Kuta-Legian-Seminyak is a great place to **shop**, and most stores stay open until at least 9pm. For basic necessities and food, check out **Matahari department store** in Kuta Square, Kuta (the smaller branch on Jalan Legian is not so interesting). There are plenty of **secondhand bookstores** on Poppies 1, Jalan Legian and the east–west stretch of Jalan Pantai Kuta.

Arts, crafts and textiles

Arin 93, Gang Kresek 5a, off Jl Singo Sari (aka Jl Bakung Sari), Kuta. Batik paintings by master batik artist Heru, plus cheaper pictures done by his students. Prices start at Rp20,000.

Batik textiles, Jl Arjuna (aka Jl Double Six), Legian. This road has more than a dozen batik textile shops and is the best place to browse and compare styles and prices.

Kaliuda, several branches along Jl Legian. A large selection of very fine weavings from Sumba, as well as a horde of wooden statues from Sumatra, Irian Jaya and Papua New Guinea.

Lumbung Batik, between Jl Raya Tuban and Jl Tanjung Mekar, Kuta. Useful fixed-price one-stop shop for traditional batik sarongs, Sumbanese hangings and *ikat* bedspreads and Lombok pottery.

Patola Ratu, Jl Legian 456, Legian. Recommended outlet for traditional woven *ikat* hangings from the island of Sumba. Also stocks all sizes of carved wooden textile hangers.

Pithe Canthrobus, Jl Melasti 88, Legian and **Pusaka**, Jl Legian 388 and Jl Pantai Kuta 20d. All branches stock traditional sarongs and unusual crafts.

Ruddin, Jl Benesari 17, Kuta. Hundreds of rayon and cotton sarongs in innovative designs.

Sumba Shop, Jl Legian, Legian. Tiny shop crammed full of bedspreads, jackets, scarves and hangings all made from Sumbanese-style woven *ikat*. Also textiles from Sabu and Flores.

Books and music

ABC Bookshop, Jl Pantai Kuta, Kuta. Secondhand outlet that deserves a special mention for bothering to keep its books in alphabetical order.

Bombocraft, Jl Pantai Kuta 8c, Kuta. Handmade musical instruments, mainly African-inspired *jimbeh* drums carved from teak and mahogany and bamboo didgeridoos.

Bookshop, on Jl Legian between Jl Arjuna (aka Jl Double Six) and Jl Dhyana Pura (aka Jl Gado-Gado), Seminyak. Good range of new books in English, mostly on Indonesia.

Fuji Jaya, Poppies 2, Kuta. Reasonable stock of secondhand books in good condition.

Mahogany, opposite *Goa 2001* on Jl Legian, Seminyak. Good range of tapes and some CDs.

Media Bookstore, 4th floor, Matahari department store, Kuta Square, Kuta. Very good range of English-language books on Bali and Indonesia, plus novels and some foreign magazines.

Men at Work, Jl Singo Sari (aka Jl Bakung Sari), Kuta. Decent selection of tapes.

Clothes and jewellery

Jonathan Gallery, Jl Legian 109, Kuta. Idiosyncratic silver and semi-precious jewellery, plus antique trinkets brought in from other parts of Indonesia. Expensive.

Kuta "Art Market", beach end of Jl Singo Sari (aka Jl Bakung Sari), Kuta. Collection of small shops and stalls selling inexpensive cotton trousers, tie-dyed beach dresses, shorts and T-shirts.

Mr Bali, several branches along Jl Legian. Popular outlet for casual menswear.

Suarti, branches on Poppies 2, in Kuta Centre on Jl Kartika Plaza, and several on Jl Legian. Distinctive modern necklaces, bracelets and earrings.

Surfwear shops, including Bali Barrel, Billabong, Blue Surf, Hot Buttered Bali, Jungle Surf, Lost Boys and Mambo, all dotted along Jl Legian. Brand-name clothes and surfing equipment.

Talismans of Power, Jl Legian, Seminyak. Dramatic silver jewellery in unusual designs.

Listings

Airline offices and agents Garuda city check-in is at *Natour Kuta Beach* on Jl Pantai Kuta, Kuta (☎0361/751179). For international air tickets, try Bali World Travel (☎0361/756262) next door.

Batik classes Batik artist Heru gives workshops at Gang Kresek 5a, off Jl Singo Sari (aka Jl Bakung Sari), Kuta (☎0361/755018). Two-day courses cost Rp50,000; five day ones are Rp100,000.

Cash advances At Bank Bali opposite *The Bounty* at Jl Legian 118, north Kuta and at several banks in Kuta Square, Kuta. There are Visa, Mastercard and Cirrus ATMs on the ground floor of the Matahari department store in Kuta Square, Kuta.

Email and Internet access The fastest, most helpful and user-friendly email access is at *Bali @ Cyber Café and Restaurant* at Jl Bagus Taruna 4 (aka Jl Rum Jungle) in Legian (daily 8.30am–11pm). Other options include Krakatoa health food shop and business centre (Mon–Fri 8am–10pm, Sat & Sun 8am–8pm), further north up Jl Legian, opposite the junction with Jl Dhyana Pura (aka Jl Gado-Gado); *Legian Cyber C@fe* at Jl Sahadewa 21 (aka Jl Menuh), Legian (Mon–Fri 10am–9pm, Sat & Sun 10am–4pm); and the convenient but annoyingly slow wartel Kambodiana in Kuta Square, Kuta (open daily 24hr).

Hospitals and clinics A number of hotels operate 24hr clinics staffed by English-speaking doctors, including SOS Natour Kuta Beach, Jl Pantai Kuta, Kuta (☎0361/751361); *Bali Intan Cottages*, corner of Jl Pantai Kuta and Jl Melasti, north Kuta (☎0361/751770); *Sri Ratu Cottages*, Jl Three Brothers, Legian (☎0361/751722). Independent clinics include the new, efficient, 24hr Legian Medical Clinic on Jl Benesari, north Kuta (☎0361/758503), and the 24hr Kuta Clinic opposite Supernova supermarket on Jl Raya Kuta, south Kuta (☎0361/754090). The nearest hospitals are in Denpasar (see p.476).

Left luggage Reliable storage at Amanda Tour, located in Century Plaza at Jl Benesari 7, north Kuta (office hours are daily 8am–9pm, but luggage is accessible 24hr; Rp1000 per piece per day).

Postal services Kuta's GPO and poste restante is on a small *gang* between Jl Raya Tuban and Jl Tanjung Mekar (Mon–Thurs 8am–2pm, Fri 8am–noon, Sat 8am–1pm). Ida's Postal Agent opposite the Poppies 2 intersection at Jl Legian 61, Kuta, is more central and keeps longer hours (Mon–Sat 8am–8pm); services here include poste restante and a fax-receiving service (fax 0361/751574). Poste/fax restante also at Amanda Tour in Century Plaza at Jl Benesari 7, Kuta (fax 0361/754146), and at Asthini Yasa Postal Agent, opposite *Glory* restaurant on Jl Legian, Legian (Mon–Sat 8am–8pm; fax 0361/752883). All the email centres also offer fax services.

Telephone and fax The government wartel is inconveniently sited down at the airport, but there are dozens of private wartels in the resort.

The Bukit and Nusa Dua

Four kilometres south of Kuta, Bali narrows into just a sliver of land before bulging out again into the **Bukit**, a harsh, scrubby limestone plateau that dangles off the far southern end of the island. While the inhospitable terrain leaves most Bukit residents in despair, its craggy shoreline is a source of great delight for **surfers** – the Padang Padang and Uluwatu breaks are rated as some of the classiest, and trickiest, in Indonesia, at their best from April through to October and, further south again, **Nusa Dua** is an immaculate resort.

Jimbaran

The tiny fishing village of **JIMBARAN**, just a couple of kilometres south of Ngurah Rai Airport, is flowering into a pleasantly peaceful little resort. About ten developments front the beach here, most of them upmarket chain hotels, but the pace is still unhurried and the sand soft and golden. Most of Jimbaran's villagers live away from the beach, down the *gang* that runs off the main Kuta–Jimbaran–Uluwatu road, cutting a swath through the heart of the village. The fruit and vegetable market thrives at the crossroads in the centre of the village and, just across from here, under a huge holy tree, stands the eleventh-century temple, Pura Ulun Siwi.

South of Ngurah Rai Airport, most of the through-traffic zips down the bypass, turning right at the Ngurah Rai statue and continuing along this major road all the way to Nusa Dua, 11km southeast. To get to Jimbaran, turn right off the bypass down one of two slip roads (one is signed Jalan Ulun Siwi). The dark-blue public Tegal (Denpasar)–Jimbaran **bemos** also follow this route, picking up passengers from Kuta on the way (see p.477).

Accommodation

Most hotels in Jimbaran are upmarket and have grounds that lead down to the beach. There are a couple of bottom-range places but they charge mid-range prices.

Bali Inter-Continental, Jl Uluwatu (☎0361/701888, fax 701777). Large, luxury beachfront hotel, offering comfortably furnished rooms, three pools, tennis courts, and several restaurants. ⑨.

Four Seasons Resort (☎0361/701010, fax 701020). One of the finest, and most expensive, hotels in Bali. Each villa here is built inside its own little traditional Balinese compound, comprising a series of three thatched pavilions – a living area, a sleeping area and a garden bathroom. ⑨.

Nelayan Jimbaran, north beachfront (☎0361/702253). Nine losmen-style rooms right on the beach road. You pay for the location, not the facilities, but rooms are decent enough. ⑤.

Pansea Puri Bali, Jl Uluwatu (☎0361/701605, fax 701320). Comprises a set of gorgeously designed individual cottage compounds, plus swimming pool and children's play area. ⑨.

Puri Bambu, Jl Pengeracikan (☎0361/701377, fax 701440). The only mid-range place in Jimbaran is 3min walk from the beach; all rooms have air-con and TV and there's a pool. ⑧.

Puri Indra Prasta, Jl Uluwatu 28a (☎0361/701552). Basic, shabby rooms, some with air-con, on the main road, about 5min from the beach. There's a pool in the garden. ⑤–⑦.

Eating

The **fresh-fish barbecues** served up by Jimbaran's beachfront warung are so good that people travel here from Kuta and Sanur just to sample them. There are two clusters of warung on the beach – one at the northern end beyond *Nelayan Jimbaran*, and the other just north of the *Keraton Bali*. Both sets have tables on the sand and offer the day's catch, grilled in front of you over smoky fires of coconut husks.

Bukit surfing beaches

Just a couple of kilometres south of Jimbaran, the road climbs up onto the limestone plateau, and it's well worth pausing for a look back across the stunning **panorama** of southern Bali. Four kilometres further south, a short distance on from the construction site for the controversial new monument known as Mandala Garuda Wisnu Kencana, the road forks at the village of **BAKUNG**, veering right for Uluwatu and left for Nusa Dua. Follow the Uluwatu road for a few more kilometres and you'll pass a couple of places to stay, patronized mainly by surfers: *Villa Koyo* (☎0361/702927; ⑥) has some upmarket rooms and *Mr Ugly's* (no phone; ④) has just a handful of basic ones. However, surfers are currently getting short shrift from the real-estate developers building the new *Bali Pecatu Indah* resort complex nearby, as it occupies the access road to the surfing beach at **BALANGAN** and this is currently out of bounds to the public.

Bajaj, Medan, North Sumatra

Gunung Rinjani from Gili Air, Lombok, Nusa Tenggara

Island near Riung, Flores, Nusa Tenggara

Orang-utan, Bukit Lawang, N. Sumatra

Bukittinggi, Central Sumatra

Minangkabau house, Central Sumatra

Pendet welcome dance, Ubud, Bali

Kuta beach, Bali

CHRIS WHITEHEAD

Komodo dragon, Komodo Island, Nusa Tenggara

STEPHEN BACKSHALL

Carved tombstone, Sumba, Nusa Tenggara

C. MARSHALL, TRAVEL INK

Crater lakes, Keli Mutu, Nusa Tenggara

LESLEY READER

Gili Islands, Nusa Tenggara

But there are plenty more top **surf spots** in the next few kilometres, including Bingin and Padang Padang, both of which are signed from **PECATU**: take the right fork for the surf spots and the longer, more scenic route to Uluwatu, or the left fork for the more direct road to the temple. **BINGIN** is accessible only via a potholed dirt track which takes you a couple of kilometres off the road, and **PADANG PADANG** is visible from the main road. Both places attract hardy groups of surfers every day, and knots of warung have sprung up along the cliffside at both locations to provide accommodation and food.

SULUBAN, location of the famous **Uluwatu surf breaks**, is signed off the Uluwatu road about 2km south of Padang Padang. These breaks are something of a surf mecca, with five separate left-handers, all of them consistent and surfable at anything from 70cm to 5m. As at Bingin and Padang Padang, there's a tiny offbeat surfers' "resort" at Suluban.

Uluwatu

One of Bali's holiest and most important temples, **Pura Luhur Uluwatu** (Rp1000 donation, plus a small fee to rent compulsory sarong and sash) commands a superb position on the tip of a sheer rocky promontory jutting out over the Indian Ocean, 70m above the foaming surf. Views over the serrated coastline to left and right are stunning and, not surprisingly, this is a favourite spot at sunset, when tour buses pour in to admire the added drama of a pink and orange horizon. Constructed almost entirely from blocks of greyish-white coral, Pura Luhur Uluwatu is one of Bali's sacred directional temples, or *kayangan jagat* (a state temple which has influence over all the people of Bali, not just the local villagers or ancestors), acting as the guardian of the southwest and dedicated to the spirits of the sea. Its festivals are open to all, and during the holy week-long period at Galungan, Balinese from all over the island come here to pay their respects. The temple structure itself, though, lacks magnificence, being relatively small and for the most part unadorned, so it's unlikely to hold your attention for much longer than half an hour.

Pura Luhur Uluwatu stands at the far southwestern tip of the Bukit, and of Bali – it's 18km south of Kuta and 16km west of Nusa Dua. Your best option is to get a dark-blue Tegal (Denpasar)–Kuta–Jimbaran **bemo** to its Jimbaran terminus and then negotiate a charter to take you on to Uluwatu; expect to pay around Rp5000 one way for this leg. Coming back from Uluwatu is more of a problem: the cheapest option is to try and hitch a ride from the temple car park; otherwise you'll have to rely on an unofficial motorcycle-taxi, which will be expensive.

Nusa Dua and Tanjung Benoa

Eleven kilometres southeast of Kuta, Bali's newest and most high-class beach resort luxuriates along a coastal stretch of reclaimed mangrove swamp. This is **NUSA DUA**, a sparklingly pristine enclave that was purpose-built to indulge the whims of upmarket tourists. The dozen or so five-star hotels boast expansive beachfront grounds and offer swimming pools, tennis courts plus several bars and restaurants. But, aside from a central shopping and entertainments complex, there's absolutely nothing else in Nusa Dua: no losmen or mid-range hotels and no markets, *banjar* or noodle stalls.

Real life, however, still happens in earnest along the narrow sandbar that extends north from Nusa Dua. **TANJUNG BENOA**, as this finger-like projection is known, still functions as a fishing village, but also boasts a rash of realistically priced tourist accommodation, including a few places in the ④ category, and a whole heap of watersports facilities as well.

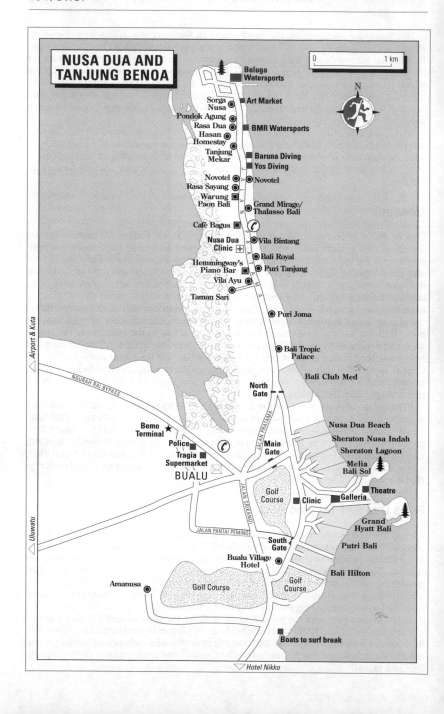

NUSA DUA AND TANJUNG BENOA

0   1 km

N

Beluga Watersports

Sorga Nusa
Art Market
Pondok Agung
Rasa Dua
BMR Watersports
Hasan Homestay
Tanjung Mekar
Baruna Diving
Yos Diving
Novotel
Novotel
Rasa Sayang
Warung Paon Bali
Grand Mirage/ Thalasso Bali
Café Bagus
Nusa Dua Clinic
Vila Bintang
Bali Royal
Hemmingway's Piano Bar
Puri Tanjung
Vila Ayu
Taman Sari

Puri Joma

Bali Tropic Palace

Bali Club Med

North Gate

Airport & Kuta

NGURAH RAI BYPASS

Nusa Dua Beach
Sheraton Nusa Indah
Sheraton Lagoon
Melia Bali Sol

Bemo Terminal
Police
Tragia Supermarket
BUALU

Main Gate

JALAN PRATAMA

Golf Course
Clinic
Galleria
Theatre

Uluwatu

JALAN SRIKANDI

JALAN PANTAI PEMINGE

South Gate

Grand Hyatt Bali

Putri Bali

Bualu Village Hotel

Amanusa

Golf Course

Golf Course

Bali Hilton

Boats to surf break

Hotel Nikko

Arrival and getting around

If you're arriving straight from **the airport** (see p.469) and staying in one of the Nusa Dua hotels, then you'll almost certainly be picked up by a hotel limousine.

The only means of **public transport** to Nusa Dua and Tanjung Benoa are the dark-blue bemos that depart Denpasar's Tegal bemo station (see p.473) and go via the eastern edge of Kuta (picking up passengers from the Jalan Imam Bonjol/Jalan Setia Budi intersection) and then via Jimbaran before racing back down the highway to terminate at the village of **BUALU**, where the main road forks right for Nusa Dua and left for Tanjung Benoa. Bemos are not allowed inside the Nusa Dua gateway, so to get to the beaches and hotels from here you'll either have to walk the one or two kilometres or flag down a taxi. Bemos do serve Tanjung Benoa, though: green ones run about once every thirty minutes between the Bualu bemo terminal and the Chinese temple at the northern end of Tanjung Benoa. Getting outgoing bemos back from Bualu to Kuta or Denpasar is an unreliable business after about 3pm and you may be forced to charter one.

In Nusa Dua, a fleet of green-and-yellow **shuttle buses** operates a free service every day from 8am to 11pm, travelling between the hotels and the Galleria shopping complex at the heart of the resort. In Tanjung Benoa, you're limited to the green public bemos that ply the main beachfront road. Alternatively, you can rent **bicycles** and **cars** from most hotels in Nusa Dua and a few in Tanjung Benoa.

Accommodation

All **accommodation** in Nusa Dua is of the highest standard. Published prices start at around US$150 per double room, but most travel agents should be able to get you a decent discount on a package deal. Tanjung Benoa caters for lower budgets, mainly offering hotels in the moderate price bracket at the north end of the peninsula and more expensive ones as you get closer to Nusa Dua.

NUSA DUA

Amanusa (☎0361/772333, fax 772335). Stunningly designed cottage compounds and ultra-luxurious facilities – with prices to match. Built beside the *Bali Golf and Country Club*. ⑨.

Bali Hilton (☎0361/771102, fax 771199). Huge, grandly designed complex with spacious, comfortable rooms, a free-form swimming pool and five restaurants. Recommended. ⑨.

Grand Hyatt Bali (☎0361/771234, fax 772038). Terraced rooms and cottages surrounded by sumptuous grounds, plus an amazing series of free-form swimming pools. ⑨.

Putri Bali (☎0361/771020, fax 771139). Some hotel rooms and some individual cottages, a few with sea view. Superbly lush gardens and a huge swimming pool with a sunken bar. ⑨.

TANJUNG BENOA

Pondok Agung, Jl Pratama (☎0361/771143). Small, stylish place with comfortable air-con rooms. The best value, though not the cheapest, accommodation at this end of Tanjung Benoa. ⑤.

Hasan Homestay, north end of Jl Pratama (☎0361/772456). A handful of terraced rooms, clean and modern if a bit dark; the cheapest place in the area. Some air-con. ④–⑤.

Puri Tanjung, Jl Pratama 62 (☎0361/772121, fax 772424). Good-value, beachfront location. All rooms come with air-con and TV, and there's a swimming pool and table tennis. ⑧.

Rasa Dua, Jl Pratama 98(☎0361/771922). Four simple but pleasant rooms in a small garden area, with bamboo furniture and partially open-air mandi. ④.

Rasa Sayang, Jl Pratama 88x (☎0361/771643). Popular and good-value small hotel in central Tanjung Benoa, offering simple rooms in a terraced block. Some air-con. ⑤–⑥.

Taman Sari, Jl Pratama 61b (☎0361/773953, fax 773954). The most stylish place in Tanjung Benoa has just ten beautifully designed bungalows, a large pool, but no beach access. ⑨.

Tanjung Mekar, Jl Pratama (☎0361/772059). Small house with fairly basic rooms. ④–⑤.

Watersports and other activities

Nearly every Nusa Dua hotel rents out some **watersports** equipment, but rates are cheaper and facilities much more extensive at the Tanjung Benoa end of the beach. Three of the best-known operators in Tanjung Benoa are Beluga, Baruna and Yos Diving, each of which does parasailing, water-skiing, windsurfing and jet-skiing, as well as a range of fishing expeditions, plus **diving** trips and courses (see p.499). Because of all the watersports facilities at Tanjung Benoa, Nusa Dua's beach is the more relaxed spot for swimming and sunbathing, though if you are staying in Tanjung Benoa you can use the **swimming pool** inside the Beluga complex (Rp5000). Nusa Dua's main **surf break**, known simply as Nusa Dua, is accessible by boat from a signposted point south of the *Bali Hilton*; it's best surfed from September to March.

Nusa Dua's eighteen-hole championship **golf course**, the Bali Golf and Country Club (☎0361/771791; green fees US$135) is spread across three areas of the resort, the main part dominating the southern end of Nusa Dua.

Eating

You'll find the cheapest and most authentic Balinese **food** on sale at the warung in **Tanjung Benoa**, most of them along the main beachfront road, Jalan Pratama, where there are also larger, more tourist-orientated seafood places. *Warung Paon Bali*, on the central stretch of Jalan Pratama, is a good in-between option, with a welcoming atmosphere and decent Indonesian and seafood dishes. **Bualu** village, at the Tanjung Benoa/Nusa Dua intersection also harbours a few fairly cheap restaurants. However, the vast majority of eating places are cloistered within the compounds of **Nusa Dua's** flashy hotels. Food here is expensive, but of a high standard, and there's a big range of options. The Galleria shopping and entertainments plaza also has dozens of topnotch restaurants.

Shopping and entertainment

Every hotel in Nusa Dua has some kind of souvenir shop on the premises, but for a proper **shopping** experience you'll need to visit the Galleria shopping plaza (daily 9am–10pm) in the middle of the resort, accessible by free shuttle bus from all Nusa Dua hotels. Spread over a huge landscaped area, the Galleria sells everything from coconut carvings to Reeboks; there's also a **supermarket** and a **duty-free** outlet here.

The Galleria is also the main venue for **Balinese dance** shows. Free performances are staged in front of a different restaurant every night from 7.30pm. In Tanjung Benoa, the *Beluga Marina Restaurant* also stages nightly Balinese dance performances during dinner.

Listings

Airline offices Garuda city check-in inside the Galleria (daily 8am–7pm; ☎0361/771444).

American Express Inside the Galleria (Mon–Fri 8.30am–4.30pm, Sat 8.30am–12.30pm; ☎0361/773334).

Exchange Available in Tanjung Benoa on the stretch of Jl Pratama between *Vila Bintang* and *Rasa Sayang*, at the Galleria, and at all Nusa Dua hotels.

Hospitals and clinics In Tanjung Benoa the 24hr Nusa Dua Clinic (☎0361/771324) at Jl Pratama 81a is staffed by English-speaking medics. All Nusa Dua hotels provide 24hr medical service. For serious illnesses you'll need to go to one of the hospitals in Denpasar; see p.476 for details.

Postal services There's a postal agent in the Galleria complex, and another one in Bualu.

Sanur

With an image that stands somewhere between the youthful hustle of Kuta and the manicured sterility of Nusa Dua, **SANUR** attracts a fairly sedate clientele to its fine white sands, peacefully lush residential streets and mainly mid-range and upmarket

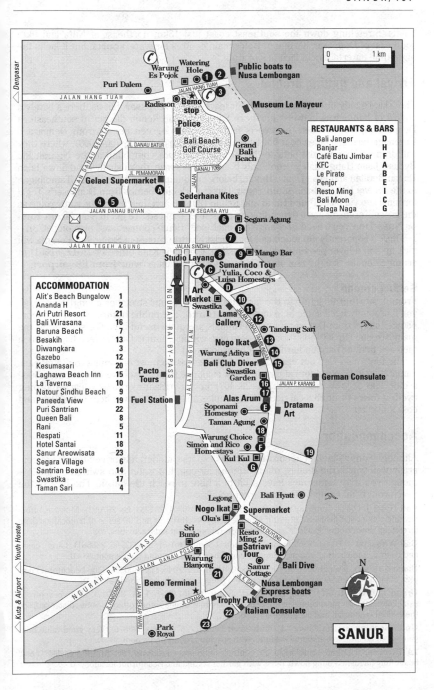

Warung
Es Pojok

Watering
Hole

Public boats to
Nusa Lembongan

Puri Dalem

JALAN HANG TUAH

Radisson
Bemo
stop

Museum Le Mayeur

Police

Bali Beach
Golf Course

Grand
Bali
Beach

JL. DANAU BATUR

JL. PEMAMORAN

Gelael Supermarket   A

DANAU TOBA

Sederhana Kites

JALAN DANAU BUYAN

JALAN SEGARA AYU

Segara Agung

B

JALAN TEGEH AGUNG

JALAN SINDHU

Studio Layang

Mango Bar

Sumarindo Tour
Yulia, Coco &
Luisa Homestays

Art
Market

C

D

Swastika
I

Lama
Gallery

Tandjung Sari

Nogo Ikat

Warung Aditya

Bali Club Diver

Swastika
Garden

German Consulate

JALAN P. KARANG

RESTAURANTS & BARS

Bali Janger	D
Banjar	H
Café Batu Jimbar	F
KFC	A
Le Pirate	B
Penjor	E
Resto Ming	I
Bali Moon	C
Telaga Naga	G

ACCOMMODATION

Alit's Beach Bungalow	1
Ananda H	2
Ari Putri Resort	21
Bali Wirasana	16
Baruna Beach	7
Besakih	13
Diwangkara	3
Gazebo	12
Kesumasari	20
Laghawa Beach Inn	15
La Taverna	10
Natour Sindhu Beach	9
Paneeda View	19
Puri Santrian	22
Queen Bali	8
Rani	5
Respati	11
Hotel Santai	18
Sanur Areowisata	23
Segara Village	6
Santrian Beach	14
Swastika	17
Taman Sari	4

Pacto
Tours

Fuel Station

Alas Arum

Soponami
Homestay

Taman Agung

Dratama
Art

E

Warung Choice

Simon and Rico
Homestays

Kul Kul

F

G

Bali Hyatt

Legong

Nogo Ikat

Supermarket

Oka's

JALAN DUYUNG

Sri
Bunio

Resto
Ming 2

Satriavi
Tour

H

Warung
Blanjong

Sanur
Cottage

Bali Dive

Bemo Terminal

Nusa Lembongan
Express boats

Trophy Pub Centre

Italian Consulate

Park
Royal

N

SANUR

Denpasar

Kuta & Airport / Youth Hostel

NGURAH RAI BY-PASS

JALAN DANAU POSO

JALAN SEKAR WARU

JL. CEMARA

hotels. Stretching down the southeast coast just 15km northeast of Kuta and 9km southeast of Denpasar, it's one of Bali's main centres for **watersports**, but it lacks the night-time entertainment facilities of Kuta.

Arrival and getting around

The island's only direct **bemos** to Sanur leave **from Denpasar**, but as there's barely a couple of kilometres between northern Sanur and the Renon district of southeastern Denpasar, travel between the two is fairly easy. Dark-green bemos from Denpasar's Kereneng terminal take about fifteen minutes to north Sanur (Rp700–1000), where they will drop passengers just outside the *Grand Bali Beach* compound at the Ngurah Rai Bypass/Jalan Hang Tuah junction only if asked; otherwise, they usually head down Jalan Danau Beratan and Jalan Danau Buyan, before continuing down Jalan Danau Tamblingan to the *Trophy Pub Centre* in south Sanur. Direct dark-blue bemos from Denpasar's Tegal terminal run via Jalan Teuku Umar and Renon (20min) and then follow the same route as the green Kereneng ones, depending on passenger requests. To get to Sanur **from Kuta or Nusa Dua** you'll need to change at Tegal (see "Bemo connections" plan on p.472).

There's apparently not much call for tourist **shuttle buses** in Sanur, but Perama will pick up and deliver passengers here if asked. Call their Kuta office (☎0361/751551) to arrange details. See the box on p.478 for information on arriving **from the airport**.

Getting around

From its northernmost tip to the far southern end, Sanur stretches a lengthy 5km, so you'll probably need some help in **getting around**. The public **bemos** which transport people to and from Denpasar's two terminals are quite useful if you're sticking to the main streets (Rp300–5000 for any journey within Sanur). Otherwise, flag down a metered **taxi**, or bargain hard with a transport tout.

The touts also rent out **cars** and **motorbikes**, as do most of Sanur's tour agencies. Sanur is an ideal place for riding **bicycles**, available from most hotels for about Rp5000 a day. The *Segara Village* (☎0361/288407) in north Sanur organizes early-morning **cycling tours** through local rice-fields, temples and markets; tours begin at 6.30am and cost Rp24,000.

Accommodation

Although Sanur's budget **accommodation** is sparse, moderately priced hotels are generally well worth the money, often offering air-con, hot water and swimming pools – though you may sometimes have a bit of a hike to reach the beach. The best of the beachfront is taken up by the upmarket hotels.

Bali Hyatt, Jl Danau Tamblingan, south-central Sanur (☎0361/281234, fax 287693). Massive, unbelievably plush establishment, offering a range of topnotch rooms and 36 acres of tropical gardens stretching down to the beach. Watersports, several pools and kids' activities. ⑨.

Bali Wirasana, Jl Danau Tamblingan 126, central Sanur (☎0361/288632, fax 288561). Large, clean and central, if unexciting, rooms; some air-con. Guests can use next door's pool. ④–⑤.

Baruna Beach, Jl Sindhu, north-central Sanur (☎0361/288546, fax 289629). Tiny beachfront complex of pleasant bungalows, all with air-con and fridge. Friendly, and good value. ⑦.

Grand Bali Beach, off Jl Hang Tuah, north Sanur (☎0361/288511, fax 287917). Huge beachfront establishment with most rooms in the central tower block, plus some cottages. Some distance from the central restaurant and shopping area. ⑨

Hotel Kesumasari, Jl Cemara 22, south Sanur (☎0361/287492, fax 288876). Very good-value bungalows, some built to traditional designs, with spacious rooms and a pool. ⑥–⑦.

La Taverna, Jl Danau Tamblingan 29, central Sanur (☎0361/288497, fax 287126). Stylish, cosy, beautifully furnished bungalows, most with garden verandahs. Beachfront location. ⑧–⑨.

Laghawa Beach Inn, Jl Danau Tamblingan 51 (☎0361/288494, fax 289353). Smartly furnished terraced rooms set in a beachfront garden, with pool. Good value for the location. ⑦.

Segara Village, Jl Segara Ayu, north-central Sanur (☎0361/288407, fax 287242). Very attractive traditional-style accommodation set in grounds with swimming pool and tennis courts. ⑧–⑨.

Simon Homestay and **Rico Homestay**, down a tiny *gang* at Jl Danau Tamblingan 164d (☎0361/289158 for *Simon*; *Rico* has no phone). Identical, sparkling-clean losmen run by two brothers; rooms are nicely furnished and well maintained. ④.

Soponami Homestay, Gang Taman Agung 4, off Jl Danau Tamblingan, central Sanur (no phone). Friendly, easy-going travellers' hangout with cheap, fairly shabby rooms. ④.

Swastika, Jl Danau Tamblingan 128, central Sanur (☎0361/288693, fax 287526). Deservedly popular place, with good, mid-range, comfortable rooms set around a garden. Two pools and some air-con. Named after the ancient Buddhist symbol, not the Nazi emblem. ⑦.

Taman Agung, Jl Danau Tamblingan 146, central Sanur (☎0361/288549, fax 289161). Huge, immaculate rooms, some with air-con. Verandah seating areas, pool and garden. ⑦–⑧.

Tandjung Sari, Jl Danau Tamblingan 41, central Sanur (☎0361/288441, fax 287930). Stunningly indulgent set of personal cottage compounds each with its own courtyard garden and shaded gazebo. Swimming pool and beachfront location. Reservations essential; very expensive. ⑨.

Watering Hole, Jl Hang Tuah 37, north Sanur (☎0361/288289). The cheapest rooms in this part of Sanur, only 250m from the beach. The better rooms have air-con and hot water. ④.

Yulia Homestay, Jl Danau Tamblingan 38, central Sanur (☎0361/288089). Friendly, family-run losmen, the longest-running and best of the three similar outfits in this cluster. ④.

The resort

Sanur's five-kilometre shoreline changes character several times along its length. A huge expanse of shore gets exposed at low tide and the reef lies only about 1km offshore at high tide. The currents beyond the reef are dangerously strong, which makes it almost impossible to swim here at low tide, but at other times of day swimming is fine and watersports are very popular. You'll find Sanur's best **sand** in front of the *Grand Bali Beach*: non-guests can rent sun-loungers and thick hotel towels on this stretch for Rp5000 a day, which also includes use of the hotel pool.

Watersports and other activities

Many of south Bali's **watersports** facilities are centred in Sanur. In general, prices are higher at the hotel-run watersport centres than at the independent places on the

---

DIVING IN SOUTH BALI

Sanur is one of south Bali's two main **diving** centres (the other is at Tanjung Benoa; see p.496), and many of the outfits that sell diving excursions from shops in Kuta and Nusa Dua have their headquarters here. It's quite a good place to learn to dive, as the local diving sites are close by. All Sanur dive centres run internationally **certificated diving courses**, including four-day open-water PADI courses and two-day advanced open-water courses.

Despite the proliferation of diving shops, **Sanur's own diving sites**, which lie just off the coast, are a bit of a disappointment. The coral isn't spectacular, and visibility is only around 6–10m, with dives ranging from 2m to 12m, but the area does teem with polychromatic fish. The average cost of a single dive is about US$40; accompanying snorkellers pay US$13.

Experienced divers usually prefer the dives off the east and north coasts. Rates for one-day **diving excursions** (including tanks and weights only) include: the reefs and wrecks of Tulamben or Amed (see p.557) for US$60; Pulau Menjangan (Deer Island, p.590) for US$80; and the islands of Nusa Lembongan (p.540) and Nusa Penida (p.543) for US$75. Two-day/one-night diving safaris to Tulamben or Nusa Penida cost around US$170.

There is one **divers' decompression chamber** on Bali, located at Sanglah Public Hospital, Jalan Kesehatan Selatan 1, in Denpasar (☎0361/227911–5).

beachfront and along the resort's main roads. All these places rent out canoes, windsurfers and jet skis, and most offer parasailing as well. The main departure point for fishing expeditions is Tanjung Benoa (see p.496), though some boats do leave from Sanur. Sanur's three main **surf breaks** – Sanur, the Tandjung Sari Reef and the Hyatt Reef – are at their best from September to March. Sanur has its own nine-hole **golf course** in the grounds of the *Grand Bali Beach* (☎0361/288511 ext 1388); green fees are US$42.

Most tourist businesses in Sanur offer a range of **sightseeing trips** to Bali's most popular sights. Numbers are generally limited to a minibus load of eight or ten people and prices kept fairly low, at around Rp30,000–50,000 per person.

Museum Le Mayeur

One of Sanur's earliest expatriate residents was the Belgian artist **Adrien Jean Le Mayeur de Merpres** (1880–1958), whose home is now open to the public as **Museum Le Mayeur**; access is via the beachfront path that turns right off Jalan Hang Tuah in north Sanur (Tues–Thurs 8am–4pm, Fri 8am–1.30pm, Sun 8am–4pm; Rp200).

Le Mayeur arrived in Bali at the age of 52 and soon fell in love with the teenage Ni Pollok, considered by many to be the best *legong* dancer in Bali. She posed for many of his pictures and by 1935 the two were married and living in this house right on Sanur beach. Much of the original structure remains – a typical low-roofed wooden building with sumptuously carved doors, lintels and pediments. Le Mayeur did most of his painting in the courtyard garden – a compact tropical wilderness dotted with stonecarvings and shrines, which features in many of the paintings and photographs displayed inside the house.

Eating

Most Sanur **restaurants** are unashamedly tourist-orientated, and standards (as well as prices) are high. The **night market** which sets up at the Jalan Danau Tamblingan/Jalan Sindhu intersection is a good place for cheap Indonesian dishes. The resort closes down quite early at night, and most tourist restaurants are loath to accept orders after 9.30pm.

Café Batu Jimbar, Jl Danau Tamblingan, central Sanur. A terrace café serving Mexican and Italian favourites, plus salads, home-baked cakes, breads and herbal teas. Moderately priced.

Kafé Tali Jiwa, in front of the *Santai Hotel*, Jl Danau Tamblingan 148, central Sanur. Sanur's best vegetarian menu, plus traditional Balinese fish and chicken dishes. Cheap to moderate.

Le Pirate, seafront, north-central Sanur. Large, mid-priced menu of wholesome dishes, including pasta and pizza, plus some Indian and Thai food. Lovely seaside location; attached to *Segara Village*.

Resto Ming, Jl Mertasari 2, south Sanur, and **Resto Ming 2**, more centrally located at Jl Danau Tamblingan 105. Seafood is a speciality here, particularly lobster thermidor and king prawns.

Segara Agung, on the beachfront next to *Segara Village*, north-central Sanur (☎0361/288574). Ideally located restaurant with a huge choice of dishes, including lots of seafood. Run as a cooperative with all profits going to local schools and clinics; call for free transport.

Sri Bunio, Jl Danau Poso. Typical *Masakan Padang* place serving spicy Sumatran dishes 24hr a day. Cheap.

Warung Aditya, Jl Danau Tamblingan, central Sanur. Homely, popular warung serving refreshingly cheap Indonesian and tourist favourites.

Warung Blanjong, Jl Danau Poso 78. Recommended restaurant that serves only Balinese dishes, both veggie and non-veggie specialities. Cheap.

Warung Choice and Bakery, Jl Danau Tamblingan 50, central Sanur. Scrumptious breads and cakes, plenty of seafood, and decent veggie dishes. Inexpensive and deservedly popular.

Nightlife and entertainment

Sanur pretty much closes down after about 10pm, when the restaurants turn away their last customers and most people seem to just go back to their hotels. There are **bars and clubs** open till the early hours, however, though the atmosphere is more formal than in Kuta and the drinks significantly more expensive. For drinks with a view, go to the seafront bars at any of the major hotels.

Bars and clubs

Bali Janger, Jl Danau Tamblingan 21, central Sanur. Flashy, cavernous disco with glitter balls but not much character. Plays mostly techno from midnight till 5am.

Banjar, beachfront end of Jl Duyung, south-central Sanur. Partially open-air dance floor with DJs playing current international dance tracks plus some reggae standards.

Mango Bar and Restaurant, beachfront end of Jl Sindhu, north-central Sanur. Informal beach bar which stages live reggae on Thursday and Saturday nights from 9.30pm.

Tandjung Sari Beach Bar, inside the *Tandjung Sari* hotel compound, Jl Danau Tamblingan 41, central Sanur. Elegant shorefront bar, known for its fiery local brew, *arak bumbu*.

The Trophy, in the *Trophy Pub Centre* at Jl Danau Tamblingan 49, south Sanur. Typical expat pub with a darts board, pool table and satellite TV. Live music every night.

Entertainment

You can see **Balinese dancing** in or around Sanur any day of the week. The **barong** is performed every morning at Pura Puseh in Batubulan (9.30–10.30am; see p.502), which can be reached by getting a dark green bemo from Sanur to Denpasar's Kereneng terminal, and then another bemo out to Batubulan (allow about 1hr in all). **Kecak** is staged every night at 6.30pm at the Taman Budaya Cultural Centre on Jalan Nusa Indah in Denpasar (see p.475); the dark-green Sanur–Kereneng bemos pass 200m from the gateway. If you don't want to travel by bemo, any Sanur tour agent will organize transport and tickets for you. Balinese dance performances are also staged free for diners at many of the restaurants on Jalan Danau Tamblingan; details are posted outside the restaurants. See p.520 for more information on Balinese dances.

Shopping

Sanur's best **shops** are found on Jalan Danau Tamblingan and its arterial *gang*. Prices are generally higher than in Kuta, but so is the quality.

Dratama Art Collection, Jl Danau Tamblingan 77, central Sanur. A huge array of batik paintings.

Kika Bookshop, next to *Café Batu Jimbar* on Jl Danau Tamblingan, central Sanur. Stocks a good range of books on Bali and Indonesia, plus some foreign newspapers and magazines.

Klick, Jl Danau Tamblingan 150, central Sanur. Idiosyncratic photo-paintings and handicrafts.

Nogo Ikat, Jl Danau Tamblingan 98, central Sanur, plus branches at Jl Cemara 29, south Sanur and at Jl Danau Tamblingan 208 in south-central Sanur. Chain of fabric shops that specializes in gorgeous lengths of *ikat* cloth sold by the metre; the main shop also has a tailoring service.

Sanggraha Kriya Asta, a few kilometres north of the *Grand Bali Beach*, on the outskirts of Denpasar (Mon–Fri 8.30am–5pm, Sat 8.30am–4.30pm; ☎0361/222942). Upmarket one-stop government handicraft centre. Call for free transport.

Sederhana, Jl Danau Buyan 73, north-central Sanur. Kites, ready-made and designed to order.

Listings

Airline offices and agents Garuda city check-in is at the *Grand Bali Beach* hotel (Mon–Fri 7.30am–4.45pm, Sat & Sun 9am–1pm; ☎0361/288243).

American Express Inside the *Grand Bali Beach* hotel in north Sanur (Mon–Fri 8.30am–4.30pm, Sat 8.30am–12.30pm; ☎0361/288449), Poste Restante, c/o American Express, *Grand Bali Beach* hotel, Sanur, Bali. For poste restante faxes, use the hotel fax number (☎0361/287917) and state clearly that it's for the Amex office. Post is kept for one month.

Cultural classes At *Segara Village* on Jl Segara Ayu (☎0361/288407 fax 287242): woodcarving, painting, batik and Balinese dance courses by arrangement.

Email and Internet access At the efficiently run Environmental Information Centre (PIL) in the lobby of the *Hotel Santai*, Jl Danau Tamblingan 148 (daily 9am–9pm).

Hospitals and clinics All the major hotels provide 24hr medical service. If your hotel does not, try the doctor at the *Grand Bali Beach* hotel (☎0361/288511) or the one at the *Bali Hyatt* (☎0361/288271). The nearest hospitals are all in Denpasar; see p.476 for details.

Postal services Sanur's main post office is on Jl Danau Buyan, north-central Sanur, and there are postal agents next to *Kul Kul* restaurant on the central stretch of Jl Danau Tamblingan and inside the *Trophy Pub Centre* at the southern end of the same road.

Telephone and fax There are plenty of private wartels in central Sanur. Direct-dial public telephones are located in the basement shopping arcade of the *Grand Bali Beach* in north Sanur.

Tourist office There is no official tourist office in Sanur; the nearest one is in Denpasar (see p.469).

UBUD AND AROUND

The inland village of **Ubud** and its surrounding area form Bali's cultural heartland, home to a huge proliferation of temples, museums and art galleries, where Balinese dance shows are staged nightly and a wealth of arts and crafts studios provide the most absorbing shopping on the island. It's also set within a stunning physical environment – a lush landscape watered by hundreds of streams, with archetypal terraced paddy vistas at every turn – all of which gives plenty of scope for leisurely hikes and bicycle rides.

Denpasar to Ubud

The thirteen-kilometre stretch of road connecting Denpasar with Ubud has become something of a sightseeing attraction in itself due to the almost unbroken string of **arts-and-crafts-producing villages** that line its course. Over the last decade, these villages have mushroomed so dramatically that they now merge into each other, coalescing into one extended crafts market. Despite the obvious commercialization, the villages all have genuine histories as centres of refined artistic activity and are still renowned for their specialist crafts.

Batubulan

Barely distinguishable from the northeastern suburbs of Denpasar, **BATUBULAN** acts as the capital's public transport interchange for all bemos heading east and northeast, but it's also an important village in its own right, home of the most famous *barong* dance troupes, and respected across the island for its superb stonecarvers. The village is a long ribbon strung out over 2.5km along the main road, defined by the bemo station in the south and the huge Barong statue at the Celuk junction in the north. The northern stretch of the village, known as **Tegaltamu**, is the most interesting, and it's here that you'll find the shops selling Batubulan's finest **stonecarvings**. Local sculptors specialize in free-standing images made either from the rough grey lava stone known as *paras*, or from smooth grey, yellow or pink sandstone.

As you'd expect in a village so renowned for its fine carvings, the main temple is exu-
berantly decorated. The main gateway to **Pura Puseh**, 200m east off the main road in
the north of the village (follow the signs for the *barong* dance held next door) is graced
by a grimacing Bhoma head and, to the right, Siwa wears a string of skulls around his
neck and stands ankle-deep in more. The plot adjacent to Pura Puseh has been given
over to a purpose-built stage, where, every morning of the year, the **barong** is performed (9.30–10.30am; Rp6000). It's quite feasible to get here by public bemo (see
"Practicalities" below) and buy tickets on the door, but most spectators come on tours
arranged through agents in Kuta or Sanur (Rp30,000–50,000 including return transport). Batubulan dancers also put on nightly performances of the **kecak dance** in a
double bill with the **fire dance** (6.30–8.00pm; Rp6000) at a stage a few hundred metres
further south down the road to Denpasar.

Taman Burung (Bali Bird Park) and Rimba Reptil (Bali Reptile Park)
Both the Bali Bird Park and the Bali Reptile Park (not to be confused with the vastly
inferior reptile park in Mengwi) are fun places for children and fairly interesting for
adults, too. The parks are right next door to each other, about 500m west of the
Tegaltamu intersection, or 3km northwest of Batubulan bemo terminal. Any bemo running between Batubulan and Ubud or Gianyar (see "Practicalities" below) will drop you
at the Tegaltamu intersection.

The **Bali Bird Park** (daily 9am–6pm; Rp14,000) is beautifully laid out with ponds,
pavilions and plenty of flowers – and has an impressive array of birds, all of them identified with English-language labels. Highlights include various **birds of paradise**
(most from Irian Jaya), as well as a couple of fluffy white **Bali starlings**, Bali's only
endemic bird and a severely endangered species (see p.589). The creatures at the **Bali
Reptile Park** (daily 9am–6pm; Rp14,000) are also informatively labelled: look out for
the eight-metre-long reticulated **python**, thought to be the largest python in captivity in
the world.

Practicalities
Batubulan's **bemo station** is at the far southern end of the village, and is well orga-
nized, with clearly signed bays for each destination. Chocolate-brown bemos from
Batubulan **to Ubud** travel directly, via Celuk, Sukawati and Mas, and take about fifty
minutes; some of these then continue to **Kintamani** via Tegalalang. Destinations east
of Batubulan are served by dark-blue-and-fawn-coloured bemos, which head for
Amlapura via Gianyar, Klungkung, the turn-off for Padang Bai, and **Candi Dasa**.
Buses also depart from Batubulan bemo station to Amlapura, following the same route,
to **Singaraja** (see the "Bemo connections" plan on p.472) and to **Nusa Dua**, via the
eastern edge of Kuta.

The Denpasar road divides at Batubulan's Barong statue roundabout; the main
artery and bemo routes veering right to Celuk (see below), and the left-hand prong narrowing into an exceptionally **scenic back road** that continues north as far as Sayan, a
few kilometres west of Ubud, and then on to Payangan and eventually to Kintamani.
This back road is only accessible with your own transport; it's a beautiful drive through
very traditional villages, with hardly any traffic.

Celuk

Strung out along the main road just east of Batubulan, in between large swaths of
paddy-field, **CELUK** is known as the "silver village" because of its reputation as a
major centre for **jewellery**. Local silversmiths have extended their homes to include
workshops and salesrooms, though they are now having to compete with far wealthi-

er outside entrepreneurs whose goods are factory-produced; head down any of the tiny *gang* leading north off the main eastbound road to watch individual artisans at work. Disappointingly, Celuk designs seem unimaginative compared to those sold in Kuta or Ubud, and are quite expensive. Batubulan–Ubud **bemos** pass through Celuk, but as the shops and workshops are spread out over a three-kilometre stretch, you'd be advised to wait for a kilometre or so before you get out, until you see the small lanes off to the left.

Sukawati

The lively market town of **SUKAWATI**, 4km east of Celuk, is a major commercial centre for local villagers and a chief stop on the tourist arts and crafts shopping circuit, especially convenient for anyone reliant on public transport, as the Batubulan–Ubud bemos stop right in front of the central marketplace. Sukawati's chief draw is its **art market** (Pasar Seni), at the heart of the village, which trades every day from dawn till dusk inside a traditional covered two-storey building. Here you'll find a tantalizing array of artefacts, fabrics, sarongs, wind chimes and basketware, piled high on stalls that are crammed together so tightly you can barely walk between them.

Batuan

Northern Sukawati merges into southern **BATUAN**, another ribbon-like roadside development, which was the original home of the Batuan style of painting (see box on p.515) and is now a commercial centre for all the main Balinese art styles. The public face of modern Batuan is dominated by **galleries**, a disappointing number of which pander to the least discriminating tour groups. There are some notable exceptions, including the I Wayan Bendi Gallery, named after a contemporary artist whose Batuan-style pictures are justifiably popular all over the world. A few examples of his work hang in the gallery (not for sale), along with a sizable collection by other artists. At the northern limit of Batuan, a plump stone statue of a prosperous-looking Buddha marks the Sakah turn-off to Blahbatuh and points east, while the main road continues north.

Mas

Long established as a major woodcarving centre, **MAS** is a rewarding place both to browse and to buy, but as it stretches 5km from end to end you'll need plenty of time or your own transport to do it justice. All Batubulan–Ubud **bemos** pass through the village. At its northern end, Mas joins up with the village of Peliatan (see p.578), on the outskirts of Ubud.

The **woodcarvers** of Mas gained great inspiration from the local Pita Maha arts movement during the 1930s, which encouraged the carving of secular subjects as well as the more traditional masks and religious images. Seventy years on, and the range of carvings on display in the Mas shops is enormous; you'll find superbly imaginative portraits of legendary creatures and erotic human figures, alongside tacky cats, dogs and fish.

Ubud

Ever since the German artist Walter Spies arrived here in 1928, **UBUD** has been a magnet for any tourist with the slightest curiosity about Balinese arts, and the traditional village of dancers and craftspeople is still apparent – the people of Ubud and adjacent villages really do still paint, carve, dance and make music, and religious practices here

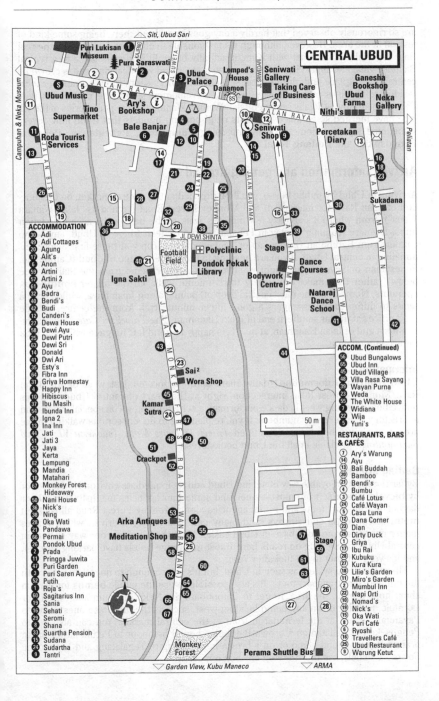

CENTRAL UBUD

Siti, Ubud Sari

Puri Lukisan Museum ①
Pura Saraswati ②③
Ubud Palace ③
Lempad's House
Seniwati Gallery
Taking Care of Business
Ganesha Bookshop
Ubud Farma
Neka Gallery
Danamon
Nithi's
Percetakan Diary ⑬
Seniwati Shop ⑨
Sukadana

JALAN RAYA
Ubud Music ⑤
Tino Supermarket
Ary's Bookshop
Bale Banjar
Roda Tourist Services ⑪

JALAN BISMA
JALAN KARNA
JALAN GAUTAMA
JL MARUTI
JALAN HANOMAN
JALAN SUGRIWA
JALAN JEMBAWAN

Campuhan & Neka Museum
Peliatan

JL DEWI SHINTA
Polyclinic
Football Field
Pondok Pekak Library
Igna Sakti
Stage
Bodywork Centre
Dance Courses
Nataraj Dance School

JALAN MONKEY FOREST ROAD/JL WANARA WANA
Sai²
Wora Shop
Kamar Sutra
Crackpot
Arka Antiques
Meditation Shop
Stage

0   50 m

ACCOMMODATION
30 Adi
49 Adi Cottages
20 Agung
17 Alit's
6 Anon
59 Artini
57 Artini 2
61 Ayu
32 Badra
40 Bendi's
42 Budi
12 Canderi's
27 Dewa House
58 Dewi Ayu
25 Dewi Putri
63 Dewi Sri
14 Donald
41 Dwi Ari
35 Esty's
64 Fibra Inn
31 Griya Homestay
4 Happy Inn
10 Hibiscus
37 Ibu Masih
54 Ibunda Inn
34 Igna 2
13 Ina Inn
44 Jati
51 Jati 3
53 Jaya
43 Kerta
62 Lempung
46 Mandia
18 Matahari
67 Monkey Forest Hideaway
50 Nani House
36 Nick's
38 Ning
28 Oka Wati
21 Pandawa
66 Permai
26 Pondok Ubud
2 Prada
1 Pringga Juwita
47 Puri Garden
3 Puri Saren Agung
52 Putih
1 Roja's
60 Sagitarius Inn
19 Sania
16 Sehati
29 Seromi
33 Shana
33 Suartha Pension
15 Sudana
24 Sudartha
8 Tantri

ACCOM. (Continued)
56 Ubud Bungalows
45 Ubud Inn
48 Ubud Village
48 Villa Rasa Sayang
39 Wayan Purna
23 Weda
55 The White House
7 Widiana
22 Wija
5 Yuni's

RESTAURANTS, BARS & CAFÉS
7 Ary's Warung
14 Ayu
13 Bali Buddah
20 Bamboo
21 Bendi's
4 Bumbu
3 Café Lotus
24 Café Wayan
5 Casa Luna
12 Dana Corner
23 Dian
26 Dirty Duck
1 Griya
17 Ibu Rai
28 Kubuku
27 Kura Kura
11 Lilie's Garden
11 Miro's Garden
2 Mumbul Inn
22 Napi Orti
10 Nomad's
19 Nick's
15 Oka Wati
8 Puri Café
6 Ryoshi
16 Travellers Café
25 Ubud Restaurant
9 Warung Ketut

N

Monkey Forest
Perama Shuttle Bus

Garden View, Kubu Maneco
ARMA

are so rigorously observed that hardly a day goes by without there being some kind of festival in the area. However, although it's fashionable to characterize Ubud as the real Bali, especially in contrast with Kuta, it actually bears little resemblance to a typical Balinese village. Cappuccino cafés, riverside losmen and woodcarving shops crowd its central marketplace and, during peak season, foreigners seem to far outnumber local residents. There is major (mostly tasteful) development along the central Monkey Forest Road (now officially renamed Jalan Wanara Wana), and the peripheries of the village have merged so completely into its neighbouring hamlets that Ubud now covers some nine square kilometres, encompassing **Campuhan**, **Penestanan**, **Peliatan**, **Pengosekan** and **Padang Tegal**.

Arrival, information and getting around

Arriving in Ubud by public **bemo**, you'll be dropped at the central market, on the junction of Jalan Raya (or main road) and Monkey Forest Road (signed as "Jalan Wanara Wana"), from where it's an easy few minutes' walk to the best of the accommodation hubs. If you're planning to stay in Peliatan on the eastern fringe of Ubud, any bemo coming from Batubulan (Denpasar) or Kintamani can drop you there first before terminating in central Ubud. If you are heading to the western edge of Ubud (Campuhan, Penestanan or Sayan), you might want to take another bemo from the market (see below) rather than make the sweaty thirty-minute walk. Of the bigger **shuttle-bus** operators, Nomad has the most central drop-off points, along Jalan Raya, while Perama tends to dump their passengers a good fifteen-minute trek from the centre, outside their offices at the far southern end of Jalan Hanoman. The *Travellers' Café*, towards the northern end of Jalan Hanoman, at no. 16, is happy to mind **left luggage** while you look for accommodation.

Information
Ubud Tourist Information (daily 10am–8pm) is located just west of the Jalan Raya/Monkey Forest Road intersection, right at the heart of central Ubud, and has notice boards giving weekly dance-performance schedules, news on special events and a directory of emergency numbers. If you're planning to do any serious walking in the area, you should buy the **map** entitled *Travel Treasure Maps: Indonesia VI – Ubud Surroundings*, available in all the Ubud bookstores.

Getting around
By far the most enjoyable way of seeing Ubud and its immediate environs is on foot or by **bicycle** (available from most losmen and some tour agencies for Rp4000–5000 per day). The transport touts and rental agencies along Monkey Forest Road all rent out **motorbikes**, **jeeps** and **jimnys**, and many can also supply a driver, which makes longer day-trips from your base in Ubud easier. Note that there's a one-way system in central Ubud, no parking on roads here (most mid-range hotels have parking spaces), and it's very difficult to get fuel after 7pm.

There is no **taxi** system as such in Ubud, but it's easy enough to negotiate rides with the omnipresent transport touts. It's also possible to use the public **bemos** for certain short hops around the area: to get to Campuhan, the Neka Museum and Sayan, for example, just flag down any bemo heading west, such as the turquoise ones going to Payangan, or ask at the terminal in front of the central market. You can also get to Pengosekan or Peliatan on a brown Batubulan-bound bemo, or to Petulu either on an orange Pujung-bound bemo or on a brown bemo going to Tegalalang and Kintamani. For more details, see the "Moving on" box opposite.

MOVING ON FROM UBUD

By bemo
All **bemos** leave from Ubud's central marketplace, either from Jalan Raya or round the corner on Monkey Forest Road. There's a regular service between Ubud and **Kintamani** (brown bemos usually), which goes via Tegalalang and Pujung, and frequent turquoise and orange bemos go to **Gianyar** (via Goa Gajah), where you can make connections to **Padang Bai** (for Lombok) and **Candi Dasa**, and to **Singaraja** and **Lovina**. Any journey south, to **Kuta** or **Sanur**, involves an initial bemo ride to Denpasar's **Batubulan** station, plus at least one cross-city connection (see the "Bemo connections" plan on p.472) unless you take the Batubulan–Nusa Dua bus, which drops you at the eastern edge of Kuta. To reach **western Bali** and **Java** by bemo, you'll need to take an equally convoluted route via Batubulan as well.

By shuttle bus
Ubud's two most reliable **shuttle-bus** operators are Perama and Nomad. **Perama's** head office is inconveniently located midway between Padang Tegal and Pengosekan at the far southern end of Jalan Hanoman (☎0361/96316), but the buses do pick-ups from designated points in the centre. Perama ticket agents include Purnama on Jalan Raya and on Monkey Forest Road, and Rona on Jalan Tebesaya. **Nomad** has offices next to *Nomad's* restaurant on Jalan Raya (☎0361/975520) and just south of the football field on Monkey Forest Road (☎0361/975824); their rates are a little cheaper than Perama's but their services are less frequent.

Both Nomad and Perama run shuttle buses from Ubud **to the airport**, which should cost around Rp5000 per person; expect to pay more if you need to go after dark. Comprehensive information on the airport can found on p.477.

Accommodation

There are hundreds of rooms available for rent in and around Ubud, and you're almost certain to find that your **accommodation** is set in gorgeously lush surroundings and that a generous breakfast is included in the price of the room.

Monkey Forest Road is the most **central**, but also the most congested, part of town, but accommodation on most of the tiny adjacent roads (eg Jalan Karna, Jalan Kajeng, Jalan Bisma and Jalan Gautama), tends to be excellent value. Staying in **Peliatan** or **Penestanan** will be more of a village experience, though Penestanan in particular is a bit of a hike from the main restaurants and shops, as are **Campuhan** and **Sayan**. **Nyuhkuning** is a good in-between option, only a pleasant ten-minute walk from the shops and restaurants of Monkey Forest Road and with lots of uninterrupted paddy-field views. For unsurpassed panoramas, though, you should opt for one of the river-side hotels in **Sayan**.

Central Ubud

Ubud's accommodation explosion has played havoc with its address system, particularly along Monkey Forest Road, where hardly a single losmen has an official road number. All Central Ubud losmen listed below are marked on the Central Ubud map (see p.505), except for the Jalan Kajeng losmen, which are on the map on pp.512–513.

Dewi Putri, Jl Maruti 8 (☎0361/96304). Large, well-furnished bungalows in a quiet little *gang* make this place very good value. Run by a family of painters. ③.

Griya Homestay, Jl Bisma (☎0361/95428). The cheapest accommodation on this idyllic hillside *gang* looking down over the terraced paddies. Large, spruce rooms, with fine views. ④.

Gusti's Garden Bungalows, Jl Kajeng 27 (☎0361/96311). Pleasant, inexpensive rooms set around a garden pool; it's a convenient and peaceful location. Some rooms have hot water. ④–⑤.

Ibunda Inn, central Monkey Forest Road (☎0361/96252). Good-value, unusual two-storey bungalows with upstairs bedroom and verandah. Some have hot water. ③–④.

Ina Inn, Jl Bisma (☎0361/96317, fax 96282). Well-maintained and nicely furnished cottages, set in
a garden on a small *gang* surrounded by rice-fields. ⑤–⑥.

Monkey Forest Hideaway, far southern end of Monkey Forest Road (☎0361/975354). Very good-
value attractively designed bungalows furnished with four-poster beds, antique chests and sunken
baths in garden bathrooms. Quiet location right next to the forest. ④–⑤.

Oka Wati's Sunset Bungalows, down a *gang* off north central Monkey Forest Road
(☎0361/96386, fax 975063). Central terraced bungalows with hot water and a pool. ⑥–⑦.

Pringga Juwita Water Garden Cottages, Jl Bisma (☎ & fax 0361/975734). Beautifully designed
bungalows with traditional-style rooms and garden bathrooms. Surrounded by a series of lotus
ponds, this is a peaceful, scenic location and there's a swimming pool too. ⑦–⑧.

Puri Saren Agung, Jl Raya (☎0361/975057, fax 975137). Superb collection of pavilions on the site
of the Sukawati family palace. Stylish, fairly traditional accommodation with four-poster beds,
carved doors and elegant outdoor sitting rooms. Some air-con. Good value and central. ⑦–⑧.

Roja's Bungalows, Jl Kajeng 1 (☎0361/975107). Small, friendly, centrally located homestay offering large rooms with character at a range of prices. ③–④.

Sudana, Jl Gautama 11 (☎0361/976435). A typical homestay: small, friendly and family-run, offering clean if slightly spartan rooms in a small garden. ③.

Ubud Bungalows, central Monkey Forest Road (☎ & fax 0361/975537). Lovely, comfortable,
detached bungalows, designed in ornate modern style; most have hot water. ③–⑤.

Ubud Village Hotel, south central Monkey Forest Road (☎0361/95571, fax 975069). Fairly stylish
mid-range place offering roomy fan-cooled cottages set in their own walled compounds: the upstairs
ones have fine rice-paddy views. Swimming pool on the premises. ⑦.

Widiana, Jl Karna 5 (☎0361/96456). Good-value basic rooms in a small family compound that's centrally located but peaceful. All rooms have fans and mosquito nets. Recommended. ③.

Western Ubud: Campuhan, Penestanan and Sayan

All accommodation listed here is marked on the map on pp.512–513.

Ananda Cottages, Jl Raya, Campuhan (☎0361/975376, fax 975375). Excellent-value cottages with
garden bathrooms and verandahs, surrounded by rice-paddies; there's a pool and restaurant. 20min
walk from central Ubud, but you can rent bicycles, motorbikes and cars. ⑦.

Londo Bungalows, Penestanan (☎0361/976548). Large, four-person cottages with kitchen, and
fine views over the paddies. Run by one of the original "Young Artists", I Nyoman Londo. ④.

Padma Indah Cottages, Penestanan (☎0361/975719, fax 975091). Small upmarket operation with
ten attractive split-level bungalows, each with garden bathroom. Swimming pool. ⑧–⑨.

Penestanan Bungalows, Penestanan (☎0361/975604, fax 288341). Good-value and comfortable
mid-range bungalows, with hot water. Swimming pool and impressive rice-terrace views. ⑥.

Sayan Terrace, Sayan (☎0361/974384, fax 975384). Awesome location overlooking Sungai Ayung.
Some good-value, mid-priced cottages, plus a few exceptionally elegant ones. Own transport essential (10min drive to central Ubud). ⑥–⑦.

Taman Bebek, Sayan (☎0361/975385 or 720507, fax 232507). Fantastic self-contained cottages, all
built to individual Balinese designs, some with attached kitchens. Most offer breathtaking Sungai
Ayung valley views. Own transport essential (10min drive to central Ubud). ⑧–⑨.

Hotel Tjampuhan, Jl Raya, Campuhan (☎0361/975368, fax 975137). Stunningly positioned cottages set on terraces that drop right down to the river, built on the site of the artist Walter Spies' former home (see p.511). Large and elegantly designed rooms, gorgeous tropical gardens, and two
swimming pools. 10min walk from central Ubud. Reservations essential. ⑧–⑨.

Southern and eastern Ubud: Peliatan and Nyuhkuning

All accommodation listed here is marked on the map on p.512–513.

Bali Spirit, southern end of Nyuhkuning (☎0361/974013, fax 974012). Superbly located upmarket
spa resort, with large stylish rooms. Free transport to Ubud. ⑧–⑨.

Family Guest House, Jl Sukma 39 (aka Jl Tebasaya), Peliatan (☎0361/974054). Exceptionally friendly place offering spotless, well-designed bungalows with comfortable furniture and garden verandahs. Some rooms have hot water. 15min walk from central Ubud. ④.

Garden View Cottages, Nyuhkuning (☎ & fax 0361/974055). Plush, nicely furnished rooms and bungalows, all with great views. Fan and hot water; swimming pool. Very good value. ⑦.

Kubu Maneco, Nyuhkuning (no phone). The cheapest accommodation in Nyuhkuning, offering clean, well-maintained basic rooms with shared bathroom. Fine paddy-field views. ④.

Nyuhkuning Hideaway (aka *Swasti*), Nyuhkuning (☎0361/974079). Large, spacious and comfortably furnished rooms, all with hot water and rice-field views. Good value. ④–⑤.

Rona, Jl Sukma 23 (aka Jl Tebasaya), Peliatan (☎0361/96229). Highly recommended good-value terraced bungalows, with comfortable bamboo beds and armchairs. Deservedly popular. ③–④.

Sari Bungalows, off the southern end of Jl Peliatan, Peliatan (☎0361/975541). Basic huts fronted by verandahs which afford superb paddy views. Some of the cheapest rooms in Ubud. ②.

Central Ubud

Extending between Jalan Raya in the north and the Monkey Forest in the south, and between Campuhan bridge to the west and the GPO to the east, **central Ubud**'s chief attractions are its restaurants and shops, but it does hold a few worthwhile sights.

Puri Lukisan

Although billed as central Ubud's major art museum, the **Puri Lukisan** on Jalan Raya (daily 8am–4pm; Rp2500) has a less impressive collection than the far superior Neka Museum, 2km west in neighbouring Campuhan (see p.511).

Set in lovely gardens, complete with lotus-filled ponds and shady arbours, Puri Lukisan (Palace of Paintings) was founded in 1956 by the Ubud *punggawa*, **Cokorda Gede Agung Sukawati** (whose descendants are still involved with the museum) and the Dutch artist **Rudolf Bonnet**. Both men had amassed a significant collection of work by local artists and almost the whole of the **First Pavilion**, located at the top of the garden, is still given over to these works. Some of these are **wayang-style** canvases, but most are early **Ubud-style**, depicting local scenes (for some background on Balinese painting styles, see the box on pp.514–515). A handful of finely crafted **wood-carving** pieces from the 1930s, 1940s and 1950s are also scattered about the First Pavilion gallery. The **Second Pavilion**, to the left of the First Pavilion, contains a pretty extensive showcase of works in the **Young Artists** style, though the place is unfortunately not very well lit. The **Third Pavilion**, to the right of the First Pavilion, houses temporary exhibitions.

Pura Saraswati

At the end of the nineteenth century, I Gusti Nyoman Lempad arrived in Ubud from the court of Blahbatuh and was employed as chief stonecarver and architect to the Sukawati royal family; **Pura Saraswati** was one of his many commissions. He set the whole temple complex in a delightful water garden, landscaped around a huge lotus pond, and dedicated it to Saraswati, the name of both a sacred Hindu river and the goddess of water and learning. An upmarket restaurant, *Café Lotus*, now capitalizes on the garden view. To get to the temple, you can either take the gateway that opens onto Jalan Raya, or go through the restaurant. A forest of metre-high lotus plants leads you right up to the red-brick entrance gate, through which you'll find a pavilion housing the two huge *barong* costumes used by local villagers for exorcizing rituals: the lion-like Barong Ket and the wild boar Barong Bangkal.

AN UBUD RICE-PADDY WALK

This is a **classic rice-paddy walk**, which takes only two and a half hours for the return trip, is flat and not at all strenuous, and affords fine views of the distant Gunung Agung. There's no shade for the first hour, so you'll need a hat, sun block and some water. With one deviation, the route is also suitable for mountain bikes.

The walk begins just past the Casa Lina shop at the western end of Ubud's Jalan Raya. Head up the grassy ramp on the north side of the road and, at the top, follow the track as it bends to the left before straightening out and heading north. Continue along the track for about 3km as it slices through gently terraced rice-fields fringed with coconut palms; you'll see scores of dragonflies en route, and plenty of **birdlife**, including, possibly, iridescent-blue Javanese kingfishers. After about seventy minutes, the track comes to an end at a sealed road. Turn right here to cross the river, then look for the **southbound track** that starts almost immediately after the bridge and runs east of the river. (If you're on a bike, you should follow the road east of the bridge, and then head back to Ubud via Sakti on the road that merges into central Ubud's Jalan Suweta.) The southbound track becomes indistinct in places, so follow the narrow paths along the top of the rice-field dykes and keep the river in view on your right. Get back on the proper track as soon as you see it emerging from the woods alongside the river, and this will take you back down to Ubud, finishing at the far northern end of Ubud's Jalan Kajeng.

Lempad's House

Until his death in the 1970s, Ubud's most accomplished artist and sculptor, **I Gusti Nyoman Lempad**, lived on Ubud's main street in a house that still belongs to his family but is now also open to the public (daily 8am–6pm; free). Disappointingly, there's little evidence of the great man on show in his former residence, as the place now functions chiefly as a gallery and showroom for a group of artists working under the "Puri Lempad" by-line. (The best collection of Lempad's work is housed in the Neka Museum, described opposite.) The pavilion at the back of the compound does, however, house a small exhibition of Lempad memorabilia.

The Seniwati Gallery of Art by Women

Balinese women feature prominently in the paintings displayed in both the Neka Museum and Puri Lukisan, but there is barely a handful of works by women artists in either collection. To redress this imbalance, British-born artist Mary Northmore set up the Association of Women Artists in Bali, out of which was born **The Seniwati Gallery of Art by Women** on Jalan Sriwedari, off Jalan Raya (daily 10am–5pm; free). Committed to the promotion, display and sale of work by women artists, the Seniwati organization currently represents about forty local and expatriate women, many of whom have pictures on show in the gallery's small but charming permanent collection. The collection covers the complete range of mainstream Balinese art styles, and the works are supported by excellent information sheets and by a staff of well-informed gallery attendants.

Campuhan and Penestanan

Sited at the confluence of the rivers Wos Barat and Wos Timor, the elongated hamlet of **CAMPUHAN** extends west from Ubud and is noted as the home of Bali's best art gallery, the **Neka Museum**. There are a couple of other noteworthy sights here too, and Campuhan also makes a good starting point for a number of **walks** around Ubud, including the picturesque route to the adjacent and very traditional hamlet of **Penestanan**. Otherwise, Campuhan comprises little more than a sprinkling of residences sandwiched between the road and the rivers, and a few losmen and hotels. Its one drawback is the ridiculously busy main road that tears through its heart, an unpleasant route for pedestrians. **Bemos**, however, roar this way too, so you might be better off catching one of these than attempting to walk; take any westbound bemo from Ubud Market (Rp300–500).

The Neka Museum

Boasting the most comprehensive collection of traditional and modern Balinese paintings on the island, the **Neka Museum** (daily 9am–5pm; Rp2500) is housed in a series of purpose-built pavilions set high on a hill overlooking the Wos Barat river valley, alongside the main Campuhan road.

The **first pavilion** attempts to give an overview of the three major schools of Balinese painting from the seventeenth century to the present day. (For an introduction to all the main Balinese art styles mentioned below, see pp.514–515) It opens with some examples of the earliest known "school", the two-dimensional **wayang-style** works from Kamasan, here represented by a couple of typical nineteenth-century pictures, as well as by modern *wayang*-style pictures from the contemporary artist **Ketut Kobot**. One of the finest **Ubud-style** paintings in this pavilion is *The Bumblebee Dance* by **Anak Agung Gede Sobrat**, which shows a traditional flirtation dance, the *oleg tambulilingan*. I **Wayan Bendi**'s *Busy Bali* is also a classic – a typically modern **Batuan-style** work that takes a wryly humorous look at the effects of tourism on the island. I **Made Budi**'s *At the Crossroads* is a similarly astute Batuan-style appraisal of the tensions that permeate modern Balinese life.

The ground-floor hall of the **second pavilion** exhibits naive, childlike and expressionistic works in the **Young Artists style**, and its upstairs gallery is devoted to pictures by **Arie Smit**, the Dutch man who is said to have inspired the young painters to pursue this style. The **third pavilion** houses a very interesting archive of black-and-white **photographs** from Bali in the 1930s and 1940s, all of them taken by the remarkable American expat **Robert Koke** who, together with his wife Louise, founded the first ever hotel in Kuta in 1936. His photographic record includes some stunning shots of village scenes, temple festivals, dances and cremations.

The small **fourth pavilion** is dedicated to the works of local renaissance man, **I Gusti Nyoman Lempad** (see opposite), who produced scores of cartoon-like line drawings inspired by religious mythology and secular folklore. Some of his best-known works are from a series on Men and Pan Brayut, a humorous reworking of the well-known folk story about a poor couple and their eighteen children.

The **fifth pavilion** focuses on works by artists from other parts of Indonesia, whose style is sometimes labelled "Academic". Outstanding works displayed here include *Three Masked Dancers* and *Divine Union*, both by Javanese-born **Anton H**. Works by Indonesian artists spill over into the ground-floor galleries of the **sixth pavilion**, and this is where you'll find the Javanese artist **Affandi's** bold expressionist portrait of fighting cocks, *Prize Fighters*. The upstairs galleries feature the paintings of Western artists who lived and worked in Ubud, including the *Temptation of Arjuna* by the influential Dutch painter **Rudolf Bonnet**.

Walter Spies' home

Descending the Campuhan hill, in the direction of Ubud, you'll pass a few homestays before reaching the elegant **Hotel Tjampuhan** on your left, 100m west of the Campuhan bridge. This lovely stylish hotel was once the home of the expatriate German artist and musician Walter Spies and, even if you're not staying here (see p.508), you're quite at liberty to explore the grounds, which slope steeply down to the Wos Barat river gully below. Non-guests can also use the pool for a Rp5000 fee. The

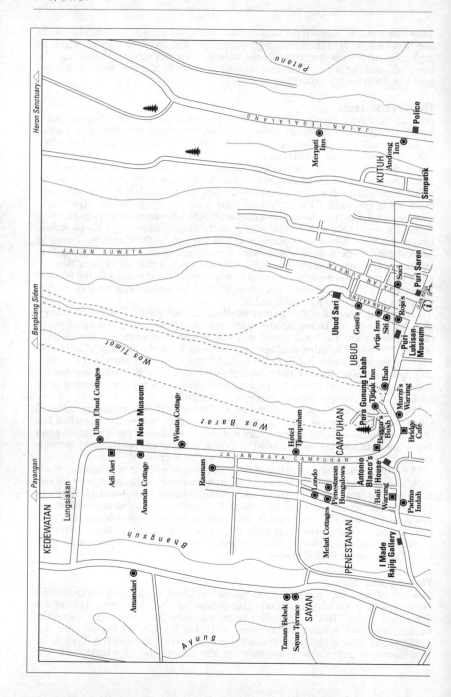

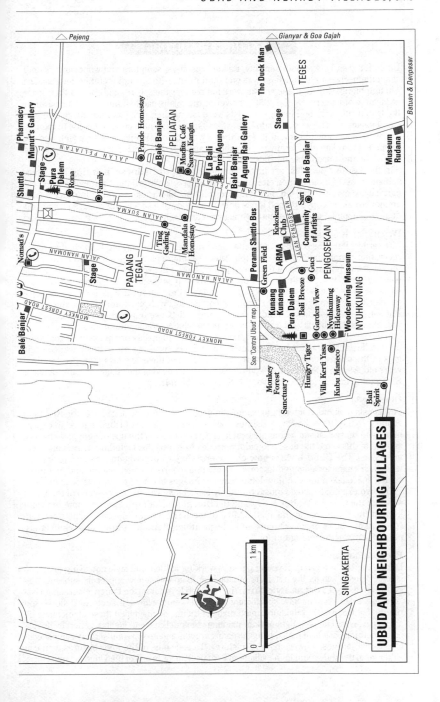

UBUD AND NEIGHBOURING VILLAGES

BALINESE PAINTING

Up until the early twentieth century, Balinese painters, sculptors and woodcarvers dedicated themselves to honouring their gods and rajahs with splendid temples and palaces. Though highly skilled, these artists were not paid for their work, and earned their living as farmers or traders. By the 1930s, however, the rajahs had lost much of their power to the Dutch colonials, and foreign tourists were taking their place as **patrons of the arts** – and paying for the work. Gradually, artists began to paint secular subjects, to express themselves as individuals and to sign their own pictures. Painting and carving became full-time and relatively lucrative occupations, and the **arts and crafts industry** is now one of the most profitable on Bali.

In the last few decades, art historians have grouped **Balinese painting** into broad schools, most of them named after the village where a style originated. Inevitably the categories are overgeneralized, but Balinese painters, like artists working in other media, are not shy about copying good ideas or even reproducing successful work, so it's not difficult to pinpoint a few representative features and techniques.

Wayang or Kamasan style

The earliest Balinese painters drew their inspiration from the wayang kulit shadow plays, recreating puppet-like figures on their canvases and depicting episodes from the same religious and historical epics that were played out on the stage. Variously known as the **wayang style**, the **classical style** or the **Kamasan style** (after the village most noted for its *wayang*-style art) – and still popular today – the pictures are packed full of people painted in three-quarter profile (both eyes visible), with caricature-like features and angular, puppet-like poses. Traditional *wayang* artists use only five different colours – red, blue, yellow, black and white – creating the characteristic muted effect.

In the seventeenth century, *wayang*-style art appeared mainly on the banners that were used to decorate temples, but the oldest surviving pictures are those that cover the ceilings of the old palace of **Klungkung** (see p.533), and these are less than two hundred years old. Most modern *wayang*-style artists are still based in the village of Kamasan near Klungkung, including the renowned **I Nyoman Mandra**.

Ubud style

Few artists took much interest in secular subjects until the early decades of the twentieth century. In the 1930s, however, Balinese painters in the village of Ubud started to experiment with more realistic techniques such as perspective and the use of light and shadow, and out of this came the desire to paint episodes from real life, including market and temple scenes. The **Ubud style** is now characterized by an overwhelming sense of activity, with each character engaged in some transaction, chore or conversation, and any intervening space taken up with tiny details such as images of offerings, insects or animals.

The two expatriate artists most commonly associated with the emergence of the Ubud style are the German **Walter Spies** and the Dutchman **Rudolph Bonnet**, both of whom lived in the Ubud area in the 1930s. Most of the best-known Ubud-style artists are represented in Ubud's major art museums; the paintings of **Anak Agung Gede Sobrat** are particularly worth looking out for.

Pengosekan style

During the 1960s, a group of young painters working in the Ubud style and living in the village of Pengosekan on the outskirts of Ubud came up with a new approach, subsequently known as the **Pengosekan style**. From the Ubud-style pictures, the Pengosekan school isolated just a few components, specifically the **birds, butterflies, insects and flowering plants** that featured, in miniature, in so many of them, and magnified these elements to fill a whole canvas. The best Pengosekan paintings look delicate and lifelike, generally depicted in soothing pastels of pinks, blues, creams, browns and greens, and slightly reminiscent of classical Japanese flower and bird pictures. To see some of the finer pictures, you can either go to the showroom in the village of Pengosekan, or to one of the Ubud art museums.

Batuan style
In contrast to the slightly romanticized visions of village events being painted by the Ubud-style artists in the 1930s, a group of painters in the nearby village of Batuan were coming up with more thought-provoking interpretations of Balinese life. Like the Ubud artists, **Batuan-style** painters filled their works with scores of people, but on a much more frantic and wide-ranging scale. A single Batuan-style picture might contain a dozen apparently unrelated scenes – a temple dance, a rice harvest, a fishing expedition, an exorcism, and a couple of tourists taking snapshots – all depicted in fine detail that strikes a balance between the naturalistic and the stylized. By clever juxtaposition, the best Batuan artists – like the Neka Museum exhibitors **I Wayan Bendi, I Made Budi** and **Ni Wayan Warti** – can turn their pictures into amusing and astute comments on Balinese society. Works by their precursors, the original Batuan artists, **Ida Bagus Made Togog** and **Ida Bagus Made Wija**, focused more on the darker side of village life and on the supernatural beings that hung around the temples and forests.

Young Artists
A second flush of artistic innovation hit the Ubud area in the 1960s, when a group of teenage boys from the hamlet of **Penestanan** started producing unusually expressionist works, painting everyday scenes in vibrant, non-realistic colours. They soon became known as the **Young Artists**, a tag now used to describe work by anyone in that same style. The inspiration for the boys' experiments is generally attributed to the interest of Dutch artist **Arie Smit**, who settled in Penestanan in the 1960s. The style is indisputably childlike, even naive, the detailed observations of daily life crudely drawn with minimal attention to perspective, outlined in black like a child's colouring book, and often washed over in weird shades of pinks, purples and blues.
   All the major museums have works by some of the original Young Artists from the 1960s, the most outstanding of whom include **I Ketut Tagen, I Wayan Pugur, I Nyoman Londo, I Nyoman Mundik** and **I Nyoman Mujung**. As for pictures by Arie Smit, the Neka Museum in Ubud devotes a whole gallery to his work.

Academic (modern) style
Any modern artist whose work doesn't fit easily into the other major schools of Balinese painting usually gets labelled as **Academic** – meaning that they have studied and been influenced by Western techniques. The best-known Academic painters tend to be men and women from other parts of Indonesia, who have settled in Bali and painted Balinese subjects in a non-traditional style. Both the Neka Museum and ARMA devote a whole gallery to these artists, and names to look out for there include **Affandi, Anton H** and **Abdul Aziz**, all from Java, the Sumatran-born **Rusli**, and from Bali, **I Nyoman Tusan** and **Nyoman Guarsa**.

house was built in 1928 and Spies tried hard to balance local style with imported sophistication. The simple two-storey thatched wooden building is still furnished with some of the artist's antiques, and the breezy verandahs and lush tropical surroundings evoke a tangible sense of its former charm.
   While in Ubud, Spies devoted most of his time to the study and practice of Balinese art and music. He sponsored two local gamelan orchestras and was the first Westerner to attempt to record Balinese **music**; he is also credited with inventing the *kecak* dance (see p.520). Spies was an avid collector of Balinese art and in 1936 helped found the locally influential Pita Maha arts group. There's currently only one of Walter Spies' own paintings on show in Ubud, at ARMA (see p.517).

Antonio Blanco's House
Some 75m further down the main road into Ubud from *Hotel Tjampuhan*, an ostentatious gateway leads you into **Antonio Blanco's House and Art Gallery** (daily during daylight hours; Rp2500), home of the flamboyant Catalan expatriate who specializes

in erotic paintings and drawings, particularly portraits of Balinese women in varying states of undress. Whatever you think of the man's artistic achievements, it's hard not to enjoy the sheer panache of this ultimate self-publicist. The gallery space has an enjoyably camp atmosphere and, likely as not, you'll encounter either the beret-clad artist or his muse, model and wife here too, as they often hold court in the central reception area.

Penestanan

Just west of the Campuhan bridge, but invisible from the main road, the hamlet of **PENESTANAN** is far more of a traditional village than its neighbour, and makes a good focus for a pleasant two-hour circular walk. It's accessible from a sideroad that turns off beside Blanco's House, but the most dramatic approach is via the steep flight of steps across from the *Hotel Tjampuhan*. The track leads up the hillside before dropping down through rice-fields into the next valley, across Sungai Blangsuh and through a small wooded area, before coming to a crossroads with Penestanan's main street. At the crossroads, go straight on for Sayan, or left for a walk through Penestanan and then back down to Blanco's House in Campuhan. Penestanan also makes a tranquil, if slightly out-of-the-way, place to stay: see p.508 for details.

Penestanan's main claim to fame is as the original home of the **Young Artists** (see p.515). The Dutch painter Arie Smit settled here in the 1960s, and set about encouraging local village boys (women rarely painted then) to paint pictures dictated by their own instinct rather than sticking to the conventional styles and themes passed down by their fathers and grandfathers. The boys came up with pictures that were bright, bold and expressionist, a style that is still followed by many painters in Penestanan today. The village now holds about a dozen art **galleries**, and is also the centre for the finest beadwork on Bali, including jewellery, belts, caps and handbags, on display in many Penestanan shops.

The Monkey Forest and Nyuhkuning

Ubud's best-known tourist attraction is its **Monkey Forest Sanctuary** (daylight hours; Rp1100), which occupies the land between the southern end of Monkey Forest Road and the northern edge of the woodcarvers' hamlet of **Nyuhkuning**. The focus of numerous day-trips because of its resident troupe of malevolent but photogenic monkeys, the forest itself is actually small and disappointing, traversed by a concrete pathway. The only way to see the Monkey Forest is on foot, but it's hardly a strenuous hike: the entrance is a ten-minute walk south from Ubud's central market, and a stroll around the forest and its temple combines well with a walk around neighbouring Nyuhkuning.

Pura Dalem Agung Padang Tegal

Five minutes into the forest, you'll come to **Pura Dalem Agung Padang Tegal** (donation requested for compulsory sarong and sash), the temple of the dead for the *banjar* of Padang Tegal. *Pura dalem* are traditionally places of extremely strong magical power and the preserve of *leyak* (evil spirits); in this temple you'll find half a dozen stonecarved images of the witch-widow **Rangda** flanking the main stairway, immediately recognizable by her hideous fanged face, unkempt hair, lolling metre-long tongue and pendulous breasts. Two of the Rangda statues are depicted in the process of devouring children – a favourite occupation of hers. Casual visitors are not allowed to enter the inner sanctuary, but in the outer courtyard you can see the ornate *kulkul* **drum tower**, built in red brick and lavishly decorated with carvings of Bhoma heads and *garuda*.

Nyuhkuning

Continuing south from the Pura Dalem Agung Padang Tegal, the track enters the tiny settlement of **NYUHKUNING**, whose villagers are renowned for their woodcarving skills. Both sides of the track are dotted with shops selling all manner of **woodcarvings**, from dolphins to elfin figurines and weeping Buddhas, most of them sculpted from coconut, hibiscus and "crocodile" wood. Prices are reasonable and the whole commercial process is much more low-key and workshop-oriented than in Mas, for example. A number of the best local carvings have been preserved in the **Widya Kusuma Woodcarving Museum**, a tiny makeshift gallery about ten minutes south of the temple of the dead (daily 10am–5pm; Rp500). Scattered in amongst the woodcarving shops are several beautifully sited small **hotels**, each one offering uninterrupted rice-paddy views; see p.508 for details.

Pengosekan, Peliatan, Teges and Petulu

The villages of **Pengosekan**, **Peliatan** and **Petulu** blend seamlessly with the eastern edges of central Ubud, and can be reached fairly easily on foot in an hour or less from the main market. **Teges** merges with the southern and eastern edges of Peliatan. It's quite possible to base yourself in these villages as there are losmen here, especially in Peliatan (see "Accommodation", listings on p.508).

Pengosekan

At the southern junction of Monkey Forest Road and Jalan Hanoman, the road enters **PENGOSEKAN**, known locally as the centre of the Pengosekan Community of Artists, a cooperative that was founded in 1969. The cooperative was so successful that most of the original members have now established their own galleries, but the spirit of the collective lives on in the **Pengosekan Community of Artists showroom**, which stands just east of the river on the main Pengosekan road (daily 9am–6pm). As with other local communities of artists, the Pengosekan painters developed a distinct style, specializing in large canvases of birds, flowers, insects and frogs, painted in gentle pastels and depicted in magnified detail; most of the work here is for sale but the selection is a bit dull.

THE AGUNG RAI MUSEUM OF ART (ARMA)

For a good selection of much meatier Balinese art, you should go instead to Pengosekan's new art museum, the **Agung Rai Museum of Art**, usually referred to as **ARMA** (daily 9am–6pm; Rp2500), which is a few hundred metres west of the river, and has entrances next to the *Kokokan Club* restaurant on Jalan Pengosekan as well as on Jalan Hanoman. ARMA also houses a very good Balinese art bookshop, an excellent library, and an open-air dance stage.

The upstairs gallery of ARMA's large **Balé Daja** pavilion gives a brief survey of the development of Balinese art (see the box on pp.514–515 for background information on Balinese art styles) and includes some **wayang-style** canvases, hung high on the walls overlooking the central well, as well as a few good examples of **I Gusti Nyoman Lempad's** pen and ink cartoons (see p.570). Two of the finest works up here, however, are Anak A Sobrat's *Baris Dance*, a typical example of **Ubud-style** art, and the popular, contemporary Batuan-style piece by **I Wayan Bendi**, *Life in Bali*, which is crammed with typical Balinese scenes – including a temple procession, a dance performance and a cockfight – and laced with satirical comments, notably in the figures of long-nosed tourists who pop up in almost every scene. The downstairs gallery in the Balé Daja houses temporary exhibitions.

Across the garden, the middle gallery of the **Balé Dauh** reads like a directory of Bali's most famous expats. In here you'll find works by Adrien Jean Le Mayeur (see p.500), Rudolf Bonnet, Antonio Blanco (see p.515) and Arie Smit (p.515). The *pièce de resistance*, though, is *Calonnarang* by the German artist **Walter Spies** (see p.511), a dark portrait of a demonic apparition being watched by a bunch of petrified villagers; this is the only Walter Spies painting currently on show in Bali.

Peliatan

The best way to approach **PELIATAN** from central Ubud is on foot via Jalan Sukma (formerly known as Jalan Tebasaya), which runs south from Jalan Raya. The upper part of Jalan Sukma is peppered with losmen, but this is still very much an undeveloped village, with rice-fields and narrow river gorges stretching beyond the roadside to east and west, accessed only by small dirt tracks. Peliatan's eastern flank, however, has a completely different character, as the main Denpasar–Ubud–Kintamani roads roars right through it. This heavily used route is lined with an almost continuous string of arts and crafts shops, including the recommended **Agung Rai Fine Art Gallery** (daily 9am–6pm). Peliatan is best known as the home of one of the island's finest **dance troupes**, and there are currently over a dozen different dance and gamelan groups active in the village, most of which perform in Peliatan and Ubud several nights a week (see p.522).

Teges

Sandwiched between Peliatan to the north and Mas to the south, the woodcarving village of TEGES is the site of a new art collection, **Museum Rudana** (daily 9am–6pm; Rp2500). The museum is about 1.5km south of the southern end of Jalan Peliatan, a ten-minute bemo ride from central Ubud, or an hour's walk. As with all the other major art museums in Ubud, this one presents an introduction to the **history of Balinese painting**, from Kamasan-style traditional calendars through Batuan-style and Ubud-style pictures to contemporary works. Many of the artists represented here also feature in the Neka Museum and at ARMA, but Rudana's fine collection of **contemporary work** in the basement gallery – which includes pieces by Made Budhiana, Nyoman Erawan and Boyke Aditya – is unrivalled.

Petulu and the white heron sanctuary

Every evening at around 6pm, hundreds of thousands of white herons fly in from kilometres around to roost in certain trees in the village of **PETULU**, immediately to the northeast of Ubud – and it makes quite an astonishing spectacle. No one knows for certain why the herons have chosen to make their home in Petulu, though one local story claims that the birds are reincarnations of the tens of thousands of men and women who died in the civil war that raged through Bali in 1966. Many of the victims were buried near here, and the birds are said to have started coming here only after a major ceremony was held in the village in memory of the dead.

To find the so-called **white heron sanctuary**, follow the main Tegalalang–Pujung road north from the T-junction at the eastern edge of Ubud for about 1.5km, then take the left-hand (signed) fork for a further 1.5km. You may be asked to give a donation just before reaching the roosting area. Lots of public bemos ply the main Pujung road, but you'll have to walk the last 1.5km from the fork.

Organized tours and outdoor activities

Ubud is well stocked with **tour agencies**, all of which offer a standard selection of organized **day-trips** in air-con minibuses for Rp30,000–50,000 per person. The most popular routes include trips to the island's holiest temple complex at Besakih, the volcano and lake at Kintamani via Goa Gajah and Tampaksiring, and the monkey forest at Sangeh. Alternatively, you could rent a car for between Rp40,000 and Rp80,000 per day and work out your own day-trip routes.

One of Ubud's more unusual attractions is its regular **Bali bird walks**, which are organized by Victor Mason from his *Beggar's Bush* pub in Campuhan (☎0361/975592). The walks depart three or four times a week at 9am and cost about US$30. The stretch of Sungai Ayung just west of Ubud is the island's centre for **white-water-rafting** and **kayaking**, and several companies currently run white-water excursions along its course; any Ubud tour agent can book you on.

Eating and drinking

With some 250 **restaurants** to choose from, eating in Ubud is a major pleasure. The quality of the food is high, and the emphasis is on wholesome ingredients. **Prices** are correspondingly higher than elsewhere, and a mandatory ten percent local government tax is added onto all restaurant bills. Most places stay open all day and shut by 10pm. There are no clubs or even full-blown bars in Ubud, and the local government has banned live-music shows of the non-traditional variety, but a smattering of restaurants do serve **beer** till fairly late: *Nomad's* on Jalan Raya stays open until at least midnight, as does the British-style pub *Beggar's Bush* in Campuhan, and *Ary's Warung* serves until around 1am.

Restaurants and cafés

Ary's Warung, Jl Raya, central Ubud. Elegant café whose wholesome menu includes wonderful brown-bread sandwiches, Middle Eastern dips and cheesecake. Stays open till about 1am.

Bali Buddha, opposite the GPO on Jl Jembawan. Comfortable chairs, delicious juices, filled bagels, tasty cakes and sandwiches. Also a notice board with yoga and language course information.

Bamboo Restaurant, Jl Dewi Shinta, central Ubud. Inexpensive and tasty authentic Indonesian dishes, with recommended seafood and some interesting veggie options.

Bendi's, Monkey Forest Road. Good selection of traditional Balinese dishes as well as Indonesian standards and travellers' fare. Inexpensive.

Bumbu, Jl Suweta, central Ubud. Delicious Indian and Balinese fare such as banana and coconut curry and chilli-fried fish, in a pleasant water-garden setting. Moderately priced.

Café Lotus, Jl Raya, central Ubud. Long-established Ubud landmark which overcharges for its rather average food, but has a great setting overlooking the Pura Saraswati lotus pond.

Café Wayan, Monkey Forest Road. Good menu of Thai and Indonesian dishes; traditional, buffet-style Balinese feasts served here every Sunday (veggie versions also available).

Casa Luna, Jl Raya, central Ubud. Stylish riverside place specializing in mouthwatering breads and cakes, but also offering great salads, Indonesian and Indian fare. Nightly videos.

Dana Corner Rumah Makan Padang, Jl Raya, central Ubud. Inexpensive and authentic Sumatran fare, including fried chicken, baked eggs, potato cakes and fish curry.

Miro's Garden, Jl Bisma, central Ubud. Lovely candlelit garden terrace, serving moderately priced international and Balinese dishes, including good nasi campur and *babi guling*.

Murni's Warung, Jl Raya, Campuhan. High-class, mid-priced curries, thick home-made soups and Indonesian specialities in a relaxed restaurant built into the side of the Wos river valley.

Nick's, southern end of Jl Bisma, central Ubud. Recommended menu of traditional Balinese food, including fish and rice cooked in banana leaves. Inexpensive.

Warung Ketut (Shadana) Vegetarian Café, Jl Raya, central Ubud. Tiny, inexpensive place, which serves the most imaginative Indonesian veggie food in Ubud. Shuts about 8pm.

TRADITIONAL DANCE-DRAMAS OF BALI

Most Balinese **dance-dramas** have evolved from sacred rituals, and are still regularly performed at religious events and village festivals, with full attention given to the devotional aspects. They are nearly always accompanied by a Balinese gamelan orchestra (see Contexts, p.966). Most tourists, however, only get the chance to see commercial shows, but these are generally very good, and well worth catching. These tourist shows are performed by expert local troupes in the traditional settings of temple courtyards and village compounds, and always comprise a medley of highlights.

There are few professional **dancers** in Bali; most performers spend their days working in the fields or in shops, donning costumes and make-up only at festival times or for the tourist shows. Almost every Balinese boy and girl is taught to dance, and the most adept are then chosen to perform at community functions, as part of the established local troupe. Personal expression has no place in the Balinese theatre, but the skilful execution of traditional moves is always much admired, and trained dancers enjoy a high status within the village. They express themselves through a vocabulary of controlled angular **movements** of the arms, wrists, fingers, neck and, most beguilingly, eyes. Each gesture derives from a movement observed in the natural rather than the human world. Thus a certain flutter of the hand may be a bird in flight; a vigorous rotation of the forearms, the shaking of water from an animal's coat.

Baris

The **baris** or **warrior dance** can be performed either as a solo or in a group of five or more, and either by a young woman or, more commonly, a young man. Strutting on stage with knees and feet turned out, his centre of gravity kept low, the *baris* cuts an impressive figure in a gilded brocade cloak of ribboned pennants which fly out dramatically at every turn. In his performance, he enacts a young warrior's preparation for battle, goading himself into courageous mood, trying out his martial skills, showing pride at his calling and then expressing a whole series of emotions – ferocity, passion, tenderness, rage – much of it through the arresting movements of his eyes. In its original sacred form, this was a devotional dance in which soldiers dedicated themselves and their weapons to the gods.

Barong–Rangda dramas

Featuring the most spectacular costumes of all the Balinese dances, the Barong–Rangda dramas are also among the most sacred and most important. The mythical widow-witch character of **Rangda** represents the forces of evil, and her costume and mask present a duly frightening spectacle. The **Barong Ket** cuts a much more lovable figure, a shaggy-haired, bug-eyed creature, like a cross between a pantomime horse and a Chinese dragon. All Rangda and Barong masks are invested with great sacred power and are treated with due respect and awe.

Barong–Rangda dramas can be self-contained as in the *calonarang*, or they can appear as just one symbolic episode in the middle of a well-known story like the *Mahabharata*. Whatever the occasion, Rangda is always summoned by a character who wants to cause harm to someone. When the opposition calls in the Barong (the defender of the good), Rangda appears, fingernails first, flashing her white magic cloth and stalking the Barong at every turn. When the Barong looks to be on his last legs, a group of village men rush in to his rescue, but are entranced by Rangda's magic and stab themselves instead of her. A priest quickly enters before any real injury is inflicted. The series of confrontations continues, and the drama ends in stalemate: the forces of good and evil remain as strong and vital as ever, ready to clash again in the next bout.

Kecak

Sometimes called the **monkey dance** after the animals represented by the chorus, the **kecak** gets its Balinese name from the hypnotic chattering sounds made by the a cappella choir. Chanting nothing more than "cak cak cak cak", the chorus of fifty or more men uses seven different rhythms to create the astonishing music that accompanies the drama. Bare-chested, and wearing black-and-white checked cloth around their waists and a single red hibiscus behind the ear, the men sit cross-legged in five or six tight concentric circles, occasionally swaying or waving their arms and clapping their hands in unison. The **narrative** is taken from a core episode of the *Ramayana*, centring around the kidnap of Sita by the demon king Rawana, and is acted out in the middle of the chorus circle, with one or two narrators speaking for all the characters. Unlike most Balinese dances, the *kecak* has no ritualistic purpose: it was invented by the German artist and musician Walter Spies in the 1930s.

Legong

Undoubtedly the most refined of all the temple dances, the **legong** is renowned for its elegantly restrained choreography. The dance is always performed by three prepubescent girls, who are bound tightly in sarongs and chest cloths of opulent green or pink, with gilded crowns filled with frangipani blossoms on their heads. When village elders and former dancers are selecting aspiring *legong* dancers, they look not only for agility and vitality, but also for grace and poise, as the spirit of the *legong* is considered the acme of Balinese femininity.

The dance itself has evolved from a highly sacred *sanghyang* trance dance (see below) and generally tells the **story** of King Laksem, who has captured a princess and is about to go to war to prevent her being rescued. As he leaves, he is attacked by a raven, an extremely bad omen, after which he duly loses the battle and is killed. The **performance** begins with a solo dance by a court lady (*condong*) dressed in pink and gold. She then welcomes the two *legong* (literally "dancers") with a pair of fans. Dressed identically in bright green and gold, the two *legong* enact the story, adopting and swapping characters apparently at random. At the climax, the *condong* always returns as the raven, with pink wings attached to her costume.

Oleg Tambulilingan

Translated as the **bumblebee dance**, the **oleg tambulilingan** is one of the most vivacious, humorous and engaging dances of the Balinese repertoire, but unfortunately, it doesn't get performed that often. It's a flirtation dance, performed by a man and woman who act as courting bumblebees sipping honey in a flower garden, the man sexually obsessed with the female, desire burning in his eyes, the female coquettish and eventually compliant.

Ramayana dance-dramas

The great Hindu epic, the *Ramayana*, is a popular inspiration for all sorts of dance-dramas, but by far the best-loved episode is the act in which Rama's queen **Sita** is kidnapped by the demon king Rawana, and whisked off to his palace. In the original poem, the **kidnapping** is the catalyst for all the ensuing action, prompting the hero, Rama (played by a woman), his brother Laksmana (also played by a woman), the monkey king Hanuman, and a motley band of retainers, to struggle through all sorts of bizarre adventures in their attempt to rescue her.

Sanghyang: trance dances

The state of trance lies at the heart of traditional Balinese dance. In order to maintain the health of the village, the gods are periodically invited down into the temple arena to help in the exorcism of evil. When the deities descend, they possess certain people, and incite them into performing dances or astonishing physical feats. One of the most common trance dances is the *sanghyang dedari* (angel deity), in which the deities possess two young girls who perform a complicated duet with their eyes closed and, in part, while seated on the shoulders of two male villagers. Although they have never learnt the steps, the duo almost invariably performs its movements in tandem and sometimes continues for up to four hours. When they finally drop to the floor in exhaustion, the priest wakes them gently by sprinkling holy water over them.

TRADITIONAL DANCE-DRAMAS OF BALI (continued)

In the **sanghyang jaran** (horse deity), one or more men are put into a trance state while the temple floor is littered with burning coconut husks. As they enter the trance, the men grab hold of wooden hobbyhorse sticks and then gallop frantically back and forth across the red-hot embers as if they were on real horses.

Topeng: mask dances

Balinese masks are extremely sacred, carved and painted with great reverence to the spirits, and in the **topeng** or **mask dance** the performer is possessed by the spirit of the mask. The storylines of most *topeng* centre around folk tales or well-known episodes from history, and every character wears a mask, which makes him or her immediately recognizable.

One of the most popular is the **topeng tua**, a portrayal of a shaky-limbed old man, whose mask is shrouded in straggly white hair and beard. Another classic tourist *topeng* is the **frog dance** which tells how a frog turns into a prince. In the **jauk**, a solo dancer portrays a terrifying demon-king. His red or white mask has huge bulging eyes, and a thick black moustache, and his hands are crowned with 30-centimetre-long fingernails. To the clashing strains of the gamelan, the *jauk* leaps mischievously about the stage as if darting through a forest and pouncing on villagers.

Wayang kulit

On an island where cinema screens and TVs haven't yet percolated through to the smallest villages, a **wayang kulit** performance, or **shadow-puppet drama**, still draws in huge crowds. The stories are familiar to all, but the sheer panache, eloquence and wit of a good puppeteer means the show is as likely to break news, spread gossip and pass on vital information as it is to entertain. A typical wayang kulit show takes place after sundown on the occasion of a wedding, a cremation or a temple festival, staged either in the outer courtyard of the village temple or in the *bale banjar* meeting area. The wayang kulit form came to Bali from Java, and its most popular stories are taken from the *Mahabharata*.

Dance

The Ubud region boasts dozens of outstanding dance and music groups, and there are up to five different **dance shows** performed every night in the area; the tourist office gives details of the regular weekly schedule and also arranges free transport to outlying venues. Tickets cost Rp7000 and can be bought either from touts or at the door. Performances start between 7pm and 8pm; arrive early for the best seats. If you have only one evening to catch a show, then go for whatever is playing at the **Ubud Palace** (Puri Saren Agung), opposite the market in central Ubud. The setting of this former raja's home (now a hotel) is breathtaking, with the torchlit courtyard gateways furnishing the perfect backdrop. For an introduction to Balinese dance-dramas, see the box on pp.520–522.

Shopping

Most Ubud shops open daily, many not closing until 8 or 9pm. For all major essentials, from suntan lotion to beer, check out Tino Supermarket on Jalan Raya.

Books and music

ARMA Bookshop, inside Agung Rai Museum of Art, Pengosekan. Best range of books about Bali.
Ary's Bookshop, Jl Raya, central Ubud. Decent stock of books on Bali and Indonesia.
Ganesha Bookshop, Jl Raya, central Ubud. Secondhand books.
Moari Music, Jl Raya, central Ubud. Specializes in traditional Balinese musical instruments.

Rona Bookshop, Jl Sukma 23 (aka Jl Tebasaya), Peliatan. Secondhand bookstore and library.
Ubud Music, Jl Raya, central Ubud. Books on Bali and Indonesia plus some tapes and CDs.

Clothes and textiles
Kamar Sutra, Monkey Forest Road, central Ubud. Stunning but expensive batik fabrics.
Nithi's Collection, Jl Raya, central Ubud. Inexpensive and idiosyncratic batik sarongs.
Pasar Seni, Jl Raya, central Ubud. Two-storey art market selling sarongs, clothes and trinkets.
Wora Shop, Monkey Forest Road, central Ubud. Fabulous traditional *ikat* hangings from Sumba.

Paintings and carvings
Agung Rai Fine Art Gallery, Jl Peliatan, Peliatan. High-quality outlet for paintings of all types.
Arka Antiques Art, Monkey Forest Road, central Ubud. Massive collection of wooden masks.
Munut's Gallery, far eastern end of Jl Raya. Recommended dealer in paintings of all styles.
Neka Gallery, opposite the GPO on Jl Raya. Upmarket commercial art gallery.
Wayan Purna, Jl Hanoman, central Ubud. Picture frames carved to order on the premises.

Souvenirs and jewellery
La Bali, Jl Peliatan, Peliatan. Painted wooden pots and boxes from Lombok.
Percetakan Diary, Jl Raya, central Ubud. Handicrafts made from hand-made paper.
Seniwati Shop, Jl Raya, central Ubud. Reproductions of pictures from the Seniwati Gallery.
Suarti, Monkey Forest Road, central Ubud. Innovative modern jewellery.

Courses and workshops

You'll find plenty of opportunities to take **courses and workshops** in Ubud, even if you're only in the area for a few days. The Agung Rai Museum of Art (ARMA) organizes **children's workshops** in Balinese painting, music, dance and mask-carving. Workshops last from 9am to 3pm and cost US$25; call ☎0361/976659 for information.

Cookery and language
Casa Luna restaurant, Jl Raya. Balinese cooking workshops every Mon & Wed.
IALF language school (☎0361/221782). Occasional month-long Indonesian-language courses.
Kubu Maneco, Nyuhkuning. Informal Indonesian language lessons arranged to order.
Napi Orta restaurant, Monkey Forest Road. Balinese cooking courses every Tues, Thurs & Sat.
Oka Wati's restaurant, off Monkey Forest Road. Language lessons in Indonesian and Balinese.
Sua Bali, Kemenuh village. Residential Indonesian language and cookery courses.
Sukadana, Jl Jembawan. Classes and courses in Balinese and Indonesian language.

Meditation, yoga and alternative therapies
Meditation Shop, Monkey Forest Road. Regular meditation sessions and talks.
Ubud Sari Health Resort, Jl Kajeng, central Ubud (☎0361/974393). Yoga, t'ai chi and shiatsu.

Music, dance and crafts
Crackpot Batik, Monkey Forest Road. Design your own batik fabrics, paintings and T-shirts.
Ganesha Bookshop, across the road from the GPO on Jl Raya. Music workshops (Tues 6pm).
Nataraja Dance School, Jl Sugriwa 20, Padang Tegal. Informal dance and gamelan lessons.
Sai^2, Monkey Forest Road. DIY batik workshop.
Ubud Batik Centre, Jl Gautama, central Ubud. Design your own batik pictures and T-shirts.

Listings

Email and Internet access The most user-friendly email access is at Pondok Pekak Library and Resource Centre on the east side of the football field, off Jl Dewi Shinta (Mon–Sat 9am–9pm, Sun 9am–3pm). Other options include Kartika wartel opposite Tino Supermarket on Jl Raya, Roda Tourist Services at Jl Bisma 3, and *Trio Café* on Jl Andong in Petulu.

Exchange Numerous tour agents on Jl Raya and Monkey Forest Road offer exchange services at reasonable rates (daily 8am–6pm). Visa cash advance available Mon–Fri 8am–1pm from Bank Danamon on Jl Raya, central Ubud.

Hospitals and clinics For minor casualties, go to the Polyclinic just east of the football field on Jl Dewi Shinta, or to the Ubud Clinic in Campuhan (☎0361/974911). The nearest hospitals are in Denpasar (see p.476). The outdoor notice board at Ubud tourist office on Jl Raya lists the home addresses of local doctors and dentists.

Libraries The Pondok Pekak Library and Resource Centre on the east side of the football field, off Jl Dewi Shinta (Mon–Sat 9am–9pm, Sun 9am–3pm), stocks books about Bali, Asia travel guides and English-language novels. ARMA (see p.517) has the island's best library about Bali.

Pharmacies The two central Ubud branches of Ubud Farma on Jl Raya and Monkey Forest Road (daily 8am–9pm) are staffed by helpful English-speaking pharmacists.

Postal services Poste restante (Mon–Sat 8am–8pm, Sun & holidays 8am–noon) at the Ubud GPO on Jl Jembawan. The real-estate office Taking Care of Business on Jl Raya, central Ubud (fax 0361/975052), will receive faxes poste restante and you can send faxes from here too. You can also send and receive faxes at any of the above-listed email bureaus.

Swimming *Andong Inn* on Jl Tegalalang, open to non-guests for Rp3000 per person, and *Hotel Tjampuhan* in Campuhan, open to non-guests for Rp5000.

Telephone and fax The Kantor Telcom (with Home Direct public phone) is at the eastern end of Jl Raya; similar rates at the two branches of Nomad wartel, one on Jl Raya and the other on Monkey Forest Road (both daily 8am–11pm). Home Direct phones also outside the GPO on Jl Jembawan and in Ubud's central marketplace. Phone cards from the tourist office, the Kantor Telcom, and the moneychanger above Ubud Bookshop.

East of Ubud: Goa Gajah, Yeh Pulu and Pejeng

Slicing through the region immediately to the **east of Ubud**, the sacred Petanu and Pakrisan rivers flow down from the Batur crater rim in parallel, framing a narrow strip of land imbued with great spiritual and historical importance. This fifteen-kilometre-long sliver has been settled since the Bronze Age, around 300 BC, and now boasts the biggest concentration of antiquities on Bali.

Goa Gajah

Thought to be a former hermitage for eleventh-century Hindu priests, **Goa Gajah**, also known as the Elephant Cave (daily during daylight hours; Rp1100 plus Rp500 for compulsory sarong and sash), has now become a major tourist attraction, owing more to its proximity to the main Ubud–Gianyar road than to any remarkable atmosphere or ancient features. To get there, either walk or drive the 3km east from Ubud's Jalan Peliatan, or take an Ubud–Gianyar **bemo**, which go right past the entrance gate.

Descending the steep flight of steps from the back of the car park, you get a good view of the rectangular **bathing pool**, whose elegant sunken contours dominate the courtyard below. Local men and women would have bathed here in the segregated male (right-hand) and female (left-hand) sections before making offerings or prayers at the holy cave. In comparison, the hillside **cave** that overlooks it seems rather unexceptional, although the carvings around its entranceway are impressive. The **doorway** is in fact a huge gaping mouth, framed by the upper jaw of a monstrous rock-carved head that's thought to represent either the earth god Bhoma, or the widow-witch Rangda, or a hybrid of the two (early visitors thought it looked like an elephant's head, hence the cave's modern name). The T-shaped cave was hewn by hand from the rocky hillside to serve as meditation cells, or possibly living quarters, for priests or ascetics, and now contains a few Hindu statues.

Yeh Pulu

The rock-cut panels at **YEH PULU** (daily during daylight hours; Rp1100, plus Rp500 for sarong and sash) are delightfully engaging, and the site is almost invariably devoid of people. This is partly due to Yeh Pulu's relative inaccessibility: get off the Ubud–Gianyar bemo at the Yeh Pulu signs just east of Goa Gajah or west of the Bedulu crossroads, and then walk the kilometre south through the hamlet of **BATULUMBANG** to Yeh Pulu. If you are driving, follow the same signs to where the road peters out, a few hundred metres above the stonecarvings.

Chipped away from the sheer rock face, the 25-metre-long series of Yeh Pulu **carvings** are said to date back to the fourteenth or fifteenth century. They are thought to depict a five-part story and, while the meaning of this story has been lost, it's still possible to make out some recurring characters. One early scene shows a man carrying two jars of *tuak* (palm wine) suspended from a shoulder pole, and another series depicts three stages of a boar hunt.

Pejeng

PEJENG'S three main temples all lie within a few hundred metres of each other on the Bedulu–Tampaksiring Road. To get to them from Ubud, take a Gianyar-bound **bemo** to the Bedulu crossroads and then either wait for a Tampaksiring-bound one, or walk the kilometre to the temples. The alternative route from Ubud, preferably by motorbike, but feasible by bicycle or even on foot, is the fairly scenic five-kilometre **back** road that heads off east from the Jalan Raya/Jalan Peliatan T-junction at the eastern edge of Ubud. Although all the major temples are clearly signposted from the main Bedulu–Tampaksiring road, you might want to engage the help of a local **guide** for the more out-of-the-way sites; they usually hang out at **Pura Penataran Sasih** and charge Rp15,000–20,000 for a full day's tour of the area.

Pura Penataran Sasih

Balinese people believe **Pura Penataran Sasih** (Rp1100 donation requested during daylight hours; sarong and sash required) to be a particularly sacred temple, because this is the home of the so-called Moon of Pejeng – hence the English epithet, **Moon Temple**. The moon in question is a large **bronze gong**, shaped almost like an hourglass, suspended so high up in its special tower that you can hardly see the decorations scratched onto its surface. It probably dates from the Balinese Bronze Age, from some time during the third century BC, and at almost 2m long is thought to be the largest such kettledrum ever cast. Etched into its green patina are a chain of striking heart-shaped faces punctured by huge round eyes.

Legend tells how the gong was once the wheel of a chariot that transported the moon through the skies. The wheel shone just as brightly as the moon itself and, when it fell out of the sky and got stuck in a tree in Pejeng, a local thief became so incensed by its incriminating light that he tried to extinguish it by urinating over it. The wheel exploded, killing the thief, and then dropped to the ground. Ever since, the Balinese have treated the Moon of Pejeng as a sacred object.

Pura Pusering Jagat

Pura Pusering Jagat (Rp1100 donation; sarong and sash required), literally translated as the "Temple of the Navel of the World", stands 100m south down the main road from Pura Penataran Sasih. Its most interesting feature is a metre-high, elaborately carved vessel for storing holy water, said to date from the fourteenth century. The vessel's exterior is sculpted with a detailed relief thought to depict the Hindu myth "The Churning of the Sea of Milk", whereby the gods and the demons vie with each other to extract and distil the elixir of eternal life.

Pura Kebo Edan

The chief attraction at **Pura Kebo Edan** (Rp1100 donation), 200m south of Pura Pusering Jagat, is a massive lifelike phallus, attached to the huge stone statue of a man, nicknamed the **Pejeng Giant**. In fact, this giant, nearly 4m tall, is said to possess six penises in all; aside from the one swinging out for all to see, one is supposed to have dropped to the ground during his very vigorous dancing, and four more are said to be hidden inside him. His principal penis is pierced from front to back with a huge bolt-like pin, probably a realistic reference to an age-old Southeast Asian practice designed to increase women's sexual pleasure.

Museum Purbakala

As the main treasure house of such a historically significant region, the government-run archeological museum, **Museum Purbakala**, 500m south of Pura Penataran Sasih (Mon–Thurs 7am–2pm, Fri 7–11am, Sat 7am–12.30pm; entrance by donation), makes unsatisfactory viewing, mainly because the objects are poorly labelled. Its four tiny pavilions house a small, eclectic assortment of artefacts found in the Pejeng area, ranging from Paleolithic chopping tools to bronze bracelets and Chinese plates, but the most interesting exhibits are the dozen **sarcophagi** at the back of the museum compound. These massive coffins fashioned from two fitted sections of hollowed-out stone probably date back to around 300 BC and range in length from 1m to nearly 3m.

North of Ubud: routes to Gunung Batur

All three major roads north out of Ubud lead eventually to the towering Gunung Batur and its huge crater. Whether you go via **Payangan** to the west, **Tegalalang** directly to the north, or **Tampaksiring** to the east, the village and rice-field scenery along the way makes it a pleasant drive. Distances along these three routes are comparable, about 40km to Batur, but the most significant tourist sights are located along the most easterly route, around the Tampaksiring area. There's little of concrete interest on the westerly route, which takes you via Campuhan (see p.510) and Payangan. The most frequent and reliable **bemo** service running north from Ubud is the brown fleet that covers the central route via Tegalalang and Pujung, though there are frequent turquoise bemos along the first section of the westerly route, as far as Payangan, some of which continue to Kintamani. For the easterly route via Tampaksiring, you need to change bemos at the Bedulu crossroads.

Tegalalang, Pujung Kelod and Sebatu

The **central route** up to Gunung Batur begins at the eastern edge of Ubud, from the point where Jalan Raya intersects with Jalan Peliatan. Turning left (north) to pass through the village of Petulu (see p.518), the road passes through the woodcarving village of **TEGALALANG** after about 7km, a strip that's lined with carvings of brightly painted birds, fish and fruit trees, most of which are snapped up for export. The views get increasingly spectacular as you continue through Tegalalang, with Bali's greatest mountains looming majestically ahead: Gunung Batur (to the north) and Gunung Agung (to the east). The sculpted rice-fields round here are also particularly eyecatching, and there's a specially signposted roadside **viewpoint** just 3km out of Tegalalang.

The northern end of Tegalalang pretty much merges into southern **PUJUNG KELOD** which, like its neighbour, also thrives on the demand for woodcarvings. Pujung's speciality are *garudas*, fashioned in all sizes from ten-centimetre-high mantelpiece ornaments to massive two-metre giants. If you continue north along the main road for another 16km, you'll reach the Batur crater rim; alternatively, a right turn about 2km beyond Pujung Kelod takes you to Tampaksiring (for Tirta Empul and Gunung Kawi; see below) via the traditional-style **bathing pools** in the village of **SEBATU**, open to the public but rarely visited by tourists.

Tampaksiring

The most **easterly route** up to the mountains takes you along the Bedulu-Penelokan road, passing through Pejeng (see p.525), before reaching **TAMPAKSIRING**, 11km further on. A fairly nondescript town that's really only interesting to tourists as the access point for nearby **Tirta Empul** and **Gunung Kawi**, Tampaksiring is nonetheless well stocked with craft and souvenir shops. The Gianyar–Bedulu–Tampaksiring **bemos** terminate in the centre of the long settlement, but the bemo service between Tampaksiring and Penelokan on the Batur crater rim (about 20km to the north) is patchy and unreliable at best, so you might have to charter one, for which you can expect to pay about Rp6000.

Gunung Kawi

A few hundred metres north of Tampaksiring's bemo terminus, a sign points east off the main road to **Gunung Kawi** (daylight hours; Rp1100; sash compulsory), the site of a series of eleventh-century tombs hewn from the rock face. It's an impressive spot, completely enclosed in the lush valley of the sacred Sungai Pakrisan and rarely visited by tour groups. To reach it, walk past the souvenir stalls and down the steep flight of three hundred steps, through a massive rock-hewn archway, to the river.

There are lots of theories about the origins and function of the Gunung Kawi tombs or *candi*, the most likely being that they were erected as memorials to a king – possibly the eleventh-century Anak Wungsu – and his queens. Before crossing the river, turn sharp left for the **Queens' Tombs**, a series of four huge, square-tiered reliefs, chiselled from the riverside cliff face to resemble temple facades. Originally, the surface of these *candi* would have been decorated with plaster carvings, but now only the outlines of the false doors remain.

Crossing Sungai Pakrisan you enter the Gunung Kawi temple complex, which contains an unusual **cloister**, complete with courtyard, rooms and cells, entirely cut from the ravine rock wall. This was probably built for the holy men who looked after the five **Royal Tombs** at the back of the temple complex. The Royal Tombs are in better condition than the Queens' Tombs, and you can see the false doors and facades quite clearly defined.

Tirta Empul

Balinese from every corner of the island make pilgrimages to **Tirta Empul** (daily during daylight hours; Rp1100; sash compulsory), signposted off the main Tampaksiring–Kintamani road, about 500m north of the turn-off to Gunung Kawi. They come seeking to cleanse themselves spiritually and to cure their physical ailments by bathing in the **holy springs**, which have been considered the most sacred in Bali ever since the tenth century, if not longer. The shallow red-brick **bathing pools** are sunk into the ground of the outer courtyard of a temple, fed by water from the springs in the inner sanctuary. Men, women and priests each have their own segregated sections in which to immerse themselves, though most modern devotees just splash their faces and smile for the camera.

THE EAST

The east of Bali is dominated both physically and spiritually by the towering volcano **Gunung Agung**, and the **Besakih** temple complex high on its slopes. The landscape ranges from sweeping rice terraces, built on the fertile soil deposited by successive volcanic eruptions, to the dry, rocky expanses of the north coast and the far east.

Formerly divided into a multitude of **ancient Balinese kingdoms**, evidence of the ancient courts remains in the now sleepy town of **Gelgel**, the Taman Gili in **Klungkung**, the Puri Agung in **Amlapura** and the **Puri Gianyar**. These relics of past glory are now surrounded by busy administrative and market towns with traffic pouring past their walls.

Most visitors come to the east for the **coast** and the area offers some of the best diving and snorkelling in Bali, **Candi Dasa**, **Padang Bai**, **Tulamben** and **Amed** being the main centres. Off the south coast lie the three islands of **Nusa Lembongan**, **Nusa Ceningan** and **Nusa Penida** with its spellbinding cliffs; only Lembongan has a developed tourist trade.

Inland, Gunung Agung and Besakih are the major tourist draws, but there are other peaks and impressive **temples**, especially Pura Kehen in Bangli and Pura Pasar Agung above Selat, where you can guarantee to escape the crowds. For the culturally curious, **Tenganan**, close to Candi Dasa, is the most welcoming of the traditional Bali Aga villages on the island, home to descendants of the early inhabitants of Bali. Along with Gianyar, this is the place to head for if you are interested in **textiles**.

The east is easily accessible by public **transport** from Kuta and Ubud and it is possible to explore the area on day-trips (Ubud is only 13km from Gianyar). But this is a relaxed and relaxing part of the country, and the best way to enjoy it is to give it a bit of time. The ideal **bases** are Candi Dasa, Padang Bai (the port for the Lombok ferries) and the section of the far east coast between Culik and Selang, the fastest-developing area of the east; outside these spots **accommodation** options are more limited. However, the lack of facilities is amply compensated for by the opportunity to experience the slow pace of rural village Bali.

Gianyar and around

The most impressive feature of the **town** is the massive white **statue**, completed in 1994, on the main road into town from the west, which shows Arjuna in his three-horsed chariot along with his godly charioteer, Krishna. After this, the rest of Gianyar feels pretty low-key.

The town centres on the main road just west of the royal palace, **Puri Gianyar**, built in 1771 but destroyed by the 1917 earthquake and largely rebuilt. Still the home of the descendants of the Gianyar royal family, it is not open to the public. A short walk away on Jalan Barata, Gianyar's **market** is a large modern structure; the main market takes place every three days but there are always some stalls here.

Gianyar is well-known for the **endek weaving** (see p.550 for more on this) produced in the factories on the western outskirts of town, just over 1km from the centre. One of the most established is Cap Cili (daily 8am–5pm) on Jalan Ciung Wenara, which has fixed prices slightly higher than the other factories, but is a good starting point. Cap Togog (daily 8am–5pm), slightly further out from the centre, on Jalan Astina Utara, is another big concern. Both places cater largely for the tour-bus market and you can watch both the preparation of the thread and the actual weaving. *Endek* cloth starts at around Rp15,000 a metre, depending on the thread used, and there is a massive range of gifts on sale too, from clothes to souvenir purses and bags: prices are competitive compared with Kuta and Sanur. Imported batik is also on sale.

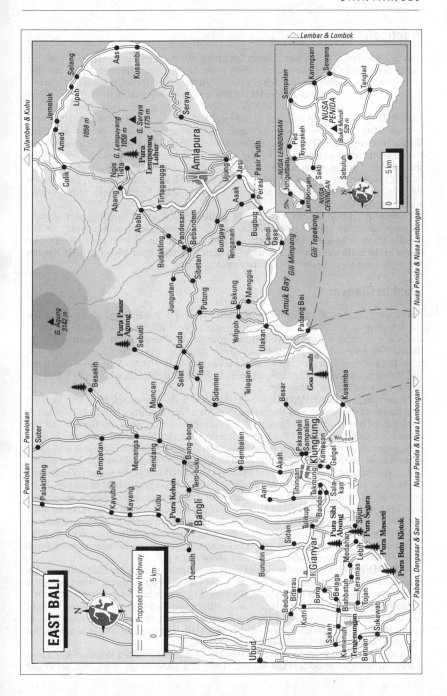

EAST BALI

N

0   5 km

= = Proposed new highway

△ Lembar & Lombok

NUSA PENIDA
Bukit Mundi
529 m

Sampalan
Karangsari
Sewana
Tanglad
Ped
Toyapakeh
Jungutbatu
Lembongan
Sakti
Sebuluh

NUSA LEMBONGAN
NUSA CENINGAN

N
0   5 km

△ Tulamben & Kubu

Aas
Kusambi
Selang
Lipah
Jemeluk
Amed
Culik
Abang
Ngis
Tista
Ababi
Budaking
Pandesari
Bebandem
Sibetan
Tirtagangga
Ujung
Jasi
Asak
Perasi
Pasir Putih
Bungaya
Tenganan
Bugbug
Candi Dasa
Seraya

AMLAPURA

1058 m
G. Lempuyang
1058 m
Pura Lempuyang Luhur
G. Seraya 1175 m

G. Agung
3142 m

Pura Pasar Agung

Besakih
Sebudi
Duda
Muncan
Selat
Iseh
Sidemen
Jungutan
Putung
Yehpoh
Bakung
Mangis
Ulakan
Telagan
Padang Bai
Amuk Bay
Gili Mimpang
Gili Tepekong

△ Penelokan   △ Penelokan

Suter
Palaktihing
Pempatan
Menanga
Rendang
Bang-bang
Tem-buku
Besar
Goa Lawah
Kusamba

Nusa Penida & Nusa Lembongan

Kayubihi
Kayang
Kubu
Pura Kehen
Bangli
Gembalan
Aan
Akah
Paksabali
Sampalan
Kamasan
Klungkung
Gelgel
Salakar
Yehunda

Sidan
Demulih
Bunutin
Titihan
Tujikup
Takmung
Banda

Nusa Penida & Nusa Lembongan

Bedulu
Biterau
Bona
Belaga
Blahbatuh
Keramas
Tojan
Sukawati
Pura Sibi Abung
Medahan
Lebih
Siyut
Pura Masceti
Pura Segara
Pura Batu Klotok

Gianyar

Kutri
Sakah
Kemenuh
Tengenungan
Batuan

Ubud

△ Paban, Denpasar & Sanur

Practicalities

Heading east **from Denpasar** (Batubulan terminal), most public transport follows the Sakah–Kemenuh–Blahbatuh–Kutri–Bitera route to Gianyar, although there are also local bemos from Blahbatuh which ply the alternative road through Bona and Jasri.

The Gianyar government **tourist office** at Jalan Ngurah Rai 21 (Mon–Thurs 7am–2pm, Fri 7–11am, Sat 7am–12.30pm; ☎0361/93401) is quite small, but does have English-language leaflets on some of the local attractions. The **wartel** just to the west is open 24hr. The most convenient banks in Gianyar to **change money** are Bank Rakyat Indonesia and BNI, both in the town centre. With Ubud so close at hand, there's no reason to stay overnight, especially as the **accommodation** options are nothing special, but if you get stranded you could try *Pondok Wisata*, Jalan Anom Sandat 10 (☎0361/942164; ③), in a side street off Jalan Ngurah Rai, or *Sari Gadung*, Jalan Dalem Rai 5 (no phone; ③), on the road along the east side of the football field, with rooms in a busy family compound.

Gianyar is rightly famous for its **babi guling** (spit-roasted suckling pig), a great Balinese speciality stuffed with chillies, rice, herbs and spices, served with rice and usually *lawar* (chopped meat, vegetables and coconut mixed with pig's blood). The shops in the main street are good places to sample it; try *Depot Melati* at Jalan Ngurah Rai 37, but get there before 2pm as they shut up early.

West of Gianyar

There are a number of interesting **villages** to the west and southwest of Gianyar, offering temples, crafts, dance performances and a waterfall. Four kilometres west of Gianyar, the small village of **KUTRI** is home to the **Pura Bukit Dharma Durga Kutri**. Well established on the tour-bus circuit, the most interesting feature is the statue of the goddess **Durga**; head up the staircase from the back of the inner courtyard and through a small forest of banyan trees to the top of the hill, where you'll find the statue shrouded in holy white cloths.

At the village of **BLAHBATUH**, 5km further south, the main road, lined with bamboo furniture workshops, meets an alternative road from Gianyar through Bona and Belaga. A few hundred metres along the Bona road, the splendid entrances of **Pura Gaduh** lead into a maze of linked courtyards. Of particular interest is a gigantic carved head with bulging eyes, supposedly the legendary **Kebo Iwa**, who is said to have created this and many other temples in the area. The village of **BONA** has a few small shops which are stuffed with a wide range of goods made from **bamboo** and the fronds of the **sugar palm**, including baskets, purses, lampshades and artificial flowers. Bona is also host to regular dance performances, and is a centre of the **trance** or **sanghyang** dances which are staged, together with the **kecak**, five times a week at 6.30pm (inquire at the tourist offices for days; Rp6000), but they are tourist rather than authentic performances. The two most famous trance dances, the *sanghyang dedari*, and the *sanghyang jaran*, sometimes known as the "Fire Dance" and performed on a carpet of coconut husk embers, are accompanied by an a cappella chorus (see pp.520–522 for more about dance).

At **KEMENUH**, 7km southwest of Gianyar, a signed road leads 2km off the main road to the **Tegenungan waterfall**, also known as **Srog Srogan**, which drops a sheer 30m into a pool where you can swim. For the more adventurous, there's a bungy-jumping operation (☎0361/758362), where you leap from a crane erected over the site. The moderately priced *Waterfall Restaurant*, at the end of the road, has an upper floor with a splendid view of the waterfall. There's one room available for overnight guests (☎0361/299265, fax 298437; ⑦).

Back on the main road, opposite the turning to the restaurant, a sideroad leads past a concentration of **woodcarving** shops. There is a good range of subject, style and

---

RANGDA

The image of the Queen of the Witches, **Rangda**, is everywhere in Bali. You will see her in dance-dramas and on masks, temple carvings, paintings and batiks. Although there is some variation in the way she is portrayed, several features are standard and all contribute to her grotesque appearance. She has a long mane of hair, with flames protruding from her head. Her face is fierce and hideous with bulging eyes, a gaping mouth, huge teeth or tusks and a long tongue often reaching to her knees. Her fingernails are long and curled, and she has enormous pendulous breasts. She wears a striped shirt and pants, with a white cloth around her waist, an important instrument of her evil magic.

Several versions of the Rangda story are enacted across the island, the most common being the **barong** and **calonarang** (see p.520 for more details of these dramas), but she always speaks in the ancient Javanese Kawi language and alternates between high whining tones, loud grunts and cackles. To the Balinese, Rangda represents the **forces of evil**, death and destruction, and she's often associated with the Hindu goddess Durga.

Rangda may have been based on a real woman, **Mahendratta**. Mahendratta was a princess from Java, who married the Balinese Prince Udayana and bore him a son, Erlangga, in 1001 AD. According to legend, the king later banished Mahendratta to the forest for practising witchcraft. When Udayana died, Mahendratta, now a *rangda* (widow), continued to build up grudges against her powerful and unrelenting son. Eventually, she used her powers to call down a **plague** upon Erlangga's kingdom, nearly destroying it. Erlangga, learning the source of the pestilence, dispatched a troop of soldiers who stabbed Rangda in the heart; she survived, however, and killed the soldiers. In desperation, the king sent for a holy man, **Empu Bharadah**, whose assistant stole Rangda's book of magic with which he was able to restore Rangda's victims to life, and eventually destroy the witch by turning her own magic on herself.

Even in performances of the story, the figure of Rangda is believed to have remarkable powers, and offerings are made and prayers said before each show to protect the actors from the evil forces they are invoking. Village performances of the drama are often a means of pacifying Rangda's anger so that she will not turn her destructive forces against them.

wood on show and, as much of the carving is done in sheds outside the shops, you can watch the work as well as tour the showrooms.

Three kilometres east of Kemenuh, at the junction of the road and bemo route north to Ubud, sits the small village of **SAKAH**, with its giant Buddha statue resembling a podgy baby in a nappy. There are a few woodcarving and art shops to pass the time in if you're waiting for a connection, but they're nothing out of the ordinary.

Bangli and around

Situated between Gianyar and the massive volcanic formations of the Batur area, **BANGLI** is set high enough in the hills to be cool; it's a spacious and peaceful market town with plenty to do for a for a day or two. It fits in well on any itinerary heading to or from Batur, but don't be fooled by its proximity to Besakih: there are no public bemos on the Bangli–Rendang road.

The Town

The main reason to visit Bangli is to see the much revered **Pura Kehen** (daily 8am–5pm; Rp1000, car Rp800), 1.5km north of the town. Rising up steeply from the road in **terraces** lined with religious statues, Pura Kehen is large and imposing – one of the gems among East Bali's temples. The fabulously carved and painted great entrance leads into the **outer courtyard** containing a massive banyan tree with a *kulkul* tower built among the branches. Also in the outer courtyard, a small compound, guarded by *naga* under a frangipani tree, contains a stone that is supposed to have glowed with fire when the site of the temple was decided. Steps lead up to the middle courtyard, from where you can look into the **inner courtyard**, with its eleven-roofed *meru*, dedicated to Siwa, and other shrines dedicated to mountain gods.

At the opposite end of town, the temple of the dead, **Pura Dalem Pengungekan**, has outside walls which depict the fate of souls in hell and heaven. The carvings are a riot of torches, pleading victims, flames and decapitated bodies. You'll also see plenty of images of the evil witch Rangda.

Practicalities

The turning to Bangli leaves the main Gianyar–Klungkung road 2km east of Gianyar. Blue public bemos wait at the junction, but if you are coming from the west you can also pick up a bemo in Gianyar, on Jalan Barata, just outside the market entrance. Buses plying between Denpasar (Batubulan terminal) and Singaraja (Penarukan terminal) pass directly through Bangli.

The Bangli government **tourist office** at Jalan Ngurah Rai 24 (Mon–Thurs 7am–2pm, Fri 7–11am, Sat 7am–12.30pm; ☎0366/91537), has a free brochure on the sights of the district. You can **change money** at Bank Rakyat Indonesia by the Trimurti statue. The **wartel**, just north of the tourist office, is open 24hr and the **post office** is at Jalan Kusumayudha 18. Bangli's **market** bursts into activity every three days.

There are several places **to stay** in town. The *Artha Sastra Inn*, Jalan Merdeka 5, is central, just opposite the bemo terminal (☎0366/91179; ③–⑥), and offers rooms in the courtyards of Puri Denpasar, the palace of the last rajah of Bangli. The more conventional *Bangli Inn*, at Jalan Rambutan 1 (☎0366/91419; ③–④), has a small restaurant, and all rooms have attached bathrooms. If you prefer to stay in a family compound, *Jaya Giri Homestay* is at Jalan Sriwijaya 6 (☎0366/92255; ②), almost opposite Pura Kehen, and *Catur Aduyana* is at the other end of town by the football field, at Jalan Lettulil 2 (☎0366/91244; ②).

During the day, the bus terminal has several stalls selling *es campur* and other **snacks** and, at night, the road beside the terminal turns into a small **night market** with the full range of sates, soups, rice and noodle dishes on offer.

Around Bangli

At **BUNUTIN**, 7km south of Bangli, **Pura Penataran Agung** (also known as Pura Langgar) is signed east off the main road. It's an attractive temple, set about 100m down the small track, overlooking a large, palm-shaded, water-lilied lake, with two small shrines built on artificial islands. The **red-brick shrine** with the two-tiered red roof is the main point of interest, having four unusual doors, one in each side. There is a local story of a seventeenth-century Hindu prince whose brother became very sick; when he went to ask advice from a traditional healer, a *dukun*, he was told about a Muslim ancestor, originally from Java, who had settled in the Bunutin area. Being told to build a temple to honour this man, the young prince designed one partly to incorporate Muslim principles, with four doorways corresponding to the directions of the four winds. The sick prince recovered, and the descendants of his family are said still to abstain from eating pork in honour of their ancestor.

Essential viewing for anyone interested in Balinese temples, the **Pura Dalem** at **SIDAN**, 3km further south from Bunutin, is just 1km north of the main

Gianyar–Klungkung road. This incredible temple of the dead drips with gruesome carvings and statues of the terrible Rangda squashing babies, while the *kulkul* tower graphically depicts the punishments that await evildoers in the afterlife, including having your head sawn off or boiled up in a vat. There are daily performances of the **barong** including the **kris** dance at 10am (Rp6000); see pp.520–522 for more on dance.

Klungkung and around

The capital of the district of the same name, **KLUNGKUNG** is a bustling trading town, with plenty of things to see both in the town and nearby. Its highlights are the remains of the royal palace, collectively known as the **Taman Gili**, which include the ancient **Kerta Gosa painted ceiling**. These murals are the only surviving examples of classical wayang painting *in situ* on the island. However, despite major restorations in the 1930s, 1960 and 1982, the pictures are decidedly grubby and the colours very faded. The centre of modern day classical-style painting is only a few kilometres south of town, at **Kamasan**, while **Museum Seni Lukis Klasik Bali**, to the west of Klungkung, just beyond Takmung, houses a collection of old classical-style paintings as well as modern works.

The Town

Klungkung centres on the crossroads, marked by the dramatic white *Kanda Pat Sari* statue which guards the four cardinal directions, beside the Taman Gili, with the Puputan Monument opposite, and the market tucked away just to the east, behind the main street.

The Taman Gili and Museum Daerah Semarapura

The **Taman Gili** (daily 7am–6pm; Rp2000), meaning "Island Gardens", has its entrance on Jalan Puputan. It is a landscaped area containing the only surviving part of the **Semarapura**, the palace of the Klungkung rulers, which was built around 1710 and largely destroyed by fighting in 1908. The Dutch attacked southern Bali in 1906, and by 1908 had subdued all the kingdoms except Klungkung and Bangli. When the Dutch set up their weapons outside the Semarapura palace in Klungkung on April 28, 1908, the *dewa agung* led two hundred members of his family and court in the traditional *puputan*. When he marched into the guns and was killed, six of his wives surrounded his body and stabbed themselves with their kris. The rest of those present were either shot down or killed themselves. The monument opposite the Taman Gili in Klungkung commemorates the *puputan*. One imposing remnant of the palace is a massive red-brick gateway, decorated with stone carvings, which marked the entrance from the outer to the inner courtyards of the palace. Legend claims that, at the time of the *puputan* in Klungkung in 1908, the wooden doors sealed themselves shut and nobody has been able to open them since.

Perched on one corner of the main crossroads, the **Kerta Gosa** (Consultation Pavilion for Peace and Prosperity) is a square open *bale* on a raised platform. It's likely the pavilion was where the king and his ministers met to debate law and other matters of importance. The **painted ceiling** is a unique example of the Kamasan style of classical painting, often referred to as the *wayang* style. There are **nine levels** of paintings, each with a specific theme or story. **Level one**, nearest the floor, shows scenes from the Tantri stories. These are an Indonesian version of the *Thousand and One Nights*, in which the girl, Tantri, weaves tales night after night. **Levels two and three** illustrate the Bhima Swarga story (part of the *Mahabharata* epic), and the suffering of souls in the afterlife as their sins are atoned for by various cruel punishments. You can be sawn in half for disobedience to your parents or have your intestines extracted through your anus for farting in public.

Level four shows the Sang Garuda, the story of the Garuda's search for *amerta*, the water of life, so that he can free his mother, Winita, and himself from eternal slavery to the thousand *naga*. **Level five** is the *palalindon*, predicting the effects of earthquakes on life and agriculture, while **levels six and seven** are a continuation of the Bhima Swarga story. **Level eight** is the Swarga Roh, which shows the rewards that the godly will receive in heaven. Unfortunately, this level is so far above your head that it's hard to see whether good behaviour is worth it. **Level nine**, the *lokapala*, right at the top of the ceiling where the four sides meet, shows a lotus surrounded by four doves symbolizing good luck, enlightenment and salvation.

The **Bale Kambung** (Floating Pavilion), almost beside the Kerta Gosa and surrounded by a moat, was the venue for royal tooth-filing ceremonies. Its ceiling is less famous than its neighbour's, but equally interesting. The six levels of paintings cover Balinese astrology, the tales of Pan Brayut (a legendary Balinese figure who produced scores of children) and, closest to the top, the adventures of Satusoma, who was a legendary Buddhist saint, adopted into a Hindu context. Satusoma's adventures consist of a series of battles and selfless acts through which he defeats evil and brings peace to the world.

The **Museum Daerah Semarapura** in the Taman Gili grounds, is worth a quick look. It contains a motley collection including kris, textiles, an old palanquin used by the royal family, and stones from the ancient monuments of Gelgel.

Practicalities

The main **bus and bemo terminal**, Terminal Kelod, is a fair distance south of the town centre; most public transport stops here. In addition, there is a small terminal just north of the main crossroads, slightly hidden away off Jalan Gunung Rinjani, where you can pick up bemos for Rendang and Besakih, which don't stop at Kelod. On several bemo routes, most notably from Padang Bai, the name "Semarapura" is used instead of "Klungkung".

The Klungkung government **tourist office** is in the same building as the Museum Daerah Semarapura (Mon–Thurs 7am–2pm, Fri 7am–noon, Sat 7am–12.30pm; ☎0366/21448), and produces a small brochure on the sights of the town. Across the road from the Kerta Gosa, the **wartel** is open 24 hours, the **post office** is just west of the museum on Jalan Untung Surapati, and there are several banks along Jalan Diponegoro to the east of the main crossroads that **change money**, including Bank Rakyat Indonesia and the Bank of Central Asia.

Most people prefer to stay in Candi Dasa and visit Klungkung as a day-trip. However, if you do want to stay, the best **accommodation** is at the *Loji Hotel*, in the eastern part of the town (☎0366/21044; ③), which has adequate rooms in a pleasant garden. Alternatively, the *Cahaya Pusaka* (☎0366/22118; ②–③) is slightly closer to the centre of town, on the opposite side of the road. Both are noisy as they are close to the main road.

Klungkung has a few reasonable, inexpensive places **to eat** and **drink**, with menus in English: the *Bali Indah*, Jalan Nakula 1, the *Sumba Rasa* on the same street, at no. 5, and the *RM Sederhana*, Jalan Gunung Rinjani 13.

Around Klungkung

There are several places worth a **trip out from Klungkung**, especially if you are on the classical-painting trail. With the exception of the beautiful black-sand beach at Siyut, all are accessible by public transport.

Museum Seni Lukis Klasik Bali

Five kilometres west of Klungkung, just beyond the village of Takmung, on the main road to Gianyar, the spacious and modern art gallery, **Museum Seni Lukis Klasik Bali** (Tues–Sun 9am–5pm; Rp5000) is a must for anyone with an interest in Balinese arts. Take any westbound bemo and get out when you see the massive Trimurti statue with mock policemen at the base. The museum contains a vast collection of historical objects and traditional art, including painting, embroidery, stone sculptures, masks and ancient doors. The top floor is a total contrast, dedicated to the works of **Nyoman Gunarsa**, the founder of the museum. Born in nearby Banda village, he is one of the foremost modern Balinese painters.

Kamasan

South of Klungkung, 500m beyond the Kelod bemo terminal, is the turning to **KAMASAN**, a tiny village packed with artists' houses, studios and small shops, and renowned on Bali as the historical and present-day centre of **classical wayang-style painting** (see p.514). This style traditionally depicts religious subjects, astrological charts and calendars, and you'll be struck immediately by the uniform colours used: muted reds, ochres, blues, greens and blacks. Many of the artists here work in family concerns, where one member of the family sketches out the work, and others make and mix the colours and fill in the outlines.

After visiting a few workshops it is surprisingly easy to pick out the better-drawn, more carefully coloured pictures. While the artists obviously want to make sales, the atmosphere is pleasant and relaxed, although be certain that you shop around and bargain hard. **I Nyoman Mandra** and **I Nyoman Tresna** are worth seeking out, and **Ni Made Suciarmi** is one of very few **female artists** working in Kamasan in what is very much a male preserve; many women mix colours and fill in the outlines, but she does the drawing too. Her work is represented in the Seniwati Gallery of Art by Women in Ubud (see p.510).

Gelgel and beyond

The ancient court centre of **GELGEL**, 4km south of Klungkung, is a village of wide streets crammed full of temples. Today it's a quiet little place with nothing but its history to offer visitors, and large numbers of its ancient stones have, in fact, been removed to museums. **Pura Dasar** on the main street is the highlight, with massive courtyards, *bale* and nine-roofed and eleven-roofed *meru* in the inner courtyard. Each year this temple is the site of the **Pewintenan ceremony**, held on the fourth full moon of the Balinese calendar (check the *Calendar of Events* produced by the tourist office for exact dates), which attracts pilgrims from all over Bali. The purpose of the ceremony is to cleanse and purify those ready to become *pemangku* (village priests).

Siyut

One of the most picturesque stretches of the south coast is at **SIYUT**, 15km from Klungkung. The beach is pure black and the bay stretches in a wide sweep for several kilometres, with the rice terraces inland forming a fabulous foreground to the bulk of Gunung Agung.

It's a good place to spend a day on the beach, but you'll need your own transport. To get to Siyut, head for Tulikup on the main Gianyar–Klungkung road and take the road that heads south just east of the football field. After a few hundred metres, turn left at the crossroads in the village centre and follow the road round to the coast (5km).

Besakih and Gunung Agung

The major tourist draw in the east of Bali, with around a quarter of a million tourists a year, is undoubtedly the **Besakih** temple complex, the most venerated site in Bali, situated on the slopes of **Gunung Agung**, the holiest and highest mountain on the island. Bus tours start arriving around 10.30am, after which the sheer volume of tourists, traders and self-styled guides make the place pretty unbearable – it's well worth coming early in the morning to get the best of the atmosphere. Besakih is the yardstick by which to measure all Balinese temples and, even if you have no special interest in them, the stark grandeur of the place will make a lasting impression.

Besakih

The **Besakih complex** (daily 8am–5pm; Rp1500, car Rp2300) consists of 22 separate **temples**, each with its own name, spread over a site stretching for more than 3km. The central temple, the largest on the island, is Pura Penataran Agung, with the other temples ranged at varying distances around it. There are many unofficial "guides" hanging around Besakih, adept at attaching themselves to tourists and then demanding large sums in payment for their services; be wary and always establish the fee beforehand.

Unless you are praying or making offerings, you are **forbidden to enter** any of the temples in the complex. However, a lot is visible through the gateways and over walls. A sarong and scarf are not strictly necessary, but you will need them if you are in skimpy clothing – sarong rental is available with negotiable prices from Rp1000 to Rp2000, but it's much easier to take your own.

To get the best out of Besakih, it's a good idea to see **Pura Penataran Agung**, the most important temple, first and then wander at will; most of the tourist crowds tend to stick to the immediate area around the central temple. The *meru* of **Pura Batu Madeg**, rising among the trees in the north of the complex, are particularly enticing, while, if you feel like a longer walk, **Pura Pengubengan**, the most far-flung of the temples, is a good couple of kilometres through the forest.

Pura Penataran Agung

The Great Temple of State or **Pura Penataran Agung** is the central and most dramatic temple in the complex, although its drama lies in size, position and the great reverence in which it is held, rather than in intricate carving.

The temple is built on seven **ascending terraces**, and altogether there are more than fifty structures including *bale*, shrines and stone thrones inside; about half are dedicated to specific gods, while the others have various ceremonial functions such as receiving offerings, providing seating for the priests or the gamelan orchestra, or as residences for the gods during temple festivals.

A giant stairway, lined by seven levels of **carved figures**, leads to the small first courtyard; the figures to the left are from the *Mahabharata* and the ones to the right from the *Ramayana*. You can look into the courtyard, although views are obstructed by the *bale* just inside the gate. This pavilion is in two parts, with a small walkway between. As worshippers process through here they symbolically sever their connection with the everyday world, praying at the *bale ongkara* before proceeding into the second courtyard – the most important in the temple. The courtyards ascend consecutively in terraces, but visitors can go no further than the top of the main stairway.

A path skirts the entire perimeter wall of Pura Penataran Agung and you can see most of the temple's terraces from it. If you're hoping to see religious ceremonies, the second courtyard is the one to watch. (The best views are from the west side.) It's the largest courtyard in the temple and contains the *padmatiga*, the three-seated lotus throne dedicated to Brahma, Siva and Vishnu, where all pilgrims pray.

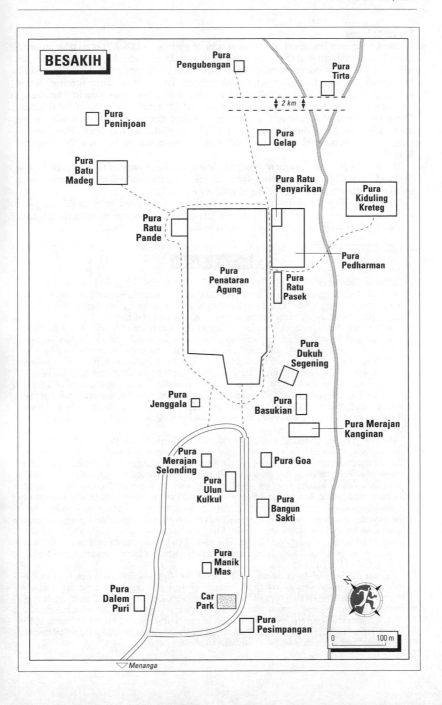

Practicalities

Without your own transport, the easiest way of getting to Besakih is to take an organized **bus tour** from one of the big resorts. If you do this, check how much time you
will have to look around; anything less than an hour is hardly worth it. By **public
transport**, you have to approach from Klungkung. Bemos leave from Terminal Kelod
in Klungkung, and from the small terminal just north of the main road in Klungkung,
although you may have to change at Rendang or Menanga, the turn-off for Besakih.
There are plenty of bemos in the morning but they dry up in both directions in the
afternoon, and after about 2pm or 3pm you'll have trouble getting back. There are no
public bemos beyond Menanga to Penelokan further north, or between Rendang and
Bangli.

The Karangasem government tourist office is on the corner of the car park beside
the road at Besakih (daily 8.30am–4pm). In the car park you will also find a wartel, a
small post office and a moneychanger with very poor rates.

If you're looking for **souvenirs**, the shops that line the road up from the car park,
and the enormous number of stalls dotted throughout the complex, offer the greatest
range of goods you'll see in one place outside Kuta, Sanur or Ubud.

1963

The year **1963** is recalled in Bali as a time of disaster, in which the gods were displeased
and took their revenge. Ancient texts prescribe that an immense ceremony, **Eka Dasa
Rudra**, the greatest ritual in Balinese Hinduism, should be held every hundred years for
the spiritual purification of the island and to bring future good fortune.

In the early 1960s, religious leaders believed that the trials of World War II and the
ensuing fight for Independence were indicators that the ritual was once again needed,
and these beliefs were confirmed by a plague of rats that overran the entire island in
1962. The climax of the festival was set for March 8, 1963, but on February 18, **Gunung
Agung**, which had been dormant for centuries, started rumbling; fire became visible
within the crater and ash began to coat the area. Initially, this was interpreted as a good
omen sent by the gods to purify Besakih, but soon doubts crept in. Some argued that the
wrong date had been chosen for the event and wanted to call it off. However, by this time
it was too late to cancel; President Sukarno was due to attend, together with an international conference of travel representatives.

By March 8, black smoke, rocks and ash were billowing from the mountain, but the
ceremony went ahead, albeit in a decidedly tense atmosphere. Eventually, on March 17,
the mountain erupted with such force that the top 100m of Agung was ripped apart. The
whole of eastern Bali was threatened by the poisonous **gas** and molten **lava** that poured
from the volcano, villages were engulfed, and between 1000 and 2000 people are thought
to have died, while the homes of another 100,000 were destroyed. In the district of
Klungkung alone, twenty percent of the arable land was destroyed. **Roads** were
destroyed, towns were isolated for weeks and the ash ruined crops, causing serious food
shortages for many months afterwards. The lava tracks are still clearly visible on the
north coast around Tianyar and Kubu. The east of Bali took many years to recover and
hundreds of homeless people joined Indonesia's transmigration programme (see p.953)
and moved to the outer islands.

Despite the force of the eruption and the position of the **Besakih complex** high on the
mountain slopes, a surprisingly small amount of damage occurred within the temples
themselves, and the closing rites of Eka Dasa Rudra took place in Pura Penataran Agung
on April 20. Subsequently, many Balinese felt that the mountain's eruption, at the time of
such a momentous ceremony, was an omen of the civil strife that engulfed Bali in 1965
(see p.468). In 1979, the year actually specified by the ancient texts, Eka Dasa Rudra was
held again and this time passed off without incident.

Accommodation options near Besakih are very limited. The *Lembah Arca* hotel (☎0366/23076; ④–⑤), on the road between Menanga and Besakih, a couple of kilometres before the temple complex, has an attractive garden, but the rooms are fairly basic and get chilly at night; the price includes breakfast and blankets. There are also a few unauthorized and unsigned lodgings (②–④) behind the shops and stalls lining the road from the car park up to the temple; ask at the tourist office for details. These places are very simple, with few private bathrooms, but are useful if you're climbing Gunung Agung or want to explore the site early or late.

There are several **restaurants** in the area catering for the tour-bus trade, though you'll find more reasonably priced food at the *Lembah Arca* (see above) and the *Taman Tirta* opposite, and at the *Rumah Makan Mawar* in Menanga, just on the left as you turn off to Besakih.

Gunung Agung

According to legend, **Gunung Agung** was created by the god Pasupati when he split Mount Mahmeru (the centre of the Hindu universe), forming both Gunung Agung and Gunung Batur. At 3014m, the superb conical-shaped Agung is the highest Balinese peak and is an awe-inspiring sight. The spiritual centre of the Balinese universe, it is believed that the spirits of the ancestors of the Balinese people dwell on Gunung Agung. Villages and house compounds are laid out in relation to the mountain, and many Balinese people prefer to sleep with their heads towards it. Directions on Bali are always given with reference to Agung, *kaja* meaning "towards the mountain" and *kelod* meaning "away from the mountain".

Climbing the mountain

If you want to climb Gunung Agung, there are two routes, both involving a long hard climb. One path leaves from **Besakih** and the other from **Pura Pasar Agung** over on the southern slope of the mountain, near Selat (see p.555). This is an extremely **sacred peak** to the Balinese and, while it is not possible to climb the mountain at certain times of the year because of the **weather**, it is also not permitted at many other times because of **religious festivals**. March and April are generally impossible from the Besakih side because of ceremonies. You will have to make offerings at temples at the start and on the way. Weather wise, the dry season (April to mid-October) is the best time to climb Gunung Agung; don't even contemplate it during January and February, the wettest months. At other times during the rainy season you may get a few dry days, but bear in mind that the weather up on the mountain can be very different from what it is on the beach.

Whichever side you climb from, you will need to set out very early in the morning if you want to be at the top to see the spectacular **sunrise** around 7am. It is essential to take a **guide** with you as the lower slopes are densely forested and it's easy to get lost. You will need to wear strong footwear, take a good torch, water and snacks to keep you going and, for the descent, a stout stick can be very handy.

From Pura Pasar Agung, it's at least a three-hour climb with an ascent of 1500m, so you'll need to set out at 3am or earlier, depending on how fit you are. This path does not go to the actual summit, but to another point on the rim which is about 100m lower. From this point you will be able to see Rinjani, the south of Bali and Gunung Batukau and look down into the 500-metre-deep crater.

From Besakih, the climb is longer, taking five to six hours, and you'll need to leave between midnight and 2am. This path starts from Pura Pengubengan, the most distant of the temples in the Besakih complex, and takes you up to the summit of Agung with views in all directions. The descent is particularly taxing from this side, too; allow four to five hours to get down.

Practicalities

There are only a few established **guiding operations** to the south of the mountain, although new ones are appearing all the time. If you want to climb **from Pura Pasar Agung**, there are guides at both **Muncan**, 4km east of Rendang, and at **Tirtagangga**, 5km north of Amlapura. (See p.556 for more on the road east of Rendang.)

I Ketut Uriada, a part-time teacher and guide, has a small shop in Muncan, where you can contact him directly. You will need to provide your own transport between Muncan and Pura Pasar Agung, although Ketut may be able to arrange a bemo charter (about Rp50,000 return trip). He can also provide accommodation (②–③) for a couple of people at a time at his house or can fix you up at the *Puri Agung Cottages* (☎0366/23037; ④–⑤) in Selat, 4km east of Muncan on the Amlapura road. Expect to pay around Rp40,000 for a guide for one person, Rp60,000 for two, Rp75,000 for three or Rp80,000 for four. You'll also need to make a contribution to the temple if you visit. Larger groups may need more than one guide and you will be expected to provide food for them.

Nyoman Budiarsa at Tirtagangga arranges transport and food from his small shop, on the right as you head north through the town. He quotes his prices in dollars, charging between US$25 and US$35 per person, depending on how many are in your party.

From Besakih, guides can be arranged at the **tourist office** and they can also help with nearby lodgings. Rp80,000 per person is a fair price from this side.

Nusa Lembongan, Nusa Ceningan and Nusa Penida

To the southeast of Bali, across the treacherous Badung Strait, the islands of Nusa Lembongan, Nusa Ceningan and Nusa Penida loom out of the ocean swell.

The nearest to the mainland and the most accessible is **Nusa Lembongan**, circled by a mixture of pure white-sand **beaches** and mangrove swamps. Seaweed farming is the major occupation, while the tourist facilities in Jungutbatu, catering for visiting **surfers**, provide the island's other main source of income. Only a few hundred metres separates Nusa Lembongan from tiny **Nusa Ceningan**, which is essentially a hill sticking out of the sea. Beyond Nusa Ceningan sits **Nusa Penida**, roughly 20km long, dominated by a high, limestone plateau with a harsh, dry landscape reminiscent of the Bukit, the far southern tip of the mainland. The island is crisscrossed by kilometres of small lanes ripe for exploring, and its south coast has some of the most spectacular scenery in Bali.

Nusa Lembongan and Nusa Ceningan

A small island, 4km long and less than 3km at its widest part, **Nusa Lembongan** is sheltered by offshore coral reefs which provide excellent snorkelling and create the perfect conditions for seaweed farming. You can walk around the island in about three hours. There are cycles for rent at Perama and the shop next to *Ketut Bungalows* (where they also have boogie boards), in Jungutbatu, but the roads are really too rough. All the accommodation is in **Jungutbatu** on the west coast and in **Mushroom Bay** (Tanjung Sanghyang) to the southwest of this, informally named after the mushroom coral in the offshore reef. Development is also under way at Celagi Empat Bay, located between these two spots. Most places have their own restaurants serving the usual Indo-Chinese options and travellers' fare. There is no post office, bank or telephone office on the island and electricity is currently produced by individual guesthouse generators, which close down around 10.30pm. The Perama office is situated

GETTING TO THE ISLANDS

Kusamba to Toyapakeh and Sampalan on Nusa Penida and Jungutbatu on Nusa Lembongan (Rp5000; 2–3hr). No fixed times; boats leave when full, but most islanders go to the mainland early in the morning and return early in the afternoon. A charter is approximately Rp50,000 one way.

Padang Bai to Sampalan on Nusa Penida (Rp4000; 1hr 30min). No fixed times, boats leave when full, starting around 7am.

Sanur to Jungutbatu on Nusa Lembongan (2 daily; 1hr 30min). Boats leave at 8am (Rp15,000) and 10am (Rp25,000), returning at 7am (Rp16,500). Buy your tickets from the ticket office near the *Ananda Hotel* beachfront in Sanur and for the return trip from the beachfront office in Jungutbatu.

If you prefer a tourist shuttle, Perama offers boats twice daily in each direction for Rp17,500; leaving at 9am and 3pm from Nusa Lembongan, and 10.30am and 4.30pm from Sanur. You need to book the day before you want to travel.

Luxury trips

Sold by tour operators in every major mainland resort; expect to pay US$80–95 for a day-cruise including lunch.

Bali Hai (☎0361/720331, fax 720334). Day-cruise to Lembongan plus a sunset dinner option.

Island Explorer (☎0361/289856, fax 289837). One-day trip to Lembongan (including a cheaper budget option) plus combined trips to Lembongan and Nusa Penida.

Nusa Lembongan Express (☎0361/724545). Slightly more economical day-trips to Lembongan.

Quicksilver (☎0361/771997, fax 771967). Day-cruise to Nusa Penida, including snorkelling off a floating pontoon and the option of a village visit.

Waka Louka (☎0361/723629, fax 722077). Day-cruise to Lembongan; longer trips also available with accommodation at Mushroom Bay.

between *Pondok Baruna* and *Nusa Indah* bungalows and also serves as the tourist information service. You can book tickets here to all the main tourist destinations on Bali and Lombok and onwards to Sumbawa. The **surf breaks** are all accessible from Jungutbatu and you can charter boats to take you to the less reachable **snorkelling** spots (ask at your losmen); one of the best is off Mushroom Bay with others at Mangrove Corner (also known as Jet Point), to the north, and Sunfish nearby. Boats will also take you to Nusa Penida where Gamat, off the coast near Sakti, and the reef off the coast at Ped are popular. Prices, which include equipment, depend on distance, and for one to two hours start at Rp7500 per person. Chartering a boat for the day costs around Rp60,000.

Jungutbatu

Spread out along the coast for well over 1km, the attractive village of **JUNGUTBATU** is a low-key place, with several losmen and a few shops selling textiles and crafts.

Most of the available **accommodation** is in simple two-storey buildings with attached bathrooms, upstairs verandahs and restaurants right by the beach. Room prices on Lembongan depend almost totally on demand. Rooms at the front with sea views are more expensive than those behind, and upstairs rooms are pricier than downstairs. The places at the north end of the beach are grouped close together, spreading out the further south you go.

ACCOMMODATION

Agung. Cheap rooms with shared, separate bathrooms in a concrete row and better rooms with fans and private bathrooms. There's a restaurant right on the beach – a great place to sit and watch the surfers – with a limited but good-value menu and videos in the evening. ②–③.

Pondok Baruna. A few hundred metres south of the main accommodation area, this small, quiet place has basic rooms looking straight onto the beach. ③.

Bungalow No. 7. At the far southern end of the beach, actually in the village, with an attractive garden and well-furnished rooms with fans. ②–④.

Mainski Inn (mobile ☎0811/394426). The liveliest and one of the biggest places, offering hot water in the more expensive rooms. It has a two-storey restaurant with an excellent range of food, including nachos, crêpes and spring rolls, and there are video shows in the evenings. The notice board downstairs offers information about the island tours of Lembongan and Nusa Penida, as well as surf safaris to Sumbawa for US$450 per person for a week. ③–⑤.

Nusa Lembongan Bungalows. Very quiet, with no restaurant, and accommodation in two-storey bamboo and thatch buildings set in a spacious compound. ③–④.

Puri Nusa (☎ & fax 0361/298613). The furthest north and one of the smartest places with new concrete-and-tile bungalows. ③–⑤.

Tarci. Next door to *Puri Nusa*, with a wide range of options, from simple rooms to attractively furnished ones with good views. ③–⑤.

Mushroom Bay

Just a few kilometres southwest of Jungutbatu, the fabulous white-sand cove of Mushroom Bay has long been a favourite snorkelling spot but has now developed facilities for visitors who want to stay longer. It's a great place, although don't expect peace once the day-trippers arrive from the mainland. *Waka Nusa Resort* (⑨) provides bed and breakfast in luxury brick-and-thatch bungalows, which can be arranged through Waka Louka luxury trips (see box on p.541). Less expensive options include *Bungalows Tanjung Sanghyang* (④–⑤), with good-quality bungalows in a brilliant location on a slight rise at the northern end of the cove, and, a couple of hundred metres inland on the Lembongan road, *Bungalows Panca Dana* (③) with cheaper, adequate rooms, but you'll need to walk to the beach. The nearby *Warung Adi* has economical Indonesian food and a variety of drinks.

To get to Mushroom Bay from Jungutbatu, either charter a boat (expect to pay Rp3000–5000 per person) or else it's an hour's hot walk. Take the first turning to the right as you enter Lembongan village on the walk over the hill from Jungutbatu; it's 1km from the turning to the cove.

Around the island

Three kilometres south of Jungutbatu, the largest town on the island, **LEMBONGAN**, is a crisscross of streets and alleyways and much busier than Jungutbatu.

The road descends through Lembongan to the coast, and the view across the shallows to **Nusa Ceningan** is lovely; the crystal-clear water over white sand is almost completely filled with frames for seaweed farming. A bridge leads across the channel, although there's little to see on the other side. The island road turns north at the coast, and mangroves begin to appear as the channel between the two islands gradually narrows, its closest point marked by two facing temples. Four kilometres of track wind their way up to the north of the island. You'll see **salt-makers' huts** here (see box opposite), and some production still continues on the island, although this has been largely replaced by more lucrative seaweed farming.

Pura Empuaji marks the northernmost point of Nusa Lembongan, beautifully situated above the mangroves with Nusa Penida rising up behind. As you leave the temple, take the right-hand turn and it's 2km back to Jungutbatu.

Nusa Penida

Tell a Balinese person you're heading to **Nusa Penida** and you won't get a positive reaction. The island is renowned as the home of the legendary evil figure of **I Macaling**, and was also formerly a place of banishment for the kingdom of Klungkung. It's still regarded as a place of evil spirits and ill-fortune, and many Balinese make the pilgrimage to the island expressly to ward off bad luck by making offerings at **Pura Dalem Penataran Ped**, home of the dreaded I Macaling.

Nusa Penida is too dry for rice cultivation and, while you'll see maize, cassava, beans and tobacco in the fields during the rainy season, there's nothing at all in the dry season. The island can only sustain a small population and many have already left as part of the government's transmigration programme (see p.953), although road improvements and construction are taking place and more development is rumoured.

As yet there are no dive operations based on Nusa Penida, but the operators on the mainland offer trips to the island's north and west coasts. There are plenty of sites, hosting enormously varied fish life, with reef sharks especially common, as well as manta rays and the occasional oceanic sunfish. For snorkelling, the site known as Gamat off the coast near Sakti, and the reef off the coast from Ped, are popular. However, the sea can be cold and difficult here, with currents over four knots, so take care.

Sampalan

SAMPALAN is the largest town on the island, with a shady street of shops, a bemo terminal, a market and the only post office, hospital and telephone office on the island. The town is spread out along the beach, and its highlight, the **Pura Dalem**, close to the cemetery near the football field, has a six-metre-tall gateway adorned with five leering Bhoma and a pendulous-breasted Rangda.

There are several **warung** in the main street, serving rice and noodles, and there is **accommodation** at *Losmen Made* (②–③). It's the white-and-red building opposite the bank in Jalan Segara, 100m west of the bemo terminal, and is small and friendly, but not that peaceful, as boats to the mainland leave from the beach at the end of the road and the loading of oil drums begins early in the morning.

Toyapakeh

Nine kilometres from Sampalan, on the northeast coast of the island, the fishing town of **TOYAPAKEH** is separated from Nusa Ceningan by a channel less than 1km wide,

---

SEAWEED FARMING

Seaweed is the source of two lucrative substances: **agar**, a vegetable gel used in cooking, and **carrageenan** used in cosmetics and foodstuffs. Seaweed grows best in areas protected by a reef so it does not get battered by strong currents but has a flow of water through it. The temperature must not get too high, the salinity needs to be constant, and at low tide the seaweed must remain covered by water. To "farm" seaweed, a simple bamboo frame is made with lengths of twine tied across it. Farmers tie small pieces of seaweed to the twine, harvesting the long offshoots every two weeks. The seaweed is then dried (8kg of wet seaweed reduce to 1kg when dry) and compressed into bales.

Areas of Nusa Penida, Nusa Lembongan and Nusa Ceningan, the Geger beach in South Bali and some areas of Lombok are big producers of seaweed, both green *kotoni* and red *pinusun* varieties. Seaweed farmers earn a good wage, around Rp200,000 a month, which compares very favourably with the Rp50,000 a month that traditional salt producers can expect to make.

but over 100m deep in places. With its lovely white **beach** and peaceful atmosphere, it's the best place to stay on Nusa Penida. There's a small daily **market** and a tiny **mosque** serving the town's Muslim population. The town's only **accommodation** is at *Losmen Tenang* (②), which has four clean rooms with attached bathrooms right next to the beach and also serves simple meals.

Pura Dalem Penataran Ped

Pura Dalem Penataran Ped, dedicated to **Jero Gede Macaling** and built from volcanic sandstone and local limestone, lies 5km east of Toyapakeh on the Sampalan road. There are few statues or intricate carvings, but the size of the courtyards and the grand entrances are impressive, emphasizing the prestige of the temple, which many regard as one of the most important in Bali. Jero Gede Macaling, also known as **I Macaling**, is feared throughout Bali. He is believed to be responsible for disease and floods, which he brings across to the mainland from Nusa Penida, landing at Lebih, south of Gianyar. The *odalan* festival here is extremely well attended by pilgrims hoping to stave off sickness and ill-fortune; every three years a larger *usaba* festival draws enormous crowds.

Around the island

The only way to see Nusa Penida is by motorcycle (ask at your guest house), although you shouldn't drive unless you are confident on very steep terrain. The island is a maze of country lanes, and signposts are few, so make sure you start early and have plenty of fuel. A full circuit is only about 70km but, allowing time to visit the major attractions, it takes most of one day. The road between Toyapakeh and Sampalan is the busiest on the island and roughly follows the coast; traffic around the rest of the island is much lighter.

Sights worth aiming for include the limestone cave of **Goa Karangsari** (Rp100), 10km south of Sampalan. The tiny entrance is about 100m above the road and opens up into an impressive cavern, which emerges after 300m onto a ledge with fine views looking out across a mango grove, surrounded by hills on all sides.

However, the real highlights are at **SEBULUH**. From the end of the road a couple of hundred metres beyond the village green, a path leads to the left between high stone walls and heads out to the coast, a walk of about 45 minutes. There are numerous paths through the outskirts of the village to the cliffs and you may be lucky enough to find a guide to take you through them, although they rarely see visitors here. The coast here is similar to the coastline at the south end of the Bukit, with dramatic limestone cliffs rising sheer out of the ocean for hundreds of metres and views that are utterly spellbinding. There are also two **temples** – one out on a promontory linked to the mainland by an exposed ridge, and the other, somewhat amazingly, sited at the bottom of an extremely narrow, incredibly exposed path that winds down the face of the cliff to a fresh-water spring at the bottom.

Candi Dasa and the coast

At the eastern end of Amuk Bay, **CANDI DASA** is a centre for snorkelling and diving, and a pleasant base from which to explore the east of Bali. Tourism began to develop at the end of the 1970s and Candi's transformation from fishing village into holiday resort is now complete, although some fishing boats remain to catch fish for the restaurants. However, throughout the 1980s, Candi's offshore reef was crushed to produce lime for cement for the building boom. The beach was left so exposed that it simply washed away. Large sea walls now protect the land, and enormous jetties protrude into the sea in the hope, largely justified, that the beach will build up against them.

The tourist developments have spread west around the bay, through the villages of **Senkidu, Buitan** and **Manggis**, where the beach is still a respectable size. Further west, just around the headland, the tiny cove of **Padang Bai** is home to the bustling access port for Lombok, and also has a small tourist infrastructure.

The entire coastal area is well served by **public transport**, both by the long-distance Denpasar (Batubulan terminal)–Amlapura buses and bemos and the local bemos on shorter runs. You can expect a ride every five to ten minutes for short hops early in the day, diminishing to every thirty minutes or so by the end of the afternoon.

Arrival and accommodation

Candi Dasa originally developed around its attractive lagoon, but hotel development now extends about 8km west into neighbouring **villages**, just to the south of the main Denpasar–Amlapura road; it's easy to get bemo drivers to drop you off where you want to go. Shuttle buses from the main tourist destinations serve Candi Dasa, and Perama has two offices in town.

Most **accommodation** is spread about 1km along the main road running just behind the beach at **Candi Dasa**. East of this central section, the **Forest Road** offers a number of quiet guest houses and hotels dotted among coconut palms. To the west, the village of **Senkidu** is about 1km from the centre of Candi Dasa, slightly detached and quiet, but still convenient for the main facilities. If you decide to stay any further towards **Buitan** you'll need your own transport to enjoy Candi's nightlife, as public transport stops at dusk. Most of the losmen listed below do not have street addresses, but all are keyed on the map overleaf.

Candi Dasa

Candi Dasa Ashram (☎0363/41108, fax 41947). The only Gandian ashram in Southeast Asia gets some of its income from renting out bungalows set in one of the best sites in Candi. Guests are free to take as much part in the daily *puja*, meditation and lectures as they wish, but must not smoke, drink or sunbathe nude, and only married couples may share rooms. Charges include three vegetarian meals a day. Booking is recommended three months in advance. Contact them directly for more information.

Geringsing (☎0363/41084). Clean bamboo and thatch bungalows set in a pretty garden offering excellent value. ②–③.

Ida Homestay (☎ & fax 0363/41096). Well-furnished, popular bungalows in the centre of Candi with a lovely garden stretching down to the sea. ④–⑤.

Kelapa Mas (☎ & fax 0363/41947). Justifiably popular, offering a range of clean bungalows set in a large well-maintained garden on the seafront. ④.

Kubu Bali (☎0363/41532, fax 41531). Excellent value in this price bracket. Bungalows are set in a lovely garden on the hillside away from the beach. Two swimming pools. ⑦–⑧.

Natia (no phone). Basic bungalows in a small, centrally located compound. ②.

Rama (☎0363/41907, fax 41778) In an excellent location between the sea and the lagoon, with various accommodation options from basic to more luxurious. ③–⑤.

Segara Wangi (☎0363/41159). Reasonable bungalows, a bit tucked away, but central and fairly priced. Seafront places are best. ②.

The Watergarden/Hotel Taman Air (☎0363/41540, fax 41164). On the hillside away from the beach, well-furnished, fan-cooled bungalows with verandahs overlooking pools, set in an atmospheric tropical garden. ⑧.

Forest Road

Bunga Putri (☎0363/41140). At the eastern end of the bay, this is the quietest place to stay. Simple rooms in small bungalows with verandahs, and great views from the restaurant. ③–④.

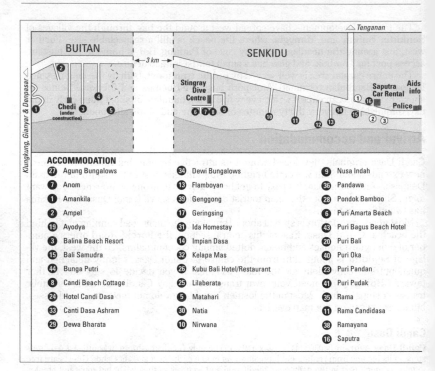

△ Tenganan

BUITAN ← 3 km → SENKIDU

Klungkung, Gianyar & Denpasar △

Chedi (under construction)

Stingray Dive Centre

Saputra Car Rental · Aids info

Police

ACCOMMODATION

27 Agung Bungalows	34 Dewi Bungalows	9 Nusa Indah
7 Anom	13 Flamboyan	36 Pandawa
1 Amankila	39 Genggong	28 Pondok Bamboo
2 Ampel	17 Geringsing	6 Puri Amarta Beach
19 Ayodya	31 Ida Homestay	43 Puri Bagus Beach Hotel
3 Balina Beach Resort	14 Impian Dasa	20 Puri Bali
15 Bali Samudra	32 Kelapa Mas	40 Puri Oka
44 Bunga Putri	26 Kubu Bali Hotel/Restaurant	23 Puri Pandan
8 Candi Beach Cottage	25 Lilaberata	41 Puri Pudak
24 Hotel Candi Dasa	5 Matahari	35 Rama
33 Canti Dasa Ashram	30 Natia	11 Rama Candidasa
29 Dewa Bharata	10 Nirwana	38 Ramayana
		16 Saputra

Genggong (☎0363/41105). Popular, good-value range of bungalows in a fair-sized compound on the beachfront. ③–⑤.

Puri Bagus Beach Hotel (☎0363/41131, fax 41290). At the end of the Forest Road with a poolside bar, flourishing garden and tiled rooms furnished with bamboo-and-rattan furniture. ⑧–⑨.

Sekar Anggrek (☎0363/41086). Simple bungalows in a small, quiet compound towards the far end of Forest Road. ③–④.

Srikandi (☎0363/41972). Good-value concrete-and-thatch place at the start of Forest Road. ③.

Senkidu

Candi Beach Cottages (☎0363/41234, fax 4111). Good-quality, top-price accommodation in an attractive compound with excellent beachside pool. ⑧–⑨.

Flamboyan (no phone). Straightforward bamboo, brick and thatch bungalows just beyond the western end of central Candi in a quiet spot, some close to the sea. If these don't appeal, *Taruna* and *Pelangi* nearby are also worth a look. ③.

Nirwana (☎0363/41136, fax 41543). A small establishment with well-furnished bungalows in a spacious garden and a good pool. ⑥–⑦.

Nusa Indah (no phone). Brick-and-tile bungalows in a quiet, relaxing spot, plus a seafront restaurant. ④.

Puri Amarta Beach (☎0363/41230). Good-value, simple bungalows along the beachfront. ③–④.

Manggis

Balina Beach Resort, Buitan (☎0363/41002, fax 41001). Offering a variety of bungalows in well-kept gardens with a pool almost on the beach. Spice Dive have a desk here. ⑦–⑨.

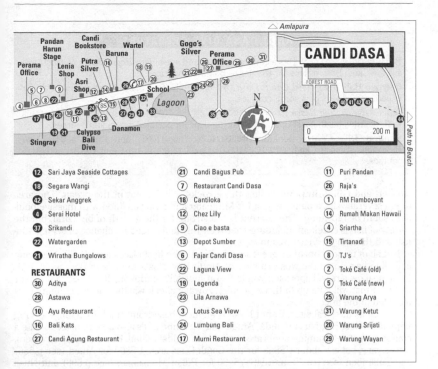

⑫ Sari Jaya Seaside Cottages	㉑ Candi Bagus Pub	⑪ Puri Pandan
⑱ Segara Wangi	⑦ Restaurant Candi Dasa	㉖ Raja's
㊷ Sekar Anggrek	⑱ Cantiloka	① RM Flamboyant
④ Serai Hotel	⑫ Chez Lilly	⑭ Rumah Makan Hawaii
㊲ Srikandi	⑨ Ciao e basta	④ Sriartha
㉒ Watergarden	⑬ Depot Sumber	⑮ Tirtanadi
㉑ Wiratha Bungalows	⑥ Fajar Candi Dasa	⑧ TJ's
RESTAURANTS	㉒ Laguna View	② Toké Café (old)
㉚ Aditya	⑲ Legenda	⑤ Toké Café (new)
㉘ Astawa	㉓ Lila Arnawa	㉕ Warung Arya
⑩ Ayu Restaurant	③ Lotus Sea View	㉛ Warung Ketut
⑯ Bali Kats	㉔ Lumbung Bali	⑳ Warung Srijati
㉗ Candi Agung Restaurant	⑰ Murni Restaurant	㉙ Warung Wayan

Serai Hotel, Buitan (☎0363/41011, fax 41015). Rooms are in a two-storey block which are well furnished and a good size. The entrance, dining and lounge areas are attractive and the swimming pool is set among the coconut palms near the beach. Regular five-day cooking schools are a speciality. ⑨.

Matahari, Buitan (☎0363/41008). 4km from central Candi Dasa, this is the best budget option in this area, with bungalows in a peaceful attractive compound. ③–④.

The resort

Candi is an ancient settlement, with its **temple**, just opposite the lagoon, believed to have been founded in the eleventh century. The statue of the fertility goddess Hariti, surrounded by numerous children, located in the lower section of the temple, is still a popular focus for pilgrims. (The name *Candi Dasa* originally derives from "Cilidasa", meaning "ten children".)

Although efforts to rebuild the **beach** here are working to a degree, even the most ardent fans of Candi admit that you don't come here for the beach. However, follow the track that passes the *Bunga Putri* bungalows at the end of the Forest Road up onto the headland. From here the path follows the top of the cliffs for a few hundred metres, but eventually descends onto a glistening black-sand beach on the other side.

Diving and snorkelling

Just off the coast of Candi Dasa, a group of small islands provides excellent **diving**, although it's not suitable for beginners as the water is often very cold and the currents can be strong. **Gili Tepekong** (also known as Gili Kambing or Goat Island) is the biggest, although only 100m by 50m; **Gili Biaha** (also known as Gili Likman) is even

---

CANDI DASA DIVE OPERATORS

Baruna (☎0363/41217). Has a counter in town and one at *Puri Bagus Beach Hotel*. These are the Candi Dasa offices for this large Bali-wide operator.

Calypso Bali Dive, *Hotel Candi Dasa* (☎0363/41537, fax 41536). Mostly offers trips for experienced divers plus some courses.

Spice Dive, *Balina Beach Resort* (☎0363/41725, fax 41001). Only southern office of this well-regarded north-coast operator, offering trips for certified divers and courses.

Stingray Dive Centre, Senkidu (☎0363/41268, fax 41062), and a desk at *Puri Bali Bungalows*, central Candi (☎0363/41063). Usual range of trips and CMAS and ADS courses.

---

smaller; and **Gili Mimpang** is just three rocks sticking out of the ocean. The area offers several walls, a pinnacle just off Mimpang and a canyon lined with massive boulders south of Tepekong. The current is too strong for the growth of big coral, but the variety of fish is excellent including (between July and August) a chance of seeing sunfish and (later in the year) manta rays.

Not all of these spots offer great **snorkelling** – the best places are off Gili Mimpang and Blue Lagoon on the western side of Amuk Bay, closer to Padang Bai (see p.551). Local boat owners will approach you to fix up snorkelling trips (Rp10,000–20,000 for 2hr in a boat that will take up to three people). Always check whether or not equipment is included in the price.

As well as the local sites, Candi Dasa is an ideal base from which to arrange **diving trips** to Padang Bai, Nusa Penida, Amed and Tulamben. It's also a good place to take a course, as hotel swimming pools are available for initial tuition. For experienced divers, prices vary, but are about US$55 for the Candi Dasa area, US$60 for Amed (see p.556) and Tulamben (see p.557), and US$75–80 for Pulau Menjangan (see p.590) and Nusa Penida (see p.543).

Eating, drinking and nightlife

There is a great variety of places to eat in Candi and generally the quality of food, especially **seafood**, is excellent. Several places have set meals for Rp6500 upwards and others have Balinese dancing to accompany your meal – look out for local adverts. Unless otherwise stated, all of the places listed below offer inexpensive to moderately priced menus and lie on or near the main road through the resort which can, unfortunately, be rather noisy.

Things are pretty quiet by 11pm and nightlife is pretty low-key in Candi. There is no disco scene and live music comes and goes – check out *Legenda* or the new *Toke Café*. Videos are the main entertainment at *Chez Lilly* and *Raja's*, while the *Candi Bagus Pub*, next door, has a pool table and darts and *Ciao e basta* has a pool table downstairs.

Balinese **dance**, including *legong, topeng* and *barong*, is performed at the Pandan Harun stage on Tuesday and Friday at 9pm (Rp6000), as long as there's a reasonable crowd.

Astawa. One of a clutch of places at the eastern end of the main road offering highly competitive prices. This one provides free peanuts with your drink, excellent *lassis* and a wide choice of well-cooked local food and seafood as well as a few Western options.

Chez Lilly. The menu features smoked Bali salmon, asparagus, profiteroles and chocolate mousse cake, as well as fish, pasta and salads. Videos are shown in the evening.

Ciao e basta. Slightly hidden away, this place has an extensive menu of superb and good-value pasta, pizza, salads and home-made ice cream.

Kubu Bali. The large dramatic kitchen at the front specializes in seafood, but also offers expensive Western, Chinese and Indonesian food in attractive surroundings. Better tables are at the back, away from the road. A big list of pricey drinks too.

Lila Arnawa. Well situated overlooking the lagoon, so slightly quieter than many, with a range of chicken, fish and Indonesian dishes.

Pandan. Seafront place with a big menu and good seafood. Watch the sunset from here with a cool drink.

Raja's. Good range of Western food as well as rice and noodle options. There's a large drinks list and nightly videos to accompany your meal.

Toke Café. The original seafront café and newer, more central place are both good value, with a large menu, including pizzas, pasta, seafood and the usual Indo-Chinese dishes. Make sure you see the steak menu, which comes highly recommended. Free welcome drink and popcorn plus good recorded sounds and occasional live music.

Listings

Bicycle rental Inquire at your losmen or at the places in the main street. Expect to pay around Rp6000 a day. Beware the main road, which is very busy.

Bookshops Several bookstores in Candi sell new and secondhand books. The Candidasa Bookstore has the largest selection and the English-language *Jakarta Post* arrives here in the afternoon.

Car and motorcycle rental You'll be offered transport every few metres along the main road, or else inquire at your accommodation. There are also plenty of rental companies around the resort with prices comparable to Kuta/Sanur: Saputra (☎0363/41083), close to the police post, is one of the larger ones. See Basics, p.38, for more information on vehicle rental.

Exchange You'll find moneychangers every few metres along the main street; rates are competitive.

Postal services Asri Shop provides a poste restante service – mail should be addressed c/o Asri Shop, Candi Dasa, PO Box 135, Karangasem, Bali – and several agents throughout the resort sell stamps.

Shopping Candi Dasa is now filling up with shops selling a variety of crafts and textiles, although the selection isn't as great as in Kuta. Asri Shop (see above, 8am–10pm) is central, sells everything and has fixed prices, which are a good guide for your bargaining elsewhere. Gogos and Putra, also in the centre of Candi, sell a good range of silver items. Nusantara Archipelago, just east of the lagoon, has an excellent selection of ceramics, paper, sculpture and other souvenirs, while Lenia has some great baskets, textiles and statues from across Indonesia. The souvenir shop at *The Watergarden* offers some of the loveliest and most expensive items in town.

Telephone and fax The wartel (daily 8am–11pm) is next to the *Kubu Bali Restaurant*. There is no fax service.

Tourist shuttle buses There are plenty of places offering shuttle buses from Candi Dasa to destinations throughout Bali and Lombok and further east to Bima and Sape. Perama (☎0363/41114) is the most established operator with plenty of departures daily.

Around Candi Dasa

It's worth making the trip out to **Pura Gomang** for good views of the area around Candi Dasa. Take an Amlapura-bound bemo for a couple of kilometres east of the resort, up the hill to the pass marked by a small shrine on the road. Concrete steps followed by a steep path head seawards from here to the temple at the top of the hill.

Six kilometres northeast from Candi, the cove of **Pasir Putih** has a 500-metre-long pure white beach sheltered by rocky headlands with good views of Gili Biaha. Take a bemo as far as Perasi, from where a track by the small shop on the corner (there's no sign) leads past paddy-fields to the coast. Two or three kilometres along the track, you reach a small temple where the path forks. The left fork leads to two black-sand beaches; the right one descends through coconut groves to Pasir Putih.

IKAT

Over half a century after Western fashions started filtering into Bali, cloth still has a **ritual purpose** on the island – worn, given or hung at important rites of passage ceremonies such as first hair-cutting and toothfiling. Bali's indigenous textile industry has always focused on the **ikat** technique, particular the weft *ikat* or *endek* of Gianyar and the double *ikat* or *geringsing* of Tenganan. It's possible to see weavers at work in both these places, as well as at the smaller weaving factories of Singaraja. Their fabrics are worn and sold all over the island, along with a whole range of batik textiles which come mainly from Java.

Easily recognized by the fuzzy-edged motifs it produces, the *ikat* **weaving technique** is common throughout Indonesia, woven either on back-strap or foot-pedal looms (or, increasingly in the wealthier areas, on semi-automatic looms) from either silk, cotton or rayon. The distinctive feature of *ikat* is, however, not so much the weaving process as the dyeing technique. The word *ikat* derives from the Indonesian verb "to tie" or "to bind", and the technique is essentially a sophisticated tie-dye process which has three variations. In **warp-ikat**, the warp yarn (the threads that run lengthwise through the material) is first threaded onto a loom frame, and then tied with dye-resistant twine into the desired pattern before being dipped into a dye vat. The binding and dyeing processes are then repeated with different colours until the final effect is achieved, after which single-coloured weft threads are woven into the patterned warp. In **weft-ikat**, the warp threads are left plain and the weft yarn (the threads running across the fabric) is dyed to the finished design. In double *ikat*, both warp and weft are dyed before weaving begins.

Nearly all the *ikat* woven in Bali is weft-*ikat*, also known as **endek**, recognizable by its predominantly geometric and abstract motifs. Weavers use mainly chemical dyes, and so colours are often bright and bold – pink, royal blue, turquoise and lime green are modern favourites. The art of embroidered *ikat*, or supplementary weft-weaving, is also practised to fine effect in Bali, where it's known as **songket**. *Songket* fabric uses threads of gold and silver metallic yarn to add decorative tapestry-like motifs of birds, butterflies and flowers onto very fine silk (or, increasingly, onto rayon or artificial silk). *Songket* sarongs are worn by the wealthiest Balinese at major ceremonial occasions. The brocaded sashes worn by performers of traditional Balinese dance are always made from *songket*, often so heavy with gold thread that you can hardly see the silk background.

Bali is quite unusual in its favouring of weft-*ikat*; warp-*ikat* is the most widely practised technique in almost every other Indonesian island. Although it's hard for a non-expert to tell the difference, you can usually hazard a guess from the textile design, which is warp *ikat* and tends to be larger and more figurative. The warp-*ikat* of **east Sumba** are particularly distinctive, and very popular in the shops of Bali, woven with bold humanoid motifs and images of real and mythological creatures such as horses, lizards, birds, monkeys, phoenixes and lions. They are usually dyed in combinations of indigo and deep red and often take the form of *hinggi* or fringed shawls. Sometimes Sumbanese weavers incorporate embroidered motifs into their fabrics; this technique, known as supplementary weft, is particularly effective on wall-hangings, where the raised designs – often of winged creatures – stand out in eye-catching relief.

Warp- and weft-*ikat* are complicated and time-consuming processes, but are nothing in comparison to double *ikat*, or **geringsing** as it's known in Bali. The *geringsing* technique involves the dyeing of both the warp and the weft threads into their final designs before they're woven together – a double-*ikat* sarong can take five years to complete. There are just three areas in the world where this highly refined weaving method is practised: India, Japan, and the Bali Aga village of **Tenganan** in eastern Bali. Not surprisingly, *geringsing* is exceedingly expensive to purchase, and over the centuries it has acquired an important ritual significance. At first glance, the *geringsing* of Tenganan is quite easily confused with the warp-*ikat* of Flores, for the Flores weavers use the same combinations of natural dyes, but the Tenganan motifs have a highly charged spiritual significance, and their geometric and floral designs are instantly recognizable to the people of Bali.

From Manggis, 6km west of Candi, a paved road heads up into the hills. There's a lovely eight-kilometre walk along a steep, quiet lane, with stunning views of the entire coastal area, to Putung on the Amlapura–Rendang road, where you can have lunch. For the return journey, bemos connect Putung with Amlapura, where you can change for Candi Dasa.

Tenganan

The village of **TENGANAN** is unique among the **Bali Aga** communities of the island in its strong adherence to traditional ways. Rejecting the Javanization of their land, the caste system and the religious reforms that followed the Majapahit conquest of the island in 1343, the Bali Aga or Bali Mula, meaning "original Balinese", withdrew to their village enclaves to live a life based around ritual and ceremony. Today, Tenganan is an extremely wealthy village, and the only place in Indonesia that produces the celebrated **geringsing** cloth. The road up to Tenganan is an easy walk from the centre of Candi but, even so, ojeks wait at the bottom to transport you the 3km up to the village. It's a major stop on the tour-bus circuit but it's easy to avoid the 11am to 2pm rush if you're staying in the area.

Tenganan's land is owned communally and the villagers do not work it, but have sharecropping agreements with other local people, leaving them free to pursue a complex round of **rituals and ceremonies**. The rituals are laid down in ancient texts and their observance is believed to prevent the wrath of the gods destroying the village.

Most of the daily rituals observed by the villagers are not open to the public, but there are so many **festival** days that the *Calendar of Events* printed by the Bali government tourist office has an entire section devoted to the events in Tenganan. The month-long Usaba Sambah festival, generally in May and June, is one of the most colourful.

The most famous product of the village is **geringsing** or double *ikat* (see box opposite), a highly valued brown, deep-red, blue-black and tan cloth. It's chiefly worn during certain rituals, given as an offering to the gods and used as a protection against evil. The village is also famous for its unusual gamelan **selonding** music, using instruments which are believed to have considerable religious power.

Padang Bai

Deriving from two languages – *padang* is Balinese for "grass" and *bai* is Dutch for "bay" – **PADANG BAI**, the **port for Lombok** (ferries run to Lembar every 2hr), nestles in a small cove with a white-sand beach lined with fishing boats. The jetty, ferry offices and car park are all at the western end of the bay, and everything is within easy walking distance from here.

Increasingly, people are choosing to stay a night or two in Padang Bai, and the village has developed into a small laid-back resort. If you find the main **beach** a bit busy, the bay of **BIAS TUGAL**, to the west, is smaller and quieter. Follow the road past the post office and, just as it begins to climb, take the track to the left. Alternatively, over the headland in the other direction, take the path from Pura Silayukti, to another small, white cove. Several places in Padang Bai rent out **snorkelling** equipment; the water in the bay is surprisingly clear, although the best snorkelling is at **Blue Lagoon**, just around the headland in Amuk Bay. You can snorkel off the beach at Blue Lagoon, but you'll see far more if you charter a boat (about Rp30,000 for 2hr); ask at *Celagi* restaurant or your guest house. The new dive operation, Geko Dive (☎ & fax 41790, alternative fax 41784; *gekodive@indosat.net.id*) is on Jalan Silayukti, and offers the full range of PADI courses and dives for the experienced, as well as providing advice about good local dives including Turtle Point, around and beyond the headland to the east of the bay, where hawksbill and green turtles are reliably spotted, as well as reef sharks and, occasionally, sunfish.

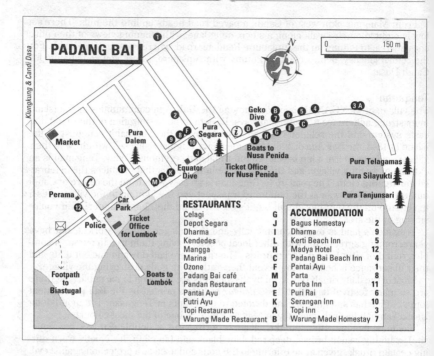

PADANG BAI

Klungkung & Candi Dasa

0 ——— 150 m

Market

Pura Dalem

Pura Segara

Geko Dive

Boats to Nusa Penida

Ticket Office for Nusa Penida

Equator Dive

Pura Telagamas

Pura Silayukti

Pura Tanjunsari

Perama

Car Park

Police

Ticket Office for Lombok

Footpath to Biastugal

Boats to Lombok

RESTAURANTS		ACCOMMODATION	
Celagi	G	Bagus Homestay	2
Depot Segara	J	Dharma	9
Dharma	I	Kerti Beach Inn	5
Kendedes	L	Madya Hotel	12
Mangga	H	Padang Bai Beach Inn	4
Marina	C	Pantai Ayu	1
Ozone	F	Parta	8
Padang Bai café	M	Purba Inn	11
Pandan Restaurant	D	Puri Rai	6
Pantai Ayu	E	Serangan Inn	10
Putri Ayu	K	Topi Inn	3
Topi Restaurant	A	Warung Made Homestay	7
Warung Made Restaurant	B		

Practicalities

Bemos arrive at, and depart from, the port entrance; orange for Amlapura, blue or white for Klungkung (also known as Semarapura). The government **tourist office** (daily 7am–8pm) is 500m further east on the beach road, Jalan Silayukti, and offers information as well as selling tours and renting cars and motorbikes. The Nusa Penida ticket office is also near here; boats leave from the beach when they are full from 7am onwards (Rp4000). Perama **tourist shuttle buses** operate from their office near the jetty in *Café Dona* and you can buy through-tickets to destinations on Bali and Lombok. There is a post office near the port entrance, many seafront restaurants **change money** and *Made Homestay* can arrange car rental (Rp40,000 daily for a Suzuki Jimny) and motorbike rental (Rp15–25,000 daily).

ACCOMMODATION

There's a choice of **accommodation** in the village and strung out along the road behind the beach; the beach places benefit from a sea breeze and are generally bigger and airier, but the ones in the village have some excellent upstairs rooms.

Bagus Homestay (☎0363/41398). Clean and friendly, with a small but pleasant garden. ③.

Kerti Beach Inn (☎0363/41391). Popular place near the beach; rooms are reasonable and have attached bathrooms. ③–④.

Made Homestay (no phone). Good-quality rooms in a small compound. ④–⑤.

Padang Bai Beach Inn (☎0363/41439). The bungalows at the front have good views across to the sea; all rooms have attached bathrooms. ③–④.

Pantai Ayu (☎0363/41396). Located in the village up behind the cemetery, this is the best of the village places, with a good view over to the beach. The better, pricier rooms are upstairs. ②–④.

Parta (☎0363/41475). Pleasant village place with good, basic rooms. ③.

Purba Inn (☎0363/41429). Simple rooms in a friendly family compound and convenient for the ferry. ③–④.

Puri Rai (☎ & fax 0363/41386). Large rooms with air-con and hot water in a two-storey building, and cheaper fan rooms in *lumbung*-style thatched places, which are better value. ④–⑦.

Serangan Inn (☎0363/41425). One of the best options in the village, with a terrace upstairs where you can sit and watch the world go by. ③–④.

EATING AND DRINKING

Seafood is the speciality in the restaurants here, with marlin, barracuda, snapper and prawns on offer, depending on the catch. You'll also find regular tourist menus featuring chicken, steaks, French fries and sandwiches, as well as rice and noodle dishes. The small places on the beach side of the road offer the perfect setting for that first cool drink of the evening. All are in the inexpensive-to-moderate price range and have happy hours, but tend to stop serving by about 9.30pm.

Kendedes. Small, friendly and close to the jetty, serving good rice, noodles and fruit juices.

Made. Small place attached to the homestay, offering simple, well-cooked food.

Mannga. A very popular place on the seafront with excellent food – the pizzas are especially good.

Marina. Last in line on the beach, with great views and very popular.

Ozone. This place is conveniently located near the accommodation in the village and has an attractive raised, sitting area.

Pantai Ayu. Tiny beachside place serving excellent barbecued fish.

Goa Lawah and Kusamba

Positioned right on the coast, **Goa Lawah** (Bat Cave; daily 7am–6pm; Rp1000, sarong rental Rp500), 7km from Padang Bai, is a major tourist draw. The temple, established around the cave in 1007AD, is quite small but much revered by the Balinese, and many drivers stop to make offerings at the small shrine on the road. The focus is the **cave** at the base of the cliff, which heaves with thousands of fruit bats. The cave is supposedly the start of a tunnel that stretches 30km inland to Pura Goa in Besakih, and is said to contain the cosmic *naga* Basuki.

Three kilometres further west, the farming, fishing and salt-producing village of **KUSAMBA** spreads about 2km along the beach (see box p.543 for more on salt production). Boats run daily to Nusa Penida and Nusa Lembongan from here, though they are very small and get loaded above the gunnels – you'd be wise to take an alternative route (see p.541). From Kusamba it's 6km west to Klungkung.

Beyond Candi Dasa

The far east of Bali **beyond Candi Dasa** offers lush rice terraces carpeting picturesque valleys, just a few kilometres from parched landscapes where cultivation is all but impossible. The main road beyond Candi Dasa cuts inland, passing close to the sleepy market town of **Amlapura**, before crossing the hills to the north coast. You can follow this route by public transport, but if you want to get further off the beaten track and explore the **far eastern end** of the island, with its remote beach hideaways and excellent snorkelling and diving, or the fabulous scenery of the **Iseh** and **Sidemen** areas, you will need your own transport.

Amlapura

Formerly known as Karangasem, **AMLAPURA** has a quiet and relaxed atmosphere which makes it a pleasant place to spend a few hours, but there's little to see. Amlapura's only sight is Puri Agung, one of the palaces of the rajahs of Karangasem.

Built in the early 1900s, **Puri Agung** (daily 8am–6pm; Rp1100) is the only one of the Amlapura royal palaces open to the public. Within the palace compound, the extremely faded highlight is the **Maskerdam building**, a corruption of the name "Amsterdam" as a tribute to the Dutch. It has intricately carved doors and furniture donated by Queen Wilhelmina of the Netherlands. The verandah is decorated with photographs and paintings, explained in the English-language guide to the palace (Rp500). In front of the Maskerdam building, the **Bale Kambang** was formerly used for meetings, dancing and dining. Royal tooth-filing ceremonies took place in the smaller **Bale Pemandesan** next door, while the **Bale Lunjuk** nearer the entrance gate was used for religious ceremonies.

Practicalities

Public transport coming into the Amlapura bemo and bus terminal completes a massive circle around the top end of town, passing the **wartel** (open 24hr), on the way up, and Puri Agung, on the way down, to the terminal. The **post office** is at Jalan Jend Gatot Subroto 25 and there are **exchange** facilities at Bank Dannamon and BNI. **Bemos** from the terminal serve Candi Dasa and Padang Bai (orange), Selat and Muncan (green) and Ujung and Seraya (blue). There are also **buses** north to Singaraja, with a few on to Gilimanuk, and around the south to Batubulan. In the afternoon Amlapura seems to die more quickly and completely than the other main towns, so travel early. Bemos to Culik and Tianyar via Tirtagangga leave from the turn-off on the outskirts of town. The staff in the **tourist office** on Jalan Diponegoro (Mon–Thurs 7am–1.45pm, Fri 6.30–11am, Sat 7am–12.30pm; ☎0363/21196), are welcoming and have a couple of pamphlets on the area and an annual calendar of events, which includes details of ceremonies at Tenganan (see p.551).

Most people stop off in Amlapura for a couple of hours on their way elsewhere. However, if you need **accommodation**, *Penginapan Lahar Mas* (②–③) on Jalan Jend Gatot Subroto, on the one-way system into town, is simple and good value.

If you fancy somewhere to **eat** other than the warung near the market and bemo terminal, the *Sumber Rasa* on Jalan Gajah Made, on the way up to Puri Agung, offers a good inexpensive range of soups, sate, steak, spaghetti, noodles and rice.

Tirtagangga

Six kilometres from Amlapura, **TIRTAGANGGA**'s main draw is its lovely Water Palace, but the town is also surrounded by beautiful paddy-fields offering pleasant walks and glorious views of Gunung Agung and Gunung Lempuyang in the distance. The refreshingly cool temperatures make this one of the best day-trips from Candi Dasa, and it's also a restful spot to stay for a night or two.

The **Water Palace** (daily 7am–6pm; Rp1100, Rp2500 for video cameras) was built in about 1947 by Anak Agung Anglurah, the last rajah of Karangasem, testament to his obsession with pools, moats and fountains. It has been damaged on several occasions, including the 1963 eruption of Gunung Agung and an earthquake in 1979. However, it has been well restored and is an impressive terraced area of pools, water channels and fountains set in a well-maintained garden. You can swim in the upper deeper pool (Rp2000) or the lower, shallower pool (Rp1000).

The **warung** on the track to the palace offer the usual rice and noodle options, while the **restaurants** at the *Kusumajaya* and the *Prima Bamboo* have the best views and serve inexpensive Indo-Chinese dishes. At the back of the Water Palace, above the car park, the *Good Karma* restaurant has a relaxed atmosphere and a good-value tourist menu, while the one attached to *Puri Sawah* is in a lovely location.

Nyoman Budiarsa's shop sells woodcarvings plus a printed map of walks to local villages and temples (Rp500), and will also arrange walking tours, trips to Pura Lempuyang and climbs up Gunung Agung (see p.539). There is a moneychanger and a postal agent on the track to the Water Palace from the main road.

Accommodation

Cabe Bali (☎0363/22045). The most luxurious accommodation in the area, with superb, bungalows, setting and atmosphere. Slightly further from Tirtagangga than the other options, but definitely worth the journey. Accessed from Temaga, it is 1km along a rough road into the paddy-fields. There is a café which non-residents can also use with a small menu of snacks and meals. ⑦.

Kusumajaya Inn (☎0363/21250). About 300m north of the centre, on a hill. The rooms have verandahs that make the most of the splendid views across the fields, but the porcupines imprisoned in a tiny cage and the uninterested staff are minus points. ③–④.

Prima Bamboo (☎0363/21316). Just north of the *Kusumajaya Inn*, with variable rooms but great views of the paddy-fields, Gunung Lempuyang and Gunung Seraya. ③–⑤.

Puri Sawah (☎0363/21847, fax 21939). About 100m beyond the Water Palace, on a track heading left from a sharp turn in the road, this place offers good-quality rooms with verandahs in a peaceful setting; more expensive ones have hot water. ④–⑤.

Rijasa Home Stay (☎0363/21873). Across the main road from the track leading to the Water Palace, this is a good-value place with an attractive garden and central location. ③–⑤.

Tirta Ayu Restaurant and Homestay (☎0363/22520). Set on the hill in the grounds of the Water Palace itself. Cheaper rooms are unexciting but others are better, including a glorious two-storey house. The room price includes admission to the swimming pools in the palace. ④–⑧.

Amlapura to Rendang

West of Amlapura, a picturesque road heads inland through Sibetan and Muncan, joining the main Klungkung–Penelokan road 14km north of Klungkung at Rendang. Public bemos do ply the Amlapura–Rendang route, but they're not frequent, and without your own transport the highlights of the area, Pura Pasar Agung above Selat and the rice paddies around Iseh and Sidemen, are very difficult to get to.

Midway between **SIBETAN** and **DUDA**, *Pondok Bukit Putung* (☎ & fax 0366/23039; ⑥) looks unpromising from the car park, but from the terrace of the restaurant the whole of the countryside down to the coast is spread out in a great panorama. A couple of *lumbung* barns (traditional Lombok barns) provide **accommodation**. There is a narrow but passable road that winds 8km down through Bakung to Manggis with gorgeous views of the entire area (see p.545).

Further west, the small village of **SELAT** offers accommodation in pleasant rooms set in a nice garden at *Puri Agung Cottages* (☎0366/23037; ④–⑤), which are on the east side of the village just before the post office. Selat also marks the turn-off to **Pura Pasar Agung** (Temple of Agung Market). It was completely destroyed by the 1963 eruption of Gunung Agung and has been rebuilt. Rising in three terraces to the inner courtyard, it's an impressive and dramatic place, at about 1200m on the slopes of Gunung Agung, and is the starting point for one of the routes up the mountain (see p.539). Even if you're not climbing Agung, though, this is a lovely spot with fabulous views.

Four kilometres west of Selat, **MUNCAN** is a quiet little village and another possible base for climbing Agung (see p.539). West of Muncan, the vistas close in and the valleys become narrower and deeper. Sungai Telaga Waja is used by several rafting companies. Four kilometres west at **RENDANG**, you pick up the main Klungkung–Penelokan road and bemos to Besakih.

Leaving the Amlapura–Rendang road at **DUDA**, just east of Selat, you can follow a beautiful route through Iseh and Sidemen to Klungkung. The views of the rice-fields along this road are among the most lovely in Bali. At **SIDEMEN**, there are two **places to stay**. The *Tabola Inn* (☎0366/23015; ⑤–⑦) is set in the middle of paddy-fields almost 3km off the road along a rough track. It has a lovely garden, small swimming pool and will arrange treks, bicycle tours and car rental. In the village, the *Sidemen Homestay* (☎0366/23009; ⑦) is much simpler, with only cold-water bathrooms, and closer to the road. Just opposite the homestay you can watch *endek* weaving on foot looms at the *Pelangi* workshop. From Sidemen the road drops down through small villages before reaching the main Klungkung–Kusamba road at Paksabali and Sampalan.

The far east

The settlements around the **far east coast** of the island are peaceful, with uncrowded beaches and good snorkelling and diving. Don't expect a post office out here, or exchange facilities, and the majority of the accommodation places do not yet have telephones. From Culik, 10km beyond Tirtagangga, you should be able to get a bemo to **Amed** and on to **Selang**, but you may have to charter it. An ojek from Culik to the furthest-flung accommodation, *Good Karma*, at Selang, will cost about Rp4000. For the remainder of the coastline you'll need your own vehicle. The coastal route from Culik around to Amlapura is 42km, but allow yourself the best part of a day.

Amed and Jemeluk
From **Culik**, the junction of the road around the far east and the Amlapura–Singaraja road, it's 3km to the picturesque, sleepy fishing village of **AMED**. About 2km beyond the village, *Amed Café and Guest House* (③) has rooms across the road from the beach. The upstairs rooms have the views, while the downstairs ones boast some seductive hammocks on the verandahs.

Less than 1km further on, the village of **JEMELUK** is the diving focus of the area, and there's a car park and a few stalls and warung along the road. Eco-Dive and the attached *AOK* restaurant arranges dives, snorkelling, tours, fishing and dolphin-watching trips and has basic accommodation (③–④). The cheapest rooms comprise mattresses on the floor of a bamboo hut with an outside bathroom. The main diving area is around the headland to the east of the parking area. A sloping terrace of coral, both hard and soft, leads to a wall dropping to a depth of more than 40m; the density of fish on the wall is high – gorgonians, fans, basket sponges and table coral are especially good, and the current is generally slow.

One kilometre further around the coast, *Amed Beach Cottages* (④–⑤) is situated by the beach with smart bungalows and a Mega Dive Centre (☎ & fax 0363/21911) offering introductory dives, dives for certified divers and PADI courses. Just beyond this, the *Kusumajaya Beach Inn* (⑤) has brick-and-tile bungalows in a compound that slopes down to the rocky beach, and 500m further on the unique *Kebun Obat Aiona, the Health Garden* (⑤) offers very simple accommodation, vegetarian food and a range of therapies. With only two bungalows, booking is advised, c/o Pos Kelling, Desa Bunutan, Abang 80852, Bali, Indonesia (no phone).

Another 2km on, perched on a headland, is the top-quality *Hotel Indra Udhyana* (☎0370/26336, fax 36797; ⑨), which offers superb accommodation in traditional buildings, and a great pool. It's the most luxurious and most expensive place on this coast.

Lipah Beach and Selang
Lipah Beach, although still peaceful, is the most developed beach in the area. There is accommodation at *Hidden Paradise* (⑦–⑧) and, just beyond this, at the newer *Coral View* (④–⑨), which are both owned by the same company (☎0361/431273, fax 423820)

and offer well-furnished bungalows in lush gardens with pools. There are several restaurants nearby: *Wawa Wewe* and *Tiying Petung* stand side by side and are great places to relax if the beach palls, and offer a range of Western and Indonesian dishes. Both have bungalows under construction (④–⑤).

Into the next bay, *Vienna Beach* (⑥) has a range of accommodation in a small, relaxed compound. There is another headland and several kilometres between here and the bay at **SELANG**, almost 12km from Culik, where *Good Karma* (④–⑤) is currently the most easterly accommodation. Bungalows are set in a glorious garden – an oasis in the midst of a parched landscape.

If you follow the road on around the coast through the village of **Aas**, you'll pass through the dry, barren country to the east of the mountains. The scenery is dramatic, with the hills sweeping up for hundreds of metres from the coast and fields at crazy angles, with terracing supported by dry-stone walls. Clinging to the side of the hills, the road twists and turns and travel is slow going.

Kusambi, Seraya and Ujung

The road leaves the coast at **KUSAMBI**, marked by a massive beacon. This is the most eastern point on Bali, and on clear days you'll be able to see Lombok just 35km across the strait. Further on, **SERAYA** is a small market town with a grand temple dominated by the looming Gunung Seraya. From here the road heads down to the coast, where rows of colourful boats line the beach, before it turns inland to **UJUNG**, 5km south of Amlapura, where you'll spot a jumble of ruins down in a dip on the right. This is another **water palace** built by the water-loving last rajah of Karangasem, Anak Agung Anglurah, in 1921. Situated among large artificial lakes, all that remains are tumbled columns, portals to nowhere and foundations. From here the road passes through attractive rice terraces, with views across to Gunung Lempuyang and Seraya before reaching the southern side of Amlapura.

Tulamben

The small, rather unattractive village of **TULAMBEN**, about 10km west of Culik, appears an unlikely target for visitors from all over the world. However, it's the site of the most famous and most popular dive in Bali, the **Liberty wreck**, which sank during World War II. Up to a hundred divers a day now visit, so it's worth avoiding the rush hours (11.30am–4pm). Night dives here are especially good.

The wreck lies almost parallel to the beach, on a sandy slope about 30m offshore, and is completely encrusted with soft coral, gorgonians and hydrozoans, with a few hard corals, providing a wonderful habitat for over 400 species of reef fish that live on the wreck and over 100 species visiting from deeper water. The wreck is now pretty broken up and there are plenty of entrances if you want to explore inside. Parts of the stern are only about 2m below the surface, making this a good snorkelling site, too. There's also a coral wall off the eastern end of the beach.

Most divers come to Tulamben on day-trips from Candi Dasa, Lovina or even further afield. However, there are plenty of local **dive operations**. Check out Mega Dive (☎0361/288192) at *Mimpi Resort*, Paradise Diving at *Bali Sorga* and Tauch Terminal at *Ganda Mayu* (☎0361/730200, fax 730385; *www.tauchbali.com*), which all arrange local dives for certified divers and run some courses. Expect to pay around US$55 for two dives at Tulamben. Snorkelling gear is also available for rent.

Practicalities

Tulamben is easily accessible from either Singaraja or Amlapura by public bemo or bus. There are several **restaurants** offering rice, noodle and pasta dishes ,and accommodation options are increasing fast, although overall it is fairly pricey and, with one exception, the places east of the village are not recommended. There are no phones up here as yet.

Bali Sorga Bungalows. Well established and just back from the beach, although it has a rather crowded compound ④.

Emerald Tulamben Beach Hotel (☎0361/462673, fax 462407). An imposing, luxury place, popular with tour groups and offering excellent facilities, watersports and well-appointed rooms. The only accommodation of this type on this section of coast, it is east of the village. ⑨.

Ganda Mayu. A good choice, close to the wreck of the *Liberty*, with straightforward bungalows set in a garden along the coast. ③–④.

Puri Aries. A new place, across the road from *Bali Sorga Bungalows* and better suited to those uninterested in the hustle and bustle of diving. ④.

Puri Madha. The most westerly place, about 200m beyond the village and the beach, very near the *Liberty*. Rooms are simple and clean but the bungalows overlook the car park, which gets pretty frantic during the day. ④.

THE NORTH AND THE CENTRAL VOLCANOES

Heading towards **the north** from the crowded southern plains and foothills, you enter another world, with a slower pace, a different climate and hugely varied countryside. The centre of the island is occupied by the awesome volcanic masses of the **Batur** and **Bedugul** areas, where dramatic mountain ranges shelter crater lakes, and small, peaceful villages line their shores. With few peaks rising above 2000m, the **mountains** don't rival Gunung Agung in stature, but their accessibility and beauty are unbeatable. Most people either come to the Batur area on a day-trip to gaze at the crater panorama, or to stay down by the lake and trek up **Gunung Batur**, the most climbed peak in Bali. The Bedugul area offers more lakes, mountains and forests, but on a smaller scale, and is regularly besieged by tour groups swarming to the stunning lakeside temple of **Pura Ulun Danu Batur**. Once through the mountain ranges, the dry northern **coast** is harsh and rugged as the mountains drop steeply to the coastal plain.

Plenty of visitors head straight for the northern coastal resort of **Lovina** which, despite its black sand, is now the largest resort outside the Kuta-Legian-Seminyak conurbation, although it still manages to retain a laid-back air. Many parts of the north are far from peaceful, though. **Singaraja**, the administrative capital of Buleleng district, is a bustling, modern city and many of the roads in the area carry a huge volume of traffic including trucks and buses.

The area is culturally rich too: the Bali Aga traditional village, **Trunyan**, nestles beside Danau Batur; the **Gedong Kirtya** in Singaraja is the only *lontar* manuscript library in the world; and the exuberant and distinctive **temple carvings and sculptures** of the north can be enjoyed in the temples at **Kubutambahan**, **Jagaraga** and **Sangsit**.

With good bus and bemo links from all directions, most of the sights in the north are fairly easy to get to on public transport, although with your own vehicle you'll be able to explore the quiet inland roads and reach some less popular places such as Danau Tamblingan and Munduk. A good range of accommodation spread throughout the region makes this an ideal touring area.

Gunung Batur and Danau Batur

The **Batur** area was formed 30,000 years ago by the eruption of a gigantic volcano. The entire area is sometimes referred to as **Kintamani**, although in fact this is just one of several villages dotted along the rim of the ancient crater. More villages are situated around **Danau Batur** at the bottom of the crater: **Toya Bungkah** is the start of the

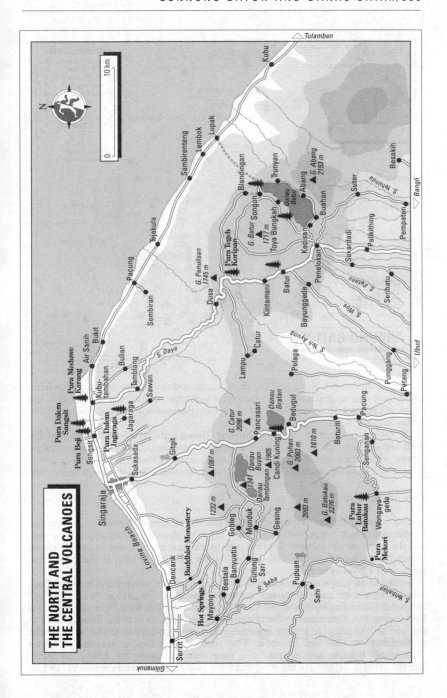

**THE NORTH AND
THE CENTRAL VOLCANOES**

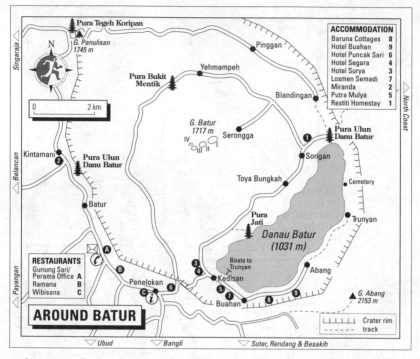

main route up Gunung Batur and the chief accommodation centre, although **Kedisan** offers some options, and is the access point for boat trips across the lake to the Bali Aga village of **Trunyan**. At the furthest end of the lake, **Songan** is one of the quietest places to stay in the area.

The highest points on the rim are **Gunung Abang** (2153m) on the eastern side, the third highest mountain in Bali, and **Gunung Penulisan** (1745m), on the southwest corner, with Pura Tegeh Koripan perched on its summit. Rising from the floor of the main crater, **Gunung Batur** (1717m) is an active volcano with four craters of its own.

The crater rim

Spread out along the rim of the crater for 11km, the villages of **Penelokan**, **Batur** and **Kintamani** almost merge with each other. If you're planning to stay up here, beware that the mist (and sometimes rain) that rolls in and obscures the view in late afternoon brings a creeping dampness, and the nights are extremely chilly; at the very least, you'll need a good sweater.

Getting to the rim is straightforward from any direction, with regular **buses** (about every 30min until mid-afternoon) between Singaraja (Penarukan terminal) and Denpasar (Batubulan terminal), via Gianyar and Bangli. The local Perama office is at the *Gunung Sari Restaurant* on the crater rim, about 2km north of the turning down to the lake in Penelokan, and there are one or two services daily to all the usual tourist destinations on Bali and Lombok. The route from Ubud is served by brown (Kintamani) **bemos**, and if you have your own transport, the roads via Suter, Tampaksiring and Payangan are good quality. If your time is short, Penelokan is included in many of the **day-trips** on offer at the major resorts, although this is usually a quick stop to admire the view from the crater rim amid serious hassle from hawkers.

There is an **entrance charge** for visiting the crater area (Rp1100 per person, cars Rp800, motorbikes Rp200; video camera Rp2500, camera Rp1000); the ticket offices are just south of Penelokan, before the final few metres up to the crater rim, on the road from Bangli and just at the junction of the Ubud and rim roads.

Penelokan

Literally meaning "place to look", the views from **PENELOKAN** (1450m) are excellent, offering a panorama of enormous scale and majesty. Danau Batur, with its ever-changing colours, lies far below, while Gunung Batur and Gunung Abang tower on either side of the lake. Over 2000 tourists in the low season and 4000 in the high are estimated to pass through Penelokan every day, attracting an entourage of aggressive **hawkers** selling all sorts of goods. The only way to really avoid the circus is to come early or late in the day, or stay overnight.

Yayasan Bintang Danu, a local organization, runs the **tourist office** in Penelokan, almost opposite the turning down to Kedisan (daily 9am–3pm; ☎0366/51730), and has notice boards giving information about accommodation, charter rates, routes up the volcano and leaflets and maps on what to see in the area.

Catering for the daytime crowd, the crater rim is packed with plush **restaurants** offering expensive buffet lunches with a view. For something cheaper, try *Ramana*; rather confusingly there are two places with this name, although both are good. One is about 300m towards Kintamani from Penelokan – it's right on the crater's rim and views are glorious. The other is a few hundred metres further on, on the opposite side of the road with good views south.

If you want **to stay** up here, *Hotel Puncak Sari* (☎0366/31394, fax 51464; ⑥–⑦) is at the junction of the road from the south and the crater rim; the views are stunning and the rooms comfortable with hot water. The **post office** and **telephone office** are 2km north of Penelokan on the road along the rim. There are several places to **change money** on the rim, including Bank Rakyat Indonesia in Kintamani.

Pura Ulun Danu Batur

Five kilometres north of Penelokan, **Pura Ulun Danu Batur** is the second most important temple on the island after the Besakih complex. It's a fascinating temple to visit as there are usually pilgrims making offerings or praying, and the mist that frequently shrouds the area adds to the atmosphere. The eleven-day *odalan* festival (see p.581) is particularly spectacular and attended by people from all over the island.

The **original temple** was located down in the crater until the 1926 eruption of Gunung Batur destroyed the whole of Batur village. Shrines and relics that could be saved were taken up onto the crater rim and the village and temple were rebuilt. The present temple structures are quite modern (inaugurated in 1935), and construction is still under way, with more than ninety shrines completed out of the planned total of almost three hundred. The temple honours **Ida Batara Dewi Ulun Danu**, the goddess of the crater lake, who controls the water for the irrigation systems throughout the island and shares dominion of Bali with the God of Gunung Agung.

Kintamani

Consisting almost entirely of concrete buildings with rusty corrugated-iron roofs, **KINTAMANI**, 2km north of Pura Ulun Danu, isn't particularly appealing, and is too far north along the rim of the crater for the best views of Danau Batur.

Famous for its breed of furry dogs and the huge outdoor market held every three days, there's little reason **to stay** here, but if you want to the best option is *Miranda* (③), about 100m north of the market on the left. The rooms are extremely basic, but the lounge cheers up when there are a few people staying and the open fire is lit. The owner, Made Senter, also works as a tour guide taking parties from the losmen down into the crater and up Gunung Batur.

Pura Tegeh Koripan

About 7km beyond Kintamani on the road towards Singaraja, **Pura Tegeh Koripan** (Rp1000), built on the summit of Gunung Penulisan, is the highest temple on Bali and one of the most ancient.

It's a climb of 333 concrete steps from the road to the top temple, **Pura Panarajon**, dedicated to Sanghyang Grinatha, a manifestation of Siwa, and god of the mountains. On this top terrace, *bale* shelter various shrines and an array of ancient lingga and worn statues from the eleventh to thirteenth centuries, predating the Majapahit invasion of the island.

Danau Batur

Home of Dewi Danu, the goddess of the crater lake, **Danau Batur** is especially sacred to the Balinese, and the waters from the lake, generated by eleven springs, are believed to percolate through the earth and reappear as springs in other parts of the island. Situated 500m below the crater rim, Danau Batur is the largest lake in Bali, 8km long and 3km wide, and one of the most glorious; the villages dotted around its shores are referred to as *bintang danu* (stars of the lake). The most popular road to the lakeside, served by **public bemos**, leaves the crater rim at Penelokan. Bemos, in theory, go as far as Songan on the western side of the lake and Abang on the eastern side, but you'll have to bargain hard to get reasonable fares beyond Toya Bungkah and Buahan.

However, the **hassles** of the lake area can make a visit here far more stressful than the stunning scenery deserves. A lot of visitors have negative experiences and, in some cases, irritation has turned into intimidation and extortion. From the moment you arrive you'll be pestered to engage a guide for the climb up Gunung Batur for sums ranging from Rp10,000 (fair) to US$60 per person; see p.560 for details of the climb. If you arrive by car, there is huge pressure to pay someone to "look after" your vehicle while you climb, sometimes followed by threats of damage to the car if you decline. The best advice is to stay cool, choose a guide with care, and climb early in your stay – they'll lose interest fast if they know you've been up. Leaving vehicles in the care of hotel and restaurants where you have stayed or eaten is also a good idea. The underlying issue here is the high unemployment in the area. Many out-of-work young men feel that hotel and restaurant owners shouldn't be the sole beneficiaries of the lucrative tourist trade and want a bite of the cherry too.

Toya Bungkah and around

TOYA BUNGKAH, 8km from Penelokan, is the accommodation centre of the lakeside area and the main starting point for climbs up Gunung Batur. The stylish hot springs, **Tirta Sanjiwana** (daily 7am–8pm), were rebuilt in 1997 amidst considerable controversy as they moved stratospherically upmarket. They look extremely good, with a cold-water swimming pool, smaller hot-water pools (US$15 for both) and a private spa area (US$20), but the current prices, and the talk of introducing a hefty entrance fee on top of the above charges, means they have moved well beyond the reach of many of the backpackers, who are the mainstay of the Toyah Bungkah economy.

Just south of Toya Bungkah, another **ticket office** collects entrance fees to the lake area (Rp1100 per person, cars Rp800, motorbikes Rp200, video camera Rp2500, camera

Rp1000), but you'll probably be stopped only if you're in your own transport. The nearest post office is up on the rim and you can **change money** and travellers' cheques at Jero Wijaya (☎0366/51249, fax 51250). Both Jero Wijaya and *Arlina's* (☎0366/51165) provide reliable **information** about the area and operate travel and tour services. They also offer guides for climbs up Gunung Abang (US$30–35 per person), Agung (US$50–75 per person), a range of local treks (from US$10), treks to Bedugul (US$30 per person) and around the Bedugul area (US$40–90). In all cases there are minimum numbers required for the trek, at least two and often four.

ACCOMMODATION, EATING AND DRINKING

Accommodation options are increasing rapidly here. **Places to stay** line the road in Toya Bungkah, with a few more down by the lakeside. Most of the losmen have inexpensive **restaurants** attached serving a good range of Western and Indo-Chinese options; freshwater fish from the lake is a local speciality. The inexpensive *Arlina's* offers a good choice and the liveliest surroundings, while the moderately priced *Amertha Restaurant* has the best position overlooking the lake and hot springs.

Arlina's (☎0366/51165). A friendly, popular setup at the southern end of town, with clean rooms, small verandahs and some rooms with unusually decorated, individual bathrooms. ③–④.

Pualam (no phone). This small, quiet losmen, close to the hot springs, has clean, well-finished rooms set around a pleasant garden. ③.

Puri Bening Hyato (☎0366/51234, fax 51248). Top-end rooms are huge with great views but the less expensive ones are poor value. There is a private hot pool (5–9pm) in the grounds. ⑥–⑧.

Tirta Yatra (no phone). A small establishment with very basic rooms and unenticing bathrooms, but the position right down on the lakeside is excellent. ②.

Under the Volcano (Nyoman Mawa). Located in the village, the rooms are clean and good value. Only cold-water bathrooms available. ③.

Under the Volcano 2 (Nyoman Mawa 2). Positioned close to the lake, the rooms are better furnished than most in the area and the more expensive ones have hot water. ③–④.

Kedisan and beyond

Three kilometres from Penelokan, there are a couple of accommodation options in the southernmost lakeside village of **KEDISAN**. The Penelokan road splits at Kedisan: the right fork leads to the jetty for boats to Trunyan and continues on to the villages of Buahan and Abang; the left fork leads to Toya Bungkah. A few hundred metres from the junction, towards Toya Bungkah, *Hotel Segara* (☎0366/51136, fax 51212; ④–⑥) has a variety of rooms and a large restaurant, while *Hotel Surya* (☎0366/51139; ③–⑥) offers rooms with cold or hot water, but is a bit shabby. Three hundred metres from the junction, towards Buahan to the right, *Putra Mulya* (no phone; ③) has simple tiled rooms but no lake view or restaurant, while, 200m further on, *Losmen Semadi* (no phone; ③) has a small restaurant and fine views across the local fields to the lake. These are convenient if you are intending to visit Trunyan, but it's further to the start of the Gunung Batur climb than accommodation in Toyah Bungkah.

Beyond Kedisan, on the eastern side of the lake, is the most attractive section of road in the crater, following the shores of the lake through Buahan to Abang. Just to the east of **BUAHAN**, 2.5km from the junction with the Penelokan road, *Baruna Cottages* (☎0366/51221; ②–③) offer basic rooms with good views of the lake and are one of the quieter places to stay. One kilometre further west, *Hotel Buahan* (☎0366/51217; ③) has no views or restaurant but has good-quality tiled cottages. From here, the road edges between the lake and the cliffs and finally ends at the tiny village of **ABANG**, where there are a couple of shops selling soft drinks. From Abang, there's a lakeside footpath to Trunyan (4km).

Trunyan

The best-known Bali Aga village in Bali, inhabited by the original people of Bali who rejected the changes brought about by the Majapahit invasion in 1343 (see p.463), the village of **TRUNYAN** and its nearby cemetery at Kuban have now become rather too much of a tourist attraction. Situated in a dramatic position right beside Danau Batur with Gunung Abang rising up sheer behind, there are two main routes to the village: by boat from Kedisan or by footpath from Abang (see above).

The **boat trip** is beautiful but chilly and takes less than an hour. Seven-seater boats leave daily from the pier at Kedisan when full (Rp5075 per person, including insurance). You can also charter boats, which will cost Rp36,000–43,000 for a maximum of seven people. Check that your boat goes from Kedisan to Trunyan, on to the cemetery, and then back to Kedisan.

The village keeps many of the ancient **Bali Aga customs**, the most notorious being the traditional way of disposing of the dead, which involves neither burial nor cremation. Bodies are placed in open pits covered only by a cloth and a rough bamboo roof and left to decompose in the air. Trunyan's tiny **cemetery** is at Kuban, just north of the actual village, and is accessible only by boat. Visit here to see a few artfully arranged bones and skulls, a towering banyan tree (supposed to prevent any smell) and some graves.

Apart from growing cabbages and onions, the village's main source of income is from tourists, and you'll be pressed for donations throughout your visit. Some people have even been pressed for a donation to be allowed to leave. You will almost certainly have to pay something to get into the village and into the cemetery, and also for a guide, if you accept his services (Rp1000 is in line with other donations on Bali, but you'll probably end up paying more here). While it's easy to suggest you stand firm on other demands, Trunyan can feel rather isolated and forbidding, so make sure you have plenty of small notes.

Songan and the rim

At the northern end of the lake, 12km from Penelokan and 4km beyond Toya Bungkah, *Restiti Homestay* (☎0366/51287; ②) in the village of **SONGAN** offers simple **bungalows** in a quiet setting, several hundred metres beyond the village towards the temple.

Not to be confused with the bigger, more important temple of the same name up on the crater rim, **Pura Ulun Danu Batur** in Songan is believed locally to be one of the oldest temples in Bali. While some of the shrines in the inner of the two courtyards are very ancient, there is much modern, but sympathetic, building under way, with a whole line of *meru* planned along the back wall.

Directly behind the temple, a small footpath winds up onto the rim of the outer crater. To the right, the path heads up towards **Abang**, passing above Trunyan and the cemetery, but this is the hard way to climb Abang and shouldn't be attempted without a guide. As you head left, several footpaths pass through small strung-out villages. There are some fine lookout spots with views down to the north coast, and back to Abang, Agung and sometimes even Rinjani, on Lombok. After about 3km, a track leads down to the village of **BLANDINGAN**, from where there's a direct path back to Songan.

Gunung Batur

With a choice of four main craters, there are several ways to approach **Gunung Batur** (1717m). With your own transport, the easiest way to get to the top is to drive to **SERONGGA**, west of Songan. From the car park, it's a climb of between thirty minutes and one hour to the largest and highest crater, **Batur I**.

If you're reasonably fit and don't have your own transport, the most common route is to climb up to Batur I from either **Toya Bungkah** or the road near **Pura Jati**. Allow two to three hours to get to the top and about half that time to get back down. If you want a longer trek, it is possible to walk around the rim of Batur I, a narrow path with sheer drops in places (allow an extra hour). The longest option involves climbing up to Batur I, walking around the rim to the western side, descending to the rim of Crater II and then to the rim of Crater III. From here you can either walk down to Toya Bungkah or Yehmampeh (about 8hr).

Climbing the volcano

Climbing Batur is a dry-season expedition (April–Oct). The path becomes extremely unpleasant in the wet, and when clouds engulf the summit there's nothing to see anyway. However, the wet season doesn't bring unrelenting rain, and you might hit a dry few days.

In daylight, you shouldn't really need a guide if you are just intending to climb up to Batur I from Toya Bungkah or Pura Jati, although you should take one for lengthier treks. In Toya Bungkah there's a sign to show you where to go, just south of the car park. From Toya Bungkah, numerous paths head up through the forest and after about an hour you'll come out onto the bare slope of the mountain. From here, follow the paths that head up to the tiny warung perched way up on the crater rim on the skyline. This is the steep bit, often slippery with black volcanic sand. Fewer people climb during the day because of the heat, and the chance that the view from the top may be clouded over.

Most people climb **in the dark** to get to the top for dawn. You'll need to leave early (4–5am), and it's a good idea to take a **guide** as it's easy to get lost in the forest in the dark. There are plenty of guides hanging around the lakeside, offering their services for the climb – agree a price beforehand, but don't pay anything until you get back, and always make clear exactly which trek you want to do. The view over the lake as the sun rises behind Gunung Abang and Rinjani on Lombok is definitely worth the effort, and gets progressively less dramatic during the day.

Organized trekking services are springing up in Toya Bungkah – as usual, personal recommendation is the best bet. Two established services are Jero Wijaya and *Arlina's* (see p.563), charging from US$10 per person for sunrise treks up Batur. Jero Wijaya treks can also be booked in Ubud (see p.518 for details) and Kuta, Sanur, Ubud or Nusa Dua pick-ups can be arranged for an additional charge.

Bedugul and the lakes

Neither as big nor as dramatic as the Batur region, the **Bedugul** and **Danau Bratan** area, nevertheless, has impressive mountains, beautiful lakes, quiet walks and attractive and important temples. There is no direct route between the two regions: Bedugul and Danau Bratan lie on a busy parallel road, 53km from Denpasar and 30km from Singaraja, nestling in the lee of Gunung Catur, with the smaller, quieter lakes Buyan and Tamblingan about 5km to the northwest.

As you approach from the south, the main Denpasar–Mengwi–Singaraja road rises up to the rim of an ancient volcanic crater at the market village of **Bedugul**, and then descends through the villages of **Candi Kuning** and **Pancasari**, skirting the western shore of Danau Bratan. It then climbs again to the pass out of the crater at **Pucak**, where it begins the steep descent to the northern plains. The entire area is frequently referred to as Bedugul or Bratan, but it's actually very spread out so it's sensible to know where you are aiming for.

In many ways, the area is a Balinese destination rather than one favoured by foreign tourists. Farmers come to **Pura Ulun Danu** on the shores of Danau Bratan to make offerings to Dewi Danu, the goddess of the crater lake, while lowland dwellers come to the **Botanical Gardens** in Bedugul for weekend picnics, and to the **leisure park** (Taman Rekreasi) on the shores of Danau Bratan, where a vast array of watersports is available.

Bedugul and Danau Bratan

The small village of **BEDUGUL**, situated above the southern shores of Danau Bratan, is the centre for many of the sights in the area and is home to one of the gems of central Bali, the **Bali Botanical Gardens**. The daily **market**, Bukit Mungsu, is small but extremely diverse and colourful. Although catering largely for the tourist trade these days, it offers a vast range of spices and plants, including orchids.

There is a **wartel** (daily 8am–9.30pm) in the market with a national and international telephone and fax service. You can **change money** at Wisma Beratan Indah, a few hundred metres north of the temple car park, but rates are much poorer than in the main tourist centres. For **shuttle bus** tickets, the Perama office is at the *Ulun Danau Restaurant* (☎0362/21191) inside the temple compound. There are two buses daily to most destinations on Bali and Lombok, but from here you'll have a stopover if you are heading to Lombok.

The Bali Botanical Gardens

A short walk south from the market area, along a small sideroad by a giant corn-on-the-cob statue, are the **Bali Botanical Gardens** (Kebun Raya Eka Karya Bali; daily 7am–5pm; Rp1000 per person, cars Rp3000, motorbikes prohibited, small parking fee), a branch of the National Botanical Gardens at Bogor on Java. The gardens cover almost 320 acres on the slopes of Gunung Pohon (Tree Mountain). There are over 650 different species of **tree** here and over 400 species of **orchids**, and the gardens are also a rich area for **birdwatching**. It is a centre for the study of the plants of the region and there is also a herbarium and a library. The office in the grounds is open for study purposes, but serious students would be wise to contact the gardens beforehand (write to Cabang Balai Kebun Raya, Eka Karya Bali, Candikuning, Baturiti, Tabanan 82191).

Accommodation

Most **accommodation** in the area is in, or near, Bedugul village, although there are a few upmarket options slightly further afield.

Ashram Guest House (☎0368/21450, fax 21101). Situated in a good position on the lakeside this is a large establishment, offering a range of options. Lovely grounds, with tennis court and a pricey restaurant. ③–⑤.

Bali Handara Kosaido Country Club (☎0362/22646, fax 23048). Accessed from the main road north of Danau Bratan, 6km from Bedugul, this luxury establishment caters mostly for the Japanese market. Facilities include a golf course, tennis courts, a health and fitness centre and a karaoke bar. The view of Danau Buyan from the bar is glorious but, unless you have your own transport, it involves a 3km walk up the drive. The golf course, which claims to be the only one in the world situated in the crater of a volcano, and the tennis courts, are both open to non-residents. Expect to pay US$10 per hour for the tennis courts and US$77.50 for a round of golf, more at weekends, with additional charges for club and shoe rental and caddy fees. ⑨.

Bukit Stroberi (Strawberry Hill) (☎0368/21265). A small compound squeezed with rooms, on a bend in the main road close to the Taman Rekreasi turn-off: it can get a bit noisy. Rooms have hot water, and there's a good inexpensive restaurant attached. ④.

Cempaka (☎0368/21402). Clean, new place behind the road to the Botanical Gardens. Accommodation is in a two-storey block and the more expensive rooms upstairs have hot water. ③–④.

Enjung Beji (☎0368/21490, fax 21022). A good new option in this price range with accommodation in comfortable cottages set in an attractive garden located in Bedugul. ⑧–⑨.

Lila Graha (☎0368/21446). Almost opposite the *Ashram Guest House*, offering reasonable value in this price range. Basic bungalows overlook the lake and have bathrooms with hot water. The restaurant is in a large old wooden colonial house. ④–⑥.

Pacung Mountain Resort (☎0368/21038, fax 21043). Some 9km south of Bedugul, before Pacung, this is a luxurious resort with a small swimming pool and splendid views. The most comfortable of the expensive places in the area. ⑨.

Permata Firdaus (☎0368/21531). Just off the road to the Botanical Gardens, this new place has clean good-value rooms with hot water in a quiet location. ④.

Sari Atha Inn (☎0368/21011). Situated north of the market, there's a choice of rooms here with or without hot water. ③–④.

Eating and drinking

In the Taman Rekreasi park, the moderately priced restaurant by the lake has an excellent position, but the service is slow. For good-value food, the warung in the temple car park are worth a try, or *As Siddiq*, about 100m north of the car park on the opposite side of the road, is a pleasant place serving Taliwang and Sasak food in addition to the usual rice and noodle options. *Strawberry Stop*, 2km towards Pancasari, does a good range of juice and drinks and also serves up the tasty strawberries that grow in the market garden behind the restaurant.

The range of options isn't so good in the evenings, and beware that most places tend to close around 8pm. The more expensive hotels all have restaurants, but if you want to eat more simply in the village try *Bogasari*, near the market, the *Anda* just across the road, or the Muslim places on the road to the Botanical Gardens.

Danau Bratan

Situated at 1200m above sea level and thought to be 35m deep in places, **Danau Bratan** is surrounded by forested hills, with Gunung Catur rising sheer behind.

Revered by Balinese farmers as the source of freshwater springs across a wide area of the island, the lake and its goddess, Dewi Danu, are worshipped in the immensely attractive temple of **Pura Ulun Danu Bratan** (daily 7am–6pm; Rp1000), one of the most-photographed temples in Bali. Set in attractive, well-maintained grounds, the temple consists of several shrines, some spread along the shore and others dramatically situated on small islands that appear to float on the surface of the lake, with the water stretching behind and the mountain looming in the distance.

The **Taman Rekreasi Bedugul** (Bedugul Leisure Park; daily 8.30am–5pm; Rp1000, cars Rp500, motorbikes Rp200), on the southern shores of the lake, offers water-skiing, parasailing and jet-skiing (expect to pay about US$10–15 for 15min for these) and rents out motorboats (US$15 for 30min). There is also a vast number of private boat operators all around the lake, both near the Taman Rekreasi and the *Ashram Guest House*, but you'll need to bargain hard. From the Taman Rekreasi you can walk around the shoreline for a few hundred metres to three **caves**, supposedly dug by Indonesian labourers for the Japanese during World War II.

To the north, the path up **Gunung Catur** (2096m) is easy to find and, unless it's a festival day, unlikely to be overrun by people. To get to the path, turn away from the lake just past the third Japanese cave and take the short track that zigzags up onto the ridge, about 20m above. It hits another, bigger path heading along the ridge; turn left onto this path and simply follow it to the top of Catur. Unless there has been a radical cleanup operation, you can simply follow the trail of plastic water bottles and other litter. The climb is through forest with some glimpses of the lake far below. Allow two to three hours' unrelenting uphill climb – in a couple of places, you'll need to haul yourself up by the tree trunks. Take plenty of water and some snacks for the way. It should take about ninety minutes to get down again.

Danau Buyan and Danau Tamblingan

The best way to explore **Danau Buyan**, 7km northwest of Bedugul, is on foot, although you can drive as far as Yehmas. Follow the side road that heads west just to the north of the Pancasari bemo terminal, between the terminal and a *kulkul* tower. This leads to the village of **YEHMAS**. After about 2km the road turns rapidly into a dirt track, which follows close to the southern shores of the lake, mostly in the forest. Keep to the biggest and most level track for another 2km and you'll come out onto the shores of the lake – if you look carefully, the *meru* of Pura Tahun are visible in the trees at the western end. Continue on the path as it heads up to the ridge and along towards the temple; within about thirty minutes the forest gives way to fields, with Pura Tahun set among them, surrounded by trees. A short track leads west from here over to Danau Tamblingan across a raised shoulder of land. However, it is extremely difficult to find and it's easy to lose your sense of direction in the densely forested terrain.

To reach **Danau Tamblingan**, there are two options, although both routes are dry-season expeditions. Take the road west from **PUCAK**, 2km north of Pancasari, which is signed "scenic route" and runs along the ridge a couple of hundred metres above the northern shore of Danau Buyan, before arriving above the western shore of Danau Tamblingan. A couple of kilometres after you first spot the lake, you'll reach the village of **ASAM MUNDUK**, where there's a small car park beside a red-walled house and shop; take the tiny track down to the lakeside from opposite the shop and within fifteen to twenty minutes you'll be at the lakeshore. Alternatively, continue past Asam Munduk to a very rough road leading down steeply to the small lakeside village of **MUNDUK TAMBLINGAN**. Just in front of the village, on the shore, **Pura Gubug**, sporting eleven-, nine- and five-roofed *meru*, is dedicated to Dewi Danu. Farmers come here frequently on pilgrimages to worship the lake goddess and pray for good harvests.

The scenic route to the north coast

From the north shores of lakes Buyan and Tamblingan, the road from Pucak turns away from the lakes as it continues west. **Munduk waterfall**, 3km from Tamblingan, is signposted on a bend in the road; from here it's a 500-metre walk to the waterfalls. At the first big fork in the path, just after the house, head left and down, but after that take all right forks. The falls are high, powerful and a far quieter, more peaceful and more attractive option than the falls at the more famous Gitgit (see p.571) on the road north to Singaraja. A kilometre further along is the village of **MUNDUK**, which is an excellent base for exploring the area. In the village, *Puri Lumbung Cottages* (☎ & fax 0362/92810; ⑦–⑨) are replicas of traditional *lumbung* (rice storage barns). They are well furnished, in lovely grounds, and are highly recommended. There's a moderately priced restaurant attached and local treks and canoeing trips can be arranged here. You can arrange a pick-up from Pancasari bus terminal or there are bemos to Munduk from Seririt during the day. At the western end of the village there are three homestays, which have small gardens from which to admire the views: *Guru Ratna* (☎0362/92812; ④) offers shared bathrooms, while *Meme Surung* (⑤) and *Mekel Ragi* (⑤) – both administered by *Puri Lumbung Cottages* – have private ones. These are not luxurious places, nor especially cheap, but breakfast is included in the price. There are several warung in the village if you want to eat elsewhere.

Singaraja and around

The second largest Balinese city after Denpasar, **SINGARAJA** has an airy spaciousness created by its broad avenues, impressive monuments and colonial bungalows set in attractive gardens. With a population of over 100,000, it's home to an interesting ethnic mix of Balinese, Muslim and Chinese. Behind the old harbour you can still see the

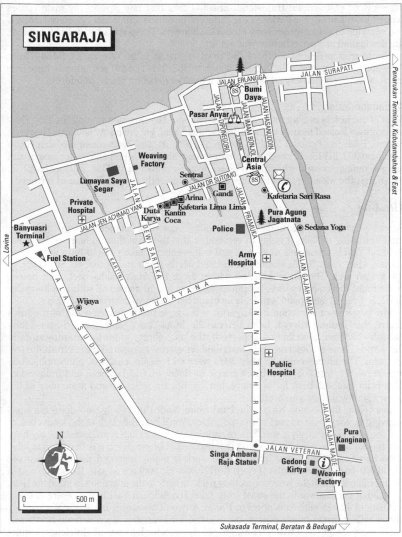

shop-houses and narrow streets of the original trading area, and most of the descendants of these earlier traders still live nearby. Jalan Hasanuddin is known locally as Kampong Bugis, and Jalan Imam Bonjol as Kampong Arab.

Arrival, information and accommodation

There are three bemo and bus **terminals** in Singaraja: **Sukasada** to the south of the town, serving Bedugul, Denpasar and points south; **Banyuasri** on the western edge of town serving the west, including Lovina and Java; and **Penarukan** to the east, operating services east around the island. Small bemos (flat rate Rp400) ply main routes around town journeying between the different terminals, but it can get complicated if you're trying to get to somewhere on the backstreets. There are a few *dokar* (negotiate the destination and price before you get in).

The **tourist office** is south of the town centre at Jalan Veteran 23 (Mon–Thurs 7am–2pm, Fri 7am–noon, Sat 7am–12.30pm; ☎0362/25141). Staff are helpful – have free maps of Buleleng district and Lovina and a booklet detailing places of interest.

Accommodation

Most of the **hotels** in Singaraja cater for Indonesian businessmen visiting the city. They are centrally located near or on Jalan Jen Achmad Yani, but are pretty soulless. However, *Sentral*, Jalan Jen Achmad Yani 48 (☎0362/21896; ③), and *Sedanayoga* on Jalan Gajah Made (☎0362/21715; ③), both offer fan rooms with an attached cold-water mandi and are welcoming enough, while the *Wijaya*, Jalan Sudirman 74 (☎0362/21915, fax 25817; ③–⑥), has the widest range of rooms and is conveniently close to Banyuasri terminal.

The City

Spread out along the coast and stretching inland for several kilometres, Singaraja can be quite confusing initially. It helps to remember that the main thoroughfare of Jalan Jen Achmad Yani is orientated west–east and will eventually take you out onto the road to Lovina, while Jalan Gajah Made is orientated north–south and heads, via Sukasada, to the Bratan area. The major junction where these two main roads meet, with hotels, restaurants, banks, post office, telephone office and night market all within walking distance, is a useful focal point and feels as much like the town centre as anywhere.

The best-known attraction in Singaraja is a couple of kilometres south of the town centre: the **Gedong Kirtya**, Jalan Veteran 20 (Mon–Thurs 8am–2pm, Fri 8am–11am, Sat 8am–12.30pm; contribution expected), the only library of **lontar manuscripts** in the world. These are ancient texts inscribed on specially prepared leaves from the *lontar* palm. The library contains over 3000 texts on religion, customs, philosophy, folklore, medicine, astrology and black magic in Balinese, Old Javanese and Indonesian. This is an establishment for scholars, but visitors are welcome and a member of the library staff will show you around.

Just behind the Gedong Kirtya, the **Puri Sinar Nadi Putri** (daily 8am–4pm) is a small **weaving factory**, built on part of the old palace. You'll hear the clack of the looms before you see what is essentially a shed where exquisite weft-*ikat* cloth is produced, mostly from silk and cotton (see p.550 for more on *ikat* textiles). A larger concern is Berdikari at Jalan Dewi Sartika 42 (daily 7am–7pm), whose work is highly regarded nationally. Scarves (Rp30,000–60,000) and lengths of cloth (Rp120,000–250,000) are on sale. It's best to visit in the morning to watch the weavers, as they pack up early in the afternoon to avoid the heat.

Walking north towards the coast from Jalan Jen Achmad Yani in the centre of town, a cluster of little streets runs down to **Pasar Anyar**, a two-storey maze of stalls and tiny shops selling pretty much everything needed for everyday life. Continue north and you'll reach Singaraja's **waterfront**, site of the ancient harbour of Buleleng. A quiet spot, backed by deserted warehouses, with views of traditional fishing villages further along the coast, it's hard to imagine the days when this was the most important and busiest port on Bali.

Eating, drinking and nightlife

The largest concentration of **restaurants** is on Jalan Jen Achmad Yani, in a small square set slightly back from the road; the Chinese restaurant, *Gandi*, is a good bet, as is *Surya*, just at the entrance, selling Padang food. Further west along the same street, there's another cluster of places which have menus in English and offer good, inexpensive rice and noodles, soft drinks and some iced desserts: *Arina* at no. 53, *Kafetaria Lima-Lima* at no. 55a and *Kantin Coca* at no. 55b. Also worth a look during the day is *Kafetaria Sari Rasa* on Jalan Gajah Made, just south of the Telkom office on the opposite side of the road. It has a small menu of cheap chicken, soups, rice, noodles and drinks. As darkness falls and the temperature drops, the **night market**, in the Jalan Durian area, springs into life. Lit by gloomy electric bulbs and parrafin lanterns, the shoppers amble between mountains of fruit and vegetables, exchange gossip or eat an evening meal at the bustling food stalls.

Listings

Banks and exchange The most central places to change money are Bank Central Asia on Jl Dr Sutomo (Mon–Fri 8am–2pm, Sat 8–11.30am), where you can also get Visa cash advances, and Bank Bumi Daya at Jl Erlangga 14 (Mon–Fri 8am–3pm, Sat 8–11.30am).

Hospitals Singaraja has three hospitals: Rumah Sakit Umum (the public hospital), Jl Ngurah Rai (☎0362/22046); Rumah Sakit Umum Angkatan Darat (an army hospital, staffed by army personnel, but open to the public), Jl Ngurah Rai (☎0362/22543); and Rumah Sakit Kerta Usada (a private hospital that also has a dentist), Jl Jen Achmad Yani 108 (☎0362/22396).

Pharmacies Many of Singaraja's medical facilities, including doctors and pharmacies, are concentrated in Jl Diponegoro.

Post office The main office with poste restante service is at Jl Gajah Made 156 (Mon–Sat 7am–4pm, Sun & hol 8am–1pm). Get mail sent to you at Jl Gajah Made 156, Singaraja 81113, Bali, Indonesia.

Telephone and fax The telephone office at Jl Gajah Made 154 (next door to the post office) is open 24 hr.

Travel agents Menggala, Jl Jen Achmad Yani 76 (☎0362/24374), and Puspasari Perdana, Jl Jen Achmad Yani 90 (☎0362/23062), both about 300m east of Banyuasri terminal, operate daily direct night buses to Surabaya (7hr; Rp22,000).

South of Singaraja

South of Singaraja, 10km along the road to Bedugul, **Gitgit waterfall** (daily 8am–5.30pm; Rp1100) is well signposted. A 500-metre walk from the road along a concrete path lined with textile and souvenir stalls, this definitely isn't the place for a quiet contemplation of the wonders of nature. The waterfall is about 40m high but falls dramatically into a deep pool, which is suitable for swimming if you can bear the audience; there are no changing rooms. There is a local belief that if you come to Gitgit with your boyfriend or girlfriend you will eventually separate.

East of Singaraja

Many of the brilliant carved **temples** to the **east of Singaraja** can be visited on a daytrip from Singaraja or Lovina. The main sights are fairly close together and all lie on regular bemo routes.

Sangsit

Eight kilometres east of Singaraja, a small road north takes you 200m to the pink sandstone **Pura Beji** of SANGSIT, highly unusual in an area where every other temple is built of grey volcanic *paras*. Dedicated to Dewi Sri, the rice goddess, it's justly famous for the sheer exuberance of its carvings.

About 400m to the northeast across the fields from Pura Beji, you'll be able to spot the red roofs of the **Pura Dalem**. The front wall of the temple shows the rewards that await the godly in heaven and the punishments awaiting the evil in hell. There is a preponderance of soft pornography here, and it isn't certain which of this is supposed to feature in hell and which in heaven. The village of Sangsit straggles 500m north from here to a black-sand working beach with a few fishing boats, shops and warung.

Jagaraga

Back on the main road, 500m east of the Sangsit turning, you come to the road that leads 4km to JAGARAGA. It was the site of an immense **battle** between the Balinese and the Dutch in 1848, which the Balinese, led by their commander Jelantik, won with huge loss of life, their 16,000 troops fighting largely with lances and kris against 3000 well-armed Dutch. The two forces met here again in 1849, when the Dutch took control of the area.

The famous temple here is **Pura Dalem Jagaraga**, where the front walls are a mass of pictorial carvings. Those on the left show a variety of village activities representing community life before the Dutch invasion; next to these are the Dutch arriving, and on the right-hand side is the much-photographed carving of two Dutch men driving a Model T Ford, being held up by bandits.

The only **place to stay** is back on the main road, about 200m east of the Jagaraga turning. *Berdikari Cottages* (☎0362/25195; ⑤–⑦) are attractive bungalows set in glorious gardens; when the planned pool is built this will be a real gem. Even if you don't want to stay, this is a good place for a moderately priced lunch, with a good range of Indo-Chinese options and drinks available.

Kubutambahan

The most spectacular of the temples in the area is **Pura Meduwe Karang** at KUBU-TAMBAHAN, 12km east of Singaraja and 500m west of the junction with the Kintamani road. The temple ensures divine protection for crops grown on dry land, such as coconuts, maize and groundnuts. It's built on a spectacular scale, with well-maintained grounds and frangipani trees galore. The terraces at the front support 34 figures from the *Ramayana* and inside, the central court is decorated with **carvings** of Balinese folk, including elderly people and mothers with babies and toddlers. In the inner courtyard you'll find one of the most famous carvings on Bali: a cyclist, wearing floral shorts, with a rat about to go under the back wheel, apparently being chased by a dog. It's possible that this depicts the Dutch artist W.O.J. Nieuwenkamp, who first visited Bali in 1904 and explored the island by bicycle. These lively carvings have a very human quality somehow missing in the other temples and, if you only make it to one temple in the north, this is the one to go for.

Around the coast

Further east, 6km from Kubutambahan, **AIR SANIH**, also known as **Yeh Sanih**, is a small, quiet beach resort that has grown up around the freshwater springs on the coast. The freezing cold **springs**, widely believed to originate in Danau Bratan, are set in attractive gardens with changing rooms (daily 7am–7pm; Rp400). Just next door, *Puri Sanih* (☎0362/23508; ④) is the most convenient **place to stay**, next to the beach and springs, with bungalows set in spacious grounds. Across the road from the springs, *Puri Rena* (no phones; ②–④) has adequate bungalows and good views from the restaurant at the front. For less expensive accommodation, head 500m east to the *Tara Beach Inn* (no phones; ③–④), which is right on the coast and offers a choice of bungalows. There's a small **restaurant** in the grounds, too. The real gem is *Cilik's Beach Garden* (☎0362/26561; bookings to *Cilik's Beach Garden*, Air Sanih, Singaraja 81172, Bali; ⑧), a few hundred metres to the east, with a superbly furnished bungalow in shady grounds right next to the beach – a lovely hideaway. Just east and across the road from the beach, *Puri Rahayu* (no phone; ④) has spotless, good-value bungalows in a small compound and a restaurant attached to it. It's another 2km to *Puri Pertiwi* (no phone; ④), with basic thatch-and-tile bungalows in a rather unkempt compound.

Lovina and around

LOVINA stretches along 8km of black-sand beach, the largest resort in Bali outside the Kuta-Legian-Seminyak conurbation. Beginning 6km west of Singaraja, the resort encompasses six villages: **Pemaron**, **Anturan**, **Tukad Mungga**, Kalibukbuk, **Kaliasem** and **Temukus**. **Kalibukbuk** is generally accepted as the centre of Lovina and it's here you'll find most tourist facilities. The reputation of Kalibukbuk as noisy, busy and spoilt is unfair, and outside of peak season (June–Aug & Dec), you can easily have a pleasant and relaxing stay. The main Singaraja–Gilimanuk road passes right through Lovina and, while some of the accommodation lines this road, most of the **accommodation** is along sideroads leading from the main road to the beach.

Activity centres mainly on the beach, with snorkelling, diving and dolphin-watching as diversions. However if you need a break from the coast, there are hot springs and a Buddhist temple nearby, and Singaraja and points east are easily accessible by bemo.

Arrival, information and getting around

Getting to Lovina is easy: inter-island buses from Java to Singaraja pass through, as do Gilimanuk–Singaraja and Amlapura–Gilimanuk services and all local buses and bemos from the west of the island. From Denpasar and the east of Bali, you'll come via Singaraja, from whose Banyuasri terminal it's a short bemo ride (Rp500). Tourist shuttle buses also serve the resort. As the accommodation is so spread out, it's worth knowing where you want to be dropped off, especially if you arrive late in the evening, as many of the buses from Java do.

Lovina's **tourist office** (Mon–Sat 8am–8pm) is on the main road at Kalibukbuk. The staff are friendly and helpful and try to coordinate information about empty beds in the busy season.

Getting around the resort on **public transport** is no problem, as you can pick up the frequent bemos (4am–9pm) that zip through between Singaraja and Seririt, although service can be erratic in the early morning and late evening. There are huge numbers of places offering **vehicles for rental** or charter (see "Listings", p.579). Rental charges are competitive, on a par with the resorts in the south. There are also **bicycles** for rent, but the Singaraja–Seririt road is very busy, traffic is fast and the heat in the north of the island doesn't make this a very pleasant option.

Accommodation

Despite its reputation as a backpackers' resort, new upmarket **accommodation** is growing all along the coast. Generally places closest to the beach are more expensive, and those on the main road are the cheapest. The busy season is from mid-June until late August and again in December, when accommodation is booked solid, and a lot of people end up spending their first night on the beach.

Pemaron and Tukad Mungga

The *Aldian Palace Hotel* on the main road is the marker for the eastern end of Lovina. Most of the accommodation here, in **PEMARON** and **Tukad Mungga**, is along sideroads leading down to the beach. It's very quiet with minimal hassle. There are no village amenities nearby and the nightlife of Kalibukbuk is several kilometres away, but you can walk 1km along the beach to the tourist facilities of Anturan. Beware of the dogs that guard the fishermen's huts.

Baruna Beach Cottages (℡0362/41745, fax 41252). Comfortable accommodation set in nice gardens, with a swimming pool only centimetres from the beach. ⑥–⑦.

RESTAURANTS

⑥	Adi Rama	⑤	John's	②	Puri Bunga
㉗	Arya's	⑭	Kakatua	㉒	Puri Taman Lovina
㉖	Bali Aga	⑳	Karma	⑪	Sea Breeze
⑱	Bali Apik	㉘	Khi Khi	⑫	Semina
⑦	Biyu Nasak	⑮	Kopi Bali	⑨	Spunky's Café
③	Djani's	⑲	Mailaku	⑧	Sunset Ayu
㉕	Flower Garden	㉓	Malibu	㉔	Surya
⑬	Gula Bali	⑰	Nick's	④	Warung Made
⑩	Harmony	①	Pondok Ayu	㉑	Wina's
⑯	Jaja Bali				

Happy Beach Inn (Bahagia; no phone). Good-value basic rooms with open-air bathrooms, conveniently located close to the beach. Small, pleasant garden and a beachside restaurant. ②.

Hepi (☎0362/41020). Fan and air-con rooms in a quiet garden setting, a short walk from the beach, and with a small pool. ③–④.

Permai (☎0362/23471). A large, clean, airy place near the beach with a good-sized pool. There's a range of options, with air-con and hot water in the more expensive rooms. The Permai diving centre is based here, so it's fairly lively when courses are going on. ③–④.

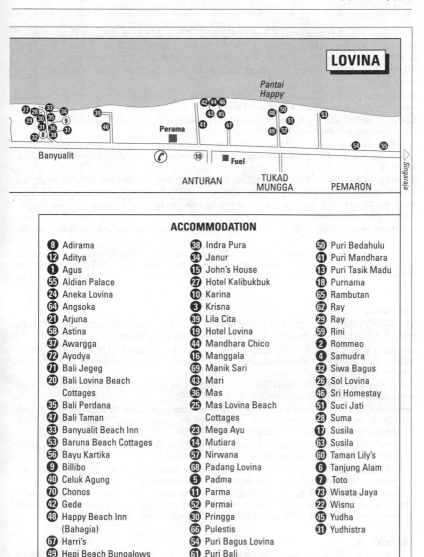

ACCOMMODATION

8 Adirama	**38** Indra Pura
12 Aditya	**34** Janur
1 Agus	**15** John's House
55 Aldian Palace	**27** Hotel Kalibukbuk
24 Aneka Lovina	**10** Karina
64 Angsoka	**3** Krisna
21 Arjuna	**39** Lila Cita
58 Astina	**19** Hotel Lovina
37 Awargga	**44** Mandhara Chico
72 Ayodya	**16** Manggala
71 Bali Jegeg	**69** Manik Sari
20 Bali Lovina Beach Cottages	**43** Mari
35 Bali Perdana	**36** Mas
47 Bali Taman	**25** Mas Lovina Beach Cottages
33 Banyualit Beach Inn	**23** Mega Ayu
53 Baruna Beach Cottages	**14** Mutiara
56 Bayu Kartika	**57** Nirwana
9 Billibo	**68** Padang Lovina
40 Celuk Agung	**5** Padma
70 Chonos	**11** Parma
42 Gede	**52** Permai
48 Happy Beach Inn (Bahagia)	**30** Pringga
67 Harri's	**66** Pulestis
49 Hepi Beach Bungalows	**54** Puri Bagus Lovina
	61 Puri Bali

50 Puri Bedahulu
41 Puri Mandhara
13 Puri Tasik Madu
18 Purnama
65 Rambutan
62 Ray
29 Ray
59 Rini
2 Rommeo
4 Samudra
32 Siwa Bagus
26 Sol Lovina
46 Sri Homestay
51 Suci Jati
28 Suma
17 Susila
63 Susila
60 Taman Lily's
6 Tanjung Alam
7 Toto
73 Wisata Jaya
22 Wisnu
45 Yudha
31 Yudhistra

Puri Bagus Lovina (☎0362/21430, fax 22627). Quality addition to the luxury end of the market. Accommodation is in large, well-furnished villas with verandahs and indoor and open-air showers. Attractive grounds and an excellent pool. ⑧–⑨.

Anturan

The main turning to the small fishing village of **ANTURAN** is opposite the petrol station and *Harmony Restaurant* on the main road and there's another sideroad, almost

1km west, which is quieter and less developed. While this area remains much quieter and more low-key than Kalibukbuk, there are still hassles, and you'll share the local beach with the villagers. This area is especially convenient if you arrive on a Perama shuttle bus, as the village is a short walk from their Anturan office where you'll be dropped off.

Bali Taman (☎0362/41126, fax 22840). A big operation with comfortable, well-furnished rooms, a swimming pool, tennis courts and pleasant grounds. ⑥–⑨.

Gede (no phone). Close to the beach in a small compound, with a range of reasonable bungalows; there's hot water in the more expensive ones. ③–④.

Lila Cita (no phone). About 300m walk from the main road and set in a garden compound right behind the beach and away from the main Anturan development. One of the quietest places along the coast. ③.

Mandhara Chico (☎0362/41476, fax 41174). Good-quality tiled rooms, some with hot water, in a small compound with seating areas close to the beach. ④–⑤.

Mari (no phone). Well positioned near the beach, with two types of room: basic cheap ones or smarter, tiled ones. ②–④.

Sri Home Stay (☎0362/41135). The rooms are very basic, but the beachside location is unbeatable. ③.

Yudha (Simon Seaside Cottage; ☎0362/41183, fax 41160). A long-time favourite that has moved upmarket with a new concrete compound and restaurant just beside the beach. The rooms are comfortably furnished and some have great views. Prices will rise when the planned pool is complete. ③–⑥.

Banyualit

The **BANYUALIT** sideroad marks the beginning of the developed part of Lovina, with a good range of places to stay, a few restaurants and some shops.

Banyualit Beach Inn (☎0362/41789, fax 41563). Well-furnished bungalows in an attractive garden setting; more expensive options have air-con and hot water. There's a good pool and a children's playground. ⑤–⑥.

Celuk Agung (☎0362/41039, fax 41379). Good-quality option in this price range. All rooms have hot water and there's a pool and a footpath to the beach. ⑥–⑧.

Janur (☎0362/41056). One of several basic places offering good budget accommodation in small compounds with attached restaurants. Similar options nearby are *Pringga* (☎0362/41281), *Indrapura* (☎0362/41560) and *Awargga* (☎0362/41561). ③.

Ray (☎0362/41088). An offshoot of the successful set-up at Kalibukbuk, this is a big, two-storey building, a short walk from the beach, with good-value rooms. ③–④.

Siwa Bagus (☎0362/41753). Located 200m west of the Banyualit turning, this place has good-quality, large bungalows in a great garden and there's a footpath to the beach. ④.

Sol Lovina (☎0362/41775, fax 41659). This is the most imposing hotel in the area, reached via its own drive from the main road, with a huge entrance area, good-quality accommodation and all the facilities you would expect at this end of the market, including a massive pool. ⑧–⑨.

Kalibukbuk

Centred around two sideroads, Ketapang and Bina Ria Street, **KALIBUKBUK** has a huge number of places to stay and to eat, some nightlife and most of the tourist facilities. The places on the main road are the ones to go for if you're on a tight budget, but the road is quite noisy. The narrow entrance to Ketapang is easy to miss; look out for *Khi Khi Restaurant* on the opposite side of the road. Bina Ria Street has the biggest concentration of buildings, and a maze of sideroads lead off from it.

Astina (☎0362/41187). A range of options, from rooms without attached bathrooms to cottages in a large, airy compound quite close to the beach at the end of Ketapang. ③–⑤.

Bali Jegeg (☎0362/41251) Good-value, budget place on the main road. Rooms have attached bathrooms and are set back a good way, so it's not too noisy. ②.

Bayu Kartika (☎0362/41055). In one of the best positions in Lovina, on the coast at the end of Ketapang. A good range of options, from fan and cold water at the bottom to air-con and hot water at the top – all are spotless and have mosquito nets. ④–⑤.

Harri's (☎0362/41152). A little gem tucked away in the backstreets off Bina Ria Street – worth searching out. ③.

Manik Sari (☎0362/41089). Accessible from the main road and Bina Ria Street, these are good-value bungalows in a convenient location with an attractive garden. ③.

Nirwana (☎0362/41288, fax 41090). A large, well-organized but rather impersonal development with a huge choice of comfortable accommodation. Lovely position in well-maintained gardens near the beach at the end of Bina Ria Street. ④–⑤.

Padang Lovina (☎0362/41302). Very popular, straightforward fan bungalows with mosquito netting set in an attractive garden in a good position off Bina Ria Street. The most expensive have hot water. ④–⑤.

Puri Bali (☎0362/41485). A variety of rooms in an attractive garden with a good-sized pool; more expensive ones have air-con and hot water. Quiet location on Ketapang not far from the beach. ④–⑥.

Rambutan (☎0362/41388, fax 41057). Halfway down Ketapang with well-furnished, clean bunga-lows set well apart in a beautiful garden. One of the nicest places in Lovina in this price range, it also has a small swimming pool and an attractive restaurant. ⑤–⑥.

Ray (☎0362/41087). Although offering good value for the location off Bina Ria Street, it's a bit hemmed in by the larger establishments nearby; upstairs rooms are more airy. ③.

Rini (☎0362/41386). Clean rooms in a quiet garden location on Ketapang. ④.

Kaliasem and Temukus

As you head west from Kalibukbuk, passing through the villages of **KALIASEM** and **TEMUKUS**, the main road gets much closer to the coast, and there are restaurants and accommodation lining the roadside. The western end of Lovina is marked by *Pondok Ayu Restaurant* on the south side of the road and *Agus* on the coast side.

Agus (☎0362/41202). A small place with good-quality rooms that currently marks the western end of the accommodation in Lovina. ③–④.

Bali Lovina Beach Cottages (☎ & fax 0362/41285). A good mid-range choice right beside the beach, with plenty of bungalows at different prices and an excellent pool. ⑦–⑧.

Billibo (☎0362/41355). These tiled, clean bungalows are close to the beachfront and have fans and cold-water bathrooms, plus mosquito screens – a definite plus in the rainy season. ④.

Krisna (☎0362/41141). Reasonable rooms with fans and attached cold-water mandi, towards the far end of Lovina and close to the beach. ③.

Parma (☎0362/41555) Attractive, clean bungalows in a small compound with tiled roofs and veran-dahs facing seawards. ④.

Puri Tasik Madu (☎0362/41376). Situated right next to the beach, the rooms are clean, comfort-able and good value. ③.

The resort

Lovina's long **black-sand beach** stretches into the distance with no bays or headlands to focus the eye. Without the huge breakers that pound the beaches on the south coast, there is nothing to draw the surfers to Lovina, and swimming around here is generally calmer and safer, although there are no lifeguards on duty. There's not a great deal to do other than enjoy the beach, although many people consider Lovina's early-morning **dolphin trips** to be the highlight of their stay.

The range of souvenirs and clothing for sale around the resort doesn't compare with Kuta, but **shopping** can be far less pressured. One place that is out of the ordinary is Benny Tantra, which sells excellent cartoon T-shirts and postcards. There's a good range of secondhand books, too: check out Ketapang and the main road in Kalibukbuk.

Snorkelling and diving

The **reef** off Lovina used to stretch at least 5km along the coast, but the anchoring of boats, fish-bombing, harpoon fishing and damage from snorkellers has decimated the coral, although it is hoped that it will begin to rejuvenate through local efforts. However, there is still an excellent range of fish. The best spot locally for **snorkelling** is off *Aditya* hotel to the west of Kalibukbuk. Your losmen can arrange trips for you or you can approach the boat skippers on the beach direct; expect to pay Rp10,000–15,000 for a two-hour trip. Most of the dive shops will take snorkellers along on trips further afield.

Situated between the main **diving** areas on the north coast of Bali – Pulau Menjangan (Deer Island) to the west (see p.590), and Tulamben (see p.557) and Amed (see p.556) to the east – Lovina is a good place to base yourself for diving. There are plenty of operators in the resort; all offer trips for qualified and experienced divers, but only some run beginners' courses. For two-dive trips to Pulau Menjangan, Tulamben or Amed, you'll pay US$45–60, and about US$40 for two local dives in the Lovina area.

DIVE OPERATORS

Baruna, on the main road in Kalibukbuk (☎0362/41084). A branch of the main office near Denpasar, offering diving trips and courses in Lovina.

Malibu Lovina Dive Centre (☎ & fax 0362/41225). A PADI diving centre operating a full range of dives for certified divers as well as PADI courses.

Permai, *Hotel Permai*, Tukad Mungga (0362/41471, fax 41224) and another counter in Bina Ria Street. Offers dives for certified divers, PADI courses and introductory dives. The early stages of courses are in the *Hotel Permai* swimming pool.

Spice Dive, Kaliasem (☎0362/41305, fax 41171; *spicedive@denpasar.wasantara.net.id*) with another shop in Bina Ria Street. A long-established operator offering courses, a range of trips (including the "Rainbow Tour" to Pemuteran to the west; see p.591) and full- or half-day introductory dives; early training is in a local pool.

Dolphin trips

Lovina has become famous, or infamous, depending on your point of view, for the dawn trips to see the school of **dolphins** that frolics just off the coast. Opinions are fairly evenly split between those who think it's grossly overrated and those who consider it one of the best things on Bali. Boats leave at 6am and the ensuing scenario is mildly comic, as one skipper spots a dolphin and chases after it, to be followed by the rest of the fleet, by which time, of course, the dolphin is long gone. If you can see the funny side, it's a good trip. Expect to pay Rp10,000 per person for the two-hour trip, and if you book directly with the skippers on the beach you'll earn their goodwill, as they'll get the full fare without having to pay commission to booking agents.

A much easier way to see dolphins, albeit concrete ones, is to visit the bold, new monument, **Patung Lumba Lumba**, at the beach end of Bina Ria Street, where they are depicted complete with black-and-white-checked *kain poleng* headscarves – it's pretty unique.

Eating, drinking and nightlife

There's a high turnover of **restaurants** in Lovina, and the favourite today may well be extinct tomorrow. The quality of food is generally reasonable, with seafood the local speciality. There's a healthy level of competition here, with plenty of good "happy hour" deals, especially around Bina Ria Street. The places recommended below are all in Kalibukbuk and are marked on the map on p.574–575.

Arya's. Offering a good range of moderately priced Western and Indonesian dishes with several vegetarian options. Many places have copied their cakes and pastries, but this is the real thing and highly recommended. Owned by the same people as *Sea Breeze*.

Bali Apik. Tucked away off Bina Ria Street, there is an excellent choice of inexpensive breakfasts and cheap pizzas during the day, as well as a large Indo-Chinese and Western menu and lots of "happy hour" specials at night.

Flower Garden Restaurant. Set well back from the main road, with a pleasant atmosphere, and lots of vegetarian options on the moderately priced menu.

Gula Bali. A quiet, attractive option on Ketapang with a moderately priced menu of Indonesian and Western food, including pizzas with a range of toppings. They also offer a good-value breakfast.

Malibu. The centre of the nightlife in Lovina, this large restaurant offers nightly videos and regular live music, free transport to and from hotels in the Lovina area, and is open until about 2am. It's inexpensive/moderate with a big range of Western food, seafood and Indo-Chinese options and a big drinks list, although drinks are pricey in the evening.

Sea Breeze. Brilliantly located on the beach, this is the spot for a sunset drink, with an excellent menu and a great selection of cakes and desserts.

Semina. A quiet little restaurant along Ketapang offering a good Indo-Chinese menu in friendly surroundings.

Nightlife

Anybody coming to Lovina expecting a thriving disco scene is in for a big disappointment. After a day relaxing on the beach, most people eat dinner slowly and head off to bed. *Malibu* is the liveliest spot and has the biggest video screen and most popular live music, although *Wina's* also offers a bar, pool table and live local rock band.

There are twice-weekly dance shows at the Panggung Terbuka stage on the main road (Rp6000), with local performers providing a standard fare of *legong*, and several restaurants offer buffets plus **Balinese dance shows** for Rp7500–9500. Look out for the flyers around town or check out the *Rambutan* bungalows, the *Semina* restaurant on Ketapang in Kalibukbuk, or the *Flower Garden* on the main road.

Listings

Banks and exchange Moneychangers (daily 8.30am–4pm) and banks (Mon–Sat 8am–2pm) are found every few metres along the main road in Kalibukbuk.

Car and motorbike rental This is available throughout the resort both from established firms and as charters from people who will approach you on the street. Expect to pay around Rp35,000 a day for a Suzuki Jimny and Rp45,000 for a Kijang, plus around Rp20,000 per day for a driver. Insurance is available with a Rp40,000 excess and will cost about Rp27,000 per day (Rp67,000 for seven days). Motorbikes are also widely available (Rp12,000–15,000 per day), as are bicycles (Rp3000–5000 per day). If you want to use an established company, try Koperasi Marga Sakti (✆0362/41061) on Bina Ria Street; Artha Transport (✆0362/41091) on Ketapang; or Perama (see Basics p.38 for general advice on car rental).

Cookery courses *Djani's* restaurant offers a range of half- and full-day Indonesian cookery courses featuring between five and eight local dishes for Rp30,000–50,000 per person (two people minimum).

Doctors There are a couple of local doctors, but they aren't around every day. The tourist office has information and can recommend doctors in Singaraja. The closest hospitals are in Singaraja (see p.571), although for anything serious you'll have to go to Denpasar (see p.476).

Police Located in the same building as the tourist office, they will also try to help you with information if the tourist office is closed.

Post office The post office is about 1km west of Kalibukbuk (Mon–Thurs & Sat 8am–3pm, Fri 8am–1pm). Poste restante is available; have mail addressed to you at the Post Office, Jl Raya Singaraja, Lovina, Banjar, Singaraja 81152, Bali, Indonesia. There are several postal agents in Kalibukbuk who will sell stamps, but the only one offering poste restante is the Perama office at Anturan (have mail addressed c/o Kantor Pos, Perama office, Anturan, Lovina 81151, Singaraja, Bali).

Telephone and fax There are wartels dotted throughout the resort. One of the largest (daily 9am–11pm) is next to *Wina's* bar on the main road in Kalibukbuk, west of Bina Ria Street, and there's one on the main road in Anturan (7.30am–10pm).

Travel agents Perama has three offices in the area, at Anturan, on the main road in Kalibukbuk, and on Ketapang (☎0362/41161; 8am–9pm), offering the full range of travel services including shuttle buses on Bali and Lombok. They can also book planes and buses to other parts of Indonesia, including Jakarta, Yogyakarta and Bromo, and rent out bicycles, motorbikes and cars. There are plenty of smaller operators offering a similar service, such as Koperasi Marga Sakti on Bina Ria Street (☎0362/41061), whose times may suit you better.

Around Lovina

Bali's only **Buddhist monastery** lies 10km southwest of Lovina and can be combined with a visit to the hot springs at Banjar. Catch any westbound bemo to **DENCARIK**, where a sign points inland to the monastery, and ojek wait to take you the last steep 5km. The **Brahma Vihara Ashrama** was consecrated in 1972; the temple complex is in a wonderful hillside setting and the lower temple contains a gold Buddha from Thailand as the centrepiece. There are carved stone plaques showing scenes from Buddha's life on all the main temples, and a colourful Buddhist grotto to the left of the top temple.

From the temple you can walk to the **hot springs** (daily 8am–6pm; Rp1000). Head back downhill and take the first major left turn. After a few hundred metres you'll reach a major crossroads and marketplace at the village of **BANJAR TEGA**. Turn left and a highly decorated *kulkul* tower will now be on your right. After about 200m you'll see a sign for the "Holy Hot Springs, Air Panas" pointing you to a left turn. From here, it's a pleasant one-kilometre walk to the springs. The area has been landscaped and is well maintained, with changing rooms and toilets. Weekends and holidays can get a bit busy, but otherwise this is a lovely spot. The pools are overlooked by a restaurant, which offers moderately priced **food** and good views. If you want to **stay** nearby, *Pondok Wisata Griya Sari* (☎0362/92903, fax 92966; ⑦–⑧) offers comfortable rooms, with good verandahs but no hot water. From the springs you can walk the 3km back to the main road, or you should be able to find an ojek. This area is the main grape-growing area in Bali and you'll see the cultivated vines in the fields next to the road; the best-quality grapes are exported to Japan and Hong Kong and the rest are used to produce Indonesian wine.

THE WEST

Sparsely populated, mountainous, and in places extremely rugged, **western Bali** stretches from the northwestern outskirts of Denpasar across 128km to Gilimanuk at the island's westernmost tip. Once connected to East Java by a tract of land (now submerged beneath the Bali Strait), the region has always had a distinct Javanese character and now boasts a significant Muslim population.

Apart from making the statutory visits to **Pura Tanah Lot** and **Sangeh Monkey Forest**, few tourists linger long in west Bali, choosing instead to rush through on their way to or from Java, pausing only to board the ferry in the port town of **Gilimanuk**. Yet the southwest coast holds some fine black-sand beaches, and some good **surf** at **Medewi**, while the cream of Bali's **coral reefs** lie off the northwest coast between **Pulau Menjangan (Deer Island)** and **Pemuteran**. Furthermore, Bali's only national park is here: over seventy percent of the land area in the west is preserved as **Bali Barat national park**, home to the endangered Bali starling.

Mengwi

Eighteen kilometres northwest of Denpasar, the small village of **MENGWI** has a glittering history as the capital of a powerful seventeenth-century kingdom and is the site of an important temple from that era. However, although **Pura Taman Ayun** (daily during daylight hours; donation requested; sarong and sash essential) now features on numerous organized tours, lauded as a magnificent "garden temple", it looks far more impressive in aerial photographs than from the ground and doesn't merit a special trip. Probably built in 1634, it was designed as a series of garden terraces with each courtyard on a different level, and the whole complex was surrounded by a moat – now picturesquely choked with weeds and lilies – to symbolize the mythological home of the gods, Mount Meru, floating in the milky sea of eternity. For the best view of the temple's layout, climb to the top of the *kulkul* tower in the southwest corner of the central courtyard.

The easiest way to reach Mengwi by **bemo** is from Denpasar's Ubung terminal, from where you can take the frequent Bedugul-bound service (30min). If you're coming from Tabanan and points further west, take any Ubung-bound bemo to the junction just before Kapal and change onto the Bedugul service.

Sangeh Monkey Forest

Monkeys have a special status in Hindu religion, and a number of temples in Bali boast a resident monkey population, respected by devotees and fed and photographed by tourists. The **Monkey Forest** (Bukit Sari; donation requested) in the village of **SANGEH** is probably the most visited of these on Bali, its inhabitants the self-appointed guardians of the slightly eerie **Pura Bukit Sari**. The temple was built here some time during the seventeenth century, in a forest of sacred nutmeg trees that tower to heights of 40m, and is best appreciated in late afternoon after the tour buses have left. During peak hours, the place can seem disappointing, but seen in waning light with only the monkeys for company the forest and the temple take on a memorably ghostly aspect.

Sangeh is on a minor road that connects Denpasar, 21km to the south, with the mountainside village of Pelaga. **Bemos** run direct to Sangeh from the small Wangaya bemo terminal in central Denpasar. This is the only way of getting to the Monkey Forest by public transport. If you have your own vehicle, Sangeh is an easy fifteen-kilometre drive northeast from Mengwi, or a pleasant forty-minute ride west from Ubud, via Sayan. Alternatively, you could join one of the numerous **organized tours** from any of the resorts, which usually combine Sangeh with visits to Mengwi, Tanah Lot or Bedugul.

Pura Tanah Lot

Dramatically marooned on a craggy wave-lashed rock sitting just off the southwest coast, **Pura Tanah Lot** (Rp1000) really does deserve its reputation as one of Bali's top sights. Fringed by frothing white surf and glistening black sand, its elegant multi-tiered shrines have become the unofficial symbol of Bali, appearing on a vast range of tourist souvenirs. Unsurprisingly, the temple attracts huge crowds every day, particularly around sunset. Even bigger crowds amass here at the time of Pura Tanah Lot's **odalan** festival.

The temple is said to have been founded by the wandering Hindu priest **Nirartha**, who was drawn to Tanah Lot by a beaming light that shone from a holy spring here. He began to preach to the local people of Beraban, but this angered the incumbent priest, who demanded that the rival holy man should leave. In response, Nirartha meditated so hard that he pushed the rock he was sitting on out into the sea; this became the Tanah Lot "island". He then dedicated his new retreat to the god of the sea and transformed his scarf into poisonous snakes to protect the place. Ever since then, Pura Tanah Lot has been one of the most holy places on Bali, closely associated with several other important temples along this coast, including Pura Rambut Siwi and Pura Luhur Uluwatu.

Because of its sacred status, only bona fide devotees are now allowed to climb the temple stairway carved out of the rock face and enter the compounds; everyone else is confined to the patch of grey sand around the base of the rock which is under water at high tide. When the waters are low enough, you can take a sip of **holy water** (*air suci*) from the spring that rises beneath the temple rock (donation requested) or stroke the docile holy coral **snakes** that are kept in nests behind the cliff face.

If you follow the **clifftop path** to the southwest (right) of the temple rock you can admire the great panorama and drop down to any number of tiny bays below, though the grey sandy beaches are prone to strong waves and aren't that inviting for swimming. After about 1km, the path veers inland, through the hamlet of **BERABAN**; follow it round to the right of the village temple to get back to the Tanah Lot car park, or veer left to rejoin the coastal path which leads to the beach at Yeh Gangga, about an hour's walk away (see opposite).

Practicalities

Though there are occasional bright-blue **bemos** from Denpasar's Ubung terminal direct to Tanah Lot, you'll probably end up having to go via **Kediri**, 12km east of the temple complex on the main Denpasar–Tabanan road. All Ubung (Denpasar)–Gilimanuk **bemos** drop passengers at Kediri bemo station (30min; Rp1000), where you can should change on to a Kediri–Tanah Lot bemo (more frequent in the morning; 25min; Rp600). Alternatively, join one of the numerous tours to Tanah Lot that operate out of all major tourist resorts.

The coastal path overlooking the temple complex is packed with pricey **restaurants**; the less expensive cafés and restaurants are further back, near the car park. The cheapest **accommodation** is in the poor-value losmen rooms (③) attached to the Puri Lukisan art studio; much more salubrious are the well-managed *Dewi Sinta Cottages* (☎0361/812933, fax 813956; ⑥–⑧), set in a tropical garden, and the similarly attractive *Mutiara Tanah Lot* (☎0361/812939; ⑦) next door. And there's the controversial new luxury hotel complex, *Le Méridien Nirwana Golf and Spa Resort*, part of the *Bali Nirwana Resort* (☎0361/244504, fax 812398; ⑨), whose construction close to such a holy temple caused a great deal of local upset.

Tabanan and the Subak Museum

Tabanan district has long been a major rice producer and the **Subak Museum** (daily 7.30am–6.30pm; donation requested) on the eastern outskirts of Tabanan district capital celebrates the role of the rice farmers' collectives, the *subak*, by describing traditional farming practices and exhibiting typical agricultural implements (for more on the *subak*, see p.466). One of the most interesting sections of the display explains the highly complex and yet completely unmechanized **irrigation system** used by every *subak* on the island – a network of underground tunnels, small channels and tiny wooden dams that's known to have been in operation on Bali as early as 600 AD.

Despite being the former capital of the ancient kingdom of Tabanan and the administrative centre of one of Bali's most fertile districts, **TABANAN** itself is only a medium-sized town with little to encourage a protracted stop. Most Ubung (Denpasar)–Gilimanuk **bemos** bypass the town centre, dropping passengers at the **Pesiapan** terminal on the northwest edge of the town, from where bright-yellow city bemos ferry people into town. The Subak Museum is poorly signposted off the main Tabanan road, in **Banjar Senggulan**, 2km east of Tabanan town centre and about 4km west of the Kediri T-junction. Coming from Ubung you may be able to persuade the **bemo** driver to drop you at the museum; if not, change onto a Tabanan bemo at Kediri or onto a town-centre bemo at Tabanan's Pesiapan terminal. Get out as soon as you see the prominent sign of the *Taman Senggulan* restaurant on the north side of the road. The museum is 400m up the hillside road opposite, flagged by a tiny sign saying *"Mandala Mathika Subak"*.

Accommodation in Tabanan is limited to the dingy outfit 1km out on the eastern edge of town, *Hotel Taruna Jaya*, at Jalan Dharma Wanasa 1 (②), across the main road from the police station; it's better to head for the nearby Yeh Gangga beach (see below) or for Lalang Linggah (Balian Beach; p.585).

Taman Kupu Kupu Butterfly Park

About 5km north of Tabanan, on the road to Gunung Batukau, the **Taman Kupu Kupu Butterfly Park** (daily 9am–6pm; Rp10,000) houses butterfly species from all over Indonesia in its small but prettily landscaped garden. Several of the butterflies are rare enough to feature on the CITES list of protected species, including the spectacular green and black *ornithoptera priamus*, which comes from Irian Jaya and has a wingspan of at least 10cm. All Tabanan–Penebel **bemos** pass the park, and they leave from the Tawakilang terminal, 2km north of Tabanan town centre on the Penebel road. To get to Tawakilang, take a town-centre bemo from either central Tabanan or from Pesiapan terminal on the eastern edge of town. Or charter a bemo from Pesiapan direct to Taman Kupu Kupu (about Rp5000 return).

Yeh Gangga beach and Tibubiyu

Heading west out of Tabanan, nearly every minor road leads straight to the coast, an as yet undeveloped stretch of black sand notable for its strong currents and weird offshore rock formations. One of the most appealing sections is at YEH GANGGA, 10km southwest of Tabanan, where the *Bali Wisata Bungalows* (☎0361/261354; ⑤–⑥) make a good base from which to explore the area if you have your own transport. The place is set in a wild shorefront garden and comprises half a dozen spacious bungalows (some with kitchen facilities), a small pool and a restaurant. The sea itself gets pretty rough and is punctuated by huge eroded rocks, but the beach stretches for kilometres in both directions. Heading southeast along the coast you can walk to Tanah Lot (see p.581) in about an hour – ask at *Bali Wisata* for precise directions. The access road to Yeh Gangga is signposted off the main road about 2km west of Tabanan town centre and goes via the small village of **Geybug** en route. Yeh Gangga **bemos** depart Tabanan's Pesiapan terminal regularly throughout the morning and early afternoon (45min; around Rp1000).

Occupying a similarly splendid spot in the village of **TIBUBIYU**, 12km southwest of Tabanan and a few kilometres west of Yeh Gangga, *BeeBee's* (no phone, fax bookings 0361/236021; ⑤) offers five beautifully designed rice-barn-style bungalows surrounded by paddy-fields with sea views from the upstairs bedrooms. The black-sand beach is ten minutes' walk away and you can borrow bicycles. To get to Tibubiyu, you'll need to go via the village of **Krambitan**, 4km north of *BeeBee's*. Turquoise Krambitan-bound **bemos** leave frequently from Tabanan's Pesiapan terminal (45min; Rp700) and, once in Krambitan, the drivers can usually be persuaded to drive the extra 4km to Tibubiyu for another Rp300 per person.

Gunung Batukau

Much of inland southwest Bali lies in the shadow of the massive **Gunung Batukau** (sometimes spelt "Bautukaru"), at 2276m the second highest mountain on the island (after Gunung Agung) and one of the holiest. All west Bali temples have a shrine dedicated to the spirit of Gunung Batukau, and on the lower slopes of the holy mountain itself stands Pura Luhur Batukau, Bali's directional temple (*kayangan jagat*) for the west, and the focus of many pilgrimages. The dense tropical forest that clothes the uppermost slopes of Gunung Batukau has now been designated as a nature reserve, and is a particularly rewarding area for birdwatching.

From Tabanan, with your own transport, you have a choice of two **routes to Batukau**. The most scenic approach starts from Tabanan town centre and takes you through some lovely flower-lined villages, via **Penebel** and the exceptionally fine rice-terrace vistas at **Jatiluwih**. West of Jatiluwih, the road eventually comes to a junction at the village of **Wangayagede**, from where it's just a two-kilometre drive north to the small car park in front of Pura Luhur Batukau. The slightly more direct route from Tabanan to Wangayagede takes you along a road that's in far better condition, but is less dramatic. It begins about 7km west of Tabanan, branching north off the main Tabanan–Gilimanuk road at **Miling**, from where it passes through **Penatahan** and on to Wangayagede.

It's currently impossible to get to Pura Luhur Batuhan by public **bemo**, though there is a Tabanan–Penebel–Jatiluwih service, and you may be able to charter the same bemo onto Pura Luhur. These leave from the bemo station at Tawakilang, 2km north of Tabanan's town centre, departing approximately hourly in the mornings (less frequently after noon). Otherwise, any tour operator will be happy to make it the focus of a tailor-made sightseeing **tour**, and most places also sell activity tours such as guided mountain-bike trips down the lower slopes of Gunung Batukau or organized hikes through the Batukau rainforests.

Pura Luhur Batukau

Usually silent except for its resident orchestra of cicadas and frogs, **Pura Luhur Batukau** (sarong and sash compulsory) does full justice to the epithet, the "garden temple". The grassy courtyards are planted with flowering hibiscus, Javanese ixora and cempaka, forest surrounds the temple on three sides, and the monuments are encrusted with moist green moss. Batukau's **bird** population finds plenty to feed on here, so you're likely to see lots of barbets, scarlet minivets and flycatchers at least. Thought to have become a holy site in the eleventh century, Pura Luhur Batukau has been rebuilt several times, most recently in 1959. Its most important shrine is the unusual seven-tiered pagoda which is dedicated to Mahadewa, the god of Gunung Batukau. To the east of the main temple compound, a large square **pond** has been dug to represent and honour the gods of nearby Danau Tamblingan (see p.568), which lies immediately to the north of Gunung Batukau. Members of local *subak* groups come here to draw holy water for use in agricultural ceremonies, and at the annual *Galungan* festivities truckloads of devotees make offerings here.

Climbing Gunung Batukau

Very few people **climb** the sacred slopes of Gunung Batukau and, during the rainy season (from Nov–March), not even the most sure-footed Balinese would attempt it. If you do decide to climb, you will definitely need a **guide** – they sometimes hang out at the temple, or can be contacted in the village of Wangayagede, 2km down the road. Expect to pay a minimum of Rp50,000 for a guide, more if you do the overnight hike. Although there are fairly well-defined paths nearly all the way to the summit (starting from the outer courtyard of Pura Luhur Batukau), many turn out to be false trails. In addition, the slopes are thickly wooded and offer few clearings from which to work out your bearings. Constant shade and low-lying cloud also make the atmosphere damp and the paths quite slippery, so you should be prepared with warm clothes and decent shoes. The usual guided climb takes about six hours to reach the summit and, though the round-trip is just about possible in one day, most people rent a tent from their guide and camp near the top.

Lalang Linggah and Balian beach

The main west coast road divides 16km west of Tabanan, at the village of **Antosari**, splitting the westbound Gilimanuk and Java traffic from the vehicles heading up to Seririt and the north coast. Ten kilometres west of Antosari, the Gilimanuk road zips through **LALANG LINGGAH**, the village closest to **Balian beach**, and a pleasant and peaceful place to base yourself for a few days. The grey-black sand beach here is popular with surfers, but the vicious current makes it far too dangerous for casual swimmers; there have been several fatalities in the last few years. For non-surfers, though, there are a number of interesting **walks** around the locality, including north along the course of Sungai Balian, or east or west along the shore. Lalang Linggah hotels can advise you on the best routes.

Lalang Linggah has two **accommodation** possibilities, beautifully set on either side of Sungai Balian estuary, about ten minutes' walk from the shore. The friendly and informally run *Balian Beach Bungalows* (☎0361/234139 ext 2842; ④–⑤) attracts surfers and family groups and offers a range of rooms, with good discounts for stays of more than one night. Across the river, 300m west along the Gilimanuk road, the *Sacred River Retreat* (also signed as *Sungai Suci*; ☎ & fax 0361/730904; ⑦–⑨) has been set up as a kind of alternative resort where the emphasis is on spiritual activities, including meditation and yoga as well as cultural activities such as Balinese painting and dancing. Its bungalows are simple but stylish, and there's a pool and vegetarian restaurant on the premises.

All Ubung (Denpasar)–Gilimanuk **bemos** and buses pass through Lalang Linggah; they take about 75 minutes from Ubung (Rp1500–2000) or about thirty minutes from Medewi (Rp1000). If you are coming from the north coast, take any Seririt–Pulukan or Singaraja–Seririt–Antosari bemo, then change onto the Ubung–Gilimanuk service.

Medewi beach

MEDEWI village sits on the main Tabanan–Gilimanuk road, 25km west of Lalang Linggah, and consists of little more than a mosque and a string of houses among coconut groves and paddy-fields. The beach is primarily a fishing beach, but there's a small enclave of shorefront bungalows which make a good short-term getaway from more crowded resorts. The black sand is fine, the current is light, and the waves are ideal for amateur **surfers**. The best **accommodation** is at the beachfront *Hotel Tin Jaya* (☎0365/42945; ③–④), which has comfortable rice-barn-style cottages, as well as simpler losmen quarters. The two unsignposted traditional rice-barn bungalows 100m further east along the road (next to the flashy *Hotel Pantai Medewi*) call themselves *Homestay Gede* (②), and are friendly, family-run and good value. Far larger, but soulless, the neighbouring *Hotel Pantai Medewi* (☎0365/40029, fax 41555; ⑥–⑧) overcharges for its cheapest rooms, but its more expensive cottages are well equipped with air-con and TV, and there's a swimming pool. All three places have good restaurants attached.

Pura Rambut Siwi

Sixteen kilometres west of Medewi, **Pura Rambut Siwi** (donation requested) is another spectacularly sited coastal temple, whose history is linked to the sixteenth-century Hindu priest Nirartha. Now the most important temple in Jembrana district, it contains a lock of Nirartha's hair, and its name translates as "the temple for worshipping the hair". The holy hair is enshrined, along with some of Nirartha's clothing, in a sandalwood box buried deep inside the central three-tiered *meru*. Descending the rock-cut steps from the temple gateway to the charcoal-black sand beach, you'll find a string of small shrines tucked into the cliff face to the left of the stairway. The first, a cave temple known as **Pura Tirta**, houses a holy freshwater spring and is guarded by a statue of Nirartha. A series of dank and bat-infested caves links Pura Tirta to **Goa Mayan Sati** (Cave of the Holy Tiger), 50m further east, but the underground complex is out of bounds to visitors, as all new priests of Pura Rambut Siwi meditate here before becoming fully ordained. All Ubung (Denpasar)–Gilimanuk **bemos** pass the turn-off for Pura Rambut Siwi, which is accessed by a 750-metre sideroad through the paddy-fields; get out when you see the sign for the temple and the cluster of roadside warung.

Negara

With its unnecessarily wide streets and large number of mosques, **NEGARA**'s town centre is reminiscent of many medium-sized Javanese towns. Its one significant attraction are the traditional **buffalo races** or *mekepung*, organized by the district authorities and held here every dry season, usually in August and again between September and November (check with any tourist office for the dates and exact location; most tour agents sell all-inclusive trips to the buffalo races). All Denpasar–Gilimanuk **bemos** pass through Negara town centre, calling in at the bemo station, 100m north of the Jalan Ngurah Rai roundabout.

Gilimanuk

Situated on the westernmost tip of Bali, less than 3km from East Java, the small, ribbon-like town of **GILIMANUK** is used by visitors mainly as a transit point for journeys to and from Java. A 24-hour ferry service crosses the Bali Strait, so few travellers bother to

CROSSING TO JAVA

Crossing the Bali Strait between Bali and Java is as easy as hopping on a bemo: there are no formalities, and **onward transport** facilities from both ports are frequent and efficient. If you're travelling quite a way into Java, to Probolinggo (for Mount Bromo) for example, or to Surabaya, Yogyakarta or Jakarta, the easiest option is to get an all-inclusive ticket from your starting point in Bali. The cheapest **long-distance buses** travel out of Denpasar's Ubung bemo station, with pick-up points in Tabanan, Negara and sometimes Gilimanuk, but there are also more expensive tourist shuttle buses and bus and train combinations operating from major tourist centres across Bali. Ticket prices always include the ferry crossing.

Ferries shuttle between Gilimanuk and **Ketapang** (East Java; see p.254) and back again every twenty minutes, 24 hours a day, and take thirty minutes including loading and docking time. Tickets must be bought before boarding – foot passengers buy them from the clearly signed desks in the terminal buildings. Seats cost Rp1000; vehicle owners pay as they drive on, and the ticket price includes the driver and any passengers: bicycles cost Rp1400; motorbikes, Rp2700; and cars, Rp10,550. Note that most car rental agencies on Bali prohibit tourists from taking their vehicles to other islands.

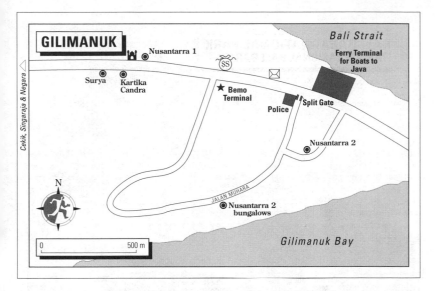

linger in the town. **Accommodation** here is poor and not at all traveller-orientated – your best option is *Nusantarra 2* (no phone; ②–④), which offers losmen-style rooms about five minutes' walk from the ferry terminal, or more expensive shared bungalows another five minutes' walk around the bay. To get there from the ferry terminal, walk a few metres to your right, then cross the road and take the first turning on your left; if you miss that one there's another access road 50m further on, beside the police station. If *Nusantarra 2* is full, try *Kartika Candra* (②), *Nusantarra 1* (②) or *Surya* (②), which are all on the main road, about fifteen minutes' walk south of the ferry terminal, less than five minutes from the bemo station. **Eating** options are limited to the warung and food carts around the ferry terminal. You can **change money** at the bank opposite the bemo terminal.

Getting to Gilimanuk by **bemo** from almost any major town in north, south and west Bali is fairly straightforward. All bemos terminate at the bemo station in the town centre, ten minutes' walk from the ferry terminal or a short *dokar* ride. From **Denpasar** (128km southwest) and the southern beaches, take either the direct dark-green bemos from Denpasar's Ubung terminal or a Gilimanuk-bound bus. From **Singaraja** (88km northeast), dark-red bemos make regular connections with Gilimanuk, as do a few buses.

Bali Barat national park

Nearly the whole of west Bali's mountain ridge is conserved as **Bali Barat national park (Taman Nasional Bali Barat)**, a 760-square kilometre area of wooded slopes, savannah, rainforest, monsoon forest, mangrove swamp and coastal flats, which is home to a range of small animals and approximately 160 species of bird – including the elusive and endangered **Bali starling**, Bali's one true endemic creature. However, over ninety percent of the parkland is out of bounds to visitors, with only a few trails open to the public.

All dark-green Ubung (Denpasar)–Gilimanuk **bemos** pass the national park headquarters at Cekik, as do all dark-red Singaraja–Gilimanuk bemos – get out at the sign announcing "Taman Nasional Bali Barat". These bemo routes also make access to trail heads a bit easier: the Gilimanuk–Denpasar road skirts the southern edge of the park,

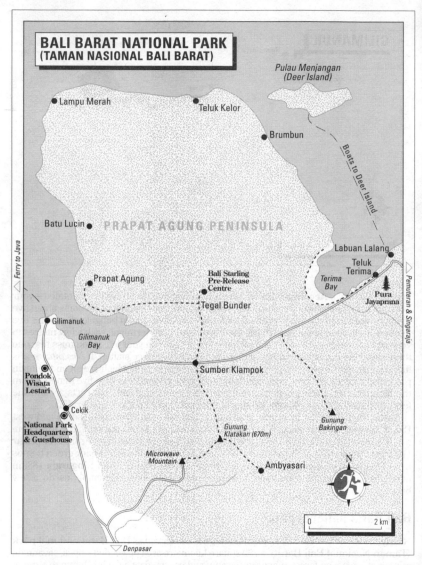

while the Gilimanuk–Singaraja road zips between the Prapat Agung peninsula in the northwest and the mountainous ridge to the east.

Practicalities

Anyone who enters Bali Barat national park has to be accompanied by an official park guide and must also be in possession of a permit. Both guides and permits need to be arranged through the **National Park headquarters** (daily except public hols

7am–5pm), conveniently located at **CEKIK**, beside the Denpasar–Gilimanuk–Singaraja T-junction, 3km south of Gilimanuk itself.

Most of the **guides** are English-speaking and fairly conversant in the flora and fauna of Bali Barat. They don't necessarily need to be booked in advance, and charge Rp25,000 for a two-hour hike for up to four people, then Rp5000 per every extra hour. If you don't have your own transport you'll also be expected to pay for bemo or boat charters where necessary. Having arranged a guide, you'll be granted a **permit**, which costs Rp2500 per person, plus a Rp500 surcharge for compulsory insurance. Permits are generally only good for one day.

It's forbidden to stay overnight within the park, but there are a few **accommodation** options within reasonable distance of the Bali Barat boundaries. Although the obvious first choice is the *National Park Guest House* (②–④), a set of seafront cottages in the compound of the park headquarters at Cekik, they have a severe problem with their water supply and regularly have to close down, sometimes for weeks at a time. Call ☎0365/61060 Monday to Saturday 7am to 2pm to check and make a reservation. If you don't mind there being no water and have your own tent, you can camp here for a nominal fee at any time of the year. The next best option is the basic, losmen-style *Pondok Wisata Lestari* (②), a walkable 2km north up the road to Gilimanuk or about Rp300 in a bemo. Alternatively, either head straight for Gilimanuk (see p.586), or further afield to Pemuteran (see p.591).

There are no warung or **food** hawkers inside the park (though a soup and noodle cart does set up outside the Cekik park headquarters everyday), so you'll need to take your own supplies for the hikes. The nearest restaurant is at *Pondok Wisata Lestari*.

If you can't face organizing guides and accommodation yourself, you could join a **tour** of Bali Barat national park, arranged through agencies in Kuta, Sanur or Ubud (from US$40 per person). *Pondok Sari Bungalows*, 28km northeast of Cekik in Pemuteran (see p.591), also does day-trips to the park.

The Tegal Bunder trail

If your main interest is birdspotting, you should opt for the **Tegal Bunder trek** (1–2hr), a 25-minute drive from Cekik. The focus of this trek is the monsoon forest around the Bali Starling Pre-Release Centre in the northwestern reaches of Bali Barat. The easiest way to explore is to drive to Tegal Bunder, but if you don't have transport you can get a bemo to the access road at Sumber Klampok and then walk the 2km. Or you could combine the Tegal Bunder trek with a jaunt through the mangrove forests of Gilimanuk Bay and arrive at Tegal Bunder by boat (see p.590).

Once through the ranger checkpoint at **Sumber Klampok**, you'll soon come to a small side-track which leads a few hundred metres to the Bali Starling Pre-Release Centre. With its silky snow-white feathers, black wing and tail tips and delicate soft crest, the **Bali starling** or Rothschild's Myna (*leucopsar Rothschildi*) is an astonishingly beautiful bird and is the provincial symbol of Bali. It is Bali's only remaining endemic creature and survives in the dry monsoon forests and savannah grasslands that characterize the northwestern peninsula of Bali Barat national park. However, it's estimated that there may now be fewer than 25 Bali starlings left in the wild, so all known haunts are out of bounds to casual observers. At the centre, the young birds (bred in captivity elsewhere) are trained for new lives in the wild and then encouraged to settle in a nearby area.

The forests of Tegal Bunder harbour a large **bird population**, and you'll see flocks of the common yellow-vented bulbul and plenty of black-naped orioles too. Other possible sightings include the pinky-brown spotted dove, the black drongo, and the tiny bright-yellow-breasted olive-backed sunbird.

Gilimanuk Bay boat trip

The Tegal Bunder trail combines nicely with a boat trip round **Gilimanuk Bay**, which takes you through the mangrove forests that line most of the shore. Boats cost Rp25,000 for two people for two hours and should be arranged through the national park guides. **Mangroves** are best seen at low tide, when their aerial roots are fully exposed to form gnarled and knotted archways above the muddy banks, and boats should be able to get close enough for you to see some of the most common creatures who live in the swamps. These include fiddler crabs and mudskippers, as well as crab-eating or long-tailed macaques, who hang out along the shore. If you get out of the boat and explore the exposed reef you'll see sea cucumbers, sea horses, and various species of crab, as well as heaps of good seashells. You might also spot some elegant dark-grey pacific reef egrets. The current off this shore is dangerously strong so it's not advisable to swim here, plus the beaches seem to end up covered with debris washed in from Java and the Bali Strait.

The Gunung Klatakan trail

The climb up **Gunung Klatakan** (a 5–6hr round-trip) is the most popular and most strenuous of the Bali Barat hikes, most of it passing through moderately interesting rainforest. The trail starts at the Sumber Klampok ranger post and for the most part follows a steep incline, via the occasional sheer descent, through **tropical rainforest** that's thick with ferns, vines and pandanus. Rattan and strangling fig abound too, as do all sorts of **orchids**, including the elegant long-stemmed white-sepalled madavellia orchid. You're unlikely to spot much **wildlife** on this trail, but you should certainly hear the black monkeys and might stumble across a wild boar or two. You could also encounter hornbills, pythons, green snakes and even flying foxes, but don't count on it.

Pulau Menjangan (Deer Island)

By far the most popular part of Bali Barat is **Pulau Menjangan (Deer Island)**, a tiny uninhabited island just 8km off the north coast, whose shoreline is encircled by some of the most spectacular **coral reefs** in Bali. The sparkling azure-tinged water is incredibly calm, protected from excessive winds and strong currents by the Prapat Agung peninsula. As you near the island, the reefs form a band 100–150m around the coastline, and this is where you'll find the best **snorkelling** and **diving**, with drop-offs ranging from 40m to 60m, first-class wall dives with plenty of crevices and grottoes, and superb visibility ranging from 15m to 50m. There's also an old shipwreck – the *Anker* – lying 7m deep off the western tip of the island, which is frequented by sharks and rays. Recent reports from snorkellers suggest that the reefs are showing signs of **damage**, and for once it's not the tourist trade that's the main culprit (though there is some anchor damage), but the dreaded crown-of-thorns starfish who seem to be munching their way through the Menjangan coral. At the moment, though, it seems that only some of the shallowest reefs have suffered.

Although the island comes under the jurisdiction of the national park, you're not obliged to go with a guide and can arrange transport across the water without first checking in at the Cekik headquarters. There are no accommodation facilities on the island, but you can camp there if you get a permit from Cekik; otherwise you'll need to stay at Cekik, Gilimanuk or Pemuteran. The departure point for Pulau Menjangan is **LABUAN LALANG**, just east of Teluk Terima, 13km from Cekik, or about two hours by bemo from Lovina or thirty minutes by bemo from Pemuteran. There's a small national park office here (daily except national holidays 7.30am–3pm), as well as several restaurants. **Boats** to Pulau Menjangan can be hired at any time of day up to about 3pm and prices are fixed at Rp60,000 for a round-trip lasting a maximum of four hours, which allows two to three hours for snorkelling and/or exploring the island. Boats hold up to ten people, take thirty minutes to reach the island, and cost an extra Rp5000 for every additional hour. You'll also be expected to pay the statutory park entrance fee of Rp2500 per person plus Rp500 insurance. You can rent masks, fins and snorkel from the warung by the jetty for Rp5000 a set.

Pulau Menjangan is also the focus of a number of day- and overnight **tours** for snorkellers and divers who are based in Kuta, Sanur, Candi Dasa, Lovina and Pemuteran. Prices for these start at around US$80 for two dives in one day (snorkellers US$40), rising to around US$180 for two-day, one-night excursions.

Pemuteran

As the road heads east from Labuan Lalang, the scenery gets more and more arresting, with the great craggy folds of Bali Barat's north-facing ridges rising almost perpendicular from the roadside. In the foreground of this amazing setting sits the small fishing village of **PEMUTERAN**, 28km east of Cekik, the location of some lovely, if rather pricey, accommodation, and a good place to base yourself for diving and snorkelling. All dark-red Gilimanuk–Singaraja **bemos** pass through Pemuteran and will drop you in front of your chosen hotel; they take thirty minutes from Labuan Lalang or eighty minutes from Lovina. If you are coming from the south coast resorts, your fastest option is to take a Perama shuttle bus to Lovina and then hop onto a bemo.

The cheapest and best value of Pemuteran's three **hotels** is *Pondok Sari* (☎ & fax 0361/92337; ⑥), whose large, stylishly designed cottages are set in a tropical garden that runs down to Pemuteran's black-sand beach. The restaurant is expensive, however, and the place regularly gets booked out by diving tours, so it's advisable to reserve ahead. *Pondok Sari* shares this stretch of beach with the more upmarket *Taman Sari* (☎0362/288096, fax 286297; ⑦–⑧), located 50m west along the shore, whose most expensive bungalows feel pleasantly indulgent and have sea views and air-con. One kilometre east of *Pondok Sari*, on its own secluded beach, stands *Matahari Beach Resort* (☎0362/92312, fax 92313; ⑨), a luxury complex of sixteen private bungalow compounds plus swimming pool and tennis courts.

All the hotels organize day-trips to local sights, including hikes through Bali Barat national park (see p.587), but the chief attraction here – apart from lying on the black-sand beach – is the **snorkelling and diving**. There are some decent reefs within easy swimming distance of the Pemuteran shore and some recommended ones are about fifteen minutes' boat ride away. The staff at Reef Seen Aquatics **dive centre** (☎0362/92339), 100m east along the beach from *Pondok Sari*, have mapped out the best local spots and will arrange boat charters to take you there (from US$10 per snorkeller or US$30 per diver, both prices including equipment). Both Reef Seen and Yos Diving, which operates out of *Pondok Sari*, also run diving and snorkelling expeditions to Pulau Menjangan (see opposite) for US$30 and US$70 respectively.

Just beyond the eastern edge of Pemuteran, the stark charcoal-grey stone of the sixteenth-century temple **Pura Agung Pulaki** peers down from a weatherworn cliff face, making a good viewpoint over the northwest coast.

travel details

Bemos and buses

It's almost impossible to give the **frequency** with which bemos and buses run, as they only depart when they have enough passengers to make the journey worthwhile. However, on the most popular routes you should be able to count on getting a ride within thirty minutes if you travel before noon; things quieten down in the afternoon and come to a standstill by around 5pm. **Journey** times also vary a great deal. The times given below are the minimum you can expect the journeys to take.

Only the direct bemo and bus routes are listed below; for all other journeys you'll almost certainly have to change at one or more of the island's major **transport hubs**. Privately run tourist **shuttle buses** run between all the major tourist centres.

Amlapura to: Batubulan (2hr); Candi Dasa (20min); Culik (20min); Gianyar (1hr 20min); Klungkung (1hr); Seraya (40min); Singaraja (Penarukan terminal; 2hr 30min); Tirtagangga (10min); Tulamben (40min); Ujung (20min).

Bangli to: Denpasar (Batubulan terminal; 1hr 30min); Gianyar (20min); Singaraja (Penarukan terminal; 2hr 15min).

Bedugul to: Denpasar (Ubung terminal;1hr 30min); Singaraja (Sukasada terminal; 1hr 30min).

Candi Dasa to: Amlapura (20min); Denpasar (Batubulan terminal; 2hr); Gianyar (1hr); Klungkung (40min).

Denpasar (Batubulan terminal) to: Amlapura (2hr 30min); Candi Dasa (2hr); Celuk (10min); Gianyar (1hr); Kintamani (1hr 30min); Klungkung (1hr 20min); Mas (35min); Nusa Dua (1hr); Padang Bai (for Lombok; 1hr 40min); Peliatan (45min); Singaraja (Penarukan terminal; 3hr); Sukawati (20min); Tegalalang (1hr 15min); Ubud (50min).

Denpasar (Kereneng terminal) to: Sanur (15–25min).

Denpasar (Tegal terminal) to: Jimbaran (40min); Kuta (25min); Ngurah Rai Airport (35min); Nusa Dua (35min); Sanur (25min).

Denpasar (Ubung terminal) to: Antosari (1hr); Bedugul (1hr 30min); Cekik (for national park headquarters; 3hr); Gilimanuk (3hr 15min); Jakarta (Java; 24hr); Kediri (for Tanah Lot; 30min); Lalang Linggah (for Balian beach; 1hr 15min); Medewi (1hr 30min); Mengwi (30min); Negara (2hr 15min); Singaraja (Sukasada terminal; 3hr); Solo (Java; 15hr); Surabaya (Java; 10hr); Tabanan (35min); Yogyakarta (Java; 15hr).

Denpasar (Wangaya terminal) to: Sangeh Monkey Forest (45min).

Gianyar to: Amlapura (1hr 20min); Bangli (20min); Batur (40min); Blahbatuh (30min); Candi Dasa (1hr); Denpasar (Batubulan terminal; 1hr); Klungkung (20min); Ubud (20min).

Gilimanuk to: Antosari (2hr 15min); Cekik (for national park headquarters; 10min); Denpasar (Ubung terminal; 3hr 15min); Kediri (for Tanah Lot; 2hr 45min); Labuan Lalang (for Deer Island; 25min); Lalang Linggah (for Balian beach; 2hr 15min); Medewi (1hr 45min); Negara (1hr); Pemuteran (1hr); Seririt (1hr 30min); Lovina (2hr 15min); Singaraja (Banyuasri terminal; 2hr 30min); Tabanan (2hr 30min).

Jimbaran to: Denpasar (Tegal terminal; 40min); Kuta (15min); Ngurah Rai Airport (10min).

Kintamani to: Ubud (40min).

Klungkung to: Amlapura (1hr); Besakih (45min); Candi Dasa (40min); Denpasar (Batubulan terminal; 1hr 20min); Gianyar (20min); Rendang (30min).

Kuta to: Denpasar (Tegal terminal; 25min); Jimbaran (15min); Ngurah Rai Airport (10min); Nusa Dua (20min).

Lovina to: Bromo (8hr); Gilimanuk (2hr 10min); Jakarta (24hr); Probolingo (7hr); Seririt (20min); Singaraja (Banyuasri terminal; 20min); Solo (17hr); Surabaya (11hr); Yogyakarta (17hr).

Ngurah Rai Airport to: Denpasar (Tegal terminal; 35min); Jimbaran (10min); Kuta (10min); Nusa Dua (20min).

Nusa Dua to: Denpasar (Tegal terminal; 35min); Denpasar (Batubulan terminal; 1hr); Kuta (20min); Ngurah Rai Airport (20min).

Padang Bai to: Amlapura (40min); Candi Dasa (20min); Klungkung (20min).

Pemuteran to: Cekik (for national park headquarters; 50min); Gilimanuk (1hr); Labuan Lalang (for Deer Island; 30min); Lovina (1hr 15min); Singaraja (1hr 30min).

Penelokan to: Bangli (45min); Denpasar (Batubulan terminal; 1hr 30min); Gianyar (50min); Singaraja (Penarukan terminal; 1hr 30min); Songan (25min); Toya Bungkah (15min).

Sanur to: Denpasar (Kereneng terminal; 15–25min); Denpasar (Tegal terminal; 25min).

Singaraja (Banyuasri terminal) to: Gilimanuk (2hr 30min); Lovina (20min); Seririt (40min); Surabaya (10hr); Yogyakarta (21hr).

Singaraja (Penarukan terminal) to: Amlapura (2hr); Denpasar (Batubulan terminal; 3hr); Gianyar (2hr 20min); Penelokan (1hr 30min); Kubutambahan (20min); Sawan (30min).

Singaraja (Sukasada terminal) to: Bedugul (1hr 30min); Denpasar (Ubung terminal; 3hr); Gitgit (30min).

Ubud to: Campuhan (5min); Celuk (40min); Denpasar (Batubulan terminal; 50min); Gianyar (20min); Goa Gajah (10min); Kintamani (1hr); Mas (15min); Peliatan (5min); Pujung (25min); Sukawati (30min).

Pelni ferries

For a chart of the Pelni routes, see pp.36–37 of Basics.

Benoa Harbour to: Ambon (*KM Dibonsolo*, fortnightly; 3 days); Biak (*KM Dibonsolo*, fortnightly; 4

days); Dili (*KM Dibonsolo*, fortnightly; 37hr); Jayapura (*KM Dibonsolo*, fortnightly; 5 days); Kupang (*KM Dibonsolo*, fortnightly; 26hr); Manokwari (*KM Dibonsolo*, fortnightly; 4 days); Sorong (*KM Dibonsolo*, fortnightly; 3 days); Surabaya (*KM Dibonsolo*, fortnightly; 15hr); Tanjung Priok (*KM Dibonsolo*, fortnightly; 39hr).

Other ferries

Benoa Harbour to: Lembar (Lombok; 2 daily; 2hr).

Gilimanuk to: Ketapang (East Java; every 20min; 30min).

Kusamba to: Nusa Lembongan (2–3hr); Nusa Penida (2–3hr).

Padang Bai to: Lembar (Lombok; 4hr); Nusa Penida (1hr 30min).

Sanur to: Jungutbatu (Nusa Lembongan; 2 daily; 1hr 30min).

CHAPTER NINE

NUSA TENGGARA

The group of islands to the east of Bali, stretching like stepping stones towards New Guinea, is **Nusa Tenggara**, which comprises a spectacularly exotic diversity of landscapes, cultures, languages and peoples. It is viewed by most Indonesians as being an obscure, sparsely populated and uncivilized region – characteristics which may indeed appeal to many travellers.

The three provinces of Nusa Tenggara (West and East Nusa Tenggara and the enclave of East Timor) occupy the majority of the Lesser Sunda islands. A volcanic northern arc runs from Lombok, through Sumbawa and the Banda Islands to Alor. The southern arc runs from Raijua off Savu through Roti and Timor; these islands have no volcanoes, consisting mainly of raised coral reef.

Lombok island is now the most popular destination in Nusa Tenggara, with scores of tourists arriving in search of the **unspoilt beaches** and thriving cultures to be found here. **Sumbawa** island is a short hop east of Lombok, and is fast becoming another big draw for surfers. The majority of travellers, however, just nip through here on their way to the **Komodo national park**, a barren, stark group of islands, which are home to the world's largest living lizards: Komodo dragons.

Flores stretches east from Komodo towards the north tip of Timor. Its lush, dramatic landscape is peppered with smouldering **volcanoes**, of which Keli Mutu, with its three coloured crater lakes, is uniquely spectacular. Further east still lies the **Alor and Solor archipelago**, the highlight of which is **Lembata**, where men set out in frail wooden sailing boats to hunt whales.

Divided **Timor** offers wild scenery and fiercely proud indigenous cultures, but travel is still limited in troubled East Timor. **Savu** and **Roti** are exposed, parched islands,

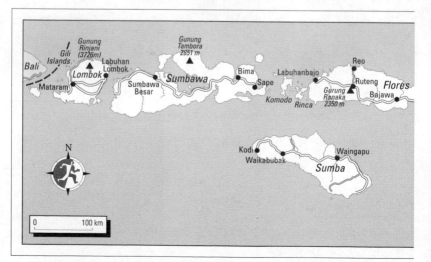

ACCOMMODATION PRICE CODES

All the **accommodation** listed in this book has been given one of the following price codes. The rates quoted here are for the **cheapest double room** in high season, except for places with dorms, where the code represents the price of a single bed. Where there's a significant spread of prices indicated (④–⑦, for example), the text will explain what extra facilities you get for more money. The 11–21 percent tax charged by most hotels is not included in these price codes.

Because of the current instability of the rupiah, accommodation prices are given throughout in their more stable **US dollar equivalents**, even for places that accept payment in rupiah.

For more on accommodation, see p.40.

① under $1	③ $2–5	⑤ $10–15	⑦ $35–60	⑨ $100
② $1–2	④ $5–10	⑥ $15–35	⑧ $60–100	and over

havens for die-hard surfers and also for anthropologists: animist traditions flourish here. In East Sumba the fine **ikat fabrics** are made and sold, while West Sumba boasts the ritual war of the **pasola** and grandiose **funeral ceremonies** equalled only by those of the Toraja of Sulawesi.

The majority of visitors to Nusa Tenggara follow obvious linear routes through the islands, often starting or finishing with the cheap, short flight from Kupang in Timor to Darwin in northern Australia, or travelling east from Bali and flying back from Flores. To make a full tour of Nusa Tenggara – from Lombok to Alor, south to Timor, looping round Roti, Savu and Sumba, and then back to civilization with a flight to Bima, Mataram or Denpasar – would take up all of your two-month visa, but more selective island-hopping is possible, with Pelni and other ferries linking the islands. Although **transport** has improved beyond recognition on Lombok, Sumbawa, Flores and most of Timor, it is still extremely primitive compared to Java and Bali. Navigating the atrocious roads of the outer islands is a challenge to say the least: boats look like salvaged shipwrecks, most services are delayed or cancelled and all journeys require serious determination.

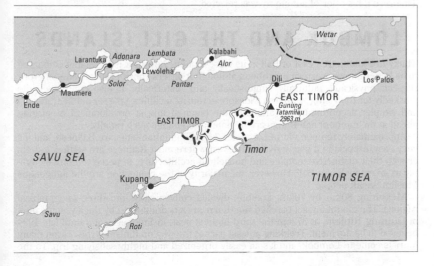

Certain parts of Nusa Tenggara are difficult to get around during the **rainy season**, particularly Flores and the Alor and Solor archipelago. The rainy season lasts from about October to March, except in the more southerly islands, where it is much shorter. The dry season is also more pronounced here, with fierce heat in Roti, Savu and Timor in the middle of the year.

Some history
The first incursions into Nusa Tenggara by outside powers were made by Chinese traders as early as the sixth century, and later by the Makarrese and Bugis peoples of Sulawesi. Traders were mainly attracted by the **sandalwood** stands of Timor, and the convenient position of ports such as Bima on the route to Java from the abundant Spice Islands. The primary commodities of spices and timber were inevitably supplemented by slaves, horses from Sumba and Timor and myriad oddities such as birds' nests, sharks' fins, and sulphur from around the archipelago. Much of Nusa Tenggara is presumed to have been under the control of the East Javanese **Majapahit empire**, founded in the thirteenth century.

In 1504, **Magellan** sailed along the coast of Flores on his way to Timor, and, later in the sixteenth century, the **Portuguese** built forts in the east at Ende and on nearby Solor, to avoid having to stay on the inhospitable malarial coast of Timor. The colonizers plundered the sandalwood forests, and brought Christianity, along with smallpox and venereal diseases. In 1859, Portuguese interests were bought out of just about everywhere in Nusa Tenggara by the Dutch. The Dutch invaded Balinese-controlled Lombok in 1894, so that the only remaining territory under Portuguese control was the tiny province of East Timor. Sumba and Timor were both briefly held by the Japanese in the World War II, but all of Nusa Tenggara (except East Timor) became part of Indonesia upon Independence in 1945.

East Timor was passed back to the Portuguese by the Japanese at the end of World War II. However, in 1974, following a major revolution in Portugal, East Timor was relinquished by its colonizers. Shortly afterwards, Indonesian forces invaded East Timor and remain there to this day. At the time of writing, though, the prospects of the region were looking more promising. In February 1998, President Habibie, in a reversal of all previous policy, pledged that Independence would be offered to the East Timorese if his offer of autonomy was rejected.

LOMBOK AND THE GILI ISLANDS

Thirty-five kilometres east of Bali at its closest point, **Lombok** is inevitably compared to its better-known western neighbour, although it differs considerably in almost every respect: physically, culturally, linguistically and historically. It also contrasts quite markedly for the visitor, with less widespread tourist facilities, sparser public transport and simpler accommodation, although the planned tourist development is surging ahead at the moment and things are beginning to change very rapidly.

Approximately ten percent of Lombok's 2.5 million inhabitants are Balinese, and it's very easy, especially if you arrive in the west where most Balinese are settled, together with their distinctive temples and household architecture, to perceive Lombok simply as an extension of Bali. However, the majority of the population are the indigenous Muslim **Sasak** people.

Measuring 80km by 70km, Lombok divides conveniently into three geographical regions. The mountainous, parched **northern area** is dominated by the awesome bulk of **Gunung Rinjani**, at 3726m the third highest peak in Indonesia, and until late 1994 believed to be dormant. Trekking at least part of the way up Rinjani is the reason many tourists come to Lombok, and it's an easily organized and highly satisfying trip. To the south of this mass, the **central plains**, about 25km wide, contain the most productive agricultural areas as well as the major road on the island linking the west and east coasts. Attractive villages perched in the southern foothills of Rinjani are easily accessible from here, and many of the island's craft centres are also in or near this cross-island corridor. Further south again is a range of low inland hills, around 500m high, behind the sweeping bays and pure white sands of the **southern beaches**, all of which can be explored from **Kuta**, the accommodation centre of the south and surfing focus of the island. There are also several groups of islands off the Lombok coast. The trio of **Gili Islands**, Trawangan, Meno and Air, off the northwest coast, are the best known to tourists, longtime favourites with backpackers in search of sea, sun and sand in simple surroundings.

GETTING TO LOMBOK

By plane
Mataram's Selaparang Airport is the only airport on the island. The only direct **international flights** are from Singapore. There are regular **internal flights** from Bali and other points in Indonesia with Bouraq, Garuda and Merpati

By ferry

From Bali
Padang Bai to Lembar (every 2hr, even hours; 4hr–4hr 30min). Ferry tickets cost Rp9000 VIP (air-con lounge with soft seats and TV), Rp5500 Ekonomi (hard seats and TV). Extra charge for bicycles Rp6200, motorbikes Rp11,700, jeeps Rp68,650 upwards. **Benoa Harbour to Lembar** (Mabua Express catamaran; 1 daily increasing to 2 daily December 23–January 5 & July & Aug, and during major local holidays; 2hr). There are three classes costing US$20–30, but none include transport at either end. Surfboards are free, bicycles Rp20,000 and baggage in excess of 20kg is charged at Rp500 per kilo. Some motion-sickness sufferers find this an uncomfortable trip. Book through travel agents or direct in Bali (☎0361/72370, fax 72521), or in Lombok (☎0370/25895, fax 37224).

From Sumbawa
Poto Tano to Kayangan, Labuhan Lombok (daily every hour 4am–9pm; 2hr). Ferry tickets cost Rp3600 Ekonomi A, Rp2300 Ekonomi B. Extra charge for motorbikes Rp6000, bicycles Rp3300, jeeps from Rp37,000.

From other islands
Pelni operates services between the islands of the archipelago, calling at Lembar on Lombok. *KM Awu* calls every fortnight on the Waingapu, Ende, Kupang, Kalabahi, Dili, Maumere, Ujung Padang (Sulawesi), Tarakan, Nunukian route. *KM Tilongkabila* also calls monthly en route to Ujung Padang, Bau-Bau, Raha, Kendari, Kolonedale, Luwuk, Gorontalo, Bitung, Tahiuna, Lirung and Davao in the Philippines and monthly to Bali and Banyuwangi. See p.35 for more information.

By bus
Java, Sumbawa and Flores to Mandalika Terminal, Sweta. Two or three services daily. Sample fares include Jakarta (two days, two nights; Rp85,000), Surabaya (20hr; Rp42,500), Yogyakarta (26hr; Rp57,500), Sumbawa Besar (6hr; Rp15,000), Bima (12hr; Rp27,500), Domphu (10hr; Rp25,000), Sape (14hr; Rp30,000), Komodo or Labuhanbajo (24hr; Rp45,000), and Ruteng (36hr; Rp50,000).

Tourist shuttle buses operate from Bali to the main tourist destinations on Lombok: Mataram, Senggigi, and Bangsal for the Gili Islands. Perama are the most established company, offering Kuta (Bali) to Kuta (Lombok; 1 daily; 12hr) for Rp30,000; Ubud to Senggigi (7 daily; 8hr) for Rp17,500; and Lovina to Bangsal (2 daily, one involves a stopover) for Rp30,000.

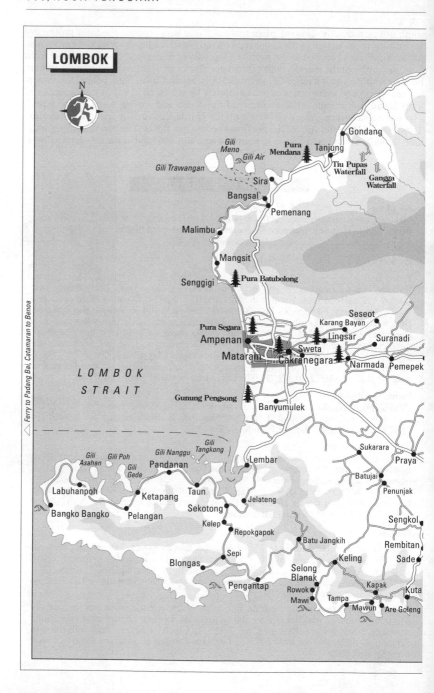

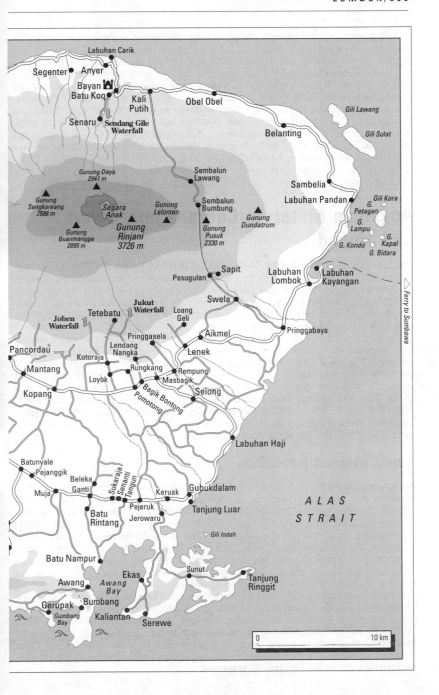

Labuhan Carik
Segenter • Anyer
Bayan
Batu Koq
Kali
Putih
Obel Obel
Senaru Sendang Gile
Waterfall
Belanting
Gili Lawang
Gili Sulat

Gunung Daya
2941 m
Sembalun
Lawang
Sambelia
Labuhan Pandan
Gili Kora
G.
Petagan
G.
Lampu
Gunung
Sengkareang
2588 m
Segara
Anak
Gunung
Lelonten
Sembalun
Bumbung
Gunung
Dundatrum
Gunung
Buanmangge
2895 m
Gunung
Rinjani
3726 m
Gunung
Pusuk
2330 m
G. Kondo Kapal
G. Bidara

Sapit
Pesugulan
Labuhan
Lombok
Labuhan
Kayangan
▷ Ferry to Sumbawa

Jukut
Waterfall
Swela
Joben
Waterfall
Tetebatu
Loang
Geli
Aikmel
Pringgabaya
Pancordau
Pringgasela
Lendang
Nangka
Lenek
Mantang
Kotoraja
Rungkang
Rempung
Loyok
Masbagik
Kopang
Bagik Bontong
Pomotong
Selong

Labuhan Haji

Batunyale
Pejanggik
Beleka
Ganti
Sukaraja
Senanti
Tangun
Keruak
Gubukdalam
Muja
Pejeruk
Tanjung Luar
ALAS
STRAIT
Batu
Rintang
Jerowaru
Gili Indah

Batu Nampur

Ekas
Sunut
Tanjung
Ringgit
Awang
Awang
Bay
Gerupak
Bumbang
Gumbang
Bay
Kaliantan
Serewe

0   10 km

With around 300,000 foreign visitors a year, the tourist presence on Lombok is nowhere near as pervasive as in Bali, but government plans to expand massively and upgrade tourist facilities are well advanced, and include the future construction of a new international airport in the Praya area. For the time being, as most visitors stick to the relatively well-beaten track – the northwest coast around **Senggigi**, the nearby Gili Islands, **Senaru** and **Batu Koq** in the Rinjani area, villages in the foothills of the mountain such as **Tetebatu**, and the south coast centring on Kuta – it's still easy to find less popular routes, remote villages, unspoilt coastline and village people still living traditional lives. Generally, **accommodation** is concentrated in the west-coast resorts and the capital, **Mataram**. Outside these places, the simple accommodation options are now being supplemented by burgeoning five-star resorts such as the new *Oberoi* development on the northwest coast and the *Novotel* in the south, although, as yet, the central, east-coast and Rinjani areas have not received the developers' attentions.

Ampenan-Mataram-Cakranegara-Sweta and around

The conurbation of **AMPENAN-MATARAM-CAKRANEGARA-SWETA**, with a population of around a quarter of a million, comprises four towns, the boundaries of which are indistinguishable to the casual visitor. At first sight rather overwhelming, the whole area measures over 8km from west to east, but a relatively straightforward local transport system allows you to get around easily, although most visitors pass through the area fairly quickly as there isn't much to see.

The conurbation is essentially laid out around three parallel roads, which stretch from Ampenan on the coast through Mataram and Cakranegara to Sweta on the eastern edge. The roads change their names several times along their length, the most northerly being Jalan Langko/Jalan Pejanggik/Jalan Selaparang, which allows travel only in a west–east direction. Its counterpart, Jalan Tumpang Sari/Jalan Panca Usaha/Jalan Pancawarga/Jalan Pendidikan, running parallel to the south, allows only east–west travel. The third major route, Jalan Brawijaya/Jalan Sriwijaya/Jalan Majapahit, two-way for most of its length, skirts to the south of these, and is useful to tourists largely as the site of the central post office.

Arrival, transport, information

Selaparang airport is on Jalan Adi Sucipto at Rembiga, only a few kilometres north of Mataram and Ampenan. There is an exchange counter, open for all international arrivals, and a taxi counter with fixed-price fares (Mataram Rp7000, Sengiggi Rp12,000, Bangsal Rp22,000, Kuta Rp36,000 – more for air-con cabs). All the major luxury hotels have booking counters here; discounts vary from day to day so shop around if you're interested. For public transport walk 200m to the main road, where you'll find bemos to Ampenan, Cakranegara and Mandalika terminal in Sweta. To get to Bangsal, head 500m to the left to a set of traffic lights on a crossroads, turn left and catch a public bus marked "Tanjung", which will drop you at Pemenang.

If you're coming across the island from the east, from Lembar in the south (see p.606 for details of transport from here) or from the airport on an eastbound bemo, you'll arrive at the new Mandalika **bus station** in Sweta, the main one on the island. Most, but not all, of the public transport from the north arrives here as well, and if you're heading on to anywhere except Senggigi you can pick up a connection here. From Senggigi, on some of the bemos from Pemenang or on a westbound bemo from the airport, you'll arrive at the terminal in **Ampenan**.

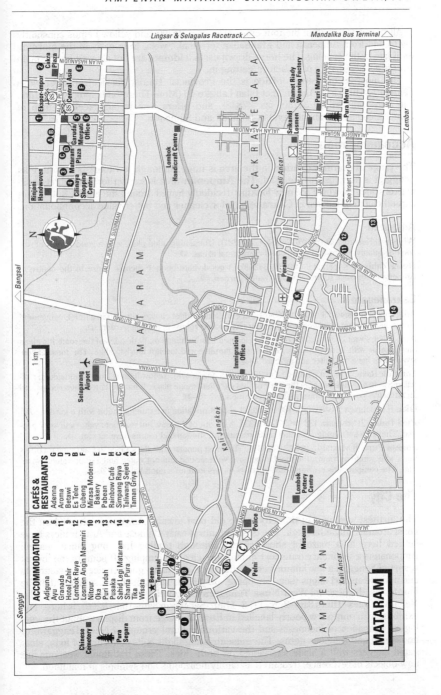

MATARAM

Lingsar & Selagalas Racetrack

Mandalika Bus Terminal

Lembar

Bangsal

Senggigi

Chinese Cemetery

Pura Segara

AMPENAN

MATARAM

CAKRANEGARA

Selaparang Airport

Immigration Office

Lombok Handicraft Centre

Slamet Riady Weaving Factory

Puri Mayura

Srikandi Losmen

Pura Meru

Perama

See Insert for Detail

Kali Ancar

Kali Jangkok

Lombok Pottery Centre

Police

Museum

Pelni

Bemo Terminal

N

0   1 km

JALAN JENDRAL SUDIRMAN
JALAN DR SUTOMO
JALAN UDAYANA
JALAN ADI SUCIPTO
JALAN HOS COKROAMINOTO
JALAN PANCA USAHA
JALAN HASANUDIN
JALAN PEJANGGIK
JALAN GEDE NGURAH
JALAN SELAPARANG
JALAN BRAWIJAYA
JALAN ERBUDAYAN
JALAN BUNG KARNO
JALAN AIRLANGGA
JALAN PANCA WARGA
JALAN RA RAHMAN HAKIM
JALAN SRIWIJAYA
JALAN MAJAPAHIT
JALAN PANJI TILAR NEGARA
JALAN SUPRAPTO
JALAN LANGKO

ACCOMMODATION

Adiguna	5
Ayu	6
Granada	11
Hotel Zahir	9
Lombok Raya	12
Losmen Angin Mammiri	7
Nitour	10
Oka	3
Puri Indah	13
Pusaka	2
Sahid Legi Mataram	14
Shanta Pura	4
Tika	1
Wisata	8

CAFÉS & RESTAURANTS

Adenna	G
Aroma	D
Betawi	J
Es Teler	B
Gubeng	F
Mirasa Modern Bakery	E
Pabean	I
Rainbow Café	H
Simpang Raya	C
Taliwang Sejeti	A
Taman Griya	K

(Insert detail)

Rinjani Handwoven

Cakra Plaza

Eksport-Impor ❷

Central Asia

Garuda/ Merpati Office

Matarama Plaza

Cilinaya Shopping Centre

All **bemo** trips within the four-cities area cost Rp300, and yellow bemos constantly ply to and from Ampenan and Mandalika terminal, Sweta, from early in the morning until late in the evening. The horse-drawn carts, **cidomo**, are not allowed on the main streets, so negotiate a price before getting in.

The most useful **tourist office** is the Provincial Tourist Service for West Nusa Tenggara, which is in Ampenan at Jalan Langko 70 (Mon–Thurs 7am–2pm, Fri 7–11am, Sat 7am–1pm; ☎0370/31730, fax 37838), and offers leaflets, an excellent map of Lombok and advice about travel in Lombok and Sumbawa.

Accommodation

The range of **accommodation** in the area is huge, although few tourists stay here as Senggigi is only just up the road. The **Ampenan** area is known for its budget backpackers' lodges, which are now looking decidedly frayed around the edges, but there's a good clutch of losmen in **Cakranegara** for cleaner and better-value accommodation.

Ampenan

Wisata, Jl Koperasi 19 (☎0370/26971, fax 21781). Unexciting, tiled place with a good variety of reasonable-quality rooms and some good communal areas. ⑥.

Hotel Zahir, Jl Koperasi 9 (☎0370/34248). A good-value budget cheapie, close to the centre of Ampenan with basic rooms around a small garden. ②.

Cakranegara

Adiguna, Jl Nursiwan 9 (☎0370/25946). An excellent budget choice, situated in a quiet, convenient street, near the bemo routes, and offering reasonable rooms in a small garden. ②.

Ayu, Jl Nursiwan 20 (☎0370/21761). This losmen has buildings on both sides of the road. It's clean and popular with businesspeople, Indonesian families and foreign tourists alike. The most expensive rooms have hot water and air-con. ③–④.

Lombok Raya, Jl Panca Usaha 11 (☎0370/32305, fax 36478). Yellow bemos from Mandalika terminal in Sweta to Ampenan pass the door of this excellent-value place. It has well-furnished rooms and an attractive pool, and comes highly recommended. ⑦–⑧.

Oka, Jl Repatmaja 5 (☎0370/22406). Budget accommodation in a quiet position with a garden. ②.

Puri Indah, Jl Sriwijaya 132 (☎0370/37633). A bit out of the way, but excellent value and very popular. There's a swimming pool and small restaurant; the top-end rooms have air-con. ④.

Shanta Pura, Jl Maktal 15 (☎0370/32649). The most popular travellers' place in Cakranegara offering a wide range of rooms, the most expensive with air-con and hot water, and a good-value restaurant. The compound is crowded, but upstairs rooms lead off a good balcony. ③–⑤.

The City

The furthest west part of **the city** is the old port town of **Ampenan**, situated on the coast around Sungai Jangkok. The descendants of early Chinese and Arab traders have settled here in a maze of shop-houses, although trading has long since ceased. Ampenan is a secondary transport hub for the city, the jumping-off point to the tourist resort of Senggigi a few kilometres up the coast, and has a good choice of restaurants and antique and art shops (see "Shopping" on p.604). The most interesting sight in the four towns, the peaceful **West Nusa Tenggara Provincial Museum**, Jalan Panji Tilar Negara 6 (Tues–Thurs 8am–2pm, Fri 8–11am, Sat & Sun 8am–1pm; R200), is here. The exhibits, with only a few poorly labelled in English, range from displays about the geological formation of Indonesia and the various cultural groups of Nusa Tenggara, to household and religious items. The museum's highlight is its collection of **kris**, elongated daggers with a blade sharpened on both sides. These traditional weapons are now objects of reverence, treasured as family heirlooms and symbols of manhood.

Merging into Ampenan to the east, **Mataram** is the capital of West Nusa Tenggara province as well as of the district of Lombok Barat (West Lombok). It's full of offices and imposing government buildings, many set in spacious grounds on broad, tree-lined avenues, but there's little to draw the visitor.

East again, **Cakranegara**, usually known as just Cakra (pronounced "Chakra"), is the commercial capital of the island, with shops, markets, workshops and hotels all aimed at Indonesian trade but more than willing to welcome tourists as well. It's also home to most of the area's historical sights. Built in 1744, the **Puri Mayura** (Mayura Water Palace), on Jalan Selaparang (daily 7am–4.30pm; Rp500), is set in well-maintained grounds, which get busy at weekends. It's pleasant enough if you're looking for a bit of relaxation in the city, although the grounds at nearby Narmada (see p.626) are far more attractive.

Across the main road, **Pura Meru**, also known as Pura Mayura, is the largest Balinese temple on the island, and was built in 1720 by Prince Anak Agung Made Karang. The temple bustles and brims with activity on festival days, but for the rest of the time is rather empty and cheerless.

The local and long-distance bus and bemo terminal used to be located at the western extremity of the city area at **Sweta**, at the junction of Jalan Sandubaya and Jalan T.R.H. Faisal, and many drivers and notices still state "Sweta" as their destination, although the new terminal, Mandalika, is 400m further east on the main cross-island road. It is surrounded by a massive **"market"** area, most of it in pristine concrete blocks and lacking the character of the traditional Indonesian market experience. For a more vibrant market experience, the small local-produce market, Pasar Sindu, on Jalan Hasanudin, about 500m north of the junction with Jalan Selaparang, or the maze of alleyways behind the main roads in the Cakranegara market area, are far more productive.

Eating and drinking

There's a wide range of **places to eat**, with an excellent choice of cuisines to choose from. Great choice and value is offered by the city's **Chinese** restaurants, and **Padang** and **Taliwang** food is also increasingly available. Anyone longing for a taste of home will be able to find something here, too.

Adenna, Jl Saleh Sungkar 33. Clean, popular, inexpensive Padang restaurant in Ampenan, convenient for the art shops and bemo terminal.

Aroma, Jl Palapa 2, Cakranegara. Excellent Chinese restaurant rather tucked away down the lane beside the *Mataram Hotel*, but worth seeking out. Inexpensive–moderate.

Betawi, Jl Yos Sudarso 152, upstairs on the corner of Jl Koperasi and Jl Yos Sudarso, Ampenan. A wide range of well-prepared and well-presented Western and Indonesian dishes. The big plus is the balcony, where you can watch life in the streets below. Inexpensive–moderate. Closed Sun.

Gubeng, Jl Wanasara Gang II, Cakranegara. A couple of alleyways east of Jl Nursiwan and its two losmen, this small, clean place offers only *soto daging*, but it's well cooked and cheap.

Mirasa Modern Bakery, Jl A.A. Gede Ngurah. Unfortunately this is only take-away, but they have excellent pizza slices, pastries, sweet breads and cakes.

Pabean, Jl Yos Sudarso 111, Ampenan. Small Chinese restaurant with large servings of basic dishes and well-cooked, inexpensive food. There are several other good options in this street if it's full; the closest is *Cirebon*, next door.

Rainbow Café, Jl Yos Sudarso, Ampenan. This small place has a limited menu, serves inexpensive food and cold beer, and plays Western music.

Shanta Pura, Jl Maktal 15. This restaurant attached to the popular losmen serves a range of travellers' fare and basic Indo-Chinese options in relaxed surroundings.

Taliwang Sejati, Jl Pejanggik 24c. One of several central, inexpensive Taliwang places in Cakranegara with a good variety of food in clean surroundings.

Taman Griya (Garden House Restaurant), Jl Pusat Pertokoan, Mataram, opposite the public hospital. A large choice of Indonesian food in a shady garden setting, but service can be erratic. Inexpensive–moderate.

Shopping

Much of **Ampenan** is awash with art and antique shops selling **crafts** from Lombok and the islands further east. They are good fun to browse and shop in, although you need to take the definition of "antique" with a pinch of salt. The majority are concentrated in Jalan Saleh Sungkar, spreading south from the turning to the bemo terminal, and in the Jalan Yos Sudarso area, north of the bridge across Sungai Jangkok. You'll find a great choice of crafts from islands east of Lombok; amulets made from bone and buffalo horn, wooden and palm boxes and textiles are all worth looking out for. Most places shut for two or three hours in the middle of the day and often on Friday afternoons too. Many shops can arrange shipping, which is priced by the cubic metre and costs around US$250–300 per cubic metre, to UK and North American destinations; Australia is slightly cheaper, and New Zealand more expensive.

A couple of local factories also produce **ikat** cloth. The process is the same as that used in Bali (see p.550) and the material produced is similar. The factories have shops attached (see below) and are good value if you want to buy cloth by the metre, but you'll get a better choice of sarongs and bedspreads on the beach at Senggigi.

An excellent one-stop shopping spot is the **Lombok Handicraft Centre** at Rungkang Jangkok, Sayang Sayang. Just beyond the Sungai Jangkok, about 2km north of Cakranegara along Jalan St Hasanudin, it has numerous small shops selling every type of craftwork imaginable, although not many textiles. You can see some of them being made, particularly the palm-leaf boxes.

Craft and textile shops

Ari, Jl Yos Sudarso 102. Extensive selection of baskets, chests, textiles, boxes and statues.

Fancy Art, Jl Saleh Sungkar 69, Ampenan. Packed full of an excellent selection of fixed-price goods including batik pictures.

Freti, Jl Yos Sudarso, Gang Sunda 18c. A good range of stuff, especially large Lombok baskets, at reasonable prices.

Gecko, Jl Saleh Sungkar 57. Some excellent things, especially the smaller items, including wooden boxes of various designs from Lombok and Sumba.

Lombok Pottery Centre, Jl Majapahit 7, Ampenan (☎ & fax 0370/33804). The shop and showroom of the Lombok Craft Project (see box), near the museum, stocks the best-quality products of the three main pottery centres on the island. Open Mon–Sat 8am–5pm.

Putu Aryasa, Jl Yos Sudarso 90. A well-displayed collection of pieces, many from Sumbawa, including metal pots, lamp-holders and smaller items.

Rinjani Handwoven, Jl Pejanggik 44–46, Cakranegara. Local factory producing *ikat* cloth and a good place to buy. Cotton is from Rp22,000 per metre; silk, from Rp75,000. You can watch the weavers until 4pm. Daily 9am–9pm.

Sasak Pottery, Jl Koperasi 102 (☎0370/31687, fax 31121). Operating shops in several hotels on the island, this is the warehouse and packing centre for overseas shipments for the largest pottery company on the island and the biggest earthenware showroom in Indonesia. Prices range from Rp5000 to Rp70,000 and shipping can be arranged. 5min from the airport; phone for a free pick-up in the city or Sengiggi area. They will also advise on good workshops to visit in the villages. Daily 8.30am–4pm.

Slamet Riady, Jl Tanun 10, just off Jl Hasanudin, Cakranegara, there is a small sign just north of *Hotel Pusaka*. Visit this *ikat* factory and shop between 8am and midday if you want to see the cloth being woven on foot looms.

Listings

Airlines All the domestic airlines have ticket counters at the airport. There are also some additional offices: Bouraq Airlines, *Hotel Selaparang*, Jl Pejanggik 40–42, Mataram (☎0370/27333, fax 33378); Garuda/Merpati, Jl Pejanggik 69, Mataram (☎0370/36745, fax 33691); PT Nitour Inc, Jl Yos Sudarso

6 (☎0370/23762); Garuda, *Hotel Lombok Raya*, Jl Panca Usaha (☎0370/37950, fax 37951). For information on international airline offices in Bali, see the box on p.478.

Banks and exchange All the large Mataram and Cakra banks change money and travellers' cheques. The most convenient if you are staying in Cakra is the Bank of Central Asia, Jl Pejanggik 67. For longer hours (Mon–Sat 8.30am–5pm) there are a couple of moneychangers on Jl Saleh Sungkar, just north of the junction with Jl Yos Sudarso. Multigraha Kelolavalas, Jl Saleh Sungkhar 1, also has a branch in Cakranegara, Jl Pejanggik 1. Bank Ekspor-Impor, Jl Pejanggik 20–22, in Cakra (Mon–Fri 8am–1.30pm, Sat 8am–10am) is the best place to get money wired from overseas (see Basics, p.24).

Boats Pelni, Jl Industri 1, Ampenan (☎0370/37212, fax 31604; Mon–Thurs 8.30am–noon & 1–3pm, Fri 8.30–11.30am & 2–3pm, Sat 8.30–11am).

Buses If you don't want to go to Mandalika terminal you can buy long-distance bus tickets from Karya Jaya, Jl Pejanggik 115d (☎0370/36065), Langsung Indah, Jl Pejanggik 56d (☎0370/34669), Perama, Jl Pejanggik 66 (☎0370/35928), and Safari Dharma Raya, Jl Pejanggik 24 (☎0370/33620).

Hospitals Catholic Hospital, Jl Koperasi, Ampenan (☎0370/21397); Muslim Hospital, Jl Pancawarga, Mataram (☎0370/23498); public hospital, Jl Pejanggik 6, Mataram (☎0370/21354).

Immigration office (Kantor Imigrasi), Jl Udayana 2, Mataram (☎0370/22520).

Motorbike rental If you know a bit about bikes and aren't worried about insurance, the main rental place is at Jl Gelantik 21, Cakranegara, a couple of hundred metres west of the *Srikandi* losmen on Jl Kebudayaan.

Police Jl Langko (☎0370/31225).

Post office, Jl Sriwijaya, Mataram. This is the main post office in Lombok and offers public access to the Internet. Open Mon–Thurs & Sat 8am–2pm, Fri 8am–11pm. For simply sending things, the post office at Jl Langko 21 opposite the tourist office is more accessible, as is the one on Jl Kebudayaan (same hours). For poste restante, the Senggigi post office is more used to dealing with tourists.

Supermarkets In the Mataram Plaza and the Cakra Plaza, both on Jl Pejanggik in Cakra (10am–9pm).

Telephone and fax The main telephone office is at Jl Langko 23, opposite the tourist office (daily 24hr), but there are also plenty of wartels in town, including Jl Panca Usaha 22b (7am–midnight), Jl Saleh Sungkar 2g (7.30am–7.30pm), and Jl Pejanggik 105 (6.30am–11pm).

Out from the city

Six kilometres south of the city, one of the three main **pottery centres** on the island, the village of **BANYUMULEK**, stretches west of the main road to Lembar. It's an easy one-kilometre walk from the junction to the place where the pottery workshops and showrooms begin, although there are cidomo serving the route. The full variety of

THE LOMBOK CRAFT PROJECT

Working in the villages of Banyumulek, Penakak and Penunjak, the **Lombok Craft Project** was established in 1988 with funding from the Indonesian Department of Industry and the New Zealand Official Development Programme with Indonesia. Women in these villages have been producing **earthenware pottery** since the early sixteenth century, passing their skills through generations from mother to daughter, using simple tools and local materials.

The aim of the project is to raise the standard of living of the potter families, who at the start of the project had a daily income of less than US$1. The project has supplied advisers and consultants in pottery, marketing, business and community development, targeting local hotels and restaurants and export markets.

The project estimates that it has directly assisted 200–300 women, but indirectly affected thousands more, as it has also sponsored literacy programmes and helped to develop better community facilities. In 1993, the potters' incomes had increased by between 300 and 500 percent, and many of the women are now establishing their own businesses.

earthenware goods is on offer and if you visit in the morning you can see the potters working. This is one of the villages involved in the Lombok Craft Project in cooperation with the New Zealand government (see box on p.605); the quality is high and they can ship items overseas for you. If you can't make it down to Banyumulek, the showroom and shop in Ampenan stocks some of the items produced here (see p.604).

A couple of kilometres north of Banyumulek, a few woodcarving workshops line the road at the village of **LABUAPI**. They specialize in the small wooden bowls, some with painted decoration, others inlaid with shells, that you'll spot in art shops across Lombok and Bali. You can see them being painted and varnished in the workshops behind the shops and prices are reasonable – from Rp5000 for small bowls to Rp45,000 for a set of larger caskets.

Lembar and the southwest peninsula

With several enticing offshore islands, the **southwest peninsula** is an exciting proposition for those who like their travel rough. This area is arid and scrubby, with only a few villages, the sparse population making its living from the sea.

LEMBAR, the gateway to the peninsula and the port for Bali, is 22km south of Mataram. Approaching by boat from Bali, the entrance to the rugged harbour is spectacular, but the village itself is insignificant. As the crow flies it's around 30km from Lembar to Bangko Bangko at the tip of the peninsula; by road, however, it's a rutted and dusty eighty-kilometre journey following the tortuous north coast. The road is only black-topped to Sekotong, after which it deteriorates badly and you'll need a powerful bike or jeep. Most of the **beaches** on the way are pure white and glorious. **Taun** is especially lovely and there is accommodation at *Sekotong Indah Beach Cottages* (☎0370/93040; ③–④). It has a small restaurant attached and a choice of rooms or cottages; you can also rent a boat to cross to Gili Nanggu from here. **Pelangan** has good snorkelling just offshore and there's a public boat to Gili Gede, while at **Labuhan Poh** there's a pearl-farming operation. **Bangko Bangko** first acquired a reputation a few years ago as a prime surfing spot (see box on p.632), but the inaccessibility of the place by road, and the fact that it has little else to offer (there's no snorkelling or coral here), means it has never developed into a resort, so keen surfers charter boats from Bali, bringing all their food and equipment with them.

There are two enticing groups of **islands** just off the north coast of the peninsula: Gili Nanggu, Gili Genting and Gili Tangkong being the closest to Lembar, and Gili Gede, Gili Asahan and Gili Poh – part of a much larger group further west, just off the coast at Pelangan. There is an accommodation place on Gili Gede (☎0370/23783; ③–④) with an attached restaurant and very little to do but relax. There are also tourist bungalows on Gili Nanggu, at *Istana Cempaka* (☎0370/22898; ③–④, including breakfast). Accommodation is in bungalows and there's a small restaurant attached. If you arrive in Lombok by ferry, you may glimpse the islands to the south as you approach the turn into Lembar harbour. To find a **boat** out to the islands from Lembar, head straight through the car park in the main port and talk to the skippers in the warung just on the shore. Expect to pay around Rp25,000 for a trip out to Gili Nanggu; otherwise make arrangements through *Sri Wahyu* losmen (see opposite).

Lembar practicalities

Bemos run between Mandalika terminal, Sweta and Lembar, connecting with the ferry and catamaran services to Bali. For details of **boat services** across the Lombok Strait, see p.597. If you're arriving at Lembar from Bali and need transport, you'll find the bemo drivers are hard bargainers; the price should be about Rp700 to Mandalika terminal, but you'll do very well to bargain them down even to Rp1500. If you arrive on the Mabua Express there is a fixed-price taxi counter in the terminal. If you share, prices will be Rp10,000 to Bangsal, Rp4000 to Mataram or Rp5000 to Senggigi, with private rentals running at Rp50,000, Rp25,000 and Rp35,000 for the same journeys.

The most local **accommodation** is the *Sri Wahyu* losmen (☎0370/81048; ①–②), on Jalan Pusri 1, Serumbung, signposted from the main road about 1.5km north of the port. The bungalows are basic but set in a garden, and there is a restaurant attached. You can arrange sailing trips from here to Gili Tangkong and Gengting (near Gili Nanggu) and Gili Sudak (near Gili Gede), starting at Rp25,000 for two people or a one-way trip to Gili Nanggu for Rp15,000 per person.

Senggigi and the northwest coast

With a reputation among travellers for being spoilt by big money and big hotels, it's a pleasant surprise to find that **SENGGIGI**, covering a huge stretch of coastline, with sweeping bays separated by towering headlands, is in reality an attractive and laid-back beach resort, offering a wide range of accommodation and restaurants, and a low-key nightlife. Although parts of the area are packed wall to wall with hotels, it's perfectly possible to have an inexpensive and relaxing stay here, and its accessibility to the airports makes it an ideal first or last night destination.

With your own transport, the road north from **Senggigi to Pemenang** (22km), hugging the spectacular coastline, makes a great day out. As you travel further north there are fine views of the Gili Islands, tiny white specks atop a turquoise sea. However, the road is very steep, with bad bends and sheer drops, and can be especially hazardous at night. The entire area from *Windy Cottages* at Manggsit to **Pantai Sira**, beyond Bangsal, has been designated *Kawasan Pariwisata*, a tourist development area, and is being developed by large hotel companies. However, this is a large area and, while central Senggigi may look increasingly like Kuta on Bali, it remains a place where you can still find total relaxation.

Arrival, getting around and information

Easily accessible by public transport, Senggigi is served by **bemos** from Ampenan terminal, every fifteen to twenty minutes throughout the day. The most convenient place to pick them up is on Jalan Saleh Sungkar just north of the turn-off to the bemo terminal in Ampenan. Fixed-price **taxis** also run direct from the airport for Rp10,000. The resort is very spread out so it's useful to have an idea of where you're heading; the southern end of Senggigi is just 5km north of Ampenan, and there are a few places spread out along the next 4km until the main concentration of hotels stretching for roughly 1km from the *Pondok Senggigi* to the *Sheraton*. Low-density development continues for another 8km to the most northerly development, *Hillberon Beach Villas*. Bemos are supposed to run as far as *Windy Cottages*, 5km north of the centre of Senggigi, but in practice these are rare, and most terminate at the *Sheraton* or the Pacific Supermarket. Many of the hotels on this stretch of road operate free shuttle services down to Central Senggigi during the day, and many restaurants offer free pick-ups in the evening. Metered blue taxis operate throughout the area from early morning to late at night; most places north of the central area will be Rp3000–5000 on the meter.

There's no **tourist office** in Senggigi. The nearest one is in Ampenan (see p.602), but the Senggigi area is lined with offices offering "tourist information", though it pays to check the information you are given as these are tour companies and primarily sell tours and transport and rent out cars, motorbikes and boats.

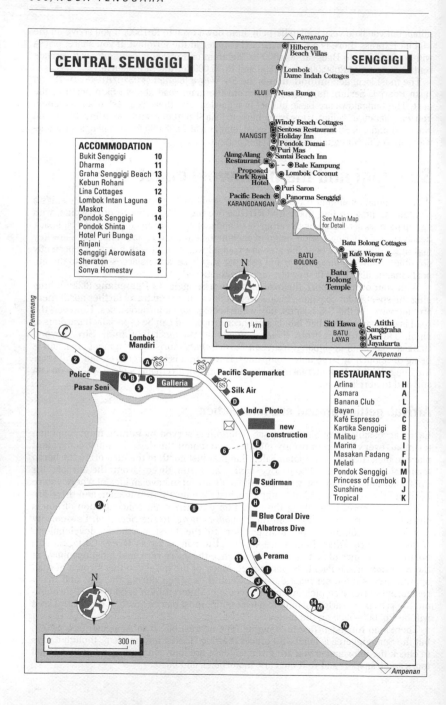

CENTRAL SENGGIGI

SENGGIGI

△ Pemenang

Hilberon Beach Villas

Lombok Dame Indah Cottages

KLUI — Nusa Bunga

Windy Beach Cottages
Sentosa Restaurant
MANGSIT — Holiday Inn
Pondok Damai
Puri Mas
Alang-Alang — Santai Beach Inn
Restaurant
Bale Kampung
Proposed — Lombok Coconut
Park Royal
Hotel
Puri Saron
Pacific Beach — Panorma Senggigi
KARANGDANGAN

See Main Map for Detail

Batu Bolong Cottages
Kafé Wayan &
BATU — Bakery
BOLONG
Batu
Bolong
Temple

N

Siti Hawa — Atithi
BATU — Sanggraha
LAYAR — Asri
Jayakarta

△ Ampenan

0   1 km

ACCOMMODATION

Bukit Senggigi	10
Dharma	11
Graha Senggigi Beach	13
Kebun Rohani	3
Lina Cottages	12
Lombok Intan Laguna	6
Maskot	8
Pondok Senggigi	14
Pondok Shinta	4
Hotel Puri Bunga	1
Rinjani	7
Senggigi Aerowisata	9
Sheraton	2
Sonya Homestay	5

△ Pemenang

Lombok Mandiri

Police

Pasar Seni

Pacific Supermarket

Silk Air

Galleria

Indra Photo

new construction

Sudirman

Blue Coral Dive

Albatross Dive

Perama

N

0   300 m

RESTAURANTS

Arlina	H
Asmara	A
Banana Club	L
Bayan	G
Kafé Espresso	C
Kartika Senggigi	B
Malibu	E
Marina	I
Masakan Padang	F
Melati	N
Pondok Senggigi	M
Princess of Lombok	D
Sunshine	J
Tropical	K

△ Ampenan

Accommodation

It's still possible to find reasonable budget **accommodation** in the resort, although you'll get more choice the more you can spend. The most attractive part of the coast is in north Senggigi, but it's very quiet and you'll have to rely on free transport from the hotels or restaurants or on taxis or bemo charters to get around.

South Senggigi

Asri (☎0370/93075). Furthest south of the three Batulayar places, with one- and two-storey basic bungalows very close to the beach. The nearby *Siti Hawa* is also worth a look. ④.

Atithi Sanggraha, Batu Layar (☎0370/31140). This is an extremely quiet place, well out of town and situated right on the beach, 4km south of central Senggigi, with well-built bungalows in a fair-sized compound between the road and beach. ④.

Batu Bolong Cottages (☎0370/93065, fax 93198). Just north of Batu Bolong temple, these are attractive, good-quality cottages in pleasant gardens, on both sides of the road; the more expensive ones have air-con and hot water. ④–⑤.

Jayakarta (☎0370/93045, fax 93043). Situated at the southern end of Senggigi, the imposing *lumbung* barn foyer with marble and rattan is the most impressive part of the hotel, although the garden is pleasant and the pool a good size. Good value for this end of the market. ⑧.

Central Senggigi

Kebun Rohani (☎0370/93018). Bamboo and thatch cottages with excellent verandahs to lounge on, set in an attractive garden on the hillside away from the sea. More expensive rooms have attached bathrooms. ③.

Lina Cottages (☎0370/93237 or 93157). The bungalows in this tiny seafront compound in the centre of Senggigi have air-con but not hot water. There's a large restaurant too. ⑤.

Maskot (☎0370/93365, fax 93236). Good-value place with pleasant grounds that stretch to the sea. The bungalows all have air-con, hot water and huge verandahs. There is no pool. ⑦.

Pondok Senggigi (☎0370/93273). This famous long time stalwart of the budget traveller has moved upmarket with a pool and some air-con and hot-water options at the top end. It's a relaxed, pleasant place to stay, with regular videos and live music in the huge restaurant. ⑤–⑦.

Pondok Shinta (no phone). Concrete rooms with pleasant verandahs set in a sizable garden just a short walk from the beach. ②.

Sheraton (☎0370/93333, fax 93140). All the facilities and comfort of an international hotel, and the best swimming pool in Senggigi (Rp20,000 for non-residents) in a beachfront location. Private villas with their own pool cost up to US$999 a night. ⑨.

Sonya Homestay (☎0370/93447) Budget rooms in a centrally located, cosy family compound. ③.

North Senggigi

Bale Kampung (no phone). Small, peaceful, budget place in Kerandangan village, easily accessible from central Senggigi. The turning is just north of *Lombok Coconut*, signed from the main road. Accommodation is in traditional bungalows set in a glorious garden; mosquito nets are provided and there's a local warung nearby. There are also a couple of basic losmen further from the main road in the village nearby. ③.

Holiday Inn (☎0370/93444, fax 93092). 5km north of Senggigi, this is the most upmarket option on this stretch of coast, with a huge compound, comfortable rooms, a giant swimming pool, plenty of activities to entertain guests and shuttle buses to central Senggigi. ⑨.

Lombok Coconut (☎0370/93195, fax 93593) Up the hillside, behind the *Lombok Coconut* restaurant, these are good-value attractively decorated bungalows with cold water and fans. There's a great little swimming pool too. ④–⑥.

Nusa Bunga, Klui (☎0370/93035, fax 93036). Over 5km north of the centre, this is a fabulous place to stay, with thatch-roofed brick cottages situated in their own small bay and a small swimming pool in an attractive garden. ⑦.

Panorama Senggigi (☎0370/93673, fax 93603). Well-furnished, well-decorated bungalows – the only places in Senggigi built to appreciate the fabulous views. The restaurant enjoys the same outlook and there's a pleasant pool. ⑧–⑨.

Pondok Damai, Mangsit (☎0370/93019). 4km north of central Senggigi, on the coast at Mangsit, this is a quiet spot with accommodation in bamboo-and-thatch bungalows. ③.

Puri Mas (☎0370/93023). A variety of bungalows with distinctive, quality furnishings, set in a lush and peaceful garden next to the beach. ⑥–⑨.

Santai Beach Inn (☎0370/93038). Right on the coast, these popular thatched bungalows are set in a wonderfully overgrown garden and have a very relaxed atmosphere. ③–⑤.

Windy Beach Cottages (Pondok Taman Windy) (☎0370/93191, fax 93193). Comfortable bungalows 5km north of central Senggigi, at Mangsit. It does get windy in the afternoons, but it's a lovely spot. The more expensive rooms have hot water. ⑤.

The resort

Life in Senggigi centres on the beach or swimming pool during the day, and the restaurants and bars in the evening. The pace is slow, and hassles from hawkers selling goods and touts offering transport, although getting worse, seem to be confined to the beach itself and the area around the supermarket. While Senggigi makes an excellent first or last stop on the island, it's also a good base for exploring further afield, although there are few sights nearby; the only local place really worth visiting is **Batu Bolong Temple**, 1km south of the centre of Senggigi. Weighed down under an excess of lurid pink paint, the shrines are spread around a rocky promontory with fabulous views in both directions along the coast.

Diving and snorkelling

Plenty of operators here cater for people who want to **dive** around the Gili Islands, but want the comforts of Senggigi and don't mind the additional cost and travel. If you're a qualified diver, expect to pay around US$55 for two dives, including the boat trip from Senggigi and lunch. Equipment rental may be included during low season. See Basics, p.56 for general information about diving. **Snorkelling** trips to the Gili Islands are run by most dive operators and also by Sunshine Tours; expect to pay US$15–20 including equipment and lunch. All of the operators have offices in Senggigi and are marked on the map.

DIVE OPERATORS

Albatross (☎0370/93399, fax 93388). Offers PADI open-water and advanced courses, as well as introductory dives (they have manuals in eight languages). Also diving trips for experienced and qualified divers, snorkelling trips to the Gili Islands and fishing trips.

Blue Coral (☎0370/93441, fax 93251). Offers PADI open-water courses in English and sometimes other languages, as well as advanced courses and diving trips for qualified and experienced divers. Confined water work is done in a local hotel pool.

Blue Marlin (☎0370/93045, fax 93043, email *bmdc@mataram.wasantar.net.id*). The main operation is on Gili Trawangan, but a full range of trips and courses is on offer from their Senggigi base at *Hotel Jayakarta,* including a range of IANTD technical courses.

Rinjani Jl Banteng 9, Mataram (☎0370/36040, fax 33972), and a counter at the *Lombok Intan Laguna* hotel (☎0370/93090 ext 8192). Offers CMAS, POSI and ADS courses in addition to dives for qualified divers.

Eating, drinking and nightlife

There's a wide range of **restaurants** in Senggigi offering international cuisine, mostly at moderate prices and generally of a high quality. They open daily, some in time for breakfast, closing around 10pm or 11pm. If you want more local food, try the small carts selling food in the streets or the Padang restaurants in the main street. The restaurants below are marked on the map on p.608.

Asmara (☎0370/93619). Set back from the main road, this tastefully furnished and relaxed restaurant offers a moderate-sized menu featuring Western, Indonesian and Sasak dishes and a massive drinks list in the moderate to expensive range. Free pick-up throughout Senggigi.

Kafé Espresso. Towards the north of the Central area offering cappuccino and espresso coffee, as well as salads, sandwiches, pasta, Indonesian favourites, *lassis* and an indulgent range of desserts. Prices are moderate.

Kafé Kokoloko. One of several seafront places in Pasar Seni with Indonesian, Sasak and Western options plus barbecued fish. Good Thai curries. The nearby *Kafé Senggigi Indah Lombok* is also worth a look.

Kafé Wayan & Bakery (☎0370/93098). About 1km from the centre of Senggigi and offering a free pick-up service in the area. An offshoot of the Ubud set up in Bali, they serve moderate to expensively priced Indonesian dishes, seafood, pizza, pasta and vegetarian food. The fresh bread, croissants and cakes are the highlight.

Lina. Large, popular restaurant attached to the cottages of the same name. There's a massive menu of soups, fish, chicken and Indo-Chinese options and the tables on the terrace overlooking the beach are a brilliant place to watch the sunset during happy hour.

Lombok Coconut (☎0370/93195). Serving pizza, pasta, burgers and salads, as well as Indonesian sate and *gado-gado*, this restaurant is located in a large *bale* just above the road, about 4km north of central Senggigi. There's free transport in the Senggigi area.

Panorama. The restaurant in the hotel of the same name with a brilliant location on the hillside. Go for afternoon tea (Rp5000) to make the most of the view.

Pondok Senggigi. Part of the hotel complex of the same name, this is a large, airy *bale* with a huge bar list and a menu offering Indonesian, Western and Sasak food at inexpensive to moderate prices. Smart but relaxed surroundings with regular live music.

Princess of Lombok (☎0370/93011). Offering a free pick-up in the area, this restaurant right in the middle of Senggigi serves moderately priced Western steak, fish and prawn dishes and tasty Mexican food.

Nightlife

The **nightlife** in Senggigi is very low-key, in keeping with the Muslim sensibilities of the local population, and there are very few venues. Licences permit music until 11pm daily and midnight on Saturday, although the *Marina* sometimes carries on until 1am or 2am. *Pondok Senggigi* has regular live music and the centrally situated *Banana Club*, one of the most popular places in Senggigi, features live bands playing covers of Western hits. Most people end up here or at the *Marina* across the road, which is a pleasant place to hang out in the evenings with regular live music, billiards, darts and board games. It also has a small dance floor but the dancing never really takes off.

Listings

Airlines and agents Silk Air (☎0370/93877, fax 93822) have a central office just south of the Pacific supermarket, and Sunshine Tours(☎0370/93232, fax 93021) are agents for Bouraq Airlines.

Boats Sunshine Tours, central Senggigi (☎0370/93232, fax 93021), sells tickets for the daily boat to Gili Trawangan (1hr 30min; Rp10,000) or Rp25,000 for a return including snorkelling.

Buses Several travel agents including Panorama (☎0370/34778 or 93020), on the main road, book long-distance buses as far as Jakarta to the west and Bima to the east, and Perama (☎0370/93007, fax 93009) offers the full range of tourist shuttles to destinations on Bali and Lombok. Sample prices are: Kuta (Bali) Rp20,000; Ubud Rp17,500; Lovina Rp25,000; Kuta (Lombok) Rp10,000; Tetebatu Rp7500.

Car and bike rental There are plenty of places renting vehicles with and without drivers. Lombok Mandiri (☎0370/93477) are competitive, with Suzuki Jimneys for Rp50,000, Kijang for Rp60,000 and motorbikes for Rp13,000. You can also rent mountain bikes from them (Rp5000), but bear in mind that the road north from Senggigi is extremely steep in parts.

Doctor Some of the luxury hotels have in-house doctors who can be consulted at the following times: *Holiday Inn* (☎0370/93444) 3–6pm; *Sheraton* (☎0370/93333) 3–11pm; *Senggigi Aerowisata* (☎0370/93210) 8am–4pm. There is also Clinic Senggigi (☎0370/93210, fax 93200) near *Senggigi Aerowisata,* who operate a 24hr call-out service. For anything serious, you'll have to go to the hospitals in the four-cities area (see p.605).

Exchange Bank Danamon and BNI are central, and there are plenty of money-exchange counters on the main street with longer hours, generally 8.30am to 7.30pm, and competitive rates.

Post office Located in the centre of Senggigi (Mon–Thurs & Sat 8am–6pm, Fri 8am–noon & 1–6pm, Sun 8am–noon). Poste restante is available here; get mail addressed to you at the Post Office, Senggigi, Lombok 83355, West Nusa Tenggara, Indonesia.

Shopping The main road is lined with shops selling Lombok crafts including textiles, jewellery, basketware and items from across the archipelago, as well as Western clothes and bags aimed at the tourist market. Pasar Seni is a collection of stalls selling a huge variety of stuff, while the nearby Galleria is a more upmarket collection of shops. Sudirman, on the main road, has top-quality items with reasonable prices and Asmara Art Shop has an excellent range of good-quality fixed-price items and is well worth a browse.

Supermarkets There are several in the centre of Senggigi. Pacific (8am–10pm) has the biggest selection, but tends to be pricier than the others. Most sell basic food, drink, toiletries and stationery as well as postcards, souvenirs and a selection of books about Indonesia. The English-language *Jakarta Post* usually arrives around 6pm.

Telephone and fax There are a couple of wartels in the centre of Senggigi and one just above the *Sheraton* with longer hours (7am–midnight).

The Gili Islands

Prized as unspoilt paradise islands by travellers in the 1980s, the **Gili Islands**, Gili Trawangan, Gili Meno and Gili Air, just off the northwest coast of Lombok, have developed rapidly in recent years to cope with the crowds of visitors.

Strikingly beautiful, with glorious white-sand beaches lapped by warm, brilliant-blue waters, each of the islands has developed its own character. Of the three islands, **Gili Trawangan** best fits the image of "party island". With its large number of places to stay, wide range of excellent restaurants and busy nightlife, it attracts the liveliest visitors, although it's still fairly low-key. To get away from it all, the smallest of the islands, **Gili Meno**, has absolutely no nightlife, and not much accommodation, although a couple of the more expensive hotels in the Gilis are sited here. Closest to the mainland, **Gili Air** offers a choice, with plenty of facilities in the south of the island, and more peace and quiet elsewhere.

Prices depend on the season and are more fluid than anywhere else on Bali or Lombok, being totally dependent on what the market will bear. A traditional bungalow costing Rp15,000 in April will rise to Rp35,000 or even more in the frantic months of July and August, while hovering somewhere in between if the crowds arrive early or leave late in the year. In the peak season (Dec & New Year, July & Aug), prices can double throughout the islands. None of the islands has a particular crime problem, but do take reasonable precautions. If you have problems, there are no police on the Gilis, but it is the role of the kepala desa, the head man who looks after Gili Air (where he lives), and Gili Meno, and the *kepala kampung* on Gili Trawangan, to deal with the situation and take you to police at Tanjung or Ampenan to make a report. It seems that when problems do arise they are sometimes dealt with rather poorly.

All of the **beaches** on the Gili Islands are public. The local people here are probably more used to seeing scantily clad Western women than in any other part of Lombok, but you should definitely cover up when you move away from the beach.

Getting to the islands and getting around

The **access port** for the Gili Islands is **BANGSAL**, 25km north of Senggigi, which has a few restaurants, some moneychangers and a Perama office (7.30am–4pm). If you get stuck, the losmen *Taman Sari* (no phone; ③–④) is just by the gate where vehicles stop on the way to the harbour. They have good-quality, clean accommodation opening onto a small garden. Bangsal is a short cidomo ride or a shadeless 1.5-kilometre walk from **PEMENANG**, 26km beyond the Ampenan-Mataram-Cakranegara-Sweta area and served by **bemos or buses** from Mandalika terminal. There are also some bemos from Ampenan. All transport between Mandalika and points around the north coast passes through Pemenang. There is no public bemo service along the coastal road north from Senggigi to Pemenang (see below for boat service from Senggigi to the islands). A gate at Bangsal stops all vehicles and most cidomo 200m from the harbour itself, so prepare to walk the final bit or bargain very hard with the drivers of the few vehicles that do ply up and down.

Boats leave Bangsal throughout the morning, when full, and take 20–45 minutes; buy your ticket at the office on the right as you head towards the beach. Blue, red and white boats serve Gili Air (Rp1200), yellow and red go to Gili Meno (Rp1500), and red and white go to Gili Trawangan (Rp1600). At both ends of the boat trip you'll get your feet wet, as the boats anchor in the shallows and you have to wade to and fro. If you arrive in the afternoon, you may have to charter a boat through the Koperasi Angkutan Laut (Sea Transportation Cooperative). Prices are Rp15,000 one way to Gili Air, Rp18,000 to Gili Meno and Rp21,000 to Gili Trawangan. From **Senggigi**, you can take the daily **Sunshine Boat** to Gili Trawangan, from Sunshine Tours in central Senggigi (1hr 30min; Rp10,000). It's not allowed to carry passengers in the opposite direction.

Perama sells **tourist shuttle** tickets to Bangsal from the main tourist destinations on Lombok and Bali. Sample prices include Rp12,500 from Kuta (Lombok), Rp22,500 from Ubud and Rp25,000 from Kuta (Bali).

Once on the islands, the **"hopping island"** boat service is extremely handy. It does one circuit, Air–Meno–Trawangan–Meno–Air, in the morning, and one in the afternoon. If you're moving from one island to another, it's cheaper to go back to Bangsal and out again, but this service is conveniently timetabled and fast, and makes a day-trip to another island a feasible option. Times from Gili Air are 8.30am and 3pm, from Gili Meno to Gili Trawangan 8.45am and 3.15pm, from Gili Trawangan 9.30am and 3.30pm, and from Gili Meno to Gili Air 9.45am and 3.45pm. Between Gili Trawangan and Gili Air the fare is Rp4000; between Gili Trawangan or Gili Air and Gili Meno, it's Rp3000.

Several operators on the islands offer shuttle tickets direct to Lombok or Bali destinations (Perama sell tickets from Bangsal). Expect prices from Gili Meno of around Rp8000 to Senggigi or the airport, Rp11,000 to Lembar, Rp16,5000 to Padang Bai, Rp19,500 to Candi Dasa, Rp20,500 to Ubud and Rp21,500 to Kuta. Fares are Rp1000 more from Gili Trawangan and Rp1000 less from Gili Air.

Snorkelling and diving

The **snorkelling and diving** around the islands is some of the best and most accessible in Lombok and, despite a lot of visitors, the reefs remain in reasonable condition. There are plans to make permanent moorings near the reefs to prevent damage from boat anchors. Fish dynamiting in the area has decreased considerably since the local population have begun seaweed farming; you'll see this in several areas around the islands. However, the use of harpoons and the removal of shells are all destroying the reef further and all visitors have a responsibility to make sure they do no harm.

All the islands are fringed by **coral reefs** which slope down to a sandy bottom at around 25m, although there are some walls. Visibility is generally around 15m. The **fish** life here is the main attraction and includes white-tip and black-tip reef sharks, sea turtles, cuttlefish, moray eels, lobster, manta rays, Napoleon wrasse and bumphead parrotfish. There are good snorkelling spots just off the beaches of all the islands; most of the best **dive sites** involve short boat trips and operators will usually also take snorkellers. Away from the shore, the currents are treacherous, so be careful.

There are **dive operations** on all the islands, with most based on Gili Trawangan. Expect to pay around US$35–45 for a two-dive trip; introductory dives are about US$55 and PADI open-water courses hover either side of US$300. You should check at the time of booking whether the price you are quoted includes equipment rental. Be especially careful over your choice of operator and **safety precautions** out here (see Basics p.56 for general tips). The nearest hospital is in Mataram and the nearest decompression chamber is in Denpasar on Bali.

Gili Trawangan

Furthest from the mainland, the largest of the islands, with a local population of 700, **GILI TRAWANGAN** attracts the greatest number of visitors. Island transport is by cidomo or you can rent bicycles (ask at your guest house; around Rp7000 per day), but as the tracks around the island are very sandy in parts walking is better than cycling. A **walk** around the island, which is less than 3km long by 2km at the widest part, takes three hours or less. There's not much to see other than seaweed in the shallows, the occasional monitor lizard and the giant cacti, ixorea, eucalyptus and palms which survive throughout the dry season, although everything greens up quite remarkably when it rains. Inland, the hundred-metre **hill** is the compulsory expedition at sunset – follow any of the tracks from the southern end of the island for views of Agung, Abang and Batur with the sky blazing behind.

Snorkelling and diving

The area towards the northern end of the east coast of the island is very popular for **snorkelling**, and most people hang out here during the day; you can amble a few metres inland to the warung that line the beach when it gets too hot. Snorkel gear is available (Rp3000–4000 a day for mask and flippers), and you can also rent boards with perspex windows set in them for viewing the sea life below.

There are plenty of dive shops on Gili Trawangan and a high resident population of **diving** instructors from overseas offering tuition and dive-guiding in all European languages. Many shops have PADI materials in several languages. It is very important to follow the guidelines given in Basics (p.56) and select your operator not only on the basis of cost. All of the operators listed here offer dives for qualified divers and many employ underwater videographers so you can buy a video of yourself down in the deep. **Albatross**, one of the longer-established Trawangan operators, is based in a shop in the market area, not on the seafront, and offers a full range of dives and PADI courses. **Blue Coral**, **AKOK** and **Dive Indonesia** (☎0370/34496) are all owned by the same company and offer a range of PADI courses. They have a swimming pool to use in the confined water stages of training. **Blue Marlin** (☎ & fax 0370/32424, *bmdc@mataram.wasantara.net.id*) are a five-star PADI dive centre and offer a full range of courses up to IDC (Instructor Development Courses) as well as IANTD (International Association of Nitrox and Technical Divers) courses and rebreather experience days. **Sea Angels** is another small operator on the island. The new Reefseekers shop on Gili Trawangan has no relationship at all with the well-regarded operator of the same name on Gili Air.

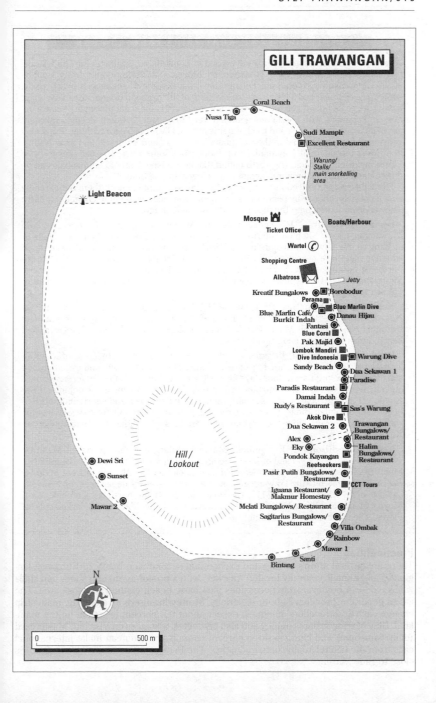

EXPLORING EAST: BOAT TRIPS FROM LOMBOK

A variety of **boat trips** are heavily advertised in Lombok, especially on the Gili Islands, travelling **via Sumbawa and Komodo to Flores** and visiting some pretty isolated spots. They involve several snorkelling stops, usually some trekking, a beach party, sometimes camping and a visit to see the feeding of the Komodo dragon, the native giant lizard. Prices include three meals a day, and transport is on boats of varying seaworthiness and comfort, with conditions generally very basic and crowded; sleeping quarters are mattresses on the deck and fresh water is not usually available for bathing. Trips vary considerably in length, and in their combination of road and sea travel and final destination. Most terminate at Labuhanbajo on Flores, but some travel by road and ferry to Flores and then sail back. It's worth noting that air transport out of Labuhanbajo can be difficult and time-consuming to arrange, so allow plenty of time.

The following is a selection of trips on offer, but you should check them out carefully and, if possible, choose by personal recommendation – names seem to change regularly. They all include watching the feeding of the Komodo dragon.

Island Adventures, PT Pemayar Rempa Wanua, in front of *Iguana Bar*, Gili Trawangan, Ozzy's Shop on Gili Air, or at any public boat ticket office on the islands or at Bangsal. Six days and five nights for US$75–110 (the price is variable depending on whether they have spaces to fill), departing from Bangsal. Includes Gili Sulat off the northeast Lombok coast, Moyo, Satonda and Banta Islands off the coast of Sumbawa, Rinca and Pulau Bidari near Komodo with trekking on Pulau Rinca. Terminates at Labuhanbajo.

Kencana Fun Sun Sea Programme, PT Suar Manik Kencana, has an office at *Natural* Warung, Bangsal. They offer a US$110, six-day and five-night programme, including Gili Bola, Gili Moyo, Gili Satonda, a visit to Wera village on Sumbawa, Red beach, Pulau Rinca and end up in Labuhanbajo.

Land Sea Adventure, Perama. Check at any Perama office (nearest offices Gili Trawangan, Gili Air, Bangsal). Trips are a mixture of boat and coach, and from Lombok start from three nights and four days for Rp200,000 and up to Rp450,000 for seven days and six nights, starting and finishing in Lombok. The trips can include camping on Gili Kondo off the northeast Lombok coast, hiking on Pulau Rinca and snorkelling off Red beach and off Pulau Bidari (Flores). Originating in Mataram, this tour is very flexible with options to suit almost everyone and can finish in Bima, Labuhanbajo or on Komodo.

Reef Expeditions, PT Lombok Mandiri, Jalan Gunung Kerinci, Mataram (☎0370/93477, fax 32497) and offices in Senggigi, the *Kontiki Restaurant* in Bangsal, Gili Meno (☎0370/32824), in front of *Gita Gili Bungalows* on Gili Air, and in front of *Sandy Beach Bungalows* on Gili Trawangan. There are twice-weekly departures for a six-day and five-night trip costing US$110, via Pulau Bidara off the northeast Lombok coast, Moyo, Satonda and Banta Islands off Sumbawa and Komodo, Rinca and Bidari Islands off Flores. The trip finishes in Labuhanbajo.

Practicalities

There are several **shops** selling and exchanging secondhand books in European languages and a small, centrally located "market" with a **postal agent** and shops and stalls where you can buy everyday necessities plus basic beach clothes and postcards. The island generator provides 24-hour electricity. **Moneychangers** all along the main strip change cash and travellers' cheques; expect about ten percent less than on the mainland. Blue Marlin changes money and also gives cash advances on Visa and Mastercard (daily 8am–5pm) and charges three percent commission. You can make international calls from the **wartel** (daily 7am–midnight). The Perama office (daily 7.30am–9pm) is close to Blue Marlin.

ACCOMMODATION

Traditional accommodation is in bamboo-and-thatch bungalows on stilts, with simple furnishings, mosquito nets, a verandah and a concrete bathroom at the back with squat toilet and mandi. Moving upmarket there are newer, bigger **concrete-and-tile bungalows**, comfortably furnished, with fans and attached bathrooms, which may include a Western-style toilet and possibly a locking cupboard or drawer. Many of the losmen have only salty water available for bathing so expect to feel a bit sticky.

The north end of the island is relatively quiet, except for the mosque, while the concentration of bungalows at the southern end is more lively and closer to the restaurants and late-night discos. There are also some developments around the southern tip and on to the west coast of the island that are pleasant and quiet. If everywhere else is full or if you fancy something a bit different, there are a few basic losmen behind the main restaurant/guest-house drag or you can always ask in the local houses about rooms for rent. At the time of writing *Vila Ombak* provided the only real hotel option on the island. There's not a great deal to choose between the different sets of bungalows, and all are marked on the map. Below are some to get you started. The price codes in this section encompass the price range throughout the year. Generally the lower price refers to the quietest times and the higher price to the July and August madness, with the months either side of this being somewhere in the middle.

Blue Marlin (Bukit Indah; ☎ & fax 0370/32324). Better-quality bungalows than most, with attractive furnishings and some options with hot water. ⑤–⑥.

Danau Hijau. Conveniently close to the harbour, these straightforward concrete bungalows are similar to many of the ones nearby, with red-tiled roofs and good verandahs. ④.

Dewi Sri. Quiet, isolated place on the west coast, a 30min walk from the harbour, with accommodation in traditional bungalows. ②–③.

Mawar 1. Inexpensive accommodation in peaceful traditional bungalows that are easily accessible from the busier areas of the island. ②–③.

Melati. Modern bungalows with lockable cupboards and drawers, fans and pleasant verandahs at the front. ③.

Nusa Tiga. Up on the peaceful north side of the island, with some traditional and some modern bungalows and a restaurant attached. ③.

Santi. Near the sea in a shady location, these well-built traditional bungalows with a brick mandi are a popular option. ③.

Sunset. One of two close-together developments on the west coast. Accommodation is in traditional bungalows facing seaward and set in a pleasant garden. ②–③.

Vila Ombak. The most upmarket option on the island. Attractive and well-furnished rooms with fans and cold-water showers set in pleasant gardens. ⑥–⑦.

EATING, DRINKING AND NIGHTLIFE

At night, the focus moves from the beach to the row of **restaurants** that line the road a few metres inland. Generally the quality and variety of the food is very good and prices are reasonable, with **seafood** the best option. Much of the fun of staying on the island is in finding your own favourite watering hole. Most of the restaurants show two or even three videos each day, which are advertised daily, and there's a surprisingly good range of new films. However, two of the favourite places, *Borododur* and *Trawangan*, have consistently good food and atmosphere but rarely show videos. The new *Vila Ombak* has the most upmarket dining experience on the island, with tables on the outdoor terrace near the water and on the balcony of the impressive two-storey main building. Prices are moderate but the value is excellent, with pizza and pasta highly recommended. Warung *Dive* in front of Dive Indonesia has a good range of salads, sate, pasta and steaks. Look out for *Sas's* warung (no sign), a small stall on the beach side of the road (shown on the map), offering cheap and excellent local food. The gado-gado is especially fine.

Parties take place nightly, with *Rudy's*, *Rainbow*, *Paradise* and *Excellent* taking turns at hosting them. They get going at about 11pm and finish around 2am to 3am. Each night's venue is clearly advertised on flyers around the island.

Gili Meno

A similar oval shape to Gili Trawangan, **GILI MENO** is much smaller, about 2km long and just over 1km wide. This is the most tranquil island of the three, with a local population of just 350, although some solo women travellers find a few of the young men that hang around particularly persistent. The **snorkelling** is good all along the east coast, especially at the northern end, where you can see blue coral and mushroom coral. It takes a couple of hours to stroll around the island. There is no postal agent or Perama office, but *Mallia's Child* offers shuttle buses to destinations on Lombok and Bali. You can **change money** at *Mallia's Child*, *Gazebo* and *Casablanca*, and there's a **wartel** at *Gazebo*. There are a few **dive operators** on the island. Albatross Dive Shop (☎0370/36040, fax 33972) near the harbour provides the same range of courses and dives as the operation on Gili Trawangan, Rinjani Dive have a counter at *Kontiki* offering CMAS, ADS and POSI courses and dives for experienced divers, and *Zoraya* (see below) also offers dives for qualified divers.

Accommodation

The range of **accommodation** options is much greater here than on the other islands, with several mid-range choices. There are some simple beach huts, but you won't find rock-bottom prices anywhere, and generally value is not as good as on Gili Trawangan. Most accommodation is spread along the east coast over a fairly small area and each set of bungalows has its own generator for electricity, except at the northern end, which is where you'll get the best budget value.

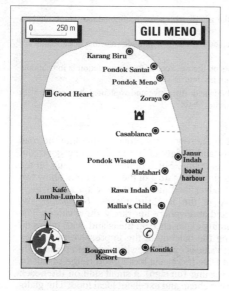

Blue Coral (Karang Biru). Quiet accommodation in traditional bungalows, but without electricity. ③.

Casablanca (☎0370/33847, fax 93482). One of the better mid-range places with a range of options and a tiny pool set about 100m back from the beach in an attractive garden. ⑤–⑦.

Gazebo (☎ & fax 0370/35975). Ten attractive and comfortable bungalows set in a coconut grove; air-con but no hot water. It's often full. Closed mid-Jan to mid-March. ⑧.

Mallia's Child (☎0370/22007). Bamboo-and-thatch bungalows in a good location near a fine beach, but the bathrooms are shared and there are no fans. ③.

Pondok Meno. Quiet accommodation in traditional bungalows, but without electricity. ③.

Pondok Santai. Traditional bungalows at the quiet northern end of the island. There's no electricity. ③.

Zoraya (☎0370/33801). To the south of the east coast, with some attractively furnished bungalows with air-con at the top end, though the nearby beach is nothing special. ⑤–⑥.

Eating and drinking

There are plenty of **places to eat** on the island. The restaurant at *Casablanca* is an attractive open *bale* in a lovely garden with a menu of moderately priced Indonesian, seafood and Western options, plus plenty of daily specials. On the west coast, *Kafe Lumba-Lumba* has Indo-Chinese and Padang food and good views of Gili Air and, if you're walking around the island, it's a convenient place for a lingering break or a sunset drink. *Good Heart* is another good place for a drink and offers standard local and travellers' fare. The restaurant in front of *Kontiki* has good beach views and a large menu of steak, seafood, rice and noodles, and the restaurant attached to *Mallia's Child* has an excellent pizza oven. All are inexpensive to moderately priced. Eat early as they all stop serving by about 9.30pm.

Gili Air

Closest to the mainland, with the largest local population (1000) of the three islands, **GILI AIR** stretches about 1.5km in each direction. It takes a couple of hours to complete a circuit on foot, and there are great views across to Sira beach on the mainland. Gili Air sits somewhere between lively, social Gili Trawangan and extremely peaceful Gili Meno.

There is a good range of **accommodation** available, from beach huts to luxurious bungalows. The conglomeration of restaurants and losmen behind the waste ground on the southeast corner is where you'll find most of the action, and the beach here is the most popular, with good **snorkelling**. Individual bungalows have their own generators which means that, especially in the more crowded southeast corner, you may well be in very close earshot of a throbbing motor. When the planned island-wide electricity supply comes to fruition these problems should be solved instantly.

Reefseekers **diving operation** (☎ & fax 0370/641008, *reefseekers-diving@mataram.was/antara.net.id*) offers dives for qualified divers, plus introductory dives and PADI courses, and also give information for snorkellers. If you do an introductory dive here you'll get a certificate allowing you to dive in other PADI-accredited operations within a short period. Reefseekers are particularly involved in conservation in the area. Blue Coral (not related to the company of the same name on Gili Trawangan) offers a similar range of dives plus courses in both English and German.

There are plenty of moneychangers around the island and the **wartel** (7.30am–9pm) is at *Gili Indah*. The full range of tourist shuttle tickets can be booked from Perama (7.30am–7pm). There is no **postal agent** on Gili Air, but postcards and stamps are available from the shops, and mail gets taken to the mainland regularly from the yellow box near Perama.

Accommodation

Coconut Cottages (Pondok Kelapa; ☎0370/35365). Away from the coast in a wonderfully peaceful coconut grove, with two standards of cottage and a small restaurant attached. ③–④.

Hotel Gili Air (☎0370/22344). The most upmarket option on the island with good-quality and well-furnished bungalows; the more expensive ones have air-con and hot water. ⑤–⑦.

Gili Indah (☎0370/36341). This is the biggest setup on the island, offering a range of accommodation in a shady compound, convenient for the harbour, but away from the hustle and bustle. ⑤–⑥.

Gita Gili (no phone). Near the coast and convenient for the harbour with a variety of bungalows. Electricity is planned. ③.

Gusung (no phone). Pleasantly located close to the east coast, with traditional well-built bungalows facing seaward. ③–④.

Lombok Indah (no phone). Simple bungalows on a quiet stretch of coast, although the attached *Legends* warung hosts weekly discos. ③–④.

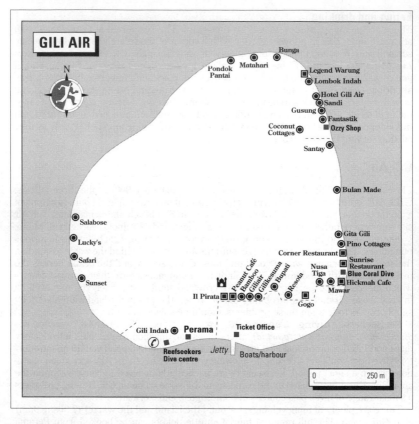

Matahari (no phone). The bungalows here are fairly close to the quiet north coast with places to sit right beside the beach. There is electricity in the restaurant, but not the bungalows. Other reasonable options nearby are *Pondok Pantai* and *Bunga*. ②–③.

Mawar (no phone). One of the cluster of accommodation places at the southeast corner of the island. Well-built cottages with mosquito nets, good verandahs and some electricity. You can also check out *Bupati's*, *Bamboo* and *Gili Kesuma (Garden)* nearby. ③.

Pino Cottages (no phone). Good cottages just on the edge of the crowded southeast corner, with a small restaurant attached. ④.

Salabose (no phone). Two standards of cottages on the peaceful west coast – the more expensive ones are well furnished and the budget ones have a good sea view. Other nearby options are *Lucky*, *Safari* and *Sunset*, all offering good budget accommodation. ②–④.

Santay (no phone). Popular, good-quality cottages in a good location set slightly back from the east coast. ③.

Eating, drinking and nightlife

There is a good range of **places to eat**, many of them attached to accommodation establishments. Most offer a range of Indonesian and Western food at cheap-to-moderate prices and Indonesian buffets are laid on by plenty of places – look for the flyers around the island. *Il Pirata* has a small Italian menu at moderate prices. The restaurant at *Hotel Gili Air* is a quality operation with a huge menu of Indo-Chinese, seafood, pasta, pizza and other Western options, and drinks including red and white wine. Prices are moderate. The warung attached to *Bulan Madu* is right on the shoreside, and is a great place for an afternoon drink. *Peanuts* café has an attractive, traditional sitting area and, so far, has not succumbed to playing loud taped music.

At the time of writing, parties were only allowed twice a week on the island, starting at 9pm or 10pm and finishing fairly strictly at midnight, alternating between *GoGo* on Saturday and *Legends* on Wednesday. Inquire at your guest house for the current situation.

The north coast

Beyond Pemenang the main coast road heads north. Two kilometres beyond the village, you'll pass a dirt road, opposite the local school, which leads to **SIRA** and the longest white-sand **beach** on Lombok. Glaringly beautiful, it's still pretty much deserted, with no tourist facilities of any kind. However, the luxury development of the area has already started nearby and is set to continue very quickly.

Six kilometres beyond Pemenang, a road and then a rough track leads 1km north to the temple of **Pura Medana**. Close to the black-sand Medana beach, the impressive temple is positioned on a promontory which has lovely coastal views. If you follow the sealed road you'll arrive at the *Oberoi* (☎0370/38444, fax 32496; ⑨), the first of many luxury developments planned for the area. Further east, a couple of kilometres before Tanjung, the only budget accommodation on the coast is at *Manopo Homestay* (fax 0370/32688; ③), an unusual place with a Sudanese owner and her exuberant, eccentric French husband, who welcomes visitors to a glimpse of the "real" Indonesia.

Almost at the northern tip of the island, the traditional village of **SEGENTER** is signed 2km inland along a broad, well-maintained dirt road. Park just outside the gate of the fenced village and a guide will meet you. You'll be taken on a village tour and inside one of the bamboo-and-thatch houses, and at the end of the visit you'll be expected to make a donation to the village and sign the visitors' book. Along with Senaru (see p.623), this is the most welcoming and interesting traditional village on the island.

Buses from Mandalika terminal in Sweta (see p.603) terminate at **ANYER**. Bemos regularly ply from Anyer via Ancak and Bayan to Batu Koq and Senaru for Rinjani. If you want to continue around the north coast, there are a few buses (morning only) that travel further east via Kalih Putih to Labuhan Lombok, or you may have to travel by bemo to **Ancak**, about 3km inland, to pick one up.

The small village of **BAYAN**, 5km south from Anyer, is generally accepted as the site of the oldest mosque in the country – at least 300 years old. You cannot enter the mosque, but even from outside it's very striking: a traditional bamboo-and-thatch building atop a stone and concrete circular citadel rising up in tiers.

East from Bayan the road winds its way through the rolling foothills of the volcano. The extensive rice-fields of the Bayan area soon give way to a much drier, dusty terrain that continues 9km to the small junction at **Kalih Putih**, from where occasional buses run to Sembalun Lawang, the alternative access point for treks up Rinjani. From Kalih Putih, it's around 10km to Obel Obel, from where you can continue on across the island to the east coast (see p.630).

Gunung Rinjani and around

From a distance, and even visible from Bali, **Gunung Rinjani** (3726m) appears to rise in solitary glory from the plains, but in fact the entire area is a throng of bare and soaring summits, wreathed in dense forest. Invisible from below, the most breathtaking feature of the range is **Segara Anak**, the magnificent crater lake, measuring 8km by 6km.

The **climb** up Rinjani is the most energetic and the most rewarding trek on either Bali or Lombok. You can ascend from either **Senaru** or **Sembalun Lawang,** where there is some accommodation, or climb the volcano as part of an organized tour (see

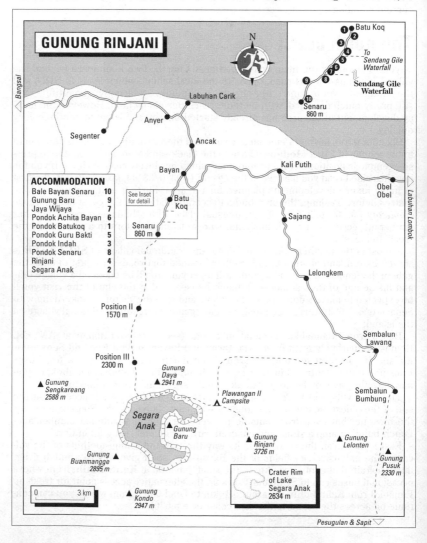

GUNUNG RINJANI

N

Bangsal

Batu Koq

To Sendang Gile Waterfall

Sendang Gile Waterfall

Senaru 860 m

Labuhan Carik

Anyer

Segenter

Ancak

Bayan

Kali Putih

Obel Obel

Labuhan Lombok

ACCOMMODATION

Bale Bayan Senaru	10
Gunung Baru	9
Jaya Wijaya	7
Pondok Achita Bayan	6
Pondok Batukoq	1
Pondok Guru Bakti	5
Pondok Indah	3
Pondok Senaru	8
Rinjani	4
Segara Anak	2

See Inset for detail

Batu Koq

Senaru 860 m

Sajang

Lelongkem

Position II 1570 m

Position III 2300 m

Gunung Daya ▲ 2941 m

Sembalun Lawang

▲ Gunung Sengkareang 2588 m

Plawangan II Campsite

Sembalun Bumbung

Segara Anak

▲ Gunung Baru

Gunung Rinjani 3726 m

▲ Gunung Lelonten

Gunung Buanmangge 2895 m

▲ Gunung Kondo 2947 m

Gunung Pusuk 2330 m

0   3 km

Crater Rim of Lake Segara Anak 2634 m

Pesugulan & Sapit

the box on p.624). The trip is only possible in the dry season, from about May to October, is not for the frail or unfit, and should not be attempted without adequate food or water. Although not all the treks need a porter or guide, you should let somebody know where you are going and when you will be back. There are conservation offices at Senaru and Sembalun Lawang to report to when you set off, but they're often deserted. There have been fatal accidents on the mountain and this is an **active volcano**; Gunung Baru in the crater lake last erupted in 1994.

Batu Koq and Senaru

The small villages of **BATU KOQ** and **SENARU** to the south of Bayan (about 86km from Mataram) are easily reached by bemo from Anyer, a few kilometres to the north – if you take an ojek, Rp1000 is a fair price. Both have **accommodation** spread out for several kilometres along the road: *Pondok Batukoq* is the most northerly and furthest from the mountain, while *Bale Bayan Senaru* lies right at the end of the road where the path up the mountain begins. Places on the east of the road generally have the best views towards the mountain. All will help you arrange your trek, rent out gear, find porters and store your stuff while you climb, and most have small **restaurants** attached, serving simple Indonesian and Sasak meals, although food and drink prices tend to be higher than in more accessible areas.

Just to the south of *Pondok Senaru*, a small path heads east to the river and **Sendang Gile waterfall**. This is a lovely spot where you can bathe, although the water is pretty chilly. Follow the irrigation channel along from here and you'll reach the road at Batu Koq; it's a pleasant walk with good views over the local fields to the north coast. Alternatively, there is an even higher and more impressive waterfall beyond the first one; ask for directions at your accommodation.

The **traditional village** at Senaru, a fenced compound with houses of bamboo and thatch set out in rows, next to the *Bale Bayan Senaru*, is worth visiting. The villagers still live a very simple life and farm the land using methods that haven't changed for centuries. Someone will appear to show you around and you'll be expected to make a donation and sign the visitors' book.

Accommodation

Bale Bayan Senaru. This is the place closest to the mountain. Basic bamboo-and-thatch bungalows in a small garden. ②.

Pondok Achita Bayan. New place with good bungalows and verandahs back and front for mountain and garden views. ②.

Pondok Batukoq. The first place you come to on the way up from the north coast. Bungalows with mosquito nets, in a small garden. ②.

Pondok Guru Bakti. Basic bungalows with excellent views of the waterfall from the rooms at the back. ②.

Pondok Indah. New place with good bungalows and fine north-coast views. ②.

Pondok Senaru. Good-quality bungalows with good views, a *bale* in the garden and a huge restaurant. ③.

Segara Anak. There are stunning views from the verandahs of the more expensive bungalows, while the cheaper ones overlook the garden. ②.

Sembalun Lawang and Sembalun Bumbung

Set in countryside that is unique in Lombok, **SEMBALUN LAWANG** is positioned in a high, flat-bottomed mountain valley virtually surrounded by hills. A steep, poorly surfaced road twists and turns 18km south from Kalih Putih (see p.621) to Sembalun Lawang. Public transport is infrequent, although buses do run from Labuhan Lombok, but realistically you'll need your own transport to get up here. There is only one **place to stay**, the *Mariia Guest House* (②), with basic rooms and an outside shared mandi. They have a limited number of tents and sleeping bags for rent, and the owner, Diralam, will give you information about the path up Rinjani or help you to arrange porters.

Four kilometres further south is **SEMBALUN BUMBUNG**, an attractive village with houses clustered around the local mosque in the shadows of the surrounding mountains. Few tourists make it this far and there's nowhere to stay. At the time of writing, there was no through-road for vehicles to traverse the 15km across Gunung Pusuk to **Pesugulan** on the southern slopes of the mountains (see p.629), although it is possible to trek. However, the road is being repaired and when completed will no doubt open the entire area up to more visitors.

Climbing Gunung Rinjani

The **summit of Rinjani**, the highest point of the region's volcanic mountainous mass, is reached by relatively few trekkers; the majority are satisfied with a shorter, less arduous trip to the crater rim and down to the crater lake. From **the rim** you can see the beautiful turquoise lake, **Segara Anak** (Child of the Sea) inside the massive crater, with the small perfect cone of **Gunung Baru** (New Mountain) rising on the far side.

RINJANI TRIPS

Although it really is easy to go to Senaru or Batu Koq and arrange the climb up Rinjani from there, many companies on Lombok arrange **inclusive trips** to climb the mountain. Prices include transport in both directions, guides, porters, accommodation, food and equipment. Don't forget that, allowing for the guide and porters, you could end up climbing in quite a crowd. Typically, there are three options on offer: one-night/two-day trips to the crater rim, two-night/three-day trips to the rim and the lake, and three-night/four-day trips that go to the summit from Sembalun Lawang, down to the lake and finish at Senaru.

In addition to the Lombok operators below it is possible to arrange trips to Rinjani from *Arlina's* at Toya Bungkah in the Batur region of Bali (see p.562). Prices start at US$280 per person.

CCT, *Borobodur Restaurant*, Gili Trawangan (☎0370/34893). Trips from US$100 per person for two people on a trip to the rim, and up to US$270 to the summit.

Discover Lombok, *Café Alberto*, Jalan Raya, Senggigi; 2km north of Ampenan (☎0370/36781). US$150 for a three-day trip.

Hati Suci, Sapit. Well situated to arrange four-night/five-day summit trips from Sembalun Lawang and finishing in Senaru. US$165 per person.

Lombok Mandiri, Jalan Gunung Kerinci 4, Mataram (☎0370/32497), and offices in Senggigi (☎0370/93477), Bangsal and on each Gili Island. Prices from US$100 each for a two-person one-night/two-day trip to the rim, to US$150 per person for the three-day/four-day trip via the summit.

Nazareth, Jalan Adi Sucipto 76, Ampenan (☎0370/31705 at *Losmen Horas*). Also in central Senggigi and in Senaru. Trips from US$150 per person in a party of two on a two-day/three-night trip, to US$240 for a four-day/five-night trip.

Rainbow, Pringgasela, central Lombok (no phone). From US$70 per person for a one-day/two-night trip to the rim, to US$120 for three nights/four days. Prices are based on two people.

Wannen, Jalan Erlangga 4, Mataram (☎ & fax 0370/31177), and in front of Indra Photo, Senggigi (☎0370/93442). From US$85 per person in a party of five for a one-night/two-day trip to the rim, to US$180 per person in a party of two on a three-day/four-night trek including the summit.

Having lain dormant since 1906, Gunung Baru erupted again in August 1994, closing the mountain for several weeks and raising fears of a major disaster. Gunung Rinjani itself has been inactive since 1901, although it puffed a bit of smoke in 1944 and 1951. Fortunately all has gone quiet again, but many of the paths in the crater, to the hot springs further south and to a waterfall behind Baru, have been destroyed.

The routes

The simplest trek is from **Senaru**, climbing to the **crater rim**. There are two offices to collect your money in exchange for permits on the way; it's Rp500 at the first, LKMD, almost at the start of the track and then Rp2000 at the forestry office further up the path. The route takes you from the village at 860m (marked on some maps as Position I), up through the forest to further **rest positions** (also called *plawangan*) with small *bale*. Rest Position II is at 1570m and Position III is at 2300m; you then leave the forest for the slog up to the rim at 2634m. It takes most people six to seven hours, not allowing for rests, to get to the rim from Senaru and usually involves a night on the mountain unless you are extremely fit and fast. Sadly the *bale* are in a very poor state of repair and not ideal for sleeping in. A tent is preferable, and vital if you plan to sleep on the actual rim.

A further possibility after climbing to the rim is to descend down into the crater to **the lake** itself, at around 2000m. The path (1hr 30min) into the crater is very steep and rather frightening at the top, but gets better further down. You can bathe in the warm water of the lake or the **hot springs** along its shores; the best-known issue is from the Goa Susu (Cave of Milk). Most people get down to the lake in one day from Senaru, stay by the shore and return the same way in another day's walking.

From the lake it's possible to climb out on a different path to a site called Plawangan II at 2900m, and from there up to the **summit** of Rinjani, a seven-hour trek. You'll need a guide for this. You should try to get to the summit for sunrise or by about 7am as it clouds over and gets very windy by 9am.

A shorter route to Plawangan II is to climb from **Sembalun Lawang** on the east side of the mountain (6–9hr), making it possible to ascend the mountain by one route and descend by another. However, relatively few people do this because of complications with porters, transport and the return of equipment they have rented. In Sembalun Lawang, the path starts under a large archway, beside a three-metre-high concrete clove of garlic which is pretty hard to miss.

Practicalities

There is spring **water** at Positions II and III from the Senaru side during and just after the rainy season, and also around the lakeshore, but check locally before you set out. It's vital to carry adequate water and food for the climb.

If you are climbing up from Senaru to the rim or down to the lake you don't need a **guide**, although a porter is a great advantage. The path leaves to the left just beyond *Bale Bayan Senaru* in Senaru and is difficult to lose. From Sembalun Lawang the path is straightforward up to Plawangan II, but check conditions with the owner of the *Mariia Guest House* in the village. To climb to the summit of Rinjani you will need someone to show you the way, usually a **porter** who will carry your gear, cook your food and pitch your tent. Prices for porters, from either starting point, are Rp15,000 a day and you must take food and water for them also.

Most of the accommodation near the mountain rents out gear. Sleeping bags are Rp5000–7000, tents Rp15,000–20,000, and stoves and cooking stuff Rp5000–10,000. The price is for each trip and you'll pay this even if you are away just one night. There are more misunderstandings about charges for gear than anything else, so make sure everyone is clear about what is agreed.

Central Lombok

Stretching for 74km from the Ampenan-Mataram-Cakranegara-Sweta conurbation in the west to Labuhan Lombok in the east, the main road across the island is the nearest thing to a highway that you'll find, and passes close to many of the most attractive places in **central Lombok**. Set high enough in the hills to be cool, and situated to make the most of the local scenery, the accommodation in the small village of **Tetebatu** and, to a lesser extent, in **Sapit**, is becoming increasingly popular. Down on the plains, **Lendang Nangka** has become something of a pilgrimage for travellers seeking the "real" village experience. Those interested in Lombok culture can make stops at the Hindu sites at **Narmada**, **Pura Lingsar** and **Suranadi**.

Narmada and the surrounding villages

Built in 1805 by the rajah of Mataram, Anak Gede Karangasem, the gardens of **Taman Narmada** (daily 7am–6pm; Rp500, swimming Rp500), served by frequent bemos to and from Mandalika terminal, Sweta (10km), are on the south side of the main road in **NARMADA**, opposite the bemo terminal and daily market (well worth a look if you are there early in the day). It's a good place to laze around, especially if you go early before the tour groups descend. The terraces and the lake are extensive and well maintained, and there's a swimming pool as well as paddle boats for rent.

Just a few kilometres north of Narmada and easily reached by bemo from there, **Pura Lingsar** (daily 7am–6pm; donation) was built around 1714 and then rebuilt in 1874. The complex is large, with a couple of lily ponds in the outer courtyards, and is a favourite local fishing spot in the evenings. Interestingly, this temple is a focus of worship for both Hindus and Muslims.

Situated about 300m above sea level, **SURANADI** is 7km north of Narmada, at the site of a freshwater spring. The **temple** here is a holy pilgrimage site for Hindus, as the Hindu saint, Nirartha, is believed to have located the springs while in a trance. If you want to stay, the rather overpriced *Hotel Suranadi* (☎0370/33686, fax 35630; ⑥–⑦) has accommodation in an attractive old bungalow with high ceilings, situated in lovely grounds with a tennis court and swimming pool – the pool is open to non-residents (Rp1500). Much simpler is the *Surya Homestay* (no phone; ④, including meals) on the edge of the village; inquire at the warung in the car park for directions. Rooms are basic, with a shared mandi, but excellent views across the fields.

Tetebatu and around

A number of new guest houses have recently sprung up in **TETEBATU**, situated on the southern slopes of Gunung Rinjani, 50km from Sweta, and surrounded by some of the most picturesque scenery in Lombok. Eleven kilometres north of the main cross-island road, the village offers stunning views across verdant rice paddies to the volcano. It's a quiet spot, but developing rapidly as a tourist centre, with a moneychanger, a Perama agent (book a day in advance) and transport rental. Some people have a fabulous stay here, while others rapidly tire of the number of children demanding money and hurling insults at the tourists. The *Pondok Bulan* (see opposite) has bicycles for rent (Rp4000 per day), but the countryside around here is extremely hilly.

To reach Tetebatu on public transport, get off the bemo or bus at **Pomotong** on the main island road and either get an ojek straight up to Tetebatu, or a bemo to **Kotaraja** and then a cidomo on to Tetebatu. Tetebatu is now one of the destinations served by Perama tourist shuttle buses from all over Bali and Lombok. Sample fares are Rp27,500 from Kuta (Bali); Rp25,000 from Ubud; Rp12,500 from Bangsal; and Rp10,000 from Kuta (Lombok).

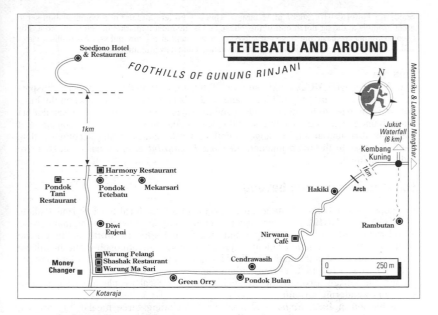

Accommodation

Accommodation choices are increasing rapidly in Tetebatu. Most are centred on the main road leading up to the *Soedjono Hotel* from Kotoraja and the road off to the east, Waterfall Street, but there are now some further-flung options. All of the accommodation places have restaurants attached, although a few simple restaurants have also sprung up in the area; all are inexpensive to moderately priced and serve the usual Indo-Chinese and travellers' fare, plus some Sasak options. At the time of writing there were no telephones in the area.

Cendrawasih. Accommodation is in the downstairs part of two-storey traditional *lumbung*-style barns, set in a flourishing garden with an attractive, raised, thatched restaurant. ③.

Diwi Enjeni. Various accommodation options with wide, comfortable verandahs set in a lovely garden, and a restaurant positioned to enjoy the views east across the fields. ②.

Green Orry. Traditional and modern bungalows in a pleasant compound plus a restaurant with good views. It is also the local Perama agent, has motorbikes for rent (Rp15,000), changes money and can provide a map of the area with suggestions for local excursions. ③.

Hakiki. Set in the middle of rice-fields, accommodation is in two-storey traditional-style barns with excellent verandahs upstairs and down. ②.

Mekarsari. Pleasant location in the fields behind *Pondok Tetebatu*, this is a small place with accommodation in bamboo-and-thatch bungalows. You may have to search for the path. ③.

Mentariku. Located 700m beyond Kembang Kuning on the Lendang Nangka road, this is well away from the other accommodation. There is a variety of traditional bungalows. ②.

Pondok Bulan .Close to the rice-fields with good views, there are traditional bamboo-and-thatch bungalows and newer concrete and tile ones, plus a large family room. Bicycles for rent. ②–③.

Pondok Tetebatu. Clean, new tiled bungalows in a small garden and a restaurant with fine views. ③.

Rambutan. 400m along a rough track in Kembang Kuning, with traditional bungalows in the middle of a rambutan orchard – the ultimate getaway. ②–③.

Soedjono Hotel (☎0370/26587 in Mataram). This hotel offers a range of accommodation set in great grounds at the far north end of the village and is the most upmarket option in the area. The cheaper rooms are basic but have attractive verandahs, and at the top end you get brilliant views and hot water. There is a moderately priced restaurant and a swimming pool. ③–⑤.

Kotaraja

The village of **KOTARAJA**, 5km south of Tetebatu, is something of a local transport hub. The name means "city of kings", and relates back to ancient times when the kingdom of Langko fell to Balinese invaders and the royal family fled here. The Kartika Art Shop, 100m beyond the crossroads on the way to Tetebatu, is the local postal agent; it has a small restaurant and a range of crafts for sale and is adding accommodation. Slightly closer to the main junction, *Renjana Restaurant* offers a basic, inexpensive Indonesian menu.

Lendang Nangka and beyond

Developed single-handedly as a tourist destination by a local teacher Haji Radiah, **LENDANG NANGKA** is a small farming community 2km north of the main cross-island road, and served by cidomo and ojek from **Bagik Bontong**. Although the scenery is not as dramatic or picturesque as Tetebatu, the atmosphere in the village is much more welcoming and friendly. This is a great place to see what Lombok life is all about and to practise your Indonesian or Sasak. There's a wealth of walks around the village through the rice-fields, and the local people are well used to strangers wandering around.

Established in 1983, *Radiah's Homestay* (③, including three meals), the original **accommodation** in the village, is still the best – a homestay in the real sense of the word. It's right in the middle of the village, but tucked away behind the school, so ask for directions. You can either stay in rooms in the family compound or in larger, newer rooms in a house in the local fields. Visitors receive a map with plenty of suggestions for local excursions and *Radiah* is also a Perama agent; you must book the day before you want to travel. There are a couple of new businesses nearby hoping to benefit from *Radiah's* popularity: the *Pondok Wira*, about 300m beyond *Radiah's* (③, including meals) on the same road, has some traditional and some modern bungalows in a garden setting, while, 100m further from the village, the *Sasak House* (③) offers *lumbung*-style cottages with good views over the fields. However, the best alternative to *Radiah* is *Pondok Bamboo* (④, including three meals), 500m north of Lendang Nangka, and signed from the road that leads to Kembang Kuning. Accommodation is in small bungalows in a quiet garden setting surrounded by fields and with good views.

East from Lendang Nangka

Further east, the village of **PENAKAK** lies just off the main road, 1500m beyond the main crossroads in **MASBAGIK**, which is marked by a bold new mosque just above the road. Look out for the Budaya Asli pottery on the north side of the main road and you'll see the turning to Penakak just before it. This is one of the three villages involved in the Lombok Craft Project (see box p.605), and the road through the village is lined with potteries. The range of goods produced, and the variety of glazes and engraving used, is enormous. The potteries also provide an overseas shipping service.

Five kilometres north of the cross-island road from **Rempung** is the local weaving centre of **PRINGGASELA**. Local women make both *songket* and *ikat* cloth here on simple backstrap looms (see p.550 for details of production), and there are several small workshops in the village. *Akmal Homestay* (③, including three meals), just north of the crossroads in the village centre, has a great atmosphere and small rooms in the family compound, with shared bathroom. They also provide guests with a highly informative map of the area. The alternative is *Rainbow Café and Cottages* (③, including three meals) who also run a cloth shop and can arrange Rinjani trekking (from US$70 per person for one night/two days).

Sapit

Situated high in the hills, at 1400m on the southern slopes of Gunung Pusuk, the small mountain village of **SAPIT** is a quiet retreat with wonderful views. Accessible from the cross-island road, either via Aik Mel or Pringgabaya, it's a fifteen-kilometre drive whichever route you take, although there is more public transport from Pringgabaya. Now the fifteen-kilometre road north across Gunung Pusuk to Sembalun Bumbung is finished, Sapit is no longer so isolated and is becoming increasingly popular, although it's very far from crowded. The road north is very steep and twisting and prone to being washed away – check in the Sembalun valley or Sapit on the current condition before setting off. There is **accommodation** at *Hati Suci* and *Hati Suci Indah* (fax 0370/22160; ③–④) nearby, with some dormitory beds and a variety of bungalows, and brilliant views across the paddy-fields to the coast and to Sumbawa. There's a small **restaurant** with a basic menu, and staff here will point you in the right direction for walks to the nearby waterfalls and hot springs, the pool and monkey forest at Lemor and, for the hardy, the fifteen-kilometre trek across to Sembalun Bumbung (see p.624).

The east

With a much drier climate, smaller population and far fewer facilities than the west of the island, the **east** tends to be left off most itineraries, although if you're heading to or from Sumbawa you'll pass through the small eastern port of **Labuhan Lombok**. While there's little to detain you long, **Labuhan Haji**, south of Labuhan Lombok, is an attractive seaside town, with lush scenery inland. To the north of Labuhan Lombok, the land is dramatically arid, giving striking views inland to the mountains, and the accommodation at **Labuhan Pandan** gives you the chance to organize a trip to the uninhabited **islands** just off the coast.

Labuhan Lombok and around

Travelling by ferry between Lombok and Sumbawa, you'll pass through **LABUHAN LOMBOK**, probably the least interesting town in Lombok, although the almost circular bay enclosed by a small curving promontory is very attractive. The **ferry terminal**, Labuhan Kayangan, is at the far end of the promontory, a three-kilometre shadeless walk along the new road around the south side of the bay; get a local bemo if you can (Rp250).

Buses run regularly from the ferry terminal along the cross-island road to and from the Mandalika terminal at Sweta (change at Kopang for Praya and the route to Kuta). To the north, buses run to and from Obel Obel and Bayan on the north coast via Sambelia; this is the way to go if your first stop on Lombok is Gunung Rinjani (see p.622). If you get stranded the best place to stay is *Pondok Lima Tiga*, Jalan Kayangan 14 (no phone; ③), about 150m from the town centre on the road to the ferry terminal. The rooms are adequate, there are places to sit in the garden and local information is provided. There are several warung along the same road that are fine for basic Indonesian food.

MOVING ON TO SUMBAWA

The **ferry to Sumbawa** departs Labuhan Lombok hourly from 4am to 9pm (see p.597 for ticket prices). It goes to **POTO TANO** on the northwest coast, a few kilometres away from the main road across the island, but there's no accommodation here. The closest is at **TALIWANG**, 30km south, or in **ALAS**, 22km east. Alternatively, you can book a **long-distance bus** ticket through to other destinations on Sumbawa from Mataram (see p.597).

North of Labuhan Lombok

Travelling north from Labuhan Lombok, you are soon out into the countryside, though the scenery quickly becomes parched and villages are few and far between. The towering mahogany trees 5km from Labuhan Lombok are welcome shade and are widely believed to be the largest such specimens in Lombok. In the area of **LABUHAN PANDAN**, look out for Pantai Pulo Lampu, a beach 14km from Labuhan Lombok. *Pondok Gili Lampu* (no phone; ③) has basic thatched cottages, some big and some small, set back some way from the beach. It is very popular at weekends but otherwise very peaceful. Three kilometres further north, there is an excellent get-away-from-it-all spot at *Siola Cottages* (no phone; ③ with all meals). The thatch-and-bamboo bungalows here have attached concrete mandi and mosquito nets provided and are situated close to the black-sand beach, with fine views to the offshore **islands** and Sumbawa on a clear day.

The closest islands are **Gili Petagan** and its satellites, with the larger **Gili Sulat** and **Gili Lawang** further north. The islands are uninhabited and the government has banned building on them, although Perama uses Gili Kondo (also known as Gili Perama) for an overnight stop on its tours. Gili Bidara and Gili Petagan have good beaches and snorkelling: you can arrange boat trips, snorkelling and fishing trips to the islands from *Siola Cottages*. Rinjani Dive bring occasional dive groups here from Senggigi, but there is no local operator.

Just north of Labuhan Pandan, the small village of **SAMBELIA** is a traditional Bugis settlement with houses built on stilts – although they are gradually being replaced by concrete-and-brick dwellings with tile or corrugated-iron roofs. The views of Gili Sulat and Gili Lawang from here around to **BELANTING** are very enticing as they appear very close, and it's easy to see their shimmering beaches across the Sanglian Strait.

Moving on around the coast towards Obel Obel, the countryside gets even drier, traffic is rare and the road begins to twist and turn through the hills which slope right down to the coast. From Padamekan, the road sticks closely to the black-sand coast. **OBEL OBEL**, about 45km from Labuhan Lombok, is a tiny oasis of green fields in among the folds of the barren hills. Ten kilometres further on is the village of Kalih Putih where the road branches south to Sembalun Lawang (see p.622), while the coast road continues to Bayan (see p.621).

The south

Largely undeveloped, the **south coast** of Lombok is extraordinarily beautiful, with kilometre after kilometre of picturesque curving bays of pure white sand separated by rocky headlands and backed by sparsely inhabited dry hills. Known to surfers for several years, **Kuta** is a low-key development with less than a dozen places to stay – this is pretty much the only accommodation on the coast. However, the inland villages specializing in pottery, weaving, basketware and carving, such as **Beleka**, **Sukarara** and **Penunjak**, are all easily accessible, as are the traditional villages of **Sade** and **Rembitan**.

The whole area, however, is in line for massive tourist development in the very near future; the coastal roads have already been improved quite dramatically, *Novotel* have opened near Kuta, and a lot of land, from Selong Blanak in the west right over to Awang Bay in the east, has been bought up by the government and private investors. Kuta, and most of the south coast, is destined to change beyond all recognition.

Praya and the craft villages

The busy market town and transport hub of **PRAYA**, 22km southeast of Sweta, is actually the capital of central Lombok (Lombok Tengah), although it lies well to the south of the island. The only **accommodation** in town is the extremely clean *Hotel Dienda Hayu* at Jalan Untung Surapati 26 (☎0370/54319; ③–④), which has pleasant verandahs to relax on and a small **restaurant** attached. To find it, turn right onto the main road at the bus terminal and after 200m turn left at the traffic lights; the hotel is up on the right. Visitors who do stay should note that Praya is a "dry" town: no alcohol is available here. The **tourist office** is at Jalan Jend Sudirman 21 (☎0370/53766), about 100m west of the bus terminal on the main road. Easily accessible by **bus or bemo** from Mandalika terminal in Sweta, most visitors change in Praya for local transport to Sengkol and Kuta (see p.632) and pass straight through.

On the road to Selong Blanak, **PENUNJAK**, 6km southwest of Praya, is one of the three pottery villages involved in the Lombok Craft Project (see p.605). Most workshops are on or near the main road and there are plenty of designs and patterns available. This is a good place to watch the potters at work if you come early in the day.

Directly west of Praya, although the route is via Puyung or Batujai, the weaving village of **SUKARARA** is firmly on the tour-bus circuit and has some enormous showrooms offering the widest range of textiles that you'll find on the island. Slick salesmen work the customers, while out on the verandah the weavers produce *ikat* and *songket* cloth using backstrap looms. The *songket* cloth tends to be more aggressively colourful than the *ikat*, whose subtle shades are produced by vegetable dyes from indigo, betel nut, pineapple and bay leaves. Look out for the traditional *lumbung* barn designs as well as the "primitive" figures. There are also a few small shops in the village, which have a more relaxed feel to them. Prices are generally reasonable, but you need to shop around, which you may not have time to do if you come on an organized tour.

MAKING SALT

On many parts of the Lombok coast, particularly around Awang Bay (and on Bali at Kusamba and on Nusa Lembongan), you'll see the salt beds and piles of white salt that indicate one of the most backbreaking occupations on the islands – salt-making. Vast quantities of salt water are still hauled from the sea in buckets and poured into specially dug **ponds**, close to the shore. When the water has evaporated, the salty, sandy residue is placed in hollowed-out **palm-tree trunks** and mixed with more sea water. The water becomes saturated with salt and a very thick brine is poured off. This is then evaporated to form salt crystals. Further stages of purification take place, and you may see large **bamboo baskets** suspended from frames at salt-making sites. The liquid from the wet salt crystals, which contains other more soluble impurities, drips down a string hanging from the baskets and forms long stalactites, leaving pure salt crystals behind.

The rainy season brings salt production to a halt and high tides can also flood the salt pools at other times. A typical family of salt producers can make around 25kg of salt a day, fetching only about Rp25–50 per kilogram, which explains why many former salt-producing areas are now turning to seaweed farming as a more lucrative way of earning a living.

East of Praya, the road to Gubukdalem is the main road across the south of the island, and most of the local **craft villages** are on or near it. With bemos plying the route, access to most of them is straightforward. To reach **BELEKA**, known for the production of rattan basketware, turn north at Ganti, about 100m east of the Batu Nampar turning. It's a busy junction, with cidomo waiting to take you the 3km north. There are a large number of shops and workshops here and the local specialities are artefacts made from grass, rattan and bamboo.

Known for its canoe-making, the village of **KERUAK**, 7km east of Sukaraja, has a few workshops east of the village, on the main road. On completion, the boats are taken by road to **TANJUNG LUAR**, 5km east on the coast. This is a vibrant fishing village with typical Bugis houses built on high stilts, with shutters instead of windows and roofs of thatch or red clay tiles. There's a small harbour and you can charter a boat here (Rp35,000) to Tanjung Ringgit on the southeast peninsula.

Kuta

The only village with any degree of tourist development on the south coast, **KUTA**, 54km from Mataram and 32km from Praya, is a tiny fishing village situated just behind the west end of the wide, white-sand, Putri Nyale beach. It's rapidly becoming the favourite choice of travellers to Lombok seeking a few days by the sea without the burgeoning tourist facilities of Senggigi or the crowds on the Gili Islands. Apart from Sunday and Wednesday, when the market takes place, the area is the ultimate in peace and quiet. The big swell here makes the sea good for **surfing** (see box), but there is no

---

SURFING ON LOMBOK

Generally the quality of the breaks is not as good on Lombok as on Bali, with the exception of Desert Point or Gili Air, but these are just too unreliable to base an entire trip around.

Most of the well-known breaks are off the **south coast**, with Kuta the ideal base for them. The resort's own breaks are **Kuta Left**, in front of the village, and **Kuta Right**, at the eastern end towards Tanjung Aan. There is also surf off the glorious **Tanjung Aan** beach (see p.635), a left-hander at the western edge, and a left- and a right-hander in the centre. Climb up Batu Kotak to get a view of what's happening on the reef.

West of Kuta, most of the bays are worth a look, although they vary in accessibility, and the surf is erratic. Around the headland, at **Selong Blanak** (see p.634), there's a good left-hander, best in the dry season. Further west, **Blongas** is less accessible, but has three good breaks – a left-hander in the east, a right in the west and another left in the centre. You'll need to charter a boat from the village to get here and it's a good spot to anchor overnight on a longer charter, but you'll have to bring everything with you. Check the local situation as the area is reported to be a shark breeding ground.

East of Kuta the best but most inaccessible breaks are off the coast of the southeast peninsula near **Serewe**. There are two good right-handers about 1.5km to the west, but you'll have to come by boat. With more breaks just inside the southern headland of **Awang Bay**, as well as further into the bay, it makes sense to base yourself at *Laut Surga* for this area if you can. You can charter boats from Awang (see p.635) on the west side of the bay to get out to the right-hander on the reef just south of the village. **Gumbang Bay**, which some people call Grupuk Bay, a short drive from Kuta, has the potential for big waves at its shallow mouth, plus smaller ones in the middle and to the east of the bay.

The world-famous break on Lombok is **Desert Point** off Bangko Bangko (see p.606), a fast but elusive left-hander with tubes that is best from June to September. The area is difficult to get to by road and there are no facilities there at all. The best option is to charter a boat, with sleeping facilities, from Bali. Elsewhere around the island, **Gili Air's** Pertama is a renowned though erratic right-hander, **Senggigi** offers a couple of breaks and there are several accessible from the beach at **Labuhanbaji**.

diving or snorkelling. The coast around the village is lovely: **Seger** and **Tanjung Aan beaches** are within walking or cycling distance, and with your own transport the whole of the south coast is wide open for exploration.

You can **change money** and travellers' cheques at *Segara Anak* and *Anda* bungalows, but expect about ten percent less for your money than you'd get in Mataram. If you want to book tourist **shuttle tickets**, the Perama office (6am–9pm) is in the grounds of the *Segara Anak*. They will also book Mabua Express tickets to Bali and provide transport to Lembar for Rp10,000. The *Segara Anak* is also a **postal agent** and you can use them for poste restante (get mail addressed to you at Segara Anak, Kuta beach, Lombok Tengah, Nusa Tenggara Barat 8357, Indonesia). The *Matahari Lombok* and *Kuta Indah* offer an international **telephone** and fax service. Ask at your accommodation or at Perama if you want to rent bicycles, motorbikes or jeeps. Expect prices of around Rp5000 for bicycles, Rp15,000 for motorbikes and Rp65,000 for jeeps per day, all without insurance (see p.38 of Basics for more information on renting vehicles).

Coming from the west, **buses and bemos** run to Praya from Mandalika terminal, Sweta. From Praya, bemos ply either to Sengkol, where you can change, or right through to Kuta. From the east of Lombok, bemos run to Praya via Kopang on the main cross-island road. Perama also offers **tourist shuttles** to Kuta from all destinations on Bali and Lombok.

Accommodation, eating and drinking

The **accommodation** here is mostly simple losmen-style, down at the east end of the beach, although there are a couple of more upmarket options and the luxury end of the market is now catered for with the newly opened *Novotel Mandalika Resort*. In Kuta itself the road runs about 50m inland from the beach and the accommodation is spread out along the coast for about 500m on the far side, so don't expect cottages on the beach itself. All the losmen have **restaurants** attached, offering cheap to moderately priced food; seafood is the speciality. *Segara Anak* has the biggest menu and is consistently good, but gets fairly busy. Only the *Mascot Pub* has live music and there is no disco scene here. *Rinjani Agung* shows nightly videos.

Anda (☎ & fax 0370/54836). A variety of bungalows in a shady garden including some new, well-built options. ②–③.

Kuta Indah (☎0370/53781, fax 54628) This is the newest place in Kuta itself, with good grounds and gleaming bungalows ranged around a pool. A short walk to the western end of Kuta beach. ⑥.

Matahari Lombok (☎0370/54832, fax 54909). Situated in the village, there are plenty of accommodation options set in a good garden with free transport to Seger and Tanjung Aan beaches. ③–⑥.

Novotel Mandalika Resort (☎0370/53333, fax 53555). Located 2km east of Kuta on Seger beach, this is the first luxury development along this coast, with accommodation in low-rise buildings in attractive grounds, a superb beachside pool and an emphasis on quiet relaxation. ⑨.

Rinjani Agung (☎0370/54849). A huge range of accommodation on offer, from basic rooms with unattached bathroom to rooms with air-con. ③–⑥.

Segara Anak (☎0370/54834). This is the liveliest place in town, with the biggest restaurant, where most people end up in the evening. Definitely the place to stay to be close to the action, with plenty of rooms on offer and a wide range of books on Indonesia on sale. ②–③.

Sekar Kuning (☎0370/54856) A good variety of rooms in an attractive garden setting. ③.

Inland from Kuta

The traditional village of **SADE**, 6km north of Kuta, is a major stop on most day-trips to the south of the island. It lies close to the Kuta–Sengkol road and is used to visitors (donation expected). It's picturesque but it feels a bit like a theme park and visitors are constantly pestered to buy things or to take photographs – all at a price.

Just up the road to the north, **REMBITAN** seems less artificial and is close to a site of Muslim pilgrimage. One of the Nine Walis believed to have brought Islam to Indonesia is supposedly buried here at **MAKAM NYATO**, and on Wednesdays pilgrims come to worship at the grave, shaded by frangipani and bayan trees.

There are two **batik workshops** on the road between Sade and Rembitan – Lombok Art Painting and Sengkol Art House Gallery (both daily 8am–6pm), producing classical scenes from the *Ramayana*, primitive motifs, traditional scenes and a huge variety of modern designs. You can sometimes see the artists at work. Prices start at Rp20,000, but you can bargain.

West of Kuta

Along the coast **west of Kuta** you can explore half a dozen or so of the prettiest beaches on the island, but bemos are few and far between so you'll need your own transport. There are few signs and not many landmarks, so be prepared for a leisurely trip and a few wrong turnings.

A couple of kilometres out of Kuta you'll pass the "MTM 64" sign; just under 1km west of this, look out for a dirt track heading off to the coast. After 2km it reaches the coastal village of **ARE GOLENG**. The beach here is about 400m long and the seaweed beds in the shallows are clearly visible. A tiny island, **Gili Nungsa**, sits out in the bay with an enticing little beach visible from the shore, and villagers' huts line the area just behind the beach; wend your way east through the coconut grove for a few hundred metres if you want to find a more secluded part of the bay.

The next beach west is **Mawan**, reached by a sealed road just beyond the "Mataram 66km" sign. The bay is very attractive, and almost semicircular, enclosed on both sides by rocky headlands. There are no houses nearby, so bring everything you need if you come here for the day.

About 2km further west, the main road reaches the coast and runs a few hundred metres inland from the gently curving **Tampa** beach. The area is not terribly attractive – the beach is backed by flat scrub and there isn't much shade – but it's pretty deserted. Continuing west, access to the beach at **Mawi** isn't easy. Take the next sealed road branching off seaward; after 1500m it degenerates into a track before ending in a stand of banana, coconut and kapok trees with a couple of houses. The people here are well used to keeping an eye on vehicles, as this is a favourite beach with surfers, but you should pay them for it. It's a few hundred metres walk to the lovely white-sand beach, separated from nearby **Rowok** by a rocky outcrop. From here, there are great views west of the coastal villages of Serangang and Torok and towards the southwestern peninsula, plus the impressive sight of Gili Lawang – three pinnacles sticking almost sheer out of the ocean.

Back on the main road, you soon reach **SELONG BLANAK**, also accessible via Penunjak from Praya (24km). The bay here has a long curving beach with rocky headlands at each end, a few canoes pulled up on the sand, some larger boats bobbing in the waters, and the striking island of **Gili Lawang** just offshore. The only **accommodation** west of Kuta is here, at *Selong Blanak Cottages* (③), a couple of kilometres inland from the beach; free transport to the beach is provided. The cottages are set in a lush garden and there's a moderately priced **restaurant** attached.

To reach **PENGANGTAP** and the beaches further west, take the signed turning north of Selong Blanak at Keling. The road detours inland away from the coast, and it's a long 15km. Eight kilometres beyond Pengangtap, the road splits at the tiny fishing village of **SEPI**. The route north climbs up giving fabulous views south and heads onto Sekotong and then Lembar (see p.606). Alternatively, you can continue west to **BLONGAS**, the end of the road, where there's good snorkelling, diving and surfing. However, it's an isolated spot and there's no accommodation in the village.

East of Kuta

The simply glorious beaches of **Seger** and **Tanjung Aan** are easily accessible from Kuta and, at a push, walkable if you have no transport; bicycles are a good idea. Seger is closest to Kuta (1km) and is now the location of the new luxury *Novotel* development, which certainly isn't inconspicuous, but neither is it as aesthetically horrible as it could have been. To reach Tanjung Aan (5km), follow the road east out of the resort and take the first sealed turning to the right. There are actually two perfect white-sand beaches here, Aan to the west and Pedau to the east, separated by a rocky outcrop, Batu Kotak. As their popularity has grown, a few hawkers now visit the beaches selling their wares and there are a few drinks stalls, but otherwise there are no other facilities.

Continuing on the road east, past Aan, the small fishing village of **GERUPAK**, just under 8km from Kuta, perches on the western shores of Gumbang Bay. The new *Kelapa Homestay* (no phone; ②) is on the right as you approach the village – it's a short walk both to the village and Tanjung Aan from here. Accommodation is in bamboo bungalows in a large compound. They've had water problems, so check in Kuta whether they are up and running before you lug all your stuff out. There are good views across the bay to **BUMBANG** on the eastern shore, and you can rent a canoe (Rp5000) or a boat with a motor (Rp10,000) to take you across. From Bumbang there's a track north to the Awang road, but you can't rely on picking up transport to take you back to Kuta.

The thriving fishing village of **AWANG**, 16km east of Kuta, is well worth the trip for the views of **Awang Bay**, a massive inlet, 10km long and 8km wide in parts. As the road descends into the village the view is stunning, you'll be able to spot the island of Linus, just off Batu Nampar at the northern end of the bay, the tiny settlement of Ekas across on the southeast peninsula (see below), and see all the way south to the open sea. You can charter boats from Awang across to Ekas (Rp30,000 round-trip) on the southeast peninsula.

SUMBAWA, KOMODO AND RINCA

East of Lombok, the island of **Sumbawa** is scorched, rough and mountainous, consisting of two sparsely populated regions. On the **west coast** are deserted paradise **beaches**, with turtle-spawning grounds and surf from **Jereweh** to **Lunyuk**. **Sumbawa Besar**, the western capital, is home to the fine sultan's palace, as well as being the jumping-off point for **Pulau Moyo** to the north, declared a national park for its spectacular coral reefs and wealth of wild animals. **Bima** province in the east has become legendary amongst surfers for the exceptional reef breaks at **Hu'u**, now also luring the boardless with its relaxed reputation. The Trans-Sumbawa highway spans the entire island, and is one of the only roads in Nusa Tenggara whose surface merits its lofty title.

The island is most frequently perceived by tourists as an inconvenient but necessary bridge between the popular destinations of Lombok and Komodo. This is a shame, as there is plenty to see here. Most places outside the regency capitals are relatively untravelled, offering unique experiences for the adventurous. Sumbawa is a strictly Muslim enclave and all the rules commensurate with visiting Islamic communities should be observed here. Wearing shorts or vests and looking generally scruffy will not win you friends: both male and female travellers should dress conservatively.

Off the east coast of Sumbawa lies the **Komodo national park**, a group of parched but majestic islands that have achieved fame as the home of a living reminder of our prehistoric past – the Komodo dragon. The south coast is lined with impressive, mostly dormant volcanoes, the north with mainly dusty plains, irrigated to create rice paddies around the major settlements. Tiny rocky **Rinca** also features dragons, but is hard to get to, and sees few visitors.

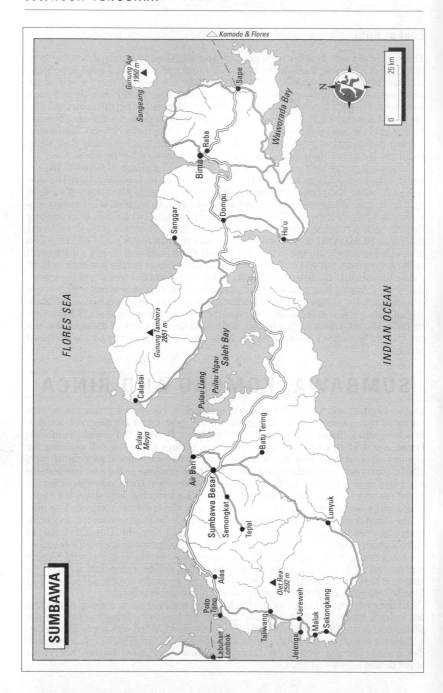

SUMBAWA

Komodo & Flores

Gunung Api
1950 m

Sangeang

Sape

Waworada Bay

FLORES SEA

Bima Raba

Dompu

Hu'u

Sanggar

Gunung Tambora
2851 m

Saleh Bay

Pulau Ngau

Pulau Liang

Calabai

Pulau
Moyo

Batu Tering

Air Bari

Sumbawa Besar

Semongkat

Tepal

Lunyuk

INDIAN OCEAN

Alas

Olet Rea
2592 m

Pato
Tano

Taliwang

Jereweh

Maluk

Sekongkang

Jelenga

Labuhan
Lombok

N

25 km

0

SUMBAWAN FESTIVALS

Whilst the widespread influence of Islam and wholesale transmigration from the congested Javan landmass has diluted the Sumbawa's indigenous culture, it is far from dead. With a little luck, spectacular **festivals** such as bone-jarring bare-fist boxing, horse and water-buffalo-racing can be seen. The **buffalo-racing** takes place before the rice is planted at the end of the rainy season: the animals drag a light plough, ridden by a tenacious male competitor, who goads them into charging down the rice paddies, then attempts to grab a coloured flag from a stick at the end of the fields. The ploughs usually disintegrate and it's a seriously high-octane occasion, great, lumbering buffalo, charging through knee-deep mud and their riders desperately clinging on for dear life.

Berempuk, **bare-fist boxing**, can be seen at some of the festivals that surround harvesting and planting. It's a particularly bloodthirsty melee of flying knuckles and gore in which young men seek to appease the spirits and drain out the "hot" aggression that's seen to reside in the villagers' blood.

The majority of travellers coming into Sumbawa arrive by ferry from Lombok (90min) to the west, or from Flores (9–12hr) via Komodo (5–7hr) in the east. These ferries connect with buses that traverse the Trans-Sumbawa highway.

Some history

Historically, the two sides of the island were subject to vastly different influences, which remain evident today. The Sumbawan people were influenced from the west, by the Balinese and the Sasaks of Lombok. The Bimans, however, owe more to the Makarese of Sulawesi and the peoples of Flores and Sumba, sharing linguistic and cultural similarities.

Most of the island is presumed to have been trading with, and at least nominally under the control of, the East Javanese **Majapahit empire**. The poet Prapança who chronicled the affairs of the dynasty, mentioned an expedition into Sumbawa, probably when the Majapahit was at the height of its powers in the early fourteenth century. Trade was based around timber resources and slaves, and Bima, with its well-protected bay, was the most important port in this area of Nusa Tenggara. The position of the island on the trade routes from the sandalwood producers to the east and also from the abundant hub of the Spice Islands, helped to elevate the islands to considerable strategic status, and the kingdom of Bima expanded to claim the majority of Nusa Tenggara. Up until the end of the sixteenth century, Bima Region was still mostly animist, ostensibly ruled by a succession of Hindu rajahs with Javanese origins but, when the Makarese of Sulawesi took control in the early seventeenth century, they converted the people to Islam.

Sumbawa was ignored by Christian missionaries and even the Dutch East India Company had only a limited stay here. The Dutch only really controlled the area at the beginning of the twentieth century, and were ousted by the Japanese in World War II, whose rule constituted a bitter period in the island's history. Soon after, Sumbawa became a part of the modern republic of Indonesia. The original sultans were not recognized by the central government, but some of their ancestors maintain some prestige as well as palaces in the two main sultanates of Bima and Sumbawa Besar.

Transmigration and the wholesale reaping of the remaining sappanwood and sandalwood forests have put huge pressure on the little land that is useable. Bima's once illustrious bay is now filling with silt as a result of over-logging: it is pouring unabated into the waters around the port and big ships can no longer call here. The region's glory days seem to be numbered.

West Sumbawa

Noticeably drier and less fertile than nearby Lombok, **West Sumbawa**, historically perceived as a vassal state to more powerful Bima, has a stark landscape of craggy hills and charred volcanoes, with dark plains of mud fields in which rice is cultivated. The west-coast **beaches** are probably the most worthwhile attraction in the whole island. **Pulau Moyo** to the north is a plentifully stocked nature reserve with good trekking and snorkelling, and there are some interesting historical sites to be found south of the capital town **Sumbawa Besar**. The town itself has little to offer, though it is a better place to stop than Bima if you have a choice, having a couple of reasonable places to eat and clean and spacious streets.

The coast

The west coast of Sumbawa offers surf, sand and solitude, although you need some time and patience to endure its appalling roads and public transport. At the extreme western end of Sumbawa lies **POTO TANO**, the ferry terminal for boats from Lombok; buses meet all incoming ferries and run south from the harbour to **Taliwang** (1hr; Rp2000), and north to **Alas** (45min; Rp2000), **Sumbawa Besar** (2hr; Rp3000) and sometimes all the way to Bima (9hr; Rp10,000).

Taliwang

TALIWANG is a charming if somewhat ramshackle village, an hour's drive south of Poto Tano, which rarely sees Western visitors but treats the few that arrive here with great hospitality. Horse drawn dokar are a more common sight than motorized vehicles, and, despite the call-to-prayer from the numerous mosques, it's a tranquil place to visit. In the backstreets, brightly painted houses are raised up to 3m off the ground on stilts, the space beneath occupied by the family's buffalo, pigs and chickens: half buried urns contain live eels and shrimp.

Taliwang is a necessary stop if you intend to visit the west coast – all trips down the western edge, even to the closest destinations, will take at least a full day from here due to the abysmal roads and relative infrequency of the public transport. A short bemo ride (Rp300) out of town and off the Poto Tano road is **Danau Taliwang**, also known as **Lebok Lebo**, a colossal lake covered in lotus flowers which has fantastic birdlife, with various birds of prey and elegant herons.

It's a small town, with two of the three losmen and eateries on the same street, so buses will drop you off at the door. The **bus station** is on the street parallel to Jalan Sudirman. The best choice for **accommodation** in town is the *Losmen Taliwang Indah* (①–②) on Jalan Sudirman. It's excellent value, with clean, spacious rooms, balcony views and a reasonable restaurant downstairs. The best meals in town are served at the *Rasate Dua Rumah Makan* across the street. They serve standard local fare and the nasi campur ayam is especially good, with a spicy piece of Taliwang's famous fried chicken.

Jereweh and the south

JEREWEH, an hour south of Taliwang by bemo (Rp500), is where the paved road dies. Despite being the area capital, it's little more than a tiny market and a few government offices, with a good white-sand beach and passable **surf**. The *Jelenga Beach Bungalows* and *Scar Surf Bungalows*, both right on the shore, offer similar, simple accommodation (① full board) and a good hangout for committed surfers.

Seventeen kilometres further on is a huge arc of **stunning beach** flanked by cliffs at the village of **MALUK**, with a slightly erratic reef break that can be magnificent about 500m offshore. You could either paddle out, or ask one of the fishermen who sometimes sit on the beach mending their nets to give you a ride. The *Rumah Makan Cassanova* is a haven for workers from the nearby American-owned Newmont gold mine, the second largest in Indonesia. It's the only place to get a cold drink and good food, though you can stay at the *Surya* or *Iwan Beach Bungalows* (②) which are both down near the seafront. Both sets of accommodation have some rooms complete with en-suite mandi, but neither has mosquito net, which are really a necessity on the coast.

SEKONGKANG, about another hour's bemo ride (Rp1000) down a fantastically dreadful track from Maluk, has an even better beach, with more shade and huge waves. The beach itself is almost always deserted, but has great snorkelling and loads of turtles, both in the sea and coming ashore to lay their eggs. The kepala desa recently had fifteen beach bungalows (②) built for tourists and surfers. From here it's a gruelling four-hour truck trip to **Tongo** (Rp3000); the beach is wonderful, and you can stay with the kepala desa. The road to **Lunyuk** is still under construction and at the moment it can only be reached by heading south from Sumbawa Besar.

Alas and Pulau Bungin

Two hours' drive to the north of Puto Tano, the quiet old port of **ALAS** is the hopping-off point for nearby **Pulau Bungin**, apparently the most densely populated place in Indonesia. The seafaring Buginese, who settled the island in 1815, built their homes on a reef no more than a metre or so above sea level, in order to be protected from marauding mainlanders. When the island was full, they merely dug up lumps of coral and rock and dumped them into the sea to expand the developable land. Nowadays, when a man wants to marry and build his own home, he must first create the land to accommodate it. Bungin is dotted with TV antennas and spanned by electricity cables, but traditional ways are strong and it's a intriguing place to visit.

If you are planning a trip to Bungin, you might need to spend a night in Alas before or afterwards, the *Losmen Anda* (①–②) near the Telkom office being the pick of the places to stay. To get to Bungin, take a dokar to the harbour for Rp300, then a motorboat (Rp1500); there is nowhere to stay on the island.

Sumbawa Besar

SUMBAWA BESAR's open streets are lined with crumbling white plaster buildings, bright-blue wooden doors adorning its many shopfronts. The old sultanate of Sumbawa, in theory always subservient to the superior power of Bima, is now the largest town on the island, and visitors looking to break up the bus-run across the island could do worse than stop here. It's quite a sprawling place with no particular centre and, apart from a small cluster of losmen on Jalan Hasanuddin near the river, accommodation is also spread from one end of town to the other.

Dalam Loka, the **Sultan's Palace**, is the only real sight of interest in town. The barn-like wooden structure, raised on great pillars, was built in 1885 by Sultan Jalashuddin and partially restored in the 1980s, the government promising to revitalize the building and turn it into a museum of Nusa Tenggaran artefacts – this grand plan has in fact totally failed to materialize. Of passing interest are **Pura Agung Girinatha**, a Balinese-style temple near the post office, and the nondescript **New Sultan's Palace**, a few blocks away from the genuine article on Jalan Merdeka.

Practicalities

Buses arriving from the west will usually come into **Barang Barat bus terminal** on the east side of town, a fifteen-minute walk south from the Sultan's Palace. Alternatively they may drop you at the more central old bus station on Jalan Yos Sudarso. The **airport** is a short dokar ride into town; if you need to buy tickets or book flights, the **Merpati office** is on Jalan Diponegro and the *Tambora Hotel* is also an agent.

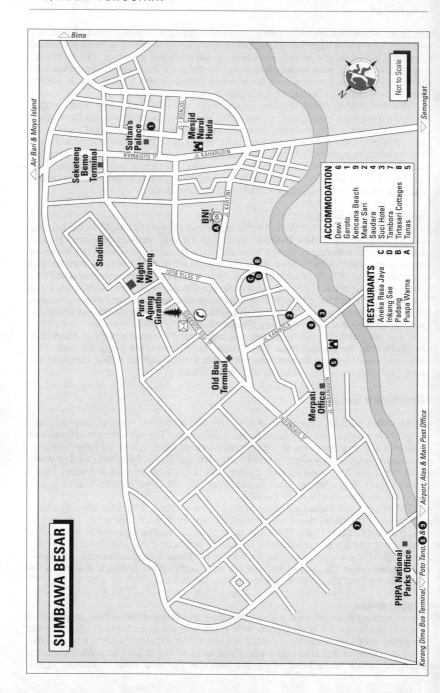

SUMBAWA BESAR

Not to Scale

△ Bima
△ Air Bari & Moyo Island
▷ Semongkat

Sultan's Palace
Mesjid Nurul Huda
JL BONJOL
JL SUDIRMAN
JL KAHARUDIN
Seketeng Bemo Terminal
JL KARTINI
BNI (SS)
Stadium
Night Warung
JL SETIA BUDI
Pura Agung Girantha
JL SOLO SUNGAI
Old Bus Terminal
JL KAMBOJA
JL DIPONEGORO
Merpati Office
JL HASANUDIN
PHPA National Parks Office

Karang Dima Bus Terminal, ▷ Poto Tano, 8 & 9 ▷ Airport, Alas & Main Post Office

ACCOMMODATION
Dewi   6
Garoto   1
Kencana Beach   9
Mekar Sari   2
Saudara   4
Suci Hotel   3
Tambora   7
Tirtasari Cottages 8
Tunas   5

RESTAURANTS
Aneka Rasa Jaya   C
Inkang Sae   D
Padang   B
Puspa Warna   A

Sumbawa Besar boasts the newest fleet of bemos in Nusa Tenggara and a wealth of horse-drawn dokar (locally known as *benhur*). The yellow bemos, *bemo kota*, do round-trips of the town; they can either be flagged down on the street or picked up at the **Seketeng market terminal**, which is on Jalan Setiabudi. Bemo Kota will drop you off pretty much anywhere, charging a flat rate of Rp200.

The **BNA bank** on Jalan Kartini 46 (Mon–Fri 8.15am–4.15pm) has the best rates for changing foreign currencies from here to Kupang. If you're heading east and have currency other than US dollars, then change enough here to see you through. A **post office** is located on Jalan Yos Sudarso, and the **GPO** opposite has international telephone, telex, telegram and fax. The regional **tourist office** (Mon–Thurs 7am–3pm, Fri 7–11am; ☎0371/21632) is about the best you'll find in Nusa Tenggara but it's still pretty dire: it's 3km out of town at the kantor Dinas Parawisata building, Jalan Garuda 1. Take a yellow bemo from the *Hotel Tambora* heading west (Rp300). There are no English-speaking staff, but they do have a handful of maps and brochures about local festivals such as buffalo racing (see box p.637). The **PHPA parks office** is on Jalan Garuda (Mon–Sat 8am–3pm; ☎0371/21358), and can provide information about Pulau Moyo, though not actual tours.

The best source of information in Sumbawa is a guide called Abdul Muis, who seems to meet every traveller who passes through Sumbawa Besar. He speaks excellent English and is the only real choice for a guide to climb **Gunung Tambora** (p.644), or visit Sumbawa's only practising animist peoples at **Tepal** (p.643). If he doesn't find you, he can be contacted through the *Tirtasari Cottages* (see below).

Moving on, early-morning buses going east to Bima and beyond leave from the Barang Barat bus terminal from 5.30am until 3.30pm to Dompu (4hr30min; Rp5000), Bima (7hr; Rp7500), Sape (8hr30min; Rp9000). For Taliwang (3hr; Rp3000) and night buses running both east and west, use the Karang Dima terminal 6km northwest of town, reachable by bemo from the town centre.

ACCOMMODATION

Quite a few places that are not mentioned here double as brothels, and one or two of them are renowned for being bug-ridden and really grotty. It's well worth checking your room very carefully before checking in.

Dewi Hotel, Jl Hasanuddin 60 (☎0371/21170). Thirty rooms ranging from good-value ekonomi to plush VIP suites with TV and bathtub, all clean and including breakfast. ③–④.

Losmen Garoto, Jl Batu Pasak 48 (☎0371/22062). Offers standard rooms with en-suite mandi and balcony views of the Sultan's Palace, but has the odd rat and lots of mosquitoes. ②.

Kencana Beach Hotel, 11km west of town, transport arranged by the *Tambora*. Comparatively expensive, but a quiet, relaxing, more upmarket place with Sumbawan-style wooden cottages near the seafront, as well as a swimming pool. ④–⑥.

Mekar Sari Losmen, Jl Hasanuddin 10. Clean, quiet and inexpensive, with friendly owners; all rooms have en-suite mandi. ③.

Suci Hotel, Jl Hasanuddin 57 (☎0371/21589). Spacious rooms with private mandi. ③–④.

Hotel Tambora, Jl Kebayan (☎0371/21555). Brand-new four-bed ekonomi rooms, right through to luxurious suites with amazing bathrooms, complete with your own personal waterfall and goldfish. The pricey downstairs restaurant does a wonderful breakfast and some good Western and Chinese food. ④–⑥.

Tirtasari Cottages, about 5km west of town at Seliperate, right on the beach; buses and bemos run from Sekateng market (☎0371/21987). The best option if you don't mind being out of town, with a variety of options to suit most budgets, including hot water and air-con in the VIP bungalows. ③–⑤.

EATING AND DRINKING

While the majority of **eating places** in Sumbawa Besar are the usual local warung serving goat stews and sate, there are two fantastic options on Jalan Hasanuddin. The larger hotels all have restaurants serving a few Western dishes plus Chinese and Indonesian food; the *Hotel Tambora*'s restaurant is pretty good but a little overpriced.

Aneka Rasa Jaya, Jl Hasanuddin 14. An excellent if idiosyncratic menu including "insipid rice", "soft corn prawn" and "Chinese bowels cooking". The food, however, is topnotch, and the beer cheap and cold.

Inkang Sae Rumah Makan, two doors down from the *Aneka Rasa Jaya* on Jl Hasanuddin. Fresh seafood, Chinese and Indonesian food, and fabulous decor, with a mural of galloping horses circling the walls. The best food in Sumbawa is slightly tempered by intermittent wailing from the upstairs karaoke bars. Most main dishes are under Rp4000, and a full meal with beer is likely to be around Rp10,000.

Padang Rumah Makan, on the opposite side of the street from *Inkang Sae*. An unimaginative name for a Padang restaurant, but decent enough food.

Puspa Warna, Jl Kartini 15. A Chinese place with excellent seafood, mainly catering for business-people but very welcoming to travellers.

Around Sumbawa Besar

Apart from **Pulau Moyo**, which receives a steady trickle of nature lovers and wealthy tourists, the sights around Sumbawa Besar tend to be the preserve of domestic tourists. Moyo is probably the most rewarding destination in Sumbawa, overrun with deer, monkeys, wild pigs and surrounded by beautiful coral reefs. Less-known sights south of Sumbawa Besar include troglodyte caves and megaliths in the **Batu Tering** area, the Dutch hill resort of **Semongkat** and the tribal villages at **Tepal**. All of these sights are well worth a visit, and remain practically tourist-free all year round.

Serious castaways should head for Pulau Liang and Pulau Dangar in Saleh Bay. They have extraordinary fishing, snorkelling and beaches, but are mostly uninhabited and have no facilities, so bring everything from Sumbawa Besar. You can charter boats from Air Bari or Tanjung Pasir.

Pulau Moyo

A few kilometres off the north coast of Sumbawa, sitting in the mouth of Saleh Bay, lies the national park of **Pulau Moyo** (entrance fee Rp2500). It's a naturalist's dream, with an abundance of animals: wild pig, snakes, monitor lizards, 21 species of bat, huge herds of native deer and hordes of crab-eating macaques, as well as plentiful birdlife, notably sulphur-crested cockatoos, orioles and megapode birds. In 1902, an Australian cattle boat was shipwrecked on the island and now cows roam free, particularly over the central grass plains. Offshore, the pristine coral gardens are well stocked with fish. The best time to visit Moyo is in June and July, though the seas are clear and quiet from April.

To hire a PHPA guide for trekking from the PHPA posts costs Rp5000 per person a day. Renting a fishing boat from Tanjung Pasir and going east to **Stama reef** is a terrific way to spend time on the island. It's only about fifteen minutes offshore, and the **snorkelling** is marvellous, with lots of sharks and turtles. There's nowhere on Moyo to rent masks and snorkels so it is best to bring your own, and fins are also advisable due to the strong currents.

A good percentage of Moyo has been commandeered by the *Amanwana Resort* (☎0371/22330; ⑨), situated on the west coast. This is one of the flashiest, most exclusive retreats in Asia: a nice option if you can spare US$750 a night. Accommodation is in spectacular tented suites, the idea being that you "rough it" under canvas but with incredible luxuries at your disposal. The resort staff arrange hunting safaris for those who would rather kill animals than watch them. Nearby is the gorgeous **Mata Jitu air terjun**, renamed the **Lady Di waterfall** after the late princess stayed here in 1995.

For a donation of about Rp5000, you can stay in much more basic **accommodation** – wooden cells with a mattress and threadbare mosquito net – at most of the four PHPA posts around the island. None of these places can provide food, and it's best to check with the PHPA in Sumbawa Besar (see p.641) as to which ones are currently open. The only post that has anything even approaching permanent guest-house status is that at **Tanjung Pasir** on the south coast, where most boats from the mainland arrive. Private rooms with outside toilet and bathing facilities are available, though at the time of writing you still need to bring your own food.

GETTING TO PULAU MOYO
To get to Moyo, take a bemo from beside Seketang Market in Sumbawa Besar to **Air Bari**, a small port settlement north east of Sumbawa Besar. Bemos run until 1pm and cost Rp2000. From Air Bari you can pick up a boat to Moyo which costs a hefty US$10; these leave infrequently, sometimes three or four times a day, at other times only once or twice a week. A charter will cost a much more reasonable US$15–25 for as many as fifteen people.

Another option is to take a regular bemo to **Labuhan Sumbawa**, the small port that serves the town and lies about 10km to the west. From Labuhan Sumbawa, charter a boat for the four-hour trip to Tanjung Pasir; it takes considerably longer, but there are far more boats to charter. Should all of this seem like too much effort, visit the **PHPA office** in Sumbawa Besar near the *Hotel Tambora* and they'll put you in touch with a tour company, who'll sort it all for you (most tours cost around US$80 a day).

Semongkat, Tepal and Roplang
Seventeen kilometres from Sumbawa Besar, high above the coastal plain and with wonderful views, lies the once grand hill resort of **SEMONGKAT**. The old **Dutch Palace** here has unfortunately been recently restored and has lost a lot of its charm, but the surroundings are still glorious and there are some refreshing freshwater **springs** and a swimming pool. Public buses run fairly frequently from Seketeng market in Sumbawa Besar (90min; 2hr).

At the summit of **Batu Lanteh mountain** lie the villages of **TEPAL** and **ROPLANG**, about 20km west of Semongkat, where the people still practise pre-Islamic animism and ancestor worship: if you stay here a while you may be lucky enough to witness one of their traditional festivals. It's a long walk up here – between six and eight hours – heading west from **Batu Dulang**, where the motorized transport from Sumbawa Besar terminates. You can hire a guide for the trek either in Sumbawa Besar or at Batu Dulang, and stay with the kepala desa in Tepal, but bring provisions, particularly fruit and tinned foods.

Batu Tering, Airnung and Lunyuk
About 25km southeast of Sumbawa Besar, near **BATU TERING** village, are a number of impressive **megaliths**, some of which possibly date from Neolithic times. Close to the Lunyuk road at **Liang Petang** are caves, which were once inhabited: a few beds, an old spinning wheel and some items of clothing still remain inside amongst the stalagmites and stalactites. The cave's present occupants are bats and snakes; there are usually guides waiting outside with paraffin lamps.

Airnung region is littered with carved sarcophagi of varying quality. Catch the daily bus to **Lunyuk** and ask to be let off at Airnung, which is about 15km south of Sumbawa Besar; to go all the way to Lunyuk will take a good three hours. Lunyuk is an excellent site for **turtle-watching**, with at least three species of turtles coming ashore to lay their eggs. The main laying season is from December to February, but can continue until June; most species come ashore at night. As in most of Asia, locals consider turtle eggs a real treat. They locate nests by following the turtle's trails (which resemble miniature tank tracks) up the beach to the buried nest, so if you're lucky enough to see a turtle laying, erasing her tracks will give her offspring an extra chance. You can stay with the kepala desa at Lunyuk.

Gunung Tambora

On April 5, 1815 the **Tambora volcano** let rip a monumental explosion. The two 4000-metre peaks had been smoking for several years, but the ferocity of the eruption took everyone by surprise. Eight days later the greatest of the force had been spent, a shroud of ash as much as 1m deep was spread over nearly a vast area of farmland, and 20,000 people were dead. The explosion was heard several thousand kilometres away; in Surabaya Sir Stamford Raffles thought it was the sound of cannonfire and mobilized troops to defend the city. The death toll in Sumbawa and the nearby islands rose to an estimated 96,000 as the thick covering of ash choked crops, and cholera, drought and famine set in. The misery was compounded by plagues of mice, which devastated food supplies and outbreaks of dysentery and smallpox.

Gungung Tambora, on the bulbous northern penisula halfway between Bima and Sumbawa Besar, is an imposing cauldron with a brightly coloured crater lake, providing stunning views as far as Lombok and Komodo. The best base for the tough **trek** up the mountain is the **Pancasila Copee Plantation**, on the lower slopes of the volcano; it's a day's truck ride from Dompu bus terminal to the plantation, via the small logging town of **CALABAI**, which lies on the coast of Saleh Bay. You can also reach Calabai by chartering a boat from Air Bari or Labuhan Sumbawa, the two ports close to Sumbawa Besar. Stay overnight either at the plantation or at the logger's guest house (②) in Calabai, which provides decent accommodation and meals. From Calabai, you can arrange a **guide** for between Rp10,000 and Rp20,000 a day; be sure to bring all your **supplies** from Bima or Sumbawa Besar. Alternatively, the large hotels in either town can set you up with an English-speaking guide. Long trousers, walking boots and a vigilant eye for leeches and ticks are all essential, and it's best to check in with the police at Calabai.

Ascending the mountain requires an arduous **hike** up to the rim, first through dense rainforest and then over treacherous volcanic rock. Once at the summit you can go down to the lake – this trip takes about three days, whereas only going to the rim and back can be done in two days.

East Sumbawa

The majority of the fine coastline of **East Sumbawa** is lined with photogenic stilted fishing villages, a reminder of the Bajo, Buginese and Makarrese seafaring peoples who have long traded with the area. Centred on its capital town of **Bima**, eastern Sumbawa has little to recommend it, except for the surfing areas around **Hu'u** on the south coast. Another place travellers head to is the port town of **Sape**, where the ferries to Komodo and Flores depart.

Bima

The slightly sad port town of **BIMA** has precious little remaining of its former glories. The streets are coated with horse dung from its many dilapidated dokar, and the buildings are characterless and dull. The port remains fairly busy, with battered wooden schooners and the occasional rusting iron cargo ship, though once it was the most important port in Nusa Tenggara. In the fifteenth and sixteenth centuries, the kingdom of Bima claimed the majority of Nusa Tenggara as its own, although this ownership probably manifested itself in nothing more than the administration of trade and allowance of occasional slave raids into the surrounding islands. Up until the end of the sixteenth century, Bima was ruled by a succession of Hindu rajas with Javanese origins, but the people were converted to Islam when the Makarrese of Sulawesi took control in the early seventeenth century.

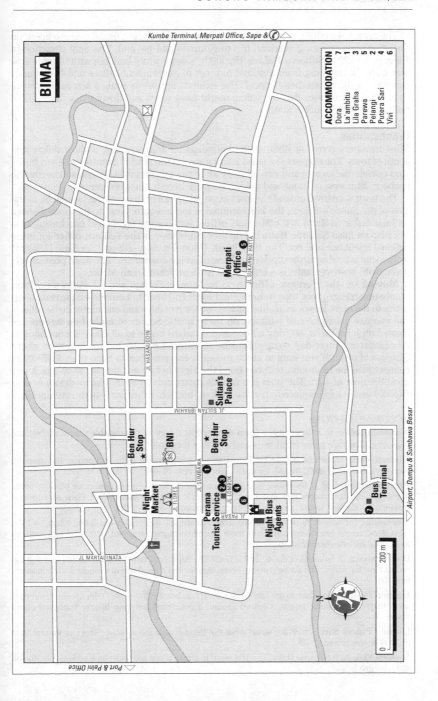

BIMA

Kumbe Terminal, Merpati Office, Sape & (C)

ACCOMMODATION
Dora 7
La'ambitu 1
Lila Graha 3
Parewa 5
Pelangi 2
Putera Sari 4
Vivi 6

Merpati Office 5
JL SUKARNO HATTA

Sultan's Palace
JL SULTAN IBRAHIM

Ben Hur Stop ★
BNI (SS)
JL SUMBAWA 1
Ben Hur Stop ★
Perama Tourist Service 2 3
JL LOMBOK 4
6
JL FLORES
Night Market
JL PASAR
Night Bus Agents

Bus Terminal 7

JL HASANUDDIN

JL MARTADINATA

Airport, Dompu & Sumbawa Besar

Port & Pelni Office

N

200 m
0

The town has nothing to lure the prospective visitor, but is a useful place to break up the otherwise agonizing overland trip to Komodo and beyond. The only attraction in Bima is the 1920s **Sultan's Palace** (Rp5000), a large white building with black beams that could be anything from a school to a set of government offices and is distinctly lacking in external aesthetic appeal. The exhibits are pretty drab, a few gaudy reconstructions of costumes that the sultan might have worn and dusty glass cases full of unmarked, unfathomable junk.

Practicalities

Most travellers arrive in Bima at the long-distance bus terminal, a short dokar ride south of town. The **airport** is a good 20km away on the road to Sumbawa Besar; buses stop outside the airport and run all the way to the bus terminal. **Ferries** arrive at the harbour, 2km west of Bima, and dokar run from here to the town centre.

The town is centred around the market on Jalan Flores; most of the losmen lie to the east of the Sultan's Palace, the bus terminal is to the south. Next to the *Hotel Parewa* on Jalan Sukarno Hatta is the **Merpati office**, for booking flights and purchasing tickets. Also on Jalan Sukarno Hatta but further out of town is the **Telkom office** for international telephone and fax. The **BNI bank** (Mon–Fri 8am–2.30pm, Sat 8am–11.30pm) by the sports field is the best place to change foreign currencies. The main **post office**, if you need poste restante, is a little out of town on Jalan Gajah Mada.

Moving on, the **Perama office** next to *Losmen Pelangi* and PT Parewa on Jalan Sumbawa arranges boat trips to Komodo, Flores and back to Lombok – a pleasant alternative to the night buses, at around Rp100,000 for two days and one night; in the off season you can get some real bargains on these boats. Scores of **night-bus agents** are located on Jalan Pasar, offering air-con and standard buses to all major destinations as far as Jakarta, a three-day journey. **Kumbe terminal** for buses to Sape is in Raba, about 5km out of town. If you want to catch the early-morning bus to Sape (2hr; Rp2000) to connect with the ferry east, tell your hotel the night before and the bus should pick you up at the door at 4am. The **port** is a two-kilometre ride away in a horse-drawn *benhur* (Rp500) and is a good place to try and pick up boats to other parts of the archipelago.

ACCOMMODATION

Accommodation in Bima ranges from downright dingy to reasonable; most places are a short dokar ride away from the southern bus terminal.

Losmen Dora, at the entrance to the long-distance bus terminal. Not a bad option: the ekonomi rooms are extremely dark, the pricier ones clean and new. ③–④.

Hotel La'ambitu, on Jl Sumbawa facing the market. By far the most salubrious place in town: brand-new standard rooms with hot water, fan and TV represent great value. Their second-floor restaurant is the best in tow, serving cold beer and passable food. ③–④.

Lila Graha, Jl Lombok 20 (☎0371/42740). Basic rooms are overpriced, small and dingy, and the "first-class" rooms just overpriced. They have a good restaurant attached, with local and Western food. Price includes breakfast. ③.

Hotel Parewa, Jl Sukarno Hatta 40 (☎0371/42652). All rooms have en-suite mandi, and the top rooms have hot water. The accompanying restaurant serves a good mix of Chinese and Indonesian fare. ③.

Losmen Pelangi, next door to the *Lila Graha*, on Jl Lombok (☎0371/42878). Inexpensive, but they seem to prefer domestic guests. Centred around a courtyard featuring bizarre feathered alarm clocks. ②.

Losmen Putera Sari, across the street from the Pelangi near the mosque. Short on natural light and a little overpriced. ②–③.

Losmen Vivi, on Jl Sukarno Hatta. The last word in cheap if you are really on a budget, usually full and a bit grotty. ①.

EATING
There are several local **rumah makan** but none offers really decent food. The restaurant of the *Hotel La'ambitu* is the best place in town, serving Chinese dishes as well as omelettes, pancakes and fried potatoes. The *Lila Graha* also has a restaurant with regular Indonesian travellers' cuisine such as fruit salads and guacamole. Another option is to try the night stalls at the market, where you can come by inexpensive sate, *soto ayam*, gado-gado, fried rice and noodles.

Hu'u

South of the large but uninteresting town of **Dompu**, on a white-sand coast with swaying palm trees is the wave rider's Mecca of **HU'U**. If you're one of the many lugging surfboards around "Indo" searching for the perfect swell, it's paradise. The waves are not for the faint-hearted or inexperienced, breaking over razor-sharp finger coral; bring a helmet and first-aid kit. Generally, **surfing** is best between May and August, with the absolute prime in June and July. It's practically impossible to get a bed during these months so bringing a tent is a good idea.

To get to Hu'u village, take a bus to Dompu from Sumbawa Besar or Bima, from where it's a one-hour trip south (Rp1500). One bus a day goes there directly from Bima, leaving at around 7.30am. As you come into Hu'u from Bima or Dompu, the first place you'll pass through is the small fishing settlement of Hu'u village. The other sets of **accommodation** lie in a cluster on the seafront about 3km from Hu'u village, the longest established being the *Mona Lisa Bungalows*, on the beach (②–③). They have decent economy rooms through to pleasant bamboo-and-wood bungalows, with or without en-suite facilities, and the restaurant, with good Western and Indonesian cuisine at reasonable prices, is very popular. Next door, the new *Hotel Amangati* (③) have clean bungalows with en-suite mandi. The *Prima Donna Lakey Cottages* (☎0373/21168; ④) are quite new and have the advantage of taking bookings in advance during high season. All of these losmen are convenient for the famous Lakey Peak and Lakey Pipe breaks. Just over 1km down the beach back towards Hu'u village and by the break of the same name is *Periscopes* (②), a friendly surf camp with the wave out front.

Sape and on to Komodo

More and more travellers are choosing to break their cross-island journey at the port town of **SAPE**. The town itself is no worse than Bima, and staying there has the advantage of allowing you a full night's sleep before catching the ferry to Komodo and Flores. Boats leave at 8am, presently every day of the week. Nearby **Gili Banta** is a good day-trip should you get stuck, with nice beaches and a burgeoning turtle population.

Accommodation here is not great – many places are dirty, infested with bedbugs and mosquitoes and many double as brothels. The best are probably the *Friendship* and *Mutiara* losmen (both ②), which are situated along the single main street that leads down to the port. *Mutiara* is right by the entrance to the port and *Friendship* is a couple of hundred metres further inland near the post office. They have genial staff and are reasonably clean. Apart from a few local warung, the *Sape Cafe* is the only option for reasonable food

At present there are two ferries to **Lahubanbajo** on Flores, stopping in **Komodo** en route in both directions every day except Friday. Take the larger ferry (Rp10,000) for a fairly painless trip: it's spacious and relatively clean with a special tourist-class deck for an extra Rp3000. The other ferry (Rp10,000) is slow, overloaded and rusty and some prefer to wait in Sape for an extra day rather than subject themselves to it. The trip from Sape to Komodo, through the tempestuous **Sape strait** is the part that is most subject to problems, and takes five hours in the large ferry or seven hours in the small one. The rest of the journey from Komodo to Lahubanbajo takes two or three hours through the cetacean-rich, sheltered calm of the **Lintah strait** (Rp4000). To go direct to Labuhanbajo costs Rp12,400 and takes nine or twelve hours. Once in the waters off Komodo there is a shuttle boat from the ferry to mainland Komodo (Rp1500).

Komodo and Rinca

Komodo island is a dry, hostile wilderness, with towering cliffs forming a forbidding skyline as you approach. Starkly beautiful as it is, the island's lack of water would have deterred tourists as it has deterred settlers, were it not for a quirk of nature that has left it the home of one of the world's most fascinating creatures. The **Komodo dragon** or *ora* as it is known locally, is perhaps the most tangible legacy of our Jurassic predecessors, a modern dinosaur which lives nowhere else but here and on a few neighbouring islands.

Rinca island, to the east of Komodo, and tiny **Motong** and **Padar**, have eluded tourism almost completely – visitors on organized tours occasionally stop for walks but they rarely stay.

Around Komodo

Komodo now receives in excess of 40,000 visitors a year, all of them offloading at the tiny **PHPA camp** at **LOH LIANG** at the east of the island, where at least one fully grown dragon is a regular scavenging visitor. In the high season, when cruise ships dump tourists here by the hundred, it can seem a bit like an adventure theme park. During the rainy season, however, you can easily find yourself alone: just you and an island full of three-metre flesh-eating predators. The *ora* are in plentiful supply, and the vast majority of tourists who visit leave contented, having seen at least one of the monsters and probably a few smaller juveniles as well. However, there are no guarantees: the majority of this huge inhospitable island remains untrammelled, and one of the dragon's prime weapons is its ability to camouflage itself.

KOMODO DRAGONS

Varanus komodoensis, the **Komodo dragon**, is the largest extant lizard in the world. Although remains of comparable size to the modern dragon have been excavated in Java and Timor, they date from the Pleistocene period, and there is no evidence that such creatures have existed anywhere other than the Komodo area for well over a million years. Unlike many rare species around the globe, the dragon is actually steadily increasing in numbers.

The dragon is of the genus *varanid*, the largest species of monitor lizard, so called because in popular folklore the lizards "monitored" crocodiles, following them to feast on the scraps they left behind. The **largest** recorded specimen of a Komodo dragon was well in excess of 3m long and weighed a mammoth 150kg. The majority of fully grown adults are a more manageable 2m and around 60kg, with the average female two-thirds the size of the males.

The dragon usually hunts by waiting hidden beside well-worn game paths, striking down its prey with its immensely powerful tail or slicing the tendons in its legs with scalpel-sharp fangs. Once the animal is incapacitated, the dragon eviscerates it, feeding on its intestines while it slowly dies. Contrary to popular belief, the dragon has neither poisonous breath or bite, but bitten creatures rapidly become infected and usually die as a result.

The PHPA charge Rp2500 for **entry** to the park, and Rp10,000 a night for **accommodation**, payable as you enter the camp: the stilted wooden cabins that comprise the accommodation are surrounded by deer, wild pigs, snakes and dragons. It is, however, pretty rough-and-ready – the coffin-sized rooms come complete with a prosperous rodent population and a selection of bugs. If the cabins are full you'll have to camp out on the floor of the restaurant, whose spacious verandah is at the centre of the camp.

While the food in the **restaurant** has improved dramatically over the last few years, don't expect luxury: basic fried noodles, omelettes and banana pancakes are usually the best they can manage. The camp rent out well-used snorkelling equipment and are close to setting up a dive facility. It's also possible to hire a PHPA **guide** from Loh Liang for a day's **trekking**: they'll take as many people as are interested for a flat Rp20,000. On all excursions around the island a guide is a necessity: they have sharp eyes and excellent knowledge of the area.

Treks and excursions

The full day's walk to the top of **Gunung Ara** from the PHPA camp, the highest point on the island, doesn't promise dragon sightings, but is absolutely extraordinary. It's an arduous, excruciatingly hot march to begin with, followed by a scorching scramble at the very top, but you'll see scores of unusual plants, animals and birdlife, such as sulphur-crested cockatoos, brush turkeys, and the megapode bird, which builds huge ground nests where its eggs are incubated in warm dung – easy plunder for juvenile dragons. The mountain walk culminates in a spectacular 360 degree panorama that takes the pain away in grand style. Don't forget to bring water and decent walking boots.

There are also regular walks from the PHPA camp, daily at 11am and 2pm, to **Banunggulung**, the river bed where the dragons used to be fed fresh goats daily, for the benefit of tourists. This practise has been discontinued, as dragons were just hanging around here and not bothering to hunt, an artificial situation that was considered to be adversely affecting their development as predators. A few especially lazy *ora* still mope around here, though, anticipating their now weekly goat sacrifice, so the forty-minute walk will usually be rewarded with a sighting or two. The guided walk costs Rp2500 per person.

The seas around Komodo, though home to spectacular coral reefs and an abundance of fish, are a far cry from the Gili Islands or Bali. The giant saltwater crocodiles that haunted estuaries in this area as little as a decade ago have all been hunted out, but riptides, whirlpools, sea snakes, sea-wasp jellyfish and a healthy shark population make these waters potentially dangerous, so stick to recommended **snorkelling** locations such as the excellent **Pantai Merah**. A day's boat trip can be bargained down to around Rp10,000 a day per person if you have a group of six or more people; the staff in the restaurant at the PHPA camp in Loh Liang can usually put you in touch with a boat owner if there no boats waiting at the pier. You can take in some of the magnificent snorkelling locations around Padar and Rinca: both the hard and soft corals are pristine in most locations and inhabited by neon-blue spotted rays, parrotfish, lobster and a bewilderment of other sea creatures. The itinerary for these trips is negotiable and can be supplemented with onshore stops for treks or beach time.

Kampung Komodo

The only permanent settlement on the island is **KAMPUNG KOMODO**, on the coast south of the PHPA camp. Once a prison colony for criminals from Sumbawa and Flores, it's a poverty-stricken, stilted fishing village that clings tenuously to survival in the most inhospitable of locations. If you choose to visit the kampung, the shuttle boat that meets the main ferry will stop here after calling at Loh Liang. Alternatively, you could include it as a destination on a day's boat charter.

TOURS TO KOMODO

For those who don't fancy night buses and basic ferries, **package tours** are a welcome possibility. Perama Tour and Travel (see p.646) have offices in Bima and Labuhanbajo, and offer tours leaving from Lembar, Senggigi and the Gili Islands on Lombok, from Bima on Sumbawa and from Labuhanbajo on Flores, subject to passenger availability. Parewa (see p.646), based in Bima, also offers similar packages. In the high season these run almost every day but in the rainy season you may have to muster your own ship-mates. Sample prices include:

Denpasar–fly to Labuhanbajo–Rinca–Komodo–Bima–fly to Bali: three days and two nights for US$450 per person.

Lombok–Pulau Moyo (Sumbawa)–Komodo–Rinca–Lombok: six days and five nights for US$225 per person.

Labuhanbajo–Komodo–Senggigi: three days and two nights for US$75 per person.

Bima–Komodo–Labuhanbajo: two days and one night for US$50 per person.

All prices include full board. You can also charter boats from any of the ports mentioned, but it's an expensive way of doing things.

If a tour includes snorkelling stops, make sure that the crew adhere to them. Also check on numbers before agreeing to the tour. On most boats, up to fifteen people is manageable but they will take up to thirty. If possible, check out the boat before paying.

Rinca

Very similar in appearance to Komodo, **Rinca** consists mostly of parched brown grasses covering steep rocky slopes, drought-resistant lontar palms and hardy shrubs providing the only real vegetation. Your chances of seeing dragons are greatly reduced as the population is less dense here, and because the only inhabitants are a few park officers there is little garbage to attract scavenging *ora*. The **PHPA camp** at **LOH BUAYA** on the northwest coast is even more basic than that on Komodo: the few rooms they have are threadbare and bug-ridden and they don't provide meals. However, you are welcome to stay here and some of the walks around the island are spectacular, with no danger of other tourists encroaching on your experience. There are no regular boats to Rinca so you will need to **charter** from Loh Liang or Kampung Komodo.

FLORES

A fertile, mountainous barrier between the Savu and Flores seas, **Flores** comprises one of the most alluring landscapes in the archipelago. When the Portuguese first encountered this dramatic island they named it "Cabo das Flores" (Cape of Flowers). While it is neither a cape nor especially famed for its blooms, it is undoubtedly endowed with a magnificent, untamed beauty that more than justifies the hyperbole. The volcanic spine of the island soars to 2500m and torrential wet seasons result in a lushness that marks Flores apart from its scorched neighbours. Thanks to the recent influx of tourists flooding into the hotspots of **Lahubanbajo**, **Bajawa** and **Moni**, facilities are improving dramatically on the island.

Despite being a mere 370km long and in some places as narrow as 12km, only Java and Sumatra have a greater number of **active volcanoes** than Flores. At the extreme east end of the island, Lahubanbajo is cashing in on its position as the jumping-off point for Komodo and fast becoming a booming **beach resort**. The islands in the bay around the port hold some fine **coral gardens**, hotels and losmen springing up to accommodate Western beachcombers. **Ruteng** is home to **Gunung Ranaka**, the island's highest peak, and has a cool climate and wonderful scenery. Bajawa is another hill town, with fascinating surrounding villages harbouring **megaliths** and traditional lifestyles, and the nearby **hot springs** at **Soe** are becoming a very popular place to soak away the aches after a long hike. The most spectacular natural sight in Flores – and possibly in all of Nusa Tenggara – is magnificent **Keli Mutu**, a unique volcano near Moni, northeast of **Ende**. The three craters of this extinct peak each contain a lake, of vibrantly different and gradually (but constantly) changing colours. In the east of Flores, high-quality **ikat weaving** is still thriving.

Some history
It seems likely that first Chinese traders, as early as the twelfth century, and then the Makarrese and Bugis peoples, made incursions here on their **trade routes** to Timor and Maluku. These traders began the slave trade, raiding the coastal towns of Flores while restocking with provisions for the long journey to Bima or Java. The people of Flores were being plundered for slaves until the late nineteenth century, which explains why so many settlements are found inland. Later, the Bugis and Makarrese began small-scale trading out of Larantuka on the eastern tip of the island.

In the sixteenth century, the **Portuguese** built forts in the east at Ende and on nearby Pulau Solor, to avoid having to stay on the inhospitable malarial coast of Timor, also taking advantage of the local materials of volcanic sulphur and cotton.

On December 12, 1992, a huge **earthquake**, with its epicentre off the north coast, killed over 3000 people and almost totally razed the tourist centre of Maumere. The quake measured 7.2 on the Richter scale, with the worst damage on nearby Pulau Babi, where the resultant *tsunami* were said to have killed almost all of the thousand inhabitants. The rebuilding process is even now still incomplete in Maumere: a cyclone only a month after the quake compounded all the problems, causing yet more damage to the buildings and crops: starvation and poverty followed.

Labuhanbajo and around

The sleepy little port town of **LABUHANBAJO** is the gateway to Flores from the islands of Komodo and Sumbawa. The boat journey from those islands is an absolute delight, past myriad tiny green islands surrounded by colourful trimarans, schools of exuberant dolphins leaping alongside the ferry. *Labuhanbajo* means "Bajau harbour", named for its Muslim Bajau fisherman, and indeed the first sight you will see of predominantly Catholic Flores is the shiny metallic mosque right by the harbour.

No longer merely a transit zone, the town is waking up to the possibilities offered by tourists, who travel vast distances to see the dragons; boatmen congregate around the harbour to conjure you away to the **deserted beach** of your choosing. The land rises at the north and south ends of the town, and these hills offer fantastic sunset views of the harbour and surrounding bay. The surrounding islands feature deserted white sands and seas alive with an endless variety of life.

Practicalities

The harbour of Labuhanbajo marks the extreme northern end of the main street, on which almost all of the losmen and restaurants are situated. **Ferries** from Sumbawa via Komodo arrive late in the afternoon and there will be touts and boats waiting to take you to losmen. The **airport** is about 2km out of town and you'll probably have to charter a bemo to get there.

To book flights and buy tickets, head to the **Merpati office**, a fifteen-minute uphill hike east of town, though people working there are vague and unhelpful. If you need to change money, head to the **Bank Rakyat Indonesia** at the south end of town; they are

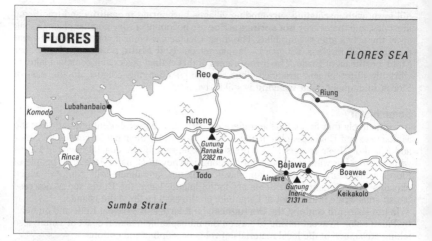

unsure about travellers' cheques, will only take prime-condition bills and give lousy rates for anything that isn't dollars. The **post office** (Mon–Thurs 7.30am–3pm, Fri & Sat 7.30–11am) is quite convenient, being next to the *Pantai Bajo Hotel*, but the **PHPA** and **Telkom** offices are a hike out of town: walk south from the harbour, passing most of the hotels, and take the second left up the hill past the **market**. For most phone calls, the **wartel** in town opposite the *Dunia Rumah Makan* is just as good a bet.

Buses heading east to **Ruteng** start running at 6.30am, and tickets can be bought from all the hotels for Rp5000. It's a four or five-hour trip along a good road to Ruteng, continuing on to Bajawa, which can take over eleven hours in total (Rp10,000). There are a few more buses in the morning and two more in the early afternoon. Buses meet the ferry for the fourteen-hour trip to **Ende** (Rp15,000). The **ferry** west to Sumbawa via Komodo leaves at 8am, and you can get tickets right up to departure.

Accommodation

Most of these **accommodation** places are located along the main street that runs parallel to the sea. Some of the **beach hotels** sit on islands off the coast within an hour's boat trip from the village. If you are going to be in the Labuhanbajo area for more than one night it's an excellent option, as most places offer a quiet getaway with unspoilt beaches and decent snorkelling.

THE TOWN

Gardena Bungalows, on a small hill set back off the main road, a 3min walk south from the port. Currently the most popular backpackers' place in town. Self-contained bungalows overlooking the bay come with mosquito nets, and breakfast is included in the price. They have a good restaurant but it's a little overpriced. ③.

Hotel Mintra, Jl Sukarno Hatta 31 (☎0385/41209). A new place with reasonably clean singles and doubles with optional en-suite mandi. ③.

Mutiara, A little further south down the main street from the entrance to the *Gardena*, but on the seaward side of the street (☎0385/41039). Rooms are basic, ranging from simple singles to a triple with air-con and mandi. There's a decent restaurant hanging right over the water, but the proximity to the road makes it noisy in the mornings. ③–④.

Pantai Bajo, close to the *Mutiara* and the next hotel if you are heading south but on the opposite side of the road (☎0385/41009). Clean rooms around a pseudo-tropical garden. In the high season it's always booked out with Dutch and Italian tour groups. ②–③.

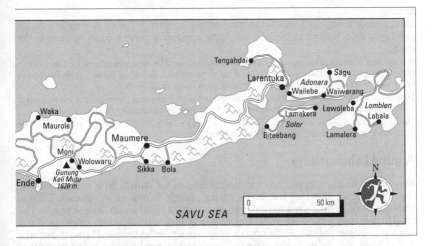

Si or **Chez Felix**, Up the road past the *Wisma Sony*. Tranquil and clean singles, doubles and triples, most with en-suite mandi and fan. ②.

Losmen Sinjai, just before the post office as you head south. Though inexpensive it's poor value and very dark and dingy. ①.

Wisma Sony, turn left immediately after the *Hotel Mintra* and continue up this hill: the *Sony* is on your right. A genuine Indonesian family-run place. What it lacks in trimmings it makes up for in homeliness, and the food is also very good. ②.

Hotel Wisata, on the main road south from the market (☎0385/41020). Standard rooms with or without en-suite mandi; the restaurant here serves breakfast and basic meals as well as cold drinks. Very clean and fresh – the owner claims they repaint the entire place every month. ③.

THE ISLANDS

Most places have only irregular electricity and running water and none have phones. However, all have restaurants, include at least breakfast in their price, and offer regular free boats or bemos to and from the harbour. The first transport in the morning is guaranteed to connect with the ferries west or the second bus to Ruteng.

Batu Gosok, on the mainland about a 30min boat ride away to the north. It has a good beach and has just undergone a major refurbishment. The pricey rooms are really quite luxurious, with en-suite mandi and air-con an option. ⑤.

Hotel Cendana, a 30min coast drive south. Reasonable rooms; the more expensive ones boast air-con, en-suite mandi and shower. ③–⑤.

Kencana Hotel, about 45min away by boat. Currently the best of the beach retreats, with a great beach and reefs that have been unaffected by reef-bombing. The hotel also has an agent in Labuhanbajo in a small hut next door to the *Gardena Bungalows*. ③.

Hotel New Bajo Beach, on the coast south of town, a 15–20min drive away. It has hot water and air-con in its top price rooms, with basic rooms also on offer, and the beach is quite clean and picturesque. ③–④.

Pungu Hotel, situated on remote Pulau Pungu, a pleasant 1hr boat trip away from Labuhanbajo port. A tranquil affair and prices include unlimited use of the hotel's snorkelling equipment and dugout canoes: prices are negotiable – especially for extended stays. ③.

Weicucu Beach, a 20min boat ride away from town and on the mainland just before the *Batu Gosok*. Attractive cottages ranging from very basic places that have little more than their shaky four walls and a battered mattress, to those with mandi and mosquito nets. The reasonable prices include three very square meals a day. The beach and snorkelling are reasonable, but the general location is beautiful with its bungalows practically sitting on the sand and lush hills rising up right behind them. ③–④.

Eating

Labuhanbajo town has a handful of good **eating** options. If you're staying at a beach hotel, you'll be limited to the accompanying restaurant, where fresh seafood is the norm.

Borobudor Rumah Makan, next to *Gardena Bungalows*. The best place for a feed in western Flores. It's a little expensive but they have great fresh seafood, including lobster, as well as steaks and good ice cream. A grilled barracuda or tuna steak costs about Rp7000.

Dewata Rumah Makan, next door to the *Borobudur*. More basic than its neighbour but still worth a try for its seafood, particularly crab and prawns and various inexpensive Indonesian dishes.

Dunia Rumah Makan, a 3min walk south of the port on the main road, on the water side of the road. Basic but wholesome, with good nasi campur.

Around Labuhanbajo

Most of the hotels organize tours to nearby islands for **snorkelling** and sunbathing, depending on whether they can muster enough people to make it worthwhile. Trips to **Pulau Bidari**, an hour's sail west of town, run to about US$9 for up to eight people. The coral here is mildly diverting, and the place is swarming with audacious monkeys. A full-day trip to **Pulau Sabolo**, further north, is recommended as the coral is much better: it costs US$20, also for up to eight people. Coral clusters can be found in just a couple of metres of water here, so it's perfect for beginners, plus there's a swim through some caves for the more experienced, and a decent chance of seeing turtles and small black-tip reef sharks. Good **scuba diving** is an option in this area, with tours organized by Dive Komodo at the *Bajo Beach* starting at US$75 a day with two tanks. With enough people and money they can also arrange trips around Komodo, Rinca and Motong, where the diving is world-class. In the strong currents of the cold, plankton-rich seas around these three islands there is an excellent chance of seeing pelagic species, including whale sharks, manta rays and cetaceans. Diving here is for the experienced only.

Other day-trip itineraries include **Pulau Kalang**, where thousands of fruit bats roost in the mangroves and leave in flocks for their daily dusk feedings, and **Batu Cermin**, the mirror rock cave. This small cavern is crammed with stalagmites and stalactites, which in some cases have met to form thick pillars, entwined by tree roots coming down through the ceiling to meet the litter-strewn floor. In the late morning, a shaft of sunlight enters through a hole in the roof and reflects off a glassy rock, to fill the cave with blinding sunlight.

Ruteng and the Manggarai district

The first large town near Labuhanbajo is **RUTENG**, 140km to the east. Surrounded by stark, forested volcanic hills, studding rolling rice-paddy plains, it's an archetypal **hill town**. The streets are spacious and spotless, adorned with beautifully manicured gardens, and the town's altitude makes it a cool relaxing place to stroll around. The **market** just outside town is flooded with plump, healthy-looking fresh vegetables, fine tobacco, coffee and all the constituent ingredients of *cirih pinang* (betel nut). The market is the central meeting point for the local Manggarai people (see the box on p.656): Ruteng is also their district capital.

Manggarai district is the largest in Flores, comprising the western third of the island. The people speak their own language and have a distinctive culture that's most in evidence in **Todo**, Pongkor and several villages on the south coast. Catholic missionaries have been in the area since the 1920s, but rarely, if ever, get to villages outside of Ruteng.

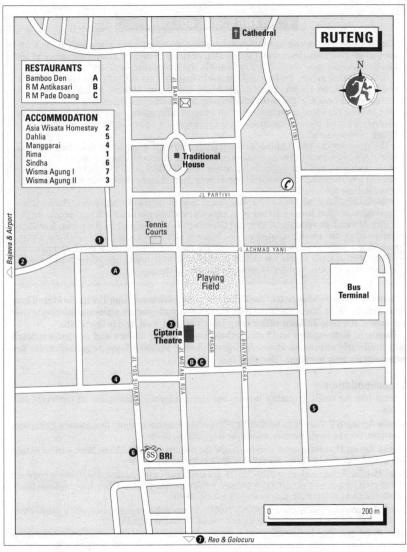

RUTENG

RESTAURANTS
Bamboo Den	A
R M Antikasari	B
R M Pade Doang	C

ACCOMMODATION
Asia Wisata Homestay	2
Dahlia	5
Manggarai	4
Rima	1
Sindha	6
Wisma Agung I	7
Wisma Agung II	3

Cathedral

JL BARUK

Traditional House

JL PARTIVI

Tennis Courts

JL ACHMAD YANI

Playing Field

Bus Terminal

JL KARTINI

Ciptaria Theatre

JL MO'ANG RUA

JL PASAR

JL BHAYANGKARA

JL YOS SUDARSO

BRI

Bajawa & Airport

0   200 m

Reo & Golocuru

Practicalities

Most buses arriving in Ruteng will drop you off at a hotel if you ask. Otherwise the **bus terminal** is relatively central and it's not much of a walk from there to most of the losmen. The airport is about 2km out of town, from where most hotels offer free buses. The main **market** is to the south of town. The **Bank Rakyat Indonesia** (Mon–Thurs 7.30am–3.45pm, Fri 7.30–11.45am & 1.30–3.45pm, Sat 7.30am–noon) is on Jalan Yos

---

MANGGARAI CULTURE

Traditions remain strong in **Manggarai**; visitors to an unknown place will still lick the ground in order to make resident spirits aware of their presence, and all the stages of life and the calendar year are marked by festivals and traditional sacrifice.

In the area's legends, the first child on earth had no anus and suffered intensely as he could not defecate. He was killed by his father, cut up into little pieces and sprinkled on the ground. Magically, the earth suddenly became fertile and crops began to spring up everywhere, his blood making food for all humans. The spilling and drinking of blood in a ritual context is therefore guaranteed to bring fertility and most festivals involve bloodletting of some sort.

The most spectacular festivals in Manggarai district involve ferocious **whip fighting** (*caci*). One combatant carries a baton and a shield, often wearing a hideous mask. The other wields an evil-looking bullwhip made from buffalo skin. The fights usually take place at **weddings** but are also held regularly in August and at New Year, right in the centre of Ruteng town.

The traditional structures of the Manggarai tend to take a circular form. The local villages have conical houses arranged in concentric circles around a round arena, in the centre of which is a sacrificial altar and totemic tree, surrounded by flat rocks. Even the rice paddies are round, divided up like spiders webs or a dartboard, with each clan receiving a slice. Most of these formations are no longer used, but a good example can still be seen at **Golo Curu**, about a three-kilometre walk uphill from the *Agung* Losmen in Ruteng town, with wonderful views all the way to the top.

Sudarso near the *Sindah* hotel. You'll find the **post office** on Jalan Baruk 6 (Mon–Thurs 9am–3pm, Fri 9–11.30am, Sat 9am–1pm, Sun 9am–noon). For international telephone calls and faxing, the new **Telkom office** is on Jalan Achmad Yani, and is open 24hr.

Buses to Bajawa, Reo and Labuhanbajo start leaving at 7am and continue sporadically until early afternoon. Buses to Bajawa (5–6hr; Rp5000) leave regularly, while Reo buses are far less frequent (2hr; Rp3000).

Accommodation

Ruteng has no real top-quality hotels, but the moderate places are all perfectly adequate.

Wisma Agung I, Jl Waeces 10 (☎0385/21080). On the road out towards Reo, about a 15min walk from town. Set in a lovely location among the rice paddies. ②–③.

Wisma Agung II, down a small street opposite the theatre (☎0385/21835). More expensive than the *Agung I*, but with larger rooms and in slightly better condition. ③.

Hotel Dahlia, Jl Bhayangkari (☎0385/21377). Located close to the market, the *Dahlia* is huge and getting even bigger, so you're unlikely to have trouble getting a room. They have sit-down toilets and sporadic hot water in the upper-category rooms. ③–④.

Hotel Manggarai, Jl Adi Sucipto 6 (☎0385/21008). A reasonable enough place with a good central meeting area (with accompanying late-night noise of TV and loud locals). ③.

Rima Hotel, Jl A. Yani 14 (☎0385/22196 or 22195). A brand-new sparkling-clean place. Most of the rooms come with en-suite mandi. Great value for money and a reasonable restaurant. ③.

Sindah Hotel, Jl Yos Sudarso (☎0385/21197). Popular with travellers, there's a good range of rooms, from budget singles and doubles to luxury rooms with en-suite shower and hot water. The manager is especially friendly and helpful. ②–③.

Eating

Only a couple of places in town offer reasonable **food**. The *Rumah Makan Pade Doang* is on the first corner as you walk north from the theatre on Jalan Motang Rua. They have cold beer and specials that include fairly fresh seafood, a rarity this far from the coast. The *Bamboo Den* is almost the next building on your right as you continue north from the theatre. It's quite appealing and has a passable selection of Indonesian food including cold sate and soto ayam. Around the bus terminal, the *Masakan Padang*, *Citra Rasa*, *Merpati* and *Garuda* do standard Padang food, the quality of which can be assessed from their window displays. The *Hotel Sindah* offers some fairly basic meals such as fried noodles and nasi campur, and has cold drinks.

Around Ruteng

TODO is a **traditional village** and seat of the (now defunct) rajah, lying about 40km south of Ruteng and well worth a visit. An irregular public bus from the main terminal in Ruteng will take you all the way (1hr; Rp1500). **Megaliths** and Manggarai houses here pepper the village, but the main attraction is a **mystical drum**, once made from the belly-skin of a Bimanese slave. To see the drum is free, but for it to be replaced in its rooftop resting place the people have to perform a sacred dance and sacrifice a chicken, for which you'll pay about Rp30,000.

WAE RENO village, right on the south coast and a three-hour trip from Ruteng, features Flores's oldest *rumah adat* (traditional house). Apparently it was originally constructed in 1718, though how much of the original structure remains is unknown. There is also great **snorkelling** at nearby beaches and **Pulau Mulus**, a short boat ride from the shore. Lots of **migrating whales** pass very close to the shore here and dolphins can be regularly seen all year round, especially in the early mornings. You can stay here with the kepala desa, or you can make it a day-trip from Ruteng; the bus journey (3hr) costs Rp3000.

Gunung Ranaka, the highest peak in Flores, lies 15km southeast of Ruteng. Take a bus to **Robo** (Rp1500) and then walk the steep 5–6km to the smoking summit; there's a road running almost to the top so you shouldn't need a guide. Less littered and larger than Labuhanbajo's Batu Cermin, there is a similar rock quartz or mica **cave** at **LIANGBUA**, north of Ruteng off the road to **Reo**. The cavern has a tiny entrance but inside is huge, glassy and, with a powerful torch, quite impressive. The bemo ride takes an hour (Rp1500); you can take the bus to Reo and ask the driver to stop at Liangbua Gua.

Beside the road from Ruteng to Bajawa sits **Danau Ranamese**, a stunning turquoise-blue lake, surrounded by forest. The locals sometimes refer to it as Little Keli Mutu, and the lake's brilliant colour and the magnificent view of the surrounding highlands falling to the sea is certainly reminiscent of its more distinguished cousin. The elevated lookout point beside the road is often used as a lavatory stop for the passengers of buses heading from Ruteng to Bajawa, so you will probably get to see it without making the effort to take a bemo or bus for the twenty-kilometre jaunt out here.

Near the north coast of the Manggarai district lies the port town of **REO**: the views on the drive from Ruteng (2hr; Rp4500) are really beautiful, with endless terraced ricefields (*sawah*) set amongst the hills. The whole town seems to have been constructed for the benefit of the mission here and as they don't get many visitors you can expect lots of stares. There are some nice beaches out of town and boats ply to Labuhanbajo – but be warned, it's a long trip. Reo has two losmen, the *Nisang Nai* (②), a little out of town amongst the rice paddies, being much the best option.

Bajawa and the Ngada district

The hill town of **BAJAWA** is one of the most popular destinations for tourists in Flores, not quite at the altitude of Ruteng 120km to the west, but still cool and surrounded by lush slopes and striking volcanoes. Bajawa is the largest town in the **Ngada district**, an area that maintains its status as the spiritual heartland of Flores. Here, despite the

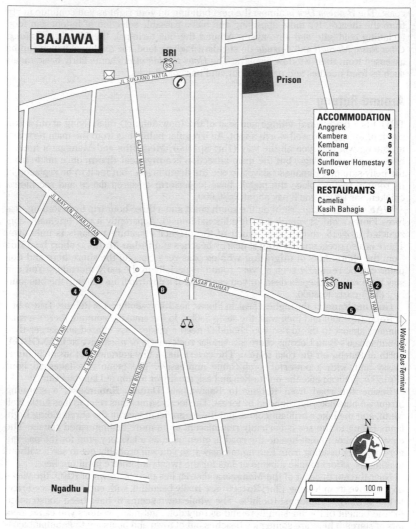

BAJAWA

BRI

Prison

ACCOMMODATION
Anggrek   4
Kambera   3
Kembang   6
Korina   2
Sunflower Homestay 5
Virgo   1

RESTAURANTS
Camelia   A
Kasih Bahagia   B

JL SUKARNO HATTA

JL GAJAH MADA

JL MAYJEN DIPARJAIAN

JL PASAR RAHMAT

BNI

JL EL TARI

JL MARTA DINATA

JL IMAN BONJOL

JL ACHMAD YANI

Watujaji Bus Terminal

N

0   100 m

Ngadhu

growing encroachment of curious travellers, indigenous animist religions flourish and the villages maintain fascinating houses, megalithic stones and interesting totemic structures. Up to 60,000 people in the Ngada district speak the distinct Ngada language, and a good proportion of the older generation speak nothing else and don't understand even basic Bahasa Indonesian.

Gunung Inerie is just one of the active volcanoes near Bajawa: it's an arduous but rewarding hike, but you can see all the way to Sumba from the summit if it's clear. Not for the faint-hearted are the local specialities of *moke*, a type of wine that tastes like methylated spirits and *raerate*, dog meat marinated in coconut milk and then boiled in its own blood.

THE RITUAL STRUCTURES OF NGADA

In the centre of the majority of villages in this district stand some of the most unusual ceremonial edifices in Indonesia, relics that pay tribute to exceptional ancestors, encapsulating their strength and influence in the present. The **Ngadhu** resembles a man in a huge hula skirt with a shrunken head, carrying a spear and a knife. The thatched skirt, which is replaced about every four years, sits atop the significant part of the structure, a carved wooden pole which is imbued with the power of a particular male ancestor. The pole is actually a forked and phallic tree trunk that has to be excavated intact and alive before being crudely carved and replanted in the village. In the village of **Wogo**, some of these posts are said to be over 500 years old and have become completely petrified.

The female part of the pairing, the **Bhaga**, is a symbol of the womb, a miniature house that is constructed in conjunction with its male partner and is always situated parallel to the Ngadhu in neat rows. The symbolic coupling is supplemented by a carved stake called a **Peo**, to which animals will be tied before being sacrificed at various ritual festivals. Apart from their role as fertility symbols, the Ngadhu and Bhaga are symbolic representations of the ancestral protection of, and presence in, the village.

Practicalities

The **bus terminal**, 2km out of town at **Watujaji**, services all long-distance routes. Regular bemos from town to the terminal cost Rp300. The **airport** lies almost 30km away near Soa, from where you'll have to charter a bemo (US$10).

The **Merpati office** is next to the market on Jalan Pasar (Mon–Sat 8am–2pm), the **BNI bank** on Jalan Hayamwuruk, and the Bank Rakyat Indonesia on Jalan Sukarno Hatta; they will only change US dollars. The **Telkom** building near the BRI is open 24hr, and the main **post office** is located slightly to the west, also on Jalan Sukarno Hatta.

When it comes to **moving on**, most buses come into town to look for passengers, but it's best to be on the safe side and go to them. Buses east to Ende (4hr; Rp5000) run pretty much all day from 7am. Tourist buses will go all the way to Moni for Keli Mutu (5hr 30min; Rp7500), heading west to Ruteng (5–6hr; Rp5000), starting at 7am but stopping in the early afternoon; the morning buses continue on to Labuhanbajo (11hr; Rp10,000).

HIRING GUIDES

The influx of tourists to the Ngada region has led to a booming **guide** industry in Bajawa. There is now a standard Rp15,000 a day charge per person for a guide, who will arrange chartered transport, a driver, entrance to all the villages and often an excellent meal of traditional Bajawan food at the guide's home village. You need a minimum of four people for a day-tour that will generally include Langa, Bena, Bela or Luba, which are close by, as well as Wogo and the **hot springs** at Soa. It's not possible to do this all in one day on your own and the tour represents excellent value for money (if you get a good guide). Obviously, itineraries are negotiable and you can easily arrange extended tours, mountain climbs or off-the-beaten-track adventures. Most of the guides speak good English, and among the best are Phillipus, Max and Lukas, who can be contacted at the *Sunflower Homestay*. When hiring a guide, take time to chat to them beforehand: most are enthusiastic and knowledgeable, but a few are impatient and dour.

Accommodation

Accommodation in Bajawa is pretty basic, but there are a few decent options. The management of the *Nusantara* are notorious for press-ganging travellers at the bus terminal, claiming it's the only losmen in town. The rooms are dirty and it's definitely one to avoid.

Hotel Anggrek, Jl Letjend Haryono (☎0383/21172). Clean rooms, most of which come with en-suite mandi and toilet. ③.

Hotel Kambera, Jl El Tari, west of the market (☎0383/21166). The larger rooms and restaurant here are decent, but it's definitely worth paying a little extra to avoid the atrocious cell-like singles. ③.

Hotel Kembang, Jl Marta Dinata (☎0383/21072). To the west of the market. The *Kembang* is a siz-able hotel, with excellent clean rooms complete with mandi and red carpets running round a care-fully manicured garden. ③.

Melati Korina, Jl Achmad Yani 81 (☎0383/21162). One of the first places you will come to on the road in from the bus terminal, almost opposite the *Camelia* restaurant. It has clean single, double and triple rooms around a spacious central lounge, and some English books to swap or borrow. ③.

Sunflower Homestay (☎0383/21230). As the road from Watujaji bus terminal reaches the out-skirts of the town, it splits at a T-junction and becomes Jl Achmad Yani, where a small path leads up to the *Sunflower*. The outward-facing rooms have nice views of the valley, and you can get good information from the guides who congregate here. ②.

Hotel Virgo, Jl Mayjen Dipanjaitan (☎0383/21061). Slightly north of the market, the *Virgo* has two delightful, huge, airy rooms, and several nondescript ones at the same price. ②.

Eating

The revamped *Restaurant Camelia*, opposite the *Korina* losmen on Jalan Achmad Yani, does fantastic guacamole and chips, *kentang goreng* and some of the best *lumpiah* (spring rolls) rupiah can buy. Near the market on Jalan Gajah Mada, the *Kasih Bahagia* has a similar menu plus cold beer. Both of these places are reasonable: it costs Rp2500 for five large spring rolls, and Rp5500 for a large *bintang*. In the market there are a few local rumah makan and stalls selling snack food; nothing very substantial, but they're the cheapest places to eat in town.

The Ngada villages

From Bajawa, the easiest Ngada village to visit is **LANGA**, which sits under the dra-matic shadow of **Gunung Inerie** and is a good example of a typical Ngada village. Tourists pass through here every day and you'll be asked to sign a visitors' book and pay a minimum of Rp1000 to take photographs. You can stay here at the *Serleon Langa Homestay* (①), not a bad place if you want to view village life but don't want to be too uncomfortable. It's also a good idea to overnight here if you want to scale Gunung Inerie; with an early-morning start from Langa you can make the three- to four-hour climb to the smoking summit before the clouds roll in. It's actually closer from nearby Bena, but if you stay there it's more likely to be on the kepala desa's floor and a good night's sleep makes the climb seem much easier. You can usually convince a villager to **guide** you to the summit for around Rp5000.

From Langa it's about another 10km, mostly downhill, to **BENA**, another village that's very popular with tourists. You'll have to walk, unless you're lucky enough to catch a ride or have chartered a vehicle. Here they have nine different clans, in a vil-lage with nine levels and nine Ngadhu/Bhaga couplings (see box p.659). It's the cen-tral village for the local area's religions and traditions, and one of the places to see **fes-tivals**; the guides in town are the best source of information about when weddings, planting and harvest celebrations will take place.

If you want to go to villages where few Westerners visit and get a real sense of the life here, you'll probably need to hire a guide from Bajawa. One walking tour that comes well recommended is best done as a two-day excursion, passing through **Nage**, **Wajo** and **Gurasina**. **NAGE** is a two- or three-hour walk from Bena, the path offering views down to the coast and the Savu sea. The village sits on a green plateau with fine views of the surrounding volcanoes, has some interesting megaliths and fine traditional structures. Every Friday evening a white ghost is said to come out of the village's megaliths and try to break into the houses. **WAJO** is just a short walk away from here and is a very pretty village with three Ngadhu/Bhaga pairings and great views of the surrounding countryside. From here it takes up to two hours to walk to **GURASINA**, the biggest village in the area, arranged on eight levels, and with a richly active ritual life. This is the best place to stay the night, probably sleeping on the floor of the kepala desa's house. Few tourists get to Gurasina and the welcome here is wonderful – they'll offer a meal of rice and vegetables and might even kill a chicken. Expect to be the centre of attention for as long as you stay.

Some of the finest **megaliths** and Ngadhu can be found at the twin villages of **WOGO**, where tin-roofed houses are springing up here and kids will ask you for pens and *gula gula* (candy). To get here, take one of the regular bemos from Bajawa to **Mataloko** (30min; Rp1000). From Mataloko, walk along the road south for about 1km and you'll come to Wogo Baru. The people moved here from Wogo Tua about thirty years ago because the old site had no freshwater source. What it does have is some distinctly eerie megaliths set in a clearing about 200m further down the road; local kids will lead you down to them. Mataloko has a decent **market** on Saturdays, with local sarongs, fruit and vegetables, and Bajawan knives which resemble kris.

Currently the most popular destination near Bajawa is the **hot springs** at **SOA**. An entrepreneurial Australian has built accommodation here, the *Flores Paradise* bungalows (③), and apparently plans to run the hot water into the showers in the pleasant, spacious bamboo rooms – it's easily the best place to stay in the area. The springs themselves, set in magnificent surroundings, are an absolute joy, especially at night or in the late afternoon, when Bajawa can get quite chilly. The hot-spring pool runs down into a river so you can happily spend all day alternating between hot and cold baths. To get here, a bus or bemo to Soa village costs Rp1000 from the bemo station in Bajawa, taking about an hour. From where the bemo stops, it's a two-kilometre walk to the springs.

AIMERE is a largish town near the south coast to the west of Bajawa; at the bustling markets on Thursday and Friday you can buy the *moke* wine and Bajawan *arak* that the town is renowned for and see the fermentation process; *arak* is more palatable, and if you add a little honey and orange juice it seems almost inviting. You can stay here with the kepala desa but the other locals will clamour to have you stay with them, and are generally more welcoming. To get to Aimere, take a bus from Watujaji bus terminal in Bajawa (2hr; Rp3500).

Near the town of **Boawae**, 40km to the east of Bajawa on the road to Ende, is **Gunung Ebulobo**, a hostile and decidedly active volcano, one of the most imposing in Flores. Adrenaline seekers can climb Ebulobo, overnighting at the *Hotel Sao Wisata* (②–③) near the church in Boawae. Hire a guide in the village the day before starting the arduous four-hour climb.

Riung and the Tujuhbelas Islands

The small town of **RIUNG** sits on Flores's lush north coast, about 60km north of Bajawa; it began as a string of seafront Bajau and Bugis fishing villages, all its houses perched precariously on fragile-looking stilts; it's a tiny community whose sole focus is the sea. Most travellers get here on one of the daily northbound buses from Bajawa or Ende, which arrive right in the centre of town. Although not of particular interest itself, Riung is the mainland route to the best beaches and snorkelling in central Flores, those of the verdant **Tujuhbelas Islands**, which stud the bay north of town.

Riung is tiny and very easy to work your way around: limited information can be gleaned from the people at the **parks office** near the church on the eastern side of town and they also rent out some pretty decrepit snorkelling equipment (Rp5000 a day). There are some white-sand beaches along this coast but if you've made it this far it's definitely worth the effort of chartering a boat out to Pulau Tujuhbelas (Seventeen Islands), which lie out in the bay north of Riung. There are actually 24 islands, but the government decided to overlook seven of them, so that the name could tie in with Independence day – August 17. **Pulau Ontoloe** has a colossal colony of fruit bats, **Pulau Rutung** has startling varieties of pristine coral, and there are six or seven other uninhabited islands that are perfect places to be cast away to. A **boat charter** to three islands with five snorkelling stops runs to around US$20, and you will be approached by willing **guides** and boatmen in town.

Practicalities

The *Pondok SVD* (③) is the pick of the accommodation in Riung, situated on the road as you come into town. It's a glorious, new place run by missionaries, all the rooms having Western toilets and showers. *The Florida Hotel* (②) is a little way out of town on the road to Ende, and the *Liberty Losmen*, *Madonna Homestay* and *Tamarin Hotel* (all ②) are fairly central and offer the same bed-and-three-meal deal.

A daily bus from Bajawa goes all the way to Riung, leaving in the early morning (3hr; Rp7500). You can also get there on the one daily bus from Ende's Ndao terminal, which leaves at 6am and takes four hours (Rp5500).

Ende and around

ENDE, the largest town and most important port on Flores, is situated on a narrow peninsula with flat-topped **Gunung Meja** and the active volcano **Gunung Ipi** at the sea end, and provides access for Keli Mutu and Moni. To the west is another volcanic peak, **Gunung Ebolobo**, and black-sand beaches stretch down both east and west coasts. Ende suffered severe damage in the 1992 earthquake that razed Maumere and killed several hundred people here. The town still seems shaken by the whole thing – ramshackle, battered and with little to attract the tourist other than banks and **ferries** to other destinations.

Both the Portuguese and Dutch have based themselves here in the past but have left no notable buildings, apart from a Dutch house whose shell remains near the village of **Nuabosi**, off the highway to Bajawa. Three or four bemos a day from Ndao terminal make this trip, which is only around 10km, and there are fantastic views of the Ende peninsula from up here. Ende's claim to fame is that President Sukarno was exiled here back in 1933: his house, **Situs Bung Karno**, can be found on Jalan Parewa, slightly northeast of the harbour. It is now a museum of sorts, with some of the original furniture and a few dull photos, unlikely to enthral the casual visitor. The **market** is near the waterfront and, apart from the usual sarongs, fruit and vegetables, they also bring in some amazing fish: huge tuna, sharks, rays and even dolphins. The **night market** is out of the centre on Jalan Kelimutu, running from late afternoon until 9pm or 10pm. They have similar produce to the day market, supplemented by food stalls and lit by candles.

Practicalities

The **airport** at Ende is in town, slightly north of Ipi harbour on Jalan Jenderal Achmad Yani; any bemos will take you into town. Travellers coming from Bajawa, Ruteng and beyond will arrive at the **Ndao bus terminal**, which is on the beach, about 2km west of the very centre of town. Bemos meet every bus and will take you to your destination of choice. Those coming into Ende from Moni, Maumere and Laruntuka will arrive in the **Wolowana** terminal, situated at the extreme east of town and a five-kilometre bemo ride from central Ende. Ipi harbour on the southeastern coast of the peninsula is used for all long-distance **boats**: the ferry's and harbour master's offices are on the road that leads down to the harbour.

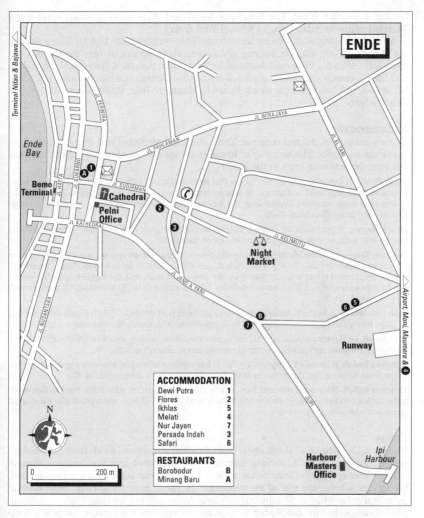

ACCOMMODATION

Dewi Putra	1
Flores	2
Ikhlas	5
Melati	4
Nur Jayan	7
Persada Indah	3
Safari	6

RESTAURANTS

Borobodur	B
Minang Baru	A

Two **Pelni ferries** call regularly at Ende. The *KM Awu* comes from Waingapu and goes on to Kupang, then back on the reverse route the next week. The *KM Pangrano* comes every two weeks and goes on to either Waingapu or Savu. There is also a ferry which does a constant loop: Ende–Waingapu–Savu–Waingapu–Ende–Kupang–Ende. It leaves from the Ipi harbour for Waingapu every Wednesday at 7pm (12hr; Rp11,200), and goes to Kupang every Thursday and Saturday (16hr; Rp17,000).

The losmen, banks and accommodation are widely dispersed, so you'll probably end up using the **bemo kota** (town bemos) fairly liberally. The best rates for foreign exchange in Ende are available at the **BNI**, which is past the airport on Jalan Jenderal Achmad Yani. If don't want to go out of town, then the **BRI** is next door to the *Dwi Putra Hotel* on Jalan Sukarno, and the **Danamon bank** (best for credit-card transactions) is behind it on Jalan Hatte. For ticket purchases and flight confirmations, contact the **Merpati office** on Jalan Nangka (closed Wed & Sat).

Moving on, westbound buses leave from Ndao terminal, the bus for Riung departing at 6am, and the Bajawa, Ruteng and Labuhanbajo service at 7am. Eastbound services leave from the Wolowana terminal for Moni from 6am until 2pm (90min; Rp2500), and there's usually one passenger truck later in the afternoon, a much cooler and sociable option, with breathtaking views. Buses to Maumere (6hr; Rp5000) start at 8am and finish at 5pm.

Accommodation

There's nothing in the top range in Ende: the Losmen *Safari* and *Dewi Putra* are as upmarket as it gets. The majority of **losmen** are spread out along the road that leads out from the centre of town to the airport.

Dewi Putra, Jl Dewantara, next door to the BRI bank (☎0383/21465). Has a choice of cheap basic rooms with external toilet and mandi, or swanky luxury ones with en-suite facilities. The sea-facing rooms have huge windows overlooking the bay and the first-floor restaurant serves reasonable Chinese and Indonesian food. ②–③.

Hotel Flores, Jl Sudirman 28 (☎0383/21075). Near to the centre of town and ludicrously over-priced, with noisy air-con. Clean and well equipped though. ④.

Losmen Iklas, Jl Jenderal Achmad Yani heading towards the airport and several doors down from the *Losmen Safari* (☎0383/21695). The original, and still the best as far as travellers are concerned. All the latest travel information is posted on the restaurant walls and the English-speaking owner can fill in any gaps for you. They have dirt-cheap, boxlike rooms through to reasonable doubles with en-suite mandi. ①–②.

Hotel Melati, on Jl Jenderal Achmad Yani close to the airport (☎0383/21311). Could do with a lick of paint; they don't have a restaurant and suffer problems with basics like running water. ③.

Nur Jayan, on Jl Jenderal Achmad Yani but nearer town than *Losmen Safari* (☎0383/21252). Brand-new, sparkling-clean and has the option of en-suite mandi. Excellent value. ②.

Persada Indah, Jl Garuda 17 (☎0383/21683). It has seatless toilets and hosepipes protruding from the walls as showers, but the owner is really friendly and it has a certain charm. ②.

Losmen Safari, Jl Jenderal Achmad Yani, a little east of the junction with Jl Adi Sucipto that leads to Ipi harbour and almost next door to the *Iklas* (☎0383/21499). Quite a clean plush place and good value, with mandi in all the rooms. ③.

Eating

There's really nothing to shout about in Ende when it comes to **food**. Both the markets provide the best cuisine, serving standard sate *murtabak* and nasi campur. *Rumah Makan Minang Baru* on Jalan Sukarno near Ende harbour serves simple Padang food, though considering the size of the restaurant the menu is pretty limited. *Depot Ende* at Jalan Sudirman 6 has similar Indonesian fare; again, nothing special. A new restaurant, provisionally called the *Borobodur,* has just opened opposite the *Losmen Nur Jayan*, serving up Indonesian staples such as nasi campur alongside seafood and a few Western dishes. *The Nur Iklas* serves travellers' favourites, cold drinks, juices and milkshakes. Around the waterfront market are a few basic warung serving goat curry, sate and nasi dishes.

Beaches and weaving villages

Ende can be stiflingly hot, being at sea level and sheltered from strong sea winds by its surrounding volcanoes. If you fancy a dip, there are reasonable black-sand **beaches** out of town in either direction. The Bajawa road runs right along the seafront, so just catch a bemo out to Ndao bus terminal and the beach begins right in front of the terminal.

The town is an ideal starting point for exploring some of the villages in the surrounding area, whose main source of income is derived from the weaving of **ikat** fabrics. **NGELLA** is a weaving village about 30km east from Wolowaru terminal in Ende and near the coast: take a bemo or truck (Rp1500). The *ikat* here is generally good quality, made from hand-spun thread with natural dyes, though it is also expensive and the women are hard bargainers. Another weaving village only 7km from town is **WOLOTOPO** – they have recently sealed the road that leads here and you can go directly in a bemo from Wolowana terminal (Rp300). From there you can walk about 3km along the seafront to the village of **NGALUPOLO**: few tourists get here and as well as weavings they have a few megaliths and traditional houses. You can stay here with the kepala desa.

Keli Mutu and Moni

Stunning **Keli Mutu** volcano, with its three strangely coloured crater lakes, is without doubt one of the most startling natural phenomena in Indonesia. The nearby village of **Moni**, 40km northeast of Ende, sits close to the mountain's slopes, and is the base for people hiking on the volcano. Moni has a definite lazy charm, nestling among scores of lush rice paddies and flanked by green slopes. The main Ende–Maumere road that runs right through the centre of town has astonishingly little traffic and often all you can hear is water babbling through the rice paddies and children splashing around in the roadside streams.

Keli Mutu

The summit of **Keli Mutu** (1620m) is a startling lunar landscape with, to the east, two vast pools separated by a narrow ridge. The waters of one are a currently luminescent green that seems to be heading for bright-yellow, the other was, a few years ago, a

---

WALKING ON KELI MUTU

Every morning at around 4am, an open-sided truck packed with bleary-eyed travellers runs from Moni up to **Keli Mutu**, returning at about 7am. The truck ride costs Rp3000, with an extra Rp1000 charged at the **PHPA post** on the way up to enter the volcano area.

Unfortunately it's impossible to photograph the three crater lakes at once: the best possible view is from the south crater rim, looking north over the two sister lakes. The trails that run around other rims are extremely dangerous. According to losmen owners in Moni, two Dutch tourists recently disappeared on a trek around the craters: divers dragged the lakes, but their bodies were never found.

A much nicer alternative to returning with the truck is to **walk** back down to Moni. As you head down the main road, two short cuts that take you through some charming local villages. The first is found at a small gap in the hedge on the right side of the road by the nine-kilometre marker, with a cardboard sign pointing to Moni. It takes you past villages where young girls weave at backstrap looms – entrepreneurs have set up stalls selling fruit and drinks all along this route, a godsend when the walk starts to heat up. If you come down on a Sunday morning you may be invited into Mass: all the women dress in fine *ikat* sarongs and there is beautiful choral singing.

The next short cut off the main road down from the summit is further down by the PHPA post and cuts off a good 4km from the road route. Both short cuts take you past the **waterfall** (*air terjun*) less than 1km from central Moni, which is a great spot for a dip after what can be a very hot walk. There is also a small hot spring near the falls. The walk takes about three hours, with alpine scenery, rolling grassy meadows flanking extinct volcanic hills, and views all the way to the sea. Practically the whole walk is downhill but always bring water and wear good walking boots. Wrap up warm for the sunrise at the summit, but make sure you can peel off layers for the descent.

vibrant turquoise, and is now deep magenta. A few hundred metres to the west, in a deep depression, is a pure-black lake – often clouds hang in wisps about the water's surface, accentuating the illusion of a witch's cauldron.

The colours of the lakes are apparently due to the levels of certain **minerals** that dissolve in them. As the waters erode the caldera they lie in, they uncover bands of different compounds and, as the levels of these compounds are in constant flux, so are the colours. In the 1960s the lakes were red, white and blue, and locals predict that within years they will have returned to these hues.

In the dialect of the region, *keli* means "mountain" and *mutu* is the spirit of the lakes. Until Christian missionaries managed to dissuade locals from the practice in the middle of the twentieth century, sacrificial animals and food offerings were regularly thrown into the waters to pacify the powerful *mutu*, who, it was believed, had the power to destroy the harvest. The people of the surrounding villages also believe that these waters are the soul's resting place: youthful souls are taken by the magenta lake, the old lounge around in the yellow-green lake and magicians, and thieves and murderers languish for eternity in the black lake.

Moni

The village of **MONI** is set out along the length of the road that runs from Ende, northeast to Maumere. Nowadays the village is almost entirely made up of losmen and restaurants, but it's still a quiet, relaxed place to spend a few days, with great walking in the surrounding hills. The **market** in Moni is on Monday morning and, though small, attracts villagers from kilometres around who come to sell *ikat*, fruit and vegetables. Behind the *Amina Moe* losmen and opposite the market is a **rumah adat**, where occasional evening dance performances are held and traders hang around trying to sell *ikat*. Expect to pay around Rp3000 to watch any performances.

There is no bank, post office or Telkom in Moni, though the owners of the *Nur Iklas* losmen in Ende are planning to open a moneychanging facility. Make sure you bring enough cash from Ende or Maumere.

Moving on, buses between Ende (90min; Rp2500) and Maumere (5hr; Rp5000) stop here about three times a day, the first one at about 11am and the last at about 3pm. All the losmen owners know the approximate times they will leave.

Accommodation

The road from Ende comes in from the north of the village and after two sharp turns heads east towards Maumere – all the accommodation is laid out along this road. The tourist explosion in Moni has led to bitter rivalries between losmen owners, who may try to persuade you that other losmen are brothels, or their owners thieves.

Amina Moe, just after *John's Homestay*. Still the travellers' favourite, more for the legendary all-you-can-eat evening buffet than for the dingy rooms. ②.

Homestay Daniel, just after *John's Homestay*, next door to the *Amina Moe*. The last of the main bunch in the village. It's basic with dusty rooms and a choice of en-suite mandi or outside facilities, but with friendly staff. ②.

Flores Hotel, A 500m walk out of the village. Not quite finished at the time of writing, but it should be terrific. The rooms are spacious and airy with en-suite mandi. ③.

Losmen Friendly and **Maria Inn,** set at the next large bend in the road after *Watagona Bungalows*, both of these losmen are recovering from being decimated after torrential rains brought down a huge tree on them, killing a Swedish couple. ②.

Hidayah Bungalows, the first place you see, on the right-hand side as you enter the main part of town. Probably the best value for money in Moni. They offer charming, well-kept bamboo huts, the host is very genuine, and the banana pancake and fruit-salad breakfast is superb. ②.

Lestari, on the right side of the road opposite the *Rona* pub. Has a huge colony of mangy dogs and dingy rooms with bare cement floors, but is an inexpensive last resort. ①.

Palm Bungalows, about 1km out of town heading towards Maumere and slightly off the main road. Set among the rice-fields, this place is tranquil and scenic. ③.

Pondok Wisata Arwanty, next on the left-hand side of the road after the *Lestari*. All rooms have outside mandi and are quite clean. ②.

Regal Jaya and **Nusa Bunga**, close together on the right-hand side coming from Ende. Nearly identical and run by the same owner: all rooms have outside mandi and are passably clean. ②.

Sao Wisata (aka **John's Homestay**). Has a 2m gnome fishing outside accompanied by kitsch concrete animals. Despite the immaculate rooms, many travellers boycott this place because of the monkey kept on a chain out back. ③.

Saoria Wisata Bungalows, right by the Keli Mutu turn-off. The most upmarket option. Comparatively expensive and a long way from the village, but clean, and most rooms have en-suite mandi and TV. ③.

Watagona Bungalows, off the road at the bend after *Arwanty* and on the right-hand side. Built to a traditional style and good value; the owner is chatty and pleasant. ②.

Eating

For such a small isolated village, the cuisine in Moni is impressive. The simple but wholesome buffet at the *Amina Moe* still draws large crowds: warn the cooks early if you want to eat so they can prepare enough food. The spread costs around Rp2500 and typically includes a variety of vegetables, croquette, fried and boiled potatoes, chicken cooked in at least two styles, rice and noodles. The *Rona* and *Chanty* pubs, both a little further up the road, can also arrange buffets of similar food if they have the customers, and with their bamboo interiors are relaxing places to enjoy an evening beer. The *Ankermi* pub is also a favourite for a view and a cold drink. They also do a few Western dishes such as spaghetti and fried potatoes. Right up by the Keli Mutu turn-off is the *Keli Mutu Restaurant*, which serves up omelettes, pancakes and guacamole. Next door to *John's Homestay*, the *Nusa Bunga* occasionally has cold drinks and the chilli chicken is delicious.

Maumere and Sikka

On the north coast of Flores, roughly equidistant between Ende and Larantuka, **MAUMERE** was once the visitor centre and best diving resort in Flores. However, the town achieved notoriety in the terrible earthquake that struck in December 1992. Even now, it's still a beaten town, with heaps of rubble and unrepaired buildings giving some parts of town the appearance of an unfinished construction site. Before the quake, many **scuba divers** were enticed by the possibility of seeing pelagic creatures such as manta rays, sharks, and schools of dog-tooth and skipjack tuna, as well as the occasional dugong (sea cow). Nowadays there's still an outside chance of seeing these huge beasts, but the majority of the dive sites have been obliterated and those that remain have fairly stunted coral growth, often covered with a blanket of silt and littered with dead, bleached-white coral heads.

Maumere is the capital of **Sikka district**, which stretches all the way to the east coast. It's especially renowned for its **weaving**, which characteristically has maroon, white and blue geometric patterns, in horizontal rows on a black or dark-blue background. Usually these are woven into hooped sarong, the more attractive female version being the one that receives most commercial attention. The male sarong is usually a black sheet interwoven with bright, shop-bought blue threads.

The entire eastern end of Flores, and particularly the two main towns of Maumere and Laratuka, is the most fervently Catholic in Flores and possibly all of Indonesia. Catholic priests from a variety of sects have been here for over four hundred years, and missionaries have made a concerted effort to educate and convert the majority of people here.

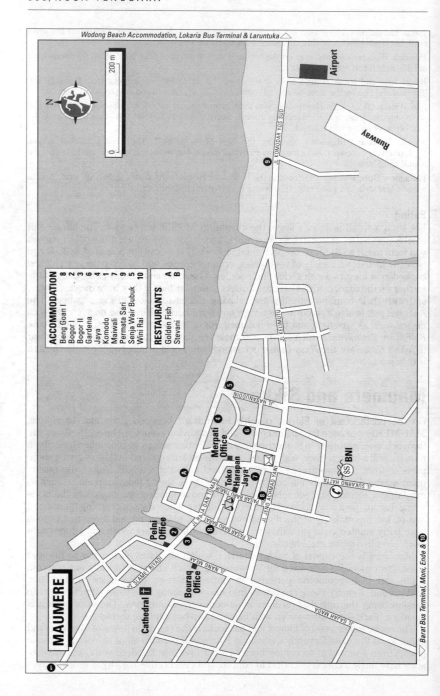

Wodong Beach Accommodation, Lokaria Bus Terminal & Laruntuka △

Airport

Runway

JL KOMODOR YOS SUD

JL KELIMUTU

ACCOMMODATION
Beng Goan I   8
Bogor I   2
Bogor II   3
Gardena   6
Jaya   4
Komodo   1
Maiwali   7
Permata Sari   9
Senja Wair Bubuk   5
Wini Rai   10

RESTAURANTS
Golden Fish   A
Stevani   B

JL. HASANUDDIN

Merpati
Office

Toko
Harapan
Jaya

BNI

JL SUKARNO HATTA

JL. PASAR BARU TIMUR

JL. PASAR BARU BARAT

JL. RAJA DAN TOMAS

Pelni
Office

JL JEND ACHMAD YANI

MAUMERE

Cathedral ✝

Bouraq
Office

JL. NANG MEAK

JL. SLAMET RIYADI

JL. GAJAH MADA

▽ Barat Bus Terminal, Moni, Ende & ⑩

Practicalities

Maumere has a square and a market at its centre, and much of the town is very close to the seafront without the water actually being visible. There are two **bus terminals**, both of which are notorious for pickpockets and con artists, so watch your pack. Buses coming from Ende and Moni arrive at **Terminal Barat** or **Ende terminal** on the southwest outskirts of town, but may drop you off in the centre. Buses from Larantuka will stop at the **Terminal Lokaria**, which is 3km east of the centre.

Two **banks** change foreign currency: the BRI is on Jalan Pasar Baru Barat, but you're usually better using the BNI on Sukarno Hatta (Mon–Fri 7.30am–2.30pm, Sat 7.30am–11am), as their rates are often better. The **post office** is on Jalan Jenderal Achmad Yani (Mon–Thurs 7.30am–3pm, Fri 7.30–11.30am, Sat 7.30am–1pm). The **Merpati** agent on Jalan Raja Don Tomas has a terrible for rude, unhelpful staff and planes that never fly: avoid having to fly out from Maumere outside of the high season. The **Bouraq** main office is pretty useless so you're better off going to their agents PT Garuda on Jalan Sutomo. The manager here owns the *Pantai Wisata* beach hotel, speaks good English and is very helpful.

Toko Harapan Jaya on Jalan Pasar Baru Timur is the best **art and weaving store** in Flores, with piles of dusty blankets and sarongs as well as some carvings and jewellery; if you have a good delve, you may find an occasional antique cloth.

Moving on, Terminal Barat serves all areas to the west and Terminal Lokaria is for eastbound buses. Both of these are a Rp300 bemo ride out of town but most long-distance buses will circle town four or five times before leaving, so you should ask locals' advice before trekking out to the terminals.

Accommodation

Maumere's **hotels** suffered with the rest of the town and are still struggling to rebuild. The out-of-town beachside establishments are without exception the best places to stay, unless of course you are only overnighting and need to head off early the next morning. If you're going east to Larantuka, however, the beach losmen at **Wodong** are on your way.

Bogor II (aka **Lareska Hotel**), opposite the *Bogor 1* on Jl Slamet Riyadi (☎0383/21137). Worlds better than its sister hotel, the sea-facing rooms have huge windows and great panoramas. It's just been refurbished and is sparkling clean and good value. Most rooms have shared mandi. ②.

Hotel Jaya, Jl Hasanuddin (☎0383/21292). Has a decent situation overlooking the seafront. Their basic rooms are pretty dark – the ones with en-suite mandi are much nicer. ③.

Losmen Komodo, Jl Nong Meak (☎0383/21523). The cheapest place in town and therefore usually full. Just a bed and four thin walls for Rp3000 a night. ①.

Hotel Maiwali, Jl Raja Don Tomas (☎0383/21220). Quite a plush place and the economy rooms represent good value for money, but beware midnight wailing from their karaoke lounge. Top rooms have air-con and TV. ③–④.

Permata Sari, Jl Jenderal Sudirman 1 (☎0383/21171). Situated well out of town and difficult to get to, but worth the effort. It has lovely bungalows with perfect Western-style bathrooms which are excellent value, through to rooms with mini-bar, hot water, TV and air-con. ③–⑤.

Hotel Senja Wair Bubuk, Jl Komodor Yos Sudarso (☎0383/21498). Large rooms with or without mandi, with amazingly kitsch decor. ③.

Wini Rai Hotel, Jl Gaja Mada (☎0383/21388). Well out on the road towards Ende, with inexpensive, standard rooms through to overpriced air-con rooms with attached mandi. ③.

THE BEACH

Anyone who has to stay in Maumere for more than one evening would be better off heading out to one of the **beach** areas. Wodong to the west with its black-sand beach is the most popular place to head to, though people who are interested in diving should go to Pantai Waiara 10km west of town, where Maumere's only dive operators are based. Diving costs US$75 at the *Sea World Club* and US$85 at the *Sao Wisata Hotel* for a full day. These prices include two or three dives and food. If you arrive the night before, they'll include a room in the price.

Ankerme Bungalows, on the beach at Wodong. At the time of writing only the restaurant had been built; the food here is far and away the best of the Wodong bunch, with regular, fresh barbecued seafood. ②.

Flores Froggies, near Wodong village on the road to Larantuka, about 28km from Maumere. Has a much nicer beach than the accommodation in the east and three sets of bungalows. It's the oldest place here and a little run-down; the rooms smell a bit damp and musty. ②.

Pantai Wisata, Nogo beach, 20min west of Maumere by public bemo #5 from Pasar Baru (☎0382/21605). Has an average beach, but a picturesque setting with views across the bay to Pulau Besar, with a nearby Bajau village in the foreground. The restaurant needs several hours' notice, but the accommodation is good, cheap and very quiet and relaxing. Touts will meet you off your bus or plane and take you there. ②–③.

Sao Wisata Hotel, Pantai Waiara (☎0383/21555). Both the *Sao Wisata* and *Sea World* serve excellent buffet meals three times a day. Breakfast is US$5, lunch US$8 and dinner US$12. The rooms at the *Sao Wisata* are not quite as upmarket as the prices would suggest, though all have fan and bath. ⑤–⑥.

Sea World Club, Pantai Waiara (☎0383/21570). Slightly cleaner and in better condition than its neighbour the *Sao Wisata*: accommodation ranges from clean bungalows with fan and shower through to rooms with air-con and TV. ④–⑤.

Wodong Bungalows, in Wodong village close to *Flores Froggies*. An excellent, quiet place to stay, offering free canoe, bike and snorkel rental. ②.

Eating

There's not a tremendous amount of choice in town, the usual profusion of cheap **warung**, several of which are centred around the market, selling identical Indonesian fare. All these places vary day by day so it's pointless recommending any – look at the food out front and choose the place with the fewest flies. Notable exceptions are the *Stevani* pub, which is on Jalan Pasar, right by the market, and the *Golden Fish Restaurant* on Jalan Hasanuddin by the waterfront. The former is about the only place between Lombok and Kupang you can get a hamburger, which are pretty tasty. They have a substantial menu, and the atmosphere can get quite raucous when it's busy. The *Golden Fish* serves fish and crustaceans fresh from tanks around the restaurant; lobster for one costs about Rp20,000.

Around Maumere

Twenty kilometres from Maumere on the road back to Ende is **LADALERO** village, based around a Catholic seminary; a bemo from the Ende terminal in Maumere costs Rp400. There's an interesting but jumbled **museum** here, maintained by the priests. It has rare *ikat*, not only from the Sikka district but from all over Flores, as well as excellent picture books (in Indonesian) on the subject, plus a profusion of weapons, pottery, ivory, coins and other bric-a-brac and a collection of small megaliths. There is no admission price but they ask for contributions.

SIKKA, on the opposite coast from Maumere nearly 30km south and slightly east, is the most-visited weaving village in the area. As soon as you walk in, the cry "turis" goes up and women drape *ikat* over every fence and bush for your appraisal. Until you walk down onto the beautiful shaded **beach**, the village seems to be devoid of men, who are relegated to sitting on the sand under the palm trees, repairing their nets and smoking. The vast majority of weaving here are of poor quality, but its possible to discover some gems. Regular bemos here cost Rp1000, and it's about 20km from Ende terminal in Maumere.

One of the most picturesque villages in the region is **WATUBLAPI**, a weaving village with magnificent panoramas to both coasts and the mountains stretching away to Larantuka and the west. A bus or bemo from terminal Lokaria for the twenty-kilometre trip southeast from Maumere costs Rp1000.

About 12km west of Maumere on the coast is **WURING**, a stilted Bugis fishing village, which has recovered remarkably from the devastation of 1992. As with most of these villages, it's a photographers' dream, with mountainous **Pulau Besar** looming in the background. Again, buses leave from Maumere's Ende terminal (Rp500).

Laruntuka

LARANTUKA is the **port** town that serves the Solor and Alor archipelagos and Timor. It's an inoffensive but uninteresting place to spend a night, as you will inevitably have to do. The four-hour drive east from Maumere takes you through some of the most perfect scenery in Flores: tropical forests, punctuated by countless volcanoes and glimpses of the sea. The town itself has an attractive setting, at the foot of the Ile Mandiri volcano, with the bare, green, mountainous islands of Solor and Adonara nestling close by in the bay.

The area from Larantuka out to Pulau Lembata shares a distinct language, Lamaholot (which sounds remarkably like Indonesian spoken with a strong Italian accent), and originally featured identical ritual-based societies. Now, however, Larantuka is one of the most fervently Catholic areas in Indonesia, renowned for its processions at Easter and Christmas. This is largely due to the huge Portuguese presence here that began in the 1500s, when Larantuka was used as a stopover for tradesmen on their routes to and from Timor and the Spice Islands.

Larantuka's Portuguese-style **cathedral**, two blocks back from the port, and the **chapel** which is west of town, are fairly unimpressive in themselves, but on Sundays are worth a visit for the uplifting singing. **Weri beach**, 6km north of town, gets busy at the weekends but is a nice place for a dip. A little way south of this beach the coastline runs so close to Pulau Adonara it seems you could almost swim across.

Practicalities

The main part of Laruntuka is centred alongside the road that runs parallel to the coast. The **harbour** lies roughly in the centre of the town, with a small market around the entrance. The harbour master's office, on the left as you enter the jetty, provides information in Bahasa Indonesia on all services, Pelni ships, ferries, speedboats and irregular cargo ships leaving from Larantuka area. Only the smaller boats leave from this harbour, however; ferries and Pelni ships leave from the pier about 5km south of town. To get there ask for a bemo to Labuhan Besar (Big Harbour).

The BNI **bank** is on the unnamed second road back from and parallel to the sea, heading towards Maumere. Alternatively, the brand-new BRI on Jalan Piere Tandean, around the corner from their more prominent but disused old building and a short walk southeast of the harbour, has fairly good rates (Mon–Fri 8am–2.30pm, Sat 8am–noon). Don't count on being able to change currency anywhere east of here except Kupang.

There is really only one place for Westerners to stay in Laruntuka: *Hotel Rulies* (☎0383/21198; ②), southeast of the pier. If you're arriving from the west ask your bus to drop you off here. It's clean and friendly enough, with shared facilities. The *Hotel Tresna* (☎0383/21072; ③) next door might take you if *Rulies* is full. Several average Padang **warung** line the main road, but by far and away the best place to eat is the *Nirwhana*, opposite *Hotel Sederhana*. It's the only place in town with cold drinks and is relatively inexpensive. The asparagus soup (Rp6500) is delicious.

MOVING ON FROM LARUNTUKA

The **Pelni ship** *KM Tatamilau* calls at Labuhan Besar twice a month, coming from Labuhanbajo, going on to Dili and from there to Irian Jaya. The *KM Siriman* also calls every fortnight, coming from Kupang and going on to Ujung Padang.

Every day, motorboats depart for **Lewoleba** (4hr; Rp4000) on Lembata, leaving at 8am and 2pm, going via **Waiwerang** on Adonara. There are regular boats to **Lamakera** and **Rita Ebang** on Solor, and **Waiwodan** on Adonara, leaving daily at 8am. Once a week on Friday mornings a boat goes direct to the whaling village of **Lamalera** on Lembata, taking eight hours (Rp7500). Ferries to Kupang leave on Mondays and Wednesdays at noon (12hr; Rp15,000).

THE ALOR AND SOLOR ARCHIPELAGO

Clustered at the eastern end of Flores, the five main islands of the **Alor and Solor archipelago** are some of the least-visited places in Indonesia, but often end up the favourite of travellers who take the time and effort to come. Adonara and Solor are the closest islands to Flores: their harsh, rocky terrain is largely deforested and there is no tourist infrastructure. They are also commonly perceived to be less interesting than the spectacular islands further to the east. **Lembata** is the island that receives most visitors – and for good reason. Its volcanoes, forests and beautiful coastlines are supplemented by fascinating indigenous cultures, particularly the unique subsistence **whaling village** of Lamalera on the south coast. Lembata's capital and largest port, Lewoleba, has a fine **market**, and the volcano of **Ile Api** smoulders impressively over the bay.

Next in the chain heading east from Lembata, but closer in proximity and culture to Alor, is the remote island of **Pantar**; there are still places here that have never seen foreigners. It has boundless natural beauty, volcanoes, beaches and spectacular coral gardens.

Alor is as far east as you can go in the Alor Solor archipelago, and is home to extraordinary animist cultures. Along with its neighbour, it has an unexplained proliferation of bronze *moko* drums in the style of the Vietnamese Dongson era, which ended around 300 AD. The islands also have many remote traditional villages, fantastic walking and some of the best **scuba diving** and snorkelling in Indonesia.

All these islands are undeveloped and still not used to Westerners: very little English is spoken, and in some places people barely speak Bahasa Indonesian. The prevalent language in the east is Lamaholot, which has a bouncing inflection and accompanying animated facial and physical expressions. On Pantar and Alor, seclusion and conflict has led to the evolution of no fewer than fifteen different languages and innumerable dialects, some spoken by no more than a few hundred people.

The recorded history of the archipelago is sparse. Chinese traders, ubiquitous in the history of most of eastern Indonesia, only started trading around the coast of Alor just before the turn of the twentieth century. The only historical site of real significance is the **Portuguese fort** on Solor, built with local slave labour under the watchful eye of Portuguese master masons: the structure's strength much impressed the Dutch when they overran it in 1613.

Most people enter the archipelago by **ferry** or **motorboat** from **Larantuka** on the east coast of Flores. From Larantuka you can get to Lembata, Solor and Adonara on relatively short motorboat trips. Getting to Alor is more difficult: there are weekly ferries from Kupang or Atambua in West Timor, and weekly flights from Kupang and Larantuka to Kalabahi in Alor. The only way to reach Pantar is by boat from Kalabahi or Lembata. There is no Western-standard accommodation in the whole of this island group and travel is hard. Be prepared for long, hot journeys, nonexistent timetables and poor food.

Solor and Adonara

Solor and Adonara, the two islands closest to Flores, though accessed by daily motorboats from Larantuka, are difficult to explore, with poor communications and accommodation, but offer plenty of scope for adventure.

Solor

Solor was once the strategic site of a **Portuguese stone fort**, built as a stop-off for trade ships to and from Timor, the remains of which can be seen in the north near **LOHAJONG** village. The walls at least were built to last, and the view is excellent – daily boats from Larantuka leave for here at noon. The place of greatest interest on the island is the whaling village of **Lamakera** on the north coast. The village has less charm than Lamalera on Lembata (see p.676), as it's ferociously poor and the few people that do still hunt do so out of motorboats, much less romantic than the wooden sailing boats of Lembata. You can stay in Lamakera with the kepala desa and go out in the boats if the seas are right. There's a good chance of seeing dolphins but much less chance of seeing whales.

The main town on Solor is **RITA EBANG** on the west coast, only a short motorboat trip from Larantuka. The town is of little interest, with two poor-quality warung and no losmen.

Adonara

Adonara, dominated by the Ile Boleng volcano, is reputedly home to some of the most violent people in Indonesia. In Lamaholot, the local language, *Adonara* means "brother's blood", apparently because of an endless series of feuds and vendettas that have resulted in countless murders and tribal wars on the island. Although Islam and Christianity are the official norm, many villages still have sacred rocks and totems and the ritual life is still thriving. The main town here is **WAIWERANG**, which has a wealth of shiny new mosques and a market on Mondays and Thursdays. The *Ile Boleng Homestay* (②–③), the only decent **accommodation** place in town, is reasonably clean and has good views looking out towards Solor; it's about 200m left out of the harbour. You can also get a sizable (if not especially tasty) meal here. A **warung** near to the harbour sells cheap but poor-quality Padang food.

Lembata

Many people come to **Lembata** (also known as Lomblen) intending on a flying visit and end up missing other parts of their trip to stay longer. It's a captivating place, frustrating to travel around but full of friendly people, beautiful landscapes and intriguing culture. Visitors arrive at the largest town of **Lewoleba** on the west coast, from where there's a weekly boat to the unmissable primitive whaling village of **Lamalera** on the south coast.

LEMBATA'S IKAT

Most of Lembata's legendary *ikat* **cloths** are made on the slopes of Ile Api volcano, from rough, hand-spun thread that becomes softer with age. Generally the designs run horizontally across the base colours of dark brown or strong magenta. Although some of the *ikat* has characters and figures such as whales, horses and elephants, these figures are not as intricate as those from Sumba, and diametric patterns are more common. Traditionally, *ikat* sarongs are a requisite part of dowries, and the prime cloths are passed down through generations, constantly spiralling in value. Genuine antique cloths, which very rarely come to market, might sell for up to US$5000, but usually they are not even seen by Westerners, being of important social significance and irreplaceable.

The island is also the home of one of the most renowned **weaving** traditions in Indonesia. The best cloths are fashioned in the remote villages on the northern coastal slopes of **Ile Api** (Fire Mountain), the volcano that looms over Lewoleba. The cloths are an essential part of "the bride price" used by a young man to secure his partner's hand. Another dowry essential is an elephant tusk – an incredible amount of ivory exists around these few islands – many of which were brought here from Africa hundreds of years ago.

Lewoleba

Despite being the main settlement on Lembata, **LEWOLEBA** is a comatose little place. It's extremely picturesque, sitting on a palm-lined bay under the shadow of the smoking volcano Ile Ape (see opposite). The town comes alive once a week for the Monday **market**; once people used to come from as far away as Timor to sell at the market, and even now they travel from Flores and the surrounding islands. This weekly event has lost a little of its edge – it used to be a regular party, with drinking and games going on until the following morning, but now tends to peter out around midnight.

The village is set a little way back from the bay, with the market as its focal point. On the seafront is a beautiful stilted **Bajo fishing village** and a small **fish market**. About 1km west of town is the harbour, for all boats in and out of Lewoleba and one of the most decrepit bemo terminals in existence. The harbour master's office opposite the port is always shut.

MOVING ON FROM LEMBATA

The fleet of ferries that service this part of the archipelago were retired here after full service on the busy routes around Java and Sumatra had rendered them too old and unreliable to use. The **schedules** change constantly, are next to impossible to find out, and nobody can give you a straight, reliable answer as to when your boat will leave, so it's essential to keep checking the details of departures with as many people of authority as you can, particularly during the rainy season.

Presently, **the ferry to Alor** leaves every three days, at some point between its arrival at Lewoleba in the afternoon and 1am. The ferry then stops for the night in Belauring, which is in the northeast of Lembata, before going on to Wairiang, at the extreme eastern tip and Baranusa on Pantar. It takes six hours from Lewoleba to Belauring (Rp6500) and then ten hours to Alor (Rp9000). The *Diana Express* is a smaller boat that leaves once a week on the same trip, usually leaving on a Wednesday morning from Belauring at 6.30am. A much better option is to find out when the ferry is coming in, and take a bus to Belauring, stay there the night and catch the ferry the next morning. The bus only takes two hours and costs Rp2000. In Belauring, stay at the *Losmen Telaga Jan* (②); it's a grotty place with fish swimming in the mandi and a cornucopia of insects, but they serve incredible Indonesian food.

Practicalities

The **bank** in Lewoleba will not change money in any form. The **post office** south of the market is usually crowded, but efficient, and the Telkom office about 1km west of the market is open 24hr. In theory, **flights** to Kupang and Larantuka leave once a week from the airfield 3km north of town, the *Rejeki* losmen being the agent for **Merpati**. In practice these flights rarely if ever run, and will probably soon be completely discontinued. It's only a short bemo ride to the airport but you're better off chartering a bemo (around Rp5000).

ACCOMMODATION AND EATING

The new **losmen** *Lile Ile* (①), exactly halfway between the harbour and the market on the bay side of the road, is a real gem. It has neat cottages with sensational views of Ile Ape and the nearby Bajo village, and you can eat superb meals with the family. You couldn't ask for a better host than the Dutchman who runs the place; if the locals don't know of the losmen then ask for "Mister Jim's". The losmen *Rejeki* (①–②) is the first building you encounter by the market when you're coming from the harbour. It's the old standby, a decent place that does terrific food: try the *spesial dengan rusa* (deer meat special), which for Rp4500 could easily feed two. The *kentang goreng* is pretty tasty too. Both of these places have mosquito nets, which is a must here as the island is notoriously malarial.

Around Lewoleba

There is a black-sand **beach** about 1km from the harbour in Lewoleba, and a better white-sand one 6km further on: you'll have to walk as there's no real road. Head west, away from the town on the path that hugs the coast.

Near **Lerahinga** village, northeast of town, you'll find excellent **snorkelling**. It's one of the few places on Lembata that has not been destroyed by fish-bombing, lava flows or coral gathering (the locals burn coral to make lime). It's about 18km from Lewoleba; ask for the bemo north to **Hadakewa**, which should go all the way there. Once at Lerahinga, the best coral is a little west of the village.

Ile Ape

While the **Ile Ape** volcano hasn't erupted on a notably violent scale for several decades, it always has at least a puff of smoke lingering around the summit. It seems a strange place to build upon, but is surrounded by **villages**, famed for their ikat weaving, but also worth visiting for the beauty of their situation and the warmth of their welcome.

Generally, a single bemo runs daily to the Ile Api region from Lewoleba, running anti-clockwise round the volcano as far as **Mawa**, the first weaving village of note. It's less than 20km from Lewoleba, but the roads are appalling and it could easily take three hours. Here, if you take some time to meet and speak with the locals, they may show you antique *ikat* cloths worth hundreds of dollars. On market days, trucks run right round to **Atawatuan**, a pretty little fishing village that appears almost Mediterranean. If you abandon the bemo here, you are committing yourself either to staying the night in a village, perhaps with the kepala desa, or making the fourteen-kilometre walk round the volcano to **Waipukang**, where you can pick up transport back to Lewoleba. This walk takes you through little-visited and beautiful villages, where the children will stream out of their classrooms, screaming with delight, and whole villages will empty to follow you.

A very hot trek from Mawa to Waipukang (5hr) leads round the dramatic far side of the volcano: the crater walls have fallen away in ancient lava flows that extend right down into the sea, and the upper slopes are a steaming, yellow, sulphurous wilderness. Make sure you bring lots of water and food as there are no warung and only a couple of kiosks all the way around the volcano. If this walk is too far, then catch the daily bus or truck to **Jontona**, coming round the volcano anticlockwise. About a four-kilometre walk round to the east from Jontona is a ceremonial village that is left derelict all year, except during the *Pesta Kacang* (Bean Festival) which takes place here in October.

If you want to climb Ile Ape, then your best base for the ascent is either **Atawatuan**, **Lamawolo** or **Tokojaeng** village, all of which are on the northeast slopes and are a one- or two-hour walk from Mawa. This is a very tough climb, which takes about five hours up and three hours down. Given that you will have to overnight in one of the villages both the night before and after, it's a three-day trip out of Lewoleba. You should be able to pay a villager a few thousand rupiah to take you to the top.

Lamalera

Even if it wasn't for the spectacular occupation of its menfolk, the village of **LAMALERA**, on the south coast of Lembata, would be well worth a visit. The people are extremely friendly, the surrounding scenery is a stunning sweep of forests and mountains, and to sit

---

THE WHALES OF LAMALERA

A visit to Lembata is not complete without riding out in search of the **whales**. Nature lovers should be warned, though, that this is not a whale-watching pleasure cruise: the people of Lembata are here to kill these magnificent beasts, an event which can be extremely harrowing to watch. Large whales take at least fifteen minutes to die, some much longer, and have been known to tow boats, attached to their harpoons, as far as Timor. Whaling takes place from May to October, never on Sundays as the people are devout Christians. They only go out in the off season if a mark is sighted from the shore or if conditions are favourable.

In the peak year of 1969, the Lamalerans took only 56 sperm whales as well as many manta rays, turtles, dolphins and other rare sea beasts. The World Wildlife Fund has carried out numerous surveys in the village and decided that their occupation has no effect on world whale stocks ,or those of other endangered species such as turtles. As with certain Inuit peoples, the whaling purely serves for the needs of a small community. Lamalera has therefore been declared a protected, subsistence whaling village and is not subject to international whaling charters or limitations.

There are few more unique or exciting experiences to be had than joining the hunt; you will be expected to take up a paddle and pull your weight as you try to overhaul the animal. The harpooner balances precariously on a flimsy platform at the front of the boat until you are within striking distance. Then he hurls the lance, leaping in after it irrespective of which creature he has speared, hoping to put his weight behind the spear and pull off an instant kill. If the animal has survived the first strike, it will reel off a couple of bundles of rope (woven from palm fronds) and drag the boat as the harpooner struggles aboard. Then they will attempt to spear it again, playing it like a game fish until it is too exhausted to fight.

The **outrigger prahus** that are used to hunt the whale are truly extraordinary vessels. Varying from 10m to 12m long and a mere 2m across, the boats are constructed in accordance with ancient statutes; the entire length of the hull is constructed without nails – instead wooden pegs are used and the beams are sealed with pitch. The sails are made from palm fronds, woven into squares and then sewn together into a large rectangular sheet. Before the boats push out at the end of the rainy season, they are blessed by the Catholic priest. The boats are generally manned by middle-aged males because the village youth shun the profession; it seems certain that the traditions will die out with the men that now follow them.

Every part of a captured whale is used by the villagers. Its meat and blubber are shared out amongst the village people according to rights and ancient lore, the boatbuilder and sail-maker both receiving a share. The parts of the whale that cannot be eaten are also used. The spermaceti is burnt as fuel, the bones are used to provide searing-hot fires to forge harpoon heads, and the teeth are carved into rings and necklaces. The only part of the animal that they ever get material compensation for is the penis, sold to Japanese traders who come by every few months to buy them for use in traditional medicines.

in the small shaded square listening to the church choir practise is a remarkably pleasant way to spend time. On Sunday afternoons the entire village turns out for a volleyball match up by the football pitch, slightly west of town: join in and you'll be an instant hero.

However pleasant Lamalera is, it's not the reason travellers come here – they come because the villagers maintain the same dangerous, barely profitable struggle with nature that they have pursued for over two centuries. The people of Lamalera hunt **whales**, not with radar and explosive harpoons but ten-metre wooden outriggers and bamboo-shafted spears (see box below).

Getting to Lamalera can be a real pain. Every Monday night, a boat destined for the village leaves from the market in Lewoleba, returning at 9am on Tuesday morning. This trip takes four hours (Rp4000) and the boat can be seriously crowded. The only other option is to take a bemo part of the way and then walk: the only regular thing about the bemo service is breakdowns. If you are lucky enough to find a truck doing the same route, it's infinitely preferable. A bemo also goes to **Boto**, which is slightly further north, leaving Lewoleba at around 1pm. From Boto, it's a 45-minute walk uphill to Puor, from there it's about a two- or three-hour walk to Lamalera, all downhill, with sensational views but a rough and rocky path.

Practicalities

There are three **accommodation** places in Lamalera, all of comparable quality and all providing three meals a day. The most popular is the *Guru Ben Homestay* (②). It's on top of the promontory that looms over the bay to the west; take the path that leads to your left coming up from the beach and follow it up about 200m. The views of the village and the morning preparations for hunting are superb. Due to the comparable outlook from their lavatory, *Guru Ben*'s has also been affectionately renamed "the poo with a view". The owner is a fluent English speaker and can tell you anything you could ever need to know about Lamalera. If you want to go out in a boat, Ben can arrange it; it's Rp15,000 a day or Rp40,000 if you want to charter their motorboat.

If you come into the village by boat, the nearest accommodation is the *White House* (②). This is the villa-like house with a balcony that overhangs the beach at the eastern end. It has huge beds in three private rooms and good food, but is in close proximity to the place where fish are dried. *Adel Beding* homestay (②) is in the centre of the village, by the shaded square. It is well kept and slightly cheaper than the other two. Wherever you stay in Lamalera, make sure you bring plenty of **mosquito repellent**.

If you can't wait for the boat back from Lamalera to Lewoleba, the only way back to civilization is to go to Boto, a village about three and a half hours' walk north of Lamalera. A bemo leaves from Boto for Lewoleba daily at 10.30am.

Alor and Pantar

Previously only a destination for a trickle of travellers, **Alor** and **Pantar** are gradually being discovered, sought after not only for their fine landscapes and traditional lifestyles but because of the phenomenal richness of the surrounding seas. It's practically impossible to spend a day on the water between the two islands without sighting whales or dolphins, and beneath the surface are some exceptional reefs, walls and slopes. Alor has become much easier to travel in over the last few years but, outside of the main few villages, it is still completely untouched by the tourist invasion. Most areas of the islands are so isolated by their rugged surroundings that at least thirteen independent tribes maintain their own distinct languages. Head-hunting and cannibalism were only officially terminated here in the late 1950s, though some areas are so remote that vestiges of the violent past remained long after.

MOKO

One of the most distinctive things about Alor and Pantar is the mysterious cache of bronze **Dongson-style drums** that have been found here. *Moko* or *nakara* as they are known locally, are a genuinely fascinating anomaly for which no satisfactory explanation has ever been found. Thousands have been dug up from shallow graves in the hard soil, some of them up to 2m in circumference and nearly 1.5m high. They are often beautifully moulded, sometimes with exquisite etchings: good examples can fetch up to Rp50million. The style of the drums is reminiscent of the pre-Christian Dongson culture of North Vietnam, and how they got here in such numbers without getting left in similar supply at sites on the way from Vietnam is unexplained. Alor has never been an especially well-known trading post or stopover for colonial soldiers and missionaries – mainly because of the violent reputation of the islanders. The drums now have particular significance in the bridal dowry: a suitor must provide the family of his intended with a good enough *moko* if he wants to secure her hand in marriage – the drums are sometimes described in terms of how many women they would buy. Probably the best existing example of a *moko* now resides in the East Nusa Tenggara museum in Kupang (see p.685).

Be warned that *moko* are now restricted items under cultural protection by the Indonesian government, and you would need permission from the Ministry of the Interior to buy one and take it out of the country.

Kalabahi

The only large town in the entire island group, **KALABAHI** has a very mellow, friendly atmosphere. It has no sights and a paucity of provision for tourists, but can still be quite a bewitching place: the bay, with its scores of lush islands, is beautiful. Pearl divers make their homes on flimsy bamboo catamarans, huge shoals of fish turn the surface of the waters into regular maelstroms, and swarms of luminous jellyfish fill dusk tides in ghostly invasions. Kalabahi itself is the only place on Alor with losmen, hotels and places to eat and, being the transport hub, is the best place to base yourself if you want to visit the sites of interest around the island.

Practicalities

The town is quite spread out, with the main harbour being fairly central and a good landmark to start from. The town stretches east and inland from here to the market and bus terminal: to the west is the ferry harbour. The **airport** is at Mali about 10km northeast of town, linked by regular buses and taxis with the town.

If you need to change money, the **BNI bank** is the only one in the whole Alor/Solor archipelago you have a chance with. They can usually be convinced to change US dollars cash, but you'll have trouble with anything else. The bank is situated on the side of a small green as you head west from the main port. From there, if you head inland (north), the **post office** is about 200m away on your right (Mon–Sat, 7am–4pm). Another 400m up this road, the red-and-white pylon of the **Telkom** office dominates the skyline. The office is open 24hr a day but there are often big queues. The main **bus terminal** and the Pasar Inpres **market** are to be found about 500m east of town. The market has a decent variety of fruit and vegetables as well as woven baskets, mats and betel-nut holders.

Most buses heading east towards Alor Besar will come through town anyway so there's no point going out to the terminal – just stand by the *Adi Dharma* or the playing field north of the harbour and they should pass. Heading to other destinations, you're best to go to the terminal. You can take a bemo from town for Rp300 or it's a fifteen-minute walk.

ACCOMMODATION

Hotel Adi Dharma, Jl Martadinata 12/26 (☎0397/21280). On the harbourfront, a 100m walk west of the main harbour gates. The most popular place in town, mainly because the owner speaks good English and is a great source of information about the area. There's a choice of singles, doubles and triples with or without fan and mandi. Rooms are very clean but some of the mandi have a flourishing cockroach population. ③.

Hotel Kenari Indah, Jl Diponegro 11 (☎0397/21119). A good Balinese-run place located close to the market. ②.

Hotel Melati, between the *Adi Dharma* and the harbour (☎0397/21075). Recently refurbished, this is a nice clean place with reasonable prices and a choice of fan or air-con. ②.

Hotel Merlina, 3km east of Kalabahi on a hill overlooking the bay (☎0397/21124). With magnificent views and the best accommodation on these islands: air-con and en-suite bathrooms are optional. Take a bemo for Rp300 from in front of the harbour gates. ④.

Hotel Pelangi Indah, Jl Diponegoro 100 (☎0397/21251). This hotel near the market purports to have all mod cons including hot water and air-con, but at the moment none of these things work. ③–④.

EATING

The best place to eat in Kalabahi is the group of **food stalls** which set up at night east of the bank. They serve excellent sate at Rp1000 for ten sticks, as well as various soups, fried rice and noodles and many other old favourites. The unnamed rumah makan on the harbour side of the *Adi Dharma* does Indonesian staples and can provide *nasi*

UNDERWATER ALOR

Only very recently has the **subaqua** potential of Alor and Pantar been recognized. Alor has a rare combination of factors that combine to create a diver's paradise. The straits between the two islands are swept with cold, nutrient-saturated waters, which bring food in for the little fish who are in turn prey for those higher up the food chain.

The one site that is earning Alor an international reputation amongst sport divers is **The Dream**: a coral-covered rocky outcrop that comes metres from the surface in the deep Pantar Strait. When the current gusts over this site at between two and four knots, the show can be quite overwhelming. Dog-tooth and skipjack tuna, Spanish mackerel, groupers and enormous wrasse glide amongst sharks, turtles and rays, and centimetres from your face.

The seas around Alor and Pantar are fairly clear: although you'll rarely get over 20m visibility, there are so many fish so close that you don't need more. In Alor Bay coming in to Kalabahi there are regular, massive and spectacular swarms of jellyfish, a sight that is utterly extraordinary on a night dive.

At the moment there is no dive operation actually on Alor, but Pitoby Watersports (☎0380/21154) run regular trips from Kupang. If you are on Alor and a certified diver, Donovan the dive master can often arrange trips for a day or more and can be contacted through the *Adi Dharma* or *Marlina* hotels. Figure on US$85 for three dives with all your equipment and food.

---

bungkus (Rp1000) to take away, along with chicken, eggs and pretty much anything else you want. The only place in town for quality food is the *Rumah Makan Tanjung*, opposite the food stalls. They serve cold beer and a few lame Indonesian dishes as well as fried potatoes. However, if you give them a day's notice, they can serve up grilled fish, lobster, chicken or whatever else you fancy. They are only open after 6pm so you might have to order the night before.

Around Alor

Close to Kalabahi is the village of **TAKPALA**, which has maintained its traditional houses and practices, mainly it seems because of the cruise-ship tour groups who come here to see dancing and singing. The invasion is usually on Monday mornings if you fancy a free show. Ask for a bemo to Takpala from Kalabahi's Inpres market, and you'll have to walk about 1km from where they drop you to get to the village. Another village that is just a bemo ride away and has thatched-roof houses is **Monbang**, about 3km east of town. *Monbang* means "snake village" and legend has it that a huge foreigner-eating serpent lives here. From Monbang you could walk the extra 1km north to **Otvai**, which is also close to Kalabahi and has staggering views over the bay, as well as many traditional houses.

East of Kalabahi and on the northern coast lies **Mali beach**. It has a good stretch of white sand and is very picturesque, but the coral here does not live up to its reputation. It's a ten-kilometre bus ride from Kalabahi bus terminal (Rp500). If snorkelling is your sport of choice, then you'd be better off heading around the northern coast of Kalabahi Bay. The first place of note on this road is **Alor Kecil**. Here they have a rather poor showcase traditional house (it has a big sign saying "traditional house" outside) and a couple of exceptional *moko* drums. The *kepala sekola* (schoolmaster) has a collection of five or six small drums, but the best are kept in a clearing inland. You will need to speak to the kepala desa and pay him about Rp5000 to get to see these amazing objects. The beach in front of the village is covered with sharp stones and broken coral and is not much good. However, if you take a boat to **Pulau Kepa** (bargain hard, and it should be about Rp1000), directly across the bay, the **snorkelling** is fantastic. Visibility is excellent and there are lots of big fish out by the northward cape and off a cove on the western side. The waters here are well-known for running so cold that they occasionally stun fish, bringing them floating to the surface; be wary of the strong currents.

Continuing round the coast, the next settlement is **Alor Besar**. The village is again very picturesque and the kepala desa keeps a good collection of drums; betel nut or cigarettes are a good exchange for a look. The snorkelling off the coast here is also good but is better at **Sebanjar**, another 3–4km north. About 100m off shore is a drop-off that runs parallel to the beach for about 1km. The currents are strong, so if you get in from the end of the beach furthest from Alor Besar, then you can just drift down the reef's entire length. The coral is spectacular and there are stacks of beautiful coloured fish. Buses run all the way round to Sebanjar from Kalabahi, but be careful when coming back: buses become very irregular in the afternoon and stop at about 3pm.

If you're looking for a bit of a trek but would like to know that you'll have somewhere to stay, then take the trek inland to **ATIMELANG**, the village that hosted one of the first Western anthropologists on Alor. Cora Dubois's *The People of Alor* was based on her experiences here in the 1930s, and much of the village is still recognizable from her descriptions. The village is an arduous but rewarding uphill **trek**, about a five-hour walk from Takpala. If you speak good Indonesian, you can make the trip alone, just asking for directions on the way. If you don't, it would be best to ask at the *Adi Dharma* losmen in Kalabahi, to see if they can put you in touch with a guide. Once in Atimelang, the friendly *kepala desa* has a reasonably comfortable room where you can stay and eat.

The best place to see Alor's own brand of **ikat** being made is on the islands of **Ternate** and **Buaya**, situated just outside Kalabahi Bay. There's also good snorkelling around these two islands and it's best to rent a motorboat for a whole day in Kalabahi: a charter will cost around US$60. *Buaya*, which means "crocodile" in Indonesian, was once populated with a huge population of fearsome saltwater crocodiles; they used to wander into Kalabahi and stroll into the market. However, during World War II the Japanese had a base on Buaya and ate the creatures. The *ikat* made on these two islands is actually quite similar to the more famous stuff being made on Lembata, but is much cheaper.

MOVING ON FROM ALOR

Ferries out of Alor depart from the western jetty, and other boats from the main harbour in the middle of town, heading to **Kupang** on Timor, **Atapupu** in West Timor, **Larantuka** and **Belauring** on Lembata, stopping off at **Baranusa** on Pantar. Once every fortnight, the Pelni ferry *KM Awu* leaves from Kalabahi, travelling alternately to Dili and Kupang. This is a far superior option in terms of comfort and time to the other ferry, and it's well worth checking at the Pelni office, slightly east of the main harbour on the road nearest the water.

There is also one Merpati **flight** weekly to Kupang; charter a bemo to the airport (Rp5000). All schedules for all modes of transport are subject to sudden and unreasonable change.

Pantar

Pantar lies between Alor and Lembata, and remains one of the least-visited paradises in Indonesia. The adventurous traveller should note that this is only because it is difficult to get to and is such an unknown quantity, definitely not because it lacks interest. There are areas on Pantar where TV, electricity and foreigners are still mysterious unknowns and where traditional life has continued unaltered for centuries. **Ferries** leave from Kalabahi on Alor to Pantar every two days (4hr; Rp5000), and ferries from Belauring on Lembata will usually stop here on their way to Alor.

The main docking point in Pantar is **BARANUSA**, a small village in a cove at the centre of the north-facing coast. It's a good place to base yourself: the kepala desa has a four-room homestay here and can provide you with basic meals, and you'll definitely be the centre of attention. From February to April there are wedding and harvest festivals here with dancing, feasting and music made with *moko* drums, gongs and bells.

From Baranusa, take one of the daily trucks to **KAKAMAUTA**, about 15km inland and on the slopes of **Gunung Situng**, an active volcano. The kepala desa here rents out a room and can provide food but, as with everywhere in Pantar, it's always best to bring your own water; they may have boiled water, but you can't count on it and it's often in very short supply. The village sits at nearly 1000m and you will be glad of your sleeping bag. From Kakamuata, you can **climb the volcano** – it only takes just over an hour to the rim, and the view of the colossal crater is spectacular. Try and get here early as the clouds may soon roll in and obscure the view. Local kids will gladly get up early to guide you, for a few thousand rupiah. The truck heading back to Baranusa generally passes through Kakamuata mid-afternoon.

Another fantastic trip from Baranusa is to the south coast. A track runs across the island through Latuna to **Puntaru**, where the beach is covered in multicoloured sand and pebbles: trucks run the entire way every day. At **Kabir** on the northwest coast, Pantar's largest village and district capital, hot springs burst up from beneath the seabed. Here you can enjoy the unusual experience of snorkelling in hot water, and the beach and coral gardens are pretty good. If you are looking for a real **snorkelling** extravaganza, rent one of the sampans that are dotted around the harbours of Baranusa and Kabir for a safari, and head out around the coast or to the islands offshore: figure on between US$10 and US$20 a day. You will of course need your own snorkelling equipment.

TIMOR

Timor sits at the extreme eastern end of the **Sunda Islands**, a chain that has its beginnings in Pulau Weh off the north coast of Sumatra and terminates just above East Timor. Unlike the vast majority of islands in this sequence, Timor is not volcanic. Nevertheless, it has an extremely mountainous backbone, its highest peak being **Tatamailau** in East Timor.

Timor's biggest natural asset was and, to a much lesser extent still is, **sandalwood**: a richly fragrant timber that has been much prized as a commodity by both European and Asian traders for centuries. The overfelling of sandalwood trees has led to minor ecological disasters, with wholesale topsoil erosion of land that was already poor, without the saving enrichment of volcanic ash. This has left great swaths of the landscape barren.

The two main cities of Timor are **Kupang** in the west and **Dili** in the east. Kupang is a sweaty, noisy maelstrom with everything that's unpalatable in Asian cities alongside the best restaurants and hotels for hundreds of kilometres. Dili could not be more different, a soulless showpiece town vaguely modelled on a Mediterranean port. The streets are broad, sparkling and sterile, filled with awful concrete-and-plaster statues dedicated to proving the patriotism of the populace.

From Kupang, most travellers head north to **Camplong** and then **Soe**, both hill towns with cool climates, fine *ikat* weavings and a few springs and waterfalls. Close to Soe is the tiny kingdom of **Boti**, a place that maintains ancient traditions and the distinctive "beehive"-style houses of the area. From either of the two towns, you can make numerous other day-trips to colourful markets, secluded tribal villages and scenic areas high in the mountains. Further north is **Kefamenanu**, also a centre of *ikat* weaving and the base for another excursion into tribal Timor in the village of **Tamkessi**. From here you can head up to the coast for a side-trip to **Oekussi**, an enclave of East Timor that managed to escape the majority of the province's troubles and remains a beautiful

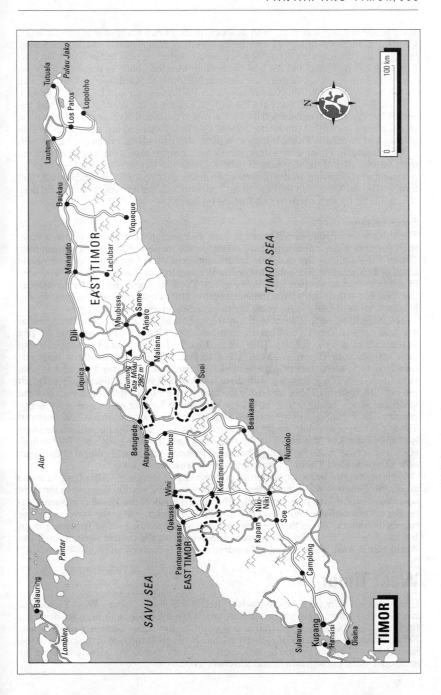

place to spend a few lazy days, with beaches, markets and traditional villages aplenty. Continuing north will bring you into the main body of East Timor. Travellers no longer require travel documents or complicated passes to enter the troubled province but travel here is still restricted and it's best to check in with the police as regularly as possible. In the hills south of Dili there are pleasant hill towns at **Maubisse** and **Ainaro**, and as you head north from Dili, you will encounter Portuguese forts in **Laga** and **Lautem**.

While the main highway that runs from Dili to Kupang is an excellent sealed road, traversed by regular, well-maintained buses, the rest of the island is crisscrossed with poor, disintegrating tracks that can be impassable after heavy rain and are susceptible to subsidence and landslides. Public transport is poor, with irregular services and tatty buses.

The **climate** in Timor differs dramatically from nearby islands such as Flores. In the most intense part of the dry season between June and October, the land is swept by monsoon winds blowing off the deserts of Australia and becomes unbearably dusty and ferociously hot. Along with Roti and Savu, Timor not only suffers oppressively arid periods, but is far enough south to risk tropical cyclones.

Some history

The indigenous inhabitants of Timor can trace their ancestry back nearly fourteen thousand years, to when a people perhaps related to the modern Atoni tribes roamed over Timor. The Atoni now live mainly in the mountains of West Timor and compose nearly a half of its population. The other major ethnic group in Timor are the Tetum, who originated from migrant peoples from Sulawesi and Flores and probably started to squeeze the Atoni out of their lands from the fourteenth century onwards. Now the Tetum mainly inhabit areas of East Timor, being the most significant ethnic group there.

The majority of early visitors to Timor were lured by the sandalwood stands that at one time covered Timor's now barren mountainsides. First the **Chinese** came as early as the sixth or seventh century. They set the tone for future visitors by supplementing their cargoes with Timorese slaves. The Europeans didn't arrive until the early sixteenth century, when the Portuguese used their garrisons on Flores and Solor to base expeditions into Timor, bringing with them smallpox and venereal diseases. The Dutch too were interested in Timor and made tentative forays into the interior in search of the wood and slaves, finally setting up a large garrison in Kupang in the mid-seventeenth century. The Portuguese never acceded their interests in the area, and in 1702 declared Timor a Portuguese colony under the control of Goa, though this declaration was fairly cosmetic and had little effect on the rule of ascendant native kingdoms. By the mid-eighteenth century, the Portuguese had been pushed east and had control of the areas now known as **East Timor**, including the small province of Oekussi.

While European influence in terms of religion and language took effect in some areas, the Timorese had earned their reputation as being sturdy, aggressive warriors who didn't succumb to pressure easily. The central areas of the island remained independent of colonialism, some of them only falling to foreign rule in the early part of the twentieth century. While the western part of Timor became part of Indonesia upon Independence in 1945, the east remained under Portugal's control right up until the World War II. East Timor's troubled modern history is covered on pp.694–696.

West Timor

Even though it is by far the most-travelled half of this divided island, **West Timor** still has vast areas where Western visitors are rare. While the landscapes here are desolate, they can also be starkly beautiful, especially in the mountains around Soe and Kefamenanau. Isolated tribal kingdoms such as **Boti** and **Tamkessi** in the centre of the island have maintained unique houses, costumes, festivals and lifestyles, fascinating for anthropologists, photographers and travellers alike.

TIMORESE CRAFTS

The best place for buying West Timorese **crafts** is in the central regions of Soe and Kefamenanau, where **ikat** and **carving** traditions are still thriving. Macabre **masks** and other primitive carvings are made from rosewood, sandalwood and mahogany. Some of the tribal peoples still hunt with blowpipes and boomerangs, rarely decorative but still good souvenirs. The most impressive of Timorese crafts are the *ikat* **fabrics** produced in the central highlands. These cloths are unusually bright, notable for the vibrant reds used as a background colour.

The *sasando* is a many-stringed **musical instrument**, most often associated with Roti but also to be found on Timor. Some have as many as 34 strings and the body is generally woven from firm *lontar* palm leaves. Another oddity that originates on Roti is the *Ti'i langga*, a bizarre cowboy-style **hat**, also woven from *lontar* leaves, that is usually adorned with a pinnacle that points heavenwards. This allows the celestial spirits a direct route to the brain, a kind of divine antenna. They are often ornamented with plastic flowers and coloured ribbons, which can look seriously incongruous on a gnarled Rotinese labourer.

Kupang and around

The dusty and chaotic streets of **KUPANG**, east Nusa Tenggara's biggest city, are a mixture of torment and relief for the average traveller. Most would praise the city's facilities and food compared to those of neighbouring islands, but the pace, noise and grime can be trying, to say the least; your seat on a typical Kupang bemo is likely to be an immense speaker with the bass turned up to full volume. However, once you've left the smog and the noise, you will probably miss the famous seafood of the *Palembang* and the chance for a few friendly drinks with the host of travellers for whom Kupang is a major hub.

The city has enjoyed a sizable influx of tourists recently, mainly those taking advantage of the quick, twice-weekly Merpati flight from Darwin in Australia to Kupang. The ferry service on the same route has been promised for a good ten years, and if it ever takes off Kupang will be even more full of backpackers.

One of the only real sights in town is the **Museum of Nusa Tenggara Timur** (daily 8am–4pm; donation) out by the bus terminal. It has an excellent collection of *ikat* from the area and a few other artefacts such as a *moko* drum from Alor and comparative drawings of all the area's traditional houses and megaliths. An easy escape from the city itself is the **natural swimming pool** 1km south of town; many travellers choose to stay in one of the nearby losmen.

Kupang's recorded history dates back to the seventeenth and eighteenth centuries, when the Dutch East India Company were active in the area. Their interest petered out once the stands of sandalwood around the city were all felled, and it was all but deserted until the beginning of the twentieth century, when missionaries began to use it as a base for expeditions into central Timor. Kupang has an additional footnote in history as the place where a haggard Captain Bligh finally ran ashore in 1789, having sailed nearly 6000km in an open boat, following the legendary mutiny on the HMS *Bounty*.

Practicalities

The **Oebolo bus terminal** services all major destinations outside of Kupang, and is the place you are most likely to arrive at. It's about 6km east of town in **Walikota** and swarms of bemos wait there to ferry passengers to the centre of town. The **El Tari Airport** is another 10km to the east; the most convenient way to get into town from here is by one of the many taxis that wait at the terminal. Alternatively, walk out to the main road and flag down a passing bemo. All bemos eventually end up at **Terminal Kota**, a bemo stand/square surrounded by shops right by the waterfront, at the heart of Kupang city.

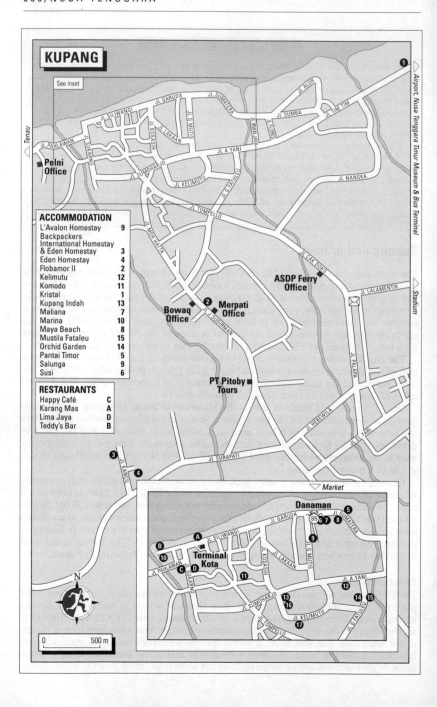

KUPANG

See Inset

Tenau

Pelni Office

JL PAHLAWAN
JL SILIWANGI
JL GARUDA
JL SUMATERA
JL ATOR
JL SUMBA
JL TIM TIM
JL FLORES
JL IRIAN JAYA
JL G MUTIS
JL LAKAAN
JL KOSASIH
JL SUKARNO
JL SUMOHARJO
JL A YANI
JL KELIMUTU
JL S FATULEU
JL NANGKA
JL TOMPELLO
JL MOH HATA
JL CAK DOKO
JL LALAMENTIK
JL PALAPA
JL HEBEWILA
JL EL TARI
JL SURAPATI
JL KANCIL

Airport, Nusa Tenggara Timur Museum & Bus Terminal

Stadium

ACCOMMODATION

L'Avalon Homestay	9
Backpackers International Homestay & Eden Homestay	3
Eden Homestay	4
Flobamor II	2
Kelimutu	12
Komodo	11
Kristal	1
Kupang Indah	13
Maliana	7
Marina	10
Maya Beach	8
Mustila Fataleu	15
Orchid Garden	14
Pantai Timor	5
Salunga	9
Susi	6

RESTAURANTS

Happy Café	C
Karang Mas	A
Lima Jaya	D
Teddy's Bar	B

ASDP Ferry Office

Bowaq Office

Merpati Office

JL SUDIRMAN

PT Pitoby Tours

Market

Danaman

Terminal Kota

N

0   500 m

Kupang is a sizable city and getting around involves endless use of the **bemos** (around town Rp400). It's best to ask a local for the bemo you will need as the system is complex and the numbers change all the time. At the time of writing, however, a few useful bemos were the #3 to the natural swimming pool, *Eden* and *Backpackers* losmen; the #15 (Baumata) for the airport; #24 for the Pasar Impres; and #5 and #6 to Oebolo bus terminal. Many out-of-town bemos now display destination names rather than numbers.

There are two tourist offices in Kupang. Both are usually out of relevant maps, brochures and, being way out of town, are not worth the effort; better information is available at the travellers' losmen.

Of the **banks**, the Danamon on Jalan Sumatera is very efficient for credit-card transactions and advances, while the nearby BNI and the Bank Dagang Negara on Jalan Jenderal Achmad Yani have better exchange rates for travellers' cheques. The main **post office** is quite a way out of town, on Jalan Palapa (Mon–Sat 7am–4pm); take a #3 or #11 bemo from Terminal Kota. The **ferry office** is close by: just head back towards town and you'll find it at Jalan Cak Doko 20. They have timetables here for all the ferries in Nusa Tenggara and can be relied on at least for the regular routes.

For boats out of **Tenau harbour**, to be found 10km to the west of Kupang, head to the **Pelni office** at Jalan Pahlawan 3. They have no English-speakers but their timetables are self-explanatory and comprehensive; the office can be found to the west of the Terminal Kota: head over the river bridge and up the following hill and it's on your left-hand side. If you are thinking about taking any **tours** around Nusa Tenggara or have problems with getting to Australia, then the best operator is Pitoby Tours and Travel Services on Jalan Jenderal Sudirman (☎0380/31044); they can organize scuba-diving tours, island-hopping, and are an agent for all the airlines flying out of Kupang.

ACCOMMODATION

Kupang is unique on Timor for the amount and variety of **accommodation** available.

Backpackers International Homestay, slightly out of town on Jl Kencil, by a large swimming pool filled with natural spring water; take bemo #3 from Terminal Kota. They offer cleanish dormitory rooms, a banana pancake or fruit-salad breakfast, and guided tours and information for their guests. ①–②.

Eden Homestay, on Jl Kencil, out of town by the natural swimming pool (☎0380/21931). Dormitories, bungalows and rooms available at reasonable rates. ①–②.

Hotel Flobamor II, Jl Sudirman 21 (☎0380/33476). Houses a dive centre and the main Merpati office. The top rooms have air-con, hot water, a mini-bar, ice machine and TV, but all in slightly crumbling rooms. ⑥–⑦.

Hotel Kristal, Jl Tim Tim 59 (☎0380/25100 fax 25104). This is the most expensive hotel around but they offer discounts during the off season. Luxuries include a large swimming pool, TV and air-con. ⑧–⑨.

L'Avalon Homestay, off Jl Sumatera and near the Danamon bank (☎0380/32278). The current backpackers' favourite. They have excellent information and the staff are real characters. Dormitory-style rooms with outside mandi are Rp4000 per person, and there are several double rooms. ①–②.

Hotel Maliana, Jl Sumatera 35 (☎0380/21879) Simple and clean: the more expensive rooms are better value, with air-con and en-suite mandi. ③–④.

Hotel Marina, Jl Jenderal Achmad Yani 72 (☎22566). Lovely and clean with delightful staff, the airy and sizable top rooms are especially good value. ③.

Hotel Maya, Jl Sumatera 31 (☎0380/32169). Quite plush for the price: has a good restaurant and all the rooms feature air-con and bathtubs. The most expensive rooms also have TV and hot water. ④.

Hotel Mustila Fataleu, Jl Gunung Fateleu 1 (☎0380/24516). Right next to the *Orchid Garden*. A bit dark and basic, but inexpensive and acceptable if everywhere else is full. ②–③.

Hotel Orchid Garden, Jl Gunung Fateleu 2 (☎0380/33707, fax 25707). The most upmarket place in town, with prices to match. It has beautiful cottages around a sculpted pool, with a tame deer that wanders into the rooms. Non-residents can use the pool for Rp15,000 per day. ⑧–⑨.

Pantai Timor, Jl Sumatera (☎0380/31651). A bit of a letdown: it looks great from the outside, but the rooms are overpriced and smell a little musty. Has a reasonable restaurant. ③.

Hotel Salunga, Jl Kakatua 20 (☎0380/21510). Mainly used by Indonesian tourists, the clean rooms and inside areas belie the tatty exterior, making it not a bad option. ③.

Hotel Susi, Jl Sumatera 37 (☎0380/22172). A lovely place, clean and quiet with pleasant communal areas and good-value economy rooms; the more expensive rooms have air-con and TV. ②–③.

EATING AND DRINKING

Kupang is one of the few places east of Lombok that you can get a real diversity of food. Plenty of **night warung** are scattered throughout the city, the largest concentration being around Terminal Kota.

Happy Cafe, Jl Ikan Paus 3. An old favourite of Kupang travellers, serving Chinese and Indonesian fare.

Intan Bakery, Jl Ikan Paus. Has a mixture of sweet bread, strangely coloured cakes and unusual pastries.

Karang Mas, Jl Siliwangi 88. Seafood and basic Indonesian dishes, perhaps a touch more expensive than you'll be used to paying; the seafront balcony is a bonus.

Lima Jaya, Jl Sukarno Hatta 15. Chinese and Indonesian food, and popular with locals for the nightclub upstairs.

Nelayan, Jl Mohammed Hatta, on the right-hand side of the road heading south from the centre of town. Not as crowded as its better-known neighbour the *Palembang*, and the meals are almost as good. Expect to pay around Rp15,000 for a full meal with several different dishes for your main course; they serve an endless variety of seafood. Open daily from about 6pm.

Palembang, Jl Mohammed Hatta 54. A terrific option: the king prawns in chilli are excellent; the lobster and grilled fish, quite superb. Everything is cooked at night on woks and barbecues right out by the pavement, the frantic bustle and flames of the open kitchen giving the place a frenetic and informal feel.

Savu Fried Chicken, Jl Mohammed Hatta, a small bamboo hut on the left-hand side of the road, heading south and before you reach the *Nelayan*. One of the healthiest chunks of chicken you will find for hundreds of kilometres, deep-fried in a variety of coatings, most costing around Rp8000. They have satellite TV.

Teddy's Bar, on the seafront at the western end of the centre. Serves burgers, pizzas and other Western fare. This is the expat hangout of Kupang, overpriced but a reasonable spot for a cold beer: they have lots of expensive imported brews. It's a good place to make contacts if you're looking to work your passage on a yacht.

Around Kupang

There are several reasonable **beaches** around Kupang: **Tablalong** is 15km west of town, clean and a better place for a swim than the more popular and closer **Lasiana beach**. To get to Tablalong, take bemo #3 to the Tabus terminal and Bemo Tablalong goes all the way there. Both beaches will be busy at the weekends. The best beaches are on the islands that sit just off Timor's western shore. **Monkey Island** has some excellent snorkelling and pristine beaches, but you'll have to charter a boat to get there which, at around US$60 for a day, should at least assure that you have the beach to yourself. **Pulau Semau** on the other hand has regular public boats departing daily: they leave whenever there are enough passengers from Tenau harbour and cost Rp5000. There is a delightful **natural spring** on the island, no cars or blaring bemos and, should you decide you feel like staying, *Teddy's Bar* have a set of bungalows (⑤), with three meals a day included. The losmen *L'Avalon* is planning to build cheaper bungalows here. The beaches on Semau are also well worth the trip. *L'Avalon*, *Backpackers*, *Eden*, *Teddy's Bar* and *Hotel Flobamor* all organize tours to these islands, which are relatively well priced and good if you fancy some company for your beachcombing.

There is a beautiful **waterfall** at **Oenesu** with two steps; one of about 15m, the other of about 7m. Reasonable Tarzan impressions can be achieved jumping from the top, but beware of the slippery banks when climbing up. It's a great place to escape the Kupang sweat: take bemo#3 to the Tabus terminal and then Bemo Oenesu. Out by Bolok Harbour, where the ferries arrive, 13km west of town, is an **underground cavern** with crystal-clear freshwater springs. It's a little creepy swimming in the pitch darkness; best bring a torch. Take the Bolok bemo and get off as it makes the final right turn down towards the port. Local kids always seem to be waiting to guide you down to the caves for a few hundred rupiah.

There's a growing crowd of young enthusiastic guides willing to take tourists to "recreation spots" near to Kupang. One popular site is the village of **Bone**, south of Kupang. It's an extremely friendly place, with a few *rumah adat*, and the people put on dances for tourists. From the village, your guide will take you the 5km to a waterfall, which is good for swimming.

Desa Oebelo, about 20km east of Kupang, is the home of a cottage industry, where the Rotinese *sasando* and *Ti'i Langga* are made (see p.685): the instrument made is excellent, if slightly fragile. About 50km north of Kupang is **CAMPLONG**. Most buses on the main Dili–Kupang road stop here, but it's worth staying a night to have a look at the surrounding area. There's one losmen here, run by the local convent, the *Oemat Honis*, which provides three meals (②). There are also a few warung around but the convent is the best place to eat if you're staying. Camplong's attractions include a natural swimming hole, a small forest called the **Taman Wisata Camplong** and a few caves. The nearby hills are a cool and scenic place to walk.

Soe and around

Once a Dutch hill station, **SOE**, 110km north of Kupang, is now a thriving town with many attractive villages in the surrounding hills. The town was taken over by the Dutch during a brutal campaign of "pacification" at the turn of the century. People come from kilometres around to the **market**, to sell everything from *ikat* to betel-nut and herbal medicines.

The most distinctive feature of the villages around Soe district is the beehive-style **traditional houses** or *lopo*. Most of these will also have another structure in front of the main house without walls, its thatched roof supported on carved pillars. This serves as a meeting place and site for the women of the family to do their daytime chores, shaded from the sun but with the benefit of the breeze. The Indonesian government actually banned *lopo* houses, because they considered them unhealthy, and, certainly if you ever have the chance to go inside one, the acrid, smoky interior feels decidedly noxious. The people of Soe, however, prefer them to their new cold, concrete abodes, and generally still build *lopo* – ostensibly for use as stores. If you're intending to visit the villages, the best way to get around outside of town is by motorbike: ask around at any of the losmen or hotels.

Practicalities

The **town** itself is fairly compact: Jalan Diponegoro is the main street, and features a Western-style supermarket, three souvenir shops, a wartel, and tourist office (open whenever they feel like it). In town, the **bemo** system is very efficient, most bemos doing a round-trip to the market and then to the out-of-town **bus station**, which lies to the west of town.

Be warned that the **BNI bank** on Jalan Diponegoro will only change US dollars cash. The **souvenir shop** next door to the *Losmen Bahagia*, has some excellent *ikat* and some of the few genuine antique masks you will find in Timor. Starting prices are very high, but if you are prepared for lengthy bargaining it's possible to get half the asking price. **Eating** out in Soe is rarely exciting. The Padang restaurant almost opposite the *Hotel Bahagia* does an excellent, fiery chicken curry, and the four rumah makan around the market dish up reasonable sate and other Indonesian staples. *Rumah Makan Suka Jadi* on Jalan Suharto serves a very limited menu of Javanese food.

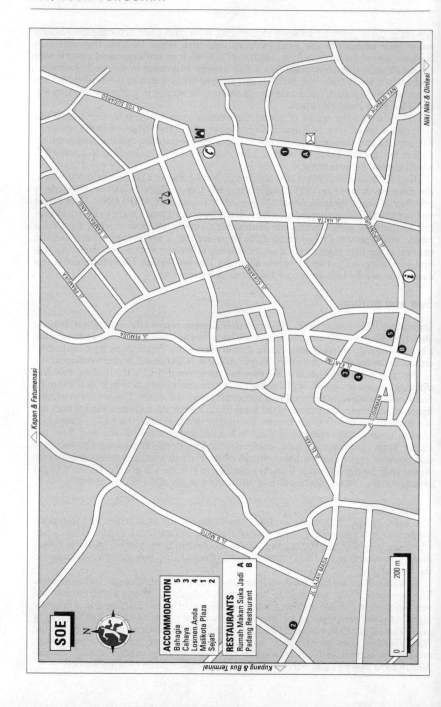

Niki Niki & Oinlasi ▷

◁ Kapan & Fatumenasi

◁ Kupang & Bus Terminal

SOE

N

ACCOMMODATION
Bahagia 5
Cahaya 3
Losmen Anda 4
Malikota Plaza 1
Sejati 2

RESTAURANTS
Rumah Makan Suka Jadi A
Padang Restaurant B

200 m
0

JL YOS SUDARSO
JL ACHMAD YANI
JL HATTA
JL DIPONEGORO
JL SAMAN GUMANG
JL PRAMUKA
JL PEMUDA
JL SUKARNO
JL KARTINI
JL SUDIRMAN
JL EL TARI
JL G MUTIS
JL GAJAH MADA

ACCOMMODATION

Most buses into Soe will drop you off on Jalan Diponegro, within walking distance of the majority of **accommodation** places.

Losmen Anda, Jl Kartini 5 (☎0391/21323). The budget-travellers' favourite in Soe. The owner, Pak Yohannes, is a rare character who speaks five languages and has a seemingly infinite supply of information and stories. The losmen itself is a kitsch masterpiece that has to be seen to be believed: Yohannes has filled the whole of the backyard with extra accommodation in the shape of a ferry and a battleship, complete with bunks, portholes and steering wheels. ②–③.

Losmen Bahagia, Jl Diponegoro 72 (☎0391/21015). A little pricey, though quite clean and with a reasonable restaurant. ③–⑤.

Bahagia II, about 2km from central Soe on the road to Kupang (☎0391/21095). Reasonably plush and with slightly unnecessary air-con (Soe is cool at nights) in all the rooms. ⑤–⑥.

Cahaya, Jl Kartini next door to the *Anda* (☎0391/21087). The *Losmen Cahaya* will usually steer you back next door as they prefer Indonesian guests, but it's a reasonable place with a choice of shared or en-suite mandi. ②.

Mahkota Plaza, Jl Suharto 11 (☎0391/21068). Opposite the disused bus terminal. It's often closed during the low season but has good clean rooms with en-suite mandi. ③–④.

Around Soe

The village of **NIKI-NIKI** is an hour's drive out of Soe on the road east to Kefamenanau; its bustling **Wednesday market** is one of the best in Timor, alive with wild produce and friendly faces. Niki-Niki was ruled by a rajah until 1912, when the Dutch conquered his kingdom. The old rajah had a reputation as a brutal tyrant who used to butcher his enemies publicly and display parts of their bodies on poles around the village. The **royal graves** are behind the old rajah's house and worth a look. There are a couple of reasonable **warung** in Niki-Niki, but no losmen.

About 8km north of Soe, **Oehala** is the site of a set of **waterfalls**, well shaded and with many pools that you can bathe (but not quite swim) in. It's a nice spot, popular with locals at the weekends, when there are direct bemos all the way down to the falls. At other times you will have to catch a bus or bemo from Soe market to Kapan and ask the driver to drop you off at the Oehala turn-off. From here it's a downhill stroll of about 45 minutes to the falls.

Directly north of Soe, **KAPAN** is another of the many towns in this area whose greatest asset is its **market**. The market here is on a Thursday and the place really comes alive, with colourful cloths, carved betel-nut holders and the usual blend of fruit and vegetables being sold. The drive up here is also very scenic, along one of the few asphalt roads in Timor off the main highway. A ninety-minute walk past Kapan is the fascinating village of **Tunua**: head towards Fatumenasi from Kapan and then take the right turn by the first settlement you come to. Near to Tunua is a huge **obelisk**, split neatly down the middle, covered with plants and topped with magical musical stones. There are several important **ritual sites** in the area that an English-speaking guide might be able to help you get to (few of the locals even speak Indonesian, so you'd have difficulty on your own). Quite a few travellers who want to really see this area in depth bring one of the young guides all the way from Kupang.

The surrounding countryside from Kapan north to **FATUMENASI** is seriously imposing, but even though it's quite green by Timor's standards there's little or no water, settlements are few and far between, and it gets ferociously hot. Fatumenasi is elevated well above sea level among the most inhospitable of mountains and gets few visitors, though it's cool at nights and a quiet friendly place to see how the majority of Timorese people live. You can stay here with the kepala desa but there are no losmen or warung. The road to Fatumenasi offers spectacular views of **Gunung Mutis**, which towers to 2470m.

BOTI

The kingdom of **BOTI** has become the "must-do" trip in the vicinity of Soe; it lies 45km to the southeast. Boti has remained independent of external influence, due to its rajah, a proud man who didn't want to see the traditions of old Timor disappear. This has led to a steady influx of curious visitors and – ironically – the place now feels like a mock-up of a traditional village. There's a weaving cooperative, a small thatched workshop that women will suddenly and miraculously inhabit as soon as your presence is verified (work ceases immediately you have seen enough), a souvenir shop and big painted direction signs so you don't get lost. It is, however, one of the few places in Timor where the men are still forbidden from cutting their hair after they have married, and the traditional houses are quite interesting. The rajah refuses to speak Indonesian (though he seems to understand it pretty well) and requires all guests to come with a guide from Soe. He particularly likes Marsellinus Besa, who is contactable through the *Losmen Anda*, as he speaks the local language and knows all the customs.

It is essential to bring **betel nut** and you will also have to pay Rp5000 to enter the village, a little less to see the weaving, and Rp10,000 to stay overnight and eat with the rajah. The rajah is not very keen on people wandering around Boti and may forbid you to go anywhere without him. As he is well into his seventies and has trouble getting out on to the porch sometimes, this can be a little restrictive.

Getting to Boti is only straightforward if you have a **motorbike**, though you'll probably have to do some pushing and walking. If you want to go by public transport, catch a bus to **Oinlassi** and then it's a three-hour walk, if you take the short cut your guide will advise you on. It's definitely not worth walking to Boti unless you plan on overnighting there.

Kefamenenau

Known as Kefa to those who can't face the full mouthful, **KEFAMENENAU** is a pleasant but anonymous little town nearly 100km north of Kupang northeast of Soe. It's a good stop on the trans-island journey, both to break up long bus rides and as a base for excursions to the surrounding countryside.

The town centre is defined by the marketplace, with the **post office** and supermarket both nearby. The **bus station** is about 2km south of town but the buses all run through town so you shouldn't need to get out there. There are several **losmen** in Kefa: the *Soko Windu* (☎0391/21122; ①) on Jalan Kartini is the cheapest place, with reasonable rooms, shared mandi and satellite TV for those who are pining for CNN. The *Cederhana* (☎0391/21069; ②) is a fair way out of town on Jalan Patimura: you'll need to take a bemo to get there – it's basic, with very small rooms and outside mandi. *Ariesta Losmen* (☎0391/21002; ③) on Jalan Basuki Rachmat has just had a facelift, and a price lift to match, providing a choice of rooms with or without en-suite mandi. The *Ariesta Losmen*'s restaurant is about the only place in Kefa with **food** to suit a tourist's palate, though there are plenty of stalls by the market and a few dodgy warung in the market area. You could also try the *Rumah Makan Padang* or the *Lumayan Sami Jaya*, both near the market.

Buses heading north to Atambua and beyond start leaving at about 7am, but there are usually only a few in the afternoons. Buses south to Kupang run almost all day.

Tamkessi

Visitors looking for a genuine insight into the animist heritage of Timor are nowadays bypassing Boti and heading 50km east of Kefamenenau to the village of **TAMKESSI**. Many travellers tend to go no further north than Soe, and so it doesn't receive so many visitors. The village is built entirely on rock, which lends it a particularly potent magic.

The houses are all of traditional design, good-quality *ikat* cloths are made here, the men still hunt with blowpipes and there are even a few boomerangs kicking about, though it's unlikely that you'll see them in use unless you ask. The village is dominated by two large rocks which you can climb them for fine views of the surrounding countryside, but make sure to ask permission from the kepala desa first.

To get there from Kefamenenau, take one of the regular buses east to **Manufui**; from there its a two-hour walk to the north. If you speak good Indonesian you'll be able to ask directions in Manufui and probably won't need a guide, otherwise you'll have to obtain a guide in Soe as nobody seems to be offering guide services in Kefa.

Ambeno-Oekussi

The regency of **Oekussi**, completely surrounded by West Timor, is historically and politically a part of East Timor, formally ruled by the Portuguese but not victim to the troubles that have shattered the main body of East Timor since the 1970s. It's a fantastically scenic trip to make from Kefa: buses run to the district capital of **PANTE MAKASSAR** (3hr; Rp5000) from 7am until midday.

It's a very traditional area – the houses are almost all beehive-style *lopo*, the roofs reaching all the way to the ground, and the men ride around in bright sarong, their legs seeming to drag along the roads from their tiny but sturdy horses. Pante Makassar is a sizable town and was the first part of Timor to be colonized by the Portuguese – they are said to have landed on the beaches near the town and there are a few reminders of their stay here, some rusting cannons along a vaguely Mediterranean seafront and the Catholic church just east of the town centre.

On the road into Pante Makassar, about 10km before you reach town, is **Tano market**, active on Tuesdays – about as picturesque an example as you'll ever see. It's on the banks of Sungai Tono, under the shade produced by gargantuan fig trees; in the distance, imposing mountains tower over the area. In Pante Makassar, about a 1km walk up the hill south of the town, is **Fatusuba**, an old garrison with some interesting ruins and a large wooden cross out front. There are also nice views of the town and the bay from here. The only **accommodation** in Pante Makassar is the *Aneka Jaya* (②), which can be found on Jalan Sukarno. It's pretty clean and the staff are delightful.

Atambua and Atapupu

ATAMBUA is the capital city of Belu Regency, which borders East Timor – the town was closed to tourists until 1989 as it was feared that Fretilin guerrillas were spilling over the border. Supposedly it's safe now, but caution is still advised if you're thinking of going off the beaten track: always check in with the police and listen to local advice.

Atambua is a large town, but pretty dull; there's nothing of note to see, but there are plenty of losmen and Padang restaurants if you want to break the long journey to or from Dili. The **bus terminal** is 1km out of town, but all buses come through town looking for custom anyway. The *Minang Rumah Makan* on Jalan Sukarno does good fresh Padang food and has some very new and clean rooms out back (②). They are also an agent for buses to Kupang (7hr; Rp12,000) and Dili (4hr; Rp6000). Just outside of town on a hill overlooking Atambua at **Ro'okfau** is a ruined Tetum settlement. Take a bemo to **Fatuketi** and then ask local kids if they can guide you for the short but strenuous walk to the deserted village. Close by is a vast cave complex, where swallow's nests are collected to make bird's-nest soup.

ATAPUPU is the port on the coast to the west of Atambua. You might be able to pick up unscheduled boats from here to interesting places around the archipelago, but the main reason to come here is for the **weekly ferry** to **Kalabahi** on Alor – it leaves at 10am every Monday and takes seven hours. You can easily get from Atambua to the ferry in the morning, and there's no need to try and stay the night before in Atapupu. Arriving in Atapupu, direct buses running all the way to Dili and Kupang can be picked up at the quayside.

East Timor

The foreign offices of most Western states advise against travel in **East Timor**, as this book was going to press there was renewed and serious conflict in the province, with paramilitaries attacking pro-independence targets. It is vital to check on the current situation before attempting to visit East Timor. A stunningly beautiful place with soaring mountains, immaculate coral reefs and undeveloped coastline, Tim Tim, as the locals call it, remains all but bereft of tourists.

Some of the highlights are found on the coastal road heading north. **Baucau** is a town with a European feel and a market of rare architectural interest. Next up the road is **Lautem**, which has some spectacular ruins, with ancient walls of crudely hewn stone. Fine examples of the bizarre traditional East Timorese house can be found at **Desa Rasa**, looking distinctly ungainly on their towering wooden stilts, and at **Tutuala** there are spectacular views, snorkelling and peace in "the losmen at the end of the world". Other areas of interest are to be found at **Same** and **Maubisse** in the highlands to the south of Dili – hill towns with stunning scenery, clear air and refreshingly cool nights.

At the time of writing, there was no requirement for **surat jalan** (travel papers), but this changes regularly. There are numerous police posts at the West/East Timor border around the province, and outside of the capital you are always advised to check in with the local police station; they'll probably just check your passport and let you go. Always listen to what the police tell you, and if they say an area is out of bounds then avoid it.

Some history

The modern **history** of East Timor began in 1904, when the Portuguese and Dutch divided Timor into provinces and East Timor was annexed from the rest of the island. The colony was all but neglected; practically the only imports were convicts and political prisoners, for whom it was a place of exile.

Portuguese control continued until the advent of World War II, when the Japanese landed here in great numbers. The allies, fearing for the safety of nearby Australia, sent thousands of ANZAC troops into the hinterlands of the province, where they proceeded to wage a highly successful guerrilla war against the Japanese. The Timorese had been instant victims of Japanese cruelty and came down on the side of the allies. They harboured the Australians and many actually fought with them against the Japanese. For this they had to endure savage Japanese retaliation: whole villages were destroyed, and crops and livestock burnt. An estimated 60,000 East Timorese were killed during the Japanese occupation, about thirteen percent of the population.

When the Japanese ceded the land to Portugal at the end of the war, things returned to the bad old days. Slave labour was reinstated, and education was still so patchy that only ten percent of the population had even basic literacy. There was no electricity or running water anywhere, and malaria was rife. However, in 1974, following the overthrow of the fascist Caetano regime, the incoming government declared that many of the colonial states were illegally occupied. East Timor was left to face its future alone, without external rule for the first time in nearly three hundred years.

Three parties formed, aspiring to lead the new country. In 1975, the first free general elections in East Timor's history resulted in a landslide victory for the **Fretilin** party, who wanted independence for East Timor, confident that they could at least rely on the support of their wartime ally Australia. They formed a transitional government, while the other two parties formed a coalition opposition. This coalition branded Fretilin as communists, an accusation that soon attracted the attention of the Indonesian government. In a series of undercover operations codenamed Komodo, the opposition sought to undermine the Fretilin, simultaneously calling for Indonesia to intervene. A small

civil war followed, from which Fretilin comfortably emerged as victors, claiming independence for the new Democratic Republic of East Timor. On December 7, 1975, Indonesian president Suharto held talks with US President Ford and Henry Kissinger. Hours after the talks were completed and Air Force One was barely off the ground back to the States, Indonesia invaded East Timor.

In the first year of the conflict, eighty percent of Dili's male population were killed. The UN general assembly and Security Council passed ten resolutions calling on Indonesia to withdraw their troops: all were ignored. The savagery of the invading regime drove the Fretilin members into the internal highlands, where they began the guerrilla war that continues to this day. The Indonesian army stifled the independence movement with political executions, imprisonments and kidnappings; torture and rape were commonplace. Those who rejected Indonesian rule were evicted from their lands, most were tortured, some were killed, others just disappeared. Little news of the invasion reached the outside world: two Australian TV crews were assassinated, Amnesty International and the Red Cross were both thrown out and banned. Amnesty reports estimate that, between 1976 and 1986, 200,000 people out of a population of 700,000 were killed.

The **Western world** was far from blameless in what has come to be described as the attempted genocide of the East Timorese. The Australians turned a blind eye to the fate of their wartime comrades, Prime Minister Gough Whitlam telling Suharto in 1974 that the dissolution of East Timor was "inevitable". Australia's largest oil companies were duly given contracts to drill for oil and gas in the Timor strait. Over a ten-year period, America and Britain provided over a billion dollars' worth of **arms** to Indonesia. In the 1978 siege on the Matebian mountains, US-produced napalm was dropped from US-supplied Bronco planes on Fretilin rebels and civilians. The British provided tanks, frigates, armoured cars, the hawk bombers that were used to strafe the Fretilin in their mountain hideaways (sold during the height of the massacres in 1978) and water cannons. The problem was highlighted as late as 1998, when Britain's "new" Labour government refused to terminate licences for exporting military hardware to Indonesia, as it would cost valuable jobs in the defence industry. The British media estimates the annual profit to British companies of these contracts at over £300 million. In 1989, the **pope** visited the province (one of the most Catholic in Asia), to bless their new cathedral. About half the population was party to a speech where he praised the East Timorese for their bravery and sympathized with their long years of suffering. Onlookers were beaten by the police, and journalists had their cameras confiscated.

On November 12, 1991, the East Timor problem was brought to world attention when a **massacre** in downtown Dili was captured on film by British journalist Max Stahl and relayed to the world's press. Around 5000 people had gathered to commemorate the execution of Sebastien Gomes, who had been shot by Indonesian troops two weeks earlier. Protesters walked through Dili to the **Santa Cruz cemetery**, where they began to pray and lay wreaths, watched by several Western journalists. Indonesian troops entered the cemetery in lines and, without provocation, opened fire on the mourners. Some of the journalists escaped after being beaten unconscious with rifle butts, but the mourners suffered a worse fate. According to eyewitnesses, after shooting had ceased in the cemetery the soldiers ransacked nearby houses, executing everyone they encountered. The badly wounded were beaten to death and the corpses were taken away in a convoy of nine trucks. It is estimated that 528 people were killed in this incident alone: the aftermath was an unprecedented series of executions, rapes and tortures.

The **Indonesian people** had no reports of the 1991 massacre, and are generally told by their media that East Timor is a troublesome, irrelevant little province that cried out for Indonesia's help then complained when they got it. It's certainly true that the general infrastructure has been dramatically improved under the Indonesians, and, though the UN has never recognized the "integration", few Indonesians sympathize with the East Timorese cause. It was with incredulity, then, that they received news that the

1997 **Nobel peace prize** was to be awarded to Bishop Carlos Felipe Ximenes Belo and Jose Ramos Horta, the two loudest voices of the East Timorese in their fight for freedom. Belo had picked up where other Catholic emissaries had left off, criticizing brutality and calling for peace. Ramos Horta, however, has been continually portrayed to the Indonesian public by their own media and government as a controversial agitator, seeking self-publicity and creating panic by sensationalizing the issues. He is also well-known for not only advocating peace, but also independence for the East Timorese. The decision of the Nobel Academy left President Suharto fuming.

East Timor was one of the most violent no-go areas during and after the downfall of Suharto, with the Timorese Catholics' anti-Indonesian sentiment being supplemented by jealous hatred for the shop-owning Muslims and Chinese. In early 1999, the Indonesian army were accused of trying to augment a civil war after admitting supplying arms to pro-Indonesian East Timorese militia, who promptly went on a rampage, massacring civilians and forcing them from their villages. The situation, while still unstable, has recently begun to look more hopeful. In January 1999, President Habibie promised to grant the province independence, if, as looks likely, his offer of autonomy is rejected. In another positive move, the jailed East Timorese resistance leader **Jose Alexandre "Xanana" Gusmao** was released from high-security prison in Jakarta and placed under house arrest, in order for him to play a role in bringing peace to the territory. The charismatic and popular Gusmao, who was arrested in Dili in 1992, looks set to play an important part in the negotiations to come and, many hope, may become the first president of an independent East Timor.

Dili and around

DILI has been rebuilt by the Indonesians, with the idea of creating a showcase town, evidence of the new, integrated East Timor. It has wide airy streets, is one of the cleanest towns you'll ever see, has a wealth of spanking-new government buildings adorned with patriotic concrete statues, and generally about as much charm as an abandoned shopping precinct. Police, government officials and swaggering soldiers – not long out of puberty – burst out of their khakis and proudly brandish huge, shiny machine guns. True, the colonial-style buildings are handsome, and the wide palm-lined bay can be quite beautiful on a misty morning, but the Dili has very little soul.

The city looks north across a wide, curving bay out to the Savu Sea, and sprawls out towards its three bus stations, all at least 2km out of the centre, which is located around the **governor's office** near the waterfront. In the immediate vicinity of this there are lots of banks, the general post office and a couple of the swankier hotels. The two main **markets** are reasonably lively, but are located well out of town in **Becora**, to the east, and **Compang** to the west.

There are several things of interest to see in and around Dili, the most spectacular being the new **statue of Christ**, which stands in the hills to the east of town, overlooking Dili Bay. The figure stands in a crucifixion-cum-benediction stance on top of a colossal globe with Indonesia at the forefront. It's a copy of Rio's better-known figure, surrounded by ghastly concrete steps, but still worth a visit. It was finished in early 1997, and opened by President Suharto in the presence of the Nobel prize winners Jose Ramos Horta and Bishop Carlos Ximenes, both of whom he completely refused to acknowledge.

Another Christian monument of note is the **cathedral**, the largest church in Southeast Asia, also opened by Suharto and blessed by the pope in 1989. It's quite a striking building, especially worth seeing if there is a service on, and can be found a five-minute walk west from the centre of town. West along the seafront from the port, you'll come to the **Motael**, a pretty little building and the oldest standing Catholic church in Nusa Tenggara. Just past this is the old **lighthouse**; there are great views from the top, but you'll have to find someone there to let you in.

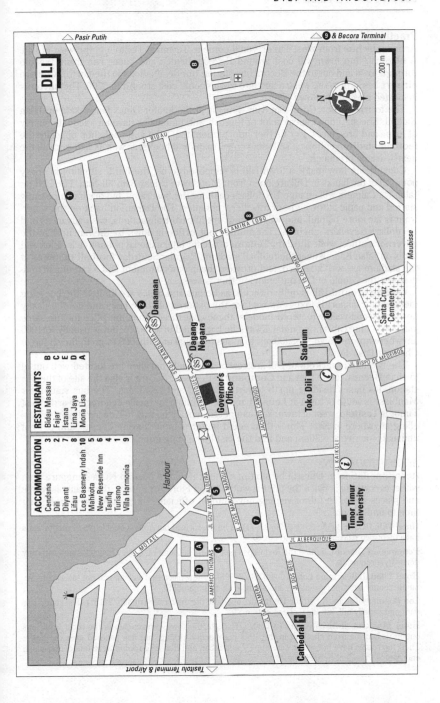

DILI

△ Pasir Putih

△ **⑨** & Becora Terminal

0   200 m

N

JL BIDAU

Ⓑ

✚

Ⓘ

JL BELAMINA LOBO

Ⓒ

▷ Maubisse

JL. 15 DE OKTOBER

Ⓓ

Santa Cruz
Cemetery

Ⓔ

JL BISPO DE MEDEIROS

Stadium

Toko Dili   ✆

Danaman

② Ⓢ

**Dagang
Negara**

Ⓢ ⑥

JL SOS BANDEIRA

**Governor's
Office**

JL HENDRIQUES

JL JACINTO CANDIDO

JL KAIKOLI

Ⓘ

Timor Timur
University

Harbour

✉

⑤

JL GOV ALVEZ ALDEIRA

JL JOSE MARICA MARQUEZ

⑦

JL ALBERQUIQUE

⑩

JL MOTAEL

Ⓐ

③ ④

JL AMERICO THOMAS

JL DA CALMERA

JL DOS REIS

Cathedral ✝

ACCOMMODATION

Cendana	3
Dili	2
Dilyanti	7
Lifau	8
Los Basmery Indah	10
Mahkota	5
New Resende Inn	6
Taufiq	4
Turismo	1
Villa Harmonia	9

RESTAURANTS

Bidau Massau	B
Fajar	C
Istana	E
Lima Jaya	D
Mona Lisa	A

△ Tastolu Terminal & Airport

Practicalities

Arriving by **bus** from West Timor, you'll come to Terminal Tasitolo to the west of Dili. A blue cab into town will cost around Rp2000; bemos and buses run from Tasitolo through town and out to the Becora bus station (for destinations to the north). Comaro **airport** lies 5km to the west; a taxi into town should cost around Rp5000. The **harbour** is located close to the town centre.

The **tourist office** (Mon–Sat 8am–4pm) is at the kantor Dinas Parawisata on Jalan Kaikoli. The staff don't speak a lot of English but, unusually, have an adequate supply of maps and brochures. For further information, the Toko Dili bookshop opposite the **football stadium** entrance, sells souvenirs, maps and books, as well as *ikat* from all the nearby island producers.

Considering how major a town Dili is supposed to be, the **bank** situation is pretty poor. All of the banks in Dili are open from Monday to Friday 8am till 4pm. The BNI on Jalan Da Calmera will change US dollars cash for the best rates, but are incompetently staffed and panic at the sight of travellers' cheques. The Danamon bank on the waterfront is far more helpful, and will execute credit-card transactions, cash advances and US dollars travellers' cheques. The **main post office** is down by the bay near to the governor's office, while the 24hr **Telkom** office for international phones calls, telex and fax is on Jalan Kaikoli near the football stadium. Regular Saturday **football matches** at the stadium are well attended, and provide cheap entertainment and a rare opportunity to see the people of Dili out enjoying themselves.

Getting around Dili is quite difficult, as bemos and buses are limited: the booming method of transport is taxis. Always take the battered old blue taxis and not the flashy new green-and-yellow metered models: these cost three times the price for the same journey. A blue cab's price must always be bargained in advance, but is usually Rp1000 anywhere around town, Rp2000 out to a bus terminal and Rp5000 to go to the statue of Christ or Pasir Putih.

The two main **markets** of Dili are reasonably lively but they are located well out of town in **Becora**, to the east and **Compang** to the west. Becora is also the site of the bus station, for buses heading north towards Baucau and Los Palos. The bus station for Maubisse is south of town at **Leusari** and the terminal for buses heading towards West Timor is **Tasitolo**, west of town. You can get tickets all the way to Kupang. If you're travelling anywhere in East Timor then you'd better plan on leaving before 8am. It's not unusual to arrive at 8.30am and find the last bus is long gone.

ACCOMMODATION

Accommodation in Dili will be a bit of a shock if you've been in Nusa Tenggara for a while: everything is twice the price it would be on Flores or Sumba, the quality is worse and places are often full of visiting government officials – it can take an awfully long time to find a room.

Hotel Dili, Jl Sada Bande 25 (☎0390/21871). A bit overpriced but quite a likable place; most rooms have their own balconies, bath and fan. ④.

Penginapan Dilyanti, behind the Red Cross post on Jl Da Calmera. A very cheap losmen with tiny dorm-style rooms. ②.

Hotel Lifau, Jl Belarmino Lobo 10 (☎0390/21998). A new place that's clean and not too expensive. Single rooms are cupboard-sized, and all have shared mandi. ③.

Los Basmery Indah, Jl Estrade De Balide, opposite the university (☎0390/22151). The rooms are dark and usually full, but it's a cheap option. ②.

Hotel Mahkota, Jl Alves Aldeia (☎0390/21662). In the town centre; this is the most luxurious option. It had the front shot out in the 1997 pre-election rioting, but has papered over the holes. Their top rooms have hot water, satellite TV and a bar, and the suite rooms were (allegedly) plush enough for President Suharto. ⑥–⑨.

Wisma Mes Adang Cendana, Jl Americo Thomas (☎0390/21141). A government-run rest house that looks a bit like a prison block. The rooms are correspondingly cell-like but it's not too expensive. Double rooms have air-con and en-suite mandi, and they also offer rooms with fridge and TV. ③–④.

New Resende Inn, Jl Bispo Madeiros 5 (☎0390/21768). Close to the governor's office, the *New Resende* is popular with foreign businesspeople, presumably enticed by a restaurant whose menu is full of expensive European and Chinese food. The poor quality of the rooms, however, belies the hefty price tag. ⑥.

Wisma Taufiq, Jl Americo Thomas (☎0390/21934). About the noisiest losmen in existence – all the rooms are above a music store. Prices are low and so are comforts. ③.

Hotel Turismo, Jl Carmona (☎0390/22029). The next most expensive hotel after the *Mahkota* but a huge drop in quality, it has rooms with or without mandi, some with TV and air-con. Aspires to represent the colonial splendour of Dili. ④–⑤.

Villa Harmonia, 3km from town heading towards the Becora bus terminal (☎0390/23595). A reasonably priced losmen with an English-speaking manager who can give you the lowdown on travel around East Timor. Rooms with shared mandi are well kept and relatively quiet. ③.

EATING AND DRINKING

While the supermarkets and bakeries of Dili are a godsend for those who've been starved of such delights, the overall restaurant scene is nothing to shout about – with a few notable exceptions. The **night warung** along the Bidau Canal have a fun atmosphere, and there are two good **bakeries** in town – one next to *Hotel Lifau* that does great banana cake, and the *Aru Bakery* near *Wisma Taufiq* on Jalan Alberquerque.

Fajar Restaurant, Jl 15 Oktober. Air-con restaurant with karaoke and an extensive menu of Chinese food with plenty of fresh seafood. A full meal is likely to cost around Rp25,000 a head.

Rumah Makan Lima Jaya, Jl 15 Oktober 10. Business restaurant with air-con, hostesses and karaoke. The menu contains lots of seafood and Chinese food. Figure on about Rp25,000 for grilled fish with rice and a beer on the side.

Miss Ollandia or **Bidau Massau**, out of town to the east, over the canal and heading towards Pasir Putih. You'll have to ask directions, as it's well hidden. Serving superb Portuguese food, seafood, meat and potato stews as well as cold imported beer, it runs to about Rp20,000 a head, which in Dili is great value.

Rumah Makan Mona Lisa, Jl Alberquerque. Serving mainly Javanese food with *nasi rames* costing around Rp7500.

Padang Istana, Jl 15 Oktober, closer to the centre of town than *Lima Jaya*. Quite flash for a Padang restaurant, with air-con and succulent-looking chicken and prawn dishes.

Around Dili

Outside of Dili, 4km to the east, is **Pasir Putih**, otherwise known as White Sands beach or Area Branca. There's a pleasant stretch of sand here and it's a good spot to come during the week at high tide. During weekends the beach is mobbed with local picnickers; at low tide it's a great soggy mud flat.

West of town at **Tacitolu**, where an altar was erected for the papal visit, is another white-sand beach. Very picturesque and a lot less likely to be busy than Pasir Putih, it's about 10km away and accessible by bus from the Lesuari terminal. At **Fatunaba** on a hill-top overlooking Dili from the east, is a freshwater pool, an understated monument constructed by the Australian army as a thankyou to the Timorese for their help in World War II. Dili actually looks much more appealing from this distance.

Pulau Atauro is a National Marine Park, an hour's speedboat ride from Dili harbour, boasting some exceptional **snorkelling** and **diving**. At the time of writing there were no organized tours to this area, though Pitoby Tours in Kupang (☎0380/21154) run occasional scuba safaris here, rating the diving off this coast as some of the best in Indonesia. You can get out to the islands by chartering boats from Dili harbour; figure on about US$30–$40 for a day in an old battered speedboat.

Baucau

The road east into the Baucau Regency from Dili passes first through **Mantutu Regency**; along the roads you will probably see patrolling soldiers and army camps. As even this coastal road is considered dangerous by the military, trips inland are strongly discouraged. **BAUCAU** is the second largest town in East Timor, a sprawling place that, despite it's size, has very little in the way of amenities. It has quite a strong colonial feel, with a few churches and other buildings having faded, pastel stucco facades. The finest sight in Baucau is the **Mercado Municipal**, the old market building, with its magnificent curved fascia, flamboyant staircases and elaborate fountain. Unfortunately they only hold markets here now on special occasions; it used to be the most dramatic market setting imaginable. The **market** is now held daily, out of town by the bus station. Another novelty near the Mercado is the local **church**, which has been built with a high thatched roof to look like a traditional East Timorese house, but instead of the customary carvings it is topped with a flashing neon cross.

There was a lot of Japanese military activity in the area surrounding Baucau during World War II, and several reminders are to be found nearby. At **Gua Tujuh** (Seven Caves), there's an excavated cave complex carved out by the occupying army, still in remarkably good condition. Bring a torch and don't attempt it if you're claustrophobic; a bus from Baucau bus station will cost around Rp1500. The **beaches** nearby are absolutely wonderful; you will probably have to charter a bemo for the five-kilometre drive down to the coast as there are no scheduled bemos – well worth it, though, as the waters are crystal-clear and the palm-lined sands utterly perfect.

Practicalities

If you are planning leaving for the north and places on the way to **Los Palos**, be warned that the last bus leaves from the terminal at 11am. Going back to Dili, they run until 3pm (Rp4000; 3hr). Baucau has no centre as such, but for the visitor the area by the Mercado and the *Flobamor Hotel* is the only area of interest. The hotel, also known as the *Baucau* (③), is a beautiful but crumbling work of colonial art – the rooms are tatty and staff struggle to put an omelette together, but it's still a pleasure staying there. Each room has a balcony and en-suite mandi and fan, with singles, doubles and triples available at the same price.

The only other option for accommodation in Baucau is to be found above the Padang restaurant, which is a short walk from here back towards the town. It is brand-new, unnamed and does not advertise its rooms, but above the restaurant they have four clean rooms with fan and mandi (③). This is also the only real place around here to get any decent **food**.

East to Tutuala

The **Lautem Regency** comprises the easternmost tip of Timor, mountainous and dry but with a fine coastline, if you can get to it. The first place you will come to on the road east from Baucau is **Laga**, a pretty fishing village with thatched houses, a fairly intact Portuguese hill fort and a bright-blue church. The first place you might want to stop is **LAUTEM**, a good four-hour drive from Baucau. This area is a real gem, a traditional village with thatched houses and people living something approaching the traditional East Timorese lifestyle, all but eradicated by the troubles. What makes the place particularly special is its setting amongst the extensive remains of a Portuguese fortified settlement. From the look of the ruins there were barracks, a chapel and scores of houses enclosed in impressive stone walls that still stand almost unbroken. Down on the **beach**, a short stroll away, are some fairly ugly Japanese bunkers and a good spot for a swim.

The next place that is worth a stop as you head north and east is **DESA RASA**, a small village that lies right on the main road about an hour from Los Palos. The attraction of the village is instantly obvious: two of the only remaining houses in the distinctive Lautem style. They are precariously balanced on high stilts, with ludicrously top-heavy roofs, and are adorned with nautilus shells and carvings. One is derelict; the other, still occupied. The whole village was full of such edifices, but Fretilin guerrillas burnt most of them down. The two houses and smaller store building that remain are said to be centuries old; certainly they are beginning to list heavily, but they are still the most interesting traditional structures in Tim Tim.

From Rasa, practically any transport heading east is going to be to **Los Palos**, so just flag anything down on the road. There's not much in Los Palos – a couple of dreary losmen and poor warung; if you get here early enough it's best to head straight on to the village of Tutuala. First go and see the police to register in Los Palos, which is mandatory. The road from Los Palos to Tutuala is a nightmare; it takes two and a half bone-shuddering hours to reach the village, and you have to register with the police twice on the way, but when you get there it's worth it.

TUTUALA is a peaceful little place, centred around a remarkably well-kept football pitch and with a population of about a hundred. The village is on the slopes of a steep hill, and at the top of is one of the most stunningly located **losmen** (③) in Indonesia. The government-run guest house towers several hundred metres over the ocean, from where, in the late afternoon as the sun sets, you can see whales feeding in the seas below. You can see all the way to Wetar and Kisar islands, and on a clear day even to Alor. The losmen itself is a beautiful Mediterranean-style villa, very basic inside, with rarely enough water for a mandi, but what it lacks in comfort it makes up for in aesthetic appeal.

About 3km to the south is **Ilikerekere**, the painted cave. It's a limestone cavern with Neolithic-style wall paintings: you'll definitely need help to find it. About a ninety-minute walk away from Tutuala to the southeast lies **Pantai Walu**, a magnificent white-sand **beach** overlooking **Pulau Jako**, a tiny uninhabited island. It's possible to swim over to Jako, or sometimes there's a boatman there who'll take you across for a few hundred rupiah. The **snorkelling** round Jako is excellent, with some huge fish and a burgeoning population of inquisitive white-tip reef sharks. The losmen is run by a government-hired porter, who will also cook you meals if you give him advance warning. Bemos back to Los Palos from Tutuala village leave at 8am and 11am; if you take the early one, you can make it all the way back to Dili in one, brain-numbing day.

Ainaro Regency

Dominated by **Gunung Tatamailau**, the highest peak in Timor, at over 2900m, Ainaro is a place of breathtaking alpine scenery with cold nights and fresh, clear air. A three-hour bus ride south from Dili brings you to the dilapidated hill resort of **MAUBISSE**, the main attraction being not only the surroundings but the town's one hotel (③). It's situated in the residence of the former Portuguese governor, elevated high above the rest of the village and with a kind of wilting grandeur to it. Nothing works, and, as in many places around Tim Tim, they are low on water, but somehow you still feel like gentry staying here. There are several **warung** in town just a short stroll away. If you want to climb Tatamailau, take a bus from Maubisse towards Ainaro for **Hatubalico**: there's a government-run rest house here, where you can stay the night before you attempt the climb. It's a good day's climb up and then back to the guest house. **AINARO** is the capital of the regency and also a spectacular hill resort. There's a fascinating old Portuguese church here, with coffee plantations on every side, one losmen and a few dodgy warung. It's an hour's truck ride from Maubisse, or five hours all the way from/to Dili.

ROTI AND SAVU

The island of **Roti**, a short ferry trip from Kupang, is becoming a regular tourist destination, the vast majority of visitors being Australian surfers destined for waves at
Nembrala beach on the west coast: the rest of the island remains all but unvisited.
Roti is relatively flat and exceptionally dry, and the main crop is a drought-resistant
palm called the **lontar**, which supplies vitamin-rich syrup as well as the fibres that
Rotinese use for everything from house-building to cutlery. These spindly trees with
their spiky crowns are ubiquitous on the island, their silhouettes against the sunset providing many photo opportunities.

Savu is about equidistant from Timor, Flores and Sumba and is extremely isolated.
Throughout the rainy season ferries rarely make it here, and the island can go months
at a time without seeing tourists. It's a place of paradisal beaches and thriving animist
cultures and remains one of the most rewarding off-the-beaten-track destinations in all
of Indonesia.

Roti

The main town on Roti is the small port of **Ba'a**, about halfway along the north-
facing coast of the island. Pelni boats dock offshore here, but ferries to and from
Kupang stop at the harbour in **Olafulihaa**, which is in a bay at the top of the island.
The majority of surfing destinations, including highly rated Nembrala beach, are
around the southwest coast, have the best accommodation and beaches and are
fantastic places to chill out, even if you're not seeking waves.

The villages in the area around **Boni** still maintain traditional ways, adhere to the
"*lontar*" economy" and have a spectacular festival in late June/early July. Triggered
by the full moon, the *hu'us* festival involves animal sacrifices, horse races and dancing – basically, two weeks of pagan knees-up.

Roti has its place in **history** as one of the success stories of the Dutch East India
Company. On their arrival in Roti, the colonizers met with little resistance and quickly allied themselves with local factions. At first the Dutch influence seemed to be taking effect gradually and progressively, but then a powerful and brutal VOC campaign established their position by force, quelling opposition and strengthening the
situation of their allies: Roti became a supply base for Kupang and some slaves were
taken. In 1729, the Rotinese rajah became a Christian, and more conversions followed swiftly. The locals came to realize that taking up Christianity, adopting
European education systems and aiding the colonists brought power and advancement, and they took up the new influence with a passion – the island remains a place
with a reputation for producing a high proportion of the nation's high-ranking officials and diplomats.

Most travellers **arrive** in Roti at the northern port of Olafulihaa on the daily ferry
from Kupang. It gets in at about 11am and there is always a crowd of buses waiting
to whisk passengers away to Nembrala (Rp5000; 4hr). The same buses will drop you
off at Ba'a, which is about halfway between the port and Nembrala. The **airport** is
near to Ba'a town: from here, your best bet is to catch one of the waiting taxis into
Ba'a and, if you want to go on to Nembrala, try to flag down a bus as it heads down
the main street. Ferries returning to Kupang leave daily at noon and buses leave
from Nembrala every morning from 7am to 8am to reach the port in time. Pelni ferries for Waingapu, Ende and Kupang leave from Ba'a – check schedules in a large
town before coming to Roti and then double-check at the Pelni office in Ba'a.

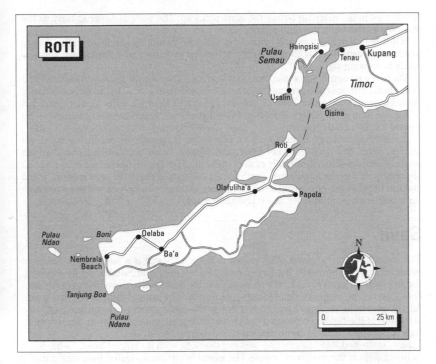

Ba'a and Boni

BA'A may be the largest town on Roti, but it's a one-street place with few advantages: it's dusty, decrepit and has no shops or good places to eat. If you are planning a trip to the traditional area of Boni or heading out on a Pelni boat to Sumba, Flores, Timor or Savu then you might have to stop here. There are several losmen in town, the best being the *Hotel Ricki* on Jalan Gereja (③), which has cleanish rooms with en-suite mandi and tiny fans. Every eating place in Ba'a is dire, the bank does not change money and the post office is on the other side of the green at the western end of town.

To get to **BONI** it's best to hire a guide and motorbike in town. You could try this from Nembrala, but it's a longer trip. Boni lies west of Ba'a and slightly off the main road, and is one of the few places left on Roti that maintains the distinctive houses with high sloping roofs and exposed scimitar-shaped, carved ridgepoles. Traditional dress is the norm: women wear only a simple sarong and the men sport the Rotinese *ti'i langga*, a woven cowboy hat with a pole pointing heavenwards. Boni's **hu'us festival** is well worth heading for if you are on Roti in June or July. At any time, though, the village is worth a visit, giving a fine insight into the island's agrarian, animist past.

Nembrala beach

Nembrala beach is a terrific **surfing** destination. The main break is called T' land, on the reef that runs offshore: it's a long ridable left that's best from April to September. At **Boa**, about an eight-kilometre bike ride from Nembrala, is a right-hander that's worth a go in the morning before the wind picks up. The wave is never as busy as the main waves can be in the high season.

Wildlife is also a feature of Nembrala, notably the dwindling stocks of turtles. These giants come ashore to lay their eggs and are rolled over, hacked up and eaten alive – a really harrowing sight.

There are presently three places to stay and eat in Nembrala: *Losmen Anugurah* (②) is the best, with ice-cold beer and enormous quantities of food. The accommodation is basic but ample. *Homestay Thomas* (②) and *Losmen Ti Rosa* (②) offer similar deals, but fail on the food front. *Andy's Nembrala* (④–⑤) is a new, overpriced set of bungalows in a good location on the beach.

Just offshore are two islands worth a trip: **Ndao** is famous for producing the finest filigree silver and gold in Nusa Tenggara; **Ndana** is an uninhabited island which swarms with wildlife – thousands of deer, pelicans, herons, monkeys and wild boar, all seemingly indifferent to humans. Turtles are a common sight in the seas around Ndana and the beaches are egg-laying sites. For either of these islands you will need to **charter** a boat from Nembrala for about Rp40,000 a day.

Savu

The stunning island of **Savu** (also known as Sabu or Sawu) is a fiercely dry, uniquely beautiful paradise sitting in the Savu Sea between Timor and Sumba. It's an exposed, flat and isolated lump of rock, where, somehow, life manages to thrive with greater success than on the fertile lands of Flores and Sumba. The annual rainfall on Savu is pitiful, the ground is stony and barren, yet due to the *lontar* palm economy, the Savunese are some of the healthiest-looking people in the region, and, along with the Rotinese, have a disproportionate representation in Indonesian public life.

Savu is divided into eastern and western districts, with its largest town, **Seba**, lying in the middle of the northwest coast. The island is circumnavigated by a single track, the only other road of note neatly bisecting it. To the west of Savu lies tiny **Pulau Raijua**, considered by the Savunese their place of origin and spiritual home: it is reputedly the driest place in all of Indonesia.

While most people on Savu now claim to be Christian, the island is actually the site of the most fervent **animism** in Indonesia. Village compounds, sacred buildings, festivals and rites are loaded with significance, so that a guide is absolutely necessary when touring Savu; otherwise, you may inadvertently offend people. In addition, always bring betel nut as an offering when you visit villages.

The only craft of note on Savu is their **ikat weaving**, rated by experts as some of the finest to be found in Indonesia. They tend to use a lot of chemical dyes rather than those made from plants, but the colours appear far more natural than on Roti and are still very appealing to the Western buyer.

Some history

Savu repelled colonial powers with remarkable ease for several hundred years. A Portuguese war expedition that stopped in search of slaves in 1676 was decimated, and the Portuguese and Dutch kept their distance thereafter. For Westerners, the biggest milestone in the history of Savu was the visit of Captain Cook's ship the **Endeavour** in 1770. Cook wrote about Savu and the *lontar* palm economy with great interest and visited several villages around the island.

Except in providing occasional soldiers for the VOC, Savu remained isolated from the outside world until 1860, when Christian missionaries landed here. Their arrival had a cataclysmic effect, bringing smallpox to the island; it's estimated that up to half of the

---

THE FESTIVALS

The main **festival** on Savu takes place between April and June. It's called the **pedoa** and as spectacle, is only second in Nusa Tenggara to Sumba's *pasola*. The *pedoa* is a thanksgiving after the planting season. It's also a special chance for young people to find a partner. The three-month ceremonies include dancing, horse races, ritual wars and stone-throwing battles.

Another notable festival is the **pehere jara** or "horse dancing" held in February. In folklore it was decreed that the stampeding sound of constantly dancing horses' hooves would drive off a plague of locusts. Now, before the sorghum is planted, on the priest's instructions young men mount their horses bareback and race endlessly around a field near Namata throwing betel nuts, which the onlookers have to try and rescue from beneath the flailing hooves. If many people fall from their horses then seeds will also fall from the sky and the harvest will be good, and the riding is therefore exhilaratingly reckless.

---

population died of the disease. Unlike on Roti, converts to Christianity received few favours and were for the most part shunned by the other Savunese. The missionaries encouraged converts to move to Sumba and Timor to dilute the spread of Islam there.

Seba

The main town and port of **SEBA** is on the west coast of Savu. It features a wide sweep of perfect beach, strewn with coloured pebbles; fisherman lurk waist-deep in the surf with throw nets and the shores are thick with gangly-topped *lontar* palms.

There are three **losmen** in Seba, the best by far being the *Ongka Dai Homestay* (②). Just walk up the street from the jetty and it's on your right. It's a gleaming new losmen with en-suite mandi, three huge meals a day and fun, friendly staff.

The best **guide** on Savu is Pak Junas Tacoy, Seba's English teacher. Junas speaks very good English, has boundless knowledge of the area and is about as friendly and accommodating a person as you are ever likely to meet. If you are staying at the *Ongka Dai Homestay* then he'll probably find you. For a seat on the back of his motorbike and his guiding abilities you should expect to pay US$20–30 a day, which sounds steep but is well worth it.

The **Rajah's Palace** (Teni Hawu) sits slightly southwest of the port. It's a grand name for the crumbling edifice, but the late rajah's wife can tell you a bit about Savu's royalty and might show you around some of the ramshackle buildings.

Ferries leaving for Kupang depart every Wednesday at 2pm (10hr; Rp12,000); the ferry to Waingapu leaves on Sundays at the same time (16hr; Rp14,000). Ferry schedules can be unpredictable, though, and they often don't run in the rainy season.

Around the island

The villages around Savu have some extremely striking traditional structures and distinctive stone **megaliths**; they are all difficult to get to by public transport and unless you intend staying a while in any of the villages then renting a motorbike is recommended; ask about vehicle rental at your losmen.

The closest village to Seba is **NAMATA**. Off the road, heading clockwise around the island, Namata has a host of Savunese houses, shaped like upturned boats as a symbol of the people's seafaring ancestry. Those whose roofs reach the ground are sacred houses for storing ritual objects and mixing magic, and are strictly taboo. Never photograph, touch or (under any circumstances) look into these houses. Namata has some of the finest examples of Savunese megaliths, oval boulders apparently rolled up to their hill-top position from the bottom of the sea and then set in brick cradles in neat groups. The village is also a good place to see **ikat weaving** and the famous stone plaque that may have been carved and presented by Captain Cook. It's a fascinating place and only a three-kilometre walk northeast from town.

In the far east of Savu, **KUDJIRATU** is the centre of the island's animism and the starting point for the *pedoa* (see p.705). You need to speak to people outside before you enter through the narrow slit in the rather spectacular black-rock walls of the kampung. At the time of writing, the kampung had just been reconstructed and was vulnerable to outside magic; visitors had to be exorcized by the *kepala adat* before being allowed inside. In the far south, **MISARA** is another fascinating traditional kampung. With three sets of megaliths and complex ritual structures, it is bounded by taboos, so watch your step. A rock here is apparently guaranteed to make you fertile. When a priest dies in Misara, a new acolyte must drink a potion of the old priest's blood and the venom from a highly poisonous fish. Those who escape violent death are ordained; this ritual last took place in 1997. A more regular ritual called the **holai** takes place here in April or May, when live animals and food are pushed out to sea bound up in *lontar* palm boats, wrapped in *ikat* as an offering to the gods. Puppies and goat kids whose eyes are as yet unopened are particularly valued offerings, as they represent helpless victims who will endure the might of the gods in place of the villagers. You can stay here with the friendly *kepala sekola* (schoolmaster), who lives just outside the main kampung.

Pulau Raijua lies to the west of Savu and is the driest place in all of Indonesia. Even the *lontar* palm will not grow here and the locals have to live on sorghum and imported food. The Savunese believe their ancestors passed through Raijua on the way from India, so the place has much significance in their ritual affairs. A handful of hardy surfers make the arduous hike across the island to **surf** the promising reef on the south coast, camping on the beach there. The surf is worth it, but there are reputed to be hordes of tiger sharks in the Raijua Straits. Boats run to **Ledeunu** on Raijua's north coast three times a week from Seba (Rp3000, 90min); there are no boats from December to February.

Surfing on Savu can be exceptionally good: in November and December, strong winds come from the southwest, bringing great surf from **Uba Ae** beach on the south coast right round to Seba.

SUMBA

Christened by the national tourist board "The Island of Spirits", **Sumba** has a genuine reputation in Indonesia for the excesses of its funerals, the wealth of its *ikat* fabrics and the thrill of the **pasola**, an annual ritual war fought on horseback. While the spectacle is still the main reason people visit Sumba, local customs, distinctive villages and fine coastline are enough to make a trip to Sumba worthwhile at any time of year.

The east of the island is rocky, parched and fairly mountainous, and has to ship most of its food from the west. The west is contrastingly fertile and green, with rolling hills and a rainy season that seems to last twice as long as that in the east. Unlike Alor and Timor, where the intensely rugged, impenetrable landscape has led to the evolution of many completely different languages in relatively small areas, the many dialects of Sumba all have a single root. Significantly, Sumba is the only island in the archipelago whose animist **religion** is officially recognized by the Indonesian government.

East Sumba, with its capital at **Waingapu**, is well-known for producing the finest *ikat* in the whole of Indonesia; in the vicinity of Waingapu are several villages where you can see the weaving process and buy finished cloths. Many of the traditional houses no longer keep their colossal roofs clad in thatch, preferring practical but miserable-

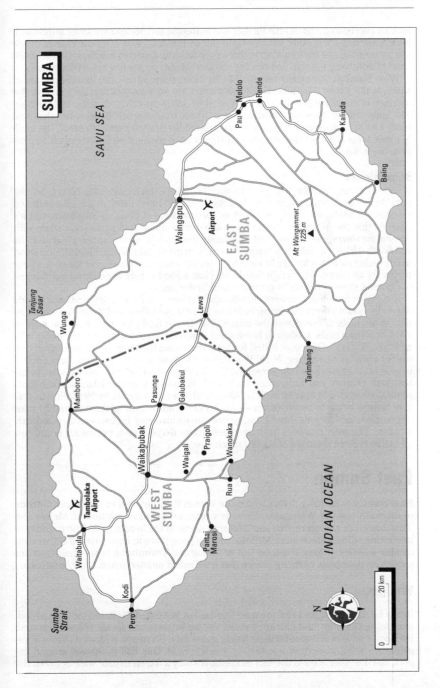

SUMBA

SAVU SEA

Melolo
Rende
Pau
Kaliuda

Baing

Waingapu
Airport

EAST
SUMBA

Mt Wangammet
1225 m

Tanjung
Sasar

Wunga

Lewa

Mamboro

Tarimbang

Pasunga
Galubakul

Waikabubak

Tambolaka
Airport

Waigali
Praigoli

Wanokaka

WEST
SUMBA

Rua

Waitabula

Pantai
Marosi

INDIAN OCEAN

Kodi

Pero

Sumba
Strait

N

0   20 km

looking corrugated iron. A little further out at **Rende** and **Melolo** are stone tombs with bizarre carvings, and other villages right out on the east coast offer the chance to see quality weaving and traditional structures near to some deserted beaches. On the south coast, **Tarimbang** is an up-and-coming surfers' Mecca with a few waterfalls inland.

West Sumba is especially remarkable for its stunning rituals, the most important of which is the *pasola*. The funerals of the district are also noteworthy; they involve the sacrifice of many animals and are preceded by stone-dragging, dancing and singing. The main town in the west is **Waikabubak**, where characteristic houses with thatched roofs soar to an apex over 15m above the ground. In this top part of the roof, the family's heirlooms and objects of ceremonial significance are kept, so that they can be closer to the heavens.

Some history

It seems unlikely that the Javanese Majapahit empire (which claimed to control Sumba until the fifteenth century), actually had any real hold here. Later, in the sixteenth and seventeenth centuries, Sumba is listed as a vassal state of Bima on Sumbawa, and it's possible that the Makarrese (who were allied with Bima) had small-scale trade with Sumba, for slaves, sandalwood and the sturdy **ponies** that were shipped as far as India and South Africa. The island is marked on early maps as "Sandalwood Island", the wood mainly being exported for use as incense in temples and shrines all over the east. These trades are all long dead, though Sumba still has a good supply of powerful but diminutive ponies, most obviously in evidence during the *pasola*.

Incursions by colonial powers onto Sumba's shores were inevitably brief and bloody due to incessant internal **warring** between Sumbanese tribes, and their ferocious hostility to attempts to overpower the island. The Dutch finally set up a garrison here in 1906, collecting taxes, trading in horses and enforcing their presence with violent military "pacification". This reign lasted for forty years until the Japanese took nominal control for a brief period during World War II. None of these invaders managed any notable degree of religious conversion amongst the Sumbanese – Christian missionaries in the twentieth century had little more luck, and the majority of the island's inhabitants remain committed to animist beliefs. Along with the missionaries in the twentieth century, Sumba began to receive a very slow trickle of **anthropologists** attracted by tales of grandiose ceremonies, head-hunting and rituals involving human sacrifice and cannibalism. The latter practices have been defunct for decades now, but the ideas and customs that created them are still very much alive.

East Sumba

East Sumba is far drier, flatter and more barren than the west of the island. Outside of the main town of **Waingapu**, there is organized **accommodation** at Melolo and Tarimbang, but anywhere else you'll have to speak to the kepala desa. The majority of interesting villages are around **Melolo**, so it's a good place to base yourself rather than making a series of long day-trips out of Waingapu. **Tarimbang** is the main spot for surfers on the island, catching waves that have rolled uninterrupted from Antarctica.

Waingapu

It may be the largest port and town on Sumba, but **WAINGAPU** is still far from a modern metropolis. Pigs and chickens roam the backstreets and locals still walk around barefoot, with *ikat* tied around their heads and waists. Waingapu is shaped like an hourglass, two small, close towns joined by a single road. One half is centred around the port, and the other around the bus terminal. It's only a fifteen-minute walk between the

VILLAGE CULTURE AND TOURISM

One of the main reasons to visit Sumba is to experience first-hand the extraordinary agrarian **animist cultures** that thrive everywhere on the island. The Sumbanese village is at the heart of all matters spiritual, quite striking in its design, its most distinguishing feature being huge clan houses topped with hat-like roofs. Most villages are set upon fortified hills, centred around megalithic graves and topped by a totem made from a petrified tree, where enemy skulls would be displayed after a head-hunting raid. Very few villages still exhibit skull trees, as they have been made illegal by the Indonesian government.

Although tradition here is still thriving, there are also many customs that are slowly fading away. Young women no longer tattoo their arms and cut holes from their earlobes when they reach maturity and, apart from the really remote villages, most women have taken to wearing blouses. Teeth-filing is also now a rarity, but male circumcision is still commonplace.

Sumbanese life is all about achieving a peaceful equilibrium with the *merapu*, the **spirits** that inhabit their surroundings and are imbued with the ghosts of dead ancestors. The most important part of life for the Sumbanese is **death**, when the mortal soul makes the journey into the superior spirit world. Dying is seen as an honour, dying in a ritual context even more so. Sumbanese **funerals** can be extremely impressive spectacles, particularly if the deceased is a person with prestige such as a village chief or priest. Even the funeral of a child will warrant the sacrifice of five or six pigs. An important person may be sent on their way with several days' worth of slaughter and feasting, the corpse buried wrapped in hundreds of exquisite *ikat* cloths. Until a hundred years ago, the wealthy would also have been kept company in their tombs by their newly sacrificed wives, horses and slaves. The government recently set limits on the numbers of animal sacrifices allowed, to prevent families bankrupting themselves, but limits are rarely observed.

The difficulty for **Western visitors** to Sumba is that traditions and taboos in Sumbanese village life are still very powerful and sit ill at ease with the demands of modern tourism. A visitor to a Sumbanese village must first take the time to share *cirih pinang* (**betel nut**) with both the kepala desa and his hosts. Betel nut is a sign of peace and of unity; Sumbanese ritual culture sets great store by returning blood to the earth, and the bright-red gobs of saliva produced by chewing *cirih* represent this blood. Historically, the only people who came into a village without betel were those who were coming in search of war and trophy heads. While the people here have mostly seen enough camera-wielding Westerners without the time, language, inclination or knowledge to indulge in such traditions and are unlikely to take them for cannibals, they still find them rude, are puzzled as to their intentions and may receive tourists with distrust or disinterest.

Many villages that are on the regular trail for group tours have supplanted the tradition of sharing betel with a simple request for money, but if you come with gifts and a little understanding you will be far more welcome.

---

two, but an endless army of bemos do the circular trip and will generally drop you off exactly where you want to go for Rp400. The bay to the west of town has a harbour at the extreme northern point of either shore: the eastern harbour serves ferries and is right at the foot of the town, the western harbour is for larger ships and requires an eight-kilometre journey all around the bay.

There's little in the town for tourists, but if there's something you need and you can't find it in Waingapu, you certainly won't find it anywhere else on Sumba. A couple of shops towards the bus terminal sell photographic film, but be sure to check the sell-by date and don't expect a great choice. There's a reasonable **pharmacy** on the linking road, and two **markets**. The market by the bus terminal is grubby but full of pushy *ikat* traders, and fantastic fruits and vegetables imported from the west. The market towards the port is just grubby. A small **Hindu temple** near to *Ali's Losmen* often has Balinese music playing and they may let you in for a closer inspection if you're polite.

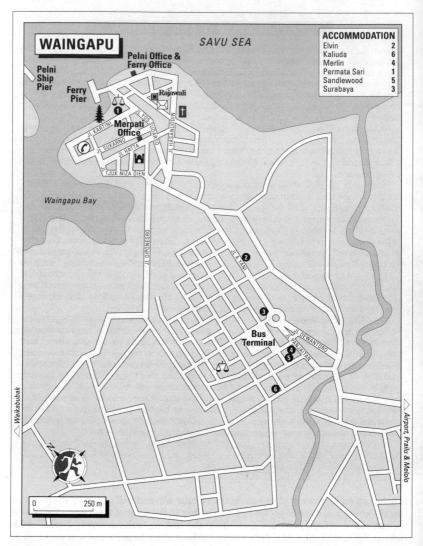

Practicalities

Most visitors to Sumba arrive in Waingapu by sea; **ferries** coming from Ende on Flores dock at the harbour on the east of the bay, a short walk from town. Pelni ferries arrive about 8km away to the west, and packed **bemos** will meet you and drop you off at hotels in town. The **airstrip** is about 10km to the southeast on the road to Rende: if there are no buses waiting to take you into town, head out to the main road and flag one down.

The **bus terminal** is in the southern part of town and can be a bit of a scrum, but there are several hotels and losmen within easy walking distance. When heading west from this terminal to **Waikabubak** (4hr30min; Rp5000), don't buy tickets from the touts without first finding out which bus will leave first and checking that it is nearly full. The offices for **Pelni** ships and **ferry** services are both down at the bottom of the hill near the east pier and can be guaranteed to give you inaccurate information on the journey of your choosing. The **Merpati office** is on Jalan Sukarno near to *Ali's Losmen*. It's worth noting that if you are planning on flying out of Sumba, do it from Waingapu rather than Tambolaka; the western airport has an appalling record for cancellations. There are three **banks** in town, but only the BRI will change travellers' cheques – it's on Jalan Achmad Yani and also arranges cash advances on credit cards. The main **post office** with poste restante is on Jalan Hasanuddin, the 24hr **Telkom** on Jalan Tjut Nya Dien.

ACCOMMODATION

The majority of **places to stay** are at the terminal end of town, only two being near the port. The hotels all offer rental cars with driver at around US$50 a day, and most can offer a selection of *ikat* for sale.

Hotel Elvin, Jl Achmad Yani (☎0386/62097). The staff are attentive, friendly and helpful. There's lots of expensive refurbishment going on here and it should be one of the better places in town when finished. ③–④.

Losmen Kaliuda, Jl Lalamentik 3 (☎0386/61264). Very close to the bus terminal, this is not a bad place – quite quiet and friendly with the option of shared or en-suite mandi. ③.

Hotel Merlin, Jl Panjaitan (☎0386/61300). Easily the plushest place in Waingapu. The rooms sparkle, most have air-con and en-suite bathrooms, and if you are feeling extravagant their top-floor restaurant is a great place for a meal. Also on the top gallery next to the restaurant is a good but expensive art shop. ④.

Losmen Permata Sari, Jl Kartini 8 (☎0386/61516). At the port end of town. Usually known as *Ali's*, this is the travellers' favourite in Waingapu. Ali himself is now big in politics and known by pretty much everyone in Sumba. Some parts of the losmen are falling apart but the proprietor is planning on building rooms (and moving upmarket). The rooms are all pretty sizable and have attached mandi. ②.

Hotel Sandle Wood, Jl W.J. Lalaimantik (☎0386/61887). This place looks a little jaded now, but still has some charm. There's a back room which serves as an art shop, stuffed full of piles of dusty *ikat* blankets; ask the manager if you want a look. Rooms range from basic with mandi outside through to full air-con, TV and en-suite bathrooms. ②–④.

Hotel Surabaya, Jl El Tari 2 (☎0386/61125). Close to the bus terminal, and tends to get noisy; the rooms are a bit dingy but passable. ②–③.

EATING

There's a very limited choice here unless you choose the **restaurants** in the hotels. A fair few warung and food carts are dotted about town, but the food is generally of a lower standard than other comparable places around Nusa Tenggara.

Hotel Elvin, Jl Achmad Yani. Has an excellent restaurant with cold beer and quite a long menu, mainly of Chinese and seafood.

Hotel Merlin, Jl Panjaitan. On the fourth floor at the top of a Himalayan staircase with fine views of the town, the food is perhaps the most expensive on Sumba: around Rp25,000 for a full Chinese meal with several courses.

Restaurant Rajawali, right by the post office on Jl Hasanuddin. While not exceptional, this is a friendly place to eat basic local food such as nasi campur and meat stews from Rp5000 a head.

Hotel Surabaya, Jl El Tari 2. Serves "black beer" and well-priced *bintang*, as well as a limited selection of Chinese food: the chicken or prawns in sambal is quite a good choice at Rp5000.

Around Waingapu

Few people come to East Sumba without checking out a few of the *ikat*-weaving villages that are its prime attraction, several of which are in the immediate vicinity of Waingapu and can be reached quickly and easily. **PRAILU** is the most visited, just a ten-minute bemo hop away. After signing in at the large traditional house you will probably be directed to, and paying Rp1000 or so, you can inspect weavings that weren't good enough to be bought by the traders. **Kwangu** is 10km from Prailu on the Melolo road, where you can see more *ikat* and a few tombs, but it's nothing special. **Lamba Napu** lies about 6km off the main road from Prailu and receives slightly fewer visitors than the other two. If you really want to buy some *ikat* in east Sumba, it's wise to take a few days purely getting some experience about the stuff, and going to these villages to see the processes is a good start.

PRAINATANG, northwest of Waingapu and on the road to **Maru**, is about the finest example of a traditional village in the east. It's beautifully set on a hill-top above a fertile plain. Not many travellers get up here; only one bus a day goes from Waingapu, leaving at 7am (3–5hr; Rp5000). If this has left then you will have to catch a bus to **Mondu** and walk the rest of the way; it's about 5km.

For the really adventurous, it's possible to continue from Mondu up to the northern cape of Sumba at **TANJUNG SASAR**, about another 40km northeast of Prainatang. Here the people are relatively untouched by the modern world, still wear clothes made from tree bark, and live in strict accordance to animist dictates.

THE SUMBANESE IKAT TRADITION

The **ikat** blankets of East Sumba are ablaze with dragons, animals, gods and head-hunting images. Each creature is associated with certain qualities: the turtle, for example, is identified with the feminine and is the most dignified and wise of creatures; the crocodile represents the masculine. Other characters such as the Chinese dragon and the Dutch lion are obvious imports, generally designed to appeal to foreign traders. The *patola rato*, a motif which originated in India, has become very highly prized. Only rajahs were allowed to make and wear cloths with this flower-like pattern. Other popular images include *andung*, or head-hunting symbols, the skull tree, and *anatau* (a corpse) in its pre-burial state.

The cloth worn by men is called the **hinggi**, and is made from two identical panels sewn together into a symmetrical blanket. One is worn around the waist and another draped across one shoulder. These are the most popular cloths for souvenir seekers, as they make great wall-hangings. The cloth worn by women is called the **lau** and is a cylindrical skirt.

The process of making *ikat* in East Sumba is especially laborious. The cotton is generally harvested in July and **spinning** continues until October. Patterns are then tied onto the vertical warp threads of the cloth, with dye-resistant string. These strings serve much the same function as wax in batik; when the cloth is dyed, the covered parts will not take up the colour and the design will be represented on them in negative. After the rains in April and May, the indigo and *kombu* (rust) dye baths are prepared and the threads are soaked. The baths must be obscured from men's eyes: they smell of rotting corpses and are taboo. The dyeing is repeated to intensify the colours and threads are re-tied so that the design can incorporate many different colours and shades. Finally, weaving begins in August, a year after the process was begun.

Ikat is one of the most traded fabrics in Indonesia, and methods to make it cheaper and easier to produce, while maintaining the high price, are commonplace. Most pieces retailing at under US$100 will use a *campur* (mix) of traditional vegetable dyes and manufactured chemical dyes. Many cloths under US$50 will use only chemical dye. Whilst most cloths use hand-spun cotton for the vertical threads, black, commercially produced threads are usually used for the horizontal weft. Bright and vibrant colours are achieved on the best cloths by repeated dippings in the dye baths, on lesser cloths with chemicals; it's not often easy to tell the difference. The attractive fading that denotes an **antique cloth** can be hastened by simple sun-bleaching or washing in rice water.

A tight weave, clean precise motifs and sharp edges between different colours are all signs of a good piece. Dealers in the towns will often give you better prices than those in the villages; generally the villagers have guaranteed sales for all their work, with a steady supply of Japanese and Balinese traders ready to pay big money for work fresh off the loom.

The east Sumban villages

The villages of eastern Sumba have made small concessions to modernity, now sporting rusty metal roofs on their houses and using concrete to build their tombs. Most of these villages are used to visitors and will request around Rp1000 as a "signing-in fee", even if you bring betel nut to offer on arrival.

East of Waingapu, and just before the larger town of Melolo, are **PAU** and **UMBARA**. Pau, though tiny, is actually an independent kingdom with its own rajah, an interesting character who is very knowledgeable about Sumba and its traditions. Umbara has a few thatched roof houses and some tombs; to see them you will be expected to pay Rp1000. Buses from Waingapu to Melolo (90min; Rp3000) run until the late afternoon and you can ask the driver to stop at Pau or Umbara.

MELOLO, 62km from Waingapu, has three high-roofed houses and a few crudely carved tombs as well as a clean and friendly **losmen** (②), which is a good place if you intend to do a fairly extended tour in the area. The next major settlement as you head east is **RENDE**. Here the house roofs are all made from tin, but are nevertheless spectacular, and doorways are adorned with unfeasibly huge buffalo horns. Rende is also the site of the finest **tombs** in East Sumba, huge flat slabs topped by animal carvings. There are buses every couple of hours direct to Rende from Waingapu (2hr; Rp3500), and occasional trucks; otherwise, catch a bus to Melolo and one of the regular bemos from there. There are also regular buses and trucks from Melolo.

South of Rende on the east coast, **KALIUDA** is a small, fairly traditional village with a justified reputation for producing the best *ikat* on the island. However, the villagers have no interest in selling individual pieces and, unless you are lucky enough to arrive at a fallow time, you won't get a good price for a cloth here. Heading west further round the coast at **BAING** is the *Palm Resort* (⑤), a **fishing** venture set up by a group of Australians who hope to draw wealthy sport fishermen out here. The surf is reasonable in the middle of the year.

About 40km out of Waingapu on the road west to Waikabubak, a turn-off leads down to **TARIMBANG** on the south coast. Here the *Martin Homestay* (② full board), with its rooms fashioned to resemble Sumbanese clan houses, caters for surfers and those looking for quiet beaches and a bit of relaxation. The surf can be outstanding and it's a nice place to hang out for a while. From here the road curves round to the east to **PRAINGKAREHA**. It's not much of a village, but there's a wonderful waterfall about four-kilometre walk from the road, with a pool at the bottom where you can swim. Several kilometres further down the Praingkareha road is another waterfall near **LUMBUNG**. This one is about a quarter of the height, but during the rainy season has a huge volume of water cascading over it and is also a great place to cool down; it's about a two-kilometre walk from the main road. For both falls you will need to ask directions or even ask someone in Praingkareha to direct you to the *air terjun* (waterfall); if they offer to guide you, a few thousand rupiah would be a suitable recompense.

West Sumba

Western Sumba has attracted eager **anthropologists** for a hundred years. It's one of the few places left in Indonesia with true commitment to its animist, spiritual past, a past that manifests itself in spectacular **rituals** and vibrant **festivals**, offering unforgettable experiences to its visitors. The largest town in the west is **Waikabubak**, which contains several enclosed kampung where life proceeds according to the laws of the spirits, just a stone's throw away from the town centre.

The extreme western districts are fast becoming the most popular destination for travellers. The **Pero** district, for example, offers some wonderful beaches and excellent

THE PASOLA

By far the best known and most dazzling festival in Nusa Tenggara, the **pasola** is one of those rare spectacles that actually surpasses all expectations. This brilliant pageant of several hundred colourfully attired, spear-wielding horsemen in a frenetic and lethal pitched battle is truly unforgettable. The only problem for the visitor is that it's difficult to predict when the event will take place; it occurs within the first two moons of the year, and is set off by the mass appearance of a type of sea worm. *Pasola* comes from the local word *sola*, which means throwing spear.

The event is a rite to balance the upper sphere of the heavens and the lower sphere of the seas, a duality reflected by West Sumbanese settlements, which have an upper village in the hills and a lower village down towards the seashore. The *pasola* places the men of each village as two teams in direct opposition; the spilling of their blood placates the spirits and restores balance between the two spheres. The proceedings begin several weeks before the main event, with villages hurling abuse and insults at their neighbours in order to get the blood up. As the day approaches, all prospective combatants must bring a chicken to their village *ratu*, who sacrifices it and examines the spirit messages in its intestines to divulge the bearer's suitability for the conflict. Should the guts bear bad signs, the owner will be forbidden from taking part.

During the full-moon period in the first or second lunar month of the year, priests keep watch on the coastlines each morning for the coming of the **nyale**. *Nyale* is the name of the goddess of the oceans, and is also given to the sea worm *Eunis viridis*, whose annual procreation sets off festivals all over the archipelago. For two days a year, the shores are turned into a maelstrom of luminous red, yellow and blue as the cavorting worms wash into the shallows to be eagerly harvested by the locals. In the month preceding this time, fishing, bathing and even surfing is strictly forbidden off the *pasola* beaches. When ashore, the worms are a rather dull brown or dark-green and black colour and have a flavour and consistency somewhere between seaweed and oysters. For best results they should be consumed raw and wriggling, but can be boiled, fried or baked, and are highly prized for their aphrodisiac qualities.

When the *nyale* arrive, they are examined by the high priests, their quality relating to the quality of the ensuing harvest, then the **fighting** commences – actually on the beaches. After a few tentative exchanges, the two teams will trek to the special *pasola* fields where the battle has taken place for centuries. The teams surge towards each other, usually led by a single warrior, who will attempt to isolate one of the opposition for a "kill". Spears fill the air and many of the combatants are startlingly accurate. Injuries are numerous and riders are often trampled underfoot. Fatalities are now relatively rare since the Indonesian government ruled that the spears must not carry sharpened tips, but it is still a potentially lethal event. This is not a circus show arranged for tourists: be aware that your safety is irrelevant to the participants, so always stay behind the guide ropes and keep a good distance if there aren't any barriers.

The *pasola* takes place in Lamboya and Kodi in February and in Wanokaka and Gaura in March; most of the hotels in town can give you a rough idea of when it will occur.

surf, combined with perfect examples of Sumbanese traditional villages, those near **Kodi** having the highest roofs in Sumba. **Wanokaka** and **Lamboya** districts, south of the western capital, host annual *pasola* festivals (see box) and have a wealth of villages dotting the countryside atop fortified hills as the land gently slopes down to the coast. There are embryonic beach resorts at **Rua** and **Marosi**, with pristine coastlines where foreigners still bewilder the locals by either frying in the sun or by sitting in the waves all day on a plastic plank. East of Waikabubak in the **Anakalang** district are the most-photographed **tombs** in Sumba.

The **ikat** of West Sumba may suffer in comparison with its eastern cousin, but there are many attractive cloths made here. More compact motifs with fewer colours are used, along with stylized symbols that often only suggest the eyes or the tail of a creature. Another important West Sumban symbol is the *mamuli*; an omega shape that is often seen in earrings or pendants and traditionally only worn by the *ratu*, the high priests of the Merapu religion. The shape represents the female vagina and uterus, enclosed by a male exterior. Also peculiar to this part of the island are **swords** with carved bone or wood handles, and grotesque masks and statues, complete with animal hair and teeth.

Waikabubak

WAIKABUBAK is a tiny town consisting of one dirt road flanked by shops, the few buildings surrounded by lush green meadows and forested hills. One of the most striking facets of the town is that several enclosed **kampung** with slanting thatched roofs and megalithic **stone graves** nestle among the more modern buildings, with their concrete and satellite dishes. The western capital bears little relation to Waingapu in the east; whereas the east spends the majority of the year on the brink of drought, Waikabubak enjoys an extended rainy season that lasts way into May, when the countryside can be drenched by daily downpours. Due to Waikabubak's slight elevation, it can get a bit chilly at night in rainy season.

One of the most important ritual sites in Sumba is to be found right in the town itself. **Tarung** kampung, on a hill-top just west of the main street, has some excellent megalithic graves and is regarded as one of the most significant spiritual centres on the island. The *ratu* of Tarung are responsible for the annual **wula padu** ceremony, which lasts for a month at the beginning of the Merapu new year in November. The ceremony commemorates the visiting spirits of important ancestors, who are honoured with the sacrifice of many animals and entertained by singing and dancing. The *ratu* enforce a month of repose before the festive final day, during which even mourning is forbidden in Tarung. There are plenty of other kampung worth seeing in and around Waikabubak, **Kampung Praijiang** – a five-tiered village on a hill-top surrounded by rice paddies – being a particularly good example several kilometres east of town. You can catch a bemo to the bottom of the hill and will be asked for Rp1500 to look around and take photographs.

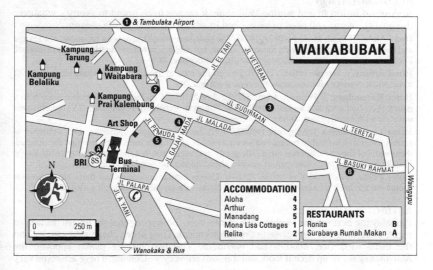

Practicalities

Most people **arrive** in Waikabubak at the **bus terminal** in the southeast of the town. Tambolaka **airport** is a good ninety-minute drive from the north of town; buses and or taxis meet arriving planes and bring passengers to Waikabubak.

Most things that you will need in Waikabubak are either on the main street of Jalan Achmad Yani, or within several minutes walk of it. At the southern end, the market and bus terminal are sandwiched together, with the 24hr **Telkom office** a few hundred metres further south. Opposite the bus-station turn-off is an interesting **art shop** full of old carvings and a few pieces of jewellery and *ikat*. The tarpaulin-covered **market**, though dirty and fly-filled is well worth a stroll. People come from all over west Sumba to buy and sell, sporting colourful *ikat* sarongs and with their mouths stained black by betel nut. The men can sometimes be seen with a distinctive headdress of two scarves, usually a white one around the ears and a red one wound under the chin and up over the crown of the head to make two horns.

The new **BRI bank** is a stone's throw west of the bus terminal and will change US dollars cash if the bills are pristine. The bus station services all areas of western Sumba, and trucks and bemos also stop here. All of these services run far too erratically to make a route listing worthwhile; buses to Waingapu usually stop running around 2pm, and you will find it difficult to get a bus anywhere after late morning. The **Merpati office**, which is often closed, is on the right-hand side of Jalan Achmad Yani on the second floor of a dusty grain store. The **post office** is to be found at the northern end of Jalan Achmad Yani where it meets Jalan Sudirman (Mon–Thurs & Sat 9am–2pm, Fri 9–11.30am).

Moving on, buses leave daily for Tambolaka airport in the early mornings and will pick you up at your hotel door in plenty of time to get there. To make sure of this, go to the bus depot which is in the back yard of the house opposite the *Hotel Manandang* the evening before you leave, and ask them to pick you up. Be warned that flights out of Tambolaka airport have an atrocious reputation for being cancelled or severely delayed, especially in the rainy season. In *pasola* season, when flights are more reliable, they are always full, and you should book months in advance. If you need to rely on leaving Sumba at a precise time then go by **ferry** from Waingapu.

ACCOMMODATION

Accommodation in and around Waikabubak ranges from grand to grotty – whatever the quality, rooms will need to be booked in advance during *pasola* season.

Hotel Aloha, Jl Gajah Mada (☎0387/21024). The beds here should have been replaced decades ago and the mandi are brimming with mosquito larvae, but *Aloha* is saved by the friendliness of its staff. For the budget traveller it is still, undoubtedly, number one. ②.

Hotel Arthur, Jl Veteran (☎0387/21112). Just off the road in from Waingapu. Quite clean and with a reasonable variety of rooms around a central garden. ③.

Hotel Manandang, Jl Permuda 4 (☎0387/21292 or 21197). A clean and comfortable place with a gaudy reception area and a giant satellite TV. The most expensive rooms have TV; the cheapest ones are a little overpriced. ③–④.

Mona Lisa Cottages, Jl Adhyaksa (☎0387/21364, fax 21042). Quite upmarket, with a number of semi-detached or individual bungalows set on a hillside about 2km from town amongst the rice paddies. Some of the cheaper ones are a little grotty and very dark, but the top ones are really lovely. Usually booked by large tour groups months ahead during the *pasola* season. ④–⑤.

Hotel Pelita, Jl Achmad Yani (☎0387/21104). Unspectacular and noisy, but there are three new rooms out the back that are quite pleasant and clean, with en-suite mandi and patios. ②

EATING

Probably the best **food** in Waikabubak comes from the warung that set up, particularly at night, along Achmad Yani close to the bus terminal. They serve cheap sate, curries and the usual fried rice, noodles and *murtabak*. The two Padang places opposite the *Manandang* serve up decent food, and the staff are very welcoming. There are some very unsanitary **warung** around the market; you may well find the proprietor putting a severed buffalo head next to your meal and starting to hack off the least palatable bits for the pot.

Hotel Manandang, The flashiest restaurant in Waikabubak, twice the price of something similar on the street. It is, however, far the most hygienic option, and their fried *tempe* is excellent.

Ronita, Jl Basuki Rahmat. Comprehensive karaoke facilities for those who want to hear a hundred Indonesian renditions of *Hey Jude*. The menu looks better than the food but it's still one of the best places in town.

Rumah Makan Surabaya, next to the BRI bank. The menu is limited but the proprietor is very friendly – the sate is pretty good and the rest of the food reasonable.

Anakalang

Anakalang district, to the east of Waikabubak, is known for being the site of the most impressive **tomb** in Sumba, which is found beside the main road at **Kampung Pasunga**. An exquisitely carved upright slab fronts the table-shaped grave, its fascia adorned with a male and female figure standing side by side and its sides carved with smaller figures. The kampung lies about 20km east of Waikabubak and is quite striking, consisting of two rows of towering parallel buildings, topped by tin roofs.

Opposite Pasunga, a sideroad leads about 1km down to **MATAKAKERI**. Unless you are lucky enough to encounter one of the irregular bemos that head this way, you'll have to walk. On the way you pass through a market, which has a part-time warung providing noodles and eggs. When you reach the village, you'll be directed to the large house at the end of the kampung, where you pay Rp1000 to look around. They do a roaring trade in *kelapa muda* (young coconut) at around Rp500 a time. Matakakeri is home to the single largest **tomb** in Sumba, but it's pretty much uncarved and not particularly interesting. From the tomb, walk around the back of the huts and follow the path for the ten-minute walk up to **LAI TARUNG**. This hill-top kampung is a good place to get a view of the surrounding countryside, with its verdant fields, hedgerows and forested hills. There are actually several different kampung on different levels, and the name "Lai Tarung" only refers to one at the summit. There's a ritual structure here, with a thatched roof resting on several carved, petrified columns – a resting place for the dead. If you share betel nut with the family who live in the one serviceable house and ask nicely, they may show you inside to see their drum, which they claim is made from human belly skin.

GALLUBAKUL is the next kampung down the main road from Pasunga and also has a few huge tombs, which you'll have to pay to see. Beyond here is the eastern part of the **Wanokaka** area, most of which lies south of Waikabubak. A few trucks infrequently venture down this way; otherwise, you'll have to walk.

Wanokaka

Travelling in **Wanokaka district** is very rewarding, as all the villages are built to traditional patterns and it's far from touristy. However, it is one of the poorest areas in Sumba; malnutrition and disease are commonplace so you should take great care to bring as many of your own supplies as possible and try to share as much as you can. Most villages will gladly take you in, but don't expect comfort.

The usual route into the Wanokaka area is to go due south out of Waikabubak. Most tourists take the left fork in this road that heads to **WAIGALI** village, popular as the site of some excellent stone **tombs**. The inauguration ceremonies for the area's *pasola* take place in the *pusat* or navel at the highest point of this village, an important religious site. From here there is a great 360-degree panorama of the surrounding countryside, and the large sacrificial altars are often caked with blood from recent ceremonies. Heading south you'll pass through several settlements. **Laihuruk** has a Saturday market when, with a little luck and determination, you may well be able to catch a truck to some very remote villages. **PRAIGOLI** is another often-visited hamlet near the south of here, famous for its large and beautifully sculpted tomb. From here you can get all the way down to the **beach**. It's a stunning walk with the coast far ahead of you, and the sea winds are usually strong enough to take the edge off the heat of the sun.

The alternate fork in the road before Waigali heading south eventually reaches **Rua** beach, about 18km from Waikabubak. You might be lucky enough to pick up transport in town or on the road near Waigali, but the wonderful views make walking or cycling a real joy, a fantastic panorama of cornfields dotted with palm trees and hill-top kampung, rolling down to the sea. There are also buses from Waikabubak to the turn-off for Lamboya, which is well south of Waigali and shortens the walk by an hour or so. On Wednesday a market is held in nearby **Padedewatu**, and you may be able to get a truck all the way to Rua. The beaches here are sensational, long stretches of empty sands with dramatic crashing surf, with forest and palm trees right down to the beachfront; it's a little too rough for safe swimming. Rua village has one budget **losmen** catering mainly for surfers. The *Ahong* homestay (③ full board) is friendly and basic and provides three large meals a day. Further round the headland, *Sumba Reef Lodge* (⑨) is an exclusive hotel with all mod cons, usually serving package tourists from Bali.

Instead of following the road from Waikabubak directly south all the way to the coast, some travellers choose to take the second major turning off towards **Lamboya**. Buses from Waikabubak will usually stop here and then it's an enjoyable five-kilometre downhill walk to **MAROSI**. A budget homestay on the way provides full board – the *Matebelu* (③), which is about 2km from a paradisal coastline where *nyale* are gathered before the *pasola*. The views from here are magnificent, and if you walk around the surrounding countryside you'll find yourself in some quite isolated settlements. The surf can be excellent, though you'll have to carry your board all the way down to the beach every day. One bus a day, the *Nusa Cendada*, leaves Waikabubak at 7am heading into this area: ask beforehand if it will go all the way to Marosi.

Kodi and Pero

In the extreme west of Sumba lie the increasingly popular areas of Kodi and Pero. The Kodi district, with its centre in the village of **BANDOKODI**, is particularly well-known for the towering roofs that top the traditional houses. There is one bus direct a day from Waikabubak to Bandokodi; otherwise you'll have to take a bus to **Waitabula** in the north and then wait for a bus to fill up for the trip around the coast.

This bus will usually take you all the way to **PERO**, a seaside village with one losmen. The village is not constructed in traditional Sumbanese style, but its rough cobbled street flanked by colourful wooden houses has a certain charm. Numerous kampung with teetering high roofs and mossy stone **tombs** dot the surrounding countryside, only a short walk away. The *Homestay Story* (③ full board) is quite clean and provides huge meals, but come prepared for the mosquitoes. To get to the beach, walk down the path outside the losmen and then either head left across the river (local kids will charge exorbitant fees to ferry you across when the tide is high) or right, down to where the most regular offshore surf breaks are. The beach to the left is very sheltered with a narrow stretch of fine yellow sand, whereas the other is far more exposed. Whichever one you choose it'll become immediately evident that the currents here are not to be messed with – the undertow can be ferocious and even with a surfboard you're not necessarily safe. If you have crossed the river to the south you could carry on around the coast to the villages of **Ratenggaro**, **Paranobaro** and **Wainyapu**. Their houses are the skyscrapers of Nusa Tenggara, the roofs towering to nearly 20m, and their coastline settings are perfect. It can be quite infuriating trying to find the villages: their roofs are visible from kilometres away but it's often impossible to find the right path unaided. Local kids will be glad to guide you – offer a few pens or candy as a thankyou.

travel details

Buses and bemos

It's almost impossible to give the **frequency** with which bemos and buses run, as they only depart when they have enough passengers to make the journey worthwhile. However, on the most popular routes you should be able to count on getting a ride within thirty minutes if you travel before noon; things quieten down in the afternoon and come to a standstill by around 5pm. **Journey times** also vary a great deal. The times given below are the minimum you can expect the journeys to take.

Ampenan to: Senggigi (20min).

Bajawa to: Ende (4hr); Labuhanbajo (10hr); Moni (5hr 30min); Ruteng (5–6hr).

Bima to: Mataram (Bima terminal 11hr); Sape (Kumbe terminal; 2hr); Sumbawa Besar (Bima terminal; 7hr).

Dili to: Atambua (Tasitolo terminal; 3hr 30min); Bacau (Becora terminal; 3hr); Los Palos (Becora terminal; 6hr); Kupang (Tasitolo terminal; 12hr); Maubisse (Leusari terminal; 2hr 30min).

Ende to: Bajawa (Ndao terminal; 4hr); Maumere (Wolowana terminal; 6hr); Moni (Wolowana terminal; 90min); Riung (Ndao terminal; 4hr).

Kupang to: Camplang (1hr); Dili (12hr); Soe (3–4hr).

Labuhan Lombok to: Bayan (2hr); Konpang (for Praya; 1hr); Sembalun Lawang (2hr 30min); Sweta (Mandalika terminal; 90min).

Labuhanbajo to: Bajawa (10hr); Ende (14hr); Ruteng (4–5hr).

Larantuka to: Maumere (4hr).

Lembar to: Sweta (Mandalika terminal; 30min).

Maumere to: Ende (Terminal Barat; 6hr); Larantuka (Terminal Lokaria; 4hr); Moni (Terminal Barat; 3hr 30min); Wodong (Terminal Lokaria; 1hr).

Poto Tano to: Alas (45min); Bima (9hr); Sumbawa Besar (2hr); Taliwang (1hr).

Praya to: Gubukdalem (1hr 30min); Kuta (1hr); Mandalika terminal, Sweta (30min).

Ruteng to: Bajawa (5–6hr); Ende (14hr); Ruteng (4–5hr).

Soe to: Kupang (3–4hr); Niki-Niki (1hr).

Sumbawa Besar to: Bima (7hr); Dompu (4hr 30min); Sape (8hr 30min).

Sweta (Mandalika terminal) to: Bayan (for Rinjani; 2hr 30min); Bima (Sumbawa; 12hr); Dompu (Sumbawa; 10hr); Jakarta (Java; 48hr); Labuhan Lombok (2hr); Labuhanbajo (Flores; 24hr); Lembar (30min); Pemenang (50min); Pomotong (for Tetebatu; 1hr 15min); Praya (for Kuta; 30min); Ruteng (Flores; 36hr); Sape (Flores; 14hr); Sumbawa Besar (Sumbawa; 6hr); Surabaya (20hr); Yogyakarta (26hr).

Waingapu to: Melolo (1hr 30min); Rende (3hr); Waikabubak (4hr 30min).

Waikabubak to: Tambulaka (1hr 30min); Waingapu (4hr 30min).

Pelni ferries

For a chart of the Pelni routes, see p.36–37 of Basics.

Bima to: Labuhanbajo (*KM Tatamilau*, monthly; 7hr/*KM Tilongkabila*, monthly; 7hr); Lembar (*KM Tilongkabila*, monthly; 7hr).

Dili to: Ambon (*KM Dobonsolo*, 2 monthly; 28hr); Kalabahi (*KM Awu*, monthly; 9hr); Kupang (*KM Dobonsolo*, 2 monthly; 12hr); Larantuka (*KM Tatamilau*, monthly; 14hr); Maumere (*KM Awu*, monthly; 19hr).

Ende to: Kupang (*KM Awu*, monthly; 10hr); Savu (*KM Pangrano*, monthly; 8hr); Waingapu (*KM Awu*, monthly; 8hr/*KM Pangrano*, monthly; 8hr).

Kalabahi to: Dili (*KM Awu*, monthly; 6hr).

Kupang to: Denpasar (*KM Dobonsolo*, 2 monthly; 1 day); Dili (*KM Dobonsolo*, 2 monthly; 12hr); Ende (*KM Awu*, monthly; 12hr); Kalabahi (*KM Awu*, 2 monthly; 2hr); Larantuka (*KM Siriman*, 2 monthly; 9hr); Savu (*KM Pangrano*, monthly; 10hr);

Larantuka to: Dili (*KM Tatamilau*, monthly; 10hr); Kupang (*KM Siriman*, 2 monthly; 9hr).

Lembar to: Bau Bau (*KM Tilongkabila*, monthly; 3 days); Bima (*KM Tilongkabila*, monthly; 24hr); Bitung(*KM Tilongkabila*, monthly; 5 days); Denpasar (*KM Tilongkabila*, monthly; 4hr); Gorontola (*KM Tilongkabila*, monthly; 4 days); Kendari (*KM Tilongkabila*, monthly; 3 days); Kolonedale (*KM Tilongkabila*, monthly; 3 days); Labuhanbajo (*KM Tilongkabila*, monthly; 31hr); Lirung (*KM Tilongkabila*, monthly; 6 days); Luwuk (*KM Tilongkabila*, monthly; 4 days); Makasar (*KM Tilongkabila*, monthly; 48hr); Raha (*KM Tilongkabila*, monthly; 3 days); Tahuna (*KM Tilongkabila*, monthly; 8 days).

Maumere to: Dili (*KM Awu*, monthly; 20hr).

Roti to: Kupang (*KM Pangrano*, monthly; 11hr).

Savu to: Ende (*KM Pangrano*, monthly; 10hr); Roti (*KM Pangrano*, monthly; 7hr).

Waingapu to: Denpasar (*KM Awu*, monthly; 26hr); Ende (*KM Awu*, monthly; 10hr/*KM Pangrano*, monthly; 12hr); Labuhanbajo (*KM Pangrano*, monthly; 11hr).

Other ferries

Bangsal to: Gili Islands (several times daily; 20–45min).

Ende to: Waingapu (Sumba; daily; 10hr).

Kalabahi to: Kupang (Timor; 3 weekly; 16hr); Atapupu (Timor; weekly; 7hr); Larantuka (weekly; 24hr).**Labuhan Lombok** to: Poto Tano (Sumbawa; hourly; 2hr).

Larantuka to: Kupang (Timor; 2 weekly; 14hr); Adonara, Solor, Lembata (2 daily; 4hr); Lembata, Pantar and Alor (every 3 days; 2 days); Lamelera, Lembata (weekly; 6–7hr).

Lembar to: Benoa Harbour (Bali; 2 daily; 2hr); Padang Bai (Bali; daily every 2hr; 4hr–4hr 30min).

Kupang to: Ende (Flores; weekly; 16hr); Kalabahi (Alor; weekly; 16hr); Laruntuka (Flores; 2 weekly; 16hr); Roti (daily; 4hr).

Sape to: Labuhanbajo (Flores; daily; 9–12hr); Komodo (daily; 5–7hr).

Senggigi to: Gili Trawangan: (daily; 1hr 30min).

Waingapu: to Ende (weekly; 10hr); Savu (weekly; 9hr).

Flights

Bima to: Bajawa (2 weekly; 1hr 15min); Denpasar (2 daily; 1hr 15min); Ende (daily; 1hr 30min); Kupang (2 daily; 2hr 10min); Labuhanbajo (4 weekly; 55min); Mataram (daily; 1hr 10min); Ruteng (daily; 1hr 10min); Surabaya (4 weekly; 2hr 20min); Waingapu (3 weekly; 1hr 30min).

Dili to: Denpasar (daily; 2hr 5min); Kupang (weekly; 1hr 20min).

Ende to: Bajawa (3 weekly; 45min); Bima (5 weekly; 1hr 30min); Kupang (6 weekly; 1hr 10min); Labuhanbajo (4 weekly; 1hr 5min).

Kupang to: Dili (weekly; 1hr 20min); Jakarta (3 weekly; 3hr 25min); Labuhanbajo (4 weekly; 2hr 45min); Larantuka (1 weekly; 1hr 5min); Leweloba (1 weekly; 1hr 50min); Maumere (daily; 55min); Roti (weekly; 55min); Ruteng (daily; 1hr 45min); Savu (weekly; 1hr 35min); Surabaya (2 daily; 2hr 5min); Tambulaka (4 weekly; 2hr 50min); Waingapu (4 weekly; 1hr 35min).

Labuhanbajo to: Bajawa (weekly; 2hr 45min); Nima (4 weekly; 45min); Ende (4 weekly; 1hr); Ruteng (3 weekly; 25min).

Mataram, Selaparang Airport to: Bima (daily; 45min); Denpasar (connecting to Jakarta; 9 daily; 30min); Kupang (daily; 5hr); Maumere (3 weekly; 3hr 30min); Singapore (daily; 2hr 30min); Sumbawa (daily; 40min); Surabaya (connecting to Jakarta; 3 daily; 45min); Waingapu (4 weekly; 3hr).

Maumere to: Bima (daily; 1hr 15min); Kupang (daily; 55min); Ujong Padang (3 weekly; 1hr 30min).

Sumbawa Besar to: Denpasar (6 weekly; 1hr 55min); Mataram (6 weekly; 45min).

Waikabubak to: Bima (3 weekly; 40min); Waingapu (3 weekly; 40min).

Waingapu to: Bima (3 weekly; 1hr); Kupang (6 weekly; 1hr 20min); Tambulaka (3 weekly; 40min).

CHAPTER TEN

KALIMANTAN

Cupped in the palm of an island arc between the Malay peninsula and Sulawesi, **Kalimantan** comprises the southern, Indonesian two-thirds of the vast island of Borneo, whose northern reaches are split between the independent sultanate of Brunei and the Malaysian states of Sabah and Sarawak. Borneo has conjured up sensational images in the outside world ever since Europeans first visited in the sixteenth century and found coastal city-states governed by wealthy sultans, whose income derived from trading trinkets and salt with inland tribes for resins, gold and gemstones – *Kalimantan* means "river of gems". Explorers who later managed to return alive from the interior confirmed rumours of a land cut by innumerable rivers

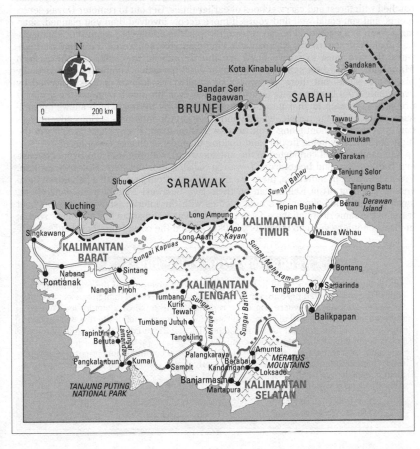

and cloaked in a silent green jungle inhabited by bizarre beasts and the infamous Dayak, pagans who collected human heads. And, until recently, the situation had changed very little, Kalimantan only emerging briefly into the limelight as the stage for Japanese–US conflict in the latter stages of World War II, and during Indonesia's Konfrontasi with Malaysia over that country's federation in 1963.

Modern Kalimantan has a tough time living up to its romantic tradition, however. Part of the problem is that, in all Kalimantan's 500,000-square-kilometre spread, there are few obvious destinations, and even the best of these often take second place to the lure of travel for its own sake. Administratively split into four unequally sized provinces, Kalimantan divides more simply into an undeveloped **interior**, with a largely Dayak population, and a more urbane Muslim **coastal fringe**, where you'll find all of the major cities. Stripped of their former status as regencies and with little obvious heritage, even the provincial capitals – **Pontianak** in Kalimantan Barat, Kalimantan Tengah's **Palangkaraya**, **Banjarmasin** in Kalimantan Selatan, and Kalimantan Timur's **Samarinda** – rarely offer much aside from their services. Get beyond them, however, and things improve: despite increasingly rapacious **logging** and **mining**, and the recent catastrophic **forest fires** in southern Kalimantan, sizable tracts of the interior remain patched with forest and carry echoes of earlier times. Get out to remoter Dayak settlements, and you could well find yourself more deeply involved than you planned, sharing a room in a traditional house, or caught up in the middle of a festival or shamanistic ritual. With few roads, Kalimantan's abundant **rivers** become the interior's highways: the two most extensive flows are the **Kapuas** in the west, and the eastern **Mahakam**, which between them total over 1100 navigable kilometres and virtually bisect the island, but there are scores of smaller, less-known options, travelled by everything from bamboo rafts to ferries. When even the rivers peg out, the properly prepared can reach further into Kalimantan's heart by **hiking**, which allows unparalleled contact with the people, wildlife and places of the interior – serious adventurers can even make a month-long **trek across Kalimantan**. Everywhere, you'll get the biggest returns by being flexible and making the most of chance encounters.

Kalimantan is well connected to the outside world, with **flights** from Brunei to eastern **Balikpapan**, and **boats** from Tewah in Sabah to northeastern **Pulau Nunukan**. From elsewhere in Indonesia, there are direct flights from Java, with a half-dozen Pelni vessels stopping off in Kalimantan on their Java–Sulawesi–Maluku runs. Once here, small aircraft link Kalimantan's bigger cities with the interior, shaving days off boat travel to the same destinations – if you can get a seat. Kalimantan has few major **roads**; in ideal conditions you can travel for 1500km around the coast from the island's south-

---

THE DAYAK

Dayak is an umbrella name for all of Borneo's indigenous peoples, who arrived here from mainland Southeast Asia around 2500 years ago and have since divided into scores of interrelated groups. Dayak **religions** trace worldly events back to the interaction of spirits: evil is kept at bay by attracting the presence of helpful spirits, or scared away by protective tattoos, carved **spirit posts** (*patong*), and courting the goodwill of the dead with lavish **funerals**. Shamans also intercede with spirits on behalf of the living, but, formerly, the most powerful way to ensure good luck was by **head-hunting**, which forced the victim's soul into the service of its captor. Head-hunting raids were often carefully planned campaigns led by warrior-magicians who invoked demons to possess their followers, granting them ferocity in battle but allowing them no rest until they had killed. Raised on three-metre-high stumps, **communal houses**, home for a clan or even a village, offered some defence against attack, as it was difficult to clamber up undetected.

Condoned by Kalimantan's sultans, head-hunting disgusted the Dutch, who made great efforts to stamp it out during the nineteenth century. Otherwise, the Dayak were well regarded by the colonial government: their honesty was legendary, and ethnographers admired their social systems, some of which defined separate **classes**. Wealth, acquired as dowries or by trading in forest products with coastal communities, was measured in bronze drums (looking more like gongs), decorative beads and Chinese dragon jars, all of which today command colossal prices from collectors. Dayak artwork too is much-sought-after, and some groups are particularly famed for their decorative designs and woodcarvings. Most Dayak still use **ladang** agriculture, in which areas of forest are clear-felled and the timber burnt to ash in order to supplement the mineral-poor topsoil; plots are farmed for a few years and then left to return to their former state. For hunting, guns have widely replaced traditional two-metre-long ironwood **blowpipes** and darts dipped in the lethal sap of the *ipoh* or **upas tree**, *antiaris toxicaria*. Fresh upas sap is white and fluid, drying as a brown, crumbly resin rendered liquid by warming – you can sometimes find older trees deeply scarred from frequent milkings. The **mandau**, a lightweight machete, is still ubiquitous as a general-purpose bush knife and was formerly the primary weapon in battle – a thinner blade attached to the back of the scabbard was for removing heads. The best blades are made from locally forged steel, though everyday versions are likely to have started life as part of a truck's suspension.

Today, all this can seem very academic. Even after slogging out to remote areas you'll often find ostensibly Christian communities whose inhabitants habitually dress in shorts and T-shirts, the dances performed at more accessible villages are stilted, and the formerly inspired crafts are now churned out as souvenirs. City dwellers are also prone to portray Dayak as wild animals, often glibly appropriating their lands for mining, timber and resettlement projects. But on their home ground the Dayak are feared for their jungle skills, abilities with magic, and the way they violently take the law into their own hands if provoked – such as in 1997, when West Kalimantan's Dayak exacted fearsome revenge against Maduran transmigrants (see p.724). There's a resurgence in the more acceptable side of tradition, too: communal houses, once banned by the government, are being restored, and public festivals like the hugely social **funerals** or the annual **Erau Festival**, a massive assembly of Kalimantan's eastern Dayak groups on Sungai Mahakam, provide an assurance that Dayak culture is still very much alive, if being redefined.

western corner right up towards the northeastern border with Sabah, with the mass of disconnected tracks probing inland from this trail often accessible to motorbikes. Reliable **all-weather roads**, however, currently extend only between Pontianak and **Sintang** in Kalimantan Barat, and from Banjarmasin to Bontang in eastern Kalimantan. The already famous **Trans-Borneo highway** across the island has actually yet to eventuate, though in 1996 a convoy of 4WD vehicles made it from Samarinda to Pontianak by following logging trails through the interior.

Crossed by the equator, Kalimantan has no real **seasons**. April through to September is the optimum time for a visit: at the height of the rains (January through to March) you'll find towns isolated by flooding, normally calm stretches of water turned to raging torrents, and planes grounded for weeks on end, while the driest months (Aug–Oct) see boats stranded by low river levels. Seasons also affect **Dayak festivals**, many of which occur during slacker agricultural periods, when people have enough spare time to participate. With only fragmentary infrastructure, Kalminatan's **costs** are higher than in most of the rest of the country, especially for transport in remote areas – fuel can be incredibly expensive. **Accommodation** is pricey, too: even simple country losmen charge US$3 a night, and it's rare in cities to find anything under US$7. Note that West and Central Kalimantan operate on Western time, while the south and eastern provinces run on Eastern time.

KALIMANTAN BARAT

Kalbar (short for "Kalimantan Barat"), or **West Kalimantan**, is Kalimantan's most densely populated province, with nearly four million inhabitants spread over 146,800 square kilometres. Unsurprisingly, given the province's relative proximity to southern China, it also has the highest ethnic Chinese population in Indonesia: a third of the population of the capital, **Pontianak**, and over two-thirds of Kalbar's second biggest town, **Singkawang**, are of Chinese origin. Of the rest of the population, nearly half are Malay with most of the rest belonging to one of the indigenous Dayak tribes, of which the Iban are the most numerous in the province.

Pontianak stands in the delta of the **Kapuas**, which at 1243km is Indonesia's longest river. Early settlers and missionaries looked upon the Kapuas as a convenient causeway to the interior of Borneo, and, as a result, the small Dayak towns that line the banks of the Kapuas, such as **Sintang** and **Putussibau**, were some of the first in Borneo to receive foreign visitors, and have a more cosmopolitan feel than many other inland settlements. The Kapuas remains an extremely busy waterway, with passenger ferries, fishing boats, *toko teapung* (the traditional floating shops of the Kapuas) and rusty little barges tugging huge trails of timber still cruising up and down the river today.

Timber remains Kalbar's number-one industry, but although the forests around the Kapuas have been seriously degraded the more remote corners of the province remain relatively untouched. The two national parks, **Gunung Palung Reserve** in the south and the nascent **Bentuang Karimun** on the border with Sarawak, contain vast tracts of primary rainforest and form the cornerstone of Kalbar's tiny tourist industry (last year only two thousand Western tourists visited Kalbar, most of whom were merely passing through on their way to Sarawak). Be warned, though, that there have been reports of chloroquine-resistant malaria in these remoter outreaches of the province.

In the first two months of 1997, the Dayak of the Kalimantan Barat undertook a campaign against the **ethnic Madurese** of the province, which took a startling and violent form. Eyewitnesses said that Dayak followed traditional pre-battle rituals, performing the *tertu* ceremony, where warriors enter a trance-like state and the spirits of their ancestors are invoked. The practice of head-hunting was also revived during the fighting. In January, 5000 Dayak, armed with machetes and *mandau* (traditional swords) stormed the villages of Sanggau Ledo, Jerak and Kampung Jawa. The army, called in to quell the unrest, was helpless in the face of such numbers, and the slaughter went unchecked: estimates of the number of deaths range from 300 to 2000. Though the region is now peaceful, underlying tension remains. The Madurese often complain of being looked over for jobs and promotion by their Dayak bosses, while the Dayak regularly complain about Madurese gangs who, they insist, are responsible for many of the crimes in the province.

Kalbar's **transport** network is improving all the time, though away from the coast and the Pontianak–Putussibau highway the roads are not sealed and often impassable in the rainy season, and public transport is unreliable all year round. Passenger ferries continue to sail up and down the Kapuas; except in the dry season, when the water level is too low.

Pontianak and around

The quaintly named capital of Kalbar (the name translates as something like "The ghost of a woman who died in childbirth"), **PONTIANAK** is a sprawling, grey industrial city of 400,000 lying right on the equator on the confluence of the Landak and Kapuas Kecil rivers. The city is at its best in the evenings, when the local kids fly their kites above the roofs, swifts flock in their thousands to find a suitable roosting spot for the night, and the sky slowly melts into a delicious golden orange hue. During the day, however, Pontianak is hot, noisy, and holds little of interest for the average sightseer.

Pontianak was founded in 1770 by an Arabian pirate-cum-trader Abdul Rahman. Its ghoulish name is a reference to the ghostly howl that early visitors to these shores heard; believing that this noise was the work of local spirits, Abdul Rahman used cannon fire to frighten them away before he landed. Initially his town was just another private fiefdom on a stretch of coastline that was dotted with them, but the discovery of gold deposits just a few kilometres to the north led to Pontianak's rapid expansion.

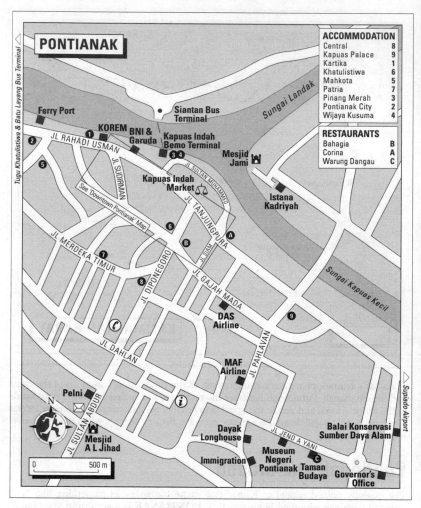

The city's provincial **museum** is one of the best of its kind in Indonesia, and Sultan Abdul Rahman's **Kadriyah Palace** and the adjoining mosque are mildly diverting too. Nevertheless, most travellers stay for only a day or so in Pontianak – just long enough to stock up on supplies and enjoy the comforts and conveniences of a big city – before heading up the Kapuas or straight on to Kuching, and in truth this isn't a bad plan.

Orientation, arrival and information

Pontianak is bisected by the north–south flowing Sungai Kapuas Kecil. On the western side of the river you'll find the Chinese quarter, the commercial heart of the city where most of the hotels, restaurants and travel agents are located. In the centre of this quarter, right on the water's edge, is the **Kapuas Indah bemo terminal**, which is connected to a second bemo terminal in **Siantan**, on the eastern side of the river, by a regular passenger ferry.

Pontianak's **Supadio airport** lies 20km south of the city centre. Bemos (Rp500) ply the route between the airport and the Kapuas Indah bemo terminal in the centre of town (every 30min), or you can catch a cab (Rp15,000).

The **ferry port** lies a few hundred metres to the north of the Kapuas Indah bemo station near the very centre of town. By contrast, the **Batu Layang bus terminal** is inconveniently located 6km north of Siantan. Regular white bemos (Rp350) leave from Batu Layang to the Siantan bemo terminal, from where you can catch a ferry (Rp150) to the western side. Please note that when leaving Pontianak there is no need to travel all the way to the Batu Layang bus terminal. All the bus companies have agents in the centre of town on the western side of the river, and buses depart from these offices.

MOVING ON FROM PONTIANAK

Nearly every tourist who arrives in Pontianak is looking to catch a **bus** straight up to **Kuching** in Sarawak, A number of bus companies run the route, which can take up to twelve hours; most departures leave either early in the morning or late at night. Buses to the **interior** – to Sintang (7hr), Putussibau (12hr) and up the coast to Singkawang (3hr 30min) – also leave frequently from these agents.

All the major cities in Indonesia are served by **flights**, as is Kuching – thrice-weekly by MAS. At the Pelni **ferry** office (see p.730) you can by tickets for services to, amongst other places, Jakarta and Kijang. **Buses** call in at the bus-ticket agents around town en route to their destinations, which will save you the inconvenience of getting to the terminal.

Information

Pontianak's **regional tourist office** (Mon–Thurs & Sat 8am–2pm, Fri 8–11am; ☎0561/36712) lies tucked away in the quiet suburbs to the west of Jalan Jend A. Yani at Jalan Ahmad Sood 25. It's really not worth the hassle to get here, unless you wish to pick up a couple of useless glossy brochures and swap a few pleasantries with the friendly but unhelpful non-English-speaking staff. For information on Kalbar's national parks, or to pick up a free two-week visitor **permit**, visit the **Balai Konservasi Sumber Daya Alam** at Jalan Rahman Saleh 33 (Mon–Thurs & Sat 7am–2pm, Fri 7am–noon). Again, no English is spoken.

Accommodation

There are plenty of **hotels** in Pontianak, though finding one to recommend is a bit of a struggle. Most of the hotels at the budget end are large, overpriced, threadbare establishments that smack of better times. The luxury end of the market offers better value for money, with the sumptuous *Kapuas Palace* leading the field.

Addresses in Pontianak can be confusing. Streets often go by two different names (for example, Jalan H.O.S. Cokroaminto is also known as Jalan Merdeka Timur, and Jalan Diponegoro is also known as Jalan Sisingamangaraja), and address numbers do not run in sequence. However, most of the locals will be able to point you in the right direction.

Central, Jl H.O.S. Cokroaminto 232 (☎0561/37444, fax 34993). Huge and hospitable Chinese-run hotel with bright and airy rooms, only let down by traffic noise from the two main roads outside. ⑤.

Kapuas Palace, Jl Imam Bonjol (☎0561/36122, fax 34374). West Kalimantan's finest hotel, a luxurious establishment set back from the Jl Pahlawan/Jl Imam Bonjol junction in the south of the city. Facilities include a swimming pool, bars, restaurants and coffee shops; every room has satellite TV and a bath or shower. ⑧.

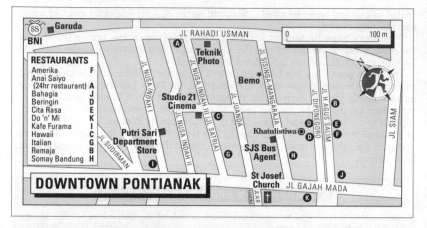

Kartika, Jl Rahadi Usman (☎0561/34401, fax 38457). Pleasant riverside hotel (most of the foundations are actually in the water) suffering, for no apparent reason, from a lack of custom. Facilities include a restaurant, tennis courts, parking, laundry and a gift shop. Try haggling for a cheaper rate. ⑥.

Khatulistiwa, Jl Diponegoro 56 (☎0561/36793, fax 34930). Huge, shabby hotel built round a central courtyard. The rooms (all doubles with attached bathrooms) are reasonably comfortable, though your sleep could well be disturbed by the long-distance lorry drivers who pull into the courtyard regularly during the night to take advantage of the services offered by the girls on the upper floors; rooms on the third floor are cheaper and quieter. ④.

Mahkota, Jl Sidas 8 (☎0561/36022, fax 36200). Luxury air-con hotel in a quiet neighbourhood just a short walk from the centre of town; facilities include a swimming pool, coffee bar and tennis courts. ⑦.

Patria, Jl H.O.S. Cokroaminto 497 (☎0561/36063). This sprawling establishment is the best of the budget bunch, despite a far-from-central location and the recent closure of its restaurant. The rooms are pleasant and all come with a bathroom, though watch out for the rats late at night. ⑤.

Pinang Merah, Jl Kapten Marsan 51–53 (☎0561/32547, fax 39032). Best of the two options in the tawdry port area. The manager speaks English and offers a variety of rooms, mostly fairly tatty, but with TV, air-con and mandi too. ④.

Pontianak City, Jl Pak Kasih 44 (☎0561/32495, fax 33781). Excellent-value hotel opposite the harbour with friendly staff and well-appointed rooms that come with TV, air-con and telephone. ⑤.

Wijaya Kusuma, Jl Kapten Marsan 51–53 (☎0561/32547). The cheapest and sleaziest hotel in Pontianak, located right in the seedy port area opposite the bemo terminal. Friendly receptionist on the ground floor, over-friendly women draped over the banisters on floors two and three; rooms dank and full of mossies – avoid it unless you're destitute. ④.

The City

Though Pontianak is bereft of compelling tourist attractions, both the **royal palace** and **mosque** of Abdul Rahman and the **Museum Negeri** (State Museum) offer enjoyable ways to spend an afternoon. If you've still got time to kill after these sights, sit on the water's edge and watch the river life go by, or have a nose around the **Kapuas Indah market**, where you'll find a couple of small Taoist Buddhist temples (watch your belongings, however, as pickpockets operate in the area). The truly restless can head up to the **Tugu Khatulistiwa**, Pontianak's "equator monument".

Istana Kadriyah and the Mesjid Jami

These two eye-catching buildings stand near each other on the eastern side of the Kapuas Kecil, just to the south of the confluence with the Landak. This area, known as the **Kampung Baris**, is the site of Abdul Rahman's original settlement and both the palace (the Istana Kadriyah) and the Mesjid Jami are his creations. Small passenger boats with a driver/rower can be rented from the eastern end of Jalan Mahakam II, in the heart of the Kapuas Indah market (Rp150 for a shared canoe, Rp500 for a rowing boat, Rp800 if the motor is switched on).

The **Mesjid Jami**, also known as the Mesjid Abdurrakhman (an Indonesian corruption of Abdul Rahman) stands right by the water's edge where the boats dock, its traditional Javanese four-tiered roof towering above the low-slung kampung that surrounds it. Indeed the yellow exterior (both the palace and the mosque are painted yellow, the traditional colour of royalty amongst the Malays) is somewhat more impressive than the rather creaky green interior, which contains little of note.

Two hundred metres to the south is the ironwood **Istana Kadriyah**, built by Abdul Rahman in 1771. The descendants of Abdul still own the *istana* today, and the son of the seventh sultan lives in one of the wings. There don't seem to be any set opening times, and indeed for long periods the *istana* remains closed to the public altogether. When it is open, visitors are treated to a rather odd, magpie collection of items, from the bust of a Dutch woman who married into the family to a large collection of mirrors, thrones, tables and other gilt furniture. It's all a little surreal, especially when one considers that this ostentatious wealth stands right in the heart of one of Pontianak's poorer districts.

Museum Negeri Pontianak

Probably Pontianak's most entertaining attraction, the **Museum Negeri Pontianak** (Mon–Thurs & Sat 8am–1pm, Fri 8–11.30am, Sun 9am–noon; Rp200) is usually overlooked by travellers, as it lies 1.5km south of the town centre on Jalan Jend A. Yani; bemos leave from the Kapuas Indah terminal (Rp350) or you can rent a becak (Rp750).

A series of kitsch concrete reliefs on the museum's facade depict the traditional lifestyles of Kalbar's two largest ethnic minorities, Malay and Dayak, with scenes of fishing, hunting, fighting and head-hunting (spot the Dayak presenting his wife with a recently severed head, for example). Inside, the exhibits are laid out by subject rather than ethnic origin (significantly, the Chinese don't feature, except in a small pottery section on the ground floor of the museum). There are no English labels, though it's pretty easy to guess from the accompanying photos what the exhibits are and what they were used for. The comprehensive collection of **tribal masks**, weapons and musical instruments gleaned from the various Dayak tribes of the interior are probably the highlight. There are also some fine examples of woven baskets, used by the Dayak for fishing, and a small selection of carved wooden blocks that were used as templates for tattoos.

Just round the corner from the museum, on Jalan Sutoyo, is an impressive but empty replica of a **Dayak longhouse**, over 50m long and 15m high, where you're free to wander around.

Tugu Khatulistiwa (equator monument)

Pontianak's **equator monument**, built in 1928 and one of the few remnants of Dutch architecture in the city, stands on its own little patch of grass by the side of Jalan Khatulistiwa on the way to the bus terminal. For some reason, the locals are inordinately proud of the rather squat-looking, twelve-metre obelisk and every March and September, on the equinoxes, when the monument casts no shadow, they flock in their thousands to witness this phenomenon, before heading back to town for a party. To see it for yourself, catch any bemo to the bus terminal from the Siantan ferry port; the monument stands about halfway along the road on the left-hand side.

Eating

Pontianak has the usual oversupply of cheap, grubby warung serving basic Indonesian snacks, particularly around Jalan Pasar Indah. Care should be exercised in these places: hygiene standards are often lower in Pontianak than in other parts of Indonesia, particularly in the dry season, when the public water supply is rationed and warung owners are forced to find their own, muckier sources. **Street stalls** congregate every night on the KOREM Place, a small concrete square by the river named after the Komando Regimen Militer building that stands behind it. Locally grown coffee is Pontianak's speciality, and all over town warung kopi (coffee houses) serve up glasses of this dark, asphyxiatingly thick brew.

Amerika, Jl H. Agus Salim 114. Popular mid-priced young hangout that specializes in frying up every edible part of a chicken. Try the liver (Rp500), gizzard (Rp250) or, for something more substantial, the entire bird (Rp7000). Not cheap, but tasty.

Bahagia, Jl H. Agus Salim 182. Vegetarian café – one of the very few in town – serving unexceptional budget fare that's fine for a lunchtime snack.

Beringin, Jl Diponegoro 113 and 149. Two mid-priced, hygienic Padang food restaurants under one name, standing within 40m of each other on the same side of Jl Diponegoro.

Corina, Jl Tanjungpura 124. Clean and quiet budget restaurant serving Chinese and Indonesian food, including a particularly tasty crab omelette for Rp4000.

Do 'n' Mi, Jl Patimura. Trendy neon-lit local hangout where green-clad staff serve well-to-do Pontianak citizens with cakes, ice creams and a few hot meals. Prices are reasonable, food is delicious, but portions are small.

Italian Steakhouse, Jl Satria 109–111. Friendly and clean restaurant with a sizable Japanese menu as well as a wide range of Western fast-food standards. Overall not bad at all, though a tad expensive.

Remaja, Jl H. Agus Salim 92. Fast food, Kalbar-style. New fried-chicken outlet that's proving very popular in the early evenings amongst Pontianak's young professionals, even though the chicken can be a little stringy and the portions on the small side.

Warung Dangau, Jl Jend A. Yani. Highly recommended and flashy little mid-priced restaurant tucked away in the Taman Budaya. Lovingly prepared Indonesian food served with a twist (their nasi goreng, for example, is embellished with prawn crackers and sate sticks).

Warung Somay Bandung, Jl Sisingamangaraja 132. Possibly the city's best warung, this no-fuss eatery serves six or seven basic meals that cost no more than Rp2500, and also provides free drinking water.

Listings

Airline offices Bouraq, Jl Pahlawan Blok D no. 3 (☎0561/37261); DAS, Jl Gajah Mada 67 (☎0561/32313); Garuda, Jl Rahadi Usman 8a (☎0561/78111); MAF, Jl Supranto 50a (☎0561/30271); MAS, Jl Sidas 8 (☎0561/30069); Merpati, Jl Gajah Mada 210 (☎0561/36568).

Bus agents PT SJS (Setia Jiwana Sakti), Jl Sisingamangaraja 155 (☎0561/34626), is one of the more popular and reliable companies, with four buses per day plying the route to Kuching Sibu and Miri. They also run buses up the Kapuas to Sintang, with a couple continuing on to Putussibau. CV Tanjung Niang, in the harbour area opposite the bemo station, is the only company operating buses (3 daily) to Nanga Pinoh.

Banks and exchange Bank BNI, Jl Rahadi Usman (8am–4pm); PT Safari moneychangers, Jl Nusa Indah III 45.

Cinema Studio 21 on Jl Nusa Indah III has four screens showing recent Hollywood films; Rp4000.

Consulate Malay consulate, Jl Jend A. Yani 42.

Disco *Kaisar*, part of the huge Istana Kaisar on the corner of Jl Sisingamangaraja and Jl Pattimur; 10pm–2.30am; Rp10,000.

Email Warposnet at the GPO; Mon–Thurs, Sat & Sun 8am–2pm, Fri 8–11am; Rp2000 for 15min.

Ferries The Pelni office is at Jl Sultan Abdur Rahman 12; Mon–Sat 9.30am–noon.

Post office Jl Sultan Abdur Rahman 49 (daily 8am–9pm). Poste restante, at the back of the building, closes at 2pm.

Telephone and fax Telkom, Jl Teuku Umar 15, has IDD, fax and reverse-charge facilities; open 24hr.

Tours Ateng Tours, Jl Gajah Mada 201 (☎0561/32683), offer a one-day tour of Pontianak, including the museum and palace, for US$25. Visits to longhouses and local fishing villages can also be arranged.

Travel agents Mitra Kalindo Samudera, Jl Diponegoro 39 (☎0561/49751), sells tickets for the daily *Ketapang Express* to Ketapang.

South of Pontianak

Surprisingly, transport connections between Pontianak and the neighbouring towns on the west coast are poor. The northern Pontianak–Sambas road peters out at the village of Supadio, just 10km south of Pontianak, and to travel any further you'll need to take a boat.

FORESTS AND FIRES

During the mid-1980s, a series of disastrous **fires** cleared thousands of square kilometres of Kalimantan's native forests but, sadly, these were only a prelude to events of a decade later. May 1997 saw the first flames of a conflagration which was to last over a year and reduce huge swaths of Kalimantan to charcoal. By August, **smoke** from the fires covered an area stretching from Thailand to western Irian, and north to the Philippines; visibility in cities in southern Kalimantan was brought down to tens of metres, and ineffective surgeons' masks were all that local people were offered against inhaling the fumes. Kuala Lumpur and Singapore were also covered in a smog-like haze, which at its worst closed airports in those cities, while expats and wealthier citizens queued to fly to cleaner climes. As President Suharto, in unprecedented move, apologized to neighbouring nations, the September 1997 crash of a Garuda airbus in Sumatra, along with numerous regional shipping collisions and the impossibility of flying relief supplies to famine-struck regions of Irian Jaya, were all blamed on the smoke.

While human attention focused on the smoke, the fires themselves were devouring sixty thousand square kilometres of **national parks**. One of the worst affected was Kutai, north of Samarinda in eastern Kalimantan, which had been already seriously degraded by the 1980s fires, along with government-approved logging and transmigrant settlements within the park. Kutai's few remaining areas of forest were effectively eradicated, along with over one hundred resident **orang-utans**. It's been estimated that, across Kalimantan, fires have either killed or destroyed the habitat of seven thousand of these apes, a third of the entire world population.

Traditional slash-and-burn agriculture was initially fingered as the **cause** of the fires, but as this has been practised for thousands of years in Kalimantan without causing such widespread devastation it can't be entirely responsible. Most likely, the 1997 fires were started by plantation companies, who, despite a ban of the practice in 1995, use **burning off** as an inexpensive way to prepare areas for planting oil palms or commercial timber. The effects of this would have been compounded by **logging**, which clears areas of damp, fire-resistant forest and leaves highly flammable debris in its wake. Logged areas are also initially recolonized by grassland, which withers during the dry season, providing excellent fuel. A major factor in the extent of the 1997 fires is that much of Kalimantan's soils are **peat**, a material which, once ignited, is capable of burning underground and so is almost impossible to extinguish.

Though the Indonesian government came under criticism for its ineffectual handling of the fires – Jakarta was south of the smoke haze, and it has been suggested that if the capital had been worse affected the response would have been speedier – the truth is that the there simply weren't enough resources available in Indonesia to deal with such a disaster. The heavy wet-season rains which naturally would have done so failed almost completely between 1996 and 1998 and, with the fires' causes still to be dealt with, it seems inevitable that the situation will occur again.

This dire transport situation can be annoying, especially if you're trying to reach the remote **Gunung Palung Reserve**, a pretty little national park 90km south of Pontianak. The park features a wide variety of flora, from thick low-lying mangrove forest to the sparse, mountain vegetation of Gunung Palung (1116m) itself, as well as a large troop of proboscis monkeys and macaques. Unfortunately, the park was ravaged by the 1997 fires (see box on p.731), and large tracts of it now lie charred and desolate; much is accessible only by boat, and with the cost of benzine so high on Borneo the total cost of the trip can be fairly exorbitant.

Getting to the park is also extremely time-consuming, to say the least. Having picked up your permit from the parks office, in Pontianak (see p.727), the next step is to catch the *Ketapang Express* ferry (see "travel details" on p.781), a journey of six hours. From Ketapang it's four hours to Sukadana by bus, 30km north back along the coast; this small town has a small KSDA office where you can hire off-duty park officials as guides (Rp25,000 per day). Telok Melano, a thirty-minute bemo ride away (Rp2000), is the last village before the park entrance; there is a small, anonymous *penginapan* (Rp10,000) and a couple of warung here. From Telok Melano you can hire one of the boatmen to ferry you to the park itself. Officially, you aren't allowed into the park without a guide, nor are you allowed to camp there – but neither of these rules seem to be rigidly adhered to. **Guides** can be hired at the park entrance, or in Telok Melano (about Rp30,000 per day).

North of Pontianak

Kalbar's second biggest town, **SINGKAWANG**, lies 145km north of Pontianak. It was originally founded as a mining settlement by the Hakka Chinese, who maintain an overwhelming presence in the town today. Crisscrossed by wide, tidy streets flanked by covered walkways, Singkawang is an attractive, easy-going town with some decent hotels and a number of excellent-value Chinese restaurants. There's little to see, though the town has a unique atmosphere, being neither absolutely Chinese nor Indonesian, and it's a useful base for exploring Kalbar's northern shores.

Of the **hotels**, the best of the budget bunch is the *Khatuliwista Plaza I*, situated in the heart of the action at Jalan Selamat Karman 17 (☎0562/31697; Rp10,000). Clean rooms, a nice elderly manager and a pleasant TV lounge on every floor make this one of the best-value places on the west coast. Its only serious rival is the *Wisata Hotel*, Jalan Diponegoro 59 (☎0562/31082, fax 32563; Rp10,000), which has a similar standard of rooms and, in the receptionist, one of the best English-speakers in town. Unfortunately, it's let down a little by its location, 2km south of the town centre. In the mid-price bracket, the *Hotel Kalbar* at Jalan Kepol Machmud 1 (☎0561/31460; Rp12,500) is very friendly, has some smart rooms and is probably the best value, though it's currently undergoing renovation work. Even if you don't plan to stay in Singkawang, don't miss out on the opportunity of tasting some excellent Chinese **food**: the *Rumah Makan Selera*, at Jalan Diponegoro 106, has some superb Chinese noodle dishes, especially the *kue tiaw* (flat noodles with seafood), and *Aquarin*, Jalan Sejahtera 70, provides the *Selera* with some healthy competition. If Chinese food doesn't appeal, try the Padang specialists *Roda Beringin*, at the northern end of Jalan Diponegoro.

The coastline around Singkawang is crammed with **beaches**. **Pasir Panjang**, a two-kilometre stretch of golden sand luxuriating just 13km south of town, is the best of these, particularly during the week, when it's deserted. Bemos leave regularly from Singkawang's central terminal on Jalan Stasiun, one block south of the *Hotel Kalbar*. There's a small picnic area at the beach's northern end, and a rather shabby hotel, the *Palapa* (☎0562/33367; Rp30,000). The accommodation on offer is nothing special, though the hotel redeems itself somewhat by organizing trips to the nearby uninhabited island of **Pulau Randayan**, a haven of peace and isolation. They charge Rp350,000 (for a maximum of 35 people); renting a fishing boat from the beach is likely to be cheaper. The *Palapa* has built a small restaurant, one bungalow (Rp85,000 per night) and two rooms (Rp30,000 each) on the island; book ahead if you're interested.

Another day-trip from Singkawang, **SAMBAS** is a two-hour bemo ride (Rp2500) north along the coast. The town acquired a degree of fame earlier this century when archeologists discovered Indian coins and Hindu statuary that proved that the Sriwijaya empire, a Hindu-Buddhist kingdom based in Sumatra during the seventh and eighth centuries, once reached at least as far as this remote corner of West Kalimantan. Today the town is one of the west coast's most picturesque, with most of the inhabitants living in the riverside kampungs that stand on stilts in the water of the Sungai Sambas basin. At the northern end of Sambas, just over the small bridge, is the muted yellow **kraton** of the Malay sultan who still rules over the town. The palace itself was built in 1812, during Sir Stamford Raffles' reign; the mosque next door was built in 1890, and is currently closed to the public.

The interior and on to the border

With its headwaters in the Muller Mountain Range of central Borneo and its mouth on Kalimantan's western shore, **Sungai Kapuas** is, at 1243km, easily Indonesia's longest river. It is is reasonably pretty, though hardly spectacular, with sawmills and timber stations rapidly replacing traditional Dayak villages all along the river bank. Most of the settlements along the Kapuas are tiny, though there are a couple of fairly sizable towns en route, such as **Sintang** and **Putussibau**, both of which were founded during the Dutch era. Many of the people who inhabit these towns and villages are non-native, having arrived in Kalbar as part of the government's *transmigrasi* programme during the 1980s and early 1990s. The Madurese, in particular, make up a considerable percentage of the population, though their presence is not always welcomed by the locals. For a glimpse of traditional Dayak settlements you need to travel beyond Putussibau, the last major settlement in West Kalimantan, to the longhouses further upstream. The hardy and adventurous may like to hire a guide and continue heading east, over the Muller mountains and into East Kalimantan.

Passenger ferries still travel between Pontianak and Putussibau, at least during the rainy season; in the dry season the waters are too shallow for all but the smallest vessels. The meandering double-decker *bandung* are the most traditional and common passenger ferries on the Kapuas, and are slow – really slow – taking up to five days to travel the 870km between Pontianak and Putussibau. The journey between Pontianak and Sintang takes only two days, and is far less arduous. The conditions on board these ferries are extremely basic, though a bed (of sorts) and food (usually fish and rice) is provided, for Rp1500.

With improvements in the condition and maintenance of the Trans-Kalbar Highway, buses have now superseded boats as the most popular and convenient mode of transport into the interior. The highway begins at Mandor, 40km north of Pontianak, and only joins the Kapuas at Sanggau, 256km east of Pontianak, though it follows the course of the river fairly closely thereafter. Buses tend to leave in the early evening, boats in the early morning; details of journey times for both boats and buses can be found in the "Travel details" on p.781.

Sintang

It seems almost surreal to find such a bustling town in the middle of Kalbar's untamed landscape, yet **SINTANG**, 325km east of Pontianak, built on the confluence of the Kapuas and Melawai rivers, has a population of over 20,000, many of whom migrated from Java and Sumatra to work in the timber and construction industries. The town, by Kalbar's standards at least, also has a fairly long and well-documented history, having

OVER THE SCHWANER MOUNTAINS: TREKKING TO KALTENG

There's a well established – if extremely demanding – trail across Kalimantan, which ascends the Kapuas from Sintang, traverses the central Muller mountains, and then follows the Mahakam from its headwaters to Samarinda. The whole journey takes around a month, with half that time spent hiking through forest, and is best arranged through an experienced agent. In 1997, three hikers made a shorter trip from Sintang to Pangkalanbun in Kalteng Province by following Sungai Pinoh to its headwaters, crossing the southwestern tail of the Schwaner mountain range, and then taking logging roads due south along Sungai Kotawaringin to their destination. None of them really knew what they were getting into, but were lucky and found first-rate guides along the way. The following is their account for those planning anything similar.

The good road south from Sintang meant that **Nanga Pinoh**, a trading post halfway up Sungai Pinoh, could be reached in two hours. By chartering a speedboat from Nanga Pinoh, we aimed to arrive in the last village upriver by the end of the following day, from where a single day's trekking would take us over the **Schwaner Mountains** to Kalteng's busy timber camps, and so down logging roads to Pangkalanbun. Our schedule proved ambitious. After seven hours dealing with fast rapids, smashed propellers, and torrential rain, our first night found us only part-way along at **Kota Batu's** floating losmen. The canoe that Daniel Madu, our guide from Sintang, chartered from here turned out to be underpowered, but we enjoyed the additional two days heading slowly upstream, despite never making it to our planned destination. As the river narrowed, the forest closed over our heads, the banks rose on either side, and, turning a corner to see a 2.5m monitor lizard basking on a rock, we felt truly captivated by our surroundings.

Our overworked engine failed on the second afternoon. Pulling in for repairs at the nearest village we found everyone riotously drunk. Offering us sleeping space on his floor, the headman explained that an elder had died that day and invited us to join the funeral party. The community house was crammed full; we squeezed inside and drank potent rice whiskey contained in enormous urns, sucking the liquid through bamboo straws. We set out again the next morning, the motor finally giving up the ghost at noon near the Pinoh's penultimate settlement, **Nanga Ora**. This was a disturbing place, with many of its inhabitants visibly malnourished. A satellite dish and TV set seemed perverse possessions under the circumstances, but these turned out to be "presents" from a timber company with interests in the area. Nanga Ora was a fortunate stop for us, however, as it was here that we heard of an exciting and little-used three-day trail into Kalteng

been one of the first Dutch towns in the interior of Borneo, and one that could also boast its own local royal family. Though the royal line died out at the beginning of the century, the **palace** still stands on the northern side of the Kapuas, where it's been converted into a small museum housing a few Dayak artefacts and some faded photos of the rajah and his family. The museum doesn't charge an entrance fee, though it's often locked and you'll have to ask one of the neighbours to fetch you the key. Just down from the palace is the local mosque, the **Mesjid Jamik**, a charming little place faced almost entirely with wooden planks.

As an overnight stop for those wishing to break the journey between Pontianak and Putussibau, Sintang is ideal: not only is the accommodation clean and, for Kalbar, fairly inexpensive, but the city is lively, friendly and easy to get around. Sintang's bus and bemo stations, as well as its tidy selection of hotels and restaurants, are all within walking distance of each other, on the southern side of the Kapuas to the west of the Melawai. The best-value **hotels** are on the waterfront, 150m due north of the bus station. The *Sesean*, at Jalan Brigjen Katamso 1 (☎0565/21011; Rp18,000), is a cheerful and reasonably smart hotel that's popular with both travellers and swifts, who nest in the eaves and make a terrible din at night; the rooms on the ground floor are quieter. Just behind the *Sesean* is the *Setian*, Jalan Brigjen Katamso 78 (☎0565/21611; ②), one of the through virgin jungle. Two men, forty-year-old Pak Gabong and younger Hendre, offered to act as guides, so we parted company with Madu.

Pak Gabong and Hendre proved to be wonderful escorts, as tough as nails and completely at home in the jungle. Both trekked barefoot, homemade rifles slung across their shoulders and machetes swinging at their sides, and shouldered all we needed for cooking and camping in plastic-bag-and-rattan backpacks. We carried our personal gear and, unaware that we would be soaking wet and muddy for the next three days, we left Nanga Ora booted and beaming in the early morning. By the afternoon we had trudged through thirty or more rivers, been torn and tripped by vines, and were covered in leeches. There were hundreds of the foul creatures, sneaking their way into our boots and clothing at every opportunity, with a tendency to gravitate towards our ankles and groins. We removed some with lighters or insect repellent, the rest we ripped off as we walked.

Our first meal was jungle cuisine — fern tips, papaya, cassava, chillies, fish and rice — but from then on the food was tasteless and monotonous, plain rice accompanied by bony, barely edible fish. The trail deteriorated too, disappearing completely by the second day after which we hacked our way through the dense, humid vegetation. Hendre and Gabong spent much of the time laughing at our incompetence, pausing now and then to set traps which would feed them on their return. Nights deep in the jungle were unforgettable, Gabong and Hendre swiftly building their shelter from expertly chopped branches, while we pitched our lightweight tent close by. The sun set a brilliant orange and mauve through the canopy, hailing a concert of bird song, calling gibbons, and hooting monkeys which lasted into the dusk. Seven was still an early bedtime despite routine 4.30am rises, so we sweated in our tent, attempting to read or play cards by torch-light.

By the end of the second day we were all beginning to feel the strains of the trek: stung by wasps, scratched by vines, and exhausted. The third day crossing into Kalteng Province proved a gruelling nine hours along steep, red, and gluey logging roads. In compensation the scenery was stunning, with dramatic skies hanging over a mountainscape drenched in rolling mists, carpeted by jungle vibrant with colour and life; rhinoceros hornbills swooped dramatically overhead, while barking deer and wild pigs ran across our path. We arrived at the **Karda logging camp** that afternoon, but, with no spare beds available, said goodbye to our guides and caught a ride in a 4WD down some scary tracks to **Beruta**, a desperately unpleasant town on Sungai Kotawaringin. We stayed in a rat-ridden brothel that night, before making the half day's bus trip south through heavily logged forests and eroded landscapes to Pangkalanbun.

Jessica Eveleigh

cheapest in town. You don't get a fan at this price, however, which in this sticky climate is a major drawback. Of better value is the *Safary*, just a little further south on Jalan Kol Sugiano (☎0565/21776; ②), where doubles come with a fan and TV.

Putussibau

A further 412km east of Sintang, the ramshackle little frontier town of **PUTUSSIBAU** was the easternmost outpost of the Dutch during the latter half of the nineteenth century. Situated at the point where the Sungai Sibau empties into the Kapuas (*Putussibau* translates as "Break in the Sibau River"), the town fairly buzzes in the morning when the riverside market is in full swing, but slowly winds down thereafter, until by sunset nearly all activity has ceased. There's little to do in Putussibau itself, though the town serves as an important base for exploration of the interior. There are also a couple of **longhouses** just a few kilometres upriver from Putussibau that still manage to retain a fairly traditional farming and fishing lifestyle, though they have been receiving tourists for years. The **Melapi I longhouse** and the **Sayut** are said to be the most impressive. Boat owners will approach you offering a guided tour of four or five longhouses: a day-trip should cost no more than Rp50,000, though add another Rp20,000 or so if you want

IBAN CULTURE AND LONGHOUSES

It's said that the **Iban** are a very egalitarian people, and it's true that the longhouse *tuai*, or **village chief**, acts as more of a figurehead than somebody who actually wields power. Traditionally the men are the hunters in the community, while the women are famous for their weaving prowess. The beautiful *pua kumba*, a ritual cloth of intricate design, can be found in Pontianak's souvenir shops, and is typical of the Iban style and flamboyant use of colour.

The Iban love a good party, the highlight of their calendar being the **gawai** (harvest festival), celebrated in May or June when the rice harvest has been gathered in. Visitors are welcome to join in the celebrations, providing they come bearing **gifts**. Western clothes, cassettes and cigarettes, and children's toys, are welcome. It's also important that you socialize with the chief's family first, and give him gifts to distribute amongst the villagers. Iban etiquette dictates that you should only enter the longhouse when invited, and should shake any proffered hands – though don't touch any other part of their body (particularly the head, even of small children). The Iban will doubtless will feed you to bursting point – it's part of their tradition of hospitality. If you're invited for a swim in the local river, don't miss out – though don't wear revealing clothes, which may embarrass your hosts.

to stay the night in one of them, and don't forget to bring presents; see the box above for more details on longhouse etiquette.

Much of Putussibau, including most of the market, stands on stilts on the riverbank. There are a couple of **hotels** here, near the large *bupati*'s house (Putussibau's *bupati*, or village head, is the most important of the six in Kalbar, and presides over Kalbar's *bupati*'s annual conference), which was once the home of the Dutch governor – the cheapest is the *Gautama* floating hotel (Rp6000). These floating hotels, known locally as *penginapan terapung*, can be found throughout Kalbar, though this is one of the very few that accepts foreigners. Don't expect much comfort, privacy or space, but if you don't mind roughing it you'll gain an interesting insight into the daily life of the itinerant market traders, fishermen and prostitutes. Overlooking the *Gautama* is the *Aman Sentosa* on Jalan Diponegoro (☎0567/21533; Rp15,000), which offers more conventional and comfortable accommodation. The centrally located *Marissa Hotel* is another fair option, with decent rooms beginning at Rp11,000.

Putussibau to Nanga Badau

To call the ochre-coloured mud-slick running between Putussibau and the town of Nanga Badau at the border with Sarawak a road is stretching things a little: the path was only made in 1997 and has yet to experience the joys of sealed roads, while most of the bridges are little more than a couple of tree trunks laid side by side. Nevertheless, there is now public transport – a bemo leaves every morning at 8am from Putussibau – and a trip along this route is never less than eventful.

There are a couple of places of interest along the way. **Danau Sentarum**, 115km west of Putussibau, is one of the largest bodies of water in Southeast Asia and contains a number of extremely rare freshwater fish. Chief among these is the arwana, a fifty-centimetre long goldfish that is so rare and prized by collectors that a single specimen can fetch up to twenty million rupiah. Naturally, these fish are now protected by law, and tracking devices have been fitted to most of them in an attempt to prevent poaching. The new road passes through the lakeside town of **Lanjak**, home to a couple of modest hotels, the pick of which is undoubtedly the smart *Penginapan Putri Kunci Ari* (no phone; Rp6000). A ferry leaves from Lanjak every morning during the wet season to **Semitau**, south of the lake on Sungai Kapuas; it takes eight hours to cross the lake and costs just Rp8000.

Forty minutes further west of Lanjak, and 3.5km north of the road along a small path that begins just before the large Mataso Bridge, the **Sendap longhouse** has become the unofficial entry point into the fledgling **Bentuang Karimun national park**. At over two hundred square kilometres, this park has the potential to be one of the greatest in Southeast Asia, particularly if, as is hoped, it links up with the neighbouring reserves in Sarawak to form a transnational sanctuary for Borneo's endangered wildlife. At the moment, however, there is no tourist infrastructure in the park and visitors have to organize their own guides and transport by haggling with the villagers in Sendap. Most of the time you'll be travelling the park by motorboat: the current estimate for a two-day, one-night excursion is Rp300,000. Sendap's *pati* (village chief), Jimbau, allows tourists to use the longhouse as a base for their treks into the park, although out of politeness you should always seek permission from him first. All visitors to the park must also have a free permit, issued by the KSDA office in Pontianak at Jalan Yos Sudarso 129.

Nanga Badau and into Malaysia

NANGA BADAU is a ramshackle little village of concrete bungalows, a half-day bus drive from Lanjak and just three hours from Sendap. The sealed highway continues east from here to the Malaysian town of Simanggung, just over the border in Sarawak. Nanga's **immigration office** (8am–5pm) lies on this road at the eastern end of town.

At the moment Nanga Badau is not a designated entry point into Indonesia, though tourists should have no trouble leaving the country from here, and exit formalities are straightforward. There's no public transport to take you into Malaysia, however, and you're not allowed to walk across, so if you caught the public bus to get here you'll have to try to hitch a lift to the Malaysian border post, where public buses leave regularly for Kuching (9hr). There's no accommodation in Nanga Badau (the nearest accommodation is in Sendap, though the immigration office may find you somewhere if you're stuck), so try to get here earlier to maximize you chances of finding a lift.

SOUTHERN KALIMANTAN

Dropping down from Kalimantan's central highlands and out to the Java Sea, **southern Kalimantan** splits into two very different parts. Until 1957 this was a single province governed by an Islamic majority settled around the southeastern city of **Banjarmasin**, but that year saw the region's Dayak population – after a brief armed struggle – granted autonomy. With the tiny river port of **Palangkaraya** as its capital, the western three-quarters of the region became the thinly populated, Dayak-controlled Kalimantan Tengah, or **Kalteng**, while the Muslim southeast continued on as Kalimantan Selatan, **Kalsel**, Kalimantan's smallest, most densely settled province. Though the process won a huge territory for the Dayak, it wasn't such a good move financially: despite its smaller size, Kalsel commands the regional economy, with Banjarmasin's port fronting one of the busiest cities in the whole of Borneo. In contrast, Kalteng remains an undeveloped backwater, whose tiny urban centres appear distinctly downmarket and with the main regional asset – timber – rapidly being stripped. But the independence movement was also about state recognition of Dayak identity, and this was certainly achieved, with the government even approving the regional religion, **Kaharingan**.

Down near the southwestern town of **Pangkalanbun**, **Tanjung Puting national park** is one of Kalimantan's biggest draws, whose primates – which include rambunctious **orang-utans** and the peculiar **proboscis monkey** – alone justify the journey here. Over in the southeast, Banjarmasin is another obvious target, a city stamped with its own assertive culture, and with the attraction of **gem mines** nearby at **Martapura**. Inland, about half of Kalteng's Dayak remain devotees of the Kaharingan faith, with villages upstream from Pangkalanbun and Palangkaraya still sporting ancient **longhouses**, memorials to the dead, and occasional massive **festivals**. More easily reached, Kalsel's **Meratus mountains** make for good hiking into the domain of the **Bukit**, less outwardly traditional than other Dayak – if no better understood.

Provincial divisions are very apparent once you start **moving around**. Kalteng's sole transport artery is the partially sealed, four-hundred-kilometre "highway" joining Pangkalanbun to Palangkaraya, traversed in dry conditions by daily buses. There are no airstrips and few roads inland, so transport here is usually by river; a general principle is that even scheduled public vessels – often desperately overcrowded *sped*, outboard-propelled speedboats – depart when, or if, they fill up. For its part, Kalsel has more roads and public transport than any other province, with the 500-kilometre Banjarmasin– Balikpapan highway skirting the west side of Kalsel's mountains and running northeast out of the region.

Pangkalanbun, Kumai and around

Stuck way down in the region's isolated southwestern corner, **PANGKALANBUN's** government offices and satellite port 25km away at **Kumai** conveniently plug an administrative and supply gap in Kalimantan's coastline. A dusty town unencumbered by sights, you'll have to stop briefly in Pangkalanbun to sort out paperwork for visiting the more engaging **Tanjung Puting national park**, reached through Kumai, or to make preparations for heading inland to **Dayak villages**.

The downtown area is a cluster of marketplaces and shops on the eastern bank of the modest **Sungai Arut**, though the river itself is obscured by buildings along the waterfront. A plywood plant and the huge numbers of diesel pumps for sale, used in working gold deposits, point to local industries, though Pangkalanbun is also romantically known as a source of *kecubung*, **amethysts**. The best stones – mined 60km west at **Sukarma** – are very dark, said to be a sign of age; polished and lustrous, they sell in lucky sets of five at Rp15,000–50,000. There are a few gem stalls at Pangkalanbun's markets – try **Pasar Baru**, about 500m east of the BNI bank along Jalan Antasari – and a bigger selection at Kecubung Antik on Jalan Santrek, which also stocks brightly coloured Dayak mementoes. Those heading **to Tanjung Puting national park** must first register with Pangkalanbun's **police** at their headquarters, 1km from the centre on Jalan Diponegoro (daily 7am–5pm; catch a bemo from the Jalan Kasamayuda–Jalan Santrek intersection). It costs nothing to do this, but you'll need your passport and a copy of the photo page; the whole process takes about ten minutes and leaves you with a registration certificate to be handed to the park authorities at Kumai (see opposite).

Pangkalanbun practicalities

Following the river's southern bank, Jalan Antasari is Pangkalanbun's main street. Orientate yourself by finding the intersection with Jalan Rangga Santrek – the BNI **bank** here (foreign exchange Mon–Thurs 8am–3pm, Fri 8–11am) is a useful landmark – which runs 70m or so south to where Jalan Kasamayuda parallels Jalan Antasari. **Arrival points** are scattered; the **airport** is 5km out to the southeast, and you'll need to charter a bemo to your destination at a flat rate of Rp10,000. **Long-distance buses** stop at their downtown offices; MP is about 500m west of the BNI on Jalan Antasari, while Yessoe Travel is on the corner of Jalan Santrek and Jalan Kasamayuda. **Boats** from Java and elsewhere in Kalimantan dock at Kumai; see p.740. Though the town is small, at Rp300 a ride Pangkalanbun's yellow **bemos** are a cheap way to get around, or negotiate fares with ojeks.

Few of Pangkalanbun's cheaper **lodgings** want foreign custom. Centrally located above a jewellery store in the backstreets off Jalan Antasari, the basic *Losmen Mawar* (③) does, but tidy, simple rooms at the *Thamarin* (⑤) on Jalan Diponegoro, and

Andika (☎0532/21218; ⑤) on Jalan Hasanudin, are a better deal – both are a couple of kilometres from the centre. Closer in on the hill above Jalan Kasamayuda, the *Blue Kecubung* (☎0532/21211, fax 21513; ⑦) is helpful, overpriced, and also takes bookings for *Rimba Lodge* in Tanjung Puting national park. All hotels serve **meals**, otherwise the usual range of inexpensive staples at stalls around the markets is supplemented by pricey Chinese fare at the *Phoenix* and a good Padang selection at *Beringin Padang*, both on Jalan Antasari.

Leaving, both bus companies advertise two daily departures for the ten-hour run to Palangkaraya (Rp30,000), while Dimendra Travel, also at the junction of Jalan Santrek and Jalan Kasamayuda, makes airline bookings to Palangkaraya, Pontianak or Java, and can find you passage aboard Pelni vessels out of Kumai. If available, **water taxis** inland leave from the **jetty** behind, and west of, the BNI bank. An ojek **to Kumai** costs Rp5000 or, before about 3pm, you can catch a bemo from Pasar Baru to *terminal bis*, then a minibus for the remaining hour-long run – about Rp1500 in all.

North to Tapinbini

Indonesian speakers on an ethnological quest will find it worthwhile exploring the headwaters of **Sungai Lamandau**, which originates 160km north of Pangkalanbun on the provincial border. The main targets here are the villages of **Bakonsu**, some 90km upstream, and **Tapinbini**, both draped in the trappings of the Kaharingan religion. There are no facilities for travellers, but it's possible to stay and eat in longhouses – see p.744 for more on Kaharingan village etiquette.

Transport is tricky. **By river**, a four-seat speedboat charter to Tapinbini will get you there in five hours, but at a cost of Rp400,000. More realistically, there's a daily water taxi to **Kotawaringin Lama** (Rp10,000), a small town about 35km up the Lamandau. From here, irregular services continue 30km upstream to **Kujan**, from where it's possible to find an ojek to cart you overland to Tapinbini (Rp20,000–30,000) – you can also reach Kujan on the weekly **bus** from Pangkalanbun's long-distance depot. The bike track from Kujan is frightful at the best of times, but then so are the boulder-ridden rapids above Bakonsu, while Tapinbini itself marks the start of a fierce stretch of cataracts. Once here, **BAKONSU** has several longhouses and, as a result of a massive funeral ceremony in June 1997, a host of traditional mausoleums and memorials to the dead; for its part, **TAPINBINI** has forests and more longhouses, two of which are reputedly three hundred years old, and the chance to organize a guide for hiking through surrounding limestone hills to weird monoliths known as **Batu Batongkat**, the Stone Sticks.

Kumai and park preparations

Connected to Pangkalanbun by a fine road, **KUMAI**'s small port, shipyard and couple of streets face across broad **Sungai Kumai** to where a fringe of mangroves and nipa palms frame the border of Tanjung Puting national park. Transport from Pangkalanbun winds up outside the **market** on the kilometre-long strip of Jalan Idris (last bemo back around 3pm); the adjacent *Aloha* and *Cempaka* **losmen** (③) are more welcoming than similarly priced accommodation in Pangkalanbun; and the **Pelni office** across the road at the **docks** can furnish tickets for the *Binaya*, which cruises past on its fortnightly circuit between Java and Sulawesi. Otherwise, continue on up Jalan Idris to organize your **national park permit** from the English-speaking staff at Departmen Kehutanan Taman Nasional Tanjung Puting (Mon–Thurs & Sat 7am–2pm, Fri 7–11am; ☎0532/61508, fax 61187). Having produced your permit from Pangkalanbun's police and another copy of your passport, you pay Rp2000 a person per day, plus Rp2000 a boat per day.

The next stage is to organize a **boat into Tanjung Puting** – access is by water only. **Speedboats** are expensive (Rp120,000 a day), scare wildlife, mangle turtles and crocodiles, and are best avoided. Slower, quieter **klotok** are six-metre-long hulls powered by an inboard engine, with enclosed mandi, open sides, a wooden roof which makes a fine vantage point, and room for four people plus two crew. Rates are fixed at Rp75,000 a day all-inclusive, but sleeping aboard sidesteps the park's pricey accommodation and, stocked with supplies from Kumai's market, the crew will cook for you. National park staff can help find a vessel, or you can head down to the jetties beside their office. Finally, ensure that you pack walking shoes, sunscreen, a hat, a torch, and anything else you might need, as there are no shops inside the park.

Tanjung Puting national park

A wild and beautiful expanse of riverine forest, coastal swamp and peat bogs bursting with wildlife, **TANJUNG PUTING NATIONAL PARK** is Kalimantan at its best. The park's fame rests on the efforts of **Dr Birute Galdikas**, who in 1971 founded **Camp Leakey** here as an **orang-utan rehabilitation centre** for animals that had been orphaned or sold as pets. As incapable of forest survival as a human baby, young orang-utans need to be taught how to forage by park staff or foster mothers, and, as the learning process takes several years, work here is very long-term. A down side of the park's popularity is that visitors only increase the orang-utans' exposure to humanity, and many youngsters prefer to hang around ranger stations to take advantage of the twice-daily feedings. None of this should stop you from visiting: few people leave Tanjung Puting with any complaints about the experience of such an easy, close contact with these animals.

Orang-utans aside, Tanjung Puting is home to *owa-owa*, the vocal, long-armed **gibbon**, and very visible troupes of Borneo's indigenous, big-nosed *bukantan*, or **proboscis monkey**. A fantastic sight as they hurl themselves through the trees with upstretched arms, habitat reduction through logging and fires have seen proboscis monkey numbers decline throughout Kalimantan since the 1980s, but they are still common enough here. Along the rivers, look for monitor lizards and **false ghavials**, a narrow-nosed crocodile which grows to about 3m, plus scores of birds; on land, **sun bears** are thrilling, if unpredictably tempered animals to encounter, while hikers need to be aware of potentially dangerous **snakes** (see Basics, p.29).

Practicalities

Tanjung Puting national park covers 4000 square kilometres south of Sungai Sekonyer, though public access is confined to just four areas along 25km of the Sekonyer and its tributaries: **ranger posts** at Tanjung Harapan and Pondok Tanggui, and **research stations** at Natai Lengkuas and Camp Leakey. There are no roads in the park, so **getting around** is primarily by boat; from Kumai a klotok takes about two hours to reach Tanjung Harapan, three hours to Pondok Tanggui, and between four and five hours to reach either Natai Lengkuas or Camp Leakey. Bear in mind that craft are prohibited from travelling after dark. **On arrival** at each stopover, you must report with your permit to park staff. Heed their **warnings**, especially about getting too close to adult orang-utans – adult males, or females with children, should be given a wide berth – and don't carry food, as orang-utans will rip bags apart to find it. Each area has fairly easy **paths** to explore, the longest of which are at Camp Leakey, while the five-day forest trail through chest-deep swamps between here and Tanjung Harapan should only be attempted by fully equipped, experienced hikers, accompanied by a ranger.

You need at least two full days in the park. If you don't sleep aboard your klotok, there are three **places to stay**, all in the vicinity of Tanjung Harapan. The ranger post here has basic **cabins** (⑤), rented out to visitors by previous arrangement through the park office at Kumai. The alternatives are sparely furnished but very comfortable rooms across the river at the brand-new wooden *Ecolodge* (fax 0532/22991; ⑦), and, five minutes upstream, the full-blown "safari camp" setup at *Rimba Lodge* (bookings through the *Blue Kecubung* in Pangkalanbun (⑧); see p.739. Both lodges have good restaurants – the only **places to eat** in the park – and can arrange **guides**, canoes and klotoks for rental. Staff at the two ranger posts and Camp Leakey also offer their guiding services at around Rp15,000 a day.

The Park

Having crossed from Kumai (see opposite), you enter the mouth of small **Sungai Sekonyer**, where an avenue of trunkless **nipa palms** gradually cede to a riverside tangle of vines and patchy forest at **Tanjung Harapan ranger post**. An **information hut** here has a good rundown on the park's ecology, the odd crocodile skull and stuffed birds – the door is kept locked to keep out inquisitive apes, but the ranger here can open it up. A few orang-utans move in for feeding at about 3pm, but not in the numbers that you'll find them elsewhere in the park; if you don't mind getting muddy, there's a five-kilometre circuit track into surrounding thickets. Just upstream, past the park's two **lodges**, is the transmigrant settlement of **TANJUNG HARAPAN**, most of whose residents have given up trying to farm the area's poor soils and now work at the **Asapai Gold Fields**, where mud churned up in the mining process has turned the Sekonyer's previously clean waters into its current soupy state.

The jungle closes in after Tanjung Harapan – lining the banks are giant lilies, pandanus (which look like a pineapple tuft growing straight out of the water on a slender trunk), and gardenia bushes with yellow flowers and bright-orange seeds. Behind them grow dense stands of tall, thin-trunked trees with buttressed roots, providing perches for vines, orchids and ferns. The next stop is **Pondok Tanggui**, whose long, solid wooden jetty is a good place to moor for the night and watch family groups of proboscis monkeys settle into the trees. A two-kilometre track leads past the ranger's office ending in woodland at an **orang-utan feeding area**, where eight or so apes receive handouts of sweetened milk and bananas at 8am and 4pm; the surrounding treetops have been stripped by the orang-utans to make beds, which is where they head when the food runs out. Cynical comparisons between this and feeding time at the zoo compete with the sight of the orang-utans' coarse red fur seen against green leaves in the morning, or watching youngsters involved in power plays over choice bits of fruit.

Past Pondok Tanggui, you veer east off the Sekonyer up **Leakey Creek**. The water immediately turns tea-coloured, clear and deep; trees almost meet overhead in the early stages, before opening up on the south bank into grassy marshland – look for triangular heads of false ghavials just breaking the water. The land around **Camp Leakey** is a mix of primary forest and open heathland; orang-utans waiting on the jetty for new arrivals give you an idea of what to expect from the local population, which includes two mature males whose overgrown cheek pouches and sheer size – one weighs 100kg – are most imposing. There's another feeding area here, and you should ask the camp's rangers to take you on a short hike into the forest proper.

Back on the Sekonyer, a final hour brings you to **Natai Lengkuas**, a research post investigating proboscis monkeys. In fact, this is the last animal you're likely to see here, as trails take you well away from the riverside study areas, but following the orange tags of the ninety-minute "Habitat Walk" through the forest you may see mahogany trees, lizards, bears, wild pigs, scorpions and roosting colonies of *kelelawar*, short-nosed fruit bats. There are no rangers to act as guides, so read the information notice above the dock and follow all of its instructions.

Palangkaraya and around

Set inland at the upper margin of southern Kalimantan's extensive marshes, **PALANGKARAYA** sprang into being in 1957, grafted onto the village of **Pahandut** as capital of the new province of Kalteng. Though the remote location seems a poor choice for what is a symbol of Dayak autonomy, everything about Palangkaraya reflects the circumstances of its foundation. Laid out 100km up the convoluted **Sungai Kahayan**, the city is both accessible to the predominantly traditional lands upstream, yet also pragmatically close enough to Banjarmasin – only a few hours away by speedboat – not to be too isolated from its economic benefits. A compromise between big-scale urban planning and small-town intimacy, most people only pass through it in transit between Pangkalanbun and Banjarmasin, but those who linger will find that Palangkaraya offers good food, interesting markets and the best starting point for a broader investigation of Kalteng's Dayak.

The City

Palangkaraya comprises ponderously organized blocks of inanimate government offices expanding westwards into the countryside, the buildings isolated by their scale and neat borders of black and white kerbing. The most interesting part of town surrounds the dock area around Jalan Dharmosugondo, where, in a pastiche of Dayak iconography, a brightly painted *sandung* and heroic bronze tableaux are overshadowed by a **clock tower**, bizarrely emerging out of a dragon jar mounted on hornbill heads. Immediately to the west, Palangkaraya's **markets** operate two shifts: early morning is the best time to mingle with crowds buying fresh meat, fruit and veggies, while youngsters hang out for booths selling sunglasses, cassettes, shoes, belts, toys and trinkets, which set up in the late afternoon, completely blocking the streets. Night-time food stalls fill any remaining gaps. It's a good place to pick up locally made **bamboo and rattan ware**, attractively patterned in purple, green and red; rain hats sell for about Rp2000, baskets and large floormats for Rp3000. **Souvenir shops** along Jalan Madura stock old porcelain, rubbery models of Dayak funeral boats, gems, carved shields and dangerous-looking archery sets. Further west, a ten-minute walk brings you to the steps leading north off Jalan Yani into **Flamboyan**, an area of wooden stalls and seedy hostels built high out over the river on boardwalks, which terminate 500m along at **Flamboyan Pier**. Back on Jalan Yani, bemo "A" runs 5km out to the **Provincial Museum** (Tues–Thurs, Sat & Sun, 8am–noon & 4–6pm, Fri 8–11am; free) on Jalan Cilik Riwut, though it's hardly worth the journey to see the few dragon jars and bronze drums sitting forlornly in oversized halls.

Practicalities

Most of Palangkaraya's services are up in the northeastern end of town off Jalan Yani. **Tjilik Riwut airport** is a kilometre further east again, and a taxi to central accommodation costs Rp5000. Arriving by river from Banjarmasin, **speedboats** terminate at Rambang Pier at the top of Jalan Dharmosugondo, while **buses** pull in 2km south across town on Jalan Soedarso, though generally deliver to hotels first. Palangkaraya's **bemos** are lettered and run fixed routes for a flat rate of Rp350; the eastern end of Jalan Yani or the streets around the markets are good places to hail one, while ojeks wait around the pier during daylight hours.

Moving on **to Banjarmasin**, speedboats and buses (both Rp25,000) leave whenever full until mid-afternoon – buy tickets at the departure points – while buses **to Pangkalanbun** (Rp30,000) are best booked a day in advance at their company offices near Rambang Pier on Jalan Dharmosugondo. See opposite for transit points if you're **heading upstream** from Palangkaraya.

Sort out **money** at the BNI on Jalan Dharmosugondo (Mon–Thurs 9am–2pm, Fri 9–11am), which handles foreign currency and has an ATM that accepts Cirrus/Maestro cards. West along Jalan Yani, the wartel office is open late for international **phone calls**, while Adi Ankassa Travel (☎0514/21480) makes flight bookings. **Information** on upriver festivals and villages can be gleaned from Pak Ariel Adrianus Ahut at the *Dandang Tingang Hotel*, or Pak Ernst Patianom at the Provincial Tourist Office, west of town along Jalan Cilik Riwut (Mon–Sat 9am–noon; ☎0536/21416, fax 31007; bemo "A" from Jalan Yani to Kantor Dinas Parawisata); both can provide guides from around Rp30,000 a day.

Eating prospects are excellent. Stalls at the night markets near Rambang Pier sell cheap soups, sates and fry-ups, but it's hard to walk past the smoky grills outside the area's open-fronted **fish restaurants**, where thick fish steaks and fillets are cooked to your order. *Sampurna*, on Jalan Jawa, is always full, as are the *Senggol* on Jalan Madura and *Almuminum* on Jalan Dharmosugondo; juicy river prawns, *pipih* – which looks like a cross between a trout and a flounder – and fatty *patin* (reputedly toxic in large amounts) are local fare. Failing this, *Sing Kar Wang* is a first-rate Chinese restaurant two minutes' distant at Jalan Bangka 87, with pricey but large portions of crispy fish, sweet and sour pork, and greens in oyster sauce.

ACCOMMODATION

Most of Palangkaraya's budget **accommodation** is set around Rambang Pier, but is generally difficult for foreigners to get into.

Dandang Tingang, Jl Yos Soedarso 13 (☎0536/21805, fax 21254). A little distant from transit points — bemo "C" from Jl Yani will get you there — but it's a pleasant place which tries hard to please, and the rooms are spacious. Air-con doubles ⑤, private units ⑧.

Dian Wisata, Jl Yani 68 (☎0536/21241). Very tidy – economy doubles with fan and shared bathroom as well as self-contained doubles available. ④.

Mina, at Rambung Pier. Nicest of local budget options, though usually "full". ③.

Sukma Indah (SIP), Jl Sumatera 12 (☎0536/21859). Grubby and due for demolition, but friendly – room no. 7 is best, with attached mandi. ④.

Yanti, Jl Yani 82 (☎0536/21634). Fair value and spotless, though some rooms are quite small. ④.

Upstream from Palangkaraya: Kaharingan country

The region upstream from Palangkaraya remains a stronghold for adherents to Kalteng's indigenous **Kaharingan faith**, and makes for an absorbing few days' excursion. The best time to visit is during **reburial ceremonies** (see box p.744), which are open to all and most frequently occur between June and August, but even if you miss the ceremonies themselves Dayak villages here generally welcome guests at any time, and retain not only impressively decorated memorials to the dead, but also some elderly traditional longhouses, or **betang**.

There are two ways into the region from Palangkaraya. With a week or more to spare, you'll get the best returns from following the Sungai Kahayan 175km up into **Ot Danum** territory around **Tumbang Kurik**, though the river's more accessible stretches below the town of **Tewah** are really not that interesting. A quicker and reliable alternative is to make a three-day return trip 130km up the **Sungai Rungan** to **Tumbang Jutuh** (*tumbang* means "the junction of two rivers"), which is within easy reach of **Ngaju** villages where tradition coexists comfortably with Christianity. Allow an extra couple of days and it's also possible to circuit the area by **hiking** through the forests between here and Tumbang Kurik. The quickest, most expensive way to travel is by chartered speedboat, but you can cut costs beyond the range of public transport by asking around for others heading your way on slower longboats, or *alkons*. Both Ot Danum and Ngaju cultures are superficially similar, with the Ngaju language widely understood across the region – in remoter corners

KAHARINGAN AND FUNERAL RITES

An animistic Dayak faith practised across interior Kalimantan, **Kaharingan** became an approved state religion in 1980 by categorizing it with Bali Hinduism – something it bears no resemblance to. Kaharingan exists in several forms, but one unifying characteristic is a multi-staged funeral, when the spirit is sent into the afterlife feeling satisfied and respected. This usually involves a **reburial ceremony**, the most elaborate of these being the **kwangkei** performed by Benuaq Dayak in Kaltim, and the **tiwah** of Kalteng. By whatever name, these ceremonies are fantastic events which last a whole month and may take years to organize – distant relatives must be invited, and the expense of hiring musicians, and buying food and animals to sacrifice, runs into millions of rupiah. Communities often collaborate, saving up their dead for a single big festival during which dozens or even hundreds of individuals are reburied.

Overseen by *basir*, the Kaharingan priesthood, the ceremony begins with a ritual purification, when the bones are dug up from their first grave and placed in a wooden coffin. Other important stages include **dances** to ancestral spirits, whose help is needed in the proceedings, and the **sacrifice of a buffalo** – formerly a slave – for each person being reburied. The animal is tied to a *patong sapundu*, a wooden post carved with a human face with the tongue lolling out, before having its throat cut; buffalo heads are later stacked in an open wooden framework. Finally, the purified bones are permanently housed in a **sandung**, an ornate hardwood mausoleum often raised off the ground like a miniature rice barn and flanked by carved and painted wooden figures, servants to the dead in the afterlife. Having spent the time between death and reburial at a sort of halfway stop between the real world and afterlife, the deceased's spirit, buoyed along by the goodwill of the mourners, navigates through a cloud of demons and reaches heaven aboard a *melambong*, a **funeral boat** guided by a hornbill and protected from roving evil by a tiger. At the end of the event, **pantar** (tall, thin poles topped by a hornbill) are raised in honour of the dead, as are similar spiky **sanggaran**, usually further embellished by having valuable Chinese jars speared on them. Long pauses – sometimes days – between separate stages in the ceremonies are filled by sociable bouts of eating, drinking and gambling at cards, dice, cockfighting (a relatively recent introduction) and *tongko*, Dayak roulette.

you'll sometimes draw a blank with Indonesian. **Guides** from Palangkaraya are best arranged through the *Dandang Tingang Hotel*, or the Provincial Tourist Office.

Palangkaraya to Tewah and Tumbang Kurik

If they fill up, speedboats (7hr; Rp25,000) and *alkon* (12hr; Rp20,000) leave Palangkaraya's Flamboyan Pier every morning for the gold-mining town of **TEWAH**, 130km up the Kahayan. This is the limit of public transport on the river, with a couple of inexpensive **losmen** – the *Batu Mas* and adjacent *Tewah* (③) – and some overgrown *sandung* to check out while you search for other passengers to share the costs of a vessel onwards. Tewah marks the southern boundary of the Ot Danum Dayak, and it might be possible to walk the 10km or so upstream to **Upun Batu**, which has some fine *sandung* and limestone scenery. Better yet is the village of **TUMBANG KURIK**, 45km northwest of Tewah on a small tributary of the Kahayan, which has more *sandung* and a splendid, run-down *betang* – you should be able to do this for Rp25,000–50,000 if you share, though a speedboat charter can cost Rp275,000. There's a homestay at Tumbang Kurik; visit the kepala desa on arrival to introduce yourself and make arrangements.

Up the Rungan to Tumbang Jutuh and beyond

From Palangkaraya, the trip **up the Rungan** starts by catching a bemo "A" from Jalan Yani to Terminal Tangkiling, 8km north of town, from where regular minibuses make the 30km run to Tangkiling township – allow Rp1800 and at least ninety minutes for the whole ride. **TANGKILING** is simply a dock on the Rungan, where you should immediately sign up for the single daily public **speedboat to Tumbang Jutuh** (Rp25,000), which leaves any time before 11am if enough customers arrive (and returns the following day, customers permitting).

The journey upstream follows steadily narrowing, ever shallower channels fringed by thin forest, arriving four hours later at **TUMBANG JUTUH**'s tall, almost vertical jetty steps. A small trading post, Jutuh is split between Muslim merchants and Christian Ngaju Dayak; there's a **ticket office** for the return journey at the docks, a single 100-metre-long cobbled street lined with clothes and hardware shops, and the unexpectedly spacious and clean **losmen** *Tiga Dara* (③) off to the right. **Meals** at the losmen are expensive, but there are several simple warung to choose from – the one by the dock is good, with a pet gibbon as an added attraction.

The reason for coming to Tumbang Jutuh is to reach the village of **Tumbang Malahoi**, 13km away; it's an easy walk, or you could charter an ojek for the day from the dock area (Rp5000). There's little forest along the way but the countryside is pleasant, with a broad stretch of rapids about 2km upstream and plenty of villages, some with *sandung*, to look at. **TUMBANG MALAHOI** is an attractive place, with a large **church** from the 1930s, excellent *sandung* and *pantar* decorated with Chinese plates and jars, and a superbly restored, fifty-metre **betang** whose massive supporting ironwood posts were sunk in 1817 – guests are inevitably invited to try to encircle them with their arms. At the time, Dayak here were headhunters, and construction of this *betang* would have required a slave to be buried under the central post. Check out the eaves above the doorway, which have some elderly painted panels, including a hunter with a rifle, patterns representing the sun and moon and mythical animals. Most impressive are the two centuries-old, skilfully carved *patong* flanking the longhouse steps, depicting figures standing upright with **tigers** atop them – strength and night vision make cats prime guardian creatures in Dayak lore. You might stay here with the kepala desa's permission, and delve deeper into local history, or organize a guide for the full-day walk east to Tumbang Kurik. Bring all supplies, as there are no stores in the village.

Banjarmasin and around

Set down in Kalimantan's southeastern corner on the closest part of the island to Java, **BANJARMASIN**'s history reaches back to when Indian traders founded the Hindu **Negara Kingdom** north of here during the thirteenth century. Within seventy years its rulers were marrying into the powerful Majapahit empire, but the fall of the Majapahit in the late 1470s saw Negara disintegrate into smaller city-states. These were reunified fifty years later after a local prince, **Samudra**, enlisted military assistance from a recently Islamicized Java and conquered the region, converting to **Islam** and shifting his capital south to near the lower **Barito River** at Banjarmasin. Abundant supplies of spices and timber from upstream soon brought the city wealth and a place in regional trade, though sixteenth-century Portuguese missionaries and British merchants found Banjarmasin and its rulers squalid and dangerous. The first real European influence came from the **Dutch**, who, having earlier tried to establish a VOC depot, managed to exert influence over the Banjarese sultanate in the late eighteenth century, after helping to drive off Bugis pirates. Their meddling in the succession provoked the **Banjar Rebellion** of 1860, when anti-foreigner factions united under the leadership of Pangeran Antasari, but his death two years later saw the revolt falter, and the Dutch took effective hold of the region in 1864.

The effects of centuries of vigorous dealings with the outside world immediately distinguish Banjarmasin from other cities in Kalimantan. This is not just another administrative centre populated by migrant profiteers, or bureaucrats and industrial experts

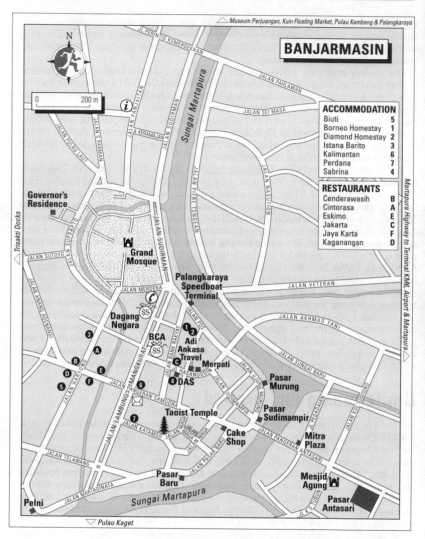

Museum Perjuangan, Kuin Floating Market, Pulau Kembang & Palangkaraya

BANJARMASIN

0   200 m

ACCOMMODATION

Biuti	5
Borneo Homestay	1
Diamond Homestay	2
Istana Barito	3
Kalimantan	6
Perdana	7
Sabrina	4

RESTAURANTS

Cenderawasih	B
Cintorasa	A
Eskimo	E
Jakarta	C
Jaya Karta	F
Kaganangan	D

Martapura Highway to Terminal KM6, Airport & Martapura

Trisakti Docks

Governor's Residence

Grand Mosque

Palangkaraya Speedboat Terminal

Dagang Negara

BCA

Adi Ankasa Travel

Merpati

DAS

Pasar Murung

Pasar Sudimampir

Taoist Temple

Cake Shop

Mitra Plaza

Pasar Baru

Mesjid Agung

Pelni

Sungai Martapura

Pasar Antasari

Pulau Kaget

serving out a posting, but somewhere with a deep, strong sense of its own identity. Over ninety percent of the city is Muslim and the streets tick in time with calls to prayer. It's easy to spend a day soaking up the atmosphere of Banjarmasin's markets, where boats remain a major form of transport, and wooden houses, built on piles as protection against daily tides, still line the canals and rivers. Hiring your own vessel is a fine way to experience the ebb and flow of life here, and will also take you down the Barito to a couple of monkey-infested islands. Not far to the east, **Martapura**'s gem mines make for an interesting day-trip, or as the first stop on the way into the rest of the province.

Orientation, arrival, information and getting around

Banjarmasin occupies flat country east of the Barito, where the last couple of kilometres of the smaller **Sungai Martapura** break up into numerous channels and streams. For a city of nearly half a million people, Banjarmasin's downtown area is remarkably small, a kilometre-broad tangle of markets, services and streets, bounded to the east by a bend in the Martapura, and to the west by Jalan Haryono. Cutting straight through the centre, Jalan Hasanuddin bridges the river to become Jalan Yani, which dips southeast out of town past the long-distance bus station as the multi-lane Martapura highway, while the longer Jalan Pangeran Samudra runs across the river into Jalan Pengeran Antasari, whose stalls, upmarket *Mitra Plaza* and colossal **Pasar Antasari** make it Banjarmasin's premier place to shop and hang out.

Arrival points are all are within the range of public transport. **Syamsuddin Noor airport** is 25km east down the Martapura highway, from where a taxi into the city costs Rp15,000 – alternatively, walk up to the highway and flag down one of the orange bemos shuttling between Martapura and Banjarmasin for Rp1200. **Long-distance buses** arrive at Banjarmasin's well-organized Terminal Km6, 6km southeast of centre on Jalan Yani; an ojek to your accommodation will cost about Rp1500, and a yellow bemo to Pasar Antasari just Rp300. **Speedboats** from Palangkaraya land you downtown, within sight of the Grand Mosque on Jalan Pos, while ocean-going transport ties up at **Trisakti Docks**, about 5km west of the centre on the banks of the Barito – bemos run into the city for Rp300.

Ojek and becak operators hang around markets or arrival points, though it's usually easier to pile aboard a **yellow bemo**. Because of one-way traffic flows through the centre, Jalan Hasanuddin is where to catch a bemo straight down Jalan Yani to the long-distance bus station, while Pasar Antasari or the western end of the Jalan Antasari bridge are the places to find bemos to anywhere else. The ideal way to see the city is by canal boat, or **klotok**, which can carry six or more people and be rented out for Rp5000–7000 an hour from the vicinity of the Jalan Hasanuddin bridge. For trips further afield, **taxis** charging Rp5000 an hour lurk in Jalan Bank Rakyat, directly behind the *Hotel Kalimantan*.

For impartial and generally sound **information**, the Government Tourist Office (Kantor Dinas Parawisata) is at Jalan Panjaitan 34 (Mon–Thurs 8am–2pm, Fri 8–11am, Sat 8am–noon; ☎0511/52982). Otherwise, staff at *Borneo Homestay* have their finger on things (see "Accommodation").

Accommodation

All of Banjarmasin's **accommodation** places are central, offer at least breakfast, and can make travel bookings.

Biuti, Jl Haryono 21 (☎0511/54493). Good mid-range option, neat and tiled, with either economy rooms or ones with fan, TV and soft mattress. ④–⑤.

Borneo Homestay, Jl Simpang Hasanuddin I, 33 (☎0511/66545, fax 57515). The only accommodation in all Kalimantan solely geared to overseas backpackers, with a travel and tour office specializing in Loksado trekking. Owner Johan Yasin is very clued up indeed, especially about what foreigners want – and how much they are prepared to pay. Beds US$5; rooms ④.

Diamond Homestay, Jl Simpang Hasanuddin II (☎0511/66100). Very friendly place, competing with the *Borneo* for the backpacker market; less of a range of rooms, but these (and their tours) are somewhat cheaper. ③.

Istana Barito (Barito Palace), Jl Haryono 16–20 (☎0511/67300, fax 52240). The next best thing in town to the *Kalimantan*, but not as smart, and its age is starting to show. Japanese, European and Korean restaurants. ⑧.

Kalimantan, Jl Lambung Mangkurat (☎0511/66818, fax 67345). Foreign business venue, with its own shopping centre, upmarket restaurants and sports facilities. ⑨.

Perdana, Jl Brigjen Katamso (☎0511/53276, fax 67988). Columns lend a colonial air to the exterior, contradicted by a traditionally Banjarese high-pitched roof. Pricier rooms are spacious and fair value. ⑥.

Sabrina, Jl Bank Rakyat 5 (☎0511/54442). Pleasantly dingy place; clean and not too stuffy. The aircon rooms are more expensive than those with fan. ⑤–⑥.

The City

As befits the capital city of a culture dominated by Islam, Banjarmasin's focus is the marble-and-bronze exterior of **Masjid Raya Sabilal Muhtadin**, more briefly known as the **Grand Mosque**, which sits in parkland overlooking the west bank of Sungai Martapura just above the city centre. Built in 1981 and one of the country's largest mosques, Masjid Raya's interior impresses by its sense of space, rather than any gaudy furnishings; you can look around outside the main prayer times, provided you dress conservatively, with legs and arms fully covered. Walk to the river here and flag down a water taxi heading 3km north to **Museum Perjuangan** (Tues–Thurs 8.30am–2.30pm, Fri 8.30–11am, Sat & Sun 8.30am–1.30pm; free), a single high-set building whose best feature is its **Banjar design**, with high-pitched roof – the display inside is a tedious collection of weapons used against the Dutch during the Independence struggle.

Following the riverbank south of the Grand Mosque, central Banjarmasin is a mosaic of **markets**, each specializing in specific merchandise. Along Jalan Ujung Murung, **Pasar Murung** has a small bird market, and marks the entrance to a wooden riverside quarter, a notoriously fire-prone labyrinth of undercover boardwalks, homes and tea kiosks. Emerging into the open again south by the Jalan Antasari bridge amongst **Pasar Sudimampir's** porcelain sellers, you'll find gem stalls west of here off Jalan Sudimampir at **Pasar Malabar**, while crossing south over Jalan Samudra takes you down into the clothing wholesalers of **Pasar Baru**. There's a small **Taoist temple** nearby on Jalan Niaga, whose caretakers tell incomprehensible tales about wartime bombings and the stuffed tiger next to the altar, but for real off-the-cuff entertainment head 1.5km east across the river down Jalan Antasari, past the Mitra Plaza and white exterior of Masjid Agung, to **Pasar Antasari**. A market and circus rolled into one, you can spend hours here among hawkers and hustlers of every description – beware of pickpockets – and watching the ever-changing setup. From sunrise, the covered market inside is packed with trays of cheap gems, jewellery, watches, wallets, medicinal spices and trinkets, with artisans polishing stones and hardware out the back; in the evening, the forecourt fills up with clothing stalls and warung, with Banjarmasin's main fruit and veg market around the back, running through until dawn. Crowds peak at the weekends after 8pm or so, but the highlight, at any time, are the **street performers**. Some are musclemen who break coconuts with their heads, chew glass or hammer nails up their noses; others are quacks who hang around selling their elixirs – one attaches medicinal leeches to various parts of his anatomy, and another regular piles up cases of poisonous snakes and sits astride a live crocodile while proclaiming the virtues of his reptile oil (a big aid to male virility) to crowds of eager men.

On the water: around Kuin floating market and Pulau Kaget

You haven't seen Banjarmasin until you've travelled the city's waterways in a klotok. Despite a gradual clearing of riverside homes around the centre, half of Banjarmasin's population spend their days on wooden porches overlooking the water. Normal conventions regarding clothing are dropped as whole streets wash and socialize in public, women in sarongs, men wearing just underpants. While a specific tour past homes in the "backstreet" canals smacks of voyeurism, there are a couple of trips to make where scenes of people's daily routine fill the background, the best being an excursion to one of

Banjarmasin's famous *pasar terapang*, or **floating markets**. The largest is at **Kuin**, where one of the Martapura's side-branches joins Sungai Barito about 4km northeast of the centre, starting daily at dawn and effectively over by 8am; it takes about half an hour to get here from the Jalan Yani bridge. As you approach the market, the canals open into the kilometre-wide Barito and you suddenly find yourself bumping around in the middle of a jam of small boats, full of shoppers who have hired a klotok between them, and dugouts paddled by old women, their bows weighed down with bunches of bananas. Vendors, some moored in midstream waiting for customers, others hunting for business by following bigger craft, sell everything – medicines, huge bricks of fermented prawn *trasi*, salted and fresh fish, and piles of pineapples, beans or watermelons. There are even **floating warung**, where you can have a breakfast of coffee and cakes by tying up alongside and hooking your choice of pastry by means of a pole-and-nail arrangement. After the market, pick up some of the contradictions of Banjarese traditions a short way downstream at lightly wooded **Pulau Kembang** (Flower Island), where both Chinese and Muslims pray for success in personal or business ventures at a small, unpretentious **shrine** to a monkey god derived from Hanuman, a Hindu deity. Recent criticism of the practice by Banjarmasin's imams seems to have had little effect, and the island is packed out at weekends, when long-tailed macaque monkeys bully visitors for a handout of peanuts.

A separate trip reaches past Banjarmasin's floating suburbs and industrial wharves out to **Pulau Kaget**, 12km down the Barito. Once the most accessible place in Kalimantan to spot **proboscis monkeys**, this island has now been cleared almost totally to plant rice, and the leaf-eating monkeys have virtually abandoned it. Still, the journey down Sungai Martapura and out to the mouth of the Barito is interesting enough, passing Banjarmasin's **shipyards**, which turned out beautiful Bugis schooners with exaggerated, curved prows until the ironwood forests upstream were logged out in the early 1990s. Plenty of schooners still dock here to load up with timber, however, and the shipyards are still kept busy refitting modern ocean-going tugs and tankers.

Eating and entertainment

Banjarese food has characteristic sweet flavours accompanied by unusually hot sambals. Fish and sates are particularly good, coming together as *katupat kandangan*, a local treat consisting of catfish sate and duck eggs covered in a spicy coconut sauce. Other Banjar dishes include the similar *ikan kipus*; *papuyu baubar* (grilled fish and pumpkin), *saluang* (crispy-fried sprats) and *soto Banjar* (a thick soup of rice, chicken, egg, carrot, fried onion and glass noodles). Sweet **cakes**, *kue*, are another Banjarese tradition, popular as a mid-afternoon snack, when men congregate around backstreet kiosks to munch on them, drink tea and chat. For cheap **warung**, try Jalan Niaga in the Pasar Baru area, and the area around Pasar Antasari; Mitra Plaza has some good-value **ice cream** and sanitized food outlets on the top floor. Street food is usually where you'll find the most authentic Banjar fare, as most of the city's **restaurants** are Chinese, but in addition to those listed below there are a couple of inexpensive Banjarese places around Pasar Antasari.

For organized entertainment, Mitra Plaza has a multi-screen **cinema** and no fewer than five **discos**; otherwise after-dark action means mingling with the crowds and people-watching.

Restaurants and warung

There are several takeaway **cake** shops along Jalan Sudimampir, but the best selection is at *Menseng Utarid*, on the corner of Jalan Samudra and Jalan Pasar Baru. Packed rooftop warung overlooking the river and the Jalan Antasari bridge above Pasar Sudimampir serve tea and Banjar pancakes, two-centimetre-thick discs coated in sugar and syrup; you have to sit on the floor and eat off low tables elbow-to-back with other patrons.

Cak Mentul, Jl Haryono. Low-key warung specializing in local-style chicken and duck, fried or roasted and served with a sweet sauce.

Cintoraso, diagonally across from the *Istana Barito* on Jl Haryono. Clean and cheap Padang food.

Eskimo, western end of Jl Samudra. Small place with Chinese-Indonesian menu; modestly priced and decent-sized portions, but incredibly slow service.

Jakarta, corner of Jl Bank Rakyat and Jl Hasanuddin. Despite the name, some of the best mid-priced Chinese food in town.

Jaya Karta, western end of Jl Samudra. Fresh Chinese-style seafood; choose prawns, fish, or live crabs and have them cooked out front in the open-air kitchen.

Kaganangan and **Cendrawasih**, opposite each other at the western end of Jl Samudra. Banjarese restaurants serving a Padang-style assortment of prawns and fish dishes, washed down with vegetable soup, tea or fluorescent-pink *es dewet*; everything is good, but avoid the sharp spines of black-skinned *pupuyu* fish.

Listings

Airline offices Office hours are Mon–Thurs 8am–5pm, Fri 8–11am & 2–5pm, Sat & Sun 9am–1pm. Bouraq, Jl Yani 343 (☎0511/52445); DAS, Jl Hasanuddin 6 (☎0511/52902); Garuda at *Istana Barito* hotel (☎0511/59063, fax 59064); Merpati, Jl Hasanuddin 31 (☎0511/53885, fax 54290).

Banks and exchange Bank Dayang Negara, near the Grand Mosque at the top end of Jl Lambung Mangkurat (Mon–Fri 8am–3.30pm), offers the best deal on all foreign exchange; further down the same road, BCA has lower rates but are also open Saturday (8–11am). Adi Ankasa Travel (see opposite) will change money and travellers' cheques outside banking hours, but their rates are poor.

Bookshops Gramedia Books, top floor of the Mitra Plaza, has a selection of standard city and provincial maps, a tiny, random assortment of books in English, and the only stock of postcards in east and southern Kalimantan outside of Balikpapan.

Buses Long-distance buses leave east of town from Terminal Km6; catch a bemo there from the Jl Hasanuddin–Jl Bank Rakyat crossroads. The terminal is nicely ordered, with minibuses and coaches all arranged in bays labelled with their destinations. Buses to Balikpapan (Rp3500–23,500) and Samarinda (Rp17,000–27,000) start leaving mid-afternoon.

Ferries Buy tickets for the crowded, forty-person speedboats to Palangkaraya (Rp25,000) from the dock near the Grand Mosque on Jl Pos. They leave when full through the morning and early afternoon and take 4–5hr to cut across the Barito, Kapuas and Kahayan rivers along canals laid down by the Dutch. Pelni's Kelimutu crosses to Surabaya several times a week from Trisakti Port; the Pelni office is about 1km southwest of the centre by Sungai Martapura on Jl Martadinata.

Hospital Banjarmasin's General Hospital is about 1.5km east of the centre on Jl Yani.

Pharmacies Apotik Kasio is diagonally across from the Istana Barito on Jl Haryono, a well-stocked chemist and clinic, with doctors on call from 5pm to 7pm.

Police Police headquarters are 2.5km out of town along Jl Yani.

Post office Jl Lambung Mangkurat, between Jl B. Katsomo and Jl Samudra. Separate buildings for letters and parcels; the staff are helpful but give the impression that they've never had to send anything overseas before.

Souvenirs Shops on Jl Sudimampir II stock a full range of Dayak crafts and weapons, plus a few pieces of porcelain and gems. Banjarmasin also manufactures its own strongly coloured tie-dyed batik, *sasirangan*, whose patterns hark back to shamanistic rituals. The best selection is at Toko Citra, some 3km east of town down Jl Yani, though you might track some down at Pasar Baru – Martapura's markets also stock them, if you're heading that way. Prices are fixed at Rp20,000–25,000 per piece, depending on quality of the cloth.

Telephone and fax There is a wartel open 24hr a day at the mosque end of Jl Lambung Mangkurat. Bigger hotels also have international call facilities.

Tours The main tours offered by agents in Banjarmasin are a short cruise of local waterways; an early-morning trip to Kuin floating market and Pulau Kembang; an afternoon proboscis-spotting at Pulau Kaget; a day-tour to Martapura and Cempaka; and three to five days hiking and rafting around Lokasado. The cruises and Cempaka tours are easy enough – and cheaper – to organize yourself, though an English-speaking guide makes them that much more interesting, and is definitely recommended if you speak little Indonesian and are heading to Loksado. Whether or not you stay there, the cheapest and most experienced tour agents in town are the *Borneo Homestay* and *Diamond Homestay* (see p.747), with a similarly competent Adi Ankasa Travel (see below) charging far more for the same packages.

Travel agents If your accommodation can't help, Adi Ankasa Travel, Jl Hasanuddin 27 (☎0511/53131), can make all accommodation, plane, bus and boat bookings.

Banjarbaru, Martapura and Cempaka

A busy country town 40km east of Banjarmasin, **Martapura** became famous in the 1660s when **Sheik Muhammad Arsyad al-Banjari** founded the blue-domed **mosque** here on his return from a forty-year sojourn at Mecca. He then settled down to spend the rest of his 102 years teaching Islamic law and compiling two enduringly famous **books**: *Sabilal Muhtadin*, the guide to daily morals which lent its name to Banjarmasin's Grand Mosque; and the *Khiltab Barincung*, a religious commentary. Since his time, Martapura has also become famous for **gems**, especially *berlian* (diamonds), mined nearby at the village of **Cempaka**, and it's the chance to see the mining operations and maybe pick up a bargain stone that draws most visitors today. Orange bemos leave Banjarmasin's Terminal Km6 throughout the day whenever full (Rp1250) and take about ninety minutes to reach Martapura; the mines are closed on Fridays, Martapura's main market day. Some 5km short of Martapura, you could call in at **BANJARBARU** for an interesting hour's browse around Hindu relics and Banjar ceremonial artefacts at **Museum Lambung** (Tues–Thurs, Sat & Sun 8am–4pm, Fri 8.30–11am & 2–4pm; Rp200).

MARTAPURA itself is basically a **marketplace** next to the mosque on Sungai Martapura. Bemos from Banjarmasin terminate in the forecourt of a white-tiled **plaza** housing gemstone and clothing stores – you can buy *sasirangan* **batik** here – behind which a camp of low canvas awnings abutting the mosque walls lends the produce and hardware markets the flavour of an Arabian bazaar. Hawkers around the plaza latch on to foreigners, often sneaking you off to one side before unravelling a twist of paper with a diamond inside, or furtively pulling a piece of agate out of an inner pocket: don't deal with them unless you can tell coloured glass from the real thing. The area's religious connotations make Martapura's gems intrinsically valuable to locals, and features that would elsewhere diminish a stone's worth can here increase it – internal flaws resembling stars or Arabic script, for instance. Even if you have no intention of buying, it's fascinating to look around the trays of coloured baubles: there are diamonds, turquoise, honey-coloured tiger's-eye, pale-blue topaz, amethysts, citrines, smoky quartz crystals, and unusual *kelulud*, or **tektites**. These black pebbles of opaque volcanic glass derive from a prehistoric meteorite impact and, for some reason, lie alongside gems at the Cempaka fields, earning them the local tag "friend of the diamond" – the two stones are often mounted together on rings. Once you've looked around the plaza, head over to the edge of the adjoining grassy park, where **showrooms** geared to tour groups and serious buyers offer a more reliable place to shop, and the chance to see **diamond polishing** out the back. Plenty of **food** stalls will keep you fed, but Martapura's single losmen refuses to take foreigners – the last bemos return to Banjarmasin after dark.

Cempaka

Green minibuses labelled "*Mart-Cemp*" depart regularly from Martapura's plaza for the fifteen-minute ride (Rp500) south to **CEMPAKA**, a village which lent its name to the local **gem-fields**. Drivers will leave you where a muddy, two-kilometre track leads off from the roadside, past a concrete diamond monument and paddy-fields, and out to the diggings. Gems of all kinds are found here, though Cempaka is famous for its **diamonds** – most are yellow and tiny, but the largest ever found here was the impressive 167-carat **Trisakti**, unearthed in 1965. The bigger, open excavations form flooded bowls where people flounder around in the water with diesel suction pumps, drawing the gravel up to ground level and dumping it in huge heaps, later to be panned for anything valuable. Most of the excavations are far smaller, however, and worked entirely by hand: a hole in the ground marks a shaft with a human chain reaching down into the water 10m below. Panning is done by putting a handful of gravel in a conical wooden vessel and swilling it around so that the heavier gems collect in the middle, and it can be an interesting process to watch when a valuable stone is found – the automatic, well-rehearsed movement of the panners giving way to sudden excitement as they examine the swill.

The Meratus mountains

Kalsel province is shaped around the 200-kilometre-long spine of the partially forested **Meratus mountains**, home of the **Bukit**, one of the most approachable of Dayak groups. Said to have been driven into these hills by the power struggles preceding Banjarmasin's foundation, the Bukit are traditionally animistic and, though few ceremonies are now performed and little is known about their original beliefs, they still enjoy a reputation for powerful magic amongst Kalsel's Muslims. Visitors to the region still have a chance to stay in square Bukit communal houses, or **balai**, bamboo-and-beam apartments which range in size from small huts to vast barns, covering twenty square metres or more. All social activities take place inside, where a sunken area in the middle, filled by a bamboo-and-palm frond shrine, acts as a stage during **festivals**. The biggest of these is the **harvest celebration** in late July or early August, whose week-long festivities kick off with twelve hours of ever-accelerating drumming, dancing and drinking. Guests – who should bring a gift – are welcome except on the penultimate day, in case they bring bad luck with them.

Around 150km northeast of Banjarmasin on the Balikpapan highway, the country town of **Kandangan** is the jumping-off point for trips to the Meratus around **Loksado**, 30km east at the foot of the mountains. A pleasant place to hang out for a day or two, Loksado also offers **bamboo rafting**, and **hikes** into the hills of anything from a few hours to several days' duration. You definitely need **guides** for longer trails and, unless you speak good Indonesian, **tours** from Banjarmasin or Barabai are the best option (if expensive, at US$100 or more for a five-day trek), though you could always just hire an interpreter, or find Indonesian-speaking guides on site, for a fraction of this sum.

To the Meratus: Kandangan and Loksado

Hourly bemos throughout the day are the most convenient way to reach **KANDANGAN** from Banjarmasin; buses from Balikpapan tend to pass through at night. If you get stuck here, recommended **rooms** include the comfortable *Hotel Bankau* (☎0517/21445; ④) or similar *Losmen Loksado* (③), both close to each other on Jalan Suprato, where you'll also find a good, cheap **restaurant**; otherwise get the first vehicle for the hour-long run to Loksado (Rp2500). You have to get out to register with the police about 10km into the journey at **Padang Batung** – bring photocopies of relevant passport pages. Six kilometres short of Loksado, the few houses along the road marking **Tanhui** are a useful orientation point for later exploring the area.

LOKSADO marks the end of the road, a small collection of buildings grouped either side of the twenty-metre-wide **Sungai Amandit**. Not a traditional village by any means – a mosque and a church lurk down the street – Loksado is nonetheless a nice base, which rouses itself for its **Wednesday market**, when entire Bukit villages from the

RAFTING THE AMANDIT

While Loksado provides a market for villagers from the hills, locals shop in Kandangan. Until the road was sealed in the mid-1990s, the only way to get there was on the Amandit, and, as the rapids along the way don't allow for big craft, people used **bamboo rafts** instead. Eight-metre-long bamboo stems, tied together at their tips and then lashed along their length to create a long, narrow, triangular vessel, these rafts are both easy to make and can be broken up and sold at the journey's end. The road has made them redundant, but the rafts are still used by tourists willing to pay for the experience. It's a long twelve hours to Kandangan, however, and most people find that the three-hour stretch to the main road at Tanhui is quite enough. If you take anything with you, make sure it's securely waterproofed (tough plastic wraps are sold in Loksado) – the rafts can't sink, but passengers and goods can fall off, water pours over you almost continually, and you'll arrive soaking wet. With the river high, it's an exciting trip: long, calm stretches overhung with trees are separated by violent rapids and cascades, the raft bouncing off boulders as the boatmen, straining every muscle, use poles to guide you through. You'll certainly be approached if you stay at Loksado; otherwise ask at the guest house for details about arranging the trip.

back of beyond come to town to sell goods – a good time to look for a Dayak guide. From the bus stop, a fine suspension bridge crosses the river into town, where early-closing warung and a dozen shops line the single street. Loksado's only **accommodation** is the row of riverside cabins comprising a guest house (④). Stay on the same side as the bus stop, and a sealed motorbike track heads off along the bank towards the mountains, past the **police post** and the open square at **Kayu Manis marketplace**.

Around Loksado

Rising steeply around Loksado through a covering of grassland, tangled undergrowth and highland forest, the Meratus mountains offer some excellent hiking. While you might see a little wildlife along the way – birds, deer, squirrels, pigs and monkeys are most likely – it's the Bukit which are the main attraction, and there are over fifty *balai* to visit, some easily reached on day-trips, others requiring more time and stamina to hike out to. **Day-trips** don't require anything very special, though it's a good idea to include snacks, an umbrella for the frequently inclement weather and a few packets of cigarettes to share around. **Hikers** should come properly prepared, but with a minimum of gear; gifts for your hosts and just two sets of clothes – shorts and a T-shirt for hiking, long pants and another shirt for the evenings – are enough. All but the shorter trails require a **guide**; the paths are clear enough, but the trick is knowing which one to follow.

Melaris and Manatui

Despite electricity, satellite TV and motorbikes, **MELARIS** is a good place to start delving into Bukit life. Just forty minutes from Loksado, take the bike track past Pasar Kayu Manis, over another suspension bridge, and then turn left and follow the power lines. Melaris is the biggest *balai* of all, with 34 families and 200 people, and the village head is the *damank*, ceremonial and cultural leader, of the entire Meratus region. You could **stay** the night here instead of at Loksado (pay about Rp5000), though the TV means that people don't sit around and talk much after dark. Ten minutes away, **Barajang** is the smaller of two **waterfalls** in the area, but it's often clogged up with garbage. For a slightly more authentic feel, the second largest *balai* is thirty minutes from Melaris at **MANATUI**, or you could head back towards Loksado and then take the path uphill for ninety minutes to **Manikili** – see p.754.

The Niwak loop

With moderate fitness and at least three days – five is better – the **circuit from Loksado** up into the mountains via the village of **Niwak** offers some excellent scenery, and overnight stops in at least two *balai*. Start 6km down the road from Loksado at **Tanhui**, from where it's an easy three-hour walk, past five villages, seven increasingly rickety suspension bridges and bamboo-grove scenery, to **BUMBIAN**, a large settlement whose kepala desa can sort out a bed (Rp5000). The next morning, the path enters rubber groves and then real forest, becoming ever steeper, muddier and tougher – look for parakeets and star-shaped red flowers of stemless ginger growing out of the ground like a fungus. A very stiff burst levels out on a high ridge, with a view of limestone cliffs and adjacent peaks rising out of forest; descending the far side, you pass a couple of small *balai* and from here the path is very slippery, passing onto cleared slopes sectioned into *ladang* plots planted with cassava, long beans, peanuts, sweet potato and rice.

Eight hours from Bumbian should see you to **NIWAK**, a single, large *balai* housing eighteen families, built in 1990 at the upper end of a kilometre-high valley. It's a lovely place to spend a couple of days, set beside a stream with tall peaks rising behind, and the people are pretty tolerant of foreign faces. The only modern appliance here is a generator used to power a rice-husking apparatus, but it's used sparingly – eight people take two days to carry a fuel drum here from Loksado – and you're more likely to be kept awake at night by pigs, chickens and dogs snuffling about under the floor. Check out the huge tree across the stream, deliberately left unfelled because it attracts honeybees, and ask someone to guide you for the forty-minute walk to **Mandin Malapan waterfall**, which drops 30m off a cliff into a shallow swimming hole, encircled by walls of greenery.

It takes another six hours to cross the ridges behind Niwak, initially ascending along a network of logs which replace paths on the slopes above the five-person *balai* of **Panggung**. There's some rainforest inhabited by gibbons at the very top, but the steep, cleared slopes on the far side make for plenty of "mud-skiing" through tall, sharp-edged grass. On the way down, a little earth mound covered in coins and shrouded in yellow silk marks the 400-year-old **grave of Ratu Mona**; local lore holds that she ruled southern Kalimantan, but committed suicide after her husband and son were killed in battle. Not far from here, the view opens up over the Amandit valley, with Loksado and the sea off in the distance, but the first stop is an hour later at **MANIKILI**, where eleven families share a slightly run-down, cramped *balai*. It's another pleasant spot, but Manikili's inhabitants are far less laid-back than Niwak's, and foreigners – especially women – can expect to be the centre of attention during their stay. If it all gets too much, another ninety minutes brings you down to the sealed Loksado–Melaris road, with either settlement only a short walk away.

The Negara wetlands

Thirty kilometres north of Kandagan, the towns of **Barabai**, **Amuntai** and **Negara** enclose the green reed-beds of the waterlogged **Negara wetlands**, site of the province's original kingdom. With the purple ridges of the mountains behind, these lowlands form a pleasant landscape of rivers and marsh, banana palms and rice-fields, rubber plantations and patches of forest; an almost continuous band of villages and towns along the highway adds the glitter of aluminium-domed mosques, buses forever slowing down to negotiate roadblocks set by villagers soliciting mosque rebuilding funds. Though hardly somewhere you'd cross Kalimantan to see, the wetlands are nonetheless a relaxing place to spend a day observing vignettes of a comfortable rural life; you can catch **bemos** here from Kandangan, or get dropped off by Banjarmasin–Balikpapan traffic.

Barabai and around

The starting point for forays into the Negara wetlands, **BARABAI** sits on a river of the same name. Buses deliver to the huge, open **terminal** on the north side of town; walk 100m down past the **market** and you'll end up on Jalan Brigjen Hasan Basri, which runs along the riverbank. Turn right and it's a two-minute walk along Jalan Brigjen Hasan Basri to **accommodation** under the traditionally pitched Banjar roof of *Hotel Fusfa* (☎0517/41136; with fan ④, with air-con ⑥), which can arrange meals, and English-speaking (but wearingly overenthusiastic) **guides**. Barabai's backstreets have plenty of old Dutch town houses, but there's not much excitement in this rather serious, conservative town: many older people speak only the rapid Banjar dialect, not Indonesian, and there's a heavy Muslim feel to the place, with a huge mosque overlooking the river and a resident pocket of ethnic Arabs. **Moving on**, buses from Banjarmasin to Balikpapan and Samarinda start turning up at the bus terminal around 6pm, bemos to Amuntai and Kandangan run all day, and the last minibus back to Banjarmasin leaves in the mid-afternoon.

Amuntai, Alabio and Negara

AMUNTAI lies an hour away to Barabai's northwest, where, 1.5km from the centre at **Paliwara**, a few grassy mounds and disjointed stonework are all that remain of a thir-teenth-century Negaran palace, **Candi Agung**. After a look, catch a bemo from Amuntai 7km southwest to **ALABIO**, whose huge Wednesday **market** alongside **Sungai Negara** is crammed with shoppers and stalls hawking rattan crafts, dried fish, buckets of river snails and, most famously, live **ducks**. A klotok, rented from below the bridge here (try for Rp5000 an hour), takes you downstream to Negara town in about two hours through a rustic replay of Banjarmasin's canals – stilt homes, outhouses, duck pens and graceful suspension bridges. If the water level is high enough, you can detour through the fields and shallow channels before Negara, where you'll see plenty of birdlife, people fishing with cast nets and wicker fish-traps.

Busy though it is, complete with a small shipyard, timber mills and the inevitable mar-ket, it's impossible to imagine that today's **NEGARA**, a kilometre-long street along the river, was once the pivot of all Kalsel, though it's an interesting place. Resounding to the chink of tiny hammers, the **Sungai Pinang** district of town is renowned for recycling metals; during World War II, gun barrels were forged here for guerrilla use against the Japanese, but the industry has since turned to producing handmade drill bits, kitchen utensils and silverware. People work in little shacks outside their houses, bellows pumped by foot; knock on front doors and ask to see the process. Down past the mar-ket, start back towards Barabai by catching a bemo 10km down the Kandangan road to **Bangkau**, a village at the southern edge of **Danau Bangkau**. Settlements around the lakeshore are the best place to see the local practice of penning **water buffalo** in *kerbau kalan*, raised ironwood enclosures that resemble islands – during the day the animals swim around and wallow, grazing. From here, there's traffic to Kandangan and Barabai until late afternoon.

KALIMANTAN TIMUR

Kalimantan Timur, or **Kaltim**, is Kalimantan's biggest and, in places, most developed and affluent region. Nowhere is this more obvious than in the coastal centres of **Balikpapan** and **Samarinda**, the only cities in Kalimantan which could be described as conspicuously wealthy. Though more accessible areas of Kaltim have been perma-nently scarred by decades of logging, parts of the mountainous interior remain very wild, and you could spend months here, whatever your interests. Samarinda itself is the terminus for cruising up the **Mahakam** on one of the world's great river journeys, while the northeast counts prime scuba diving on beautiful **Pulau Derawan** among its attractions. Head to the interior, to the upper Mahakam or isolated **Apo Kayan** region around the border with Malaysia, and there's the chance to meet the Dayak on their home ground – a guaranteed adventure, however you attempt it.

Historically, scattered relics are all that remain of Kaltim's early **Hindu kingdoms**, which were established in the Mahakam basin as early as the fourth century and expanded a millennium later by political refugees from Java. Their demise followed the subsequent spread of Islam, and by the seventeenth century Kaltim was divided into rival **Muslim sultanates**, the most influential of which was based on the lower reaches of the Mahakam in the **Kutai** region. Rich, yet far from omnipotent – their capitals were occasionally the target of pirate raids, and their rule was always nominal in the interior – the sultans held onto power throughout the colonial era, though they lost all effective control when **Japan invaded** from Sarawak in 1942 and began milking Kaltim's oilfields to power their Pacific campaigns. After the war, Independence saw the sultans formally stripped of their status, and their regencies merged to form Kaltim province, though their names – and some former **palaces** – survive as administrative districts.

Samarinda is Kaltim's transport terminus, with regular road traffic south into Kalsel, north along the coast, and inland to towns on the Mahakam's lower reaches; this is also where public river ferries depart up the Mahakam, and where most of Kaltim's internal flights originate. Balikpapan handles domestic and international flights, while both Samarinda and Balikpapan are major seaports; elsewhere, private and public craft come in handy for exploring Kaltim's lesser-known rivers. There are endless possibilities for **hiking** too, but, despite the lengthy border with Malaysian Borneo, the only official overland crossing is into Sabah via **Pulau Nunukan** – see p.781.

Balikpapan

Staked out over Kalimantan's richest petroleum deposits, **BALIKPAPAN** has always been a company town. The Dutch founded Balikpapan's mass of purpose-built services and housing in 1897, and two years later the city's first **oil refinery** was up and running. Occupied by the Japanese during World War II, and the scene of heavy fighting when Allied troops evicted them in 1945, the city's fortunes have otherwise waxed and waned along with international fuel prices: business has boomed since the Gulf War ended years of stagnation in 1991, and Balikpapan's 350,000 residents currently enjoy a tidy and busy city, with plenty of traffic, a few high-rises, and large numbers of expatriate oil workers from the US and Australia. Arriving by air from Brunei for your first look at Indonesia, however, you may wonder why you bothered – with its Western ambience, Balikpapan is probably best experienced after a long sojourn in Kalimantan's interior, when its above-average facilities can be properly appreciated.

Orientation, arrival and city transport

Occupying a ten-square-kilometre corner of land bordered by the Makasar Strait to the south and Balikpapan Bay to the west, Balikpapan's commercial district surrounds three-kilometre-long Jalan Yani, with the nearest thing to a downtown hub at its southern intersection with Jalan Sudirman. **Sepinggan airport** is 8km east of the city (15min by taxi; Rp9000); unless you look like an oil worker, touts here expect that you'll be heading directly to Samarinda (2hr; Rp35,000). Arriving from Brunei in northern Borneo, sixty-day tourist visas are issued with no problems. The **Banjarmasin bus terminal** is on the west side of Balikpapan Bay, opposite the city at the hamlet of **Penajam** and connected to it by a ferry to the **Kampung Baru dock** on Jalan Mong Insidi (Rp2000). Buses from Banjarmasin continuing to Samarinda, however, cross the

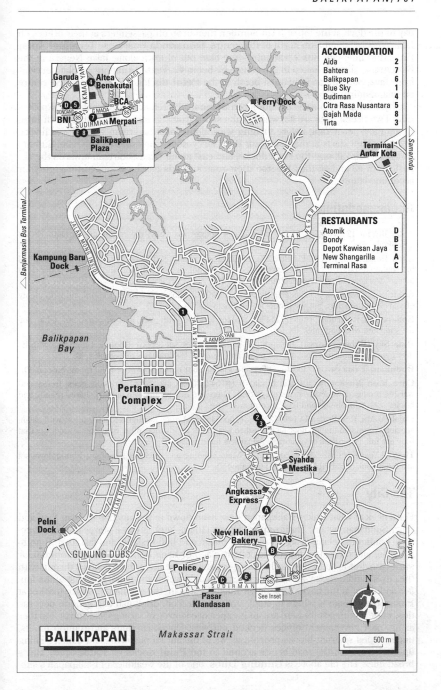

ACCOMMODATION

Aida	2
Bahtera	7
Balikpapan	6
Blue Sky	1
Budiman	4
Citra Rasa Nusantara	5
Gajah Mada	8
Tirta	3

RESTAURANTS

Atomik	D
Bondy	B
Depot Kawisan Jaya	E
New Shangarilla	A
Terminal Rasa	C

BALIKPAPAN

Makassar Strait

0   500 m

bay to the dock at the top of Jalan Somber, then drop off passengers at their offices on Jalan Negara, about 5km north of the centre. **Samarinda buses** use **Terminal Antar Kota** (the Inter-city Bus Terminal) some 6km out of town along Jalan Negara in the Batu Ampar district, linked to the centre by bemo #3. Vessels running regular services from Java, Sumatra and Sulawesi berth at the **Pelni docks**, 2.5km west of the centre on Jalan Sudirman.

City transport consists of numbered **bemos**, which follow fixed routes for Rp350 a ride. Two useful ones are #3, which runs south from Terminal Antar Kota down Jalan Negara and Jalan Yani, before turning west along Jalan Sudirman to the Pelni docks, and #6, which starts at the Kampung Baru ferry dock, runs south along Jalan Suprato and Jalan Minyak past the Pelni docks, and east along Jalan Sudirman towards the airport. Both #3 and #6 then reverse their routes. **Taxis** can be arranged through your accommodation.

Accommodation

Aida, Jl Yani 12 (☎0542/31011). Balikpapan's budget mainstay; the rooms are threadbare but acceptable. ④.

Altea Benakutai, Jl Yani, PO Box 299, Balikpapan (☎0542/33022, fax 31823). The city's original international-standard hotel: well presented with a pool, sauna and gym, and targeted squarely at foreign workers on expense accounts. ⑨.

Bahtera, Jl Sudirman, PO Box 490, Balikpapan (☎0542/22563, fax 31889). Central and with plenty of marble in the lobby, but the rooms are ordinary for the price. ⑦.

Balikpapan, Jl Garuda 2 (☎0542/21490). Hill-top location, with plain, neat air-con rooms, a bar, coffee shop and weekend rates. ⑦.

Blue Sky (Bahana Surya), Jl Suprato 1 (☎0542/22268, fax 35895). Upmarket high-rise with its own gym and sauna, overlooking the pipes and flame of Balikpapan's oil complex. ⑧.

Budiman, Jl Yani (☎0542/36030). Quiet and gloomy, but reasonably priced. All rooms air-con. ⑦.

Citra Rasa Nusantara, Jl Gajah Mada 76 (☎0542/25366, fax 35236). Friendly guest house and warung hidden down a side street off Jl Yani. There are tiny rooms with fan and shared mandi, and pricier ones with air-con and their own mandi. ④–⑥.

Gajah Mada, Jl Sudirman 14 (☎0542/34634, fax 34636). A good location and a fair price, with clean, spacious rooms on the top floor facing out to sea. Book in advance; otherwise they always say that they are full, regardless of vacancies. All rooms have mandi. ⑥.

Tirta, Jl Yani 8 (☎0542/22772, fax 22132). Main building and pricier self-contained bungalows set around a pool. Standard hotel room/bungalow ⑦.

The City

For a peek at what makes Balikpapan tick, head down to the junction of Jalan Yani and Jalan Sudirman, where **Balikpapan Plaza** (10am–late) is three storeys of duty-free-style boutiques selling designer clothes, music and hi-fi systems and fast food. If nothing else, air-con makes this an excellent place to hang out; by day the ground-floor **supermarket** is packed with shopping expatriates, at night the balconies throng with the city's middle-class youth, who gather to people-watch and make the most of the fun-fair and disco at the back. West down Jalan Sudirman, the morning produce market at **Pasar Klandasan** is where to stock up on fresh fruit, dried fish and general necessities, while clothing stalls here are an inexpensive source of sarongs and shirts. Further along, past government offices decked out with Dayak carvings and rooftop motifs, undeveloped seafront blocks provide views of distant oil platforms and tankers lining up offshore, then the road bends around to the **Pelni docks** on **Balikpapan Bay's** broad inlet. The hill above is **Gunung Dubs**, one of the wealthier of Balikpapan's suburbs, whose winding lanes and groves of banana and cunjevoi pleasantly complement the mildewed colonial houses. From here you can look down on the gargantuan **Pertamina oil complex** to the north, whose countless kilometres of rounded silver piping assume organic qualities at night, lit up by sporadic breaths of orange flame spouting from the refinery, all reflected in the dark waters of the bay.

Eating and entertainment

There's a decent range of **food** in town, including some stylish, good-value restaurants. For Western fare, try hotel menus at the *Altea Benakutai, Blue Sky* and *Mirama*. Entertainment is largely limited to **nightclubs** patronized by Westerners at the foreign-oriented hotels, and a couple of **cinemas**: the Glora, down towards the GPO on Jalan Sudirman, delivers a daily dose of Hong Kong and Western action pictures; while the Antasari, at the southern end of Jalan Yani, has soft-core Indonesian romances.

Restaurants

There are a string of cheap **warung** opposite Cinema Antasari on Jalan Sutoyo. Terminal Rasa, near the Glora cinema on Jalan Sudirman, is a huge, airy canteen with various stalls offering all the usual staples.

Atomik, long-running Chinese favourite, with frog, pigeon and snails pepping up a mid-priced menu of standard stir-fries.

Bondy, Jl Yani. An unexceptional exterior conceals a wonderful split-level, open-air courtyard out the back, where you can eat superbly grilled seafood in real comfort for about Rp20,000 a head. The best place to dine in town.

Depot Kawisan Jaya, just west of the Balikpapan Plaza on Jl Sudirman. The finest goat and venison sates in Kalimantan, though house specialities are various types of grilled fish. Fill up for Rp10,000.

New Hollan, Jl Yani. Bakery, café and restaurant, with steak, cakes, doughnuts and cheerfully named ice-cream sundaes.

New Shangrila, Jl Yani 29. A popular Chinese restaurant with check tablecloths and a skilled way with crab, fried prawn balls and spicy tofu.

Listings

Airline offices Bouraq, Jl Sudirman (☎0542/31475); DAS, Jl Yani 33 (☎0542/24286); Garuda, Jl Yani 19 (☎0542/22300, fax 35194); Merpati, Jl Sudirman 22 (☎0542/24452); Royal Brunei, at the *Hotel Bahtera* (☎0542/26011).

Banks The BCA, 200m east of *Hotel Bahtera* on Jl Sudirman, has good rates but only accepts Visa travellers' cheques; otherwise, use the BNI, also on Jl Sudirman, opposite the *Hotel Gadjah Mada*. ATMs outside the Balikpapan Plaza take Cirrus/Maestro cards.

Boats Pelni's *Kambuna* stops twice a month on a Java–Sulawesi circuit, with the *Kerinci* and *Tidar* also calling at Tarakan and Nunukan, and the *Umsini* running right through to Ternate in Maluku. Tickets and timetables are available through their offices at the harbour on Jl Minyak or from tour agents (see p.760).

Bookshops Gramedia, 2nd floor, Balikpapan Plaza, is Kalimantan's best-stocked bookshop; English titles include a few coffee-table albums, guides, an assortment of writings on Borneo and standard city and provincial maps for Kalimantan and Indonesia. English-language magazines and newspapers are sold at the *Hotel Altea Benakutai*.

Buses Buses to Banjarmasin (Rp13,500–23,500) leave through the day from the far side of Balikpapan Bay; catch a ferry there for Rp2000 from the Kampung Baru dock on Jl Mong Insidi. Buses for Samarinda (Rp3500) depart hourly from morning to late afternoon from Terminal Antar Kota, 6km north of the centre on Jl Negara. Tickets can be bought at departure points, and there should be no trouble getting on the next departure on either routes.

Hospital Public Hospital (Rumah Sakit Umum) is halfway up Jl Yani (☎0542/34181).

Pharmacies Pharmacies and evening consultations at Apotik Vita Farma, at the junction of Jl Yani and Jl Martadinata, and Apotik Dayakindo, further down Jl Yani. The supermarket at Balikpapan Plaza stocks aspirin, cough medicines, plasters, and so on.

Police Jl Wiluyo (☎0542/21110).

Post Big hotels will hold mail for you if you have a reservation; the GPO with poste restante, parcel post and EMS counters is at Jl Sudirman 31.

Souvenirs For a broad range of local rattanwork, Banjar and Samarinda batik, Dutch coins, Dayak crafts from all over Kalimantan, Chinese porcelain, gemstones and even fossils, head to Syahda Mestika, Jl Yani 2, or Borneo Arts, Jl Yani 229. Most items are made for the tourist trade, but collectors might look out for old decorative Kenyah wooden baby-carriers, strings of ceramic beads once used as currency among Dayak groups and green-glazed celadon crockery.

Telephone and fax The main wartel office is across from the *Hotel Altea Benakutai* on Jl Yani.

Tours and guides All but the cheapest hotels can make transport bookings. For this and hiking expeditions, Sungai Mahakam cruises, diving at Pulau Derawan, or private guides, try Angkassa Express at Jl Yani 12 (☎0542/35363, fax 34626), or their desk at the *Blue Sky Hotel* (☎0542/414590); they take most credit cards, but offer a ten-percent discount for cash payments on airfares.

Samarinda

Some 120km north of Balikpapan, **SAMARINDA** sprang to life during the eighteenth century after a raiding party of Bugis pirates from Sulawesi founded a settlement on the lower reaches of the **Sungai Mahakam**. Positioned 50km upstream from the sea, where the Mahakam is 1km wide and deep enough to be navigable by ocean-going cargo ships, Samarinda has become increasingly prosperous since large-scale **logging** of Kaltim's interior began in the 1970s, its western riverfront abuzz with mills turning the huge log rafts floated down from upstream into plywood and planking. The city has also long provided jobs, markets and amenities for communities along the Mahakam, benefits that new air links have recently brought within reach of more isolated regions across the province. There's not much to see here, but as the source of Sungai Mahakam ferries and flights to Dayak strongholds on the Upper Mahakam and Apo Kayan Samarinda makes a good place to stock up for trips into Kalimantan's wilds – or to recover on your return.

Orientation, arrival and city transport

Hemmed in by hills, the bulk of Samarinda occupies the north bank of the Mahakam. The centre is a three-square-kilometre mesh of broad streets and alleys running back from waterfront **Jalan Gajah Mada**, bordered initially by Jalan Awang Long to the west and Jalan Sangaji to the east. Most services are near to the river in the vicinity of **Pasar Pagi**, along **Jalan Khalid** and **Jalan Panglima Batur**. South of the river, semi-rural suburbs are connected to the centre by ferries from near Pasar Pagi – the only **bridge** across the Mahakam is 5km to the west.

Samarinda's **airport** is 2km north of the centre, surrounded by suburbs. Taxis into town charge Rp5000, or you can just turn left at the gates, walk 100m to Jalan Gatot, and wave down a city bemo heading south to Pasar Pagi. **Buses** from the north terminate 5km northeast of the city at Terminal Bontang, from where you catch a brown bemo to the centre. Arriving on a bus originating at Banjarmasin or Tenggarong you'll land up on the south bank of the Mahakam at Terminal Banjarmasin; cross over the road to the pier and catch a boat directly across to Pasar Pagi (Rp500). Buses direct from Balikpapan or Kota Bangun, however, end up beyond the bridge, 5km west of the city at Terminal Balikpapan – as do **Mahakam river ferries**, which stop at the Sungai Kunjang docks. At either, green bemos await to cart you downtown. All **ocean-going vessels** use the docks immediately east of the centre along Jalan Sudarso.

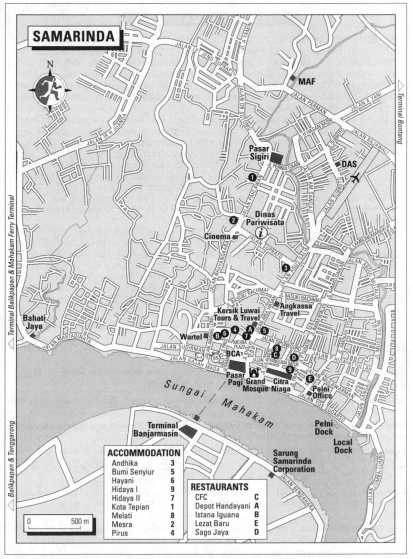

Samarinda's colour-coded **bemos** cost Rp400 a ride and run between particular areas rather than following strict routes – tell the driver your destination as you embark. Jalan Awang Long is a good place to find one heading north, while either side of Pasar Pagi on Jalan Sudirman or Jalan Gajah Mada is where to hail westbound traffic. **Ojeks** wait around Pasar Pagi and the Mesra Plaza; **taxis** can be found west of Pasar Pagi on Jalan Veteran, or at the rank on Jalan Pangalima Batur.

LEAVING SAMARINDA

One of the main reasons for coming to Samarinda is to arrange a ticket out. **By air,** there's little problem getting a seat on major routes to Berau, Tanjung Selor, Tarakan or Balikpapan, but it is vital to book flights to **Datah Dawai**, on the Upper Mahakam, and various airstrips in the **Apo Kayan** – handled by DAS and MAF respectively – well in advance (see p.782 for details). Bemos don't run to the airport, but stopping orange or brown ones heading north up Jalan Awang Long you might eventually find a driver willing to take you there for about Rp1000.

Buses to Banjarmasin (Rp17,000–27,000) depart from mid-afternoon onwards from Terminal Banjarmasin, across the river on Jalan Bendahara, and it's best to buy a ticket at least a few hours in advance. **Minibuses to Tenggarong** (Rp2000) leave all the time from outside Terminal Banjarmasin until the late afternoon: just wave one down. For **Balikpapan** (Rp3500), either catch a bus to Banjarmasin, or a green bemo from outside Pasar Pagi on Jalan Gajah Mada 5km west to Terminal Balikpapan, where buses heading upriver to **Kota Bangun** (Rp4000) also depart – Balikpapan buses leave hourly, but those to Kota Bangun are less frequent. For **Bontang** (Rp3700) and **Sengata** (Rp8700), take a brown bemo from Jalan Bhayangkara 5km northeast to Terminal Bontang, where there are departures at least until early afternoon.

Sungai Mahakam ferries leave from Terminal Sungai Kunjang, upstream from the city past Terminal Balikpapan – catch a green bemo from behind Pasar Pagi on Jalan Gajah Mada, and see p.781 for full ferry details. **Marine docks** are along Jalan Yos Sudarso, on the east side of town. Independent services to Berau and Tarakan leave from the far end of the street, with Pelni's *Leseur* and *Binaiya* using the western dock for an average three trips a month to Tarakan and Nunukan, and one a month to Kumai, on Java–Sulawesi circuits. The Pelni office (☎0541/41402) and timetables are on Jalan Sudarso.

Accommodation

Most hotels offer at least travel booking and basic tourist information services; bigger ones have their own restaurants, bars and tour companies.

Andhika, Jl Agus Salim 37 (☎0541/42358, fax 43507). Sometimes rowdy Muslim establishment, but clean and generally sound. ⑤.

Bumi Senyiur, Jl Diponegoro 17–19 (☎0541/41443, fax 38014). Opulent venue for international tour groups. Standard rooms ⑧, suite ⑨.

Hayani, Jl Pirus 31 (☎0541/42653). Cool, tidy and quiet; all rooms have a mandi. ⑤–⑥.

Hidayah I, Jl Mas Temenggung (☎0541/31408, fax 37761). Nice central location, with decent rooms but snotty staff. Fan ⑤, air-con ⑥.

Hidayah II, Jl Khalid 25 (☎0541/31166). Cheaper rooms have clanking ceiling fans, water stains down the walls and dirty red cloth over the windows; more expensive berths come with attached mandi. ④–⑤.

Kota Tepian, Jl Pahlawan 4 (☎0541/32510, fax 43515).Wood-panelled inside and out to vaguely resemble a Swiss chalet; the rooms are a little gloomy as a result, but comfortable enough. ⑦.

Melati, Jl Sulawesi 4 (☎0541/41043, fax 31512). Small but over-the-top marble exterior topped with a red neon "hotel" sign; modern and comfortable inside. Fan ⑥, air-con ⑦.

Mesra, Jl Pahlawan 1 (☎0541/32772, fax 41017). The most prestigious accommodation in Kalimantan, with acres of parkland, its own radio transmitter, medical facilities, golf course and tennis court. Not bad value, considering. Economy rooms ⑨, cottages ⑨.

Pirus, Jl Pirus 30 (☎0541/41873, fax 35890). Banjarmasin's best-value accommodation, ranging from basic rooms with fans and shared mandi to self-contained, air-con comforts. ④–⑤.

The City

Full of bustle, slightly ramshackle and lined with open sewers and low-roofed shops, Samarinda's streets exude the atmosphere of a typical tropical port. Despite the city's origins, most residents are of Banjar descent, mixing with an ever-changing transient population: upcountry workers and transmigrant villagers here to party or shop, sailors and merchants from Sulawesi and Java and students from all over eastern Kalimantan.

For an insight into what Samarinda once looked like, head north to **Pasar Sigiri** and Jalan Pernia Gaan, where the canal behind the market remains crowded with rickety wooden housing in every shade of brown, boats pulled up on the muddy banks, washing hung out to dry and children playing in the water. Further south, the green dome and untiled concrete spires of Samarinda's own **Grand Mosque** dominates the riverfront view along Jalan Gajah Mada, though nearby **markets** are far busier. **Pasar Pagi** is the standard Indonesian maze of overflowing stalls and tight spaces, with a choice range of just about everything you could ever need for daily living; shops nearby are strangely divided between gold stores and chandlers with rudders, bells and *ketingting* props hung up outside. Just up the road on Jalan Khalid, **Mesra Plaza** shopping centre is not as attractive as Balikpapan's, but it's still somewhere to see and be seen. East between Jalan Gajah Mada and Jalan Panglima Batur, **Citra Niaga** is a purpose-built bazaar, whose layout of cheap clothing and souvenir stalls and shops around a central open-air plaza won an architectural award; the plaza sometimes hosts evening song-and-dance sessions, featuring modern pop as well as traditional Banjar and Bugis pieces.

Catching a ferry (Rp500) from the dock behind Pasar Pagi carries you across the Mahakam to **Seberang** district, a string of small country villages grown together and totally different in feel to downtown Samarinda. Landing opposite the mosque at the main jetty, walk up to Terminal Banjarmasin and then turn east down Jalan Bendahara, where wooden houses are built on poles over the water. A short way along you pass a small grove of carved wooden posts marking a cemetery, then look for a small sign on the right advertising the presence of the **Sarung Samarinda Corporation** about 500m further on, which produces silk sarongs hand-woven in Bugis "tartan" styles. Further east again, the road runs past what appears to be a dilapidated Dayak longhouse, before fizzling out 1km later in a Muslim kampung.

Eating and entertainment

The bigger **hotels** all have Indonesian and Western restaurants; *Bumi Senyiur* also sports a café with impeccable pastries, while the *Mesra*'s 24hr coffee bar sells sandwiches, burgers and Western breakfasts. Samarinda's **nightlife** runs to disco-bar pickup joints, the least sleazy being the *Blue Pacific* in the Kaltim Building at Citra Niaga. You might also catch some after-dark revelry outdoors at the Citra Niaga Plaza, and the Makila information centre on Jalan Pirus puts on regular evening performances of Kenyah Dayak dancing – drop by during the day and ask what's on. The multi-screen **cinema** across from the *Hotel Mesra* on Jalan Bhayangkara shows the usual Western and Hong Kong action movies.

Restaurants

There are cheap **warung** on Jalan Sulawesi, Jalan Jamrud north of Pasar Pagi and Jalan Khalid, opposite Mesra Plaza, with another row on Jalan Awang Long. There's also a small, sanitized café on Jalan Mutiara selling a limited range of juices, rice and soto, and rooftop warung at the Mesra Plaza offering chicken soup and gado-gado with views out over Samarinda's rusting iron rooftops to the Mahakam.

CFC, Jl Sulawesi. Bakery, coffee shop and franchized fried chicken joint in one, with nice ice creams and sticky doughnuts.

Depot Handayani, Jl Abul Hasan, opposite Jl Diponegoro. An evening sate stall sets up out front, but sit down and treat yourself to something off their main menu: grilled river prawns, *lontong*, vegetables in peanut sauce and yellow rice.

Istana Iguana, Jl Awang Long 22. This Chinese-run place with nice open-plan bamboo decor specializes in seafood. Some dishes are a bit bland, but *cha udang kacang ment* is the highlight, if available: prawns cooked with chillies, peanuts and mint.

Lezat Baru, Jl Mulawarman 56. The best Chinese food in town with a long list of favourites, but lacks atmosphere unless you go in a group, and portions can be on the small side.

Sago Jaya, Jl Panglima Batur. Noisy and popular Padang restaurant; crowded out after dark.

Sari Bundo, Jl Khalid, near Mesra Plaza. Good-tasting, inexpensive Padang fare, but their chicken is as tough as a boot.

Listings

Airline offices Bouraq, Jl Mulawarman 24 (☎0541/41105); DAS, Jl Gatot Subroto 92 (☎0541/35250); MAF, Jl Rahuia Rahaya, northwest of the airport off Jl Let Jend Parman (☎0541/43628); Merpati, Jl Sudirman 23.

Exchange The BCA on Jl Sudirman has fair rates, with counter no. 2 for foreign exchange. ATMs are on the corner of Jl Sulawesi and Jl Panglima Batur.

Guides You'll need to find a guide in Samarinda if your Indonesian is poor and you're heading further upstream than Long Bagun on the Mahakam, or into the Apo Kayan. Choosing an experienced, bilingual guide is vital if you are going to have one at all, and the best are accredited by the Dinas Pariwisata – test them by discussing your intended route in detail before committing yourself. Some work through hotel tour companies, such as that at the *Mesra*, but most are freelancers, and you'll save money by tracking them down yourself. The Dinas Pariwisata or *Hotel Pirus* are good places to find one; seek out Andi Subagio at the *Pirus*, or the experienced and knowledgeable Sarkani Gambi – ask at the *Mesra* for his whereabouts. Expect to pay Rp35,000 a day plus food and lodgings, or Rp50,000 a day all-inclusive.

Information and maps Dinas Pariwisata (Provincial Tourist Office) is at Jl Harmonika 1, off Jl Suprato (☎0541/41669, fax 37696). On a good day they are thoroughly informed about costs, transport and accommodation throughout the province – ask for Pak Rosihan. Alternatively, Makila, Jl Pirus 168 (☎0541/75121), is an independent venture with Dayak contacts. For basic city and more detailed provincial maps, try the bookshops at the corner of Jl Pangalima Batur and Jl Sulawesi.

Pharmacies Supermarkets at the Mesra Plaza and Apotik Tanjung Batu just north of Ankassa Travel on Jl Abul Hasan, stock various brand-name remedies; Rumah Sakit Bhakti Nugraha on Jl Basuki Rachmat (☎0541/41363) comes recommended for anything more serious.

Police Jl Bhayangkara, about 200m south of the cinema (☎0541/41340 or 41516).

Post office Corner of Jl Gajah Mada and Jl Awang Long.

Souvenirs The souvenir shop near the BCA on Jl Sudirman sells silk sarongs made across the river at the Samarinda Sarung Corporation. For Dayak carvings, beads, blowpipes and baby carriers, try the row of run-down shops 1.5km out from the centre along Jl Martadinata. Most of the stuff here is made for the tourist trade, and sometimes not even by Dayak; arrive unexpectedly and you may catch staff assembling beadwork themselves. Bahati Jaya, at Jl Martadinata 16, is better than most, with a range of tribal artefacts and Chinese ceramics.

Telephone and fax 24hr wartel on Jl Awang Long, across from the *Istana Iguana* restaurant, with a smaller office in the Citra Niaga plaza (8pm–midnight).

Travel agents and tours Borneo Kersik Lluwai Tour & Travel, Jl Hasan 3 (☎0541/41486, fax 36728) are helpful, and can arrange most airline (including Royal Brunei, but not MAF) and Pelni tickets, private Mahakam cruises, and trips to Pulau Derawan. Also good are Angkassa Travel, Jl Abul Hasan (☎0541/42098), though they don't deal with MAF or DAS.

Sungai Mahakam

Borneo's second longest river, the **Mahakam**, winds southeast for over 900km from its source far inside the central ranges on the border between Kaltim, Kalbar and Malaysia, before emptying its muddy waters into the Makassar Straits through a complex, multi-channelled delta. Cruising upstream from Samarinda, the river gradually evolves through its distinct Lower, Middle and Upper reaches, cutting through a tableau which describes Kalimantan's entire history. In its first half, the **Lower Mahakam** loops over a broad region of marshes, where forests have long since ceded to disjointed woods and farmland, and towns along the bank stand in memory of defunct kingdoms. Beyond the marshes, the transitional **Middle Mahakam** is under increasing pressure from mining and logging operations, but still with some wild corners echoing to the cries of the hornbill. Continuing west, mountains begin to rise up, and entry into the **Upper Mahakam** is through a series of formidable **rapids**, a barrier which has preserved much of the region's forests and, to some extent, ethnic traditions intact.

Against this constantly mutating background, it's the Mahakam's **people** which make the journey upstream so worthwhile. Pushed to its fringes by more recent settlers – almost all settlements downstream from Long Iram are Muslim – the Mahakam nonetheless remains a stronghold for **Bahau**, **Benuaq** and **Kayan** Dayak, alongside **Kenyah**, more recently arrived from their Apo Kayan homelands. It's best not to have too romantic a notion of what you'll see, but there are endless chances to get below the surface of Dayak culture here, not least during festivals, or by staying in *lamin*, communal **longhouses**. Closest to Samarinda, the Lower Mahakam is the most touristy area, and there's an established three-day circuit taking in the historic town of **Tenggarong** and Benuaq Dayak settlements at **Tanjung Issuy** and adjacent **Mancong**. With a week to spare, scanty forest and less cosmetic communities inland from the Middle Mahakam townships of **Melak** and **Long Iram** are within range; ten days is enough to include a host of Kenyah and Benuaq villages between Long Iram and **Long Bagun**, where the Upper Mahakam begins. Getting beyond Long Bagun can be difficult, if you even make it at all: it takes at least two days to run the rapids as far as the Upper Mahakam at **Long Lunuk** – though you could cheat and **fly** directly here from Samarinda – and another day or more to reach the Kayan village of **Long Apari**, the last settlement on the river, some 90km short of the Mahakam's source. Long Apari marks the start of an **overland trek** west into Kalbar and the headwaters of the Kapuas, but even if you don't get this far there are plenty of other hiking trails from the river's Lower and Middle sections out of the Mahakam basin and into adjacent regions, not to mention over a dozen major **tributaries** to investigate.

Practicalities

Bring as little as possible with you. A change of clothes, wet-weather gear, and essentials such as a torch and first-aid kit are all you should need for the Lower and Middle Mahakam, as there's accommodation, places to eat and well-supplied stores at towns along the way. Self-sufficiency is required in the Upper Mahakam and other remoter areas, especially with food (even if you end up giving it away as gifts to your hosts) though you'll generally find room and board with locals. Don't bother with a tent or cooking gear unless you're planning to trek out of the region, but decent footwear is vital for even short walks; a sleeping bag also comes in handy for the cool heights of the Upper Mahakam. There are **no banks** on the Mahakam capable of changing money. Assuming that you have a rudimentary grasp of Indonesian, **guides** are not essential for the Lower and Middle reaches, but they certainly are if you're going beyond Long Bagun and can't speak the language, or if you're planning serious hiking

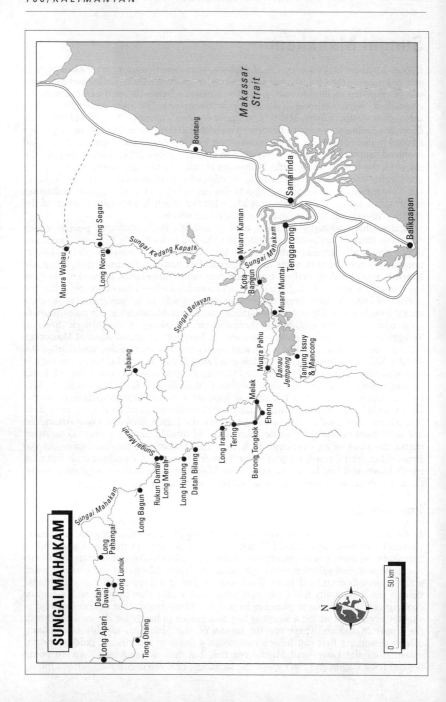

SUNGAI MAHAKAM

at any stage. Samarinda is a good place to hire a guide, though there are a few opportunities to pick one up along the way.

Note that, while overall the Mahakam flows southeast, the extreme twisting and
looping of its course means that you'll often find that boats travel in all sorts of impossible directions. **Place names** can also be confusing, with the common prefixes *Muara*
and *Long* both indicating a river junction. December through to March is the wettest
period of the year, with fabulous electrical storms against heavy skies, while July
through to October is the driest.

Mahakam transport

Public ferries are the cheapest way to tackle the Lower and Middle reaches of the
Mahakam, their crowded decks forcing you into contact with fellow travellers. Broad,
flat-bottomed and about 20m long, they are roofed over but open at their sides; passengers sit on the floor, though night services provide a bedroll (and sometimes even
TV) on an upper, enclosed, level. Toilets are a simple bucket-and-hole affair at the back;
some ferries also serve hot drinks and basic snacks, though hawkers and dockside
warung at stops along the way are the main source of food.

Ferries leave Samarinda's Terminal Sungai Kunjang every morning for towns as far
upstream as Long Iram and, when the water is high enough, Long Bagun; all services
pause for half an hour or so at Tenggarong, making this a good alternative starting
point. As all ferries depart at roughly the same time, if you get out at any stage you'll
have to stop over for 24 hours until the next batch arrive. When you board, take your
shoes off and put them in the overhead rack, squeeze yourself into a space on the deck
(away from the exhaust, if you have any choice), and wait for somebody to collect your
fare. If you plan to disembark before the boat's ultimate destination, make sure that the
pilot, not the ticket collector, knows where you want to get off. To catch a ferry from
smaller settlements you stand on the jetty – or whatever is available – and hail passing
traffic; locals know roughly at what time the regular services troll by, though the further you get from Samarinda, the less accurate any schedules are.

A more luxurious option for seeing the Mahakam are **private houseboats**, which
can be rented for about Rp150,000 a day through agencies in Samarinda and
Balikpapan, and come complete with guides, cooks and private cabins.

For village-hopping and detours off the Mahakam, you'll need assistance from smaller **ces** or **ketingting**, ubiquitous narrow-hulled speedboats capable of seating about
four people. They're rented out by the day and, as the price of fuel increases as you
head away from the coast, so does the cost of rental. Check the condition of your *ces*
before hiring it, and never travel in one after dark, as logging debris – including whole
rafts of felled timber – make deadly obstacles. Rougher stretches of the Mahakam are
covered by ten-seater **longboats** powered by up to three outboard engines.

Away from the water, **buses** link Samarinda to Tenggarong and Kota Bangun, and
are a useful short cut for heading upstream – or if you run out of patience with the

---

FERRY FARES AND JOURNEY TIMES FROM SAMARINDA

The following **schedule** from Samarinda is a guide only. Fares vary depending on ferries'
individual facilities, and journey times are affected by the size of the motor, the number of
stops along the way, and how much rain there has been – with the river in full spate, it can
take five days to reach Long Bagun. Conversely, coming back downstream with the current can shorten the trip back to Samarinda from Long Bagun to just 24hr.

Tenggarong 3hr; Rp1000	**Melak** 24hr; Rp8000
Kota Bangun 10hr; Rp3500	**Long Iram** 30hr; Rp10,000
Muara Muntai 14hr; Rp5000	**Long Bagun** 40hr; Rp15,000

ferries on your way back to civilization. To head straight into the heart of Dayak territory, however, you can **fly** directly from **Samarinda to Datah Dawai** on the Upper Mahakam: though bad weather often causes delays, this is actually cheaper than taking a ferry to Long Bagun and then battling through the rapids in a longboat. DAS in Samarinda charge just Rp75,000 return, a subsidized fare which needs to be booked a month in advance – though paying double will find you a seat on the next flight.

Tenggarong

As the ferry leaves Samarinda early in the morning you settle into your deck space surrounded by upriver villagers returning home; women who've travelled down to the city to give birth improvise cradles from sarongs and sling their infants from the ceiling out of the crush, rocking them gently to send them to sleep. The river here is broad, slow and smooth, sawmills and villages pepper the banks, and *ces* zip past at twice ferry speed, their passengers holding umbrellas against the spray and sun. Groves of coconut and spindly kapok trees punctuate the regular sprinkle of villages and sudden cleared spaces filled by shipyards or the hulking machinery of timber and coal operations. Rooflines rise to satellite dishes and mosque domes, low wooden stilt buildings backing onto the water, each with a flight of stairs – or notched palm-trunk – descending to a private outhouse at river level, where people spend the day endlessly washing themselves, their teeth and their clothes.

TENGGARONG is 45km and three hours upstream – or just an hour by road – from Samarinda. This small country town was, until 1959, the seat of the **Kutai Sultanate**, whose territory encompassed the entire Mahakam basin and adjacent coastline. Originally known as **Kartanegara**, the sultanate was founded downstream in the fifteenth century, when Muslim raiders annexed the older Hindu **Mulawarman Kingdom**; Tenggarong itself was established three hundred years later, after Bugis pirates forced the sultan to shift his capital further inland. The former palace and contents are on display just up from the docks at **Museum Negeri Mulawarman** (Tues–Thurs, Sat & Sun 8am–4pm, Fri 8–11am & 1.30–4pm; Rp300) on Jalan Diponegoro. The original wooden structure burnt down in 1935 and was replaced by this angular Dutch-designed building. The front door is guarded by a statue of the strange **Lambu Suana**, a griffin with a scaly body and elephant's head; inside, the collection kicks off with Art Deco tile portraits of sultans in the entrance hall, and a bedroom assembly – including an over-the-top bridal bed trimmed in silver, red velvet and brass – off to the right. Further on, the Mahakam's Hindu period is illustrated by statuary from the basin's northern fringes, and replicas of fourth-century conical stone *yupa* found upstream near Muara Kaman, whose cursive inscriptions are Indonesia's oldest written records. Dayak pieces include explanations of Benuaq weaving, and some examples of Kenyah beadwork and grotesque *hudoq* masks used by the Bahau. Outside, all nineteen of Kutai's sultans are buried in the adjacent **cemetery**, while the forecourt often hosts **Dayak dancing** on Sundays.

Practicalities

History aside, Tenggarong is simply a far more relaxed – and cheaper – place to stay than Samarinda. The **docks** are on the downstream end of town on Jalan Sudirman, which runs 250m north along the river, over a small canal, and on as Jalan Diponegoro past **Seni Tepian Pandan marketplace** and the museum. **Minibuses** to Samarinda orbit the roundabout near the docks, while Tenggarong's **tourist information centre** is at the back of the marketplace, and can advise on all aspects of the Mahakam. Try and catch the **Erau Festival** in late September, when Dayak groups from all over the province descend for a week-long performance at the showgrounds outside of town, a fantastic display of traditional costumes, dances and ceremonies.

Accommodation includes the clean and welcoming *Penginapan Anda II*, near the canal at Jalan Sudirman 63 (☎0541/61409; ④), offering simple rooms with shared mandi and self-contained, air-con units, while additional comforts such as TV and hot water are available at *Timbau Indah*, 250m south of the docks towards Samarinda at Jalan Muksin 15 (☎0541/61367; ⑤). Overlooking the river about 50m beyond the museum, *Rumah Makan Tepian Pandan* is a great place to tuck into Chinese and Indonesian **food**; there are also several good Banjar warung between the docks and canal on Jalan Sudirman.

Muara Kaman, Kota Bangun and detours

About four hours from Tenggarong, the handful of dirt lanes which comprise the township of **MUARA KAMAN** were once the focus of the powerful Hindu **Mulawarman Kingdom**, though, aside from the name and a few enigmatic stone relics off in the scrub 2km inland, almost nothing is known about the Mulawarman. The only reason to stop here – in which case, seek **accommodation** at the *Penginapan Martapura* (③) – would be to detour north to Dayak communities along **Sungai Kedang Kepala** (Severed Head), where you'll find the recently settled Kenyah villages of **Long Noran** and **Long Segar**, where you can sleep in a *lamin* for Rp5000. Beyond here, the town of **Muara Wahau** has overland connections back to Samarinda, or further north up the coast. Seasonal ferries run from Muara Kaman to Muara Wahau for around Rp15,000; otherwise you'll have to rent a *ces* for about ten times this price.

Back on the Mahakam, the river narrows perceptibly as it continues to **KOTA BANGUN**, a large, well-supplied town. Four hours from Samarinda by **bus**, ferries dock on the north bank, where you'll find 500m of sealed road, and **meals** and **beds** either off to the left at *Penginapan Mukjizat* (③), or ten minutes' walk along to the right at the surprisingly comfortable *Sri Bangun Lodge* (⑤). Kota Bangun offers further detours off the Mahakam, this time 120km northwest along **Sungai Belayan** to **TABANG**; *ces* are the only way there, but Kota Bangun is big enough that you should eventually be able to find others to share costs. Tabang itself is another Kenyah community, and offers the possibility of trekking westwards through densely forested **Punan** territory to the upper **Sungai Merah**, which enters the Mahakam way upstream near Rukun Damai (see p.774). Nomadic hunters, the Punan are the least known of all Kalimantan's Dayak; they are wary of strangers, and if you plan to hike west from Tabang it's essential that you first find a Punan guide to smooth the way.

Muara Muntai and around

The Mahakam continues to narrow beyond Kota Bangun, and there's a definite thickening of the forest along the banks as the river enters the flat, marshy regions of the basin's lakelands. This is the first place that you're likely to see **hornbills**, big black birds with outsized curved beaks, honking, flapping and coasting across the treetops in the late afternoon light. Symbolic of the Dayak as a people, one species, the helmeted hornbill, has a solid beak once much in demand in China as ivory for carvings.

Around four hours from Kota Bangun and fourteen from Samarinda, **MUARA MUNTAI** sits due north of **Danau Jempang**, the town raised over the surrounding swamps on piles, with the interconnected wooden **boardwalks** which serve as streets rattling as motorbikes tear along them. Turn left from the dock and *Penginapan Nita Wardana* is about 50m along on the right, with *Sri Muntai Indah* just a bit further; both have tiny rooms with fans and essential mosquito nets (③). Incredibly hot and sticky during the day, not much happens in town until ferries start arriving after dark – even the couple of warung don't seem to want business – and there's nothing to distract from negotiating a visit to **Benuaq** settlements on the far side of the lake with *ces* operators at the dock (Rp20,000).

Danau Jempang, Tanjung Issuy and Mancong

Right out from Muara Muntai, watch for the slate-grey backs and tiny dorsal fin of **pesut**, freshwater dolphins; woods lining the channels leading from the river to the lake harbour proboscis monkeys (for more on which, see p.740). Once through these, Jempang's hundred square kilometres of reed beds, waterfowl and fishermen open up, and it takes about an hour to reach **TANJUNG ISSUY**, a small township of gravel lanes, timber houses and fruit trees built on a slope overlooking the water. Turn right off the jetty, past a couple of lumber yards, stores and workshops, and follow the street around to *Losmen Wisata*, a restored Dayak **lamin** maintained as tourist accommodation (④). It's not that "authentic", but the place is surrounded by carved wooden *patong* posts, and tour groups get Benuaq **dances** performed for them, excellent photo opportunities that draw crowds of local spectators. Out the back is a six-tier **mausoleum** where Tanjung Isuuy's founder was laid to rest in 1984, decorated with carvings of dragons, hornbills and scenes from the **kwangkei reburial ceremonies**. The losmen has coffee and tea, with evening servings of chicken curry at *Rumah Makan Jempang Sejahtera* just down the street. There's also an unrestored *lamin* with bigger *patong* to check out near Tanjung Issuy's mosque, or spend the day a couple of hours' walk or *ces* ride south through farmland at **MANCONG**, a pretty Benuaq village built on boardwalks like Muara Muntai, whose own two-storey *lamin* can house 200 people. Heading on **up the Mahakam** from Tanjung Issuy, you could either return to Muara Muntai, or hire a *ces* to take you across the forested northwest corner of Danau Jempang and back to the Mahakam west at **Muara Pahu** (Rp30,000).

The Middle Mahakam: Melak and around

The Mahakam's middle reaches are defined by a steady raising of the landscape as the river begins to edge into the first outrunners of central Borneo's granite and limestone plateaus. Initially, this isn't very obvious, though a few hills rise around **MELAK**, a small Muslim town about ten hours beyond Muara Muntai, servicing **gold mines** in the vicinity. A convenient jumping-off point for exploring the surrounding forest and villages, Melak comprises two surfaced roads, one running along the riverbank, and the other heading inland from the docks. A knot of stores and services surround their intersection, with *Etam Kutai* offering decent **meals** and Dayak souvenirs, and the clean *Penginapan Bahagiai* and *Rahamat Abadi* providing simple **accommodation** (③). Villages and townships further inland from Melak also have accommodation, with a network of dirt roads running through the region and on to the upstream Mahakam port of **Tering** (see opposite).

Transport out to local sights includes ojeks from the docks, or minibuses, which wait for passengers at the **market square** about 100m downstream. An ojek charter costs upwards of Rp15,000, depending on how far you want to go; minibuses run to particular destinations for Rp2000 or so if they fill up, or can be rented from around Rp40,000.

Inland to Kersik Luway Forest Reserve, Barong Tongkok and Eheng

It's a bumpy motorbike ride on dirt roads 19km southwest of Melak to hot, sandy heathland at **Kersik Luway Forest Reserve**, where shady "islands" of dense vegetation conceal spongy mosses, trailing vines of carnivorous **pitcher plants**, and over sixty species of **orchid**. Most famous is the lightly scented *anggrek hitam* or **black orchid**, which unfurls a pale-green flower with a mottled black centre between January and April. Guides are on hand to show you around – Rp1000 repays their help.

Eighteen kilometres west from Melak, Benuaq **villages** surround the transmigrant settlement of **BARONG TONGKOK**, making it a good place to settle for a while. The 250-metre-long main road comes in from Melak, passes Barong Tongkok's **market** and **minibus compound**, and forks as it runs uphill and out of town. A smaller road before the market leads off alongside a **playing field**, where you'll find basic **beds** at the *Losmen Anggrek Hitam* (③); the Padang warung at the bus compound provides the only **food**. A **Catholic church** on the far side of the playing field identifies a Dayak quarter, with two brightly painted and wonderfully lively *patong* of former Dutch priests at the church gates. Following the road past the playing field brings you to the tiny Benuaq village of **Lei**, where reburials see days of dancing and gambling, and the carving of a dragon *patong* and wooden mausoleum for a late village head. **Moving on**, ojek and minibuses can run you back to Melak, 35km north to Tering and the Mahakam, or out to other Benuaq villages.

The best of these lie southwest of Barong Tongkok. A surprising **museum** (closed Fri) sits 7km down the road at **MENCIMAI**, a tiny hut by the roadside concealing some fine Benuaq artefacts and a detailed rundown of agricultural practices, while a further 8km brings you to **ENKUNI**'s tidy *lamin*. Another 10km due west of Enkuni, **EHENG** has a **cemetery** with more mausoleums, and also one of the most authentic *lamin* in the region, a 75-metre-long assembly of hardwood, rattan and bamboo raised 3m off the ground and reached by a traditional ladder made from a notched pole. Inside, an open gallery runs the length of the building, where people sit during the day; the living quarters for each of the *lamin*'s thirteen families are partitioned off behind a wall. Residents have become used to visitors breezing quickly in and out of Eheng, and offer a flurry of tourist trinkets; to get more out of the place, ask the kepala desa if you could stay overnight (offer about Rp5000).

Tering

TERING, five hours upstream from Melak by ferry or just ninety minutes by road, is doing very well supplying the nearby **Kelian Equator Mining** – better known as P.T. KEM (pronounced "Petakem") – gold mine. The town is bisected by the Mahakam, with river ferries and roads winding up on the south bank at **Tering Sebarang**, where you'll find muddy streets, a Muslim population, and a hugely busy Saturday market. A *ces* from the dock here can whisk you straight across the river to **Tering Lama** (Rp1000), a quieter **Bahau Dayak** village where a Catholic mission has been based since the 1920s. Considered a downriver offshoot of the Kayan, the Bahau are best known for their **rice-planting festivals**, in which performers dressed in palm fronds and wearing huge-nosed **hudoq masks** dance to snare the goodwill of the agricultural goddess Hunai. Tering Lama's large meeting house patterned in green, red, black and white sits just above the landing stage, and there are dozens of human *patong* around the place – including a two-metre-high figure with mirror eyes, supporting a satellite dish. Tering Lama is the first place that you are likely to see older Dayak with **tattoos and stretched earlobes**, decorations seldom seen nowadays. Foreigners are often grabbed and taken to see a collection of antique pieces stored in a private house here: *hudoq* masks, posts which once supported Tering's defunct *lamin*, and ceremonial costumes. A *ces* can run you upstream **to Long Iram** in about an hour (Rp25,000), or you can **walk** there through overgrown *ladang* and open woodland in an easy three hours: turn left from above Tering Lama's landing stage and walk 50m upstream through the village, then follow the footpath and power lines heading north into the countryside.

Long Iram

Marking the furthest point on the Mahakam that passenger ferries can reach year-round, **LONG IRAM** has been a government post since colonial times, and retains a small military barracks and government offices. A sleepy, Muslim place on the surface, the town borders Benuaq and Bahau lands; make local connections here and you can find yourself witnessing some unusual events (see the box overleaf). If you've got this

The girl was sick – did we want to see a *basir*, a Dayak shaman, cure her? Having immediately said yes hours before, we now felt awkward standing outside a stranger's home after dark on the edge of Long Iram, the master of the house listening to our introductions before politely inviting us in. We sat down in a front room while the girl's brothers came and checked us out, proffering cigarettes and glaring at these tourists invading a family affair – at least, that's how we felt, though perhaps everyone was just nervous. Something was out of place; surely this was a Muslim family, with lines from the Koran written in gold above the door? Yes, but the girl was ill because someone unknown, probably motivated by jealousy, had paid a *basir* to evoke the spirit causing her sickness. Only another *basir* could send this spirit back to plague whoever had originally sponsored the curse.

Ushered into the plain room where the ceremony would take place, we sat cross-legged on the bare wooden floor in what little space wasn't taken up by other spectators, a bed and the *basir*'s paraphernalia. In one corner of the room, a dozen plates of cooked rice, meat and vegetables were neatly arranged on banana leaves in a split bamboo tray, the whole assembly scattered with flowers and decorations made from shaved wood. A heavy black drape the size of a curtain hung down all the way from the ceiling to just above the floor, while a man in military fatigues tied a long piece of rattan cable diagonally across the room, so that it stretched about a metre off the ground like a tightrope. Through a doorway into the kitchen, the parents and brothers could be seen talking with two men, one short, muscular and dark, the other tall, wiry and moustached. The *basir* and his assistant, said someone, another anomaly as it was obvious that neither were local Bahau or Benuaq Dayak, who were pale-skinned. No, they were Muslim Banjarese from 500km south in Kalsel, but were descended from the Bukit Dayak of that province. It didn't matter. Their principles were the same.

Wailing suddenly came from the kitchen, then the father came in carrying the girl in his arms. Nobody had been too specific about her illness, and, having expected to see someone perhaps be pathetically sick with fever, her appearance was shocking: she was in her mid-teens, dressed in a shirt and trousers and, as it became immediately clear, was completely deranged. Placed on the bed she squatted on her haunches, hands and arms horribly twisted up at her sides, and crowed harshly at everyone. A whisper from next to me: the spirits which cause this type of illness always adopt the form of an animal – this

far you'll also want to spend a few days arranging transport and guides to escort you around Dayak villages upstream.

Long Iram's main street is a sealed road running for several kilometres along the north bank of the Mahakam, though the stores which make up the tiny town centre surround the ferry dock. The track from Tering Lama joins the main street about 500m upstream from the docks near long Iram's **police station**; arriving by river, climb the tall steps to the road and turn right (downstream), where you'll find all **accommodation** within a two-minute walk. Nearest is spartan *Losmen Susanti* (③), while further along you'll find spacious rooms at *Losmen Wahtu* (④). Opposite the *Susanti*, Long Iram's sole **restaurant**, *Java Timur*, offers good evening meals, while stalls around the docks provide tea and cakes during the day. If you're after a **guide** for the area, ask for Rudi Yanto; he's Muslim, but genuinely interested in the Dayak, and can wrangle fair *ces* rates. With time to kill, some big trees, hornbills and giant red squirrels lurk in a patch of woodland 1km or so downstream from Long Iram's docks, while a couple of **lakes** about 3km down the Tering track are home to monkeys and kingfishers.

Upriver to Long Bagun

Beyond Long Iram the Mahakam squeezes between forested hills and cliffs. In drier months (July–Nov) the water is too shallow for ferries, while heavy rains see the river was a chicken. The *basir* would try to dislodge the spirit from the girl, then take it on himself and overpower it, frightening it away. A sudden uproar came from the bed, as the girl started to bash her head against the wall. Her brothers leapt up with pillows, trying to restrain her, but she screamed and butted them off, then calmed abruptly as the *basir* entered the room holding a freshly killed fowl by the feet. Its throat had been cut, and, his back to the bed, he sprinkled blood over the plates, turned around, and invited her over to inspect the food. Still squatting and holding her hands like folded wings, she jumped down and sniffed around the plates, but soon lost interest and returned to the bed, where she rocked back and forth, crooning quietly. The *basir* seemed satisfied; this was clearly the way things should proceed. Picking up a glass jar from the edge of the room, he removed a twist of paper from it, which he placed in a crucible and lit before sitting on the floor under the black drape and drawing the cloth about him.

Nothing happened for a while, then the assistant unwound the cloth to reveal the *basir* sitting in a trance; face screwed up, he rose slowly to his feet and started making senseless, chicken-like noises to the girl. She responded, and their exchange went on until the girl again lost interest, though the *basir* continued long after she stopped responding and seemed completely oblivious to his surroundings. A lull followed, while both the *basir* and his assistant went into a huddle under the cloth, then things suddenly got violent. The girl started screaming and bashing her head again, and the *basir* rocketed up, grabbed the drape, and began swinging wildly around on it, crashing into the spectators. As we scattered to the sides of the room the girl became more and more hysterical, lashing out at everyone; while the *basir* still oscillated above, his assistant dragged her roughly off the bed, held her down and sucked grotesquely at her midriff. Suddenly he sat up and spat out a stone – the spirit's physical form, dislodged from her belly – and with a shriek she stopped thrashing and lay still on the floor. The assistant, eyes closed, crawled over to the rattan cable and, in a seemingly impossible balancing act, stretched out along its length and stayed there for the next hour. Things went quiet; now unconscious, the girl was laid out on the bed, while the *basir* had returned to earth and was sitting on the floor, muttering softly, gradually bringing himself back to the present. We sat and watched for a long time while both men recovered, then the girl sat up, got off the bed and walked out of the room – the first time she had stood upright in six weeks.

David Leffman

swell rapidly and race past town, making Long Bagun anything between ten hours and two days away, depending on the current. Even if passenger services are running, it's better to cover this stretch by *ces* (Rp150,000–200,000), stopping off to explore **villages** along the banks; it's polite to introduce yourself to the kepala desa, who can sort out accommodation or simply assist your investigations. Times below refer to *ces* travel, not ferry.

Sungai Kelian and Datah Bilang

An hour upstream from Long Iram, detouring along **Sungai Kelian** takes you past a half-dozen shantytowns where private enterprises are busy unearthing alluvial deposits for **gold** flakes, excavating huge muddy quarries. Pumps suck up the watery slush, which is then cascaded down a stepped trough lined with **carpet**; being heavier than anything else, grains of gold settle into the pile and are trapped, while most mud washes out – independent panners sit downstream from the quarries' outflows, picking up missed bits and pieces. Weekly treatment of the carpets' trapped sludge with mercury and cyanide removes the gold, but has also killed off all of the Kelian's fish life.

Back on the Mahakam, lumber camps have yet to strip all of the forest, and more extreme slopes above the river are covered in huge trees, ferns and vines, rock ledges and small waterfalls breaking through the canopy. Another hour brings you to flatter country around **DATAH BILANG**, a **Kenyah** village settled between 1972 and 1975 by migrants from a (then) economically isolated Apo Kayan. Like all Dayak villages along this stretch, Datah Bilang is extremely tidy and, though people here are Catholic and live in ordinary houses instead of *lamin*, traditional ways are still followed. The Kenyah have a stratified society, with aristocrats still held in considerable respect by lower classes. Once considered amongst the fiercest of head-hunters, today they are best known for their **artistry**, evident in their architecture, weaving, carving and decorative beadwork. Government attention has made Datah Bilang a good place to catch official ceremonies: dressed in full war regalia, men weave a strange, slow-motion **sword dance** performed in a half-crouch, encircled by a gently swaying ring of women holding fans of hornbill feathers. The two large wooden **meeting halls** here are supported by posts carved into faces and spirit figures; check out the **murals** inside, one of which details the story of the migration from the Apo Kayan, and the rafters, where festival masks and carvings are stashed. There are also a couple of tall *patong* of dragons and warriors in the village, one outside the upstream meeting hall, the other on the edge of the playing fields – a monument to Suharto's visit here during the 1970s. Stretched miniature roofs across the river mark a **cemetery** (Dayak spirits are unable to cross water). Datah Bilang's sole **losmen** is the *Cahaya Sidenreng* (③), whose manager has a collection of Dayak curios and connections with a tattoo artist, and there are a couple of **warung** at the docks whose basic repertoires occasionally stretch to deer curry.

Long Hubung, Long Merah and Rukun Damai

LONG HUBUNG is the next likely stop, a Bahau village an hour beyond Datah Bilang with two suspension bridges and the extremely basic *Losmen Benitha*. Autumnal rice-planting **festivities** are performed here, *hudoq* masks and all, and the kepala desa can tell you if any other rituals are imminent. The same distance upstream again, you pass **Sungai Merah** on the north bank, just past which is **LONG MERAH**, whose meeting hall is a riot of wildly ornate **Bahau carving** – supporting posts inside and out are alive with animal and human figures, some implausibly sexual. Long Merah is one end of a cross-country hike up the Merah and over to **Tabang** (see p.769); April is a good time to look for a Punan guide here, as they come downstream to trade after the rains. Further on from Long Merah, **RUKUN DAMAI** is essentially a Kenyah settlement with two *lamin*, whose long-lobed, tattooed residents will proudly show you their ceremonial finery and dragon-jar dowries while children stare on. From here on the forest comes and goes, but below Long Bagun a spectacular hundred-metre-high **limestone cliff** rears up on the north bank, streaked in yellow, white and grey.

Long Bagun

A messy trading post 583km upstream from Samarinda, **LONG BAGUN**'s appeal stems from its position right on the edge of the Mahakam's wilds. Divided into **Long Bagun Ilir** downstream and **Long Bagun Ulu** upstream, Ulu is where you'll find **stores** offering a thin display of essential supplies, and a **mattress** on the floor at *Penginipan Artomorow* (③); the only warung is down at the docks. Across the Mahakam, a small wooden enclosure above the river at the Sumalindo Timber Company houses a surprising relic of the Mulawarman Kingdom in a **stone cow sculpture**, a metre-long carving of the Hindu god Nandi. Locals say that it was originally found a short way northwest at **Batu Majang**, and can predict floods by turning its head upstream.

If Long Bagun is as far as you're going, ferries or *ces* take only about five hours to ride the river back to Long Iram. Otherwise, you'll have to ask around for longboats heading on through the rapids **into the Upper Mahakam**; Rp40,000–50,000 is the usual price for a seat on the 140-kilometre, two- to four-day ride through to the next large settlement at Long Pahangai, though you'd have to pay ten times this to charter an entire longboat yourself. Days can be spent in Long Bagun waiting to set off, with April through to July the best time to travel. **Overland treks** from Long Bagun include a ten-day, moderately hard trail running southwest through thick forest and **Ot Danum** villages to **Puruk Cahu** on **Sungai Barito**, from where you can find ferries south to Banjarmasin in Kalsel Province. **Guides** can be arranged through Kosmos Trekking in Long Bagun Ulu; plan on Rp150,000–200,000 to Puruk Cahu.

The Upper Mahakam

It's an exciting and exhausting run through the rock-strewn rapids above Long Bagun, as, with the jungle closing in around you, twin-engined longboats capable of travelling 50km an hour on calm water are brought nearly to a standstill by the force of the river. Don't underestimate the **dangers** involved in the journey: this violent stretch claims twenty lives a year, and pilots often deposit passengers on the banks while they negotiate the worst sections, or may enlist your help in hauling the longboat through the foam. If your boat **capsizes** in rapids with you aboard, try to hang onto the hull until the current carries you down to a calmer stretch, then swim to shore. Once through, all of the Upper Mahakam's villages are Dayak, and on arrival you should announce yourself to the kepala desa and, if necessary, the police too – either of whom can be invaluable in helping to find transport and accommodation.

Long Pahangai to Long Apari and Kalbar province

Interspersed with calm stretches, the rapids continue all the way to **LONG PAHANGAI**, an administrative centre where the Norwegian ethnographer **Carl Lumholz** based himself for a time during World War I while studying the Upper Mahakam's tribes. Long Pahangai's population comprises various **Kayan** groups, who settled here after fleeing roving Kenyah, who had themselves been forced south by Sarawak's fierce Iban Dayak. There's a run-down *lamin* at Long Pahangai, and a Catholic mission who might be able to organize a bed if asked politely.

Half a day upstream, **LONG LUNUK** is ordinary in itself, but services the Upper Mahakam's **airstrip** nearby at **Datah Dawai**. Flying in from Samarinda, confirm your return flight at the airstrip and ask around to see if anyone is heading your way and might share longboat costs. Another half-day from Long Lunuk takes you past the Kayan village of **Long Bluu** to **Tiong Ohang**, where there are more *lamin* and a final day's ride on the river to **LONG APARI**, the Mahakam's last village. There's an excellent *lamin* here and a century-old, four-metre-high dragon *patong*, plus surrounding forests and hills to explore, and locals may act as guides for trips out of Kaltim Province. It's a two- to four-day trek west across a 1900-metre range into **Kalbar province** at **TANJUNG LONGKONG** on a tributary of the **Sungai Kapuas**, from where it's possible to continue downstream by foot and boat to Pontianak (p.725).

Interior Kaltim: the Apo Kayan

While the coastal fringes become ever more tamed, Kaltim's **interior** seems initially to be everything that Borneo's reputation promises. Though you'll find the red scars of logging roads, forests extend to the horizon as a dark-green haze, interrupted where the occasional bare grey ridge pokes skywards and convoluted brown rivers reflect the sun as they run towards the sea, while down below Dayak communities exist as they have done for centuries, hunting, farming and performing traditional rites. This is the last expanse of wilderness in Kalimantan, and if you've come looking for Borneo's traditional heart, you'll find it 300km northwest of Samarinda in the highlands of the **Apo Kayan**, so isolated from the rest of the province that it can take four months to reach here overland by following rivers and tracks from the coast.

Even ardent trekkers, however, find that it's better to **fly** into the Apo Kayan on **missionary aircraft**, and burn up energy after arrival. The two operators are **Dirgantara Air Service** (DAS) and **Missionary Air Fellowship** (MAF); while both run fairly regular schedules, travel on a specific day is by no means guaranteed as planes are small, and **cancellations** (most often due to bad weather) are frequent. Mission staff and locals – who pay subsidized fares – receive priority over visitors.

After arrival, there are various ways to **get around**. Trails link many villages; Dayak almost always build near rivers, so **canoes** and **ces** are another common mode of travel. Some people will show you around for free, but you should plan to pay about Rp20,000 a day for a **guide**, on top of transport costs. **Accommodation** is with officials or local families, for which you should also either pay or give about Rp5000 worth of goods. Without overloading yourself, bring everything you'll need for the trip along from the coast – supplies here are limited and very expensive. It's always **wet** in the Apo Kayan, and, with the highlands here rising to around 2000m, often cool at night.

The Apo Kayan

Based around the headwaters of Sungai Kayan, the **Apo Kayan** was originally inhabited by Kayan Dayak, who were mostly displaced south during the nineteenth century by Sarawak's aggressive Iban and neighbouring Kenyah groups. In the 1890s, the Dutch founded a **garrison** on the Apo Kayan at **Long Nawang**, in a move to counter what they saw as British expansionism from Sarawak; **missionaries** followed, engineering a peace treaty between the Apo Kayan's still-warring tribes in 1924. Stability lasted until the **Japanese** took Long Nawang eighteen years later; the garrison was later revived during the 1960s *Konfrontasi* with Malaysia and ensuing "communist" insurgency within Indonesia, when the army held tight rein over the whole area. By this time population pressures had caused a huge **migration** of Kenyah from the Apo Kayan to government-sponsored settlements in the Mahakam basin.

Despite all this, even a few days here offers a fascinating insight into a way of life which, on this scale at least, has all but vanished elsewhere in Kalimantan. **Flights** arrive in the Apo Kayan several times a week from Samarinda and Tarakan; the most used airstrip (served by DAS) is a half-day journey from Long Bawang at **Long Ampung**, though MAF fly on a regular basis to Long Nawang and a handful of other locations.

Long Ampung, Long Nawang and around

The ninety-minute flight from Samarinda leaves you unprepared for arrival at **LONG AMPUNG**, a fair-sized settlement on the banks of **Sungai Boh** whose couple of well-constructed **meeting houses** covered in elaborately curly roof decorations are typical of Kenyah designs – a couple of tigers and a hornbill (both guardian figures in Dayak lore) are among the less abstract motifs. A wide, shadeless track runs west along the river from here, making **LONG NAWANG** a hot five-hour walk away. Still the seat of the Apo Kayan's administration, Long Nawang is the Apo Kayan's biggest settlement and boasts a couple of stores, a school and police and army barracks; you should introduce yourself to the district *camat* here, who can help with guides and canoe rental. You'll need a boat to reach **LONG BETOAH**, a pretty village to settle down in for a few days, six hours or so to the northwest of Long Nawang, though rapids along the way make this a doubtful trip in drier weather. Much closer in, **NAWANG BARU** is just a short walk south of Long Nawang, with brightly decorated rice barns, a Dayak cemetery, and two *lamin* to check out.

The northeast

Kaltim's **northeast**, comprising the 500-kilometre coastal strip between Samarinda and Kalimantan's open border with Malaysian Sabah, is an area of fragmentary forests, islands, river deltas and mountains, administered by self-contained towns, which seem to have sprung up out of nothing. Daily **buses** follow a fine road for 145km north from Samarinda's Terminal Bontang past **Bontang's** refineries to **Muara Wahau**. Beyond here, the road becomes an unreliable, dry-weather-only track, and you'll probably have to **fly** or travel by **boat** to reach further destinations: there's **Berau**, springboard for underwater realms surrounding **Pulau Derawan**, and **Tanjung Selor** and **Tarakan**, last stops on the way out of the country into Malaysia.

Bontang to Berau

BONTANG is a sprawling township built around Pertamina's huge **liquid gas refinery**, two twisting hours by road from Samarinda. Along with neighbouring Sengata, Bontang used to be a staging post for trips east into **Kutai national park**, one of the easiest places in the world to see genuinely wild **orang-utans**. Unfortunately, the park was almost entirely destroyed during the appalling 1997–98 **forest fires** (see p.731), with 140 apes left homeless and likely to end their days as pets. It's possible, however, that patches of jungle survived the blaze, and it might be worth stopping at Bontang to check on access. Bontang's **bus station** is 3km south of the centre, a short bemo ride from the **Forestry Department**, Departmen Kerhutanan Kantor Taman Nasional Kutai, just off the main road on Jalan Mulawarman (Mon–Thurs 8am–3pm, Fri 8–11am & 1–3pm; ☎0548/21191; some English spoken). They'll tell you the latest state of affairs, and supply permits and guides. If you need to spend the night at Bontang, there's the clean *Losmen Rahayu* (③) in rural suburbs about a ten-minute walk further down Jalan Mulawarman, or catch a bemo to *Hotel Kartika*, Jalan Yani 37 (☎0548/21012; ④), though a disco makes this a noisy prospect. Heading on **from Bontang**, buses run back to Samarinda (2hr; Rp3700) and through the national park to Sengata (2hr; Rp5500) until mid-afternoon, and during drier months there are daily kijang from the bus station north to Muara Wahau and Berau (12–24hr; Rp40,000).

Over the Sambaliung mountains: Muara Wahau

The journey between Bontang and Berau is spectacular, circling the northeastern edge of the Mahakam river basin before entering a huge spread of rainforest where karst formations weathered into incredible, shark-toothed escarpments spring 1300m out of the canopy as the **Sambaliung mountains**. Thirty kilometres of sealed road north of Sengata, **Sepasu** marks where the route to Berau diverges west for 100km to **MUARA WAHAU**, from where you can catch ferries down past Dayak settlements to Muara Kaman on Sungai Mahakam (see p.769). Outside of Muara Wahau, Hindu sculptures have been found at the **Kongbeng Caves**, whose stalactites and stalagmites are under threat from cement companies mining the hills for limestone. From here the road follows Sungai Wahau northeast, then crosses between the pinnacles of the **Sankulirang Forest Reserve** to the Dayak villages of **Muara Lasan**, **Merasak** and **Tumbit**, and on up the Sungai Kelai valley to Berau.

Berau

Three hundred kilometres north of Samarinda, **BERAU** – alias **Tanjung Redeb** – occupies a prong of land where two minor flows converge to form **Sungai Berau**. Still

50km from the sea, Berau has long been a trading port, recently favoured as the site of a now declining wood-pulping industry, and you need to stop off here in order to catch marine traffic heading on up the coast to Pulau Derawan and Tarakan. The town was also once the seat of **two sultanates**, visited in the late 1880s by **Joseph Conrad**, then mate on the trading vessel SS *Vidar*, whose brief meeting with two "worn-out European" merchants named Willems and Almayer formed the basis for his novels *Almayer's Folly* and *An Outcast of the Islands*.

Berau's languid pace picks up after dark with open-air stalls and a party atmosphere along the Jalan Yani riverfront. For something to do, catch a *ces* across from the east end of Jalan Yani to the old **sultan's palaces**, now private buildings, which face each other and the town across the waters. To the north, there's a small display of period pieces at **Keraton Gunung Tabur**, rebuilt after Allied bombs destroyed the building during the World War II Japanese occupation, and a sacred cannon south at **Keraton Sambaliung**, which apparently protected this palace from a similar fate. With more time to spare, it's also possible to head upstream along the Segan to overnight at **TEPI-AN BUAH**, a Kenyah Dayak settlement founded during the 1960s; there are no long-houses or traditional buildings here, but coinciding with one of the occasional festivals would make the trip worthwhile. A **public ferry** to Tepian leaves several times during the week, and takes three hours (Rp10,000).

Practicalities

Berau's central core is a small grid of streets running back from the wharves and stores, fronted by 150-metre-long, riverbank Jalan Yani. Larger boats use the **port** at Jalan Yani's western end, where you'll also find the **Pelni office**; smaller vessels tie up further east along the waterfront. **Buses** from Bontang and Sengata terminate about 1km across town in the Jalan Guna market, while the **airport** is a ten-minute bemo or ojek ride to the south. Running back from the Samarinda docks off Jalan Yani's western end, Jalan Antasari is where you'll find Berau's **accommodation**: right behind the docks, *Losmen Sederhana* (☎0554/21353; ⑤) is fine, the *Kartika* is a dive, but cheap (④), and Berau's best rooms are found at the *Hotel Citra Indah* (☎0554/21171; ⑤). **Food** can be scarce during the day, but the *Citra Indah* has a restaurant and there are plenty of evening warung along Jalan Yani.

Heading on, Pelni's *Awu* runs monthly from the port **to Tarakan**, as part of a huge Sulawesi–Flores–Timor loop. Other boats to Tarakan or Samarinda leave several times a week from the Jalan Yani waterfront, where owners post departure times on trees alongside their vessels; fast craft to Tarakan charge Rp40,000 and take five hours, slower tubs cost Rp25,000 and take ten. **For Pulau Derawan**, catch a Tarakan boat to the halfway point of Tanjung Batu and proceed from there (see below), or charter a **speedboat** direct to the island for Rp200,000. If they're running, **buses to Tanjung Selor** or Bontang leave early from the Jalan Guna market; buy tickets at the stop (Rp40,000 either way). Berau–Tarakan vessels don't stop off at Tanjung Selor, so if you can't get there by bus you'll have to go to Tarakan first and take a ferry from there. The *Sederhana* and *Citra Indah* can organize all **flights**.

To Pulau Derawan

Shallow seas and reefs surrounding islands 40km east of the mouth of the Sungai Berau have gained a well-deserved reputation in **scuba-diving** circles recently, though you don't have to be a dedicated diver to enjoy the islands' pretty arrangement of sand, coral and palm trees. **Pulau Derawan** is the easiest place to base yourself, with access from here to other islands in the group.

Speedboats from Berau get to Derawan in a couple of hours, but it's far cheaper to catch a Tarakan-bound ferry to the mainland fishing village of **TANJUNG BATU**, which looks over to where the islands hover temptingly against the skyline; there's accommodation and food at the simple *Losmen Famili* (③). Low-key touts at Tanjung Batu's dock can run you over to the island of your choice for about Rp25,000, though it's also possible to arrange a ride with fishermen here, who ask far less.

Pulau Derawan, Sangalaki and around

A tiny rise of coarse white sand and coral rubble stabilized by coconut trees, **PULAU DERAWAN** is a delightful place. The village here includes a mosque, adjacent **losmen** (bed and board ③) and the **Derawan Dive Resort** (bookings through the *Hotel Benakutai* in Balikpapan; resort phone ☎0551/23275, fax 23274; bed and board ⑦; all-inclusive dive packages ⑨). Non-guests can arrange **scuba** or snorkelling through the resort (around US$50 per person); Derawan's waters are especially good for seahorses, nudibranchs and other invertebrates, as well as small reef sharks, barracuda and hulking Maori wrasse.

Southeast of Derawan, **PULAU SANGALAKI** is similar to Derawan but uninhabited except for its own wooden cabin **dive resort**, run by Borneo Divers in Sabah (bookings through Borneo Divers, Rooms 401–412, Floor 4, Wisma Sabah, Kota Kinabalu; ☎+60-88/222226, fax 221550; all-inclusive packages ⑨). Coral outcrops near Sangalaki's **lighthouse** attract cuttlefish and **green turtles**, whose local population is one of the biggest in the world, coming ashore year-round to lay their eggs in the sand. Across a channel from Sangalaki, **KAKABAN** is an extinct volcano with good wall diving, where you are likely to encounter big schools of pelagic fish, and an internal **lake** with some strange, stingless jellyfish. Northeast of Kakaban, **MARATUA** is the biggest island of all, thin and bent, with some tiny settlements ashore and exceptional drop-offs into the deeps, patrolled by barracuda, sharks and manta rays.

Tanjung Selor

With forests edging down from upstream and little more to the town than blocks of government buildings, **TANJUNG SELOR** is the backwater to end them all, marking where Kalimantan's roads finally give up the ghost, having run – on a good day – all the way from Pangkalanbun, 1500km away in southwestern Kalteng province. Isolated some 90km north of Berau on **Sungai Kayan**, this neat, moribund township is actually the administrative capital of the vast **Bulungan district**, which spreads for 67,000 square kilometres northeast to the Malaysian border. It's a nice setting, but there's no reason to visit Tanjung Selor unless you want to try and arrange a trip upstream to remote Kenyah and Punan settlements and a **World Wide Fund for Nature** study area at **Long Alango**. If you've time to kill, there's a riverfront **Chinese temple**, past which *ces* wait at a wooden **dock** to cart you across the river to where **Gunung Putih**, the White Mountain, rises behind the site of Bulungan's now-vanished sultan's palace. It's more of a hill really, but a good place to explore, with a steep cliff and caves facing town.

Practicalities

Tanjung Selor sits on the western bank of the Kayan, with the mid-point of a two-kilometre-long road along the river marked by a pillar topped with a hornbill. Another road runs inland from here, curving left past a mosque, a couple of **restaurants**, and out to the **airstrip**. Problems with weather and the road from Berau makes arrival via speedboat from Tarakan more likely; vessels running between Berau and Tarakan do not call in. The **speedboat docks** and **ticket office** are south along the waterfront (services to Tarakan take 1–2hr and leave until 3pm; Rp10,000), and Jalan Skip is where to find the **bus stop** and DAS office (☎0552/21182). **Accommodation** includes the friendly *Penginapan Lamin*, near the hornbill pillar (☎0552/21439; ④), and the equally good Chinese-run *Gracias*, north past the temple (☎0552/21074; ⑥).

Those planning to head **upstream to Long Alango** need first to sort out logistics at the WWF ("Weh-weh Eff"), whose riverfront **office** is marked by their panda logo. River travel to Long Alango takes between three days and a week; with luck, you might be able to catch public **boats** all the way to Long Alango, but otherwise you'll have to **fly** in with MAF – arrange this through their offices in Tarakan – or charter a longboat from the local river baron, Pak Moming, who typically charges around five million rupiah for the return trip in an eight-person vessel.

Tarakan, Nunukan and border crossings

A 24-kilometre spread of low hills just off the coast northeast of Tanjung Selor, **Pulau Tarakan** floats above extensive **oil** reserves: offshore rigs dot the horizon, while the west-coast town of **TARAKAN** is surrounded by smaller-scale "nodding donkey" pumps, patiently drawing oil out of wells and piping it into storage tanks above the harbour. The Japanese captured the island in January 1942, digging themselves into caves and putting up a hard struggle before being dislodged three years later by Australian troops armed with flamethrowers during operation **"Oboe"**. Intended less to recover Tarakan's oil than to establish a fighter-plane base in eastern Borneo, Oboe was a pointless campaign, as Tarakan's airfield was destroyed during the assault and subsequent landings at Brunei and Balikpapan had to rely on carriers for support. Today, with plenty of money passing through town, Tarakan is a surprisingly brisk, busy place, just a stone's throw from **Pulau Nunukan** and the open **border with Malaysia**. The oil industry means good wages both for Indonesians and the handful of Westerners stationed here, and the town enjoys an obviously high standard of living, its shops and supermarkets overflowing with goods – some of which appear to have trickled illicitly over the border.

Practicalities

Tarakan has just two main roads, set at right angles to each other. Paralleling the coast, Jalan Sudarso runs north from the port area for a couple of kilometres, where it's crossed by Jalan Sudirman, which runs east for a similar distance into the suburbs. Their **intersection** serves as a town centre, though services are quite widely scattered. The **airport** is 2km north of town, where taxis charge Rp5000 to accommodation, while all marine traffic docks at the southern end of Jalan Sudarso: ferries from Berau and Tanjung Selor at the **jetty** about 1.5km south of the intersection, passenger services on the Samarinda–Nunukan route at Tarakan's **port**, 500m further down near the end of the road, where you'll also find the **Pelni office**. Bemos around town are plentiful and cost Rp300 a ride.

There are numerous **places to stay**, mostly east down Jalan Sudirman within 150m of the centre. *Hotel Wisata*, Jalan Sudirman 46 (☎0552/21347; ⑤), is a good standby, while the adjacent *Orchid*, Jalan Sudirman 171 (☎0551/21664; ④), is cheap and grotty, with Tarakan's best-value rooms a little further along at the tidy *Barito Timur*, Jalan Sudirman 129 (☎0551/21181; ⑤). Right at the intersection on Jalan Sudarso, the *Kartika* is a fine Chinese **restaurant**, as are the *Cahaya* and *Anneka*, both along Jalan Sudirman. For **supplies**, there's a huge produce market at the Jalan Sudirman–Jalan Sudarso intersection, and a supermarket selling everything from decks of cards to Swiss chocolates opposite the *Orchid* hotel on Jalan Sudirman. Good exchange rates and ATMs can be found at the BNI **bank** just south of the intersection and across from the **police station** on Jalan Sudarso. For local **information**, including day-trips to Dayak villages and trekking inland from Tanjung Selor, contact English-speaking Pak Herry at the *Orchid* hotel.

Moving on, Wisma Murni Travel at the *Hotel Wisata* (☎0551/21697) can book **flights** to Samarinda, Nunukan and Balikpapan. DAS, opposite the *Hotel Orchid*, Jalan Sudirman 9 (☎0551/51578), or MAF at the *Hotel Barito Timur* (☎0551/51011), are the people to contact for travel to the interior Apo Kayan or Long Alango regions. At the jetty you'll find tickets and **ferries** for Tanjung Selor (about 5 daily; Rp10,000), Berau (several weekly; Rp25,000–40,000) and Nunukan (about 2 daily, 15,000); it's the port for Pelni's *Kerinci, Tidar, Awu, Leuser* and *Binaya* services to Samarinda, Balikpapan, Berau, Nunukan, Sulawesi and Java.

Nunukan and into Malaysia

Only 100km and half a day north of Tarakan, **NUNUKAN** is a busy, sleazy town on an island of the same name, right up against Malaysian **Sabah**. Crossing is straightforward: Nunukan's **Immigration Department**, Kantor Imigrasi, is about 200m from the port on the main road into town, and opens at 8am; it can take a few hours to sort out the paperwork, so if you get stuck overnight catch a bemo to the downmarket *Losmen Nunukan* (③) or, slightly better, *Idabus* (③). Once exit formalities are complete, *Samudra Expres* leaves Nunukan in the early afternoon and putters along the coast for a couple of hours to **TEWAU** in Sabah, where you'll be processed quickly by Malaysian officials.

travel details

Buses

Balikpapan to: Banjarmasin (10 daily; 12–14hr); Samarinda (10 daily; 2hr 30min).

Banjarmasin to: Balikpapan (10 daily; 12–14hr); Barabai (frequent; 4hr); Kandangan (frequent; 3hr 30min); Martapura (frequent; 1hr 30min); Palangkaraya (several daily; 5–7hr); Samarinda (10 daily; 14–16hr).

Kumai to: Pangkalanbun (several daily; 1hr 15min).

Palangkaraya to: Banjarmasin (several daily; 5–7hr); Pangkalanbun (4 daily; 10hr).

Pangkalanbun to: Kumai (several daily; 1hr 15min); Palangkaraya (4 daily; 10hr).

Pontianak to: Putussibau (early morning & evening; 12hr); Kuching (Sabah; 7 daily; 12hr); Singkawang (every 30min; 3hr 30min); Sintang (early morning & evening; 7hr).

Putussibau to: Lanjak (daily 8am; 5hr 30min); Nanga Badau (daily 8am; 7hr); Pontianak (8 daily from 8am; 12hr); Sintang (8 daily; 6hr).

Samarinda to: Balikpapan (10 daily; 2hr 30min); Banjarmasin (10 daily; 14–16hr); Bontang (several daily; 2hr); Kota Bangun (several daily; 3hr); Sanggata (several daily; 4hr); Tenggarong (many daily; 1hr).

Semitau to: Pontianak (3 daily; 11hr); Putussibau (2 daily; 5hr); Sintang (3 daily; 3hr 30min).

Sintang to: Nanga Pinoh (hourly; 90min); Pontianak (8 daily; 8hr); Putussibau (daily 6am; 6hr); Semitau (3 daily; 3hr 30min).

Pelni ferries

For a chart of the Pelni routes, see pp.36–37 of Basics.

Balikpapan to: Pantoloan (*KM Kerinci*, 2 monthly; 14hr); Parepare (*KM Tidar*, 2 monthly; 19hr); Surabaya (*KM Kerinci*, 2 monthly; 45h/*KM Kambuna*, 2 monthly; 45hr/*KM Umsini*, 2 monthly; 45hr/*KM Tidar*, 4 monthly; 24–40hr); Tanjung Priok, Jakarta (*KM Kerinci*, 2 monthly; 2–3 days/*KM Kambuna*, 2 monthly; 3 days); Ternate (*KM Umsini*, 2 monthly; 41hr); Toli-Toli (*KM Kambuna*, 2 monthly; 24h/*KM Kerinci*, 2 monthly; 24hr); Ujung Padang (*KM Kerinci*, 2 monthly; 19hr/*KM Kambuna*, 2 monthly; 17hr/*KM Umsini*, 2 monthly; 16hr).

Banjarmasin to: Surabaya (*KM Kelimutu*, 3–4 weekly; 24hr).

Berau to: Nunukan (*KM Awu*, 2 monthly; 24hr); Tarakan (*KM Awu*, 2 monthly; 24hr).

Kumai to: Semarang (*KM Lawit*, 2 monthly; 24hr/*KM Leuser*, monthly; 24hr; *KM Binaiya*, 2 monthly; 24hr); Surabaya (*KM Tilongkabila*, monthly; 24hr/*KM Binaiya*, 2 monthly; 24hr); Tanjung Pandang (*KM Lawit*, 2 monthly; 3 days).

Nunukan to: Tarakan (*KM Tidar*, 2 monthly; 5hr); Ujung Padang (*KM Awu*, 2 monthly; 42hr).

Pontianak to: Natuna (*KM Bukit Raya*, monthly; 31hr); Semarang (*KM Tatamailau*, 2 monthly; 34hr/*KM Lawit*, 2 monthly; 32hr); Serasan (*KM Bukit Raya*, 2 monthly; 20hr); Tanjung Priok, Jakarta (*KM Ambulu*, every 3 days; 11hr/*KM Lawit*, weekly; 33hr); Tarempa (*KM Bukit Raya*, monthly; 40hr).

Samarinda to: Surabaya (*KM Binaiya*, 2 monthly; 3 days).

Tarakan to: Balikpapan (*KM Tidar*, 2 monthly; 20hr); Nunukan (*KM Awu*, 2 monthly; 7hr); Pantoloan (*KM Tidar*, 2 monthly; 15hr); Ujung Pandang (*KM Tidar*, 2 monthly; 35hr/*KM Awu*, 2 monthly; 51hr).

Other ferries

Berau to: Tanjung Batu (for Pulau Derawan; 2–3 weekly; 4hr); Tarakan (3 weekly; 10hr).

Lanjak to: Semitau (daily 8am; 8hr).

Palangkaraya to: Banjarmasin (frequent; 5hr); Tewah (daily; 8hr); Tumbang Jutuh (from Tangkiling, daily; 4hr).

Pontianak to: Jakarta (*Kapuas Expres*, twice weekly, 19hr); Ketapang (*Ketapang Expres*, daily 8am; 6hr); Putussibau (*Kapal Bandung*, weekly; 5 days); Sintang (*Kapal Bandung*, weekly; 3 days).

Putussibau to: Pontianak (*Kapal Bandung*, weekly; 4 days); Sintang (*Kapal Bandung*, weekly; 36hr).

Samarinda to: Kota Bangun (several daily; 10hr); Long Bagun (seasonally 1 daily; 40hr–4 days); Long Iram (1–2 daily; 30hr); Melak (several daily; 24hr); Muara Kaman (several daily; 6hr); Muara Muntai (several daily; 14hr); Tenggarong (several daily; 3hr).

Semitau to: Lanjak (speedboat daily 9am; 3hr 30min; passenger ferry 9am; 8hr).

Sintang to: Putussibau (*Kapal Bandung* weekly; 2 days/*Bunut Utama* speedboat 3–4 weekly; 6hr).

Tarakan to: Berau (3 weekly; 10hr); Nunukan (6–12hr; daily); Tanjung Selor (several daily; 1–2hr).

Flights

Balikpapan to: Banjarmasin (daily; 40min); Berau (2 daily; 2hr); Brunei (2 weekly; 1hr 30min); Jakarta (3 daily; 2hr); Palu (daily; 45min); Pontianak (6 weekly; 4hr); Samarinda (2 daily, 40min); Surabaya (3 daily; 1hr 15min); Tarakan (2 daily; 2hr); Ujung Pandang (daily; 2hr).

Banjarmasin to: Balikpapan (daily; 40min); Jakarta (4 daily; 1hr 45min); Palangkaraya (daily; 40min); Pangkalanbun (6 weekly; 2hr); Surabaya (4 daily; 1hr 10min).

Berau/Tanjung Redeb to: Balikpapan (2 daily; 2hr); Samarinda (2 daily; 1hr 30min); Tarakan (2 daily; 40min).

Palangkaraya to: Balikpapan (daily; 2hr); Banjarmasin (daily; 40min); Pangkalanbun (daily; 2hr); Surabaya (2 daily; 1hr 50min).

Pangkalanbun to: Banjarmasin (6 weekly; 2hr); Palangkaraya (daily; 2hr); Pontianak (daily; 2hr); Semarang (daily; 3hr).

Pontianak to: Balikpapan (4 weekly; 2hr 35min); Ketapang (3 daily; 1hr); Kuching (3 weekly; 1hr 45min); Medan (3 weekly; 3hr 35min); Pekanbaru (3 weekly; 2hr 50min); Putussibau (5 weekly; 1hr 25min).

Samarinda to: Balikpapan (2 daily; 40min); Berau (2 daily; 1hr 30min); Datah Dawai (3 weekly; 1hr 35min); Long Ampung (5 weekly; 1hr 50min); Melak (3 weekly; 55min); Tanjung Selor (3 daily; 2hr); Tarakan (3 daily; 2hr).

Tarakan to: Apo Kayan (3 weekly; 2hr); Balikpapan (3 daily; 2hr 40min); Berau (2 daily; 40min); Samarinda (3 daily; 2hr); Tanjung Selor (daily; 15min); Tewau (3 weekly; 40min).

CHAPTER ELEVEN

SULAWESI

Sulawesi sprawls in the centre of the Indonesian archipelago, its bizarre outline a foretaste of the many peculiarities that make this one of the country's most compelling regions. Occupying a marine corridor where the influences of Java, the Philippines and Papuan Maluku overlap, the island is saved from being an untidy mixture of these neighbours by its shape, a 1000-kilometre letter "K" with the upright arm swept eastwards. Formed by tectonic shuffles uplifting and rotating two long, parallel landmasses together to create four separate peninsulas, nowhere in Sulawesi is much more than 100km from the sea, though an almost complete covering of mountains not only isolated these peninsulas from one another, but also made them difficult to penetrate individually. Invaders were hard pushed to colonize beyond the coast and, despite echoes of external forces, a unique blend of cultures and habitats developed.

Even now, Sulawesi's division into three parts – the south, centre and north – is very apparent. **Southern Sulawesi**, comprising the two peninsula provinces of **Sulawesi Selatan** and **Sulawesi Tenggara**, is geographically the least extreme region, its lower reaches comprising conveniently flat coastal fringes and relatively small-scale limestone hills. The most settled part of the island, the south, is home to most of Sulawesi's fifteen million inhabitants, and the obvious location of its capital, the energetic port of **Ujung Pandang**. Rich in history, the southern plains rise to the mountain fastness of **Tanah Toraja**, attractively fertile home to one of Indonesia's most securely self-aware ethnic groups. Beyond here lies **Sulawesi Tengah**, Central Sulawesi Province, whose crumpled interior provides for some quality **trekking**, while those after a more languid experience can soak up sun and scenery at **Danau Poso** and the **Togian Islands**. Sulawesi's final third, **Sulawesi Utara** (North Sulawesi Province) is a volcanic tail of land covered in coconut plantations and thick rainforest, the peninsula topped by the unique people and still-smoking cones of the **Minahasa highlands**. Offshore, each region also has its own archipelagos, strewn with everything from unlikely evidence of contact with distant empires to simply beautiful beaches. Here you'll find superlative **scuba diving**; new sites are being pioneered continually, but the venue of the moment is **Pulau Bunaken**, out from the northern city of **Manado**. Sulawesi also sits on the western side of **Wallacea** (see box on p.974) and is spotted with some exceptional **wildlife reserves**, where you can spend days on humid jungle tracks looking for unusual creatures.

Formerly focused on Tanah Toraja, **tourism** has discovered the rest of Sulawesi over the past decade, and though this has brought certain irritations – worst are rising **costs** and a tendency to be quickly pigeonholed by locals – the infrastructure has improved greatly, especially with regard to **getting around**. The southern peninsula's **highways** reach up into Sulawesi Tengah, though north of Parepare there's hardly a straight stretch anywhere, and travel involves endless, nausea-inducing slaloms. Nor can the southeastern peninsula or Sulawesi Utara be reached easily overland, though roads elsewhere are well covered by public transport – freelance kijang and minibuses are often faster and cheaper than scheduled buses. Where these fail you'll find **ferries**, even if services are unreliable. Tanah Toraja and all outlying provincial capitals (**Kendari** in Sulawesi Tenggara, **Palu** in Sulawesi Tenggah, and Manado) are also connected by direct **flights** to Ujung Pandang, if seldom to each other. Crossed by the equator, Sulawesi shares its **weather** patterns with western Indonesia, with August

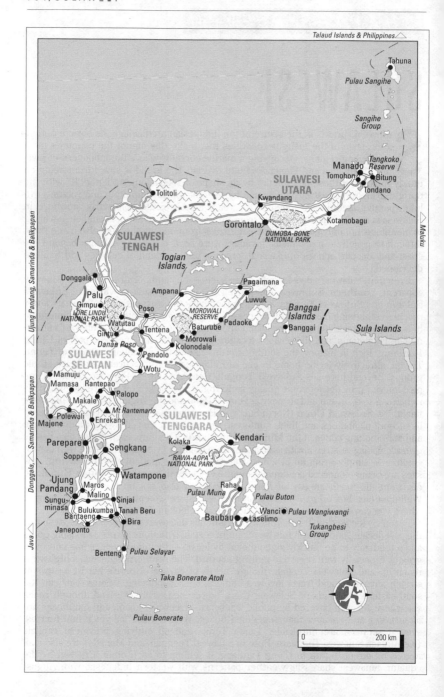

ACCOMMODATION PRICE CODES

All the **accommodation** listed in this book has been given one of the following price codes. The rates quoted here are for the **cheapest double room** in high season, except for places with dorms, where the code represents the price of a single bed. Where there's a significant spread of prices indicated (④–⑦, for example), the text will explain what extra facilities you get for more money. The 11–21 percent tax charged by most hotels is not included in these price codes.

Because of the current instability of the rupiah, accommodation prices are given throughout in their more stable **US dollar equivalents**, even for places that accept payment in rupiah.

For more on accommodation, see p.40.

① under $1	③ $2–5	⑤ $10–15	⑦ $35–60	⑨ $100
② $1–2	④ $5–10	⑥ $15–35	⑧ $60–100	and over

---

through to November the driest time of year, and December to April the wettest. Tourism peaks with the European summer holidays (June–Sept) and Christmas, so April is the best time to see things at their greenest and least crowded.

Some history

Thirty-thousand-year-old remains from caves near the southern town of Maros provide the earliest evidence of human occupation in Sulawesi, but it's likely that the peoples here today are descended from the bronzeworking cultures which arrived in Indonesia from the Asian mainland after 3000 BC. By the time the **Portuguese** first marked Sulawesi as the "**Celebes**" – an name with endless possible origins – on their maps during the sixteenth century, the island was ethnically divided much as it is today, with the south split between the highland **Torajans** and the lowland **Bugis**, various isolated tribes in the central highlands, and the Filipino-descended **Minahasans** in the far north. Both Minahasans and Bugis had contacts with the rest of the Indonesian region through their ports, the north coming under the influence of the sultan of Ternate, while the south was part of the decaying Hindu Majapahit empire. They were also the first to be affected by European contact, as the next few centuries saw the Portuguese and their **Dutch** successors build forts, meddle in local politics and introduce **Christianity** to the north of the island just as **Islam** swept the south and coastal communities elsewhere. But for a long while the Dutch considered Sulawesi only inasmuch as its involvement in maritime trade affected their concerns elsewhere, and it wasn't until the late nineteenth century that they decided to bring the whole island under their thumb.

By this time the north had already proved compliant to the European presence, but southern Sulawesi was not so malleable. The Dutch had achieved a loose hold over the Bugis states in 1825, but an attempt in 1905 to make Sulawesi's kingdoms sign a declaration of obedience to Holland sparked furious resistance, and the south took two years of bloody warfare to subjugate. Not surprisingly, the **Japanese** were welcomed as liberators on arrival in 1942, and the south rose again when the Dutch returned in 1946. This time, even north Sulawesi joined in the revolution before coming to terms with colonial powers, who needed their support – or at least didn't want them at their backs – for what became an exceptionally brutal campaign against the Bugis. Independence in 1950 wasn't the end of trouble, either: economic discontent led to widespread guerrilla action, which snowballed during the next decade under the pro-Muslim-state **Darul Islam** banner, and then the **Permesta** movement – the word being a telescoping of the Indonesian for "United Struggle". Support for Permesta focused in the north, where it formed dangerous ties with Sumatran rebel groups before being finished off by a full-scale military campaign in the early 1960s.

SOUTHERN SULAWESI

Southern Sulawesi descends from the island's highest mountain, **Gunung Rantemario**, out to some of its remotest islands. The **south peninsula** is thoroughly infused with the outgoing character of its famously quarrelsome **Bugis** population, whose squabbling split the region into competing states and left Sulawesi's modern capital, **Ujung Pandang**, surrounded by the ghosts of former kingdoms, where you'll still find traditional shipbuilding communities and palaces occupied by royal descendants. As Muslims, the Bugis also had confrontations with their pagan neighbours, especially the **Torajans**, whose inaccessible homeland in the region's mountainous north allowed them to resist conversion, and where beautiful scenery coupled with unusual architecture and festivals today make **Mamasa** and **Tanah Toraja** some of the most rewarding parts of the country to delve into indigenous culture. Off to the southeast, only the lower third of **Sulawesi Tenggara** province is really accessible and, broken up into a group of islands as it is, you'll need some time to cover the attractions here, which include cave art and a scattering of remote coral reefs.

Transport is as plentiful as anywhere in Sulawesi, with good roads around Ujung Pandang, the south peninsula, and Mamasa and Tanah Toraja. Very much more isolated, Sulawesi Tenggara has to be reached by air from Ujung Pandang or ferry from the eastern town of Watampone, though once there you'll find roads out to the sights and regular ferries connecting the main islands.

Ujung Pandang and around

Set down at Sulawesi's southwestern corner and facing Java and Kalimantan, **UJUNG PANDANG** is an animated, determinedly unpretentious port city geared up as a transit point and business centre. It's also dauntingly large, hot and crowded, but, in terms of specific attractions, it has more than the average provincial hub. There's good food and a visibly lively history to investigate and, with Ujung Pandang's docks and airport an increasingly vital bridge between eastern and western Indonesia, a growing number of visitors are spending time in town. More than anything, Ujung Pandang offers an introduction to Sulawesi's largest ethnic group, the **Bugis**, seafarers whose twanging pronunciation fills in the spaces between the city's traffic noise. Apt to turn to piracy if the need arose, the Bugis are considered headstrong and short-tempered by other Indonesians, and continue to export their goods and presence well beyond Sulawesi in **prahu**, distinctive vessels with steep, upcurved prows.

Ujung Pandang traces its history back five hundred years or more to the rise of **Makassar**, a grouping of western Bugis states whose central position on the Indonesian maritime trade routes won it a huge amount of trade. To protect their harbours, these states constructed a string of coastal defences, most notably **Ujung Pandang fort** and the nearby fortified town of **Somba Opu**. By the mid-seventeenth century, the accumulated wealth and military skills of its Muslim ruler, **Sultan Hasanuddin**, had brought the Makassan state of **Gowa** (whose capital was just south of Ujung Pandang) to the ascendancy right across southern Sulawesi. This also made them direct rivals with the Dutch, who wanted all regional trade to funnel through their base at Malacca, a Malaysian holding recently acquired from the Portuguese. Trying to destabilize Gowa, the Dutch found an ally in the rival eastern Bugis kingdom of Bone; they helped the kingdom to defeat Gowan forces in 1667. The subsequent **Bungaya Treaty** ceded Ujung Pandang to the Dutch (which they renamed **Fort Rotterdam**), closed Makassan ports to foreign merchants, and exiled the Gowan royalty to Somba Opu – until fears over that town's defences prompted the Dutch into razing it two years later, dismembering the Makassan empire.

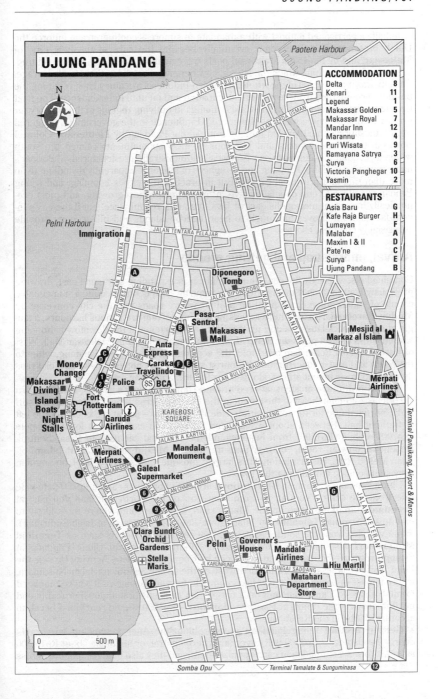

UJUNG PANDANG

N

Paotere Harbour

Pelni Harbour

Immigration

ACCOMMODATION

Delta	8
Kenari	11
Legend	1
Makassar Golden	5
Makassar Royal	7
Mandar Inn	12
Marannu	4
Puri Wisata	9
Ramayana Satrya	3
Surya	6
Victoria Panghegar	10
Yasmin	2

RESTAURANTS

Asia Baru	G
Kafe Raja Burger	H
Lumayan	F
Malabar	A
Maxim I & II	D
Pate'ne	C
Surya	E
Ujung Pandang	B

Diponegoro Tomb

Pasar Sentral

Makassar Mall

Mesjid al Markaz al Islam

Anta Express

Caraka Travelindo

Money Changer

Makassar Diving

Island Boats

Night Stalls

Police

BCA

Fort Rotterdam

Garuda Airlines

KAREBOSI SQUARE

Merpati Airlines

Merpati Airlines

Mandala Monument

Galeal Supermarket

Clara Bundt Orchid Gardens

Stella Maris

Pelni

Governor's House

Mandala Airlines

Hiu Martil

Matahari Department Store

Terminal Panaikang, Airport & Maros

0   500 m

Somba Opu   Terminal Tamalate & Sunguminasa

Initially a garrisoned outpost with a mandate to suppress commerce and enforce the Dutch presence, Fort Rotterdam eventually became the core of the new **city of Makassar**, and by the 1830s Makassan ports were again at the centre of a broad trading network – something which the Dutch, now beneficiaries, did nothing to discourage. The city was made capital of the whole of eastern Indonesia a century later, retaining the position through the Japanese wartime occupation and on until Independence. The next decade was rough, however, as growing demands in outlying regions of the country for greater autonomy, and a watering down of PKI influence in the government, triggered the Permesta revolt of 1957, led initially from Ujung Pandang by **Lieutenant Colonel Sumual**. Government forces and judicious political appointments calmed the south within a year, but the aftermath saw Sulawesi's administration restructured, Makassar's name reverting to Ujung Pandang and its sphere of influence apparently dwindling to no more than that of a provincial capital. But in practice the city is booming, and Ujung Pandang's million-strong population live in the largest, fastest-growing, and most economically important metropolis east of Java. It's not a restful place, but if the city's in-your-face attitude proves too much to bear, nearby islands and hill scenery provide surprisingly complete escapes.

Arrival, information and getting around

Contained elsewhere by the sea, Ujung Pandang is expanding south and east, drawing previously well-separated towns within its suburbs. The centre is quite a manageable couple of square kilometres, pivoting around where roads into the city converge on **Medan Karebosi**. North of here across Jalan Ahmed Yani are various harbours, a tangle of grubby back-lanes making up the Chinese quarter, and the downtown shopping and business district of **Pasar Sentral**, also known as Sentral or Makassar Mall. West of Karebosi, Fort Rotterdam overlooks the seafront on Jalan Ujung Pandang, while to the south and east a concentration of tourist services and hotels cedes to official residences and government offices along Jalan Jendral Sudirman.

Arrival points are mostly scattered around Ujung Pandang's fringes. **Hasanuddin Airport** is 25km northeast of the city near the town of Maros, where taxis charge a stiff Rp17,500 fixed fare for the forty-minute ride into the city – pay at the booth on the left of the exit hall. Between about 6.30am and 6.30pm you can also opt for a pete-pete (Rp700) or bus (Rp1500) from just beyond the terminal car park to Pasar Sentral. Depending on your route, you may pass the mighty **Mesjid al Markaz al Islami** on Jalan Mesjid Raya, eastern Indonesia's largest mosque and Islamic school, an angular, grey-stone edifice built during the 1990s.

Ujung Pandang's two main **bus stations** are both about 5km and a Rp350 pete-pete ride from the centre: coming in from Rantepao or the north will land you east at **Terminal Panaikang**, also on the Maros road; from the south you're most likely to end up at **Terminal Tamalate** on Jalan Gowa Raya (an extension of Jalan Sudirman). Some vehicles from the south coast might favour smaller depots such as **Terminal Mallengkeri**, also on Jalan Gowa Raya, or 10km southeast of Ujung Pandang at **Sungguminasa** – both are linked to the city by frequent pete-pete. Arriving **by sea**, the Pelni harbour is less than 1km northwest of the Pasar Sentral on Jalan Nusantara, where a mass of becaks and a few taxis compete for your business. If you've managed to hitch a ride to Ujung Pandang on a cargo boat or Bugis prahu, you'll probably end up 3km north of the centre at **Paotere Harbour** – Rp1500 should rent you a becak to accommodation in the Karebosi area.

Getting around Ujung Pandang is unproblematic. After a standing fare, **taxis** charge by distance – Rp3000 will cover anywhere central, or negotiate about Rp10,000 an hour. Your accommodation can organize them, and they also tend to hang out across from the *Marannu* hotel on Jalan Sultan Hasanuddin. Bemos are here called **pete-pete**, charge Rp350–700 depending on distance, and terminate either at Pasar Sentral or in the vicinity of Medan Karebosi. The best way to find one to your destination is to shout it or the street name at drivers, who will either wave you on board or point you in the direction of other vehicles. Ujung Pandang's **becak** drivers are masters of irritation and incompetence, hard to shake off if you don't want them and often ignorant of your destination if you do. Pasar Sentral and the GPO are good places to find one, and a fare of Rp500 per kilometre is reasonable.

For **information**, your hotel desk or the airport information counter should be able to at least provide you with a map of the city. The **tourist information office** is right at the back and upstairs at the government offices at Jalan Balai Kota 11 (Mon–Thurs 7am–2pm, Fri 7–11am, Sat 7am–1pm), where the pleasant, hopeless staff will urge you to visit Bira and Rantepao whatever your actual inquiry.

Accommodation

Ujung Pandang has no lack of places to stay, though few of the cheaper places will take foreigners. Even so, mid-range rooms – here, ⑤–⑥ for a double – are fair value. Most **accommodation** places at least give travel advice or have their own agents; pricier ones also have pools, laundry services, shops, and discos/karaoke halls. Hotel food, however, tends to be overpriced, and you're better off eating out.

Delta, Jl Sultan Hasanuddin 43 (☎0411/312711, fax 312655). Casual hotel recently smartened with a blue-glass-and-tile face-lift to attract commercial travellers; comfortable, spacious rooms with all conveniences. ⑦.

Kenari, Jl Latumahina 30 (☎0411/874250, fax 872126). A new, topnotch hotel and the *Makassar Royal*'s only real competitor, trying hard and with nearly as fine amenities and ocean views. ⑧.

Legend, Jl Jampea 5 (☎0411/328203, fax 328204). The city's budget standby, with basic, sticky dorms and doubles, a good central position, helpful staff, and heaps of information about the rest of Sulawesi. Shared mandis only. ③.

Makassar Golden, Jl Pasar Ikan 50–52 (☎0411/314408, fax 320951). Ujung Pandang's best hotel is no more expensive than other luxury places in the city, but has finer views and better service than any. Rooms ⑧, seafront cottages ⑨.

Makassar Royal, Jl Daeng Tompo 8 (☎0411/328488, fax 328045). Not cheap, but quiet, good-value rooms with air-con, bathrooms and TV. ⑥.

Mandar Inn, Jl Annuang 17. A bit of a hike southeast from the centre, but a very helpful, clean and friendly hostel. ③.

Marannu, Jl Sultan Hasanuddin 3–5 (☎0411/315087, fax 321821). Charmless concrete exterior and a gloomy interior, though rooms are fine and the staff attentive. Merpati stick their delay victims here. ⑥.

Puri Wisata, Jl Sultan Hasanuddin 36–38 (☎0411/324344, fax 312783). A nicely placed, very welcoming and well-run hotel. Older rooms with fans, and doubles in the new wing with air-con. ⑤–⑥.

Ramayana Satrya, Jl Bawakareang 121 (☎0411/442478, fax 442479). A couple of kilometres due east of the centre (transport from the airport or Terminal Panaikang passes the door), but pleasantly informal and good value, with a mix of foreign and Indonesian visitors sharing two tiers enclosing a courtyard. All rooms have at least fans and mandi; take precautions against mosquitoes. Ekonomi doubles plus rooms with air-con and TV. ④–⑤.

Surya, Jl Botolempangan 21 (☎0411/322651, fax 311498). Tiled, pleasant place; all rooms with air-con, hot water and TV. ⑥.

Victoria Panghegar, Jl Sudirman 24 (☎0411/328888, fax 312468). Airy, exceptionally well-organized, clean and tidy hotel aimed at foreign tour groups. ⑧.

Yasmin, Jl Jampea 5 (☎0411/320424, fax 328283). Friendly business venue with good new facilities and free airport pick-up. ⑦.

The City: Fort Rotterdam and around

A monument to Sulawesi's colonial era, **Fort Rotterdam** on Jalan Ujung Pandang (daily 7.30am–6pm, free; museum Tues–Sun 8am–1pm, Rp200) would be worth a look even if it wasn't also the quietest spot in the city centre. The site has been a defensive position since 1545, when the tenth Gowan king, Tunipa Langa, first raised a fort here with Portuguese assistance and named it **Jum Pandan** (from which the name "Ujung Pandang" derives) after pandanus trees growing in the vicinity. Enlarged a century later, the Bungaya Treaty saw the fort become Dutch property in November 1667 under the command of **Cornelius Speelman**, who rechristened the complex Fort Rotterdam in memory of his home town. A rebuilding of the walls in stone was followed by the addition of solid barracks, residences and a church, and the fort remained the regional Dutch military and governmental headquarters until the 1930s. Falling into a disrepair after World War II, when the Japanese used it as a college, restoration provided a face-lift in the 1970s, and renovated eighteenth-century buildings now house new government offices and a **museum**.

High, thick, and forming a protective square with drawn-out corners, Rotterdam's **walls** are perhaps the most impressive part of the entire fort; orientate yourself by climbing them and promenading along the top, where you'll get a fine view of the tall, white buildings inside, their steep roofs tiled in grey slate. On the northwest side, **Speelman's House** – actually dating from after his death in 1686 – is the oldest surviving building, and nestles next to one half of **La Galigo museum** (Rp500). Named after a Bugis prince featured in a lengthy romantic poem, the museum has its moments, but brief captions make it hard to put exhibits into context: the most relevant item is a prehistoric megalith from Watampone South across a courtyard, where the **church** stands alone; the other part of the museum illustrates local skills in silk weaving, agriculture and boatbuilding, with some fine scale models of different types of prahu.

South of the fort

South of Fort Rotterdam, Jalan Ujung Pandang runs down along the seafront as Jalan Penghibur, a picturesque place to watch the sunset over the Makassar Strait and one which the city's hotels have taken full advantage of. This esplanade — also known as **Pantai Losari** — is famous for its **evening food stalls**, which stretch way down south and are a good deal more romantic places to eat than the upmarket bars and restaurants which overlook them. Parallel and just east of Jalan Penghibur, **Jalan Somba Opu** is known across Indonesia for its **gold shops**; other stalls sell silk from Sengkang, intricate silver filigree in the Kendari style, and potentially antique Chinese porcelain, all priced at about three times what you'd pay elsewhere. The street's southern end is crossed by Jalan Mochtar Lufti, down which you'll find the **Clara Bundt Orchid Gardens** at no. 15a. A privately owned nursery rather than a public space, visitors are welcome to look around this tranquil corner of the city, shadecloth protecting row upon row of planter pots and orchids held in bamboo frames. The type and quantity of flowers depends on the season, but look for purple hybrids, golden "dancing ladies" and long-petalled spider orchids.

Medan Karebosi and beyond

Medan Karebosi is a scruffy, spacious patch of green surrounded by trees, venue for daytime football matches or military parades, and the source of much local gossip concerning the activities of its transvestite prostitutes. The shaded fringes along Jalan Ahmed Yani also attract street performers and panacea-sellers with megaphones. To the south, the space is continued by broad Jalan Sudirman; about 200m down here you'll encounter the **Mandala Monument**, whose thirty-metre tower rising out of a colonial-style building flanked by flaming bamboo is a weird concoction even by

Indonesian standards. Continuing along Jalan Sudirman, the grounds of the **Governor's House**, about a ten-minute walk beyond the Mandala Monument on the corner of Jalan Sungai Saddang, sports a small aviary built around a fig tree, the grass kept short by a herd of deer while a lonely cassowary stalks the tennis court. Jalan Sungai Saddang itself is becoming a popular middle-class shopping district, with a string of cosmetically neat businesses and plazas centred around the glossy new Matahari department store about 1km further east.

The area **north of Medan Karebosi** is a mix of down-to-earth commercial districts and twisting alleys which were the heart of eighteenth-century Makassar. Northwest of Karebosi, and bordered by north-orientated Jalan Nusantara and Jalan Irian (the latter also labelled Jalan Sudirohusodo on street signs), the **Chinese quarter** is worth a look for its half-dozen **temples**, decked in dragons and brightly coloured decor, which cluster along the lower reaches of Jalan Sulawesi. Cross east over Jalan Irian and you'll find circling pete-petes, crowds, and leather-belt, wallet and fruit hawkers which make up the chaotic melange surrounding **Pasar Sentral**. In the middle of it all, **Makassar Mall** is a crowded, multi-storey firetrap of a fabric warehouse full of beggars and pickpockets, where cheap cotton, silk and synthetics are sold by the metre. Push northeast through this onto Jalan Diponegoro, where **Makam Pengeran Diponegoro** marks the final resting place of Prince Diponegoro of Yogyakarta. Exiled to Sulawesi by the Dutch after instigating the five-year Javan War of 1825, he was imprisoned at Fort Rotterdam in 1845 and died there a decade later. He and his wife are buried side by side in a large but plain multi-tiered **tomb** up against the western side of this small Islamic cemetery.

From Pasar Sentral you can also catch a pete-pete heading 3km north up Jalan Sudarso to where **Bugis prahu** from all over Indonesia unload and embark cargo at **Paotere harbour** (Rp350 admission). Though the smell and lack of sanitation can be a bit much on a hot day, it's quite a spectacle when the harbour is crowded, the red, white and green prahu lined up along the dock wall with much shifting of bales, boxes, barrels and jerry cans on backs and carts. The adjoining streets are one of the most attractively squalid parts of the city: tattooed sailors on shore leave roam around blearily, vendors display fresh and grilled fish on banana leaves, and shops sell huge mats of spongy tree bark, spices, and cloth from all four corners of the archipelago.

Eating and Entertainment

Ujung Pandang's after-dark **entertainment** is Western-orientated, with popular sessions at the *Makassar Golden* hotel's *Zig-Zag Disco* – the hotel also sometimes has live bands at the weekend. To see what locals do with their time off, spend a few hours one weekend out at Pulau Kayangan. One **bar** worth patronizing for sunset views and evening atmosphere is the *Taman Safari*, on the corner of Jalan Penghibur and Jalan Haji Bau, south of the Stella Maris hospital. The most comfortable **cinemas** are the Makassar, just west of Pasar Sentral on Jalan Bali, and Studio 21, Jalan Ratulangi (a continuation of Jalan Sudirman), with daily screenings of recent Hollywood and Hong Kong releases, and weekend late-night specials.

Eating out in Ujung Pandang involves plenty of **seafood**; other specialities such as *soto makassar* – a soup made from buffalo offal – don't appeal to everyone. For unequalled atmosphere and the lowest prices, try the after-dark alfresco stalls opposite Fort Rotterdam on Jalan Ujung Pandang where, lit by hissing pressure lamps and protected from the elements by a tarpaulin, you share benches with other diners while cats scavenge around your ankles. Rice, tea, and a big plate of either prawns, duck, squid or fish, grilled or fried to your order, will set you back Rp3000. Another fine evening spot is the sea wall above Pantai Losari along Jalan Penghibur, whose kilometre-long string of mobile food carts sell more seafood, fried rice, noodles, bananas and cakes than you could ever hope to eat, with the sunset and glowing dusk as wallpaper. In all these places, popular vendors have the best food. **Restaurants** are pricey compared with the rest of Sulawesi, though portions are healthy; the biggest drawback is that most have similar Chinese-style menus, leading to monotony if you're in town for any length of time. **Western food** at the bigger hotels is not recommended, though there's a *KFC* above the Galael supermarket on Jalan Hasanuddin, featuring erratic supplies of French fries, and the Colonel's original *sambal* sauce recipe.

Restaurants

Asia Baru, Jl Gunung Salahutu 2. Inexpensive fish restaurant, whose menu classes items according to size and quantity of bones. Open daily 11am–2pm & 5–10pm; very busy at weekends.

Kafe Raja Burger, corner of Jl Merapi and Sungai Saddang. Indonesian versions of pizza and burgers, as well as usual rice-orientated selection. Seasonally specializes in durian.

Lumayan, Jl Samalona. Bugis-run restaurant offering well-priced servings of staples such as sate, excellent grilled fish, and nasi campur.

Malabar, Jl Sulawesi 290. Indian restaurant with functional decor and no vegetable, let alone vegetarian, courses. Otherwise, a short but very tasty menu offering crisp, light *martabak* (meat-stuffed roti), aromatic sate and curries, and chicken korma or *kebuly* rice specials served noon to midnight on Friday. Fractionally more expensive than the average rumah makan.

Maxim I, Jl Sulawesi 42, corner of Jl Serui. Mid-range, sociable Chinese restaurant doing brisk trade in takeaways, and the finest pineapple chicken in Sulawesi.

Maxim II, Jl Sulawesi 78, north of Jl Serui. Expensive version of its nearby sister; some very authentic recipes, swish decor, and even chopsticks. Nice place for a treat.

Pate'ne, Jl Sulawesi. Though full of Bugis patrons and describing itself as an east Javanese establishment, the menu betrays this restaurant's Chinese ownership. Big, noisy, enjoyable atmosphere, cheap and filling fish, soup and noodle staples.

Surya, Jl Nusakambangan 16. Nothing but shellfish and rice here; great crab and mid-range prices.

Ujung Pandang, Jl Irian 42. Pricey seafood restaurant with comfortable furnishings; chargrilled fish or giant prawns are best, but staff can get pushy if they don't think you've ordered enough.

Listings

Airline offices Hasanuddin airport is the busiest in Eastern Indonesia, with flights to Maluku, Irian, Nusa Tenggara, Java, Kalimantan, and beyond Indonesia. Most airline offices open Mon–Fri 8.30am–5.30pm, Sat 8.30am–12.30pm. Garuda, Jl Slamet Riyadi 6, just north of the post office (☎0411/322543); Malaysia, ground floor of the *Marannu* hotel, Jl Sultan Hasanuddin 3–5 (☎0411/319934); Mandala, Kompleks Latanette Plaza, Jl Sungai Saddang, near the Matahari Plaza (☎0411/325592, fax 314451), to Manado and Surabaya; Merpati, Jl Hasanuddin, opposite the *Marannu* hotel (☎0411/442471), and also Jl Gunung Bawakareang 109, near *Ramayan Satrya* hotel (☎0411/442474, fax 442480), all destinations in Sulawesi.

Airport bus Between 6am and 6pm; catch the thrice-hourly Maros bus from Jl Cokroaminoto on the west side of Pasar Sentral and tell the driver you want to be dropped at the airport (Rp1500). At other times, a taxi costs about Rp10,000.

Banks and exchange Main branches of most banks are along the northern side of Medan Karebosi, and give very variable rates of exchange. BCA have good rates; the BNI, bad. Elsewhere, 24hr Cirrus/Maestro ATMs are located at the Bank Universal, about 500m south of Medan Karebosi along Jl Sudirman, and at the BNI south of Fort Rotterdam on the corner of Jl Penghibur and Jl Ali Malaka. The best moneychanger in town is Haji La Tunrung, in the building by the seafront at the southern end of Jl Nusantara.

Bookshops There's a good range of English-language novels, maps and guidebooks at Promedia, on the top floor of the Matahari Department Store on Jl Sungai Saddang.

Buses Buses for Sengkang, Parepare, Tanah Toraja and many other destinations right up to Manado leave from Terminal Panaikang, 5km east of the city; catch a pete-pete from Pasar Sentral. For the south coast, including direct buses to Bira and Pulau Selayar, use Terminal Mallengkeri, Terminal Tamalate, or Sunguminasa's bus station, all of which can be reached by red pete-pete from the northeast corner of Medan Karebosi on Jl Sudirman (Rp400).

Diving Hiu Martil (Hammerhead Shark), Jl Latimojong 150, over a pizza shop near the corner with Jl Sungai Saddang (☎0411/322368, fax 314170); and Makassar Diving, in the POPSA compound diagonally across the road from the fort at Jl Ujung Pandang 3 (☎0411/326056, fax 319842). Both operators take qualified divers on day- or weekend trips to the Speermonde archipelago, northwest of Ujung Pandang, and have tiny, difficult-to-locate offices – it's best to arrange things by phone. Rates start at US$50 for two dives, including weights, tank, boat, dive guide and food; about US$26 extra for full gear rental. There's a two-person minimum, but solo divers can join in if a group is going already. Lack of large fish is compensated by stretches of good fringing coral, plus deep walls at distant Pulau Kapoposang and a couple of World War II wrecks.

Ferries The Pelni office is at Jl Sudirman 38 (☎0411/331401, fax 331411). Tickets (Mon–Fri 8am–4pm) on ground level; top floor for timetables. Connections here to ports all over Sulawesi, plus Java, Sumatra, Kalimantan, Bali, Nusa Tenggara, Maluku and Irian.

Hospitals Stella Maris, Jl Penghibur (☎0411/854341). Your best chance in southern Sulawesi for correct diagnosis and treatment by English-speaking staff.

Immigration Jl Seram Ujung 8–12 (☎0411/831531). Officials here can be obstructive, and it's not the easiest place in Indonesia to get a visa extended.

Pharmacies Apotik Kimia Firma, Jl Ahmed Yani, and Apotik Via Farma, south of Galael supermarket on Jl Sultan Hasanuddin, are large establishments open 24hr.

Police Main office is on Jl Ahmed Yani.

Post office Jl Slamet Riyadi, southeast of Fort Rotterdam (daily 6am–6pm). Stalls outside sell postcards, envelopes and an occasional copy of the *Jakarta Post*.

Shopping Matahari Department Store, Jl Sungai Saddang, is the city's premier source of Western-style clothing, home appliances, stationery and groceries. Another good supermarket is Galael, across from the *Marannu* hotel on Jl Sultan Hasanuddin.

Souvenirs Indonesian Handicraft Centre, Jl Somba Opu 28, and Toko Mas Benteng, Jl Somba Opu 86, both have a good general stock, or try Asdar Art, Jl Somba Opu 207, Nostalgia Art's Gallery, Jl Pattimura 8 (at the north end of Somba Opu), and Toko Subur, Jl Somba Opu 114, for porcelain and ethnic artefacts.

Telephone and fax Aside from bigger hotels, there are international wartel booths on the western side of Medan Karebosi on Jl Kajaolaliddo, and also on Jl Bali, west of Pasar Sentral.

Travel agents All tour and transport bookings from Anta Express, Jl Irian 34a (☎0411/318648, fax 313910), or Sena, Jl Jampea 1a (☎0411/318373, fax 323906). Caraka Travelindo, Jl Samalona 12 (☎0411/318877, fax 318889), also organize upmarket, four- to eight-day tours to Tanah Toraja and south Sulawesi, the Bada Valley, and Minahasa.

Around Ujung Pandang

Ujung Pandang's environs could hardly be described as undisturbed, but, as few Indonesian cities this size boast extensive archeological remains, tropical islands and forests within 40km of their centres, these are something to take advantage of. A short ride south of town are the well-displayed foundations of the old Gowan port **Somba Opu**, along with royal remnants at **Gowa Tua** and **Sungguminasa**. Offshore, the sandbars and reefs of the **Speermonde archipelago** offer fairgrounds and fragmentary coral, while inland is a steep-sided, 150-kilometre-long plateau extending from Bantaeng on the peninsula's south coast to Parepare in the northwest. Surrounded by dry plains, these eroded limestone hills – ancient coral reefs, now quarried for cement – hide some unexpectedly lush pockets of scenery east of the city at **Malino** and northeast at **Bantimurung** via the town of **Maros**, also the jumping-off point for exploring Sulawesi's prehistory at **Laeng-Laeng**.

Somba Opu

Somba Opu is a former trading settlement which grew up 7km south of Ujung Pandang at the mouth of **Sungai Jenberang** as part of the Makassan coastal defences. To get there, catch a pete-pete labelled either "Cenderawasih" or "C/Wasih" from Jalan

Ahmed Yani down Jalan Cenderawasih to the **Abdul Kadir** terminus (Rp300). This leaves you by a wooden bridge spanning a river, where you can either rent a waiting becak or stroll across and ask directions for the one-kilometre walk.

At the peak of Gowa's power in the early seventeenth century Somba Opu was the largest Makassan port, a well-fortified town of several square kilometres, with warehouses stocked by traders from all over Asia, and royal residences protected by walls 7m high. Siltation has since moved the site more than 1km inland, but it was Dutch determination to break the Bugis trading empire that brought Somba Opu down in 1669, after fierce fighting. Now surrounded by vegetable plots and grazing buffalo, ongoing excavations have restored an 150-metre stretch of Somba Opu's western **ramparts**, where you can see the rammed-earth and red-brick construction and climb the reinforced corners which once supported watchtowers. Supplementing the remains, the area also incorporates full-scale **wooden replicas** of south Sulawesi architecture: a thirty-metre-long Mandar dwelling from the northwest coast stands out, raised high off the ground on posts. There's a **museum** here, too (open if the caretaker sees you; donation), identifiable by its grey-blue walls and the cannon outside. The exhibits include an ingeniously displayed aerial view of Somba Opu in its heyday, bricks decorated with animal tracks and incised patterns, Dutch musket balls from their 1669 attack, and a Gowanese spear-blade of similar vintage.

Gowa Tua and Sungguminasa

Red pete-petes from the northeast corner of Medan Karebosi on Jalan Sudirman take forty minutes to cover the ten-kilometre highway running southeast to the town of **Sungguminasa** (Rp400), passing more royal relics along the way – tell the driver where you want to go and get dropped off nearby. Some 8km towards Sungguminasa, a small signpost labelled "Hasanuddin Tomb" points east off the highway into the vanished bounds of **Gowa Tua**, Old Gowa, once the Makassan state's spiritual core. Dodging down the semi-rural lanes, you pass first the stocky, grey **Syeh Yussuf Mosque**, named after a seventeenth-century Islamic mystic whose whitewashed pyramidal tomb lies in the adjacent graveyard; bearing right after this brings you in about fifteen minutes to **Tamalate cemetery**, planted with frangipani trees and reserved for the Gowan royalty. The biggest mausoleum here belongs to the ill-fated **Sultan Hasanuddin** who died in 1670, one year after the fall of Somba Opu marked the close of Gowa's fortunes. Just east of here on a rise is **Batu Pelantikan**, the stone where Gowan royalty were crowned, while off to the southwest is **Tempat Tomanurung**, the point where the goddess Tomanurung arrived on earth to found the Gowan royal line. Conspicuously unheralded, a separate alley from the Sungguminasa road leads to a further cemetery and the tomb of **Arung Palakka**, the king of Bone (see p.800), who colluded with the Dutch to overthrow Gowa. As Hasanuddin's nemesis, Arung Palakka is understandably unpopular in Ujung Pandang, and it's something of a mystery why he was buried here, though east in Watampone – the only place where Palakka is considered a hero – they say that it was so that he could continue his fight with Hasanuddin in the afterlife.

Arrival at **SUNGGUMINASA** itself is signalled by the statue of a Bugis horseman, but otherwise there's nothing to separate this town from the rest of the suburbs that have flanked the highway from Ujung Pandang. Pete-petes terminate at Sungguminasa's bus station, from where it's a couple of minutes' walk to **Balla Lompoa**, the former **Sultan of Gowa's Palace** and now a museum (closes 2pm; free). Deprived of all real power, the Gowan state actually survived into recent times, and the last king was crowned in 1947. Built of wood in the traditional style, Balla Lompoa is only some sixty years old, but its curators take great pride in their exhibits. Antique ceremonial clothing almost crumbles under your stare, and there are documents written in angular

Makassan writing, said to have been invented in 1538 by Gowa's harbour master, Daeng Panatte. **Bugis script**, on which Makassan is based, originated a century earlier; the 23 bent and curved characters represent sounds such as *ka, ga, nga, nka*, with attached dots, circles and "elbows" modifying pronounciation. A **map** shows the Gowan view of their empire in 1660 enclosing Irian, Lombok, north Australia, and half of Kalimantan, while a **royal family tree** illustrates the tangled relationships binding the different Bugis states. Photos of the Gowan regalia – stored safely elsewhere – include a 1.7-kilogramme, solid-gold crown, while a token from 1814 provides a memento of Britain's brief occupation of Sulawesi, given by the British to Rajah Lambang Parang "in friendship and esteem & in testimony of his attachment & faithful services".

The Speermonde archipelago

While Ujung Pandang's offshore ecology labours under city garbage and the widespread practice of bombing for fish, the hundred or more islands and reefs of the **Speermonde archipelago** still have much to offer. Spread northwest of the city for 80km, there's fair snorkelling around the further islands, and **divers** should try to reach remote **Kapoposang**, where there are sharks, shallow coral in reasonable condition, and deep walls – see p.793 for dive operators. The islands are best reached by giving in to the touts and **chartering a boat** at about Rp30,000 for a half-day from the harbour opposite Fort Rotterdam on Jalan Ujung Pandang. Cheaper public ferries – except weekend services to Kayangan – are unreliable, and can leave you stranded overnight.

The two easiest islands to reach are **Lae-lae** (15min) and **Kayangan** (45min), but there are drawbacks: Kayangan sets the scene, with a tacky day-resort whose cabins are rented by the hour, loudspeakers blaring pop music, and vast throngs at weekends. Far better is **Samalona** (1hr), also popular but less tourist-orientated, despite the Rp2000 landing charge. The island itself is a bit dowdy, but the beaches are clean, and during the week you can sunbathe in peace or snorkel over patchy reef outcrops. If you'd like to spend the night, *Wisma Pulau Samalona* (⑤) has reasonable cottages. **Barang Lompo** (30min) is a partly vegetated sand islet covered with houses belonging to a fishing village; there's not much coral left, but it is anyway more interesting to have a look around this self-supporting community. The domain of local fishermen, **Kodingareng** and **Barang Caddi** have far fewer facilities but better reef, and are both about an hour away – take food and water.

Malino

Set about halfway to the top of 2560-metre Gunung Bawa Karaeng amongst a refreshing landscape of pine trees and rice-fields, **MALINO** is one of the nicer legacies of Dutch rule in Sulawesi. Originally a haunt of the Gowan aristocracy, it was the Dutch who developed the town as a popular retreat from the baking lowlands. There's early-morning transport from Terminal Tamalate or Sunguminasa (Rp2000), and the seventy-kilometre, two-hour journey from Ujung Pandang means that it's possible to make a return trip in one day, but Malino is really somewhere to unwind and spend at least a night. The weekend is best, as there's a big Sunday-morning **market** here where Malino's excellent fruit gets an airing; most **accommodation** and eating options are basic, though the *Celebes* on Jalan Hasanuddin (☎0417/21183; ⑥) offers comfortable bungalows. Malino can get decidedly nippy at night, and is often very damp, so come prepared. An easy four-kilometre walk east of town takes you to the **Takapala waterfall**, a narrow band of water dropping 50m or so into the side of a paddy-field; for something more adventurous, try the four-hour hike to the peak of Bawa Karaeng from **Appiang**, a village about 10km east of Malino. It's not a difficult trail, but it's a good idea to take a guide from Malino – ask at your accommodation place – to prevent you from losing the way between Appiang and the summit.

Maros, Leang-Leang and Bantimurung

The market town of **MAROS**, its stalls crowded with mangoes and bananas, lies about 30km northeast of Ujung Pandang, an air-con ride in the "Patas" **buses** (Rp1500), which depart three times an hour between 6am and 6pm from Pasar Sentral on Jalan Cokroaminoto – the **last bus** back to Ujung Pandang leaves Maros around 7pm. There's nothing to keep you in Maros itself, but the road to Watampone runs east across the hills from here, with turn-offs along the way to prehistoric remains at Leang-Leang, 15km distant, and waterfalls at Bantimurung (11km). The bus from Ujung Pandang leaves you near Maros's **pete-pete terminal**, where there are frequent departures to Bantimurung and far less regular services **to Leang-Leang**, both for around Rp500. If you're in a hurry to reach the latter, either charter a vehicle (at Rp10,000 an hour), or take a Bantimurung-bound pete-pete to the Leang-Leang junction and walk the rest of the way, but be aware that this involves a five-kilometre hike in the blazing sun.

LEANG-LEANG – the name means simply "caves" – is a handful of houses and a tile factory at the northern end of a valley, the flat plain planted with rice and backed by looming limestone walls. Just before the village, **Taman Purbakala Leang-Leang**, the Caves' Archeology Park (Rp200), encloses an area where thousands of years ago humans occupied a natural network of tunnels hollowed into the hillside. The first is **Pettae cave**, a small cleft decorated with red ochre hand stencils and pictures of long-since extinct wildlife; further back and reached up a ladder is the larger, bat-ridden **Pettakere cave**, whose low passage walls include more stencils and some recent graffiti – bring good shoes and a torch. Stone blades known as **maros points** found here indicate 2500 BC as a minimum date of occupation of these caves.

Back on the Maros–Watampone road, 5km past the Leang-Leang turn-off, a giant concrete monkey marks the entrance to **Bantimurung** (Rp2000), a lovely area of woodland and waterfalls where you can unwind in peace during the week or join sociable mobs scoffing ice creams and cooling off at weekends. The park is immediately damp, green and shady, with marked paths winding off along minor gorges. **Goa Mimpi** is a kilometre-long, electrically lit cavern (Rp1000; take a torch in case of power failures) right through a hillside, but the best part of the park is **Bantimurung waterfall**; steps up the side follow the river upstream to another cascade – beware of undertows if you go swimming. Aside from plentiful **butterflies**, look for kingfishers, birds of prey and dark-grey **flying lizards** (see p.838), most likely sunbathing with wings fanned out on tall trunks.

The south coast and Pulau Selayar

Along Sulawesi's agriculturally starved **south coast** people turned to the sea for their livelihood and became Indonesia's foremost sailors and shipwrights, industries still enthusiastically pursued around the village of **Tanah Beru**, with good beaches at the nearby resort of **Bira**, and peaceful, little-visited **Pulau Selayar** only a short ferry ride away. From Ujung Pandang, **buses** to Bira (5hr; Rp8000) and other south-coast destinations leave early in the morning from Terminal Tamalate, and also from Sungguminasa's bus station. If you can't find anything heading further than Bulukumba, go there first and then hop on local kijang to your destination. Terminal Tamalate is also where to find morning buses all the way to **Benteng** on Pulau Selayar (about 11hr; Rp15,000, includes ferry). Bina Bakti and Nusamukti Lestari are good bus companies; note that the ferries themselves cross from either Bulukumba or Bira, depending on seasonal winds. There are **no banks** capable of exchanging foreign currency in the region.

To Tanah Beru

An hour from Ujung Pandang, the 190-kilometre coastal road to Bira bears southeast just before the pottery centre of **Takalar** and enters the dry, chronically poor **Janeponto region**. For the next 60km or so, right through to the government offices and a huge bus station/marketplace which comprises the district capital of **JANEPONTO**, the bus passes kampung made up of eccentric wooden houses, with goats and slow-moving ponies eking out a living amongst parched hillsides tufted with corn and *lontar* palms. Extracting salt from seawater is the main industry at shoreside settlements; people seem to spend most of their days pumping water into square-sided evaporation ponds, scraping off the whitened crust and storing the finished product in roadside warehouses. Paddy-fields and fishing outriggers pulled up on beaches with furled sails soften the scenery further on around **BANTAENG**, whose mango trees shade tidy gardens – look for street signs written in Bugis characters. Comfortably shabby **BULUKUMBA** is the next town, 155km from Ujung Pandang; buses are slowed by *bendi* carts and the main square is decorated with models of Bugis prahu. **Moving on**, vehicles to Tanah Beru and Bira, back to Ujung Pandang, and north via Sinjai to Watampone leave from depots off the main square; Bulukumba's **port** is about 2km east of town, and pedestrians catching seasonal traffic to Benteng can buy tickets here. If you get stuck in town, **beds** at the basic *Sinar Fajar*, Jalan Sulthan 27 (☎0413/81068; ③), and food at *Karya Saudara Restaurant*, Jalan Sulthan 10, are acceptable.

Tanah Beru

It's about 20km from Bulukumba to **TANAH BERU**, where the landscape is far less forbidding and the atmosphere is, if not redolent of wealth, at least not of poverty either. A pretty hamlet stretching for a couple of kilometres along the beach, Tanah Beru's status as Indonesia's foremost traditional shipbuilding centre seems at first rather unlikely, but a wander soon uncovers front yards piled with sawdust, boats of all sizes lying on the sand and in the water in various stages of completion, and much carving, sawing and assembling going on underneath the palms. **Prahu** come in various **styles**, such as bulky **pelari**, used for heavy cargo, and more graceful, mid-sized **pinisi**, the form most commonly seen in southern Sulawesi. Both share unique oar-shaped and seemingly awkward side-mounted rudders, though some features have been absorbed from other cultures over the years: the *pelari*'s broad stern is modelled on sixteenth-century Portuguese vessels, and the *pinisi* shape owes quite a bit to turn-of-the-century European schooners. While still equipped with at least one mast, prahu also no longer rely solely on sails, and carry powerful engines. Until recently, vessels from southern Sulawesi used the prevailing winds to spend the year ranging east to Aru and west to Singapore; today, the main trade route has constricted to a Sulawesi–Java–Kalimantan circuit. **Construction** of a prahu is a prolonged process, the building involving no plans, only basic tools, and a great deal of superstition and ritual – including the sacrifice of a goat, whose forelegs are strung up on the stern of newly floated ships. Preferred timbers, such as the ironwood *kayu ulin*, are now in very short supply in Indonesia, let alone locally, and Tanah Beru's materials come from the Palopo district, 250km north.

Tanah Beru is a fascinating place to spend half a day, but a number of foreigners have gone a step further and actually commissioned their own vessels, planning to settle in the village for the two years or so it takes to construct an eighteen-metre hull. Locals are accommodating, but very few Europeans have the tact and patience necessary to endure both the slow pace of work set by conservative traditions, and the struggles with officialdom, which such a project entails. In his book *Makassar Sailing* (Oxford), adventurer G. Collins recounts the gargantuan efforts it took to have a prahu built at Bira during the 1930s, and, judging by the reports of Westerners living at Tanah Beru in 1997, nothing has changed. If you fancy stopping over, the Bulukumba–Bira road passes through as Jalan Sultan Alauddin, with an intersection grouped with warung and stores part way along defining the village centre. Local kijang circle here, with simple **accommodation** at the *Losmen Anda* and a backstreet market that sometimes sells dolphin along with fish of all descriptions.

Bira and around

About 15km east of Tanah Beru, **BIRA** is an unassuming group of wooden homes painted green and blue and raised on stumps. Shipbuilding is here a thing of the past, and,
though the village retains a reputation for woven cloth, there's nothing to see as such
and visitors generally continue to the powdery sand at **Paloppalakaya Bay** (also
known as **Bira beach**), 4km south. Between the two is **Panrang Luhuk**, the tiny port
for seasonal **ferries to Pulau Selayar**, which cross to the north tip of the island
around 2pm (5hr; bus to Benteng Rp11,500). A few kijangs and minibuses orbit a
Bulukumba–Bira–Paloppalakaya Bay route throughout the day.

The **beach** at Paloppalakaya Bay is a narrow strip of blindingly white sand below
which a dry headland overburdened with tourist accommodation overlooks the Selayar
Strait and tiny Pulau Lihukan. Shallow water off the beach is for safe swimming, ending in a coral wall dropping into the depths about 150m from shore. Snorkellers can see
turtles and graceful, three-metre-wide manta rays here, with exciting diving deeper
down featuring strong currents, cold water and big sharks. All accommodation rents
out snorkels and fins, and *Anda Bungalows* has scuba gear and packages for qualified
divers starting at US$60. Another way to spend some time is to rent a boat (Rp7500 a
day) and visit Lihukan, or buy a hand line in the store up the road and go fishing for
small fry – trying to catch tuna or sharks on a hand line is exhilarating, but definitely
not a relaxing day out.

Orientation is simple: the road from Bira runs past the port and straight down to the
headland, with what few services there are clustered at its end above Paloppalakaya
Bay. The pick of the cheaper **places to stay** includes *Riswan Guest House* (④), a nice
traditional Bugis house on a breezy hill-top with all meals included; *Riswan Bungalows*
(cabins ④); and *Anda Bungalows* (☎0413/82125; cabins ③). More upmarket are *Bira
Beach Hotel* (☎0413/81515; chic cabins with sea views ⑥), with a travel agent and the
only public **telephone** in the area; and *Bira View Inn* (☎0413/82043; bungalows with
ocean views ⑥). As there is virtually no fertile soil around Bira, **food** is straightforward,
but cooks try hard to vary the fish-and-rice standby or make it interesting; the clean
Melati is the sole alternative to hotel kitchens.

Pulau Selayar and beyond

A hundred-kilometre ridge pointing south towards Flores, **Pulau Selayar** has great
esoteric appeal. Planted with pomegranates, the north of the island is a stony continuation of the mainland, but there are waterfalls and patchy tropical woodlands in the
south, the latter thick enough to shelter cuscus and deer. There are some good beaches too, empty aside from long walls of bamboo fish traps, and the island is ringed by
coconut plantations and small villages, with the only settlement of any size, Benteng,
halfway down Selayar's west coast. Little is known about the island's early history,
though the **Layolo**, now found mainly in the south and interior, are said to be the oldest of Selayar's five ethnic groups. Bugis traders from Makassar introduced Islam in
1605, naming the island **Tanah Doang**, the Land of Prayer. Selayar's kingdoms paid
tribute to Gowa before its fall, when the island became a vassal state of the Sultan of
Ternate in distant Maluku; the Dutch chased the Malukkans out a century later, set up
a government post at Benteng, and tried to offset Selayar's declining cotton industry
with **copra** – still the primary, not very profitable, source of income.

Whether you cross directly from Bulukumba, or land at the north of the island from
Bira and bus down the west coast, all traffic winds up at **BENTENG**, an informal, tropical
town with a scattering of colonial-era buildings and sandy backstreets. As you'd expect, the
market between Jalan Haji Hayung and Jalan Sukarno-Hatta overflows with seafood, with
catches unloaded on the beach behind in the morning: giant cuttlefish, emperor trout and

spider shells accompany veggies and very little fruit. Indonesian speakers can arrange with boat owners for beach-and-snorkelling excursions a couple of kilometres offshore to the northern end of **Pulau Pasi**, or there are a couple of trips to be made by pete-pete or foot **around Benteng**. A half-day walk east from town takes you to **Gantarang**, a fortified village whose ancient stone walls are still maintained; the mosque here is of antique design and claims to date back to the early seventeenth century.

Benteng's main square faces east out to sea over a stone jetty, with most essentials on three parallel roads running north from here: Jalan Sukarno-Hatta along the seafront; Jalan Haji Hayung, 50m back; and Jalan Sudirman. The seldom-staffed **tourist office** is in the old Dutch controller's house, on the eastern side of the square, but a better source of **information** is Pak Arafin, at Jalan Haji Hayung 102 (☎0414/21388, fax 21813). A retired teacher who speaks English, he acts as an interpreter and organizes trips to forests, caves and waterfalls, as well as sleepovers in villages, and excursions to nearby islets for Rp40,000 a day. **Accommodation** is limited to the clean *Hotel Berlian* at Jalan Sudirman 45 (☎0414 21129; plain doubles with mandi ③); the *Selayar Beach* (Jalan Sukarno-Hatta) is closed at present. The *Berlian* can provide **meals**, but *Rumah Makan Crystal* on Jalan Haji Hayung is better, and there are also coffee houses nearby, whose patrons will be most amused to find a Westerner joining them for breakfast. Before discussing you, they'll ask if you understand *bahasa Selayar* – you could reply *soh'dhi*, "a little". **Transport** around the island is by pete-pete from behind the market on Jalan Sukarno-Hatta, with **buses** back to Ujung Pandang leaving in the morning from their agencies on Jalan Haji Hayung – there is no bus depot.

A relic of old Selayar lies 3km south of Benteng at **MATALALANG**, half a dozen buildings and a glassed-in pavilion containing a metre-high, narrow-waisted **bronze drum**. This is **Gong Nekara**, a beautiful example of Bronze Age artistry: four frogs sit up on the rim of the tympanum, while the sides are finely chased in friezes of peacocks, elephants, palm trees, birds, fish, and highly stylized human figures with plumed headdresses in a boat. Of a form typical to southwestern China two thousand years ago, when they were a symbol of aristocratic power, Gong Nekara's presence on Selayar is a mystery. Locals say that the drum was an heirloom of the local **Putabangun kingdom**, brought to the island by the kingdom's founder **Wi Tenri Dio**, a Palopo prince whose mother was Chinese. Used in rainmaking ceremonies, the drum was lost after being buried in the seventeenth century to protect it from Malukkan raiders; rediscovered in 1868, it was acquired by the sultan of **Bontobangun**, whose decaying palace is next door. The drum is plainly visible from outside the pavilion, though for a closer look keys (Rp2500) are kept at the adjacent government office, whose three staff are masters of bureaucratic delay.

A BACK DOOR TO FLORES

Around 300km of sea separate Pulau Selayar from the north coast of Flores (see pp.650–672), and it's feasible to travel the distance on local vessels, though you'll need to be patient and very flexible with both timetables and destinations. If it's simply the chance to see somewhere remote that interests you, there's marginally more traffic to **Taka Bonerate**, Indonesia's largest coral atoll. Also known as the **Macan Islands**, Taka Bonerate is about 90km due east of Selayar's southern tip, and shouldn't be confused with Pulau Bonerate, 150km southeast. Taka's main islands are **Latombu**, **Tarupa** (both with homestay accommodation) and **Rajuni**. People here make a living from collecting *trepang* (sea slugs) to sell to the Chinese; a boat from Tarupa was recently caught poaching in Australian waters. Getting to Taka Bonerate or Flores from Selayar involves waiting at Benteng until transport turns up, though there may soon be regular dive expeditions to Taka Bonerate operating from Bira and Selayar – ask *Anda Bungalows* in Bira or Pak Arafin in Benteng for the latest details.

The central kingdoms

The centre of Sulawesi's two-hundred-kilometre southern peninsula is the heart of the Bugis' world. Long split into **feuding kingdoms**, the seventeenth century saw the state of **Bone** (based around the modern city of **Watampone**) brought to supremacy with Dutch military aid, following which princes from the rival states felt a lack of opportunity at home and left Sulawesi to earn the Bugis a piratical reputation abroad as they sought plunder across the region's seas. Holland put these insurgents down with difficulty, only to see their holdings in Indonesia taken by the British during the Napoleonic wars, and then endured yet another uprising – led this time by their former ally, Bone – when they resumed ownership of Sulawesi in 1817. It took another ninety years, and the systematic routing of Sulawesi's rebel kingdoms, for the Dutch position to become secure, if only briefly. A few Bugis rulers reinstated during the 1930s became figureheads for Independence movements, first under the Japanese during World War II, then against the return of the Dutch, relinquishing their power to the Indonesian government as recently as 1955.

It's easy to soak up some of this past, even if you're just in transit through the region. While a network of Dutch-inspired irrigation canals hover in the background, the foremost targets are the historically proud towns of Watampone, from where ferries depart to Sulawesi Tenggara, and **Sengkang**, the latter set on the shores of a gradually shrinking system of **freshwater lakes**. Everywhere, you'll find local **architecture** – whether simple homes, or one of the several surviving **sultans' palaces** – is a record of the Bugis **class system**, buildings identifying their owner's status in the construction of their triangular end gables: royals' gables were divided into five sections, nobles' into four, and so on down to commoners and slaves. Roofs are also typically decorated with two upright wooden prongs known as **tandung tedong**, buffalo horns, denoting strength, calmness and patience.

From Ujung Pandang's Terminal Panaikang, it's about 150km to either Sengkang or Watampone, both routes covered by buses throughout the day. Watampone can also be reached by kijang from Bulukumba on the south coast, via Sinjai.

Watampone

Once the capital of **Bone**, southern Sulawesi's strongest state, **WATAMPONE** owed its days of glory to an alliance with the Dutch that destroyed the rival Makassan empire – though from the Bone perspective the move was justifiable. Having been unwillingly absorbed by Gowa in the early seventeenth century, Bone triumphed twenty years later under its larger-than-life leader **Arung Palakka**, one of the most vivid characters in Sulawesi's history, and a towering 2m tall. Palace politics saw Palakka forced into exile in his youth, though after returning in the 1660s he spent the rest of his life expanding Bone's empire, accumulating titles – Arung Palakka just means "Lord Palakka", the most common abbreviation of his lengthy full name – and wearing out his twenty wives in the quest for an heir. Bone remained the dominant power in southern Sulawesi for a century after Palakka's death in 1696 and, though the Dutch finally muscled in around 1905, their puppet rajah sponsored a rebellion.

Now a static, faded town, Watampone's main appeal is its history, amply illustrated in sites surrounding a small **public square** up in the old quarter. On the north side, **Museum Lapalawoi** (daily 8am–noon; donation; English-speaking guides sometimes on hand) on Jalan Thamrin is maintained by **Andi Mappassissi**, grandson of the last Bone king. Amongst more mundane silver *sireh* sets and dinner services, look for Bone's sacred sword and shield, gold wedding ornaments, a magical kris, and a document in Dutch outlining the terms of the alliance between Bone and Holland, accompanied by two interlocked iron rings symbolically representing the strength of the deal. Contemporary portraits of a long-haired, muscular and half-naked Arung Palakka are the basis of a wild **statue** outside; Palakka's five kilogramme **gold chain** is kept locked away at the **Bupati's residence** across on the west side of the square, outside of which you might see **transvestite priests** – formerly palace officials known as *waria* or *bissu* in Indonesian – teaching children traditional dance steps. About ten minutes' walk south down Jalan Sudirman and west along Jalan Sukawati, **Bola Soba** (Audience Hall) and **Saoraja Petta Ponggawae** (Palace of the King's Army Commanders) are two lifeless, well-maintained antique ironwood buildings; much more entertaining, and proving that there's more to Watampone than nostalgia, is a wander around the town's excellent **market**, down near the bus station. It's a real Arabian-style bazaar; vendors call you over to their booths and lean-to stalls to inspect Muslim prayer rugs, veggies, piles of scented, dried spices, and cones of palm sugar. A **goldsmiths' quarter** sits at the market's core, where you can see artisans making fine bracelets – and deepening the colour of poor-quality items with nitric acid.

Practicalities

Watampone's **bus station** and market area are on the edge of town, about 1km southwest of the public square. Becaks and ojeks are plentiful and not too hard to bargain with, though nowhere is too far to walk to. **Accommodation** prospects include the relatively expensive *Wisma Wisata* (☎0418/21362; doubles ⑥), fairly convenient for the bus station on Jalan Sudirman 14, but there are two better-value, more characterful options east off the square: *Wisma Bola Ride* (③ with mandi, ② without), Jalan Merdeka 8, is an airy Dutch house from 1930s with original furnishings and tiled floor; while the slightly cheaper and rather more plainly furnished *Wisma Merdeka* (③) is nearby at Jalan Merdeka 4. Running north off the northwestern corner of the square, short Jalan Mesjid offers several **stores** and **places to eat**, the best of which are good Chinese-Indonesian menus at the *Ramayan* or the *Victoria*, while the *Dynasty* cake shop is the place for a snack breakfast. There's also a **post office** near the museum on Jalan Thamrin, and a wartel on the east side of the square.

Heading on, buses and Kijang run direct to Bulukumba, Ujung Pandang, Sengkang, and Parepare, though station touts expect Westerners to be heading south and herd you towards Bulukumba-bound vehicles. **For Sulawesi Tenggara**, catch a pete-pete heading 7km east from outside Museum Lapawawoi to the port of **Bajoe** (Rp750), where you'll find a **ticket office** and a long, warped stone jetty. Three ferries daily make the eight-hour crossing to Kolaka, departing between 5pm and 9pm, with bare seats Rp7500 and padded ones in an air-con room at Rp13,700. Tickets are usually still available about ninety minutes before departure.

Goa Mampu, Sengkang and Danau Tempe

Halfway along the sixty-kilometre road between Watampone and Sengkang, the township of **Uloe** marks the turning west to **Goa Mampu**, the largest limestone caverns in southern Sulawesi. Lured by tales of the fossilized remains of a lost kingdom, **James Brooke** – later Rajah Brooke of Sarawak – investigated the caves in 1840, only to find that the statues he was hoping for were stalagmites. Split into upper and lower galleries, the encrusted rock formations are impressive in their own right, however, and you'll only need to extend your journey by an hour for a quick examination. Pete-pete or ojek make the five-kilometre run from Uloe to the caves in ten minutes, where guides with torches await your custom.

Sengkang

SENGKANG is a pretty town on the shores of **Danau Tempe**, a shallow, seasonally fluctuating lake with floating villages and a healthy bird population. Once the seat of the **Wajo kingdom**, the town is a pleasant stop on the road north, with the lake and an emerging **silk industry** to investigate, and a number of Western expats working in the gas industry stationed here. Sengkang itself is fairly functional and shouldn't take up much of your time: the kilometre-long town centre is on the east side of **Sungai Walanae** (though the river isn't visible from the main streets), which flows north into Danau Tempe. The main road zigzags south through the centre under various names, with the **bus station** on Jalan Kartini, within a short walk of all amenities. For **somewhere to stay**, *Pondok Eka*, Jalan Maluku 12 (☎0458/21296; ③), is friendly, but cheaper rooms come with unwanted vermin; *Hotel Alsalam Dua*, Jalan Emy Saelan 8 (☎0458/21278; ④), is cleaner and nicer; while higher prices and a longer walk to the *Hotel Apada*, Jalan Durian 9 (☎0458/21053; ④), are compensated by spacious grounds and aristocratic Bugis owners. Accommodation can organize **tour guides** for lake trips (something Indonesian speakers can arrange for a fraction of the cost by going to boatmen and bargaining) and tours of the silk industry – impossible alone – for a steep Rp40,000. The *Apada* also has a fine, costly, **restaurant**; otherwise, *Rumah Makan Sulawesi*, on Jalan Latain Rilai, is where to head if you arrive late looking for a beer and generous helpings of grilled fish and chicken sate. Down the hill on Jalan Mesjid Raya, *Warung Sengkang* has cheaper portions of fried chicken, plus fossils and local memorabilia in the glass case at the back. For the best *soto makassar*, try the dirty, enormously busy place next to *Warung Marodadi*, across road from the bus station. There's a wartel and BNI **bank** amenable to travellers' cheques on central Jalan Sudirman. **Moving on**, Parepare is two or more hours away, alternative roads circuiting Danau Tempe to the north via **Pangkajene**, or to the south via the attractive, bat-ridden town of **Soppeng** – after the late September harvest, look for troupes of brightly outfitted ponies carrying heavy white bags of husked rice back to villages along the roadside.

SENGKANG'S SILK

Sengkang's flourishing **silk industry** was established in the last decade with help from local officials and support from Thailand. Set up in the airy space under traditional Bugis houses, it's fascinating to follow the entire process from caterpillar to glossy sarong, but as each stage is handled by independent home industries scattered all over the town and surrounding kampung, you need a couple of hours and a guide to show you around. In the first stage, pale-green caterpillars spend three weeks chomping their way through piles of mulberry leaves, before spinning a silk cocoon. When complete, the cocoon is boiled to kill the caterpillar and dissolve the glue binding it together, then the single strand – over 1km long – is ingeniously unravelled using aubergine leaves and wound onto a spool. Spun into thread, the raw silk is tied into lengths, then dyed; in the case of *ikat* designs, the colours are painted by women dyers who work cross-legged on the floor, their brush hands permanently stained. They pass their finished work onto weavers, who might take a week just to set up an *ikat* loom, and another actually to produce a bolt of the brightly coloured tartan or chevron patterns favoured by the Bugis. The final stage is the selling, with a quality *ikat* going for Rp25,000 a metre – not cheap, but half of the price you'd pay in Ujung Pandang. Unless you know how to check quality by the way threads fray, ask your accommodation to point you towards reputable dealers, as some stores in town sell silk–rayon mixes as the real thing.

Danau Tempe

Danau Tempe and smaller lakes nearby are the diminishing remains of a gulf which once cut the southern peninsula in two. Fed by Sungai Wallanae, the lake level is capricious, sometimes flooding violently, or drying up completely, as it did in October 1997, beaching whole communities and their **floating houses**. If the water level is high enough (the lowest period is September through to the December rains), taking a brightly painted *lopi* – a dugout with an outboard – from the riverbank on Jalan Sudirman is a great way to spend a morning. Passing castnet fishermen and Bugis homes with filigree flared roof adornments and tall stilts along the river, the lake unfolds suddenly in front of the boat, a vast, open space. This is where you'll start to see Tempe's renowned **birdlife**: terns, white egrets, long-legged stilts, black ibis, spoonbills and herons all hunt food in their own fashion, some using the bamboo walls of **fish farms** as perches. These farms are Danau Tempe's equivalent of fields, the villagers first gathering huge mats of floating aquatic grasses, which attract fish with shade and food. The mats are initially contained in loose-sided bamboo pens, which are tightened up after a week or two to prevent fish escaping; trapped fish are then left to grow fat on the grasses before harvesting. In amongst all this is the floating village of **Salo Tengah**, a group of some dozen bamboo, rattan and thatch homes built on buoyant platforms of bamboo, the houses tethered as protection from shifting winds, though the whole village might move in the face of a storm or floods. These dangers are guarded against by **flags** on the roof, with yellow offering protection from flooding, white from storms, and red from fire. Tours will usually include a visit to a home at Salo Tengah, something you should not otherwise do without an invitation.

Parepare to Mamuju

With abrupt limestone escarpments in the background, the fine road running north of Ujung Pandang and Maros races inexorably up towards the Torajan highlands in the north of the province. Routes diverge some 150km along at **Parepare**, southern Sulawesi's second largest port, the point at which most people continue northeast to Rantepao and Tanah Toraja; continue northwest along the coast, however, and you'll find transport ascending from **Polewali** to the less travelled side of the highlands at Mamasa, and some unspoilt coastal scenery before the road terminates at **Mamuju**, a Mandar fishing town. **Buses** to Parepare and Polewali depart from Ujung Pandang's Terminal Panaikang at least until early afternoon, or you can also reach Parepare on local transport from Sengkang.

Parepare

Somewhat earthquake-prone, **PAREPARE** inevitably invites comparisons with its sister city Ujung Pandang, five hours to the south. Sharing similar locations on west-facing harbours, in fact the two couldn't differ more in character, and Parepare's lack of both sights and the capital's manic atmosphere make it a far friendlier spot to spend an evening mingling with the crowds. This quiet pace is slightly at odds with Parepare's position as a bottleneck for highway traffic from all over Sulawesi, and ignores the importance of the city's **port**, which connects Parepare to multiple destinations in Java and Kalimantan.

Overlooked by dry hills and with the sea immediately west, central Parepare is a small grid of narrow streets and mildewed colonial buildings with car-wheel rims sunk into the plasterwork forming decorative motifs. Jalan Panggir Laut and Jalan Andi Cammi both follow the shore, with Jalan Hasanuddin and Jalan Baumassepe parallel and further inland. Jalan Baumassepe runs south past a broad **sports field**, out of the centre, and down to the Ujung Pandang highway, while Jalan Hasanuddin bypasses the very Islamic-looking **Mesjid Raya** before becoming northern Jalan Baso Patompo. Arrival by road will land you at least 2km out of town; catch a "Balai Kota" pete-pete to the centre. The **bus terminal** is south on the road to Ujung Pandang, while transport from Sengkang or Polewali uses the eastern **Mapade** and northern **Kilometre Dua** terminals respectively. The **port** and **Pelni office** are obligingly more central on Jalan Andi Cammi, with ticket agents and blackboard schedules for alternative maritime services on Jalan Baso Patompo. Parepare's best **accommodation** is in the *Hotel Gandaria*, Jalan Baumassepe 171 (☎0421/21093; ③), a clean gem; *Hotel Gemini*, Jalan Baumassepe 451 (☎0421/21754; ③), is nearly as good. Less appealing, despite an elegant colonial exterior, *Hotel Siswa*, Jalan Baso Patompo 3 (☎0421/21374; ③ with fan, ④ with air-con), has nice staff but the budget rooms are very grubby.

The breezy seafront and harbour are picturesque in the late afternoon, with plenty of prahu and the occasional bigger passenger ferry or cargo ship in dock. Further out are huge **fishing platforms** built of giant bamboo poles, and three-pole frames with nets underneath and their owners patiently waiting above to haul in the catch. A prahu **shipyard** – mostly dealing in repairs – hides off the northern end of Jalan Panggir Laut, where there's also a popular **night market** with stocks of shoes, fruit, toys, cakes and seafood – check out tuna, shining like muscular torpedoes, and multi-hued dorado. Karaoke nightclubs and cheap **warung** dot the area, with excellent chargrilled fish and giant prawns at the black-glassed *Restaurant Asia* and less formal, open-fronted *Warung Sedap*, next to each other and opposite the *Hotel Siswa* on Jalan Baso Patompo. Sort out **money** at the BNI (with a Cirrus/Maestro ATM) on Jalan Veteran, north of the sports field; rates at the moneychanger on Jalan Hasanuddin aren't especially good, but they're open late, closing briefly for evening prayers. Your accommodation can advise on **onward transport**; as an alternative to slogging out to the terminals, some services can be hailed as they pass through the centre, and night buses to Ujung Pandang and Tanah Toraja accumulate around the *Hotel Siswa* in the afternoon.

Polewali, Majene and Mamuju

Northwest of Parepare, the coastal road and buses continue for 250km via Polewali and Majene to Mamuju, with ambitious dreams afoot to stretch the bitumen all the way through to Palu, in Sulawesi Tengah. Two hours from Parepare, **POLEWALI** is the administrative capital and springboard for the **Mamasa region** (see below); the town's unfocused amenities cluster in two separated satellites, though all essentials are in the southern section, where the highway runs through as Jalan Ahmed Yani. Here you'll find warung and the fair-value *Hotel Melati* (☎0428/21075; ③), diagonally opposite where transport departs for Mamasa.

Pinched between steep mountain sides and the sea, the coastal road beyond Polewali traverses the beautiful homeland of the **Mandar**, who, like the more outgoing Bugis, are famed shipbuilders and fishermen. They have a capital of sorts in the small town of **MAJENE**, whose sea wall and attached boatyards are worth a wander, with pre-Islamic **graves** sporting unusual headstones in the nearby village of **Cillallang**, and beds at *Wisma Cahaya* (☎0422/21105; ③) on Jalan Rahman. Beyond Majene, the seascapes continue to where the best part of the road evaporates at **MAMUJU**, though few find the scenery an adequate reason to make the long haul to this hot, disappointing backwater town.

Mamasa and around

Cocooned in a cool, isolated valley 1200m up in the mountains above Polewali, the **Mamasa region** – also known as **Western Toraja** – comes as a pleasant surprise. A landscape of terraced hills and rice terraces make for fairly easy hiking along narrow paths to a huge number of traditional villages, most of which feature extraordinary architecture and noticeably friendly people. Though culturally similar to their eastern neighbours in Tanah Toraja – for more on whom, see pp.807–818 – Mamasa is a far poorer district and its heritage is much lower-key; consequently, the hordes of foreigners are absent, and the area is welcoming without catering overly to mass tourism.

The only settlement of any size in the valley is **Mamasa**, reached either along a two- to four-day hiking trail from Tanah Toraja (see p.814) or **by road** from the coast via Polewali, covered by buses from Ujung Pandang and Rantepao. Vehicles also originate in Polewali itself, leaving whenever full; opt for a bus if possible, as minibuses are very cramped, and mechanically on their last legs. The 95-kilometre road is steep and sometimes closed by landslides but otherwise fine, and the trip from the coast takes five hours on a good day.

Mamasa

MAMASA is a spacious village of wooden houses beside Sungai Mamasa, where electricity and telephones still very recent arrivals. The **marketplace** and most amenities are along Jalan Ahmed Yani, with everything else – homes bordered by roses and hibiscus, a few stores selling bananas, soap powder and chillies, and a coffee-roasting plant – scattered around the perimeter of a large and unkempt **football field** where dogs and stunted horses sport in the morning. A **mosque** sits in the shadows between the market and river, but Mamasa is predominantly Christian, and a white stone **church** dominates the slope above town; from up here Mamasa's few score buildings sit on the edge of a sprawl of paddy-fields and bamboo thickets. The twice-weekly **market** on Thursday and Sunday is Mamasa's sole organized entertainment, but it's a good one, with people from distant hamlets often dragging their wares – including the heavy, boldly coloured **sambu blankets**, for which Mamasa is famed – into town on horseback. Locals know what Westerners will pay and seldom haggle, even if you hike out to the villages where the blankets are made: coarser blankets cost about Rp35,000, and better examples are Rp50,000. To see some older pieces – including cloth from India, once regularly imported by coastal Bugis and believed to have influenced some local designs – *Losmen Marapan*'s owner has a small **museum** of Mamasan antiquities.

Budget **accommodation** includes *Losmen Gereja*, the church guest house (②), a nice, bare couple of bungalows down near the river on the northern side of town; and *Losmen Marapan* and *Losmen Mini* (both ③), offering cosy rooms in old wooden houses near the market on Jalan Ahmed Yani. The *Marapan*'s drawback is that it's in line of fire of the mosque. Slightly more upmarket, *Mantana Lodge* (④), around the corner from the market on Jalan Emy Salean, is good value with larger rooms, though the tiling can make it cold at night. For **food**, *Mantana*, *Marapan* and *Mini* serve Indonesian meals as good as any in town; *Rumah Makan Pada Idi*, between the *Marapan* and *Mini*, has coconut chicken or sates of low cost and unpredictable quality (it's sometimes excellent), while two warung dealing in coffee and cakes complete Mamasa's gastronomic possibilities. **Leaving**, there's transport back to Polewali every day, and to Ujung Pandang or Rantepao most days; your accommodation can find out departure times and arrange a pick-up, or organize **horses and guides** for the trail to Tanah Toraja.

Mamasa trails

Walking trails surround Mamasa, allowing for hikes of anything between a couple of hours and three days or more. Most involve a bit of legwork, as villages are set on isolated hillocks surrounded by terraced fields, all linked by muddy footpaths. Scenery aside, one of the big attractions here are **traditional houses**, similarly covered in carvings and adorned with buffalo horns like those in Tanah Toraja. Lacking the extreme roof angles and bamboo tiles typical of buildings further east, a few are large and clearly very old, adding immense character to the villages they adorn. Elsewhere in the fields, look for seemingly purposeless bamboo **windmills**, and ingenious water-driven mechanisms for scaring birds from crops.

Home-made **maps** available in Mamasa – *Losmen Marapan*'s, for instance – are useful indicators of paths between villages, but don't distinguish between easily discernible tracks and those completely invisible without local knowledge. Some trails return to Mamasa, others terminate south of town at various points along the Polewali road, such as the open-air **hot springs** 3km south of town at **Mese Kada** – looking like a grubby swimming pool, but somewhere to relax with locals after a hard day out. Bemos run in both directions along the Polewali road (not all go as far as Polewali) at least until mid-afternoon, though you may have to wait a while. For day-trips you'll need footwear with a good grip, a torch, something to keep the rain off, food and drink, and a packet of cigarettes to share around; biros are good gifts for children, though they always ask for money or sweets. There are a few **campsites** if you plan to stay out overnight – in which case you'll need a pullover to keep out the chill – though it's more interesting to negotiate accommodation with locals.

The Loko circuit

There's a great four-hour **circuit from Mamasa** via **Loko**, involving much cross-country tracking. From Mamasa, aim across the river for **Tusan**, a cluster of unexceptionally traditional thatched houses about fifteen minutes from Mamasa's market. A shed on the far side of the village provides panoramas south down the valley, distant mountains looming black and grey, peaks fringed in forestry plantations. Past here are some newish graves and two churches, before **TONDOK BAKARU**, whose wobbly houses are said to be the oldest in the valley. The most interesting is towards the far end of village, a much-patched and restructured home under a twenty-metre roof covered in ironwood shingles – a sign of status – with elaborate, if weather-worn carved panels of buffalo, geometric patterns, and birds.

Bearing left into a creaking bamboo grove after Tondok Baru, follow a path downhill, across a covered bridge, then uphill again to **Rantebonko**. At this point the Loko trail simply vanishes into the fields, and you'll need continual help to know which of the instep-wide tracks to follow. But it's worth the effort: **LOKO** perches like an island on a hill-top, with fields dropping straight off the eastern side into the valley, sacrificial stones fronting its heavily carved houses, buffalo horns adorning their front posts. A patch of lawn acts as a **campsite** just outside Loko, and a trail leads 8km west from the village to where **Mambulillin waterfall** tumbles off the hillside. Alternatively, continue south from Loko to **Taupe**, but the track is in no way clear and has some exhausting, if short, gradients. **TAUPE** itself is not that engrossing, though there's a huge new meeting hall and a good lookout point. From here, there's a further 5km of cross-paddy weaving to the Polewali road via **Asango**, or a direct trail **back to Mamasa** which fizzles out midway, leaving you to chose your own path down the river, over an extremely basic bamboo bridge, and into town behind the market.

Around Rante Balla Kalua

Mamasa's most-celebrated *sambu* weavers live southwest of town around the village of Rante Balla Kalua. Start by taking a bemo 9km down the Polewali road to **RANTE SEPANG**, where you'll see women working away on looms under the houses; cross Sungai Mamasa over a good suspension bridge and follow the path uphill for ten minutes to simply ornamented homes at **Sumua**. A kilometre further on, past **Tumangke**, a half-dozen **house graves** face west towards the hills – simple open wooden frames with aluminium roofs covering burial mounds, and strewn with offerings of cigarettes, betel nuts and bottles. Though these graves are traditional in style, one with carved images of the deceased, others display crucifixes. At this point the path bears right to **RANTE BALLA KALUA**, a large village of fifty or more homes surrounded by tall trees at the upper end of a small valley; among thatched dwellings of split rattan and bamboo is a row of three fine old houses and accompanying rice barns adorned with buffalo horns, pig-jaws stacks, and drums. Weavers or their agents will find you, invite you to sit down and start bargaining, but are easy enough to refuse if you're not interested. A short walk downhill leads to more of the same at **BATARIRAK**, where you can stay in one impressive old building with dozens of ancestor carvings and horns. At this point there are two alternatives to backtracking simply to Rante Sepang: either spending ninety minutes – if you don't become thoroughly lost – following the usual obscure rice-field course northeast to **Lumbatu**, where a further hour will take you across to the Polewali road at Asango; or a similar length of time for a nice trail southeast of Batarirak, via more graves and buffalo-horn-bedecked houses at **Buntu Balla**, and back to the Polewali road some 14km from Mamasa at **Pena**.

Rambu Saratu and on to Tanah Toraja

Mamasa's easiest trek follows the vehicle road for 3km north from town to alternative accommodation and a splendid traditional house at Rambu Saratu, past postcard-pretty scenery of vivid green fields and mountain slopes receding into blues and greys. After about half an hour you'll see a turning west across the river to **Kole** and the valley's premier **accommodation** at *Mamasa Cottages* (⑥), whose **hot springs** are technically guests-only – though staff are generally so engrossed in TV that they're unlikely to notice you. Another ten minutes and you're at **RAMBU SARATU** (also known as **Rante Buda**), a name meaning something like "a hundred possibilities", referring to the number of interconnected families in this village. The main building here is magnificent, easily the finest traditional house in the whole Mamasa district: the body is 25m long and the roof – supported by a huge pole where it stretches out over the forecourt – extends this considerably, with every possible space on the front wall intricately carved. The interior is partitioned into a small front room for greeting guests (look up and you'll see some odd antiques stashed in the rafters) opening into sleeping quarters and kitchen. Visitors are often encouraged to spend the night here by the caretaker and his wife, who speak some English.

Beyond Rambu Saratu, there's a **hiking trail** 70km east **to Bittuang** in **Tanah Toraja**, possible either simply on foot or using ponies to help carry your gear – not really necessary. The walk spreads comfortably over three days, with regularly spaced kampung along the way growing used to the trickle of foreign faces, the homestays charging around ③ for room and board. Following the road north past Rambu Saratu to **Timbaan** (26km from Mamasa), most of the first day is spent climbing steadily through pleasant rural scenes against a backdrop of low terraced hills, though the last 8km after **Pakassasan** features a pass through the range with patches of forest. The next day follows the trail across two rivers (with a good swimming spot 13km along at the second) before a steep stretch to **Paku** (50km), while the final day enters pine plantations east of Paku, crosses another pass, then descends to the trailhead at **BITTUANG** (66km). Here you'll find more basic accommodation, a further two-day hiking track north to **Pangala** (see p.817), or a daily bemo for the forty-kilometre run to **Makale** (p.809).

Tanah Toraja

Some 250km north of Ujung Pandang, a steep wall of mountains marks the limits of Bugis territory and the entrance into the highlands of **Tanah Toraja**, a gorgeous spread of hills and valleys where fat buffalo wallow beside lush green paddy-fields and where the people enjoy one of Indonesia's most confident and vivid cultures. Ostensibly Christian, trappings of the old religion are still an integral part of Torajan life: everywhere you'll see extraordinary **tongkonan** and **alang**, traditional houses and rice-barns, while the Torajan social calendar remains ringed with exuberant **ceremonies** involving pig and buffalo sacrifice. Nor, even in a brief visit, is all this difficult to explore, as Torajans are masters at promoting their culture, positively encouraging outsiders to experience their way of life on its own terms. With easy access, Tanah Toraja is planted firmly on the agenda of every visitor to Sulawesi, though tour groups tend to concentrate on key sites and it takes only minimal determination to find more secluded corners and spend an afternoon chatting, or days hiking, in places that see far fewer Western faces.

Tanah Toraja's main towns are the district capital of **Makale**, and larger **Rantepao**, 18km further north along the Sungai Sadan valley. Rantepao's range of services make it the favoured base for tourists, the bulk of whom descend for the major **festival season** between July and September, though the only really quiet time is from February to perhaps May. Expect hot days and cool nights; there is a "dry" season between April and October, but this is relative only to the amount of rain at other times, so bring non-slip walking boots and a waterproof jacket or umbrella. **Moving around**, there are endless opportunities for hiking between villages, and a range of roads and vehicles spanning out across the hills above Makale and Rantepao, though surfaces tend to be rough and travel's rather slow.

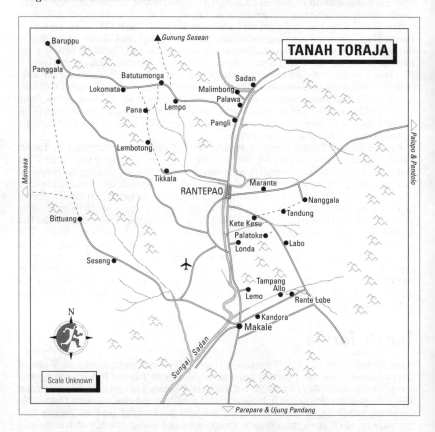

THE TORAJANS

Anthropologists place Torajan origins as part of the Bronze Age exodus from Vietnam; Torajans say that their ancestors descended from heaven by way of a stone staircase, which was later angrily smashed by the creator **Puang Matua** after his laws were broken. These laws became the root of **aluk todolo**, the way of the ancestors, which at its most basic divides the world into **opposites** associated with **directions**: north for gods, south for humanity, east for life, and west for death. Rather than an overall Torajan state, each kampung had its own hereditary leaders (**class** remains markedly important in Torajan society), and achieved fame through the ferocity of its blowpipe-toting warriors. Fortified villages were positioned on hill-tops as protection against **raiding parties** seeking heads and captives – the latter kept as slaves or sacrificed at funerals.

Not entirely isolated from the outside world – the need for coffee and slaves fuelled lasting trade, intermarriage and warfare between the Torajans and Bugis – Tanah Toraja managed to avoid contact with Europeans until the twentieth century. Then in 1905 the Dutch ordered Sulawesi's leaders to recognize Holland as their sovereign state, treating any refusals as a declaration of war. Torajans were amongst the many dissenters, the warlord **Pong Tiku** of Baruppu holding out for two years before being captured and executed. The new rulers introduced Christianity, which has proved increasingly popular since the 1970s, though if you've just spent the day visiting freshly built tongkonan or at a funeral watching buffalo being sacrificed, it seems at first that *aluk* still underpins Torajan life. In fact, only a fraction of Torajans now follow the old religion, the strict practice of which was prohibited after headhunting and raunchy life-rites proved unacceptable to colonial and nationalist administrations. Though **to minaa** – the Torajan priesthood – still set the agricultural calendar and officiate at ceremonies, festivals have been largely stripped of their religious meanings to become social events, a chance to display wealth and status and reinforce secular rather than spiritual ties.

Getting to Tanah Toraja

Tanah Toraja is known as **Tator** in the local idiom, and you should look for this on transport timetables. Daily Merpati **flights** from Ujung Pandang to Makale are very unreliable, and the surest way to Tanah Toraja is by **bus**, with Makale and Rantepao connected to points all over Sulawesi. From Ujung Pandang, buses leave day and night from Terminal Panaikang, the good road and range of coaches making the eight-hour journey fairly comfortable. First following the lowland plains, the road starts climbing about 70km north of Parepare at aptly named **ENREKANG** (Place to Ascend): not only does Sulawesi's highest peak, **Bulu Rantemario**, rise 3455m to the east, but this is also the site of the mythical celestial stairway linking the earth to the heavens – the remains are now known as "Porn Mountain" from the shape of its rock formations. Sixty kilometres further on, the road levels out at Makale before heading up along the Sadan valley for the final 18km to Rantepao.

Makale and around

MAKALE is a small town studded with churches and administrative offices set around a large pond and public square. Jalan Merdeka enters from the south into the square, while Jalan Pong Tiku exits north from the pond towards Rantepao; a sprinkling of monuments include a model of the Eiffel Tower welcoming the ubiquitous French package groups to Tanah Toraja, and an equine statue of Pong Tiku. Every six days, Makale's large **market** fires up after about 9am, drawing people from all over southern Tanah Toraja to buy pigs, jerry cans of palm wine and other necessities. Long-distance traffic continues to Rantepao and there's little reason to stop overnight here, but if you fancy a change or simply miss the last bemo onwards at some point, Makale's **accommodation** includes the inexpensive *Losmen Litha* (③) right on the square on Jalan Pelita (also the agent for **buses back south**), and better-value *Wisma Bungin* (③) on Jalan Pong Tiku; up near the mosque, the nasi campur-orientated *Idaman* is the cleanest **place to eat**. Moving on, **bemos** to Rantepao and other destinations – including **Bittunag**, trailhead for the three-day walk west to Mamasa – leave the square whenever full between dawn and dusk. Makale's **airport** is 5km northwest at **Rantetaya**, and taxis for Makale or Rantepao meet flights; Merpati's office is in Rantepao.

Villages along an eight-kilometre road **east of Makale** offer a quick introduction to Tanah Toraja, and are far less visited than better-known sites between here and Rantepao. A couple of kilometres from Makale, look for **hanging graves** and the remains of a hillfort of doubtful vintage on cliffs at **KANDORA**, while a track leading north after some 5km leads to some oddly shaped **megaliths** at **RANTE LOBE**, and more hanging graves with **tau-tau**, statues of the dead, at **TAMPANG ALLO**. For more about these features, see "Touring Tanah Toraja", pp.814–818.

Rantepao

RANTEPAO is a prosperous market town on the rocky banks of **Sungai Sadan**, home to both the Sadan Toraja and, for half the year, swarms of foreigners. However unfavourably you view this, Rantepao has excellent facilities and local contacts, while a couple of sites within walking distance will keep you interested for as long as it takes to orientate yourself and decide in which direction to head off into the countryside. And while you're doing this, the town offers intrinsically Torajan scenes: chilly mornings with men wrapped in blankets and shivering, smoking furiously; smartly dressed women with Bibles tucked under their arms off to church on Sunday; teenagers gathering in single-sex groups under streetlamps in the evening, watching each other furtively. West of the exhibition grounds and away from the couple of main streets, stalls supply locals' day-to-day needs – heavy stone rice mortars, plastic chairs, noodles, fish (couriered up from the coast by motorbike every morning), fresh noodles and tempeh, and chillies, with a warung or two for fried bananas and coffee. Further south, there's a **football pitch** off Jalan Mederka, and games seem to have taken up where warfare left off – weekend matches draw huge crowds, whose victory roars and cheers of encouragement can be heard kilometres away. Rantepao's main **market** – the biggest in Tanah Toraja and located 2.5km northeast of the centre at Terminal Bolu – is a must, even if they usually bore you; where else could you pick up a bargain buffalo then celebrate your purchase with a litre or two of palm wine? As at Makale, it operates on a six-day cycle, and an entry fee of Rp2000 is demanded of foreigners – you could argue the point that you're there to buy, not sightsee. Around the edge of the market are various woodcarvers and carpenters, also worth a look; one specializes in ornamental buffalo heads, another in parts of rice barns.

An easy hour's **walk from Rantepao** follows Jalan Singki west across the river, and then bears right into the fields along the Sadan's west bank. Across the paddy, hamlets such as **Pa'bontang** are marked by stately tongkonan, but look for where a white mausoleum at **TAMBOLANG** stands below a cliff-side niche sporting rows of tau-tau and coffins. It's all a bit it neglected, but perhaps this is more "authentic" than other sites which have been smartened up for tourists. A path leads briefly south from here and then climbs through woodland to the summit of **Bukit Singki** and a view over Rantepao; the top – the remains of a lookout post of Pong Tiku vintage – is terraced in dangerously loose stones, and planted with cassava and papaya.

Arrival, orientation and information

Rantepao stretches for 1km along the eastern bank of the Sadan, just where the river bends sharply in from the east to flow south down the valley. The central **crossroads**

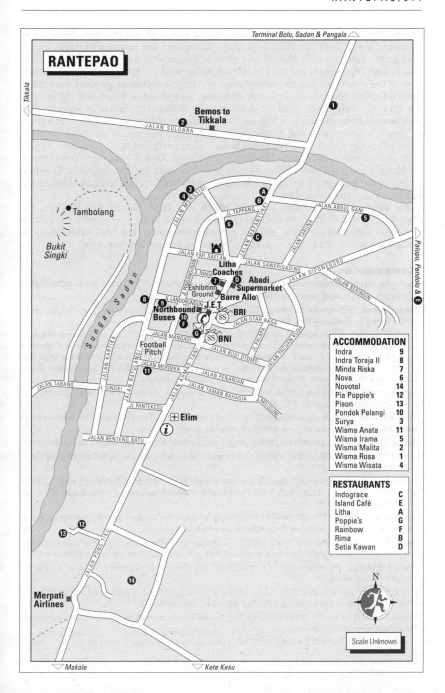

are marked by a miniature tongkonan on a pedestal: north from here, Jalan Mapanyukki is a short run of souvenir shops, bus agents and restaurants; Jalan Ahmed Yani points south towards Makale past more of the same to become Jalan Pong Tiku; east is Jalan Diponegoro and the Palopo road; while westerly Jalan Landorundun heads over to the riverside along the bottom edge of a large **exhibition ground**, covered in forlorn-looking ceremonial platforms. **Arriving**, long-distance buses will either drop you off at accommodation, or in the vicinity of the exhibition ground or crossroads; likewise **bemos** from the south or Palopo. Bemos from northern and northwestern parts of Toraja, however, may well terminate either on Jalan Suloara, immediately north of town across the Sadan, or at **Terminal Bolu**, 2.5km northeast from the centre. People walk everywhere around town, but bemos leave Jalan Ahmed Yani every few minutes for Makale, and just as often from riverside Jalan Mongsidi for Terminal Bolu. **Leaving**, long-distance bus agents surround the centre, with Jalan Andi Mapanyukki becoming one long bus station after dark.

For **information**, Rantepao's **tourist office** is at Jalan Ahmed Yani 62 (Mon–Fri 8am–4pm; ☎0423/21277), on the Makale side of town. Many tour agents and restaurants with guide services also give out general information, but don't expect them to divulge the venue of a festival unless you've agreed to buy their services.

Accommodation

Rantepao's **accommodation** is varied, plentiful, and scattered all over town, often down side-lanes you'd otherwise overlook.

Wisma Anata, Jl Merdeka 15 (☎0423/21356). Welcoming, slightly run-down guest house, quiet except during football matches. ④.

Hotel Indra, Jl Londurundun 63 (☎0423/21583, fax 21547). Chain of three closely grouped mid-range hotels, whose room prices and standards rise the closer you get to the river. *Indra City* offers a good deal (⑤); *Indra Toraja I* (⑥) and *Indra Toraja II* (⑦) are overpriced considering what this will get you elsewhere, though the latter has nice riverside rooms and a garden, Torajan dance nights, and a treasure trove of paperback novels in various languages.

Wisma Irama, Jl Abdul Gani (☎0423/21371). A big tiled place, clean and with huge garden, bordering budget to mid-range prices. ⑥.

Wisma Malita, Jl Suloara 110 (☎0423/21011). Extremely tidy, well-run backpackers' haunt; rooms come either with shared mandi, or with their own hot water. ③–④.

Minda Riska, Jl Niaga 18 (☎0423/25290). New, central place with decent singles and doubles. ④.

Nova, Jl Tappang (☎0423/23320). Rather grubby and with no frills, but cheap and popular with budget travellers. ③.

Novotel, off the Kete Kesu road about 3km south of Rantepao (PO Box 80, Rantepao; ☎0423/27000, fax 21666). The height of luxury; full-sized tongkonan "chalets", swimming pool, and tennis court overlooking rice-fields. ⑧.

Pia Poppie's, Jl Pong Tiku 27 (☎0423/21121). One of Rantepao's older upmarket offerings: quiet, comfortable and nicely placed at the southern boundary of town. ④.

Pison, Jl Pong Tiku 8 (☎0423/21221, fax 21344). Across from *Pia Poppie's* and fairly similar; ordinary rooms set behind a nice spacious courtyard with rice barn to sit under in the afternoon. ③.

Pondok Pelangi, Jl Pengangunan 11 (☎0423/21753). Central, backstreet homestay, a little bit cramped but fair value. ④.

Surya, Jl Mongsidi (☎0423/21312). Along with neighbouring *Wisma Wisata* – and a fraction better – this is one of the nicest homestays in town and often booked out. ③.

Wisma Rosa, Jl Sa'dan 28 (☎0423/21075). Elderly place with a small garden and faded, comfortable rooms. ③.

Wisma Wisata, Jl Mongsidi 40 (☎423/21746). Plain cabins overlooking a small garden and stretch of river. ③.

Eating, drinking and entertainment

Rantepao spoils you for **food**, with everything from market snacks – try *soko* for breakfast, rice steamed in banana leaf, shredded coconut and *sambal* – to warung and restaurants serving reasonable Western fare. Most places along Jalan Ahmed Yani and Jalan Andi Mapanyukki cater exclusively to tourists, stay open late, and can produce Torajan specialities such as *papiong* (meat grilled in bamboo tubes), *mengrawang* (sate) and *bale tongkonan* (fish cooked in banana leaves), with a couple of hours' warning. Torajans have two favourite beverages: locally grown arabica **coffee**, and **balok**, or palm wine, both a vital part of the daily routine. *Balok* is traditionally sold frothing in bamboo tubes, though the festival season sees markets stocked with five-litre jerry cans to keep up with demand, and its flavour – somewhere between lager and Alka-Seltzer – is actually quite encouraging.

Eating aside, Rantepao offers little nightlife. **Bars** such as the *Tiku Linu*, upstairs above the souvenir shops on Jalan Andi Mapanyukki, have loud music and are popular with Torajan youth, and foreigners who venture in are made welcome. Rantepao's cinema closed down years ago and they're still awaiting a replacement, possibly up at the main market – ask around for the latest.

RESTAURANTS

Indograce, Jl Andi Mapanyukki. Inexpensive Chinese food in spacious and bright surroundings, and the coldest beer in town, but the glass front makes it a bit like a goldfish bowl.

Island Café, 3km north of Rantepao past Tallunglipu ("Pangli" bemo). Riverside open-air restaurant with a mix of Indonesian and pricey Western dishes.

Litha, Jl Andi Mapanyukki. Good food, particularly Torajan items, and some of the lowest restaurant prices in town, but staff regard customers as a nuisance.

Poppie's, Jl Ahmed Yani 117. Dingy lighting and high prices, but the menu is good, including Torajan, Indonesian, Chinese and European items – the only place in Sulawesi you'll see Wiener schnitzel on a menu.

Rainbow, at *Pondok Pelangi*, Jl Pengangunan 11. Slow service, but a fine kitchen; try the garlic beans and chewy buffalo sate. Inexpensive.

Rima, Jl Andi Mapanyukki. Low priced Indonesian and Torajan menu, and their chicken with lime sauce is something to write home about. Waiters doubling as guides can be a bore about pushing their services.

Setia Kawan, Jl Andi Mapanyukki 32. Slightly pricey Indonesian-Chinese place, but the roomy, cool setting makes it a favourite spot for Westerners to sit for an hour over a coffee or cold drinks and peruse the newspapers.

Listings

Airlines Merpati are in a high-rise shack about 1.5km south of Rantepao, the last building on the western side of the road. There's no computer link here, and confirmations are rendered extremely unreliable by a static-inhibited radio link with Ujung Pandang. Your accommodation place can organize transport to the airport, about 13km southwest.

Buses For Parepare and Ujung Pandang, use Litha, across from the Abadi supermarket on Jl Andi Mapanyukki, who run basic, comfortable and luxury buses (daily 7.30am–9pm). Departures north to Pendolo, Tentena, Poso and Palu are handled by a small depot just west along Jl Landorundun. Mamasa buses come and go with demand; anyway, there is no vehicle road directly between Rantepao and Mamasa, and Tator–Mamasa buses travel via Parepare and Polewali.

Guides If nobody else you meet offers their services, accommodation, tour agents and some restaurants can all organize guides from around Rp40,000 a day. *Rima* restaurant has a mafioso-like clique who get very defensive if they find you've visited a ceremony with anyone else, but can be good otherwise.

Hospital The best doctors are at Elim Hospital, Jl Ahmed Yani.

Maps Travel Treasure Maps put out a very colourful and useful "Tanah Toraja" sheet, showing distances, villages, important sites and giving heaps of local information. The Abadi supermarket or *Setia Kawan* restaurant are the cheapest places to buy a copy.

Money The BRI and BNI on Jl Ahmed Yani offer good exchange on currency and travellers' cheques (but ignore their seldom-updated display boards), and most tour agencies and larger hotels can change money. Rantepao's official moneychangers are not reliable, however, often renegotiating rates or revealing substantial service fees after you've signed your travellers' cheques.

Pharmacies Rantepao's pharmacies, on Jl Andi Mapanyukki, have very old stock.

Post office Jl Ahmed Yani. Daily 7am–6pm.

Souvenirs Shops on the eastern side of exhibition grounds along Jl Andi Mapanyukki offer carefully aged items clearly made for the tourist market – model tongkonan, bamboo flutes, local necklaces and headbands in orange, black and white beads, plenty of porcelain and coins, plus *ikat* and sarongs from Flores and Bali. Barre Allo has locally made knives with fine wooden scabbards and hilts, and also the best carvings, including panels salvaged from old buildings, worth a look even if you don't want to buy.

Telephone and fax Rantepao's exchange on Jl Ahmed Yani opens 8am–late. Toraja Permai Tours and Travel, next to the Abadi supermarket on Jl Andi Mapanyukki, are useless as a tour agent but have good phone rates for local and international calls.

Tour agents Best of the many available operators is JET, Jl Landorundun 1–3 (☎0423/21145, fax 23227).

Touring Tanah Toraja

There's a morbid attraction to many of Tanah Toraja's sights, which feature ceremonial animal slaughter, decaying coffins and dank mausoleums spilling bones. Fortunately, the people and landscape are very much alive, and there's nothing depressing about spending time here, nor are these key sights obligatory viewing. There's a good deal to be said for just picking somewhere on the edge of the map and hiking off into the distance. Torajaland's sixty-odd villages make it impossible to give a comprehensive rundown on the area, though almost all have tongkonan and rice barns, and you might find yourself at any number of otherwise insignificant places if a funeral is in progress. View those listed below simply as a starting point, and note that **entry fees** of a few thousand rupiah are becoming common at sites around Rantepao. If you overdose on landscape and culture, try a three-day trekking and **white-water rafting** excursion through the 1500-metre-deep Sadan Gorge with Sobek Tour (Torango Buya, Jalan Pongtiku, Rantepao; ☎0423/21336; US$285 inclusive). About half the trip is spent on the water, shooting twenty sets of rapids.

One of the decisions in Tanah Toraja is whether you'll need a **guide**. If you speak a little Indonesian they are seldom necessary for hiking or visiting villages, though outsiders should really have an **invitation** to visit a ceremony, which guides with connections can provide. As more participants means greater honour, however, it's also possible to turn up at an event and hang around the sidelines until somebody takes it upon themselves to act as your host. Guides can add considerable depth to the sights, but they vary in quality; almost all, however knowledgeable, are pushy over gifts for themselves and can be irritatingly self-aware, churning out a mash of semi-anthropological interpretations. With luck, you'll meet people during your stay who will offer to show you around as a friend.

Bemos to just about everywhere originate at Rantepao's Terminal Bolu, though those heading south can be hailed on Jalan Ahmed Yani. While it's possible to flag down a constant stream of bemos on the Makale road, you may find only one a day heading to remote corners such as Baruppu, so the further you're going, the earlier you should start looking for transport. Accommodation and tour agents also rent out **bicycles** (Rp7000 a day), **motorbikes** (Rp30,000), or **minibus and drivers** (Rp60,000) if you don't want to rely on public transport. **Hikers** heading off to villages should carry cig-

CEREMONIAL RITES AND WRONGS

Witnessing a traditional ceremony is what draws most visitors to Tanah Toraja, particularly during the "peak festival season" in the agriculturally quiet period from June to September. The atmosphere at these events is very sociable, and Torajans are tolerant of crowds of Westerners invading proceedings with long lenses poking all over the place, but there are some things to bear in mind. Take a **gift** for your hosts – a carton of cigarettes, or a jerry can of *balok* – and hand it over when they invite you to sit down with them. Gift-giving is an integral part of Torajan ceremonies, an expression of the reciprocal obligations binding families and friends, and close relations of the hosts may contribute a brace of buffalo or pigs. Do not sit down uninvited, or take photos without asking (though permission is invariably given); dress modestly, and wear **dark clothing** for funerals – a black T-shirt with blue jeans is perfectly acceptable, as are thong sandals. Most importantly, spend **time** at any ceremony you attend, as too many tourists just breeze in and out, bored by the long lulls in the proceedings. Instead, use them to play cards, drink coffee and *balok*, and just gossip with your hosts as *papiong* pop in the background. In this regard, small affairs are more intimate and rewarding, though large funerals are certainly splendid.

Ceremonies are divided into *rambu tuka*, or **smoke ascending** (associated with the east and life), and *rambu solo*, **smoke descending** (west and death); all *rambu tuka* events begin in the morning, while the sun is rising, and *rambu solo* start after noon, when the sun is falling westwards. A typical *rambu tuka* ceremony is the **dedication of a new tongkonan**. Tongkonan design is credited to Puang Matua, the upcurving roof symbolizing the shape of the sky – though, as an example of how modern Torajans have reinterpreted their beliefs in the light of anthropology, some say that roof shape derives from when ancestral Torajans used their overturned boats as shelter when they first arrived in Sulawesi. It would be hard to overstate the tongkonan's symbolic importance: for example, they face north, so the front door is a gate between human and divine worlds, and are aligned north–south, defining a borderline between life and death. **Carved panels** of patterns, cockerels, buffalo, horses and birds all have their own meanings, as do the red, black, white and yellow **colours** used. And, if nothing else, a traditionally built tongkonan is a sure sign of wealth – even the simplest costs upwards of thirty million rupiah – and the lavishness of its dedication is a further indication of its owner's prestige: the ceremony is called **mangrara banua** if just pigs are sacrificed, and **merok** if buffalo are involved. Lasting a single day and not a huge event compared with a funeral, the dedication of a noble's house nonetheless draws a big slaughter and crowds.

The biggest of all Torajan ceremonies are **funerals**, the epitome of a *rambu solo* occasion. Known as **aluk to mate**, funerals are performed to send the spirit of the deceased (which remains near the body after death) to **Puya**, the Torajan afterlife. The scale of the event is determined by the dead's class, and – what with financing the event and the need to assemble relatives from afar – invariably takes place long after death. Spread over several days, the ceremony is held in a special field, with purpose-built spectator accommodation erected around the perimeter, and two platforms or towers facing each other at either end, all decorated in gold, red and yellow trim. The funeral starts with the moving of the oval coffin from the south room of the deceased's house – where it will have lain since death – and parading it with much jostling and shouting to the platform, where photos of the dead are displayed. Pigs and **buffalo** provided by close family are trotted out too, and later dispatched to feed guests. Torajans measure their wealth in buffalo, spend hours every day grooming and washing their animals, and might save up for years to buy a really fine one – much-coveted piebalds cost eight million rupiah or more. At the end of the first afternoon you'll see **buffalo fights**, *mapasi laga tedong*, where, amid much discreet betting, the buffalo are led up to face each other, heads raised and turned aside as if in scorn. Then they charge suddenly, spectators going wild and running in as close as possible before the loser turns tail and gallops off to whoops and jeers, scattering the crowd. Northeast of Rantepao buffalo fights are followed by the all-male pursuit of

sisemba, Torajan kick boxing, where pairs hold hands, using each other as pivots to execute cartwheeling kicks and belt the living daylights out of their opponents. Kicking the fallen is forbidden, but otherwise there are no "illegal" moves and injuries are common.

The following day – or days, if it's a big funeral – is spent **welcoming guests**, who troop village by village into the ceremonial field, led by a noblewoman dressed in orange and gold, bearing gifts of *balok*, pigs trussed on poles, and buffalo. Formal introductions make everyone – including the tax inspectors at the gate – aware of how many people have come and what they've brought, thereby increasing the respect being paid to the deceased. **Ma'badong singing** starts up at some point, with a group in black forming a ring, and chanting a soulful song as they sway and move in a slow rotation, the ring growing as others mourners join in. The day after all the guests have arrived, the **major sacrifice** takes place: slaves can get away with just one buffalo, but the nobility must sacrifice at least 24, with 100 needed to see a high-ranking chieftain on his way. Horns decorated with gold braid and ribbons, the buffalo are tied one by one to a post and their throats slit, the blood caught in bamboo tubes and used in cooking. Dogs prowl and flies swarm as the heads are stacked up and the meat hacked into chunks and distributed to guests, the *to minaa* calling out names and throwing pieces down from the second platform. Finally, the coffin is laid to rest in a west-orientated house-grave or rockface mausoleum, with a **tau-tau**, a life-sized wooden effigy of the deceased, positioned in a nearby gallery facing outwards, and – for the highest-ranking nobles only – a megalith raised in the village **rante ground**.

arettes, if only to initiate conversations along the way. Many places are close enough for day-trips, or at least to catch a bemo out to and hike back, though you'll also find a few homestays around the countryside, or you may be offered private accommodation – in which case, it's polite to offer further small gifts.

Rantepao to Makale

Tanah Toraja's most famous sites lie off the eighteen-kilometre Rantepao–Makale road, worthy attractions despite the flow of tourists. Just south of Rantepao, a concrete statue of a pied buffalo marks the four-kilometre road east to four much-restored tongkonans at **KETE KESU**. The central one is said to be the oldest in the district, and it's a fine spot to get a first close look at the structure and decoration of tongkonan and alang, built facing each other as "husband" and "wife". An adjacent rante ground sports a dozen megaliths, the tallest about 3m high, with a path leading up the hill past hanging and no-longer-hanging coffins mortised into side of the truncated peak. Some coffins are shaped as animals, with fallen skulls and bones artfully arranged, and tau-tau of various vintages are protected by a grille in a suitable overhang. Less-visited sites beyond Kete Kesu include views from the clifftop village of **PALATOKE** (9km from Rantepao), whose hanging graves are said to have been positioned by a race whose gecko-like hands allowed them to climb up here without ladders.

Back on the Makale road, a signpost at 5km prompts you east towards **Londa**, a fifteen-minute walk from the highway. A shaded green well underneath tall cliffs, overhung with a few coffins and a fantastic collection of very lifelike tau-tau, Londa boasts two **caves** whose entrances are piled high with more coffins and bones, all strewn with offerings of tobacco and booze. **Guides** with pressure lamps (Rp3000) are a necessity for venturing inside the bat-ridden labyrinth, where tunnels slippery with guano weave off into the earth.

At around 7km from Rantepao, a trail heads up to a **swimming hole** in the forest at **Tilangnga**, a refreshing target on a hot day. Around halfway to Makale, another road runs 1km east to **LEMO**, past a church curiously designed in the shape of a boat. Lemo is famous for the sheer number of its much-photographed tau-tau, set 30m up on a flat cliff-face; they're not as sophisticated as those at Londa but more expressive, mutely staring over the fields with arms outstretched. There are also several dozen square-doored mausoleums bored straight into the rock face, a type of burial site more common further north and said to be a comparatively recent innovation.

East to Nanggala, and north to Sadan

If you're pushed for time, you can see almost all the main features of Torajaland at **MARANTE**, a spread-out village 6km east from Rantepao on the Palopo road. Close to the road are a fine row of tongkonan, one with a monumentally carved dragon's head out the front; behind, a path leads to where tau-tau and weathered coffins face out over a river – some of the coffins are large and very old, adorned with dragon and buffalo motifs. **NANGGALA**, about 11km along the Palopo road and then 2km south, is a stately village whose dozen brilliantly finished tongkonan are a splendid sight. There's a very pleasant five-hour walk due west to Kete Kesu from here, via **Tandung** village, patches of pine forest and a couple of small lakes.

For something a bit different, spend a day making the slow haul from Rantepao's bemo terminal **north to Sadan**. Seven kilometres along the way you pass **PANGLI**, famed for its *balok* and home village to the great nineteenth-century Torajan chief, **Pong Massangka**. Not much further, a rante ground with thirty upright stones marks the short track to **PALAWA**, a well-presented village whose tongkonan are embellished with scores of buffalo horns stacked up their tall front posts, while in the hills beyond the village are **babies' graves**, wooden platforms in the trees. Five kilometres more brings you to a fork in the road: east is **SADAN** itself, with another market every six days; west is riverside **MALIMBONG**, famous for its **ikat** (see p.550), which you can watch being made.

Northwest to Batutumonga, Pangala and beyond

The area northwest of Rantepao surrounding **Gunung Sesean**, the region's highest peak, is quite accessible but not overly explored, and different in feel to the Torajan lowlands. There's a smattering of morning traffic about 17km to Lempo; the road climbs through semi-cultivated forest out onto hill terraces scattered with coffee bushes and house-sized boulders, some hollowed into mausoleums with heavily carved stonework around the doors. **LEMPO** has a great series of moss-ridden tongkonan; there are views off the three-kilometre road between here and Batutumonga, with **accommodation** in the area providing the perfect rural base. Before Batutumonga, a sign on the roadside points to basic bamboo rooms at friendly *Mama Siska's* (③ including meals); *Mentirotiku* (④), a little further along and right on the road, is a smart, pretentious affair with an expensive restaurant overlooking the valley, and cosy accommodation in tongkonan or cabins. Around the corner is **BATUTUMONGA** itself, comprising a school, a church with tongkonan-like roof, the necessary football pitch, village stores, and further comfortable cabin/tongkonan **homestays** at *Londurunden* (③) or *Mama Rima's* (③).

Gunung Sesean's 2328-metre **summit** can be reached in a couple of hours from Batutumonga; your accommodation place can point you to the nearest trails, which lead sharply up through a smudge of forest and onto open heath. All tracks converge at a south-facing ridge overlooking the Sadan valley and Rantepao far below, then continue climbing through the heath before plunging into thickets. The first peak brings you suddenly into the open again and is a splendid spot to stop, with swifts wheeling above your head and the main peak on your left usually tufted in cloud. It's another steep half-hour from here to the summit, with more vistas and a cliff dropping vertically away at your feet. Another fine walk from Batutumonga can take you **back to Rantepao** in under four hours; take the road through Batutumonga until you see about thirty small megaliths in a ring, then follow the footpath opposite downhill. This brings you to a hamlet where you'll have to turn sharp right across the fields to where a broader trail continues down to woodland at **PANA**, the site of some very old, well-camouflaged graves, and a big rante ground with four-metre-high megaliths. From here the track onwards is unmistakable – you may even find bemo to Rantepao, but it's worth walking. Not far along the road is **Lembotong**, a kampung famed for its **blacksmiths** – look for roadside forges ringing with hammering, the finished products hung up for sale out front. The remainder of the walk down to the flat fields below is less interesting, and you end up at **TIKKALA**, a nondescript spread of homes where you'll find bemos for the seven-kilometre ride back to Rantepao's Jalan Suloara.

The rest of the road northwest of Batutumonga is harder to cover. Six kilometres from Batutumonga, a massive boulder along the roadside at **LOKOMATA** has become an apartment building for the dead, with about sixty mausoleums. It's another 15km from here to **PANGGALA**, the last place you could reach on scheduled public transport from Rantepao (about 3hr). A nice mountain village, there's well-organized **accommodation** and information available at *Wisma Sandro* (③), with a two-day hiking track south to Bittuang on the Mamasa trail (see p.805). Ask for directions to Pong Tiku's **tomb**, rumoured to be nearby; his last stand against the Dutch was at the end of the road at **BARUPPU**, where remains of his fort can still be seen. The Dutch brought in cannon, which made short work of the Torajan defenders, who had only spears and tubes full of crushed chillies to spray into the faces of anyone scaling the walls. One story says that Pong Tiku escaped from Baruppu, but was later ambushed by the Dutch while attending his mother's funeral. He was executed in Rantepao in 1907 – shot while bathing, says one tale, the only time he was without his magically bulletproof clothing.

Sulawesi Tenggara

The province of **Sulawesi Tenggara** is joined to the rest of Sulawesi by a crumpled mountain range that makes overland access impossible. South of the mountains, the flatter end of the peninsula breaks up into some sizable islands, the largest being **Muna** and **Buton**. Muslim since the early seventeenth century, much of the region was governed by the powerful **Sultan of Wolio**, whose formidably defended royal complex survives at **Baubau** on Pulau Buton. Elsewhere, you'll find an undercurrent of pre-Islamic belief, which becomes tangible in rural areas such as **Mabolo** on Pulau Muna, where expressive **cave paintings** illustrate pagan times. There's also some scenery and an underpatronized wetlands national park to soak up in passing, but for **scuba divers** Sulawesi Tenggara's ultimate destination lies southeast of Pulau Buton where the land fragments further into the Banda Sea as the **Tukangbesi group**, whose reefs are amongst the best in Indonesia.

The province's only **airport** is at its capital, **Kendari**, with a daily Merpati flight from Ujung Pandang. For around a tenth of the airfare, it seems sensible to travel by **ferry** from Bajoe (Watampone) to Sulawesi Tenggara's western port at **KOLAKA**, and then catch a Kijang for the 120-kilometre ride to Kendari – about a twelve-hour journey in all. But though the ferry crossing is none too bad, landing at Kolaka in the early hours of the morning to be loaded into the back of a suicidally driven kijang for a five-hour ride is an experience to avoid. As alternatives, Kendari, **Raha** (on Pulau Muna) and Baubau are viable ports with regular Pelni and freighter traffic to Ujung Pandang and up Sulawesi's eastern coast. Getting around, there's surprisingly good access throughout the province on local Kijang and bemos, with a daily air-con speedboat moving both ways between Kendari, Raha and Baubau. Food and accommodation are generally more **expensive** here than elsewhere in Sulawesi, and **currency exchange** is only possible in Kendari and Baubau, where it's a prolonged process – try and bring enough to see you through.

Kendari and around

Five hours by road from Kolaka on the eastern side of the mainland, **KENDARI** is Sulawesi Tenggara's largest settlement, though there's little of substance here. The city stretches along **Kendari Bay** with its two centres – western **Pasar Mandonga** and eastern **Kota** – linked by a seven-kilometre main road, which changes its name at every opportunity. Pasar Mandonga consists of a market, a cluster of businesses and a bemo terminal south of a large main-road **roundabout** along Jalan Silondae; Kota comprises a kilometre or two of the main road, with key services and another market, culminating at Kendari's **port**. If you don't arrive here, the **airport** is forty minutes southwest of Pasar Mandonga, and waiting taxis charge about Rp10,000 to anywhere in Kendari. **Kijangs from Kolaka** drop off about 8km west of Pasar Mandonga at **Puwutu** (Terminal Kolaka), where bemos frequently depart to town. Fixed-fare bemos run continually between Pasar Mandonga and Kota through the day, though the absence of clear orientation points along the main road makes finding destinations confusing at first – tell bemo drivers exactly where you want to go.

Accommodation places are spread all over Kendari. In Kota, the pick of the town's accommodation is *Hotel Cenderawasih*, where terrace units overlook the bay at (main road) Jalan Diponegoro 42 (☎0401/21932; air-con doubles ⑤, triples with fan ④; all rooms with mandi). Also in Kota, *Hotel Hamdamin* (③), on a hill above the port on Jalan Tekaka, is the cheapest place in Kendari likely to take foreigners, though it takes some finding and a walk from the main road. West of Kota on the main road, *Kendari Beach Hotel*, Jalan Hasanuddin 44 (☎0401/21988; ⑥), offers cavernous, quietly mouldering, overpriced rooms, but its very reasonably priced **restaurant** and terrace bar are fine places to while away a sultry evening. Set back from Pasar Mandonga's traffic circle, *Wisma Duta*, Jalan Silondae 1 (☎0401/21053; ③), has bungalow-style rooms with a small garden, though cheaper rooms are poor value. For somewhere **to eat** in Kota, try the *Ayam Goreng* on main road Jalan Sukarno: a typical, open-fronted Chinese place whose manager spends most of his time at his desk playing with a mountain of cashew nuts. Pasar Mandonga's options include the *Aden* on Jalan Silondae – for sit-down coffee and cream cakes, sponges, and sticky Bugis treats such as *lempar*, a mix of sago, palm sugar and coconut – and the *Marannu*, a flash and expensive Chinese restaurant also on Jalan Silondae.

Most of Kendari's **services** are in the Kota end of town, where on Jalan Hatta you'll find the Telkom office, BNI **bank** (foreign exchange Mon–Fri 8.30am–2pm), with a Cirrus/Maestro ATM, and local cashew nuts, pearls and hand-woven cloth at Citra Permai, diagonally across the road from Telkom. For more of this, as well as the gold and silver **filigree jewellery** for which Kendari is famed – undeniably skilful work, though ugly – visit Toko Diamond Kendari, opposite the market on Jalan Silondae at Mandonga. Helping out with advice on less well-known locations, the **provincial tourist office**, Dinas Parawista, is 2km south of Pasar Mandonga, just off Jalan Ahmed Yani at Jalan Tepau Ningu 2 (Mon–Thurs 7am–2pm, Fri 7–11am; ☎0401/26634); ask for English-speaking Dr Burhanuddin.

Leaving Kendari, **ferry tickets** for Pelni and Andhika Express, who operate the daily Kendari–Raha–Baubau service, are available at numerous agents near the dock. There's also a twice-weekly **ferry to Wangiwangi** in the Tukangbesi group (p.822). The Merpati office is near the docks at main road Jalan Sukarno 85 (Mon–Sat 7am–4pm, Sun 7am–2pm; ☎0401/21896), and can organize a shared taxi to the airport. Also on Jalan Sukarno, Cahaya Ujung have **night buses** through to Watampone.

Around Kendari

Kendari may not require much of your time, but with a spare day it's worth making the tedious journey 65km southeast of town to the delightful **Air Terjun Moramo**, where a river cascades from a small plateau over a series of limestone terraces, each forming natural swimming pools surrounded by teak forest. A couple of shelter sheds and week-end stalls are the only artificial intrusions; get there by taking a bemo from Pasar Mandongo 3km south to Pasar Baru, change vehicles for **Lapuko**, and there rent a bemo or ojek for the last 15km to Moramo. An hour offshore from Kendari, **Pulau Hari** – the Island of Sun – has a fine beach and splintered reef, the best place to check out local marine life; boats can be chartered by the day from the wharf 100m west of Kendari's port, and are not bad value for two or more people.

Requiring far more advance planning and determination to visit, those with a yen for the great outdoors should consider exploring the peat swamps and forest at **Rawa-Aopa national park**, roughly 70km west of Kendari by road. This is the only place in southern Sulawesi you can see anoa, though crocodiles, snakes, monkeys and birds are more likely to cross your path. You need at least three days, must be prepared to travel by foot and canoe through the park, and to pay for a **guide** and **permit** from Sulawesi Tenggara's forestry department – Kendari's tourist office can make all the arrangements.

Pulau Muna: Raha and around

It takes about two and a half hours to make the crossing from Kendari to **RAHA** on **Pulau Muna**, the ferry travelling due south between steep, thinly vegetated headlands as it follows the deep blue channel. First impressions of Raha are of the sun blazing down on a shadeless **jetty**, and a small town with half the animation of a Mexican border post during siesta; nor is there much to experience here once everybody has said "hello mister" to you a dozen times. From the jetty, Jalan Sudirman and a cluster of shops are immediately south, while Jalan Ahmed Yani runs 1km north along the seafront, past a couple of colonial-era buildings and a **post office**, to Raha's market and **bemo terminal**; look here for vehicles to sites around Raha. A small office opposite the bemo terminal sells **ferry tickets** for Kendari and Baubau, and can advise on the availability of berths aboard the single Pelni vessel to call here. Raha's **accommodation** is fair value, but check first on screens and nets in your room as mosquitoes are a problem. *Hotel Tanti*, off Jalan Sudirman at Jalan Sutomo 18 (☎0403/21168; ③), has spotless rooms with fans, shutters and mandi; *Hotel Alia*, Jalan Sudirman 5 (☎0403/21218; ④), is a similar, motel-like affair; while *Hotel Nappabale* overlooks the sea on Jalan Ahmed Yani (☎0403/21276; ④). All the **places to eat** are along Jalan Sudirman, and include *Rumah Makan Nikmat*'s single table and (quite good) take-it-or-leave-it menu, plus a variety of Chinese dishes in the back of the *Hawaii* general store and inexpensive grilled fish with peanut sauce and soup at *Cahaya Pangkap*.

Lagoons and caves

Fortunately, Raha's surroundings compensate for the town. Sunday is the big day for families to picnic and teenagers to get drunk 15km south of Raha at the exquisitely toned **Nappabale and Motonunu lagoons**. Encircled by forest, swimming is safe here and canoes can be rented by the hour to paddle over the water into a low-ceilinged **tunnel** connecting the two lagoons. It's a fine day out – but for a glimpse under the everyday skin of Sulawesi Tenggara pay a visit to **Liang-liang Mabolu** (Mabolo Caves) a journey which begins at the kampung of **MABOLO**, half an hour west of Raha. Bemos go this way fairly regularly, but make it clear if you don't want to charter a vehicle because drivers at the terminal will assume you do. At Mabolo, take your pick of the trails behind the houses on the south (left) side of the road; the paths themselves are clear, but there are many to chose from, so keep asking directions or hunt around for guides. Hike through a Muslim **cemetery** – note the stalactite headstones – and then off under the shade of sprawling groves of **cashew trees** (*menta*), whose nuts are hidden under a swollen, purple-green, cyanide-laden husk. You emerge into an open countryside of scrub and dry-stone walls separating the brown fields between villages, an abundantly poor area whose porous soil makes water a critical concern during the dry season, when children spend their days staggering out to public tanks on the main road with jerry cans.

Soon the path weaves between an increasing number of ever-larger, rough-sided limestone hillocks; look for the first **paintings** on a hillside on your right, a clear group of **horses** with one human figure, perhaps holding a sword. Horses were a vital part of life in pagan times on Muna, and ritual horse-fighting is still performed in villages around Raha. Press on from here to the minuscule whitewashed mosque at **Kampung Liang Kabori**, where elderly **Pak Lahadha** waits in ambush to escort foreigners to the caves. The first of these, **Liang Toko**, is perhaps 20m deep and 15m high, floored in boulders covered with green algae, and has some large ochre paintings of three more horses, fat and clearly male, being ridden by small human figures. Around the other walls are more people, **ships**, and what look like sun symbols, with these themes repeated around the corner at **Liang Kabori** – look for two human figures with taloned hands and feet. A couple of **shrines** at the caves point to a religious significance which has survived Islam.

Pulau Buton and the Tukangbesi group

At over 150km long, **Pulau Buton** is the largest island in all Sulawesi. Its northern end is heavily forested and there are villages steeped in animist tradition, where children run screaming at the sight of foreigners, but a lack of roads effectively limits exploration to the vicinity of the southern city of **BAUBAU**. Especially if you've worked you way down through Kendari and Raha, Baubau's size, order and sense of purpose is unexpected: this was the seat of the **Wolio Sultanate**, whose founder, Wakaka, was a grandson of Kublai Khan. Here, as on the mainland, the seventeenth century was portentous: Islam arrived; an invading army led by the Dutch East Indies governor general, **Antony van Dieman**, was beaten off; and Arung Palakka of Bone sought sanctuary on Buton while fleeing the wrath of Gowa's Sultan Hasanuddin, whose forces were defeated here by the Dutch in 1667. The Wolio line proved resilient, and, though Baubau became the seat of a Dutch controller in the nineteenth century, the sultanate survived until 1960.

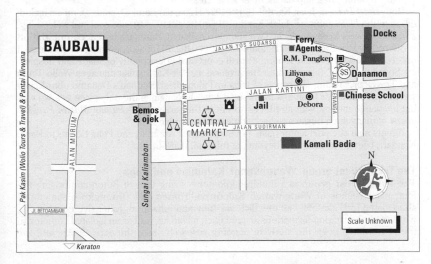

Baubau's centre, a busy dockside area, makes for a good wander past the few century-old European-style buildings along Jalan Kartini, where the solid **jail** and more refined shutters and arched windows of the former Chinese school at the corner of Jalan Kenanga stand out. Back off Jalan Sudirman, **Kamali Badia** is a wooden three-tiered Bugis palace dating back to the 1920s, and would have been impressive in its day, though it's now run-down. About 500m further west off the end of Jalan Sudirman, Baubau's **central market** is all you'd expect given the city's position on trade routes between Java and Maluku: a tight square of busy stalls selling imported fruit and veggies, spices from the Spice Islands, gold, silk, ships' chandlery, and locally cast **brass-ware**. When you've had a sniff around, catch a bemo or ojek from the market 2km south to Baubau's **Keraton**, the largest and most impressive pre-Dutch construction in Sulawesi. This was Wolio's stronghold, an entire hill-top citadel ringed by 3km of stone walls, now fully restored, where the sultan, his wives, family and servants all lived. You'll need a good hour to circuit the walls, past rusting cannon (some stamped with the VOC logo), and to check out the various royal tombs and dwellings, which include **Benteng Wolio**, the last sultan's home and now a museum with period furniture, heavy wooden decor, and family paintings. The most obvious landmark up here is a lichen-covered "**flagpole**" of unknown provenance, though it looks like the mast and crow's-nest of an eighteenth-century European vessel. Next to this is a square-sided, blue-and-white stone **mosque** dated to 1712, the oldest unrestored example in Sulawesi; while opposite is the neat, two-storey controller's house. **Outside town**, the most popular place to unwind, sunbathe and snorkel (though the reef is a long way offshore) is the sandy **Pantai Nirwana**, about 11km west – again, catch an ojek or charter a bemo from the market.

Baubau practicalities

The Kendari–Raha ferry and Pelni vessels stop at Baubau's north-facing **docks**, with the town centre immediately west. Jalan Yos Sudarso runs along the waterfront, paralleled by Jalan Kartini and Jalan Sudirman; Sudarso and Kartini join up near the market to cross a small iron **bridge** over the narrow **Sungai Kaliambon**, and then curve south in the direction of the Keraton as Jalan Katamso. Five hundred metres along, Jalan Katamso is crossed by Jalan Betoambari, which heads west again in the direction of Pantai Nirwana. Ojek and becak meet all ferries.

Both *Hotel Debora*, Jalan Kartini 15 (☎0402/21203; ekonomi ④, suite ⑤; meals included), and the *Hotel Liliyana*, Jalan Kartini 18 (☎0402/21197; ③), are cool and welcoming, and a short walk from the dock. Two kilometres distant, Baubau's best **accommodation** is offered by Pak Kasim Jalan Betoambari 92 (☎0402/21189; ③), evening Bugis meals if ordered, whose fine house around a small courtyard offers plenty of shade and hospitality. Styled "Notaris" (lawyer) after his profession, Pak Kasim also manages Wolio Tours and Travel, organizing all aspects of trips to Tukangbesi. Baubau's Danamon **bank**, just west of the docks off Jalan Yos Sudarso on Jalan Kenanga, is the only place in town willing to change money, with all **places to eat** in the same area – *Rumah Makan Pangkep* is one of many such businesses, serving excellent grilled fish.

Agents near the port along Jalan Yos Sudarso sell Andhika and Pelni tickets to Raha, Kendari, Ujung Pandang and beyond, at minimal mark-ups.

The Tukangbesi group: Wangiwangi, Kaledupa and Hoga

The **Tukangbesi group** is a hundred-kilometre string east of Buton comprising the four major islands of **Wangiwangi**, **Kaledupa**, **Tomea** and **Binongko** – sometimes abbreviated to Wakatobi – all of which are hilly and inhabited. Extensive **coral reefs**, which include fringing formations around each island, as well as an isolated complex to the south, have been the study of ongoing research since the early 1990s, and the

Tukangbesi group have recently been drawing a steady trickle of scuba enthusiasts willing to put up with simple living and prolonged travel in order to pioneer diving in this largely unexplored area. Whether you travel via Baubau, or catch the Kendari–Wangiwangi ferry, it's best to organize everything in advance with Wolio Tours and Travel in Baubau – see opposite for details.

From Baubau, there's a daily 4am bus (picks up from accommodation) to the port 70km east at **Laselimo**, where a ferry takes ninety minutes to reach Wanci on Pulau Wangiwangi. WANCI is a large fishing village with the distinctly average *Losmen Samudra* (③), but you should arrive in time to catch a smaller barge onwards to **Pulau Kaledupa** (4hr), where you'll find a few toko and homestay accommodation. From here, ask at the docks for an outboard-driven "johnston" to run you across to **Pulau Hoga**, about five square kilometres of sand, scrub and coconut trees five minutes east of Kaledupa. Assuming you've already arranged things, you can stay in **cabins** here (known as *Wakatobi Dive Resort*; ④ all-inclusive), snorkel and dive the nearby reefs, and visit the **Bajau fishing village** of **Sampela**, raised over the sea on stilts between Kaledupa and Hoga. It's worth bearing in mind that the return journey to the mainland takes two days, with a night in Wanci, as the Wanci–Baubau ferry leaves first thing in the morning, before you arrive from Kaledupa. The direct Wanci–Kendari ferry runs twice a week, but the crossing can be very rough, so it's better to travel the long way round via Baubau.

SULAWESI TENGAH

Though the peaks are of no great height, **Sulawesi Tengah** – the island's second largest province, and one which includes Sulawesi's physical centre as well as parts of the northern, and all of the eastern, peninsula – is almost completely covered in mountains, terrain made all the more impenetrable by what survives of its forests. As the influence of Portugal, Holland and Ternate waxed and waned down on the coast, Sulawesi Tengah's highlands remained more remote than those of Toraja or Minahasa, whose inhabitants were at least aware of the outside world: the **Mire** people of the eastern peninsula had their first contact with foreigners in 1992, when a mission aircraft spotted huts in the jungle. Even the road from southern Sulawesi is barely a decade old, and local infrastructure remains minimal. Nonetheless, there's superlative **hiking** through two wilderness reserves: **Lore Lindu**, where you'll encounter the remains of a vanished megalithic culture, and **Morowali**, domain of the nomadic Wana. Stay on the main roads, and you'll experience little of the highlands beyond the backdrop surrounding **Danau Poso**; instead, your view of this otherwise landlocked region will be confined to the coast, where a five-hundred-kilometre road follows the southern line of **Tomini Bay** between the easterly provincial capital, **Palu**, the transport hub of **Poso town**, and western port of **Luwuk**. None of these should slow you down for long, though out in the bay itself the **Togian Islands'** seascapes lull almost everyone into extending their stay, besides providing a stepping stone into Sulawesi Utara.

There are daily **flights** from Ujung Pandang and Manado to Palu, and plenty of public transport into the province from Ujung Pandang or Rantepao via the coastal towns of Palopo and Wotu. Arriving from the north you will most likely land at either Poso or on the eastern peninsula at **Pagaimana**, both terminals for ferries from Gorontalo. In theory, it's also possible to travel by road down the north peninsula from Gorontalo to Palu or Poso, though even in ideal conditions this is at least a two-day ordeal. Once here, you'll find that long-distance buses seldom stop except at main towns, and between these points it's always easier to make use of short-range minibuses and Kijangs.

The Poso Valley: Pendolo and Danau Poso

The highway from southern Sulawesi winds up into the ranges at **Mangkutana**, buses taking a couple of hours to reach a sign welcoming you to Sulawesi Tengah before the road starts a downhill run into the hundred-kilometre-long **Poso Valley**. Domain of the **Pomona**, a Christianized offshoot of the Torajans, the valley's flooded upper reaches form **Danau Poso**, drained by a river that flows out of the top end of the lake past **Tentena** and follows the valley north to the coast at **Poso town**.

Set on the lake's sandy southern shore and pretty well bang in the centre of Sulawesi, the village of **PENDOLO** is a practical spot to break your journey – it's a long haul whichever direction you're heading in. Nicely insubstantial, the village comprises just a few houses, a market, and a large church where the highway kinks around the lake, with a scattering of low-profile **accommodation** stretching a kilometre or two to the east. The best places to stay in Pendolo itself are *Pondok Wisata Victory* (③) and *Pondok Masamba* (③), which both enjoy beachside locations on Jalan Pelabuhan; further east, *Pendolo Cottages* (③) has nicer wooden cabins with balconies facing north over the water. All supply filling meals and advice on boat rental and hiking around the lake. **Moving on**, minibuses leave early for Mangkutana (where you can find more of the same to Palopo), or Tentena – trying to flag down long-distance buses heading beyond these points is a waste of time. The road north is tortuous, however, and unless the weather is rough you're better off catching a morning **ferry** across the lake to Tentena in three hours. Seasonal water levels dictate which of Pendolo's two **jetties** are in use; one is in the town, the other 2km east near *Pendolo Cottages*.

Some 35km long, **Danau Poso** fills a 450-metre-deep rift between two mountain ranges with clear-blue water, the shoreline a mixture of steep rock faces, and sandy bays backed by forest. There are rough trails along both sides of the lake, though the main Pendolo–Tentena road stays well clear of the eastern shore, and you'll need to venture out onto the water to appreciate the scenery fully. Some accommodation has basic snorkelling gear for you to goggle at crabs, eels and fish, and is also where to ask about renting a boat (around Rp10,000 an hour, depending on horsepower) for broader explorations. A good trip to the western shore takes in **Bancea reserve**, famed for the quantity and variety of its **orchids**; there's a fifteen-kilometre, five-hour hike back to Pendolo from here, or you could continue across the lake to **TOLAMBO**, a fishing village with nearby caves, a waterfall, and beaches patrolled by wading birds.

Tentena and around

Surrounded by clove, cocoa and coffee plantations, **TENTENA** sits right where the lake empties into Sungai Poso through a V-shaped barrage of eel traps. A scruffy Christian town, which perks up for three days of dancing and boat races during the annual **Danau Poso festival** in late August, Tentena's character is salvaged by its location and services, besides being a necessary staging post for transport west to **Gintu** at the southern end of Lore Lindu national park. As at Pendolo, exploring the lake is the main pastime, but make sure you also spend half a day at **air terjun Salopa**, an enchanting **waterfall** up against the hills 15km west of town. If you don't want to rent a minibus through your accommodation place for Rp40,000 – not a bad deal if you can get a group together – catch a bemo from the far side of the bridge for the twenty-minute haul to **Tonusu**, then walk the last 4km through fields and groves of fruit trees festooned with the zigzag climbing stems of vanilla orchids. Entry into the forest is sudden; there's a caretaker here who takes your Rp1000 admission fee and gravely requests that you sign his book before pointing you along the path to the falls. Alive with butterflies and birds, these tumble for over 4km down the mountain range, the pale-blue, lime-rich waters glazing rocks and sculpting pools. Unofficially you can spend the night here, sheltering in a tent or using one of the tumbledown wooden huts at the base of the falls; come prepared for damp conditions and bring a fuel stove rather than counting on finding firewood.

Everything you'll need in Tentena is in a close grid of streets on the eastern side of covered, well-maintained **Pomona Bridge**. Next to the bridge you'll find a **post office**, market and shops, with most **places to stay** south of here off Jalan Yos Sudarso. Inexpensive options in the vicinity include basic but clean beds at *Pondok Remaja* (③), on Jalan Sudarso, and *Moro Seneng* (③), just around the corner on Jalan Diponegoro; in a higher bracket, helpful management and airy rooms make *Hotel Victory*, Jalan Diponegoro 18 (☎0458/21165; ③), one of the best choices in town, while *Natural Cottages*, Jalan Yani 32(☎0458/21356; ④), has unobstructed views over the lake. Tentena's only place with pretentions to luxury is *Wisma Ue Datu* (☎0458/21222; ⑤), across the bridge and 150m north, whose thatched cabins overlook the river. *Hotel Victory's* **restaurant** has the most hygienic kitchen, but spicy Padang fare at *Moro Seneng* (the warung is on Jalan Sudarso) tastes better and is far cheaper; *R.M. Danau Poso*, immediately on the western side of the bridge, seldom has food, but the river-side balcony makes it ideal for a coffee. The Ebony Visitor Information, two streets behind *Pondok Remaja* on Jalan Setia Budi, is where to find advice, transport and **guides** for trekking around the regional reserves, with alternatives offered by *Natural Cottages* and *Hotel Victory*.

Leaving, the good road to Poso during daylight hours has a continual stream of minibuses from Tentena's **bus terminal**, 2km north of town. There are also departures at least daily to Pendolo, and to **Kolonodale** for access to Morowali, but for anywhere beyond Poso, or direct services to Rantepao or Ujung Pandang, go first to Poso and look for further transport there. The **ferry to Pendolo** leaves around 4pm from the shore off Jalan Yos Sudarso, arriving at 7pm, and the spray-soaked crossing is cool enough for a shirt.

To Lore Lindu and Kolonodale

Sturdy Toyota **jeeps** for the eighty-kilometre, four-wheel-drive-only track west from Tentena to Bomba and Gintu in **Lore Lindu national park** can be arranged through Tentena's information services from Rp150,000, or more cheaply (Rp40,000) by approaching the drivers of these badly battered vehicles in town and negotiating directly. Jeeps make a couple of runs a week in dry weather, when the journey takes at least seven hours; after heavy rain, convoys have been known to spend a week on the trail. You can also **walk** from Tentena to Gintu in three days, for which you'll need a tent, warm clothing and all supplies, as there are no settlements or shelters along the way.

The 180-kilometre road east from Tentena is a far more run-of-the-mill, six-hour bus ride, which ends at **KOLONODALE**, a small town of stilt houses and shops clustered around a port on the southwestern shore of **Tomori Bay**, whose blue waters are studded with rocky islands. A stop for Pelni ferries heading up the east coast between Baubau and Bitung, Kolonodale is also a transit point for Morowali Reserve, east across the bay; there's down-to-earth **accommodation** near the docks at *Losmen Sederhana* (②), with better facilities at either *Penginapan Lestari* (④), five minutes' walk away along Jalan Sudarso, or *Penginapan Rejeki Jaya* (③), the same distance down Jalan Hasanuddin. If you haven't arranged things already in Tentena, a **guide service** at the *Sederhana* can organize a boat across to the reserve. For more about Lore Lindu and Morowali, see p.830 and p.836.

Poso

POSO is an orderly administrative centre on the south side of **Tomini Bay**, a vast expanse of water encircled by Sulawesi's eastern and northern peninsulas. A port, and its location at the junction of Sulawesi Tengah's main roads, have also turned Poso into a transport black hole, and you'll certainly get sucked through here at some point. It's therefore disappointing to find that Poso offers no distractions, and once you've sorted your next move there's no reason to hang around.

The town covers a couple of square kilometres either side of **Sungai Poso**, which flows west into the bay. On the northern side you'll find the **port** at the end of Jalan Sudarso, which runs south for 500m to a riverside **roundabout**. Minibuses from Tentena, and some services from the eastern peninsula, terminate at the **bus depot** about 2km east of here, while Jalan Kalimantan crosses the river into the southern side of town. About 200m down Jalan Kalimantan, Jalan Sumatra branches west for 1km, passing a knot of services before heading out of town past bus company offices and the **main market** – you might get dropped off here if you're coming in from Palu. **Bemos** run between the eastern bus depot and market all through the day (Rp350), as do ojeks. The most handy **accommodation** is south of the river: *Hotel Alugoro* at Jalan Sumatra 20 (☎0452/23736; rooms with fans and mandi ③ per person) is great value and almost always full, its overflow handled by the less salubrious *Beringin* (②) opposite. North of the river on Jalan Agus Salim, *Hotel Kalimantan* (☎0452/21420; ③) and *Hotel Bambu Jaya* (☎0452/21570; ④) are quieter and a little run-down, but comfortable. Poso's **post office** and Telkom are also both north of the river on Jalan Urip Sumoharjo, as are **moneychanging facilities** at Bank Dagang Negara, Jalan Hasanuddin 13. **Information** is on hand at the Dinas Pariwisata at the junction of Jalan Sumatra and Jalan Kalimantan (☎0452/21211), where the voluble and well-informed Pak Amir offers advice on everything the province can offer. **Eating out**, try the *Pemuda*, next to the *Beriengin* on Jalan Sumatra, for fine nasi goreng, coffee and sweet-and-sour prawns; *R.M. Lelanga Jaya*, just outside the dock gates on Jalan Sudarso, has expensive Chinese meals, cold beer and good seascapes, or try the *Pangkep*, on the roundabout on Jalan Sudarso, with excellent chargrilled seafood.

On from Poso

Bemos to Tentena, and **buses** for the east peninsula towns of Ampana, Pagaimana and Luwuk, and all points south to Ujung Pandang, leave Poso from the eastern bus depot. For Palu, use one of the bus companies on Jalan Sumatra. There are a few options if you're heading for the **Togian Islands and Gorontalo**, including the putative weekly **ferry** direct from Poso to Gorontalo via Ampana, Wakai, Katupat and Dolong. The current schedule is chalked up outside the port on Jalan Sudarso, where you can also buy tickets, but in practice this service is both uncomfortable and very unreliable, and there are better alternatives from Ampana (for the Togians) and Pagaimana (Gorontalo). Those heading **to Lore Lindu** can take advantage of a daily Kijang service (Rp13,000) for the ninety-kilometre, six-hour journey west from Poso to **Watutau** in the park's northeastern **Napu Valley** (p.833), with Lore Indah, Jalan Enggano 23, in the Kaya Manya district of town – ojeks, or Poso's Dinas Parawisata, can get you there in time to sign up for the mid-morning departure.

Western Sulawesi Tengah

Western Sulawesi Tengah is very different from the green and central Poso Valley, the mountain range in the background capturing the clouds and rendering the **Palu Valley** beyond one of the driest areas in Indonesia. Here you'll find the capital city of **Palu** surrounded by fields of bleached brown grass and prickly-pear cactus, though the coast at **Donggala** is more attractive, with good beaches and clean water. In contrast, the mountains that receive all the rain are perennially verdant, rich in wildlife, forests and enigmatic **megaliths**, which sprout along a series of stepped valleys in the **Lore Lindu national park**. Lore Lindu is the reason most people find themselves in this part of Sulawesi as, despite Palu's status, the west is otherwise something of a dead end, with only subjectively reliable roads heading up into the northern peninsula.

Palu

At the base of the northern peninsula and the mouth of the Palu Valley, there has been a town on the site of **PALU** for centuries, but the city only gained its current importance during World War II, developed by the Japanese as a supply centre. Trade is still keeping the city ticking over, and a moderate pace and pleasant people – including a noticeable Christian **Kaili** minority, the valley's original inhabitants – make Palu an easy place to pass a day.

Arrival, orientation and information

Palu is set on **Sungai Palu**, which cuts the city in two as it flows north into the bay. The city covers a fair few square kilometres, but the **centre** is a small area on the eastern bank around the junction of Jalan Sudirman and Jalan Hasanuddin, which crosses west over the river into a commercial district along Jalan Gajah Mada and Jalan Bonjol. **Arrivals** on Pelni vessels from Ujung Pandang, Bitung, Kalimantan or Java land 30km north of town at **Pantaloan harbour**, while **Mutiara Airport** is 7km southeast – microlets or taxis will be waiting. Long-distance buses and vehicles from Gimpu

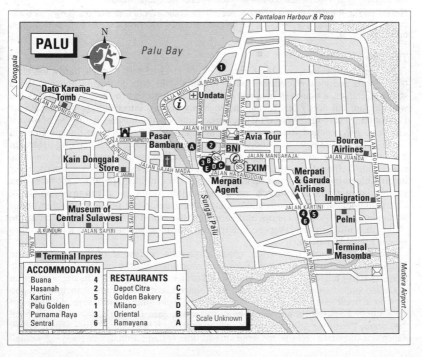

generally wind up at **Terminal Masomba**, 2km southeast of the centre, though some companies disembark passengers at their various offices around the suburbs. You can reach anywhere within the city boundaries by waving down **microlets** (bemos) already heading in the required direction; fares are fixed at Rp400, but, as drivers adapt their routes to fit the passengers' needs, rides often involve lengthy tours of the city.

Good **information** from knowledgeable, English-speaking staff is on hand at Palu's **tourist office**, Jalan Raja Moili 11 (☎0451/21795, fax 26810; Mon–Fri 9am–2pm), where you can also arrange PHPA permits for Morowali or Lore Lindu; their fees for private transport to the reserves (Rp150,000–300,000) and guiding (US$25 per day) are extortionate, however.

Accommodation

Palu has basically two aggregations of **places to stay**, geared to specific budgets: you'll find cheaper lodgings in the **city centre**, with a collection of mid-range hotels 1km southeast along **Jalan Kartini**, not too far from Terminal Masomba.

Buana, Jl Kartini 8 (☎0451/21475). Nondescript but neat hotel with a good Padang restaurant; all rooms with air-con and TV. ⑤.

Hasanah, Jl Cut Nyak Dien 19c (☎0451/22225). Small, friendly, family-run place with simple but roomy doubles and a mostly local clientele. ④.

Kartini, Jl Kartini 12 (☎0451/21964). Old but decent rooms off a central courtyard; fan and mandi Rp20,000, air-con, shower and TV. ⑥.

Palu Golden, Jl Raden Saleh 1 (☎0451/21126). Tour-group hotel set on the waterfront due north of the centre, with a fine pool, all conveniences and international pretensions and prices. ⑥.

Purnama Raya, Jl Wahidin 4 (☎0451/23646). Popular budget standby; the rooms are a bit stuffy but it's close to everything and the management speaks some English. ④.

Hotel Sentral, Jl Kartini 6 (☎0451/22789, fax 22418). Standard Chinese-owned affair with a booking agent, coffee shop, top-floor karaoke hall and attached supermarket. All rooms with air-con, mandi and TV. ⑤.

The City

Palu's centre thrives on small businesses: shops stocked with clothes, hardware, electrical goods and locally produced pottery, while stalls outside private houses offer a string of chillies, a bunch of bananas or other home-grown produce. The markets are well stocked but pretty functional, and dismally divided into concrete booths; **Pasar Bambaru**, west of the river on Jalan Cokroaminoto, is the busiest, with piles of *rono*, a tiny dried fish crushed and used as a garnish, and excellent October durian. Deep in the dry season you have to wonder that anything grows here at all; looking upstream from the Jalan Hasanuddin bridge, men scrub their bikes and cattle in the toe-deep river while behind them the valley is squeezed dry between the mountains, their heights blued by distance and dust. Across the river, a fifteen-minute walk takes you past a large Catholic **church** on Jalan Gajah Mada to a **mosque** on Jalan Cokroaminoto, whose smooth white minaret and dome are presently hidden under scaffolding. The mosque claims to be amongst the oldest in Sulawesi, founded in the sixteenth century by the Javanese Imam **Dato Karama**, whose **tomb** is a further 2km west off Jalan Diponegoro.

For an insight into the region, catch a microlet southwest of the centre to the **Museum of Central Sulawesi** (Tues–Sun mornings; Rp200) on Jalan Sapiri, whose front lawn has full-sized concrete copies of Lore Lindu's megaliths. Inside, a selection of stuffed fauna mounted in a forest diorama share space with ceramics, including a pottery jar shaped as a bust, with its face "tattooed", clothing of *kulit kayu*, soft and not very sturdy **bark cloth**, and some beautiful **silks**, *kain Donggala*, woven in the local fashion and featuring animals, plants and an unusual "chessboard" *ikat* pattern. Other designs incorporate cottons and gold thread; this cottage industry is enjoying a small

Martapura market, Kalimantan

Buffalo racing, Sumbawa, Nusa Tenggara

Detail, old rice barns, Tanah Toraja, Sulawesi

Stilt village, Lembata, Nusa Tenggara

Asats (fish on jetty), Irian Jaya

Stone boat, Sangliat Dol, Maluku

Tau tau (effigies), Tanah Toraja, Sulawesi

Batak dance puppets, North Sumatra

Dani tribesman, Irian Jaya

Wardo waterfall, Pulau Biak, Irian Jaya

Paddy-field, near Lempo, Tanah Toraja, Sulawesi

boom in villages around Donggala, having been banned by the Japanese during World War II. There are also wooden coffins and clay burial jars from the Poso Valley's **Pamona** population, while archeological odds and ends in a separate hall illustrate fragments of Donggala's past: best are some peculiar jewellery and whips cast in bronze, as well as tiny cult figurines with hideous faces and rampant genitals.

Eating

Palu has some good food, and occasionally you'll even find **local dishes** such as *utakelo* (vegetables with coconut milk) and *Palu mara* (fish with turmeric, tomatoes and chilli) on restaurant menus. For snacking, the chocolate and cream **cakes** at the *Golden Bakery* on Jalan Wahidin can't be beaten, and to eat with locals it's worth tracking down the nocturnal **grilled-fish stalls** near the cinema on Jalan Heyun and overlooking the bay on Jalan Moili.

Depot Citra, Jl Hasanuddin Dua. A big, noisy, sociable canteen serving *cap cai*, nasi/*mie goreng*, sate, grilled prawns and iced fruit drinks.

Milano, Jl Hasanuddin Dua. Not so brilliant pasta and burgers, but fantastic ice cream.

Oriental Jl Hasanuddin Dua. Authentic Chinese menu with fish stomach, shark fin and *trepang* soups amongst expensive exotics, but also less pricey tofu and crab dishes.

Ramayana, Jl Wahidin. Very good Chinese-Indonesian fare, including a chicken in chilli sauce which leaves your lips buzzing. Food is cooked out the front.

Listings

Airlines Offices open Mon–Fri 8am–4pm, Sat & Sun 8am–2pm. Bouraq, Jl Juanda 87 (☎0451/22995), to Ujung Pandang, Manado and Kalimantan; Merpati and Garuda at Jl Mongsidi 71 (☎0451/21172), to Ujung Pandang. There's also a Merpati agent on Jl Hasanuddin. Mutiara airport is 7km southeast of the centre; taxis cost around Rp5000.

Banks and exchange Good rates for cash at Bank Exim, Jl Hasanuddin; and for travellers' cheques, go to the BNI on Jl Sudirman.

Buses Terminal Inpres, on the southwest side of town, is where to find bemos for Donggala. Buses to all destinations between Manado and Ujung Pandang depart from Terminal Masomba, southeast of the centre. You can also go direct to bus companies: Jawa Indah (Jl Hasanuddin, across from Merpati and the Exim bank) for all stops to Ujung Pandang, Alugoro (office 2km north of city on Jl Sudarso) for the Palu–Poso–Luwuk stretch. Come prepared, however, to find that provincial services are not as advertised – for instance, a ticket to Tentena or Luwuk can see you turfed off the bus in Poso if there are not enough customers to make the full trip worthwhile. Very few visitors ever travel the 500km road north from Palu to Gorontalo and Sulawesi Utara, a rough, two-day excursion in the back of a bus along the inner curve of Tomini bay, as the experience is rendered unnecessary by less excruciating bus-and-ferry connections from the eastern peninsula. If you're heading to Lore Lindu national park, there are at least two buses each morning to Gimpu, 100km south of Palu at the start of the walking trail to the Bada Valley, and there's also less regular transport to Wuasa in the eastern Napu Valley with *Napu Star* – ask at the tourist office (see opposite) for their details.

Ferries The Pelni office is at Jl Kartini (☎0451/23237).

Hospital Hospital Undata, Jl Suharso 33 (☎0451/21270).

Immigration Jl Kartini (☎0451/21433).

Post office The most central branch is on Jl Sudirman (daily 7am–6pm); the GPO itself is several kilometres southeast of the centre on Jl Mohammed Yamin.

Shopping If you can't find what you need at the markets or shops around the centre, Sentosa supermarket, on the corner of Jl Mongsidi and Jl Kartini, has a host of imported chocolates, kitchenware and stationery. For local flavour, *kain Donggala* is sold at Rp100,000 a piece from a small, anonymous store west of the river on Jl Jambu, though from the outside the shop seems to stock only medicinal honey-and-egg drinks – the tourist office can help locate the store (see opposite).

Taxis Taxis congregate at the junction of Jl Sudirman and Jl Hasanuddin Dua, and drivers assume that all foreigners are heading for Donggala.

Telephone and fax International phone and fax services at the Telkom office on Jl Ahmed Yani are supposedly available around the clock.

Travel agents and tours Avia Tour, Jl Moh Hatta 4 (☎0451/26985, fax 22895), for all airlines and Pelni bookings. Katrial Travel, Jl Hasanuddin 10 (☎0451/23236), come recommended for their experience with guided tours into Lore Lindu and Morowali; count on US$100 a day, all-inclusive, for up to four people.

Donggala and around

The sleepy port of **DONGGALA**, 40km north of Palu at the mouth of the bay, was once the busiest town in the region, for centuries a regular stop on the trading routes between Sulawesi, Kalimantan and India. Elevated to the status of local capital under the Dutch, a siltation-prone harbour and Japanese influence saw Donggala lose the title to Palu, and its wharves finally closed to passenger shipping during the 1980s. A peaceful town, then, the gentle hills nearby planted with coconut trees and the streets reeking of drying copra and cloves, it's the perfect place to unwind for a few days, checking out the shallow-draft Bugis schooners in the harbour, or enjoying the shallow seas hereabouts. **Minibuses** take under an hour to get here from Palu's Terminal Inpres, dropping you at the bus terminal just short of Donggala, where a dokar or ojek can cart you into town. Alternatively, a **taxi** from Palu can deliver direct to accommodation, which, excepting no-frills *Losmen Bhakti* (②) on Jalan Samauna, are all about 2km north of town at **Tanjung Karang**, a rocky headland with some gorgeous beaches. If you want to **scuba dive**, *Prince John Dive Resort* (⑥; price includes everything except beer) has all the facilities and its bungalows overlook the reef; otherwise, there are cheaper, but good options, nearby at *Natural Cottages* (⑤ including meals, open to negotiation) and *Harmoni Cottages* (⑤).

Lore Lindu national park

Southeast of Palu, the land rises to a forested plateau, 2500 square kilometres of which is given over to **Lore Lindu national park**, itself based around 2355-metre **Gunung Nokilolaki** and the catchment areas of the Palu and Lariang rivers. Much of the park is thinly settled, the most accessible regions being the southern **Bada Valley**, central **Besoa Valley**, and the eastern **Napu Valley**, each rising higher than the other and linked by trails. Natural attractions aside, the valleys also feature impressively physical **megaliths**, including male and female stone **statues** of anything between 50cm and 4.5m in height, and **kalamba**, large, cylindrical stone basins. Probably raised a millennium ago, these *megalitik* predate Lore Lindu's current settlers, and nothing is known positively about their purpose. Christianity now predominates, and villages here come complete with dogs and churches, all of which have clock towers with the hands painted on at the time of Sunday service.

The most popular route through the park, taking in some good forest, river crossings and a big bag of statues, starts south of Palu at the village of **Gimpu**, and then follows the Lariang south and east to the Bada Valley settlements of **Gintu** and **Bomba**, exiting the region via a rough vehicle road over the mountains to Tentena. In ideal conditions, Palu to Bomba takes four days, but six would be both more realistic, and allow enough time to have a good look around. One drawback to this trail is that it actually skirts around the park, and for a closer look at Lore Lindu's interior you should consider extending your trip north from the Bada Valley, through to **Doda** in the Besoa Valley, and then over to the Napu Valley and the villages of **Watutau** and **Wuasa**, from where there's regular traffic on to Poso or back to Palu – about an extra four days in all.

Practicalities

Assuming you speak rudimentary Indonesian and are prepared to reach Lore Lindu on foot or by local transport, you'll find **guides** and tours from Palu, Poso or Tentena are unnecessarily expensive, especially along the well-defined and serviced Palu–Bada Valley–Tentena trail. You do need guides for locating megaliths, and for the tracks to Doda from either Gimpu or Bomba, but these are far cheaper to engage on site – about Rp15,000 a day. There are a few formal **lodgings** within the park, but you can also call on village hospitality where these are lacking by presenting yourself to the village head, who will probably put you up himself for a fee. The only time that you're likely to end up **camping out** is if you decide to walk between Bomba and Tentena, for which you'll need a tent, stove and food. **Meals** usually come with accommodation and there are very few places to eat in the area, though food is very plain and even if you're not camping you won't regret bringing some goodies with you. Boiled **water** in villages is safe to drink, but any collected along trails needs to be purified; carry a decent-sized water bottle, as the valleys can be exposed and very hot, especially in the July to October dry season. Conversely, nights are cool, even chilly enough for a heavy shirt in the Besoa and Napu valleys, while heavy rain – possible at any time – swells streams and turns the fields and tracks into quagmires, making hiking between villages or out to megaliths a much more difficult and lengthy operation. All this means that **distances** and **walking times** are unpredictable, and most of those given below are minimum personal estimates.

Palu to Tentena: the Bada Valley

Buses from Palu's Masomba terminal take about five hours to reach trailheads at **GIMPU**, a tidy collection of homes and stores at the end of the bitumen 100km south of Palu, whose inhabitants subsist by collecting rattan and planting cocoa. There's homestay accommodation here, and transport back to Palu in the morning. The Bada Valley trail starts with an eight-hour walk southeast along the Lariang to **MOA**, a pretty village whose friendly homestay and surrounding dry forest of solid, grey-barked **eucalyptus trees** and big butterflies might encourage you to hang around for a day. From here, in another full day's walk east you'll ford the river to **Tuare**, and then climb over the ridges and down into the Bada Valley at Gintu.

Orientated east–west right on the southern tip of the national park, the **Bada Valley** is a broad, fifteen-kilometre-long oval basin surrounding Sungai Lariang, its shallow slopes given over to rice and slash-and-burn cultivation. South of the Lariang, Gintu is pretty central to the valley, with another half-dozen kampung and a score of megalithic statues scattered on both sides of the river in the 7km east of here to the village of Bomba. Either settlement makes a good base: **GINTU** has two fine losmen (③ with all meals) and a bitumen road along the south side of the river to **BOMBA**, a slightly nicer prospect with coconut trees, a couple of small stores, and a one-kilometre walk north to tiny twin rooms with mandi, breakfast and dinner at *Losmen Ningsi* (④). As always, your accommodation can produce guides and also arrange a seat in a jeep to Tentena (Rp40,000).

To explore Bada **north of the river**, start by backtracking over the Lariang 1km from Gintu to **Lengkeka** village, where there are **hot springs** five minutes' walk uphill. Four statues lie off the path in the 3km east between Lengkeka and kampung **Sepe**; most interesting are **Oba**, a tiny, dumpy figure, and the reclining **Mpeime**. Southeast of Sepe is **Palindo**; at 4.5m high, the biggest megalith in all Lore Lindu – even so, impossible to find on your own – whose clearly carved, stylized face betrays nothing concerning the cause of a startling erection. From Sepe it's forty minutes further east to a waterfall at **Kolori**, where trails diverge east to the Besoa Valley, and a twenty-minute walk south over the Lariang to Bomba across a deathtrap of a suspension bridge – one hundred scary metres of missing planks, broken cables and no handrails. **South of the river**, you'll find easily the small statues at Gintu itself and 3km east at **Bewa**, though there are four more hidden in the scrub along a track which loops 7.5km south between the two villages; one of these, known as **Dula Boe**, is unique in having the body of a buffalo. In a grove fifteen minutes' walk east of Bomba, another carving worth seeing is two-metre-high **Lanke Bulawa**, a rare female statue.

Whether you walk in three days, or spend at least eight hours bucking around on a plank across the back of a jeep, the road **from Bomba to Tentena** is quite an adventure. The first stage ascends into the mountains along very steep, muddy and rutted tracks, where every ridge scaled means a hair-raising plunge on the far side to a gully spanned by tree trunks or branches, though a couple of solid bridges cross bigger creeks. A highland scrub of bushes, pitcher plants and stunted trees right on top of the range marks the halfway point, and once past this the gradient levels out somewhat as the road follows crests through cloud forest, the trees draped with wisps of old man's beard; look for **knobbed hornbills**, with their heavy yellow beaks, and long-tailed, deep-blue **bearded bee-eaters** – both common enough here, but found only on Sulawesi. The last third of the journey winds down the western side of the Poso Valley on a wide road, gaps in the canopy allowing occasional views over Danau Poso. Once you hit the bitumen at the base of the range, it's another twenty minutes or so to Tentena.

Bomba to Doda and the Besoa Valley

The thirty-kilometre trail between Bomba and Doda is harder than anything the Bada Valley has to offer; mostly uphill, with plenty of gullies and narrow paths with crumbly edges to negotiate. You'll need at least ten hours, and come prepared to camp out. From Bomba, cross the river to Kolori, then turn east over a stream into marshy fields beyond **Lelio** and start climbing into woodland above the Lariang, where the river cuts a steep gorge between the hills, especially impressive after the flat flow through the valley. At first the walk is only semi-shaded and hot, but you reach the forest proper by the mid-point **waterfall**, a good spot to cool off and have lunch. There's jungle most of the way from here to Bomba, with huge mountain pandanus, silvery trunks climbing out of a mass of supporting roots, long-stemmed heliconia growing like ginger alongside the path, and a couple of big fig trees. The last hour is spent descending a low saddle through the Besoa Valley's paddy-fields and streams, and then down a broad track to Doda.

Set at a 1200-metre altitude, the **Besoa Valley** runs north along a tributary of the Lariang, a much greener and somehow tidier bowl than Bada, with a huge number of *kalamba* basins found here. A large public-square-cum-playing-field surrounded by houses, **DODA** is at the southeast side of valley, with the path from Bomba entering the square near the kepala desa's house. Here you're obliged to pay a steep Rp15,000 per person for **board and lodging** – there's no alternative – though washing in the river with cattle is good fun. Negotiate guiding services for the valley with either the kepala desa, or Doda's English-speaking schoolteacher, and check out the **museum** next to the kepala desa's home, where a traditional bamboo rice barn and wooden, A-frame **tambi** house sit on thick supporting posts. There are three megalithic sites in the valley: **Pokekea** is the biggest single grouping of megaliths in the park, with two figures and a dozen or more *kalamba*, but it's 7km west and you can see just as much closer to Doda. At **Tadulakoh**, a twenty-minute walk over muddy fields, a half-dozen *kalamba* stand exposed on a slope, accurately sculpted cylinders 1.5m across and similarly deep with slightly bulging sides, some grooved in wide bands. A few **lids** lie beside the basins, carved with flat central "nipples" and probably weighing a tonne or more, with a sole two-metre-high male statue overlooking the site. The third location is 3km southeast of Doda near **LEMPE**, whose kepala desa will arrange for somebody to show you to the megaliths, which are spookily surrounded by forest on the hills behind the village. The first is a recently propped-up statue with a moss-covered body and very distinct face, set in a tiny clearing from where trails lead deeper into the vegetation to two lidless *kalamba*, filled with water, the guide bounding along barefoot, casually pointing out passion-fruit vines and tunnels made through the undergrowth by anoa.

The Napu Valley

There's a decent 31-kilometre mud road from Doda to Watutau in the **Napu Valley**, and, though Doda's kepala desa may recommend that you charter a jeep (Rp150,000) or at least hire a guide, it's an easy eight-hour walk along an obvious track. Follow the road out of Doda and bear sharply right at the fork about 3km further on; flat fields cede to a steep road under a light forest canopy. Over the top, the road quickly drops into the Napu Valley, where you'll need to ask directions at every village you pass through in order to stay on track for Watutau. The indescribably warped and twisted covered wooden bridges along the way are another good reason to make this journey on foot.

Lying north–south along the headwaters of the Lariang, only the western side of the twenty-kilometre long Napu Valley is actually inside the national park, and it's all thoroughly farmed and settled. **WATUTAU** lies across the river at the southern end, a single sandy street; the kepala desa is a serious man who offers bed and breakfast for a donation. A satellite dish outside his home is the first in the village and at night the entire household gathers to watch the soaps, sprawled amongst a sea of cobs from the year's maize harvest. There are more **hot springs** and five **megaliths** in the valley, including a 1.5-metre-example outside the kepala desa's house, and one with prominent ears off across the fields; try and get out early on in the morning, when a thick mist covers everything. From Watutau, a twenty-kilometre sealed road runs flat **to Wuasa** at the northern end of the valley, past another megalith right by the roadside at **Wangga**, a metre-high male with a broad smile. **WUASA** is a large settlement by local standards: a grid of gravel streets, a big church and a couple of tiny mosques, a few toko selling fuel and essentials, **accommodation** (③) at *Losmen Mes Penda* or *Losmen Citra*, two places **to eat**, and daily **buses** out on the *Napu Star* for Palu (6hr) and *Lore Indah* for Poso (5hr). If you're heading over the range to Poso, ask the driver to stop on the lower slopes of the valley at **Batu Nonkoh**, an atypical roughly shaped *kalamba* with eyes and nose carved into its side, and also on the hillsides above, where there are grand views back over Napu – villages dotting brilliant-green fields.

The eastern peninsula and islands

Most of the 300-kilometre-long eastern peninsula is exceptionally rugged, the majority of peaks topping 2000m. While the adventurous can see something of this by hiking into the undeveloped **Morowali Reserve**, most of the area's attractions lie offshore. The main road from Poso skirts along the north coast to the ports of **Ampana**, springboard for the maritime pleasures surrounding the **Togian Islands**, and **Pagaimana**, departure point for the crossing to Gorontalo and Sulawesi Utara. South across the peninsula's thin neck from Pagaimana, **Luwuk** is a staging post into Morowali Reserve, and also out to the seldom-visited **Banggai Islands**. There are no **banks** at all in the region, so stock up first in Poso or Gorontalo.

Ampana

Five hours east of Poso along a road crossed by a handful of flood-prone rivers, **AMPANA** is a dusty little hole whose bus station, market and Pertamina fuel storage tanks are the focus of a tumbledown **port area** from where most Togian traffic departs. There's a private **homestay** (③) around the side of the bus station – family members often collar Westerners as they arrive – otherwise, walk about 500m west past the port, market, and over a small bridge to Jalan Kartini, where you'll find reasonable rooms at *Losmen Irama* (doubles with fan, mandi and breakfast ③) and *Hotel Plaza* (③). On the corner of Jalan Kartini, verandah tables at *Rumah Makan Mekar* (6am–11pm) catch breezes, while surly staff serve up coffee, beer and extremely palatable Indonesian

food. Ask at the port about **ferry schedules** – there's transport to Wakai most days from here – though some boats to Bomba leave from an anonymous beach about 3km east of town, best reached by dokar or ojek. Ampana isn't really the sort of place to hang around in unnecessarily, but with a spare half-day it's worth hiring a longboat from the docks for the short ride east to **Tanjung Api**, the Fire Cape, where there are a couple of interesting beaches to picnic at, and blue-burning **volcanic gasses** seeping up through the sands.

The Togian Islands

The **Togian Islands** form a fragmented, 120-kilometre-long crescent across the shallow blue waters of Tomini Bay, their steep grey sides undercut by tides and weathered into sharp ridges capped by coconut palms and hardwoods. The soil is poor, so people make a living from the sea, fishing from vessels ranging from eight-metre catamarans with little off-centre huts and sails on each hull, to smaller craft outrigged with thigh-thick bamboo – some opportunists even spear fish with home-made goggles and guns made from wood, rubber and glass. Not all the Togians are inhabited, and **fauna** on remoter islands includes monkeys, the weird babirusa, and huge coconut crabs, *kedang kenari*, though their popularity as a novelty cuisine with visitors has made them rare. Offshore, the ubiquitous yellow buoys of Japanese and Australian pearl farms are testament to the bay's pristine waters, and the exceptional **snorkelling and diving** around the islands features fever-sharp visibility, turtles, sharks, octopus, garden eels, and a mixed bag of reef and pelagic fish species. On the down side, there are also nine depots in the Togians dealing in the live export of seafood to restaurants in Asia; many of these operations employ cyanide sprays, which stun large fish but kill everything else – including coral.

TOGIAN TRANSPORT

The lack of information about **inter-island transport** in the Togians is only partly due to deliberate fudging by private operators, who want your custom for themselves. The truth is that even scheduled public services are notoriously unreliable, either through a lack of customers on any particular day, the incessant mechanical failures on the large passenger vessels, or the reluctance of the owners of smaller craft to put to sea in anything but perfect conditions. Aside from the weekly Poso–Gorontalo ferry, which stops in Ampana and then travels Wakai–Katupat–Malenge–Dolong–Gorontalo before returning along the same route, at the time of writing you could (with luck) count on the following:

* Ampana–Wakai/Wakai–Ampana: 5 weekly; Rp2500.
* Ampana–Bomba/Bomba–Ampana: daily; Rp2500.
* Wakai–Bomba/Bomba–Wakai: daily; Rp2500.
* Wakai–Katupat/Katupat–Wakai: 3 or more weekly; Rp1500.
* Wakai–Kadidiri/Kadidiri–Wakai: daily; free/Rp2500 depending on accommodation at Kadidiri.
* Wakai–Malenge/Malenge–Wakai: 1–2 weekly; Rp2500.

Elsewhere, there's bound to be something along eventually if you can afford to wait, or you can **charter** a motorized outrigger at about Rp10,000 an hour – damp, but not necessarily expensive if you can find others to share costs. It's also possible to rent ten-person ferries for **island cruises** at around a million rupiah for five days; conditions are hardly luxurious but you can set your own schedule. Contact either Tune Mohammad, Jalan Nusantara 4, Ampana (✆0464/21267); Poso's Dinas Pariwisata; or Rudy Ruus, Jalan Pulau Seram, Nusa Indah 8, Poso.

From west to east, **Batu Daka, Togian** and **Talata Koh** are the Togian's three main islands, together forming a tightly grouped, sixty-kilometre-long chain, each island separated from its neighbour by a narrow channel. The main settlements here are **Bomba** and **Wakai** on Batu Daka, and **Katupat** on Togian Wakai is something of a regional hub, with transport out to smaller islands such as **Kadidiri**, off Togian, and **Malenge**, due north off Talata Koh. Further east of this main trinity are another two large islands, **Walea Kodi** and **Walea Bahi**, with the main town of **Dolong** on Walea Kodi. There are no vehicle roads or widespread electricity in the Togians and, with all travel by boat, you'll find it pays not to be on too tight a schedule – see the "Togian transport" box opposite. With little time or money, it's a good idea to confine yourself to one area, and make use of various day-trips or shared transfers offered by your accommodation. Tourism in the islands is budget-orientated, though lodgings are often surprisingly good; **meals** are usually included in room price. Be conservative with **water**, which has to be shipped in to many places. July through to September are the coolest months, when winds often interrupt ferries and make for poor diving; at other times Tomini is rated as the calmest bay on earth, its waters often glassy-smooth.

Around the islands

Three hours from Ampana and at the western end of Batu Daka, **BOMBA** comprises two dozen houses and a mosque facing north across a pleasant bay. There's a long **beach** 5km west of town, but it's the sea which warrants a visit here, with the Togians' best snorkelling an hour distant at **Catherine reef**. The coast roundabout is interesting, too, with the possibility of seeing **crocodiles** in remote inlets, and some islets east of Bomba completely covered by villages, their sides reinforced with hand-cut coral ramparts. In Bomba itself, dockside *Losmen Poya Lisa* (③) is a fine **place to stay**, but the alternatives are just that bit better: immediately offshore on a hump of rock and trees, *Sicilia Bungalows* (③) has friendly management and a monopoly on views; opposite *Sicilia* is a small stretch of sand and cabins (③) on little **Pulau Poya**; or try the unusual *Tandongi Homestay* (③), built out in the bay over a reef. Entrepreneurs at the dock can run you across to the place of your choice, and your accommodation will arrange boat trips to suit guests' needs. Ferries back to Ampana and on to Wakai leave Bomba most mornings – if they don't run aground on the reef just out from the jetty.

At the eastern end of Batu Daka, about five hours from Ampana and two from Bomba, **WAKAI** is similar to the dock area at Ampana, though with far better accommodation at the white timber *Togian Islands Hotel* (④). Slow and expensive, the restaurant here is Wakai's best; there are also a few warung and well-stocked stores around the dock. New arrivals from Ampana heading **to Kadidiri** should go straight to the hotel for transfers. Half an hour by motorized outrigger from Wakai, **Kadidiri** is one of the nicest of the islands, 3km long and with fine beaches and ample lodgings. The highest-profile accommodation is *Kadidiri Paradise Bungalows* (③), whose safety-conscious **scuba** team charges a flat US$25 per dive for all-inclusive trips to nearby reefs such as **Taipi Wall**, with additional transport costs if you want to visit the submerged wreck of a B-24 fighter plane or volcanic **Pulau Una-Una**. Food in *Paradise* is abysmal, however, and non-divers should head one beach over to the hillside *Wakai Cottages* (③) or *Kadidiri Cottages* (④). Just offshore, there are secluded cabins on **Pulau Taipi** (④); both these and *Paradise* are run by Wakai's hotel and, if you stay at either, transport between Wakai and Kadidiri is free (otherwise, it's Rp2500). Shallow coral around Taipi makes for good skin-diving, and, if you want some solitude, tracks through undergrowth lead across to Kadidiri's isolated southern beaches.

On Pulau Togian's central northern coast, **KATUPAT** village was a tourist core before Kadidiri got going, but few visitors make it here now – a Friday market means that you're most likely to find transport heading this way on Thursday morning. A sleepy hundred metres of coral-rubble streets strewn with goats and drying copra runs east into mangroves and a coconut plantation, with the couple of stores at the jetty specializing in soap, tobacco and tins of sardines. Over the water, *Losmen Bolilanga Indah* looks fine but receives bad press from all who stay there; ask around instead for transport across to little **Pulau Pangempa**, about 200m offshore, where you'll find *Fadhilar Bungalows* (③ full board; nice staff), fair snorkelling, beaches and monitor lizards. A good four hours northeast of Katupat off the top of Talata Koh – but probably more reliably reached directly from Wakai – ten-kilometre-long **Malenge's** primary forests make it one of the best spots in the Togians to hunt for wildlife. *Losmen Malenge Indah* (③) and *Rudi's* (③), both near the jetty, are recommended **places to stay** and organize hiking and snorkelling; *Honeymoon Beach* (③), with its eccentric owner, is less so.

The only easy way to reach the eastern Togians is on the weekly Ampana–Gorontalo ferry, which puts in at **DOLONG** on **Walea Kodi**. Dolong is somewhere to experience Togian life beyond tourism; you can of course rent boats to local reefs, but to get treated like a celebrity walk 4km west across the island to the remote village of **Tutung**, where foreign faces are, to put it mildly, a rare sight. There are no losmen in Dolong, so you'll need to locate and make arrangements with Umrah, the hospitable kepala desa. Further east again, **Walea Bahi** is right off any regular transport routes, though it's rumoured that cabins will shortly be opening up at **Tanjung Kramat**, on the forested southeastern tip. Accessed from Pagaimana, facilities will include a **dive operation** concentrating on some exceptional reef walls off **Pulau Dondoia**, a square of white coral sand topped by a single tree.

Pagaimana, Luwuk and beyond

Five hours east of Ampana, **PAGAIMANA** is a small Bajau town with a dense collection of houses built over the water next to a busy port for the overnight **ferry to Gorontalo** (see p.838), which departs on alternate days. Leaving, the cheapest option for the crossing is to buy an ekonomi fare (Rp12,000) at the harbour, and then negotiate a cash donation with the purser for a mattress on the floor of the air-con first-class room. The crossing takes about ten hours and is not too bad, though vessels tend to roll heavily even in the lightest swell. If you've just arrived from Gorontalo, you'll be grabbed and ushered towards a host of minibuses heading to Luwuk, Ampana and Poso; take your pick.

Three hours from Pagaimana and thirteen from Poso, **LUWUK**, the east peninsula's largest town, looks south across the Seleng Straits to the **Banggai Islands**. A relaxed place to spend the evening in transit, there are good rooms and food at *Hotel Ramayana*, Jalan Sutaryo 7 (☎0461/21152; ④), and cheaper beds at the *City* (③) on Jalan Gunung Mulia. Moving on, morning **buses** head all the way back west to Palu, and along the southern coast to trailheads for Morowali Reserve. From the **port**, Pelni stop here on their east-coast run, and there's also a nightly **ferry** for the nine-hour run southeast past large **Pulau Peleng** to **BANGGAI**, the main town on the island of the same name. Only about a dozen tourists visit Banggai each year and facilities are rudimentary, but there's losmen and hotel accommodation, supposedly good snorkelling, the high-set former **palace** of the Sultan of Banggai, and the possibility of hitching a ride on cargo vessels and fishing boats heading east to Maluku.

Morowali Reserve

One Sulawesi's wildest corners, boundaries of the **Morowali Reserve**, 100km southwest of Luwuk at the base of the eastern peninsula, enclose every terrain from coastal swamp to mountainous heathland. Home to butterflies, birds and a broad slice of Sulawesi's endemic mammals, Morowali is also the haunt of several thousand **Wana**, nomads who use blowpipes and poison darts for hunting, and have so far resisted gov-

ernment attempts to settle them. Unless you arrange a tour into Morowali with operators in Tentena, Poso or Palu, you need to be able to speak Indonesian and come fully
equipped for hard hiking and minimal comforts. There are various ways to tackle
Morowali: **from Luwuk**, a daily bus runs to **Padaoke** (also known as Donggi), where
you can catch a public boat or, if the road is open, another bus, to **BATURUBE**, just
outside the eastern edge of the reserve. Baturube has two losmen and a bimonthly
market attended by Wana drifting in from the wilds; hikers should stock up here with
presents – **salt** and rough-smoking *leta* or *adidie* **tobacco** (sold in bamboo tubes at
about Rp1000 a slice) are much appreciated in the interior. Baturube's kepala desa can
help to find essential **guides** for the reserve at Rp15,000 a day, or try to track down
Nasip Njee or Yonathon, both highly experienced escorts and sources of information.

From Baturube, there's a tough ten-day trek north through virgin forests **to**
Tobamawu on Sungai Bongka, with transport on from here to **Tamponompo** on the
Ampana–Poso road; almost all of this is actually outside the reserve, but it's the best
area to find wildlife and groups of Wana. A shorter option, which takes you **into the**
reserve itself, heads west along a vehicle track from Baturube to the village of **Tokala**
Atas, from where you can hike or catch a ride on an ojek to **Tarongo**. It's a long day's
hike from here to **KAYUPOLI**, a relatively modernized Wana village at the centre of
the reserve where you can base yourself for day-trips south to **Ranu lakes**, strangely
still, twinned pools surrounded by forest. Another day south of Kayupoli, villagers in
kampung around the mouth of the Morowali estuary can organize transport across the
bay to **Kolonodale** and the road to Tentena – ask for Pak Nawir.

SULAWESI UTARA

A narrow trail of active volcanic ranges continuing out across the Celebes Sea as a scattered group of islands, isolation from the south and close contacts with outside powers
has always marked **Sulawesi Utara** apart from the rest of Sulawesi. Not that the
province is unified: the western side, including the city of **Gorontalo** and the former
Bolaang-Mongondow regency, is Islamic, while at the peninsula's tip, around the
provincial capital of **Manado**, the ancestors of the **Minahasans** island-hopped down
from the Philippines, converting to Christianity during the nineteenth century. What
both areas share is a strong legacy of Dutch influence, which became so entrenched
that the region was nicknamed "Holland's Twelfth Province", its people even widely
supporting Dutch attempts to resume control of Indonesia after World War II. A sense
of being different continued beyond Independence, when in 1958 the north became the
last stand of the **Permesta revolt**, the military-backed uprising against increasing
Javan influence in regional affairs which had started the year before in Ujung Pandang.
But within a matter of months, and before Permesta's support of similar groups in Java
and Sumatra could lead to unified opposition against his rule, Sukarno had **bombed**
the revolution into submission, though Permesta guerrillas (with covert aid from the
US) continued sporadic resistance until 1961.

While most of this is academic, Sulawesi Utara also abounds with natural attractions.
Particularly if you've just arrived from the drier southern peninsula, it's striking just
how fertile the north's volcanic soils are; one of the most lasting impressions of the lowlands here is of millions of mature **coconut trees**, and much of what isn't given over to
palm plantations or rice is covered instead in **rainforest**. The province's two most
accessible reserves, **Dumoga-Bone** east of Gorontalo, and **Tangkoko** near Manado,
are the easiest places in Sulawesi to find wildlife, with sightings of the island's unusual
mammals and birds almost guaranteed. For their part, the gently cultivated
Minahasan highlands south of Manado have live **volcanoes** to climb and, as the
heart of Minahasan culture, offer a different picture from the coast. Offshore, waters

SULAWESI'S FOREST FAUNA

Sulawesi's forests support a healthy diversity of **wildlife**, some of it unique to the island and much becoming increasingly rare, requiring dedication and luck to track down. The largest endemic mammal is the sheep-sized **anoa** or dwarf buffalo, a sharp-horned inhabitant of thick forest which, despite its small stature, is extremely fierce and greatly feared for its habit of attacking unprovoked – take care if you cross paths with one. The less aggressive **babirusa** (deer-pig) is an extraordinary beast, a thinly haired hog with two sets of upcurving tusks, one pair spreading out from the lips and the other forming what looks like a double horn growing up through its forehead. Sadly, the babirusa's liking for villagers' crops, and the fact that Christians consider it good eating, has made it scarce, likely to be spotted only in remote areas. The tail-less **black macaque** (*monyet hitam* in Indonesian) is more widespread and, with a stretched face, bright-orange eyes and a cheerful upright tuft on top of it's head, is an entertaining resident of northern Sulawesi's national parks. Native birds include parrots, pigeons and the **knobbed hornbill**, whose large black body is set off by a curved yellow beak and blue wattle, but the biggest fuss is made over the chicken-sized **maleo**, a pied, plump fowl with a curious lumpy "helmet". The maleo is a **megapode**, a family of birds found in Asia and Australasia who build mound nests where their eggs incubate in the heat of decaying leaves; male birds (whose mouths are natural thermometers) tend the nests, adding or removing compost as necessary to keep the eggs at the right temperature. Maleos are widespread, but have become endangered as their eggs are greatly valued for food. Other animals worth looking out for, though found elsewhere in Asia, include **kuskus** and **lorises** (*kukang*), both resembling small, slow-moving bears and difficult to see in the forest canopy, and the enchanting **tarsier** (*bangka*), a mug-sized primate with a squat body, feathery tail, long fingers with padded tips, enormous ears and eyes, and a round head that it can turn through 180 degrees. Common in lowland forest margins, tarsiers spend the day dozing in bamboo clumps, and at night spring around in shrubs chasing insects. Often ignored, **flying lizards** (*cecak trebang*, or *bunglon*) are at first sight dull-grey, bony little lizards, which habitually sit immobile on tree trunks in open woodland. Catch them at the right moment, however, and you'll see them suddenly flick out a little white "banner" from their chin, and spread their **wings** (extensions of the lizard's ribs) for sunbathing, as a territorial display or to glide from tree to tree like a paper dart.

and vertical coral walls around **Pulau Bunaken** have been attracting scuba divers for the last decade, and are in themselves enough reason for any enthusiast to spend a week or more up here. Far less well-known are the **Sangihe and Talaud Islands** between Manado and the Philippines, though with time they are easy enough to reach either as part of a round-trip, or as a last stop on the way out of Indonesia.

Roads onto the northern peninsula are none too good, but Sulawesi Utara is otherwise well connected to other parts of Sulawesi and Indonesia, as well as Singapore and the Philippines, with two airports and four major harbours servicing Pelni and local passenger ferries. Transport within the province is reliable, with a 400-kilometre **highway** between Gorontalo and Manado, and plenty of sealed roads elsewhere.

Gorontalo and Bolaang-Mongondow

Arriving in **Gorontalo** from either the south or elsewhere in Sulawesi Utara, you'll find a couple of surrounding historic and scenic sights, but it's the wilds of **Dumoga-Bone national park** that really warrant a stop. A small area of the western side of Dumoga-Bone can be explored easily from Gorontalo, with greater access to the less-frequented eastern end of the park through the village of **Doloduo** in the **Bolaang-Mongondow district**, reached off the Gorontalo–Manado road via the town of **Kotamobagu**.

Gorontalo and around

GORONTALO is a pleasant Muslim city, its centre a set piece of whitewashed, veran-dahed and wooden-shuttered Dutch bungalows. Colonial associations run deep here; many older people in Gorontalo speak perfect Dutch and English, and the statue of pro-Independence guerrilla **Nani Wartabone** stands ignored on the southern side of town, more of a necessary patriotic nod to the government than a heartfelt memorial. The place exudes a sleepy charm; by late morning shutters are pulled tight against the heat and everything closes down until about 4pm and, with dokars clip-clopping around and the streets littered with broken horseshoes, you can almost step back fifty years amongst Gorontalo's lanes.

Sited just east of unimpressive **Sungai Bolango**, Gorontalo's **city centre** is a standard net of a dozen or so streets more or less centred on **Mesjid Baitur Rahim**, a multiple-domed mosque and tall, smoothly tiled minaret set at a wide crossroads. Jalan Basuki Rahmat runs north of here, though the main road out of town in this direction is paral-lel Jalan Sam Ratulangi, two blocks further west; Jalan Sultan Botutihe heads east, past a **hospital**, south are businesses along Jalan Ahmed Yani, while Jalan Hasanuddin points west through Gorontalo's commercial district and over the river. Ferries from Poso, Ampana and Pagaimana in Sulawesi Tenggara dock 7km southeast at Gorontalo's **port**, and all long-distance **buses** wind up 3km north at **Terminal Andalas**. Kijangs, micro-lets and ojeks service these points of arrival; the city's **microlet terminal** is 1km north at **Pasar Sentral** on Jalan Sam Ratulangi, a busy acre of covered stalls selling fresh pro-duce, coconut shredders, betel nut and cakes. Dokar, at Rp300–600 depending on dis-tance, can be rented all around downtown Gorontalo, although the area is so small there's no need to look for one unless you're impossibly encumbered with luggage.

Most **places to stay** are south of the mosque and within easy walking distance of it. A favourite is *Hotel Melati* at Jalan Gajah Mada 33 (☎0435/21853; dorm ③; doubles ④). You tend to get ushered towards a very tidy, mosquito-infested new wing set around a garden, but there's far more atmosphere (and mosquito nets) in the older colonial house next door, complete with period furniture and Rembrandt prints. *Hotel Wisata*, at Jalan 23 Januari 19 (☎0435/21736; fan ④, air-con ⑤), has a gloomy interior but is quiet and clean; there are big rooms and aged fittings at *Penginapan Teluk Kau*, Jalan Sungai Parman 42 (☎0435/22093; ③); and mid-range comforts at friendly *Hotel Saronde*, Jalan Walanda Maramis 17 (☎0435/21735; fans ④, air-con and TV ⑤). All **banks** are on Jalan Ahmed Yani; the BNI offers bad rates, but has an ATM and is the only place in town accepting American Express travellers' cheques. The **post office** is on the corner of Jalan Ahmed Yani and Jalan 23 Januari, while the Telkom office is just west of here on Jalan 23 Januari. For something **to eat**, night stalls south off Jalan Hasanuddin on Jalan Pertiwi have endless assortments of buns, jackfruit soup, rice and noodle dishes, with some fine sate at the tiny *Warung Kita*, across from the mosque on Jalan Suprator. *Toko Brantas*, also near the mosque on Jalan Hasanuddin, is Gorontalo's best cake shop and always sells out early, and the attached restaurant is good for cheap food. For something better, head north off Jalan Sultan Botutihe to the *Boulevard* on Jalan Merdeka, a Chinese establishment with cold beer, juicy grilled fish and sweet chicken with pineap-ple and chillies, and a full-on karaoke. For a lively dose of sleaze, check out the *Nikita*, upstairs at the corner of Jalan Pertiwi and Jalan Haryono, a popular **disco-bar**.

The **harbour** is twenty minutes from the Pasar Sentral microlet terminal, though some hotels also arrange pick-ups for their guests. Services leave at night; there's a weekly ferry through the Togians to Ampana and Poso, and a direct crossing to Pagaimana every other day – inquire at your accommodation about schedules and buy tickets a couple of hours in advance at the harbour (see Kwandang p.840 for all Pelni departures). **Buses** to everywhere between Manado and Ujung Pandang leave from Terminal Andalas; catch a microlet or ojek from Pasar Sentral.

Danau Limboto, forts, hot springs and jungle

A twenty-minute microlet ride west from Pasar Sentral takes you to the shores of shallow, gradually contracting **Danau Limboto**. There are excellent views over the 56-square-kilometre basin from **Benteng Otanaha**, a series of three circular stone **forts** arranged on a stony, dry hill-top at the eastern edge of the lake, possibly built in the sixteenth century by the Portuguese and later used by local warlords. Microlets to the village of **Dembe** (Rp500) leave you where stairs climb to the turret-like walls, whose blocks are held together by a mixture of cement laced with maleo eggs. The lake sprawls below into the hazy distance, its marshy fringes a patchwork of fish farms, aluminium village roofs, and the soft, dark green of palm tops.

In the other direction, **Lumbongo hot springs** lie 17km east of Gorontalo at the edge of Dumoga-Bone national park, crowded at weekends (when transport is plentiful) and otherwise deserted. Microlets in this direction leave at irregular intervals from outside Gorontalo's hospital on Jalan Sultan Botutihe, and you'll have to bargain down ridiculous asking prices for the thirty-minute journey – the springs are about 1km off the main road, and drivers charge extra to take you right to the gates. Entry to the springs – which fill a couple of swimming pools at the foot of a steep, wooded mountain range – is Rp1000, but those intending to hike 3km beyond them to a series of **waterfalls** inside the national park are supposed to call in first at the **ranger station** (just before the entrance) for a **permit**. This is also valid for entry into Dumoga-Bone's eastern end, if you're heading that way, and the ranger himself is glad to chat about wildlife and the possibility of five-day traverses of the park (Rp250,000). The path to the waterfall is rocky and easy to follow, crossing nine streams and taking you through some respectable forest; clearings with pools along the way allow a view of the treetops, and are good spots to look for butterflies, reptiles, birds and monkeys. The last microlet **back to Gorontalo** passes along the main road at about 6pm, but is often full – don't leave things this late.

Kwandang, Kotamobagu and Dumoga-Bone national park

Two hours north from Gorontalo, the Manado road crosses the peninsula to the far coast at **KWANDANG**, where it's a short microlet hop from the tiny centre to Kwandang's **Pelni harbour**, port of call for a monthly service to Palu, Ujung Pandang, Kalimantan and Java. There are also two more **forts** of Portuguese stamp just south of town, though neither are worth a special visit; **Ota Mas Udangan** is a pile of rubble, with renovations fleshing out the remains of **Benteng Oranje**.

The highway continues 300km east from Kwandang and on up to Manado, but about halfway along a secondary road cuts inland at **Inobonto** to **KOTAMOBAGU**, one-time capital of the Bolaang-Mongondow sultanate, a hideout for Permesta rebels, and now a friendly market town. Eight hours from Gorontalo, buses pull in to Terminal Tiga Bonawang at the northern edge of town, where microlets will ferry you to the mosque, market, stores and active, scruffy streets that make up Kotamobagu's centre. The pick of the **accommodation** here are *Hotel Ramayana* on Jalan Adampe Dolot, the approach road to the centre (☎0434/21188; ③), and *Hotel Ade Irama*, closer in on Jalan Ade Irama (☎0434/21216; ④); warung near the mosque and a couple of Padang and Indonesian canteens on Jalan Ahmed Yani provide **food** – try the *Nasional* or *Surya*. Set aside a day in Kotamobagu and catch a minibus 25km east via **Modayang** to **Modoinding** village on the western side of **Danau Mooat**, a flooded volcano crater ringed by forest. Trails from behind Modoinding's church lead west up 1780-metre-high **Gunung Ambang** – check with locals to make sure of the track. A couple of hours should see you at the apparent summit; thick vegetation means no views, but steaming, sulphurous vents and the jungle compensate. **Leaving Kotamobagu**, buses to Gorontalo or Manado leave Terminal Tiga Bonawang in the morning, mid-afternoon and evening, with shared kijang to Doloduo and Dumoga-Bone best organized early on in the day.

Doloduo and Dumoga-Bone national park

The paddy-field colours along the fifty-kilometre, well-watered **Dumoga Valley** south-west of Kotamobagu terminate with the drier, darker tones of **Dumoga-Bone national park**, a 1900-square-kilometre reserve created as much to protect water-catchment areas as to provide a safe haven for Sulawesi's dwindling populations of endemic fauna. About two-thirds of the way into the journey and just past **DUMOGA**, the village of **IMANDI** marks a detour 7km south to a **maleo nesting ground**, the best place in the region to encounter this elusive bird – though reports suggest that sightings are rare even here. You might be able to arrange for a Kijang from Kotamobagu to take you to the site, or hunt around for an ojek at Imandi.

All transport terminates at **DOLODUO**, a dusty T-intersection on **Sungai Kasingolan**, from where vehicles back to Kotamobagu and Manado leave in the morning. Ask around in Doluduo for inexpensive **homestay** accommodation with "Niko", or catch one of the frequent microlets plying the ten-kilometre road west to **Camp Wallacea** (⑨; meals extra) at the gateway to the park. A former research post, *Wallacea*'s facilities are fine, but attempts to chisel the last rupiah out of guests is a major irritation – look out for the service charge, which they forget to mention until settling the bill. Your accommodation can arrange an obligatory **guide** into Dumoga-Bone for a flat Rp17,500, irrespective of whether you spend forty minutes or four hours in the jungle; bear in mind that unless a group comprises "family members", each person has to pay.

Fortunately, Dumoga-Bone's interior is impressively wild, with circuit tracks fording shallow Sungai Kasingolan behind *Wallacea* into a margin of vines and bamboo clumps, which gradually merge with a mix of mature fan palms and mighty rainforest trees, fig trunks reaching 40m skywards while their buttress roots form complex tangles at ground level. Steamy heat and crunchy leaf litter make for tiring stalking, and abundant rattan means boots, legs and arms can take a scratching. Wildlife is best seen at dawn; birds find the break in the canopy over the river a convenient highway between the trees, and you can spot native pigeons, racquet-tail parrots and hornbills within a minute's walk of *Wallacea*'s walls. Further into the forest, you might catch tarsiers nestling down for the day, get checked out by an inquisitive black macaque or two, or glimpse snakes and jungle fowl – wild chickens – tearing off into the undergrowth at your approach.

Manado, Minahasa and beyond

Mainland Sulawesi's final 120km descends north off the volcanic plateau of the **Minahasan highlands** and out over a string of sand-and-coral islands, which start immediately offshore inside **Bunaken Marine Reserve** and reach right on up to the **Sangihe-Talaud group** towards the Philippines. On the western shore, **Manado** is the north's largest city, well positioned for trips up into the hills, out to sea, or across the peninsula to more mountains, forests, and the port of **Bitung**.

Manado

Capital of Sulawesi Utara, **MANADO** is a cosmopolitan place, its blended population of islanders, Minahasans, Chinese, Indonesians and Westerners reflecting a long history of absorbed influences. Facing west over **Manado Bay**, there was already a settlement called **Wenang** here before the Portuguese and Spanish introduced Catholicism during the sixteenth century, but the city's current name seems to have been in vogue by the time that the VOC evicted the Iberians and built the now-defunct **Fort Amsterdam** against Ternate's claims on the area a hundred years later. Today Manado projects a prosperous, self-respecting air, managing to be modern without having fallen victim to the cheap concrete constructions that overwhelm so many of Indonesia's cities, and you don't have to look hard to find backstreets with neat houses and gardens.

Practicalities

Downtown Manado is a couple of blocks of markets, squares, roundabouts and intersections on the north side of the city immediately below a shallow, silted **harbour**, with other businesses and services south of here along the first kilometre or so of Jalan Sam Ratulangi, which runs parallel with seafront Jalan Pierre Tendean. **Sam Ratulangi airport** is 12km northeast, where taxis and touts for accommodation and dive operations meet new arrivals. Long-distance **buses** stop on Manado's southern outskirts at **Terminal Malalayang**; minibuses from the Minahasa highlands arrive southeast at

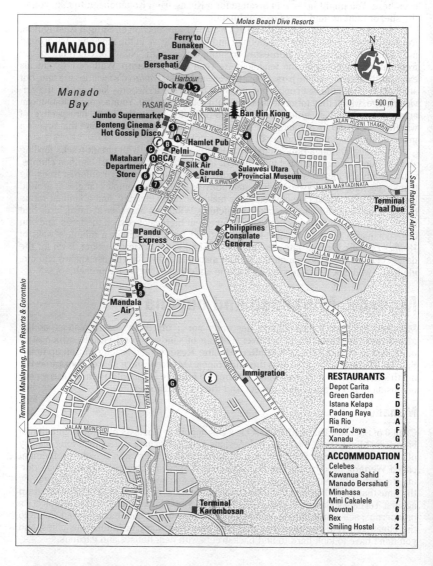

RESTAURANTS

Depot Carita	C
Green Garden	E
Istana Kelapa	D
Padang Raya	B
Ria Rio	A
Tinoor Jaya	F
Xanadu	G

ACCOMMODATION

Celebes	1
Kawanua Sahid	3
Manado Bersahati	5
Minahasa	8
Mini Cakalele	7
Novotel	6
Rex	4
Smiling Hostel	2

Terminal Karombasan; those from Bitung (the regional Pelni port) wind up east at **Terminal Paal Dua** – see the "Useful microlets" box below for transport from all arrival points into the city. Manado has no becaks, but an inordinate quantity of numbered and labelled **microlets** converge downtown at the top of Jalan Sam Ratulangi at **Pasar 45** ("Pasar Empat Lima"), an area of back-lane stalls, supermarkets and ferry agents next to the **dock**. Otherwise, **taxis** are on hand outside the Matahari and Golden department stores about 500m south of Pasar 45 on Jalan Ratulangi.

Seek **information** at your accommodation. Manado's tourist office (Dinas Pariwisata), 4km southeast of the centre off Jalan 17 Augustus (☎0431/864911), hands out brochures but offers no practical advice.

USEFUL MICROLETS

Airport–Paal Dua: microlet "Paal Dua".
Terminal Malalayang–Pasar 45: microlets #1, #2, #3 and #4.
Terminal Karombosan–Pasar 45: microlet #9 or #13, or "Wanea".
Terminal Paal Dua–Pasar 45: microlet "Paal II-Pasar 45".

ACCOMMODATION

Manado has plenty of central, fair-value lodgings, all with restaurants relative to their facilities and able to provide at least basic information about the city and surroundings. There are also a handful of **dive resorts** outside the city offering good deals for divers – see box below.

Hotel Celebes, Jl Rumambi 8 (☎0431/870425, fax 859068). Backing onto the harbour, within 100m of Pasar 45, this is new; the tiled, four-storey building has ekonomi singles smaller than a monastic cell (Rp21,000), and better air-con doubles with TV and mandi. ⑥.

DIVE RESORTS

If you're in Manado to **dive**, and are prepared to spend a little in order to do it with any comfort and safety, you can find accommodation-and-scuba packages with the following resorts. All are on the coast 5–10km either side of Manado; packages include airport transfers, or catch a taxi from the centre to the place of your choice. **Prices** below are per person, per day for double/twin-share rooms, two dives, boat and guide, weight belt and all meals. For gear rental rates, plus the cost of dive trips from the mainland without accommodation, see "Diving" in the Manado Listings on p.846.

Barracuda Dive Resort, Molas Dusun II (☎0431/854279, fax 864848). Newish operation, with bungalows facing mangroves and mountains 5km north of the city at Molas Beach. Boats are a little cramped, but good standards and a fair deal. US$85.

Manado Seagarden, PO Box 1535, Manado (☎ & fax 0431/861100). Clean, motel-like rooms 5km south of Manado at Malalayang; well-maintained dive gear and a knowledgeable Italian instructor. US$75.

Manado Underwater Explorations (Murex), PO Box 236, Manado (office on Jalan Sudirman 28; ☎0431/866280, fax 852116). Small, friendly and relaxed resort 7km south at Desa Kelasay, with helpful staff and fine food; dive gear in good condition but dated. US$75.

Nusantara Dive Centre (NDC), PO Box 15, Manado (☎0431/863988, fax 863707). 5km north at Molas Beach, big grounds and fine facilities make NDC the most established dive resort in Manado; some rental equipment is a bit worse for wear, but dive guides are excellent – ask for Daeng. US$100.

Hotel Kawanua Sahid, Jl Sam Ratulangi 1 (☎0431/867777, fax 865220). Manado's most prestigious business hotel; good restaurants, but otherwise nothing more than a pretentious, overpriced landmark. ⑨.

Hotel Manado Bersahati, Jl Sudirman 20 (☎0431/855022, fax 857238). "Traditional" wooden exterior with balcony; inside a little confined but spotless and one of the best budget deals in town, offering bicycle rental and good local information. Small singles and doubles, plus bigger rooms with air-con and mandi. ④–⑤.

Hotel Minahasa, Jl Sam Ratulangi 199 (☎0431/862059); 1500m south of Pasar 45 on microlet #1, #2, #3 and #4 route. Unusually atmospheric, older hotel with attentive staff and peaceful grounds. ⑥.

Hotel Mini Cakalele, Jl Korengkeng 40 (☎0431/852942, fax 866948). Old, tidy and friendly, with quieter rooms out the back facing onto the garden. Doubles with mandi ⑤.

Novotel, Jl Pierre Tendean (☎0431/855555, fax 868888). Brand-new tower block offering all the services and comforts you'd expect from this international hotel chain, including its own wharf and dive operation. ⑨.

Hotel Rex, Jl Sugiono 3 (☎0431/851136, fax 867706). Very clean and fairly priced, if somewhat cramped. Singles Rp9000; doubles with fan Rp15,000, with air-con ⑤.

Smiling Hostel, Jl Rumambi 7 (☎0431/868463). Right next to the harbour; helpful, laid-back staff, low prices and an informative notice board compensate for dingy rooms. Dorm or single ③.

The City

Start a tour of Manado on the north side of the harbour at the city's most active market, **Pasar Bersahati**, where a blaring loudspeaker is, for once, not calling the faithful to prayer but announcing **fish prices** as boats unload their catches on the beach behind. In 1997, the contents of one vessel returning from a deep-water trawl around Manado Tua sent shock waves through the icthyological world when a **coelacanth** – an exceptionally rare "living fossil" fish only known previously from the Comoro islands off East Africa – was offered for sale. At least one more has been netted since, adding new importance to the preservation of Manado's marine habitat.

Though you're unlikely to see such wonders, the **market** presents a squalid, bustling scene, the angles of the three-storey building swamped under a mass of humanity; blue shoals of microlets circle in the forecourt, spangled street magicians balance heavy rocks on bottle necks or perform sword tricks while shifty urchins eye spectators, and men parade with fighting cockerels tucked under their arms. The **harbour** itself is rimmed by a sea wall, the water a shambles of floating and semi-submerged boats, island ferries and outrigger canoes. Heading south towards the centre from here takes you through **Pasar Ikan Tua**, the old fish market, a scrap of wasteland covered in shacks selling hardware; bear east and you'll soon arrive at the yellow walls and red trim of the **Ban Hin Kiong temple** on the corner of Jalan Panjaitan and Jalan Sutomo. An indication of Manado's wealthy Chinese population, this recently restored, nineteenth-century Taoist complex with fairy lights and elegant dragons crawling along the rooftop is the focus for lunar new year festivities, usually in February.

Weaving past the markets and shops southwest of the temple, and the gold shops along Jalan Walanda Maramis, the top end of Jalan Sam Ratulangi is marked by a complex traffic flow around **Victory monument**, a tableau of seven concrete soldiers painted garish green and yellow. Southwest again, Jalan Pierre Tendean is Manado's wide boulevard, whose northern end seems to have been earmarked as the site of future upmarket tourist development. It's a bit barren at present, though Manado's poor have taken advantage of the situation and built corrugated-iron shanties in vacant blocks facing the sea, pulling their boats up the steep sea walls on bamboo slipways. Further down, a few bars and mobile warung open up in the afternoon, and there are always a handful of people in the vicinity soaking up the fine views of the sunset and nearby islands. A thirty-minute walk east of here past a half-dozen **churches**, or about the same time in a microlet from Pasar 45, the dusty halls of the **Sulawesi Utara**

Provincial Museum on Jalan Supratman (open when the staff arrive; Rp750 or Rp500 for a guide) might appeal to history buffs, but the contents are otherwise of minor interest – a coral diorama and *waruga* mausoleums from the Airmadidi region are amongst the few topical items here.

Eating and Entertainment

Manado's latest entertainment trend is "English pubs", which inside are normal bardisco-karaoke affairs. *Depot Carita Pub & Karaoke* on Jalan Pierre Tendean has fast food, imported beer and impeccable sunset views; *Hamlet Pub & Karaoke*, Jalan Sudirman 37, specializes in cocktails; while the two most popular discos in town are *Hot Gossip* and *Borneo*, both on Jalan Sam Ratulangi and packed nightly with a sweaty, young crowd. The Benteng **cinema** on Jalan Sam Ratulangi is the most central, with mainly Western releases.

Minahasan cooking features **dog** (*rintek wuuk* in Minahasan, usually shortened to *rw*, or "airway"), **rat** (*tikkus*) and **fruit bat** (*paniki*), generally unceremoniously stewed with blistering quantities of chillies – though deep-fried bat wings make an interesting side dish. Wash it down with *tuak*, palm wine, or a distilled tipple known as **sopi** and marketed under the Cap Tikkus (Rat Brand) label. Most of Manado's restaurants serve more familiar Indonesian fare, though there is one Minahasan place in town, and others along the range road to Tomohon (p.848). **Cheap warung** are legion around Pasar 45 and Jalan Sudirman, and you can sit down to European-style **pastries** and coffee at *Hotel Kawanua Sahid* and *Bakeri Batavia*, the latter between supermarkets on Jalan Sam Ratulangi. Try the markets for *tuak, sopi* and fresh fruit – salak, mangoes and huge pawpaws – with groceries also on hand at the Matahari, Golden and Jumbo **supermarkets**, all once again south of Pasar 45 on Jalan Sam Ratulangi.

RESTAURANTS

Green Garden, Jl Sam Ratulangi 52. Extremely busy, airy, open-sided Chinese establishment with moderate prices, good soups, seafood and *sayur lohan* (monks' vegetables).

Istana Kelapa, Jl Pierre Tendean. Imported beer, grilled fish and sea views.

Padang Raya, Jl Sam Ratulangi, across from Telkom. Above-average Padang meals; some dishes are extremely hot.

Ria Rio, Jl Sudirman 3. Cheap, fresh, tasty seafood, simple decor and noisy patrons.

Tinoor Jaya, Jl Sam Ratulangi 169. Check tablecloths and a breezy upstairs setting for consuming Minahasan specialities; the fruit bat here looks as if the animal was hit by a grenade – fragments of bone, skin and chunky black meat – but very tasty.

Xanadu, Jl Sam Ratulangi, about 3km south of the centre. Upmarket Chinese restaurant with expensive food and dim lighting; good *ikan mas* and spicy bean-curd dishes.

Listings

Airlines Some accommodation, but no airlines, run minibuses to the airport; otherwise take a microlet from Terminal Paal Dua, or a taxi. Airline offices open Mon–Fri 8am–4pm, Sat & Sun 9am–1pm. Garuda, Jl Diponegoro 15 (☎0431/864535, fax 851390), to Ujung Pandang; Mandala, Jl Sam Ratulangi 206 (☎0431/851324), to Ujung Pandang; Merpati, Jl Sudirman 132 (☎0431/864028, fax 851525), to Ternate; Silk Air, Jl Lasut (☎0431/863744, fax 853841), to Balikpapan and Singapore.

Banks and exchange BCA, Jl Sam Ratulangi, across from Matahari store (Mon–Fri 8am–2pm, Sat 8am–noon), is fast and efficient, with fair exchange rates and cash advances on Visa or Mastercard.

Buses Long-distance buses to Kotamobagu, Doloduo, Gorontalo and beyond depart from Terminal Malalayang; Paris Express have air-con and Marina have older buses. Services to Minahasan highlands depart from Terminal Karombasan through the day, as do those for Airmadidi, Girian and Bitung from Terminal Paal Dua.

Consulates Philippines Consulate General, Jl Lumimuut 8, PO Box 1079, Manado (☎0431/862181, fax 855316).

Diving Day-trips from the mainland with two dives, boat, dive guide, weight belt, air and lunch cost from US$65. Hiring a suit, gauges, BCD, and mask, snorkel and fins will set you back a further US$30; certification courses and night dives can also be arranged. Aside from Manado's dive resorts (p.843), a recommended option is Blue Banter, Floor 2, Novotel, Jl Piere Tandean (☎0431/862135, fax 863545), with good equipment, facilities and dive crew. Diving costs on Pulau Bunaken are far lower than Manado, but first read the account opposite.

Ferries Pelni, opposite Telkom on Jl Sam Ratulangi, is a gloomy office with one photocopied schedule under cracked glass, but they can organize tickets out of Bitung. For tickets and schedules for boats from Manado to Tahuna on Sangihe island, Lirung on Pulau Talaud, and Ambon, try agents in the streets between Pasar 45 and the dock.

Hospital Public hospital 6km south of city beside Terminal Melalayang (☎0431/853191); take mikrolet #1–4 from Pasar 45 – there's a better hospital in the hills at Tomohon (see p.848).

Immigration Jl 17 Augustus (☎0431/863491).

Post office GPO Manado Jl Sam Ratulangi 21.

Shopping Golden, Matahari and Jumbo supermarkets have all supplies; there's also a top-floor bookshop with a few maps at the Matahari. For cheap bags, shoes, clothes, watches and hats try Pasar 45. Specially designed "Dive Manado" T-shirts from Toko Karawang, Jl Walanda Maramis.

Telephone and fax Telkom, Jl Sam Ratulangi 4, has a fax sevice and international phones; opens early.

Travel and tour agents Where possible it's easier to go direct to airlines or Pelni, but you can also make bookings through Kartika Mapalus, tucked away next to the Jumbo Supermarket; Maya Express, Jl Sudirman 15 (☎0431/870111, fax 870603); Dian Sakatho Tours and Travel, Jl Sam Ratulangi (☎0431/860003); and Pandu Express, Jl Sam Ratulangi 91 (☎0431/851188, fax 861487).

Bunaken Marine Reserve

Northwest of Manado, a 75-square-kilometre patch of sea is sectioned off as **Bunaken Marine Reserve**, where **coral reefs** around the reserve's four major islands drop to a forty-metre shelf before falling into depths of 200m and more, creating stupendous reef **walls** abounding with so much life that at times you hardly know where to start looking. Blue-green Napoleon (maori) wrasse and coral-crunching humpheaded parrotfish are two of the largest fish here, usually encountered over deep water; barracuda materialize disconcertingly for a closer look, while divers are frequently buzzed by schools of trevally and tuna, and the odd shark. Turtles, manta rays, whales and dolphin put in an appearance, too, though pods of the latter are more often seen from boats around the islands than met underwater. Smaller creatures include gaping morays; at shallower depths look for vividly coloured nudibranchs, camouflaged scorpionfish, mantis shrimps with razor-sharp forelegs, and black-and-silver banded sea snakes, which remain totally indifferent to your following them around as they forage in crevices for fry. Set aside concerns about snakes and sharks and avoid instead the metre-long Titan triggerfish, sharp-beaked and notoriously pugnacious when guarding its nest; and small, fluorescent-red anemone fish, which are prone to giving divers a painful nip in defence of their territory.

Promoted as Indonesia's official scuba centre, loosely enforced management plans and the soaring popularity of the marine reserve are starting to take its toll on conditions here, particularly around **Pulau Bunaken**, whose prime sites receive the most attention from visitors and tend to eclipse the potential of nearby **Siladen**, **Manado Tua** and **Montehage** islands. Fortunately, it looks as if local dive shops are starting to cooperate over conservation, and with luck Bunaken will start to receive more than paper protection in the near future.

Visiting and diving the reserve

Organizing a trip to Bunaken Marine Reserve is complicated by a good deal of mud-slinging about the quality of specific operations. Much depends on your budget and personal expectations, but basically you can visit the reserve in two ways, both of which allow for snorkelling and diving: either on **day-trips** from Manado, which can be arranged privately or through dive operations, or by staying at **budget accommodation** within the reserve on Bunaken or Siladen islands. As regards what type of **dive operation** to use, if you need any training, qualified assistance or reasonable rental gear, opt for one of the pricier, professional operators in Manado itself. If you are already certified, preferably have your own equipment, and accept that you are not hiring a divemaster or instructor, but only a dive guide of unknown competence, then save money by shopping around on Pulau Bunaken. In either case you must assume responsibility for checking out the **reliability** of rental gear and **air quality**, the two biggest causes for concern here.

The best **weather conditions** are between June and November, with light breezes, calm seas and visibility underwater averaging 25m and peaking beyond 50m. Try to avoid the westerly storms between December and February – though on calm days you'll see a fair amount even then, and fewer visitors means that it's a good time to push for deals – and less severe, easterly winds from March until June, when upwellings can make for cold water and reduced visibility.

Pulau Bunaken and around

About an hour by ferry out from Manado, **Pulau Bunaken** is a low-backed, five-kilometre-long comma covered in coconut trees and ringed by sand and mangroves. There's a **public ferry** (Rp2500) from the dock behind Manado's Pasar Bersehati daily at 8am (get there 30min early), or plenty of private boat owners hanging around the harbour wall offering their services to foreigners (Rp40,000). Either way, you end up at **Bunaken village** on the island's southeastern tip, from where the ferry returns to Manado at 7.30am. Here you'll be met by touts attached to one of Bunaken's **homestays**, who will tell you that anywhere other than the business they represent doesn't exist, or is full; places below draw generally good press and are clustered in two groups within a couple of kilometres of the village, providing rooms with shared mandi (④ per person), cottages with own mandi (④ per person), all meals and some snorkelling gear. On the east coast, **Pangalisang beach** is quiet and, though some feel that the reef is patchy and the sand compromised by too many mangrove trees, adventurous skindivers can test their lungs on some fine drop-offs here; recommended places to stay include *Daniel's, Lorenzo's* (top food), *Doris* and *Tuwo Kona*. Western **Liang beach** is the most popular spot, with fewer trees and Bunaken's best coral 100m offshore; *Papa Boa, Yulin, Tante Nona* and *Ibu Konda* are pick of the homestays here. All of Bunaken's accommodation is **illegal**, incidentally, as marine park status means that there should be no tourist facilities at all on the island. Accepting that locals need to make money, however, the government looks the other way as long as only the budget market is catered to here, and official businesses in Manado are not challenged – hence the absence of "real" scuba schools on the island. With this in mind, you'll find that **dive operators** come and go; at the time of writing Randi Montalalo and Ronni were the best on Bunaken – you should try to track them down through your accommodation. Two dives start from US$40 all-inclusive, but anyone planning some serious dive time should try to negotiate reductions through bulk deals – establish clearly what your deal includes, and make sure you fix prices in advance, preferably in writing. Rental gear on Bunaken is in short supply and bad repair.

Off the west beach between Bunaken village and Liang beach, **Lekuan** 1, 2 and 3 are exceptionally steep, deep walls, and the place to find everything from gobies and eels to deep-water sharks. Further around on the far western end of the island, there are giant clams and stingrays at **Fukui**, while **Mandolin** is good for turtles, occasional mantas and even marlin, and **Mike's Point** attracts more sharks and sea snakes. On shore, there are a few seafood restaurants on Liang beach, with women selling fruit and shells outside – collected elsewhere, they say, should you ask – and tracks over the middle of the island, which you can follow to a couple of isolated little sandy coves on the north shore.

The reserve's **other islands** can be reached by chartering a boat from Manado or Bunaken, and sometimes feature on dive trips from the mainland. Just east of Bunaken, tiny **Siladen** has better beaches, fewer visitors, and *Martha's* homestay (④ all-inclusive); westerly **Manado Tua** features a prominent, steep-sided cone, with a tiring trail to the top. Seven kilometres north of Bunaken, **Montehage** is the biggest island in the reserve, with a Bajau village on its north end. There's also a potentially good dive site here, known as **Barracuda Point** for the numbers of these fierce-looking fish often seen hanging motionless in the current, but if the barracuda don't show there's nothing else to see.

The Minahasan highlands

The green, volcanic highlands rising 20km south of Manado are home to the **Minahasans**, a people who colonized this corner of Sulawesi from the Philippines some two millennia ago. Minahasan legends, however, name the goddess **Lumimuut** and her husband (and son) **Toar** as the ancestor of **seven clans**, which, though they cooperated in many ways through the ages – the word *Minahasa* derives from a term meaning "unity" – never had an overall ruler. The success of **Protestantism** since its nineteenth-century introduction to the highlands means that little survives of traditional Minahasan life, though head-hunting was practised and the dead were buried in stone mausoleums called **waruga**. First contacts with the West came when the Spanish tried to foist a puppet king on the highlands during the seventeenth century, but the Minahasans allied with the Dutch and kicked them out, and were subsequently left much to their own devices until Holland itself subjugated the north with the abrupt **Tondano War** of 1809. The new rulers introduced coffee cultivation and schooling, simultaneously finding this remote land useful as a quarantine for **political trouble-makers** from elsewhere in the archipelago – Javan War instigator Prince Diponegoro and his general Kyai Modjo were exiled here, as was their fellow countryman Imam Bonjol. **Japanese occupation** during the 1940s was a low point, the population put to forced labour digging caves and tunnels against Allied air raids, but things have picked up since Independence, particularly during the **clove** boom of the 1970s, when Minahasa had the highest per-capita income of any rural district in Southeast Asia. There's been a fall in prices since then, but the highlands remain a refreshingly confident place, whose people make the most of any excuse to enjoy themselves; get out to the smaller villages up here for one of the countless minor festivals through the year, and soak up the local style of music, dancing and drink.

Minibuses from Manado's Terminal Karombasan climb the winding range road to the **western highlands** at **Tomohon**, from where there's transport to everywhere else in Minahasa. On the way, stop at **Tinoor** for a Minahasan meal at one of the **restaurants** built looking out down the hillside to the coast; try the *Tinoor Indah*, for some of the best views and tastiest grilled pig – not to mention rat – that the region has to offer. There's also a route running up **from Airmadidi**, on the Manado–Bitung road, to the **eastern highlands**, which focus around **Tondano** town and its adjoining **lake**. Microlets cover all but the smallest roads, where dokar take over; come dressed for cool nights, morning mists and hot days.

Tomohon and volcanoes
The approach to **TOMOHON**, 30km from Manado and the highland's second town, is through 5km of flower nurseries between the rumbling, highly active cones of **Gunung Lokon**, abode of the Minahasan deity Pinondoan, and the slightly shorter **Gunung Malawu**. A busy, friendly, breezy, strongly Christian place, the town clusters about a **crossroads** whose four streets align with main compass points, where you'll find a **supermarket**, BCA **bank** amenable to travellers' cheques, and **Bethesda Hospital**,

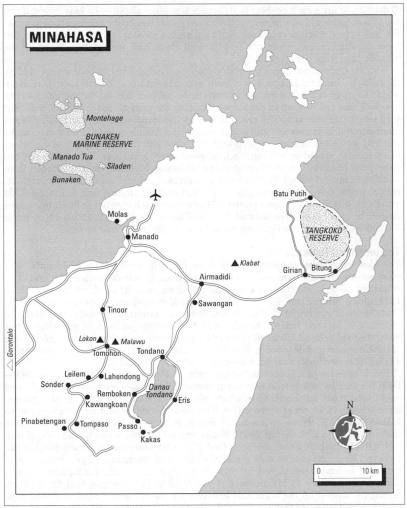

MINAHASA

Montehage

BUNAKEN
MARINE RESERVE

Manado Tua

Siladen

Bunaken

✈

Molas

● Manado

Batu Putih

TANGKOKO
RESERVE

▲ Klabat

Airmadidi

Girian ● Bitung

△ Gorontalo

● Tinoor

● Sawangan

Lokon ▲ ▲ Malawu

Tomohon ● Tondano

● Leilem

● Lahendong

Sonder ● ● Remboken

● Kawangkoan

Danau
Tondano

● Eris

Pinabetengan ● ● Tompaso

Passo ●

Kakas

N

0   10 km

the province's best. Immediately east of the crossroads, all **transport** around the eastern highlands, across to Tondano, and back to Manado congregates in the vicinity of Tomohon's **market**, where Westerners go to be disgusted by the sight of charred-black dogs and rats, and to buy excellent coffee – Tuesday, Thursday and Saturday are the main times. **Accommodation** lies back towards Manado; either get dropped off on the way here or catch a blue microlet or **taxi** from opposite the hospital. About 1500m along the main road is the tidy *Palm Tree Homestay* (③), or there are three places to stay about 2km from Tomohon at **Kakaskasen Dua** village, on the very foothills of Gunung Lokon. Get out at **Gereja Pniel**, a large, iron-roofed church, and follow the lane opposite 500m west to a choice of accommodation at the wooden, high-set *Happy Flower* (☎0431/352787; single ③, double with air-con ⑤), similar *Lokon Bunga Asri* (③ single,

④ double), or the smarter cabins at *Volcano Resort* (⑤) – all prices include meals. If you want them, **guides** at your accommodation can escort you up the volcanoes, help locate five bulky stone **waruga** in Kakaskasen's back lanes, similar to those at Sawangan (for more on which, see opposite), or find the trail out to **Kali waterfall**, reached off the Manado road from **Kinalow** village.

With energy, you can knock off both volcanoes in a day. The two-hour ascent of 1580-metre-high **Gunung Lokon** starts from accommodation at Kakaskasen Dua, from where a variety of tracks eventually converge on old lava flow on the mountain's eastern flank, and follow it up to rubble surrounding the crater – not a difficult walk, but very slow going after rain. The crater is a 500-metre-broad steaming pit stinking of sulphur, covered in brown ash and edged in obsidian boulders; poisonous fumes make climbing inside a dangerous undertaking. Lokon's south rim rises steeply to the mountain's summit, scaled by a tiring track of loose scree, and views from the grassy top encompass Manado Tua and Tomohon. For **Gunung Malawu**, catch a microlet from Tomohon's market a few kilometres east past acres of aubergines, cauliflowers and carrots, to where drivers will leave you at the start of the hour-long path to the top. Thin woodlands along the way open up to a 1311-metre summit covered in fire-prone grasslands. The crater is sheer-sided and deep, and winds, cloud and crumbly edges make the entire trail around the rim very hazardous – a slip here would be fatal.

The western highlands

The road south from Tomohon heads down through the **western highlands**, with more vulcanism some 7km along at **Gunung Linau**, in Minahasan lore the first of all volcanoes to be created. A sealed, kilometre-long road uphill from the church at **Lahendong** passes a rim-side restaurant (with cold drinks) and views into the semi-cultivated interior and bright blue-green disc of **Danau Linau**, the broad crater lake. The mountain is dormant but still ticking, with **hot springs** on its southern slopes, just down the road before **Leilem** village; a cracked footpath leads through a hostile terrain of bubbling mud and desolate grey rubble streaked with yellow, the ground covered in a crunchy crystallized crust with steam oozing out of the soil.

Five kilometres past Leilem and at the centre of Minahasan **clove** production, **SONDER** is a wealthy little retreat of wooden houses in the chalet-like Minahasan style, and might soon enjoy a financial renaissance after the IMF's recent breakup of a government scheme to suppress clove prices. The same distance south again brings you to **KAWANGKOAN**, where **caves** (more like large tunnels) built to store ammunition under Japanese orders during World War II, and now standing empty, can be explored with a torch. Push on from here for a final 10km past **Tompaso** to **Pinabetengan village**, and it's a forty-minute walk uphill to **Watu Pinabetengan**, a large, oblong slab of rock said to have been hurled here by an eruption of Gunung Linau, and a site of immense importance to Minahasans. It was at Watu Pinabetengan that the goddess Lumimuut divided up the highlands between Minahasa's seven clans, and the stone became a rallying point through the ages where leaders met to reject formally the idea of kings and to present a united front against invaders. Associations and the walk make the journey worthwhile, as the rock itself is covered with concrete, recent graffiti and an ugly pavilion, and the faint archaic symbols carved on one side are almost invisible.

The eastern highlands: Tondano and the lake

Ringed by hills, Minahasa's **eastern highlands** form a flat, green, grassy basin around fifty-square-kilometre **Danau Tondano**, with **TONDANO** town on its northern tip. A small high street with a market at one end and a minibus terminal at the other, and smelling – as does everywhere up here – of cloves and horses, Tondano is prettier but less active than Tomohon; there's **accommodation** here at the tidy *AsriBaru* (④), a couple of warung along the high street, and **memorials** to local heroes Sam Ratulangi, a pro-Independence fighter who governed Sulawesi briefly before his death in 1949, and Sarapung and Korengkeng, Minahasan leaders during the 1809 anti-Dutch Tondano war, which was fought around the lake.

Starting in town, you can travel down both sides of Danau Tondano by microlet, though the south end is infrequently serviced and it's best to allow most of a day to get right around the perimeter; out on the lake is an ever-changing scenery of fish farms, pole houses reached along rickety bamboo bridges, and dark-blue water whipped with white crests raised by the afternoon winds. Halfway down the west shore is the pottery centre of **REMBOKEN** and **Sumaru Endo**, a tourist complex with pedal boats, food and naturally heated hot spas, all very popular at the weekends. There are more thermal pools south of Remboken at **Passo**, whose fields are strung with plastic bags to keep birds away, then the road leaves the lakeside for **Kakas** before heading up the eastern side to **ERIS**, a quiet town opposite Remboken where it's possible to rent a boat out to **Likri islet**, a speck of rock out in the middle of the water.

Sawangan and waruga

North of Tondano, it takes around ninety minutes for minibuses to follow the twenty-kilometre twisting road down the range to Airmadidi on the Manado–Bitung highway. About 5km from Airmadidi is **SAWANGAN** village, where a short lane off the road ends at **Taman Purbakala Waruga-Waruga**, a cemetery with a difference. Here stand over a hundred *waruga*, Minahasan sarcophagi, gathered from across the region during the 1970s and all predating an 1828 Dutch ban on their use; two-metre upright stone boxes with spreading, roof-shaped lids, arranged in rows like fossilized mushrooms. Most of the boxes are plain, but the lids are heavily carved with male and female figures, some naked, others seemingly attired in Western-style clothing; other motifs include birds, cattle and dragons. Pieces of porcelain, spiky (and improbably heavy) bronze armbands, iron axes and even a few bone fragments which looters missed are on show at a small **museum** nearby, whose caretaker laboriously produces keys and a donation box when foreigners arrive.

The northern tip: Airmadidi, Tangkoko and Bitung

The fifty-kilometre highway running east across the peninsula from Manado to Bitung is covered by frequent minibuses from Terminal Paal Dua. About halfway along, **AIRMADIDI** is where to look for traffic heading south into the highlands at Tondano, but the town also sits below the province's highest peak, **Gunung Klabat**. Minahasan lore has it that Klabat was once Gunung Lokon's summit until villagers, feeling that Lokon was too tall, sliced the top off and carried it here. It's a solid six-hour climb on a sometimes dodgy path from Airmadidi's police station to Klabat's 1995-metre-high apex; start at midnight and catch the sunrise over Minahasa.

Past Airmadidi and forty minutes from Manado, **Girian** is the jumping-off point for the mix of dry woodlands and full-blown rainforest of **Tangkoko-Batuangus-Dua-Saudara Reserve**, named after the three mountains around which the park is formed and usually abbreviated to just Tangkoko. A battered bus leaves Girian late morning along the two-hour, twenty-kilometre potholed track to **BATU PUTIH** village, which faces the sea at the northern edge of the reserve. Get out a couple of kilometres short of Batu Putih at Tangkoko's **entrance**; there's a **homestay** (④, meals included) on the main road here, but it's more fun to follow the two-kilometre access track into the reserve itself, which ends where a **bunkhouse** (④, meals included) sits on a shaded shingle beach between the sea and the forest. The **ranger** will catch up with you at some point, request a Rp750 entry fee, and offer his considerable abilities as a **guide** at Rp15,000–20,000, which includes a short evening walk after tarsiers, and a longer dawn circuit for the black macaques and hornbills which are Tangkoko's pride. You're pretty

TO THE SANGIHE-TALAUD ISLANDS AND THE PHILIPPINES

The 500-kilometre straits separating mainland north Sulawesi and the Philippines is dotted with the seventy-odd **islands** of the **Sangihe-Talaud group**, whose Filipino people were subjected to the shifting spheres of sultanate and Western influences since the sixteenth century. Though there are regular boat connections with both Indonesia and the Philippines, the islands are remote in feel, planted with cash crops such as coconut and cloves, and with all but the biggest settlements being basic fishing villages; you need to speak Indonesian and have plenty of time, but you'll find friendly people, white beaches and good coral, plus the chance of continuing your journey beyond Indonesia. There are two main groups: southernmost are the loosely scattered **Sangihe Islands**, with the capital of **TAHUNA** on Pulau Sangihe itself within a two-hour bemo ride of waterfalls and jungle at **Tamako**, where you'll find losmen **accommodation** at *Rainbow* or *Fret's*. Northeast of Sangihe, and within about 150km of the Philippines, the **Talaud Islands** are a compact little group, with the main settlement of **LIRUNG** on central **Pulau Salibau**. Lirung's accommodation places include *Penginepan Sederhana* or the *Chindy*; rent small craft for a fifteen-minute run out to the tiny, uninhabited **Sara Islands** for a day in paradise.

There are three passenger boats a week each way between Manado and Tahuna, one a week between Manado and Lirung, and a monthly Pelni liner from Bitung calling in to Tahuna, Lirung, and **Davao** in the **Philippines**. Check with the Philippine consulate in Manado first, but at the time of writing Filipino immigration would board the boat on arrival in Davao and generally hand out three-week visas on the spot.

---

certain of encountering all these creatures, as the ranger knows where to look and tears off through the undergrowth, so bring plenty of film. Particularly memorable are close encounters with families of **black macaques**, which stay up in the branches until the chunky lead male has nerved himself up to climb down; then you're suddenly surrounded by twenty or more animals, youngsters romping and adults foraging and clouting them to order. Look too for **flying lizards**, which display around the bunkhouses in the early morning, and keep your fingers crossed for glimpses of maleos scratching up leaf litter – though sightings usually turn out to be the related and similar-looking scrub fowl. One thing to protect against are **mites**, *gonone*, whose burrowing causes an infuriating rash; insect repellent or tiger balm kills them and lessens the irritation. Buses return **to Girian** at some point in the morning, or stop any passing vehicle and ask for a lift.

Back on the main road, minibuses from Manado wind up at **Terminal Mapalus**, from where a microlet will carry you the final 5km into **BITUNG**. A hot grid of a town servicing the **port**, if there are no ships in dock Bitung seems a bit pointless. The **Pelni port** is along Jalan Jakarta, with departures down Sulawesi's east coast to Ujung Pandang and Kadidiri, and further afield to Java, Kalimantan, Maluku, Irian and the Philippines; organize tickets and timetables either in Manado or try the Pandu Express office here at Jalan Sukarno 5 (☎0438/30480).

There are a handful of places to **eat** along Jalan Sudarso – the *Remaja Jaya* is a pricey Chinese place serving big portions – but Bitung's accommodation is pretty dire and new arrivals should catch a microlet from Jalan Sukarno back to Terminal Mapalus, where minibuses to Tondano and Manado await. Alternatively, **scuba divers** could head 5km north up the coast from Bitung to seafront lodgings at **Kungkungan Bay Resort** (⑦; full dive facilities) and explore the unusual marine life of the **Lembeh Strait**; be warned, however, that cold waters and strong currents make this an option for seasoned divers only.

travel details

Buses

Ampana to: Luwuk (daily; 8hr); Pagaimana (daily; 5hr); Palu (daily; 15hr); Poso (daily; 5hr); Ujung Pandang (daily; 26hr).

Gorontalo to: Kotamobagu (daily; 8hr); Manado (daily; 12hr); Ujung Pandang (daily; 2–4 days).

Manado to: Gorontalo (daily; 12hr); Kotamobagu (daily; 4hr); Tomohon (daily; 1hr); Ujung Pandang (daily; 2–4 days).

Palu to: Ampana (daily; 15hr); Luwuk (daily; 22hr); Pagaimana (daily; 20hr); Poso (daily; 10hr); Rantepao (daily; 21hr); Ujung Pandang (daily; 29hr).

Parepare to: Polewali (daily; 2hr); Rantepao (daily; 4hr); Sengkang (daily; 2hr 30min); Ujung Pandang (daily; 5hr); Watampone (daily; 5hr).

Poso to: Ampana (daily; 5hr); Luwuk (daily; 12hr); Pagaimana (daily; 10hr); Palu (daily; 10hr); Pendolo (daily; 5hr); Rantepao (daily; 13hr); Tentena (daily; 2hr); Ujung Pandang (daily; 21hr).

Rantepao to: Mamasa via Parepare (infrequent; 11hr); Palu (daily; 21hr); Parepare (daily; 4hr); Pendolo (daily; 8hr); Poso (daily; 13hr); Tentena (daily; 11hr); Ujung Pandang (daily; 8hr).

Sengkang to: Parepare (daily; 2hr 30min); Watampone (daily; 2hr 30min); Ujung Pandang (daily; 6hr).

Ujung Pandang to: Ampana (daily; 26hr); Benteng (daily; 11hr); Bira (daily; 5hr); Bulukumba (daily; 5hr); Gorontalo (daily; 2–4 days); Mamasa (most days; 15hr); Manado (daily; 2–4 days); Palu (daily; 29hr); Parepare (daily; 5hr); Pendolo (daily; 16hr); Polewali (daily; 7hr); Poso (daily; 21hr); Rantepao (daily; 8hr); Sengkang (daily; 6hr); Tentena (daily; 19hr); Watampone (daily; 5hr).

Watampone to: Bulukumba (daily; 4hr); Parepare (daily; 5hr); Sengkang (daily; 2hr 30min); Ujung Pandang (daily; 5hr).

Pelni ferries

For a chart of the Pelni routes, see pp.36–37 of Basics.

Baubau to: Ambon (*KM Rinjani*, 2 monthly; 24–30hr/*KM Tatamailau*, monthly; 29hr/*KM Bukit Siguntang*, monthly; 24hr/*KM Lambelu*, 2 monthly; 24hr); Bitung (*KM Ceremai*, 2 monthly; 26hr); Davao, Philippines (*KM Leuser*, monthly; 4 days); Denpasar (*KM Tatamailau*, monthly; 36hr/*KM Tilongkabila*, monthly; 65hr); Gorontalo (*KM Leuser*, monthly; 2 days/*KM Tilongkabila*, monthly; 2 days); Jayapura (*KM Ceremai*, 2 monthly; 4 days); Kolonodale (*KM Tilongkabila*, monthly; 24hr/*KM Leuser*, monthly; 24hr); Lirung (*KM Tilongkabila*, monthly; 3 days); Luwuk (*KM Tilongkabila*, monthly; 35hr/*KM Leuser*, monthly; 33hr); Manokwari (*KM Rinjani*, 2 monthly; 3 days/*KM Ceremai*, 2 monthly; 3 days); Sorong (*KM Rinjani*, 2 monthly; 3 days/*KM Ceremai*, 2 monthly; 2 days); Tahuna (*KM Leuser*, monthly; 3 days); Ternate (*Km Ceremai*, 2 monthly; 39hr/*KM Lambelu*, 2 monthly; 2 days); Ujung Pandang (*KM Rinjani*, 2 monthly; 16hr/*KM Tatamailau*, monthly; 20hr/*KM Ceremai*, 2 monthly; 14hr/*KM Tilongkabila*, monthly; 17hr/*KM Bukit Siguntang*, 2 monthly; 14hr/*KM Lambelu*, 2 monthly; 14hr).

Bitung to: Balikpapan (*KM Kambuna*, 2 monthly; 2 days/*KM Umsini*, 2 monthly; 36hr); Baubau (*KM Ceremai*, 2 monthly; 26hr); Davao, Philippines (*KM Leuser*, monthly; 38hr); Kendari (*KM Leuser*, monthly; 2 days/*KM Tilongkabila*, monthly; 2 days); Kolonodale (*KM Leuser*, monthly; 36hr/*KM Tilongkabila*, monthly; 3 days); Kwandung (*KM Umsini*, 2 monthly; 10hr); Lirung (*KM Leuser*, monthly; 24hr/*KM Bukit Raya*, monthly; 12hr); Luwuk (*KM Leuser*, monthly; 24hr/*KM Tilongkabila*, monthly; 24hr); Pantaloan/Palu (*KM Kambuna*, 2 monthly; 34hr); Tahuna (*KM Leuser*, monthly; 10hr/*KM Tilongkabila*, monthly; 24hr); Ujung Pandang (*KM Umsini*, 2 monthly; 2 days/*KM Ceremai*, 2 monthly; 2 days).

Gorontalo to: Baubau (*KM Leuser*, monthly; 2 days); Bitung (*KM Leuser*, monthly; 11hr/*KM Tilongkabila*, monthly; 11hr); Davao, Philippines (*KM Leuser*, monthly; 2 days); Denpasar (*KM Tilongkabila*, monthly; 4–5 days/*KM Leuser*, monthly; 4–5 days); Kendari (*KM Leuser*, monthly; 36hr/*KM Tilongkabila*, monthly; 36hr); Kolonodale (*KM Leuser*, monthly; 24hr/*KM Tilongkabila*, monthly; 24hr); Luwuk (*KM Leuser*, monthly; 9hr); Raha (*KM Leuser*, monthly; 41hr/*KM Tilongkabila*, monthly; 41hr); Ujung Pandang (*KM Leuser*, monthly; 3 days/*KM Tilongkabila*, monthly; 3 days).

Kendari to: Bitung (*KM Leuser*, monthly; 2 days); Denpasar (*KM Tilongkabila*, monthly; 3 days); Gorontalo (*KM Leuser*, monthly; 36hr); Luwuk (*KM Leuser*, monthly; 24hr); Ujung Pandang (*KM Leuser*, monthly; 27hr/*KM Tilongkabila*, monthly; 27hr).

Pantaloan/Palu to: Balikpapan (*KM Kambuna*, 2 monthly; 11hr/*KM Kerinci*, 2 monthly, 11hr/*KM Tidar*, 2 monthly; 2 days); Bitung (*KM Kambuna*, 2 monthly; 34hr); Parepare via Kalimantan (*KM Tidar*, 2 monthly; 3 days); Surabaya (*KM Kerinci*, 2 monthly; 56hr/*KM Kambuna*, 2 monthly; 56hr/*KM Tidar*, 2 monthly; 4 days); Tarakan (*KM Kerinci*, 2 monthly; 24hr/*KM Tidar*, 4 monthly, 24hr); Ujung Pandang (*KM Kerinci*, 2 monthly; 30hr/*KM Kambuna*, 2 monthly, 30hr/*KM Tidar*, 2 monthly; 17hr).

Parepare to: Balikpapan (*KM Tidar*, 2 monthly; 3 days); Pantaloan (*KM Tidar*, 4 monthly; 14hr–3 days); Surabaya (*KM Tidar*, 2 monthly; 24hr; *KM Binaiya*, 2 monthly; 41hr); Samarinda (*KM Binaiya*, 2 monthly; 24hr); Tarakan (*KM Tidar*, 2 monthly; 2 days); Ujung Pandang (*KM Tidar*, 2 monthly; 50hr).

Raha to: Bitung (*KM Leuser*, monthly; 55hr); Gorontalo (*KM Leuser*, monthly; 45hr/*KM Tilongkabila*, monthly; 45hr); Luwuk (*KM Leuser*, monthly; 33hr/*KM Tilongkabila*, monthly; 33hr); Ujung Pandang (*KM Tilongkabila*, monthly; 24hr/*KM Leuser*, monthly, 24hr).

Ujung Pandang to: Ambon (*KM Rinjani*, 2 monthly; 41hr/*KM Tatamailu*, monthly, 51hr/*KM Bukit Siguntang*, 2 monthly; 36hr/*KM Lambelu*, 2 monthly; 36hr); Balikpapan (*KM Kerinci*, 2 monthly; 19hr/*KM Kambuna*, 2 monthly; 21hr/*KM Umsini*, 2 monthly; 16hr); Banda (*KM Bukit Siguntang*, 2 monthly; 2 days/*KM Rinjani*, 2 monthly; 2 days); Baubau (*KM Rinjani*, 2 monthly; 16hr/*KM Tatamailau*, monthly; 20hr/*KM Ceremai*, 2 monthly; 14hr/*KM Leuser*, monthly; 24hr/*KM Bukit Siguntang*, 2 monthly; 14hr/*KM Lambelu*, 2 monthly; 14hr); Biak (*KM Ceremai*, monthly; 4 days); Bitung (*KM Umsini*, 2 monthly; 50hr/*KM Ceremai*, 2 monthly; 48hr); Denpasar (*KM Tilongkabila*, monthly; 2 days/*KM Leuser*, monthly; 2 days/*KM Tatamailau*, monthly; 40hr); Dili (*KM Awu*, 2 monthly; 2 days); Fakfak (*KM Tatamailau*, monthly; 3 days); Gorontalo (*KM Leuser*, monthly; 3 days); Jayapura (*KM Rinjani*, 2 monthly; 5–6 days/*KM Ceremai*, 2 monthly; 4–5 days); Kupang (*KM Awu*, 2 monthly; 3 days); Kwandang (*KM Umsini*, 2 monthly; 36hr); Manokwari (*KM Ceremai*, 2 monthly; 4 days/*KM Rinjani*, 2 monthly; 4 days); Maumere (*KM Awu*, monthly; 30hr); Nias (*KM Kambuna*, 2 monthly; 4–5 days); Nunukan (*KM Awu*, 2 monthly; 60hr); Padang (*KM Kambuna*, 2 monthly; 3–4 days); Parepare (*KM Tidar*, 2 monthly; 60hr); Sorong (*KM Ceremai*, 2 monthly; 3 days/*KM Rinjani*, 2 monthly; 3–4 days/*KM Umsini*, 2 monthly; 3–4 days);

Surabaya (*KM Kerinci*, 2 monthly; 24hr/*KM Kambuna*, 2 monthly; 24hr/*KM Rinjani*, 2 monthly; 24hr/*KM Umsini*, 2 monthly; 24hr/*KM Tidar*, 2 monthly; 24hr/*KM Bukit Siguntang*, 2 monthly; 24hr/*KM Lambelu*, 2 monthly; 24hr); Tanjung Priok (*KM Kerinci*, 2 monthly; 45hr/*KM Kambuna*, 2 monthly; 48hr/*KM Ceremai*, 2 monthly; 40hr/*KM Bukit Siguntang*, 2 monthly; 48hr/*KM Lambelu*, 2 monthly; 48hr); Tarakan (*KM Awu*, 2 monthly; 50hr/*KM Tidar*, 2 monthly; 2 days); Ternate (*KM Umsini*, 2 monthly; 38hr/*KM Ceremai*, 2 monthly; 52hr); Toli-Toli (*KM Kambuna*, 2 monthly; 41hr); Tual (*KM Rinjani*, 2 monthly; 2–3 days/*KM Bukit Siguntang*, 2 monthly; 2–3 days).

Other ferries

Ampana to: Bomba (daily; 3hr); Dolong (1 weekly; 12hr); Gorontalo (1 weekly; 18hr); Katupat (1 weekly; 8hr); Wakai (daily; 3hr).

Baubau to: Kendari (daily; 5hr); Raha (daily; 2hr).

Gorontalo to: Bomba (1 weekly; 12hr); Pagaimana (3 weekly; 10hr); Wakai (1 weekly; 8hr).

Kendari to: Baubau (daily; 5hr); Raha (daily; 2hr 30min).

Kwandang to: Balikpapan (1 monthly; 30hr); Bitung (1 monthly; 10hr); Pantaloan/Palu (1 monthly; 18hr); Surabaya (1 monthly; 3 days); Ujung Pandang (1 monthly; 48hr).

Manado to: Ambon (regular; 48hr); Bunaken (daily; 1hr); Lirung (1 weekly; 20hr); Tahuna (3 weekly; 12hr).

Poso to: Ampana (1 weekly; 6hr); Dolong (1 weekly; 18hr); Gorontalo (1 weekly; 24hr); Katupat (1 weekly; 14hr); Wakai (1 weekly; 12hr).

Raha to: Baubau (daily; 1hr 30min); Kendari (daily; 2hr 30min).

Flights

Kendari to: Ujung Pandang (1 daily; 1hr).

Makale to: Ujung Pandang (1–3 daily; 1hr).

Manado to: Palu (1 daily; 1hr 20min); Singapore (3 weekly; 5hr); Ternate (1–2 daily; 2hr); Ujung Pandang (1–3 daily; 1hr 35min).

Palu to: Balikpapan (1 daily; 40min); Manado (1 daily; 1hr 20min); Ujung Pandang (2 daily; 2hr).

Ujung Pandang to: Ambon (1 daily; 2hr 45min); Balikpapan (6 weekly; 1hr 10min); Denpasar (2–4 daily; 1hr 20min); Jakarta (5–7 daily; 1hr 10min); Kendari (1 daily; 1hr); Makale (1–3 daily; 1hr); Manado (1–3 daily, 1hr 35min).

CHAPTER TWELVE

MALUKU

S cattered over the ample space separating Sulawesi from Irian, the thousand or more islands comprising the province of **Maluku** seem at first rather insignificant, many too small to feature noticeably on maps of the region. Yet Maluku has been known to the outside world for longer than anywhere else in Indonesia: these were the fabled Spice Islands, whose produce was in demand everywhere between here and Europe two thousand years ago, and the search for which fired the great sixteenth-century European voyages of exploration which saw the globe circled for the first time.

Maluku clusters into three main regions. The provincial pivot and seat of its capital is **Ambon**, which, together with much larger and wilder **Seram** and **Buru**, and the pinprick specks of the **Bandas**, form **Central Maluku**, a compact area which offers everything from hardcore trekking to lackadaisical sunbathing. There's a similar variety in **North Maluku**, with the relatively urbane centres of **Ternate** and **Tidore** almost invisible off the west coast of giant **Halmahera**, itself virtually undeveloped but the scene of Japanese–US conflicts during World War II. Completely different in character, **Southeast Maluku**'s islands share interlinked cultures and lower profiles: the pleasant **Kei Islands** are the doorway here, a stepping-stone towards a rougher, more mysterious **Aru**, and the neglected and apparently ordinary **Tanimbars**.

A backdrop of pristine beaches, volcanoes jutting out of the sea, tall mountain ranges, and thick forests make it a place to enjoy the great outdoors. Low-key commercial fishing ensures some immaculate **diving and snorkelling**, while those after **wildlife** can clock up both Asian and Australasian species, including deer and kangaroos, birds of paradise and cassowaries. Because of European depredations, however, Maluku's most obvious heritage is not its **indigenous cultures** but the remains of its colonial outposts. This is not to say that, underlying a basic Christian south/Muslim north division, there are no traditional beliefs, just that you'll have to dig a little to uncover them – Seram's **Nuaulu** people are one of Maluku's many groups who still live a hunter-gatherer existence, while ceremonial **megaliths** can be seen on the Tanimbars and even in Ambon.

Maluku is connected to the rest of Indonesia by air through Ambon and Ternate, and on regular Pelni loops via Sulawesi, Irian, Timor and Java. With over eight hundred thousand square kilometres of ocean to traverse, however, **getting around** requires time and flexibility. **Flying** is notoriously unreliable. Airline offices are unable to book anything but outward tickets; small aircraft and a lack of radar require good weather both at your starting point and destination, and high costs for locals mean that services are often cancelled for want of passengers. In practice, count on making long hauls within Maluku by **boat**: Pelni link the three main island groups, beyond which you'll have to share minimal deck space with other passengers and livestock on cargo freighters. Shorter runs are covered by inter-island **ferries** and **speedboats**, with endless opportunities to charter or hitch rides on a variety of vessels. You'll find a few vehicles and tracks on most islands, but **local transport** is often by boat too, hopping between coastal villages – only a few islands have enough roads for comprehensive **bus travel**.

In early 1999, since this chapter was researched, Ambon has seen several weeks of ethnic violence. It is essential for travellers to check on the current situation before visiting Muslim regions of Maluku.

On a daily basis, Maluku's **weather** is local and, with an average rainfall exceeding two metres a year, wet – **monsoonal winds** also whip up the seas for much of the time. The central and southeastern islands have a drier trend from August to October, with the wettest months between November and April, while the reverse is true in the north. There's no trouble finding food and places to stay, but isolation makes Maluku a relatively **expensive** area, compounded by poor exchange rates for both cash and travellers' cheques – use **credit card** advances to obtain international rates. **Banks** in Ambon and Ternate are the only places in all Maluku handling foreign exchange, which means carrying huge wads of cash further afield. **Language** might be another problem; you'll find English-speakers in Ambon, Ternate, and, to a lesser extent, Kei, but

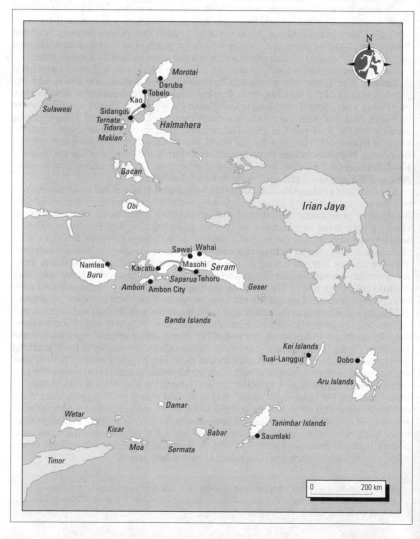

elsewhere a working knowledge of Bahasa Indonesia is essential – even if you sometimes find yourself more fluent in this than locals. For a highly recommended account of travel and the natural history of the region during the mid-nineteenth century – much of it still valid – read *The Malay Archipelago* by **Alfred Wallace** (see p.974).

Some history

Human remains from caves in southeastern Maluku indicate that the region has been inhabited for at least 30,000 years, though current cultures owe more to bronze-age migrations from the Southeast Asian mainland which introduced metallurgy, distinctive house styles, and headhunting around two millennia ago. It's possible that even this early the region was a source of spices – specifically Bandanese **nutmeg** and **cloves** from north Maluku – which were in high demand for their preservative and medicinal properties. Certainly, cloves were known in China and Rome during the second century, and ancient bronze **Dongson drums** of Chinese origin, found in several places in Maluku, were possibly one currency of the spice trade. But neither the Chinese nor Romans knew the location of the islands, and for over a thousand years overseas markets were supplied indirectly through Javan, Indian and Arab intermediaries – the latter introducing Islam to northern Maluku by the fifteenth century. By this time Maluku was further involved in the lucrative export of **pearls, sea slugs** and **bird of paradise** feathers to China via Timor and Sulawesi, exchanging these products for gold, ivory and fabrics.

Meanwhile, in medieval Europe, nutmegs and cloves had become so valuable that the race was on between nations to discover their origin – and corner the market. The **Portuguese** were first, locating Banda, Ternate and Ambon soon after capturing Malacca (in Malaysia) in 1511, followed a decade later by the **Spanish**. But their arrogant behaviour having soon exhausted local goodwill, the two powers spent the rest of the century bullying for shares in the spice trade, rather than controlling it. Their main contributions were to leave behind dozens of defensive stone **forts**, and to introduce Christianity to the central and southeastern islands. In the early seventeenth century, Spain and Portugal's political decline in Europe saw their Maluccan interests usurped by the aspiring nation of **Holland**, which had itself broken away from Spanish rule in the 1570s.

The Dutch proved very different from their somewhat inept predecessors. With Ambon as their headquarters, by the 1660s the **VOC** – Vereenigde Oostindische Compaigne, or United East Indies Company – had ruthlessly eliminated foreign rivals and achieved an iron grip on the Bandas and Ternate. To ensure their monopoly, they banned private production of spices, responding to dissent by decimating island populations and destroying their plantations. While this brought immense profits for the **Heeren XVII**, the VOC's seventeen-strong board of directors, Maluku lost its major source of income, traditional trade networks collapsed, and the islands were depopulated through war and famine. Even a more liberal regime instigated by the Dutch government after the VOC's ignominious ruin in the late eighteenth century couldn't resuscitate the region; by the 1820s spice plantations overseas, established from smuggled seedlings, had lowered world prices and made dreams of monopolies redundant. Stripped of resources, Maluku slid into economic decrepitude which lasted beyond the 1942–45 **Japanese occupation** – when the islands were the base for assaults on Australia – and subsequent independence struggles, which included attempts to set up the secessionary **Republik Maluku Selatan**, South Maluku Republic, in 1950. The Dutch upheld their cause and, when Java forcefully suppressed the insurrection, gave **asylum** to 40,000 RMS supporters in Holland. Having been drawn under the Indonesian umbrella, Maluku's basic infrastructure has gradually improved, and pearl, copra and cocoa industries are flourishing, but the province's two million residents still bear their historical scars – most islands remain minimally developed, and only a fraction of the world's cloves and nutmegs grow here today.

CENTRAL MALUKU

Comprehensive connections to the rest of Indonesia mean that **Central Maluku** is the first stop for most newcomers to the province. Functional and relaxed, **Ambon City** is a good place to get your bearings, with easy side trips around **Pulau Ambon** and out to the nearby **Lease group**. In contrast, high mountains and thick forests give seasoned hikers a chance to test their mettle on tough trails between villages in Seram's **Manusela national park**, and also in the interior of **Buru**, both only a few hours from the city. Further away, but easier to come to grips with, the charming **Banda Islands** are somewhere to unwind amongst milder scenery. This is the simplest part of Maluku to **get around**, with regular flights, ferries and passenger ships leaving Ambon for all corners of the province, and a relatively generous number of local roads.

Ambon City

The rise of the modern, active hub of Maluku – **AMBON CITY** – during the late sixteenth century marked the end of a sixty-year attempt by Portugal to secure a base on the island. Driven out of Ambon's Muslim north, the Portuguese retired to the more amenable animist villages of the southern **Leitimur peninsula**, and in 1575 chose a site overlooking **Ambon Bay** for their **Fort Nuestra Senhora da Anunciada**, around which the town of **Amboina** coalesced over the next few decades as a marketplace for Bandanese nutmeg and goods from central Maluku.

The **Dutch** arrived in 1605, dispossessed the Portuguese without a struggle, and renamed the fort **Victoria**. It was from here that the VOC (whose intolerance of competition led them to execute eighteen members of an English trade mission to Ambon in 1623) and their Dutch Government successors ran Maluku for over three hundred years, interrupted briefly during the early-nineteenth-century Napoleonic wars when Britain took over. As the region's only approved trading post, by the 1850s Amboina had become quietly prosperous, its busy streets and offshore coral gardens drawing praise from visiting Europeans.

The **Japanese** brought World War II to Ambon in January 1942, easily overrunning the Dutch and Australian defence forces stationed here. The city's predominantly Christian residents suffered badly during the war, both at the hands of the occupiers, and when the city was destroyed in late 1944 by Allied air raids. Rebuilt over the next decade in charmless grey concrete, modern Ambon is hardly the **Kota Manise** –

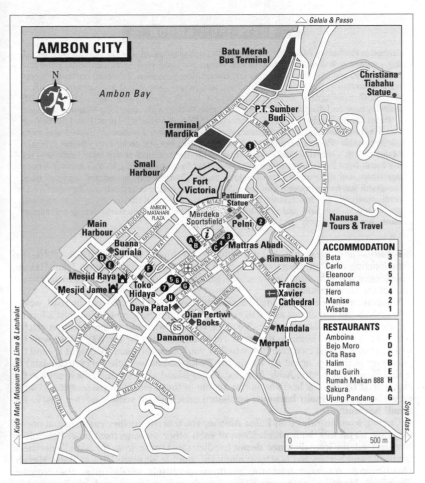

AMBON CITY

Galala & Passo

Batu Merah
Bus Terminal

Christiana
Tiahahu
Statue

Ambon Bay

P.T. Sumber
Budi

Terminal
Mardika

Small
Harbour

Fort
Victoria

Pattimura
Statue

AMBON
MATAHARI
PLAZA

Merdeka
Sportsfield

Pelni

Nanusa
Tours & Travel

Main
Harbour

Buana
Suriala

Mattras Abadi

Rinamakana

Mesjid Raya

Mesjid Jame

Toko
Hidaya

Daya Patal

Francis
Xavier
Cathedral

Dian Pertiwi
Books

Danamon

Mandala

Merpati

ACCOMMODATION

Beta	3
Carlo	6
Eleanoor	5
Gamalama	7
Hero	4
Manise	2
Wisata	1

RESTAURANTS

Amboina	F
Bejo Moro	D
Cita Rasa	C
Halim	B
Ratu Gurih	E
Rumah Makan 888	H
Sakura	A
Ujung Pandang	G

0   500 m

Kuda Mati, Museum Siwa Lima & Latuhalat

Soya Atas

Pretty City – of its tourist brochures. Nonetheless, along with the services and distractions you'd expect from a provincial capital of 80,000 people, you'll find an easygoing atmosphere, a worthwhile **museum**, and a good number of English speakers, many of them relatives of the South Maluku Republic's supporters who sought sanctuary in Holland in the 1950s.

Orientation, information, arrival and transport

The city streets form an irregular mesh between the waterfront and hills on the south side of Ambon Bay. The centre is small, boxed in between the **two harbours** at either end of 500-metre-long Jalan Sudarso, with the commercial heart in parallel Jalan Ratulangi and Jalan Patty. Immediately east you'll find **Fort Victoria** and the **Merdeka sportsfield**; west is a small **Muslim quarter**, and ill-defined suburbs edge up the hills behind town and follow the main roads either way along the coast. Doling out

---

BOATS FROM AMBON

Ambon is the hub of Maluku's marine traffic, but organizing a ticket out can be frustrating – expect to find outdated timetables, vague staff and endless run-arounds. Pelni and Perentis vessels use the main harbour; everything else uses the small harbour, except regular **ferries** to the Lease Islands, Buru and Seram (see island accounts for details of these). All travel agents can book Pelni tickets, and the host of small agencies around the main harbour on Jalan Sangaji just might be able to help with other long-distance services.

Pelni run to Banda, Tual (Kei), Dobo (Aru), Namlea (Buru), Ternate and beyond on the *Rinjani, Lambelu, Bukit Siguntang, Tatamailau* and *Dobonsolo*. Slower and very uncomfortable, **Perentis freighters** from Ambon cover just about every island group in Maluku, with a schedule and ticket office inside the terminal at the main harbour – try the kiosk here if the ticket office is closed. The Pelni office should also know Perentis timetables, but it's a waste of time asking them. There are no scheduled services from the **small harbour**; instead, you have to check the notice board outside for what's currently available, or – much more reliably – ask boat crews if they're going your way, and pay on board. Freelance boats to and from the outer islands increase during the annual **clove harvest** (roughly Aug–Nov).

---

brochures and varyingly helpful advice, Ambon's **tourist office** (Mon–Fri 8am–lunchtime) is on the ground floor of the government offices on Jalan Hairun. Supplement this with a jumble of regional information from the notice board across the road at the *Halim* restaurant.

Pattimura Airport is diagonally across the bay, 30km from the city by road, where new arrivals are sometimes asked to register with immigration officials – just a formality. **Taxis** to town cost around Rp25,000, or you can walk out to the road and catch a passing red #31/#33 bemo to the city's Terminal Mardika for Rp1000. Either way, the journey takes at least forty minutes, whether you follow the main road right around the perimeter of the bay, or cut across on the **Poka-Galala vehicle ferry** (6am–late) to within 5km of the centre. Aside from local inter-island ferries, which dock outside the city, arrival **by sea** will land you in the middle of town, either on passenger and large cargo boats at the **main harbour**, or aboard unscheduled vessels further east at the **small harbour**.

Coming from elsewhere on Pulau Ambon, you'll arrive further east again at one of two **bus terminals**, both within 250m of each other on waterfront Jalan Pelabuhan. Furthest out, the **long distance depot** handles most traffic from the island's northern peninsula and Seram, and is strung along the road in separate bays at **Batu Merah**. Shorter-range transport from the southern peninsula winds up at the crowded **Terminal Mardika**, where you'll find numbered, coloured, and labelled **mobils** (minibuses) to nearby destinations (about Rp500 per ride). Walking is the most convenient way of **getting around** Ambon's immediate centre, however – just beware of one-way systems when crossing the roads. Otherwise, **becaks** painted red, yellow or white on successive days cruise backstreets (Rp500–1000), but are not allowed onto main roads or into bus terminals. Hotels can arrange **taxis**, or hire a Kijang direct from the operators on Jalan Perintah.

Accommodation

Ambon has no cheap bargains, but mid-range hotels are good value and, if you're going to be passing through town a good deal, make a comfortable base where you can leave surplus gear. The price always includes roti and coffee breakfasts, with meals as an optional extra.

Beta, Jl Reawaru (☎0911/53463). Ambon's budget venue; basic cubicles on three floors, served by eccentric staff who give the impression that guests are a nuisance. ④.

Carlo, Jl Latumahina 24 (☎0911/42220). Bright, welcoming guest house. Rooms come with fan or air-con. ④–⑤.

Eleanoor, Jl Rhebok 30 (☎0911/52834). Unimposing friendly homestay with decent-sized rooms, all with attached mandis. ④.

Gamalama, Jl Rhebok 27 (☎0911/53724). Popular, cool, quiet, single-floor guest house. Rooms with fan ④.

Hero, Jl Reawaru 76 (☎0911/55973, fax 52493). Ambon's best deal, with decent-sized rooms and helpful staff. All rooms have air-con and mandi. ⑤.

Manise, Jl Supratman 1 (☎0911/54144, fax 41054). One of several places with the same name; a tidy business hotel with full facilities and a restaurant offering Ambon's only passable Western food. ⑦.

Transit, out near the airport on Jl Leimena-Tawiri (☎0911/61415). Saves the fare to and from town if you are staying only one night in Ambon, but not especially good otherwise. Clean doubles with air-con. ⑥.

Wisata, Jl Mutiara 67 (☎0911/53567, fax 53592). Fully air-con rooms with TV and showers in a pleasantly gloomy building which lies a bit too close to the sights and scents of the Mardika Terminal. ⑤.

The City

Orbited by one-way traffic flows, the scruffy space of **Merdeka sportsfield** is a good place to start a tour of downtown Ambon. At the eastern end, a snarling, big-toed **statue** offers a concrete caricature of Thomas Matulessy, better known as **Pattimura**, Ambon's foremost hero. A protégé of Britain's brief hold on the islands during the early nineteenth century, Pattimura organized a fierce revolt against the Dutch in 1817 on the nearby Lease Islands (see pp.868–870), but was captured and later hanged on this spot.

To the north, VOC cannons and a gold-painted soldier outside **Fort Victoria** proclaim continuing use by the military; entry and photography are prohibited but you can look in through a whitewashed stone arch to see barracks and another, less sprightly gateway beyond. Following the fort's remaining dirty brown-brick walls northwest takes you past a seedy array of dodgy bars, prostitutes, sailors and dark, rank lanes, to emerge amongst rare caged birds from Seram and Buru in the **market** area near the **small harbour** on Jalan Pelabuhan. Moving west, the junction with Jalan Sudarso forms a traffic bottleneck, where competing music stores blasting out the latest songs and shops hawking washing powder, tobacco, fruit, hardware, car-tyre shoes and chandlery mark the fringe of Ambon's shopping district along Jalan Ratulangi and Jalan Patty. At their far ends you'll find Jalan Sangaji heading south from the entrance to the main harbour past the ugly, prominent **Mesjid Raya**, the focus of Ambon's small **Muslim quarter**; next door along Jalan Babullah, the older **Mesjid Jame** is far nicer, painted green and attractively styled. Ambon's larger, multidenomination Christian population count the newly rebuilt **Francis Xavier Cathedral**, south of the sports field on Jalan Pattimura, as their most impressive place of worship, decorated with hefty statues of the apostles and a dynamic rendition of a crab handing **Saint Francis Xavier** a prayerbook. Patron saint of missionaries, Xavier co-founded the **Jesuit order** in the early sixteenth century and visited Maluku during his travels through Southeast Asia.

Despite sad associations, two hillsides in Ambon's iron-roofed suburbs are worth the walk (or short mobil ride from Terminal Mardika) for views over the city and bay. A couple of kilometres northeast at **Karang Panjang**, you'll find a statue of a romantically windswept **Christiana Tiahahu**, who fought in Pattimura's revolt and starved herself to death after her father was hanged alongside Pattimura. A little further southwest of the centre, **Gunung Nona**'s TV towers and 220-metre-high peak rise behind the district of Kuda Mati – Dead Horse – whose name relates to the tale of a young girl who, along with her mount, became lost and died up here.

Museum Siwa Lima

Those set on exploring Maluku should first head 5km west of Ambon's centre to **Museum Siwa Lima** (open mornings Tues–Sun; Rp200); catch a Taman Makmur or Amahusu mobil from Terminal Mardika to the main road gates, then walk 500m uphill to the entrance. Among straightforward displays of traditional weapons and textiles, look for unique spiky "sun" earrings from Babar, squatting, elongated wooden *tongkat* **ancestor carvings** from Tanimbar with characteristic almond eyes and exposed genitals, and pagan Ambonese charms handed over by church converts – snake eggs, a metal cockerel and a *doti*, a miniature wooden boat used in black magic. **Dioramas** of regional scenes feature **sago** production, walk-through limestone burial caverns from Maluku Tenggara, and a bamboo-and-biscuit-tin **sopi still** – standard equipment for all Maluccan moonshiners. Almost half of the museum is given over to southeastern ethnography, with particularly fine *walut* **amulets** in stone and wood – look for the human-lizard figure. A few contemporary guns, cannons and European illustrations of sea battles between Dutch frigates and local *kora-kora* warships round out the display, alongside red earth pottery from Aru and Ternate – northern Maluku is poorly represented otherwise.

SAGO

The starchy pith of a spiky species of palm tree, **sago** remains a major staple throughout Maluku, though it's considered rustic fare nowadays and those who can afford to prefer to eat rice. It's an easy food source: sago palms grow wild and need little tending, and a single day's harvesting produces enough food to feed a family for several weeks. The mature, four-metre-high trees are felled, the trunk split along its length, and the pith scraped, beaten, boiled and strained until only edible starch remains – hikers often come across remains of this process on forest tracks. Sometimes just baked into marshmallow-sized **cakes** and stored, sago is also served in drinks, or as a gelatinous mass which has to be slurped off the plate. Don't expect to find this delicacy on restaurant menus, though you'll often be offered sago in villages and can buy packets of the dried, almost tasteless cakes in most towns.

Eating and drinking

For snacks, backstreet stalls around the centre are the cheapest places to find seasonal **fruit**, such as rambutan, mangosteen and loquats, backed by an anaemic selection at the **supermarket** on the ground floor of the Ambon Matahari Plaza on Jalan Ratulangi. **Coffee houses** along the lower end of Jalan Sangaji are mostly Muslim male hangouts, open early for post-prayer customers; more secular options such as the *Zig-zag* and *Hitam-Putih* cafés on the top floor of the Plaza serve strong coffee to loud music. Maluccan treats, including Bandanese toffee-and-almond biscuits and packets of dried sago cakes, are on hand at stores like Toko Hidaya, on the corner of Jalan Patty and Jalan Sangaji. You'll find most of Ambon's **restaurants** offering similar, halal Chinese-Indonesian food, with a certain proportion of anything you order unavailable. For purely Christian items such as **pork** and local specialities like **dog**, you'll need to make enquiries at the group of small warung on Jalan Rhebok, just west of Jalan Sultan Hairun.

Restaurants

Amboina, Jl Patty. Fine bakery and fair-priced restaurant with the best sweet-and-sour chicken in Ambon. Also offers reasonable burgers and hot dogs, but often closed for no apparent reason.

Bejo Moro, Jl Sangaji. A fine warung with coffee, cakes and Indonesian staples at low cost.

Halim, Jl Sultan Hairun. Favoured expat and tourist haunt, pricey but with ice-cold beer and big portions of good food. Expect to be approached by guides and souvenir hawkers during your meal.

Pondok Cita Rasa, Jl Reawaru. Bamboo walls, chequered tablecloths and a quality of food and service which changes daily. Potentially excellent crisp fried fish or squid and decent sates.

Ratu Gurih, Jl Sangaji. Popular Muslim seafood restaurant, best for inexpensive grilled fish and prawns – you can even ask for small, medium, or large portions. Vegetables treated as side orders.

Rumah Makan 888, Jl Perintah. Cheap, clean warung with unpretentious nasi campur and excellent rendang.

Sakura, Jl Sultan Hairun. A lower-key, less expensive version of *Halim*, open in the evening only.

Ujung Pandang, Jl Perintah. Unusually charming, inexpensive restaurant with warung-style menu and tables flanking a small garden at the back.

Listings

Airlines Larger planes to Ternate and Ujung Pandang are fairly reliable; otherwise, don't get too excited over what timetables promise, and read the chapter introduction on p.855, for the vagaries of flying in Maluku. Travel light: smaller inter-island flights have a 10kg baggage allowance and very steep excesses. Mandala, Jl Yani (☎0911/45995), flies to Ujung Pandang; Merpati, Jl Yani 19 (☎0911/52481) to Ujung Pandang, Banda, Seram, Langgur (Kei), Dobo (Aru) and Saumlaki (Tanimbar); and Citra Air flights to Kei and Ternate are available through P.T. Sumber Budi, Jl Mutiara (☎0911/51942). There is no Garuda office.

Banks and exchange Ambon is the only place you can officially change money in central or southeast Maluku. The best – but not good – deals for cash or travellers' cheques are offered at the Danamon bank on Jl Diponegoro, where you can also arrange credit-card advances at less usurious rates. At the time of writing, there were also ATMs accepting international cards at the BNI on Jl Ulupaha, and the BCA on Jl Pattimura, though these may now be defunct. A poor alternative is to exchange US dollar notes at the *Manise* hotel or *Halim* restaurant.

Bookshops There's a book exchange at an unnamed shop on Jl Said Perintah, just east of Daya Patal travel agent. Other possible sources of English-language maps, magazines and occasional pulp novels are the stationers upstairs at Ambon Matahari Plaza and Dian Pertiwi Books, opposite the Danamon bank on Jl Diponegoro.

Cinemas Showing big international releases, Ambon's smartest is Studio 21, upstairs at the Ambon Matahari Plaza on Jl Ratulangi. More popular Chinese action flicks screen at the Amboina, nearby on Jl Patty.

Diving Ambon Dive Centre, 15km out at Latuhalat (☎0911/62101, fax 62104); and Nelma Dive Club, about 5km from the centre at Jl Soar Sopacua 50 (☎ & fax 0911/44659) have sound rental gear, good guides and two-dive packages from about US$60 a day.

Ferries The Pelni office is opposite the Pattimura statue, south side of Merdeka sportsfield (☎0911/48219 or 52049). The front desk is open daily for enquiries; the ticket office is open Mon–Fri 8.30am–4pm.

Guides Bilingual guides for exploring Ambon, Saparua, Seram, and beyond can be arranged for around Rp40,000 a day through the tourist office, the competent Hendrik Maruanaya at Nanusa Tours and Travel, Jl Rijali 53 (☎0911/55334, fax 52593), or freelance operators such as Oce or Iwan Anaktototy at *Halim* restaurant. If you're planning a major excursion, such as a hike through Seram's Manusela national park, assess your guide's abilities on something minor first – some are fine interpreters, but you wouldn't necessarily rely on their organizational skills.

Hospitals Ambon's dire public hospital is 3km southwest at Kuda Mati (☎0911/43438). A slightly better alternative, and rated by locals as the cheapest hotel in town (Rp10,000 a night including food) is the church-run Rumah Sakit GPM on Jl Rhebok (☎0911/52373), though still verminous and noisy. English-speaking doctors can be summoned through your accommodation place; call-out fees are around Rp35,000.

Immigration Jl Kayadoe, about 2.5km west along the coast in the suburb of Kuda Mati (☎0911/53066).

Permits for national parks are available from Balai Konservasi Sumber Daya Alam or BKSDA, also known as "Kanwil Kehutanan", Jl Kebun Cengkeh (☎0911/43619). Catch a green Kebun Cengkeh mobil from Terminal Mardika for a twenty-minute ride into the eastern suburbs. Some people have problems with the staff here, others find them obliging and prompt. You need your passport and about half an hour while they type up the forms; permits are free, but you may be asked for administration fees – the price of a packet of cigarettes is enough.

Pharmacy Apotik Pelita Farma, Jl Setia Budi (☎0911/42519), is open around the clock.

Police Jl Batu Meja (☎0911/52310).

Post office Jl Pattimura. Main counter open daily 8am–8pm, with poste restante pickup around the back; Internet access Mon–Sat 8am–3pm.

Shopping Four-storey Ambon Matahari Plaza on Jl Ratulangi has a well-stocked supermarket, everyday clothing and household wares, a print-film processing booth and upmarket fashion stores. More of the same – often at lower prices – can be found in the surrounding streets.

Souvenirs Maluccan mementos include: pearls from Aru; bizarre sculptures of boats made from cloves; framed pictures of birds of paradise and religious scenes montaged from mother-of-pearl slivers; and Tanimbarese textiles, attenuated carvings and jointed wooden belts. Shops along Jl Patty, such as Toko Mas Sulawesi, sell the lot. For jewellery, statues and cloth from southeast Maluku, try Rinamakana, across from the post office at Jl Pattimura 17, whose collection of antiques has been appropriated by the church for religious reasons. A regional product you'll see on sale everywhere is *minyak kayu putih*, an aromatic balm made from pale green eucalyptus oil – Toko Abadi, on the corner of Jl Patty and Jl Sangaji, is well stocked.

Telephone and fax Long-distance and international wartels can be found near the main harbour on Jl Sangaji, on the ground floor of the Ambon Matahari Plaza, and at the western end of Jl Rhebok.

Travel agents For all flights and Pelni bookings contact Daya Patal, Jl Said Perintah 11/27a (☎0911/53344, fax 53287) or Mattras Abadi, Jl Latumahina 1/29 (☎0911/52652, fax 53740). For Pelni tickets only try Buana Suriala, near the main harbour on Jl Sangaji.

Pulau Ambon

Pulau Ambon consists of **two mountainous peninsulas** joined in the east by a thin isthmus. At 20km long, southern **Leitimur** is the smaller but, with Ambon City embedded halfway along its coast, the more settled of the two, and easy to explore. Looming dark green across the bay, **Leihitu** is twice Leitimur's bulk, with a rougher, less populated interior and a limited road network which has yet to reach the peninsula's far west. After the city's functional air, it's surprising how vivid the rest of the island can be,

---

DIVING AMBON

The best months to dive Ambon are October and November, with roughest seas in April and May, but you'll find good sites year round; see Ambon City "Listings", overleaf, for dive operators. **Leihitu** has the best pickings, with steep walls at Tanjung Setan north of Hitu, and fine reefs around the remote westerly islands known collectively as Pulau Tiga. Less demanding locations off Tulehu on the east coast include scanty soft corals at Pulau Pombo, and **underwater hot springs** at Batu Lompa. **Ambon Bay**, though degraded in recent years, still offers moderate visibility and easy access to several shallow coral outcrops populated by juvenile reef fish, lobsters, morays, rays and nudibranchs. More exciting is the **wreck** of the *Akuila M. Rufia*, a massive cargo boat which was bombed during the 1960s Permesta revolt and now lies at 15–45m opposite Waiame – few fish, but a monstrous buzz of a dive. **Leitimur's south coast** has two excellent spots: caves off Airlouw, near Latuhalat, and a **tunnel** through the reef wall and up to the surface at Hukurila, where southeasterly currents sometimes attract schools of **hammerhead sharks**.

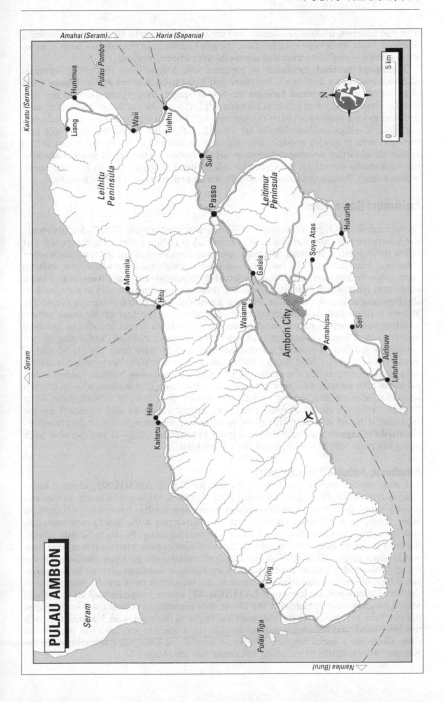

PULAU AMBON

Seram

Amahai (Seram) △   △ Haria (Saparua)

Kairatu (Seram) △

Pulau Pombo

Hunimua

Liang

Waii

Tulehu

Suli

Leihitu Peninsula

Passo

Leitimur Peninsula

Hukurla

Soya Atas

Galala

Mamala

Hitu

Waiame

Ambon City

Amahusu

Seri

Airlouw

Latuhalat

Seram

Hila

Kaitetu

Uring

Pulau Tiga

Namlea (Buru) △

5 km

N

0

with fine beaches, traditional villages, and the odd colonial relic all within easy striking distance. Most Ambonese are Christian, though Leihitu's north coast has been Muslim for centuries – you'll find traces of animism everywhere, however.

Transport around Leitimur is plentiful and leaves from the city's Terminal Mardika from dawn until late – the most you'll pay here is about Rp750. **Buses** from Batu Merah depots **around Leihitu** are less frequent, though transport up the east coast is steady, and travel as far as **Kaitetu** (Rp1500) on the north coast shouldn't be a problem as long as you start early enough to catch the last bus back – ask before boarding. Both Mardika and Batu Merah are chaotic at first, but ask around and you'll find the right vehicle quickly enough. Day-trips are possible to all the places below, with a scattering of formal **accommodation** as an alternative to the city. If you get stuck in the backblocks overnight, seek out the village head (kepala desa) to arrange somewhere to stay, though this can occasionally cause problems with the authorities.

Leitimur: Soya Atas

Orange minibuses leave Terminal Mardika until mid-afternoon (Rp500) for the steep, five-kilometre run from the city centre to **SOYA ATAS**, a pretty village perched just below the summit of **Gunung Sirimau**; morning sees the bus full of garrulous women returning from market. The road ends at the village gates, from where you walk up stone steps to the cluster of gardens, colonial-style bungalows, shady trees, and general peace and quiet which characterizes Soya; there's also a **church** said to date back to the Portuguese era. A ten-minute walk on a new concrete path up through the village follows a ridge past overgrown coconut plantations to the **top of Sirimau**, where swiftlets and sunbirds dart around while you gaze down across the city to Leihitu's moody peaks. Soya is considered a centre of ritual and tradition, and a ring of low shrubbery up here surrounds **sacred stones**, said to have been the literal seat of Soya's ruler; behind, a brief flagged path ends in front of a buried **urn**, which is always full of water however dry the season. There's also a **Japanese bunker** hidden in forest about 20m away: Soya's jungle was a refuge for Australian soldiers who went bush after the Japanese invasion, when villagers risked their lives to protect them – the brother of Soya's current kepala desa was caught doing so and executed by the Japanese. One of several **trails** from here descends through the undergrowth to **Hukurila village** on the south coast – a guide is recommended – or you can walk back along the main road to the city from Soya in an hour.

Amahusu, Airlouw and Latuhalat

The road west of Ambon City follows the bay for 7km to **AMAHUSU**, where it kinks sharply around the *Tirta Kencana* **hotel** (☎0911/42324; ⑥), scene of much Antipodean revelry when the annual **Darwin–Ambon boat race** finishes here in July/August. At other times, it's worth downing an afternoon beer or two at the hotel's expensive outside bar, while the sun settles over Leihitu. Continuing along the bay to **Seilale** village, the road drops down across low hills to the drier south coast, where a minor road eastwards takes you to **AIRLOUW**. A few hundred rupiah here gets you admission to the rocky beach and a look at **Pintu Kota** (City Gate), a headland pierced by a square-sided hole. West, the main road continues to the breadfruit trees and coconut palms of the three-kilometre-long kampung **LATUHALAT**, where footpaths trail off to various walled beaches – sandy **Santai** is the nicest, and crowded to critical mass on Sundays, but you have to haggle over the entrance fee. Right on the main road, **Namalatu beach** has little sand, and seasonally savage swells, but a warung and bar right next to the **dive shop** are a social magnet. The most friendly of Latuhalat's **homestays** is the *Europa* (☎0911/62105; ⑤ including breakfast and afternoon tea).

To Leihitu

Heading east from Ambon City, you first pass the beautifully green **Commonwealth War Cemetery** at **Tantui**, the last resting place of two thousand soldiers from New Zealand, Australia and elsewhere, who died defending Maluku in 1942. Then comes **Galala**, from where you can either catch a **ferry** every few minutes to the **Pattimura University** and the airport road, or continue another 5km to Leihitu at **PASSO**, the nexus between north and south peninsulas – roadsides here are thronged by people waiting for the right bus. From Passo, the **east coast road** runs another 20km to Liang, while the **road west** heads either to the airport, or across the ranges to Hitu and the northern coast.

The east coast

Four kilometres from Passo, past Japanese bunkers guarding neat groves of spice and coconut trees, is **SULI** and the ever-popular **Natsepa beach**, whose *Vaneysa Paradise* (☎0911/61451; ⑤) provides beds, scenery and meals. From here the road cuts north-east over low hills to **TULEHU**, its busy **harbour** full of fishing boats, wooden houses, and a mess of fast-food shacks. On the north fringe you'll find **Hurnala Port**, with daily departures **to the Lease Islands and Seram** (pp.868–870); ask around for snorkelling charters to what remains of the coral at the south end of **Pulau Pombo**, a small, uninhabited island off to the northeast. Tulehu also has several **hot springs** – including an offshore submarine vent – with the best in the forest about 3km from the main road via a path from the police station.

Ten minutes by bus beyond Tulehu is **WAII**, an attractive village at the base of 1030m **Gunung Salahutu**, famed for its mascot *belut*, sacred **eels**. A five-minute walk inland through the village takes you to a narrow, fifty-metre-long natural pool, where there's nothing too sacred about the sight of villagers of all ages splashing around in the clear water, washing teeth and clothes. The eels share a cave at top end of the pool with a couple of dozen large fish, reluctantly venturing into view with the offer of a raw egg. Past Waii, the last 10km of road forks, with the right branch ending at **HUNIMUA**, another public stretch of sand and departure point for the daily **ferry to Kairatu** in western Seram (p.870), and the north branch continuing to **Liang** village.

Hitu and the north coast

Around thirty minutes by bus from Passo on a winding road, two-street **HITU**'s mosques proclaim Islam, while its jetty handles local traffic to Seram. Before the Dutch muscled in and razed the old town in 1646, Hitu was the most important harbour on Ambon, a regular stop-over for Arab spice merchants since the thirteenth century. There's nothing to see today, but catch an ojek or irregular buses 5km east to **MAMALA**, whose **Idul Fitri celebrations** feature *pukul sapu* dancers, who slash each other with sharp palm fronds and are later healed by a magical oil. Seek a guide here for the two-hour return hike across Satan's Cape to the remains of Portuguese **Benteng Kapalaha**.

Half an hour's drive west of Hitu, Christian **HILA** was another colonial outpost, site of a temporary Portuguese customs house and the longer-lasting **Benteng Amsterdam**, where the Dutch spied out illegal traffic along the coast. A restored, six-metre-tall, thick-walled blockhouse, Benteng Amsterdam was also the seventeenth-century abode of **Rumphius**, a German botanist and historian who wrote much about Ambon; ask around to be let in. The adjacent stone and beam **Imanual Church** dates from 1780; a tower toppled in the 1918 earthquake, but it's otherwise in fine condition. It's a ten-minute walk from here to **KAITETU**, Hila's Muslim sister village, whose thatched, fifteenth-century **Mesjid Wapauwe** originally overlooked the town from

Mount Wawane, until it was moved, allegedly by sorcery, to its present location. Both villages are noticeably poor compared to those on the south peninsula; prickly pear cactus hedges keep wandering goats out of the bananas and maize, while most houses are simple split rattan-bamboo affairs, more elaborate dwellings built up of plastered coral blocks, all decorated by sprays of orchids. There's **homestay accommodation** at Kaitetu (③), buses for the ninety-minute run back to the city until early afternoon, and, in good conditions, up to three buses a day ply the thirty-kilometre, rough road west to **URING**, where there's a fifteen-metre waterfall.

The Lease Islands

Immediately east of Ambon, the four **Lease Islands** (pronounced "Lei-asser") are easy to reach and make for an attractive trip, with nicely green hills and the usual complement of sand and sea. Last stop before the nutmeg-producing Banda Islands off to the southeast, the Leases were key to Dutch plans to monopolize the spice trade; **forts** scattered around the coastlines kept an eye on marine traffic and acted as bases for controlling insurrection seeping through from an untamed Seram. The islands also became the theatre for the 1817 **Pattimura rebellion**, the key sites of which give an excuse to explore; as on Ambon, there's a good deal of local tradition and superstition mixed with imported beliefs.

Fat, X-shaped **Saparua** is, at 20km across, the largest of the Leases, where you'll find the main town and most of the attractions. A bus from Ambon's Batu Merah depot can get you to Hurnala Port at Tulehu, where there's a daily morning and afternoon **ferry to Saparua** (90min; Rp5000). A faster, unnerving, option from Tulehu are the private **speedboats** (1hr; Rp5000) which leave whenever full from the eastern side of town; bus drivers can drop you off at the right spot. Start early and it's quite feasible to day-trip to Saparua, though stay longer and you'll find good accommodation and the chance of organizing transport to the smaller **Haruku, Nusa Laut** and **Molana Islands**.

Saparua and beyond

The scenic, 35-kilometre-trip from Tulehu to **SAPARUA** passes bulky Haruku and the sliver of Pulau Molana to the western kampung of **HARIA**, Saparua's **port** – low tide arrival means wading ashore, so wear suitable footwear. Check the current frequency and times of **boats back to Ambon**, and then, if you've a few minutes to spare, seek out Haria's *baileu*, a thirty-metre, open-sided, thatched **traditional meeting hall**, close to the high-profile Gethsemani church. It was here in May 1817 that Pattimura allegedly made a declaration of independence from Dutch rule, though this sounds suspiciously like a retrospective amendment of history. Saparua's most comfortable accommodation is nearby at **Laino resort** (diving/snorkelling can be arranged; ☎0931/21114, fax 21600; cabins ⑥) – charter a boat or mobil from Haria for the short ride.

Alternatively, hop on a public mobil and head 5km east to **KOTA SAPARUA**, the island's hot, sleepy capital, where single-storey, shuttered houses flank two 200-metre-long parallel streets and a handful of connecting lanes. At the west end you'll find the **mobil terminal**, the market, the *Piala* coffee house, where they've seen enough Westerners to expect you to want unsweetened coffee, and the *Rumah Makan Andlas*, the only place offering full meals. For somewhere to stay, walk east for five minutes along the lower Jalan Benteng to big, airy **rooms** at *Penginapan Lease Indah* (☎0931/21105; ③; no meals). Kota Saparua's upper street is worth a quick look round; there's another *baileu* and a metre-wide stone "**altar**" similar to the sacred stones at Soya Atas on Ambon, but the main point of interest here is **Benteng Duurstede**, just past the *Lease Indah*. The VOC built this large fort in 1690, and, apart from damage inflicted by US bombs trying to oust the Japanese in 1944, it has survived in good

THE PATTIMURA REVOLT

The **Pattimura revolt**, which lasted from May until November in 1817, followed the resumption of Dutch rule in Maluku after a decade of caretaker British government during the Napoleonic wars. The British had proved lenient overseers, and Maluccans had no affection for the Dutch, who had forbidden them to grow or trade spices, and used them for forced labour. On May 14, 1817, Pattimura – a former British army sergeant – and his followers met on Mount Saniri behind Haria to organize resistance: two days later they had overrun Benteng Duurstede, sparing only the five-year-old son of the Resident. A Dutch retaliatory force arrived from Ambon on May 20, but, their *kora-kora* transports foundering in heavy swells, were massacred in hand-to-hand fighting as they tried to land at **Waisisil beach**. Retiring to Haria in triumph, Pattimura spent the next few months encouraging skirmishes, as fighting spread around the Leases, and across to Seram and Ambon. There were no more decisive battles, however, and the rebels suffered increasingly insupportable losses and waning local support through Dutch raids on innocent villages. In November, Pattimura and three of his generals were apparently betrayed by Booi's chief and handed over to the Dutch. They were hanged the following month in Ambon.

condition; a donation gets you access to watchposts around the walls, five heavy cannon, and views across to the Ouw peninsula, Pulau Nusa Laut, and palm frond tufts above Waisisil beach. There's also a **jail** off to one side, with airholes rather than windows in the walls, and a hall with dioramas of scenes from Pattimura's rebellion.

Around the island

Four roads fan out from Kota Saparua to the corners of the island, and there's no problem finding (or chartering) mobils from town before late afternoon. **Southwest**, you almost immediately pass murky **Waisisil beach**, where a **memorial** marks Pattimura's victory. The road ends twenty minutes later at **BOOI**, a fishing village whose streets are ranged up a steep hillside overlooking the sea. Follow stone stairs up past a well and you'll find a walking track through the undergrowth to the top of **Booi Hill**, Pattimura's last stand, or walk down to the coast past houses whose verandahs are lumbered with fishing nets and outrigger canoes awaiting repairs. Below, Booi's deep bay has a narrow shingle beach shaded by nut trees, with villagers combing dead coral flats for shellfish.

Heading **east from Kota Saparua**, there's an overgrown **cemetery** with aged, Dutch-style mausoleums, and about 10km of anonymous landscapes and coastal villages with tight streets, sleeping dogs and sea almond trees. The road evaporates at **OUW**, origin of Saparua's popular red-glazed **pottery** which you'll find drying on racks along the main street; look too for the overgrown ruins of **Benteng Hollandia**, sacked on November 10, 1817 by rebels – including, according to some sources, **Christiana Tiahahu** (see p.861).

The road **northeast to Nolloth** diverges from the Ouw road a short way out of town; this is a less populated, lower-lying part of the island where mangroves, sago palms and saltwater creeks hold sway. It's around 5km to **MAHU**, where a path alongside the large Catholic church leads coastwards to the decent but overpriced *Mahu Dive Lodge*, known locally as **Kelapa Indah** (packages include two dives and accommodation; ☎0911/53344, fax 54127; ⑨). Staying on the main road for the final 5km to **NOLLOTH** lands you in a quiet coastal kampung where children play with catapults on the sand.

Haruku and Nusa Laut

Charter boats, arranged direct with owners or through accommodation, are the only reliable way to visit Lease's other islands, though you may find transport from Haria on Wednesday and Saturday, when shoppers visit Kota Saparua's market. There are no guest houses on the other islands.

Rounded, tall and marginally smaller than Saparua, **HARUKU** is known chiefly for **sasi lompa**, a blood-drawing dance similar to that performed at Hitu on Pulau Ambon (see p.867), which is held every three years at **Pelauw village** on Haruku's north coast. Otherwise, there's at least one more **fort** to track down, and some fine snorkelling, with more ruins and better coral out at **NUSA LAUT**, a far smaller island off Saparua's southeastern point.

Seram

A moody eyebrow glowering north over a more urbane Ambon, **Seram** is, at 350km long, Maluku's second largest island. And, despite the onslaught of loggers, it remains one of the wildest: this is the home of the region's most traditional people, including the distinctive red-turbaned **Nuaulu**, whose influential cults and *kakehan* organizations spread their rituals, headhunting and religion to Ambon and the Lease Islands. In addition, Maluku's highest mountain ranges and dense monsoonal forests protect plenty of deer and Seram's legendary **birdlife**, which includes rare endemics such as *kakatua seram*, the salmon-crested cockatoo, along with more widespread ecclectus parrots, here called *bayan*, and the large, flightless **cassowary** – the latter possibly introduced centuries ago as a food source.

Closest to Ambon, southern Seram offers the bland district capital of **Masohi** and nearby ferry port of **Amahai** as places to get established before heading further afield. Along a scenic north coast, **Sawai** and **Wahai** are good hideaways with quick trips to forest fringes, and also access into the rugged interior of **Manusela national park**; self-sufficient **hikers** heading here first need a **permit**, and perhaps a guide, from Ambon – see p.863 for details. **Buses** ply the decent south coast road between westerly **Piru** and eastern **Tehoru**, and up through the centre to tiny **Saleman**; elsewhere you'll be catching speedboat **ferries** between coastal settlements, or trekking.

Getting to Seram

Merpati post a weekly **flight** to Amahai, but it seldom leaves. More reliably, there are direct early morning **buses** from Ambon City's Batu Merah depot daily to either Masohi or Saleman (also known as **Saka**). It's eight to twelve hours and Rp15,000 to either destination, involving a **ferry** crossing (90min) between Hunimua on Ambon and **Kairatu** in western Seram, the port for **WAIPIRIT** town. You might want to leave the bus at Waipirit (**beds** at the *Hotel Agatis* come recommended; ④), and day-trip to snorkelling beaches and a waterfall at **Rumahkai**, or detour up the west coast to **PIRU** and try and locate the remains of the Dutch **Harder Vlik fortress**. Stay on the bus at Waipirit, and it's between three and five hours to either Masohi or Saleman.

A faster alternative for reaching Masohi is to catch the **hydrofoil** which runs twice a day from Tulehu, forty minutes northeast of Ambon City, to Amahai (around 2hr) – Ambon's tourist office should have current schedules. Of real esoteric interest, there's also a weekly, 48-hour ferry from Tulehu to **GESER**, the only settlement on a tiny crescent **atoll** of the same name off Seram's far eastern tip. Once the haunt of pirates, a century ago Geser had become trading post for all sorts of goods from Irian and the rest of eastern Indonesia; today there's said to be a Dongson drum in fine shape somewhere on the island.

Masohi and southern Seram

Ambon excepted, **MASOHI** is capital for all of central Maluku, and, like most purpose-built administrative posts throughout Indonesia, is exceptionally tidy and totally life-less. Founded in 1957, you'll find absurdly wide, virtually empty roads dwarfing wandering schoolchildren and government staff alike, and what little activity there is revolving around the **bus station** and attached **market**. Install yourself at either *Hotel Masohi Indah* (④) or *Penginapan Sri Lestari* (③), both a short way east of the bus station on Jalan Soulisa; eat at the hotel or the very decent *Surabaya* restaurant next door to the *Sri Lestari*. Masohi's **tourist office** at the *Kantor Bupati* on Jalan Imam Bonjol (open mornings Mon–Sat; ☎0914/21462), more or less behind the *Sri Lestari*, is a helpful source of information if you can locate the staff, some of whom speak English. **Moving on**, vehicles leave Masohi's bus station every few minutes east to Amahai (Rp350), with early morning departures further east to Tehoru (for access to Hatumetan and southern Manusela national park; Rp15,000), west to Waipirit, and north across the island to Saleman-Saka (for boats to Sawai, Wahai, and northern Manusela; Rp10,000).

Amahai, Bonara and beyond

Twenty minutes by road from Masohi, **AMAHAI** is a small, comfortably spread community of football pitches, churches and neat wooden houses with picket fences. Mobils terminate at the market next to the **hydrofoil port**, where there are morning and afternoon departures to Ambon. Near the Ebenezer church, a donation gains admission to the tiny **Museum Seram**, whose energetic owner accompanies you around his delightfully gory home-made exhibits illustrating Seram's traditional life – ritual cannibalism, death and puberty rites, barehand wrestling with wild beasts, skull cults – all the while delivering a stream of anecdotes about history and customs.

To attempt first-hand dealings with the Nuaulu, catch a Sepa-bound mobil from Amahai for the hour-long run east past the **airstrip** and nicely vacant, grey-sand beaches to **BONARA**, Seram's most accessible **Nuaulu village**. This is not an easy place to visit, however, as older villagers want nothing to do with foreigners. Under no circumstances should you just barge in here; either take a guide from Masohi's tourist office, or seek permission to look around from Bonara's Indonesian-speaking kepala desa, if he's available, or adult villagers – a small gift, and sharing cigarettes, will help. Even so, you'll probably be forbidden to take photos and may still be shooed away, but with luck you may see Bonara's old wooden meeting house, raised on stumps and meticulously thatched, several other traditional buildings, and sacred stones curiously roped down to the ground.

Ten minutes beyond Bonara is Sepa, where, if you haven't caught the bus in Masohi, those heading for the southern reaches of Manusela national park can find transport 70km east to **TEHORU**. There's **accommodation** in Tehoru at *Penginapan Susi* (③), and speedboats for the thirty-minute run to **Hatumetan**, Manusela's trailhead.

Northern Seram: Saleman to Wahai

It takes two hours to follow the road due north across Seram from the Waipirit–Masohi highway to the beach at **SALEMAN-SAKA**, a dusty few houses, stores and single **losmen** from where **boats** depart to everywhere else along Seram's north coast. Arriving in October, the first thing you'll notice is the smell of **durian**; there are whole forests of this pungent fruit up here, and locals seem constantly to be gorging themselves. There's little to do at Saleman except wait for **ferries** east **to Sawai and Wahai** to arrive; buses then fill up with southbound passengers and head off. If you get bored, ask around to find if anyone else is heading your way, and negotiate a longboat **charter**.

Seram's north coast is very beautiful, dotted with sandy bays and coconut plantations above which forested slopes descend steeply into the sea from distant peaks. About an hour's run from Saleman, you round some sheer grey cliffs and arrive at **SAWAI**, a

Muslim town of a hundred houses tightly packed into a tiny cove. Ask the boat to drop you at *Lisar Bahari* **guest house** (④ including meals), a very comfortable waterside location whose owner can arrange guides for local trails and canoes to nearby reefs, where there's average **snorkelling**. A walk through Sawai reveals a central mosque and public washing spots before the path continues east over a small headland, through a durian forest (beware of falling fruit), and down to a Christian enclave. Ask here for **Pak Julius**, a first-rate **guide** who at Rp20,000 a day can take you up into the ranges overlooking Sawai or on a gentler, twenty-kilometre round-trip through lowland forests to an impressive waterfall – pigeons, hornbills and deer are common. With ten days to spare, it's also possible to walk from Sawai right across Manusela national park to Manusela village and down to Seram's south coast – *Lisar Bahari* can set this up.

An hour further along the coast from Sawai is **WAHAI**, the north's largest town and favoured **starting point for Manusela**. Your best contact here is the well-known Pak Eddy, who speaks no English, but arranges reliable guides and can sort out delivery of park permits to the relevant authorities. The cheapest **beds** are at the basic *Sinar Indah* (②) or nicer *Penginapan Taman Baru* (③ including meals).

Manusela national park

Nearly 1900 square kilometres of central Seram's lowland swamps, vine forests and high altitude heaths are gazetted as **Manusela national park**, an eminently exciting place to hike through. Wildlife is one draw; another is Manusela's **Alifur people**, who live on sago, slash-and-burn agriculture and **hunting** – it's not unusual to encounter spiked deer traps along the trails, or a freshly-skinned pelt and antlers hanging in the trees. Different Alifur groups don't get on well amongst themselves but are, on the whole, friendly to outsiders, though you'd be well advised to take local superstitions seriously while you're here. At least three mountains in the park – including **Gunung Binaya**, Maluku's 3027-metre apex – are considered the sacred abode of spirits.

Various **routes** traverse the park between Wahai in the north and southern Hatumetan, the easier direction to travel as some of Seram's ranges have exceedingly steep southern faces, best tackled as descents rather than climbs. One option is to follow logging tracks and forest trails southwest from Wahai to **Roho**, then turn southeast via **Kanike** and **Maraina** to the halfway point at **Manusela village**; another is to hike or catch a boat east along the north coast from Wahai to **Pasahari**, follow **Sungai Wae Isal** south to **Kaloa**, then continue to Manusela via **Hatuolo**. Set in an elevated valley, **MANUSELA** is a friendly place, worth a stop to rest up and look around before spending a final couple of days negotiating the 1750-metre ridges of the Merkele range, and a difficult, slippery descent down the far side to Hatumetan. Either route is about 70km long, and takes around a week.

Park practicalities

Trails through Manusela are clear but not easy, so you need to be fit and properly prepared. Ambon's BKSDA issues obligatory **permits** (see "Permits" in Ambon Listings on p.864), and you should end up with three copies: one each for the police and PHPA at your chosen trailhead, and one for yourself. If you can't speak Indonesian, you'll also need to bring an interpreter from Ambon, though Masohi's tourist office just might be able to find a bilingual guide. Indonesian speakers will find it much cheaper to engage **guides** – who are essential – on site at around Rp20,000 a day. There are no supplies to be had on the trail, and **accommodation** is a matter of camping out and staying with villagers, so bring a tent, all your own **food** and cooking gear. **Water** collected along the way needs to be purified. Manusela's **weather** is always wet, and cold enough at altitude to need a sleeping bag and warm evening wear.

Pulau Buru

Eighty kilometres west from Ambon, **Pulau Buru** is chiefly known as a source of **minyak kayu putih**, or katjupat, an astringent oil distilled from eucalyptus leaves, and the fact that it served as a **prison island** for political troublemakers after Indonesia's 1965 coup. Oval, and covering some 2000 square kilometres, the island also has abundant natural attractions, long exploited by logging companies and just beginning to draw intrepid Western visitors. Buru's northern half is very dry, though extensive coastal mangroves here attract migratory shorebirds, with the southern half of the island cloaked in monsoonal rainforest, home to giant plants. Two **hiking** targets are **Danau Rana**, a high-altitude lake in Buru's geographical centre, and northwesterly **Gunung Kaplamada**, the island's highest point at a respectable 2730m; trails to either will bring you in contact with **traditional peoples** of the interior.

Trips are best organized through guides in Ambon, such as Nanusa Tours and Travel – see Ambon "Listings" on p.863. On the top side of northeasterly Kayeli Bay, **NAMLEA's** 10,000 inhabitants make it Buru's largest settlement by far, reached **from Ambon** by a weekly Merpati **flight**, twice a month on **Pelni's** *Lambelu*, or several times a week by **ferry** from Galala, 5km east of Ambon City. The latter crossing takes eight to ten hours, and, as the ferries are the same type used to cross Ambon Bay, you wouldn't want to make the trip in high seas.

The Bandas

Isolated in the open water some 150km southeast of Ambon, the **Banda Islands** are a small-scale tropical idyll. There's no rugged grandeur here, just the manageable beauty of a dozen or so hunchbacked volcanic islands emerging from the deep blue Banda Sea, only one of which is larger than a couple of square kilometres, and whose highest point requires hours, not days, to conquer – if you even get around to it. **Bandaneira** is the capital, still dressed in the solid European architecture raised when this tiny island was the focus of the world trade in **nutmeg**, overlooked by conical **Gunung Api**, whose slopes will keep you occupied for a morning. Cupped around both, **Banda Besar** (also known as Lonthoir) offers more colonial leftovers, as do the other main satellite islands – southeasterly **Rozengeim** (Hatta), and western **Ai** and **Rhun**. Around the coast you'll find superb **beaches** and **coral**, with a sprinkle of uninhabited islets to keep you busy long after you tire of the obvious sights; put to sea and you'll often see dolphins and turtles.

All traffic to the Bandas stops at Bandaneira. **From Ambon**, Merpati fly in five times a week, while Pelni averages one trip a week aboard the *Rinjani*, *Bukit Siguntang*, or *Tatamailau*. The *Rinjani* and *Bukit Siguntang* also call in at Bandaneira on their return legs **from Irian and Southeast Maluku**. Once here, travel between islands is on local boats; the only roads are on Bandaneira.

Some history

It's unclear when nutmeg first became a cash crop in the Banda Islands, but by the time the Portuguese cruised by in 1512, nutmeg cultivation was so profitable that all available land in the islands was dedicated to it. At the time, the Bandas existed as a loose alliance of **orang kaya**, or influential headmen, rather than having any unified government or king, a situation which the Portuguese found difficult to manipulate and so contented themselves with simply trading for spices. The Dutch, on the other hand, set out to govern right from their earliest landings in 1599. Unlike the Portuguese, they built

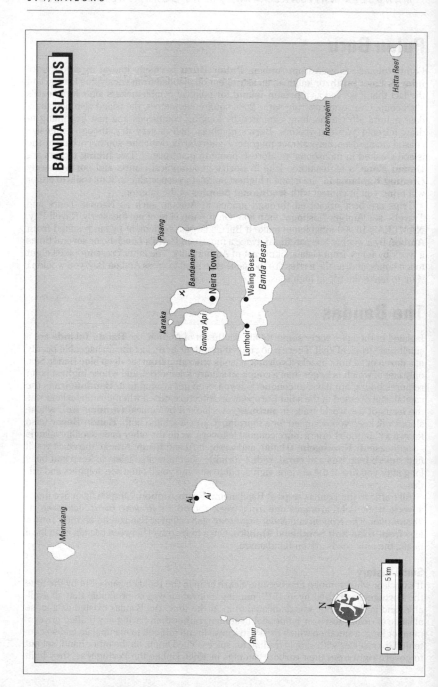

BANDA ISLANDS

Hatta Reef

Rozengein

Pisang

Bandaneira

Karaka

Neira Town

Waling Besar

Banda Besar

Gunung Api

Lonthoir

Manukang

Ai

Ai

Rhun

N

0   5 km

<table>
<tr><td>

NUTMEG

The **nutmeg**, *pala* in Indonesian, is the seed of an evergreen tree which grows wild in India, Indonesia and Australia. Only in Maluku, however, are nutmeg so large and fragrant, and the best of all originated from the Bandas. Planted in the shade of *kenari* or coconut groves, the trees grow to 20m and crop twice a year; the ripe **fruit** resembles a pale green apricot which splits open to reveal a glossy seed wrapped in scarlet tracery. This tracery, or aril – which attracts **nutmeg pigeons** (*pombok*) who eat the fruit and scatter the seeds – is peeled off and dried as **mace**, while the brittle seed shell is easily cracked to get at the nutmeg inside. Fresh nutmeg smells intensely soapy and aromatic, and is quite toxic in large quantities; in Maluku, the fruit itself is also boiled down to make **nutmeg jam**, which tastes nothing like nutmeg and a little like strawberry.
</td></tr>
</table>

forts, and, incorrectly assuming them to hold absolute power over their villages, wrangled from the *orang kaya* the **Euwig Verbond**, or Eternal Compact, which granted Holland a lasting monopoly of the spice trade. This was totally ignored by the Bandanese traders, however, who continued to deal with whoever they liked – including the British, who, much to Holland's irritation, had occupied the western islands of Ai and Rhun. A decade of scuffles between the Dutch, the British, and Bandanese followed, but in 1619 the VOC tired of diplomacy and sent two thousand troops under **Jan Pieterzoon Coen** to the Bandas with orders to enforce Holland's claims. Coen achieved this by slaughtering the Bandanese *orang kaya*, an act which sparked a mass migration of the islands' residents, and then distributing the now-vacant plantations to Dutch **perkerniers** (managers), who imported **slaves** to work them. In this manner, the Dutch controlled the world supply of nutmeg for over a century, a business which bought even the relatively poorly-paid *perkerniers* elegant dwellings.

After the spice trade's eventual collapse, the Bandas vegetated, Dutch interest in the islands shifting to their use as a dustbin for troublemakers. The two most famous twentieth-century exiles were anti-colonial activists **Mohammed Hatta** and **Sutan Syarhrir**, who later took a hand in national government alongside Sukarno. Since Independence the Bandas have remained undeveloped, though nutmeg plantations are back in the hands of locals, and low-key tourism is beginning to add some activity to the atmosphere of genteel poverty.

Bandaneira: island and town

Small enough to wander around in half a day, **Pulau Bandaneira** covers just three square kilometres, most of which is occupied by the lazy lanes of **Neira town**. This is a colonial post long gone to seed: pedestrians saunter along the narrow, shady streets and on all sides old buildings stand patched, restored, or simply crumbling, and people sit gossiping on their verandahs, peeling home-grown sea almonds and nutmegs. Always visible above the roofs, Gunung Api and Benteng Belgica (the biggest of the island's two **forts**) make good reference points while you wander, though it's unlikely you'd become lost. The town's **centre** lies around western Jalan Pelabuhan and the **main port**, with an **administrative area** in the streets between Benteng Belgica and seafront Jalan Kujali.

Neira town

Start a walk around Neira on Jalan Pelabuhan, whose now small **market** and quiet shops once drew spice merchants from Java, India, China and Europe. The best survivor from those days is the **Heavenly City temple**, a Chinese edifice in multicoloured trim, used today more by visiting Taiwanese fishing crews than local ethnic Chinese.

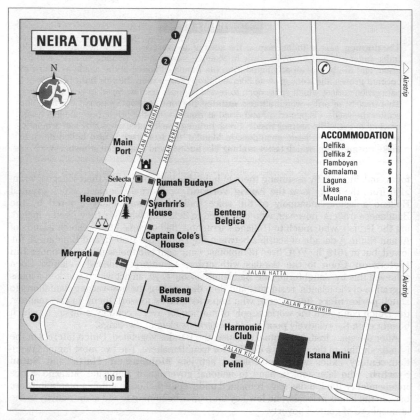

NEIRA TOWN

N

Main Port

Selecta

Heavenly City

Merpati

Rumah Budaya

Syarhrir's House

Captain Cole's House

Benteng Belgica

Benteng Nassau

Harmonie Club

Pelni

Istana Mini

JALAN PELABUHAN

JALAN GEREJA TUA

JALAN HATTA

JALAN SYARHRIR

JALAN KUJALI

Airstrip

Airstrip

ACCOMMODATION	
Delfika	4
Delfika 2	7
Flamboyan	5
Gamalama	6
Laguna	1
Likes	2
Maulana	3

0   100 m

Further along you pass a **mosque** (the majority of the Banda Islands' 20,000 souls are Muslim) and the port area, before arriving outside the **Maulana hotel** (see p.878), owned by local big wheel Des Alwi. Ask here about the next screening of Pak Alwi's footage of Gunung Api's 1988 eruption – a gem.

One street back, Jalan Gereja Tua is named after a squat, nineteenth-century **church**, focus for torchlight parades and night-long singing at Easter and Christmas. Just north are some of Banda's finest surviving colonial town-houses, complete with porticoes and columns: one is labelled as the **House of Captain Cole**, a British marine who captured Neira from the Dutch in 1810. Opposite, **Syarhrir's House** is an empty few rooms with an aged caretaker and mementos of the statesman, who, along with Hatta, was exiled by the Dutch to Neira in the mid-1930s and played a key role in post-war Independence negotiations. Hatta went on to become Indonesia's vice-president, but differences with Sukarno's leadership later forced both he and Syarhrir from the political scene. More interesting is the adjacent **Rumah Budaya**, Banda's **museum** (no fixed times; donation), where lurid paintings of colonial atrocities hang above cases of Portuguese and Dutch coinage, weapons and vast quantities of glass and ceramic bottles. Don't miss the decorative bronze cannons out the back, some with playfully modelled crocodiles, their tails vanishing into the fuse hole.

The forts and waterfront

Up on a rise above Neira, **Benteng Belgica's** severely restored walls and towers still convey the unflinching authority that the Dutch imposed on the Bandas. Built in heavy stone, the fort dates from the 1620s, partly a symbol of power, partly intended to discourage the British from expanding their tenuous holdings in the region. An unusual, **pentagonal plan** brings the whole island and surrounding straits within clear cannon range, incidentally providing dramatic views of Gunung Api and the town. The **entrance** is on Jalan Hatta (no fixed opening hours; Rp10,000).

Below Belgica, cross Jalan Syarhrir and you're amongst the remains of **Benteng Nassau**. Founded in 1607, this fort was where Coen oversaw the execution of 44 of the Bandas' *orang kaya* by Japanese mercenaries on May 8, 1621 in response to trade violations, an act which earned him a mild reproach from the VOC's directors. It's a complete ruin, with remains of the walls now enclosing a patch of kapok trees and grass, where children play football in the afternoon. A tunnel through the south wall leads to waterfront Jalan Kujali, and a minute or so east along here brings you to the ornamental plaster lions and stylishly proportioned lines of **Istana Mini** (literally "Little Castle"), the VOC governor's house. A few doors along, the freshly restored **Harmonie Club**, Bandaneira's colonial hotspot, faces a long, open-sided **kora-kora shed**; there's a chance to catch these fifteen-metre-long traditional canoes in action during inter-island **races** in April.

Practicalities

Bandaneira's **airstrip** is at the north end of the island, where accommodation touts meet arrivals with offers of free transport. Or it's a twenty-minute walk into town – with the 10kg Merpati baggage allowance, you're unlikely to be weighed down. The **Merpati office** on Jalan Pelabuhan (Mon–Sat 8am–early afternoon, except when a flight is due) is a place of constant confusion. Sort out your ticket back to Ambon as soon as possible, and anticipate overbookings and delays by signing up for several flights. If no seats are available, go on all available waiting lists, and come back regularly to check. Travelling by sea, the **main port** is on Jalan Pelabuhan, but the **Pelni office**, with ticket sales and a departure board for Pelni and Perentis vessels to Ambon, Kei and Tanimbar, is down on Jalan Kujali.

Eat at your lodgings, or try out the simple alternatives on Jalan Pelabuhan: *Selecta* is the best, with bubblegum-flavoured pineapple ice cream and *jus pala*, a nutmeg drink. Stores along Jalan Pelabuhan sell home-made almond biscuits and nutmeg jam. **Accommodation** is mostly central, and waterfront locations have superb views of Gunung Api. With the exception of the *Maulana* and *Laguna* hotels, prices below include all meals.

ACCOMMODATION

Delfika (☎0910/21027). Central colonial house opposite the museum on Jl Gereja Tua, with a small garden. ④.

Delfika 2 off the southern end of Jl Pelabuhan (☎0910/21127). New, with fine views and facilities, but slack staff. All rooms have fan and bathroom. ④.

Flamboyan Jl Syarhrir (☎0910/21233). Neat guest house with a quiet, shady garden at back. Doubles ④.

Gamalama at the corner of Jl Gereja Tua and Jl Kujali, near Benteng Nassau (☎0910/21053). Good value favourite, tidy and clean. Double with fan ④.

Laguna top end of Jl Pelabuhan (☎0910/21018). Run by *Maulana* as a downmarket alternative, but similarly overpriced and under-patronized. ⑤.

Likes top end of Jl Pelabuhan, past *Hotel Maulana*. Quiet homestay, with same views of Gunung Api as *Maulana*, but a fraction of the cost. ④.

UNDERWATER BANDA

Most visitors are quickly hooked by the Bandas' magical submarine scenery, a blend of sand flats, fringing reefs and thirty-metre **coral walls** whose inhabitants have yet to fall foul of commercial fishing. The sheer quantity of marine life here is astounding: shallower reefs seethe with banded sea snakes, surgeonfish, anthias, trumpetfish and prowling coral trout, all surrounded by clouds of butterfly-like blue triggerfish. Over deeper water you'll see bigger game: bumpheaded parrotfish and maori wrasse, turtles, schools of trevally, chevron barracuda and unicorn fish – only sharks are rare.

One of the best **snorkelling sites** is on the northwest side of **Gunung Api**, where lava from the 1988 eruption flowed into the sea, killing the coral. It has since grown back at a rate which has baffled marine biologists – huge plates of *acrapora* here look centuries old – and is a wonderful spot for young reef fish. Around the corner, **Pulau Karaka** is a pretty block of black rock, palms, pandanus and sand, perfect for finning out from into the channel between here and Bandaneira. Better yet is **Karnofol beach** on the eastern side of Banda Besar, with excellent shallow coral and a drop-off to patrol for deep-water fish. Prime **dive sites** include **Tanjung Burang**, the northeastern tip of Banda Besar, which features currents, walls covered in sea-squirts, huge barrel sponges, abundant pelagic species and a five-metre-long tunnel; **Pulau Pisang** has more of the same, plus big scorpion fish and morays. Further out, experienced divers rate sites around **Ai and Rhun Islands** as the best in Maluku.

Maulana past the port at the upper end of Jl Pelabuhan (☎0910/21022).Neira's only place with pretensions to luxury, but absurdly expensive and usually empty. Also runs the Bandas' sole dive operation, with even more expensive accommodation/dive packages. ⑦–⑨.

Gunung Api, Banda Besar and beyond

Irregular **transport to other islands** departs when full from Neira's **local dock** behind the market on Jalan Pelabuhan, where you can also haggle a boat charter, if your accommodation can't help out. Outrigger canoes cost a few thousand an hour, while a ten-person, outboard-powered longboat with canopy is around Rp50,000 for the day. Lodgings also provide **snorkelling gear** and a **handline** for Rp5000 or so, and then you're all set for a pleasurable day in the water, with a lunch of freshly grilled fish on the nearest beach. Des Alwi's monopoly – and the insistence that you stay at one of his hotels – makes **diving** extremely expensive, though you might find it worthwhile to deal directly with the divemaster. The dive shop is opposite the *Maulana*; count on US$100 (in dollars cash) for two dives, plus gear hire.

Gunung Api

Almost close enough to touch from Bandaneira, **Gunung Api** has a long history of activity, the last eruption in 1988 causing the evacuation of nearby islands and sending a tongue of lava down the mountain's northwestern slopes. All the same, as long as you are fairly fit and wear a decent pair of boots, **climbing** Gunung Api is safe enough; athletes have reached the 660-metre-high summit in forty-five minutes, but count on three hours for the return trip. Pack some water and arrange for a canoe to take you over from the Jalan Pelabuhan market to the **pavilion** at the base of the mountain before dawn, which will see you at the top before the day heats up.

A few minutes from the beach brings you to a **second pavilion** and the start of a flight of almost useless **steps**; by the time they evaporate around the halfway mark you're already losing your footing on a carpeting of loose scree. From here it's an exhausting scramble, following gullies up a slippery, forty-five-degree slope through stands of spindly, loose-rooted saplings, until the going eases slightly near the top. You arrive stained with ash and grit, amongst a landscape of steaming rubble and sulphurous smells, with grand views out over the Bandas and to Seram. Take great care around the peak: the rim is undercut and drops vertically into the main crater, a grey-and-red streaked maw disappearing into the bowels of the mountain.

Banda Besar and the western islands

Just southeast of Bandaneira, **Banda Besar** is a ten-kilometre-long crescent, the largest island in the group. **Lonthoir** is the main town, connected by boats from Neira's market until mid-afternoon; leave it too late and you'll have to charter a return. **Benteng Hollandia** stands on a crest above town at the top of 300 stairs, the fort built after Coen took the island in 1621. Nothing much is left beyond an overgrown wall or two, but views are good, and there's a nicely maintained **perkernier's residence** along the way, now used as a meeting house. The last *perkernier* in the Bandas, Wim van den Broeke, still manages a nutmeg plantation 5km further north along the coast at **Waling Besar village**, reached in an hour or so via a footpath from Lonthoir. Fluent in English and Dutch, he's an interesting man to talk to, and can show you the various stages of nutmeg cultivation on a tour of his land. There's nowhere to stay on Banda Besar, but for a few days' of peaceful indolence try heading to **Pulau Pisang**, a banana-shaped isle off Banda Besar's northern tip. The *Mealina* **homestay** here has four beachside cabins (④ including meals), a short beach and average snorkelling which improves away from shore.

Two of the Bandas' **western islands** are also worth a visit. Despite nutmeg groves galore, another fort and more *perkernier* relics, **AI**'s splendid beaches make it a fine place to do nothing at all, with the bonus of often being clear and sunny when a deluge descends on Bandaneira. Ai was held by the British at the beginning of the seventeenth century, until their garrison was massacred during a Dutch assault in 1616. There's decent all-inclusive **accommodation** here at *Penginapan Weltevreden* (④) and *Penginapan Revenge* (④), both in **Ai village**, where you might also be able to negotiate a quick trip west again to **RHUN**. This island's claim to fame is that the British gave it to the Dutch under the 1667 **Treaty of Breda** (which ended the second of four Anglo-Dutch wars in Europe), in exchange for Dutch-owned Manhattan Island – now downtown New York City.

NORTH MALUKU

Stuck out on the fringes of modern Indonesia, **North Maluku** was once the most sought-after destination on earth. For over a thousand years, this was the source of the entire world supply of **cloves** – and the scene of centuries of bitter conflict between local rulers and Europeans for control of the spice trade.

Of the region's three hundred islands, the most important are tiny **Ternate** and **Tidore**, both seats of rival **Muslim sultanates** and dwarfed by irregulary-shaped **Halmahera**. The Portuguese were in business here from 1512, establishing a trading base on Ternate at the invitation of its ruler. All went well until the remnants of Magellan's expedition heralded the arrival of the Spanish a decade later, sparking predictable competition between the Europeans and inevitable demands for trade monopolies. When these failed to materialize, both sides tried to force the issue with a spree of kidnappings and assassinations which culminated in the murder of Ternate's **Sultan Hairun** by the Portuguese in 1570. The ensuing uprising drove the Portuguese out of Ternate, though the Spanish held on in Tidore until being eclipsed by the Dutch VOC in the early seventeenth century. The VOC insisted on its own monopoly, installed a puppet sultan on Ternate to ensure it got one, suffered a new rebellion, and decided that the north was too distant from its base in Ambon to police effectively. To solve the problem, they established clove plantations on Ambon, then ordered their **eradication** on all other islands. Though not entirely successful, the plan was effective, and, deprived of a purpose, the north sunk into obscurity until **World War II** saw a massive Japanese presence on Halmahera and neighbouring **Morotai**, the latter taken by the US in the final year of the war. Steeped in this turbulent past, the towering volcanic cone of Ternate is the seat of the north's capital, **Ternate Town**; across a narrow strait, Tidore is a larger, more rustic carbon copy. Each have enough to keep you busy for a day, with onward connections to seldom visited outlying islands. A more obvious target from Ternate, Halmahera is largely undeveloped, though the road up the northern peninsula to **Tobelo**, port for Morotai, gets you within reach of war relics, rare birds and some decent coral.

Wherever you are coming from, Ternate is the entry point for the north. **From Ambon**, there are almost daily flights on Citra Air and Merpati – one of the most reliable services in the province, though often a bumpy ride – with Pelni's *Lambelu* cruising in twice a month via Namlea on Buru and Bitung in northern Sulawesi. **From Sulawesi**, Merpati fly in daily from Manado, with the *Lambelu*, *Umsini* and *Ciremei* crossing from Bitung three times a month; the *Ciremei* and *Umsini*'s return legs also link Ternate to Sorong in **Irian Jaya** twice a month.

The clove islands: Ternate, Tidore and beyond

If cloves brought fame to north Maluku, volcanic fertility ensured that a string of four relatively small islands off Halmahera's west coast – **Ternate**, **Tidore**, **Makian** and **Bacan** – were the centre of this fame. Called **cengkeh** in Indonesian, cloves are the astringently-scented buds of the nicely-named *syzigium aromaticum*, a tree related to myrtles. The unopened, pale-green flower buds are picked and left to dry a dark brown; today they are ground up for *kretek* cigarettes, or put to various medicinal and culinary ends, but it was their ability to make preserved meat palatable which once made them so precious. This value may be hard to appreciate in an age of ready refrigeration, but there was no question previously: by the seventeenth century, wealth from the clove trade made Ternate's sultan the most powerful ruler in eastern Indonesia, his status and war parties demanding tribute from a territory reaching from Borneo to Australia. It's also notable that the Dutch, who were hardly known for their sympathy towards those they governed, had enough respect for Ternate and Tidore's sultans to pay them a moderate compensation when they banned clove production in the region.

Little more than large volcano cones, Ternate and Tidore are ringed by roads and easy to visit: Ternate town's ready facilities make it a good base, while both islands have tough trails up their smouldering peaks, relics of their sultancies, and an absurd number of forts left over from colonial times. Makian and Bacan are more distant, with fewer facilities and attractions – unless simply getting off the beaten track appeals in itself.

Ternate Town

The largest settlement in north Maluku, **TERNATE TOWN** sprawls over a few kilometres of Ternate's east coast, its relaxed residents seemingly unfazed by the hugely solid presence of the **Gamalama volcano** looming above. The town's central core is a nicely dishevelled collection of colonial buildings and tiny back lanes, reeking of drying cloves, wandering livestock and open sewers, and its busy markets pull in people and produce from all over the region. Locals jostle with Papuans, Minahasans from north Sulawesi, and villagers from Tidore and Halmahera for fresh fruit (pineapples and carambola are excellent), honey, cheap watches, miracle oils, rings set with Bacan agates and antique coins – many are fakes.

Overlooking all this, **Benteng Oranye** is the most substantial fort in Maluku, founded in 1606 as the product of an unlikely Dutch–Ternatean alliance. At the time, the Spanish had invaded Ternate, and the deposed prince **Ali** sent an embassy to the newly arrived VOC in Ambon asking for assistance. The Dutch agreed to help, snuck over to Ternate and, using local labour, built Oranye's prototype in a couple of months. Never seriously menaced by the Spaniards, who were losing interest in the region anyway, Oranye was greatly expanded over the next decade and, for a short while, became the VOC's headquarters. Greatly run-down and strewn with piles of rubbish, the fort retains an imposing presence, surrounded by thick, four-metre-high walls where a few VOC cannon are still in place; it currently serves as a military barracks, though open to the public.

If you don't want to walk, mobils from Oranye can cart you out to a couple of other sites just north of the centre. A few minutes away is the red layered roof of **Mesjid Tua**, a mosque built in 1606 under orders of Sultan Saidi Barakati, and the oldest functioning building on the island. From here, it's another 2km to the **Kedaton**, the former sultan's palace and now a **museum** (open mornings; donation). The site of the regency for seven hundred years, the present building is a nice colonial mansion about a century old; remove your shoes, stub out cigarettes and put away your camera before entering. The high-ceilinged front hall sports alloy chandeliers, moody paintings of previous monarchs, a portrait of the current sultan, **Mudafar**, and glass cases neatly filled with regal memorabilia and tribute staffs from subject nations – dents in some of the pieces of armour here suggest a more than decorative function. A small central dais ornamented with cowries, water and flowers is the basis of a **ceremony** held three times a week which, along with the **royal crown** and kris held in an adjacent locked room, help keep Gamalama inactive.

Two kilometres north again, **Benteng Toluku** (daylight hours; donation) is the site of the first foreign outpost on these islands, established in 1512 by a party of Portuguese under **Fransisco Serrao**. Shipwrecked off Ambon, Serrao's expedition was later rescued and invited to Ternate by **Sultan Bolief**, where Serrao ended his days as an advisor to the court. Toluku itself is a VOC construction of about a century later, reputedly built from ballast stones from Dutch ships. Recent restorations have encased the building in an ugly concrete shell, but the views over the town to Halmahera are fantastic.

Practicalities

Ternate's centre lies between Benteng Oranye and the **port**, connected by 500-metre-long Jalan Pahlawan Revolusi. The **airport** is 5km north of town, where arrivals are greeted by Kijang drivers wanting a steep Rp5000 – walk to the main road and pick up a mobil for Rp500. For trips beyond the centre, you can hire **bendis** for short hops at the corner of Jalan Revolusi and Jalan Nukila, while the island's **mobil terminal** is outside Oranye between Jalan Revolusi and Jalan Bosoini – Rp500 covers local destinations.

Most services are along Jalan Revolusi. Without exception, **banks** give terrible rates for cash and travellers' cheques, but are the only places in Maluku, aside from Ambon, which handle foreign exchange. Bilingual staff at Ternate's **tourist office**, down towards the port (Mon–Fri 8.30am–4pm; ☎0921/22646), dole out roughly accurate pamphlets and advice, and can arrange expensive guides for island tours and climbing Gamalama. The *Bonanza* on Jalan Nukila, and *Hawaii* on Jalan Revolusi, are the pick of Ternate's **coffee houses**, with superb cakes; evening **warung** around the centre deal in soups, noodles and *nasi pulok*, a rice, coconut and sugar confection. For a filling **meal**, head to *Restoran Garuda* on Jalan Revolusi, which can supply cold juices and large portions of Chinese-style dishes such as squid with tofu and Nanking chicken.

ACCOMMODATION

Hotel El Shinta, Jl Revolusi (☎0921/21059). Pleasantly gloomy; the cheaper rooms are a bit tatty. Fan ④; air-con ⑤.

Hotel Indah, Jl Bosoiri 3 (☎0921/21334). Ternate's best mid-range deal; meals cost Rp10,000 extra. Doubles with fan or air-con. ③–④.

Hotel Merdeka, Jl Merdeka 19 (☎0921/21120). Small, homestay-like place with nice staff. Stuffy rooms with fan or air-con. ③–④.

Neraca Golden Hotel, Jl Revolusi 30 (☎0921/21668). More upmarket, business-oriented version of *Nirwana*; all rooms have hot water, air-con and TV. ⑤.

Hotel Nirwana, Jl Revolusi 58–60 (☎0921/21787, fax 21487). Rooms fine but otherwise a sleazy number, with attached bar, disco and hostesses. Fan doubles ④.

Wisma Yamin, Jl Ahmad Yani, opposite the harbour. The best of cheap lodgings in this area, for the budget-conscious only. ②.

Moving on from Ternate

The main departure point for **boats to Tidore**, **Bacan** and **Halmahera** is 3km south of town at **Bastiong**; there are actually **two docks** here about 250m apart, so tell mobil drivers where you want to be dropped off, and see individual island accounts for ferry details. **Leaving the north**, there are roughly daily **flights** to Manado with Boraq (at the *Neraca Golden Hotel*, Jalan Revolusi; ☎0921/21327), and to Ambon with Merpati/Citra Air (Jalan Basoiri 81; ☎0921/21651) – Merpati no longer fly to Kao and Galela on Halmahera, or Daruba on Morotai. Pelni's *Ciremai*, *Lambelu* and *Umsini* all call in at Ternate on their fortnightly circuits between Java, Sulawesi and Irian; the *Lambelu* heads south via Ambon. Head office and timetables are on the right as you enter the port area; the **ticket office** is just outside the port on Jalan Ahmad Yani.

Gamalama and Pulau Ternate

Not surprisingly, Ternate's attractions are mostly volcanic, though there are also a few beaches and historical remains to check out. A sealed, forty-kilometre coastal road circles the island, with a shorter stretch up Gamalama's eastern slopes; kampung on the way comprise whitewashed homes, interspersed with patches of sago, coconuts, cassava, maize, nutmeg and, of course, cloves – almost half the island is planted with them. **Mobils** from the Oranye terminal run on demand throughout the day, though decreasing in frequency the further you get from town; you really need to **charter** a vehicle (Rp40,000 for the day) for a full circuit. There is **no accommodation** outside of Ternate Town.

Gamalama

Gamalama is the all-pervasive body of Pulau Ternate, its 1721-metre crown often clear in the early morning, but otherwise cloud-covered. The volcano is far from dormant, averaging an eruption every decade and last coughing out a plume of ash in 1994; the biggest recorded event was during the 1770s, when a massive explosion created the crater lakes at the north end of the island and killed 1300 people. The tiring ascent from the roadhead above Ternate town at **MARIKURUBU** village takes five hours, so **hikers** should set aside a full day for the return trip, pack plenty of water, start early, and first check on current conditions – and pick up a **guide** – at the tourist office in town. On the way to Marikurubu, **Tongole village** is the start of a short track to the unique, ten-metre **Afo clove tree**, planted in 1602 and still producing bumper crops.

Around the island

Some 6km north of Ternate town, the road crosses a great dark mass of degraded, sharp-edged lava known as **Batu Angus** (literally "Burnt Rock"), which spilled out from Gamalama and down to the sea during the 1712 eruption. It's rough stuff to clamber over, but if the peak is visible you can see where smaller recent eruptions have cleared the mountain's upper forests. Just before the island's northern tip, **Sulamadaha** is a small, slightly scruffy, black-sand **swimming beach** facing **Pulau Hari**, whose peak looks as if it would be a satisfying scramble if you could find transport across. Not far down Ternate's west side, a footpath uphill from the murky beachside lagoon of **Tolire Kecil**, around 15km from town, ends at **Tolire Besar**, an impressively deep, sheer-sided **crater lake**. With binoculars you can spot **crocodiles** hiding in the waterlilies below, and there's a track of sorts through grassland and light forest around the perimeter.

From here it's a bumpy ride south to where gentle swells roll in at **Taduma beach**, just past which overgrown ruins at **KASTELLA village** mark the site of **Benteng Rosario**, the Portuguese fort where Sultan Hairun was stabbed to death by his captors on February 28, 1570. Friezes on an accompanying monument detail the murder and subsequent siege which ended peacefully with the Portuguese eviction from Ternate in 1575.

A further 8km brings you to the southern point of the island at **Gambesi Beach**, beyond which the road climbs past the entrance to **Danau Laguna**, another crater lake with slippery trails down to the water for picturesque scenes of Gamalama rising above semi-cultivated shores – sadly, more crocodiles and a lack of trails limit exploration. Back on the main road, there are cheap fry-ups, local sago dishes and great seascapes over to Tidore from cliffside tables at the *Rumah Makan Florida*; a pile of rubble one hundred metres down the road mark the remains of **Santo Pedro**, a **Spanish fort** dating from their brief invasion of Ternate in 1606. From here it's 5km back to town via the shipyards and ports at **BASTIONG**, where **Benteng Kalumata** (closes early afternoon; donation), a square, seventeenth-century Dutch stronghold, has been considerably restored.

Tidore

Barely a kilometre south of Ternate, **Tidore** makes for an enjoyable day-trip from its sister. Always rivals, the two islands were similarly caught up in the intrigues of the spice wars, Tidore's weaker sultanate boosting its strength by offering sanctuary to European refugees from Ternate in exchange for military aid. The policy saw Spanish and Tidorean forces deposing Ternate's sultan in 1606, and, though the victory was brief, the Spanish presence on Tidore discouraged Dutch conquest for some sixty years. Yet somehow Tidore never quite got ahead; the sultanate was dissolved in the early twentieth century, and today the island is a quiet version of Ternate, less touristy and also more traditional.

The island is slightly larger than Ternate, and also based around a volcano: 1730-metre **Keimatabu**. Regular **speedboats** (10min; Rp1500) cross during daylight hours between Ternate's Bastiong port and Tidore's northwestern corner at **RUM**, where you'll find plenty of mobils heading south along the thirty-kilometre coastal road to Tidore's capital, **Soasiu**. Before touts force you on board, however, consider hopping on a local boat for the short trip to sand and snorkelling around **Pulau Maitara**, or making the hour-long walk east around the headland to **thermal springs** at **COBO**.

With the sea on one side and Keimatabu on the other, it's a scenic drive to Soasiu through endless kampung such as **Bobo**, settled by the sultan's Papuan slaves. Leave the bus just short of Soasiu at the **Sonyine Malige museum** (opens on demand; donation), an unimposing building with cannons on the porch and the "**hairy crown**" of Tidore's sultan inside, trimmed with cassowary feathers and, as in Ternate, accredited with volcano-pacifying properties. Some effort is needed to find the last pieces of Spanish **Benteng Tohula** on a nearby rise. Back on the road, it's another couple of kilometres to where mobils wind up in the market at **SOASIU**, Tidore's rather austere hub. There's good **accommodation** here at *Hotel Jangi* on Jalan Indonesia (☎0920/21131; ③), plenty of warung around the marketplace, and further transport up to the attractive village of **GURABUNGA**, Tidore's spiritual centre and starting point for assaults on Keimatabu – another hard, full-day slog.

Bacan

Eighty kilometres south of Ternate, **Bacan** never featured very strongly in Maluku's history, despite its size – over 50km across – and being a major source of cloves. Buying into local politics through marriage alliances with other sultanates, Bacan became a backwater station for European powers from the Portuguese onwards, who all dutifully built encampments but otherwise contributed little to the island. Covered in a mixture of plantations and wild forest, Bacan is still largely neglected, known in biological circles as the eastern limit that **monkeys** occur, and locally famed for fine **agates**.

Ternate's Bastiong harbour is the departure point for overnight **ferries** (12hr; Rp20,000) and a morning **fast boat** to Bacan (5hr; Rp30,000); buy tickets and confirm times in advance. About a third of the way to Bacan you pass **MAKIAN** island, whose central **Kie Besi** volcano blew itself apart in July 1988 after nearly a century of dormancy – islanders are slowly returning. You arrive on Bacan's east coast at **BABANG**, with a fifteen-kilometre mobil ride west to the main settlement **LABUHA**, where *Pondok Indah* (③) or *Penginapan Borero* (④) offer **food** and **accommodation**. Labuha has a good market, and the obligatory colonial footnote in the form of atmospherically overgrown **Benteng Barnevald**, raised by the Dutch in the seventeenth century.

Halmahera and Morotai

Maluku's largest island, **Halmahera** comprises 17,000 square kilometres of mountains in four backswept peninsulas. The central-west was the domain of the **Jailolo sultanate**, absorbed by Ternate during the sixteenth century, and the east coast was occupied by Japanese during World War II, but the rest of Halmahera never had much contact with the outside world. Despite shrinking forest cover, the island's interior is still inhabited by hunter-gathering tribes and unusual wildlife, including rare birds and the *katouri*, a large, tabby-patterned native **wildcat** (possibly a civet). Though a small fraction of the island is easily accessible, even a few days on Halmahera gives you a chance to touch on all these points, and the option to cross over to **Morotai**, an island off Halmahera's northeastern coast which served as a stepping stone for US forces during the Pacific campaign.

Plentiful transport crosses from Ternate to Halmahera's western shores at **Sidangoli**, the island's biggest port. From here, vehicles follow a 180-kilometre road up the east side of Halmahera's bulbous northern peninsula to **Kao** and **Tobelo**, port for Morotai, with access from these towns to war relics, volcanoes and jungle. **Speedboats** from Ternate town run on demand from the sea wall opposite the BNI bank on Jalan Revolusi (40min; Rp5000); or there's the slower, more stable morning **ferry** from Bastiong harbour (1hr 30min; Rp5000). At Bastiong, you'll be swamped by touts selling **Kijang tickets** for the Sigangoli–Kao–Tobelo road, or you can sort out transport on arrival in Sidangoli.

Halmahera: Sidangoli to Kao

From the water, first impressions of **SIDANGOLI** are none too promising, with piles of logs being towed behind barges to the town's large, smoking **wood-pulp plant**. But, though most people hop on the first available vehicle north, Sidangoli is actually the easiest place from which to probe into Halmahera's dense rainforest. The town itself is small: turn right out of the port and it's less than a kilometre, past the speedboat dock, to the **bus terminal** where Kijang to Kao and Tobelo await new arrivals off the ferry. Adjacent *Penginapan Sidangoli* (③) is the best **place to stay**, with basic meals available at *Rumah Makan Fany*. **Birders** should catch a local mobil 20km out to **BATU PUTIH**, where guest-house accommodation can supply guides for forest forays after rare rosy-breasted pittas and **Wallace's standardwing**, an indigenous bird of paradise whose buff-coloured males sport a metallic blue bib, trail white "standards" and dance a courtship ritual featuring a strange parachuting display. Back in Sidangoli, the ferry returns **to Ternate** around 10.30am, and speedboats make the crossing all day.

After a smooth start through the forest between Sidangoli and Halmahera's east coast, the road to Kao loses its surface and winds past grey coves, cleared land around kampung, and timber and mining camps. It's not a bad journey, however, and only takes three hours to the halfway stop at **MALIFUT**, recognizable from a rusting World War II-vintage **destroyer** offshore. Then you're at **KAO**, a quiet jumble of dusty lanes facing Halmahera's rugged eastern arm over the long sandy stretch of Kao Bay. It's hard to believe now, but during the war there were 100,000 Japanese troops stationed here, maintaining a large fleet and an airstrip where bombers left for raids over Australia. Memories remain in the form of two more hulks a kilometre offshore, and a "**Japanese fort**" – actually a gun emplacement – 2km from town, where four cannon still point skywards amongst banana palms. There's some good **hiking** between villages in the hills behind Kao, and an area **map** to copy at Kao's police station; the police like to talk to foreigners and find passports interesting, so take your time and play along. Simple cells at the friendly *Penginapan Dirgahayu* (③ including food) typify Kao's **accommodation**, where they'll also help with guides, boat charters, snorkelling gear and transport bookings on to Tobelo or back to Sidangoli.

Tobelo

Another couple of hours on a fine road from Kao lands you at **TOBELO**, the north's main marketplace and port for Morotai and the northeastern peninsula. A transit point, there's little to do here except stock up, and perhaps organize a trip offshore to nearby **Pulau Tagolo**, said to have a pretty reef on its west side. Running due north, Tobelo is a busy line of stores flanking a 500m stretch of the main road, with an orientation point at the halfway **crossroads**: the **market** area is immediately south of here, the **port** 100m east. You'll find inexpensive **accommodation** south of the crossroads at the *Alfa Mas* (☎0924/21543; ③); in a pricier bracket, rooms 200m north at the *President Hotel* (☎0924/21231; ⑤) lose out to inclusive meals and the seafront sundeck at the *Pantai Indah* (☎0924/21068, fax 21064; ⑤), immediately behind the *President*. For **eating out**, head just north of the crossroads to the *Padang Raya*.

Moving on, Kijang and mobil for **Galela** leave continually from the crossroads, where you'll also find buses back to Kao until the early afternoon. Various stores advertise as agents for Kijangs **back to Sidangoli**; these leave around 4am to meet the Ternate ferry, so book the day before. Ferries and speedboats **to Morotai** depart daily from the port.

To Galela and Danau Duma

Vehicles hurtle along the new Tobelo–Galela road, dodging ox carts and making the forty-kilometre run in thirty minutes. Though seldom visible behind the coconut groves, the inland here is dominated by the bald, deeply ridged cone of **Gunung Dukono**, rated as the most active crater in Indonesia – Dukono has been rumbling continuously for sixty years, regularly spitting out lava bombs and last erupting in the late 1970s. Around the nineteen-kilometre mark, you cross over a bridge and pass a small **seismology office** on the right at **MAMUYA**, which can advise about the five-hour riverside trail up nearby **Gunung Mamuya**, a less feisty but similarly active vent.

Mobils wind up by the market at **GALELA**, simply a knot of houses surrounding a small port. From here, backtrack 500m to kampung **PUNE**, where you'll find a concrete track heading coastwards opposite the large church to where two more **Japanese** cannon (*meriam Jepang*) sit attractively amongst a vegetable plot. One is still in place under palm trees, its barrel used as a see-saw by local children, the other is stashed against a house. Back in Galela, walk or catch a mobil from the market a couple of kilometres up the road to **Danau Duma**, the largest of five crater lakes in the vicinity. There's a fifteen-kilometre road around the lake, though most traffic can only take you 5km through a mix of Christian and Muslim kampung to **Duma village** on the south shore. The coconut-covered north shore is less settled, with some square-sided Japanese "caves" – ammunition stores – the scene of recent interest in the search for a legendary horde of gold. Another road splits northwest from the lake to a huge, Chinese-owned **banana plantation** at the foot of the thickly forested ridges which screen north Halmahera's interior.

Morotai

Fifty kilometres northeast of Tobelo on the rim of the Pacific Ocean, **Morotai** stares into a vast, empty horizon. Occupied by the Japanese in 1942, this mountainous island was captured by US forces on September 15, 1944, in part of a larger scheme to retake the Philippines. The US needed an airstrip in the region: Kao was too heavily defended, so General MacArthur, under the philosophy of "hitting [the Japanese] where they ain't", chose Morotai instead. Caught entirely unawares, the five hundred Japanese stationed here offered no resistance, despite US landing craft getting bogged down on the beach in soft sand.

Wartime relics, some good diving and snorkelling, and just the rather bizarre environment, all make Morotai worth the trip over. A daily **speedboat** (Rp10,000–15,000) and five **ferries** a week (Rp7,500) leave Tobelo around 9am to **Daruba**, Morotai's main town; buy **tickets** on the morning of departure at the speedboat or portside ferry ticket office. Crossing times range from two to four hours, depending on vessel and conditions; as usual, avoid speedboats in rough swells.

The island

Down on Morotai's southwestern coast, **DARUBA** may not be the remotest town in Indonesia, but in this direction it is the last, laden with a shifty, end-of-the-road atmosphere. A stone jetty and wide, muddy main street sit under a low hill where a church and mosque battle for high ground, with just about every building incorporating scrap metal from the war – walls and gates made from flattened fuel drums and fences made from sand tracks. A big mixture of people live here, from local fishermen to Chinese storekeepers and Bugis timber workers from southern Sulawesi, a situation which renders the local version of Bahasa Indonesia occasionally unintelligible with borrowed words. Walk up from the dock, turn left, and you're at a **crossroads** which passes for the centre of town: down towards the water is a vague marketplace with vegetables and fish, a video-screen **cinema** and **accommodation** at *Penginapan Ampera* (③ including meals). Or continue straight ahead from the crossroads, and it's 100m to the better *Penginapan Tonga* (③ including meals). Daruba's stores are well supplied with essentials, and there are a few warung and coffee-and-cake houses. A quiet place during the day, there's plenty of after-dark partying in the best frontier-town tradition – just follow the noise. Seek **guides** for excursions through your accommodation, and avoid freelancers, who are only in it for the ride. All vessels **back to Halmahera** leave in the early afternoon.

The main road out of town runs uphill from the crossroads past a **post office**, then turns right to Daruba's **police station**, where military buffs should ask for permission to visit the **airfield**, currently under martial law. Five kilometres from town and built by the US in October 1944, it features parallel runways, an unusual configuration only made possible by the reliability of prevailing winds. There are more wartime associations 35km inland from Daruba at **Gunung Nakamura**, a mountain named after a Japanese soldier who went bush when the US invaded and lived undetected in the jungle until 1973. Barito Timber have a logging camp here; ask around Daruba for the personnel manager, Mr Hassan, who speaks a little English and might be able to arrange a trip.

Hire **boat and snorkelling gear** for local reef and islets through accommodation (Rp100,000 for the day), or **divers** can seek out Richard at Toko Moro Jaya, a haberdashery near the crossroads, who has full scuba equipment – check it all first. The water close to shore is murky after rain, but clears further out. Nearby **Pulau Sumsum** is a mangrove-fringed island said to have been MacArthur's temporary headquarters, with reports of a Catalina **aircraft** in 15m of water just to the north, and downed Mustang fighter planes off **Pulau Babi**. Yet to be found are the remains of the *Seawolf*, a US **submarine** accidentally sunk by an American destroyer after the assault. For pure pleasure, **Pulau Dodolo** is a sandy island past Sumsum with a lagoon used for agar-agar cultivation, fair snorkelling over shallow coral, and outer reef walls with barracuda and sharks.

SOUTHEAST MALUKU

A collection of three low island groups 600km from Ambon, **Southeast Maluku** has, from a European perspective, always assumed a minor position in the province's history. With an economy revolving around exchanges in slaves and marine produce with central and western Indonesia rather than spices, the islands were occupied but otherwise ignored by the Dutch, and were too distant from anywhere to attract much attention even during twentieth-century upheavals. Today, class systems, ancestor worship, and boat cults have been superficially supplanted by widespread Christianity, but those prepared to take unpredictable rewards as compensation for days of hard travel will find Southeast Maluku is unquestionably worth the effort it takes to get around. Only an overnight trip from the Bandas, the beaches and laconic inhabitants on the **Kei Islands** are gradually attracting a few visitors; these are notably absent, however, further east towards Irian at **Aru**, a thickly forested, geologically weird group whose remote villages and Australasian fauna need initiative to investigate. Off to the southwest of Kei, the **Tanimbars** and an associated island-string stretching west to Timor have strong cultural traditions, even if these are at first hidden under a mantle of modern values.

From Ambon, there's little problem getting to **Tual-Langgur** in the Keis, with several flights weekly on Merpati and Citra Air, and the **Pelni** ships *Bukit Siguntang*, *Rinjani* and *Tatamailau* averaging one trip a week via Bandaneira on their Java–Irian circuits. At the time of writing, the separate weekly flights from Ambon to **Dobo** (Aru) and **Saumlaki** (Tanimbar) were so unreliable as to be effectively inoperative. **From Irian**, the *Bukit Siguntang* and *Rinjani* return to Ambon via Dobo and Kei; the *Tatamailau* heads back to Java via Dobo and Saumlaki. Once here, **ferries** and Pelni link Tual, Dobo and Saumlaki, though extensive travel is likely to involve at least one trip on the swarm of **freighters** which circuit the region – cheap, if also slow and foul. Rough seas and phenomenal **rains** can occur through most of the year: March and November are the calmest months, with big swells across the region in June and July. Before you go, read Nico de Jonge and Toos van Dijk's excellent *Forgotten Islands of Indonesia* (Periplus), and note that southeast Maluku has **no banks** capable of foreign currency transactions, almost nobody speaks English, and that you should take particular care to guard against **malaria**.

The Keis

A group of two hundred mostly minute islands, the **Keis** were formerly a trade entrepôt and a renowned boatbuilding centre, with hereditary land ownership and a strongly structured social system which persists to this day – marriage between Christian and Muslim is more acceptable here than marriage between classes. The Keis focus on what is generally called **Kei Kecil**, though this is actually a pair of flat islands – northern **Dullah**, and larger Kei Kecil itself – totalling 50km in length between them and joined by a short road bridge. Here, the twinned centres of Tual and Langgur form the **capital** of southeast Maluku, but exquisite **beaches** around Kei Kecil far outshine the town, from where it's possible to get out to the island's less developed southern end. Lying either side of Kei Kecil, tiny **Tanebar-Kei** to the southwest, and the elongated, high, easterly **Kei Besar** offer wilder scenery and a glimpse of pre-colonial times. This is one place in the southeast where you'll find a few English speakers: widespread support in the Keis for the 1950 Republik Maluku Selatan cause saw many islanders seek sanctuary in Holland when the movement was overrun, and they are now returning to visit, if not settle.

Kei Kecil: Tual and Langgur

On opposite sides of a marine channel, Tual and Langgur together form a useful and functional service centre; there's little need to stay here longer than it takes to get oriented. **TUAL** is based around the Keis' main **harbour** and adjacent **market** on Pulau Dullah, from where Jalan Pattimura runs due south from the harbour, past a mosque and a kilometre-long string of small shops, to a **bridge**. On the other side is **LANGGUR** and Kei Kecil proper: just over the bridge and left, **Pelabuhan Motor** is the ferry terminal for Kei Besar, while the main road runs past 3km of administrative buildings, churches and schools to the **airport** and **Terminal Pasar Baru**, departure point for traffic around Kei Kecil. For **local transport**, mobils marked "Langgur" run from before dawn to after dark between Tual's harbour and Terminal Pasar Baru (Rp350), and you can hail them at any point along the way. You can also **charter** empty mobils at either end (Rp8000 an hour).

The most convenient **accommodation** is in Tual at the spacious *Mirah Inn*, just uphill from the mosque on Jalan Sadsustubun (☎0916/21172; ③), the manager speaks English and can organize beds at *Coaster Cottages* at Ohoililir beach (see p.890). Alternatives are the dingy *Penginapan Linda Mas*, a fifteen-minute walk beyond the *Mirah* on Jalan Rhebok (☎0916/21271; ③); or flashy *Rosemgen*, a mobil ride over the bridge in Langgur (☎0916/21477; ⑤). You could try wrangling a bed at *Toko Cahaya Pamana*, who are shy of foreigners (③); it's a harbourside haberdashery next to the BRI bank on Jalan Pattimura, with clean rooms above the shop.

With spare time, visit tiny Toko Ina, across from Gatra Perkasa Tour and Travel on Jalan Pattimura in Tual. The Arab owner has a quite amazing collection of local **antiquities**, including a courtyard full of Portuguese-era cannon. Tual's market and shops have everything else you'll need, with IDD **telephones** at the wartel outside the harbour. For **food**, the *Minang Jaya* at the harbour end of Jalan Pattimura is the pick of Tual's often flyblown warung, but if you're after something special, try reasonably priced chilli squid, sauced tofu and crispy fried fish at *Rumah Makan Fajar*, about a kilometre south of the bridge in Langgur (any mobil will drop you off). Avoid becoming too involved with English-speaking **guides** in town; some are undoubtedly knowledgeable, but you'll be better off without them.

Moving on from the Keis

Up near the harbour, the **Merpati office** (8am–1pm) takes bookings for the more or less daily Merpati and Citra Air flights back to Ambon; the weekly connection to Dobo

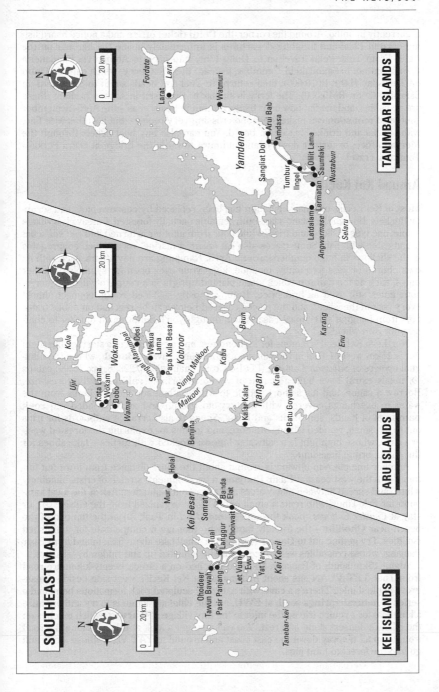

is currently in limbo. Around the corner, the **Pelni ticket office** and a notice board list-ing current Pelni and freighter departures is immediately inside the harbour on the right. From Tual, Pelni travel on to Dobo (7hr) and back to Ambon via Bandaneira (22hr), but not to Saumlaki in Tanimbar; instead, there's a **ferry**, which runs **to Dobo** on Thursday (14hr; Rp10,000), then returns to Tual and heads south **to Saumlaki** on Saturday (36hr; Rp15,000). The ferry is similar to that used in Ambon harbour: there are no cabins, and the flat bow door bangs around in heavy seas – the April–September southeast **monsoon** can make the Dobo crossing very rough – but it's otherwise fine, with snacks and drinks for sale on board. You can also buy boat tickets through the Merpati office, or further down Jalan Pattimura towards the bridge at Gatra Perkasa Tour and Travel.

Around Kei Kecil

Most of Kei Kecil's original vegetation has been replaced by **cassava** plots and scrub-by thickets, though the island's far south remains partially forested. Cassava is a village staple; one type is sliced and fried, while flour from another is turned into *roti kai*, a flat bread eaten with fish. Some places also eat *lawar*, a marine worm which congregates in the shallows in huge numbers around April. Kampung are tidy affairs, each with its own church or, less frequently, mosque; keep your eyes open for symbols of earlier times, such as the **cannon** which stand planted upright in a couple of village squares, sometimes still used as brideprice. Bumpy, mostly surfaced **roads** connect almost every part of the island, and the places covered below can be reached on public trans-port from Langgur's Terminal Pasar Baru, though you'll find it much quicker to char-ter your own wheels.

Northern Kei Kecil is famous for its **beaches**, and a good place to start testing them out is 15km west of Tual at the village of **Ohoideer Tawun Bawah**, where the bilin-gual owners of *Savanah Cottages* (PO Box 168, Tual; ☎0916/22328, fax 22390; cabins ④, meals extra) have built a couple of very comfortable **cabins** on the foreshore. Borrow a canoe, and it's a short paddle to where a bamboo ladder climbs from the water to overhangs covered with century-old graffiti and archaic, faded red **rock paintings** of hands, sun motifs and boats. *Savanah* also arrange outboards for trips out to the small, wooded islands offshore, and guides for exploring the forested west-ern cape, whose highlight is a saltwater **lagoon** stocked with turtles – take shoes for the sharp, brittle limestone.

Another fine place to unwind is around about the same distance from town but fur-ther down the west coast at **Pasir Panjang**, a two-kilometre stretch of crisp, blindingly white sand spread between blue waters and a coconut plantation. Ask at the local kam-pung for Pak Tinus, who rents a small **cabin** (food organized from the village; ③), or stay at *Coaster Cottages* (book through *Mirah Hotel* in Tual; ③) at the top end of the beach near **Ohoililir** – the friendly family who manage it compensate for unfinished facilities. Try getting out to **Danau Ngilngof**, a small lake about 5km inland from Pasir Panjang, whose crocodiles were once reputedly whistled up and ridden by villagers.

About 15km south of Panjang, and also reached on a direct, twenty-kilometre road from Tual, **LET VUAN** sits about halfway down Kei Kecil's west side beside a man-grove-choked inlet. There's a **cave** with naturally sculpted rock formations here, and a series of **natural springs** south at **EWU**, but the chief attraction is to try and organize a longboat for a return trip up the inlet to the tiny village of **Warwut**, which touches on the island's densest stand of forest. You can also get a look at this by taking the road from town all the way down the east coast and around to **YAT VAV**, whose locals still go into the forest to hunt pigs.

Tanebar-Kei and Kei Besar

From Kei Kecil it's possible to make side-trips to two islands which are visibly steeped in old beliefs. About 45km to the southwest, the sole settlement of **Atnebar** on diminutive **Tanebar-Kei** is said to house powerful magic and sports the remains of village guardian figures, long vanished elsewhere in the region. Getting there is not easy, however; make enquiries through beachside accommodation on Kei Kecil.

A more straightforward prospect, **Kei Besar** rises immediately east of Kei Kecil, an eighty-kilometre mountainous ridge with a couple of roads and plenty of tradition. **Caste** still plays a part in daily life, and you'll see villages partitioned by stone walls to keep the aristocracy and lower classes apart. At least two **ferries** daily make the twenty-kilometre trip from Langgur's Pelabuhan Motor to **BANDA ELAT**, Kei Besar's main town, which was settled by seventeenth-century refugees fleeing Dutch atrocities in the Bandas – the local language is actually Bandanese, not *Bahasa Kei*. Elat is more or less halfway along the narrow island – the *Hotel Adios* here comes recommended as **somewhere to stay**, there's a big **waterfall** just east at **Mulurat**, and the highest point in southeast Maluku – a whopping 801m – a dozen kilometres north via **Somrat**. One of Kei Besar's most interesting villages is 18km southeast of Elat (there are regular mobils) at coastal **OHOIWAIT**, where you'll find homestay **accommodation** and a big stone staircase running up the hill, with rumours of two old **cannon** hidden in nearby forests. It's also possible to explore **northern Kei Besar**, much of which has been proposed as a nature reserve, though you need to be self-sufficient. Catch the daily boat from Banda Elat up to the west coast village of **MUN**, where donations to the church allow you to stay and cook for yourself at a stone guest house. Assuming you have a tent, seek out guides in Mun for the three-day walk around Kei Besar's forested, largely undeveloped north tip and down the east coast to **Banda Ely** and **HOLAL**, where there's irregular road transport back to Elat.

Aru

Floating in the Arufura sea between Kei and Irian, everything about **Aru** is intriguing. A 180-kilometre bed of uplifted coral with an apex of just 200m, narrow but deep **marine channels** cut Aru's main body into segments, the largest of which form the islands of **Wokam**, **Kobroor** and **Trangan**. Dutch attention was first drawn to the Arus during the mid-seventeenth century, when they collected sago here to feed their plantation slaves in the Bandas, but they found it a much tougher place to administer than the rest of Maluku. Certainly, there was wealth to be had by tapping in to local trade in pearl shell, *trepang* (sea slug) and bird of paradise plumes, but, as these products concerned Chinese and Muslim customers, the Dutch didn't have much success in marketing them, or in dislodging local businessmen. Shortly before they were found to be bankrupt, the VOC abandoned their handful of forts here in 1794 declaring that running the Arus was a "real nuisance" – in fact, their administrator had just been murdered.

Visitors today are unlikely to face anything so severe, but the islands remain an exciting place to travel around. Surrounding clean seas have recently attracted commercial fishing and – until a virus started disturbing oysters – **pearl farming**, but Aru's interior remains almost totally covered in unexplored forests. **Dobo**, Aru's major port and settlement on the small western island of **Wamar**, is the entry point, from where local boats give access to main-island **villages** where you can hire guides for hiking inland. Aru's population is a Papuan–Indonesian mix, the majority of the people professing Christianity, though this is a recent import and you'll occasionally encounter animistic tendencies and sites. Out in the villages there's also the chance to see locals **hunting**

PLUMES OF PARADISE

Featured on the old Rp20,000 note, the **greater bird of paradise**, *Paradisaea apoda*, the largest of the family, is found only in Aru and New Guinea. There are various forms, but on Aru breeding males have a glossy russet body, with a green face, bright yellow cap and a huge, almost fluffy cascade of golden feathers arching out from the back. Between May and October, they gather in favourite display trees, using level branches like a catwalk to squawk, swish plumes and parade around in competition with each other – not, apparently, to attract a mate, so much as to establish a pecking order. At present, they're fairly common within their limited range, and with the right contacts you've a good chance of seeing them here. Called **cenderawasih** in Indonesian, the greater bird of paradise is also known as *burung bodoh*, the stupid bird, because its loud "wok-wok-wok-wok" call makes it easy to track down. Aru is also home to the rarer and even more outrageously coloured **king bird of paradise**, *Cicinnurus regius*, which sports riotous crimson and white plumage, embellished by bright blue legs and two wire-like pennant feathers trailing out from the tail.

Used in Indonesia and beyond for headdresses, the **trade** in bird of paradise plumes was already well established by the time the survivors of the Magellan expedition brought examples back to Europe for the first time in the 1520s. Though completely illegal, the business continues today, and it's possible you'll see "skins" – dead birds – for sale in Dobo. They're generally shot from the ground with a thin-bladed arrow which doesn't damage the feathers, but a live bird fetches Rp250,000 – four times the going rate for skins – and so hunters sometimes hide behind blinds in adjacent trees and use blunt-headed arrows to stun the birds.

for pig, deer and cassowary, or to spend time tracking down some of Aru's more unusual wildlife, which includes giant **birdwing butterflies**, the nocturnal **green tree python** – at least the adults are green, though the young are a bright lemon yellow – and two spectacular **birds of paradise**. In doing so, you'll be following in the footsteps of the Victorian naturalist Alfred Wallace, who lived here for six months in 1857, and a more contemporary David Quammen, whose book *Song of the Dodo* (Touchstone, US) retraces Wallace's steps while explaining his theories of biogeography.

Merpati provisionally fly in **to Dobo** once a week via Tual, though it's more likely you'll arrive aboard Pelni's *Bukit Siguntang*, *Rinjani* or *Tatamailau* (all of which also visit from Irian), or the weekly Tual–Dobo ferry. Once here, **transport around Aru** involves off-the-cuff hitching or chartering. There are no facilities for visitors outside of Dobo, and you won't get far without some conversational Bahasa Indonesia, as it's vital to be able to talk to villagers so that they can help you explore.

Wamar, Dobo and around

From out at sea the Arus appear flat as pancakes, with Dobo on **Pulau Wamar** marked from afar by a tall radio tower. Arriving, the jetty is too fragile for the *Bukit Siguntang* and *Rinjani*, which moor in the channel between Wamar and Wokam while passengers are chaotically ferried to shore in smaller craft.

Set on a small spur of land on Wamar's northern side, **DOBO** is a town of coral-block and wood construction, its three muddy, parallel streets – featuring an absurd one-way system – running south for a few hundred metres from the port. Almost every building is a Chinese-owned **store**, all doing fierce trade in everything from rice to ghetto-blasters; drying on sheets outside you'll see smoked, charcoal-grey *trepang*, and batches of **sharks fin**, export items aimed at Chinese palates. A bounty of Rp600,000 a kilo for prime-quality fins has made sharks locally extinct, however, so fishing crews often sneak down into Australian waters. If they get caught their boats are burned and they're flown home – an adventure which some recall dreamily, enthusing about three big meals a day and endless coffee in Darwin's detention centre. Hang out at Dobo's **telephone exchange**, popular for the contents of their two massive fridge-freezers – the only ice cream and cold beer in the region. For **accommodation** and food, there's the central *Hotel Venezia* (④), basically an upmarket brothel for pearl businessmen; the mosquito-ridden *Losmen Lima Saudara* (③) on stilts over the water; or the *Penginapan Fany* (☎0917/21432; ③) which, though 2km from town, is a welcome retreat after the rigours of Aru's outlying islands – catch a mobil there for Rp350. Meals here are mighty, and the manager can suggest targets elsewhere in Aru, and set up boat charters and lifts.

Moving on, the ethnic Chinese control all regional business, with trading posts in many villages, so Dobo's stores are as good a place as the harbour to make enquiries about hitching on boats **around Aru**. For a **charter**, you won't get a better deal than that offered by Johnny Limber, who lives opposite the Kantor Pos on Jalan Mayor Abdulla and rents a stable, diesel-powered prahu which sleeps five plus two crew to look after you at US$30–50 per day – he also has extensive **scuba gear** if you know what you're doing. **Leaving Aru**, check with the Merpati agent at Toko Sumber Mas on the likelihood of flights to Tual and Ambon. The Pelni office (mornings Mon–Sat) is down a side street: their three vessels connect to Ambon and Irian, with the *Tatamailau* heading direct to Saumlaki, with regular Perentis freighters to Saumlaki travelling via Aru's southwestern coast. Buy tickets for the weekly Tual–Saumlaki ferry at the harbour.

Short trips from Dobo

There's not much to see on Wamar, but **ruins** on nearby islands make for interesting excursions, even if you've otherwise had enough of these things. You'll only need a couple of hours for the **Dutch fort** across the channel on Pulau Wokam: ask around in Dobo to rent a shallow-draught *ketinting* – Rp10,000 should be enough – and aim for **WOKAM**, a small village sheltered by palm-frond windbreaks directly opposite Dobo, whose kepala desa keeps a registry of visitors. From here you can either walk or motor around the coast to **KOTA LAMA** (Old Town), a half-dozen huts on the western beach about 5km from Wokam, where villagers are usually happy to escort you out to the site. Three **wells** and remains of a **church** (complete with arched windows) stand pretty well intact amongst a coconut grove, but the fort itself has been largely reclaimed by vegetation, though substantial parts of the surrounding wall and what were presumably barracks and a watchtower survive. The fort was occupied until the late eighteenth century, when its garrison was besieged by locals angry at Dutch interference in the local economy; older people remember seeing cannon and skulls amongst the rubble years ago – there are still VOC **coins** kicking around – and tell stories of ghosts. Back in the sunlight, there's exceptional **diving** on the reef directly out from Kota Lama.

With a day, and a decent boat from Dobo's harbour, you should be able to make a return trip to **UJIR**, a village on an island of the same name about 20km north of Wamar. Ujir's **Muslim** villagers are not immediately welcoming to Westerners, but if you're lucky the kepala desa will allow you to visit the very strange remains of a mosque built around an earlier "Portuguese" fort, itself apparently based on even older Hindu-era foundations.

Around the Arus

Very few of Aru's **villages** are inland, most of them occupying bald limestone hummocks right above the saltwater, their wooden houses supported by poles morticed straight into the rock. The procedure on arrival is to seek out the kepala desa and explain your presence, ask permission to stay, and arrange a price for accommodation (if needed) and **guides**. These are hunters who are glad to be paid for doing what they would do anyway, and inevitably take bow and arrows along in case you encounter game. Before heading off with them, make it very clear what you are after – specific animals, for instance – and discuss the best places and times to go. You'll find people are often quite reserved, as few have had any dealings with foreigners, but show an interest and guides respond, going out of their way to point out animals and wild-food plants, or teaching you how to use a bow.

One of the easiest areas to get started is along **Sungai Manumbai**, the channel between Wokam and Kobroor, whose western end is 30km from Dobo. Frequent marine traffic passing through makes it as accessible as anywhere in Aru, and there's plenty to see in the surrounding forests. Further afield, southerly **Pulau Trangan** is another good option, its centre totally untouched and with a remote **marine park** off to the southeast. **Hitching around** Aru is not as difficult as you'd expect, but it is time-consuming. Boats from Dobo use the channels as short cuts across to Aru's eastern side, and can drop you off on their way. The problem here is that, unless you can arrange with the same boat to pick you up, you'll have to take pot luck with passing craft in order to move on, though village-hopping on local longboats is also possible. If you've the money, **chartering** saves time, allows flexibility and gives you a place to sleep, and the crew can cook for you. Whichever way you travel, stock up beforehand from Dobo's markets, as villages are ill-equipped to lavish food on unexpected guests.

Along Sungai Manumbai

A couple of hours due east of Dobo takes you into the mouth of the Manumbai, which oscillates gently northeast for 40km to Aru's far shores. Once around the first bend you could be on a river; villages perch on the steep, undercut limestone banks, while behind all is jungle. A mid-stream island 10km along marks a fork in the channel at **PAPA KULA BESAR**, a pretty kampung with short trails following limestone streams to other villages, riverside scenes of children fishing with arrows, and canoes returning at sunset loaded down with jerrycans filled at nearby freshwater springs. It's not the most friendly of places, however, and the kepala desa does his best to intimidate, but there are some interesting **caves** 9km south; you'll need to negotiate for guides and a *ketingting* upstream to the start of the trail (around Rp45,000 in total). For what is virtually level ground, it's a tough three-hour slog to the caves, the path muddy, rocky, flooded, and tangled with undergrowth by turns; if you've energy enough to look, you'll see butterflies, sago palms, giant buttressed trees, turmeric and torch gingers along the way. The caves are in an area of forested outcrops: one near an abandoned kampung has a bathing pool inside; another, where archeologists have found signs of occupation dating back millennia, bores 50m through a hill. Some caves were used for burials within living memory, and there are the remains of a *rumah adat* – possibly the site of **Wallace's camp** – in the vicinity, but it's unlikely you'll be shown either.

Back on the Manumbai, it's another hour to the south bank settlement of **WAKUA LAMA**, a far more easy-going place than Papa Kula. Facing Wokam's solid jungle wall, there are good walking trails from Wakua across mite-infested grassland (where you might encounter **kangaroos**) and into Kobroor's varied, well-stocked forests, and an excellent freshwater **bathing hole** within easy canoe range, where locals will be absolutely bamboozled at your presence. If it's **greater birds of paradise** you're after – here called **loblobai** – ask at the village for Bapak Gusti, who knows where they hang out and, at the right time of year, can take you over to Wokam to watch them displaying at dawn. Once you've been paddled up a short mangrove creek, their favourite tree is a twenty-minute walk into the woods, and to see them perform as the sunlight just brushes the treetops is worth whatever it has taken you to get to Aru. It's also just possible that Bapak Gusti or others may know the whereabouts of **fanen**, the **king bird of paradise**. Two hours further east from Wakua Lama, there are also the completely overgrown remains of another **Dutch fort** at **DOSI**, a relatively substantial trading post near the far end of the Manumbai.

Pulau Trangan

Most of southern Aru comprises **Pulau Trangan**, the Arus' largest island at around 80km in length. Aru's least known region, Trangan's southern coastal villages are thick with porcelain and antique French cognac bottles, relics of an age when traders sought exchanges for local turtle and pearl shells. Many villages also display shed-like **animist shrines** filled with turtle shells and dugong (manatee) bones facing the water, their contents ensuring the renewal of game. In addition to the usual run of wildlife, coastal fringes here are stacked with estuarine **crocodiles**, virtually hunted out elsewhere on Aru.

On Trangan's northwest tip about four hours from Dobo, **BENJINA** is the Aru's commercial fishing centre, and also site of a naval base. Police and military here can be heavy-handed with foreigners, but Benjina is otherwise a good place to find transport southeast along the sixty-kilometre **Sungai Maikoor** between Trangan and the segments of **Maikoor** and **Koba**, with similar scenery to that along the Manumbai. Three days from Dobo off Trangan's southeastern side, a **marine park** around **Enu, Jeh, Mar** and **Karang** islands is a vital laying ground for green and hawksbill **turtle** populations, and, at the right time of year, there should be good diving down here.

The Tanimbars

Closer to Australia than Ambon, the sixty-odd islands which make up the **Tanimbars** have pretty well always been left to their own devices. A century ago, warfare and headhunting dissuaded much interaction with the outside world, but today the minimal infrastructure, poor services and lack of industries on the Tanimbars seems more deliberate. When the government sold off Tanimbarese forests to a Chinese timber company in the early 1990s, the locals obtained a court injunction against them, and the official response seems to have been to let the Tanimbars rot. The effects are everywhere: the state shipping line calls in just once a month, the district capital wallows in an atmosphere of sloth, and funds to maintain the islands' main road have never been forthcoming, the surface having long-since degenerated into a rough, potholed strip, impassable after rain.

Having said all this, and despite cannibalism, protective ancestral carvings, and ceremonies to celebrate the union of the earth and sun being a thing of the past, there's a huge amount happening under the surface here. **Megaliths** are the most solid reminders of an all pervasive **boat cult**, which has Tanimbarese villages ordered according to assigned positions on a vessel, such as rowers, captains, helmsman, and even frigate birds. There are strong traditions of craftsmanship too: sacred **antique gold** artefacts are owned by many families, with **weaving and carving** still widely practised. Festivals such as Independence Day and Christmas are a chance to see **dancing**, where dancers wearing fine sarongs, gold earrings and pendants, and bird of paradise headpieces mimic fighting, or ritual activities such as weaving. In very rare instances you may see full-scale affairs with entire communities assuming their hereditary positions in a "boat dance" recounting the islanders' voyages to settle the Tanimbars, or performances held to reinforce ties between specific villages.

At 100km long, **Yamdena** is by far the Tanimbars' biggest island, with runners-up **Larat** to the north and **Selaru** to the south. All traffic to the Tanimbars heads to the southern end of Yamdena at **Saumlaki**, the district capital. **From Ambon**, the only direct transport are Perentis freighters and Merpati's one flight a week; there's also the weekly ferry **from Tual**, while Pelni's *Tatamailau* calls in once a month **from Dobo**. There's limited transport on and around the islands, and you'll need to be patient to travel very widely – September through to November is probably the driest time of year, when both sea and road conditions are optimum for getting about.

To Yamdena: Fordate and Larat

On the way to Saumlaki, boats visit the **northern Tanimbars,** passing **Pulau Fordate** – usually hidden under rainclouds and considered by Tanimbarese as their ancestral home – before calling in at **LARAT,** a busy centre for the north with perhaps two thousand inhabitants. It's a nice location: the town sits on a sheltered bay, a community of wooden buildings backed by the inevitable church-on-a-hill, with immaculately-clad schoolchildren being poled across from nearby kampung in the early morning. Things have certainly changed from the 1880s, when a steely-nerved **Anna Forbes** found Larat at war with its neighbours, surrounded by bamboo palisades and dismembered corpses – check out her *Unbeaten Tracks in Islands of the Far East* (see p.978) for the full story. From Larat, it's an uneventful trip south to Saumlaki, boats hugging Yamdena's eastern or western coast depending on which provides shelter from the prevailing winds.

Saumlaki

Facing west across a bay at the bottom end of Yamdena, **Saumlaki** is a torpid community of four thousand souls based around a **port** and **market** area. There's nothing wrong with the town, but the only time you'll see any activity here is during Christian festivals, or when boats from Australia cross the finishing line in the annual **Gove–Saumlaki yacht race** in September. Running north–south, the 250-metre main road is Jalan Bhineka, with the market square halfway along enclosed by **Yamdena Plaza**'s empty shell. **Arrival points** are 1.5km south of town at the **airport,** or immediately behind the market, where a long stone **jetty** leads out to the dock. Saumlaki's three **places to stay** are all along Jalan Bhineka. The clean and tiled *Harapan Indah* (✆0918/21019; singles with fan ③, air-con doubles ⑤) has an oceanside verandah and exceptional food; *Penginapan Ratulei* (③) is a friendly, basic homestay, unfortunately located right next to the pink and white mosque; and there's the *Pantai Indah* (④), a compromise between the two. The market is good for fish and whatever fruit and vegetables are in season – citrus, aubergines, gourds, corn, papaya flowers, soursop – while stores in the area sell essentials, and you'll find a couple of **coffee houses** and Padang warung along Jalan Bhineka. English-speaking Ronie will probably catch up with you at some point; he's well-connected, but don't let him arrange anything unless you want to pay about ten times the going rate.

Vehicles for the rest of the island congregate at Yamdena Plaza. Short-range mobils cost Rp1000 a person; buses up the east coast charge Rp15,000 to Arui Bab; and Kijangs can be chartered from Rp10,000 an hour, depending on road conditions. Ask at the port, or the tiny **harbour** beside the mosque, for **local boats** around Yamdena and nearby islands. **Leaving,** Merpati are at the *Harapan Indah* (✆0918/21017; mornings are a good time to catch them in) – it can, apparently, be hard to find a seat unless you're staying at the hotel – while Pelni's backstreet office (daily from 10am) is easily overlooked near the market. A board at the port entrance lists all vessels: there's the Tual ferry, the *Tatamailau* to Timor and Java, and a stream of Perentis boats on Timor/Tual/Ambon circuits.

Pantai Leluan and Olilit Lama

One way to pass half a day is by following the 5km sealed road **south from Saumlaki** to a couple of seafront locations; mobils leave the Plaza whenever full, or it's an easy walk through open countryside. Just outside of town, there's a view across western Yamdena from the hilltop "suburb" of **Olilit Baru,** then it's another 3km to where the road **forks:** bear right here for **Pantai Leluan,** a pleasant sandy **beach** with coconut trees and concrete tables, popular on Sundays. Continue straight on at the fork, and the road reaches a blustery rise, with a fantastic seascape of open blue water and contorted, wind-sharpened islets spread beneath you, before descending to **OLILIT LAMA**. Once a centre for the old religion, you're greeted at the outskirts by a grotto with a concrete tableau of the Resurrection, and the village itself is an unremarkable arrangement of houses and earth streets, with brightly painted outrigger canoes pulled up above the beach. You could be in for a surprise if anyone invites you into their home, however – a few older people have ceremonial relics squirreled away, while others keep **ancestor skulls** under crucifixes on the mantlepiece, benevolent spirits guarding over their descendants.

Around Yamdena

Central Yamdena is forested, completely uninhabited – except by ferocious **wild cattle** – and very difficult to visit, as the maritime-oriented Tanimbarese show it little interest. A 100-kilometre "highway" links Saumlaki with villages along Yamdena's **east coast**, but just how far you'll get, how long it will take, and how much it will cost are determined by the road's chronically poor condition. On a good day, public buses make the 60km run to **Arui Bab** via **Tumbur** and **Sangliat Dol** – whose ancient **stone boat** is the most obvious highlight of a trip to Tanimbar – in around two hours, but at other times you may find yourself spending most of a day trying to extricate your chartered, high-clearance KIJANG from the mud. One way around this is to use **speedboat taxis**, which leave more or less daily between September and April to various points along the east coast from **ILNGEL**, about 5km north of Saumlaki. In the opposite direction, it's also possible to organize boats to a few small **islands** off Saumlaki – though this is a dangerous proposition in rough conditions – and around to **Latdalam** on Yamdena's southwest coast. Always take some money and a few necessities along in case you get stranded by weather or transport lacunae, and, at all villages, make a courtesy call to the kepala desa, who can help organize people to show you around or sort out accommodation.

The east coast: Tumbur, Sangliat Dol and Arui Bab

The east coast road doesn't touch on Yamdena's forests, rather the cleared plantations and plots between kampung, though you can sometimes see treetops inland. Around 20km from town, **TUMBUR** is a centre for **woodcarving**, a traditional skill revived recently by the Catholic church to produce spindly-limbed figures for souvenir, rather than pagan, purposes.

After Tumbur the road degenerates, with another 30km to **SANGLIAT DOL**. If you can manage it, however, the best way to arrive at the village would be by sea, landing on the beach from where a disintegrating, but impressive, **staircase** ascends steeply to the village square. Here, surrounded by houses and overlooked by one of the largest churches you'll see outside of Ambon, is a twenty-metre **stone boat** which Sangliat Dol's villagers say brought their ancestors to this spot. Built of rectangular blocks, the boat forms a barrel-bellied **platform**, still used for **dances** during festivals (or, at other times, with Rp300,000 and a few days' warning); check out the rudder and three-metre-high **prow**, carved with swirls and fish. Fifty years ago every kampung on Yamdena possessed such a boat, though Sangliat Dol's is the last intact example. Photographs are allowed with the permission of the *kepala adat* – the head of tradition – who charges Rp10,000 and seeks the spirits' approval with a gift of *sopi* (replaced in this dry village by lemonade). Exactly which spirits are involved isn't clear, as the invocation begins in the ritual Larat language, but concludes with the Lord's Prayer in Indonesian. The rest of Sangliat Dol consists of simple bamboo-slat houses, though up near the road there's a modern building whose roof has a **sculpture** of a dog's head at the front, and the tail at the back, which nobody will explain. If the bridge hasn't washed out, try to get 7km up the road from Sangliat Dol to **ARUI BAB**, where another stone boat with a more elaborately carved prow marks the site of the old village, now in woods alongside the new.

Southern islands and Latdalam

A couple of **islands** due south of Saumlaki make for an interesting day-trip. Around 10km out, **Nustabun** is a small sandy island anchored around rocks, inhabited by seabirds. Surrounding coral has been bombed, but a few fragments populated by stingrays and small fish survive about 50m offshore where the water deepens. To the west, the kilometre-broad **Angwarmase** rises cake-like from the waters, with steep southeastern cliffs sloping back to a low and sandy rear. Seasonally occupied by Selaru islanders, who fish and process copra here, Angwarmase is primarily known for its pink **orchids**. The orchids are held sacred by islanders, who rough up anyone caught stealing these valuable plants and insist on another *sopi* ritual – this time with the real thing – before guiding you through the tangled, sharp-rocked foothills to where the flowers grow.

Extend your trip by crossing over to western Yamdena at **Latdalam**, whose 3000 residents make this village only marginally smaller than Saumlaki. Local fishing boats line the foreshore, though otherwise Latdalam is a dull place at first, with drab, evenly spaced rectangular houses and a single **store**. Actually, the village is still organized along traditional lines, with families occupying their nautical "positions" in relation to one another, and it's also a good place to see the **weaving** of *kain* on hand looms. A short walk takes you to the edge of forest, just inside of which are a couple of springfed **pools**; the mens' is framed in concrete surrounds, but the womens' is more natural. With a guide from Latdalam and a day, it's also possible to hike 15km east from here, through undergrowth and across at least two rivers, to **Lermatan** village, and then get a local prahu across the bay to Saumlaki.

Yamdena to Timor

The 300-kilometre strait between Yamdena and Timor is strewn with islands, culturally related to the rest of southeastern Maluku and with some of their traditions still intact. Though there are no passenger liners, freighters make the crossing all the time, stopping off at some otherwise extremely isolated places. Moving west, the first of the four main groups is **Babaar**, a mountainous island and the last place in Maluku to practice old **goldsmithing** skills, where craftsmen still cast ceremonial earrings. Bypassing the northern **Damar Islands**, and continuing westwards to the tip of Timor past **Sermata**, **Moa** and **Leti**, tiny **Kisar** has two Dutch **forts**, one of which, Vollenhove, was built in 1668 to defend the island against Portuguese raids from the mainland.

travel details

Buses

Masohi to: Amahai (frequent; 20min); Kairatu (several daily; 5hr); Saleman-Saka (several daily; 3hr); Tehoru (several daily; 4hr).

Sidangoli to: Kao (several daily; 2hr 30min); Tobelo (several daily; 5hr).

Pelni ferries

For a chart of the Pelni routes, see pp.36–37 of Basics.

Ambon/Pulau Ambon to: Bandaneira (*KM Rinjani*, 2 monthly; 10hr/*KM Bukit Siguntang*, 2 monthly; 10hr); Denpasar (*KM Dobonsolo*, 2 monthly; 2–3 days); Dobo (*KM Bukit Siguntang*, monthly; 30hr); Jayapura (*KM Dobonsolo*, 2 monthly; 60hr/*KM Rinjani*, 2 monthly; 4 days); Kupang (*KM Dobonsolo*, 2 monthly; 29hr); Namlea (*KM Lambelu*, 2 monthly; 5hr); Surabaya (*KM Rinjani*, 2 monthly; 60hr/*KM Dobonsolo*, 2 monthly; 3 days); Ternate (*KM Lambelu*, 2 monthly; 36hr); Tual (*KM Rinjani*, 2 monthly; 19hr/*KM Bukit Siguntang*, 2 monthly; 18hr); Ujung Pandang (*KM Bukit Siguntang*, 2 monthly; 36hr/*KM Lambelu*, 2 monthly; 33hr/*KM Rinjani*, 2 monthly; 33hr/*KM Tatamailu*, monthly; 2 days).

Bandaneira to: Ambon (*KM Rinjani*, 2 monthly; 7hr); Dobo (*KM Bukit Siguntang*, monthly; 24hr);

Sorong (*KM Rinjani*, 2 monthly; 33hr); Tual (*KM Rinjani*, 2 monthly; 10hr/*KM Bukit Siguntang*, 2 monthly; 10hr).

Dobo to: Dili (*KM Tatamailau*, monthly; 2 days); Saumlaki (*KM Tatamailau*, monthly; 26hr); Timika (*KM Tatamailau*, monthly; 16hr); Tual (*KM Tatamailau*, monthly; 8hr).

Saumlaki to: Dili (*KM Tatamailau*, monthly; 26hr); Dobo (*KM Tatamailau*, monthly; 24hr); Tual (*KM Tatamailau*, monthly; 15hr).

Ternate to: Bitung (*KM Umsini*, 2 monthly; 10hr/ *KM Ceremai*, 2 monthly; 7hr); Sorong (*KM Ceremai*, 2 monthly; 16hr/*KM Umsini*, 2 monthly; 17hr).

Tual to: Dobo (*KM Tatamailau*, monthly; 8hr);

Other ferries and speedboats

Amahai to: Pulau Ambon (daily; 2hr).

Ambon/Pulau Ambon to: Amahai (daily; 2hr); Kairatu (daily; 2hr); Namlea (3 weekly; 10hr); Saparua (daily; 1hr 30min).

Dobo to: Saumlaki (weekly; 36hr); Tual (weekly; 14hr).

Saumlaki to: Dobo (weekly; 36hr); Tual (weekly; 36hr).

Ternate to: Sidangoli (several daily; 30min–1hr 30min).

Tobelo to: Daruba, Morotai (daily; 3–5hr).

Tual to: Dobo (weekly; 14hr); Saumlaki (weekly; 30hr).

Flights

Ambon to: Bandaneira (5 weekly; 1hr 30min); Dobo (weekly; 4hr); Langgur (weekly; 3hr); Saumlaki (weekly; 2hr); Sorong, Irian Jaya (daily; 1hr 20min); Ternate (7 weekly; 1hr 40min); Ujung Pandang, Sulawesi (daily; 1hr 45min).

Bandaneira to: Ambon (5 weekly; 1hr 30min). Saumlaki (*KM Tatamailau*, monthly; 15hr).

Dobo to: Ambon (weekly; 4hr); Langgur (weekly; 1hr).

Langgur to: Ambon (daily; 3hr); Dobo (weekly; 1hr).

Saumlaki to: Ambon (weekly; 2hr).

Ternate to: Ambon (7 weekly; 1hr 40min); Manado (daily; 50min).

CHAPTER THIRTEEN

IRIAN JAYA

rian Jaya is one of the world's last great wildernesses: maps of the area still show stretches as wide as 300km without any relief data at all. In 1996, emissaries from two unknown tribes emerged from the Asmat jungle. One tribe began its first tentative steps towards communication with the outside world, the other slipped back into the jungle and has not been heard of since. From the towering glacial highlands of its spine to the sweaty mangrove swamps of the coast, Irian Jaya is a tantalizing place for explorers.

The island of **New Guinea**, the second largest in the world, is neatly bisected down its north–south axis, the eastern portion comprising independent Papua New Guinea and the western half, Irian Jaya, belonging to Indonesia. It is surrounded by thousands of other smaller islands that pepper the southwestern corner of the Pacific. The whole area is known as Melanesia which means "Black Islands", either a reference to the dark skin of the inhabitants, or to the distinctive volcanic black ash that makes up much of its soil. Melanesians comprise one percent of the world's population, but speak twenty five percent of its languages; in Irian Jaya alone there are between 250 and 300 different languages, some spoken by only a few hundred people. This is due to extreme isolation, the harshness of the terrain and the ceaselessly warlike nature of the tribes, all of which have combined to maintain small, fiercely insular communities.

The majority of visitors will arrive, after a night flight from Java, in the capital city **Jayapura**, or on **Biak**, with its fabulous birdlife and fascinating coral reefs: travelling around Irian Jaya takes a lot of planning (see box opposite), and these are the best places to do it from. From Jayapura there are daily flights to the **Baliem Valley**, the highland plain that is home to the Dani tribes, and which features the most highly dramatic scenery imaginable. The jungles of the **south** are also a draw for travellers, as is the **Asmat region**, with its wonderful primitive art. On the **Bird's Head peninsula**, there are stunning ancient cave paintings near **Fak Fak**, gorgeous lakes near **Manokwari** and **Nabire**, and the untouched coral reefs of the **Cenderawasih national park**.

The **climate** of the region varies greatly, some parts of the island receiving heavy rainfall every day of the year. On the highest mountains, such as 5030-metre Puncak Jaya, this precipitation takes the form of snow, and **glaciers** can be up to 40m thick,

ACCOMMODATION PRICE CODES

All the **accommodation** listed in this book has been given one of the following price codes. The rates quoted here are for the **cheapest double room** in high season, except for places with dorms, where the code represents the price of a single bed. Where there's a significant spread of prices indicated (④–⑦, for example), the text will explain what extra facilities you get for more money. The 11–21 percent tax charged by most hotels is not included in these price codes.

Because of the current instability of the rupiah, accommodation prices are given throughout in their more stable **US dollar equivalents**, even for places that accept payment in rupiah.

For more on accommodation, see p.000.

| ① under $1 | ③ $2–5 | ⑤ $10–15 | ⑦ $35–60 | ⑨ $100 |
| ② $1–2 | ④ $5–10 | ⑥ $15–35 | ⑧ $60–100 | and over |

TRAVELLING IN IRIAN JAYA

Even if you're going to stick to Biak or the well-worn Baliem trails, a trip to Irian Jaya requires more **planning** than any other destination in Indonesia.

The first complication is the **surat jalan** – literally your "walking papers" – or travel permit. Mainly because the Indonesian government wants to keep tabs on all visitors and keep them out of sensitive areas, you must acquire this permit from the police on your arrival in Irian, with signed permission for each and every one of the small districts you wish to visit. Many places are completely out of bounds, and the police may not be sure about which ones. The rule of thumb is to apply for every feasible destination, as you can't add places to your surat jalan outside of the large towns (Biak, Jayapura, Timika and Sorong). If there is an area you want to get to, which you think might be problematic, it's best to clear it with the minister of tourism in Jayapura first (see p.910).

Photography in Irian is also a different proposition to other parts of Indonesia. No matter what they say, most X-ray machines at airports are not film safe; take films out and have them searched by hand. Military installations and personnel should never be photographed, and take great care when photographing people; in areas where photography is rare it can cause great distress, and in areas where it is common, permission and cash are expected first. Film is difficult to get hold of; the big towns have some, usually very old stock, and slide film is just about impossible to find.

Prices in Irian are a shock to travellers who have come from the rest of Indonesia. A lousy fleapit hotel costs twice as much in Irian as a reasonable guest house anywhere else; food and fuel are also **expensive** as they have to be imported. Chartering transport and hiring guides, however, are likely to be the greatest expenditure, as much as US$50 for a day in a paddle canoe, or US$500 in a motorized outboard.

Malaria is rife in the jungles of the south and the Bird's Head peninsula, and strains are resistant to usual brands of malarial prophylactics; see Basics (p.28) for advice on this.

The **OPM** (Organisas Papua Merdeka) or Free Papua Movement is far from dead, and is still particularly active in the jungles of the Lorentz reserve and parts of the Bird's Head; kidnapping foreigners is their means of drawing attention to their cause. Most travel writers who have written about Irian tell of lucky escapes at the hands of indignant chiefs, unsettled locals and gun-toting police. Common sense is your best precaution.

even though the mountains are practically on the equator. The southern coastal plain contains some of the world's largest and most impenetrable **swamplands**. The rainfall here is intense, and tides can flood miles inland, leaving vast mud flats on their retreat. To the east, near the town of Merauke, the land is much like that in the Northern Territory of Australia, with eucalyptus trees clinging to harsh, red soil. Several hundred miles inland are tropical **rainforests** of gigantic buttress-rooted trees, the tallest tropical trees in the world, cut through with myriad streams, rivers and waterfalls. As the tropical rainforest climbs to become **cloud forest**, the fauna becomes more alpine, with ferns, shrubs, grasses and mosses.

Some history

Despite numerous attempts by Western explorers to tame Papua, the colossal island all but repelled them right up until the latter part of the twentieth century. The extraordinary remoteness and hostility of its landscape, combined with reports of vicious cannibals to deter even the most committed of adventurers. It seemed to early pioneers that the island had no prospect of mineral deposits – coconuts and timber were too difficult to farm profitably and trade in bird of paradise feathers and crocodile skins was far too arduous.

Papua's early history is of a succession of budding landing parties meeting intense opposition. The Dutch came first in 1597: Willem Janz landed and lost six of his men; Carstenz tried in 1623 and his party was decimated; and Captain Cook barely set foot

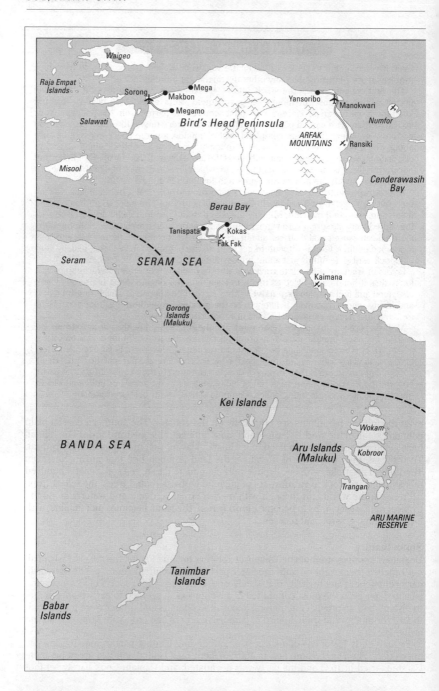

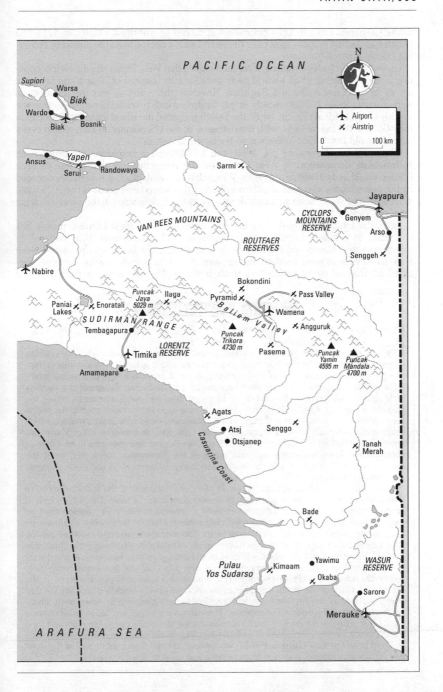

at the Casuarina coast in 1770 before being forced to withdraw. Finally, in 1714, the Dutch East India Company took over the island with a decree from the Sultan of Tidore, but mainly ignored the place.

On Indonesian **Independence**, it seemed logical that West Papua should itself become independent. After all, it was a world away from Java: the capitals of Jakarta and Jayapura are as far apart as London and Baghdad. However, there was no way the Indonesians were going to let such a vast, mostly empty landmass with potential natural resources be meekly ceded to tribal rule. So, while the Dutch prepared the island for union with Papua New Guinea, the Indonesians, with the collusion of the US, planned to ensure that every part of the old Dutch East Indies would become Indonesian.

Eventually, on November 19, 1969, the UN passed a resolution to endorse an **Indonesian occupation** of West Papua, on the understanding that a Vote of Free Choice would be held within six years. When this vote took place, it was stage-managed by the Indonesians, who selected, then bribed or threatened every one of the 1025 tribal delegates, and West Papua was ceded entirely to the Indonesians, to be renamed Irian Jaya, or "Victorious Irian".

Since the Indonesians took over in 1963, resentment amongst Irianese people has continued to escalate. Initially, programmes to clothe and house the "natives" in Indonesian-style homes and clothing were begun benignly, but when the results were slow, tribal villages were bombed and napalmed, and local leaders were tortured, executed or dropped out of helicopters to their death. The cleansing, or pacification of

---

IRIAN'S WILDLIFE

Irian Jaya's **wildlife** differs widely from that found in the rest of Indonesia, with a dazzling variety of species and some spectacular oddities.

Papua's **marsupials** include cuscus, feather-tail possums and bandicoots. The echidna or spiny anteater is a burrowing, toothless creature with a great, long snout that it uses to suck up ants and earthworms: it is practically blind, and black with protruding white spines. Many marsupials live on plant sap, nectar or insects, but the **quoll** is a particularly vicious little predator that feeds on birds, reptiles and small mammals. About the size of a domestic cat and with big dark eyes, its cute appearance hides a ferocious predatory instinct. The mbaiso **tree kangaroo** is a black-and-white tree-living creature which emits a characteristic whistle, measures about 1.5m long and weighs 15kg. It was discovered in 1994 by Dr Tim Flannery, making it the largest new mammal to be found in recent times. Irian is also the possible home of the Tasmanian Tiger, the "most frequently seen extinct species" in the world, which also happens to be the world's largest carnivorous marsupial.

Irian's **birds** are fabulously attractive. In the dense shadow of the forest, they have developed extravagant showy plumage to ensure they attract a mate. Due to the lack of sizeable carnivores, several birds have evolved as ground dwellers. The **maleo fowl**, or megapode bird, a turkey-like creature with big powerful feet for burrowing, incubates its eggs by means of a giant rotting compost heap. The megapode bird and crowned pigeon (the largest and probably most beautiful pigeon extant) can laboriously fly short distances if threatened, but the island's largest inhabitant (other than humans), is an entirely ground-bound bird, the **cassowary**. It stands over 1.5m tall and possesses immensely powerful claws; its head is iridescent electric blue with a solid bony protuberance on the crown and a turkey-like, wattled red neck. Its spray of stringy black feathers are used to adorn the hats of the highlanders, and jungle dwellers pierce their noses with single feathers which curl upwards like antenna. The cassowary's eggs are laid in shallow nests on the forest floor and look like giant shiny avocados; the males guard the eggs and then the offspring for several months after hatching. The world's only known poisonous bird is found here: the **New Guinea Pitohi**, whose feathers and flesh contain one of the most powerful toxins around, poached from berries and used to deter predators.

native people in Irian, paved the way for the largest **transmigration** scheme the world has ever seen. The people who took up the government's offer of a plot of soil and a plane ticket to Irian found themselves ditched on infertile land, or crammed into bitterly depressing townships. The empty, colossal bulk of Irian that had seen no external influence or noticeable population increase in thousands of years, was suddenly inundated with four million new inhabitants in little over a decade. In places where they mixed with the natives, the Javanese took over Irianese enterprises and lands, while elsewhere, the government shunted Irianese off their land to make way for mining and timber interests. As towns started to expand around the plunder.of Irian's resources, people from Maluku and Sulawesi started the trek east and to populate towns like Sorong and Jayapura, further disinheriting the native population.

The Anti Slavery Society in its recent *Plunder in Paradise* paper, estimates that at least 300,000 Papuans have lost their lives to the Indonesian tyranny, that 15,000 are refugees in New Guinea and that there are thousands without homes or land.

Sentani and Jayapura

The vast majority of visitors to Irian will first arrive at **Sentani**'s airport, which also services Irian's capital town of **Jayapura**. Sentani is 30km away from Jayapura and it takes about ninety minutes to reach the city by public transport from the airport. Sentani is a smaller and quieter place to stay, but travellers will have to call at the capital to arrange a **surat jalan** (see the box on p.901). Jayapura is also the central point for visiting travel agents, exchanging foreign currencies and getting visas for Papua New Guinea, but it's usually possible to arrange **flights** around Irian from Sentani.

Although Jayapura is the biggest settlement in Irian, its entire municipality, taking up most of the north coast, boasts a population of only 168,000. There is almost no industry here and everything but a few foodstuffs is imported at great expense by boat or plane from other areas of Indonesia. Travelling essentials such as medicines and camera film should all be brought with you. The north coast is not quite as malarial and steamy as the south, but is extremely hot; the rainy season lasts from December to March and the average temperature is just under 30°C.

Sentani and around

Around 15km inland from the northern coast and 30km west of Jayapura, **SENTANI** is the central transport hub of Irian, with the largest and busiest airport. As planes circle to begin their descent into Sentani, they afford a breathtaking view of one of the north's most impressive features, **Danau Sentani**. Unfortunately, the lake is not actually visible from any part of Sentani town, which is not much more than an airport with a few buildings thrown up around it. The hills that slope sharply down to the town's perimeters are totally deforested, and due to the lack of binding tree roots, the topsoil has disintegrated and the ground has collapsed into ugly, torn rockfaces that look much like open-cast quarries.

However, just beyond these hills are peaks as dramatic as knife points, covered with thick forest. It's possible to get to some good **beaches** from Sentani, two hours' drive northwest around **Depapre**. The lake is also well worth a visit, though there are no organized tours and you will have to arrange a motorized canoe yourself.

Practicalities

The **airport** is located in the south of the town and most facilities and hotels are within easy walking distance; the **minibus** (here known as taksi) **terminal** lies 1500m to the west. Garuda and Merpati have offices at the airport, and though they'll probably insist

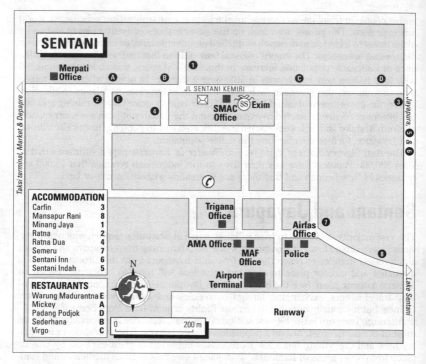

that you go to Jayapura to buy your ticket, you can check on availability, reserve a seat and find out about cancellations here. There is an **information office** and a branch of Bank Exim, both rarely open. The police station is at the main entrance to the airport, but at the time of writing you could not get a **surat jalan** here. It's always worth checking though, as this would save a trip into Jayapura.

If you plan to head straight **to Jayapura** on arrival at Sentani airport, then the easiest way is just to hop in a taxi outside the terminal (35min; Rp25,000). If you want to take public transport or are not in a hurry, then you can walk out to Jalan Sentani Chimera (600m to the north) and flag down a taksi heading east. This will terminate at Abepura terminal (30min; Rp800), but if you tell the driver you are going to Jayapura he'll drop you off just before, from where you can catch a taksi on to Entrop (20min; Rp500). Again, you need to get off just before the terminal, and take another taksi into the centre of town (15min; Rp350).

The **Telkom** office in Sentani is on the way north from the airport to the main road and is easily located by its red-and-white communications mast. They are open 24hr and are relatively efficient, though prices are subject to sudden and unexplained fluctuations. The **post office** (Mon–Sat 8am–5pm) is on the main road to Jayapura, Jalan Sentani Chimera, and has poste restante. There is a **Bank Exim** just east of here on the same road, which will change dollars cash and some brands of travellers' cheques.

ACCOMMODATION

Most **hotels** in Sentani are pretty close to the airport and will send staff to wait at the terminal to greet incoming flights and ferry passengers to their hotels. Places here are generally quieter than those in Jayapura, but slightly more expensive.

Carfin Hotel, Jl Flafon (☎0967/91478). Next door to the Onomi Christian Church at the eastern end of Jl Sentani Chimera. Prices here include full board; it's a clean place with lots of shiny glass and ceramic tile. Each room has a TV and air-con and the restaurant features karaoke. ④.

Mansapur Rani, Jl Yabaco 113 (☎0967/91219). Close to the airport: turn right out of the terminal gates and it's a five-minute walk. This is a good place to leave baggage if you are travelling around Irian and plan to depart from Sentani. Rooms are no more than adequate, but come with fan and en-suite mandi. ③.

Minang Jaya, Jl Bestur Post (☎0967/91067). Down a small side road off Jl Sentani Chimera, between *Rumah Makan Mickey* and the Bank Exim. It's simple, a little dilapidated and mainly frequented by Indonesian army personnel, but the staff are charming and willing to please. ③.

Hotel Ratna, Jl Pln Sentani 2 (☎0967/91435). The standard singles here are the cheapest to be had in Sentani, small and cramped but reasonably well kept and clean. Air-con rooms are poor value by comparison. ④.

Hotel Ratna Dua, Jl Kalurakan (☎0967/92277 or 92496). Features beautiful, sizeable rooms with gleaming white-tiled floors around a central restaurant. The price includes a breakfast of tea, coffee, fruit and sweetmeats. Out the back is a remarkable aviary, where birds are kept before export to private collectors around Asia. It's a bleak, dung-spattered chicken-wire affair, but usually full of startling lorries, parrots, parakeets and a few mambruk and raja cockatoos. ⑥.

Hotel Semeru, Jl Yabasco (☎0967/91447). The closest place to the airport, just a three-minute walk east of the gates. Has decent, clean rooms with fan or air-con; all rooms have en-suite mandi. ④.

Hotel Sentani Indah, Jl Raya Hawaii (☎0967/91900). Flashy brochure photos of this place were clearly taken of a completely different hotel; from the road this three-star joint looks more like an airport terminal, but it'll be quite plush inside once finished. All the rooms are arranged around a large swimming pool with a sunken bar. There are also tennis courts and a fitness room is on the way. All rooms have satellite TV, hot water and fridge and there is an additional ten percent tax charged on everything. ⑧–⑨.

Sentani Inn, Jl Raya Sentani (☎0967/91440). In Hawaii, an area just east of Sentani town and on the road to Jayapura. The rooms here smell a bit musty and it's a bit of a haunt for local drinkers, though generally quite quiet and relaxed. ④.

EATING

Rumah Makan Mickey, at the western end of Jl Sentani Chimera opposite the junction with Jl Pln Sentani. The most popular place and the restaurant where you are most likely to meet other foreigners in Sentani: it's a favourite of missionaries and adventurers who've spent too long eating cassava and sago grubs and are in need of a hamburger. A reasonable cheeseburger here costs Rp4750 and a hot dog Rp3000; they also serve Indonesian food and some Chinese dishes. The chicken cooked with mushrooms is especially good, served in a thin tomato sauce with baby vegetables.

Padang Podjok On the mountain side of Jl Flafon and 50m further east of the *Sari*. An upmarket Padang place with air-con and satellite TV. Their standard dishes of curried potatoes, prawns, fish and chicken with varieties of vegetables are a little overpriced; figure on around Rp10,000 for a full meal.

Sederhana, heading east along Jl Sentani Chimera from *Mickey*. A Padang restaurant that specializes in spicy food. About 50m further east of the *Sederhana*, are the *Tanjung* and *Mutiara*, also Padang restaurants. Have a look at the food displayed in the windows before sitting down to eat, unlike traditional Padang restaurants they don't just bring everything to your table but you have to select what you want beforehand.

Hotel Sentani Indah, in Hawaii, east of Sentani town and on the road to Jayapura. Does the best food around the Sentani area, with the option of buffet breakfast (US$8) lunch (US$12) and evening meal (US$15). All of the food is Western-style.

Rumah Makan Virgo, on the northern side of Jl Flafon, closest to the mountains. They have a similar menu to *Mickey* but the execution is slightly lacking and their European food such as hamburgers is often unavailable. On the opposite side of the road are the rumah makans *Sari* and *Lily*. They serve central Javanese food for Rp5000 in basic warung surroundings.

Warung Madurantna Sentani, about 20m down Jl Pln Sentani from *Mickey*. Serves Javanese food: their deer sate and excellent *ikan bakar* are cooked over hot coals outside the front door. Ask for freshly cooked sate rather than the stuff they've had sitting around out back for hours.

Danau Sentani, Waena and the beaches

The most rewarding excursion in the Sentani area is to **Danau Sentani**. Standing 75m above sea level and with an area of 15.3 square kilometres, the lake is an exceedingly beautiful expanse of island-studded azure and cobalt blue, teeming with catfish and gurami and framed by the looming green lower slopes of the Cyclops mountains. The best way to see the lake is to take a taksi from Sentani down to **Yahim harbour** and then try and find someone with a motorized dugout canoe – no more than a hacked-out tree trunk with an outboard nailed to the back. The usual rate for an hour's charter of one of these boats is about $12, though you would need a little longer than an hour to get out to a few islands and take a swim. A good island to head for is **Apayo**, one of the few places in the Sentani area where the people still practise sculpture and distinctive paintings on bark canvasses. The paintings are characterized by stylized geckos and snakes painted in natural pigments, and resemble Australian aboriginal art.

East of Sentani and on the lakeside is **DOYO LAMA** village, renowned for a nearby black boulder, covered with faint, ancient carvings and believed to have magical powers. It's possible to get to the village by taksi from Sentani. *Yougga Cottage* (☎0967/71570; ④), about 23km from downtown Jayapura and accessible by taksi from Abepura, is a **restaurant** and small **guest house** on the shores of the lake. All rooms come with breakfast and en-suite mandi and the restaurant has reasonable Indonesian and Chinese food. Gelanggang Remaja, the youth centre, is a sort of recreation area at the lakeside where locals come at weekends to fish and canoe on the lake. It's also accessible from Abepura.

To see the lake from a distance, the best lookout is at the **MacArthur Monument**, 325m up Gunung Ifar. The plaque on the monument cites this spot as the headquarters of General Douglas MacArthur's "Reckless task force" during the Pacific War. The monument is about 6km from Sentani and, at the weekends, taksis will run right up to it. At all other times you'll probably have to charter a taksi: take care to check in with the guard on the way up to the monument, who may want to see your passport or surat jalan if you have one.

The village of **WAENA**, a twenty-minute taksi ride east of Sentani, has a couple of worthwhile attractions. The **Taman Budaya** (Cultural Park) has some mock-ups of traditional Irianese houses; they're rather exaggerated replicas and not a particularly good representation of the buildings you'll see around Irian, but it's free to get in. The **museum** next door (daily 8am–4pm; Rp200) is much better: a large map shows where every one of Irian's 250 languages are spoken and others depict the geology and history of Irian (mostly in Indonesian). There are several *bisj* poles and decorated skulls from the Asmat region, some fine Baliem Valley stone axe-heads and several ammonites and mammoth shark's teeth. Other relics document Irian's more recent past, with samurai swords, bayonets and shells from American servicemen, and pistols and cannons left behind by the VOC. To get there, take a taksi from Sentani to Abepura and ask the driver to stop at the Museum Negeri.

To the northwest of Sentani there are a few good **beaches** in Depapre district, most notably **Pantai Amai**. It's no more than 15km from Sentani, but takes over an hour to reach in a crammed taksi. You will be dropped off at the harbour in Depapre, from where the usual course is to hire a boat over to Amai. It costs around $10 for a boat that can seat about fifteen, and at the weekend you may be able to share a boat with locals also heading over to the lovely white-sand beach.

Jayapura and around

Huddled in a narrow valley between jungle-covered hills, **JAYAPURA** is Irian Jaya's capital city and major port town. If you're arranging a serious tour around Irian, you will probably have to take advantage of the city's poor amenities. Most people acquire their

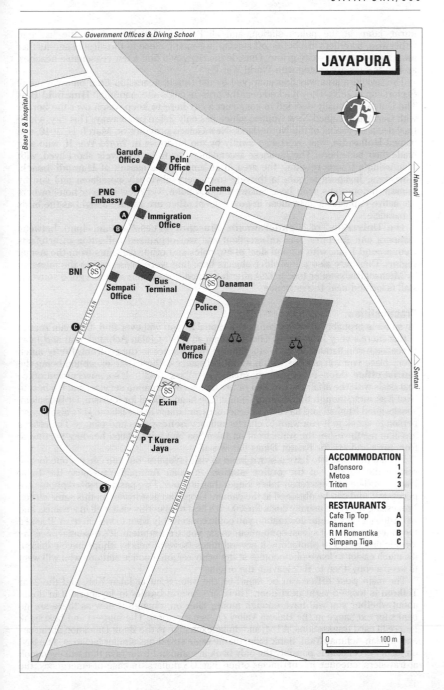

JAYAPURA

Government Offices & Diving School

Base G & hospital

Hamadi

Sentani

Garuda Office

Pelni Office

Cinema

PNG Embassy

❶

Ⓐ
Ⓑ

Immigration Office

BNI $S

Sempati Office

Bus Terminal

$S Danaman

Police

Ⓒ

❷

Merpati Office

Exim $S

Ⓓ

P T Kurera Jaya

❸

JL PERTEKAN

JL ACHMAD YANI

JL PEMBANGUNAN

ACCOMMODATION

Dafonsoro	1
Metoa	2
Triton	3

RESTAURANTS

Cafe Tip Top	A
Ramant	D
R M Romantika	B
Simpang Tiga	C

0   100 m

surat jalan at the police station, and all Pelni ferries leave from the harbour. Otherwise, travellers are better off staying in Sentani, close to the airport and further away from Jayapura's city grime. Outside the city you'll find a few reasonable beaches, as well as sites associated with World War II.

The Jayapura area was first surveyed by the Dutch steamship *Etna* on a voyage of exploration in 1858. They docked near the present city's site, naming it **Humbold Bay**. The Dutch eventually decided to construct a city here to keep watch over the border with German-occupied New Guinea, which lies only 20km or so away. This city, which they declared capital of the Netherlands New Guinea province on March 17, 1910, and named **Hollandia**, was overtaken swiftly by the Japanese in World War II, who also made their base here. The Japanese ascendancy was to be relatively short lived, with MacArthur's troops retaking the area in an amphibious assault at **Hamadi beach**. Nowadays, Jayapura is quite a thriving town, very obviously populated and run by migrant Indonesians from Java, Sulawesi and Maluku. Very few shop or hotel owners are native Papuans, and Irianese in government office are as rare a sight as the birds of paradise.

The **University of Cenderawasih Museum** (Tues–Sat 8am–4pm) between Jayapura and Abepura, has an excellent and well-organized collection of artefacts from around Irian, with a good deal of *bisj* poles and other carvings from the Asmat region. There are also a few older objects here that were presented to the museum by Michael Rockefeller (see p.929) after his expeditions in the south. A good souvenir stall is located near the entrance.

Practicalities

Jayapura is probably about as compact a capital as you will ever find, the main reason is that there's very little there. The two main streets of Jalan Achmad Yani and Jalan Percetakan run parallel to each other and at right angles to the seafront. Pretty much every place you will need is within walking distance of here, one exception being the **tourist office** (Mon–Fri 8am–5pm; ☎0967/35923, fax 37435). It's a government office that deals with the affairs of tourism rather than an information service, and it's best to treat it as such, though the staff are helpful. The head official for tourism, Dr Baasalem, speaks good English and has a lot of brochures and maps of the island. He's also a good person to speak to if you want to charter military **helicopters** and planes. The offices are 3km northwest of the waterfront on Jalan Soa Siu: take a taksi heading northwest from town and ask for Kantor Dinas Parawisata.

It is not necessary to have a **surat jalan** to visit Jayapura, but you can get one for the rest of the country at the **police station** on Jalan Achmad Yani near the Bank Danamon. The process rarely takes longer than an hour. Two passport-sized photos are necessary, and can be obtained at the camera shop 50m southwest on this same street. Processing the form usually costs Rp2000. It's best to plan this visit well in advance, and write down every single destination you could conceivably want to visit in Irian. If asked for your profession, it's least contentious to say you are a student. It's essential once the form is processed to photocopy it several times (several nearby shops have copiers); it's much easier to leave photocopies at the many regional police stations who will want to keep a copy, than to risk leaving the original.

The main **post office** can be found on the waterfront at Jalan Koti, and the 24hr **Telkom** is located right next door. There are several **banks** in Jayapura: if in doubt about whether you will have enough money later on, change it now as there are no banks for exchange in the Baliem Valley or Asmat region. The biggest and best bank for credit card transactions, ATM, and dollar exchange is the Bank Danamon at the sea end of Jalan Achmad Yani. Bank Exim on the same street has similar facilities. The BNI on Jalan Percetakan is possibly the only bank in mainland Irian Jaya that will even look at travellers' cheques in currencies other than US dollars. In case of emergency, the hospital is located 3km east of town. Catch a taksi heading northeast around the bay and ask for the rumah sakit umum.

The **Papua New Guinea consulate** is at Jalan Percetakan 28, by the *Hotel Dafonsoro* (Mon–Fri 8am–9pm). To obtain your three-month **visa** (Rp20,000), you'll need to show a return plane ticket for Papua New Guinea, and provide your passport and two passport-sized photos. All these details are subject to regular change.

There are several **travel agents** in Jayapura, of which the PT Kurera Jaya is the longest established and most efficient. They are at Jalan Achmad Yani 39 (☎0967/31583, fax 32236) and sell all tickets for Garuda, Bouraq and Merpati and are far better for information and tickets for Pelni boats than the out of town Pelni office. They do not however deal with the "pioneer" airlines, the small companies which mainly transport cargo around the region. They accept Visa and MasterCard, sell postcards, and arrange diving, rafting on the Baliem river as well as numerous walking and bird-watching tours around Irian. They also handle trips for the Lumba-Lumba Diving Club, whose main buildings are 4km out of town. Dives around the local area are about US$55 for two tanks. The **Merpati Office** is at Jalan Achmad Yani 15 (Mon–Thurs 8am–3pm, Fri 8am–noon, Sat 8am–1pm, Sun 10am–noon).

ACCOMMODATION

Jayapura doesn't have any good-value **accommodation**, and quite a few of the smaller hotels can be real fleapits. Even in the larger, smarter hotels it's essential to check your room before you agree to check in.

Hotel Dafonsoro, Jl Percetakan 20–24 (☎0967/31695 or 31696). All the rooms here have hot water and air-con, though some smell very musty. ⑤–⑦.

Hotel Jayapura, Jl Olahraga 4 (☎0967/33216). The cheapest hotel in town, with tiny windowless rooms: it's a bit like sleeping in a Turkish bath. ③–④.

Hotel Kartini, Jl Perintis 2 (☎0967/31557). Easily the best place for budget travellers, so it's usually full. The staff are friendly, the rooms kept very clean, and it's one of the few places with natural light in the rooms. ③.

Hotel Metoa, Jl Achmad Yani 14 (☎0967/31633). All of the rooms here have air-con and hot-water baths, and the top rooms are luxurious; all are pristine clean and well equipped. ⑦–⑧.

Hotel Sederhana, Jl Halmahera 2 (☎0967/31561). Has a good situation close to the seafront, and very basic doubles without mandi through to air-con options with TV and en-suite mandi. ④–⑤.

Hotel Triton, Jl Achmad Yani 14 (☎0967/33218 or 33171). All rooms here have air-con and colour TV, but are very much in need of refurbishment; the staff are unwelcoming. ⑤–⑥.

EATING

Night warung along Jalan Irian, at the waterfront and at the end of Jalan Achmad Yani, sell the usual Indonesian snacks, as well as *ikan bakar*, sate and various soups and stews.

Café Tip Top, Jl Percetakan 32. This is a great place for coffee and cakes and a chat with some of the locals.

Cafeteria Bahari, Jl Setiapura 10. Clean, cool and well-presented. They provide a variety of dishes such as mixed tofu and fried chicken, and can provide feasts for several guests if you give them advance notice.

Hotel Dafonsoro, Jl Percetakan 20–24. Serves Indonesian-style beef, pork and seafood dishes for around Rp15,000. A small, cold Bintang beer is Rp4400.

Malioboro, Jl Achmad Yani 2. Looks a lot like a standard warung but has the food and prices of a far more upmarket joint. They dish up Indonesian and Chinese food: the sweet-and-sour prawns or chicken is excellent and costs Rp8000.

Hotel Metoa, Jl Achmad Yani 14. Stocks a good variety of well-prepared Indonesian foods at high prices and European dishes such as hamburgers, stuffed tomatoes and seafood. A rump steak comes in at Rp40,000.

Pramont Rumah Makan, Jl Koti 124. A dark, air-con restaurant with karaoke and hostess girls, and an extensive menu of seafood: loads of dishes using squid, abalone, crab and fish cooked in a variety of Chinese and Javanese styles. The seafood prices depend on the day's catch but sweet-and-sour or chilli chicken costs Rp6000–13,000.

Prima Gasten, opposite the *Hotel Metoa*. A bakery serving excellent coffee, cold drinks and a variety of cakes, puddings and sandwiches.

Around Jayapura

Most of the attractions in the Jayapura area are coastal, with a few decent beaches and some pleasant seaside villages. Nearby **HAMADI** was the scene of MacArthur's historic World War II landings, but is now a lazy seaside suburb of Jayapura. The market here is well worth a look: it's a busy bric-a-brac affair, flooded with souvenirs. The beach is a short walk away and is no great shakes, with littered sands and murky water, but is a quick and easy escape from Jayapura. A few rusting hulks of old tanks and a commemorative statue lie nearby. Across Yotefa bay from Hamadi is **ENGROS**, a picturesque fishing village with houses perched on precarious stilts. The road that runs round the bay to this village continues east into New Guinea, but border crossings are completely forbidden. Hamadi is about 5km from Jayapura and taksis run here every few minutes. On the road between Hamadi and Jayapura are the *Pacific* (☎0967/35427; ④) and *99* (☎0967/35689; ③) hotels, both overlooking the sea and with reasonable air-con rooms with en-suite mandi. In Hamadi itself, the *Hotel Asia* (☎0967/35478; ③) has basic rooms with fan or air-con, and the upmarket *Hotel Mahkota* (☎0967/32997; ⑦), wildly overpriced for rooms with air-con and TV but no hot water. The *Mahkota*'s restaurant has sea views and a mix of European and Indonesian foods; figure on about $10 for a full meal.

A far better and cleaner beach then Hamadi's can be found at **Tanjung Ria**, otherwise known as Pantai Base G: it's about 4km north of Jayapura and can get very crowded over the weekends. Public transport only goes there at the weekends, so at other times you'll have to charter a taksi or get as close as possible and then walk. The beach itself has no coral, but about ten minutes' boat ride offshore is a fantastic reef that starts at a depth of around 5m and plunges down to about 30m. It's festooned with hard corals and plenty of exotic sea creatures dart about: blue spotted rays, bumphead parrot fish, clown fish and the odd white-tip reef shark. Further north at **Pasir Lima** is another good slope, with barracuda, rays, surgeonfish and triggerfish. To get to these reefs, you will either need to find a knowledgeable local boat owner, or contact the Lumba-Lumba Dive Club, through PT Kurera Travel in Jayapura (see p.911).

Several farms in the Jayapura area raise **crocodiles** for their skins and meat. These beasts were, not so long ago, thriving inhabitants of Danau Sentani and the estuaries of north-coast rivers but have now been hunted to near extinction. The best known crocodile farm is **Bintang Mas**, established in 1986; ask your taksi driver from Abepura Terminal to Sentani for *Taman Buaya*, and he should drop you off within walking distance. They claim to have 35,000 crocodiles here, 2500 of which are the estuarine variety: some of the males are as much as 6m in length.

The Baliem Valley

Today's visitors to the **Baliem Valley** will have their first glimpse of it from the plane, as the undulating jungle-covered mountains abruptly plunge into an unexpected and remarkable landscape. All of a sudden, from flying over a vast wilderness of uncharted forests, harsh cliff-faces fall away to a cultivated plain: a chess board of terraced fields, divided by rattan fences to keep the pigs out and the crops segregated. Sprinkled over the valley floor are jumbled assemblies of thatched *honai* huts. Occasional crude, dusty roads and snaking streams carve up the plains, and Sungai Baliem slowly meanders across it before falling into fierce rapids in the southeastern **Baliem Gorge**.

Nowadays the majority of visitors to **Jayawijaya regency**, as it is known, come here to encounter the inhabitants of the valley, the Dani. These proud people have managed, in the face of continued government and missionary pressure, to maintain a culture of incredible depth and beauty. Whilst the warlike nature of the Dani lives on only symbolically in dance and festival, for the most part they still live by the same methods as have existed in the valley for thousands of years. They mostly shun Western clothes, the men dressing solely in a penis gourd (*horim*), with pig teeth pushed through their noses and their bodies decorated in clay-and-grease warpaint.

Some history
In 1938, the millionaire Richard Archbold was on a reconnaissance mission for the American Museum of Natural History, when he first saw the Baliem Valley from his seaplane. He returned and landed on Danau Habbema some months later, with porters, soldiers and tonnes of equipment, and set to walk across the valley. Their reception by the natives varied from almost frenzied welcomes to showers of spears and arrows, but Archbold's party found the inhabitants to be at a remarkable stage of agricultural development, with stone-and-wood terracing making steep valley walls into viable fields, and crop rotation and irrigation in use. Though the Archbold expedition was a tremendous success, it was not until after World War II that another entered the valley, and not until the 1960s that the missionaries and Indonesian officials started to trickle in.

THE TRIBES OF THE BALIEM

The people of Jayawijaya regency can be subdivided into many different groups, but the three broadest tribes are the Dani, Western Dani or Lani, and the Yali. **Dani people** are instantly recognizable, because they use the thin end of a gourd for their *horim*: the length of the gourd encloses the penis and points it upwards in a permanent erection. Dani headdresses are made of cockerel feathers in a fetching circular crown, often with longer, more elaborate feathers falling down to frame the face. Once these were made from the furs of the cuscus, but now the more vibrantly coloured cuscus are all but extinct.

Dani **women** wear knee-length skirts, traditionally made of grass, and usually go barechested. All women are considered to be witches in the highlands, with powerful magic that increases with age. Aged women, it is believed, can put curses on men, causing them to become infertile and die horrible deaths.

The **Yali**, who come from the east of the Baliem, have a different kind of *horim*. They use the thick end of the gourd but it points straight out at right angles to the body from beneath a rattan skirt, which appears to be made of strung together hula hoops whose size ascends towards the ground. The **Lani** cover their heads in a palm tree-like spray of cassowary feathers, which spills over the head and hair. Their *horim* are also made from the thick end of the gourd but are secured around the waist by a wide, brightly coloured sash. Often the top of their gourd is used as a pouch for keeping money or tobacco in.

Even during freezing cold evenings, valley peoples remain practically naked, hugging themselves with folded arms and coating their bodies with insulating pig fat to keep warm. Pigs themselves are central to the highlanders culture, and very much a part of the family they are owned by. Pigs sleep in the *honai* with their owners and, if a sow dies, it's customary for the piglets to be suckled by a woman of the household.

The traditional **weapon** of the valley is the bow and arrow. A four-pronged arrow is for shooting birds, three prongs are used to shoot fish, a single bamboo is used on pigs, and a single shaft of wood or bone is for people. Around the Baliem Valley, the highlanders have a very distinctive diet, dominated by sweet potato but supplemented by fruits such as pandanus and *buah merah*. The latter is a large spiky pod, the insides of which are crushed and boiled; it tastes a bit like dark chocolate.

In 1969 and 1977, the Dani people revolted against Indonesian rule: the government was trying to force them to adopt Western clothes and discard their cultural practices. The Indonesians also began huge logging commissions in Dani areas, which have now almost entirely cleared the Baliem Valley of forests. The Dani **uprising** was brutally suppressed, with many people killed, villages bombed, and tribal leaders publicly tortured and executed.

The summer of 1997 saw the beginning of one of the harshest periods in the memory of the peoples of the central highlands. The El Niño weather system was blamed for the terrible destruction all over the island, with Papua New Guinea having to receive supply drops from Australia and much of Irian Jaya's normally drenched forests drying up. **Fires** started by slash-and-burn farmers raged out of control, and locals started more fires as they thought the smoke in the sky would become cloud and cause rain. Such a vast amount of smoke poured into the air that for months the haze blocked out the sun, and visibility in Wamena was down to a few hundred metres. Merpati didn't fly into Wamena for many weeks at a time, and missionary mercy flights were also grounded, completely stranding unfortunate travellers. By the end of 1997, after four rainless months in the usually lush valley, over 500 people had starved to death in the immediate area of Wamena. While this situation was certainly intensified by El Niño, summer smoke haze and its knock-on effects have become quite regular over recent years. Whilst the thickest smoke has been in Kalimantan and northern Sumatra, it's much more of a problem for travellers here, as almost all travel is by air. It may soon be the case that July to September become months when travellers should steer well clear of travel in Irian.

Wamena and around

At first sight, the town of **WAMENA** appears to be the only blot on the wonderful rural landscape of the Baliem Valley, with characterless tin-roofed buildings, clapped out old minivan taxis and deep slurry-filled drainage trenches along its streets. However, the streets themselves are spacious, as the valley people, used to living in small isolated communities, are loath to live crammed together. Missionary houses lie on manicured lawns behind white picket fences, amongst the strolling, naked Dani and their ubiquitous pigs. The town's **climate** is excellent, cold enough so you need a blanket at night and rarely suffering the daytime swelter of sea-level towns such as Jayapura. An additional bonus for walkers is the heavy, refreshing wind that rushes into the valley in the afternoons.

The **marketplace**, too, is a real attraction – certainly it's a bit grotty, but it boasts a fascinating selection of produce. Stalls are stocked with the healthy looking vegetables from the surrounding fields and are supplemented by such oddities as *horim* penis gourds and the other accoutrements of the valley people. The market is still alive with Dani and Lani peoples in traditional dress – expect to pay around Rp1500 if you want to take a photo of someone, and more if they are done up in "warpaint" for the purpose of being photographed. Stallholders also sell a variety of snakes, frogs, Baliem river goldfish and cuscus, all destined for the dinner table. Sometimes you will even find the sad corpses of endangered species such as the spiny echidna, wrapped in palm packages.

The market was completely burned down recently; it may have been an accident, but many people say it was destroyed deliberately by Dani people, angry at their increasing disinheritance at the hands of migrant Indonesians. Pretty much all of the shops around the market and the bigger businesses are being taken over by opportunists from Sulawesi, Maluku, Java and Sumatra; the Dani see them getting rich and their own situation stagnate, and are understandably resentful. The Dani and occasional Lani people cannot afford the exorbitant taksi fares from their villages, and have often walked for days to sell a few, poor bundles of produce, but all the people you see running warung, shops and driving taksis, are Indonesian. Generally speaking, this aggres-

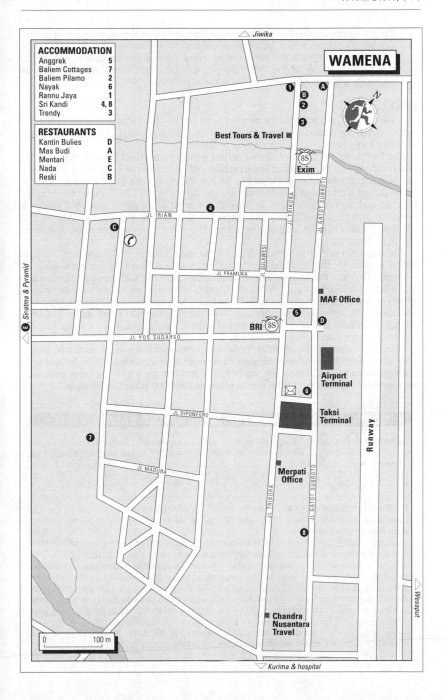

△ Jiwika

WAMENA

ACCOMMODATION
Anggrek	5
Baliem Cottages	7
Baliem Pilamo	2
Nayak	6
Rannu Jaya	1
Sri Kandi	4, 8
Trendy	3

RESTAURANTS
Kantin Bulies	D
Mas Budi	A
Mentari	E
Nada	C
Reski	B

Best Tours & Travel ■

(SS) Exim

JL TRIKORA

JL GATOT SUBROTO

JL IRIAN

JL SULAWESI

JL PRAMUKA

MAF Office

BRI (SS)

JL YOS SUDARSO

Airport Terminal

JL DIPONEGRO

Taksi Terminal

Runway

JL MADURA

Merpati Office

JL TRIKORA

JL GATOT SUBROTO

△ E, Sinatma & Pyramid

△ Wesaput

Chandra Nusantara Travel

0   100 m

▽ Kurima & hospital

sion has not swung against tourists yet, as they are seen as a potential source of income to many, but it's always well to be aware of the unrest in Wamena.

Several of the **villages** in the surrounding valley, such as Jiwika, give an insight into the agrarian way of life of the valley people; a bizarre additional attraction are the ancient, blackened mummies on display in these villages.

Practicalities

Just about all visitors arrive at the **airport** here, and its conspicuous runway is the best landmark for orientation in Wamena. It runs from the northwest to the southeast, and the town spreads away from the runway to the west.

The first thing you'll have to do on arrival is have your **surat jalan** stamped by the police officer who runs a small **information office** inside the terminal. He is one of the best sources of information in the Baliem Valley, speaks good English, and has accompanied all the high-profile tours around the valley (BBC, National Geographic, international surveying teams). In his office is a list of all of the qualified guides in Wamena, with their specialities and languages recorded. If you intend taking a long trip then it's best to vet your guide here first. The office is open when major flights are due in to Wamena.

The **taksi terminal** is right in front of the main airport buildings, and the **post office** is next to the terminal on Jalan Timor (Mon–Thurs & Sat 8am–2pm, Fri 8–11am). They are not tremendously reliable; they have no scales and just guess how much letters weigh and cost. A fair stroll away, but easily identifiable by its red-and-white communication masts, is the **Telkom** office, supposedly open 24hr but often non-operational. Near to the huge, sparkling new church is the BRI **bank** on the corner of Jalan Yos Sudarso and Jalan Timor; they change US dollars cash for a lousy rate and will break large rupiah notes down into denominations more practical for use when trekking. The Bank Exim on Jalan Trikora is pretty much the same, and won't touch other currencies or travellers' cheques. **Transport** around town is either by foot or by pedal-powered **becak**. These are easily hailed and charge Rp500 for most town journeys: perhaps Rp1000 out to the tourist office and Rp3000 round to Wesaput.

MOVING ON FROM WAMENA: AROUND THE BALIEM VALLEY

Battered **minibuses** and **jeep taksis** (that have to be flown in from Jayapura), depart from the taksi terminal, leaving when they are crammed full to bursting. Especially long journeys such as those to end-of-the-road destinations such as Bokondini (5hr; Rp15,000), Pit River (6hr; Rp15,000), Pogga (3hr; Rp7000), Tagime (4hr; Rp13,000), and Pondok Yabbagaima for Danau Habbema (4hr; Rp10,000), leave daily early in the morning and must be booked a day in advance. Ask around the terminal for information. **Taksis** to destinations like Kurima (1hr; Rp2000) leave almost every hour, as do those to Uwosilimo for Jiwika, Waga Waga and Akima. Those to nearby Wesaput and Sinatma leave regularly when full.

Since the valley opened up to tourists, the most popular way of getting around has been to walk out to a destination with an airfield and then catch a mission **flight** back. This method is, however, becoming less and less viable. The pioneer and missionary airlines are generally far too busy to be taking commercial passengers, and are for the most part pretty sick of tourists using their mercy flights as holiday transport. Plane schedules are already overstressed – even the workers themselves need to book flights several weeks in advance – and if you can get a flight to the area you want to go to, at the time you want to go, then you'll be extremely lucky. However, if you're desperate, the missionary airlines, and Pioneers Airfas, Trigana and Manunngal, all have offices in or around Wamena's terminal, and it may be worth asking if they can help you out.

ACCOMMODATION

Because of Wamena's altitude, it can get cold at night, and luxuries such as hot water and heaters are important. **Accommodation** options in town are limited, which at present, with the lack of foreign visitors, is not a great problem. However, should tourism begin to pick up again, and during large festivals in the area, accommodation should be booked well in advance. An alternative to staying in town is the losmen at **Wesaput** (see p.919) across the runway, which is cheap, quiet and well designed.

Baliem Cottages, Jl Thamrin 5 (☎0969/31370). This collection of bungalows are nicely designed, comfortable traditional houses, arranged around well-kept gardens and a restaurant. The bathrooms have no roofs, so theoretically you could take a bath under the stars, however they're presently not equipped with hot water so it probably wouldn't be as indulgent as it sounds. This is the only place in the Baliem Valley that openly sells beer, though at Rp15,000 for a small Bintang you'd have to be pretty desperate. ⑤.

Baliem Palimo, Jl Trikora (☎0969/31043 or 32359, fax 31798). Probably the nicest place to stay in Wamena: the staff are friendly and some speak English. Standard rooms don't have hot water, but the more expensive rooms do, along with satellite TV and their own little private garden and minibar. Bathrooms come with a private rainforest, complete with waterfall, flowers and trees, the roof open to the stars. ⑤–⑥.

Hotel Nayak, Jl Gatut Sabroto 1 (☎0969/31067). Suite rooms here have TV and bath, but no hot water; standard rooms are relatively clean and well kept but are only a few hundred yards away from the runway, with all its daytime racket of planes and taksis. The central areas of the hotel are all charming – the restaurant has a high roof and is hung with Asmat carvings, although food is erratic: it may be possible to eat here if the hotel is full. ④–⑤.

Rasu Jaya, Jl Trikora 109 (☎0969/31257). Standard rooms all have dark and grimy mandi and are pretty threadbare for the price tag. Economy rooms are almost identical but half the price and much better value. ④.

Sri Kandi Hotel, Jl Irian 16 (☎0969/31367). The owners here are friendly and speak a little English, and rooms are reasonable although a little lacking in natural light. ④–⑤.

Hotel Syriah Jaya, Jl Gatut Subroto (☎0969/31306). About 200m walk south of the airport. The rooms are dark and musty with paper-thin walls, but it's the only budget option in town. ③.

Hotel Trendy, Jl Trikora 91 (☎0969/313264). There's nothing particularly striking about this place: it has average rooms with en-suite mandi and doesn't provide breakfast. ④.

EATING

The **rumah makan** in Wamena serve almost identical food, the choice obviously being limited to what the valley can produce, but wonderful prawns, goldfish and crayfish are plucked daily from Sungai Baliem, and the specialty hot lemon/orange juice is a joy on cold valley evenings. For the cheapest food in town, the market is literally surrounded on all sides by Padang-style **warung**. These serve dried river fish as well as boiled eggs or fried chicken in delicious, but occasionally fiery, sambal sauces. Stalls around the market dish up *murtabak*, *bakso* and *soto ayam*.

Baliem Pilamo, Jl Trikora. The restaurant is complete with its own indoor waterfall and serves tasty soups: the macaroni and the chicken and corn are particularly good.

Kantin Bu Lies, next to the airport. Serves decent but expensive Padang food. Their fried chicken is tasty and the prawns are also good. In the evenings, there's a barbecue out front, serving superb goat sate.

Mas Budi, around the corner from the *Hotel Trendy*. The most popular place in town for foreigners, missionaries and wealthier locals. Their speciality is prawns and crayfish at Rp10,000–13,000, and they also serve a variety of Indonesian and Chinese food.

Mentari, Jl Yos Sudarso 46. About 2km out of town out by the tourist office. Easily the best restaurant in the Baliem Valley, it's sparkling clean and constructed of wood from floor to ceiling, with not a scrap of Formica or lino in sight. Succulent shrimp sate fresh from Sungai Baliem costs Rp10,000, and goldfish costs from Rp8000–12,000.

Reski, Jl Trikora next to the *Hotel Trikora*. A friendly place with sound cooking, that's inexplicably always empty. It's a little cheaper than the *Mas Budi* but with a very similar menu.

Shinta Prima, Jl Trikora 17. Next door to Chandra Tours and Travel. It's mainly a karaoke bar, and generally resounds with the wails of Indonesian businessmen. There is an extensive menu with a bit of a disparity between prices: *fu yung hai* is expensive at Rp6000, shrimp sate a positive bargain at Rp9000.

Around Wamena

JIWIKA lies 20km northwest of Wamena and is serviced by regular taksis from the terminal (Rp2000; 1hr): it's a *kecamatan* (administrative capital), which attracts tourists to its nearby showcase villages and strange blackened mummies. Jiwika has one losmen, the *La'uk Inn* (③), a beautifully kept little place with nice gardens and a charming Javanese manager who speaks a little English. They can arrange food with a little notice and have rooms both with and without en-suite mandi. About 100m further up the road from the losmen and on the right-hand side, is a signpost, pointing up a dirt track to the "momi". In the traditional kampung at the end of this track, an **ancient mummified corpse** is kept, its knees hunched up to its chest and its taut flesh sooty black. The village is a real tourist trap, and it costs about Rp3000 to bring the mummy outside or Rp2000 for you to enter the *honai* and see it inside. Don't believe the guest book, which shows other guests have paid tens or hundreds of thousands to see it; they add extra noughts after you leave.

From behind the market in Jiwika, a path heads up the mountainside to **Iluemainma**, a brine spring 1800m above sea level and just over an hour's hike out of the village. Here the women harvest salt by soaking banana stems in the water. These are later burned and the salty ash used to flavour food. If you continue on the main road towards the crossroads town of Uwosilimo, you come to the **Kontitlola Caves**, near the village of **Waga Waga**: the tunnel-like cavern is adorned with stalactites and stalagmites and has a river flowing through it. On the way back to Wamena, the main road passes close to **Akima** village, which also has a mummy, incongruously stuck together with sticky tape.

WESAPUT

On the eastern side of Wamena, the other side of the runway from the town, lies **WESAPUT** village, the turn-off marked by an orange clock tower – without a clock. There are a few traditional *honai* houses by the end of the road and the locals generally dress traditionally in *horim* and grass skirts, but they're very camera conscious. Just show that you've got a camera and you could be assaulted by locals, chanting "seribu, seribu, seribu" (Rp1000, 1000, 1000). On a more pleasant note, Wesaput is an essential trip for its **museum**, the **Palimo Adat** (Rp1000 donation). It's a beautifully laid-out building, built to resemble a *honai*, and contains a variety of Baliem curiosities such as weapons and traditional clothing. The caretaker/curator speaks only Indonesian but if you have a trekking guide, it's normal for him to accompany you here and translate.

Behind the Palimo Adat is a **suspension bridge**; it's a good spot for a swim if you can brave Sungai Baliem, as the water is slow-moving and deep here. Beyond the bridge, a path leads to **Pugima** village. It takes just over thirty minutes to walk there along a good flat path. The walk is far from taxing, and though the scenery isn't as magnificent as in the mountains, it's a good way to view the Dani's agrarian lifestyle. Just off this path is a large cave, fairly musty smelling and damp but satisfyingly spooky.

Taksis come all the way to Wesaput from Wamena, circumnavigating the northwestern end of the runway, and cost Rp400. It's often quicker to walk right across the middle of the runway on the path that starts at the fire station than to wait for a taksi to fill up. If you hear the klaxon which warns of a plane's arrival, do like the locals and run. You can also cut across the fields at the northwestern end of the runway, and then walk down the road. Before you reach Wesaput and on the right-hand side of the road you'll come across the *Wiosilimo Losmen* (③). They have several rooms in slightly kitsch reproductions of *honai*, the walls decorated with mosaic animal murals made from bits of dried plant. It's a nice quiet place to stay, all the rooms have their own mandi and patio and the owners will give you transport to and from town in the evenings to the restaurant of your choice (though you will probably have to help push start their truck).

Trekking in the valley

The Baliem Valley is changing fast, and although Wamena and the nearby villages are still vastly different to anywhere else in Indonesia, you won't experience the really extraordinary aspects of Dani life and culture unless you get off the beaten track. Due to the paucity of roads and the expense and infrequency of flights, this means a lot of **walking** and significant **planning**: see the box overleaf. For information on transport around the area, see the box on p.901, and Travel Details on p.944.

Northern Baliem

To the north of the valley, standing 4750m above sea level, **Gunung Trikora** is Irian's second-highest mountain after Puncak Jaya. Nestling in its northern shadow, **Danau Habbema** is about the most beautiful and mysterious expanse of water in the highlands, mirror smooth, deep and icy cold, and usually framed by perfect blue skies and rocky hills. The air is thin and pure up here, the pleasant warmth of the day changing the instant the sun dips below the horizon to chill nights, with bright stars above. Due to the movements of the OPM (see p.901), this area is sometimes closed to tourists, though travel companies can usually get you a special permit. Danau Habbema is not worth visiting in June and July, when it generally dries up.

Danau Archbold is another exciting and beautiful area to head for, particularly noted for its bird and animal life and named after the first white man to see the valley from the air. It's situated at a lower altitude than Habbema, and has dense forests in its environs, stocked with cuscus, cassowaries and birds of paradise. The best way to visit this little-known and stunningly beautiful area, is to fly to **Kelila** or **Bokondini**, both situated in the northwest of the Baliem Valley, and then trek northeast for several days to the lake.

Eastern Baliem

The areas to the east of the valley, home to the **Yali people**, are becoming increasingly popular for those with the time and money for adventure tours. The Yali are renowned for fierce adherence to custom, bizarre traditional dress and ritual war festivals. Some of the tribes here were cannibals right up until the 1970s, having reputedly eaten two of the highest profile missionaries in the area. The Yali are now the only people who still build wooden towers to keep watch over surrounding territory and warn of advancing enemy tribes. Yali villages are the favourites of many photographers as spectacular festivals and mock battles can be arranged here (for a price).

The Yali region is only accessible by plane and by foot, the usual arrival point being the largest village of **Angguruk**. The village has a mission station, and one of the more frequently used runways in the central highlands: the people here are quite used to Western faces and you will probably be led hand-in-hand with delighted local schoolchildren to the house of the *kepala sekola* who has a room put aside for unexpected tourist guests.

From Angguruk, you'll have to walk out to the surrounding villages, and, if a flight can't be arranged, you'll have to walk all the way from Wamena: a minimum of five days.

PLANNING A TREK

Apart from a few treks in the Baliem Gorge and along other well-forged trails that can be done alone, a **guide** and **porter** are necessary. Most nights will be spent in tribal villages where nobody speaks Indonesian, let alone English, or you may need to bed down in a rough shelter hacked out of the jungle, which most guides are expert at constructing. To be comfortable you will need more food and water for the trip than you can carry for yourself, and if this doesn't convince you to take a guide, bear in mind that main trails are crisscrossed by side tracks that could take you off into the middle of nowhere.

Finding a guide is not a problem: as soon as you land in Wamena you'll be under siege from guides all looking to take you off on treks. It's a little more difficult to find a good guide. All those who are registered with the police and speak foreign languages are listed in the police office in the airport terminal (see p.916), so that's a good place to start. Generally speaking, a guide should **cost** $10–15 a day, though they may charge more for longer treks, and will expect all food and transport to be paid for. Porters and cooks will usually be found by the guide and will cost about $5 a day.

If you go to one of the many **travel companies** in Wamena or Jayapura and arrange a tour through them, you're likely to get a good guide, but prices are usually higher. Chandra Nusantara Tours and Travel at Jl Trikora 17 (☎0969/31293, fax 31297; Jayapura agent ☎0967/31370) has an excellent reputation and is owned by a fluent English-speaker who really cares about how his clients enjoy their treks. They run tours that head as far away as the tree-living Korowai tribes on the brink of the Asmat region, two-week trips to Yali or Lani country, and can even organize special **permits** for visiting Gunung Trikora and Puncak Jaya, when they are officially closed to tourists. Sample **prices** are US$360 for five days in Dani country; US$475 for a nine-day encounter with the western Lani, US$1500 for eighteen days to Korowai and Nomina, and nearly US$3000 for a twenty-day adventure including reaching the peak of Puncak Jaya. All prices are based on seven people participating, and include food, transport from Wamena, accommodation and guides, but may be extra if a plane charter is necessary.

Long treks of a week or more in the Jayawijaya area require even more planning. After the terrible droughts and famine of 1997–98, you cannot count on being able to buy food in the villages. The market at Wamena is a reasonable place to purchase food, although (as long as you do not get charged for excess luggage) it is much, much cheaper to bring supplies from Jayapura. For trekking, the best food is packet noodles, rice and canned sardines in tomato sauce. You can usually buy a few vegetables along the way, and fish, eggs, chicken, snakes or frogs to spice it up.

Other **necessities** will depend on your destination. Anywhere in the valley or around the valley walls you'll need a sleeping bag, fleece, long trousers and, preferably, a woolly hat. If you intend to take a serious trek out of the valley and into the lowlands, then a mosquito net is an absolute must: you can buy them for a few thousand rupiah in Jayapura's market. A **water-purifier** (see p.25) is a real bonus, as is a bottle of flavoured cordial to hide the taste of boiled or iodine-tinged water. Insect repellent with a high percentage of deet, applied all over, will deter fleas, ticks and bed bugs. Though the jungle shelters most guides will construct are excellent, you can improve their water resistance (and keep yourself and your pack dry while walking) with a poncho. Shaking out your boots each morning is essential; they're more likely to be inhabited by cockroaches than scorpions and snakes but it's best to be cautious.

Western Baliem

The western Baliem Valley is home to the **Lani people**, and is notable as the place where Sungai Baliem drops underground into a cavern system, to reappear by the town of **Tiom**. According to guides in Wamena, this stretch of subterranean tunnel was surveyed in 1996 by an American team, who lowered themselves down the raging Baliem on dinghies attached to ropes. However, it is difficult to see how, as the 100-metre-wide Baliem seems to vanish in a whirlpool up against a limestone wall.

This area boasts some of the most spectacular **scenery** in Jayawijaya, forested cliffs plunging down to the valley floor, and gullies thick with jungle carving up the hillsides to form razor-edged ridges. The road is passable by taksi through **Pyramid**, where there is a large Protestant missionary set-up, a church and a weekly market held on Saturdays, to Pit River and on to Tiom where the road ends. From Tiom there are two "major" walking paths that skirt the valley edges and head right up to Bokondini and Kelila in the north. Any walk that attempts to bridge these two areas will take weeks rather than days.

Southern Baliem

South of the Baliem Valley lies the magnificent scenery of the **Baliem Gorge**. Here, tumultuous Sungai Baliem leaves the broad flat plain it has flowed across for some 60km, and tears violently into the steep gorge, with waterfalls and scree-covered rock-faces, and villages precariously perched on cliffside promontories. The area is relatively regularly visited, but still retains a raw, natural appeal, especially when you venture beyond the canyon walls.

The people who live here are **Dani**, the most prevalent of the peoples in the central highlands and possibly the most welcoming. Spending nights in a thatched *honai* to a lullaby of gently grunting pigs may not be especially comfortable, but is certainly an experience you will not easily forget. Most of the internal Baliem Valley in the south has been deforested with slash-and-burn techniques, and is not as enjoyable to trek through. However, the route into the gorge and surrounding mountains is stunning.

KURIMA AND AROUND

The paved road from Wamena now runs all the way to the administrative centre of **KURIMA**: taksis run to the village from 7am until the early evening (Rp2000; 1hr). At Kurima, where the gorge begins, an **airstrip** and **mission** have been cut into a precipitous rockface, 300m above the valley floor.

Just northwest of Kurima at Sugokmo, you can take a trek uphill and west to **Wulik** village. It's a tough three-hour trek for which you'll be rewarded with a magnificent panorama of the valley and a nearby waterfall. From here you can trek round to **Tangma**, a six-hour walk, mostly through dense forest, for which a guide is a must: the scramble down is extremely steep and difficult.

Tangma is arranged around a rarely used airfield where the houses are more modern than the *honai* of nearby settlements. It's wise to stay here with the *kepala sekola*, whose house is at the bottom of the runway. Alternatively, you could push on through **Wamarek** village to areas where several waterfalls tumble down the steep gorge sides. Raging Sungai Baliem is crossed here on a safe, but nonetheless heartstopping **suspension bridge**, ninety minutes' walk from Tangma. During the height of the rains, when the river is in full force, the waters actually lap about the boards as each step causes the slats to lunge downwards. Next to the bridge are the remnants of the old bridge that collapsed a few years back, just to add a touch of apprehension.

From here it's another two to three hours' trek to **Wusurem**, a smaller and more traditional kampung, where you can stay the night, again with the *kepala sekola*. If you speak a bit of Indonesian it's perfectly feasible to do this trek without a guide. Another option is to hire someone in each village as a guide/porter to take you on to the next place, which will be infinitely cheaper than getting a guide from Wamena, and a good way of distributing your money to people who would not normally benefit from tourism. However, if you intend to go on any further than Wusurem, you'll probably have to carry too much food to make this method, or going solo practical.

From Wusurem, the usual route is to continue on to Wet, and then **Passema** or **Soba**. The scenery along this route is dramatic, great ravaged cliff faces torn by landslides, earthquakes and waterfalls. Scree-covered slopes tumble down to the Baliem and its tributaries, with dark green vegetation clinging to any plausible holds. It's possible to make Passema in a day from Wusurem, but Soba will take two days, overnighting in **Werima** village. Both Passema and Soba are set at altitude in stunning scenery, but suffered greatly in the famine and are desperately poor. The airstrips and missions here were set up in the Sixties, and both villages are centred around the airstrips, built more like Swiss log cottages than Baliem *honai*. The dark, planked walls are surrounded by flowerbeds, their windows and gables edged in gay purple and blue paint. It's quite an experience to land at one of these "airstrips", which are little more than small, grassy football pitches.

If you don't fancy backtracking from Wusurem, you can **return to Kurima** on the eastern side of the river. It's a solid day's hike, with the first part through stunning gorge scenery. The latter part however is a little desolate, as the forests are being cleared, presumably for agriculture, with the dreaded slash-and-burn techniques. When you stop to rest, the silence will be cut by the methodical thud of axes coming down on the few remaining trees in this area of the valley. Occasionally a loud crack and then a wrenching creak will be followed by the workmen's whooping chorus.

YALI COUNTRY AND BEYOND
Another exciting alternative, an extensive undertaking but one of the most rewarding treks south of the Baliem Valley, is to head right over the rim of the valley into **Yali country**. Trails from Wusurem and Kurima head over the top of stunning 3600-metre **Gunung Elit**, and then descend for four tough days through wild palm-tree forests to Angguruk, the capital of the Yali tribes (see p.913).

Other possibilities include following the 60km route east described by Benedict Allen in *Into the Crocodiles Nest*, which took him through the mission stations of Ninia, Lolat, Korupun and Sela.

Several tour companies now arrange near month-long treks which continue south from Soba to Holowun, Sumo and Dekai, before taking to canoes and heading into the **Korowai** and **Kombai regions** north of Senggo. These are amongst the most exciting places to visit anywhere in the world and this trip, though extremely expensive and demanding, is a holy grail for explorers. If you arrange the trek independently it will cost upwards of $50 a day per person for everything, and then you will have to arrange your own transport out of Senggo. Only two guides based in Wamena even claim to have experience of this route, and neither speak English. Travel companies charge about $80 a day.

Asmat and the south

The **south** of Irian Jaya features vast areas of inhospitable, untrammelled wilderness. It's possible to fly for hours over the **Asmat region** and see nothing but lightly undulating oceans of jungle and alluvial swamps cut through with vast, meandering brown rivers, with not so much as a glimmer of life. At ground level however, it's a completely different story. Nervous crocodiles duck beneath the water's surface at a canoe's approach, and fabulous birds and reptiles provide flashes of iridescent colour amongst the mossy boughs. The area is known for the **woodcarving** of its few indigenous inhabitants, the **Asmat people**, who construct huge communal **longhouses**, living on sago and animals hunted from the surrounding jungles.

There are two large towns on the south coast of Irian: **Merauke** to the east of the Asmat jungle, and **Timika** to the west. Merauke is quite a decent destination, with Australasian landscapes and wildlife, while Timika is an unpleasant town which has sprung up around **Tembagapura**, the Freeport company's gold-and-copper mine. Generally speaking, if you want to explore this region, you'll need to spend some time in one or both of these places. Between the two lie miles of forests, punctuated by occa-

TRANSPORT IN THE ASMAT REGION

Most travellers enter the Asmat region on the unreliable twice-weekly flight from Merauke to Senggo, and hire longboats from there out into the jungle or down to Agats. At the time of writing, the Merpati office in Merauke (see p.924) ran **flights** from there to Jayapura (daily 8am), Tanah Merah (Fri), Senggo (Wed), Bade (Tues & Thurs) and Kimaam (Wed). Apart from the Jayapura flight, which uses a large aircraft, you cannot rely on any of these. If they do by some miracle go on the right day, it won't be until many hours after departure time, and the smaller planes' susceptibility to bad weather means a very high proportion either get turned back before landing or just don't take off at all.

The flight into Ewer airstrip, which lies very close to Agats and is wonderfully convenient, has not been used commercially for many years. Charter and missionary planes still land here, as well as the occasional flying boat and a couple of Merpati flights during the Asmat festival in August, but for the average traveller, Ewer airport is not an option.

Senggo is probably the most frustrating and expensive place to leave in the whole archipelago. The Javanese merchants who control Benzine and oil sales for the longboats that provide the only practical method of transport here, also control the prices through intimidation: the local Irianese are too scared to talk to you and prices are ludicrous. Even if a boat is already heading to your destination, they would rather go empty than take you along for less than a full charter price. Sample prices include: to the Basman area (7hr in a 15hp boat; $110/5hr in a 40hp boat; $230), to Atsj (6–9hr; $195–290), to Agats (4–8hr; $215–345). For any trip that crosses a seaward river mouth, a 15hp boat is not recommended as they really struggle against the current.

If you are going upriver from Senggo, a **daiyung** (paddle canoe) is far less noisy and gives you some peace to enjoy the incredible sights and sounds of the jungle. It does, however, take an eternity to get anywhere and it's difficult to find people to take you on an extended trip. To get to Basman for the Korowai region takes four days and three nights, and you'll have to sleep rough for at least one of those nights. Coming back, it's much easier to find a boat and takes three days if you paddle hard.

sional tiny villages and a few fair-sized settlements. **Agats** is the focus for visitors to the Asmat, right between the two main towns, an amazing riverside village raised entirely on stilts above the mud and the centre for the culture and art of the area.

However romantic a trip into **the jungle** of the Asmat region may seem, it should not be undertaken lightly. It bears no resemblance to travel in any other part of Indonesia: there's no tourist infrastructure, transport is dangerous and exorbitantly expensive: unless you invest substantial time and money, you'll see nothing much at all. However, if you have the patience and cash, you can access one of the world's few genuine frontiers. In the backwoods are peoples who probably still practise cannibalism, wonderfully exotic birds and vast stands of jungle. Access to the Asmat area is generally either by plane into Senggo (inland in the east), or by boat into Agats, or Otsjanep or Atsj (all on the south coast).

Merauke and the Wasur national park

MERAUKE is a dusty dry settlement that's somewhere between a typical Indonesian outpost and an Australian outback town. Its main street is lined with wire-mesh-fronted stores and blue wooden houses with shaded verandahs, alongside Padang restaurants. The town is at the southernmost point in Irian Jaya, as far east as you can go in Indonesia, and is surrounded by wide expanses of flat, grassy savannah, fading to great stretches of tidal sand and mudflats. Beyond this, innumerable rivers crisscross thick rainforest which covers flat land, rarely raising more than a few metres above sea level. This area comprises the near 690 square kilometres of the **Taman Wasur national park**, protected by the WWF for its exceptional birdlife and Australasian animals.

Merauke was set up in by the Dutch in1902, because the English in New Guinea were complaining about cross-border head-hunting raids by the Marindanim tribes who inhabit the areas to the north. The pious Dutch dully "pacified" and then attempted to convert these tribes, and Merauke became what it is today: the easternmost outpost of the Indonesian archipelago.

Practicalities

The vast majority of visitors to Merauke will arrive at **Mopah airport**, about 3km east of town, generally by the once-daily morning flight from Jayapura. From here, charter a minibus taxi from the terminal (Rp7500). Alternatively, walk out to the main road and flag down one of the blue minibuses heading west. This road is Jalan Raya Mandala, which becomes the main street of Merauke town, where most of the hotels, restaurants and other sites of interest are situated.

The sandy streets are traversed by a surfeit of new **minibuses**, so short of custom that they'll take passengers to the door anywhere in town for Rp500. If your **surat jalan** is checked on your arrival at the airport, you don't need to report to a police station in Merauke. However, if you arrive by boat it might be advisable to report to the main police station on Jalan Raya Mandala. **Tourist information** is handled at the Kantor Dinas Parawisata, Jalan Achmad Yani 1 (☎0971/22588). Nobody here speaks English, though the staff are very friendly and may even give you a tour around town on the back of a motorbike. This is a good place to organize trips around the national park, and to get information about the Asmat region.

The **post office** can be found on Jalan Brawijaya (Mon–Fri 8am–4pm) and there are branches of **Bank Expor Impor** and the **BRI**, both on Jalan Raya Mandala, which will change dollars cash only. There are two good **art shops** in Merauke, the Ude Atsj on Jalan Parakomando 42, being easily the best. Their speciality is Asmat woodcarvings, shields, figures and spears, though they also sell pricey Baliem curios.

Moving on, the **Merpati office** in Merauke is at Jalan Raya Mandala 163, on the way into town from the airport, and the manager, Pak Ronny, will do anything humanly possible to make sure that you get on a flight if there is one.

ACCOMMODATION

Due to Merauke's temperature, a fan at least is a necessity and air-con is very welcome. Few people arrive here direct from other parts of Indonesia without having passed through Jayapura, so the poor value and standard of the **accommodation** shouldn't come as much of a surprise.

Akat Hotel, Jl Prajurit 111 (☎0971/22944). Exceedingly friendly and helpful staff; their central lounge area has satellite TV and all rooms have en-suite mandi. Cheaper rooms have fans, the others air-con. ③–④.

Asmat Hotel, Jl Trikora 3 (☎0971/21065). This hotel offers reasonable rates for its basic accommodation, but is often full with parties of government officials. ③–④.

Marind Hotel, Jl Biak 73 (☎0971/21375). The cheaper rooms here are an absolute rip-off: filthy and fanless. However, the top rooms and the central lounge area are well laid out and pleasant, and all rooms have en-suite mandi. ③–⑤.

Megaria Hotel, Jl Raya Mandala 166 (☎0971/21932). All rooms here have air-con, hot water and TV, and the bathrooms are decked out in pristine dark blue tiles, with bath and shower. ⑤.

Nirmala Hotel, Jl Raya Mandala 66 (☎0971/21932). Has a choice of rooms, with or without air-con, hot water and en-suite mandi: the price includes a simple breakfast. ④–⑤.

Penginapan Murah Sederhana, Jl Angkasa (☎0971/21533). Most Merauke people, including those in the tourist office and other hotels, will swear this place does not exist – it does. It's a very, very basic place that's a little dark and grotty inside, but possibly the only true budget option on the south coast of Irian. ②.

EATING
The **food** in Merauke is really not all that special, but if you've just spent a few days in the jungle, it'll seem like paradise. Venison and kangaroo meat sometimes turn up in the restaurants, as does a reasonable variety of seafood.

Merapi Jaya, Jl Raya Mandala 69. A standard, slightly overpriced Padang restaurant. All the food is available for you to look at in the outside window before you commit to entering.

Nusantara, Jl Raya Mandala 189. If you're desperately in need of fried rice or an omelette, then this is the place to stock up. They generally serve the average Indonesian staples.

Serumpun Indah, Jl Raya Mandala. Right next door to the *Megaria Hotel*, this serves terrific Padang food – excellent curry sauces with chicken, beef, squid, prawns, crab. A full meal costs between Rp5000 and Rp15,000 a head.

The Wasur national park

The **Wasur national park** is particularly enticing to bird lovers, with an estimated 419 species, 74 of which are found nowhere else. The park straddles the southern part of the border between Papua New Guinea and Irian Jaya, and is a world away from the lush, dark caverns of the island's vast jungles. The plain that encompasses Wasur is more reminiscent of the Australian outback; it was only separated from the Australian landmass 8000 years ago, when the Torres Strait was engulfed by rising sea levels. Because Australia and New Guinea were so recently connected, the species are almost identical where climate and habitat allow. Wasur has herds of **wallabies** and **kangaroos**, kookaburras, huge bustards, cranes and flocks of pelicans that coast low over the plains and swarm about the lakes. In addition, a monotreme (egg-laying mammal) echidna related to the duck-billed platypus flourishes here, feeding on the inhabitants of Wasur's omnipresent towering red termite mounds with its powerful claws and thirty-centimetre tongue. The **world's longest lizard**, Salvatori's monitor, is also a resident. The Komodo dragon is much heftier than Salvatori's, but the latter is far longer, growing up to 5m from tail to flickering tongue; it is mainly arboreal, living in the woods that border the grasslands. Of these trees, acacias, gum trees and eucalyptus are the most common, and the scrub beneath them bristles with Australian snakes such as the deadly taipan.

Wasur is best explored on **horseback** or **motorcycle**; horses can be hired in the villages of Wasur, Ndalir or Yanggandur on the outskirts of the park. There are park offices at Ndalir and Wasur, where you will have to register and **pay** Rp5000. You'll probably have to charter a **taksi** from Merauke to get to these places. Alternatively, visit the tourist information and WWF offices in Merauke; both can help to set you up with a motorbike, and the guides may even offer to take you themselves on the back of a bike, though this is very uncomfortable, over dreadful roads. **Accommodation** is either under canvas of your own providing, or in small villages along the main trails.

Senggo

Lying well northeast of Merauke, **SENGGO** is the next stepping-stone to the Asmat region: it's a bleak place, so far inland as to be utterly remote, but with enough deforestation to lack the charm of a jungle village. It sprawls between two kampung, one clustered around the grass airstrip and the other at the river harbour, with a few houses and kiosks along the footpath that joins them. The airstrip part of town is slightly higher than the harbour, and contains the missionary buildings and hospital – Australian homestead-style wooden buildings among pristine lawns, landscaped with palm trees and flowers.

The *Kasim Homestay* is also near the airstrip, charging Rp30,000 a night per person for very basic rooms (④). From here, a path leads downwards about 2km to the river. Just before reaching the wooden harbour, Senggo's other homestay is on the left-hand side: it's unnamed but obvious, as it's the only building more than a single storey high. They have two double rooms here, at Rp25,000 full board or Rp15,000 without food (③). The owner cooks up rice, noodles, fish and meat, which is a considerable improvement on the fare of the town's only warung. There have been several reports of thefts from both of these losmen, so bring your own lock for the rooms and keep your valuables with you at all times.

Kombai and Korowai

A visit to the tree-living peoples of the **Kombai** and **Korowai** regions, which lie west and north of Senggo respectively, is a unique experience. Beyond the "pacification line", no more than 20km to the west of the mission village of Yaniruma, lie the "Stone Korowai", tribes of warlike tree-inhabitants who had no real contact with the outside world and attack anyone who ventures towards their territory with poisoned arrows and spears. To the east of here, between the Dairam Hitam and Eilanden rivers, are a score of tiny settlements, where the natives live as much as 20m up in the jungle canopy, naked except for the cassowary feathers protruding like whiskers from piercings in their noses, and greet visitors with suspicion and wonder.

Villages such as **Yaniruma** and **Wanggemalo** were built by missionaries and government agencies to attempt to lure the Kombai and Korowai people out of the trees. Such places are completely alien to the natives, who are used to living in territories that have belonged to their clan for generations. Inside these territories the people live in households of patrilineal descent in groups of tree houses that may number as few as two or three. The people are traditionally polygamous and exogamous, that is they take many wives, all of whom are from external villages. Marriage is a massive undertaking, involving elaborate transactions and bride prices. Korowai people are all primitive horticulturists, tending sago and banana groves near their tree houses. The women raise domestic pigs, while the men hunt for wild pigs, cassowaries, snakes and anything else that adds protein to their poor diet. In areas close to main waterways, a kind of pidgin Irianese-Indonesian is spoken, which is sufficient to maintain contact with traders.

Depending on how far the river is navigable at the time of year you arrive, the best course of action is to head for the mission villages of **Binerbis**, **Basman** or Yaniruma on the central Dairum Kabur river, or **Sepanape** or **Sirape** on the northern Eilanden river. From Basman, it's a six-hour walk to Muh, which is right on the boundary of Korowai. Kurfa, Ferma and Yapupla villages are all sensational examples of Korowai life. It's wise to approach the area with great **caution** and common sense. In the week we visited the area, missionaries told us headhunters killed fifteen men, women and children, in a single raid on a village in the Stone Korowai region. The same missionaries are certain that cannibalistic practises still exist in these areas.

Agats and around

At the mouth of the Aswetsj river on Irian's south coast, **AGATS** is a peculiar mixture of rustic romance and outright squalor, depending on the whim of the tides. Its rickety kiosks tower either above litter-strewn mud or murky lapping waves, perched on precipitous thick stilts. The pavements are precarious plankways, that range from sturdy ironwood boardwalks to creaking deathtraps. However, somehow it manages to have much more charm than apparently similar Asmat towns such as Atsj and Otsjanep. There's only electricity for a few hours at night, so fans and cold drinks are unfortunately hard to come by.

The **Asmat festival** is based here at the beginning of October, and is one of the few times when you won't be the only foreigner in Agats. The festival involves canoe racing, dancing and a carving competition. All accommodation in Agats will be booked up

ASMAT ART

Asmat art takes several forms, mostly mangrove and ironwood carved into shields, drums, spears, canoe paddles and prows, "soul ships", ancestor sculptures, masks and a kind of totem pole called *bisj*.

The **bisj** pole is the most regarded of the Asmat artforms, and is often over 5m tall, carved from a whole, fully grown mangrove. One heavy plank root is left intact, to form a sort of flag shape at the top of the pole. This is called the *tjemen*, which means penis, and is an intricate fretworked phallic shape protruding from the figure at the top of the pole. The main length of the pole is made up of carvings of famous headhunter ancestors (whose spirit is invested into the figures), one sitting on the head of another. Many of these poles have canoes at the base, suggesting that the pole is itself a development of the soulship. Several poles are made together for a special *bisj* ceremony, a pledge to avenge these ancestors' deaths. No death for the Asmat is by natural causes: either people are killed by enemy tribes, or they die because of the black magic of malignant neighbours, so all deaths must traditionally be avenged. When the ceremony is completed, the pole is thrown into the sago orchards, where it decomposes, allowing the spirits to be released into the sago. When the sago is eaten, the power of the dead ancestor is transported back into the person who consumes it.

Shields are made from the buttress plank roots of the mangrove, and, as with other Asmat carvings, are painted in three colours. The background is usually white, made from chalk mixed in water. Tattoos and bones on the decorative figures are painted in red, mixed from the soil; hair is stained black with charcoal. The **stylized creatures** depicted are connected with cannibalism. The praying mantis is revered as it actually eats its own kind, but as trees are analogous to people in Asmat lore, any animals that eat the fruit (which equates to the brains) of a tree, are also potent symbols. The raja cockatoo, flying fox and hornbill are all used liberally in carvings, and warriors dress up to resemble these animals when on revenge raids, with red eye-patches for the cockatoo and feathers in their hair for the hornbill.

Masks are less common than many of the other forms, as they are not sold for the tourist market. Really more of a full body suit, they consist of a bodice made from cord or rattan basketry, painted red-and-white and with a suitably dramatic face. After a villager dies, a dancer will come out of the forest in a mask, to dance one last time in the place of the deceased. He is then chased into the longhouse, to begin the symbolic journey to the spiritworld. This journey is then continued by the soulship, a small bottomless canoe carving filled with carved figures, which is left outside the door of the longhouse to ferry the deceased to the afterlife.

Under the guidance of the missions, and to cater to the tastes of those who come to buy carvings for export to souvenir stalls in Bali and Java, certain very modern interpretations of these traditional forms have evolved. Most popular is a three-dimensional melee of climbing figures that has developed from the *bisj* pole. Canoe prows and flat paddle-handle carvings have been extended to form beautiful flat friezes, generally in symmetrical shapes, and ancestor sculptures are now being made to last, rather than to rot in the sago groves.

months in advance, but you'll always be able to find families willing to let you stay, or you could camp. It's also one of the few times in a year that commercial **flights** from Timika and Merauke will come here, arriving five minutes away by boat at Ewer, seaplanes landing on the river right in front of town.

The Town

Asmat's major draw is its **museum**, about 300m to the southeast of the helipad. Similar *bisj* poles and shields can be seen at local art shops, but the huge **rattan masks** and **trophy skulls** are fascinating. The most appealing part of the museum is the collection of modern carvings that have won commendation in the annual competition held during the Asmat festival. These are derived from the old forms, but are generally infinitely more appealing to the Western eye, with cleaner, less crude work and remarkable subjects. Some illustrate local stories, others show macabre images from the days of cannibalism, often with darkly humorous caricatures.

Next to the BRI bank is an **art shop** which sells high-quality carvings to American and Japanese bulk buyers. Their prices are very high, but they are willing to bargain. Opposite the *Losmen Pada Elo* are two more art shops: the one on the left sells poor quality work, while the other sells a good variety of shields and figures at reasonable prices. From here, if you walk towards the helipad and then take the first left, there is another shop right by the river – the friendly owner will take time to help you find exactly what you want from his mounds of pieces, and his prices are good. Another shop can be found by the dormitories before the Pusat Asmat, which is located down the second left turning out of town, and after the new dock.

The **Pusat Asmat** (literally navel, or centre of the Asmat) was set up by missionaries to assist **artists**, providing a space where they can live and work in comparatively comfortable circumstances. The central building is a tatty but charming wooden hall, adorned with friezes and *bisj* poles. Most of the year it's almost empty, but during the festival the place throngs with people, cooking around open hearths while they whittle away at wonderful carvings; it becomes a magical place to spend a few hours, chatting and watching the artists work.

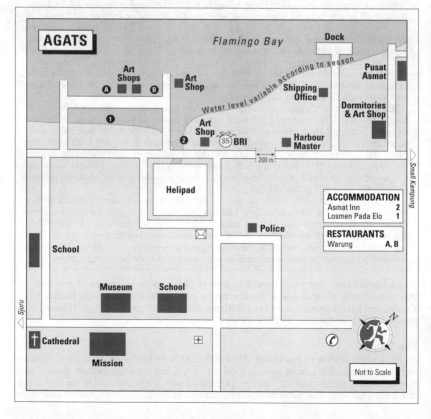

MICHAEL CLARK ROCKEFELLER

The son of the then governor of New York, **Michael Clark Rockefeller**, first visited Irian Jaya in 1961, as a photographer and sound technician for the Harvard-Peabody expedition studying the lives of the Ndani peoples of the central highlands. After his work was completed, he and a friend headed south into the Asmat swamps and were immediately captivated by the astounding primitive art they found there. Twenty-three-year-old Michael decided to return later that year, to study and collect some of this art for the New York Museum of Primitive Art. Two months into this trip, on November 18, 1961, Rockefeller's flimsy canoe capsized at the mouth of the Betsj river. The two Asmat guides swam for shore, leaving Michael and his companion, Rene Wassing, clinging to the upturned hull overnight. The next morning, Michael struck out for shore, with an empty petrol can for flotation, and was never seen again.

Governor Rockefeller himself flew out to Agats to oversee a mammoth search of the area, but it was utterly fruitless. The world's media revelled in the story of a millionaire's son eaten by cannibals, but it's equally likely that strong tides, sharks or crocodiles were responsible. However the cooking-pot theory has many adherents. Lorne Blair visited the Asmat area in the early 1980s to research part of his wonderful book *Ring Of Fire*, and was pretty much obsessed with the theory that Michael Rockefeller had been eaten by cannibals, coming to the conclusion that the villagers of Otsjanep (see p.930) were responsible. His reasoning was that it was revenge for "pacification raids" by white Dutch soldiers, who had massacred all of Otsjanep's tribal leaders a few years earlier, in an attempt to stamp out cannibalism. Like many adventurers who come here, Blair seemed keen to believe in this more dramatic version of the tale, a story of rare theatre from the dying days of exploration.

Practicalities

Everyone arrives in Agats by **boat**, most of which pull up at the foot of the stilts that hold up the main street. From here it's a matter of metres to either of the two losmen. The boardwalks run parallel to the river, and head off 1km southwest to the village of **Sjuru** and northeast to the **new dock**, which has a shipping office nearby which can be handy for information about boats in and out of Agats.

Heading away from the river and the main street, you'll come to a large flat wooden platform. This is used as a **helipad** and for dances during the festival. The **post office** is at the corner furthest away from the main street. Don't be lulled by the fact that there is a branch of the BRI near to the helipad; it has no foreign exchange or credit card advance. If you're anywhere in the 600-kilometre stretch between Merauke and Timika, you'll be living on the rupiah you bring in with you. About 500m to the east of the helipad is the **Telkom building** for domestic and international phone calls. Their service is quite reliable but, as you would expect, very expensive.

MOVING ON FROM AGATS

Moving on is likely to be more of a problem than arriving in town. In the early 1990s, the Pelni ferry *KM Tatamailau* started calling monthly in Agats, but at the time of writing it was sailing straight past. Infrequent cargo boats may take you on to Timika or Merauke, but again, don't hold your breath. There is one boat that monthly plies the route from Merauke to Senggo, stopping off at several villages en route, but it runs to an unpredictable schedule, is often out of service, and is squalid and dangerous on high seas. The missionaries may be able to help you out and it is worth checking with their office near the museum to see if they have any **flights**, otherwise you may have to **charter** a plane or boat. Bear in mind that to charter a motorboat to Timika (the most common escape for those who are really stuck), may cost 1.5 million rupiah.

ACCOMMODATION AND EATING
There are two **losmen** in Agats, with total room for about 35 guests. You should have no problems getting a room, except during October, when the festival means most rooms will be prebooked. Along with all the residential properties in Agats, the losmen have real problems with water. Their only supply is run off from their roofs, which, given the almost continual rainfall here, is usually more than enough. However, just a few dry days mean that all water has to be carted along the boardwalks in barrels from a small tributary. The *Asmat Inn* (④–⑤) is the best losmen in town, clean and relatively cool, decked out in dark wood and with artworks dotted around the foyer. Their basic rooms come with choice of mandi in or outside. The *Losmen Pada Elo* (④) is right on the main boardwalk and can get a bit noisy. Each room has only two beds and a bit of tatty lino, and no mandi or fan.

Both losmen provide breakfast and can get basic **meals** for you. Opposite the *Pada Elo*, is a small **warung** selling rice with fish, chicken and vegetables for between Rp3000 and Rp8000. Around the corner and opposite the art shop is a similar place. Strictly speaking Agats is a "dry" town and alcohol is frowned on; some of the stores will sell you whisky but at high prices.

Nearby villages

Only 1km down the boardwalks southwest of Agats is **SJURU** village, really more like a suburb of Agats. The village has a single *jeu* (longhouse), which you can enter and take photos of for a donation of around Rp2000. Sjuru is probably the best place to go to rent *daiyung* (paddle canoes), great for a day's paddle in the jungle (around $30 a day).

Southeast of here, **YEPEM** is just about reachable in a day by paddle canoe, or it's ninety minutes by Jonson (motorized canoe). Yepem is an attractive village where locals fish, and net prawns, crabs and other river fare. At low tide, village boys play on the steep mud banks, sledding down them in tiny dugout canoes and splashing around in the slime. There is also some quality carving done here.

A full day's paddle south of Yepem, or an hour in a Jonson, **PER** village is renowned for the quality of its friezes and *bisj* style climbing figures. From here, many travellers go on to **Owus**, about 10km upriver, where they make fantastic *bisj* poles and have a new losmen, and **Beriten** which has a perfect *jeu*. Up the Betsj river from here is **ATSJ**, the biggest and one of the least pleasant villages in the Asmat area. Much like Agats, the whole town is raised up on stilts with tin roof shacks rather than wooden *jeu*. However it is surrounded by sawmills and deforested mud swamps, and its boardwalks are covered with rusting oil barrels and broken engines. If you get stranded, there is quite a nice losmen in Atsj, with en-suite mandi and fan in every room (④).

Continuing south from Atsj, you come into the area known as the **Casuarina Coast**, where the people wear only traditional clothes and are far less often contacted. The area was named for its huge casuarina trees, which are unfortunately being rapidly logged and are disappearing. You'll definitely need a 40hp Jonson boat to visit the area; it'll take five hours from Agats to **OTSJANEP**, the nearest large village. Otsjanep itself is not much to look at, very much a mission station with some grass lawns, very unusual in this part of Asmat, and a modern church. It's amazing how much Otsjanep must have changed since the Blair brothers stopped here researching *The Ring Of Fire*; they walked in on a tribal war.

Timika

Although **TIMIKA** is older than the Freeport mines, it feels now much like an overspill town for the rich "copper city" **Tembagapura**, located some 70km away in the mountains. The immediate surrounding countryside is a fairly bleak sandy floodplain that gets dusty and dry during the middle of the year. The town itself is pretty sleazy and unfriendly, and there are several bars and less salubrious hotels with extortionate prices which are best avoided. Timika is, however, a place you'll find difficult to avoid if you're visiting the south of Irian, and it's a possible gateway to Irian Jaya from the rest of Indonesia.

If you're coming from the Asmat region, then Timika's saving grace is its restaurants and the incredible and incongruous *Sheraton Hotel*, which offers five-star luxury. The **mines** themselves contain the world's largest reserves of gold and copper, and create a total daily profit of well over US$1,000,000. They remain the subject of continued misery among indigenous peoples: a tiny proportion of the employees of copper city are Irianese, most being imported from other parts of Indonesia. Tribal lands were claimed by the Indonesian government with barbaric stringency and widespread slaughter, and the waste from the site continues to pollute the surrounding land. For this reason, Timika has been the site of numerous protests and riots, some of which have resulted in armed response from the Indonesian army. In 1997 for example, fifteen protesters armed with bows and arrows were gunned down by the military. Timika remains a place to be vigilant.

Practicalities

Most visitors arrive in Timika at the airport, located about 4km to the northeast of town; there are Merpati flights daily to and from Sentani. Occasionally, minibus taksis head into town, otherwise motorbike taxis will take you for about Rp1500. Boats arrive at **Amamapare port**, about 15km southeast of Timika – regular taksis connect the port and town, or you can hire a motorbike taxi. The **Pelni** ferry *KM Tatamailau* stops in Timika once a month on its way to Merauke.

At the centre of Timika town is the **market**, which has a few Padang-style restaurants but doesn't sell much of interest. The **post office** is located at Jalan Yos Sudarso 17 and is infinitely more reliable than any of the others in the south of Irian, and the **Merpati** office can be found on the outskirts of the market. The Freeport mines are off limits, except to those who have professional reasons and **permits** for visiting the area, which can only be obtained in Jakarta.

ACCOMMODATION

There are no budget **hotels** in Timika: a couple of hotel/brothels will give you a bed full of lice where you may be robbed, but the price will be little less than those of the decent hotels listed.

Losmen Amole, Jl Pelikan 14 (☎0901/321125). A reasonably quiet and well-kept place, though some rooms smell a bit musty. All have mandi and fan and electricity only in the evenings. ④.

GSBJ Komoro Tame, Jl Cenderawasih 2 (☎0901/321962). A super-plush place with a large pool; all rooms come with hot water, spring beds, parabola TV, breakfast and laundry. Tends to fill up at the weekends with mine workers. ⑦.

Jasa Hotel, Jl Yos Sudarso 14 (☎0901/321911). The entranceway to the *Jasa Hotel* is through a noisy billiard hall and arcade. The rooms all have parabola TV and air-con, but are a little dark and dingy. ⑤.

Lawamena, Jl A. Yani (☎0901/321128). A good clean place where all the rooms have fan and en-suite mandi. ④.

Marannu, Jl Yos Sudarso 48 (☎0901/321312). All the rooms here have mandi and fan, the floors are clean and tiled and it's cheaper than in town. ④.

Sheraton Hotel, on the outskirts of town near the airport (☎0901/394949, fax 394950). Has everything you would expect from a Sheraton: tennis courts, a pool, health centre, several bars and restaurants. In addition, it's a beautifully designed and grandly decorated building. ⑨.

EATING
Timika is close to the sea, and **seafood** is definitely the best buy here. Chicken and beef are extortionately expensive, but many places cook reasonably priced prawns, crab and squid on coals out in front of their shop.

Amole Jaya, Jl Freeport 66. If the restaurant is open, it serves staples such as *cap cay* and *fu yung hai*, but they're a little pricey.

Cafe 61, Jl Yos Sudarso 25. The best restaurant in town, dishing up excellent seafood barbecued out front for around Rp10,000. The crab and asparagus soup is really special at Rp7500.

Kebun Sirih, Jl Alsani. Squid and fish are cooked out front on the griddle for between Rp6000 and Rp15,000. Most of the food is fresh and very tasty.

Kharisma, Jl Tamara 93. Speciality of the house is *garo ricu ayam*, a hearty piece of chicken, fried in a very hot and spicy sauce – delicious, but expensive at Rp15,000.

Seafood Lestari, Jl Yos Sudarso 14. Serves reasonable *ikan bakar* and standard Indonesian dishes. Next door, the *Jakarta 99* is an identical place.

Warung Bangkalan, Jl Komp Pasar 103. Serving barbecued fish and Padang food; there are several similar places around the market but this is the best.

Puncak Jaya, the Lorentz reserve and the Paniai lakes

The most potent attraction near Timika is **Puncak Jaya**, the highest peak in Southeast Asia (5030m) and one of only three snow-capped equatorial mountains in the world. Unfortunately, although it's a tantalizingly short distance away, it's very difficult to access Puncak Jaya from here, as it would mean crossing Freeport mine property, which is very politically sensitive. The usual starting point for an ascent is Illaga village to the east, usually reached by plane from Wamena. A climb of Puncak Jaya, sometimes known as Carstenz peak, takes eight days each way, and you won't get a **permit** unless you go with an established tour company: try Chandra Nusantara Tours and Travel at Jalan Trikora 17 in Wamena (☎0969/31293, fax 31297; Jayapura agent ☎0967/31370).

To the east of Timika is the massive **Lorentz reserve**, one of the best protected, most remote stretches of rainforest remaining in the world; it comprises an amazing 34 different ecosystems, from mangrove swamp to banks of snow. The area stretches over some 15,000 square kilometres, and is the largest conservation area in Indonesia. Over half of all Irian's birds and mammals live here, 639 species of birds and 123 species of mammals, including tree kangaroos and possums. It's accessible by longboat from Timika's port, but it should be noted that it was while studying in the northeastern highland section of Lorentz that Dan Start and his colleagues were kidnapped and frogmarched through the jungle for four months by the OPM. An expedition into this area will need to be planned extensively in advance; with enough notice and money, tour companies in Jayapura can plan tours for you.

To the northeast of Timika and near **Enoratali** is the beautiful area of the **Paniai lakes**. The valley around these lakes is much like a smaller version of the Baliem, with pygmy peoples living stone age agrarian lifestyles. A nearby mountain reserve features abundant mammal- and birdlife. This area suffered greatly from Indonesian pacification in the 1970s, and was additionally decimated when imported Javanese pigs (gifts from the Indonesian government supposedly to placate the locals) were found to be riddled with a type of tapeworm completely alien to Irian. These imported gifts spread disease through the entire populace causing widespread deaths. Paniai was, at the time of writing, off-limits to Westerners; when it opens again it may be easier to reach from Nabire (see p.938).

The Bird's Head Peninsula

The **Bird's Head Peninsula** (Vogelkop in Dutch, Kepala Burung in Indonesian) contains some of the least explored areas in the world, with mountain ranges, lakes and forests leading down to swamps in the south. It's a very difficult area to visit, much of it being subject to continual conflict between Indonesian forces and the Pemka wing of the OPM, based around Manokwari. Trying to get a **surat jalan** to most of the peninsula's regencies is a constant headache, and outside of the main towns you'll find no transport or tourist infrastructure at all.

The largest town in the Bird's Head is **Sorong**, a settlement with few redeeming features, based around harvesting oil and timber. However, you'll have to stop here if you wish to visit the **Raja Empat Islands** or **Pulau Waigeo**, which feature intact stands of forests, home to the marvellous birds of paradise. **Manokwari** is the second biggest town in the Bird's Head, and the location most favoured by missionaries. There are some beautiful tropical islands in the vicinity, with white-sand beaches and teeming coral reefs, but probably the biggest attraction is the **Anggi lakes**, which lie to the south in the **Arfak mountains**. The scenery of the lakes, which sit in valleys high above sea level, is utterly spectacular, and the surrounding forests are renowned as the home of some exquisite butterflies. If you plan to visit **Cenderewasih Bay**, then you'll probably have to base yourself in **Nabire**, a small, quiet coastal town with excursions to beaches, waterfalls, deserted islands and Irian's only hot springs. Cenderawasih Bay is a fine bird-watching site, and the diving is terrific. However, don't expect any dive schools to facilitate things for you: if you want to dive here, then you're going to have to sort the whole thing out yourself.

The **Bomberai peninsula** lies at the throat of the Bird's Head, a southwestern chunk of mountains and forest below massive Bintuni Bay. **Fak Fak** and **Kaimana** are the two towns of note in the peninsula, both unusually pleasant for largish Irianese

---

BIRDS OF PARADISE

In 1522, Magellan landed in Seville with several **birds of paradise** skins he had purchased in Maluku. The birds' legs had been removed by trappers, and Europeans immediately seized on the idea that they were actually built this way, and were born in the air, spending their entire lives aloft and supping on dew. This myth was not properly dispelled until 1824, when Rene Lesson became the first Westerner to see the birds alive. Shortly after, in 1884, when German rule commenced in northeast New Guinea, 50,000 bird of paradise pelts were shipped to Europe to adorn women's hats. This trade continued right up until 1924, when legislation was passed to protect the birds, which by then were almost extinct.

There are 43 species of birds of paradise in the world, and New Guinea has 38 of them. Most of these species are notable for the male's extravagant tail plumage that can be well over double the length of the body: the King Of Saxony bird of paradise has similar feathers, but they cascade from behind its head, while others have huge chest pouches or coloured linings to their mouths. The purpose of these outlandish accoutrements is to attract a female of the same species in the darkness of the forest canopy, and is usually complemented by a courtship dance and song. Some, such as the raggiana, hang upsidedown from branches like bats, others clear a hole in the leaves above to create a brilliant shaft of sunlight to dance in. The male birds gather together at special courtship trees called leks, and drab females cluster around to choose the most handsome mate. Normally hard to detect in the jungle's half light, they return habitually to show off on the same stage and are thus easy prey for vigilant poachers.

towns, and notable for nearby cave paintings, similar to those produced by Australian aborigines. Unless you're **flying** around the region, getting between any of these towns will either take a very long time or will be horrifyingly expensive, most probably both. The Pelni ferry *KM Tatamailau* links all the major towns once a month, and the *KM Ceremai* and *KM Dobonsolo* ply routes along the north coast fortnightly. There are occasional smaller boats and cargo ships, all of which will redefine your idea of discomfort.

Sorong and around

SORONG is nobody's idea of a seaside resort town, a glum stretch of tin-roofed shacks fronted by littered shores, which melts away into glummer transmigration settlements. The second largest city in Irian after Jayapura, Sorong, which was located on nearby Doom Island until 1965, became something of a boom town after Dutch Shell started drilling for oil nearby in 1932. Other industries such as logging followed, and have now taken over as the oil stocks diminish. Now pearl farming is one of the biggest businesses in the area, with numerous Japanese pearl farms, including that at **Pulau Kabra**, which is the largest in New Guinea.

Most visitors will arrive by air, at the **airfield** on Pulau Jeffman, which is a set Rp10,000 speedboat trip from Sorong town. From the pier you can walk to most places in town, but there are also plenty of taksis available: the dock for **Pelni ferries** is a short walk west of here. A **surat jalan** is not strictly necessary for Sorong town, but if you intend to visit anywhere else around the area you'll need one. Check in upon arrival at the **police station**, on Jalan Basuki Rahmat. The Expor-Impor **bank** on Jalan Arfak Kamp Baru and the Bumi Daya on Jalan Achmad Yani, will both change money, but as yet have no facilities for credit card advances. The **post office** is also on Jalan Achmad Yani, situated slightly closer to the port, and both **Garuda** and **Merpati's** offices can be found at the extreme eastern end of Jalan Achmad Yani.

Accommodation

Sorong has a variety of **hotels**, some as close to budget as you will find in Irian.

Batanta Beach Hotel, Jl Barito (☎0951/21569). Close to the port, the *Batanta* offers small but reasonable rooms, with a choice of en-suite mandi and fan. ④.

Cenderawasih Hotel, Jl Sam Ratulangi 54 (☎0951/21966). Quite a plush establishment; all rooms have air-con and bath. Has a large restaurant with occasional karaoke. ⑤.

Hotel Indah, Jl Yos Sudarso 4 (☎0951/21514). The closest place to the port, with some very reasonably priced rooms. Good views from the sea-facing rooms in the upper storeys. ③.

Hotel Manise, Jl Jend Sudirman (☎0951/21456). The town's one real budget hotel. It's not especially well kept and the rooms are tiny, but it's about the cheapest place in Irian. ②.

Sahid Mariad Hotel, Jl Achmad Yani (☎0951/23535). The last word in luxury in the Bird's Head. All rooms come with hot water, satellite TV, and air-con. Expect to meet all the town's expats in the restaurant at night. ⑧–⑨.

Eating

Night **warung** near the port serve sate and *ikan bakar* over barbecues outside the shops; there are also places serving nasi campur and fried noodles around here. The major hotels have expensive **restaurants** with limited European and Chinese food, often in air-con rooms with hostesses and karaoke.

Dafior, Jl Misol 84. Has great sea views and a good selection of Chinese food at reasonable prices.

Irian beach, Jl Yos Sudarso. Specializes in baked fish, squid and prawns. All dishes can be served sweet and sour, or barbecued. A whole fish costs around Rp12,000.

Marino, Jl Sam Ratulangi 26. A good selection of Indonesian and Chinese food, including crab and prawn dishes at around Rp8000.

Miami Lido, Jl Yos Sudarso. Standard inexpensive mix of Indonesian staples and Chinese favourites such as *fu yung hai*.

Nearby beaches and islands

Cassowary Point, 8km to the north of town, has the best accessible beach on the mainland, with a reasonably intact coral reef. You'll need to charter a taksi for around Rp10,000, except at the weekends when locals pour down there to picnic and there's plenty of public transport. Better beaches can be found twenty minutes away at **Pulau Matan** and ten minutes away at **Pulau Buaya** (Crocodile Island). The former is the best bet, with beautifully clear water and clean, white-sand beaches lined by thick forests.

The village of **Klayili**, 5km west from Sorong or ten minutes by taksi, has a nearby hot spring surrounded by forest. The water is said to have healing properties, and, altogether, it's a lovely spot for a dip. At **Sansapur**, a five-hour speedboat trip north around the coast, is a stunning **beach** which has a reputation as a turtle-breeding and egg-laying ground. The surrounding countryside is also alive with birds and jungle.

The **Raja Empat islands** to the east of the Bird's Head Peninsula – Batanta, Waigeo, Salawati and Misool – are all sanctuaries for birds of paradise, but they aren't accessible by public transport, so you'll have to charter a boat from Sorong harbour. The nearest spot on Batanta takes about four hours by speedboat from Sorong, some of the further islands will take several days. In addition, bird-watchers can feast their eyes on exotic species such as terek sandpipers, hooded pittas, singing stralings, various honeyeaters, and puff-backed meliphagas: the red and Wilson's bird of paradise are also endemic to Waigeo and Batanta.

Manokwari and around

Surrounded by dark green hills and deep blue sea, **MANOKWARI**, at the eastern edge of the peninsula, has more to maintain a visitor's attention than most towns of comparable size in Irian. Its surrounding islands, beaches, mountains and lakes provide some very enjoyable **excursions**, and the facilities that have sprung up to cater for Manokwari's burgeoning missionary population make it a good place to base yourself. The town first received the Word from Ottow and Geisler, two Protestant priests from Germany who set up a mission here in 1855 and, despite their low conversion rate, the town has been a hub for pioneer pastors ever since. Alfred Russell Wallace (see p.974) also had a brief stay here, studying birds in the 1850s. During World War II, the highlanders who lived in the mountains south of here were air-dropped rifles by the Allies in the hope that they would fight off the Japanese, who had made several bases here and lived in many cave encampments around Manokwari. Legend has it that, not satisfied with just shooting the enemy, the tribes decided to eat their corpses, terrifying the invaders, who soon withdrew.

Practicalities

Most visitors will either arrive at the **Rendani Airport**, ten minutes out of town, or at the Pelni dock which is about as central as it is possible to get, and walking distance from most hotels. From the airport you can either take a taxi which should cost between Rp5000 and Rp10,000, or walk out to the main road and flag down a minibus taksi heading into town.

It's best to report to the local **police** at Jalan Bhayangkara before heading off into the wilderness, as they'll want to check your **surat jalan**. Information about the area can be gleaned from the **tourist office** (Mon–Sat 8am–3pm) on Jalan Condronegro, where the staff have a bundle of leaflets and are always delighted to see foreigners. There are several **banks** in Manokwari, but the Expor-Impor (Mon–Fri 8am–2pm) on Jalan Yogyakarta is the only one that has facilities for foreign exchange. The 24hr **Telkom office** can be found on Jalan Kota Baru, and there are several wartels around town. The **post office** is located on Jalan Siliwangi.

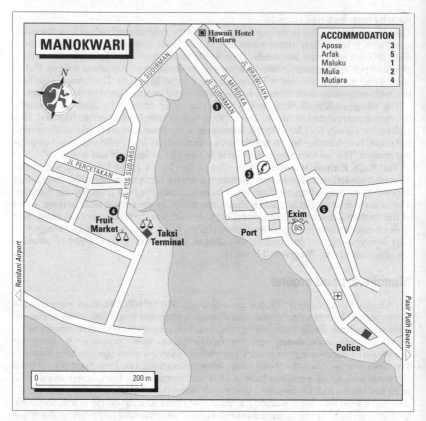

ACCOMMODATION

Apose	3
Arfak	5
Maluku	1
Mulia	2
Mutiara	4

If you're planning to trek in the reserves of the **Arfak mountains**, you'll first require a permit from the **WWF**, whose offices are at Jalan Trikora Wosi on the way to the airport. The tourist office is useful for helping with arranging trips, and there are several tour operators in town, offering package deals for bird and butterfly watchers, marine enthusiasts and mountaineers. Their charges are high, but as travel around here can be a real headache to organize, you might well decide it's worthwhile. Rante Madik Tours can be found at Jalan Yos Sudarso (☎0962/21397), and Cahaya Alam Agung Tours are at Jalan Kota Baru 39 (☎0962/21153). There are also a few souvenir, and **arts and crafts** places, the best known and most established being the Cinta Alam, above the market on Jalan Pasar Sangeang. They sell Asmat carvings, lots of old porcelain and occasional pinned dead butterflies.

ACCOMMODATION

Most of the **hotels** are in Kota, the part of Manokwari town that hugs the eastern shore of Doreri Bay. Most accommodation is mid-range, but some are unusually good value for Irian.

Losmen Apose, Jl Kota Baru (☎0962/21369). One of the cheapest places in town, with a choice of private or shared mandi. All rooms come with fan. ③.

Arfak Hotel, Jl Brawijaya (☎0962/21293 or 21195). Once a resort for Dutch officials, the *Arfak* retains a certain colonial presence, and has the added advantage of views over Dorerei Bay. ④.

Hotel Maluku, Jl Jend Sudirman (☎0962/21948). Has a choice of passably clean rooms, from those with shared bath and fan to ones with TV and air-con. ③.

Hotel Mulia, Jl Yos Sudarso (☎0962/21320). Friendly and efficient staff, clean rooms and breakfast make this the best deal in Manokwari. ③.

Hotel Mutiara, Jl Yos Sudarso (☎0962/21782). The most luxurious place in town, with air-con, TV, hot water and breakfast included. ⑤–⑥.

EATING
The best-value **food** is to be found at night stalls that set up near the market on Jalan Pasar Sangeang and around the taksi terminal. Here you can get excellent *ikan bakar* and sate for a few thousand rupiah.

Hawaii, Jl Sudirman. Serves Indonesian and Chinese food, with some seafood. The crab and corn soup is excellent at Rp8000.

Hotel Mutiara, Jl Yos Sudarso. Not surprisingly the best place in town, with air-con and music some evenings. Mainly Chinese food, though there are also a few Western dishes, and it's all quite reasonably priced.

Sea Food New Garden, Jl Trikora. A good selection of barbecued seafood: ignore the menu and ask what's good and fresh that day.

Around Manokwari

The most popular destination in the immediate vicinity of Manokwari is **Pasir Putih** beach, 3km to the east of town; regular taksis from the terminal in town will take you there. The water is quite clear and the sands are lined by thick forest. **Taman Gunung Meja** (Table Mountain Park), is a pleasant excursion, offering excellent views of the city and Dorerei Bay. A trail from close to the *Arfak Hotel* will take you uphill to the **Monument Jepang** in Table Mountain Park, which commemorates the first Japanese landings in the area. There are some rich areas of forest around here, full of birds and butterflies and with good paths and occasional views out over the coast.

Other excursions include the nearby islands of **Mansinam** and **Leman**, which, with their coral gardens and gorgeous beaches, are the archetype of a tropical paradise. The former is the site of the first missionary landing in the Manokwari area, and has a monument to the two unfortunate priests who perished here having converted nobody. Off the west coast of Mansinam, is a submerged **Japanese wreck** which makes for sensational snorkelling if your lungs are powerful and the waters clear.

Further afield (perhaps too far to warrant a journey in itself), is **Danau Kabori**, 25km from Manokwari on the road to the transmigration settlement of **Ransiki**, and serviced rarely by public transport. It's a good spot for fishermen and there's some good walking in the area.

The Anggi lakes

The most dominant and impressive sight around Manokwari are the **Arfak mountains** which lie to the south, and, in the valley they enclose, the **Anggi lakes**. The valley contains many groups of traditional peoples which, though they have been converted to Christianity, are still fascinating to visit. The valley is a particularly fine place to trek, with a cool, breezy climate and stunning panoramas. The forests along the lower mountainsides feature some fantastic butterflies, huge multicoloured creatures of fantastic beauty. The birdlife too is extravagant, with mountain firetails, honeyeaters and lorries flocking out to feed at dawn.

Even the lakes are at altitude, so bring a sleeping bag and some warm clothing: as soon as the sun goes down the temperature falls, usually to around 4°C at night. A small **airstrip** at Anggi near **Sureri village**, the largest in the area, services the highland area. The flight in itself is fabulously exciting: you skirt over the rim of near 3000-metre mountain ridges in a twin Otter, plunging down to the lakeshore. Merpati and MAF both make the trip from Manokwari twice weekly ($14), but if you are feeling more energetic you can walk from Warmeri, 40km from Manokwari on the east coast of the peninsula, or Ransiki (see p.937) in about three days. You'll need an additional entry on your **surat jalan** for the Arfak mountain area.

Nabire and Cenderawasih Bay

The mellow, seaside town of **NABIRE** at the extreme south of Cenderawasih Bay, with its friendly locals and fine coastline, is one of the more charming towns in Irian. It's the capital town of Paniai district that includes the Paniai lakes and most of **Cenderawasih Bay**, an area that has the potential to be one of Asia's great scuba-diving locations, with hundreds of kilometres of fringing reefs, but is still utterly without provision for casual visitors. At the moment, most visitors who want to explore the Cenderawasih **national reserve**, for bird-watching or trekking, have to do so by taking expensive organized tours out of Manokwari or Jayapura.

Some of the major islands in the reserve are **Anggromeos**, which has fine beaches and coral reefs as well as substantial indigenous birdlife, **Rumberpon** which offers more of the same and scores of giant sea turtles which come to the protected areas to breed and lay their eggs, and **Wairondi**. To get anywhere in the reserve or Cenderawasih Bay as a whole, you'll need to charter a boat; the best places for this are Ransiki, Nabire and **Wasior**, a small village on the east coast of the Bird's Head. Wasior has a small airstrip serviced weekly by Merpati and occasionally by MAF. There are also boats here from Ransiki. Nabire is accessible by daily Merpati flights from Biak and Jayapura, and the Pelni ferry *KM Tatamailau* and Perentis boat *Ilosangi* both stop here. There is organized **accommodation** in Nabire, but in Wasior and Ransiki you will have to improvise.

The Bomberai Peninsula

For those with a lot of money, time and patience, the **Bomberai Peninsula**, the throat of the Bird's Head, is a rewarding destination. The coastal scenery is astounding, with stark white-and-grey limestone cliff-faces and islands cloaked with tangled vegetation, the soft rock cut dramatically by wind and tides. The pretty towns of **Fak Fak** to the northwest and **Kaimana** to the southeast are quiet little settlements that see few foreign faces. From these towns the most usual excursions are by boat or foot, to see the **painted cliff-faces** that have fascinated explorers since their discovery three centuries ago. Much like some of the aboriginal art of Australia, these astounding paintings show human and animal figures, boomerangs and abstract designs, but the most frequent image is that of a human hand, created by blowing pigment over the hand like a stencil. Most of the paintings can be found in caverns on offshore islands or on seafacing cliffs, though some of the finest examples are inland. All of them take some getting to.

This region was the first to be **colonized** by the Dutch in all of Irian, who made their base at Fak Fak in the late seventeenth century. Because of its proximity to Maluku, the Bomberai Peninsula was under the sway of the Sultan of Tidore for many centuries. Thus it has had more influence from Islam than Christianity, and the towns have mosques and a higher proportion of practising Muslims than any other place in Irian.

Fak Fak

The town of **FAK FAK** is extremely charming, with a strong colonial Dutch feel; it's situated on a hillside leading down to **Tambaruni Bay**, and is surrounded by limestone hills, dotted with rivers and caves. It also has one of the world's most terrifying **runways**, a tiny airstrip that's been hacked into a precipitous rocky ridge, with gut churning drops to either side. On the northern coast of the peninsula is **Kokas**, a smaller village close to many of the rock art sites. A road from Fak Fak is nearing completion, but if you can't take a minibus you'll need a Jonson dugout and a guide – you should be able to find someone through one of the losmen – to find all of these places: the best rock art site is several days' walk away in the Fak Fak mountains. Another good trip from Fak Fak is to **Maredred waterfall**, a beautiful twenty-metre cataract tumbling into an icy pool. It can be reached in about fifteen minutes by boat from town.

PRACTICALITIES

On arrival, you should register your **surat jalan** with the **police**, at their offices on Jalan Tambaruni. The **tourist office** is up on the hillside, at Jalan Diponegro, and though they speak no English, the staff can be quite useful in helping you to set up a **tour** to see surrounding areas. The **post office** is also on a steep hill, at Jalan Letjen Haryono, with the 24hr **Telkom** on Jalan Cenderawasih. The bank for foreign exchange is the Expor-Impor, located on Jalan Izak Telusa, which is the main, coastal street of the town.

There's not a great deal of choice in terms of **accommodation**, but there are so few visitors that you shouldn't have any trouble finding a bed. The *Hotel Marco Polo*, just off Jalan Izak Telusa, is probably the best place to stay (☎0967/22218; ③–④); they have quite basic rooms with fan and decent views. The *Tembagapura* at Jalan Izak Telusa 16 (☎0967/22136; ③–④) is another option, featuring a choice of rooms with air-con or fan, all with en-suite mandi. The only other place here is the *Sulinah*, near the police station at Jalan Tambaruni 93 (☎0967/22447; ③–④); their rooms are reasonable and well kept and they offer full board for a decent price.

The *Marco Polo* and *Tembagapura* both have good **seafood restaurants** and the *Amanda* at Jalan Izak Telusa serves Indonesian and Chinese meals.

Kaimana

KAIMANA may be tiny and remote, but it's a minor legend in Indonesia, as a well-known popular song tells of the town's magical sunsets, said to be the most beautiful in the world. It's another Muslim settlement, serviced by **Utarom airstrip** and with more fantastic side trips possible, to see cave paintings, coral reefs, beaches, orchid groves and forests filled with birds and butterflies. Merpati has regular flights into Kaimana from Biak, Timika, Sorong, Nabire and Fak Fak, and the Pelni ferry *KM Tatamailau* is scheduled to stop here monthly but in reality often just sails straight past. There are two reasonable hotels here: the *Selatan Indah* on Jalan Brawijaya (☎0957/21230; ④–⑤), and the *Diana* on Jalan Trikora (☎0957/21053; ③–④).

Pulau Biak

Pulau Biak is about the only place in Irian whose charms are easily savoured. It's the first stop for most planes from Java and the rest of Indonesia, and its beaches, coral reefs and waterfalls are only hours away from the main airport. By contrast, adjoining **Supiori** and the surrounding islands such as **Yapen** and **Numfor** are much more difficult to visit, with no tourist infrastructure and little transport, and so their lagoons and forests, filled with brilliantly coloured fish and birds, remain practically undiscovered by tourists. Less than a degree south of the equator, Biak is hot and sticky, and during the rainy season of January to June it rains practically every day, though this actually provides some relief from the humid swelter.

Biak had great strategic significance during **World War II**, when the Japanese occupied the island. The Americans invaded in 1944, and the Japanese retreated to massive cave systems which they had turned into functioning subterranean towns. They launched raids on the US forces from the cover of the caverns, the Americans responding by pumping gas into the tunnels and igniting it, blowing most of the occupants away. Many of the remaining Japanese committed *hari kari*, realizing they were about to be defeated. There are still reminders of the war in many places in these islands: decrepit tank shells, sunken wrecks and caves filled with oily wartime debris.

The island group's main town is **Kota Biak**, located on the south coast of Pulau Biak. There are no other large towns here, though there are a scattering of smaller settlements, most of which are also coastal. The highlights of a journey to Biak are generally beaches, reefs and waterfalls, of which the islands have an abundance. The **Padaido Islands** off Biak's southeastern coast feature great snorkelling and diving, and the northern part of Pulau Biak and Supiori have several stunning **waterfalls** such as **Warsa** and **Wardo**, cascading out of thick tropical jungle. In addition, in the vicinity of Biak and Bosnik towns are an excellent **bird and orchid park**, a huge **crocodile farm** and some of the World War II **caves**.

Kota Biak

At the centre of the south coast of Biak lies **KOTA BIAK**, the only sizeable settlement in this entire island group. Though it is not of much interest in itself, it's an excellent base for exploring the islands. It's also worth considering as an alternative base to Jayapura if you're intending forays into the northern part of Irian: the airport services most of the mainland towns and you can get a **surat jalan** here. The island's main attractions aren't far away and it's a fairly relaxed port town, with some good restaurants and hotels.

Practicalities

If you're arriving from the **airport**, just walk out to the road and flag down any bemos heading west – the town is only a couple of kilometres away. The **main road** which comes into town from the airport starts as Jalan Mohammed Yamin, then becomes Jalan Achmad Yani and finally turns into Jalan Sudirman. The road is parallel to and only a stone's throw away from the sea, and pretty much everything you'll need is along either it or the side road, Jalan Imam Bonjol. You don't actually need a **surat jalan** for Biak, but you'll need one for the nearby Yapen and Numfor islands. You can also get a surat jalan to cover you for travel around all of Irian at the **police office** on Jalan Diponegro: take two photographs.

The **tourist office** (Mon–Sat 8am–2pm) is about halfway between the airport and town on Jalan Mohammed Yamin 58 (☎0961/21663), and is accessible by bemos joining the two; staff here are very friendly and helpful, but have limited resources. The main **post office** (daily 8am–6pm) is slightly further back towards town, also on Jalan Mohammed Yamin – there's a poste restante service. The modern 24hr **Telkom** building can be found on Jalan Yos Sudarso, about a ten-minute walk east of **Bank Exim**. This bank is the most prominent in Biak, but not necessarily the best place to change money. It's well worth checking the rates at the BNI and Danamon (Mon–Fri 8am–4pm, Sat 8am–noon) on Jalan Imam Bonjol, before changing foreign currencies. Generally the Danamon has best rates for US dollars, Australian dollars and Singapore dollars cash and they also handle credit card advances, while the BNI may be able to process traveller's cheques with a little cajoling. For buying air tickets and reserving flights, the **Merpati** office is near the airport, and the **Garuda** office downtown at Jalan Sudirman. The latter has friendly English-speaking staff who will do whatever they can to help you out.

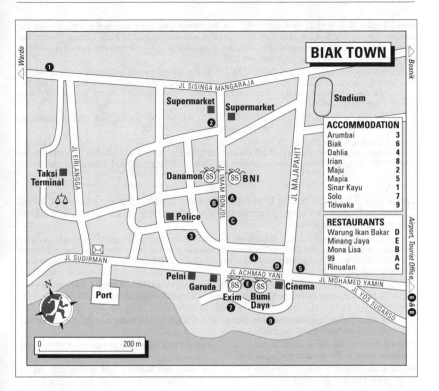

ACCOMMODATION

The best **hotel** in the island group is the *Biak*, not actually in Biak town, but in Bosnik, a 45-minute taksi ride down the coast to the southeast. On the whole, the quality of accommodation in Biak is excellent when compared with the rest of Irian, but still more expensive than the rest of Indonesia.

Arumbai Hotel, Jl Selat Makassar 3 (☎0961/21835, fax 22501). The standard rooms are good value, the top rooms exceedingly plush and priced accordingly, with satellite TV, air-con, hot water; there's a swimming pool. ⑦–⑧.

Biak Hotel, Jl Yaspan, PO Box 138 (☎0981/81005, fax 81003). Four-star luxury a 45-minute drive southeast of Biak town; they are desperate for custom and eager to discount prices. Facilities include landscaped gardens and a huge pool, a disco, sailing, dive shop, fitness centre, tennis courts and several restaurants. All rooms have air-con, hot water, TV and fridge. ⑦–⑨.

Hotel Dahlia, Jl Selat Madura 6 (☎0961/21851). As the price is always for a room with two beds, it's cheap for two people but expensive for one. The rooms smell a little damp but all have mandi and fan. ④.

Hotel Irian, Jl Mohammed Yamin, PO Box 137 (☎0961/21939). Right opposite the airport if you need somewhere to collapse after the cross-archipelago flight. Has a good bar, gardens and sea view, and all rooms have en-suite mandi and a choice of air-con or fan. ⑤–⑥.

Hotel Maju, Jl Imam Bonjol 45 (☎0961/21841). The basic rooms here are decent value, with attached mandi. Air-con rooms all have TV with satellite and bilingual option, but at the price are a little drab and scuffed. ④–⑤.

Hotel Mapia, Jl A. Yani 23 (☎0961/21383). All the rooms here have attached mandi, though the cheapest are not much of a deal as they have no fan, a necessity in sweaty Biak. Luxury rooms have air-con and are pretty cavernous. The hotel bar is sculpted like a hollowed-out pumpkin, and is a nice if rather expensive place for a cold beer. ④–⑤.

Losmen Sinar Kayu, Jl Selayar 1 (☎0961/21613). The economy rooms with outside mandi are the best value in town, well kept and clean around very well-crafted wood-beamed halls. Ekonomi rooms with en-suite mandi, on the other hand, are rather threadbare and musty; the air-con rooms are very overpriced. ③–④.

Losmen Solo, Jl Wolter Monginsidi (☎0961/21397). Inexpensive rooms with shared mandi; all have fans. The best, quietest rooms are the ones nearest the sea. ③.

Hotel Titiwaka, Jl Selat Madura 13 (☎0961/22005). The price here includes three square meals a day, plus transport to and from the airport. All rooms have hot water, air-con and satellite TV with bilingual function. They arrange a variety of trips around the island and rent masks and snorkels by the day. ⑥.

EATING

The **food** in Biak is the best in Irian Jaya, with some fantastic Padang places and lots of Chinese restaurants serving up excellent seafood. Beer here is also much more affordable than on mainland Irian.

Bakmi Jakarta, Jl Sedap Malam. Aside from the notoriously grumpy proprietress, this is an excellent place, with inexpensive Chinese food and an extensive menu, including about thirty different ways of cooking noodles. A good portion of lobster costs Rp25,000, and the crab and asparagus soup is excellent (Rp6000).

Ice Cream Palace, *Hotel Arumbai* Jl Selat Makassar 3. Overpriced Indonesian food, but a good spot for a hamburger or fishburger; fried chicken and fries, pizza and ice cream are all also on the menu.

Warung Ikan Bakar, opposite the *Hotel Mapia* on Jl A. Yani. A very basic warung that sells excellent fresh seafood, barbecued out front.

Minang Jaya, in the arcade on Jl A. Yani, just before the Bank Exim. Serves quality Padang food: the *ayam bakar* is exceptional and costs Rp8000.

Mona Lisa, Jl Imam Bonjol. Opposite the *99*, this place has karaoke and air-con, and serves Chinese food at average prices.

99, Jl Imam Bonjol. Full air-con and darkened windows, rated by the locals as the best Chinese and Indonesian place in town.

Ratu Kuring, Jl Selat Makassar 55. Serves excellent fried chicken for Rp3500. The hostesses are very friendly and they have an air-con eating lounge.

Rinualan, Jl Imam Bonjol 22. A good Padang place with several different curry sauces: hygienic and swish.

Salam Manis, Jl Imam Bonjol. Next to the BNI bank, this place has cheap cold drinks, and a limited menu of nasi goreng variations at very reasonable prices. Fish and mixed vegetables costs Rp5000.

Umum Jakarta, Jl Imam Bonjol 10. A well-cooled place with immaculate white tile floors, Chinese-run and selling both Chinese and Indonesian cuisine. Prices are high but the food is tasty. Fried beef in oyster sauce costs Rp14,000; fried chicken in *cai sim* is especially recommended and costs the same.

Around the island

The only other settlement of any size on Biak is **BOSNIK**, not much more than a sprawling fishing village, but the site of the last word in luxury, the *Biak Hotel*. They have a dive shop (☎0981/81050, fax 81051) that can organize a variety of tours in the immediate vicinity, charging US$75 a day for two dives, with all equipment and lunch provided. Some of the best spots for **snorkelling** are also near here: **Saba beach** in front of the hotel has a good spot to the side of the small pier, and **Barito village**, about 5km east from the *Biak Hotel*, has some great spots. At Barito, there's a fantastic drop-off with schools of lionfish, barracuda and occasional Napoleon wrasse and sharks.

The best places for snorkelling and diving are in the **Padaido Islands**, which lie to the southeast of Bosnik. Unfortunately, unless you charter a boat, they're very difficult to access. On Wednesdays and Saturdays when there's a market in Bosnik, you may be able to get a boat with the locals – on other days if you're on the beach and you see a boat heading off just ask them where they're going and try to hitch a lift. The charter option is very expensive, perhaps Rp200,000 for a day, however if you're into snorkelling then it's well worthwhile. The islands of Pakreki, Mansurbabur, Mapia, Rurbon and Patodui all have excellent reputations for their reefs and fishlife, but almost all of the Padaidos are bound to have something to offer.

All of the three attractions below are accessible by catching a minibus from Biak Kota to Bosnik (30min; Rp1000) and asking to be let off at the relevant site. If you're interested in military history, head for **Gua Jepang**, about 6km east of Biak town, one of the caves that the Japanese hid in to evade American detection, leading ultimately to their incineration. It's best visited at dusk, when no other visitors are around, and the bats, monitor lizards and snakes that inhabit it all come out to feed. The caves are filled with rusting oil drums nestling amongst bulbous limestone outcrops, intertwined with tree roots that hang down in ropes from the cavern roof high above. Pay Rp5000 at the house and museum opposite the entrance, and walk through the graveyard of old bomb shells, plane propellers and destroyed jeeps and down a flight of steep slippery steps into the cave. The **Japanese War Memorial** is a couple of kilometres away from the caves at the seafront, and consists of a large concrete bowl with several memorial plaques and picnic tables alongside a beautiful palm-lined stretch of sand with the skeleton of a beached shipwreck. To one side is a tunnel where the remains of several Japanese victims are kept inside steel boxes, adorned with flowers and photos of the dead. Bones and fragments of clothing are clearly and macabrely visible inside the lidless boxes. The **Taman Burung dan Anggrek** (opening hours dependent on the whim of the keepers; Rp2000) is an excellent bird park on the way to Bosnik from Biak. Two huge, fully grown cassowaries roam free around the park, alongside birds of paradise, mambruk and assorted birds of prey.

Other destinations around Biak have far less reliable public transport, and will generally involve long waits for battered minibuses to take you over deeply-rutted roads. However, the far corners of Biak are not often visited and offer some rewarding destinations. Probably the best excursion is to **Wardo** in the northwest of Biak. The road splits just before the village: take the left fork in the road and carry on down to Wardo village. Here the river flows into the sea in a beautiful estuary, and a bridge high above the river makes a sensational diving board. From Wardo village you can hire a motorboat or paddled outboard to take you upriver through the jungle to the Wardo **waterfall**. Prices are high, but it's a great trip (2hr; Rp25,000), with snakes and lizards on the boughs and brilliant birdlife.

Pulau Yapem

Only a quick flight or day's boat ride from Biak, **Pulau Yapem** remains extremely untouristy, seeing few Westerners. The only town of any size here is **SERUI**. There's a daily Merpati flight from Biak to Serui, and the Pelni ship *KM Tatamailau* goes from Jayapura to Serui and then on to Nabire once a month. Upon arrival in Serui, report with your **surat jalan** to the police station on Jalan Bhayangkara. There are three hotels here, the cheapest being the *Bersaudara* on Jalan Jend Sudirman (☎0981/31420; ③). They have decent rooms with choice of en-suite or shared mandi and fan. Of the several **restaurants** in Serui, the *Banuwa Beach* at Jalan Pantai Banawagoro is probably the best, serving Chinese, Indonesian and even a few European dishes. Their speciality is baked fish, which costs around Rp9500 for a whole fair-sized specimen.

The island is renowned for its birdlife, and has huge stands of orchid-filled tropical forests and coastal mangrove swamps. Some of the attractions around the island include **Haribi Waterfall**, some 20km from Serui, and stunning **Danau Sarwandori**, 5km from the town.

travel details

Getting to Irian from Indonesia's capital city of Jakarta, will take you across two time zones and take a minimum of eight hours flying; the only realistic way to get to the region is by **plane**. There are no roads to speak of in Irian Jaya, apart from a few in the Baliem Valley and around the major towns, meaning that you can only get around by plane, boat or foot.

Pelni ferries

For a chart of the Pelni ferries, see pp.36–37 of Basics.

Agats to: Timika (*KM Tatamailau*, monthly; 24hr); Merauke (*KM Tatamailau*, monthly; 32hr).

Ambon to: Sorong (*KM Dobonsolo*, monthly; 22hr).

Biak to: Jayapura (*KM Ceremai*, 2 monthly; 18hr/*KM Dobonsolo*, monthly; 19hr); Manokwari (*KM Ceremai*, 2 monthly; 10hr/*KM Dobonsolo*, monthly; 10hr).

Fak Fak to: Kaimana (*KM Tatamailau*, 2 monthly; 9hr); Sorong (*KM Rinjani*, 2 monthly; 29hr); Tual (*KM Rinjani*, 2 monthly; 11hr).

Kaimana to: Fak Fak (*KM Tatamailau*, monthly; 12hr); Timika (*KM Tatamailau*, monthly; 20hr).

Manokwari to: Biak (*KM Ceremai*, 2 monthly; 9hr/*KM Dobonsolo*, monthly; 8hr); Nabire (*KM Rinjani*, 2 monthly; 11hr); Sorong (*KM Ceremai*, 2 monthly; 11hr).

Merauke to: Agats (*KM Tatamailau*, monthly; 24hr).

Nabire to: Serui (*KM Umsini*, 2 monthly; 8hr).

Serui to: Jayapura (*KM Rinjani*, 2 monthly; 15hr/*KM Umsini*, 2 monthly; 18hr); Nabire (*KM Rinjani*, 2 monthly; 8hr).

Sorong to: Ambon (*KM Dobonsolo*, monthly; 22hr); Manokwari (*KM Dobonsolo*, monthly; 16hr); Ternate (*KM Ceremai*, 2 monthly; 20hr).

Timika to: Agats (*KM Tatamailau*, monthly; 24hr); Merauke (*KM Tatamailau*, monthly; 32hr).

Flights

Merpati and Garuda have flights into Irian from Java and Bali. These flights originate in Denpasar or Jakarta, and usually stop in Ujung Pandang before arriving in either Biak then Jayapura or Timika then Jayapura.

Biak to: Fak Fak (weekly; 2hr); Jayapura (twice daily; 1hr); Manokwari (daily; 1hr 10min); Nabire (3 weekly; 1hr 15min); Numfoor (2 weekly; 50min); Serui (6 weekly; 35min); Sorong (4 weekly; 1hr 10min); Timika (4 weekly; 1hr 5min).

Jayapura to: Manokwari (4 weekly; 2hr 10min); Nabire (5 weekly; 1hr 50min); Serui (weekly; 2hr); Tanah Merah (weekly; 1hr 40min).

Kaimana to: Fak Fak (6 weekly; 1hr); Nabire (4 weekly; 1hr).

Manokwari to: Anggi (2 weekly; 35min); Fak Fak (weekly; 1hr 25min); Wasior (weekly; 1hr 5min).

Merauke to: Bade (2 weekly; 55min); Kepi (weekly; 1hr 25min); Kimam (weekly; 1hr 10min); Senggo (weekly; 1hr 40min); Tanah Merah (weekly; 1hr 15min).

Nabire to: Enarotali (3 weekly; 40min); Fak Fak (4 weekly; 2hr 30min); Illaga (2 weekly; 1hr 5min); Kaimana (4 weekly; 1hr).

Sorong to: Ambon (6 weekly; 1hr 5min); Fak Fak (5 weekly; 1hr 5min); Kaimana (4 weekly; 2hr 30min); Manokwari (weekly; 1hr 10min); Nabire (4 weekly; 4hr); Timika (weekly; 3hr 30min).

Timika to: Ambon (4 weekly; 3hr 10min); Biak (4 weekly; 55min); Fak Fak (weekly; 3hr); Jayapura (6 weekly; 1hr); Kaimana (weekly; 1hr 30min); Sorong (weekly; 4hr 30min); Ujung Pandang (2 weekly; 2hr).

Wamena to: Apalapsili (weekly; 50min); Bokondini (weekly; 45min); Karubaga (2 weekly; 35min); Kelila (weekly; 30min); Mulia (2 weekly; 45min); Tiom (weekly; 30min).

THE HISTORICAL FRAMEWORK

Prior to the colonial era, the history of Indonesia is the aggregation of separate histories. The country is, after all, a modern invention: until the Dutch subsumed most of the islands under the title the "Dutch East Indies" towards the end of the nineteenth century, the Indonesian archipelago was little more than a series of unrelated kingdoms, sultanates and private fiefdoms whose histories, though they overlapped occasionally (and, given their proximity to each other, inevitably), remained distinct.

A second obstacle to overcome is the lack of decent historical records and other evidence. Few contemporary accounts were written, most of those that were have perished, and almost all early buildings, being made of wood, have either burnt down or rotted away.

The guide chapters have more information on the specific histories of each island, and the following account merely describes generic trends – the first inhabitants, the arrival of Islam, the beginning of sea trade and so on – that affected most or all of the archipelago.

BEGINNINGS

Hominids first arrived in Indonesia about eight hundred thousand years ago. Excavations in 1890 by Dutch-born paleontologist Eugene Dubois uncovered parts of the skull of *Pithecanthropus*

erectus, since renamed *Homo erectus erectus* – or **Java Man** as he's now more popularly known – in the tiny village of Sangiran near Solo.

Homo sapiens first made an appearance in about 40,000 BC, having crossed over to the Indonesian archipelago from the northern parts of Southeast Asia – the Philippines, Thailand and Burma – using land bridges exposed during the Ice Ages that temporarily connected the archipelago with the mainland. Later migrants brought with them specialized knowledge of rice irrigation and animal husbandry, sea navigation and weaving techniques. From the seventh or eighth centuries BC, the **Bronze Age** began to spread south from Southern China. Important centres for Bronze Age skills arose in Annam and Tonkin in what is now northern Vietnam, famed for their bronze casting, particularly of drums, decorated with animal, human and geometric patterns. The drums have been found throughout Indonesia, as have the stone moulds used in their production.

EARLY TRADERS AND KINGDOMS

One of the methods of rice cultivation brought by the early migrants was the **sawah**, or wet-field cultivation, which suited the volcanic soil of Java and, to a lesser extent, Bali, perfectly. This method of cultivation, however, is extremely labour-intensive, and in early Indonesia required co-operation between villages in order for it to succeed. This inter-village co-operation necessitated a degree of organization and leadership and, inevitably, an established hierarchy emerged between the villages. These tiny first-century AD village federations gradually evolved into the first **kingdoms** in the archipelago.

Trade with other islands – and, later, with India, China and the rest of Southeast Asia – also began at this time. Some historians believe that these merchants arriving from India were the first to bring Hinduism to the archipelago. The people of the Indonesian archipelago, once exposed to Hinduism, quickly converted to the faith. Early Hindu inscriptions from around the third century AD have been found in places as far apart as Sulawesi and Sumatra, and early Indonesian rulers were usually portrayed as incarnations of Shiva or Vishnu. By the fifth century, a myriad of small Hindu kingdoms, such as the fifth-century **Tarumanegara** kingdom in West Java, peppered the archipelago.

THE SRIWIJAYA, SALIENDRA AND SANJAYA KINGDOMS

The **Sriwijaya** kingdom, based in Palembang in South Sumatra, was the most successful of the early Indonesian kingdoms. For approximately four hundred years, beginning in around the seventh century AD, it enjoyed unrivalled power, controlling the Melaka Straits – and the accompanying lucrative trade in spices, wood, camphor, tortoise shell and precious stones – and extending its empire as far north as Thailand and as far east as West Borneo. Sriwijaya also enjoyed a reputation as a seat of learning and religion, with over a thousand Buddhist monks living within the city, studying Sanskrit and Buddhist scriptures.

Despite this power, the town of Sriwijaya was not a huge place, little more than a strip of houses stretching for a kilometre or so along the banks of Sungai Musi. Influence was confined to the region's coastal ports; as the basis of the Sriwijayan's wealth and power was the trade that passed through the straits, they had little incentive to head inland and subjugate the people of the interior.

Thus, whilst the Sriwijayans enjoyed supremacy around the coasts of Indonesia, small kingdoms began to flourish inland. In particular, the rival **Saliendra** and **Sanjaya** (the latter sometimes known as Mataram) kingdoms began to wield considerable influence in their homeland on the volcanic plains of Central Java. Unlike the Sriwijaya's, these two rival kingdoms could boast huge populations, which they mobilized to build monumental structures such as the magnificent temple at **Borobudur**, built by the Buddhist Saliendras, and the manifold temples of **Prambanan** that owe their existence to the Hindu Sanjaya Empire.

While the Sriwijaya Empire enjoyed by far the greater wealth and influence than either of these dynasties, and its territories extended for much further, the coastal location left it vulnerable to attack from overseas. The hold over the more remote outposts was extremely tenuous too: apart from paying a regular tribute to the Sriwijayans, the rulers of the more remote corners of the empire were allowed to rule without interference. The Sriwijayan empire was thus little more than a collection of small kingdoms and, as a result, following a devastating attack perpetrated by the **Cholas** of southern India in the twelfth century, it broke up completely into its component parts. The Saliendras and Sanjayas too, after engaging in internecine fighting for centuries, found their control wilting as new empires emerged in the east of Java.

THE MAJAPAHIT EMPIRE

The **Majapahit Empire** enjoyed unrivalled success for almost a hundred years, from its foundation in 1292 to the death of its greatest king, **Hayam Wuruk**, in 1389. Based in Trowulan in East Java, the Majapahit (whose name means Bitter Gourd) were a Hindu people who enjoyed their greatest successes under the guidance of their charismatic prime minister and general, **Gajah Made**, a former royal guard who rose to power after putting down an anti-royalist revolt in 1323. During his lifetime, the Majapahit enjoyed at least partial control over a vast area covering Java, Bali, Sumatra, Borneo, Sulawesi, Lombok and Timor. It was the first time the major islands of the Indonesian archipelago had been united, however loosely, under one command.

The Majapahit Empire is usually referred to as Indonesia's **golden age**, and it's true that during Gajah Made's term of office the empire wielded considerable influence over much of East Asia, conducting mutually beneficial relations with the courts of China, Vietnam, Cambodia and Siam. As well as economic prosperity, the Majapahit empire also saw the first flowering of Indonesian culture. The *Nagarakertagama*, an ancient historical text from Central Java, was written at this time, and though little is known about the lifestyle and political organization of the Majapahit royal house, it is believed that the courtly traditions still found in Indonesia were borrowed from it. The success was continued by Hayam Wuruk – the grandson of the founder of the Majapahit dynasty, Vijaya – who ascended to the throne in 1350, while Gajah Made was still serving as prime minister, and reigned for 39 years.

Hayam's death, however, precipitated the slow collapse of the empire. The arrival of Islam on Java and a massive revolt in the north of the island soon after Hayam's demise left the empire weak and in disarray, and although it managed to survive for over a hundred years longer on its new home in Bali, it was never to regain its former power.

THE ARRIVAL OF ISLAM

Islam first gained a toehold in the archipelago as early as the fifth century AD, during the rule of the Buddhist Sriwijaya Empire. Merchants from **Gujarat** in India who called in at Aceh in northern Sumatra were the first to bring the message of Mohammed, followed soon after by traders from Arabia, who went on to found small settlements on the east coast of Sumatra.

From Sumatra, Islam spread eastwards, first along the coast and then into the interior of Java and the rest of Indonesia (Bali, Flores and Irian Jaya excepted), where it syncretized with the Hindu, Buddhist and animist faiths that were already practised throughout the archipelago. The faith also spread to **Melaka**, which had become the pre-eminent port in the region.

The first Islamic kingdoms in the archipelago emerged not on Sumatra, however, but on neighbouring Java. Small coastal sultanates grew in the vacuum left by the Majapahit. The **sultanates** of **Demak**, **Cirebon**, **Jepara** and finally **Banten** (in west Java near Jakarta) took it in turns to take control of the north coast. This was also the period of the **Wali Songo**, nine holy men, who, from their bases on the north coast, spread the word of Islam throughout Java and beyond.

THE PORTUGUESE AND THE SPICE TRADE

The first Europeans to exploit Indonesia's abundant natural resources arrived in the sixteenth century. It proved to be impeccable timing. A united Indonesia, that had almost emerged under the Majapahit Empire less than a hundred years before, would probably have been able to repel any attempts by European traders to muscle in on the lucrative **spice trade**. As it was, the Majapahit, severely weakened by attacks from the nascent Islamic states emerging on the north coast of Java, could offer no resistance, and though these Islamic states, and the **Gowa** and **Makassar** kingdoms of southern Sulawesi – the first Indonesian power to trade regularly with Aborigines from Australia and Papua New Guinea – flourished briefly towards the end of the sixteenth century, none of them were sufficiently powerful to offer any real opposition to the Europeans.

The **Portuguese** were the first Europeans to arrive. Portuguese ships, following in the wake of **Vasco de Gama's** trailblazing journey around the South African cape in 1498, began appearing in the seas around Indonesia in the early sixteenth century. As with the Dutch who followed eighty years later, the Portuguese weren't in the Indonesian archipelago for the glory of the empire, but simply to get rich as quickly and expeditiously as possible. What drew them to Indonesia were its immense natural resources and, in particular, the unique produce of the **Moluccas (Maluku)**, which soon became known as the **Spice Islands**. Pepper, nutmeg, **cloves**, **mace**, **ginger** and **cinnamon** were all produced on the Moluccas. They were the ideal cargo, being light and compact and with a long shelf life. They were also extremely highly prized in sixteenth-century Europe, where they were used to preserve meat and hide the taste of semi-decayed food, as well as being a vital ingredient in early medicine.

To ensure a smooth passage through the archipelago, and to provide an ideal springboard for an invasion of the Moluccas, the Portuguese, under **Alfonso d'Albuquerque**, attacked and took control of the once-invincible port of Melaka in 1511. The Moluccas fell to **Magellan**, Albuquerque's sidekick, the following year. From then on the Portuguese operated a virtual monopoly over the spice trade that lasted until the latter part of the sixteenth century.

Despite this, most of the Indonesian islands were unaffected by the Portuguese presence, and life outside of the Spice Islands continued as before. But the Portuguese had left the door open to other European powers to explore the Indonesian archipelago. Portugal's traditional enemy, the **Spanish**, with the help of Magellan (who, having quarrelled with the Portuguese king following his return from the Moluccas, defected to Spain in 1512) established themselves to the north in the Philippines in 1521, from where they fought a ferocious and long-running battle with the Portuguese over the ownership of the Spice Islands. (Incidentally, one of Magellan's ships, the *Vittoria*, which visited the Moluccas on its return to Spain, was the first ship to circumnavigate the globe.) The Portuguese and Spanish finally signed a peace accord in which the Spanish were pronounced rulers over the Philippines, while Portugal kept the Moluccas.

THE DUTCH CONQUEST OF INDONESIA

In 1580 Portugal was annexed by Spain, and their iron grip on the spice trade relaxed. The Spanish themselves were defeated by the British a few years later in 1588, opening the way for the **Dutch**, themselves part of the Spanish Empire at this time, to explore the Indonesian archipelago. Their forays began in 1595, when **Cornelius de Houtman** led an ill-starred expedition of four ships to Java. When they returned two years later, only 89 of the original 249 crew were left; most had fallen victim to scurvy. They had had to burn one of their ships for want of crew, and while in West Java they had also managed to upset the local Bantenese, killing one of their princes. Nevertheless, the expedition had brought back a small profit for its investors, and a second expedition the following year proved much more successful, reaping four times the amount invested. Soon Dutch fleet followed Dutch fleet round the southern capes of South America and Africa, with each bent on exploiting the seemingly endless trading possibilities that the archipelago offered.

Rivalry with the British at this time was intense. By 1600, the Dutch, by now the supreme European trading power in the region, felt it necessary to amalgamate the various Dutch fleets operating in the archipelago into a monopoly organization, to prevent the local sultanates from trading directly with the Chinese and British. Thus in 1602, the **United Dutch East India Company (VOC)**, was founded, with monopoly control over trade with the Moluccas. To further ensure that they maintained control over the spice trade, the Dutch invaded and occupied the Banda Islands, part of the Moluccas, in 1603. It was the first overtly aggressive act by the Dutch against their Indonesian hosts. Two years later, the VOC successfully chased the Portuguese from their remaining strongholds on Tidore and Ambon, and the Dutch annexation of Indonesia began in earnest. Trading vessels were now being replaced by war ships, and the battle for the archipelago commenced.

THE VOC AND THE MATARAM EMPIRE

By the end of the first decade of the seventeenth century, the VOC had begun to build,

almost by accident, a loose but lucrative empire. Although their motives remained purely pecuniary, and their influence over much of the archipelago was still small, they were given considerable responsibility by the Dutch government, who authorized them to be their official representatives in the archipelago. As John Crawfurd, the British resident in Java from 1811 to 1816, wrote of the early VOC:

The first Dutch adventurers to the East were a set of rapacious traders, who found themselves unexpectedly called upon to exercise the functions of politicians and sovereigns.

At the helm of the VOC at this time was the ruthless **Jan Pieterzoon Coen**, an aggressive leader who once stated that there could never be trade without war, nor war without trade. Indeed, it appeared that his one goal was to prove this maxim. Having already wiped out two-thirds of the Bandanese during the invasion in 1603, Coen set about raising the prices of nutmeg and clove artificially high by destroying vast plantations on the island, thus devastating the livelihood of Banda's already decimated population.

Coen then turned his attention to Java, and in particular **Jayakarta** (now Jakarta) which he decided would be the ideal location for the capital of the ever-expanding VOC territories. Having been granted permission to build a warehouse at Jayakarta by the local sultan, Fathillah, the Dutch converted it into a fortress. Besieged by both an angry Bantenese population and the British, the Dutch retaliated, razing the city and renaming it **Batavia**. Further strategically important territories were acquired soon after, including **Melaka**, the last Portuguese stronghold in the region, in 1641, and **Makassar**, one of the last remaining British territories, in 1667.

Unlike previous trading powers, however, the VOC were not content with control over the sea trade, and turned their sights inland too. Java by this time was in the grip of the small but highly influential Islamic **Mataram Empire**, the last of the great home-grown empires of Indonesia (and different from the Mataram, or Sanjaya, empire, which was Hindu). Though the Mataram's territories extended little further than the plains of Central Java and the northern shores, its rulers, beginning with **Sultan Agung**, who ruled between 1613 and 1646, were treated almost as deities by their subjects. However, the royal house of Mataram was often riven with internal squabbling. During the early years of the eighteenth century the region was paralyzed by **Three Wars of Succession**, as different members of the royal house struggled for superiority. The last of these (1746–57) brought about the division of the empire into three separate sultanates, two at Solo and one at Yogyakarta. The only winners of these hugely destructive wars were the Dutch, who, by playing off one rival against the other, had successfully divided the Mataram's power base, making it all the easier for them to subjugate the entire territory.

Though they were now the first rulers of a united Java, by the end of the eighteenth century things had definitely taken a turn for the worse for the VOC. The Treaty of Paris (1780) permitted free trade in the East, and the VOC's fortunes dwindled as a result in the face of huge competition from the British and French. The expense of running an empire, financing battles for further territorial gains and maintaining law and order over their dominions was proving prohibitive too. In 1795 the Dutch government, investigating the affairs of the company that for 99 years had represented their interests in the Far East, found mismanagement and corruption on a grand scale. The VOC company was **bankrupt** – indeed, it had last been in the black way back in 1724. The Dutch government decided to pull the plug on the VOC there and then; the company struggled on as a purely private concern for another four years, eventually expiring in 1799 with debts of 134,000,000 guilders. The Netherlands government took possession of all VOC territories, and thus all of the islands we regard as Indonesia today formally became part of the **Dutch colonial empire**.

GOVERNOR DAENDALS AND THE ARRIVAL OF THE BRITISH

In 1795, the French, under Napoleon, invaded and occupied Holland. Amongst the French battalions was a small legion of patriotic Dutchmen who believed that they were liberating their country from the hands of despotism into which it had fallen. One of their number was Herman Willem Daendels. To thank him for his part in the success of the invasion, Napoleon's brother, Louis, the new King of Holland, sent Daendels to act as governor-general of the East Indies.

Known for his ferociousness and contempt for local Indonesian aristocracy, Daendals ruled over the archipelago for just three years, during which time he built all sorts of fortifications to fend off attacks by the British who, under the leadership of **Sir Thomas Stamford Raffles**, were showing a renewed interest in the islands. Troops were recruited from Ambon, Madura, Bali and Makassar to help with the defence, and fortresses were built along the Javanese coast – but all to no avail. With diminishing supplies and a lack of reinforcements from either France or Holland, the British found they were able to pick off the islands one by one, and duly landed at Batavia in August 1811 with a fresh fleet of up to 10,000 men.

Raffles' tenure in the archipelago lasted for just five years before he was forced to hand back the territories under a new peace deal signed with the Dutch. His time in the archipelago, however, left a lasting impact. Raffles was one of the first Europeans to take an interest in the ancient monuments that littered the island – among them Borobudur and Prambanan – and he ordered surveys of every historical building. As well as this he conducted extensive research into the country's fascinating flora and fauna.

The British also unwittingly sowed the seeds of revolution during their stay. By passing over the valid claims of **Prince Diponegoro** to the throne of the sultanate of Yogyakarta, in favour of his pro-British younger brother, they not only upset the royal households of Java, who disliked outsiders meddling in their affairs, but also, in the disaffected Diponegoro, created a charismatic leader for the anti-colonial cause.

THE RETURN OF THE DUTCH

The Dutch returned to Indonesia in 1816 and were soon embroiled in a couple of bloody disputes against opponents of their rule. One of the most serious of these was the **Paderi War** in Sumatra. Led by three Islamic holy men who had been inspired by a recent pilgrimage to Mecca, the Paderi movement started out as a crusade against lax morals amongst the Sumatran people, and had nothing to do with the Dutch. By the time the Dutch arrived to retake control of the archipelago, however, the Paderi had already moved across the centre of the island from their base in Padang, converting the southernmost Batak tribes to their ultra-orthodox (by Indonesian standards) brand of

Islam, where alcohol, gambling, cockfighting and smoking were forbidden. With the arrival of the Dutch in southern Sumatra in 1819, war between these two forces was inevitable; just two years later the Dutch and Paderi engaged in a ferocious seventeen-year battle for central and southern Sumatra, with the Dutch finally winning a decisive victory at Daludalu in 1838.

The Dutch probably would have won a little sooner had they not had to concentrate most of their efforts on a second war that centred around Yogyakarta in Central Java. Led by Prince Diponegoro, the local Indonesian aristocracy, including fifteen out of Central Java's 29 princes and 41 out of 88 senior courtiers, had united with the peasants to launch guerrilla attacks against Dutch strongholds. The Dutch suffered some notable defeats during the five-year **Javanese War** (1825–1830), and only by tricking Diponegoro into peace negotiations in Magelang – where he was unsportingly arrested and sent in exile to Makassar – were they able to resume control over Java. The war had cost the lives of over two-hundred thousand Javanese, mainly through starvation, and eight thousand Dutch troops.

EXPANSION AND EXPLOITATION

Having finally regained control over their old colonies, the rest of the nineteenth century and the beginning of the twentieth saw the Dutch attempting to expand into previously independent territories. Their early efforts met with limited success: the **Balinese** only surrendered in 1906, a full sixty years after the Dutch had first invaded, whilst the war in Aceh, which the Dutch had first tried to annex in 1873, dragged on until 1908, costing thousands of lives on both sides. By 1910, however, following the fall of **Banjarmasin** in 1864, **Lombok** in 1894 and **Sulawesi** in 1905, the Dutch had conquered nearly all of what we today call Indonesia; the only major exception, **Irian Jaya**, finally accepted colonial rule in 1920.

This expansionism coincided with renewed Dutch attempts to increase the exploitation of their Indonesian territories – policies which provoked more anti-colonial sentiment in Indonesia and outrage back in Holland. Following the debilitating battles in Java and Sumatra, the Dutch in Indonesia were facing bankruptcy and needed an instant return on their investments in the archipelago. Unfortunately, the policies they

implemented to try and achieve this were ineffectual at best, and at worst downright cruel.

The first of these policies was the so-called **Cultural System**, implemented in 1830 following the war with Diponegoro. Under this scheme, local farmers in Java had to give up a portion of their land – usually two-fifths, though sometimes as much as half was appropriated – to grow lucrative cash crops that could then be sold back in Europe for a huge profit. This system replaced land rent, though the farmers were still liable to the land tax on all of their land.

The Cultural System was not implemented everywhere, and in some districts farmers were unaffected; in other areas, however, farmers starved as the land used for cash crops was too great, and the remaining land too small to grow enough rice and other staple foodstuffs to subsist on. The primary aim of the Dutch was achieved: the islands staved off bankruptcy and Indonesia became a major world exporter of indigo, coffee and sugar. Unfortunately, their profits were reaped at the expense of the indigenous farmers, some of whom starved to death. In effect, Java had become one giant plantation.

The **Liberal System** (1870–1900) was a reaction to the exploitation of these farmers and a response to the new laissez-faire school of economic thought. Under this system, only local farmers could own land, although foreigners could lease it from the government for up to 75 years. The aim of these reforms was to open the islands up to private enterprise and the free market and to end the exploitation of the local population, while at the same time increasing local demand (by improving the purchasing power of the new farmers), thus maintaining the profits accruing to the Dutch.

Unfortunately, the liberal period coincided with some pretty devastating natural and economic disasters. **Coffee-leaf disease** began to spread in the 1870s, and a **sugar blight** in 1882 hit Cirebon and moved east throughout Java. Sugar beet from the West Indies and Africa flooded the European market at this time too, lowering prices and leading to economic depression throughout the islands. Even without this hard luck, however, it is still doubtful whether the Liberal System would have achieved all of its goals. Policies moved very slowly, and, by maintaining the monopoly on coffee production – the most profitable crop – the Dutch prevented local farmers from enjoying the kind of windfalls they had been expecting. The farmers were still being exploited, and, as the Dutch made further territorial gains in the archipelago, farmers from neighbouring islands outside Java began to be exploited too.

As the harsh realities of the Liberal System continued, a vocal, altruistic minority in the Dutch parliament began pressing for more drastic policies to end the injustices in Indonesia. Their motives were admirable, but unfortunately their ideas on how to change the system were both patronizing and misguided. The policies, implemented during the first few years of the twentieth century, gave rise to what is now called the **Ethical Period**. During this time, radical irrigation, health care, drainage and flood control programmes were started, and **transmigration** policies, from Java to the outlying islands, were introduced. But transmigration, as is still seen today, while temporarily alleviating over-population on Java, brought its own set of problems, with the displaced often ending up as the victims of ethnic violence in their new homelands. The irrigation programme, although fairly successful in increasing arable land, also had the consequence of ensuring that Indonesia remained an agrarian country, unable to reap the massive profits that were accruing to industrialized nations. Though the ideas behind the Ethical Period were laudable, at the end of the day the Indonesians were still treated as inferiors by the Dutch, and progress was slow.

THE INDEPENDENCE MOVEMENT

Though widely seen as a flop, the Ethical Period, and in particular its emphasis on education, did have far-reaching and unforeseen consequences. Though education amongst Indonesians was still the preserve of a rich minority, it was from this minority that the leaders of the **Independence movement** would emerge in the generations to come. Educated Indonesians were not only better at pinpointing the injustices of colonial rule, but were more able to articulate their grievances to their Dutch masters.

The **Islamic Association**, or **Sarekat Islam**, founded in 1909, was the first of these nationalist movements. Originally formed by an educated elite to protect Indonesians against Chinese dealers, the group received a lot of popular support among the peasant population. Out of the Sarekat Islam came the **Indonesian Communist Party**, or **PKI** (Perserikatan Kommunist Indonesia), which shared many of Sarekat's goals. Following a series of PKI-organized strikes and civil disruptions a few years later, however, the PKI leaders were arrested and the organization was to play little part in the revolution that followed.

A third party, the **Partai Nasional Indonesia** (PNI), founded a few years later in 1927 by **Achmed Sukarno**, grew to become the biggest of the independence organizations. With a huge following amongst the uneducated masses, the PNI aimed to achieve independence through non-co-operation and mass action, and quickly became a major threat to Dutch domination, so much so that the Dutch outlawed the party four years after its foundation, throwing its leaders, Sukarno included, in prison.

After 1927, and with the Dutch cracking down hard on any anti-colonial organizations, the independence movement gained little momentum: new nationalist parties came and went (including one, the **PNI Baru** – new PNI – which was led by former PKI member **Muhammed Hatta**); Sukarno was released from prison in 1933, then promptly re-arrested in the same year and exiled to Flores, while Hatta was apprehended in 1934 and exiled to Boven Digul. Without their natural leaders, the movement faltered and grew fractious. In an attempt to move forward once more, another Independence party, the **Partai Indonesia Raya**, changed tack, opting to win independence through co-operation with the Dutch rather than the disruption and dissent which had so far met with little success. It was felt that the Dutch, under threat both in Europe and the Far East from the rising tide of fascism, would be more amenable to the idea of independence if, in return, they were guaranteed the support of the Indonesians against the Japanese army. The Dutch, however, continued stubbornly to refuse all Indonesian offers, and the independence movement was thwarted once more. On May 10, 1940, Hitler invaded Holland and the Dutch government fled to London. The issue of Indonesia's independence was now on ice.

THE JAPANESE INVASION

The **Japanese** made no secret of their intention to "liberate" Indonesia. Indonesia's seemingly indefatigable supply of oil, rubber and bauxite had always been vital to the Japanese economy, and Japanese traders had a good working relationship with their Indonesian counterparts. Indeed, when the Japanese did finally invade, in January 1942, most Indonesians saw the Japanese army as liberators, rather than just another occupying force. This welcome ensured the success of the invasion, and less than two months later, on March 8, 1942, the Dutch on Java surrendered.

The three-and-a-half-year **occupation** was a mixed blessing for Indonesians. While the Japanese were every bit as ruthless as the Dutch whom they had replaced, this had the effect of politicizing the masses, adding more fuel to the fires of independence. The Japanese also encouraged the independence movement – particularly towards the end of World War II, when defeat at the hands of the allies became a foregone conclusion – helping to train and prepare the indigenous population for the inevitable struggle ahead. One man in particular, a Japanese vice admiral and fervent pro-nationalist by the name of **Maeda Tadashi**, conspicuously sided with the independence movement, and diverted money from the Japanese navy to fund lectures and rallies given by the recently-freed Sukarno and Hatta.

By 1945, dozens of **"youth movements"**, reactionary groups dedicated to the country's independence, had sprouted up throughout Java. The Japanese, meanwhile, began manoeuvring the old guard – Sukarno, Hatta *et al* – to the forefront of the nationalist movement, no doubt feeling that they would find it easier to negotiate and do deals with the old campaigners rather than the hot-headed youth groups. The "Investigating Body for Preparatory Work for Indonesian Independence", a committee that included most of the established nationalist leaders, was founded by the Japanese in 1945. It was from these meetings that Sukarno came up with his doctrine of **Pancasila**, the "five principles" by which an Independent Indonesia would be governed: belief in God, nationalism, democracy, social justice and humanitarianism. From this, the committee was able to draw up the country's first constitution.

Despite these preparations, when the Japanese finally surrendered to the Allied forces, on August 15, 1945, there was a short hiatus. Maeda was keen to transfer the power to the Indonesian people, with Sukarno at their head, as quickly as possible, before either the Allies returned to Indonesia or the youth groups took it upon themselves to assume control. That night Sukarno and Hatta were kidnapped by one of these youth groups, **Menteng 31 Asrama**, in an attempt to force them to declare Independence outside of the orderly arrangements laid down by the Japanese. Maeda, however, managed to persuade them to return both of the hostages, and that night all three – Sukarno, Hatta and Maeda – were safely ensconced in Maeda's house, where they drafted a Declaration of Independence. Menteng 31 Asrama hoped for a fiery declaration full of inflammatory phrases and revolutionary sentiments, but on August 17, 1945, Sukarno read a simple, unemotional declaration to a small group of people outside his house in Menteng. The Republic of Indonesia was born, with Achmed Sukarno as its first president and Muhammed Hatta as vice-president.

THE REVOLUTION

Announcing that they were now an Independent republic was one thing; ensuring that it stayed that way was quite another. Under the terms of the surrender agreed with the Allies, the Japanese had no right to hand over Indonesia to the Indonesian people. **Lord Louis Mountbatten** arrived in mid-1945 with several thousand British troops to accept the surrender of the Japanese occupying force. Their presence only added to an already tense situation, and skirmishes between the British troops and the Indonesians were frequent. The Japanese, realizing that they had obligations to the Allies in the terms of surrender, tried to retake towns that they'd previously handed over to the local people. The situation was getting out of hand. Some intense, short-lived battles occurred between Japanese and Indonesian forces, and later between Indonesian and British, including a particularly horrific ten-day fight for **Surabaya**. Throughout this time the British tried to remain neutral, planning to withdraw only when the Dutch were in a position to resume control and sort the mess out for themselves. By November 1946, 55,000 Dutch troops had arrived and the British finally left the archipelago.

The war with the Dutch, however, continued for the next three years. It was a curious affair, with diplomacy giving way to all-out war and vice versa. The situation looked to be heading rapidly towards stalemate, until pressure from outside the archipelago exerted itself on the Dutch. The world was turning against their campaign in Indonesia, finding their attempts to re-establish a colonial empire anachronistic in the twentieth century. The US was particularly strong in its criticism, threatening the Dutch with economic sanctions unless they pulled out of the war. The Dutch finally withdrew in December 1949, and sovereignty was handed over to the new Republic of Indonesia.

While it's fair to say that the Indonesians had won a great victory, it would be wrong to think that the revolution was fought by a totally united Indonesian people against imperialist oppressors. The islands, while more united than ever before, had poor communications, and some islands, particularly those ruled by leaders who had grown wealthy under the Dutch regime, viewed the declaration of Independence with something akin to disappointment. Even within the revolutionary vanguard there was little consensus on how the republic should be run and what form it should take. When Independence was finally won, these differences – strategic, ideological and religious – rose quickly to the surface to dog the first steps of the republic.

GUIDED DEMOCRACY AND THE LAST YEARS OF SUKARNO 1957–65

According to Sukarno, **guided democracy** was an attempt to create a wholly Indonesian political system based on the traditional, hierarchical organization of Indonesian villages. Sukarno considered the Western form of democracy as divisive, a system that led to too much political infighting and rarely to a universally acceptable outcome. In Sukarno's idealized view of traditional village life, however, decisions were made with the consent of everyone, and not simply the majority – though this unanimous agreement was only to be found with the considerable help and influence of the village elders. In guided democracy, the various political factions would still have their say, though Sukarno would now play the part of village chief, with all the power that entailed.

To many, the term guided democracy was a euphemism: despite the name, democracy featured little in Sukarno's new political system, and the measures introduced under guided democracy can be seen as the first step on the road to **authoritarian rule**, removing power from the elected cabinet and investing it instead with the presidency. These measures included the establishment of the Kabinet Karya (Business Cabinet), made up of a selection of non-elected representatives of all the main parties (including the PNI, the NU, the army and, a few years later as their influence grew, the PKI), to replace the existing, democratically elected cabinet that was dissolved in 1960, and the founding of the Supreme Advisory Committee, another non-elected body, with Sukarno as the self-appointed chairman, that made decisions on national policy.

Sukarno adorned his new political system with a smattering of newly coined terms to describe the ideas behind guided democracy, chief amongst which was **Nas-A-Kom**, made up of the three essential parties of his co-operative government – *nasionalisme*, *agaman* and *komunisme*, or nationalism, religion and communism, representing the major parties (the nationalist PNI, Islamic NU party and communist PKI) which formed his new government. Sukarno would bandy terms such as Nasakom about, promising in his speeches to "Nasakom the armed forces" and, in the long run, even Nasakom every public body in the country.

Unsurprisingly, many people, both within and outside government, were suspicious of Sukarno's real motives in introducing guided democracy, and lengthy protests in Sulawesi (where the first of two attempts on the president's life took place in 1960) and Sumatra marred the early years of guided democracy. For a brief while a breakaway parliament, the PRRI, founded by disgruntled former politicians who had had their authority diminished under guided democracy, emerged in the Sumatran city of Bukittingi.

THE RISE OF THE COMMUNISTS

It was around this time that Sukarno began to forge strong ties with the **Soviet Union**. The Soviets appreciated Sukarno's Marxist leanings and his aggressively anti-Western foreign policy, and began pouring money into the country to finance the Konfrontasi (see next page) against the neo-colonial state of Malaysia. The increasing Soviet influence had far-reaching consequences for Indonesian politics too. Sukarno still relied on maintaining a delicate balance between the various factions in his cabinet to maintain control. Even before the period of guided democracy, the communist PKI could boast the support of almost a third of the electorate; the influence that Soviet doctrine had over Sukarno made the president more sympathetic towards the communists' views, and further swelled their support at ground level.

Perversely, the rise in power of the **Indonesian army**, the communists' natural enemy, also increased the PKI's power. Thanks to a law allowing them to confiscate the last few Dutch interests that remained on the archipelago – such as the Royal Mail Steam Packet Company which controlled much of the inter-island shipping – the army had grown wealthy. This increasing prosperity, combined with their successful annihilation of the rebel PRRI government in 1958, had done much to increase the army's standing in society. Indeed, by the 1960s, Sukarno had begun to look upon the army's Chief of Staff, **Colonel A.H. Nasution**, as a challenge to his authority and a serious rival for his role as president. Inevitably, therefore, Sukarno and the PKI began siding with each other against the army. This in turn led to the polarization of the entire parliament, with different factions forming temporary allegiances in an attempt to defeat a mutual enemy, with Sukarno and the communists on one side, and the army and its unlikely allies – including the NU and PNI – on the other.

This fractious situation continued throughout the first half of the 1960s. The political fighting in parliament was mirrored by pitched battles between the various factions on the streets of the capital, and law and order began to break down. Nevertheless, if it wasn't for the drive, political nous and impassioned speeches of President Sukarno, many believe that democracy in any form would never have got off the ground in Indonesia.

KONFRONTASI

Sukarno made no secret of his desire to wreak revenge for all the humiliations and poverty Southeast Asia had suffered at the hands of Western imperialists. To this end, and to distract his people from the economic crisis his wayward financial policies had engendered, he began a crusade to rid the region of the last vestiges of Western colonialism. After both diplomatic and military effort, the Dutch were ousted from their last remaining Indonesian territory – Irian Jaya – in 1963, and in the same year Sukarno launched

the bruising **Konfrontasi** ("Confrontation") against Malaysia, who he saw as a mere puppet state of their erstwhile British rulers. At stake in the Konfrontasi were the northern Borneo states of Sabah, Sarawak and Brunei, which had initially been reluctant to join Peninsular Malaysia and Singapore in the newly-formed Malaysian federation. However, Sukarno was unwilling to commit too many troops to fight battles in the jungles of Kalimantan when, thanks to a failing economy and increasing inter-party friction, there was increasing unrest on Java and other islands. As a result, their ambition to bring Sabah, Sarawak and Brunei into the Indonesian republic failed, and the Indonesians under new president Suharto finally gave up the Konfrontasi (they never dignified the struggle by calling it a war) in 1965.

In hindsight, the decision to take up arms in an ultimately fruitless battle against his country's northern neighbours was one of Sukarno's gravest mistakes. The Konfrontasi weighed heavily on Indonesia's fledgling economy, and, as funds were diverted to the cause, subsidies were withdrawn from several areas of the public sector, leading to annual **hyperinflation** of at least one hundred percent throughout the early 1960s. The Konfrontasi also alienated the West at a time when the country needed them – or at least their cash – most of all. This only forced the Indonesians more and more into the arms of the Soviets until, less than twenty years after throwing off the yoke of Dutch imperialist rule, the Indonesians found themselves financially dependent on another foreign power.

THE COMMUNIST COUP, 1965

By mid-1965, Sukarno's health began to fail and his grip on power weakened, leading to a flurry of activity from each of the various factions in the cabinet as they jockeyed for position, ready to take advantage should the ailing president finally call it a day. Sukarno's eventual demise, however, was accelerated by the events of late September, events which not only precipitated his fall from power, but saw the rise to prominence of the man who would eventually replace him: General Suharto.

Nobody is really sure what happened on the night of September 30, 1965. What is known for certain is that, at about midnight, a number of leading generals were taken from their homes at gunpoint to Halim airport. Those who refused to co-operate, such as General A. Yani, were shot immediately. Those who went to Halim Airport suffered the same fate; their bodies were later discovered down a nearby well. Their abductors were a group of communist-inspired renegade army divisions and other leftist sympathizers. These **revolutionaries** were later to claim that they were only preventing an army-led coup that was due to occur later that same night – a claim that has never been substantiated. Of more significance, however, was the presence of President Sukarno at Halim. Although the rebels claimed that he was only taken there as a precaution, ready to fly out at the first sign of army insurrection, it was hard not to feel that Sukarno was somehow in cahoots with the communists, and that the idea of an army coup was a complete fabrication, invented by Sukarno and the PKI as an excuse for their extermination of senior figures in the armed forces.

The rebels managed to occupy Medan Merdeka in the middle of Jakarta, and thus controlled the telecommunications centre and the presidential palace situated nearby. Their success was shortlived, however. General Suharto, a veteran of the Irian campaign and a senior member of the Indonesian army, rounded up those generals who weren't kidnapped and began to plan a strategy to retake Jakarta and quash the coup. In the event, this proved surprisingly easy. Suharto managed to persuade many of those holding Medan Merdeka to retreat back to their base at Halim Airport, and, as he garnered further support, more of the coup participants fled, until Medan Merdeka was under his control completely.

The **failure of the coup** had disastrous consequences for both the communist PKI and Sukarno. Over the next five years, the communists became the victims of a massive Suharto-led purge. It was also the beginning of the end of Sukarno's rule. Though he lived until 1970, his grip on power had almost completely slipped by the end of 1965, and for the remaining year of his presidency he ruled in name only, as General Suharto manoeuvred himself to the top of the political ladder.

SUHARTO TAKES CONTROL, 1965–67

In the months immediately following September 1965, Sukarno must have felt that his grip on power was still pretty secure. Some of his keenest rivals in the armed forces had been mur-

dered, and his part, if any, in the events of that night had not been discovered. Unfortunately for Sukarno, he underestimated the political guile of his new rival, **General Suharto**. While Sukarno sought to prove that the coup was just another turbulent moment in the ongoing revolution that was his rule, Suharto, using the powers granted to him by Sukarno to restore order, began a campaign against the communist PKI party and their sympathizers, rounding up the ringleaders of the coup, anybody connected with the PKI and, eventually, anybody whose political ideology leaned more to the left than right. As more communists were arrested and killed, so violence and anti-PKI demonstrations filled the streets of the capital and elsewhere, allowing Suharto to remain in effective control of the country until they subsided.

The slaughter of communist sympathizers continued until the early months of March 1966. It was the bloodiest episode in Indonesia's history: most experts today reckon that at least 500,000 people lost their lives, although the official figure was a more modest 160,000. A similar number were thrown into jail where, up to a decade later, at least 100,000 languished without ever having been convicted or even charged. It was just as Suharto wanted. He had enjoyed a few months in power, had totally crushed the anti-army PKI and, as the main beneficiary of PKI support, Sukarno's grip on power had been severely weakened. The army was now the dominant force in Indonesian society and politics.

Sukarno, on returning to power, tried desperately to save his beloved guided democracy, reshuffling the cabinet in an attempt to weaken the power of the armed forces. In response, Suharto encouraged a renewed outbreak of violence, compelling Sukarno to hand over the controls to Suharto once again, just as he had in the aftermath of the initial communist uprising of September of the previous year, in order to quell these latest disturbances.

It was a simple tactic, but it worked. On March 11, 1966, Sukarno was informed that unidentified troops (positioned there, so it turned out, by Suharto himself) were surrounding his palace, and in panic the president fled to Bogor. Once there, Sukarno was persuaded to sign a document giving Suharto full authority to restore order and protect the president by whatever means necessary. It was just the invitation Suharto required.

The next day, anti-Suharto members of the cabinet were arrested. The following year the MPRS (the People's Consultative Assembly, Indonesia's parliament), was purged of any pro-Sukarno elements and the man himself was asked to explain the mismanagement and corruption of his rule. Pro-Suharto Adam Malik was made minister for foreign affairs, and quickly set about restoring relations with the West and loosening existing ties with communist China. The debilitating Konfrontasi, the last obstacle to renewing relations with the West, ended in May 1966, with a peace treaty signed in December of that year, and soon aid from the West began pouring back into Indonesia, rescuing the ailing economy and providing essential relief to thousands of the poorest in Indonesian society. Suharto now had popular support to go with his burgeoning political power, and, in the new bourgeoisie that emerged as the economy improved, he found a powerful and secure foundation for his regime. The final *coup de grâce* to Sukarno's twenty-one-year reign occurred on March 12, 1967, when the MPRS stripped Sukarno of all his powers and named Suharto **acting president**.

Indonsia has never had a more charismatic leader than Sukarno, and there were times during his twenty-year rule when his popularity reached unprecedented levels. He embodied the conflicts and contradictions inherent in Indonesian society. A devout Muslim who nevertheless clung to the timeworn superstitions of traditional Javanese religion, whose fondness for alcohol and extramarital affairs are the stuff of legend, and whose political allegiances gravitated, throughout his career, towards the secular tenets of Marxism – the anomalies in Sukarno's personality mirrored the contradictions of the country he governed.

Unfortunately, policy decisions, most of which were of national importance were seldom granted the same level of care and attention to detail that he lavished on his public image. It was typical of Sukarno that, while the country struggled to clamber out of the economic trough of the 1960s, he frittered away millions building colossal monuments in his beloved Jakarta: the Monumen Nasional in the centre of Medan Merdeka, the Free Irian Monument in Lapangan Benteng and the Mesjid Istiqlal – the largest mosque in Southeast Asia – were all built during his rule and still stand testimony to his wastefulness.

Ultimately, Sukarno was at heart a revolutionary. In order to rule effectively, he required Indonesia to be in a state of permanent revolution: fighting wars on all fronts, undertaking radical changes of government, and even entire political systems. His ideas, beliefs and speeches were that of the zealous revolutionary – perfectly suited for the turbulent years of 1945–46, but of limited use in the years that followed when stability and order were required.

THE NEW ORDER

Suharto's first few years in power were seen as a brave new dawn, and there seems no doubt that he did bring some benefits to Indonesia. Suharto dubbed his new regime the **New Order**, to distinguish it from the chaos of the "Old Order" of Sukarno's presidency. It was an apt choice of words: after the turbulent years of Sukarno's rule, Suharto managed to restore a measure of order to society unseen since the Dutch era. The **economy** improved beyond all recognition too: even inflation, which had dogged almost every year of Sukarno's rule, was brought under control. The new links forged with the West also brought significant benefits, both financially and politically. Furthermore, Suharto managed to create a **pluralistic society** where religious intolerance had no place; providing people belonged to one of the five main faiths, their religious beliefs were respected. (This tolerance, however, did not stretch to those who held traditional animist beliefs, for they worshipped more than one god. Nor did it stretch to atheism, which in Suharto's eyes equated with communism. During the late 1960s there was a rush of conversions to Islam and Christianity by people frightened of being labelled communists.)

There was a price to pay for the blessings of the Suharto era. The religious tolerance Suharto promoted in society was not matched by any political tolerance on his part. Instead, his people were forced to live under a suffocating **dictatorial regime** and take part in the charade of the so-called "festivals of democracy", the "elections" that took place every five years. With the restrictions placed on the opposition parties, the re-election of Suharto was a foregone conclusion.

Throughout his term in office, Suharto promised to bring about greater political freedoms, but these never materialized. Critics of

Suharto's New Order found themselves languishing in jails alongside those arrested in the aftermath of the September 1965 coup – jails where torture was the rule rather than the exception. Improvements in the country's economy too, while significant, tended to benefit only the privileged minority, while a huge underclass developed in rural areas and in slum districts on the outskirts of large cities. There was also widespread **corruption** throughout society, from the president down. The scale of Suharto's nepotism, bestowing privilege, power and lucrative monopolies on his children and cronies, was breathtaking.

Throughout the late 1960s, Suharto continued his persecution of all things communist, tracking down existing PKI units in jungle hideouts in West Kalimantan. He also consolidated his position within parliament by simplifying the political system: where beforehand there had been a multitude of political parties, Suharto reduced them to just three: the **PPP** (United Development Party) made up of the old Islamic parties; the **PDI** (Indonesian Democratic Party) made up largely of the old nationalist party, the PNI; and the government's own political vehicle, **Golkar**. Political expression and criticism of Suharto's heavy-handed techniques were suppressed. Opposition parties were impotent, and participation in the government-controlled five-yearly elections gave Suharto a veneer of democratic legitimacy he clearly didn't deserve.

THE 1970S AND 1980S

Suharto, encircled by a close and trusted band of loyal followers, now had complete control over the country, a country which had expanded its boundaries during the mid-1970s. **East Timor**, independent since a revolution in Portugal had emancipated the tiny former colony in 1974, collapsed into civil war the following year as various factions failed to agree on whether the territory should become part of Indonesia. In the event, the decision was taken out of their hands by the Indonesians themselves, who invaded on Suharto's orders in December 1975. Despite strong condemnation from the United Nations, and regular Amnesty International reports of human rights abuses in East Timor, the US and Europe were unwilling to upset their new Southeast Asian ally. East Timor was incorporated into the republic of Indonesia the following year.

The oil crisis of the 1970s raised the price of oil, then Indonesia's most lucrative export, significantly. This windfall lasted until the oil price collapsed in 1983, allowing the government to use the **oil revenue** to create a sound industrial base founded on steel and natural gas production, oil refining and aluminium industries. Welfare measures were introduced, with 100,000 new schools built. With breakthroughs in pesticides and improved farming methods, the 1980s also saw an increase of fifty percent in agricultural production, avoiding the food shortages many had predicted for the country following the postwar population explosion.

Yet these were minor triumphs in the face of the country's overwhelming poverty. The beneficiaries of Suharto's economic miracle were a small but wealthy minority who lived in air-conditioned luxury in the big cities, while the majority continued to struggle, eking out a meagre existence in the rural areas of the country. The people who belonged in this disaffected underclass, though numerous, lacked the organization and influence necessary to change matters, and Suharto knew it. As long as the middle and upper classes continued to support his regime, his position was safe.

SUHARTO'S DOWNFALL

For over three decades, Suharto had managed to concentrate power almost exclusively in his own hands. This political stability had raised confidence among foreign investors, enabling the economy to grow steadily throughout his tenure. But even such suffocating control and economic prosperity could not mask the growing disapproval of Suharto's government. The previously supportive middle classes were tiring of his brazen **nepotism** and the unbridled corruption of his government, and, although there was never any direct challenge to his authority, resentment against the regime grew throughout the 1990s.

Nevertheless, Suharto would probably have survived for a few more years if it wasn't for the **currency crisis** that hit the region in the latter part of 1997, a crisis triggered by a run on the Thai baht. In a few dramatic months, the rupiah slipped in value from Rp2500 to the US dollar to nearly Rp9000. Prices of even the most basic of goods such as fuel and food rose five hundred percent.

Suharto recognized the seriousness of the situation and contacted the IMF for aid. The IMF, however, promised to help only after certain conditions had been met. Suharto had been backed into a corner. Refuse to comply and his country faced ruin. Agree to the IMF's terms, which included removing his family and friends from a number of senior and lucrative posts, and his hold on the country would be seriously undermined. Suharto eventually decided to comply with the IMF's demands, but then committed political suicide by appointing a cabinet full of his own cronies – including his old golfing partner – following the last "festival of democracy" in May 1998. Foreign investors lost all confidence in Suharto, and the rupiah went into freefall. Pressure on Suharto was also growing from his own people, as many took to the streets to protest against his incompetence and demand greater political freedom. These demonstrations, initially fairly peaceful, grew more violent as the people's frustration increased, until a state of lawlessness ensued. For over a week, riots took place in all the main cities, buildings were set on fire and shops looted. The **Chinese community**, long resented in Indonesia for their domination of the economy and success in business, were targeted by the rioters for special persecution. Over 1200 people died in the mayhem that followed the May elections, until, on May 21, 1998, Suharto stepped down and his vice-president, B.J. Habibie, took over.

THE FUTURE

Though Suharto's resignation quelled the riots in the short term, few believed that the appointment of **Habibie**, a close friend of Suharto's for many years, would end the public's dissatisfaction with the political situation. Despite promises to introduce sweeping reforms, many believed Habibie was dragging his feet over a number of issues, and, in early November 1998, more rioting occurred. The rioters – largely students – wanted to see a number of measures taken instantly, including the removal of the army from parliament, an end to corruption within government, the bringing to trial of

Suharto on charges of mismanagement and corruption, and a return to democracy. In the days leading up to a special session of parliament convened by Habibie to address these issues, fifteen protesters were shot dead in the capital by the army. Further protests took place in a number of other cities, but as yet Habibie has failed to deliver. The cry for **"Reformasi"**, first heard in May, grows more voluble by the day.

Nobody expected Indonesia's transition to democracy to be an easy one after so many years of totalitarian rule. And indeed, the country is currently in the grip of a mixture of fear, intrigue and hope. Occasionally this manifests itself in the form of **religious intolerance**: a number of churches have been burnt down and Christians killed in a series of attacks, prompting revenge killings by Christian gangs. Adding to the tension is the recent phenomenon of the so-called Ninja murders. Over the last year, almost two hundred Muslim clerics have been brutally killed. Nobody knows who is behind the slaughter – dubbed the Ninja murders because of the assailants' black costumes and face masks. Again, the murders have prompted a spate of revenge killings.

Nevertheless, 1998 also brought signs of hope for those who believe in political freedom as the way forward for Indonesia. The fervour with which the protesters have made their demands suggests that they won't be satisfied until full political freedom has been won. In another significant move, people now openly express their support for reform and, just as importantly, their dissatisfaction with the government. Even the press is enjoying a freedom of expression it has never enjoyed before. A number of valid **political rivals** to Habibie have emerged in the last year too, including Megawati Sukarnoputri – the daughter of Sukarno and the leader of the Indonesian Democratic Party (PDI), and Amien Rais, head of the National Mandate Party (PAN).

As Indonesia approaches the end of the century, it is to be hoped that, whoever wins out in this latest bout of unrest, the new millennium will bring the country much-needed stability and peace.

RELIGION

Every citizen in Indonesia professes, officially at least, to one of five major faiths: Islam, Buddhism, Hinduism, Catholicism and Protestantism. Yet the Islam you'll find in Indonesia is very different from the Islam you'll find in West Asia or the Indian subcontinent, and likewise the other major faiths in the archipelago bear striking differences to their counterparts in other parts of the world.

This is because religion in Indonesia is dynamic, not dogmatic; by gaining a foothold in the archipelago, each of the major faiths has undergone major changes. These changes may have been introduced deliberately – to make the new religion more attractive to the local population and thus ensure its long-term survival – or they may just be the natural result of introducing a new faith into a region that already has very deep-rooted beliefs of its own. For example, Hinduism in Indonesia, brought over to the archipelago in the first few centuries AD, has significant elements of **indigenous animism** (once the predominant faith in the archipelago) grafted onto the more orthodox faith that you'll find in India. Thus converts to the new religion need not forsake their old animist beliefs entirely, but instead can continue to adhere to them, within the framework of Hinduism. Similarly, Islam, brought over a few centuries later by merchants from Gujarat in India, has aspects of Hinduism, Buddhism and animism – the three major faiths that had preceded it in the archipelago – incorporated within its rituals and beliefs.

These changes to the major religions still continue to this day, though nowadays the alterations usually arise through political pressure, rather than from a desire to appeal to potential converts as before. For example, as part of it's code of national law (Pancasila), the Jakarta administration also requires that all Indonesian faiths be **monotheistic** – a proviso that doesn't sit easily with either **Hindu** or animist tenets. By emphasizing the role of their supreme deity, Sanghyang Widi Wasa (who manifests himself as the Hindu trinity of Brahma, Siwa and Wisnu), the Hindu Council of Bali (which, uniquely in Indonesia, is 93 percent Hindu) convinced the Ministry of Religion that Bali was essentially monotheistic, and in 1962 Balinese Hinduism was formally recognized by Jakarta. As a result, a host of new Balinese temples were dedicated to a unifying force – Jagatnata or "Lord of the World".

Outside of Bali, Indonesia has a predominantly **Muslim** population, though with significant **Buddhist** (the Chinese populations in the large cities and in West Kalimantan), Hindu and animist minorities (in Irian Jaya, Sumatra, Kalimantan and other remote outposts). **Christianity** is not particularly widespread in Indonesia. The Batak of North Sumatra, the Ambonese, Florinese and a few tribes in Irian Jaya and Kalimantan are the only pockets of Christianity, despite three hundred years of Dutch rule. Nevertheless, the Christian minority is a powerful one; those who converted under the Dutch were offered the opportunity to receive a European education, and this has ensured that the Christians form a disproportionate presence in the elite of the army, government and business.

ANIMISM

Animism is the belief that all living things – including plants and trees – and some non-living natural features such as rocks and waterfalls, have **spirits**. **Ancestor worship** – the practice of paying tribute to the spirits of deceased relatives – is also common throughout the archipelago. As with Hinduism, the animistic faiths teach that it is necessary to live in harmony with these spirits; disturb this harmonious balance, by upsetting a spirit for example, and you risk bringing misfortune upon yourself, your household or your village. For this reason, animists consult, or at least consider the spirits before almost everything they do, and you'll often see small offerings of flowers or food left by a tree or river to appease the spirits that live within. Spirits can also be called upon for favours: to cure sickness, for example, or to bring rain or guarantee a fine harvest. As such, the witch doctors, or **dukun** in Indonesian, who traditionally act as the go-between between the temporal and spirit world, rank high in the village hierarchy.

Animism is still the predominant faith in some of the villages of the outlying islands, particularly Sumatra, Kalimantan and Irian Jaya. The rituals and beliefs vary significantly between each of these islands. Many of these ancient animist beliefs, permeate each of the five major religions, and many Indonesian people, no matter what faith they profess, still perform animist rituals. Indeed, it was widely reported that President Sukarno, during the revolution of 1946, spent an entire day praying to his ceremonial kris to gain courage and fortitude.

ISLAM

Indonesia is the largest **Islamic nation** in the world. Initially brought over to **Aceh** by traders from Gujarat in the eighth century, the religion slowly filtered down to the rest of the archipelago in the centuries that followed. Its progress is reflected in the religious make-up of the islands today: the northernmost province of Aceh, which received Islam directly from India, is still the most orthodox area, whereas Muslims in the rest of the archipelago follow a style of Islam that has been syncretized with other, older religions, such as animism, Buddhism and Hinduism. Indeed, so different is the Indonesian take on Islam compared to the orthodox faith as followed in Arabia, that a follower of the latter would probably find the former idolatrous, and even blasphemous.

The youngest of all the major religions, the beginnings of Islam are fairly well-documented. Born in 570 AD, **Mohammed**, an illiterate semi-recluse from Mecca in Arabia, began, at the age of forty, to receive messages from **Allah** (God) via the Archangel Gabriel. On these revelations Mohammed began to build a new religion: Islam or "Submission", as the faith required people to submit to God's will.

His early proselytizing met with limited success in his hometown, and in 622 AD, Mohammed, accompanied by his followers, the **Muslims**, or "Surrendered Men" (as they had surrendered themselves to God's will), abandoned Mecca for Medina. There he built up a massive following, and returned in triumph to Mecca in 630 AD.

Soon after Mohammed's death in 632 AD, the religion he had founded split into two over an argument over succession, with the **Sunni** Muslims preferring an elected leader, and the **Shi'ites** preferring the caliphate to be hereditary. Since that initial split, the two factions have drifted further apart in matters of dogma and ritual, to a point of irreconcilability.

To many Westerners, it comes as something of a surprise to find how close the Islamic faith is to Christianity: the ideas of heaven and hell and the creation story are much the same, and many of the prophets – Abraham, Noah, Moses – appear in both faiths. Indeed, Jesus is an Islamic prophet too, although Muslims believe that Mohammed is the only true prophet, to whom everything was revealed.

The Islamic religion is founded on the **Five Pillars**, the essential tenets revealed by Allah to Mohammed and collected in the **Koran**, the holy book which Mohammed dictated before he died. Essentially, Mohammed preached that all Muslims should base their lives on these five rules. The first is that one should profess one's faith in Allah with the phrase "There is no God but Allah and Mohammed is his prophet". It is this sentence that is intoned by the muezzin five times a day when calling the faithful to prayer. The act of praying is the second pillar. According to Mohammed's teachings, praying can be done anywhere, and not just in a mosque, though the same ritual should always be performed: Muslims should always face Mecca when praying, the head must also be covered, and a ritual set of ablutions, including the washing of feet and hands, should be carried out before starting. The third pillar demands that the faithful should always give a percentage of their income to charity, whilst the fourth states that all Muslims must observe the fasting month (Ramadan; see p.51). The fifth pillar demands that every Muslim should make a pilgrimage to Mecca at least once in their lifetime. Those who do are known as *haji* (*haja* for women) and are accorded great respect in Indonesia.

ISLAM IN INDONESIA

Nearly all Indonesian Muslims are followers of the **Sunni** sect. Indeed, in Indonesia the argument is not between Sunni and Shi'ite, but between those who practice a more orthodox form of the religion, the **Santri Muslims**, and those who follow a mystical, homegrown form of Islam which combines elements of Hinduism and animism, and which has more in common with the spiritual Sufi faith of Eastern Turkey and Iran. A good example of the latter can be found in Central Java, where the sultans of Yogyakarta and Solo, though they will insist they practise a fairly orthodox brand of Islam, put on puppet festivals where tales from the Hindu classics, the *Ramayana* and *Mahabarata*, are performed. Traditionally, the sultan of Solo is also believed to have close ties with the Goddess of the South Seas, Loro Kidul, and every year the sultan visits the goddess's home at Parangtritis where he prays to the goddess and leaves offerings. Indeed, according to popular legend, the Islamic faith was initially spread throughout Java by the **Wali Songo** (Nine Saints), nine holy men who were supposedly blessed with supernatural powers.

There are other differences between the Indonesian-style Islam and that practised by the rest of the Islamic world. Indonesian women tend to be accorded far more respect, with veils and women in full purdah a rare sight. Indonesian men are only allowed two wives, as opposed to four in Arabian countries, though just one wife is the norm. Islam in Indonesia is also a lot **less political** than in many other parts of the Islamic world – the country is, after all, a secular state – though this may be about to change. Suharto, for all his faults, did at least try to keep Indonesia faithful to its pluralistic concepts as laid down in the Pancasila. Despite growing pressure from Islamic groups, the archipelago remained a pluralist state throughout his lengthy term of office. President Habibie, however, is seen as an aggressive defender of "the faith", and was once president of the Association of Muslim Intellectuals. Currently, the status quo from Suharto's reign has been preserved, but as Habibie consolidates his position and his confidence grows, a more Islamic form of governance may well be adopted.

THE MOSQUE

The mosque, or **mesjid** as it's known in Indonesia, is simply a prayer hall. Most towns have at least two mosques: one for Friday prayers, the *jami mesjid*, and the *musalla*, which is used every day except Friday. In addition, you'll find rooms set aside for praying in hotels, airports and in train and bus stations. Visitors are nearly always allowed to tour around the mosque, though obviously not during prayer times.

Though different parts of Indonesia have developed their own idiosyncratic mosque design – the multitiered, or *joglo* roofs of the older Javanese mosques (which, it is believed, grew out of the Hindu Meru shrines of Bali) being a classic example – each conforms to the same basic layout that you'll find in mosques all over the Islamic world. Stand by the gateway to

any mosque and you'll notice the same features: a **courtyard** at the front, often with a **fountain** or washroom to one side where worshippers can perform their ritual ablutions before proceeding into the mosque to pray; the mosque itself, which is normally just one large room or hall; and a **minaret**, or *menara*, from where the muezzin used to call the faithful to prayer five times a day. More often than not these days, the muezzin doesn't actually climb the minaret, but calls the faithful via loudspeakers attached to the top of the minaret, and in many cases there's no muezzin at all, the call to prayer being performed by a prerecorded cassette.

The interior of the mosque is usually very simple. The congregation sit or kneel on the carpeted floor when praying, so there is usually very little furniture within the mosque, save, perhaps, the **mimbar** – the pulpit, from where the Friday sermon is delivered. The direction of Mecca, which the faithful must pray towards, is indicated by a small niche, or **mihrab**, in what is known as the **qibla** wall (usually the wall nearest the mimbar). The decor of the mosques adheres to the strict iconoclastic rules of Islam, with no images of any living creatures inside a mosque. Nevertheless, the walls are occasionally enlivened – sometimes, particularly in Banda Aceh and Medan, beautifully so – by elaborate geometric patterns or verses from the Koran.

HINDUISM

Despite certain obvious similarities, Balinese Hinduism, or **Agama Hinduism** as it's usually termed, differs dramatically from Indian and Nepalese Hinduism. At the root of Agama Hinduism lies the fundamental understanding that the world – both natural and supernatural – is composed of **opposing forces**. These can be defined as good and evil, positive and negative, pure and impure, order and disorder, gods and demons, or as a mixture of all these things – but the crucial fact is that the forces need to be balanced. Positive forces, or **dharma**, are represented by the gods (*Dewa* and *Bhatara*), and need to be cultivated, entertained and honoured – with offerings of food, water and flowers, with dances, beautiful paintings and sculptures, fine earthly abodes (temples) and ministrations from ceremonially clad devotees. The malevolent forces, **adharma**, which manifest themselves as earth demons (*bhuta, kala* and *leyak*) and cause sickness, death and volcanic eruptions, need to be neutralized with elaborate rituals and special offerings.

To ensure that malevolent forces never take the upper hand, elaborate **purification** rituals are undertaken for the exorcism of spirits. Crucial to this is the notion of **ritual uncleanliness** (*sebel*), a state which can affect an individual (during a women's period for example, or after a serious illness), a family (after the death of a close relative, or if twins are born), or even a whole community (a plague of rats in the ricefields, or a fire in village buildings). The focus of every purification ritual is the ministering of **holy water** – such an essential part of the religion that Agama Hindu is sometimes known as *agama tirta*, the religion of holy water. As the main sources of these life-giving waters, Bali's three great mountains are also worshipped. Ever since the Stone Age, the Balinese have regarded their **mountains** as being the realm of the deities, the sea as the abode of demons and giants, and the valleys in between as the natural province of the human world. From this concept comes the Balinese sense of direction and spatial orientation, whereby all things, such as temples, houses and villages, are aligned in relation to the mountains and the sea.

Finally, there are the notions of **karma**, reincarnation, and the attaining of **enlightenment**. The aim of every Hindu is to attain enlightenment (*moksa*), which brings with it the union of the individual and the divine, and liberation from the endless painful cycle of death and rebirth. *Moksa* is only attainable by pure souls, and this can take hundreds of lifetimes to attain. Hindus believe that everybody is reincarnated according to their karma, karma being a kind of account book which registers all the good and bad deeds performed in the past lives of a soul. Karma is closely bound up with caste and the notion that an individual should accept rather than challenge their destiny.

GODS AND DEMONS

All Balinese gods are manifestations of the supreme being, **Sanghyang Widi Wasa**, a deity who is only ever alluded to in abstract form by an empty throne-shrine, the *padmasana*, that stands in the holiest corner of every temple. Sanghyang Widi Wasa's three main aspects manifest themselves as the Hindu trinity: **Brahma**, **Wisnu** and **Siwa**. Each of these three gods has different roles and is associated with specific colours and animals. Brahma is the Creator, represented by the colour red and often depicted riding on a bull. His consort is the goddess of learning, **Saraswati**, who rides a white goose. As the Preserver, Wisnu is associated with life-giving waters; he rides the **garuda** (half-man, half-bird) and is honoured by the colour black. Wisnu also has several avatars, including Buddha – a neat way of incorporating Buddhist elements into the Hindu faith. Siwa, the Destroyer or, more accurately, the Dissolver, is associated with death and rebirth, with the temples of the dead and with the colour white. He is sometimes represented as a phallic pillar or lingam, and sometimes in the manifestation of Surya, the sun god. Siwa's consort is the terrifying goddess **Durga**, whose Balinese personality is the gruesome widow-witch Rangda, queen of the demons. The son of Siwa and Durga is the elephant-headed deity **Ganesh**, generally worshipped as the remover of obstacles.

Brahma, Wisnu and Siwa all have associated lesser deities or **dewi** (**dewa** if male), many of them gods of the elements and of the physical world. The most famous of these, and certainly the most widely worshipped, is **Dewi Sri**, the goddess of rice.

The forces of evil are personified by a cast of **bhuta** and **kala**, invisible goblins and ghosts who inhabit eerie, desolate places like the temples of the dead, cemeteries, moonless seashores and dark forests. Various strategies are used to repel, confuse and banish the *bhuta* and *kala*. Most entrance gates to temples and households are guarded by fierce-looking statues and demonic images designed to be so ugly as to frighten off even the boldest demon. Many gateways are also blocked by a low brick wall, an *aling-aling*, as demons can only walk in straight lines, and so won't be able to negotiate the necessary zigzag to get around the wall. These demons can also be appeased and placated with offerings just as the gods can – the difference being that the offerings for these demons consist mainly of dirty, unpleasant, unattractive and mouldy things, which are thrown down on the ground, not placed respectfully on ledges and altars.

In addition to the unseen *bhuta* and *kala*, there are the equally fearful **leyak**, or witches, who take highly visible and creepy forms, transforming themselves into such horrors as headless chickens and riderless motorbikes. *Leyak* can transform themselves effortlessly from one form to another, and most assume the human form during the daytime. Even in their human form, *leyak* cannot be killed with knives or poisons, but they can be controlled and disempowered by harnessing white magic, as practised by shamanic *balian* (traditional healers), or by priests.

THE TEMPLES

The focus of every community's spiritual activity is the **temple** or *pura* – a specially designed temporary abode for the gods to inhabit whenever they so desire, open and unroofed so as to invite easy access between heaven and earth. Every *banjar* or small village is obliged to build at least three temples, each one serving a specific role within the community. At the top of the village stands the **pura puseh**, the temple of origin, which is dedicated to the founders of the community. For everyday spiritual activities, villagers worship at the **pura desa**, the village temple, which always lies at the heart of the village. The essential triumvirate is completed by the **pura dalem**, or temple of the dead, at the *kelod* (unclean) end of the village, which is usually dedicated either to Siwa, or to the widow-witch Rangda.

Bali also has nine directional temples, or *kayangan jagat*, which are regarded as extremely sacred by all islanders as they protect the island as a whole and all its people. The *kayangan jagat* are located at strategic points across the island, especially on high mountain slopes, rugged cliff-faces and lakeside shores.

Nearly all Balinese temples are designed around three courtyards, each section divided from the next by a low wall punctuated by a huge, and usually ornate, gateway. The outer courtyard or **jaba**, holds the secular world at bay. The middle courtyard, **jaba tengah**, acts as a transition zone between the human and the divine world, and generally contains pavilions for the preparation of offerings and the storing of temple paraphernalia. The extremely sacred inner courtyard, **jeroan**, houses all the shrines, and is the focus of all temple rituals. All offerings are brought here, prayers are held in front of the shrines, and the most sacred dances are performed within its confines. The *jeroan* is quite often out of bounds to the lay community and opened only during festivals.

Every *pura* contains a whole collection of small structures, each one devoted to a specific purpose. *Gedong* is the generic term for the squat, often cube-shaped shrines that are generally made of brick, with thatched roofs. Each *gedong* is dedicated to a particular deity or ancestor, and sometimes contains a symbolic image. The elegant pagoda-style shrines that tower over every temple wall are known as *meru*, after the sacred Hindu peak **Mount Meru**, home of the gods. There is always an odd number of roofs (three, five, seven, nine or eleven), the number indicating the status of the god to whom the temple is dedicated.

TEMPLE FESTIVALS

Aside from the daily propitiation of the household spirits, Agama Hindu requires no regular act of collective worship from its devotees. The temple's **anniversary celebration**, or *odalan*, is a three-day devotional extravaganza held at every temple either once every 210 days (every Balinese calendar year), or once every 365 days (the *saka* year). The purpose is always the same: to invite the gods down to earth so that they can be entertained and pampered by as many displays of devotion and gratitude as the community can afford. In the days before the *odalan*, the *pemangku* (priest) dresses the temple statues in holy cloths, either the spiritually charged black and white *kain poleng*, or a length of plain cloth in the colour symbolic of that temple's deity. Meanwhile, the women of the community begin to construct their offering towers, or *banten*, and to cook ceremonial food.

Odalan celebrations start in the afternoon, with a procession of women carrying their offerings to the temple. At the *pura*, the offerings are taken into the inner sanctum where the *pemangku* receives them and then blesses the devotees with holy water. Sometimes the gods will temporarily inhabit the body of one of the worshippers, sending him or her into a trance and conveying its message through gestures or words. Elsewhere in the temple compound, there's generally some performance going on: the local gamelan orchestra play, and often sacred dances are performed as well, particularly the *pendet* or offertory dance and perhaps a *barong* as well. After dark, a shadow play, wayang kulit, is often staged.

MUSIC

The shimmering sounds of the gamelan have fascinated and delighted Western visitors to Indonesia for half a millennium. Sir Francis Drake, who visited Java in 1580, described music "of a very strange kind, pleasant and delightful" – which sums up most people's reaction. The structural complexity of the music alongside its sonorous and ethereal sound gives it a lasting fascination. From the beginning of the twentieth century, composers as diverse as Debussy, Messiaen, Britten and John Cage were inspired by the music and, in recent years, there's been an enthusiastic growth of gamelan ensembles in Britain and the US. Javanese gamelan is predominantly slow and refined, whereas Balinese is fast and quixotic – and there are many other types besides.

The popular music scene in Indonesia is one of the most robust and exciting in Southeast Asia, from the bewildering range of folk and popular styles throughout the islands, to the world of *kroncong*, *dangdut*, *jaipongan* and more.

GAMELAN

A **gamelan** has been described as "one instrument played by many people". It's an ensemble of tuned percussion, consisting mainly of gongs, metallophones and drums. Gamelan **instruments** may be made of bronze, iron, brass, wood or bamboo, with wooden frames, which are often intricately carved and painted. The term "gamelan" covers a wide variety of ensembles ranging from the bronze court gamelans of Central Java to the bamboo village orchestras in Bali.

CENTRAL JAVA

The largest **bronze gamelans** in Indonesia are found in **Central Java**. A complete Javanese gamelan is made up of two sets of instruments, one in each of two scales – the five-note *laras slendro* and the seven-note *laras pelog*. The two sets are laid out with the corresponding instruments at right angles to each other. No two gamelans are tuned exactly alike, and a Javanese musician will often prefer the sound and feeling of a piece played on one gamelan to another. Larger bronze gamelans are traditionally given a name, such as "The Venerable Rain of Love".

All the instruments in the gamelan have a clear role to play, and this is reflected in the **layout** of the ensemble. Various hanging and mounted gongs are arranged at the back of the gamelan and provide the structure and form of the music. In the middle, the metallophones play the central melody. At the front are the more complex instruments, which lead and elaborate the melody. These include metallophones, a wooden xylophone, spike fiddle, bamboo flute and zither. The full ensemble also includes vocalists – a male chorus and female solo singers – and is led by the drummer in the centre of the gamelan.

The large **gong** (*gong ageng*) at the back of the gamelan is the most important instrument in the ensemble and it's believed that the spirit of the gamelan resides within it. A large gong can be over 1m in diameter and is made from a single piece of bronze. The skilled gongsmiths of Central Java are highly respected and receive orders from the whole of Java and Bali.

Although a large gamelan may be played by as many as thirty musicians, there is neither a conductor nor any visual cues, as the players all sit facing the same way. Musical notation, although now used extensively in teaching, is never used in performance. Gamelan musicians learn all the instruments and so develop a deep understanding of the music plus great sensitivity and flexibility in ensemble playing. During an all-night **wayang kulit** you may see musicians changing places, and special guests are sometimes invited to play. Gamelan is a communal form of musicmaking – there are no soloists or virtuosos – and although the female singers tend to use microphones they are not considered soloists in the Western sense.

Some of the finest gamelans in Java are housed in the courts, including a number of **ceremonial gamelans**; some of the ceremonial gamelans are believed to be magically charged. The gongs are the most sacred instruments, and are given offerings of flowers and incense before performances. The largest and loudest, known as **Gamelan Sekaten**, are still played once a year in the palace mosques of Solo and Yogya. These large gamelans were built in the early days of Islam in Java to draw people in to the mosques. To this day a pair of Gamelan Sekaten are played almost continuously for a week during the **sekaten festival**, to commemorate the birth and death of the prophet Mohammed. The powerful sound of these gamelans draws huge crowds into the mosques, where calls to prayer mingle with gamelan music, incense, offerings, and the hubbub of the fair outside.

But gamelan music is played by a wide range of people in Central Java. Most village halls and neighbourhoods in major towns have a gamelan for use by the local community. The majority of schoolchildren learn basic gamelan pieces and can continue their studies in conservatories and academies of performing arts in the major towns of Solo and Yogyakarta. Gamelan music accompanies many types of dance and theatre, ranging from lively village **ketoprak** performances to the refined palace **srimpi** dance. The radio station (RRI: Radio Republik Indonesia) employs professional studio musicians and broadcasts a wide range of gamelan music.

BALI

Most villages in **Bali** boast several gamelans owned by the local music club. The club members meet in the evenings to rehearse, after earning their living as farmers, craftsmen or civil servants. Gamelan playing is traditionally considered a part of every man's education, as important as the art of rice growing or cooking ceremonial food. Children play too, and learn by sitting in their father's laps as they rehearse.

The **village gamelan** is kept in a public place, and rehearsals usually draw an interested audience of onlookers who offer comments and suggestions. Many villages have a distinctive style or speciality: Peliatan is known for the refinement of its courtly *legong* dance and music, Sukawati for the complexity and brilliance of its *gender* playing. It's said that people can find their way around the island in the dark by recognizing the distinctive tones of the local gamelans shimmering across the ricefields.

When the Dutch took control of Bali in the early twentieth century, the island's courts all but disappeared. This had an enormous impact on the musical life of the island. The court gamelans had no function outside the palace walls and were sold or taken to the villages where they were melted down to make new gamelans for the latest style that was taking Bali by storm: **kebyar**.

The word literally means "like the bursting open of a flower". *Kebyar* originated in north Bali and replaced the slow, stately court pieces with fast, dynamic music, full of dramatic contrasts, changes of tempo and sudden loud outbursts. It was not long before Bali's most famous dancer, **I Mario**, choreographed the first *kebyar* dance, in which the intricate and beautiful movements of the dancer's eyes, head and hands mirror the dazzling display of the music. It is this dynamic new virtuoso style that makes much Balinese gamelan music today sound so different from the Javanese form.

Kebyar has influenced other ensembles in Bali: the most stunning example being the all-bamboo **joged bumbung**, Even the "gong" is made from bamboo. *Joged bumbung* is very popular in West Bali, where it developed in the 1950s from a small bamboo ensemble used to accompany lively village dances.

Where Javanese music is quiet, contemplative and restrained, Balinese is loud, sparkling and extrovert. It is, after all, outdoor music. Like the elaborate temple carvings and paintings, the music is intricately detailed. Just as the harmony of village life depends on the delicate balance of opposing forces, so in the gamelan the instruments appear in pairs, even the drums, which are called male and female.

The rhythmic vitality of Balinese music comes from lively interlocking patterns played on various pairs of instruments. These patterns, called **kotekan**, are played on the bronze *gangsas* (similar to the Javanese *gender* but struck with hard wooden mallets), a pair of drums and the *reong* (a row of small kettlegongs in a frame, played by four people).

Apart from the rhythm, there's another kind of beat in Balinese gamelan music. The various pairs of instruments are tuned slightly "out"

BALI

Bali: A Suite of Tropical Music and Sound
(World Network, Germany).
Volume 35 in WN's ambitious global survey. The ideal introduction to the varied sounds of Balinese music, beginning with frogs and cicadas. Includes many of the lesser-known gamelan styles – *gambuh*, *selunding*, *jegog*, *joged bumbung* and *kecak*. The only thing missing is the straight *kebyar* sound, but there's plenty of that to be found elsewhere.

Gamelan Semar Pegulingan Saih Pitu: The Heavenly Orchestra of Bali (CMP, Germany).
The "love gamelan", the ethereal, tinkly sound of this sort of ensemble, accompanied the king while he slept with the queen. Gamelan, flutes and drums in a lovely clear recording of a 29-strong ensemble from Kamasan, eastern Bali. The best Semar Pegulingan recording, with good sleeve notes.

Gamelan Semar Pegulingan (II) (JVC, Japan).
Semar Pegulingan group from Peliatan village. Another exquisite recording without the bamboo flutes but with atmospheric insects in the background. Poor notes in English.

Jegog of Nagara (King, Japan).
The best *jegog* disc around. Thunderous sound, lots of atmosphere and the competing of two groups from west Bali. Turn it up loud and enjoy the thrill.

Music for the Gods (Rykodisc, US).
Recordings made (mostly in Bali) in 1941 by Bruce and Sheridan Fahnestock, weeks before World War II and subsequent tourism changed the island forever. These unique recordings include Semar Pegulingan, *kebyar*, a *gender* quartet for wayang and *kecak*, plus three tracks of fascinating stuff from the island of Madura.

JAVA

Gamelan of the Kraton, Yogyakarta
(Celestial Harmonies, US).
The most atmospheric and beautifully recorded of Javanese gamelan discs. Here the court musicians play grandiose ceremonial pieces, elegant dance repertoire and the extraordinary music, peculiar to the Yogya kraton, of the *bedhaya* dance with added snare drums and brass. Excellent.

Gamelan of Surakarta (JVC, Japan).
This is the best introduction available to the Surakarta style of Javanese gamelan. Three pieces played by the Surakarta School of Indonesian Arts (STSI), from serene music with choral singing to dynamic and varied instrumental playing co-ordinated by the virtuoso drumming of Rahayu Supanggah, the composer. The final piece, composed to accompany traditional dance drama, reveals gamelan as a living, developing tradition.

WEST JAVA

Flutes and Gamelan Music of West Java
(Topic Records, UK).
A rare glimpse of gamelan music from Cirebon, a city on the north coast of West Java, as well as a selection of *kecapi suling*. It features Sulaeman, a player of the Sundanese *suling* with a recording career stretching back to the days of 78s.

Java – Pays Sunda, 2: L'art du Gamelan Degung (Ocora, France).
One of the definitive recordings of gamelan *degung* currently available in the West, with a fine representation of pieces from the classical repertoire as well as new compositions. Features the bamboo flute playing of Ono Sukarna.

Tembang Sunda (Nimbus, UK).
Mellow performances from male and female vocalists, Imas Permas and Asep Kosasih, accompanied by zither and flute. Refined classical repertoire plus more easy-going love songs. Translations included.

OTHER

Banyumas Bamboo Gamelan (Nimbus, UK).
The only widely available recording of Banyumas *calung* music, the Javanese bamboo gamelan. Traditional dance pieces with vocals and some more contemporary styles drawing on *jaipongan* and *dangdut*. Great frog imitations on track no. 3.

Lombok, Kalimantan, Banyumas: Little-Known Forms of Gamelan and Wayang
(Smithsonian Folkways, US).
Part fourteen of SF's extensive survey of Indonesian music features *wayang sasak* from Lombok, a theatrical form related to Balinese *gambuh*; masked and shadow theatre music from South Kalimantan (Borneo); and *jemblung* from Banyumas which comprises amazing vocal imitations of gamelan.

NEW GAMELAN MUSIC

Asmat Dream (Lyrichord, US).
More for gamelan or new music specialists perhaps, but ample illustration of the radical experiments underway with gamelan and other traditional instruments. Includes music by four Sundanese composers including Nano S.

Music of K.R.T. Wasitodiningrat (CMP, Germany).
Rebab player and composer Wasitodiningrat was associated with the Paku Alaman court gamelan of Yogyakarta. The eight compositions on this disc are within the traditional framework of Central Javanese gamelan.

Thanks to Penny King and Maria Mendonça for help with the discography.

with each other, so that when two instruments are played together, there is a "harmonic beating". This gives the sound of the Balinese gamelan its characteristic shimmering quality.

WEST JAVA (SUNDA)

The island of Java is inhabited by several ethnic groups. The Javanese live mainly in Central and East Java, while the main inhabitants of **West Java** are the Sundanese, which is why that region is often known as Sunda.

The sound of **degung** is arguably the most accessible of all gamelan music to Western ears. Its musical structures are clear and well-defined, and the timbres of the instruments blend delicately with one another without losing any of their integrity or individuality. The ensemble is small, consisting only of a few instruments, but includes the usual range of gongs and metallophones found in all gamelan. However, the very special character of *degung*, which uses its own five-note version of the *pelog* scale found in Java, owes much to the additional presence of the **suling** and is regarded as something of a signature for Sundanese music. In fact, no other instrument more perfectly exemplifies the musical heart of Sunda or better conjures up the traditional picture of gentle, picturesque paddyfields and restful, idyllic village life.

Degung is unique to Sunda, and was developed during the last century. Deriving from a court tradition, it has a more exalted place among the performing arts than gamelan *salendro* – although the best musicians frequent the circles of both – and is now mainly used in concert form for wedding receptions and other social events. Nevertheless, examples of *degung* for *tari topeng* (masked dances) exist, and, more recently, augmented forms of the ensemble have been used to accompany performances of wayang golek. In addition, it has made inroads into popular culture through **"pop Sunda"** (using Western pop instruments) which achieved immense popularity during the 1980s through the hands of composers such as **Nano S.** (see p.971).

EAST JAVA

As you travel progressively eastwards, the prevailing musical style becomes marked by increasing dynamism and aggressiveness. Whilst it is true to say that groups performing in the province's capital city of Surabaya often play pieces in a mixture of styles, those from rural areas, particularly from around the town of Malang, are usually more genuinely **East Javanese** in expression.

Perhaps the most dramatic element of East Javanese gamelan music, and certainly one not found outside the region, is that of the **gamyak drum**. Larger than the Central Javanese equivalent, its drumheads are made from buffalo rather than goat skin, and the piercingly-sharp sound produced is immediately recognizable. It is especially associated with the *ngremo* dance – the drumming for which is considered some of the most technically demanding anywhere in Java – and various forms of *tari topeng* (masked dance) popular around Malang. In addition, *tayuban* – dances where male spectators may request pieces from the gamelan and, for a small gratuity, dance with one of the *tandhak* (female dancers) present – have helped steer the popular gamelan repertoire away from the classical refinement associated with Central Java. Once common throughout Java, these are rowdy affairs and only continue to exist in areas where Islam has a limited influence on daily life. As a consequence it is still popular in the Tengger region, where the prevailing religion synthesizes elements of Hinduism with pre-Hindu beliefs.

By Jenny Heaton and Simon Steptoe

POP

There are any number of rock groups, rappers, boy's groups and pop singers and a growing dance-floor scene for which the name "house" has been co-opted. It seems that every region has it's own house music – Bali House, Java House, Batak House from Sumatra and so on. But this is not to discount the ongoing popularity of the more identifiably home-grown **pop music**: *kroncong, dangdut, jaipongan, degung, pop-Sunda, mandarin, pop-batak* and *qasidah*.

KRONCONG

Kroncong (pronounced ker-ong-chong), can trace its roots back several centuries to when the Portuguese were establishing trade links with Africa and South Asia. The arrival of European instruments laid the basis for what later became the first major urban-folk style. By the early 1900s, *kroncong* was mainly associated with the lowlife of the cities, but began gaining national popularity in the 1930s through its use by the new Indonesian film industry. During the independence struggle, many inspirational patriotic songs were set to *kroncong* music.

Then a typical ensemble consisted of two *kroncong* (three-string ukuleles), guitar, violin, flute, percussion and, variously, a cello played pizzicato or a double bass accompanying a singer, usually female. The distinctive *kroncong* rhythm is set up by the two ukuleles – one known as the *cik*, the other as the *cuk* – playing alternate strokes of the beat. The medium-pace tempo, the diatonic melodies and the languid, crooning singing style invite comparison with east African Taarab music and even Portuguese Fado. The most celebrated *kroncong* number, *Bengawan Solo*, was written by composer and singer Gesang in 1943. It's about the beauty of the river in Solo and is probably the most famous and most covered of Indonesian pop songs. In and around Solo, there's also a regional style of *kroncong* called **langgam jawa** in which the *pelog* (seven-note) scale and textures of gamelan music are imitated by the *kroncong* ensemble. It has an enchanting and sentimental sound.

GAMBANG KROMONG

Gambang kromong developed out of the type of *kroncong* music featured in an urban folk theatre form called *komedi stambul*, popular in the early decades of the twentieth century. If you travel to the town of Tangerang, about two hour's drive from Jakarta, you may be able to catch the modern-day equivalent called *lenong*, or get yourself invited to a wedding. In either case the music will be *gambang kromong* played on a bewildering array of Chinese, Indonesian and Western instruments. A typical ensemble can bring together two-string fiddle, bamboo flute (*suling*), xylophone (*gambang*), pot-gongs, drums and percussion from the Javanese gamelan, plus one or more Western instruments such as trumpet, keyboards, electric bass guitar, clarinet or Hawaiian guitar. Melodies weave in and out and against the *loping* percussive backdrop, sounding at times like a Dixieland Jazz band jamming with a gamelan. Highly recommended.

DANGDUT

Dang-dut-dang-dut-dang-dut-dang-dut. You can't mistake it and you'll hear it everywhere you go. **Dangdut**, Indonesia's equivalent of

danceable Latin music, has been thriving since the mid-1970s. It grew out of *kroncong* and *orkes Melayu* (Malay) – the sort of music typified by Malaysia's P. Ramlee – but its most obvious influence is that of Indian film song. As with many Indonesian musical terms, *dangdut* is an onomatopoeic word derived from the rhythm, usually played on the *gendang* (a pair of bongo-like drums tuned to sound like *tabla*). So that you know your dang from your dut, count in fours and hear the low dang note struck on the fourth beat and the high dut note struck on the first beat of the following bar. Alongside the *gendang*, a typical group consists of electric guitar, bass, mandolin, drum kit and keyboards. But the real stars, of course, are the singers: glamorous men and women singing of love found, lost and wanted or of moral issues, family matters – the everyday and fantasy life of the *dangdut* audience.

Following on from the *orkes Melayu* crooners like Munif and Ellya Agus, came the first superstars of *dangdut*. **Rhoma Irama** and **Elvy Sukaesih** are still known today as the king and queen of *dangdut*. They made many successful recordings as a duo in the early Seventies, and both have many million-selling albums to their credit. Rhoma Irama has always been identified as a "working class hero". Starting out as a long-haired rebel, he found his true artistic direction after his *haj* to Mecca. He went on to star in several films and still tours regularly with his Soneta group, putting his inspirational messages over with all the paraphernalia of a full-blown rock-show.

JAIPONGAN

Just occasionally in the *dangdut* dancehalls, the drum machines and bendy guitars may be interrupted by a percussion-based style with an unpredictable tempo. This will be **jaipongan**, a style that has no detectable Western influence, using only instruments from the Sundanese gamelan tradition.

The *rebab* (a two-stringed bowed fiddle) plays the introduction, as the *khendang* (a large two-headed barrel drum) improvises in free time underneath; then, with whooping cries, the rest of the orchestra enters. The *khendang* sets to building and releasing tension through a cyclical pattern marked by a single stroke on a large gong, while a smaller gong, a *kempul*, beats out one-note bass-lines. The mellow sounds of the *bonang rincik* and the *panerus* (sets of pot-shaped gongs) play stately cyclical melodies as the *saron* (a row of seven bronze keys set over a resonating box) hammers out faster arpeggios. The *rebab* anticipates, accompanies and answers the singer (*pesindhen*) as she floats like a butterfly through tales of love, money and agriculture, while throughout, various members of the orchestra indulge in more whooping, wailing and rhythmic grunting known as *senggak.*

It was in Bandung that *jaipongan* first appeared in the mid-1960s, and by the end of the decade it had become a national dance-craze, and all without an electric guitar in sight. *Jaipongan* is still popular today and in recent years the distinctive drumming style has been co-opted by several *dangdut* artists.

DEGUNG, KECAPI SULING AND POP-SUNDA

Wistful, melancholic, meditative, the sound of **degung** embodies the feeling Indonesians describe as "Sakit Hati". The literal English translation is "sick liver", but of course that is losing some of the romantic inference. In Bahasa Indonesia, the poetic organ of affection is the liver rather than the heart, and "Sakit Hati" describes a feeling of longing and sadness.

Gamelan degung developed as a court music deemed the most suitable for playing while guests were arriving at social occasions, and modern *degung* music performs a similar function today. It has found a whole new audience, particularly among tourists in Bali, where *degung* cassettes provide the ambience in many cafés and restaurants. It is peaceful, harmonious background music characterized by gentle percussion, delicate improvising on the *suling* and soft arpeggios played on the *bonang* and *saron* and underpinned by the warm tones of the hanging gongs which give the music its name.

Kecapi Suling is an instrumental form developed from another court tradition of sung entertainment music called *tembang Sunda.* A typical ensemble consists of a *suling* accompanied by two or three *kecapi* – a zither or koto-like instrument of varying sizes and number of strings. Each string has a separate bridge to facilitate tuning between various modes. *Kecapi Suling* utilizes the pentatonic scales known as *pelog* and *sorog.* When singing is included, the haunting melodies carry poetic and sometimes mysterious images sung in Sundanese.

A mark of quality to look out for is the name of **Nano S.** on the cassette cover. This amazingly prolific composer is also responsible for some of the best examples of the **pop-Sunda** style, where *degung* meets modern technology. Sequenced drum and bass patterns accompany the traditional-style melodies, and often all the Sundanese instruments are replaced by synthesized sounds.

QASIDAH MODERN

Qasidah is a classical Arabic word for epic religious poetry, traditionally performed by a story-teller-singer, accompanied by percussion and chanting. Indonesian Muslims practise their own versions of this, improvising lyrics in local languages that address contemporary concerns and moral issues.

Qasidah modern places this in a pop-song form, adding electric guitars, mandolin, keyboards, violins and flutes. Rhythms and melodies from *dangdut* and Arabic pop are used, while the lyrics frequently offer moral advice to young lovers, extolling a virtuous life and warning against corruption and other temptations. Sometimes the lyrics even tackle environmental issues such as pollution, nuclear power and cigarette smoking.

The pioneers of *qasidah modern* are **Nasida Ria**, a nine-woman orchestra from Semarang who have released over 25 albums and have twice toured Germany. One of their albums is available on the Berlin-based Piranha label. At home they perform chiefly at Muslim weddings throughout Java or occasionally at open-air rallies sponsored by religious groups, where the proceedings are opened by a sermon or two before the orchestra take the stage. In their colourful head-scarves and close-fitting dresses that cover them from head to foot, they manage to look simultaneously alluring and modest, and the occasional heavy-metal posturing of the guitarists is also conducted with great decorum.

If the strong Arabic influence of this music is to your taste then you might want to plan a trip along the north coast of Java to **Surabaya**, home of Gambus music.

GAMBUS

Gambus is the Indonesian word for the Arabic lute, the *oud,* but it is now used to denote both a style of music and the orchestra that plays it.

KRONCONG AND DANGDUT

Music of Indonesia Vol 2: Kroncong, Dangdut and Langgam Jawa
(Smithsonian Folkways, US).
Part of Philip Yampolsky's ambitious series), and certainly the most approachable for newcomers. Beautiful *kroncong* tracks, with good *dangdut* selections from the Soneta Group with Rhoma Irama, Elvy Sukaesih and others. Excellent sleeve notes.

Street Music of Java (Original Music, US).
Wonderful recordings made in the late Seventies of more homespun versions of *kroncong* and *dangdut*, plus *ronggeng* dances and zither music. Java has lots of street musicians playing in market areas.

Hetty Koes Endang Keroncong Asli
(Musica, Indonesia).
Currently available only in Indonesia, recorded in the early Eighties, but still sounding fresh. This is high quality *kroncong* by the most versatile of popular singers, accompanied by the greatest orchestra of the time, Orkes Kroncong Bintang Jakarta.

Rhoma Irama Begadang 1975–1980
(Meta, Japan).
A good introduction to the rock-influenced style of the man still known as the king of *dangdut*. Features some of his most famous songs including the great *Santai (Relax)*.

Elvy Sukaesih Raja dan Ratu (Rice Records, Japan).
Featuring Rhoma Irama and Elvy Sukaesih, these are sparkling pop gems from the early Seventies from the king and queen (*raja* and *ratu*) of *dangdut*.

JAIPONGAN AND POP-SUNDA

Hetty Koes Endang The Best of Sundanese Pop Songs (Musica, Indonesia).
Only available in Indonesia, but an essential buy if you're there. Sweet, haunting melodies with pop arrangements. Includes the multi-million selling hit *Cinta*.

Jugala Orchestra The Sound of Sunda
(GlobeStyle, UK).
A cross section of modern *degung* and other popular music. To be played "after 6pm in a peaceful environment, while your guests are arriving for dinner or when your love-object has left you". Strongly recommended.

Detty Kurnia Coyor Panon
(Wave, Japan; Flame Tree, UK).
Detty Kurnia is the daughter of a famous Sundanese gamelan player and is pop-Sunda's brightest star, singing both pop and traditional styles. A first-class collection of songs betraying the influence of *degung*, *jaipongan*, *calung* and more. Highly recommended, although currently unavailable.

Yayah Ratnasari & Karawang Group
Break Pong (Meta Co, Japan).
This female vocalist and band are one of the best current *jaipongan* outfits, based in the Sundanese town of Karawang. An unusual recording; they obviously had lots of fun adding a drum machine to their traditional percussion set-up.

TRADITIONAL

Sing Sing So: Songs of the Batak People
(JVC, Japan).
The Batak are famed for the beauty of their folksongs, justifiably so, on the strength of these performances. The tunes are rather European in character with a strongly lyrical line but distinctly Southeast Asian warmth. Solo songs accompanied by Western-style guitar, wonderful instrumental tracks of wooden gamelan and flute and choral numbers sounding distinctly evangelical. Very approachable.

CONTEMPORARY

Djaduk Ferianto & Kua Etnika
Nang Ning Nong Orkes Sumpeg
(Galang Comm, Indonesia).
Djaduk Ferianto and his group use instruments from all over the archipelago to create their own "world music". So far only available in Indonesia, this is an exciting new direction from Yogyakarta. Traditional violins, flutes, percussion and metallophones interact with modern keyboard sounds and global rhythms. Recommended.

Moluccan Moods Orchestra Wakoi
(Piranha, Germany).
A band of expatriates based in Holland, led by guitarist Eddy Lekransy until his death in 1988. Moluccan songs given a contemporary jazz-funk treatment. Guitar, keyboards, sax, flutes and percussion plus wonderful harmony singing from the three female vocalists.

Sabah Habas Mustapha Denpasar Moon
(Wave, Japan; Piranha, Germany).
A wonderful disc from 1994. *Dangdut* and Sundanese styles performed with musicians in Jakarta with global rhythms and English lyrics. Great for reminiscing about those fleeting holiday romances and strongly recommended even if you've never set foot there.

Nasida Ria Keadilan (Piranha, Germany).
The leading exponents of *qasidah modern*. Hugely successful nine-member, all-female band from Central Java with a moralistic message. An enjoyable, bouncy mix of Arabic and *dangdut* styles sung with plenty of synthesizer plus flute and violin.

The *oud* was brought to Indonesia along with Islam, and much of the music and dances associated with it were introduced by settlers from the Yemen. Visit the Arab quarter in Surabaya, and you may hear the voice of **Oum Kalthoum** wafting out of one of the shops in the bazaar, or it could be Surabaya's own diva, **Soraya**. You may also hear what sounds like a typical modern pop production from Saudi or Kuwait, but it is more likely to be one of the local stars of the *gambus* modern scene – **Muhdar Alatas** or **Ali Alatas** (no relation).

Many *gambus* songs are lifted straight from imported Arabic cassettes and given a local stamp. Some retain the Arabic texts, many are rewritten in Bahasa Indonesia. All the hallmarks of great Arabic pop are there: rolling rhythms on the *derbuka* and the *oud*, sinuous melody lines on flute and violins and, regardless of the language, much silky ornamentation of the vocal lines from the singer. Although loved by millions, *gambus* is hardly known outside Indonesia and there are still no recordings available internationally.

By Colin Bass

ENVIRONMENT
AND WILDLIFE

Indonesia's environment and wildlife reflect the country's unique position as a series of island stepping stones between the Southeast Asian mainland and Australia, comprising some of the last great expanses of prime tropical wilder-ness on earth. While it's possible to visit areas which have hardly changed since they were first seen by Europeans in the mid-nineteenth century, it's also true that Indonesia's natural history – in common with that of Asia, Africa and South America – is also under severe threat from the modern world.

HABITATS AND INHABITANTS

Although all of Indonesia is equatorial, resulting in locally stable temperatures and rainfall, varied geology has created a huge range of habitats. Most famous, perhaps, is the country's position on the "Ring of Fire", a tectonic fault line responsible for creating much of the archipelago in the first place, and centring the world's greatest concentration of active **volcanoes** in Java and Bali. Elsewhere, older ranges have eroded to form the **alluvial lowlands** of Sumatra, Kalimantan and Irian. Southern Kalimantan's **peat beds** are compressed, ancient forests, and uplifted fossil reefs are the basis of the porous **limestone** hills of southern Sulawesi and southeastern Maluku. And, as

WALLACE AND WALLACEA

Born in 1823, **Alfred Russell Wallace** was a largely self-educated naturalist who spent his early professional life hunting wildlife in Europe and the Amazon for museum collections. In 1854 he began what was to become a 22,000-kilometre, eight-year expedition to Indonesia (engagingly recounted in his book *The Malay Archipelago*), amassing 125,000 specimens and discovering countless new creatures for science. During his travels in Indonesia, Wallace noticed how similar animals varied between islands, and began to wonder if isolated environments might allow identical forms to gradually **evolve** over time into completely different species. This prompted his 1858 thesis, *On the Tendency of Varieties to Depart Indefinitely from the Original Type*, which he sent from his north Maluku base to the foremost biologist of the day, **Charles Darwin**. Unknown to Wallace, Darwin had formulated a similar theory 25 years earlier whilst in the Galapagos islands; fearing the negative reception such a notion would receive in creationist Victorian England, however, he had kept his conclusions private. The two now made a joint public announcement, but, with Wallace still in distant Indonesia, it was Darwin whose name became fixed in the public mind as the inventor of evolu-tionary theory following publication in 1859 of his classic *On the Origin of Species by Means of Natural Selection*.

Not begrudging Darwin his fame – he even dedicated *The Malay Archipelago* to him – Wallace spent the rest of his ninety years refining his views on **biogeography**, the factors affecting the distribution of species throughout the world. Most importantly, he identified Indonesia as a crossover point between Oriental and Australasian fauna, and drew a definite line running north through the region between Bali and Lombok, and Borneo and Sulawesi, either side of which species were predominantly either Oriental or Australasian. A straightforward idea in itself, **Wallace's Line** became the subject of a complicated set of revisions, clarified in the 1920s by the creation of **Wallacea**, which sidesteps definite boundaries by encapsulating Sulawesi, Nusa Tenggara and Maluku as a biological **transition zone** between Asia and Australasia. With wildlife and plants from both regions to draw upon, as well as a huge number of species found nowhere else – over 240 endemic types of bird, for example – Wallacea remains one of the richest hunting-grounds on earth for anyone interested in natural history.

Indonesia's thousands of islands encompass terrain ranging from sandy beaches to snow-clad mountains, you'll also find a broad slice of the world's environments represented within this single country: montane heathland, temperate, tropical and even deciduous forests, savannah and semi-arid grassland, and coastal sand flats fringed by swamps.

When it comes to flora and fauna, Indonesia splits into three **biological zones**. The western section, from Sumatra to Bali, was once connected to the Asian mainland during lower ice-age sea levels, which allowed **Oriental** species to cross and colonize. Over in the east, Irian Jaya and parts of Maluku were similarly once joined to Australia, and so are home to mainly **Australasian** species. The region in between, which contains a mixture of Oriental, Australasian and unique species, is known as **Wallacea** after the naturalist who first recognized the division – see the box opposite. In addition, the abrupt volcanic formation of many islands results in typically steep **underwater** drop-offs, encouraging abundant coral reefs with a staggering range of marine life.

SOME FLORA

Indonesia has the most extensive coastal **mangrove swamps** in tropical Asia, concentrated in Irian Jaya and Kalimantan. Though not the prettiest of trees, mangroves are specially adapted to living in salt water, many species having distinctively arched and buttressed roots, and they aerate the typically thick, sticky mud that they live in. Another salt-tolerant tree, the **nipa palm**, has a trunk which grows almost completely underwater in brackish estuaries, with just the tall fronds showing. Indonesia has a palm tree for almost every situation: cultivated coconuts; thorny rattan, which look like vines but are actually a climbing palm and are used all over the country in furniture, houses and household goods; sago from Maluku, the pith of which is turned into tapioca; tall, elegant arecas, source of the stimulating betel nut; and lontar fan palms, a hardy species equally at home in Maluku's swampy lowland forest and drier parts of Sulawesi and Nusa Tenggara, where trees stand widely spaced across the grasslands.

Indonesia's rainforests are pretty well everything you would expect them to be, varying from steamy, swampy lowland jungle thick with bamboo, vines, gingers, ferns and lianas, to high-altitude cloud forests where trees are whiskered in **orchids**, carnivorous pitcher plants, patches of moss and strands of old man's beard. Western Indonesian forests are dominated by dipterocarps, a family of trees found from Asia through to Africa which includes teak and meranti, both valuable timbers. Of no commercial use, **rafflesia** is a rainforest parasite found mainly on Java and Sumatra, whose family includes the largest, tallest, and smelliest fruiting bodies of any plants. Further east, forest giants are more likely to be quandongs, whose spherical blue seeds litter the ground in Aru and parts of Irian, or figs, some of which start off life as a seedling at the top of another tree before encircling and strangling the host. The myrtle family is also well represented in Wallacea and the east: there are some massive gum trees as far west as central Sulawesi, while both cloves and aromatic ti-tree oil (once famous as Makassar oil) are derived from myrtle trees native to Maluku. Right over in southeastern Irian Jaya, the country becomes downright Australian, an open savannah peppered with wattles and sclerophyl.

SOME FAUNA

One feature of western Indonesia are **large mammals**, whose populations dwindle rapidly as you move east through the archipelago. Along with five kinds of deer, the forests of Java and Sumatra are the last place you've a chance to see wild tigers, rhino or elephants in Southeast Asia. There's a range of primates here too, including chunky macaques, long-armed gibbons and the orange-furred orang-utan of Kalimantan and Sumatra; Kalimantan's riverine forests are also home to the big-nosed proboscis monkey, a vegetarian ape which enjoys swimming.

Deer hang on in parts of Wallacea, along with a few monkeys such as Sulawesi's black macaque, but are overshadowed by some plain unusual animals such as Nusa Tenggara's giant **Komodo dragon**, a three-metre-long monitor lizard, and Sulawesi's mysterious babirusa, a horned pig-like beast with no known relatives. This region is also renowned for its **birdlife**, including endemic hornbills, parrots, pigeons and megapodes, grouse-sized birds which incubate their eggs in a specially-constructed mound of rotting leaves and soil. You'll also start to encounter a trickle of distinctly Australian animals in Wallacea – cockatoos for instance – which becomes a flood further east in Irian: most distinctive are the **marsupials**, or pouched mammals, who give birth to a partially formed embryo which is nurtured in a special pouch. Indonesian representatives include forest-dwelling, slow-moving cuscus possums found as far west as Sulawesi, with grassland-loving wallabies and kangaroos, along with arboreal **tree kangaroos**, confined to Irian and nearby islands. Looking like a long-nosed porcupine or hedgehog, Irian Jaya's ant-eating **echidnas** are even stranger, one of only two egg-laying mammals (the other is eastern Australia's platypus). Lowland vine forests in Irian and eastern Maluku are also the stomping ground for the ostrich-like cassowary, while full blown Irianese rainforest hides over twenty species of **birds of paradise**, unquestionably the most spectacularly-adorned of all birds – if also some of the hardest to actually see.

THREATS

The biggest threats to Indonesia's environment are modern economic and human pressures. Worst hit are those areas which, until now, have been by their very natures the least touched: primary rainforest and the marine environment.

Forests across the archipelago are rapidly retreating, cleared either to create new farmland, or to provide commercial timber. The problem here is not so much the logging itself, but rather the methods employed, which tend to strip forests back to bedrock either by dragging chains or simply setting **fire** to the trees. The latter method was almost certainly to blame for igniting the massive 1997–98 conflagrations in Kalimantan's forests (see p.731), which had been degraded to a lesser extent during the 1980s. In the short term, burning enriches the soil for cultivation – a method traditionally used on a far smaller scale by Kalimantan's Dayaks – but the nutrients are soon exhausted and, unless left to grow wild again, are not replaced. A side effect of logging is that it opens up new areas to **mining**, which, whether on a small or large scale, is an industry notorious for not clearing up after itself – witness the heavy-metal-laden Sungai Sekonyer in Kalimantan's southwest.

Once their habitat has gone, there's little chance for wildlife. Obvious species such as tigers or elephants may survive in zoos, but this ignores the demise of smaller, less appealing animals. And extinction in the wild may be permanent, even if the animal itself thrives in captivity and suitable reserves are later established. Young orang-utan, for instance, need a lengthy education to teach them how to live in the wild; unless raised there, it's unlikely that they can be reintroduced at a later stage. Other factors affect successful reintroduction: the **Bali starling** is a common-enough cage bird, but attempts to re-establish a viable population in western Bali have been stymied by **collectors**. The demand for cage birds in Southeast Asia is a major drain on many species, particularly in Maluku and Irian Jaya – populations of endemic parrots have declined rapidly in recent years.

While Indonesia's **seas** themselves remain clean, encouraging a healthy pearl industry, fishing practices are beginning to have a serious impact. The popularity of **reef bombing** is fading in the face of government pressure, but **drift-netting** seems to be on the increase, a method which – like bombing – catches everything, whether commercially useful or not. Unlike bombing, however, a good deal of commercial fishing in Indonesia is run by Japanese, Korean, Chinese, Singaporean and Taiwanese companies, who have no interest in preserving local fish stocks. The acute demand for shark's fin has seen populations almost wiped out in southeastern Maluku, and an increasing number of Indonesian vessels are being caught fishing in Australian waters as a result.

CONSERVATION AND THE FUTURE

Indonesia has an impressive number of **national parks** and **reserves** covering every imaginable habitat, which, although they are not inviolate, provide an excellent basis for preserving the archipelago's range of environments. The problem lies with ensuring that protection within these reserves is enforced, a difficult task considering that many are extremely remote from major population centres and that effective policing is therefore almost impossible. Remoteness, and the practical difficulties involved in simply tracking down and seeing wildlife – even common species – in thick undergrowth, has also limited the commercial potential of **eco-tourism**. This means that most Indonesian reserves are not financially viable, and that government protection is altruistic – and so vulnerable to other pressures.

It's likely that the effect of Indonesia's economic downturn on it's natural heritage will be two-sided. Development projects, such as the construction of new roads to, or through, wilderness areas, will slow down; at the same time, there will be an ever-growing need to earn export income from mining and timber resources. As Indonesia faces the twenty-first century, it remains to be seen how far its commitments to its environment are compromised by the country's uncertain economic future.

BOOKS

While plenty has been written on the culture, temples and arts and crafts of Bali, there is relatively little coverage of the rest of Indonesia. Early visitors produced a clutch of fascinating first-hand accounts of a now vanished world, and many of these are available through the OUP Asia imprint. Periplus is a specialist on the region and produces a range of excellently written and photographed works about Indonesia, including a six-volume ecology series, cookbooks, a host of travel guides, and adventure guides on the best places to go diving, birding and surfing.

Many of these books are published by Indonesian publishers – you may be able to order them from bookshops in your own country, but most are available in Indonesia. Where two publishers are listed, these are British/US publishers. UP denotes University Press.

TRAVEL

Benedict Allen *Into the Crocodile's Nest* (Palladin). Allen treks alone through Irian's forests in search of a certain tribe, fails dismally and has to add Papua New Guinea to his trip in order to fill a book.

David Attenborough *Zoo Quest for a Dragon* (o/p). A youthful Attenborough's erratic travels through the archipelago during the 1950s as a wildlife collector and filmmaker, peaking with the capture of a Komodo dragon – even if authorities wouldn't let him ship it to England.

Nigel Barley *Not a Hazardous Sport* (Penguin). Humourous, double-sided culture-shock tale, as the anthropologist author visits Indonesia for the first time and persuades craftsmen from Sulawesi to return to London with him in order

to build a traditional Torajan rice barn in the Museum of Mankind.

Vicki Baum *A Tale from Bali* (OUP Asia). Occasionally moving and always interesting semi-factual historical novel based on the events leading up to the 1906 *puputan* in Denpasar. Written from the notes bequeathed to the author in 1937 by a Dutch doctor who had lived and worked in Sanur for several decades.

Lawrence and Lorne Blair *Ring of Fire* (Bantam). Possibly the definitive account of a tour around the Indonesian archipelago. The photos are great, the tales are occasionally tall and certainly not lacking in drama, atmosphere and a genuine passion for the country and its inhabitants.

Carl Bock *Head Hunters of Borneo* (OUP Asia). Taken with a pinch of salt, Bock's account of his trek into the unknown wilds of Kalimantan during the 1870s is an excellent read, though he gets carried away by the gorier side of Dayak tradition.

Peter Carey and G. Carter Bentley (eds) *East Timor at the Crossroads* (Cassell). A mixture of scholarly essays and personal accounts of the East Timor problem. The material is – as you might expect – mostly seen from the East Timorese perspective, but it remains an excellent, non-sensationalist document and well worth studying.

Anna Forbes *Unbeaten Tracks in Islands of the Far East* (OUP Asia). Island life in remote corners of Maluku and Nusa Tenggara as observed by the resourceful wife of nineteenth-century naturalist Henry Forbes, as she battles rough living, bouts of malaria, and the attempted murder of her husband.

Louise G. Koke *Our Hotel in Bali* (January Books, New Zealand). The engaging story of two young Americans who arrived in Bali in 1936 and decided almost immediately to build a hotel on Kuta beach, the first of its kind. The book describes a Bali that was just beginning to attract tourists, and is an affectionate account of the locals, expats and visitors involved with the *Kuta Beach Hotel* from 1936 to 1942. It also includes some great black-and-white photos from the time.

Carl Lumholtz *Through Central Borneo* (OUP Asia). A dry cultural sketch of Kalimantan's Dayak tribes in the early twentieth century by this seasoned anthropologist.

Anna Matthews *Night of Purnama* (o/p). Evocative and moving description of village life and characters of the early 1960s, focusing on events in

Iseh and the surrounding villages from the first eruption of Gunung Agung until the Matthews left in 1963. Written with affection and a keen realization of the gap between West and East.

George Monbiot *Poisoned Arrows: An Investigative Journey Through Indonesia* (Joseph). The author travels through some of the less well known areas of Irian Jaya, researching the effects of the Indonesian government's transmigration policy, and uncovers startling poverty and, in some places, deep hatred of the central government. Monbiot paints a grim picture of the new settlements to contrast sharply with the rural idyll of life before interference.

Hickman Powell *The Last Paradise* (OUP Asia). Highly readable reflection of an American traveller's experiences in Bali in the late 1920s. Interesting accounts of village customs and temple festivals plus a few spicy anecdotes.

Tim Severin *The Spice Island Voyage* (Penguin Carroll & Graf). Rather downbeat account of Severin's travels around Maluku in the 1990s, following Wallace's trail in a traditional boat and finding Indonesia's wildlife and people on the brink of collapse.

Mark Shand *Skullduggery!* (Penguin). By the man best known for travelling across India on an elephant, with Goldie Hawn in tow. *Skullduggery!* is a 1990s *Boys Own*-style adventure, as Shand and a group of bored British dilettantes go to the Asmat region of Irian looking for headhunting trophies – and nearly leave their own behind.

Neville Shulman *Zen Explorations in Remotest New Guinea: Adventures in the Jungles and Mountains of Irian Jaya* (Summersdale). Not a drop of rain escapes without some obscure explanatory proverb or quotation, but even if you find his determination to find the zen in everything irritating, you can't escape the author's genuine delight and enthusiasm for his journey and his surroundings.

John Joseph Stockdale *Island of Java* (Periplus, Singapore). Travelogue describing the author's journey through Java during the first year of British rule in 1811. The book includes some interesting anecdotes regarding the tribulations of travel in the nineteenth century, but overall this tome is of interest to students and fans of Indonesian history.

K'tut Tantri *Revolt in Paradise* (o/p). The extraordinary story of an extraordinary woman.

British-born artist and adventurer Muriel Pearson – known in Bali as K'tut Tantri and in Java as Surabaya Sue – tells the astonishing tale of her fifteen years in Bali and Java. First living in close association with the raja of Bangli, then building one of the first hotels on Kuta beach, K'tut Tantri finally became an active member of the Indonesian independence movement, operating an underground radio station and smuggling arms and other supplies between the islands, for which she suffered two years' imprisonment and torture at the hands of the Japanese invaders. A fascinating, if in places somewhat embellished, account of Bali and Java between 1932 and 1947.

Adrian Vickers (ed.) *Travelling to Bali: Four Hundred Years of Journeys* (OUP Asia). Thought-provoking one-stop anthology which includes accounts by early Dutch, Thai and British adventurers, as well as excerpts from writings by the expat community in the 1930s, and the musings of late twentieth-century visitors. The editor's extensive introductions to the pieces make interesting reading, but the extracts themselves merely whet the appetite.

Harry Wilcox *Six Moons in Sulawesi* (OUP Asia). Immediately after World War II, a battle-weary Wilcox spent six months recuperating in Sulawesi's Tanah Toraja highlands and wrote this warmly affectionate, sometimes gushy, portrait of the people he found there.

HISTORY

Nigel Barley (ed.) *The Golden Sword: Stanford Raffles and the East* (British Museum Press, UK). Originally written to accompany an exhibition about Raffles, this is an excellent, well-illustrated introduction to the man, his life, work and the full extent of his fascination with all the countries he explored – Indonesia features largely.

Edwin M. Loeb *Sumatra, its History and People* (o/p). Classic 1935 account, and one of the few in-depth studies of the island. Perhaps too detailed and involved for the average reader, and parts of the analysis have even been proved wrong since the book was published. Worth reading, however, if only because the book's introduction remains the best overview of Sumatra in existence.

M.C. Ricklefs *A History of Modern Indonesia Since c.1300* (Macmillan). Acknowledged as the most thorough study of Indonesian history, Ricklef's 300-page account is written in a rather dry and scholarly style, and with its comprehensive index is probably best used as a textbook to dip into rather than as a work to be read from start to finish.

John G. Taylor *Indonesia's Forgotten War: The Hidden History of East Timor* (Zed Books/ Humanities Press). Clear and incisive account of the disastrous events in East Timor, from the fifteenth century up to the present day, with the final chapter looking at possible future scenarios.

CULTURE AND SOCIETY

Miguel Covurrubias *Island of Bali* (Kegan Paul International/Routledge and Chapman Hall). The Mexican artist and amateur anthropologist describes all aspects of life on Bali in the 1930s, from the daily routines of his adopted village household to the religious and philosophical meanings behind the island's arts, dramas and music. An early classic (first published in 1937) that's still as relevant and readable sixty years on.

Fred B. Eisemann Jr *Bali: Sekala and Niskala Vols 1 and 2* (Periplus, Singapore). The fascinating and admirably wide-ranging cultural and anthropological essays of a contemporary American, thirty years resident in Bali. His pieces encompass everything from the esoteric rituals of Balinese Hinduism to musings on the popularity of the clove cigarette. Essential background reading for any interested visitor.

David J. Fox *Once a Century: Pura Besakih and the Eka Dasa Rudra Festival* (Penerbit Sinar Harapan, Citra, Indonesia). Fabulous colour pictures, and an erudite but readable text, make this the best introduction to Besakih both ancient and modern. Also includes careful and sympathetic accounts of the 1963 Eka Dasa Rudra festival and the eruption of Gunung Agung.

A.J. Bernet Kempers *Monumental Bali: Introduction to Balinese Archaeology and Guide to the Monuments* (Periplus, Singapore). A fairly highbrow analysis of Bali's temples and ruins, written by a Dutch ethnology and archeology professor. Worth reading if you have a serious interest in the historical sites.

Gregor Krause *Bali 1912* (January Books, New Zealand). Reprinted edition of the original black-and-white photographs that inspired the first generation of arty expats to visit Bali. The pictures were taken by a young German doctor and give unrivalled insight into Balinese life in the early twentieth century.

Hugh Mabbett *The Balinese* (January Books, New Zealand). An accessible collection of short anecdotal essays on various aspects of contemporary Balinese life, from a look at the role of Bali's women to a discussion on the impact of tourism. *In Praise of Kuta* (January Books, New Zealand). Affectionate and very enjoyable portrait of Kuta in the 1980s, with lots of attention paid to the characters who live, work and visit Bali's most exuberant resort.

V.S. Naipaul *Beyond Belief – Islamic Conversions Among the Converted Peoples* (Little, Brown and Company). Account of Naipaul's travels to four Islamic nations, the first chapter of which deals with his time in Indonesia where he meets, among others, Abdurrahman Wahid, leader of the Islamic Nahdatul Ulama Party. Overall, a worthwhile and absorbing investigation into the current state of Islam that also touches on the political and socioeconomic situation of the country.

Michel Picard *Bali: Cultural Tourism and Touristic Culture* (Archipelago Press, Singapore). Fascinating, readable but ultimately depressing analysis of the effects of tourism upon the people of Bali. Required reading for serious students of what is going on on the island.

Adrian Vickers *Bali: A Paradise Created* (Periplus, Singapore). Detailed, intelligent and highly readable account of the outside world's perception of Bali, the development of tourism and how events inside and outside the country have shaped the Balinese view of themselves as well as outsiders view of them.

NATURAL HISTORY

Guy Buckles *Dive Sites of Indonesia* (New Holland). Exhaustively researched, attractive and up-to-date guide for potential divers with good sections on Bali and Lombok. Especially strong on the practical details.

Coates, Bishop, Gardner *Birds of Wallacea* (Dove). Almost portable, nicely illustrated single volume covering all 700 species recorded from Nusa Tenggara, Sulawesi and Maluku.

Cubitt & Whitten *Wild Indonesia* (New Holland). Plenty of good pictures and text in this overview of Indonesia's natural history, including coverage of main island groups and national parks.

Fred and Margaret Eisemann *Flowers of Bali* (Periplus, Singapore). Slim, fully illustrated handbook describing fifty of the most common flowers growing in Bali, with Latin, English, Indonesian and Balinese names given where possible.

Paul Jepson and Rosie Ounsted *Birding Indonesia: A Bird-watcher's Guide to the World's Largest Archipelago* (Periplus, Singapore). Excellent introduction to the subject with plenty of good photographs, clear descriptions and practical detail. Suitable for beginners and experts.

John MacKinnon *Field Guide to the Birds of Java and Bali* (Gajah Made UP, Indonesia). The most comprehensive field guide of its kind, with full colour plates, useful pointers for amateur spotters, and detailed descriptions of the 494 species found on Java, Bali and smaller offshore islands.

Victor Mason *Bali Bird Walks* (Insight Pocket Guides). Delightful, highly personal offbeat guide book to the Ubud area, which focuses on the flora and fauna, particularly the birds. The book describes over a dozen walks of varying lengths and difficulty, highlighting notable things to look at en route. Available from Ubud bookshops or from the author's bar and restaurant, *The Beggar's Bush*, in Campuhan, west Ubud.

Victor Mason and Frank Jarvis *Birds of Bali* (Periplus, Singapore). Informal, illustrated introduction to the 120 most commonly sighted birds in Bali; slim, easy-to-digest volume by Ubud expatriate and committed birder.

Kal Muller *Underwater Indonesia: A Guide to the World's Best Diving* (Periplus, Singapore). This is the must-have handbook for anybody planning to dive in Indonesia. Written by experts, it is exquisitely photographed and supplemented with clear, useful maps.

Mary Nightingale *New Guinea, An Island Apart* (BBC Books). Excellent photographs and analysis of the unique and extraordinary Papuan flora and fauna, including generous sections on Irian Jaya.

David Quammen *The Song of the Dodo* (Pimlico, UK). The author retraces many of Alfred Wallace's footsteps in Maluku as he updates Wallace's notions of biogeography. Very accessible, and a heartfelt tribute to Wallace's life and work.

Wendy Veevers-Carter *Riches of the Rain Forest* (OUP). User-friendly introduction to both common and unusual rainforest flora, including figs, rattans, durian and the extraordinary rafflesia.

Alfred Russell Wallace *The Malay Archipelago* (OUP o/p). A thoroughly readable account of the eight years that Wallace – whose independent discovery of the theory of evolution by natural selection prompted Charles Darwin to publish his more famous *Origin of Species* – spent in Indonesia collecting and studying wildlife during the mid-nineteenth century.

FICTION

Joseph Conrad *Almayer's Folly, An Outcast of the Islands*, and *Victory* (all Penguin). In his time as a sailor, Conrad visited Indonesia several times and later set some of his novels there. These – the first two set in Kalimantan, the third in Surabaya and the remote island of Sam – are atmospheric pieces revolving around self-destructive characters forced into each others' company by circumstance.

Vern Cook (ed.) *Bali Behind the Seen: Recent Fiction from Bali* (Darma Printing, Australia). Interesting and insightful collection of short stories by contemporary Balinese and Javanese writers. Many of the stories explore the ways in which Bali is changing, highlighting the tensions between the generations and their different outlooks on traditions, families and Westernization.

Victor Mason *The Butterflies of Bali* (Periplus, Singapore). Gentle cultural thriller about four expats who discover a Balinese village that's been hidden from the modern world for decades. The novel includes plenty of interesting detail on traditional rural Bali, but the quaint, elaborate writing style can get annoying.

Michael Wiese *On the Edge of a Dream* (Michael Wiese Productions). The story of two young Americans who settle for a while in a Balinese village in 1969. The most interesting parts of the novel show how the boys get drawn into – and spooked by – the island's spirit world and black magic.

ARTS, CRAFTS AND ARCHITECTURE

Antonio Blanco *Fabulous Blanco* (Blanco Fine Arts Foundation, Bali). The lavishly produced autobiography and retrospective catalogue of contemporary Ubud's most flamboyant expatri-ate artist, the Catalan-born creator of countless erotic paintings and surreal mixed-media collages and poems. Published as a limited edition and available from the artist's home in Campuhan, Ubud (see p.515).

Jacques Dumarcay *Borobudur* (OUP Asia). Sister publication of *The Temples of Java*, below, concentrating specifically on Indonesia's most famous monument. The sections dealing with the reliefs of the temple and their interpretation are most informative and entertaining. *The Temples of Java* (OUP Asia). Slim but entertaining rundown of all the major historical temple complexes in Java, beginning with the earliest temples (on the Dieng Plateau) and continuing in chronological order through to Ceto and Sukuh. The book's at its best when analysing the developments in architecture and the interpretation of the reliefs and statues that adorn the temples.

Fred and Margaret Eisemann *Woodcarvings of Bali* (Periplus, Singapore). Slim but interesting volume about one of Bali's finest crafts, with particularly good sections on the history of the craft and on the types of wood used.

Edward Frey *The Kris: Mystic Weapon of the Malay World* (OUP Asia). Small but well-illustrated book outlining the history and making of the kris, along with some of the myths associated with this magical weapon. Although intended more for the collector than the visitor, this is an excellent introduction to help you appreciate what you see in the museums.

John Gillow and Barry Dawson *Traditional Indonesian Textiles* (Thames & Hudson). Beautifully photographed and accessible introduction to the *ikat* and batik fabrics of the archipelago, whether you are thinking of buying or just enjoying them in museums.

Brigitta Hauser-Schaüblin, Marie-Louise Nabholz-Kartaschoff and Urs Ramseyer *Balinese Textiles* (British Museum Press, UK). Thorough and gloriously photographed survey of Balinese textiles and their role within contemporary society. Includes sections on the more common fabrics such as *endek*, *songket* and *kain poleng*, as well as introductions to some of the much rarer weaves including the *geringsing* of Tenganan.

Rio Helmi and Barbara Walker *Bali Style* (Thames & Hudson). Sumptuously photographed

glossy volume celebrating all things Balinese, from the humblest bamboo craftwork to some of the most fabulous buildings on the island. A good souvenir and an inspiration for potential visitors.

Garret Kam *Perceptions of Paradise: Images of Bali in the Arts* (Yayasan Dharma Seni Neka Museum, Bali). Ostensibly a guide to the paintings displayed in Ubud's Neka Museum, this is actually one of the best introductions to Balinese art so far published, with helpful sections on the traditions and practices that have informed much of the work to date. Plenty of full-colour plates and wider references as well.

Jean McKinnon *Vessels of Life: Lombok Earthenware* (Saritaksu). Fabulously photographed and exhaustive book about Sasak life, pottery techniques and the significance of the items they create in the lives of the women potters.

Idanna Pucci *Bhima Swarga: The Balinese Journey of the Soul* (Bulfinch Press). Fabulously produced guide to the *Mahabharata* legends depicted on the ceiling of Klungkung's Kerta Gosa. Illustrated with large, glossy, colour photographs and a panel-by-panel description of the stories, which makes the whole creation much easier to interpret.

Hans Rhodius and John Darling *Walter Spies and Balinese Art* (Tropical Museum, Amsterdam, distributed in Britain by IBD Ltd). Biography of the German expatriate artist and musician Walter Spies, which discusses, in brief, his early life and influences and then takes up the controversial debate over the extent of Spies' influence on modern Balinese art, asking whether the received view is actually a colonialist view of art history.

Anne Richter *Arts and Crafts of Indonesia* (Thames & Hudson). General guide to the fabrics, carvings, jewellery and other folk arts of the archipelago, with some background on the practices involved.

Haryati Soebadio and John Miksic (eds) *Art of Indonesia* (Taurus Parke Books). Huge coffee-table book packed with gorgeous photographs of the collection at the National Museum in Jakarta. An excellent, though pricey introduction to the archipelago and its variegated cultures.

Tara Sosrowardoyo, Peter Schoppert and Soedarmadji Damais *Java Style* (Thames and Hudson). Sumptuous volume in this glossy series, brilliantly and evocatively photographed, with illuminating descriptions of buildings and design all across the island, from ancient to modern.

Michael Tenzer *Balinese Music* (Periplus, Singapore). Well-pitched introduction to the delights and complexities of the gamelan, by an American composer who did a six-month stint at Batubulan's KOKAR high school of music and dance. Sections on theory, practice and history as well as interesting anecdotes from expert Balinese musicians.

Made Wijaya *Balinese Architecture: Towards an Encyclopedia* (Sanur, Bali). Off-beat, large format, limited edition which documents domestic, official and religious architectural styles. Designed to resemble an architect's scrapbook, with all sorts of inserts, photocopies, and photographs stuck on to the pages. Expensive, but appealing.

FOOD AND COOKERY

Heinz von Holzen and Lother Arsana *The Food of Bali* (Periplus, Singapore). Sumptuously illustrated paperback on all aspects of Balinese cuisine, including the religious and cultural background. The bulk of the book comprises recipes for local specialities – everything from snail soup to unripe-jackfruit curry.

Sri Owen *Indonesian Regional Cooking* (St Martin's Press, US). Relatively few recipes, but an otherwise excellent book with plenty of theory, techniques and background to Indonesian cuisine.

Jacqueline Piper *Fruits of South-East Asia: Fact and Folklore* (OUP Asia). Although only 94 pages long, this is an exhaustive, well-illustrated book, introducing all the fruits of the region together with the influence they have had on arts and crafts and the part they play in religious and cultural practices.

LANGUAGE

The national language of Indonesia is Bahasa Indonesia, although there are also over 250 native languages and dialects spoken throughout the archipelago. Until the 1920s, the lingua franca of government and commerce was Dutch, but the emerging independence movement adopted a form of Bahasa Malay as a more suitable revolutionary medium; by the 1950s this had crystallized into Bahasa Indonesia. Now taught in every school and widely understood across Indonesia, Bahasa Indonesia was a crucial means of unifying the new nation. The indigenous languages of Bali (see p.987) and Lombok (see p.988), are still spoken in the islands' villages.

Bahasa Indonesia is written in Roman script, has no tones and uses a fairly straightforward grammar – all of which makes it relatively easy for the visitor to get to grips with. The pocket-sized **phrase book** *Indonesian: A Rough Guide Phrasebook* makes a handy, comprehensive travelling companion, and includes an exhaustive dictionary of useful words as well as pronunciation details, some cultural hints, and information on grammar. Otherwise, try the *Berlitz Indonesian Phrase Book and Dictionary*, which can be supplemented by a ninety-minute cassette tape. Of the numerous **teach yourself** options, Sutanto Atmosumarto's *Colloquial Indonesian: A Comprehensive Language Course* (Routledge), including two 60-minute tapes, makes the best investment – an easy to follow step-by-step guide, complete with listening comprehensions, written exercises and situational dialogues. Once you're in Indonesia, you might want to get hold of the portable, though definitely not pocket-sized, **dictionary** *Kamus Lengkap Inggeris–Indonesia, Indonesia–Ingerris* (Hasta Penerbit).

GRAMMAR

Bahasa Indonesia uses the same subject-verb-object **word order** as in English. The easiest way to make a **question** is simply to add a question mark and use a rising intonation. **Nouns** have no gender and don't require an article. To make a noun **plural** you usually just say the noun twice, eg *anak* (child), *anak-anak* (children). **Adjectives** always follow the noun. **Verbs** have no tenses. To indicate the past, prefix the verb with *sudah* (already) or *belum* (not yet); for the future, prefix the verb with *akan* (will). For example, *saya sudah makan* means I have already eaten, *saya belum makan* I haven't eaten yet, and *saya akan makan* I will eat.

PRONUNCIATION

VOWELS AND DIPTHONGS

a as in a cross between f**a**ther and c**u**p

e sometimes as in **a**long; or as in p**ay**; or as in g**e**t; or sometimes omitted (*selamat* pronounced "slamat")

i either as in bout**i**que; or as in p**i**t

o either as in h**o**t; or as in c**o**ld

u as in b**oo**t

ai as in f**i**ne

au as in h**ow**

CONSONANTS

Most are pronounced as in English, with the following exceptions:

c as in **ch**eap

g always hard as in **g**irl

k hard, as in English, except at the end of the word, when you should stop just short of pronouncing it. In written form, this is often indicated by an apostrophe, for example, *beso'* for *besok*.

CONVERSATION

Selamat is the all-purpose greeting derived from Arabic, which communicates general goodwill. If addressing a married woman, it's polite to use the respectful term *Ibu* or *Nyonya*; if addressing a married man use *Bapak*.

Mau ke mana? (literally "want to where") is the usual opening gambit in any conversation, and means "where are you going?" The proper reply is *mau ke...* (want to go to...) followed by your intended destination. Other good answers are *saya jalan jalan* (I'm just walking) or *saya makan angin* (literally "I'm eating the wind"). The next question will be *darimana?* (from where) and relates to your nationality. Other keywords to listen out for in questions about nationality are *negera* (country) and *asal* (native). The response should be *dari Amerika/Ingerris/Ferancis* and so on.

You will probably also be asked *sudah kawin?* (already married?) and *sudah ada isteri* or *suami?* (already have wife/husband?). The proper response is either *ja* (yes) or *belum* (not yet); marriage is a natural goal for all Indonesians so a straight no answer is too blunt. From here you

will be asked if you have kids: *sudah ada anak?* If the answer is yes they'll want to know how many and how old – the suffix for years is *tahun*. When asking your age, people will use one of the "you" pronouns, with *berapa tahun?* (how many years). To answer say; *saya duapuluh tahun* (I am twenty). Another concern of Indonesians is your religion. Listen out for questions with the word *agama* (religion) in them, such as *Agamamana?* The response might be generally *Agama Catholik*. Whatever you do, don't try and tell anyone you have no religion; in Indonesia this equates with communism, which is still utterly derided.

You may be asked if you can speak Indonesian: *bisa berbicara bahasa Indonesia?* The usual response is *saya belum lanca* (I'm not yet fluent) or *sedikit sedikit* (just a little); the less confident should go for *ma'af tidak bisa* (sorry not at all).

COMMON WORDS AND PHRASES IN BAHASA INDONESIA

GREETINGS AND BASIC PHRASES

Good morning (5–11am)	Selamat pagi	I don't want it/No thanks	Tidak mau
Good day (11am–3pm)	Selamat siang	What is this/that?	Apa ini/itu?
Good afternoon (3–7pm)	Selamat sore	What?	Apa?
Good evening (after 7pm)	Selamat malam	When?	Kapan?
Good night	Selamat tidur	Where?	Dimana?
Goodbye	Selamat tinggal	Why?	Mengapa?
See you later	Sampai jumpa lagi	Who?	Siapa?
Have a good trip	Selamat jalan	How?	Berapa?
Welcome	Selamat datang	Boyfriend or girlfriend	Pacar
Enjoy your meal	Selamat makan	Foreigner	Turis
Cheers/Enjoy your drink	Selamat minum	Friend	Teman
How are you?	Apa kabar?	Men/women	Laki-laki/perempuan or wanita
I'm fine	Bagus/Kabar baik		
Please (requesting)	Tolong	Another	Satu lagi
Please (offering)	Silakan	Beautiful	Cantik
Thank you (very much)	Terima kasih (banyak)	Big/small	Besar/kecil
You're welcome	Sama sama	Clean/dirty	Bersih/kotor
Sorry/Excuse me	Ma'af	Cold	Dingin
No worries/Never mind	Tidak apa apa	Expensive/inexpensive	Mahal/murah
Yes	Ya	Fast/slow	Cepat/lambat
No (with noun)	Bukan	Good/bad	Bagus/buruk
Not (with verb)	Tidak (sometimes pronounced tak)	Hot (water/weather)	Panas
		Hot (spicy)	Pedas
What is your name?	Siapa nama anda?	Hungry/thirsty	Lapar/haus
My name is...	Nama saya...	Ill/sick	Sakit
Where are you from?	Dari mana?	Married/single	Kawin/bujang
I come from...	Saya dari...	Open/closed	Buka/tutup
Do you speak English?	Bisa bicara bahasa Inggris?	Tired	Lelah
		Very much/a lot	Banyak
I don't understand	Saya tidak mengerti		
Do you have...?	Ada...?		
I want/would like...	Saya mau...		(continues overleaf)

PRONOUNS

When addressing people, two multipurpose respectful tags you cannot overuse are *bu/ibu* (for women) and *pak/bapak* (for men) In Java use *Mas* instead for men.

You	*anda* is the most neutral and safest; *engkau* and *kamu* are familiar; to be superpolite use *tuan* (sir), *bu* or *pak*. To a young child use *adik*.	We/us/our	*kita*
		We (but not the person you're addressing)	*kami*
		They/them/their	*mereka*
		This/these	*ini*
I	*saya*	That/those	*itu*
He/she	*Ia/dia*		

GETTING AROUND

Where is the...?	*dimana...?*	Fuel (petrol)	*Bensin*
I would like to go to the...	*Saya mau pergi ke...*	Horse cart	*Dokar/cidomo*
... airport	*lapangan terbang*	Motorbike	*Sepeda motor*
... bank	*bank*	Motorbike taxi	*Ojek*
... beach	*pantai*	Taxi	*Taksi*
... bemo/bus station	*terminal*	Ticket	*Karcis*
... city/downtown	*kota*	To drive	*Mengendarai*
... hospital	*sakit*	To walk	*Jalan kaki*
... hotel	*losmen*	To come/go	*Datang/pergi*
... market	*pasar*	How far?	*Berapa kilometre?*
... pharmacy	*apotik*	How long?	*Berapa jam?*
... police station	*kantor polisi*	How much is the fare to...?	*Berapa harga karcis ke...?*
... post office	*kantor pos*		
... restaurant	*restoran/rumah makan/ warung*	Where is this bemo going?	*Kemana bemo pergi?*
...shop	*toko*	When will the bemo/ bus leave?	*Bila bemo/bis berangkut?*
...telephone office	*wartel/kantor telkom*	Where is this?	*Dimana ini?*
...tourist office	*kantor turis*	Stop!	*Estop!*
...village	*desa*	Here	*Disini*
Bicycle	*Sepeda*	Right	*Kanan*
Bus	*Bis*	Left	*Kiri*
Car	*Mobil*	Straight on	*Terus*
Entrance/exit	*Masuk/keluar*	Near	*Dekat*
Ferry	*Ferry*	Far	*Jauh*

ACCOMMODATION AND SHOPPING

How much is...?	*Berapa harga...?*	Money	*Uang*
...single room	*...kamar untuk satu orang*		
...double room	*...kamar untuk dua orang*		
Do you have a cheaper room?	*Ada kamar yang lebih murah?*		
Can I look at the room?	*Boleh saya lihat kamar?*		
To sleep	*Tidur*		
To buy/sell	*Membeli/menjual*		

NUMBERS

Zero	*Nol*	Four	*Empat*	Eight	*Delapan*
One	*Satu*	Five	*Lima*	Nine	*Sembilan*
Two	*Dua*	Six	*Enam*	Ten	*Sepuluh*
Three	*Tiga*	Seven	*Tujuh*		

NUMBERS (continued)

Eleven	*Sebelas*	Thirty, forty, etc	*Tigapuluh, empatpuluh, etc*	Two thousand, three thousand, etc	*Duaribu, tigaribu, etc*
Twelve, thirteen, etc	*Duabelas, tigabelas, etc*	One hundred	*Seratus*	Ten thousand	*Sepuluhribu*
Twenty	*Duapuluh*	Two hundred, three hundred, etc	*Duaratus, tigaratus, etc*	One hundred thousand	*Seratusribu*
Twenty one, twenty two,etc	*Duapuluh satu, duapuluh dua, etc*	One thousand	*Seribu*	One million	*Sejuta*
				Two million	*Dua juta*

TIME AND DAYS OF THE WEEK

What time is it?	*Jam berapa?*	Year	*Tahun*
When does it open/close?	*Kapan dia buka/tutup?*	Today/tomorrow	*Hari ini/besok*
It's... three o'clock	*jam tiga*	Yesterday	*Kemarin*
... ten past four	*jam empat lewat sepuluh*	Now	*Sekarang*
... quarter to five	*jam lima kurang seperempat*	Not yet	*Belum*
... six-thirty	*jam setengah tujuh* (literally "half to seven")	Never	*Tidak pernah*
		Already	*Sudah*
... in the morning	*... pagi*	Monday	*Hari Senin*
... in the afternoon	*... sore*	Tuesday	*Hari Selasa*
... pm/in the evening	*... malam*	Wednesday	*Hari Rabu*
Minute/hour	*Menit/jam*	Thursday	*Hari Kamis*
Day	*Hari*	Friday	*Hari Jumaat*
Week	*Minggu*	Saturday	*Hari Sabtu*
Month	*Bulan*	Sunday	*Hari Minggu*

BALINESE

The Balinese language, Bahasa Bali, has three main **forms** (and dozens of less widespread variations) – High (*Ida*), Middle or Polite (*Ipun*), and Low (*Ia*) – and the speaker decides which form to use depending on the caste of the person he or she is addressing and on the context. If speaking to family or friends, or to a low-caste (Sudra) Balinese, you use **Low Balinese**; if you are addressing a superior or a stranger, you use **Middle or Polite Balinese**, if talking to someone from a high caste (Brahman, Satriya or Wesya) or discussing religious affairs, you use **High Balinese**. If the caste is not immediately apparent, then the speaker will traditionally open the conversation with the euphemistic question "Where do you sit?", in order to elicit an indication of caste, but in the last couple of decades there's been a move to popularize the use of the polite Middle Balinese form, and disregard the caste factor wherever possible.Despite its numerous forms, Bahasa Bali is essentially a spoken language, with few official rules of grammar or syntax and hardly any textbooks or dictionaries. However, there is a useful if rather basic **primer** for any interested English-speaker, called *Bali Pocket Dictionary* by N Shadeg (Yayasan Dharma Bhakti Pertiwi), which is available from some bookshops on the island. All phrases and questions given below are shown in the Middle or Polite form.

USEFUL PHRASES

What is your name?	*Sira pesengan ragane?*	What is that?	*Napi punika?*
Where are you going?	*Lunga kija?*	Yes	*Inggih, patut*
Where have you been?	*Kija busan?*	No	*Tan, nente*
How are you?	*Kenken kebara?*	Child	*Putra, putri*
How are things?	*Napa orti?*	Family	*Panyaman, pasa metonan*
(I'm/things are...) fine	*Becik*		(continues overleaf)
I am sick	*Tiang gele*		

BALINESE (continued)

USEFUL PHRASES (continued)

Food	Ajeng-ajengan, tetedan	Three	Tiga
Friend	Switra	Four	Pat
House	Jeroan	Five	Lima
Husband	Rabi	Six	Nem, enem
Rice	Pantu, beras, ajengan	Seven	Pitu
Wife	Timpal, isteri	Eight	Kutus
Bad	Corah	Nine	Sia
Big	Ageng	Ten	Dasa
Delicious	Jaen	Bad	Corah
Good	Becik	Big	Ageng
Small	Alit	Delicious	Jaen
To come	Rauh, dateng	Good	Becik
To eat	Ngajeng, nunas	Small	Alit
To go	Lunga	To come	Rauh, dateng
To sleep	Sirep sare	To eat	Ngajeng, nunas
One	Siki, diri	To go	Lunga
Two	Kalih	To sleep	Sirep sare

SURVIVAL SASAK

The language of Lombok is **Sasak**, a purely oral language which varies from one part of the island to another. Realistically, Bahasa Indonesia is more practical for travellers, but even a few words of Sasak are likely to be greeted with delight. The following – transcribed for the English-speaker – should get you started.

There's no Sasak equivalent to the Indonesian **greetings** *selamat pagi* and the like. If you meet someone walking along the road, the enquiry "Where are you going?" *Ojok um bay?* serves this purpose – even if the answer is blatantly obvious.

USEFUL PHRASES

Where are you going?	Ojok um bay?	Delicious	Maik
Just walking around	Lampat-lampat	Fast/slow	Betjat/adeng-adeng
I am going to Rinjani	Rinjani wah mo ojok um bay	Heavy/light	Berat/ringan
Where is...?	Um bay tao...?	Brother/sister	Semeton mama/semeton
How are you?	Berem bay khabar?	nine	
I'm fine	Bagus/solah	Child/grandchild	Kanak/bai
... tired	... telah	Daughter/son	Kanak nine/kanak mame
... frightened	... takoot	Friend	Kantje
... thirsty	... goro	Husband/wife	Semame/senine
... hungry	... lapar	How many children	
... hot	... beneng	do you have?	Pira kanak de?
And you?	Berem bay seeda?	None	Ndarak
What are you doing?	Upa gowey de?	One	Skek
Nothing	Ndarak	Two	Dua
See you (I'm going)	Yak la low	Three	Telu
No problem	Nday kambay kambay	Four	Empat
Go away!	Nyeri too!	Five	Lima
Today	Djelo sine	Six	Enam
Tomorrow	Djema	Seven	Pitook
Yesterday	Sirutsin	Eight	Baluk
Big/small	Belek/kodek	Nine	Siwak
Dark/light	Peteng/tenang	Ten	Sepulu

GLOSSARY

For food glossaries, see Basics pp.41–45, for useful Indonesian phrases see pp.985–987, and for a brief guide to Balinese and Sasak, see p.988.

Adat Traditional law and custom.

Air terjun Waterfall.

Alkon Type of longboat.

Alun-alun Town square.

Andong Horse-drawn carriage.

Angkuta Minibus transport that plies routes inside a town's limits.

Anklung Musical instrument from Bali and Java, made from suspended bamboo tubes.

Arak Palm liquor.

Arjuna The most famous of the five Pandawa brothers, stars of the *Mahabharata*.

Baileu Meeting hall.

Bajaj Motorized rickshaw.

Balai Dayak meeting hall.

Bale Open-sided pavilion found in temples, family compounds and on roadsides, usually used as a resting place or shelter.

Balian (or *dukun*) Traditional faith healer, herbalist or witch doctor.

Balok Palm wine.

Banteng Wild cattle.

Bapak Father, also with its shortened form "pak", the usual address for an adult male.

Basir Dayak shaman.

Batik Cloth made by covering designs with wax, dying the whole cloth, melting off the wax (which has been protected from the dye) then reapplying the wax and redying.

Batu tulis Inscriptions in rock.

Becak Three-wheeled bicycle taxi.

Bemo Minibus.

Benhur Horse drawn carriage (after the Charlton Heston epic).

Bensin Petrol.

Benteng Fortress.

Bhaga Traditional structure built to commemorate female ancestors.

Bhoma (or **Boma**) The son of the earth, who repels evil spirits and is most commonly represented as a huge open-mouthed face above temple gateways.

Bis Bus.

Bisj Totem pole.

Bissu Transvestite priests.

Brem Rice wine.

Bukit Hill.

Bunga Flower.

Bupati Village head.

Camat District head.

Cidomo Horse-drawn cart used as a taxi on Lombok.

Cirih (pinang) Betel nut, a mild narcotic originally of ritual significance, chewed by many women (and some men) up and down the archipelago, which stains the mouth and teeth bright red.

Dalang Storyteller/shaman, the operator of Javanese wayang kulit.

Danau Lake.

Dayak Indonesian term for the indigenous peoples of Kalimantan.

Debus player Self-mutilating Sundanese performer.

Desa Village.

Dokar Horse-drawn carts.

Doktor gigi Dentist.

Dongson Ancient bronze drums of Chinese origin.

Dukun Traditional healer.

Ekonomi Inexpensive option.

Endek (or **ikat**) Cloth in which the weft threads are dyed to the final pattern before being woven.

Galungan The most important Bali-wide holiday, held for ten days every 210 days in celebration of the triumph of good over evil.

Gamelan Indonesian orchestra.

Ganesh Hindu elephant-headed deity, remover of obstacles and god of knowledge.

Garuda Mythical Hindu creature – half-man and half-bird – and the favoured vehicle of the god Wisnu; featured in numerous sculptures and temple reliefs and as a character in several dance-dramas.

Gereja Church.

Gili Small island or atoll.

Gorengan Street vendor selling deep-fried snack food.

Gua Cave.

Gunung Mountain.

Hajj Pilgrimage to Mecca.

Hinggi Cloth shawl or sarong.

Ibu (bu) Mother, usual address for any adult woman.

Ikat Distinctive and complex weaving style.

Jaipongan West Javan dance originally practised by prostitutes and incorporating elements of Pencak Silat.

Jalan Street.

Java man *Homo erectus erectus*; prehistoric inhabitant of Java, the fossilized remains of which have greatly influenced international theories of evolution.

Jimbeh Type of drum.

Kain Type of cloth.

Kamar kecil/way say Toilet.

Kampung Village.

Kantor Office, as in kantor telkom (telecom office) and kantor pos (post office).

Kebun Gardens.

Kepala desa/Kepala kampung Village head man.

Kepala sekola Schoolmaster.

Konfrontasi Sukarno's 1960s campaign against the West and Malaysia.

Kraton Walled royal residence.

Kretek Clove cigarettes.

Kris Traditional dagger, with scalloped blade edges, of great symbolic and spiritual significance.

Kulit kayu Cloth made out of beaten tree bark.

Kuningan The culmination day of the important ten-day *Galungan* festivities.

Legong Classical Balinese dance performed by two or three pre-pubescent girls.

Lontar Spindly palm tree whose nectar is gathered by certain peoples of the east for sustenance, and whose dried leaves have been used for manuscripts for centuries.

Lopi Dugout canoe.

Lopo Beehive shaped houses of West Timor.

Losmen Simple accommodation, usually family-run.

Lumbung Traditional Lombok barns.

Mahabharata Lengthy Hindu epic describing the battles between representatives of good and evil, and focusing on the exploits of the Pandawa brothers – the inspiration for a huge number of dance-dramas, paintings and sculptures.

Mandi Traditional scoop-and-slosh method of showering, often in open-roofed or "garden" bathrooms.

Meru Multi-tiered Hindu shrine with an odd number of thatched roofs (from one to eleven), which symbolizes the cosmic mountain Mahameru.

Mesjid Mosque.

Microlet Form of public transport.

Moko Dongson-style drums found in Alor.

Ngadhu Male equivalent of *Bhaga*.

Odalan Individual temple festival held to mark the anniversary of the founding of every temple on Bali.

Ojek Motorbike taxi.

Ora Komodo dragon.

Padmatiga Throne.

Pancasila The five principles of the Indonesian constitution: belief in one supreme god; the unity of the Indonesian nation; democracy; social justice; and humanitarianism. Symbolized by an eagle bearing a five-part crest.

Pasar baru New market.

Pasar senggkol Night market.

Pasar seni Literally art market, usually selling fabrics and sometimes artefacts and souvenirs.

Pasola Sumbanese ritual war.

Patola Ikat motif of regular stylized patterns, often used on cloths for regal persons.

Pelni National ferry company.

Pemangku Village priests.

Pencak silat Indonesia's martial art.

Penginapan Accommodation, sometimes a little less plush than a losmen.

Perada Type of textile.

Pete-pete Bus.

Pinisi High-masted wooden Bugis or Makassar schooner.

Pondok Guest house.

Prahu Traditional wooden fishing boat.

Pulau Island.

Puputan Ritual fight.

Rafflesia The world's largest bloom, pollinated by flies and with a strong smell.

Raja King or person of highest stature.

Ramayana Hugely influential Hindu epic, essentially a morality tale of the battles between good and evil – the source material for numerous dance-dramas, paintings and sculptures.

Rangda Legendary widow-witch who personifies evil and is most commonly depicted with huge fangs, a massive lolling tongue and pendulous breasts; features in carvings and in Balinese dance performances.

Raya main or principal, as in Jalan Raya Ubud – the main Ubud road.

Rumah adat Traditional house.

Rumah makan Restaurant.

Rumah sakit Hospital.

Sandung Mausoleum.

Sanghyang Trance dance.

Sarong The anglicized generic term for any length of material wrapped around the lower body and worn by men and women.

Sasak Native of Lombok.

Sawah Terraced ricefield.

Selat Strait.

Shophouse Shuttered building with living space upstairs and shop space on ground floor.

Songket Silk brocade often woven with real gold thread.

Sungai River.

Tau-Tau Torajan death carving.

Teluk Bay.

Toko Shop.

Topeng Wooden masks, and dances that use them.

Transmigration The controversial government policy of relocating people from overcrowded Java to other parts of the country.

Tsunami Japanese word meaning pressure wave, usually related to earth tremors and volcanic eruptions.

Tuak Palm wine.

Wallacea The area to the east of the archipelago studied by Alfred Russell Wallace, marking the transition between Asian and Australasian flora and fauna.

Waria Transvestite priests.

Warpostel Private postal service.

Wartel Private telecom office.

Waruga Sarcophagus, Sulawesi.

Warung Foodstall or tiny streetside restaurant.

Warung kopi Coffee house.

Wisma Guesthouse.

INDEX

Stay in touch with us!

ROUGH*NEWS* is Rough Guides' free newsletter.
In three issues a year we give you news, travel
issues, music reviews, readers' letters and the
latest dispatches from authors on the road.

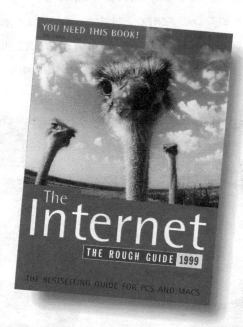

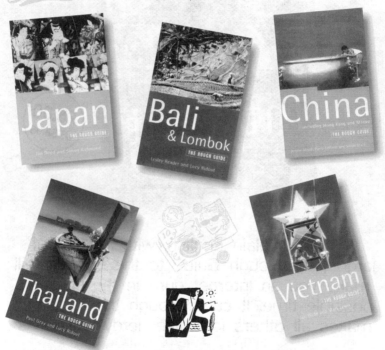

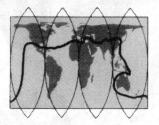